THE
GRIMOIRE
ENCYCLOPAEDIA

THE GRIMOIRE ENCYCLOPAEDIA VOLUME 1
Copyright © David Rankine 2023
Cover artwork © Rosa Laguna
Interior images provided by the author.
All Rights Reserved Worldwide.
Hardcover edition printed by Biddles, Nortfolk.

ISBN 978-1-914166-34-1 (HB)
ISBN 978-1-914166-36-5 (PB)

10 9 8 7 6 5 4 3 2 1

Except in the case of quotations embedded in critical articles or reviews, no part of this book may be reproduced or transmitted in any form or by any means, electronic or mechanical, including photocopying, recording, or by any information storage and retrieval system, without permission in writing from the publisher.

David Rankine has asserted his moral right to be identified as the author of this work.

A catolgue for this title is available from the British Library.

First published in 2023
Hadean Press Limited
Unit 30, Mantra House, South Street
Keighley, West Yorkshire, BD21 1SX
England
www.hadeanpress.com

THE GRIMOIRE ENCYCLOPAEDIA

A convocation of spirits, texts, materials, and practices

VOLUME 1

DAVID RANKINE

As for any man, even of any foreign land, whether of Nubia, Cush, or Syria, who shall remove this book, carrying it off from me – their corpse shall not be buried; they shall not receive cool water; their incense shall not be inhaled; no son or daughter shall wait upon them to pour water offerings to them; their name shall not be remembered anywhere on earth; they shall not see the rays of the solar disk. But, as for any servant who shall see this book, when he has caused that my soul and my name be enduring with praises – there shall be done the like for him after death in exchange for what he has done for me.

Bremner-Rhind Papyrus

'Freedom of information' of somebody's livelihood, research, and hard work is a spurious, ignorant, and frankly insulting argument, and to that end, the foregoing curse from ancient Egypt is for anyone who produces or distributes illegal electronic or paper copies of this book.

This book is dedicated to:

Joseph H. Peterson, whose tireless dedication, generosity of spirit, and superb scholarship through his books and website has provided an invaluable body of work on the grimoires.

&

Stephen Skinner, whose numerous excellent works (many on grimoires) since the 1970s have firmly established his position as one of the most significant contributors to the modern occult revival.

Acknowledgements

I must give especial thanks to the following people:

My beautiful and multi-talented wife Rosa Laguna for giving form and life to my idea for the cover design so perfectly, and putting up with numerous excited rants as I discovered new grimoires and insights, as well as my sleep-talking about the book and early morning starts to record material my unconscious mind processed during the night.

My dear friend and wonderful editor Erzebet Barthold for her encouragement and support, and for being such a great editor and sounding board; and her partner in Hadean wonderment, Chris Carr, for his work on the illustrations.

My co-author in assorted grimoire books and good friend Stephen Skinner for reading the manuscript and offering excellent suggestions and insights to further improve it.

The best grimoire librarian out there, Dan Harms, for his meticulous attention to detail, insights, and suggestions for additional material to improve the book.

I would like to thank all the scholar magicians and academics whose contributions have expanded the field of grimoire magic in recent decades. These include (but are not limited to): Aaman Lamda, Aaron Leitch, Adam McLean, Adley Nichols, Alan Thorogood, Alexander Cummins, Alexander Eth, Alison Chicosky, Andreas Erneus, Andy Mercer, Armada Winter, Arundell Overman, Benedek Lang, Brian Johnson, Carroll 'Poke' Runyon, Charles Burnett, Chris Carr, Christopher Lehrich, Claire Fanger, Claudia Rohrbacher-Sticker, Colin Campbell, Daniel Clark, Dan Harms, Daniel Walker, Darcy Kuntz, David Halperin, Deborah Harkness, Don Karr, Don Skemer, Edward A. Smith, Egil Asprem, Francis Ashwood, Frank Klaassen, Frater Acher, Frater Ashan Chassan, Gal Sofer, Gary Nottingham, Georg Dehn, Gideon Bohak, Gösta Hedegård, Hereward Tilton, Humberto Maggi, Ioan Couliano, Ioannis Marathakis, Jake Stratton-Kent, James Clark, James R. Davila, Jason Miller, Jean-Patrice Boudet, José Leitão, Joseph H. Peterson, Joseph Lisiewski, Julien Véronèse, Juris Lidaka, Katrina Bels, Kevin Wilby, Lauren Kassell, Liana Saif, Marvin Meyer, Mat Hadfield, Meh Osim, Merlin Cox, Michael Bailey, Michael Albion Macdonald, Michael Putman, Mihai Vârtejaru, Naomi Janowitz, Nicolás Álvarez Ortiz, Owen Davies, Pablo Torijano, Peter Forshaw, Phil Legard, Puk Speckens, Rafael Princk, Rebecca Lesses, Reda Ben Adam, Richard Kieckhefer, Robert Mathiesen, Robert Turner, Rosa Laguna, Rufus Opus, Simon Dyda, Sophie Page, Stephen J. Zietz, Stephen Skinner, Steve Savedow, Stian Kulystin, Vajra Regan, Valerie Flint, V. Velius.

Contents

Abbreviations xiii
Introduction 1
Before the Grimoires 4
Spirit Hierarchies 13
The Practice of Conjuration 18
Timeline 29
Encyclopaedic Entries 38
  Bible 39
  Greek Magical Papyri 42
  Supplementum Magicum 53
  Testament of Solomon 57
  Ancient Christian Magic 59
  Sepher ha-Razim 64
  Sword of Moses 68
  Shi'ur Qomah 71
  Picatrix 73
  De Lapidibus 77
  Liber Prestigiorum 79
  Liber Lunae 81
  Ars Notoria 83
  Ars Almandel 88
  Sepher Raziel 91
  Sworn Book of Honorius 95
  Summa Sacre Magice 98
  Elucidation of Necromancy 102
  Book of the Seven Rings of the Planets of Messalah 104
  Book of Consecrations 106
  Munich Handbook of Necromancy 107
  Annulorum Experimenta 109
  Book of Wisdom of Apollonius of Tyana 111
  Hygromanteia 113
  The Book of Angels, Rings, Characters and Images of the Planets 117
  Liber Runarum 119
  Le Grand Albert 120
  Key of Solomon 122
  Necromancy in the Medici Library 128
  Steganographia 129
  De Nigromancia 131
  Herpentil texts 133
  De Septem Secundeis 135
  Antipalus Maleficiorum 136
  Art of Drawing Spirits into Crystals 140
  Three Books of Occult Philosophy 141
  Cambridge Book of Magic 147

Galdrabók   149
Le Livre des Esperitz   151
Sepher Shimmush Tehillim   152
Magia Naturalis   153
Fourth Book of Occult Philosophy   154
Heptameron   156
Arbatel   158
Secrets of Solomon   160
Pseudomonarchia Daemonum   162
An Excellent Booke of the Art of Magicke   163
Secret of Secrets   164
Book of Oberon   167
Book of the Offices of Spirits   171
Enchiridion of Pope Leo III   173
Discoverie of Witchcraft   175
Crafte of Conjurynge   177
Archidoxes of Magic   178
De Heptarchia Mystica   179
Book of Abramelin   181
Antiphoner Notebook   184
Boxgrove Manual   186
Tuba Veneris   187
Tabula Bonorum Angelorum Invocationes   188
Key of Necromancy   190
Magia Naturalis et Innaturalis   192
Magical Calendar   196
Grimoire of Arthur Gauntlet   197
Goetia   200
Theurgia-Goetia   203
Ars Paulina   206
Of Angels, Demons & Spirits   209
Book of Gold   213
Janua Magica Reserata   216
Nine Celestial Keys   219
Book of Treasure Spirits   221
Pneumatologia Occulta   224
Theomagia   226
Grimoire of Pope Honorius   229
Semiphoras and Shemhamphorash   233
Book of St Cyprian the Sorcerer's Treasure   235
Sepher Maphteah Shelomoh   239
Sepher Rezial Hemelach   241
Petit Albert   245
Egyptian Secrets of Albertus Magnus   248
Grimoire of Armadel   257
Ars Phytonica   260
Grand Grimoire/Red Dragon   261
Veritable Magie Noire   263
A Collection of Magical Secrets   267

Clavis Inferni 268
The Magus 269
Grimorium Verum 272
Dictionnaire Infernal 274
Black Pullet 275
Complete Book of Magic Science 277
Verus Jesuitarum Libellus 278
Sixth and Seventh Books of Moses 279
Black Dragon 281
Grimoire Sympathia 283
Supreme Black Red & Infernal Magic 285
Secret Grimoire of Turiel 286
Sworn and Secret Grimoire 287
SPIRIT LIST 288
GLOSSARY 714
BIBLIOGRAPHY 715

Abbreviations

1 Chr	1 Chronicles
1 Cor	1 Corinthians
1 Kgs	1 Kings
1 Sam	1 Samuel
1 Th	1 Thessalonians
1 Tim	1 Timothy
2 Chr	2 Chronicles
2 Cor	2 Corinthians
2 Kgs	2 Kings
2 Mac	2 Maccabees
2 Sam	2 Samuel
2 Th	2 Thessalonians
3BOP	*Three Books of Occult Philosophy*
67M	*Sixth and Seventh Books of Moses*
9CK	*Nine Celestial Keys*
AAAA	*Almuchabosa Absegalim Alkakib Albaon*
Abm	*Abramelin*
ACM	*Ancient Christian Magic*
ADS	*Art of Drawing Spirits into Crystals*
AE	*Annulorum Experimenta*
Alex	*Alexandria*
Alm	*Almandel*
AM	Ashmolean Musem
Amos	Amos
AN	*Antiphoner Notebook*
AoM	*Archidoxes of Magic*
ArA	*Ars Almadel*
Arb	*Arbatel*
ArP	*Ars Paulina*
ArPh	*Ars Phytonica*
B7R	*Book of the Seven Rings of the Planets*
Bar	Baruch
BARC	*Book of Angels, Rings, Characters and Images of the Planets*
BD	Black Dragon
Ben	Ben Sira
BM	Boxgrove Manual
BN	Bibliothèque Nationale
BoC	*Book of Consecrations*
BoG	*Book of Gold*
BoMS	*Book of the Mightiest Spirits*
BoO	*Book of Oberon*
BOS	*Book of the Offices of Spirits*
BoSC	Book(s) of Saint Cyprian
BoTS	*Book of Treasure Spirits*

BoW	*Book of Wisdom*
BP	*Black Pullet*
BSM	Berlin Staatliche Museen
C	Century
CBMS	*Complete Book of Magical Science*
CBoM	*Cambridge Book of Magic*
ClI	*Clavis Inferni*
CoC	*Crafte of Conjuring*
CoMS	*A Collection of Magical Secrets*
Dan	Daniel
dCL	*De Consecratione Lapidum*
Deut	Deuteronomy
dHM	*De Heptarchia Mystica*
DI	*Dictionnaire Infernal*
dN	*De Nigromancia*
DoW	*Discoverie of Witchcraft*
dSS	*De Septem Secundeis*
EBAM	*Excellent Booke of the Arte of Magicke*
EM	Egyptian Museum
EoN	*Elucidation of Necromancy*
EPL	*Enchiridion of Pope Leo III*
ES	*Egyptian Secrets (of Albertus Magnus)*
Est	Esther
EUM	*Embodiment of the Unnatural Magic*
Ex	Exodus
Ez	Ezekiel
GA	*Grand Albert*
GAG	*Grimoire of Arthur Gauntlet*
Gbk	*Galdrabók*
Gen	Genesis
GG	*Grand Grimoire*
GMPP	*Great Magical Papyrus of Paris*
GoA	*Grimoire of Armadel*
Goe	*Goetia*
GoeR	*Goetia Rudd edition*
GoPH	*Grimoire of Pope Honorius*
Gr	*Greek*
GS	*Grimoire Sympathia*
GV	*Grimorium Verum*
HB	Holy Bible
Heb	Hebrew
Heid.	Heidelberg
Hmn	*Heptameron*
Hos	Hosea
HS	*Herpentills Salomonis*
Hyg	*Hygromanteia*
Isa	Isaiah
Jer	Jeremiah
JMR	*Janua Magica Reserata*

ABBREVIATIONS

Job	Job
Jud	Judith
Judg	Judges
KoN	*Key of Necromancy*
Kopt.	Koptisch (Coptic)
KoSA	*Key of Solomon* Abraham Colorno text family
KoSR	*Key of Solomon* Rabbi Solomon text family
KoSU	*Key of Solomon* Universal Treatise text family
L.	Leiden
LdE	*Livre des Esperitz*
Lev	Leviticus
LL	*Liber Lunae*
LP	*Liber Prestigiorum*
LR	*Liber Runarum*
Matt	Matthew
MC	Magical Calendar
Mic	Micah
MHN	*Munich Handbook of Necromancy*
Mich.	Michigan
MNeI	*Magia Naturalis et Innaturalis*
MOAS	*Magia Ordinis, Artium et Scientiarum abstrusarum*
MRC	*A Most Rare Compendium*
MS	Manuscript
MSS	Manuscripts
NA	*Notary Art*
ND	No date
NKB	*Nigromantisches Kunst-Buch*
NML	*Necromancy in the Medici Library*
NH	*Nag Hammadi*
Num	Numbers
O.	Ostracon (ribbed pottery)
oADS	*Of Angels, Demons & Spirits*
Oxy.	Oxyrhyncus (papyri)
P.	Papyrus
PA	*Petit Albert*
Pet	Peter
PGM	Greek Magical Papyri (also PDM)
Pic	*Picatrix*
PmD	*Pseudomonarchia Daemonum*
PO	*Pneumatologia Occulta*
Prv	Proverbs
Ps	Psalm
Rev	Revelations
Rom	Romans
SaS	*Semiphoras and Shemhamphorash*
SBH	*Sworn Book of Honorius*
SBRM	*Supreme Black, Red & Infernal Magic*
SGT	*Secret Grimoire of Turiel*
Shem	Shemhamphorash

ShR	*Sepher ha-Razim*
SM	*Supplementum Magicum*
SMS	*Sepher Mephteah Shelomoh*
SoM	*Sword of Moses*
SoS	*Secrets of Solomon*
SoSW	*Secrets of Solomon* (Wellcome MS 983)
SQ	*Shi'ur Qomah*
SR	*Sepher Raziel*
SRH	*Sepher Rezial Hemelach*
SSG	*Sworn and Secret Grimoire*
SSM	*Summa Sacre Magice*
SST	*Sepher Shimmush Tehillim*
Stg	*Steganographia*
SZH	*Der Schlüssel von der Zwang der Höllen*
T.	Tablet
TBA	*Tabula Bonorum Angelorum Invocationes*
tSoS	*The Secret of Secrets*
tM	*The Magus*
ThG	*Theurgia-Goetia*
Thm	*Theomagia*
Tob	Tobit
ToS	*Testament of Solomon*
ToSC	*Testament of Solomon Recension C*
Ts	Titus
TV	*Tuba Veneris*
VJL	*Verus Jesuitarum Libellus*
VMN	*La Véritable Magie Noire*
Wis	Wisdom
Zec	Zechariah
Zeph	Zephaniah

Introduction

When I began this work I did not realise the scope of my undertaking, nor did I appreciate the numerous realisations that would come from such a panoramic study. Themes run through the grimoires consistently, with a wealth of variations which flavour the individual grimoires subtly like an immense collection of spices. What is clear is that there are three main themes running parallel through the grimoires, with greater or less importance in individual works. These themes are spirit conjuration, divination, and simple charms/spells for dealing with the hardships of daily life and seeking to improve it.

Although there is a consistency and coherence found throughout many of the grimoire practices, the terminology used does vary. The practice of calling a spirit may be described as an acite/ascite, adjuration, call, citation, clepe,[1] coercion, commission, conjuration, evocation, exorcism, invocation, narration, or summoning. It is important to remember that the use of language over time changes, and some of these terms, although they may be used differently now, had a specific context in grimoire practice.

As the material in this work demonstrates, the major influences into the grimoire tradition were Greco-Egyptian, Jewish, and Arabic magic, set in the framework of Christian theology. As the tradition was influenced by earlier practices, so too has it influenced more recent ones. The modern British tradition of Wicca draws much of its practices from the grimoires, to the extent that it could be described as a simplified version of grimoire practice plus folklore with a pagan overlay.[2] American folk magic drew heavily from British (and German) sources, such as *Theomagia*, *Three Books of Occult Philosophy*, and the *Fourth Book of Occult Philosophy*, with Psalm texts like the *Sixth and Seventh Books of Moses* and *Sepher Shimmush Tehillim*[3] being particularly influential in traditions like the Pennsylvania Dutch. French sources unsurprisingly influenced Canada, and the Bibliothèque Bleue[4] texts were significant in spreading their content beyond Europe, notably to the Caribbean. Works like the *Grand Albert* and *Petit Albert*, *Black Pullet*, *Red Dragon*, *Grimoire of Pope Honorius*, *Enchiridion of Pope Leo*, and *Key of Solomon* were all frequently referenced. Of these the *Petit Albert* stands out as arguably the most commonly mentioned and influential, however even more (at the time) obscure texts could find their way across the world. An example of this is material from the *Grimoire of Armadel* appearing in a Palo Mayombe notebook in the Library of Havana.[5] Iberian Cyprianic texts and Allan Kardec's Spiritism stand out at the strongest influences into South America, with reference to other works like the *Grimorium Verum*.

The influence of astrology in the grimoires is significant. As well as the pervasive influence of the seven Classical planets and the twelve signs of the zodiac, there is a significant level of reference to the thirty-six decans and twenty-eight mansions of the moon. As with astrology as a whole, these influences date back long before antiquity to the earliest civilizations of Sumer and Egypt. Astrology would develop from here and spread into India and throughout the

---

1 Old word for 'call'.
2 For a more comprehensive study of this see Rankine (2023) *Wicca's Grimoire Roots*, and Rankine & d'Este (2008) *Wicca: Magical Beginnings*.
3 Printed in English as *The Secrets of the Psalms* by Godfrey Selig in the early twentieth century.
4 A popular imprint of French booklets and books produced from the early eighteenth century onwards. They were notable for their cheap cost and blue rice paper covers which gave them their name.
5 I am indebted to José Beceiro for drawing this to my attention.

antique world. The deities of the thirty-six decans are replaced by demons in the grimoires, but the principle of ruling spiritual creatures remains the same.

The first century CE Greek astrologer Dorotheus of Sidon is best known for his five volume verse work known as the *Pentateuch*. Fragments of this work survive in Greek, and as was often the case, it was translated into Arabic where it had a major influence on Arabic astrology. The work deals extensively with natal astrology and electional/horary astrology and is considered the single most important influence on Arabic natal astrology. What is also hugely significant about the work of Dorotheus is that he was the first known Greek person to record the system of the twenty-eight mansions of the Moon. It must also be stressed that Dorotheus was influenced by Indian astrology, and the Mansions of the Moon are clearly derived from the system of the twenty-seven *nakshatras* (lunar mansions) found there.

Although I have strived to use gender neutral terminology in this work, the historically recorded predominance in the grimoires is male. This is not to say that women did not practice grimoire magic, as clearly they did from literary evidence. A few grimoires do make references to female practitioners, as the following examples demonstrate.

The *Abramelin*, in the chapter on 'The age and the qualities that you need', specifies that women can perform the operation. It states 'In regard to women, virgins are the fittest. Others should avoid the work because of their impurity.'[6] Although the prejudice against sex and menstruation of the time period is evident in the work, at least they are included.

The *Cambridge Book of Magic* makes a distinction in the divination of the thumb, stating 'Say the six names in the right of the child, and if a woman in the left ear of the child'. This clearly refers to the practitioner as two sentences previously the child is qualified as a man or maid child of nine years of age.

In the *Secrets of Solomon* a character is created using the practitioner's blood, preferably on a red jasper or bloodstone for use in the rituals. The practitioner's initials are incorporated into the character. Men are told to carry it in their right pocket, and women in the left pocket or between the breasts.

The *Grimorium Verum*, in its description of the construction of the lamen, qualifies the differences in construction if the practitioner is male or female, stating, 'If you are a female, carry them on the left side, within your bosom, like a reliquary'.[7] Another example of the reference to male and female is found in the visionary feast conjuration. Here it states, 'If a woman performs the ceremony. Three gentlemen will come, but if a man performs the ceremony, three ladies will come.'[8]

An aspect of the grimoires which must be discussed is their religious nature. This is most prominent in earlier works like the *Sworn Book of Honorius*, and as the centuries passed becomes more implicit than explicit in many later grimoires, especially with those that focused more on demons rather than angels. Nonetheless, there is in this religiosity an assumption of belief and faith in the Christian worldview and its associated spiritual hierarchies and realms. There is also a belief in the power of the Bible as the core text of Christianity, and in the power of words, especially those drawn from its pages.

In his *Commentary on the Sefer Yetsira*, Isaac the Blind (1160-1236 CE), one of the great Kabbalists, describes language as the way to retrace the path of emanation. Divine force can be given form in written language and seals and sigils, and used by the practitioner in spoken form to conjure spirits. If we perceive language as a divine conduit, then conjuration, prayer, song, and ritual intonation all become pathways to the divine, both within and without.

---

6 Dehn, 2015:115.

7 Peterson, 2007:8.

8 Peterson, 2997:45.

Conjuration and talismanic magic thus both share the qualities of reception of divine force, and emanation of the divine force. This is a perception which is entirely in keeping with the nature and practice of the grimoires.

The revival of interest in the grimoires over the last few decades demonstrates an increase in awareness and appreciation for their value and scope, as well as their role in continuing practices from antiquity through to today. This work aims to provide an overview and reference guide to the tradition in a way that has not previously been attempted.

> All this that the Lord made me understand by His hand on me,
> I give you in writing—the pattern of all the works.
>
> I Chronicles 28:18-19

BEFORE THE GRIMOIRES

The origins of individual grimoires are often shrouded in mystery, due to the authors of most of the texts being unknown, making it very difficult to place the texts in the correct context and determine their provenance. However, we can trace the main roots of the grimoires by looking at earlier texts which had a significant input on the material and practices contained in the grimoires, and consider historical figures whose contributions have been recorded.

What is a Grimoire?

The word grimoire is believed to be derived from the Old French *grammair*, and is used to literally represent a grammar of magic, or workbook of information and techniques. The books or manuscripts commonly known as grimoires were generally written in the period from the thirteenth to eighteenth century. The grimoires were an essentially European phenomena, despite the external influences which contributed to their creation. Thus the grimoires are usually found in English, French, German, Greek, Hebrew, Italian, or Latin versions, with occasional texts in other languages such as Arabic, Czech, Dutch, Portuguese, and Spanish.

The core components usually found in grimoires are the creation of the magic circle, consecration of the magic tools, spirit lists (being the angels, demons, or other creatures summoned), conjurations of the said spirits, and other correspondences or pertinent information, such as details of purification of the practitioners and their paraphernalia (and sometimes its construction). Some works, like a number of the variants of the *Key of Solomon*, replaced spirit lists and conjurations with lists of amulets and talismans, with details of their creation and consecration. Nonetheless, there are still common themes with both the conjurations and amulets/talismans being used for similar purposes, such as. protection and acquisition.

Both of these terms encompass a range of purposes, with protection including health, property, whilst travelling, pregnancy protection, protection from attack, etc. Likewise acquisition may include wealth, success, love, sex, favour with a powerful figure, knowledge, good harvest, etc.

Although the popular perception of the grimoire tradition is of a heavily Jewish and Christian framework, upon inspection of different grimoires it is clear that in addition to the earlier texts which influenced the practices, there are also many influences from classical religions and folk practices. The clearest indicator of this influence is the number of deities from old religions who occur in the grimoires, sometimes by their own names and at other times in bastardised forms, such as the Roman and Greek deities Apollo, Diana, Hades, Pluto, Python, and Serapis, as well as other ancient deities like Astarte (Ashtoreth), Baal (Bael), and Horus (Hauros), and classical mythical creatures like Cerberus and the Phoenix (Phenex).

The Roots: Proto-Grimoires and Early Magical Texts

A number of works spanning the period from the second century BCE through the twelfth century CE may be seen as major influences on the material subsequently found in the grimoires. The ongoing and derivative nature of such magical texts and the amuletic tradition which was interconnected with them is also significant in the diversity of material which they incorporated.

The Greek Magical Papyri (*Papyri Graecae Magicae* or PGM) is the name given to a collection of magical texts found together which span the period from second century BCE to the fifth century CE. To these are added the collection of texts in *Supplementum Magicum* volumes 1 and 2, which contain material from the same period. The Greek Magical Papyri are characterised by the syncretisation of deities and spiritual creatures from numerous ancient pantheons including Babylonian, Christian, Egyptian, Gnostic, Greek, Jewish, and Mithraic. They also contain practices which are seen as key components of the grimoires, particularly the conjuration of spiritual creatures through repeated coercion, followed by a dismissal when the task is completed or agreed to by the spirit. Another theme seen in many of the charms and spells is that of planetary and zodiacal attributions (such as the thirty-six decans), which would also later feature prominently in some of the grimoires. They also contain practices concerning the use of the human skull as a spirit home (*Hygromanteia*, *Book of Oberon*, *Ars Phytonica*), and lead curse tablets (*Book of Oberon*, *Book of Treasure Spirits*).

Another significant collection of material is that published by Meyer and Smith in *Ancient Christian Magic*. This work spans the period from the second to the twelfth century CE, and contains numerous charms, spells, and conjurations written in Coptic and Greek. The flavour of the material is more Christian, with heavy Gnostic and Jewish influences. However, there is also a crossover with the material found in the PGM, such as the use of the seven Greek vowels and some of the same voces magicae.[9] There are also long angelic conjurations and phrases which hint at the influence of the Jewish system of Merkavah mysticism.

Two early Jewish texts of particular note are the second century CE *Testament of Solomon*[10] and the fourth century CE *Sepher ha-Razim* (*Book of the Mysteries*). The *Testament of Solomon* tells the story of the subjugation of sixty-one demons by King Solomon, who uses a magical ring given to him by the archangel Michael to bind them and learn the name of their controlling angels. The *Testament of Solomon* not only includes spirits of all thirty-six decans, but also emphasises the use of a controlling angel to bind the more chaotic nature of the demon to the service of the magician.

Sepher ha-Razim is largely planetary in nature, and contains conjurations of numerous angels and also the use of a wide range of paraphernalia including engraved metal lamellae, an ancient Greek practice which can be seen later in the grimoires in the form of the engraved pentacles. Another feature of *Sepher ha-Razim* is the use of the so-called Celestial Script, which is also found on contemporary amulets from this period and the following centuries.

A theological text from the late fifth century CE would also have a significant effect on the grimoire tradition. The *Celestial Hierarchies* of Pseudo-Dionysus the Areopagite was the first text to detail the hierarchy of nine orders of angels which would form the basis of the hierarchies found in orthodox Christianity, the grimoires, and the Kabbalah. This work stands out as a significant example of Christian Neo-Platonism.

---

9 'Voces magicae' are words of unknown origin and meaning, which are often included in charms to focus power and heighten the awareness of the practitioner.
10 See the chapter in the Encyclopaedic Entries.

In 2005 it was suggested there may have been an influence from the Merkavah tradition on the grimoires.[11] Recent work on *Summa Sacre Magice* proves this supposition, with material drawn from texts including *Shi'ur Qomah* and *Sepher ha-Razim* found in it. Whilst the Merkavah tradition has been commonly associated with the period from the third to eighth centuries CE, work in recent decades shows it flourished parallel to the grimoire tradition, and a degree of cross-fertilisation is unsurprising. Rebiger explored a group of seven manuscripts from the fourteenth through the sixteenth centuries CE written in Ashkenazi, Byzantine, Italian, and Sephardic scripts, demonstrating the geographical and cultural extent to which Hekhalot texts proliferated.[12] It is also interesting to note that some of these texts contain elements reminiscent of the *Sword of Moses*, which may suggest synergy with other strands of Jewish magic and evolution within the tradition. Hekhalot texts often demonstrate large amounts of hymnology.[13] The *Shi'ur Qomah* (*Measure of the Body* [of God]) is a Jewish text which dates to between the sixth and ninth centuries CE. The text, often found bound with *Sepher ha-Razim* and *Hekalot Rabbati*, describes the body of God, giving measurements for each part, and divine names for each part of the body as well.

The *Sword of Moses* may also be mentioned here, as this tenth century CE text (which may date back as far as the fourth century CE) has some similarities to the grimoires that would follow, with numerous angels to be conjured to gain the sword (a long string of divine names used in the charms), and a long list of possible acquisitive and protective results which can be achieved using the text. The sword itself is an example of the practice of hymnology being used outside of the Hekhalot texts.

The Development of Lapidaries

The earliest lapidary of note which influenced those to come was the *De Lapidibus* of Theophrastus (372-287 BCE), 'the father of botany', which classified around seventy different stones. Although more scientific in his approach and largely lacking in mythological material, he was influential on the works that would follow, especially Pliny's *Natural History*.

De Virtutibus Lapidum (*The Virtues of Stones*) was written in Greek by the Alexandrian Jew Damigeron in the second century BCE. Only Latin translations have survived, and it is better known through the fifth century CE Latin translation by 'Evax'. This work is important in its focus on Greco-Egyptian magical attributions to stones, with an emphasis on planetary associations.

An important early work which was not specifically a lapidary is the *De Materia Medica* of Dioscorides (50-70 CE). Focusing on remedies using a wide range of plants, he also includes around two hundred 'stones' (i.e., hard materials) with their attributions in part five. Significantly for later use of stones in amulets and incenses, Dioscorides made the distinction between stones that could be powdered and used, and those harder stones which needed to be worn in amulets close to the skin.

Shortly after Dioscorides, Pliny the Elder wrote his epic ten book, thirty-nine volume *Historia Naturalis* (Natural History, 77 CE). The basis for the later concept of encyclopedias, this hugely influential work included a volume on precious stones (volume thirty-seven), which like Dioscorides, recorded oral traditions of magical attributions which had probably circulated for centuries.

---

11 Rankine, 2005:15.
12 See Rebiger 2013:685-713.
13 Angelic adjuration through the repetitious use of prayer and strings of divine names.

The *Cyranides* (first to fifth century CE) is a six-volume work attributed to Hermes Trismegistus which discusses the magical attributions of animals, plants, and stones. Through the Latin and Arab translations of this work it exerted an influence on the lapidaries and bestiaries of the medieval period. The amuletic descriptions of image and type of stone can also be seen as having an influence on the Arabic tradition of image magic that would so strongly influence some of the grimoires.

Pliny's work was quoted heavily by Isidore of Seville (560-636 CE) in his twenty volume *Etymologiae* (including 'on stones' in book sixteen). This encyclopedic work by the Spanish archbishop, described as the 'last classical scholar', was the main Latin preserve of classical writings until the later waves of Arabic to Latin translations during the twelfth century renaissance, and would also introduce the full stop, comma, and colon to writing.

The Development of Herbals

The frequent use of plants in the grimoires and books of secrets draws focus to the works which preserved medical and folkloric knowledge of plants. The most significant herbal in Europe from its creation until the twelfth century was the *Herbarium Apuleii Platonici* (fourth to fifth century CE), or *Herbal of pseudo-Apuleius*. This work of one hundred and thirty-one chapters drew heavily on Pliny's *Natural History* and the *De Materia Medica* of Dioscorides. Each chapter focused on one plant, and gave an illustration along with uses and folklore.[14]

Herbal knowledge was a strong feature of Anglo-Saxon lore, and this can be seen in works such as the *Leechbook of Bald* (900-950 CE) which has a far wider scope than any other herbals prior to the Italian Renaissance, and has been described as the first medical treatise written in western Europe belonging to the modern age. Another important Anglo-Saxon work was the *Lacnunga* (tenth to eleventh century CE). This work repeated material from the *Leechbook of Bald*, as well as a number of charms in old English. Of these the 'Nine Herbs Charm' and 'Lorica of Laidcenn' are of particular note.[15]

The possible origins of the Solomonic pentacles

Lamellae are thin strips of metal on which the ancient Greeks wrote protective magical charms. They were generally made of gold, silver, copper, or bronze,[16] and together with the lead defixiones (curse tablets), comprise the metal corpus of the ancient Greek magical texts. Lamellae were commonly inscribed with a sharp bronze stylus onto very thin sheets of metal foil, and often rolled up and worn on the body (as phylacteries).

Common features inscribed on lamellae include charaktêres and voces magicae. Repetition of names and vowels occurs, as does the use of shapes such as wings and diminishing triangles (*schwindeschema*). The text may vary from a couple of lines to well over a hundred in length.

As well as Greek, Hebrew is found in divine names and short excerpts from Biblical quotations which often contain divine names, Latin, and Coptic. Egyptian gods, who made the cultural shift into Greek culture, also occur, as do Gnostic references. Various archangels

---

14 Although the earliest copies have not survived, there are copies dating from the the sixth century onwards, such as Harley MS 585, which also contains a copy of the *Lacnunga*.

15 This old Irish charm (seventh century CE) calls on Jesus and numerous angels to protect the parts of the body from demonic attack.

16 Tin and lead are also mentioned, see Kotansky, 1994:xvi.

are mentioned, with their names written in Greek; one interesting fourth to fifth century CE example simply gives the names Michael, Gabriel, Raphael, and Ouriel (Uriel) on a gold lamella.[17]

The fact that almost all the planetary metals were used for the lamellae may be significant. The common materials are those most frequently attributed to the Sun (gold), Moon (silver), Venus (copper), and bronze (Mars as its planetary alloy), and the others are also planetary, being those of Jupiter (tin) and Saturn (lead). The only missing planet is Mercury, whose planetary metal by its unique liquid nature is unsuitable for making charms unless it is combined into an alloy or amalgam, or substituted with another metal.

Although this is speculation, it is tempting to see these metal lamellae as the prototypes for the later medieval Solomonic pentacles made in planetary metals. Kotansky (1994:xix) suggests a link in this chain, saying:

> In the 5th and 6th centuries we see a slow but steady drop off and decline in the quality of writing and overall productivity of amulets in general. The lamellae, it seems, are becoming replaced by a new series of bronze suspension-amulets: mostly a special category of Solomonic amulets probably widely used by the now nominally Christian population.

Both the use of planetary metals and Hebrew biblical quotes are standard in Solomonic pentacles. It is also worth considering a specific sub-set of the lamellae, the Orphic-Dionysian gold funerary lamellae, buried with the dead as both amulet and reminder of the passwords to be given on the underworld journey towards the perfection promised through cult initiation in life.

Moving towards the Grimoire

The commonly accepted division of philosophy in the Middle Ages was into the Seven Liberal Arts. These are named as Arithmetic, Astronomy, Dialectic, Geometry, Grammar, Music, and Rhetoric. However, in the early Middle Ages some variants to this scheme present an interesting glimpse into the beginning of the grimoire tradition.

The Jewish Spanish physician and astronomer Petrus Alfonsi (1062-1110?) replaced Rhetoric with Medicine, and Grammar with Necromancy or Philosophy.[18] This inclusion of Necromancy amongst the Liberal Arts is not unique, as Constantine the African (d.1098 CE), one of the pioneering translators of Arab medical texts into Latin, was said to be educated in a range of subjects including necromancy.[19] Both Alfonsi and Constantine converted to Christianity, and brought their experience of the Jewish and Islamic world and scholarship into the shaping of medieval science.

The term 'necromancy' was interpreted in more than one way. Isidore of Seville (560-636 CE) in his twenty volume *Etymologiae* had defined necromancers as 'those by whose incantations the dead, having been resuscitated, seem to divine the future and reply to questions put to them.' This text was incredibly important as a reference work through the

---

17 Kotansky, 1994:104-106.

18 'Those who admit the possibility of prophecies say that it is necromancy; those who do not, say it is philosophy ... and those who do not study philosophy say that it is grammar.' Disciplina Clericalis, early twelfth century CE.

19 'Grammar, dialectic, rhetoric, geometry, arithmetic, mathematics, astronomy, necromancy, music, and physics.' Petrus Diaconus, *De viris illustribus* (written between 1137-59 CE).

Middle Ages; however, in the works of Albertus Magnus, a different definition is seen. In his *Speculum Astronomiae* (mid-thirteenth century CE), widely regarded as the most authoritative book on the categorisation of astrology and magic of the age, he qualified necromancy as work using talismans and also suffumigations and invocations. Magic using characters, names, and exorcisms was additionally considered necromancy, though of a lesser evil.

Necromancy can be seen in this definition as working with spirits, using conjurations or exorcisms, and suffumigations. Magnus states that the spirits deceive magicians by God's permission. This description clearly fits most of the grimoires, so the previous connection to the Liberal Arts is an interesting one.[20] Albertus considered works which employed talismans without the 'unholy' additions he described as licit, mentioning in particular the *De Imaginibus* of Thābit ibn Qurrah.

Thābit ibn Qurrah[21] (826/835-901CE) was a Sabian mathematician, astronomer, physician, and translator, who lived in Baghdad in the second half of the ninth century CE. Born in Harran in Upper Mesopotamia, he moved to Baghdad and became part of a circle of scholars translating Greek texts into Arabic. He was trilingual, speaking Syriac, Greek and Arabic, and his work was hugely significant in the development of Arabic science. At the end of his life, he became a court astronomer for the Abasid Caliph al-Mu'tadid (reigned 892-902 CE).

His work translating and revising the works of such luminaries as Archimedes, Euclid, and Ptolemy led to him reforming the Ptolemaic system and calculating accurately the length of the sidereal year (to within two seconds). Originally coming from a stellar-worshipping movement (the Sabians), it is not surprising that he should have written a hugely important treatise on planetary talismanic image magic, *De Imaginibus*.[22] Like most of his one hundred and fifty or so works it did not survive in its original form (less than a dozen did). However, it was translated into Latin where its influence would be felt in the development of the grimoire tradition.

Two different translations of *De Imaginabus* into Latin were made in the twelfth century, by Adelard of Bath (1080-1162 CE) and by John of Seville (unknown, flourished 1135-53 CE). Adelard of Bath's translation, *Liber Prestigiorum*, dates to the late 1120s and contains a number of elements not found in the other translation, including suffumigations, magical rings, and prayers to spirits. The *De Imaginabus* of John of Seville is slightly later (1135-1153 CE) and is a more modest and acceptable text within the religious environment of the time.

Adelard of Bath has been described as 'the first English scientist'. Born in 1080 CE, he travelled extensively, first to France where he studied in Tours and then taught in Laon. From there he travelled to Spain, Sicily, and Syria, and then on to Palestine. During these travels he would study with Jewish and Arabic scholars, as well as Petrus Alfonsi (in England). By 1126 CE he had returned to England and was translating Arab texts on astronomy, and teaching astronomy to a young King Henry II. Adelard was by his own admission a student of magic, who consulted with a witch to learn incantations, as stated in his *Questiones Naturales*. This work also explores the concept of 'same and different' found in Aristotle's *Physics* and Plato's *Timaeus*, stating 'the power and efficacy of the green of his emerald ring he wears is stronger than that of his green cloak, although the cloak is much larger'.[23] This discussion can be seen as a precursor to the doctrine of sympathetic magic expressed centuries later by Paracelsus in *Archidoxes of Magic*.

---

20 The concept of using magic to learn the Liberal Arts very quickly would form the basis of the *Ars Notoria*.

21 His name was Latinised to Thebit Bencora when referred to in translations of his work.

22 The text is lost and is referred to by the Latin name ascribed to it.

23 Translation in Burnett 1998:95.

In his work *Speculum Astronomiae*, Albertus Magnus named *Liber Prestigiorum* as the worst of the astronomical texts which he considered abominable due to the inclusion of suffumigations and incantations of spirits. He was however more accepting of John of Seville's later *De Imaginibus* translation which omitted these. In comparison to *Liber Prestigiorum*, at least fifty-six copies or fragments of this work are known to have survived.

A contemporary of Adelard was Robert of Chester (possibly Robert Castrensis) who flourished 1140-1150 CE. Robert travelled to Castile to work on translating Arabic works into Latin, and made a significant contribution to the proliferation of key texts. As well as translating *Liber Lunae* into Latin, he also translated *Liber de compositionae alchemiae* (*The Book of the Composition of Alchemy*), the first known Latin work on alchemy available in Europe in 1144.

The first known Arabic astrological texts translated into Latin occurred in the tenth century and were known as the *Alchandreana*. These texts were translated in Italy, and had spread to Spain and France before the eleventh century. Named after a mysterious philosopher, Alchandreanus, it has been suggested that this name was a corruption of al-Kindi. Al-Kindi (801-873 CE) was born in Kufa and educated in Baghdad, where he was one of the most significant figures in the house of wisdom translating Greek texts into Arabic. Known as the 'father of Arabic philosophy', the works of al-Kindi were hugely influential on a range of subjects including astronomy, astrology, mathematics, philosophy, and cryptography.

Abū Ma'shar (787-886 CE) is another relevant figure in the transmission of texts and practices from late Antiquity through the Arabic world to Europe. Born in Balkh, Kurasan, he has been referred to as the greatest astrologer of the Abbasid court in Baghdad. A Persian philosopher, astrologer, and astronomer, he was a contemporary of Thābit ibn Qurrah, who drew on the work of earlier Greek, Islamic, Mesopotamian, and Persian scholars. He was heavily influenced by the works of Aristotle and al-Kindi, and wrote a number of practical astrological manuals. Some of these would be translated into Latin by both Adelard of Bath and the mysterious John of Seville,[24] and they would influence the work of subsequent significant figures like Albertus Magnus, Roger Bacon, and Pico della Mirandola.

The work of John of Seville leads to a largely ignored but incredibly important area of transmission of the material which influenced the grimoire tradition – Spain. The work of Spanish translators as the main entry point to Europe of the classical Greek works which had been preserved in Arabic translations cannot be overstated. As well as the transmission of astrological knowledge, this includes the tradition of astral magic, the influence of the stars on the human body and through gemstones as receptacles of that influence and in talismans. When exploring this influence, the name which stands out is that of King Alfonso X.

Alfonso X ('the Wise', 1221-84 CE) was the king of Castile, Leon, and Galicia from 1252-84 CE. He encouraged and promoted learning, having Arabic, Christian, and Jewish scholars in his court. Alfonso sponsored the translation of numerous Arabic (and also Hebrew and Latin) works into Castilian, which he sought to establish as the language of higher learning.

Alfonso liked to personally oversee translations, and a number of these were by his personal physician, the Jewish scholar and Rabbi Yehuda ben Moshe. Amongst the earliest works carried out in his scriptorium were the *Picatrix, Lapidario, Liber Razielis, Libro de Astromagia*[25] and *Libro de las formas et las ymagenes*.

The translation of the *Picatrix* into Castilian in 1256 CE was the first non-Arab version, and from here it would soon be translated into Latin and become more widely known. *Lapidario*

---

24 *Kitab al-mudkhal al-kabir ila 'ilm ahkam an-nujjum* (848 CE), was translated into Latin (*Introductorium in Astronomiam*) by John of Seville in 1133 CE. An abridged version titled *Kitāb mukhtaṣar al-mudkhal* was previously translated by Adelard of Bath. John also translated the astrological manual *Kitāb tahāwīl sinī al-'ālam* (*Flowers of Abu Ma'shar*).

25 MS Reg.Lat.1283 Part A, Napoli.

was a collection of lapidaries, which were a prominent accompaniment to the astrological works of the time. *Liber Razielis* (*Book of Raziel*) clearly predates the subsequent works of the same name, which are not all related, being quite distinct texts, found in Hebrew, Latin and English in the following centuries. This *Liber Razielis* serves as the source of angelic names in the two anthologies mentioned below.

The *Libro de las formas et las ymagenes* (*Book of the images and forms* [which are in the heavens]) (1276-9 CE) dealt with the influence of heavenly images on the human body (melothesia) and the magical powers of certain stones received from the influence of the stars.[26] Much of this work was drawn from the *Picatrix*, *Liber Razielis*, and *Lapidario* along with other texts to provide a comprehensive anthology of astral images. Although the text has not survived, evidence demonstrates that it was copied and crossed borders. The 1373 CE catalogue of the library of King Charles V of France contains this reference: 'Thirty-nine paper quires of the book of the forms, figures and images which are in the heavens, translated from Spanish into French by Pierre Levant... by order of my lord, the Duke of Berry'.

Libro de Astromagia (c. 1280 CE) was another compilation work, also drawing from *Liber Razielis* and the *Picatrix*, together with the works of Abū Ma'shar, and a number of unidentified sources.[27] Addresses to angels or spirits in some of the operations make it clear this work was not just a collection of astral images. This book also travelled, as another entry in the 1373 CE catalogue describes 'A book of astronomy, which seems to be of the Ars notoria, written in Spanish, perfectly decorated with figures and with fine colours of Bolognese illumination'. Further references make it clear that the text in question is the *Libro de Astromagia*.

Lapidaries, books describing the magical properties and attributions of gemstones, were an important companion to astrological works in the tradition of astral magic. The lapidaries also served as 'one of the main delivery systems for both licit and illicit magical texts',[28] as seen in the transmission of the *Almandel* in copies of *De Consecratione Lapidum* (thirteenth century). Of these the most significant was *De Lapidibus* by Marbodius of Rennes (which among others heavily influenced *De Consecratione Lapidum*). Marbodius of Rennes (1035-1123) was a poet, hagiographer, and hymnologist who became the bishop of Rennes. He wrote widely, though the best known of his works was *De Lapidibus*, a hexameter verse lapidary describing sixty stones. This Latin text was widely disseminated,[29] being the first of his works to be published (Vienna, 1511) and by the fourteenth century it had been translated into Hebrew, French, Italian, Provençal, Danish, and Irish.

Looking further East to the Byzantine Empire, we encounter the works of Michael Psellus (1018-96 CE). Psellus was an advisor, professor, and monk, who translated and commented on numerous classical works, ensuring their survival. Of these, particularly significant are his translation and commentaries on the works of Aristotle, the *Corpus Hermeticum*, and the *Chaldean Oracles*. His writings, while publicly Christian and critical of Classical philosophies and practices, are full of overt sympathy and keen understanding of their contents. His interest in astrology, theurgy, and pagan practices nearly resulted in him being excommunicated, hence the public caution in his work.

Psellus' work *On the Operation of Dæmons* takes the form of a dialogue between Timothy and Thracian, discussing Platonic and Neo-Platonic concepts of the nature of dæmons. Stephen Skinner expressed the value of this work very lucidly, stating, 'Psellus was the bridge between

---

26 Only one fragmentary manuscript survives of this work, El Escorial Real Biblioteca ms h-I-16, which gives the table of contents, hinting at much interesting material sadly lost.
27 A partial version of this manuscript survives as MS Vatican BAV Reg. Lat. 1283a.
28 Regan, 2018:280.
29 At least one hundred and fifty manuscripts of it survive.

Neo-Platonic, Gnostic and Hermetic texts and the theology, philosophy and dæmonology of the late Byzantine era: a bridge between the classical view of the dæmon as a beneficial guiding spiritual presence, and the later Christian view of demons as intrinsically evil fallen angels.'[30]

As can be seen, the grimoires grew from the syncretic practices of Antiquity, with a range of influences particularly from Arab, Greek, and Jewish texts and cultures. The range of material found in the numerous grimoires can be seen as reflecting the diversity of sources which fed into them, as will be shown in the following chapters.

Essential Reading

Bremmer, Jan N., & Veenstra, Jan R. (eds) (2002) *The Metamorphosis of Magic from Late Antiquity to the Early Modern Period*. Connecticut: David Brown

Burnett, Charles (1996) *Magic and Divination in the Middle Ages. Texts and Techniques in the Islamic and Christian Worlds*. Aldershot: Variorium

Faraone, Christopher A. & Obbink, Dirk (1991) *Magika Hiera: Ancient Greek Magic and Religion*. Oxford: Oxford University Press.

Gager, John G. (1992) *Curse Tablets and Binding Spells from the Ancient World*. Oxford: Oxford University Press.

Greenfield, Richard (1988) *Traditions of Belief in Late Byzantine Demonology*. Amsterdam: Hakkert

Kent, Jake-Stratton (2010) *Geosophia: The Argo of Magic*. London: Scarlet Imprint

Luibheld, C. (trans) (1987) *Pseudo-Dionysus: The Complete Works*. New York: Paulist Press

Mirecki, Paul A. & Marvin W. Meyer (2002) *Magic and Ritual in the Ancient World*. Leiden: Brill

Ritner, Robert K. (1993) *The Mechanics of Ancient Egyptian Magical Practice*. Chicago: University of Chicago

Shaked, Shaul (ed) *Officina Magica: Essays on the Practice of Magic in Antiquity*. Leiden: Brill

---

30 Skinner, *Introduction to Collisson*, 2010:11.

Spirit Hierarchies

Life creates hierarchies. From ant-hills to wolf packs, nature orders itself for efficiency and propagation. An important function of such hierarchies is skill specialization. As part of nature, the same is seen in human society, and it is logical to expect (and find) the same principles occurring with spirits.

There is a hierarchy at the top of the spirit hierarchies in grimoires, which is implicit, but rarely mentioned. This is the Christian Trinity of God, Jesus, and the Holy Spirit (only God in Jewish texts). Also mentioned in some of the earlier texts as one of the 'rulers' at the top of the hierarchy is the Virgin Mary. These are the beings to which all the spirits below are subservient, and whose names are used as signs of authority in conjurations, on paraphernalia, pentacles, etc.

When considering the spiritual creatures found in the grimoires, angels and demons are the most prevalent. Fairies, elementals, genii loci, and others also occur on occasion.

Demons present an example of the synergistic nature of the grimoires. They may be seen as the fallen angels serving under the Devil as described in the Christian tradition. A common theological view from late Antiquity into the Middle Ages was that demons could not be compelled by magic, and that they deceived those who called upon them in order to gain adoration and worship. This differs from the grimoires, which argue that demons are subject to God's power, and that power can endow the magician with the authority to compel them. It is possible this perspective was influenced by the Arabic magical texts, where the use of prayer and the supremacy of Allah (God) are fundamental to working with spiritual creatures.

Demons may also be seen as the daimons (or daemons) of the Greco-Roman world, powerful spiritual creatures who may be neutral, good, or evil. Gods, heroes, and ghosts were sometimes described as daimons, further adding to the diverse associations and bringing the dead and the divine into the spectrum of daimon identity. Additionally, daimons were associated with humans as guiding the destiny of the individual they were attached to, and in this function may be seen as a source of the later idea of the guardian angel.[31]

Contrary to the Christian viewpoint, daimons were acknowledged as effective at magic without divine intercession. Interestingly, in opposition to the mainstream, there were voices presenting the demon more in line with the views of the daimon from antiquity. In the early fifteenth century, German theology professor Johannes of Francofordia commented that, 'the demon is the best physician, very understanding of the nature of things like stones, of herbs and the like'.[32]

The association of the Agathos Daimon (Good Daimon), who had a wide-ranging worship, with the serpent may have contributed to negative connotations in the early Christian mindset. In addition, the association of daimons with the sublunary realm, below the celestial, as intermediary dwellers between divine influence and human action could have also added to this 'demonisation'. The wide-ranging imprecation of daimons on curse tablets, which focused on malefic and erotic magic,[33] in the early centuries of the Christian era could only further have influenced their association with the malefic in the minds of the early Christian Church.

---

31 'They were transformed by Zeus into daimons, guardians over mortals', Hesiod, *Works & Days*, 8 BCE.
32 Quoted in Hansen, 1901:71-82.
33 For which see particularly Gager, 1992.

By the late fourth century CE St Augustine had extended the view of demons as malefic entities engaged in a divine struggle with good, an apocalyptic war in which demons were responsible for diseases and all manner of ills and woes.[34] Whilst a few writers in the following centuries would question these views, the mindset of the founding fathers of the Christian Church set the common perception of demons for the centuries to come. It is only in recent decades that people have started to question and challenge these views and argue for a more balanced perspective of demons and daimons.

The Angelic Hierarchy

Janua Magica Resarata presents the most comprehensive listing of the angelic hierarchy. Interestingly it also includes the Enochian spirits[35] and the top of the infernal hierarchy.

At the top of the heavens are the eighteen fiery regions – the Superior and Celestial Heavens wherein reside the seven Great Archangels who dwell in the presence of the divine: Metatron, Raziel, Tzaphkiel, Tzadkiel, Michael, Raphael, and Gabriel. Under these are the nine Orders of Angels:

1. The Superior Hierarchy

Seraphim (Chaioth haQadosh) under Metatron/Methratton

Cherubim (Auphanim) under Raziel

Thrones (Aralim) under Tzaphkiel/Cassiel, who also rules the Olympic Spirit Aratron, the Planetary Spirit Zazel and the Planetary Intelligence Agiel

2. The Middle Hierarchy

Dominations (Chasmalim) under Tzadkiel/Sachiel, who also rules the Olympic Spirit Bethor, the Planetary Spirit Hismael and the Planetary Intelligence Yaphiel

Potestates or Powers (Seraphim) under Khamael/Samael, who also rules the Olympic Spirit Phaleg, the Planetary Spirit Bartzabel and the Planetary Intelligence Graphiel

Virtues (Malachim) under Michael, who also rules the Olympic Spirit Och, the Planetary Spirit Sorath and the Planetary Intelligence Nakhiel

3. The Inferior Hierarchy

Principalities (Elohim) under Haniel/Anael, who also rules the Olympic Spirit Hagith, the Planetary Spirit Kedemel and the Planetary Intelligence Hagiel

Archangels (Bene Elohim) under Raphael, who also rules the Olympic Spirit Ophiel, the Planetary Spirit Taphtartharath and the Planetary Intelligence Tiriel

Angels (Cherubim) under Gabriel, who also rules the Olympic Spirit Phul, the Planetary Spirit Schad Barschemoth ha-Shartathan and the Planetary Intelligence Malkah be-Tharshisim ve-ad Be-Ruachoth Shechalim

---

34 See e.g. *On the Divination of Demons*, Augustine, late C4 CE.

35 This, along with the use of an Enochian divine name in the *Book of Treasure Spirits*, suggests that practice of the Enochian system continued after John Dee's death. For how long is unknown, but it does present an interesting avenue of research and demonstrates the revival of Enochian by the Golden Dawn was perhaps not as ground-breaking as has been credited.

The twelve Zodiacal Presidential Angels are also under the seven great Archangels, as are the twenty-eight Mansions of the Moon, each with its Presidential Angel, and the seventy-two Shemhamphorash Angels, who rule the Quinaries (5° angles).

Additionally there are the Militia of Heaven, containing seven other orders. These are:

The Doctrinal Order
The Tutelary Order
The Procuratory Order
The Ministerial Order
The Auxiliary Hierarchy
The Receptory Order of Souls
The Order of Assistants

Below the eighteen fiery heavens are the thirty Airy or Inferior regions of the Heavens (the Aethyrs), wherein reside the ninety-one Aerial Princes, who rule over the four Angelic Rulers of the Watchtowers, each ruling six Seniors, each ruling sixteen Angels, each ruling countless spirits.

Below all these angelic regions are the infernal spirits. These are ruled by the three Kings of the infernal hierarchy – Lucifer, Beelzebub, and Sathan.

Sathan rules the four Kings of the Air, better known as the Demon Princes, each of whom has a subordinate demon bishop and numerous demons. The demon princes are:

Oriens in the East, under whom is the Demon Bishop Theltryon
Amaymon in the South, under whom is the Demon Bishop Boytheon
Paymon in the West, under whom is the Demon Bishop Sperion
Egyn in the North, under whom is the Demon Bishop Mayerion

Under each of the Bishops are many named spirits, such as Vassago, Belial and others, and under them numberless demons.

Greek Hierarchy

The *Hygromanteia* contains a planetary hierarchy which is three tier, consisting of a classical planetary deity, angel of the hour, and demon of the hour, conjured in that order. As the different manuscripts have many variations in names, I am not including multiple lists of one hundred and sixty-eight[36] angels and demons each here.

Jewish Angelic Hierarchy

Jewish proto-grimoire texts list angelic hierarchies based on the seven heavens. *Sepher ha-Razim* has the seven heavens, with some of them containing encampments or steps, each with differing numbers of angels with different functions.

---

36 One for each hour of the day, for each day of the week, hence 7x24 = 168. They are however all listed in the Spirit List chapter.

Heaven	Encampment	Step	Function	Number
1	1		Healing	72
	2		Wrath and Anger	80
	3		Foretelling	36
	4		Favour	44
	5		Answers in the Night	62
	6		Might	37
	7		Dreaming	44
2			Fire and Moisture	
		1	Silencing	9
		2	Love	12
		3	Nullifying Intentions	14
		4	Disquiet	16
		5	Fire	12
		6	Healing	17
		7	Fiery and Watery Might	11
		8	Protection (Pregnancy)	16
		9	Martial	14
		10	Truth and Rescue	15
		11	Bestowing Authority	15
		12	Righteousness and Healing	20
3			Extinguishing bath-house fires, illusion of fire, winning horse races	69
4			Fire and Water, leading to Helios to ask questions	31+35
5			Glory, asking questions for the ruled month	12+
6			Fire	36+30
7			Location of Throne of Glory	?

Demonic Hierarchies

The ruling triumvirate of Lucifer, Beelzebub, and Satan is found in a number of grimoires. In some this is extended to also include Astaroth, giving four spirits at the top of the hierarchy, though sometimes with Lucifer as supreme.

There is a role which could be described as vizier (or facilitator in modern terminology) seen in some of the grimoires. This is a role usually fulfilled by Tantavalerion and Scirlin.

SPIRIT HIERARCHIES

Under the ruling group are the four kings of air in the directions – Oriens, Amaymon, Paymon, and Egyn (with some variation in names). These kings have other demons/spirits under them as counsellors and messengers, some of whom are described as kings in their own right. The *Book of Treasure Spirits* gives a good example of this.

The lower hierarchies vary considerably between grimoires and regions, to the extent that there are a significant number of demon kings, princes, and other ranks. This is a subject which deserves a book in its own right, as study of it will undoubtedly reveal much about the circulation of ideas and ideologies within the material transmitted between grimoires.

Book of Treasure Spirits

(Note ^{K} indicates the spirit is described as a king.)

Direction	King of Air	Presidential Counsellors	Messengers
East	Oriens	Niophryn Barbas Sibarbas Alilgon	Baal^K Temel Belfarto Marage
South	Amaymon	Alick Berith Mala	Emlon^K Ocarbidaton^K Madicon^K Marage
West	Paymon	Gordonizor Tams	Balferth Belial^K Baruson^K Rombulence Alphasis Mirage
North	Egyn	Vassago Othiy Um Anaboth	Merage

The Practice of Conjuration

'The Spirit will never come to you without being called from the heart at the same time as by the mouth, and proves once more that you must be resolute and unwavering in your Will.'[37]

Although this book is a serious and scholarly treatment of many of the grimoires, it is appropriate to provide some explanation of how they were used. It should be understood that most grimoires were the practical records of magicians, focused on method and practice (and on occasion theology and philosophy). They were not created for publication, hence the manuscript form of the originals. As printing became more popular, published works did proliferate, but still maintained a similar content style. It is for that reason this chapter has been added. For those who are more concerned with the history, social, or bibliographic background, this chapter could with some advantage be skipped.

Given the central nature of conjuration to the grimoire tradition, a discursive template on the sequence of preparation and practice for conjuration is provided. **This is not the only way or the best way**. This template draws on the author's over forty years experience, at the time of writing, of practicing grimoire conjuration to offer some guidelines and advice the reader may find useful. It is not a definitive A-Z of conjuration.

Experience shows that it is not a good idea to start changing a system until you are competent in that system and fluid in its practices. On this note, experience suggests it is often better to add to, rather than take away from, an existing structure. It is also important to bear in mind that just because something is not mentioned, that does not mean it should be excluded (e.g., a text may not mention cleanliness, purification, or consecration, but they should still be part of the process). Many grimoires (especially those from the seventeenth century onwards) were written to include material the author or compiler felt was essential for their own reference, and so much is assumed about the knowledge of the reader, as the reader was themselves.

All of the preparation for a conjuration, including the fasting, purification baths, confession, prayers, consecrations, circle construction, etc., add to the magical momentum of the operation.[38] The greater the momentum, the greater the chance of a successful outcome. Anything which reduces the momentum, such as leaving out preparations, should be recognized as such, and avoided if possible. Another contributory factor to magical momentum is the mental discipline that comes from years of daily practice, such as concentration exercises, meditation, visualization, breath work, body work. This mental discipline is valuable both in performing conjuration and in skrying with spirits. Apart from increasing the clarity and acumen of the practitioner, these practices also help in switching off the internal dialogue. Over time this ability becomes something the practitioner can do at will, and is a recommended state for conjuration work. Having no internal dialogue allows the practitioner to recognize and identify mental spirit communication without falling into the trap of confusing internal ego dialogue for a message from the spirit.

---

37 *The Black Dragon*.

38 I am indebted to Alison Chicosky for her observations on momentum, and Mat Hadfield and Stian Kulystin for their observations in the discussion we had regarding the essentials of practice, all of which gave me the impetus to add this section.

Experience also shows that the things we think are the most obvious are the ones we should definitely discuss, as what is obvious to one person may not be so to another. As a practical aside, if you are going to work with unfamiliar materials, e.g., writing on vellum using a quill and ink, or even lighting charcoal blocks, it is worth practicing first and making sure you have competency in the required skill. Making your first attempt within the framework of the conjuration, where attention to detail counts, can lead to mistakes when you least want them.

The Three Ps for the Template for Conjuration:
Planning, Preparation, and Practice.

Planning

The first decision to be made is why do you want to perform a conjuration? What is the purpose of the conjuration, and does it require a conjuration to achieve the desired outcome? It is no coincidence that many grimoires include simple charms to achieve results which facilitate maintaining quality of daily life.

The form of the conjuration then needs to be considered – will it be the more elaborate, religious, angelic form of a grimoire like the *Sworn Book of Honorius*, or the more pared down, demonic form of a work like the *Grimorium Verum*?[39] The style and which spirit one intends to work with will obviously be a huge factor in the process.

Timing

Once the choice of which spirit and which grimoire has been made, the serious planning begins. Timing is key and there may be several factors to consider. Some grimoires include lists of good and bad days for performing conjuration, or particular times of day for different spirits or classes of spirits, so these should be taken into account. There are also some spirits attributed to specific times, such as individual hours of the day or night. Beyond the timings specifically mentioned in the grimoire being worked, relevant planetary timings such as the planetary hours, planetary days, and positive astrological aspects should also be examined.

If possible it is worth ensuring the days before and after the conjuration, as well as the day itself, should be taken off work (if relevant). Having this time free gives more time to focus on the preparation, reduces what needs to be done while fasting, and also allows time for recovery afterwards if needed.

A list of ingredients should also be prepared. This includes any tools and paraphernalia, candles, incense, oil, and any other *materia magica*. When considering any plant ingredients required, if possible it is preferable to gather these yourself, and take into account any special gathering times which may be relevant.

Notes on Herb Gathering

There may be specific instructions for gathering particular herbs in the grimoire you are working with, but regardless there are a number of guidelines which have been employed for many centuries that are worth keeping in mind. These are: (1) use the left hand if possible and

---

[39] If you have not performed conjuration before, I would recommend starting with the Olympic Spirits or Planetary Intelligences. The style is simpler and the spirits generally more ameliorable as a first contact.

preferably wear white, (2) do not face into the wind or look behind you whilst picking, (3) do not use iron tools unless specified, (4) address the plant and explain why it is being picked, and make an offering (e.g. tobacco, alcohol, silver coin, bread, milk, etc.), (5) once picked, wrap the plant in white (natural) cloth and do not let it touch the ground, (6) unless otherwise specified dawn is a standard herb-gathering time.[40]

Preparation

During the preparation, all of the items you will be using need to be gathered or made, and also consecrated. Depending on the circumstances, the magic circle may also be prepared prior to the conjuration. If it is an outdoor conjuration it is worth considering making the magic circle on four pieces of suitable material which can be connected, as seen in some of the grimoires. This way you have a magic circle that is ready to use and avoid any problems with making a magic circle on the earth which might be easily broken. Of course the magic circle should also be made during times appropriate to the nature of the conjuration. If the magic circle is being drawn on the floor in an inside room, the same principles of timing apply. The activation of the magic circle is one of the first actions that take place during the conjuration process.

Tools

Whilst it may not be practical to make all the items required, they do need to be gathered. Items such as swords and knives can be purchased and suitably consecrated. Items such as wands, phylacteries, and seals can be made, and in so doing you further contribute to the magical momentum of your work. The usual constraints of appropriate timing and a magic circle should be applied to any tool construction to enhance this as much as possible.

Rehearsal

Reading through the conjuration(s) beforehand a few times is recommended, especially if they are long. This both gives an idea of the flow of the conjuration, and also alerts you to any phrasing or words that might trip you up when you perform it. If words seem awkward or trip you up repeatedly, replacing them with an equivalent word for better flow can be done. Updating the language of a conjuration is valid if it does not alter the nature of the conjuration. However, it is not recommended to replace the divine names with deities from other pantheons, as the names are there for good reason. The divine names (including Jesus) represent the power to which the spirits ultimately answer, and so substituting them is not advisable. If you are able to memorise the conjuration then this has the benefit of enabling you to stay alert for any signs of activity, and not have to worry about light levels. This is not essential as a number of grimoires do refer to reading the conjuration, but if you have a good retentive memory you may find it an added plus to the magical momentum.

Consecrations

Every item present inside a magic circle (and the circle itself) should have been consecrated. *The Key of Solomon* is a great source for many consecrations, but as a product of its time, certain items are not present for that reason. It is easy to overlook things that are part

---

40 For more detail on this and working with herbs generally, I would strongly recommend the excellent *Mastering Herbalism* by Paul Huson (1974, but republished in 2001 and more widely available in this slightly expanded edition).

of who we are, particularly if they are always with us, such as glasses or contact lenses. For this reason I created a consecration to be performed for these items prior to conjuration (see below). The same can also be true of taking personal jewellery for granted. My preference is to not wear any jewellery that is not specifically relevant to the conjuration (i.e., magical rings, phylacteries, etc.), but for those who choose to keep any jewellery on (especially difficult to remove items like some piercings), it should all be consecrated prior to the ceremony. Also remember that if you have items like chairs to sit on, these also should have been consecrated.[41] The consecration consideration also applies to items used in the preparation that might not be present in the magic circle for the conjuration, such as the pestle and mortar for making incense, the jars the incense is stored in, etc.

Consecration of Glasses/Contact Lenses

Oh, God! who art the author of all good things, strengthen, I beseech thee, thy servant, that I may stand fast, without fear, through this dealing and work; enlighten, I beseech thee, oh Lord! my dark understanding, so that my spiritual eye may be opened to see and know thy spirits through this object of clear vision: (place preferred hand on glasses or tray of lenses) and thou, oh object of clear vision, be sanctified and consecrated, and blessed to this purpose, that no evil phantasy may appear in thee truly, and without the least ambiguity, for Christ's sake. ✠ (Make cross over glasses/lenses with preferred hand) Amen.[42]

Fasting

Fasting, or abstinence, is mentioned in a number of grimoires as part of the preparation to conjuration, and needs serious consideration. First is the duration of the fast: the normal suggestions are seven or three days. For either of these, checking with a medical professional before starting them (a doctor, not a friend who thinks they know it all) is strongly encouraged, especially if you have any pre-existing medical conditions.

Seven days of consuming *only* water is strongly discouraged. If you have ever done this, you will know that by the end of the week your mind is wandering and your body is confused. This is not a state to be performing conjuration in, and should be avoided. However starting the abstinence at seven days is a good idea. At the seven-day period, begin the abstinence from alcohol, caffeine, drugs (except those prescribed by your doctor), fish, meat, nicotine, swearing, and sexual activity (including masturbation), so that at the three-day mark (or one-day mark), the full fast may begin. My rule of thumb is three days for angels and demons, one day for Olympic spirits, planetary intelligences, and planetary spirits. For these days you should only drink water and eat nothing. If this is going to be a struggle or you find yourself starting to get a little mentally fuzzy, drink pure apple juice[43] to keep your blood sugar up. Personally, I recommend including the apple juice; it has always worked well for me.

There is a second type of fast to include which is a product of the modern world: the electronic fast. As the physical fast works to purify the body, so the electronic fast works to purify the mind. For the seven days prior to the conjuration, avoid social media, gaming, and television as much as possible. Ideally this should be a complete abstinence, though if you

---

[41] Chairs are shown in the magic circles in several grimoires, so this is not an unusual item to find if you are doing the conjuration indoors. They are particularly useful if standing for several hours may be uncomfortable for any of the practitioners.

[42] Adapted from the consecration of the crystal in Trithemius' *The Art of Drawing Spirits into Crystals*.

[43] Or a different natural, pure juice if you cannot drink apple.

need to check emails this is fine. Certainly avoid gaming, watching television, or binging on Netflix, and indulging in social media like Facebook, Instagram, TikTok, etc.

Remember that fasting is a purificatory process, and you should commit fully to it as part of the process of building magical momentum. Another abstinence which is mentioned in the grimoires as part of this process is abstinence from swearing. Swearing and cursing can be seen as profaning the mouth which you will be using to utter sacred names. Avoid swearing, and consider gargling each day with holy water as part of your purification to prepare your mouth for the conjuration. In *Experimentir-Buch* the practice of placing a small piece of frankincense resin in the mouth before conjuration is mentioned. This may have been to act as a purification of the words being spoken.

Sigils and Seals

All the evil Daemons had names and sigils placed upon them by the Highest Creator when previously they were Angels and Stars in heaven; and through these same names and sigils it is wholly necessary to summon and compel them, by which means we are able to summon even the good angels.[44]

This quote from *Tuba Veneris* emphasises the relevance of using seals and sigils during conjuration. These should be made (in a magic circle) prior to the practice at appropriate times. In my research I found a prayer by Sir Thomas Middleton, included below, which may be recited over the sigil or seal as part of its preparation.

A Prayer before the putting of any Sigil[45]

'O Almighty Lord and everlasting God, by whose power both the heavens and the Earth with all things therein contained were made, by whose providence all things both in heaven & Earth are governed Who givest virtue to every Creature, that thou hast made as to plants, stones, herbs, & all for the use of man (who in thee doth live, move, & hath his being) yea & to words, prayers, signs & sigils dost give especial virtues, & especially to thy own great Names, for expelling of evil spirits & healing diseases, give thy special blessing unto these sigils which in thy Name we do apply unto this thy Servant, let those virtues equal the virtue of Gideon's Sword that vanquished the Philistines, of Judith that cut off the Babylonian's head, the strength of Sampson's arms, the strength of David; let his prayers that made them (who bear a place in the Celestial Choir) be now heard in remembrance, & let our weak prayers, have access unto thy throne of Grace, & so for prayer with thy Sacred Majesty that these Sigils may receive that virtue from thee, that was humbly supplicated at the making of them, and Let this thy Servant find & feel the effectual workings of them, to the Recovering of health both of body & mind, & preserving from the Like or any other evil, both of body & mind hereafter, & grant this O merciful father for Jesus Christ his Sake in whose blessed Name we do humbly & heartily beg it, of thee, in that prayer which he hath taught us.'

---

44 *Tuba Veneris*.
45 Sloane MSS 3822, folio 35, 1739?

Prayer and Confession

Daily prayer during the period of fasting helps focus the mind on the coming conjuration. The Penitential Psalms were collated by Cassiodorus in the sixth Century CE and are chanted every day during Lent. They are Psalms 6, 31, 37, 50, 101, 129, and 142. Dee used them as part of the preparation for his work, and they are often used in the period prior to conjuration in the same way.

The confession is mentioned in a number of grimoires, and can cause a knee-jerk reaction in some people. The confession is said by yourself on the day of the conjuration, and does serve important functions. The confession acts as a reminder to avoid ego inflation, and also to clear the mind of distractions. Before bathing on the day of the conjuration is a good time to perform the confession, so you go into the conjuration in humility with a pure mind and pure body. Beyond the rite, it is also a reminder of the importance of compassion, which is one of the most powerful virtues the practitioner possesses.

PRACTICE

The sequence of a conjuration follows a number of steps. All the practitioners will already have bathed, prayed, and prepared themselves and have all the required items to hand.

- Enter, seal, and activate the magic circle, including asperging and censing.
- Anoint the crystal or mirror and prepare the seer.
- Perform any preparatory prayers.
- Perform conjuration.
- Engage with spirit and record answers.
- Give license to depart to spirt and any others attracted.
- Open magic circle, record results, and eat.

Activation of the Magic Circle

When all the practitioners are inside the magic circle, the conjurer marks the circumference of each band of the magic circle clockwise with the tip of the sword, seeing it burning with a white fire (the other practitioners should also be concentrating on this). This is commonly done from East to East, though this is not set in stone. Then any names in the band(s) of the magic circle should be traced with the tip of the sword and intoned as this is done. Any symbols such as crosses, pentagrams, and sigils should also be traced.

When this is complete, I recommend the practice described in the *Sworn Book of Honorius*, of drawing two circles in the air above the outer band of the circle,[46] as high in the air as you comfortably can, again from East to East (or however you did the circles on the ground), saying:

'I put the Seal of Solomon over me for salvation and defence, in order that it protects me in the face of the enemy. In the name of the Father and the Son and the Holy Spirit. Amen.'

This serves the function of giving a more three dimensional feel to the magic circle, extending it from a two-dimensional circle to a three-dimensional cylinder.

---

46 For those rare circles that do not have a band, draw the second circle 6in/15cm outside the first.

Incense Prayer

This prayer is to be spoken when fumigating the magic circle with incense. The prayer emphasises the use of fragrance and its virtues in attracting spirits, making the space comfortable for them, masking any background smells, and invigorating the practitioners. The reference to keeping the vision true prior to skrying is an important one.

> Have mercy on me O God according to thy loving kindness, according to the multitude of thy tender mercies.
>
> Blot out my transgressions, cleanse me from my sin, and bless both me, and these thy creatures of kinds, and increase thy virtue, force and might in these odours, that no enemy nor vain visions, nor false delusions enter into them, but through thy virtue, truth, and might, make them helpful to unto me through ✠ Jesus Christ ✠ our Lord, so be it done, Amen, fiat, Amen.[47]

A practical alternative to incense which may be preferable in some circumstances is to use oil burners instead. For this you use appropriate essential oils, or blends of essential oils (ideally matching the recipe if one is specified) diluted in water and released via the burners during the ceremony. The key factor in suffumigation is that the fragrances are pleasing to the spirits, and so using oil burners to release the fragrance achieves the same result without clouds of smoke, or the deterioration in quality of fragrance that occurs as the burning incense reaches the plant material. The absence of smoke can be helpful if you are indoors (remember smoke detectors need disabling if you are burning incense), especially if any of the practitioners suffer from asthma or other bronchial or breathing issues which could be triggered by copious amounts of smoke.

If the spirit being called has a seal or particular attribution (planetary, zodiacal, etc.), then this can also be carved into the candles so that it is released with the fragrance emphasising the connection to the spirit and its seal. If this is a tea light or regular candle, the temperature is not so high that the release of the seal as the candle burns will be painful to it, like the burning of the seal in coercion.

Anointing the Crystal

In *The Secret of Secrets* mention is made of anointing the glass with mugwort juice. Mugwort has a long history of use in skrying, and being made into a tea to aid with psychism and lucid dreaming. Another option is to put a thin film of olive oil over the crystal, as is done in *onykhomanteia* (fingernail divination) to enhance receptivity. Alternatively making a fluid accumulator using an olive oil base with mugwort juice and holy water and using this to anoint the crystal gives the benefits of all combined.

Preliminary Prayer

A preliminary prayer before starting the conjuration can add to its magical momentum. The following is an example from the *Book of Treasure Spirits*.

A Prayer to be said before the calling forth of Elemental or Infernal Powers, or Spirits of Darkness.

> O most high, Immense, Immortal, Incomprehensible, and Omnipotent Lord God of Hosts, the only Creator of Heaven & Earth, & of all things contained therein;

---

[47] Adapted from a prayer in *The Secret of Secrets*, with a couple of minor word changes being the only adjustments made.

who, amongst all other admirable works of the Creation, hast made Man, according to the express Image of thy self, dignifying him with more divine, Celestial & Sublime Excellency, & superior part and participation, cohering with the most high & sacred Godhead, Angels, Heavens, Elements, & Elemental things, & given him an Imperial Sovereignty, over all Sublunar things in the Creation, both Animal, Vegetable, Mineral & Elemental: and next even to thy self under the Heavens, as a benefit and prerogative proper only to Man, & to no other Creature: And who hath likewise given to Man, a Sovereign power over all sublunar Spirits, both Aerial, Terrestrial & otherwise Elemental, residing in Orders & Mansions proper, & other wandering Spirits out of Orders or Mansions proper, both of Light & Darkness, & also Infernal Spirits, & subjected them to his Obedience & Service, whensoever he shall Command, Constrain, Call forth & move them to visible appearance, in order thereunto.

Now then O most high & heavenly God we thy humble Servants, reverently here present in thy holy fear, do beseech thee in thine infinite Mercy & paternal goodness, that all Sublunar Spirits both Elemental and residing in Orders, & otherwise wandering out of Orders, both of Light & Darkness, & also Infernal Powers, may at the reading & rehearsal of our Invocations, Conjurations & Constraints, & by thee commanded, & compelled, & constrained, obediently and peaceably to move & appear visibly, in fair & decent Form: & Shape, & in no wise hurtful, dreadful, terrible or affrightful, or otherwise in any violence or violent manner unto us, & here before us in these Glass Receptacles, or otherwise, to appear out of them here before us, in like serene, fair & decent manner, as shall be most convenient & necessary for any action, thing or matter, that they are called for to such appearances; & to serve & obey us, & to fulfil & go forth in our will, desires & Commandments in all & every several & particular matters & things respectively, wherein their Office & Orders are concerned, or whereunto in any wise they properly appertain; & also to depart from our presence, & obediently & peaceably to return to their Orders & Places of residence, when they have conformed & fulfilled all our Will and Commandments; And that we shall discharge them for the time present, & time future; or shall accordingly give them Licence so to do, and also to be ready from time to time at our Call, & at all times to appear visibly unto us, & to serve & obey us, & to fulfil all our requests whatsoever we shall command them, & also to return to their Orders in peace, when we shall give them Licence to depart thereunto, without violence, injury, harm, prejudice or other mischief or mischievous matter to be done unto us or this Place, or to any other person or places whatsoever. Amen. The Lord bless us & keep us, the Lord make his Face shine upon us, & be gracious unto us: the Lord lift up his Countenance upon us, & give us his Peace.

Conjuration of the Skryer[48]

I conjure you, seer
By the Father ✠ and Son ✠ and Holy Spirit ✠, to whose name all knees are bent and

---

48 Taken from a divination in the *Munich Handbook of Necromancy*, with a minor adaption replacing 'boy' with 'seer'. The translation from the Latin and adaptation of the flow are my own. I have omitted a phrase at the end as it pertained to discovering a murder and is not appropriate here. The anointing of the eyes with holy anointing oil as an aid to spirit vision is given in *De Nigromancia*.

all voices proclaim Hosanna, [Anoint eyes of seer with chrism49]
I conjure you,
By the holy Mary ✠ always virgin,
By the angels ✠ and archangels ✠,
By the four seniors ✠,
And by the thousands of martyrs who stumbled in the name of Christ ✠,
And by holy John the Baptist ✠,
And by all the patriarchs ✠ and prophets ✠,
And by the twelve apostles ✠,
And by the four evangelists ✠,
And by the seventy disciples ✠,
And by all the saints who are holy men ✠ and holy women ✠,
And by all the powers of almighty God ✠, celestial, terrestrial, and infernal, so that whatever you see, you see truly through the power and grace of almighty God ✠.

Conjuration

The process of conjuration usually calls on divine (or infernal) power, as the top of the spiritual hierarchy to which the conjured spiritual being belongs. The conjuration may include reference to acts and/or powers and attributes of this supreme power, as well as a description of the gateway image[50] of the spiritual creature being called. The divine names used, particularly in hymnology where there are strings of names, may be seen as acting as a reservoir or battery of divine power which the practitioner draws upon as part of the process.

It is important to be aware that you may need to repeat the conjuration several times. If the spirit does not attend after the first recitation of the conjuration, repeat it. The conjuration should be spoken in a clear, firm and steady voice.

Important note for practice – whenever you see a cross in the text in grimoire conjurations, it means make the sign of the cross with your hand. If the text does contain crosses, you may wish to hold the sword in your hand under the book (or place it in a scabbard if worn), leaving a free hand with which to make the crosses. An alternative to this is to hold the sword downwards by the cross-bar so it is in the shape of a cross, thus making the cross with a cross.

In the original grimoires divine names and spirit names are often written in red or bold, indicating extra emphasis is to be placed on them. This is usually done by intoning these names rather than speaking them. Additionally, if you are reciting Psalms, especially in Latin, you may find singing them improves the atmosphere and your personal exhilaration.

With the emphasis of the voice in conjuration, the question of singing and the use of music in the grimoires is an obvious one. An intriguing reference is found in section seven of the *Cambridge Book of Magic* ('A general rule for the working of necromancy'). In the magic circle construction it states 'Take the sword or the hallowed chalk and draw the outermost circle, and round about *sing* of this wise while thou drawest the circle.'[51] The charm 'To have coins as often as we please' in *Secrets of Solomon* also refers to singing to the lyre, combining both singing and use of a musical instrument.

Several grimoires mention the use of musical instruments. Bells are used as part of the conjuration in the *Hygromanteia, Magia Naturalis et Innaturalis,* and *Pneumatologia Occulta*. A ram

---

49 It is hugely important that the oil be on the eyelids in minimal quantity; any oil in the eyes may result in extreme pain and the need to stop the whole conjuration.

50 A gateway image is the form by which a spiritual creature is perceived, acting as an agreed interface between the spirit and the conjuror. This concept may be seen in statues, charms, art, and literature.

51 Italics mine, for emphasis.

horn is used for the same purpose in *Sixth and Seventh Books of Moses*, and a whistle in the *Sworn Book of Honorius* and *Secrets of Solomon*. *Magia Naturalis et Innaturalis* indicates that music is pleasing to the spirits and encourages the practitioners, saying, 'if you and your partner who is with you can play music mellifluously, then do it incessantly as thus they appear sooner'. The theme of playing music to attract spirits is also well documented in fairy folklore.

Checking the Contact

When you perform a conjuration, it can draw the attention of other spirits as well as the one you are seeking to connect with. On the appearance of the spirit, it should be asked something like:

'Are you the same, whom we have moved & called forth to visible appearance here before us at this time, known by the name (N)?'[52]

Then, if it answers, continue, and if not repeat the question. Then it will tell its name or depart. Note if it refuses and is unfriendly, and not the spirit you were conjuring, you may choose to perform a banishing. *Janua Magica Resarata* gives a detailed description of the process.

When the spirit contact has been established the conjurer should ask their questions if they are seeking information, or obtain an oath from the spirit to perform the task asked of it. As spirits can be as tricky as lawyers, be sure to specify a timeframe for any task to be performed within, and have a list of questions prepared so you are not distracted from your objectives.

After the spirit contact and information is provided, or agreement for a task made, the license to depart is the last stage of the conjuration. Some grimoires have these, but many do not. However it is an essential component and the license to depart should always be performed. The license to depart is not only for the spirit that has been conjured, but also any others which may have been attracted or turned up. Here follows an example:

The Licence to depart

'O thou Spirit N: because thou hast very diligently answered our demands, & was very willing to come at our (first) Call, We do here Licence thee to depart unto thy proper place, without doing any harm, injury or danger to Man or Beast (depart I say) & be ever ready to come at our Call, being Exorcised and Conjured, by the sacred rites of Magick, We charge thee to depart peaceably & quietly, And the Peace of God be ever continued between us & thee. Amen.'[53]

Afterword

Sometimes, for no obvious reason, a conjuration does not appear to work, even when everything seems to have been done correctly. This could be because the spirit is otherwise occupied, or something was missed. This is not cause for being disheartened; conjuration does not have a guaranteed one hundred percent success rate. In such instances the fourth P comes in to play – Persistence. After checking through your records and assessing if there is anything that can be improved, choose a suitable date and perform the conjuration again.

Another consideration is that sometimes it seems like nothing has happened, and then you get the answers you were looking for in a dream. Spirit communication in dreams is not uncommon, as it is an easier interface for contact between them and us. As such it is

---

52 N is the common abbreviation used in many grimoires to denote the name of the spirit, which is substituted in appropriately.
53 *Book of Treasure Spirits*.

particularly important to record your dreams in the run-up to a conjuration, and in the days following.

It may be noted that I have not included the cursing sequence for recalcitrant spirits found in some grimoires such as the *Goetia*. This is because in over forty years I have never needed to use the sequence, as I have always found that co-operation works much better than coercion/compulsion.

Essential Reading

Leitch, Aaron (2005) *Secrets of the Magical Grimoires*. Woodbury: Llewellyn. Strongly recommended reading for a wide-ranging perspective on working with a range of grimoires.

Miller, Jason (2022) *Consorting with Spirits. Your Guide to Working with Invisible Allies*. York Beach: Weiser Books. Excellent practical work on working with spirits. Essential reading whether you are new or have been practicing for decades.

Nottingham, Gary St. Michael (2015) *Liber Terribilis: being an instruction on the Seventy-Two Spirits of the Goetia*. Glastonbury: Avalonia. Good primer work for the *Goetia* which can be applied to other conjurations as well.

Savedow, Steve (2022) *Goetic Evocation*. West Yorkshire: Hadean Press. Great work on working with the Goetic spirits. The information and perspectives in this work are valuable for working with other grimoires.

Skinner, Stephen (2021) *Techniques of Solomonic Magic*. Singapore: Golden Hoard Press. Important and detailed study which elucidates the Solomonic strand of the grimoires and working them.

Skinner, Stephen & Rankine, David (2005) *Keys to the Gateway of Magic*. Singapore: Golden Hoard Press. Includes a lot of very useful information regarding behaviour prior to conjuration, and the nature of spirits, as well as the spirit testing sequence.

Timeline

This timeline demonstrates the development of the grimoire tradition and includes early influential works. Note that the dates are of the first known manuscript or publication; this does not mean it is the original date as many manuscripts have been destroyed or lost over the centuries.

Date	Work	Language	Comments
C12 through C2 BCE	Hebrew Bible/Old Testament	Hebrew, Greek, and Aramaic	Core work of Christian theology
C8 BCE	*Odyssey* and *Iliad*	Greek	Epic and influential poems by Homer
C6 BCE	*Ketef Hinnom Scrolls*	Hebrew	Oldest surviving Old Testament fragment
C2 BCE	*Dead Seas Scrolls*	Hebrew	Earliest surviving collection of Old Testament fragments
C2 BCE	*De Virtutibus Lapidum*	Greek	Early Greco-Egyptian lapidary by Damigeron
C2 BCE through C7 CE	*Greek Magical Papyri*	Greek, Demotic, and Coptic	Large collection of spells, charms, and conjurations
C2 BCE through C6 CE	*Supplementum Magicum*	Greek	Collection of magical papyri and amulets
C1 CE	*New Testament*	Greek and Aramaic	Core work of Christian theology
50-70 CE	*De Materia Medica*	Greek	Work on healing by Dioscorides with attributions of plants, including stones
77 CE	*Historia Naturalis*	Latin	Encyclopedic work by Pliny the Elder, includes a volume on precious stones
C1 through 2	*Cyranides*	Greek	Work on magical attributions of animals, plants, and stones
C2	*Sepher Yetzirah*	Hebrew	First and most important Kabbalistic text
C2-3	*London-Leiden Papyrus*	Demotic Egyptian	Late magical papyri found as PDM XIV

C2-3	*Testament of Solomon*	Hebrew, Greek, Arabic	First known dating
C2-12	*Ancient Christian Magic*	Coptic	Collection of Coptic magical papyri
Early C4	*Sepher ha-Razim*	Hebrew	First known dating
C4	*Codex Vaticanus*	Greek	Oldest surviving Bible
C4-5	*Herbarium Apuleii Platonici*	Latin	Influential herbal
Late C5	*Celestial Hierarchies*	Greek	Origin of the angelic hierarchies by Pseudo-Dionysus the Areopagite
Early C7	*Etymologiae*	Latin	Encyclopedic work by Isidore of Seville, includes work on stones
C8-10	*Sword of Moses*	Hebrew and Aramaic	Jewish magical text, referenced in other works
C9	*Shiur Qoma*	Hebrew	Jewish Merkavah text
Mid to late C9	*De Imaginibus*	Arabic	Work on planetary image magic by Thābit ibn Qurrah, original lost
C10	*Sepher Shimmush Tehillim*	Hebrew	Jewish Psalm text
900-950	*Leechbook of Bald*	English	Significant herbal work
Mid C10	*Ghāyat al-Hākim*	Arabic	The original *Picatrix*
c.1050	*On the Operation of Dæmons*	Greek	Discursive text by Michael Psellus
1061-81	*De Lapidibus*	Latin	Lapidary by Marbodius
1126-30	*Liber Prestigiorum*	Latin	Translation of *De Imaginibus* by Adelard of Bath
1135-53	*De Imaginibus*	Latin	Translation by John of Seville
1144	*Liber de compositionae alchemiae*	Latin	Translation of first alchemical work available in Europe by Robert of Chester
1145	*Liber Lunae*	Latin	Translation from Arabic by Robert of Chester
C13	*Sepher Rezial Hemelach*	Hebrew	First references

TIMELINE

1220–1240	*Almandal*	Latin	First mention by William of Auvergne
1225	*Ars Notoria (Notary Art)*	Latin	First MS
C13	*Almandal*	Latin	First appearance in *De Consecratione Lapidum*
Mid C13	*Speculum Astronomiae*	Latin	Classification of astronomy and magic attributed to Albertus Magnus
1253	*Lapidario*	Castilian	Collection of four different lapidaries
1256	*Picatrix*	Castilian	First non-Arab translation
1258	*Picatrix*	Latin	First Latin translation
Pre 1259	*Liber Razielis*	Latin	First Latin MS of *Sepher Raziel*
1259	*Sepher Raziel*	Castilian	Translation lost
c.1260	*Speculum Astronomiae*	Latin	Albertus Magnus cataloguing work
1276–9	*Libro de las formas et las ymagenes*	Castilian	Compilation including parts of *Picatrix*, *Liber Razielis Lapidario*, and others
1280	*Libro de Astromagia*	Castilian	Compilation including parts of *Picatrix*, *Liber Razielis* and others
1290	*Zohar*	Aramaic	First publication by Moses de Leon
1310	*Clavicula Salomonis*	Latin	First mention by Peter of Abano
1311	*Liber Visionum*	Latin	First MS of John of Morigny's adaption of *Ars Notoria*
1343	*Sworn Book of Honorius (Liber Iuratus)*	Latin	First known MS owned by Ganellus
1346	*Summa Sacre Magice*	Latin	Huge significant grimoire compilation and work by Ganellus
C14	*Elucidation of Necromancy*	Latin	Likely date of creation
Late C14	*Liber Lunae*	Latin	First known surviving MS

Early C15	*Book of the Seven Rings of the Planets of Messalah*	Latin	First known MS
c.1400	*Liber Consecrationum*	Latin	First known MS
Early to mid C15	*Munich Handbook of Necromancy*	Latin & German	Only known MS
C15	*Annulorum Experimenta*	Latin	First known MS
1440	*Book of Wisdom of Apollonius of Tyana*	Greek	First known MS
1440	*Hygromanteia*	Greek	First known MS
1441–45	*Book of Angels, Rings, Characters and Images of the Planets*	Latin	Only known MS
1447	*Liber Runarum*	Latin	First known MS
1493	*Le Grand Albert*	Latin	First publication
1494	*Fasciculus Rerum Geomanticarum*	Latin	Only known MS, published as *Necromancy in the Medici Library* (2020)
1500	*Steganographia*	Latin	Trithemius
1500	*Le Grand Albert*	French	First French edition
1505	*Herpentills Salomonis*	Latin	First publication
1508	*De Septem Secundeis*	Latin	Trithemius
1508	*Antipalus Maleficiorum*	Latin	Trithemius
1509–10	*Three Books of Occult Philosophy*	Latin	Manuscript written by Agrippa
1511	*De Lapidibus*	Latin	First publication
1517	*De Arte Cabalstica*	Latin	First publication by Pico della Mirandola
Early C16	*Sword of Moses*	Hebrew and Aramaic	First known complete edition in *Sefer Shoshan Yesod Ha'olam* by Rabbi Yosef Tirshom
Early C16	*Art of Drawing Spirits into Crystals*	Latin	Trithemius, MS lost, published in *The Magus* (1801)
1533	*Three Books of Occult Philosophy*	Latin	First publication

1532–1558	*Cambridge Book of Magic*	Latin	Only known MS
1550–1650	*Galdrabók*	Latin	First known MS
C16	*Key of Solomon*	Latin	First known MS in Latin
C16	*Key of Solomon*	Italian	First known Italian MS
C16	*Key of Solomon*	German	First known German MS
C16	*De Nigromancia*	Latin	First known MS
C16	*Almuchabosa Absegalim Alkakib Albaon*	Latin	First known MS
Mid C16	*Book of Consecrations (Liber Consecrationum)*	English	First known English translation
Mid C16	*Le Livre des Esperitz*	French	Only known MS
1551	*Sepher Shimmush Tehillim*	Hebrew	First publication
1552	*Sepher Yetzirah*	Latin	First translation by Gulielmus Postellus
1558	*Magia Naturalis*	Latin	First publication by Giambatista della Porta
1558	*Zohar*	Hebrew	First translation published
1559	*Fourth Book of Occult Philosophy*	Latin	First publication
1559	*Heptameron*	Latin	First publication
1559	*Arbatel*	Latin	First publication
1559–1630	*Secrets of Solomon*	Latin	Date range for first MS
1563	*Pseudomonarchia Daemonum*	Latin	First publication
1564	*Sepher Raziel*	English	First known English translation
1565	*Heptameron*	French	First known French publication
1567	*An Excellent Booke of the Arte of Magicke*	English	Only known MS
1567	*Heptameron*	German	First known German publication
1572	*Key of Solomon*	English	First dated English MS
1577	*Secret of Secrets*	English	Only known MS
1577–83	*Book of Oberon*	Latin	Only known MS

1583	*Book of the Offices of Spirits*	Latin	First MS in *Book of Oberon*, likely to be decades older
1584	*Enchiridion of Pope Leo III*	French	First publication
1584	*Discoverie of Witchcraft*	English	First publication
1590	*Crafte of Conjurynge*	English	Only known MS
1591	*Archidoxes of Magic*	Latin	First posthumous publication
1592	*De Heptarchia Mystica*	English	First copy of MS by John Dee
Late C16	*Antiphoner Notebook*	English	Only known MS
Late C16	*De Nigromancia*	English	First known English translation
Late C16	*Book of Saint Cyprian*	Portuguese	First known manuscript mention
Early C17	*Of Angels, Demons & Spirits*	English	Only known MS
C17	*Book of Gold*	French	Only known MS
C17	*Key of Solomon*	Dutch	First known Dutch MS
1600	*Boxgrove Manual*	English	Only known MS
c.1600	*Tuba Veneris*	Latin	First known MS, attributed to John Dee
1605	*Antipalus Maleficiorum*	Latin	Posthumous first publication
1605-8	*Tabula Bonorum Angelorum Invocationes*	English	First MS, John Dee
1606	*Steganographia*	Latin	Posthumous first publication
1608	*Abramelin*	German	First known MS
1609	*Der Schlüssel von der Zwang der Höllen*	German	First known publication
1612	*Magia Naturalis et Innaturalis*	German	First known MS
1620	*Magical Calendar*	Latin	First engraving
1630-6	*Grimoire of Arthur Gauntlet*	English	Only MS
Early to mid C17	*Janua Magica Reserata*	English	First known MS

TIMELINE

1641	*Goetia*	English	First known MS bound with others as *Lemegeton*
1641	*Theurgia-Goetia*	English	First known MS bound with others as *Lemegeton*
1641	*Ars Paulina*	English	First known MS bound with others as *Lemegeton*
1641	*Ars Almadel*	English	First known MS bound with others as *Lemegeton*
1641	*Nine Celestial Keys*	English	First known MS
1642	*Thirty-Two Paths of Wisdom*	Latin	First publication by Joannes Rittangelius
1649	*Book of Treasure Spirits*	English	Only known MS
1651	*Three Books of Occult Philosophy*	English	Translation by John French published
1655	*Arbatel*	English	Translation by Robert Turner published
1655	*Heptameron*	English	Translation by Robert Turner published
1656	*Archidoxes of Magic*	English	Translation by Robert Turner published
1660	*Pneumatologia Occulta et Vera*	German	Date given as origin of text
1662–1664	*Theomagia*	English	First publication
1665	*Fourth Book of Occult Philosophy*	English	English translation by Robert Turner
1665	*Discoverie of Witchcraft*	English	Edition with extra chapters published
1670	*Grimoire of Pope Honorius*	French	First publication
1686	*Semiphoras and Shemhamphorash*	Latin	First publication
C18	*Embodiment of the Unnatural Magic*	German	First known publication
Early C18	*Experimentir-Buch*	German	First known MS
1700	*Sepher Maphteah Shelomoh*	Hebrew	First known MS
1701	*Sepher Rezial Hemelach*	Hebrew	First publication
1706	*Le Grand Albert*	French	Most complete edition

1706	*Petit Albert*	French	First publication
1725	*Egyptian Secrets of Albertus Magnus*	German	First publication
1725	*Magia Ordinis, Artium et Scientiarum abstrusarum*	Latin	First known MS
1725	*Book of the Mightiest Spirits*	German	First known MS
1725	*Abramelin*	German	First publication
1734	*Sixth and Seventh Books of Moses*	German	First publication of pamphlets
1743	*Nigromantisches Kunst-Buch*	German	First known publication
Mid C18	*Grimoire of Armadel*	French	First known MS
1750	*Ars Phytonica*	German	German transcription
1750	*Grand Grimoire/Red Dragon*	French	First publication
1788	*Sepher Shimmush Tehillim*	German	Translation by Godfrey Selig
1790	*Véritable Magie Noire*	French	First publication
c.1795	*A Most Rare Compendium of the Whole Magical Art*	German and Latin	Only known MS
1796	*A Collection of Magical Secrets*	French	Only known MS
1797	*Clavis Inferni*	Latin, Greek, and Hebrew	Only known MS
C19	*Book of Saint Cyprian*	Portuguese / Spanish	First publications
1801	*The Magus*	English	First publication
1805	*Libellus St. Gertrudis*	German	First known MS
1810	*Key of Solomon*	Czech	First known Czech MS
1817	*Grimorium Verum*	French	First publication
1818	*Dictionnaire Infernal*	French	First publication
1820	*Black Pullet*	French	First publication
1821–26	*Zauber Bibliotek*	German	Six-volume set by Georg Conrad Horst, includes *Pneumatologia Occulta*

TIMELINE

1834–50	*Complete Book of Magic Science*	English	Date range for Hockley's creation
1845–9	*Das Kloster*	German	Twelve volume set by Scheible, contents include *Abramelin, Arbatel, Grimoire of Pope Honorius, Sixth and Seventh Books of Moses, Semiphoras and Shemhamphorash, Verus Jesuitarum Libellus*
1846	*Verus Jesuitarum Libellus*	Latin	Published in *Das Kloster*
1849	*Magia Naturalis et Innaturalis*	German	Published in *Das Kloster*
1849	*Sixth and Seventh Books of Moses*	German	Published in *Das Kloster*
1863	*Dictionnaire Infernal*	French	Illustrated edition
1868	*Grimorium Verum*	Italian	First Italian edition
1869	*Egyptian Secrets of Albertus Magnus*	English	First English edition
1875	*Verus Jesuitarum Libellus*	English	Translated by Herbert Irwin
1880	*Sixth and Seventh Books of Moses*	English	First English edition
1887	*Black Dragon*	French	First publication
1906	*Grimoire Sympathia*	English	Frist publication
1916	*Supreme Black, Red & Infernal Magic*	Spanish	First publication
1960	*Secret Grimoire of Turiel*	English	First publication
2021	*Sworn and Secret Grimoire*	English	First publication

Encyclopaedic Entries

The grimoires are magical texts set within an Abrahamic cosmology (mainly Christian but with some Islamic and Judaic) which focus on spirit contact through conjuration and divination, usually with a magic circle, and commonly include a spirit list. Whilst there have been many excellent books written in different fields of magic in the last twenty years, few of them fit this criteria (the obvious exception being Jake Stratton-Kent's *Sworn and Secret Grimoire* which is included). Around ninety of the following subchapters are on grimoires; the other ten are texts from before the grimoires that were important to the development of the tradition, or contemporary works that contributed to its proliferation or clarification (e.g., *Antipalus Maleficorum*). Modern works which develop themes found in texts such as the Greek Magical Papyri are generally developments of that tradition and are not included here.

One hundred griomoires seemed a good end point for the first edition. The second edition will be expanded; at the time of writing approximately twenty chapters are drafted of Arabic texts and obscure texts as well as other texts which contributed in some way to the tradition as a whole.

The Holy Bible

Date: C12-2 BCE (Old Testament), C1 CE (New Testament).
Language: Hebrew (Hebrew Bible/Old Testament), Greek and Aramaic (New Testament).
Influences: Semitic mythologies, particularly including Canaanite and Ugaritic.
Provenance: The Hebrew Bible was written from C12 BCE to a final form around C2 BCE. The New Testament was written in the latter half of C1 CE.
MSS: Ketef Hinnom Scrolls (two silver amuletic scrolls containing earliest recorded extract, the priestly blessing from Numbers 6:24-26, C7 CE) Dead Sea Scrolls (C2 BCE, fragmentary but containing parts of every book except Esther from the Hebrew Bible). The earliest copies of the Bible, in Greek, are known as the four great uncials.[54] They are Codex Vaticanus (Bibl. Vat. Gr. 1209) (C4 CE), which is the oldest known copy of a (largely) complete Bible; Codex Siniaticus (British Library Additional MS 43725) (C4 CE), which is the first Bible containing the complete New Testament; Codex Alexandrinus, which is another early largely complete Bible (British Library Royal MS 1 D V-VIII) (C5 CE); and Codex Ephraemi Rescriptus (BNF Greek MS 9) (C5 CE), which contains some of the Old Testament and most of the New Testament. There are numerous later manuscripts of the Bible.
Circle: N/A.
Tools: Altar, Ark of the Covenant, Censers, High Priest's Breastplate, Serpent Wand, Urim and Thummim.[55]
Spirit List: Abaddon, Amon, Apis, Artemis, Asherah, Ashima, Asmodeus, Astarte, Atargatis, Azazel, Baal, Baalzebub (Beelzebub), Babylon, Behemoth, Bel (Marduk), Beliar (Belial), Chemosh, Dagon, Dionysus, Dioscuri, Gabriel, Hermes, Holy Spirit, Legion,[56] Leviathan, Lilith, Michael, Milcom, Molech, Nanea, Nebo (Nabu), Nisroch, Rahab, Raphael, Rephan, Satan,[57] Tammuz, Unknown God, Wickedness, Wisdom (Shekinah), Zeus.

The Text

The Bible is the elephant in the room in the grimoire tradition. As the sacred foundational text of Christianity, it contains and expounds upon the theology which underlies the grimoire tradition. Biblical figures and their exploits are frequently referenced in conjurations, and textual quotes are used extensively in prayers, conjurations, magic circles, and pentacles. Despite this, the Bible receives relatively little attention or discussion considering the importance it holds.

The Hebrew Bible, or Tanakh,[58] was comprised from different sources over a period of centuries, into a largely established from by the C6 CE. It is divided into three main sections. The first of these is the Torah ('teaching'), containing Genesis, Exodus, Leviticus, Numbers, and Deuteronomy (also later known as the Pentateuch or Five Books of Moses). These texts focus

---

54 Uncial is a majuscule (upper case) script.
55 The form and use of these items are unknown. They are thought to have been used for a yes/no answer in divination.
56 Strictly speaking this name is for a group of demons.
57 Referring to a non-specific spiritual creature (or even person) who takes the role of adversary (the meaning of Satan). This is why multiple Satans are referred to at times, e.g., in the Aramaic curse bowls (which also mention multiple Liliths). Later theology would see this word equated with the devil (Gk. Diabolos).
58 Tanakh is formed from the first letter of each of the three parts, T(orah), N(evi'im) and K(etuvim), giving an early example of the form of gematria known as notariqon.

on the narratives of creation and the foundation of Judaism along with instructions and rules. The second section is Nevi'im ('prophets'), containing the lives, prophecies, and anecdotes of the major prophets in Joshua, Judges, Samuel, Kings, Isaiah, Jeremiah, and Ezekiel, and the minor prophets Hosea, Joel, Amos, Obadiah, Jonah, Micah, Nahum, Habakkuk, Zephaniah, Haggai, Zechariah, and Malachi. The third section, Ketuvim ('writings'), focuses on theology and poetry (both devotional and erotic) and contains Psalms, Proverbs, Song of Songs, Ruth, Lamentations, Ecclesiastes, Esther, Daniel, Ezra, Nehemiah, and Chronicles.

The Old Testament is comprised of the material from the Hebrew Bible, restructured in places. It contains thirty-nine books in Protestant versions, and forty-six in Catholic ones. Seven books were removed by Martin Luther as not fitting in with the doctrines he espoused. These remain in the Catholic Bible and are known as the deuterocanonical books.[59] Both Protestant and Catholic bibles contain the same twenty-seven books in the New Testament. The term Old Testament was first used by the Greek bishop Melito of Sardis in C2 CE. The New Testament was first listed in its complete form in 367 CE by Bishop Athanasius of Alexandria.

Old Testament books in sequence: Genesis, Exodus, Leviticus, Numbers, Deuteronomy (the Pentateuch); Joshua, Judges, Ruth, 1 Samuel (1 Kings), 2 Samuel (2 Kings), 1 Kings (3 Kings), 2 Kings (4 Kings), 1 Chronicles, 2 Chronicles, Ezra, Nehemiah, [Tobit], [Judith], Esther, [1 Maccabees], [2 Maccabees], Job, Psalms, Proverbs, Ecclesiastes, Song of Solomon/Song of Songs (Canticles), [Wisdom], [Ben Sira/Ecclesiasticus], Isaiah, Jeremiah, Lamentations, [Baruch], Ezekiel, Daniel, Hosea, Joel, Amos, Obadiah, Jonah, Micah, Nahum, Habakkuk, Zephaniah, Haggai, Zechariah, Malachi.

New Testament Books: Matthew, Mark, Luke, John, Acts, Romans, 1 Corinthians, 2 Corinthians, Galatians, Ephesians, Philippians, Colossians, 1 Thessalonians, 2 Thessalonians, 1 Timothy, 2 Timothy, Titus, Philemon, Hebrews, James, 1 Peter, 2 Peter, 1 John, 2 John, 3 John, Jude, Revelation.

Genesis, containing the creation myth, is one of the most significant of the Old Testament books. Lines from the opening verses are used at times in conjurations and on magical seals. Additionally, it forms part of the foundation of Kabbalah, both in its symbolism and influence on the theology and symbolism set out in *Sepher Yetzirah* and discussed in later texts like the Zohar.

Exodus sets out the paraphernalia of the Temple, along with recipes such as the incense and holy oil (used as the standard oil in grimoires where one is not stated). Leviticus contains instructions to the Israelites, such as the burnt offerings, grain offerings, communion services, purification services, special cases for purification offerings, reparation offerings, communion sacrifices, ceremony of ordination, conduct of the priests, ritual purity, impurity, and prohibitions.

Numbers includes material on purification, including the use of hyssop and water, the bronze serpent (Nehushtan), and offerings at the feasts. Deuteronomy discusses instructions for the Israelites, and the Deuteronomic code. Joshua includes the use of ram horns to bring down the walls of Jericho. 1 Samuel has the interesting episode of the witch of Endor summoning the shade of Samuel. 2 Samuel includes the Song of Thanksgiving (which reappears slightly reworded as Psalm 18) and the introduction of Solomon. 1 Kings describes the building of the temple. 1 Chronicles also includes a song derived from a number of Psalms (105:1-15, 96:1-13, 106:1).

Tobit has the first named angel appearance in the Bible (Raphael), as opposed to previous references to the angel of the lord. Job contains a chapter on where Wisdom is to be found,

---

59 Indicated in the list of books by being in square brackets.

ascribing a feminine nature to wisdom, implying the Shekinah (Job 28);[60] and descriptions of the primal chaos beings Behemoth and Leviathan (Job 40).

Psalms contains one hundred and fifty individual psalms which quickly entered into Jewish folk magic, with references for apotropaic, coercive, and healing magic evident by the C3 CE, and lines from them are also found in the PGM. They had a huge influence on the grimoire tradition, perhaps most visibly in the pentacles of the *Key of Solomon*, the Shemhamphorash seals of Rudd's *Goetia*, and the *Abramelin*.[61] Works dedicated entirely to working magic with the psalms were also created, such as *Sepher Shimmush Tehillim* and the *Book of Gold*.[62] It should be noted that the introductions to the individual psalms often mention playing specific instruments and sometimes refer to them as songs. The psalms are often referred to by their incipit, i.e., the opening line, as a way to identify them. One interesting theme found in some of the psalms is battle magic, perhaps continuing this practice from ancient Egypt.[63]

Proverbs sees further references to the feminine wisdom, including identification as the first being with God, i.e., the Shekinah. She reappears in the books of Wisdom and Ben Sira. Ezekiel gives a detailed description of the holy living creatures (angels), and an example of sympathetic battle magic (Ez 4-5).

Of the gospels, the most commonly quoted is Mark, especially the incipit (1:1) 'In the beginning was the Word'. The New Testament focuses on the life of Jesus (the four gospels) and other contemporaries. It also emphasises the Holy Spirit as a distinct entity. Jesus (and to an extent the Holy Spirit) are referenced heavily in the grimoire tradition, and he is prominent in many charms, especially historiolae. The Virgin Mary is found in earlier grimoires like the *Sworn Book of Honorius* and *Ars Notoria* but is largely absent from grimoires written after C14 CE.

Essential Reading

There are numerous editions of the Bible in print and online, so I am not listing a specific edition here.

'Priests of the Tabernacle', from Bible Pictures and What They Teach Us by Charles Foster

---

60 For detailed discussion of the development of the Shekinah, and her relationship to Asherah and other early wisdom goddesses, see Rankine & d'Este (2011) *The Cosmic Shekinah: A Historical Study of the Goddess of the Old Testament and Kabbalah*.
61 For discussion of this see Rankine 2010:11-15.
62 Both of these works have their own subchapters giving more details.
63 See Ritner (1993) *The Mechanics of Ancient Egyptian Magical Practice*.

Greek Magical Papyri (Papyri Graecae Magicae, or PGM)

Date: C2 BCE – C7 CE.
Language: Greek, Demotic and Coptic.
Influences: Babylonian, Christian, Egyptian, Gnostic, Greek, and Jewish elements are syncretised throughout the text; *Book of the Dead, Testament of Solomon, Odyssey, Iliad*.
Provenance: Part of the Chaldean 'wizard's hoard' obtained by Jean d'Anastasi (1780-1857).
MSS: P. Berol inv. 5025 (I, C4/5 CE);[64] P. Berol inv. 5026 (II, C4 CE); Louvre no. 2396 (III, C4 CE); P. BN Suppl. Gr. no. 574 (IV, C4 CE); P. London 46 (V, C4 CE); P. Holm p.42 (Va, ND); P. London 47 (VI, C2/3 CE); P. London 121 (VII, C3/4 CE); P. London 122 (VIII, C4/5 CE); P. London 123 (IX, C4/5 CE); P. London 124 (X, C4/5 CE); P. London 125 (XIa, C5 CE); P. London 147 (XIb, C3 CE); P. London 148 (XIc, C2/3 CE); P. Lugd. Bat. J384 (XII, C4 CE); P. Lugd. Bat. J395 (XIII, C4 CE); P. London Demotic 10070 (XIV, C3 CE); P. Lugd. Bat. J383 (XIV, C3 CE); P. Alex. Inv. 491 (XV, C3 CE); Louvre no. 3378 (XVI, C1 CE); P. Gr. 1167 (XVIIa, C4 CE); P. Gr. 1179 (XVIIb, C2 CE); P. Gr. 574 (XVIIc, ND); BSM BGU III.955 (XVIIIa, C3/4 CE); BSM BGU III.956 (XVIIIb, C3/4 CE); BSM P. Berol. Inv. 9909 (XIXa, C4/5 CE); BSM P. Berol. Inv. 11737 (XIXb, C4 CE); BSM P. Berol. Inv. 7504 + P. Amh. Ii Col II(A) + P. Oxy. Inedit (XX, C1, BCE); BSM P. Berol. Inv. 9566 verso (XXI, C2/3 CE); BSM BGU IV.1026 (XXIIa, C4/5 CE); BSM P. Berol. Inv. 13895 (XXIIb, C4 CE); P. Oxy. 412 (XXIII, C3 CE); P. Oxy. 886 (XXIVa, C3 CE); P. Oxy. 887 (XXIVb, C3 CE); P. Oxy. 959 (XXVa, C3 CE); P. Un. Bibl. Freiburg unnumbered (XXVb, C6 CE); P. Cairo 10434 (XXVc, ND); P. Florence unnumbered (XXVd, ND); P. Oxy. 1477 (XXVI, C3/4 CE); P. Oxy. 1478 (XXVII, C3/4 CE); P. Oxy. 2061 (XVIIIa, C5 CE); P. Oxy. 2062 (XXVIIIb, C6 CE); P. Oxy. 2063 (XXVIIIc, C6 CE); P. Oxy. 1383 (XXIX, C3 CE); UCL P. Haw. 312 (XXXII, C2 CE); P. Tebt. II.275 (XXXIII, C3 CE); P. Fay. 5 (XXXIV, C2/3 CE); PSI I.29 (XXXV, C5 CE); P. Oslo I,1 (XXXVI, C4 CE); P. Oslo I,2 (XXXVII, C4 CE); P. Oslo I,3 (XXXVIII, C4 CE); P. Oslo I,4 (XIX, C4 CE); P. Gr. 1 (XL, C4 CE); P. Gr. 339/P. Rain. 4 (XLI, C5/6 CE); P. Gr. 331/P. Rain. 8 (XLII, C6 CE); P. Gr. 335/P. Rain. 9 (XLIII, C5 CE); P. Gr. 328/P. Rain. 10 (XLIV, ND); P. Gr. 334/P. Rain. 11 (XLV, C6/7 CE); P. Gr. 332/P. Rain. 12 (XLVI, C5 CE); Vienna inv. no. 8034/P. Rain. 2 (XLVII, ND); Vienna inv. no. 8031/P. Rain. 6 (XLVIII, C6/7 CE); Vienna inv. no. 8035/P. Rain. 7 (XLIX, ND); Vienna inv. no. 8033/P. Rain. (L, C6 CE); P. Gr. 9.418 (LI, C3 CE); P. Gr. 9.429 (LII, C3 CE); Ann Arbor cryptogr. Pap. (C1/2 CE); Giessen inv. no. 266/P. Iand. 87 (LVIII, C4 CE); P. Cairo 10563 (LIX, C2/3 CE); P. Brux. In. E6390, 6391 (LX, C6 CE); P. Brit. Mus. 10588 (LXI, C3 CE); P. Warren 21 (LXII, C3 CE); P. Gr. 323 (LXIII, C2/3 CE); P. Gr. 29273 (LXIV, C4 CE); P. Gr. 29272 (LXV, C6/7 CE); P. Cairo 60139 (LXVI, C3/4 CE); P. Cairo 60140 (LXVII, ND); P. Cairo 60636 (LXVIII, C2/3 CE); P. Mich. III, 156 (LXIX, C2 CE); P. Mich. III, 154 (LXX, C3/4 CE); P. Mich. III, 155 (LXXI, C2/3 CE); P. Oslo III, 75 (LXXII, C1/2 CE); P. Harr. 55 (LXXVII, C2 CE); P. Heid. 2170 (LXXVIII, C3 CE); P. Gr. I, 18 (LXXX, C3/4 CE); P. Oxy. 1866 (LXXXI, C4 CE); P. Vars. 4 (LXXXII, C3 CE), P. Princ. II.107 (LXXXIII, ND), P. Princ. II.76 (LXXXIV, C3 CE), P. Harris 56 (LXXXV, C1/2 CE), P. Rein. II.89 inv. 2176 (LXXXVI, C4 CE), P. Erlangen 37 (LXXXVII, C4 CE), P. Princ. III.159 (LXXXVIII, C3/4 CE), P. Lund Univ. Bibl. IV.12 inv. no. 32 (LXXXIX, C4 CE), P. Med. Inv. no. 23 (XC, C4/5 CE), P. Michael 27 (XCI, C3/4 CE), P. Merton II.58 (XCII, C3 CE), P. Ant. II.65 (XCIII, C5 CE), P. Ant. II.66 (XCIV, C5 CE), P. Ant. III.140 (XCV, C5/6 CE), P. Palau Rib. Inv. 126 (XCVI, C4/5 CE), P. Köln inv. 1886 (XCVII, C3/4 CE), P. Köln inv. 1982 (XCVIII, C3 CE), P. Köln inv. 2283

---

64 The Roman numeral refers to the PGM number, followed by the date of the papyrus when known.

(XCIX, C5/6 CE), P. Köln inv. 2283 (C, C5/6 CE), P. Köln inv. 3323 (CI, C5 CE), P. Oxy. 2753 (CII, C4 CE), P.S.A. Athen. 70 (CIII, C2 CE), PUG I.6 (CIV, C3 CE), P. Berol. 21227 (CV, C3/4 CE), P. Berol. 21165 (CVI, C3/4 CE), P. Köln inv. 5512 (CVII, C3/4 CE), P. Köln inv. 5514 (CVIII, C3/4 CE), P. Oxy. 50.4 B23 J(1-3)b (CIX, C4 CE), P. Wash. Univ. inv. 181 (CX, C2/3 CE), P. Wash. Univ. inv. 139 (CXI, C4/5 CE), P. Wash. Univ. inv. 242 (CXII, C4/5 CE), P. Amst. Inv. 16 (CXIII, C5 CE), P. Yale inv. 989 (CXIV, C3/4 CE), P. (Mag.) Gaál. ined. (CXV, C4 CE), P. Laur. inv. 54 (CXVI, C6 CE), P. Mon. Gr. Inv. 216 (CXVII, C1 CE), P. Palau Rib. inv. 200 (CXVIII, ND), P. Laur. III.57 (CXIX, C3 CE), P. Laur. III.58 (CXX, C3 CE), P. Med. inv. 71.58 (CXXI, C3/4 CE), P. Berol. Inv. 21243 (CXXII, C1 BCE – C1 CE), P. Cazzaniga nos 1-6 (CXXIIIa-f, C5 CE), P. Cazzaniga no. 7 (CXXIV, C5 CE), P. Cazzaniga nos 8-13 (CXXVa-f, C5/6 CE), P. Laur. III/472 (CXXVI, C5 CE), P. Yale inv. 1206 (CXXVII, C3/4 CE), P. Heid. G. 1386 (CXXVIII, C5 CE) P. Berol. 21260 (CXXIX, C3 CE), P. Mich. Inv. 6666 (CXXX, C3 CE), P. Louvre E3229 (PDM supplement, C3 CE).

Circle: N/A.

Tools: Censer, ebony staff, garments, knife, lamps, linen garments, phylacteries, rings, sandals, sword, tripod, wreaths.

Spirit List: Abaōth, Abrasax, Achrichiour, Adonaios (Hades), Adrasteia, Aē, Agathos Daimon, Aierōnthi, Aikos, Aion, Aktiōphis, Albalal, Alekto, Alkyone, Ammon, Amoun, Amphiaraos, Anag Biathi, Aniel, Anouth, Anubis, Aphyhpis, Apollo, Ararmachēs, Arbrathiabra, Ariste, Arouēr, Artemis, Asklepios, Asstraelos, Athena, Atropos, Azaēl, Azariēl, Aziēl, Balsamēs, Bast, Bathiabēl, Bimadam, Binchōōōch, Bouēl, Bythath, Chadraoun, Charon, Chichrōalithō, Chnoum, Chōnsou, Chorborbath, Chphyris (Khephra), Chrepsenthaēs, Circe, Danoup/Chrator Berbali Balbith Iaō, Echommiē, Edanōth, Enaezraēl, Eorasichē, Ephialtes, Erebos, Ermichthathōps, Erou Rombriēs, Eschakleō, Ezriēl, Gabriel, Garta, Genna, Harbathanōps Ioaoi, Hamst, Hapy, Harkentechtha, Harpokrates, Hebe, Hekate, Heknet, Helioros, Helios, Helios-Mithras, Hephaistos, Hera, Heriey, Hermekate, Hermes, Hestia, Hike (Heka), Hor-Amoun, Horus, Hyesemigadōn, Iao Sabaoth, Imhotep the Great, Ioēl, Iouēl, Iphiaph, Irraēl, Isis, Isis-Sothis, Istraēl, Ixion, Jesus, Kairos, Kattiēl, Kerberos, Khonsu, Klotho, Kommes, Kore, Lachesis, Lailam, Lēmnei, Marmar, Marmaraōth, Mechran, Megaira, Menebain, Menescheēs, Mercheimeros, Mesargiltō, Metmouriēl, Michael, Mihos, Min, Mithra, Mithras, Mnevis, Moira, Mouriatha, Mut, Nabrishotht, Nariēl, Neboun, Neboutosualēth, Neith, Nemesis, Nemormoth, Nemouēl, Nephthys, Nouphiēr, Nous/Phrenes, Opet, Orbeēth, Orgogorgoniotrian, Orion, Osiris, Osiris-Re, Osiris-Khenty-Amenti, Osor Mnevis, Osor Nobechis, Osor Nophris/Osoronnophris (Osiris), Otos, Ouranos, Ouriēl, Pakerbeth, Pan, Panmōth, Parammon (Hermes), Pithiēl, Phoibos (Apollo), Phōs-Auge, Phōx, Phre, Physis, Pluto, Pronoia, Pshoi, Ptah, Rabchlou, Rabiēēl, Raphael, Re/Ra, Re-Khephri-Atum, Roubēl, Roumbouthiēl, Sachmoune, Saesechel, Samas, Saoumiēl, Sarapis, Sarbitha, Sarnochoibal, Satis, Selene, Semea, Semesilam, Seth-Typhon, Shlate Late Balate, Shu, Sisiaho, Sobek, Sokar, Souriel, Spora, Tabiym, Tagrtat, Telzē, Themis, Thoth, Thouri, Thouriēl, Thymenphri, Tichnondaēs, Triphis, Tyche, Typhon, Wepwawet, Xanthis, Zebourthaunēn, Zeus, Zeus-Iao-Zen-Helios, Zizaubiō, Zouriēl.

The Text

The PGM are an incredibly important collection of texts that provide a key surviving example of the types of magic practiced in antiquity. Most texts from this period were suppressed and destroyed, so the material collected in the PGM is invaluable in demonstrating the continuity of practice over a period of eight or nine centuries.

Examining the contents of the PGM, it is evident that human nature does not change that much, and the themes are similar to those seen later in the grimoires. By far the most common objective is love rites of attraction, followed by healing/health rites. Divination methods and dream revelations/sending are common themes (bowl and lamp particularly so). Amulets and talismans are also common, often as phylacteries. There is significant interaction with the dead, especially for defixiones, as well as with the divine, seen in invocations and rites for a 'god's arrival'.

A number of the PGM contain quotes from Homer (*Iliad, Odyssey*), in a similar manner to that later seen with Biblical quotes in the grimoires. Hexameter verse is a common feature in the charms, and there are also a number of historiolae spread through the texts, most commonly from Egyptian myths. As Judge notes (1987:340), 'practitioners of magic aimed to harness to their ends every known source of supernatural power'. Considering this, the spirits include Egyptian, Greek, Sumerian, and Gnostic gods and goddesses, Jewish divine names and angels, and assorted daimons. Of these the most common are the Greek deities Helios, Hermes, Zeus, Selene and Hekate, and the Egyptian gods Anubis, Horus, Isis, Osiris, Seth, Thoth, and Typhon, as well as the gnostic Abraxas. There are also a range of composite deities, syncretizing two or more gods or goddesses, and even a deity-archangel syncretism (Osiris-Michael).

The *London-Leiden Papyrus* is one work which was ripped in two, and each part ended up in a different museum. Purchased in Thebes by Anastasi in the early nineteenth century, he sold one part to the Dutch government, and the other part was bought later for the British Museum. It is a significant work as it is one of the latest Egyptian magical papyri written in Demotic Egyptian, and is found as PDM XIV. It is also significant because several of the Greek glosses in it made it one of the texts which helped in the deciphering of a number of hieroglyphics.

The material in the PGM is a collection of magical handbooks (collections of spells and prayers) and individual spells, charms, and prayers. The text contains:

PGM I (magical handbook) – rite for acquiring an assistant daemon (includes two vowel *schwindeschema*,[65] one of them inverted) (1-42);[66] the spell of Pnouthis (to acquire an assistant daimon) (42-195); prayer of deliverance (195-222); invisibility spell (222-231); memory spell (232-247);[67] invisibility spell (247-262); Apollonian invocation (lamp divination) (262-347).

PGM II (magical handbook) – spell for revelation (1-64); alternative spell for revelation (includes Santalala schwindeschema, headless figure wielding laurel sprig and wand, with divine names and vowels in body) (64-184).

PGM III (magical handbook) – cat ritual for many purposes (involves cat drowning as vessel, includes three human figures, one with cat head) (1-164); oracular request (165-186); spell for revelation (includes tripod drawing) (187-262); foreknowledge charm (263-275); horoscope (275-281); foreknowledge spell (282-409); memory spell (410-423); copy from a holy book (foreknowledge and memory spell) (424-466); memory spell (467-478); foreknowledge charm (479-483); another foreknowledge charm (to detect a thief) (483-488); another spell to detect a thief (488-494); spell to establish a relationship with Helios (494-611); spell for gaining control of one's shadow (612-632); spell for a direct vision (includes Ablanathanalba schwindeschema) (633-731).

---

65 A schwindeschema, or disappearing pattern, refers to an inverted triangle which reduces the number of letters from the original word down to a single letter. The most famous of these is Abracadabra. It ia a common motif in ancient Greek charms.

66 The line numbers for each individual spell, rite, prayer, etc., are given for convenience and clarity.

67 Although not named, the use of Hermaic ink would suggest this spell is associated with Hermes.

PGM IV (magical handbook) – spell for revelation (1-25); initiation (26-51); spell for revelation (52-85); phylactery for those possessed by demons (86-87); another to Helios (divination using a boy) (88-93); love spell of attraction (Isis historiolae) (94-153); Nephotes to Psammetichos (instruction on bowl divination) (154-285); spell for picking a plant (286-95); wondrous spell for binding a lover (includes charaktêres) (296-466); charm to restrain anger (467-468); charm to get friends (469-470); verses from Homer (471-473); verse from Homer (474); the Mithras Liturgy (475-829); verse from Homer (830); charm to restrain anger (831-832); charm to get friends (833-834); astrological text (835-849); charm of Solomon that produces a trance ('Solomon's collapse') (850-929); charm that produces a direct vision (930-1114); hidden stele (prayer) (1115-1166); stele that is useful for all things, even delivering from death (1167-1226); rite for driving out daimons (1227-1264); Aphrodite's name (love spell (1365-1274); Bear charm (1275-1322);[68] another bear charm (1323-1330); bear charm (1331-1389); love spell of attraction performed with the help of heroes or gladiators or those who have died a violent death (1390-1495); love spell of attraction over myrrh (1496-1595); consecration for all purposes (1596-1715); Sword of Dardanos[69] (love spell) (1716-1870); fetching charm (1872-1927); King Pitys' spell of attraction over a skull-cup (uses armara incense) (1928-2005; Pitys' spell of attraction (2006-2125); a restraining seal for skulls (2125-2139); Pitys the Thessalian's spell for questioning corpses (2140-2144); divine assistance from three Homeric verses (2145-2240); document to the waning Moon (2241-2358); business spell (2359-2372); charm for acquiring business (2373-2440); love spell of attraction (2441-2621); slander spell to Selene (2622-2707); another love spell of attraction (2708-2784); prayer to Selene (2785-2890); love spell of attraction (to the planet Venus) (2891-2942); love spell of attraction through wakefulness (uses kyphi incense) (2943-2966); spell for picking a plant (herb gathering instructions) (2967-3006); charm of Pibechis for those possessed by daimons (using the name of Jesus) (3007-3086); oracle of Kronos, called 'little mill' (3086-3124); spell for favour (3125-3171); dream producing charm using three reeds (3172-3208); saucer divination of Aphrodite (3209-3254); spell to induce insomnia (3255-3274).

PGM V (magical handbook) – oracle of Sarapis (uses young boy) (1-53); direct vision spell (54-69); spell to catch a thief (includes two inverted mixed vowel *schwindeschema* with an eye of Horus between them) (70-95); Stele of Jeu the hieroglyphist[70] (96-172); another way to catch a thief (172-212); Hermes' ring (uses kyphi) (213-303); binding defixio with the dead (304-369); compulsion spell with Hermes (370-446); instruction concerning a magical ring (447-458); another way (spell for many purposes (459-489).

PGM Va – spell for direct vision (1-3).

PGM VI – prayer for encounter with Helios

PGM VII (magical handbook) – Homer oracle (dice divination) (1-148); to keep bugs out of the house (149-154); days and hours for divination (155-167); Demokritos' 'table gimmicks' (167-186);[71] favour and victory charm (186-190); spell for binding a lover (191-192); for scorpion sting (charaktêres on papyrus) (193-196); for discharge of the eyes (197-198); for migraine headache (199-201); another (for migraine headache) (201-202); for coughs

---

68 The Bear in these charms refers to the constellation of Ursa Major, identified as a goddess, as were other constellations like the Pleiades. It is also sometimes identified with Typhon, Artemis, and Hekate.

69 It has been suggested that this spell is a precursor to the *Sword of Moses*, but the main similarity is in the word 'sword' being in the title. This charm includes a gold sword-shaped lamella containing a few names, which is given to a partridge to swallow that is then killed, which has a parallel in one part of the Sword of Moses in giving a silver lamella to a cock to swallow and killing it.

70 This is the text popularised by Aleister Crowley as the 'Bornless One'.

71 This is a good example of the material later found in books of secrets, showing that tradition also has its origins in Antiquity.

(203-205); another for coughs (206-207); for hardening of the breasts (208-209); for swollen testicles (209-210); for fever with shivering fits (211-212); for daily fever and nightly fever (213-214); Stele of Aphrodite (spell for favour, includes charaktêres) (215-218); phylactery for daily fever with shivering fits (218-221); request for a dream oracle from Besas (222-249); request for a dream oracle (250-254); another to the same lamp (255-259); for the ascent of the uterus (260-271); astrological calendar (272-283; orbit of the Moon (horoscope) (284-299); spell of uncertain purpose (300); love charm (300a-310); phylactery (311-316); another phylactery (317-318); charm for direct vision (319-334); charm for a direct vision (335-347); divination by means of a boy (348-358); request for a dream oracle (359-369); spell against every wild animal (370-373); charm to induce insomnia (374-376); another charm to induce insomnia (376-384); cup spell (love) (385-389); victory charm for the races (390-393); coercive spell for restraining (394-395); spell for silencing, subjecting, and restraining (396-404); love spell (405-406); dream spell (407-410); spell for causing talk while asleep (411-416); restraining spell (417-422); to win at dice (423-428); restraining spell (429-458); love charm (459-461); love charm (462-466); love spell of attraction (467-477); spell for dream revelation (478-490); spell for protection (490-504); meeting with your own daimon (505-528); victory charm (528-539); lamp divination (540-578); phylactery against daimons, phantasms, sickness and suffering (includes ouroboros image with charaktêres in it) (579-590); prayer of invocation (591-592); fetching charm for an unmanageable woman (593-619); from the Diadem of Moses[72] (invisibility and love spells) (619-627); rite involving a magical ring (healing, Asklepios/Imhotep) (628-642); cup spell (love) (643-651); spell to induce insomnia by means of a bat (652-660); love spell (661-663); request for dream revelations (664-685); bear charm (686-702); request for dream oracle (uses 30-letter name in two wings) (703-726); charm for a direct vision of Apollo (727-739); request for a dream oracle (740-755); prayer (756-794); Pythagoras' request for a dream oracle and Demokritos' dream divination (includes charaktêres) (795-845); shadow on the Sun (revelation spell) (846-861); lunar spell of Claudianus (862-918); Hermes' wondrous victory charm (919-924); courtroom curse (925-939); charm to restrain anger (includes drawing surrounded by four wing of voces magicae) (940-968); a good potion (love) (969-972); love spell of attraction (973-980); love spell of attraction (981-993); spell of uncertain purpose (only first part in fragment) (993-1009); divination by a dream (1009-1016); spell for favour and victory (1017-1026).

PGM VIII – binding love spell of Astrapsoukos (1-63); request for a dream oracle of Besas (includes crowned figure) (64-110).

PGM IX – spell to subjugate and silence (includes image of two figures) (1-14).

PGM X – love spell (1-23); charm to restrain anger (includes charaktêres) (24-35); Apollo's charm to subject (includes drawing of foot) (36-50).

PGM XIa – Apollonius of Tyana's old serving woman (includes charaktêres on ass skull) (1-40).

PGM XIb – table gimmick to make drunks look like they have donkey snouts (1-5).

PGM XIc – love spell (1-19).

PDM XII (PGM XII)[73] (magic handbook) – invocation (1-5); a ring to cause praise (6-20); prayer for a revelation of a remedy for a disease (21-49).

PGM XII – rite to produce an epiphany of Kore (1-13); Eros as assistant daimon (14-95); Himerios' recipes (96-106); charm of Agathokles for sending dreams (107-121); Zminis of Tentyra's spell for sending dreams (121-143); request for a dream (144-152); spell for a

---

72 The Diadem of Moses seems to be the name of a larger text these spells are taken from.

73 Also listed as PGM XII. Note that the D stands for Demotic, indicating the language change from Greek. Hence the numbering restarting for the Greek text following the Demotic. Later in the text more Demotic spells are included which have dual numbering.

divine revelation (153-160); spell to release from bonds (160-178); spell for restraining anger (179-181); spell for gaining favour (182-189); request for a dream oracle spoken to the Bear (190-192); to make a tincture of gold (193-201); a ring (201-269); a little ring for success and favour and victory (270-350); Demokritos' 'sphere' (351-364); charm for causing separation (365-375); charm to induce insomnia (376-396); to gain favour and friendship forever (397-400); interpretations (401-444); spell for separating one person from another (445-448, PDM xii.50-61); another separation spell (includes image of Seth) (449-452, PDM xii.62-75); another separation spell (453-465, PDM xii.76-107); a spell to cause a woman to hate a man (466-468, PDM xii.108-118); a fetching spell (469-473, PDM xii.119-134); love spell of attraction (includes picture) (474-479, PDM xii.135-146); another love spell of attraction (480-495, PDM xii.147-164).

PGM XIII – initiation ritual and magical handbook, called 'Unique or the Eighth Book of Moses' (1-343); second different version of the initiation ritual (and Eighth Book of Moses) (343-646); third different version of the initiation ritual (partial copy of Eighth Book of Moses) (646-734); collection of miscellaneous spells including initiation (the Tenth Hidden Book of Moses) (734-1077).

PDM XIV (magical handbook) – a vessel divination (1-92); spell for revelation (93-114, PGM XIVa.1-11); spell for vision (security of shadows) (115); another spell for vision (116); a 'god's arrival' (117-149); an inquiry of the lamp (150-231); a 'god's' arrival (232-238); the vessel inquiry of Khonsu[74] (239-295; a vessel inquiry to see the barque of Pre (solitary) (295-308); a spell for causing favour (309-334); love spell (335-355); another love spell (355-365); the method (spell for separating man and woman) (366-375); various recipes into which the shrew-mouse goes (376-394); vessel divination (395-427); two love potions (428-450); spell for going before a superior (451-458, PGM XIVb.12-15); lamp divination (459-475); lamp divination (475-488); another lamp divination (489-515); another lamp divination (516-527); vessel divination (528-553); spell for dog bite (554-562); spell for removal of poison (563-574); spell for removal of bone stuck in the throat (574-585); spell for dog bite (585-593); spell for sting (594-620); spell for removal of bone stuck in the throat (574-585); spell for dog bite (585-593); spell for sting (594-620); spell for removal of bone stuck in the throat (620-626); vessel divination (627-635); love potion (636-669); introduction to a collection of spells (670-674); a spell to cause evil sleep (675-694, PGM XIVc.16-27); vessel divination (695-700); vessel divination (701-705); spell against evil sleep (706-710); prescription to cause evil sleep (711-715); another spell to cause evil sleep (716-724); another spell to cause evil sleep (724-726); three prescriptions to cause evil sleep (727-736); a prescription to cause evil sleep (737-738); a spell to cause death (739-740); a spell to cause blindness (741); another spell to cause evil sleep (742); another spell to cause evil sleep (743-749); lamp divination (750-771); a method (love spells) 772-804); another vessel inquiry (805-840); another method (solitary vessel inquiry) (841-850); another vessel inquiry (851-855); inquiry of the Sun (856-875); here is another inquiry of the Sun (875-885); recipes involving herbs (886-896); list of herbs and minerals (897-910); spell to cause evil sleep (911-916); prescription to cause evil sleep (917-919); information concerning minerals (920-929); a prescription (love spell) (930-932); information concerning minerals (933-934); prescription for a watery ear (935-939; information concerning salamander and herbs (940-952); a prescription to stop blood (953-955); test of pregnancy (956-960); two prescriptions to stop blood (961-965); information concerning herbs (966-969); two prescriptions to stop liquid in a woman (970-977); another prescription to stop liquid in a woman (978-980); another prescription to stop liquid in a woman (981-984); gout prescription (985-992); another prescription for gout (993-1002);

---

74 Note that this may refer to the lunar timing (waxing) as Anubis is the god who is greeted after the conjuration.

amulet for gout (1003-1014); prescription for unidentifiable ailment (1015-1020); prescription for a stiff foot (1021-1023); another prescription for a stiff foot (1024-1025); love spell (1026-1045); love spell (1046-1047); love spell (1047-1048); love spell (1049-1055); spells involving voces magicae (1056-1062); love spell (1063-1069); spell to send dreams and make a woman love (1070-1077); request for revelation (1078-1089); fetching spell (1090-1096); spell to heal an eye disease (1097-1103); recipe concerning eye ointment (1104-1109); spell (and ointment) to open eyes for divination (1110-1129); love spell (1130-1140); spell for lamp divination (1141-1154); love spell (1155-1162); spell for vessel divination (1163-1179); fragment from invocation (1180-1181); spell to cause madness (1182-1187); love spell (1188-1189); another love spell (1190-1193); another love spell (1194-1195); another love spell (1196-1198); spell for lamp divination (1199-1205); love spell (obsession) (1206-1218); spell for fever (1219-1227).

PGM XV – charm to bind a lover (1-21).

PGM XVI – charm to bind a lover (1-75).

PGM XVIIa – love spell of attraction (includes double wing formation forming diamond of voces magicae) (1-25).

PGM XVIIb – prayer (1-23).

PGM XVIIc – amulet (includes charaktêres) (1-14).

PGM XVIIIa – amulet for headache (1-4).

PGM XVIIIb – fever amulet (includes *schwindeschema* surrounded by spell written in triangular form, and wing formation of Gorgophonas)(1-7).

PGM XIXa – love spell of attraction (includes *schwindeschema* with wing-like formations on either side) (1-54).

PGM XIXb – love spell of attraction (1-3); love spell of attraction over a dog (4-18).

PGM XX – spell for headache (1-4); charm of the Syrian woman of Gadara for any inflammation (4-12); charm of the Thessalian Philinna for headache (13-19).

PGM XXI – invocation (1-29).

PGM XXIIa – iatromagical[75] recipes: for hemorrhage[76] (1); for bloody flux (2-9); for pain in the breasts and uterus (9-10); contraceptive (11-14); for a sufferer of elephantiasis (15-17); favour and love spell to Helios (18-27).

PGM XXIIb – prayer of Jacob (1-26); request for a dream oracle (27-31); request for a dream oracle (32-35).

PGM XXIII – fragment of the *Kestoi* of Julianus Africanus (1-70).

PGM XXIVa – Oracle (1-25).

PGM XXIVb – love spell (1-15).

PGM XXVa-d – amulets (include charaktêres).

PGM XXVI – *Sortes Astrampsychi* (1-21) (omitted).

PGM XXVII – victory charm (1-5).

PGM XXVIIIa – spell for scorpion sting (1-7).

PGM XXVIIIb – spell for scorpion sting (1-9).

PGM XXVIIIc – spell for scorpion sting (1-11).

PGM XXIX – prayer (poem) (1-10)

PGM XXXa-f – oracle questions (omitted).

PGM XXXIa-c – oracle questions (omitted).

PGM XXXII – love spell of attraction (1-19).

PGM XXXIIa – love spell of attraction (1-25).

PGM XXXIII – fever amulet (large *schwindeschema*) (1-25).

---

75 Iatromagical, i.e., they are on the threshold of medicine and magic, and combine elements of both.
76 Uses line from Homer's *Iliad*.

PGM XXXIV – fragments from a novel (1-24).

PGM XXXV – charm for favour and victory (includes charaktêres and drawings of human heads) (1-42).

PGM XXXVI – charm to restrain (includes figure with names and voces magicae in and around figure) (1-34); charm to restrain anger and to secure favour (includes figure holding snake, possibly tattooed, with vertical charaktêres on either side) (35-68); love spell of attraction (includes figure holding whip in right hand, smaller figure under left hand) (69-101); divination by fire (love spell) (includes figure and four wing formations) (102-133); love spell of attraction (134-160); charm to restrain anger, and for success (161-177); charm to break spells (includes charaktêres and figure) (178-187); love spell of attraction (includes charaktêres) (187-210); prayer to Helios, charm to restrain anger and for victory and favour (211-230); charm to inflict harm (includes figure holding sword and severed head) (231-255); charm to break enchantment (includes charaktêres) (256-264); charm of uncertain purpose (264-274); charm for gaining favour (includes charaktêres) (275-283); Pudenda key spell (283-294); love spell of attraction (295-311); charm to open a door (312-320); contraceptive spell (320-332); love spell of attraction over myrrh (333-360); love spell of attraction (361-371).

PGM XXXVII – spell of uncertain purpose (1-26).

PGM XXXVIII – love spell of attraction (1-26).

PGM XXXIX – love spell of attraction (includes two figures surrounded by two wing formations) (1-21).

PGM XL – curse (1-18).

PGM XLI – amulet (1-9).

PGM XLII – amulet (includes vowel strings and charaktêres) (1-10).

PGM XLIII – amulet against fever (includes wing formation next to divine names) (1-27).

PGM XLIV – amulet against fever (includes vowel strings and two wing formations of Michael) (1-18).

PGM XLV – amulet (1-8).

PGM XLVI – request for revelation (1-4); spell to silence and subject (4-8).

PGM XLVII – amulet against fever (1-17).

PGM XLVIII – amulet (1-21).

PGM XLIX – amulet (includes charaktêres).

PGM L – oracle (1-18).

PGM LI – charm to inflict harm (1-27).

PGM LII – love spell (1-9); love spell (9-19); spell to induce insomnia (20-26).

PGM LII-LVI – spells of uncertain purpose (omitted).

PGM LVII – rite to acquire an assistant daimon (1-37).

PGM LVIII – spell to inflict harm (1-14); spell of uncertain purpose (15-39).

PGM LIX – phylactery (1-15).

PGM LX – amulet (includes charaktêres) (1-5).

PDM LXI – spell for revelation (1-30); spell of uncertain purpose (30-41); spell of uncertain purpose (42); remedy for an ulcer of the head (43-48, PGM LXI.1-5); remedy for the head (49-57); for an erection (58-62, PGM LXI.6-10); spell for a dream revelation (63-78); way of finding a thief (79-94); spell of giving praise and love in Nubian (95-99); the red cloth of Nephthys (100-105); prescription for a donkey not moving (106-111); prescription for making a woman love (112-127); love spell (128-147); love spell (148-158); love charm (159-196, PGM LXI.1-38); love spell of attraction (197-216, PGM LXI.39-71).

PGM LXXII – love spell of attraction (1-24); saucer divination (includes charaktêres) (24-46); oracle (with dice) (47-51); horoscope (52-75); spell to inflict harm (includes drawing of horns-up crescent and vowel wing formation underneath) (76-106).

PGM LXIII – love potion (1-7); spell to make a woman confess the name of the man she loves (7-12); spell of uncertain purpose (13-20); spell of uncertain purpose (includes charaktêres) (21-24); contraceptive (24-25); contraceptive (26-28).

PGM LXIV – charm to inflict harm (includes drawing) (1-12).

PGM LXV – spell to prevent pregnancy (includes charaktêre) (1-4); for migraine headache (includes charaktêres) (4-7).

PGM LXVI – charm to cause separation (includes drawing of two figures) (1-11).[77]

PGM LXVII – love spell (1-24).

PGM LXVIII – love spell (1-20).

PGM LXIX – victory spell (1-3).

PGM LXX – charm for favour (1-4); charm of Hekate-Ereschigal against fear of punishment (4-25); against fear and to dissolve spells (26-51).

PGM LXXI – phylactery (1-8).

PGM LXXII – rite concerning the Bear (1-36).

PGM LXXIII-LXXVI – oracle questions (omitted).

PGM LXXVII – charm for getting a revelation (1-24).

PGM LXXVIII – love spell of attraction (includes drawing) (1-14).

PGM LXXIX – charm to restrain anger (1-7).

PGM LXXX – charm to restrain anger (1-5).

PGM LXXXI – greetings to deities (1-10).

PGM LXXXII – recipes for ingredients fragment (1-12).

PGM LXXXIII – for fever with shivering fits (references several biblical verses) (1-20).

PGM LXXXIV – fetching charm (includes *schwindeschema*) (1-21).

PGM LXXXV – for daimon possession (1-6).

PGM LXXXVI – amulet (1-2); uncertain rite (3-7).

PGM LXXXVII – fever amulet (1-11).

PGM LXXXVIII – fever amulet (includes *schwindeschema*) (1-19)

PGM LXXXIX – phylactery for fever, phantoms, daimons, etc (1-27).

PGM XC – rite or phylactery (includes charaktêres) (1-13); salve for fever (includes charaktêres) (14-18).

PGM XCI – fever amulet (includes *schwindeschema*) (1-14).

PGM XCII – charm for favour (1-16).

PGM XCIII – sacrificial rite (1-6); rite (7-21).

PGM XCIV – voces magicae (1-3); drying powder made with saffron for sharp eyesight (4-6); for excellent health (7-9); a phylactery for fever (includes charaktêres) (10-16); for those possessed by daimons (17-21); for the eyes (22-26); for tumours (includes charaktêres) (27-35); for strangury (36-38); another for migraine headache (39-60).

PGM XCV – spell for subjugation (1-6); concerning the mole (epilepsy charm) (7-13); a remedy for all cases of epilepsy (14-18).

PGM XCVI – amulet (1-8).

PGM XCVII – spell against eye disease (1-6); another spell (7-9); another spell (10-13); for every disease (15-17).

PGM XCVIII – amulet (includes inverted *schwindeschema* of the vowels) (1-7).

PGM XCIX – amulet (1-3).

PGM C – amulet (includes charaktêres) (1-7).

PGM CI – fetching charm (1-53).

PGM CII – request for a dream oracle (1-17).

---

77 Daniel suggests this spell is motivated by homosexual jealousy. See Daniel, 1991:119-120.

PGM CIII – fetching charm (1-18).
PGM CIV – amulet for fever with shivering fits (1-8).
PGM CV – invocation of Sarapis (1-15).
PGM CVI – amulet for fever with shivering fits (includes serpent ouroboros image) (1-10).
PGM CVII – fetching charm (includes charaktêres) (1-19).
PGM CVIII – fetching charm (1-12).
PGM CIX – curse (1-8).[78]
PGM CX – horoscope (1-12).
PGM CXI – instructions for making magical figures (1-15).
PGM CXII – amulet for scorpion sting (1-5).
PGM CXIII – amulet for scorpion sting (includes scorpion image) (1-4).
PGM CXIV – amulet for attack by daimons and for epilepsy (1-14).
PGM CXV – amulet for fever with shivering fits (1-7).
PGM CXVI – invocation of Typhon-Seth (includes two *schwindeschema* separated by two wing formations) (1-17).
PGM CXVII Fragments – fetching charm (1-23).
PGM CXVIII – magical scroll (omitted).
PGM CXIXa – fragment from formulary (1); love spell through touch (2-3); fetching charm (4-6); charm to subject (7-11).
PGM CXIXb – for fever with shivering fits (1-5).
PGM CXX – amulet for inflammation of the uvula (wing formation) (1-13).
PGM CXXI – phylactery for a variety of evils (1-14).
PGM CXXII – an excerpt for enchantments (1-5); enchantment using apples (5-25); love spell (26-50); for headache (51-55).
PGM CXXIIIa – voces magicae (includes figures and charaktêres) (1-23); erotylos[79] (24-47); for childbearing (48-50); for sleep (includes charaktêres) (51-52); for strangury (includes charaktêres) (53-55); for a shivering fit (includes charaktêres) (56-68); for victory (includes drawing) (69-72).
PGM CXXIIIb – voces magicae.
PGM CXXIIIc – voces magicae.
PGM CXXIIId – voces magicae.
PGM CXXIIIe – repeat of CXXIIIa 24-47.
PGM CXXIIIf – repeat of CXXIIIa 24-47.
PGM CXXIV – charm to inflict harm (includes charaktêres) (1-5); charm to inflict harm (includes figure) (6-43).
PGM CXXVa-f – fragments of spells.
PGM CXXVIa – spell to cause separation (1-21).
PGM CXXVIb – spell to cause separation (1-17).
PGM CXXVII – fragment of formulary of iatromagical prescriptions (1-12).
PGM CXXVIII – phylactery for fever (1-11).
PGM CXXIX – fragment of unidentifiable spell (1-7).
PGM CXXX – for a shivering fever (includes vowel *schwindeschema*) (1-13).
PDM Supplement – spell for sending a dream (1-6); spell for sending a dream (7-18); spell for sending a dream (19-27); spell for sending a dream (28-40); spell for sending a dream (40-60); spell for sending a dream (60-101); spell for sending a dream (101-116); spell for sending

---

[78] Although this is called a love spell in Betz, Faraone convincingly argues that this is in fact a defixione. See Faraone, 1988:279-286.

[79] A stone, the 'love stone', referred to by Pliny in *Natural History*, Book 37.

a dream (117-130); a 'god's arrival' of Osiris (130-138); spell for subjection (138-149); a 'god's arrival' of Thoth (149-162); spell for finding your house of life (162-168); spell for reciting a document (168-184); fragments of rites and formulae (185-208).

Essential Reading

Betz, Hans Dieter (ed, trans) (1992) *The Greek Magical Papyri in Translation. Volume One: Texts.* Chicago: University of Chicago Press. Fantastic text of spells, charms, and conjurations from antiquity.

Chicosky, Alison (2022) *The Secrets of Helios. Unlocking the Practical Uses of PGM IV:1596-1715.* West Yorkshire: Hadean Press. Excellent short practical work which serves well as a lead-in to the practices of the *PGM*.

Faraone, Christopher A. & Tovar, Sofia Torallas (2022) *The Greco-Egyptian Magical Formularies: Libraries, Books and Individual Recipes.* Michigan: University of Michigan Press. Excellent academic study revisiting the PGM from the latest perspectives.

Skinner, Stephen (2021) *Techniques of Greco-Egyptian Magic.* Singapore: Golden Hoard Press. Excellent scholarly presentation of the material in the PGM in a coherent and accessible format, making it much more useable.

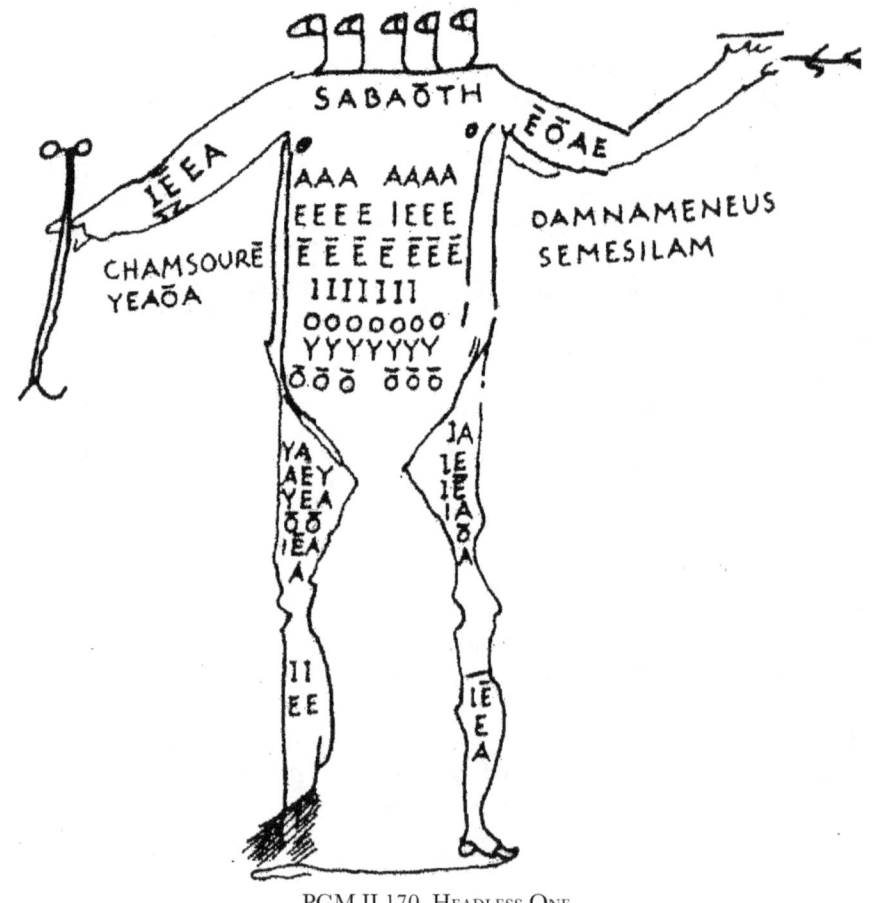

PGM II.170, Headless One

Supplementum Magicum

Date: C2-6 CE.
Language: Greek (small amount of Latin, Aramaic, and Coptic).
Influences: Greco-Egyptian, Roman, Jewish, and Christian magical practices.
Provenance: Book published in 1989-91 consolidating material contemporary to the PGM from C2-6 CE.
MSS: Listed individually in the text below.
Circle: N/A.
Tools: N/A as all are written charms.
Spirit List: Abaal, Abêl, Adonaios, Adonis, Aion, Ammon, Anaêl, Ananke, Anubis, Aphrodite, Apis, Ariêl, Arsenouphis, Artemis, Azaziel, Baal, Barouch, Baubo, Bes, Brimo, Ebriêl, Êlêlyth, Erebos, Ereschigal, Gabriel, Gê, Helios, Hekate-Artemis, Herakles, Hermes-Thoth, Horus, Horus-Apollo, Iarbath, Ieremiel, Isis, Kemouêl, Kerberos, Kneph, Kypris, Louêl, Michael, Mithras, Neith, Nephthys, Nourêl, Obach, Olamtêr, Osiris, Ouriel, Persephone, Phabriêl, Photuel, Pluto, Raphael, Sarapis, Seth, Souriel, Toumiel, Typhon-Seth, Zeus, Zeus-Helios.

The Text

Supplementum Magicum is hugely significant, as it expands on the material given in the Greek Magical Papyri (with which it shares much parallel material), presenting the additional material in a more coherent manner. The practices and charms are written in Greek (with one in Latin, and several in Aramaic and Coptic), though it is of Egyptian provenance, and combine Christian and pagan material. This results in the juxtaposition of Jewish and Christian divine names and angels with Greco-Egyptian gods. It is interesting to see that, by this time, the grouping of Gabriel, Michael, Raphael, and Uriel as a working group of archangels is already clearly in place.

The charms are divided into protective charms (Pagan and Christian sections), erotic charms, curses (Pagan and Christian), charms to win favour, and divinatory charms. They are recorded on a variety of materials, largely papyrus, but also including clay vessels and terracotta shards, linen, lead tablets, tin sheets, silver plates, gold plates, wooden tablets, and hematite amulets. A substantial number of the charms are iatromagical.

The nineteen Pagan protective charms listed are from: P. Laur. III.58 (C3 CE), for inflammation of the uvula (contains a schwindeschema); T Köln inv.7 (C3 CE), for protection from fever; P. Mich. inv. 6666 (C3 CE), for protection from illness and fever (includes schwindeschema, sun wheels, and lunar crescent); PUG I.6 (C3 CE), for protection from quotidian fever;[80] P. Oxy. XLII.3068 (C3 CE), charm against tonsillitis; Inscr. Mus. Louvre 204 (ND), hematite falcon amulet for protection from evil, sorcerers, and the wrath of gods and daemons; P. Köln inv. 1982 (C3 CE), for general protection (includes upward schwindeschema of the seven vowels);[81] P. Haun. III.50 (C3-4 CE), charm of uncertain purpose, possibly amulet against dysuria[82] (has large letters theta, kappa, and pi, surrounded by their own letters and vertical lines of the same letters under each, ending in an inverted semi-circle); P. Michael 27 (C3/4 CE), for protection from quotidian fever (includes schwindeschema of palindrome word ablanathanalba); P. Berol inv. 21165 (C3/4 CE), protection from shivering and all

---

80 Malaria with daily spasms.
81 When the seven vowels are mentioned, it refers to the seven vowels in the ancient Greek alphabet.
82 Painful urination.

fevers (includes ouroboros and charaktêres); P. Princ. III.159 (C3/4 CE), protection from fever (includes schwindeschema of name Zagourepagoure); P. Gaál (C3/4 CE), protection from fever; P. Lund IV.12 (C4 CE), protection from fever, including magically induced; P. Erl. 15 (C4 CE), protection from shivering and fevers; P. Palau Rib. Inv. 126 (C4/5 CE), for protection for the wearer; P. Wash. Univ. inv. 242 (C4/5 CE), protection from scorpion stings; P. Amst. I.15 (C5 CE), protection from scorpion stings (includes scorpion image); P. Lugd. Bat. XXV.9 (C5 CE), protection charm from illness (includes charaktêres); P. IFAO III.50 (C6 CE), protection from suffering and fevers (includes charaktêres).

The seventeen Christian protective charms listed are from: P. Köln Inv. 2861 (C4/5 CE), healing charm (includes charaktêres); P. Köln VI.257 (C4/5 CE), protection from shivering and all fevers (includes charaktêres and schwindeschema of ablanathanalba); P. Amst. 126 (C4/5 CE), protection from pains of the head and temple (migraine?) and all fevers; P. Haun III.51 (C5 CE), protection from fevers calling on Jesus (includes charaktêres); PSI Inv. 319 (C5 CE), exorcism of demons, calling on Solomon; P. Prag. I.6 (C5 CE), protection from fever calling on Jesus; P. Berol Inv. 21911 (C5 CE), protection charm for eye ailments (includes *Psalm 90:1*); P. Vindob. Inv. G 42406, protection for sinner (includes charaktêres); P. Heid. Inv G 1386 (C5 CE), protection from fever calling on Jesus; P. Princ. II.107 (C5/6 CE), protection from fever, interestingly calls on the dead amongst the divine names and Michael; P. Coll. Youtie II (C5/6 CE), protection from all evil; P. Turner 49 (C5/6 CE), protection from illness, fever, headaches, and evil; P. Heid. Inv. G 1101, for healing from migraine and eye discharge (includes charaktêres); P. Köln Inv. 2283 (C5/6 CE), charm to heal all illnesses, has ankh on the reverse; P. Köln Inv. 851 (C6 CE), healing from fevers and all illness by Jesus and the white wolf (Horus-Apollo); P. Lugd. Bat. XiX.20 (C6 CE), protection by Jesus from all fevers (lots of crosses included); P. Heid. inv. Lat. 5 (C5/6 CE),[83] protection charm including John 1.1 and parts of Psalm 20 (verses 3-7 in no-sequential order).

The fifteen erotic charms are: T. Heid. Arch. Inst. Inv. F429a & b (C2 CE), love charm placed on grave of named person (with mummy picture); T. Genav. Inv. 269 (C2 CE), sex binding charm (with pictures); T. Berol Inv. 13412 (C3 CE), love charm calling on Baal and the dead (corpse-daemon); P. Princ. II.76 (C3 CE), love charm (includes charaktêres, schwindeschema, and has lock of hair attached); T. Leid. Demarée (C3/4 CE), love charm; PSI I.28 (C3/4 CE), lesbian love charm which calls on a daemon to inflame the target via a bath-house; P. Köln Inv. 5514 (C4 CE), love charm; P. Köln Inv. 5512 (C3/4 CE), love charm (includes thirty-six signs which may correspond to the decans); P. Köln Inv. 3323 (C5 CE), love charm (sealed in a pot with two wax figures); T. Cairo Mus. JdE 48217 (C2/3 CE), love charm focusing on chthonic gods and spirits; T. Louvre Inv. E 27145 (C2/3 CE), love charm focusing on chthonic gods and spirits; P. Mich. Inv. 6925 (C2/3 CE), love charm focusing on chthonic gods and spirits (includes multiple schwindeschemas);[84] T. Köln Inv. 1 (C2/3 CE), binding love charm focusing on chthonic gods and spirits; T. Köln Inv. 2 (C2/3 CE), another binding love charm focusing on chthonic gods and spirits; O. Köln inv. 409 (C2/3 CE), love charm with chthonic spirits.

There are seven pagan and four Christian curses, these are: T. Louvre Inv. AF 6716 (C1 CE), curse calling on the dead and chthonic gods; T. Köln Inv. 4 (C3 CE), curse against athletes; Audollent DT.38 (C2/3 CE), rambling curse calling on chthonic gods; T. Cairo Mus. JdE 36059 (C3 CE), curse of muteness (includes schwindeschema with upward word wings on either side; P. Oxy. Inv. 50.4B 23/J (C3/4 CE), curse to make a person change their mind; P.

---

83 Note this is the only included example in Latin rather than Greek.

84 The preceding grouping of love charms calling on chthonic gods and spirits have a near identical wording with different family names, suggesting this may have been a popular charm, or was used extensively by the same practitioner.

Reinach II.88 (C4 CE), wrath-restraining curse (includes magical symbols, schwindeschema); O. Bodl. II.2180 (C4/5 CE), restrainer of wrath and victory charm; P. Ups. 8 (C6 CE), curse against enemies; P. Hamb. I.22 (C6 CE), curse to strike down enemies; P. IFAO s.n. (C6 CE), curse to strike down a woman and her family; P. Vindob. G16685 (C5/6 CE), curse to punish someone.

There are two charms to win favour: P. Merton II.58 (early C3 CE), charm to win favour; T. Köln Inv. 8 (C2/3 CE), success charm. There are two divinatory charms, Museo del Vicino Oriente Inv. 181/665 (C3 CE), bowl for liquid divination (lekanomanteia) containing schwindeschema of long palindromic word; T. Moen s.n. (C3/4 CE), charm calling a daemon into a child seer. There are also three charms of uncertain provenance, O. Mil. Vogl. Inv. 85 (C1/2 CE), fragmentary words or reverse of a schwindeschema of ablanathanalba; O. Cairo inv. CP 25/8/37/1-2 (C3 CE), shows figure of woman and child with few words, possibly fertility or domestic well-being charm; P. Palau Rib. Inv. 3 (C2-5 CE), figure of the god Seth with a bow and arrow and words suggesting it is a charm to spread discord.

The final section contains formularies. These are: P. Wash. Univ. II.74 (C2/1 BCE), partial text about making different animal figures; P. Monac. II.28 (C1 BCE), fragmentary love charm and uncertain fragments; P. Berol. Inv. 21243 (C1 BCE), three love charms and a headache charm; P.S.A. Athen. 70 (C1 BCE – C1 CE), love charm calling on a daemon to act on the target; P. Genav. inv. 186 (C2 CE), spells against insomnia and sciatica; P. Genav. Inv. 293 (C2 CE), fragmentary instructions to sacrifice a pig and call on deities for unknown purpose; P. Yale II.134 (C2/3 CE), contains six charms: to relax an erect penis, to pick someone up at the baths, for amorous dalliance, to cause a fight at a banquet, to turn wine sour, for frequent sex; P. Bon. 3 (C2/3 CE), fragments of Homeric oracle results from divination rolling a die three times; P. Köln inv. 1886 (C2/3 CE), six iatromagical fragments of five eye charms and one against every illness; P. Oxy. LVI.3834 (C3 CE), six assorted short charms: two to promote conception, to induce a prophetic dream, to restrain wrath, against legal adversaries, against fever (fragment); P. Reinach II.89 (C3 CE), two fragmentary recipes; P. Berol. Inv. 21260 (C3 CE), uncertain charm fragment; P. Laur. III.57 (C3 CE), five short charms and three medical charms: a love charm, a touch charm, a charm to drive the beloved, subjugation charm, charm to win favour, against wounds, undetermined, against fever; P. Lit. Lond. 171 (C3 CE), two charms: for having sex with a concubine, and for having a lot of sex; P. Yale II.130 (C3/4 CE), protective charm for a woman; P. Oxy. XLVI.3298 (late C3 CE), dream request; P. Oxy. LVI.3835 (C3/4 CE), five spells for identifying a thief; P. Berol. inv. 21227 (C3/4 CE), hymn to the great god; P. Oxy. inv. 72/65 (a) (C4 CE), two iatromagical charms: against erysipelas[85] and red eruptions; O. Ashm. Shelton 194 (C4 CE), two fragmentary charms against scorpion stings; P. Oxy. XXXVI.2753 (C4 CE), part of a dream request to Bes;[86] P. Laur. IV.149 (C3 CE), two recipes; P. Med. I.20 (C4/5 CE), charm with a lot of angels called (includes charaktêres); P. Noviomagensis Inv. 2 (C4/5 CE), lamp divination (lychnomancy); P. Ant. II.66 (C6 CE), thirteen healing charms: of uncertain purpose, a drying powder for the eyes, for easy childbirth, for fever, of uncertain purpose, against demonic possession, to protect or heal the eyes, against tumours, of uncertain purpose, against strangury,[87] against migraine, against wound effects, of uncertain purpose; P. Laur. IV.148 (C5 CE), two spells

---

85 Upper skin infection causing red, raised skin.

86 Note several lines of the request are identical to those found in the so-called Headless One (the Stele of Jeu), which is not surprising given the identification of Bes as the Headless One amongst some Egyptologists.

87 A blockage or irritation at the base of the bladder which causes pain and a desire to urinate.

to separate a couple; P. Mil. Vogl. Inv. 1245-50, 1252-53 (C5/6 CE),[88] uncertain charm, for easy labour, to sleep, against strangury, against shivering, uncertain, to win at games (includes figures and charaktêres); P. Mil. Vogl. Inv. 1251 (C5/6 CE), spell to secure favour, spell for calling in customers, uncertain charm (includes figure and charaktêres); P. Mil Vogl. Inv. 1254-62 (C5/6 CE), uncertain charms (some Aramaic words, figures, some charaktêres); P. Ant. III.140 (C5/6 CE), subjugation spell, charm to cure lunatics and lung problems; P. Ant. II.65 (C5 CE), fragment dealing with animal sacrifice.

Essential Reading

Daniel, Robert W. & Maltomini, Franco (eds & trans) (1989 & 1991) *Supplementum Magicum* Volumes 1 & 2. Köln: Westdeutscher Verlag. Excellent academic work with copious notes on translations and references to contemporary works.

✠ ἰc πατήρ ✠ ἰc υἱόc ✠ ἐν
πνεῦμα ἅγιον· ἀμήν.
αβλαναθαναβλα
βλαναθαναβλα
λαθαναναβλα
αθαναβλα
θαναβλα
αναβλα   θεραπεύ-
ναβλα   cατε
ἅγιε   αβλα   Τείρονα,
χαρακ- βλα   ὃν ἔτε-
τῆρεc   λα   κεν
        α   Παλλαδία,
ἀπὸ παντὸc ῥίγουc,
τριτέον, τεταρτέον

HEALING CHARM FROM P. KÖLN VI.257

---

88 This and the following two entries are in Coptic and Aramaic, with the different hands and style indicating their production in a workshop for documents.

Testament of Solomon

Date: C2-3 CE, with recensions in the Middle Ages/Renaissance.
Language: Hebrew, Greek, Arabic.
Influences: Unknown.
Provenance: Key proto-grimoire of unknown origin.
MSS: Dionysius Monastery MS 132 (C16); Recension A – Holkham Hall MS 99 (C15), BN Paris Supp. Graec. MS 500 (C16); Recension B – BN Paris Anciens fonds Grec MS 38 (C16) (Colbert 4895), Andreas Convent MS 73 (C15); Recension C – Vienna Codex philos. Graec. MS 108 (C16), Harley MS 5596 (1440) bound with *Magical Treatise* (recension A and C), Ambrosian Library MS 1030 (C16), Bologna University MS 3632 (C15), Parisinus Graec. MS 2419 bound with *Magical Treatise* (C15), Bononiensis Uni. MS 3632.
Circle: N/A.
Tools: Black-handled knife (Recension C), ring.
Spirit List: Recension A: Abezithibod, Adonael, Adonaeth, Afarot, Agchonion, Akton, Alath, Allazool, Alleborith, Anatreth, Anoster, Arael, Arotosael, Asmodeus, Asteraoth, Atrax, Autothith, Azael, Balthial, Barsafael, Baruchiachel, Bazazeth, Beelzeboul, Belbel, Bianakith, Bothothel, Brieus, Buldumech, Crest of Dragons, Deception, Distress, Enenuth, Enepsigos, Envy, Ephippas, Error, Harpax, Hekate,[89] Hephesikireth, Iameth, Iathoth, Iax, Ichthion, Ieropael, Iudal, Jealousy, Katanikotael, Klothod, Kumeatel, Kunospaston, Kurtael, Lamechiel, Lascivious Spirit, Lix Tetrax, Mardero, Marmarao, Marmarath, Metathiax, Michael, Naoth, Nefthada, Obizuth, Onoskelis, Ornias, Oropel, Pheth, Phnunoboeol, Phthenoth, Power, Rabdos, Raphael, Rath, Rathanael, Roeled, Rorex, Ruax, Sabrael, Saphathorael, Sphandor, Sphendonael, Strife, Uriel, Uruel, Winged Dragon, Zoroel; Recension C: Amemon, Ampatzout, Anet, Apolen, Asiel, Asmodeo, Astaroth, Asteroth, Atanianous, Belet, Boul, Darogan, Eltzen, Enodas, Karap, Kastiel, Krinel, Lasarak, Latzepher, Lenel, Loupet, Machoumet, Magot, Makatak, Meinget, Myragkous, Myratziel, Nabel, Napalaikon, Napour, Oel, Oriens, Ouleos, Paltaphote, Paltiel Tzamal, Panon, Parel, Pelon, Phakanel, Pharan, Potzeties, Rhaamet, Rhoapt, Sansoniel, Saparatzel, Saratiel, Satael, Setariel, Soupiel, Tarseus, Tougel, Tzerepones, Tzianphiel.

The Text

The *Testament of Solomon* (or *ToS*) occupies a unique position in the grimoire tradition. It dates back to around the second century CE, but there are three main recensions or groups of manuscripts, the last of which date to around the fifteenth century.

The *ToS* tells the story of King Solomon's construction of the Temple. One of his servants is being harassed by a vampiric demon, and Solomon prays to God for help. God sends the archangel Michael who gives him a ring engraved with a pentagram, which gives him power over all demons. Solomon then summons the demon, and binds it, and forces it to call a number of other demons, each of whom he binds to help build the Temple and forces to name themselves and the way to deal with them.

After all the demons are bound, one of the demons predicts the death of one of Solomon's servants in three days. This comes to pass and Solomon has a discourse with the demon on the behaviours of demons. This is followed by a visit from the Queen of the South who Solomon aids, binding another demon. The text ends with Solomon, lured by his lust for a Shunammite woman, sacrificing five locusts to Moloch, and being abandoned by the Spirit of God. Solomon warns all readers of the ToS not to repeat his mistakes.

---
89 Not specifically named but identified through the references.

The *ToS* can be considered one of the original proto-grimoire sources, providing the first spirit catalogue or list, together with the means of controlling the demons. In many cases this is via the assistance of a confounding or thwarting angel. This theme is seen later in the grimoires, e.g., in the angels of the hours controlling the demons of the hours in the *Hygromanteia*, the use of the Shemhamphorash angels in Rudd's *Goetia*, the planetary intelligences controlling the planetary spirits, etc.

Recensions A and B of the ToS are revisions of the original document (lost to time), with some variants in the material contained in them. The spirit list in Recension C, the last of the manuscript families, is very different to that found previously in A and B but shares many spirits with the texts of the *Magical Treatise*, which it was sometimes bound with. It is significant that the spirits are each given with their seal, like those in grimoires from the following century such as the *Goetia*.

Essential Reading

Conybeare, F.C. (1898) *The Testament of Solomon*, in *The Jewish Quarterly Review* 11.1, New York. The article which brought the *ToS* into prominence in the Anglophile world.

Johnson, Brian (2019) *Testament of Solomon Recension C*. West Yorkshire, Hadean Press. A small but comprehensive study of the significant Greek recension C texts of the *ToS* from the fifteenth century, with original translation and significant useful notes.

McCown, C.C. (ed) (1922) *The Testament of Solomon*. Leipzig: J.C. Hinrichs'sche Buchhandlung. The most complete study to date, covering many of the manuscripts (all known at that time) and exploring the variants between the recensions.

Ancient Christian Magic

Date: C2-12 CE.
Language: Coptic.
Influences: Egyptian mythology, Gnostic mythology, Greek Magical Papyri, Bible.
Provenance: Collection of Coptic texts from C2-12 CE.
MSS: Many papyri contained within, listed in text.
Circle: N/A.
Tools: Text written mainly on papyrus, also other materials like lead and other metal sheets, human and animal bones.
Spirit List:[90] Abbachiaox, Abiout, Abrasax, Abrasaxael, Abrax, Abraxiel, Achab, Achael, Acharah, Achorbou, Achoubael, Adawn, Adon, Adonael, Adone, Ael, Akalata, Akentael, Akrael, Akramata, Akutael, Akuel, Altheros, Amachem, Amanael, Amanou, Amarael, Amman, Amoel, Amuath, Amun, Anaboel, Anael, Ananael, Anaoth, Anapuel, Anatalael, Anatel, Anathael, Anax, Anlel, Anramuel, Antrakuel, Anubis, Aoiel, Aou, Aphael, Aphrodite, Aphropaic, Aphrodite, Apiel, Apollo, Apophantes, Aracha, Arachael, Arael, Aram, Aranael, Aratachael, Aratha, Arathael, Archon, Ariel, Arimatha, Arinatael, Armozel, Arnael, Arophtebel, Arphael, Artemis, Arthamiel, Artolan, Artolar, Artole, Aruel, Asamuth, Asaroth, Asel, Asentael, Asmodeus, Asuel, Atha, Athael, Athariel, Athena, Athiel, Athrak, Auriel, Authrounios, Azael, Bael, Baktiotha, Bal, Banchooch, Banithe, Bantal, Banuel, Barbarouch, Barbelo, Bariana, Bariel, Barouch, Bathuel, Bathurael, Bathuriel, Bel, Belouch, Bersebour, Beth, Betha, Bok, Boriel, Bunes, Chabroel, Chamachal, Chamarmariao, Charon, Cherinael, Cheroubin, Chooch, Chouncheoch, Chous, Choucho, Christuel, Chu, Cyprian, Daveithe, Davithea, Dedael, Doruel, Eia, Eiael, Eidiel, Eieio, Eiphiel, Ekenel, Eknel, Eleleth, Elouch, Emiel, Eneriel, Ennael, Ephemeranion, Ephesech, Ephnix, Eptiel, Eraphael, Eriel, Ermukratos, Erphanouel, Esparte, Ethael, Exiel, Gabriel, Ganuel, Garmaniel, Gereel, Harmosiel, Harmozel, Hathor, Hormosiel, Horus, Hraguel, Hraphael, Hrophot, Icho, Iochael, Isis, Israel, Jesus Christ, Kardiel, Karnabiel, Karnabot, Kasis, Kenel, Keria, Kimphas, Kronos, Kouchos, Kukkuel, Labdiel, Labtiel, Lamei, Lanach, Lauriel, Lelael, Lohep, Lonuel, Louchme, Louloukaksa, Macharael, Mael, Maiel, Maiman, Manachoth, Manael, Manuel, Mar, Mareupel, Mariel, Marinthael, Marioth, Marmar, Marmarael, Marmaraoth, Marmariel, Maroutha, Marouthael, Marthael, Marthiel, Maruel, Masthel, Meliton, Merael, Merusel, Mesemiasim, Meuchiel, Michael, Mikael, Mikroel, Mimmechabatouthel, Minianto, Mirotheos, Moira, Mosul, Murophael, Naias Meli, Naltrothothr, Namer, Nanoel, Neater, Nechiel, Nephael, Nerael, Nuriel, Ochael, Olalborim, Olithiel, Orasiel, Oriel, Oriskos, Oroiael, Orpha, Orphamiel, Osiris, Osul, Ouliat, Oupiel, Ourael, Ouchou, Ousiel, Outriel, Pakathiel, Pamathiel, Paonel, Paplin, Papothiel, Paramera, Parithoel, Parthoel, Paruthel, Patriel, Pechiel, Pechoel, Pemadel, Pemnamouel, Pemoel, Perachamiel, Periel, Persomphon, Perthathaniel, Peskinther, Petbe, Phael, Phanuel, Phariel, Phausiel, Phiel, Philopael, Phoraeim, Phourani, Phourat, Phukta, Piak, Pirael, Pithiel, Plemos, Praiithel, Priel, Prikael, Priphiel, Priroel, Proeiel, Promiel, Prophiel, Proteth, Prothiel, Psatael, Pserathael, Psilaphael, Psotomis, Psourouthioun, Rabuel, Rael, Raguel, Rakuel, Raphael, Ruel, Rumiel, Runuel, Ruphos, Sabael, Sachoiel, Saint Leontius, Saint Philoxenus, Saint Phocas, Saint Serenus, Saint Zachariah, Salaman, Salamex, Salani, Salpiax, Sanael, Saoth, Sappathai, Sarael, Sariel, Sarinael, Sasael, Sasmiasas, Satan, Satanael, Sebt-Hor, Sechrer, Sedekiel, Semanuel, Serapis, Seroael, Shafriel, Shanamael, Siak, Sisinaei, Sitoriel, Sntael, Sochot, Solomon, Solothiel, Somuel, Sophia, Sourouchchata, Srael, Sraguel, Sramael, Sraphoel, Stoel, Subba, Suel,

---

[90] Note the presence of many Gnostic spirits in this collection of texts. Also, a number of names are very similar, which may suggest their possible corruption over time.

Suriel, Suruel, Susael, Tael, Takuel, Tartarachous, Tatriel, Tauriel, Tekauriel, Temeluchos, Thaisara, Thalamora, Thanael, Thaoth, Thaotha, Thathiel, Thauruel, Theriel, Thesoha, Theumatha, Thimiael, Thol, Thoran, Thoth, Thrakai, Thriel, Throel, Tophou, Torothora, Tremael, Trophos, Tsel, Tupopsta, Umnuel, Uranos, Uri, Wepwawet, White Wolf, Xanael, Xiphiel, Yak, Yaldabaoth, Yao, Yaoel, Yao Sabaoth Adonai, Yeremiel, Yoel, Yohau, Yoiriel, Yonael, Yoniel, Yonuel, Yoranael, Yothael, Youlach, Zarathiel, Zartiel, Zedekiel, Zetekiel, Zeus, Zorokothora Melchisidek.

The Text

Ancient Christian Magic contains texts written by Coptic Christians living in Egypt over a period of a millennia. It is worth noting that a number of the texts (4-37) are Christian texts that Betz chose to omit from the Greek Magical Papyri, and some of the texts are from the same. Some of the charms are historiolae, usually focusing on events with Jesus as the protagonist, and some of them are Gnostic. As well as Gnostic influences, Egyptian and Greek deities are also found in some of the charms, emphasizing the cultural cross-fertilisation that occurred. The last few chapters each contain a prayer with a number of different uses for the prayer. Amongst the texts are an early example of the life story of Saint Cyprian of Antioch, and the letters between Jesus and King Abgar, which would appear later in the grimoires. Amongst the numerous angels, the texts also contain early (or maybe first recorded) appearances of angels who subsequently appear later in sources like the *Hygromanteia*.

The texts contained are: a woman's complaint against neglect (Old Coptic Schmidt Papyrus, c.100 CE); invocation of Egyptian and Jewish deities for revelation (GMPP: 1-25, C4 CE);[91] Isis love spell (GMPP: 94-153, C4 CE3);[92] spells and healing legends for medical problems (P. Oxy. 1384, C5 CE); amulet to heal eye ailments (P. Berol 21911, C5 CE); healing ostracon (ostracon from Egger collection, C7/8 CE); healing spell using the *Gospel of Matthew* (includes human figure and words in form of cross) (P. Oxy. 1077, C6 CE); amulets for help from God and the saints (P. Berol. 11858, C6/7 CE); spell for healing and protection using biblical quotations (P. Berol. 9096, ND); spell invoking Christ for protection against illness and ill treatment (P. Cairo 10263, C4/5 CE); amulet to heal and protect Joseph[93] from fever (includes Erichthonie as a schwindeschema) (P. Köln 851, C7 CE); amulet to heal and protect Megas (P. Amsterdam 173, C4/5 CE); healing amulet for a woman (P. Vitelli 365, C5/6 CE); another healing amulet for a woman (P. Berol. 21230, C5/6 CE); amulet to protect Aria from fever (P. Oxy. 924, C4 CE);[94] amulet to heal and protect Joannia from fever (P. Oxy. 1151, C5 CE); amulet to protect a woman from pain and distress (P. Rainer 5, C6/7 CE); amulet to protect Silvanus and give him good health (P. Berol. 954, C6 CE); spell to drive out demons (GMPP: 1227-64, C4 CE);[95] amulet to protect against the mischief of evil spirits (P. Gr. 337, C6 CE);[96] protective spell using the Lord's Prayer and the Exorcism of Solomon (P. Ianda 14, C5/6 CE); spell for protection against evil spirits (P. Cairo 67188, C6 CE); spell for protection against headless powers (Zereteli-Tiflis 24, C6 CE); amulet for protection against a headless power (Edward Collection, C5/6 CE); amulet to protect the entrance to a house from vermin (includes

---

91 PGM IV:1-25.

92 PGM IV:94-153.

93 A number of the amulets are for specifically named individuals.

94 Note the Holy Spirit is referred to as 'Mother' as part of the Trinity in this amulet.

95 PGM IV:1227-64.

96 Interestingly the text on this amulet includes reference to 'all of you who swore before Solomon', suggesting the creator may have been aware of the *Testament of Solomon*.

wing form triangle of Aphrodite's name) (P. Oxy. 1060, C6 CE); amulet to protect a house and its occupants from evil (P. Oslo 1.5, C4/5 CE); spell seeking relief from the wrongs of Theodosios (Hermitage, C4 CE); spell for a person seeking vengeance (P. Vienna G 19929, C6 CE); Mesa's curse against Philadelphe and her children (Amulet text, C4 CE); oracular text (P. Oxy. 925, C5/6 CE); oracular text (P. Oxy 1150, C6 CE); oracular text (P. Oxy. 1926, C6 CE); oracular text (P. Harris 54, C6 CE); oracular text (P. Berol. 21269, C6/7 CE); oracular text (P. Berol 13232, C5+); invocation of divine power to bring success and good luck (P. Prag. 1 Wessely, 300 CE); Biblical names of power and their translations (P. Heid. G 1359, C3/4 CE); a Gnostic fire baptism (Bruce Codex, C4 CE); spell for ascending through the heavens (Bruce Codex, C4 CE); the Gospel of the Egyptians (Nag Hammadi Codex III, C4 CE);[97] the First Stele of Seth (Nag Hammadi Codex VII, C4 CE); prayers, hymns, and invocations for transcendent initiation (Nag Hammadi Codex VIII, C4 CE); book of ritual spells for medical problems (P. Mich. 136, ND); spells for medical problems and the protection of a house (P. Vienna K 8303, C11/12 CE); spell for various diseases (P. Berol. 8324, ND); spell to heal a foot (P. Vienna K 8638, C10 CE); spell using legends about Horus and Abimelech to bring sleep (P. Berol 5565, C6-8 CE); another spell using legends about Horus and Abimelech to bring sleep (or sex?) (P. Schmidt 1, C4-7 CE); spell for relieving the pain of childbirth and stomach pain (P. Berol. 8313, ND); amulet to heal and protect a woman (includes Sator palindrome) (P. Vienna K 7093, C10 CE); amulet to heal and protect Poulpehepus from fever (includes Sator sequence) (P. Oxy. 39 5B 125/A, C11 CE); amulet to heal and protect Phoibammon from fever (Moen amulet, ND); another amulet against fever (includes seven pentagrams) (P. Heid. Kopt. 564, C7-12 CE); amulet to heal Ahmed from fever, evil eye, and other problems (P. Heid. Kopt. 544, c.541 CE); amulet against snakebite (includes Sator square) (P. Yale 1792, C6/7 CE); spell for a cup of healing (P. Berlin 8319, C8 CE); spell for healing with water, oil, and honey (Oriental MS 5899, ND); a monk's prayer for good health (P. Yale 2124, ND); invocation of the Sun for protection (three creature drawings at end) (P. Köln 20826, C5-8 CE); invocation of god for protection (Freer frag. 10, C9 CE); spell for protection against illness and evil (includes Sator palindrome) (P. Vienna K 8302, C6/7 CE); amulet to protect Philoxenos from all evil (Robert Nahman text amulet, ND); ritual spell to heal and protect (P. Berlin 11347, C8/9 CE); exorcistic spell to drive evil forces from a pregnant woman (includes figure, Ablanathanalba, A, O, wing formations, attribution of the seven Greek vowels to archangels, the Sator square words) (Oriental MS 5525, ND); spell for healthy childbirth (Rylands 100, ND); spell for protection during childbirth (P. Michigan 1190, C5 CE); spell for the well-being of a child (P Vienna K 70, C10/11 CE); spell for protection against reptiles (P. Rylands 104, C7/8 CE); spell for protection against violent attack (Oriental MS 4721, ND); spell, with Gnostic characteristics, to protect from filthy demons (Oriental MS 5987, ND); Rossi's 'Gnostic' tractate against the powers of evil (includes long angelic spirit list with rulerships, Gabriel conjuration, and complex figure) (BN Turin, ND);[98] spell using a Horus legend for erotic purposes (P. Schmidt 2); erotic spell of Cyprian of Antioch (includes complex figure and detailed telling of the Cyprian legend) (P. Heid. Kopt. 684, C11 CE); erotic spell to attract a woman (P. Yale 1791, C6/7 CE); another erotic spell to attract a woman (P. Berlin 8314, ND); another erotic spell to attract a woman (P. Berlin 8325, C9 CE); another erotic spell to attract a woman (Heid. Kopt. 518, ND); another erotic spell to attract a woman (P. Hay 10376, C6/7 CE); spells for sex and business (P. Hay 10414, C6/7 CE); spells for favour, honour, and passion (P. Hay 10434, C6/7 CE); spell for gathering to a business, for menstrual flow (drawing of a boat, many figures and signs) (P. Hay 10122, C6/7 CE); spell for mutual love between a man and a woman (P. Mich. 4932f,

---

97 From the Sethian Gnostic text *Holy Book of the Great Invisible Spirit*.
98 Original destroyed in a fire in 1904.

C5/7 CE); spell to make a woman become pregnant (Pierpont M662B 22, C7 CE); spell for a man to obtain a male lover (Ashmolean 1981.940, C6 CE); sexual curse to leave a man impotent and protect a woman from sexual advances (Chicago Oriental 13767, ND); another sexual curse to leave a man impotent and protect a woman from sexual advances (P. Heid. Kopt. 682, ND); another sexual curse to leave a man impotent and protect a woman from sexual advances (Strasbourg Coptic MS 135, ND); curse against Victor (the twin), David, and Papnoute (Oriental MS 5986, ND); a widow's curse against Shenoute (Munich Copt. P. 5, C7 CE); curse against several violent people (P. Lichačev, C4/5 CE); Jacob's curse against Maria, Tatore, and Andreas (Coptic MS C (P) 4, C5/6 CE); curse against perjurers (P. Berlin 10587, C10 CE); curse of a mother against her son's female companion (Oriental MS 6172, ND); curse to make a man tongue-tied (Cambridge T-S 12.207, C10+);[99] Abdallah's curses to weaken Mouflehalpahapani (figure surrounded by text) (P. Berlin 8503, C8 CE); lead curse tablet against the health of Kyriakos (Köln T 10, C6/7 CE); bone curse to make Apollo burn (on human rib) (Florence 5645, ND); bone curse to bring the powers of darkness down upon Aaron (Cairo A & B, C10 CE); spell for a bone and corpse (Liverpool Inst. Arch. Text, C6/7 CE); Mary's curse against Martha (Aberdeen text, C4/5 CE); Jacob's curse to give someone an ulcerous tumour (IFAO Cairo papyrus, C4/5 CE); Victor's curse to silence Semne (Würzberg 42, C10 CE); invocation of a power for blessing and cursing (P. Köln 10235, C6 CE); Apa Victor's curse against Alo (P. Mich. 3565, C6 CE); curse against a woman's face and work (P. Heid. Kopt 681, late C10 CE); curse to bring seventy different diseases upon a victim (several figures surrounded by text) (P. Yale 1800, C6/7 CE); possible curse through the power of Shafriel (has figure of eight-rayed star) (P. Yale 882(A), C6/7 CE); curse against Joor and his wife (P. Mich. 1523, C4/5 CE); curse to separate a man and a woman, using necromancy and a blade-shaped parchment (Louvre E14.250, C10 CE); curse to harm a person through the use of wax dolls (P. Hied. Kopt. 679, C11 CE); curse to disable the body of an enemy (figures and numerous charaktêres) (P. Berlin 8321, ND); spell for the return of a stolen object and a curse upon the thief (Vienna K 8304, C10-11 CE); spell invoking Bathuriel and other heavenly powers (Cairo 49547, ND); invocation of Orphamiel (O. Moen 34, ND); spell of summons, by the power of God's tattoos (Rylands 103, ND); spell for power to dominate adversaries (P. Berlin 8322, C7-9 CE); spell for invoking Michael and the heavenly powers for business and other purposes (includes vowel schwindeschema) (Moen 3, C9-12 CE); spell invoking a thundering power to perform every wish (H.O. Lange, C7 CE); spell invoking Aknator the Ethiopian to perform every wish (includes three figures surrounded by text) (Coptic Mus. 4959, C9-11 CE); spell invoking the divine to accomplish whatever is requested (Coptic Mus. 4960, C6-8 CE); spell for a good singing voice (P. Berlin 8318, C8 CE); another spell for a good singing voice (P. Yale 1791, C6/7 CE); spell to bind or silence a dog (Oriental MS 1013A, C8 CE); amulet with words and names of power (P. Mich. 3023A, ND); another amulet with names of power (P. Mich. 3472, ND); collection of oracles (Vatican Copt. P. 1, C7/8 CE); the London Hay cookbook (Hay 10391, C6/7 CE); a cookbook from Cairo (Cairo 45060, ND); spell to obtain a good singing voice (includes human figure and charaktêres) (Oriental MS 6794, C7 CE); spell for good fishing (image of man fishing) (Oriental MS 6795, C7 CE); a prayer made by Mary and a prayer for power, with additions (includes alpha schwindeschema) (Oriental MS 6796, C7 CE); spell to cast out every unclean spirit (has drawing of the crucifixion) (Oriental MS 6796, C7 CE); the Coptic hoard of spells from Michigan university (P. Mich. 593, C4/6 CE); the Coptic book of ritual power from Leiden (includes the letters between Jesus and Abgar) (Leiden Anastasi 9, ND); the praise of Michael the Archangel (P. Heid. Kopt. 686, late C10 CE).

---

99 This is a Cairo Genizah fragment written in Arabic and Coptic.

ENCYCLOPAEDIC ENTRIES 63

Essential Reading

Meyer, Marvin W. & Smith, Richard (eds) (1999) *Ancient Christian Magic: Coptic Texts of Ritual Power*. New Jersey: Princeton University Press. Superb work containing numerous charms and demonstrating the relevance and cross-fertilisation of magical practice in late Antiquity into the early Medieval period.

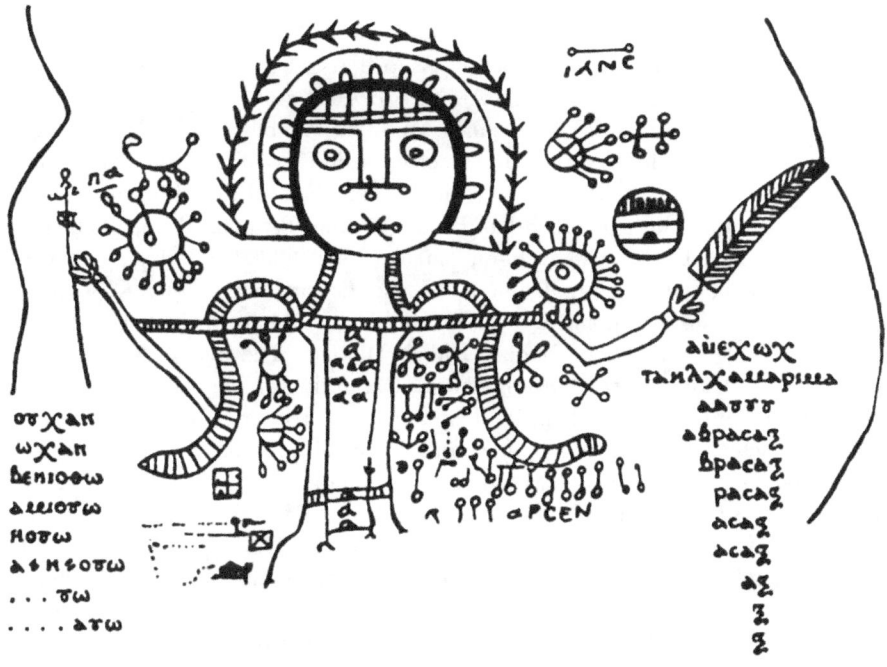

Image from Rossi's Gnostic Tractate

Sepher ha-Razim (The Book of the Mysteries)

Date: Early C4 CE.
Language: Hebrew, Arabic, Latin.
Influences: PGM, Enoch literature.
Provenance: Early Jewish magical text, translated into Arabic by C10 in Cairo, and into Latin in the Court of King Alfonso X in mid C13.
MSS: Hungarian Academy MS 224 (C8-9; Florence Plut. 44.13 (C13); JTSL MS 12; JTSL MS 14; JTSL MS 163; Jerusalem 8° 476; Schoken Kabbalah MS 3; fragments in Cairo Genizah (generally C11-12) including Oxford MS Heb. 18/30, MS Heb. D 62/50, MS Heb. E 67/32-33, MS Heb. F 45; Cambridge T-S K 1/13, K 1/97, K 1/98, K 1/102, K 1/145, K 21/95, NS 135, NS 246/26, NS 298/72, T-S Arabic 31/183, 33/9, 43/84, 43/223, 43/260, 45/12; JTSL ENA 2673/23, ENA 2750; Dropsie College Genizah Collection 437, Leningrad Antonine 238.
Circle: N/A.
Tools: N/A.
Spirit List: Aaazial, Aabdial, Aabr, Aadmun, Aadnnial, Aagial, Aali,[100] Aalzial, Aamial, Aamnial, Aanbal, Aannial, Aanshal, Aaqb, Aaqhial, Aaqrial, Aaulph, Aaur, Aauzial, Aazial, Aazmal, Aazrial, Aazy, Abba, Abial, Abibal, Abimud, Abrasks, Abrh, Abrial, Abrih, Abrita, Abrkial, Aburm, Achal, Achial, Achmuda, Achsp, Adir, Adlial, Adnial, Adq, Adrk, Adrun, Aduma, Adunial, Adut, Agdln, Aglgltun, Agmial, Agra, Agrial, Agrital, Ahgiih, Aial, Aikrit, Ailial, Aimik, Ainik, Aisturti, Aitmial, Akal, Aknsp, Akpp, Akr, Akzan, Al, Alaashh, Alaazr, Alal, Alial, Aliss, Alminial, Alnitkal, Alnu, Alpi, Alpial, Alpntus, Alprt, Alsdq, Alun, Amap, Amial, Amikal, Aminal, Aminual, Amlial, Amnchial, Amngnan, Amnhr, Amnial, Amrial, Amstial, Amuk, Anaur, Anbur, Andgnur, Angial, Anmri, Anqiu, Anuk, Anup, Apikh, Apnial, Aprial, Aprksi, Apshrial, Aptial, Aqilih, Aqrba, Aqrial, Aqudu, Aral, Aranial, Arbial, Ardq, Arduda, Argla, Armat, Armial, Armud, Armunis, Armut, Arnub, Arpda, Arq, Arqni, Artlidi, Artmiktun, Arunur, Arush, Ashbh, Ashbur, Ashdda, Ashlba, Ashmdaa, Ashpr, Ashpur, Ashrial, Ashtib, Ashtnuil, Askiri, Asmaaual, Asmigdun, Asppial, Astial, Astirup, Astrimi, Asttial, Astun, Asturin, Asymur, Atdshu, Atgla, Atkial, Atnni, Atr, Aual, Aubr, Aubshal, Audhal, Audial, Augrbbu, Auhial, Aumial, Aumigra, Aumrhi, Aumtun, Aunbib, Aupri, Aur, Aurial, Aurit, Aurpnial, Aurpnil, Aurnh, Aurnial, Autut, Azial, Azlibn, Azuti, Baashial, Bariba, Bbital, Bbsbau, Bghial, Bhchml, Bhdrk, Bhnirial, Biual, Bkpi, Blnial, Blqur, Bmriut, Bnrial, Bnsh, Braut, Brgal, Brgmi, Britur, Brkial, Brkib, Brqial, Brshsal, Brtubial, Bruq, Btuar, Bubukuk, Burtias, Bvmdi, Bwal, Chdial, Chgl, Chgra, Chilial, Chlilal, Chlian, Chlshial, Chlsial, Chlual, Chmmial, Chmqial, Chnial, Chrhal, Chrial, Chsdial, Chshndrnus, Chsial, Chsnial, Chtnial, Chtpial, Chustual, Chzal, Daaihu, Dainut, Daubit, Dbal, Dbbal, Dbrial, Dbubaur, Dchgial, Dghial, Dgrial, Dgugra, Diam, Dibqial, Didial, Didnaur, Didriuk, Digl, Digra, Dimhn, Dimtmr, Dinmur, Diqna, Diraz, Ditrun, Dknsur, Dkrial, Dlgial, Dlglial, Dlkt, Dlqial, Dlrial, Dmal, Dmimial, Dmna, Dmnai, Dmnshr, Dmual, Dmula, Dmumial, Dnhl, Drmial, Drudial, Drumial, Dshnchia, Dshuua, Dukmsal, Dumial, Dunrnia, Durial, Gaashial, Gaupr, Gba, Gblial, Gbrial, Gchlial, Gdgl, Gdial, Gdrial, Gdudial, Girshum, Glgla, Gmti, Gnts, Graaih, Grchta, Gsqial, Gulan, Gulial, Gurial, Gushpnial, Gzrial, Hdrial, Hdrnial, Helios, Hgdiab, Hhgrit, Hmk, Hmnkial, Hnial, Hrmaial, Hrmnaa, Hrmur, Hsaaial, Hshtk, Hsniplpt, Hstr, Htnial, Hud, Hud Hud, Hudial, Hudih, Hunmura, Hupniaun, Iaashal, Iabuk, Iabutiau, Ialal, Iamnuk, Iarn, Ibnial, Ichsi, Ichspt, Ichzial, Idaat, Idrial, Idual, Ihal, Ihual, Iiqr, Ikmtu, Ikstr, Ikptini, Ildng, Ikti, Ilial, Imumial, Irshial, Ishaaial, Ishmi, Ishmrial, Isrial, Iuqmial, Iussh,

---

100 This name is listed twice in this encampment.

Iuun, Iutnh, Kbir, Kdial, Kdir, Kdumial, Kildh, Klmiia, Klmniia, Klnh, Klptun, Klubial, Kmshial, Kmshu, Kntun, Knur, Kpniia, Kpun, Krba, Krbi, Krbtun, Krdi, Krhal, Krimka, Kriophoros (Hermes), Krital, Krkus, Krm, Krqta, Krsun, Krth, Ksil, Ktbral, Kuzziba, Lbial, Lchsun, Lgch, Lhba, Lhgial, Lhtqup, Libbal, Libral, Librnk, Linnial, Llp, Lmial, Lmushy, Lpum, Ltmial, Ltsrpal, Marinus, Marit, Maut, Mbum, Mchshina, Mdnial, Mhrial, Mial, Migal, Mkmikal, Mksabu, Mksial, Mlgdm, Mlkial, Mlkih, Mlmial, Mltchial, Mnhal, Mnhral, Mnitial, Mnmlk, Mnurial, Mpnial, Mpnur, Mqpa, Mrbnial, Mrgial, Mrial, Mriut, Mrmin, Mrmraut, Mrmrin, Mrmual, Mrnisal, Mrsum, Msgial, Mshtub, Msrial, Msrush, Mtnal, Mual, Mukal, Muktial, Mural, Mus, Mushial, Mutar, Naanh, Nbimal, Nbrial, Nchlial, Nhial, Nimmus, Ninshia, Niplial, Nkbrial, Nkmra, Nmdial, Nnrial, Npli, Nppmiut, Nqrial, Nrhal, Nrntq, Nrumial, Nsbrial, Nshchial, Nshmial, Nshr, Ntial, Ntnal, Ntpial, Nudniia, Nuhrial, Nurial, Paaur, Pchdrun, Pdhal, Pdutial, Pgrial, Pial, Pitpri, Pkhur, Plaual, Pnial, Pnimur, Ppal, Pptsh, Praatup, Pral, Prchgal, Prdial, Prial, Prian, Pribial, Prikinu, Prnigal, Prnin, Prnus, Prsial, Prsumun, Prual, Prug, Prukh, Prupial, Prush, Prutial, Przirum, Psal, Pshshial, Psiksuk, Pskial, Pskr, Pspial, Pstmr, Ptchial, Ptchih, Ptkia, Ptrupi, Ptual, Ptunial, Pual, Pubun, Pukbus, Purtnial, Qchnial, Qdmial, Qdshial, Qlilial, Qitr, Qlaaial, Qmnial, Qnal, Qnumial, Qrba, Qrstus, Qrukns, Qrumial, Qrunidn, Qshtial, Qsmial, Qspial, Qstsdial, Qtchnial, Qtipur, Qtibia, Qudshial, Quial, Qumial, Qunaqrial, Qup, Quz, Raadnial, Ralkh, Rbaaial, Rbal, Rbnia, Rbsal, Rchbia, Rchbial, Rchgl, Rdqial, Rdrial, Rgbial, Rhtial, Ripipis, Rkilal, Rlbial, Rmgdl, Rmial, Rnchial, Rnzial, Rpdial, Rppial, Rqhti, Rshial, Rsput, Rumapi, Rzial, Sabial, Sbbial, Sbibal, Sblh, Schal, Schruri, Sdrial, Sdrkin, Sgrial, Shaaipial, Shaapial, Shaaqmuh, Shaasial, Shawal, Shbaaqni, Shbial, Shbiudaa, Shbkiria, Shbqial, Shchial, Shdqi, Shdqial, Shdrlial, Shgrial, Shial, Shiraium, Shkinttk, Shknial, Shlhbin, Shlmial, Shlqial, Shmial, Shmihud, Shmshial, Shnnal, Shpiqual, Shplial, Shptial, Shptp, Shrial, Shrmial, Shshmaa, Shtqial, Shukdun, Shuprial, Sikbrdum, Siqmh, Sktbaq, Sksial, Slbidm, Slchial, Smiail, Smikal, Smkial, Smkih, Smnial, Snial, Spipial, Spnig, Sprial, Spum, Srk, Srpial, Srsial, Srugial, Srukit, Srura, Stal, Strial, Strtu, Susial, Suua, Taanbun, Taay, Taazma, Tagishun, Tbgial, Tbl, Tdhdial, Tgmlial, Tgrial, Thpial, Thrial, Thzrial, Tiamial, Tigrh, Tilh, Timnhrq, Timugu, Tirli, Tirum, Tkt, Tkurks, Tlbaap, Tlhbm, Tlial, Tlgial, Tmkial, Tmnial, Tmpnih, Tmr, Tnimial, Tqu, Trgch, Tripun, Trkial, Trmial, Trquih, Trspu, Trsunial, Trtm, Truaur, Trurgr, Truhun, Tsial, Ttbal, Ttqhh, Tub, Tubial, Tupumus, Tuqpial, Tuqpirs, Uiutn, Upathna, Zbdial, Zbitur, Zchzchal, Zhal, Zkrial, Zlqial, Zmbut, Zrgri, Zunnum, Zzial.

THE TEXT

According to its origin story, *Sepher ha-Razim* was presented by the archangel Raziel to Noah before the Flood. He used it and it was passed through the generations to Solomon. *Sepher ha-Razim* is an early Jewish magical work with parallels to parts of the Talmud, the Enoch literature (*Books of Enoch*) and Hekhalot texts. Indeed, six of the seven manuscripts were bound together with two Merkavah texts, *Shi'ur Qomah* and *Maseket Hekhalot*, showing the close connection. The structure of the work is divided into seven sections, each for one of the heavens or firmaments (clearly mirrored in the later Hekhalot texts of the Merkavah tradition). A number of fragments of the text are found in the *Cairo Genizah*, demonstrating the continuity of this material over many centuries. From its structure and content, *Sepher ha-Razim* could arguably be considered the first grimoire-style text. The translation of the text into Arabic and Latin and elements of it being found in *Summa Sacre Magice* also support the view that the influence of *Sepher ha-Razim* on the grimoire tradition was greater than has previously been credited.

Each section of heaven includes a list of angels for that heaven, making this text a huge angelic spirit list. There is a strong emphasis on purification when working with these angels. For each heaven, the text describes both the heaven and the appearance of the angels, providing a clear visual basis for the practitioner to work with.

The seventy-two angels of the first encampment are healing angels, with the practice of how to call on them and give people healing described. The eighty angels of the second encampment are angels of wrath and anger, who deal with war, torment, and death. Their practice includes revenge on enemies, creditors, and ships, and focuses on sevenfold symbolism using water and pottery shards with conjurations. The thirty-six angels of the third encampment are angels of foretelling. They can reveal events of the coming year including harvests, disasters, wars, and other major events. This is done with slips of papyrus in oil in a flask and focuses on threefold symbolism and the Sun. The forty-four angels of the fourth encampment bestow favour, and are called upon to petition nobles, judges, and kings. They can also influence the wealthy and women to gain their favour. These techniques use a slaughtered lion cub with its heart and blood. The sixty-two angels of the fifth encampment operate during the night and aid with answers from the moon, stars, ghosts, and spirits. The charms include love conjurations, both homosexual and heterosexual, charms for acts of kindness, conjuring ghosts to speak to (calling on Hermes), and calling on spirits. The thirty-seven angels of the sixth encampment are angels of might, who are called on to return fled slaves, thieves, or fugitives. The forty-four angels of the seventh encampment are in charge of dreaming.

The second heaven or firmament contains angels of fire and of moisture, and spirits of fear and dread. There are twelve steps in the heaven, with angels on each. The nine angels of the first step work to silence whoever the practitioner desires, be it a judge or the citizens of a city or others. The twelve angels of the second step are called upon to put the love of a man in a woman's heart. The fourteen angels of the third step are called to nullify the intentions or thought of powerful enemies.[101] The sixteen angels of the fourth step are angels of disquiet and stop men from sleeping. The twelve angels of the fifth step are angels of fire. The seventeen angels of the sixth step are angels of healing, called on for curing a stroke caused by witchcraft or evil spirits. The eleven angels of the seventh step are angels of fiery and watery might. They are called upon to expel all dangerous animals from a city or quell a rising river or sea. The sixteen angels of the eighth step rule the spirits that wander in the earth and protect from evil spirits, especially for pregnant women carrying and in their labour. The fourteen angels of the ninth step are martial and can protect a man from harm in war. The fifteen angels of the tenth step reward truth, and are called upon to rescue friends from difficulties or bad judgements. The fifteen angels of the eleventh step bestow authority and are called on to restore someone to their previous position (e.g., judge, noble, etc.). The twenty angels of the twelfth step are angels of righteousness and healing. They are called on to cure migraines, or to bind migraine spirits.

The third heaven is described as containing storerooms of mist from which thunder and lightning comes. Three angel princes rule, served by nineteen, twenty-six, and twenty-one angels respectively. They are called on to extinguish a bath-house fire, to ensure horses win races no matter their condition, or to create an illusion of fire. The fourth heaven contains the bridal chamber of the Sun, and lists the thirty-one fiery angels who lead him through the day and the thirty-five watery angels who lead him through the night. These angels are called to guide the practitioner to Helios to ask questions of life and death, good and evil.

---

101 Note there is a sequence of letters in Malachim script included in the text in this section and engraved on the silver lamella used for the charm, also for the angels of the sixth step, and the angels in the third heaven.

The fifth heaven contains angels of glory, and has twelve princes who each rule a month of the year. These angels are called on to discover what will happen in the month they rule. The sixth heaven contains mighty fiery angels, with two rulers of East and West of thirty-five and twenty-nine encampment heads respectively. The seventh heaven is the location of the Throne of Glory and storehouse of souls. The chapter contains a long devotional prayer to God, which completes the text.

Essential Reading

Morgan, Michael A. (1983) *Sepher ha-Razim: The Book of the Mysteries*. California: Scholars Press. Excellent study with English translation of the text derived from the source manuscripts.

Charaktêres charm to extinguish fire third firmament.

Sword of Moses (Harba de-Moshe)

Date: C8-10? (Based on contemporary references.)
Language: Hebrew & Aramaic.
Influences: *Cairo Genizah*, *Hekhalot* literature.
Provenance: Parts of the *Sword of Moses* occur in the *Cairo Genizah* and other Jewish magical manuscripts. First full version in *Sefer Shoshan Yesod Ha'olam* by Rabbi Yosef Tirshom (early C16). First published by Moses Gaster in 1896, transcribed from Gaster MS 177.
MSS:[102] Paris Jacques Mosseri VI 13.2 (C10-11), Cambridge T-S NS 70.130 (C11-12), New York JTSL ENA 2643.5 (C11-12), New York JTSL ENA 3373 (C11-12), New York JTSL ENA NS 2.11 (C11-12), New York JTSL ENA NS 89 (C11-12), MS Genève 145 (formerly MS Sassoon 290 (1510-30), Or MS 10678 (formerly Gaster MS 188) (C18), Gaster MS 177 (C19).
Circle: N/A.
Tools:[103] Belt, clay vessels, knife, lamp, lead plate, lion skin, pottery shards, red plate, scarf, silver plate, tin plate, unglazed jug.
Spirit List: Abulal, Adulal, Ahyw Psqtyh, Akaultu, Alusi, Amuhael, Aniquel, Arel, Arfose, Arias, Ariel, Asbeor, A'shael, Asqryhw, Asrael, Asshy, Asmoy, Assi/Assih/Apragsih, Ataf, Atuesuel, Aul, Avzhia,[104] Aziabel, Aziel, Azliel, Barbuel, Bedunim, Bualu, Chymchy, Corowe, Diema, Drsmiel, Ebuhuel, Elubatel, Gabriel, Gefowe, Gorhon, Gubril, Guziel, Hagyr, Haniel, Hdrzywlw, Iabiel, Ittalainma, Kadukuliti, Kalabusi, Kaluku, Katuel, Kawisu, Kebutzi, Labatu, Labusi, Latabusi, Lawisu, Lebatel, Lebusi, Legioh, Maktiel, Marbuel, Mbriel, Meachuel, Mechuel, Mephistopheles, Mhyhwgtzt, Michael, Mittron, Mrgywal, Mtnisl, Mzpwpyasayal, Naamwsnyqttyal, Nesanel, Orowor, Pchdwttgm, Prziel, Psdiel, Puchon, Puziel, Qswaappghyal, Qtgnypry, Quato, Quiheth, Quorthonn, Ra'asiel, Rampel, Raphael, Shqd Chwzy, Shtryshwyh, Shwtgyayh, Shytynychwm, Sofiel, Ta'aniel, Tafel, Talbusi, Thebor, Tmsmael, Trsiel, Tubatlu, Tubo, Tulatu, Tulef, Tuwalu, Tuwisu, Tzqtzwrwmtyal, Ubekutusi, Ubesu, Ubisi, Wegulo, Welor, Wethor, Wewor, Woreth, Woryon, Xexor, Xomoy, Xonor, Xysorym, Yadiel, Yisriel, Yofiel Trgiaob, Yrzon, Ywote, Yzazel, Zahbuk, Zenay, Zhsmael, Zsniel, Zuwey.

The Text

The text of the *Sword of Moses* divides into three main parts. The first part deals with the three-day practice of prayers, purification and adjuration to gain power over the thirteen angelic princes of the sword, and thus the power of the sword. The second part of the text is the sword itself, which is a huge string of around eighteen hundred words, most of which are unintelligible voces magicae, with intelligible sections at the beginning and end.

The third part is a list of one hundred and forty charms/recipes which use segments of the sword to achieve their purpose. Each charm gives the materia magica and part of the sword to be used for the desired effect. The range of purposes for the sword is wide, as would be expected from such a large magical text, and mirrors the themes found throughout the later grimoires. The purposes include healing (a large number), agriculture, causing harm and killing, communicating with the dead, control over spirits and animals, divination, enhancing

---

102 Most of these manuscripts are fragmentary but are included here for a more complete representation.
103 In this instance the tools are items used with sword charms.
104 Azhia is described as the Angel of the Presence and that the Shekinah is always with him, which fits earlier descriptions of Metatron.

knowledge and memory, escaping danger, financial success, governance, grace and favour (gaining and removing), love and sex, rescue from distress, self-protection, and war. Many of the charms use water, dust, or are recorded on amulets.

The charms are: to seize and bind a man and woman so they will be with each other, and to annul spirits and blast-demons and satans, and to bind a boat, and to free a man from prison; to destroy high mountains and pass safely through sea and land, and to go into fire and come out, to remove kings, and to cause an optical illusion, and to stop up a mouth, and to converse with the dead, and to kill the living, and to bring down and raise up and adjure angels to abide by you, and to learn all the secrets of the world; for a spirit that moves in the body; for a spirit that causes inflammation; for a spirit in the whole body; for a demon; for a spirit of terror; for diphtheria; for earache; for any kind of eye pain; for a cataract; for grit in the eye; for blood that runs from the head; for a *Palga* spirit; for hemicrania spirit and for a spirit that cuts the skull bone; for a spirit that blocks up the bone; for an earache; for deafness; for skin conditions and impotence; for jaundice; for pain in a nostril and for a nostril spirit; for pain in the stomach and the intestines; for scabs; for problems concerning the testicles; for a person hurt by an evil sorcerer; for drinking uncovered liquids; for a person bitten by a snake or any reptile; against any reptiles and distress charms; for a woman who sees menstrual blood not at the proper time; for every pain in the mouth; for skin conditions; for aching sciatic nerve; for retention of urine; for haemorrhoids; for a person who has swelling and for one who has gonorrhoea; for *nishma*;[105] for heavy blows and for a wound caused by an iron knife and any wound that it should not inflame; for cough and stomach ache; for a diseased gall bladder and excrement problems; for the liver of a sick person; for a diseased spleen; for a spirit that dwells in a woman's womb; for a woman that miscarries; for a man whose hair does not grow; to adjure a heavenly prince; to remove a magistrate from his prominent position; to cure a sore; for *burdes*;[106] for no rain to fall on your roof; if you wish to see the sun; that an angel dressed in white will answer you whatever you ask him, and even make a woman follow you; for a person who wishes to descend into a fiery furnace; if you see a king or a ruler and you wish him to follow you, or that everyone upon whom you decree will come to you, even if it concerns a woman; if you wish to reverse them; for any charm you wish to untie, also you can use it to release a man from prison; to catch fish; to make a woman follow you; to make a man follow you; for trees that do not produce fruit; for white rot that afflicts fruit; for a *merubya* spirit; for a person bitten by a rabid dog; for fever or sons of fever; for someone who is walking and gets lost; if you wish to borrow something from someone; one more if you wish a woman to follow you; if you wish to know whether you succeed in your journey or not; if you wish to release a man from prison; to disperse an assembly; if you wish to kill a person; if you wish to send a sore to afflict someone; to send a dream against someone; if a snake follows you; to detain a ship at sea; and if you wish to release it; if you wish to close an oven or a basin or a pot so that foods will not be put in them; if you wish to untie them; if you wish to cross over the sea as on dry land; if you wish to curse a person; if you wish to speak with the dead; if you wish to kill a lion or a bear, hyena or any harmful animal; if you wish to magically bind them; if you wish to open a door; if you wish to kill an ox or cattle; if you wish to inflame love in someone's heart; if you wish to make someone demented; if you wish to destroy someone's house; if you wish to banish someone; if you wish to make someone hated by others; if you wish to cause a women to abort; if you wish to make someone sick; if you wish to know concerning a sick person whether he will die or recover; if you wish to hold a lion by its ear; if you wish for your fame to go forth in the world; if you wish the earth to contract before you;

---

105 Unknown term.
106 Another unknown term.

if you wish a person to be cured from haemorrhoids and not to be sick again; for every kind of dripping; for poison; for hailstones that descend from the sky; if you wish to enter before a king or nobles; for blight that afflicts the field; for worms that afflict fruit; to release a man from prison; for land that does not produce fruit; for a sick person who is weak and you do not know why he is weak; to stir up a battle; if you wish to impose your terror over all people; if you wish light to shine for you when it is dark; if you wish to tie eyes from afflicting evil; if you wish to send a sword and it will fight for you; if you wish them to kill each other; and if you wish them to calm down; if an adversary lays hold of you and wishes to kill you; to cause an optical illusion so as not to be seen; if you fall into fire and you wish to ascend out of it; if you fall into a deep pit without knowing; if you are drowning in a deep river; if a rock or a landslide falls on you and you are trapped under it; if the authorities lay hold of you; if a band of marauders attacks you; if you wish to untie them; if you walk in valleys or mountains and there is no water to drink; if you are hungry; if you wish to summon the Prince of Man to you; if you wish to remove him; if you wish that any heavenly prince will teach you what he knows; if you wish to walk upon water; if you wish to become wise; if you wish to learn immediately everything that you may hear; if you wish to make someone forget all that he knows; if you wish to send an evil demon against your enemy; to send a spirit; for catching thieves; when you wish to release them; to close up your house against thieves; to seal a house from marauders; to seal yourself from an evil spirit, also to excommunicate them; for all other things that are not referred to explicitly.

Essential Reading

Gaster, M. (1896) *The Sword of Moses*. London. First translation of the *Sword of Moses* into English. Dated but useful.
Harrari, Yuval (1997) *Harba de-Moshe: A New Edition and a Study*. Jerusalem: Jerusalem University. Excellent study of the development of the *Sword of Moses* with a new translation of the text.
Roth, Harold (2022) *The Magic of the Sword of Moses*. Newbury: Weiser Books. Excellent scholarly and practical work which makes it accessible whilst also providing context and development of the text.

הידסטא
אוטא דימא דאימא הינן
טלאין טלאוס פאמוטום
אטופלמא

HEALING SPELL FROM THE *SWORD OF MOSES*.

Shi'ur Qomah (Measure of the [Divine] Body)

Date: C9 CE.
Language: Hebrew.
Influences: Torah, especially Psalms and Song of Solomon, *Hekhalot Rabbati*.
Provenance: Mystical texts of the Merkavah tradition.
MSS: Guenzberg MS 90 (C14), BL MS Oriental 6577 (C14-15), Guenzberg MS 131 (C15), Oxford MS 1791 (C15), JTS MS 1892 (C15), Mossayef MS 145 (C15), Florence MS Plut. 44.13 (C15-16), Munich MS 40 (C15-16), JTS MS 8115 (C15-16), JTS MS 1990 (C16), Oxford MS 1102 (C16, fragment), Cambridge MS Add. 405 (C16-17), Oxford MS 1816 (C16-17, fragment), JNUL MS 381 (C16-17), Oxford MS 1960 (C17-18), JTS MS 2130 (C19), Oxford MS 2257, Oxford MS 1915, Oxford Heb. C 65 (Genizah fragment), Sassoon MS 522 (Genizah fragment), British Library MS 10384 (ND), British Library MS 10675 (ND), Munich MS22 (ND).
Circle: N/A.
Tools: N/A.
Spirit List: Metatron, Tzadadraban, Yofiel.

The Text

Shi'ur Qomah is a liturgical/theurgic text in the Merkavah tradition, which due to its consideration of the size of the body of God, would have been seen as an heretical, or at the least, radical text. Its structure and flow is suggestive of a manual of prayer, with phrasing which could be used for inducing mystical communion.

There are arguments for the composition date of the urtext[107] being as far back as C2 CE, which are more substantial for around C5 CE onwards (Cohen 1983:51-52), but definitive evidence gives a C9 CE date. The idea of divine names for the parts of the body existed in earlier cultures, and may be seen in Mesopotamia.[108]

It is worth noting that a number of the copies of *Shi'ur Qomah* were bound together with *Sepher ha-Razim* and *Hekalot Rabbati*. The former two being bound together may be a contributory factor to material from both appearing later in *Summa Sacre Magice*. The text has variants seen in different recensions with differences. These recensions (described below) are *Sepher Hash'iur* (*Book of the Measurement*), *Siddur Rabbah* (*Great Prayer Book*), *Merkavah Rabbah* (*Great Chariot*), *Sepher Razi'el* (*Book of Raziel*), *Sepher Haqqomah* (*Book of the* [Measure of the] *Body*).

Sepher Hash'iur begins with the measurements, qualifying the divine measurements into more mundane expressions (lines 1-23). Next the measurements continue, but with divine names given with the measurements for the corresponding body parts. At line 33 Metatron is referred to by Rabbi Aqiba[109] as having told him the seventy divine names on the heart of God (lines 34-41). From here the measurements and names move up the neck to the parts of the head (lines 41-58), before returning to body measurements (lines 59-67). The following lines give the names of his crown, his (rain)bow, his sword, his throne of glory, and the seat of his glory (68-71).

Siddur Rabbah begins with Rabbi Ishmael recounting a description of God given to him by Metatron. In this Moses is described as being most venerated of the patriarchs in heaven,

---

107 Original text from which others are derived.
108 E.g., first millennium BCE hymn 'Limbs of Ninurta'.
109 It is interesting that in Merkavah tradition, Akiba was the only one, of the group of four Rabbis who sought to reach the presence of God, to do successfully and to both survive and remain sane.

and reference is made to the Shekinah (lines 1-48). Rabbi Ishmael subsequently describes a vision he had of God and his angels, and a sequence of alternative names of Metatron given (52-55), followed by measurements and names of God's body parts (56-105). A description of God follows (106-114) and the measurement of *parsangs*, the unit of measurement (115-121).

Merkavah Rabbah also begins with Rabbi Ishmael saying he saw God on his throne and speaking to Metatron (1-6) and declaring a great seal and Metatron also calling a series of divine names (6-20). A series of alternative names of Metatron are given (21-25) and he describes the heaven (26-30) before giving a long divine name string (31-46). Next, God is praised (47-52) and the body measurements and associated divine names are given (53-171), including the seventy names in the heart of God (71-82) and seventy-two letters on his forehead (105-110), ending with a description of God (172-175). Rabbi Ishmael then declares the glory of God and describes the qualities that may be gained from reciting the divine names (176-185). These are: to make the face glow and the body be attractive (186), to create fear and have a good name (187), for peaceful dreams and to remember the Torah (188), to remember all memories (189), to awaken for the world to come (190), for forgiveness for sins before the Throne of Glory (191), to not be inclined to evil and be protected from demons, damagers, spirits, and robbers (192), for protection from evil men, animals, and snakes (193), for protection from scorpions and imps and to stop the mouths of any who plot evil against you (194). The text then ends with more phrases praising God (195-214).

Sepher Razi'el begins with a lovely sequence of praise of God (1-27). This continues with Rabbi Ishmael addressing Metatron about the virtues of God (28-93), including a sequence of titles of God and prayer and exaltation of God. Rabbi Ishmael then gives the measure of the body (94-210) including the 70 names on the heart of God (119-126) and the seventy-two letters on his forehead (144-146). Next are the names of his crown, his (rain)bow, his sword, and his throne of glory including the names of the holy creatures of the legs (211-239). The praises of the holy creatures and Metatron to God and how they conduct these follow (with reference to the Shekinah and a Psalm of David), and a long sequence of praise to God into which the practitioner incorporates their name (240-4231).

Sepher Haqqomah also begins with a praise sequence to God (1-11). Rabbi Aqiba gives the measure of God (12-22), continuing into a long sequence of titles of God (23-46). Rabbi Ishmael then speaks to Metatron (47-51), and then gives the measure of God (52-113), including the seventy names on the heart of God (64-72) and seventy-two letters on his forehead (86-89). A description of God then follows (114-124), along with the names of his crown, his (rain)bow, his sword, his throne of glory including the names of the holy creatures of the legs, praises to God, and descriptions of the holy creatures (125-219).

Essential Reading

Cohen, Martin Samuel (1985) *Shi'ur Qomah: Text and Recensions*. Tubingen: J.C.B. Mohr. Excellent study with the texts in Hebrew and English and copious notes.

Cohen, Martin Samuel (1983) *Shi'ur Qomah: Liturgy and Theurgy in Pre-Kabbalistic Jewish Mysticism*. Tubingen: J.C.B. Mohr. Another excellent study exploring the roots and development of the text.

Picatrix (Ghāyat al-Hākim or Goal of the Wise)

Date: Mid C10 CE.
Language: Arabic, Castilian, Latin, German.
Influences: *De Imaginibus, Rasa-il, Flos Naturarum* (Latin version), Aristotle, numerous other Arabic works (the author claims over two hundred!).
Provenance: Translated from Arabic into Castilian in 1256, possibly by Yehudā ben Moshē. The Latin text may be as early as 1258 (possibly by Aegidius de Thebaldis) and contains additional material from *Flos Naturarum*.[110] The original Arabic text was attributed to the Spanish-based Islamic astronomer and scholar al-Majriti (c. 950-1007), but this has been disputed and discounted.
MSS:[111] Weimar MS O 95 (C14/15), Cracow MS 793 (1459), Vienna MS 3317 (1466), BN Lat. 10272 (late C15), Darmstadt MS 362 (1509), Florence BNC Magliabechi XX 20 (1536), Florence BNC Magliabechi XX 21 (1536), Darmstadt MS 1410 (early C16), Bodleian Canonicus Lat. 500 (C16), Prague MS 2483 (C16), BN Lat. 17871 (C16), BN MS Lat. 13016 (early C17), BN MS Lat. 13017 (early C17), Sloane MS 3679 (early C17), Sloane MS 1302 (1647) owned by Simon Forman, Richard Napier, Elias Ashmole and William Lilly; Sloane MS 1305 (C17) (Latin); Sloane MS 1309 (C17) (Italian), BA MS 1033 (C17), BN MS Lat. 10273 (C17), BN MS Lat. 7340 (late C17), Hamburg Mag. Fol. 188 (C18) (Lat).
Circle: N/A.
Tools: N/A.
Spirit List: Adilas, Aktarya, Albowarees, Andalees, Antoor, Aooda, Arhawthaas, Ashbeel, Awdoras, Ayinmoos, Baayel, Badalimaas, Bahatores, Bahimoos, Bandalos (Abdulas, Atiyefas, Dahifas, Dahimas, Ghadees, Maghnamos, Tahimarees[112] Bandoras, Barhawt. Barhoyas (Amiras, Dahdees, Darees, Helees, Hiytes, Mahodees, Sahees), Barmolees, Barolas, Basras, Batirolees, Batiydyas, Bayalos, Betaeel, Bihynolsaser, Bikataroos, Bitaeel, Bodyees, Brimas (Ciyoos, Diriyoos, Doroos, Khroos, Tahitoos, Tamus, Tos), Briyanos, Brohoyas, Daghdiyos, (Ardaghos, Dahidmas, Ghidyos, Haghedes, Handighyos, Maghras, Mahandas), Daitoos, Damahos (Dahidas, Darees, Darmas, Faroos, Maghees, Matees, Tamees), Didas (Ablimas, Arhos, Baslamos, Dahtarees, Damayis, Ghiylos, Hiylos), Diwas, Femalos, Gharnos (Daghayos, Hadees, Maranos, Minalos, Multas, Rabees, Tiymas), Handaroos, Hartiyoon, Herkeel, Hiyadees, Hiyakos, Kafinas, Kidmoos, Madees, Madloos, Mancoraas, Manhorees, Mantoris, Manurayis, Matinos, Milyoras, Obohees, Oliyos, Rafael, Rubaeel, Sarghatoom, Shams, Silyaeel, Sliyobaroon, Susip, Swatlees, Tawados, Utarid, Vidoraas, Wandolas, Yamoora, Yanayel, Zahra.

The Text

The *Picatrix* is a compilation work. The author states he read two hundred and twenty-four books on the subject in the process of gathering the material contained within it. A number of works are referred to, most of which do not appear to have survived to the present. Much of the text is concerned with the construction of talismans (charms might be a better term for

---

110 The identity of the author of the original text and the early translators is still being debated. David Pingree's suggested translators have been used, as he was probably the greatest expert on the text.

111 Destroyed MSS or those with small fragments of the text are not included, such as Plut 89. Sup 38 or Vaticanus Palatinus latinus 1354 (1470).

112 The spirit names in brackets refer to the seven parts which are collected to make the complete spirit of a planet, in this case Bandalos. Each set of bracketed names will refer to the preceding spirit.

many of them). Many of these charms use different types of animal blood, brains, and other parts in their construction, and animal sacrifice is also a common theme; however, the plethora of talismans in the book are not its real legacy. The discussion of talismans, and the concepts behind them, and the working of magic, are of greater significance. The work in the *Picatrix* incorporates elements from diverse cultures including those of ancient Egypt, Mesopotamia, India, ancient Greece, and others. This is particularly evident in the strong presence of Neoplatonic theurgy woven into the Islamic devotion to Allah as the Supreme Being.

The magic contained in the *Picatrix* rarely relies on spirits like most grimoires do. It is astral, or image, magic, and focuses on the astrologically appropriate creation of talismans empowered by the divine influences of the heavens, specifically the seven classical planets. The first two books require careful study and are likely to be of far more value to the student than the latter two, which have so many recipes that would not be legal to create in modern society and offer considerable risks to the health of the practitioner.

The text begins with a prologue setting out the raison d'être of the book and explaining the nature of the four volumes within. Book one begins with a chapter discussing Allah and his wisdom,[113] and then a chapter discussing magic and the nature of talismans. Chapter three discusses astrology and the seven classical planets. Chapter four introduces the twenty-eight mansions of the Moon, giving their astrological positions in the zodiac and the works to be done with their respective talismans, as well as good and bad lunar timings for their construction. Chapter five gives examples of talisman uses and the appropriate astrological timings corresponding to them, and ends with a discussion of the construction of talismans and the wording to be used. Chapter six discusses the degree to which things exist in the universe, and how man is a reflection of the universe (the principle of 'as above, so below'). Chapter seven discusses the nature of humans and their capacity for wisdom and growth. Chapter eight explores rankings in nature and how different qualities are embodied through this.

Book two deals with celestial images. In chapter one the author explains how the writings of Ptolemy inspired his interest in talismans and how a knowledge of nature and metaphysics are required for the art. Chapter two discusses the symbolism of images and the importance of astrology. Chapter three looks at the Sun and the Moon and their relationship to each other and the world below, as well as the changing nature of the Moon's effects with its cycle. Chapter four discusses the importance of eight in talisman making and the associated qualities of the twenty-eight mansions of the Moon. Chapter five discusses the main races which have contributed to talismanic lore, especially the Indians. It also explores ideas of imagination, perception, and revelation. Chapter six explores that all things increase or decrease, and how this is incorporated into talismans, particularly with regard to the movements of the planets. Chapter seven is a very interesting discussion of difference and similitude. It also explores divisions of quantity as factors included in preparation of talismans. Chapter eight considers combination, especially in regard to the four elements, their qualities and manifestations. Chapter nine lists some simple talismans. Chapter ten lists the rocks and stones of the planets, as well as giving the symbols of the planets, and planetary images for each of them and a number of planetary talismans.[114] It also describes the rings for the planets, and numerous images engraved on different stones and their effects for each planet. Chapter eleven discusses talismans more, and gives the images for the three phases of each zodiacal sign (the decans) and their qualities. Chapter twelve explores the thirty-six decans more, and the qualities attributed to each of them. It also considers the

---

113 Note that the Latin text replaces Allah with God and essentially Christianises the text to make it acceptable.

114 The author quotes two otherwise unknown texts here, *The Interpretation of Spiritual Talismans* (curiously attributed to an author called Picatrix) and *The Benefits of the Rocks of Mercury*.

phases of each planet and their colours and qualities, and discusses important works by other authors he has read and been influenced by.

Book three begins with a short introduction about the three realms of earth, air, and heaven, and the significance of harmony in the creation of talismans. Chapter one looks at associated symbols of the planets, such as places, professions, body parts, languages, jewels, animals, and plants. Chapter two deals with the zodiacal signs. Chapter three refers to a text by Aristotle called *The Book of Lamps and Banners*, and gives more planetary images, with more colour and fragrance references. It continues with the construction of the supporting materials for the zodiacal signs, and a discussion of different geographical areas and what they are good for supplying. Chapter four begins with a discussion of dividing the Quran using the seven planets. This leads into a complete chapter list with the planetary attributions of each. Chapter five discusses divisions, into the elements, and into animal, plant, and mineral, and how these fit in with the talismanic art. There is a digression into an example the author saw of a charm being used, followed by a discussion of talisman making. Chapter six discusses the four spirits which embody spiritual power, their nature and presence in old writings of Aristotle and Hermes. Chapter seven revisits the qualities associated with the planets and what to work with them for, and the nature of the individual planetary powers. The process of invocation for each of the planets is then covered. The practices of the Sabians and some of their rites are discussed. Chapter eight refers to the Nabateans, and gives a prayer of theirs to the Sun, and one to Saturn. Chapter nine discusses the planetary spirits as composed of seven parts which unite to form the whole spirit. Invocations/feasts for each of the planets are then described. Chapter ten details the production of four magical beads to be used in amulets. There are then a number of other talismans, including several for love/sexual attraction, to gain the support of a king, to turn a king against somebody, to cause enmity in a couple, as well as how to unbind bound talismans. Chapter eleven contains more charms, and starts with one to tongue-tie a malicious person. There are talismans for pleasant or disgusting food and incense, for separation, to create desire, four talismans to spread hostility and separation, seven talismans to remove desire, seven food talismans to kill a person, ten potions that cause fatal sickness, the talisman of the imagination (requires a fresh human body!), a potion to see different things, talismans to cause delusion and hallucination, talismans to blind, and those to prevent a person talking or hearing, to spread hatred and hostility between groups of people, for sleeping (four), for death (two), for rotting body parts, for protection from poison and evil effects, to resemble an animal, and to cause one to go insane and not be able to leave the home area. Chapter twelve entreats the reader to be faithful and honest to themselves, love Allah, and understand the flow of will.

Book four covers the talismans of the Nabateans, Kurds, and Al-Habasah people. Chapter one is again a philosophical discourse on the nature of the soul. Chapter two contains invocations of the Moon in the zodiacal signs (Aries is missing), and conjurations of the planetary spirit kings with their animal sacrifices. Chapter three begins with pseudo-historical discussion about statues and rivers and people. It continues with an invisibility charm, followed by a bunch of sayings. Chapter four contains forty-five aphorisms said to be from a book called *Secret of Secrets*, which give advice on the planets and their interactions. This is followed by ten aphorisms attributed to Ptolemy giving advice regarding the fine details of the talismanic art. Discussion referencing Aristotle, Hippocrates, and Plato follows, along with more on astronomy. Chapter five begins by listing the ten sciences required for charms. These are (1) farming, caring, and navigation; (2) knowledge of leading troops, war tricks, horse training, veterinary matters, and refining weapons; (3) civil knowledge including grammar, language, literature, and laws; (4) policies, of city, community, and house; (5) knowledge of morals; (6) knowledge of mathematics, including algebra, geometry, astronomy, engineering, and music; (7) knowledge of logic; (8) medicine; (9) knowledge of nature; (10) knowledge of the after nature. The chapter continues with discussion of love and the soul, and a detailed description of human conception. Chapter six gives Indian recipes for planetary incenses, as well as Moses' incense (Exodus), consecration incense, Indian incenses for Mercury and Saturn, spirit protection incense, and Indian solar oil. Chapter seven begins with charms of the laurel tree, discussion of the hollyhock and the mandrake, a charm with the Abraham tree, discussion of myrtle and olive, assorted other charms which are more akin to book of secrets material, some poisons, and folklore on a number of plants (both real and mythical). Chapter eight continues with more stories of alleged properties of various plants and substances and folkloric anecdotes. Chapter nine has more talismans, some of which are quite fantastical, and ends the book with the seven admonitions of Pythagoras and a final praise to Allah.

Essential Reading

Atallah, Hashem (trans) & Kiesel, William (ed) (2002, 2008) *Picatrix (Ghayat al-Hakim) Goal of the Wise*. Seattle: Ouroboros Press. Two volumes. Good study of the text, and first translation from Arabic into English, bypassing the translation errors through multiple language translation. The main flaw is the lack of an index.

Attrell, Dan (trans) & Porreca, David (trans) (2019) *Picatrix: A Medieval Treatise on Astral Magic*. Pennsylvania: Pennsylvania State University Press. This work is part of the superb Magic in History series put out by this publisher. Translated from the Latin with more emphasis on codifying the practices and providing a scholarly overview of the material.

Warnock, Christopher & Greer, John Michael (2018) *The Complete Picatrix: The Occult Classic of Astrological Magic*. Lulu.com. Well written work with a lot of context and explanation, translated from the Latin edition.

At the time of writing an edition translated from the Arabic by Liana Saif has been announced for publication. This edition is likely to be the most definitive.

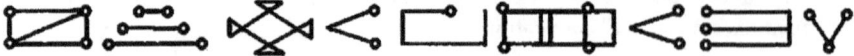

Characters of Roquiel

DE LAPIDIBUS (ON GEMSTONES)

Date: 1061-1081.
Language: Latin. By C14 translated into Hebrew, French, Italian, Provençal, Danish, and Irish.
Influences: *Materia Medica* of Dioscorides (C1 CE); *De Lapidibus* by Evax (C5 CE), translated from *De Lapidibus* of Damigeron (C2 BCE); *Etymologiae* Book 16 by Isidore of Seville (drawing on Pliny's *Natural History* Book 37, C1 CE).
Provenance: Written by Marbodius of Rennes. First published in Vienna in 1511.
MSS: At least one hundred and fifty MSS survive. Sometimes bound with other works, e.g., *Liber Lune* in Harley MS 80 (C15).
Circle: N/A.
Tools: N/A.
Stone List[115] Agate, Alectorius[116] Almandine, Amber, Amethyst, Androdragma[117] Apsyctos[118] Asbestos, Beryl, Calcofanus[119] Cameo[120] Carnelian, Ceraunus[121] Chalcedony, Chelidony[122] Chelonite[123] Chrysoelectrum,[124] Chrysolith (Topaz), Chrysoprase, Coral, Crystal (Quartz), Diadochus[125] Diamond, Dionysia[126] Eaglestone[127] Emerald, Enidros[128] Epistites[129] Exacontalitus[130] Exebenus[131] Gagate (Jet), Gagatromeus[132] Galactite[133] Gegolitus[134] Gelacia[135]

---

115 As this is a lapidary, the spirit list is replaced with a stone list of all the named stones which were described as having magical properties. Note that a number of the stones were mythical, and in some instances suggestions have been made as to what they might have been.

116 Also known as a capon stone, due to being a stone found in the gizzard of a capon.

117 A black square stone.

118 Also called absinctus, a red-veined black stone. Possibly lignite.

119 An unknown stone.

120 Not a stone, but a style of engraving, especially of gems, where the figure is in raised relief, as opposed to intaglio which is carved into the material.

121 Also known as a thunderstone, said to be formed where lightning strikes the ground. Is a name for nephrite jade

122 A stone said to develop in the bellies of swallows.

123 Red and green stone, possibly snakestone.

124 An unknown stone.

125 Said to be similar to a beryl.

126 A hard black gem with red patches.

127 Name given to hollow geodes.

128 Also called enhydros, a perfectly round and smooth white stone that 'weeps' tears with magical properties.

129 Also called Vulcan stone, an unknown form of red gem.

130 Harlequin opal.

131 A white gem.

132 Unknown stone listed by Damigeron and described as fawn-coloured.

133 Also called galaxia, a gem bisected by red or white veins.

134 Also called tecolithos, said to resemble an olive pit.

135 Also called chalazias, a white hard stone, possibly white quartz?

Gerachite[136] Heliotrope, Hematite, Hyena[137] Iris[138] Jacinth[139] Jasper, Liparea[140] Lygurius[141] Magnetite, Malachite, Medus,[142] Onyx, Opal, Orites,[143] Paederos,[144] Pantheros,[145] Peanita,[146] Pearl, Peridot, Prase, Pyrite, Sadda,[147] Sapphire, Sard, Sardonyx, Selenite, Topaz.

The Text

Marbode's *De Lapidibus* was the most significant lapidary of the Middle Ages. As such, its influence can be seen in attributions found in many of the grimoires, and through the writings of Agrippa. Comprised of seven hundred and thirty-two hexameter verses, it describes the qualities of sixty stones, many of which are mythical. In the text the tradition of lapidaries from ancient Greece is preserved, giving a direct link back to a part of the magic of the classical world. Marbode drew from a range of available sources, referencing the *De Lapidibus* of Theophrastus, Evax, who translated the *De Virtutibus Lapidum* of Damigeron, and the writings of the Persian philosopher and polymath Avicenna (980-1037CE).

Essential Reading

Lecouteux, Claude (2012) *A Lapidary of Sacred Stones: Their Magical and Medicinal Powers Based on the Earliest Sources*. Vermont: Inner Traditions. Good reference work with more than eight hundred entries referring back to all the major lapidaries including Marbodius and earlier classical sources.

Riddle, John (ed) M. & King, C.W. (ed) (1977) *Marbode of Rennes' (1035-1123) De Lapibibus*. Wiesbaden: Franz Steiner. Academic work with text and commentary, also includes his other minor works on stones.

---

136 Also called Falcon stone, a streaked black stone.

137 A stone said to come from the petrified eye of a hyena.

138 Possibly rainbow quartz.

139 Orange-red variety of zircon.

140 An undescribed stone of marvellous powers from Libya.

141 A stone said in the ancient world to form from solidified lynx urine, widely believed to be amber.

142 Also called Medius or Medea, another magical green or black gem said to be discovered by Medea. Possibly tourmaline?

143 A round stone that may be black, green or coppery with white patches.

144 Purple-blue shaded opal.

145 A multi-coloured stone. Possibly opal.

146 Another unknown stone.

147 Magical green or black gem of unknown provenance.

Liber Prestigiorum (Book of Talismans)

Date: 1126-30.
Language: Latin.
Influences: Babylonian, Greek, Egyptian, Sabian, and Neo-Platonic philosophies and practices.
Provenance: Translated from C9 text *De Imaginibus* of Thābit ibn Qurrah by Adelard of Bath.
MSS: Avranches MS 235 (1145-55), fragment in Cambridge K.K 1.1 (1234) part in Vatican BAV pal. Lat. 1401 (1300-38), Lyons MS 328 (1393), Unknown location Conte de Sarzana MS XX (1510), St Petersburg BAN Q.537 (1512).
Circle: N/A.
Tools: N/A.
Spirit List: Described as 'shining spirits of the planets' without being named, i.e., planetary spirits.

The Text

Liber Prestigiorum was the first known Hermetic text (attributed to Hermes Trismegistus) to enter the West. With influences from Babylonian, Greek, Egyptian, Sabian and Neo-Platonic philosophies and practices, this text is a vital part of the subsequent development of the Grimoire Tradition. Six copies or partial copies of the manuscript are known to have survived. The *Picatrix* has sections in common with *Liber Prestigiorum*, and also refers back to Thābit ibn Qurrah, demonstrating their common root in his *De Imaginibus*. It is significant that *Liber Prestigiorum* is found bound together with the same pair of astrological manuscripts, *Ysagoga Minor*[148] of Abū Ma'shar and the *Centiloquium* of pseudo-Ptolemy, providing a more complete guide to its use and practice.

The text begins with the assertion that the practitioner should be skilled in astrology and confident in themselves. This is followed by a melothesia, i.e., attribution of the planets for rulership of parts of the body. Then comes instruction on the construction of talismans for a number of purposes. The text is divided into two sections, for gaining love, and for causing harm and other purposes. These are: gaining the love of your equal; gaining the love of your son; gaining the love of the king; regaining the love of your spouse; causing hatred between people; causing all-out war between people; regaining stolen money; increasing your wealth; winning a lawsuit; protecting a place against misfortune; destroying a city; and driving scorpions out of a city. The use of the appropriate planetary metals for the talisman is detailed, these being bronze, gold, lead, silver, or tin.[149] An appropriate planetary image is inscribed on the talisman, which is suffumigated with appropriate fragrances, a prayer is recited over it, and it is buried where it will be most efficacious. The text ends with some miscellaneous information.

John of Seville's slightly later translation of the *De Imaginibus* (1135-53 CE) is a more modest and acceptable text within the religious environment of the time, omitting reference to spirits and the suffumigations.[150] Pseudo-Albertus Magnus did not categorise this as a

---

148 This work details the rulers of the constellations and planetary hours, and the influence of planetary spirits on animals, minerals, and vegetables. See Aakhus 2012:152.
149 These are the same metals used in ancient Greek practice to construct lamellae; see chapter 'Before the Grimoires'.
150 See e.g., British Library Harley MS 80 (C13-15), MS Royal C.XVIII (C14).

negative text in his influential *Speculum Astronomiae* (Mirror of Astronomy)[151] like he did *Liber Prestigiorum*, meaning it was able to circulate more widely as a licit text.

Essential Reading

Burnett, Charles (1996) *Magic and Divination in the Middle Ages. Texts and Techniques in the Islamic and Christian Worlds*. Aldershot: Variorium. Excellent study by the acknowledged expert in the field. Includes a plethora of contextual material.

---

151 This work was highly influential, especially for cataloguing texts according to their illicit or licit content.

LIBER LUNAE (THE BOOK OF THE MOON)

Date: 1145.
Language: Latin.
Influences: *Kitāb al-makhzūn* (*The Hidden Book of Aristotle*).
Provenance: Translated from Arabic by Robert of Chester in 1145.
MSS: York Austin Friars MS A8 362 (pre-1400, not surviving), Digby MS 226 (late C14), Vatican Barb lat 3589 (1430), Harley MS 80 (C15), Firenze II.III.24 (C15), Corpus Christia MS 125 (C15), Sloane MS 3826 (C16), Oriental MS 6360 (C16), Darmstadt MS 1410 (1550).
Circle: N/A.
Tools: N/A.
Spirit List: [Abrakiim, Abranodomilim, Abrashim, Abratim, Adiamenim, Aladim, Amaamilim, Amikhilim, Anailim, Andalashim, Aqashimadi, Aqrapirim, Arihaylim, Badaylin, Belgahalidim, Beqshdeilim, Blaknaratim, Dabnotirorin, Diqomeylim, Gaporim, Genithokim, Haqoilim, Hartninay, Hiraminim, Kearldim, Lairayozim, Lanagotim, Latzandonim, Madarilim, Manenim, Mangororam, Montaginim, Nehelim, Panaplor, Qamshilindim, Qarmayndim, Quntzilim, Shaamam, Sharailim, Sharahitzinim, Shethakam, Tayriomim, Teibinenim, Tzetahotim, Wipoliyapa, Yadalim, Yamaghash, Yatzarpnishim, Yebrunkhelim,][152], Abrayel, Affayelin, Ameyl, Amonayelin, Amymaryil, Azareil, Badadeyl, Badrayeylyn, Bahalim, Barcayl, Batraiel, Berharim, Cadnaelin, Canariel, Dareyl, Durayl, Farcelin, Fariel, Gabriel, Hoasaresin, Lagha, Laghoo, Lahagenim, Laiagelm, Laiaselesyn, Lalakim, Lamitrorosh, Langbali, Lanporish, Lashepet, Lashepim, Layafurin, Machiel, Madualim, Manopiqon, Melkailin, Nalkatan, Noreil, Priolam, Uabalkanarithin, Uorayeylin, Wel, {Abramathin, Abrancasai, Abranorin, Abras, Achithim, Adiamenim, Andalasin, Andonin, Angarozan, Aninei, Arieisin, Azafirin, Azardin, Balkanaritin, Barionin, Barthaylin, Begehalodin, Bifulica, Borcolin, Candanegin, Cannamdin, Carnnamdin, Cemeil, Charochin, Comeil, Deibenim, Farbarakin, Feresin, Gaforin, Genira, Hacsemin, Heizamamin, Iaciz, Jachehay, Janozothin, Labelas, Langas, Larabusin, Mamenim, Manderilin Matnairelin, Mediesin, Mezetin, Mimgogm, Neilin, Rasaidin, Reanei, Saeosin, Saphianim, Sarajemin, Soe}[153].

THE TEXT

Liber Lunae first appears as a translation from Arabic into Latin by Robert of Chester in 1145. This may well be the work referred to by William of Auvergne, Bishop of Paris (1180-1249) as the *Book of the Images of the Moon* which sought to work magic by the name of God. Although the first known surviving manuscript is from the fourteenth century, earlier versions existed. It is also clear that it was influenced by early Arabic works which date back to the ninth century.

The text of *Liber Lunae* appears in several forms. Amongst these is the Hebrew *Sepher ha-Levanah* (Book of the Moon) which is sometimes included with *Sepher Maphteah Shelomoh*. From the text it is clear that *Sepher ha-Levanah* does not predate *Liber Lunae* and was a Hebrew translation from a similar source.[154]

Liber Lunae begins with the preamble and instructions from Hermes, which include suffumigating and reciting the angelic names seven times over talismans. The fifty-five names are then given. This is followed by the descriptions of the twenty-eight mansions of the Moon,

---

152 Angel name list from *Sepher ha-Levanah*.
153 Angel name list from *Liber Lunae*.
154 Karr, 2017:19.

their names and virtues, and zodiacal attributions (signs, etc.). The theme for each mansion indicates the nature of the work: separation, discord, and hatred for the first mansion; hope, love, and friendship for the second; joining together for the third; adversity, desolation, loss, and evil for the fourth; alliance and friendship for the fifth; peace and love for the sixth and seventh; ships, floods, and waters for the eighth; profit for the ninth; fortunate Venusian work for the tenth; profit through destruction for the eleventh; building positive things for the twelfth; joining together for the thirteenth; alliance, love, and friendship for the fourteenth; destruction for the fifteenth and sixteenth; discord, tribulation, and impediment for the seventeenth; silence and binding people for the eighteenth; fornication, sedition, allegation, and lust for the nineteenth; love and concord for the twentieth; co-operation and silence for the twenty-first; ending good things in the twenty-second; good things in the twenty-third and twenty-fourth; binding in the twenty-fifth; alliance, co-operation, and friendship in the twenty-sixth; separation, departing, binding, or infirmity for the twenty-seventh; influencing highly ranked people for the twenty-eighth.

The next part deals with working with the fifty-five lunar angels and discusses the importance of suffumigations. After this the text focuses on the hours of the day and night and the operations to be conducted during them, with four additional operations added at the end. The nature of the operations is similar in many ways to the themes covered in the mansions. The final part concentrates on the planets, their symbols, kameas (magic squares), virtues, rings, images, and operations. The kameas are discussed for different uses of each individual kamea, giving their use as talismans in themselves (rather than the later Agrippa use for derivation of spirit seals). This makes the final section of the book very interesting from a planetary talismanic perspective.

ESSENTIAL READING

Karr, Don (2017) *The Book of the Moon – Liber Lunae*. Sourceworks of Ceremonial Magic Volume 7. Singapore: Golden Hoard Press. Excellent study of this important early work.

MERCURY KAMEA FROM *LIBER LUNAE*

Ars Notoria (The Notary Art) & Liber Visionum

Date: 1225.
Language: Latin.
Influences: Possibly Jewish and/or Greek influence.
Provenance: Copies were owned by several significant Renaissance figures including Dr. Hartmann Schedel (1440-1514), Duke Albrecht V of Bavaria (1528-1579), Dr. John Dee (1527-1608), Simon Forman (1552-1611), Robert Fludd (1574-1637), Ben Jonson (1572-1637), William Lilly (1602-1681), Elias Ashmole (1617-1692), Robert Turner (1626-1666), Thomas Rudd (1583-1656), Sir Hans Sloane (1660-1753).
MSS:[155] Yale Mellon 1 (1225), Erfurt Quarto 380 (1230), BNF Lat. 7152 (1239), Sloane MS 1712 (1250), Turin E.V.13 (1250-1275), BNF 1565 (C13), BNF 7373 (C13), Heilsbronn 153 (C13), Klosterneuburg CCl 759 (C13), Klosterneuburg Cod. 950 (C13), Digby 218 (C13/14), Klosterneuburg CCl 221 (C13/14), Vorau Cod. Voraviensis 186 (C13/14), Bodleian Liturg. 160 (pre 1315), Graz 680 (1315), Vatican BA Lat. 3185 (1340-1350), Munich CLM 276 (1350, some German), BNF Lat. 9336 (1350-1375), BL Additional 18027 (1373), Scots Abbey Vind. 140 (1377), Cracow JB 2076 (C14), Erfurt Math 14 (C14), Graz 1016 (C14), Leiden Cod. Vulcaniani 45 (C14), Munich CLM 268 (C14), Munich CLM 30010 (C14), St Nicholas Hospital Library CC 216 (C14), St Nicholas Hospital Library CC 232 (C14), Vatican BA Lat. 6842 (C14), Vatican Pal. Lat. 957 (late C14), Vienna 15482 (1400), Prague 267 (1431), McMaster 107 (1461), Ashmole 2871 (C15), Bodley 951 (C15), Digby 29 (C15), BML Plut. 89 sup. 35 (C15), Merton Med. 999 (C15), Sloane MS 513 (C15), Sloane MS 3008 (C15), Weimar F. 374/2 (C15), Guelf. 47.15 Aug. 4° (C15), Edinburgh R.O. Cr.3.14 (mid C15), Erfurt Quarto 28a (late C15), Munich CLM 28858 (late C15), BNF Lat. 7153 (1554), BNF Lat. 7154 (1554), Ashmole 1416 (C16), BNF 7170A (C16), Kassel 4° Chem. 96 (C16), Prague 1866 (C16), Rev. A. B. Hunter 39 (C16), Sachsen-Anhalt 14 B.36 (C16), Sloane MS 3826 (C16), Sloane MS 3853 (mid C16), Sloane MS 3846 (1564), Ashmole 1515 (late C16), Harley MS 181 (late C16), Yar. Var. 34 (1600), Trinity O.9.7 (1600), Trinity 1419 (1600), Bodley 8908 (1601), Sloane MS 3825 (1641), Wellcome MS 4653 (1660), Munich CLM 17711 (C17), Sloane MS 3648 (C17), Harley MS 6483 (1712), Vienna 11340 (1748), Bibliothèque de l'Arsenal MS 824 (C18), Leipzig 829 (C18), Wellcome MS 1581 (1820, French), Glasgow Ferguson 50 (1826, French), Amsterdam BPH 242 (ND), Augsburg 4° Cod. 55 (ND), BL Oriental 14759 (ND), Bologna A.165 (ND), Firenze Ambrosiana B8 Sup. (ND), George A. Plimpton 180 (ND), Plut. 17 Cod. III (ND), Royal Library Gl. Kgl. S.3499 (ND), Salzburg Cod. M I 24 (ND), Sloane MS 3822 (ND), Steitenstetten 273 (ND), Stolb. Wernig Za 74 (ND), Vatican Pal. Lat. 957 (ND), Vienna 11281 (ND), Vienna 11321 (ND), Vienna 13859 (ND).
Circle: N/A
Tools: The *Notae*.
Spirit List: Abba, Anacor, Ancor, Anylos, Banai, Basyaccor, Behemnos, Boros, Camael, Caphar, Cemas, Chahelype, Chemamoht, Chyma, Cramos, Debehal, Dehel, Demeham, Depymo, Depymon, Deyhel, Deyn, Eliphamasay, Elomnit, Exchauruht, Exhauthes, Exluso, Exmegan, Exmegon, Gabriel, Garbona, Gebeche Gehanamos, Gelamaguar, Gelonucoa, Genahyha, Gerabcai, Gerguolyhon, Germyohal, Gezede, Guabriel, Guamasyemahe, Habracha, Hachar, Hagyhoty, Halamas, Halamothona, Hallamon, Halmasython, Hamasy, Hamos, Hamyhel, Hamynos, Hamynosya, Hanatar, Hanatayhar, Hancomagos, Hapochohon, Harabar, Haraman, Harays, Harsanaraht, Haryolomo, Hasa, Hassyhethas, Hatanazar, Hathanaym, Havechylem, Hazamyhathos, Hazaryobal, Hazathor, Hazihadas, Hazyhaccor,

---

155 MSS are in Latin unless otherwise noted and include MSS of *Liber Visionum*.

Hebero, Hechondos, Hegrozamyhel, Hel, Helenothos, Helphleges, Helsa, Helymaht, Helymoht, Helymyhot, Helynon, Helythos, Hena, Heremegos, Heseculaty, Heseleagy, Hesonas, Hezegrathos, Hiatregilos, Hosiel, Hostyhol, Hosuatyn, Hosymagalon, Hozor, Hymon, Hyne, Hyquirros, Hysichar, Jamyrum, Jasamana, Jechar, Jecushuo, Jemamoht, Jemehiz, Jesamanay, Jesbar, Jechon, Jeroham, Jesenemay, Jethomezos, Jethosama, Jomaraht, Joroyhel, Josey, Lamaho, Lamehc, Landabamy, Lemay, Lemythan, Logos, Machadon, Machalay, Machar, Machromechon, Maraht, Massatholon, Mechelyptos, Medagamos, Megalos, Megehon, Megnon, Megon, Mephython, Messay, Michael, Mlechial, Monyham, Myhon, Myhotheophy, Myretagyl, Mysahel, Navagen, Neysa, Oragon, Otheos, Pamphilius, Panatheneos, Paryneos, Patyr, Phareht, Pharene, Phateneynehos, Pheheneos, Phlegothes, Phosegemeha, Phosmo, Phoste, Phothos, Pomelyhon, Prohos, Rachion, Raphael, Rasamen, Rasaym, Regay, Resaym, Sabayhon, Sacromatyhel, Sadama, Saguar, Sahacabary, Samarahos, Samelos, Samyos, Sandamyhar, Saromalay, Sasamalyhon, Sathamaht, Secramalan, Secray, Sehan, Sechay, Semahabal, Semegay, Semezehel, Semohy, Semynaphaz, Senazamar, Serasopho, Seruhc, Servehyhon, Socthac, Solarcham, Sordazal, Tahegilihos, Thacserar, Than, Tharinela, Themahehugos, Themamoht, Themos, Theodony, Thephehohal, Therechamzon, Thesara, Thetynchos, Thezemon, Thoramodor, Ythasym, Zadama, Zasamaht, Theos, Zadaynahc, Zaguhel, Zallamay, Zamanzathas, Zatahel, Zechar, Zechas, Zerobehel, Zerubehel, Zezaymanay, Zostihon, Zynconzon.

The Text

The Notary Art stands alone as a unique form of grimoire magic, designed for rapid learning. The subjects covered are the seven liberal arts of grammar, dialectic (logic), rhetoric, arithmetic, geometry, music, astronomy (and astrology), as well as chiromancy, general arts, Greek, Hebrew, hydromancy, medicine, memory, music, new arts, nigromancy, philosophy, pyromancy, theology, the mechanical arts, and the exceptive arts (divination and magic).

It is traditionally claimed to have been received by King Solomon from God via the angel Pamphilius. Although attributed, as are so many grimoires, to Solomon as the recipient, it is not part of the Solomonic stream of grimoires. The other pseudepigraphical attribution is to Apollonius of Tyana as the author of the *Golden Flowers* (*Flores Aurei*), which forms part of the text. After the *Key of Solomon*, it is the most prolific text, with at least one hundred and ten known manuscripts (including fragments, references to destroyed copies, and copies of *Liber Visionum*).[156]

The earliest known manuscript (Yale Mellon 1) can be traced to Bologna in northern Italy.[157] From here, it proliferated across Europe, used by monks and students as an aid to their learning, as well as finding its way into Royal and aristocratic libraries. Criticisms from contemporary figures like William of Auvergne and Albertus Magnus did nothing to diminish its popularity. Despite questions over its religious validity, copies were made and passed on, with one of the prayers even being used by St Anthony of Padua (1195-1231). The first printed editions of the *Ars Notoria* appear around 1620 in *Opera Omnia*, a collection of works which included the *Three Books of Occult Philosophy* of Agrippa (to whom the work is credited despite the inclusion of other works he did not author). Robert Turner produced an English

---

156 Skinner suggests there could be as many as fifty manuscripts currently unknown due to incorrect cataloguing (2019).

157 Although this is the first known source, it is worth noting that it was sometimes referred to as 'the art of Toledo', due to the reputation of this city as a centre for black magic and divination. See Veenstra, 1998.

publication of the *Ars Notoria* in 1657, translated from *Opera Omnia* and critically omitting the *notae*, making it unusable for practice.

The techniques involve purification, contemplation, and prayer, requiring a period of months, and have the intricate *notae* (illustrations which give their name to the practice) as foci. A significant adaptation of the *Ars Notoria* was created by the fourteenth-century monk John of Morigny.[158] John used the system without proper preparation, resulting in demonic visions. Disturbed by this he created a simplified form which is commonly called *Liber Visionum*, which omitted the *notae* and focused on the Virgin Mary, including material for acquiring the beatific vision of her. The full title is *The Book of Flowers of Heavenly Doctrine Book of the Grace of Christ*, and there were three compilations of it. These were the old compilation (one MS, 1311), the new compilation (at least twelve MSS, 1315) and the third compilation (six MSS).

A version of the *Ars Notoria* (omitting the *notae*) was included as the fifth and final work in the *Lemegeton*. It is unrelated to the other four works, and despite some claims to its relevance, it is essentially an irrelevant addition to the rest of the texts therein. It is important to note that many of the prayers from the *Ars Notoria* were used in the *Sworn Book of Honorius*.

The text contains: prologue, Part 1 *Flores Aurei* – of what efficacy words are; an explanation of the Notary Art; [chapter 1] the first precept, here begins the first oration, *Hely Scemath*,[159] a spiritual mandate of the precedent oration; the oration *Theos Megale*, here begins the exposition of the oration; the words of these orations cannot be wholly expounded; of the triumphal figures, how sparingly they are to be pronounced, and honestly and devoutly spoken; the expositions of the lunations of the Notary Art; he sheweth how the precedent oration is the beginning and foundation of the whole Art; the oration, *Assaylemath Assay*; the second part of the precedent orations, which is to be said only once, *Azzaylemath Lemath*; this oration hath no exposition in the Latin; of the efficacy of that oration which is inexplicable to human sense; [chapter 2] here he sheweth in what manner those Notes differ in Art, and the reason thereof; the oration. *Lameth Leymach*; how this oration is to be said in the beginning of every month, chastely, and with a pure mind; here followeth the prayer we spake of before, to obtain a good memory; here following is the prologue of the precedent oration, which provoketh and procureth memory, and is continued with the precedent Note; here beginneth the prologue of this oration; here he sheweth some other virtue of the precedent oration; here followeth an oration of great virtue, to attain the knowledge of the Physical Art; here begins the oration of the Physical [Medical] Art, *Ihesus fili*; another part of the same oration; here follows an efficacious preface of an oration; [chapter 3] here he sheweth how every Note of every Art, ought to exercise his own office, that all figures have their proper orations; a certain special precept; here begins the oration, *Lamed Rogum*; the beginning of the oration; here is also a particular exposition of the foregoing oration; the first of these orations which we call spiritual, the virtue whereof teacheth Divinity, and preserveth the memory thereof; the election of time, in what lunation these orations ought to be said; here followeth the beginning of this oration, *Achacham Yhel*; this is the beginning of the second part of that oration, *Aglaros Theomiros*; the third part, *Megal Ariotas*; the fourth part, *Hely Latur*; then the parts being commemorated as is directed, add also the following oration; how the Latin orations are not expounded by the words of the orations; here he speaketh of the efficacy of all these; in this chapter he sheweth the efficacy of the subsequent oration, it being special to obtain Eloquence; in this chapter he setteth down the time and manner how the oration is to be pronounced; an oration of great virtue for General and all Liberal Arts, *Gemot Geel*; no man that is impeded or corrupted with any crime ought to presume to say this oration; this is a prologue or exposition of the precedent

---

158 For a detailed discussion of this see Fanger 1998:216-249.

159 For the different orations which are lists of words, the first two words of each are listed to distinguish them.

oration, which ought to be said together; after a little space of silence begin to say this oration seriously, *Semet Lamen*; how every several art hath its proper note, *Semot Lamen*.'

Part 2, of the Liberal Arts or Trivium; of the liberal sciences and other things, which may be had by that Art; of the liberal sciences and other things which may be had thereby; he declareth what notes the three first liberal Arts have; here Solomon sheweth, how the angel told him distinctly, wherefore the Grammar hath three Figures; the reason why the Dialectical Art hath two Figures only; the reason why Rhetoric hath four Figures; at what times and hours the Notes of these three liberal Arts are to be looked into; how the Grammatical Notes are to be looked into in the first Moon; here followeth the knowledge of the Notes; of the logical notes; how the Logical Notes are to be inspected, and the orations said thereof; how we must beware of offences; how the Notes ought to be inspected, at certain elected times; three chapters to be published, before any of the Notes; how the Proper Notes are to be inspected; what days are to be observed in the inspection of the Notes of the four Arts; of the inspection of General Notes; how the first three chapters are to be pronounced before orations; how the fifth oration of Theology ought to be rehearsed upon these orations; the first orations at the beginning of the Notes; Notae of Grammar, the 1st oration, the 2nd oration, the 3rd oration, the 4th oration, here is made mention of the Notes of all Arts; Notae of Dialectic (Logic), the 5th oration, the 6th oration; Notae of Rhetoric, the 7th oration, the 8th oration, the 9th oration, the 10th oration, the 11th oration, the 12th oration; Quadrivium, Notae of Arithmetic, the 13th oration, the 14th oration, the 15th oration; definitions of several Arts, and the Notes thereof, 16th oration [Geometry], 17th oration [Theology]; how diverse months are to be sought out in the inspection of the Notes; Notae of Philosophy, 1st oration, 2nd oration, 3rd oration, 4th oration; how these notes are to be said every day once before the general Notes, and the Notes of the liberal Arts; 6th oration; Notae of Theology, 7th oration; special precepts of the Notes of Theology, chiefly of the 1st, 2nd, and 3rd Notes; how Solomon received that ineffable Note from the angel; how the precepts are to be observed in the operation of all Arts; these precepts are specially to be observed.

Part 3 Artem Novem/Ars Nova;[160] orations prologue; 1st oration, Theology; 2nd oration, Eloquence; 3rd oration, Astronomy; 4th oration, Works of Celebration, *Otheos Athamaziel*; 5th oration, Memory; 6th oration, strengthening the interior and exterior senses; 7th oration, Eloquence, Memory, and Stability; 8th oration, to recover lost wisdom; 9th oration, to obtain the grace of the Holy Spirit; 10th oration, to recover intellectual wisdom.

Part 4, Supplementary Gloss and full text of main prayers; say these orations from the first day of the month, to the fourth day, *Theos Megale*; hereby is increased so much Eloquence, that nothing is above it, *Thezay Lemach*; the third part, the sign Lemach, *Lemach Sabrice*; for the Memory; the conclusion of the whole work, and confirmation of the science obtained; the benediction of the place; to perform any work; some other precepts to be observed in this work; the process follows; other precepts; then silently say these orations.

Part 5, on the Figure of Memory; the manner of consecrating the Figure of Memory; four days the Figure of Memory ought to be consecrated with these orations; the oration following ought to be said as you stand up; the following oration hath power to expel all lusts.

---

160 This is in no way connected to the 'Ars Nova' in the *Lemegeton*, though one can speculate that the same title being used may have contributed to the inclusion of the abbreviated and notae-free *Notary Art* as the final part of that work.

Essential Reading

Skinner, Stephen & Clark, Daniel (2019) *Ars Notoria: The Grimoire of Rapid Learning by Magic.* Singapore: Golden Hoard Press. Sourceworks of Ceremonial Magic Volume 11. Excellent study of the *Ars Notoria*, with colour images of all the Notae, also includes the *Golden Flowers of Apollonius of Tyana.*

Skinner, Stephen (2021) *Ars Notoria: The Method, Version B Medieval Angel Magic.* Singapore: Golden Hoard Press. Sourceworks of Ceremonial Magic Volume 12. Great companion volume which explores the practice of the *Ars Notoria* in depth, making it practical in a coherent manner.

Véronèse, Julien (2007) *L'Ars Notoria au Moyen Age: Introduction et edition critique.* Firenze: SISMEL, Edizioni del Galluzzo. Academic critical edition of the text.

Ars Notoria BNF Paris ms Latin 9336

Almandal / Ars Almadel (The Almadel Art)

Date: 1220-40/1641.
Language: Latin, German, English.
Influences: Lost Arab source, earliest Latin translation lost. *Vinculum Salomonis, Ars Notoria*.
Provenance: Unknown author. Munich Cgm. 407 in the hand of the merchant Claus Spaun. Sloane MS 3825 is first known copy of *Ars Almadel*. Harley MS 6483 by Thomas Rudd, copied by Peter Smart (1712); NWU MS 65 in hand of Thomas Simpkins (1713); Ebenezer Sibley (1752-99) (late C18); copied by Frederick Hockley (1808-85) (1828), copied by Henry Dawson Lea (1809-63) as Wellcome MS 3203.
MSS: Almandal:[161] Vatican MS BAV Reg lat 1106 (C13); Corpus Christi MS 243 (C13-14); Wellcome MS 116 (C14); Vienna codex Vincob 3400 (1469); Florence II.iii.24 (C15); Florence Plut. 89 sup. 38 (C15); Halle ULSA B14 B.36 (late C15); Paris Coxe 25 (late C15); Vatican BA lat. 3180 (late C15); Freiburg BR Hs. 458 (1490-1509, German); Munich Cgm. 407 (1496, German); BNF Allemand 160 (1500, German); MS Genève 145 (formerly MS Sassoon 290 (1510-30, Hebrew); BL Oriental MS 6360 (C17, Hebrew); Leipzig Cod. Mag. 60 (1751, German); Berlin MS Germ. Fol. 903 (c.1580, German); Jerusalem AMST Ros 1808 A9 (C18, Hebrew). **Ars Almadel:** Sloane MS 3825 (1641); Sloane MS 3824 (1649); Sloane 3648 (1649); Sloane 2731 (1686); Harley MS 6483 (1712 from earlier copy); Northwestern University MS 65 (1713); Wellcome MS 3203 (1843).
Circle: N/A.[162]
Tools: Almandal (wax), candleholders (four), censer, gold seal, robes, silver stylus.
Spirit List: *Almandal*: Abonay, Allayn, Almeos, Alnay, Alpha, Alphaneos, Alpharaym, Alybyn, Alymos, Anabo, Anaphyn, Anas, Anay, Anaym, Anabbeyl, Anrach, Anthychoy, Armon, Arnech, Arphel, Arymyel, Asser, Ay, Barachiel, Beremon, Bisseros, Coroczay, Ecabel, Eheomynt, Erynhel, Ezay, Gelomyoro, Gereon/Geon, Gabriel, Halay, Heloy, Helyffan, Helyson, Heros, Hyros, Lanalay, Lubras, Lybes, Mercy, Michael, Monosy, Mynuel, Nayzaday, Onay, Ornochynta, Pamphirius, Panthanay, Patience, Patra, Peace, Pneumathon, Prince, Ramana, Raphael, Rathan, Ruluxidye, Safrax, Salnet, Salny, Strength, Thanay, Vereon, Yarceth, Yatham, Yhethamey, Yssa, Ytach, Zaan, Zabon, Zadanay, Zarneach, Zedebomoy.

Ars Almadel: Alimiel, Alphariza, Armon, Barchiel, Borachiel, Captiel, Deliel, Eliphimasai, Elomnia, Gabiel, Gabriel, Gediel, Gedobonai, Gelomiros, Genon, Gereinon, Geron, Hellison, Lebes, Saranana.

The Text

There are two distinct phases of the *Almandal*[163] (earlier, Arabic-influenced text mentioning djinn or shayatin[164] and the *Almadel* (later, Christian-influenced text with angels). William of Auvergne gives the first recorded reference between 1220-40 CE in a way that describes

---

161 Unless otherwise stated, the *Almandal* manuscripts are in Latin. All *Almadel* manuscripts are in English.

162 The *De Consecratione Lapidum* copies mention a circle but it is absent in all other texts.

163 Note from the Arabic 'al-mandal' meaning circle. It has been suggested the roots of this practice may lie in India, and that the use of the word 'mandal' is derived from the Sanskrit word mandala, a symbolic representation of the universe. This would fit with the symbolic actions performed, where in this case the practitioner is literally assuming the role of God, communicating via angels in the universe (the almandal).

164 Islamic name for demons.

some of the practice and clearly indicates he is taking about the *Almandal*. It is thought to have been translated in the C12 CE from a lost Arabic text. The *Almandal* is often associated with Solomon, and a gloss added to Codex Vincob 3400 tells the story of an angel (a Seraph) rewarding the king for his wisdom after his judgement of the two women arguing over the baby by giving him the secrets of the *Almandal*.

The earliest three extant copies are all found included in manuscripts of *De Consecratione Lapidum*. Trithemius listed a work entitled *Almadel* attributed to King Solomon in *Antipalus Maleficorum* (1508). Agrippa also lists the Almadel with the Pauline Art and the Notary Art in his *Three Books of Occult Philosophy*. From these sources it is clear that this was a well-established practice long before its inclusion in the *Lemegeton*, and the version contained therein is a simplified version of earlier practices.

The almandal is six-inch or fifteen-cm square and made of wax, coloured according to the Altitude used, as are the robes worn by the practitioner and the four candles burned at the corners of the almandal. The divine names and symbols are written on with the silver stylus, preferably before sunrise on a Sunday. For timing the hours of the Sun on Sunday are described (i.e., first, eighth, fifteenth, and twenty-second) and this should be during the appropriate sign for the Altitude. A sequence of four conjurations follows the set-up of the altar.[165]

The angels are described in some detail so their appearance can be matched when they appear after the incense has been burned beneath the almandal. The angels are called on for a range of purposes, including assistance with birth; regulation of profits, money, and goods; with movement in the heavens and the flow of water in seas and rivers; enlightening the mind; teaching the liberal arts, astrology, and theology; with politics; and with passion and love. The rite is also said to bring clarity of mind to the practitioner.

The sequence ends with the departure of the angel, who assures the practitioner that they are now brothers and friends, and the text states that the practitioner will now love the angel above all others. This can be viewed as a redemptive act, placing the magician in the hierarchy of angels and so assured a heavenly resting place.

The *Ars Almadel* begins with instructions on how to construct the Almadel, a wax tablet inscribed with divine names and figures, the image of which is provided in the text. The colour of wax used for the Almadel depends on which of the four Choras (or Altitudes) are worked with. One third of the wax is used for this, and the other two thirds to make four candles and four supports for the Almadel. A gold (or silver) seal is also constructed to use on the Almadel during conjurations.

The four Choras, associated with the four directions, are described, giving the associated angels, appropriate timings, and qualities they bring. A description of their appearances and the appropriate incense to burn follow this. A note on timing and an invocation follow, completing the short but interesting practice in this work. This later version also introduces using a crystal as a shew-stone, which is absent in earlier versions. The earlier version has twelve Altitudes, with zodiacal attributions, which is heavily reduced in the later version to the four directional Altitudes (though the zodiac is still implied in the four groups of angels). Three of the four Altitudes are derived from the earlier text (first, second and eighth), with the fourth being added from an unknown source.

---

165 In the *De Consecratione Lapidum* version these are four prayers addressed to Michael, Gabriel, Raphael, and Pamphirius. The latter angel does not appear anywhere else, and it is tempting to equate it to Pamphilius from the *Ars Notoria*; Regan also does this, see 2018:299.

Essential Reading

Peterson, Joseph H. (2001) *The Lesser Key of Solomon: Lemegeton Clavicula Salomonis*. Maine, Weiser Books. An excellent book exploring the history of the *Goetia*, with the complete Manuscript of Sloane MS 3825, the earliest known copy. Peterson's work is the definitive study of the earlier manuscripts of the *Lemegeton*.

Regan, Vajra (2018) '*The De Consecratione Lapidum: A Previously Unknown Thirteenth Century Version of the Liber Almandal Salamonis*', in Journal of Medieval Latin 28:277-333. Fabulous scholarly work tracing the Almandal back to earlier manuscripts and providing text and detailed contextualization.

Skinner, Stephen & Rankine, David (2007) *The Goetia of Dr Rudd*. Singapore, Golden Hoard Press. The complete manuscript of Harley MS 6483, this book also explores the roots of the *Goetia* and associated figures. Together with Peterson's edition the two works provide a complete reference to the *Lemegeton*.

Veenstra, Jan R. (2002) *The Holy Almandal: Angels and the Intellectual Aims of Magic*. Leuven: Peeters. Detailed academic work exploring the Almandal tradition and its influence.

Véronèse, Julien (2012) *L'Almandal et l'Almadel latins au Moyen Âge: introduction et édition critique*. Firenze: SISMEL, Edizioni del Galluzzo. Critical academic work which explores the earlier Almandel texts and development into the later Almadel.

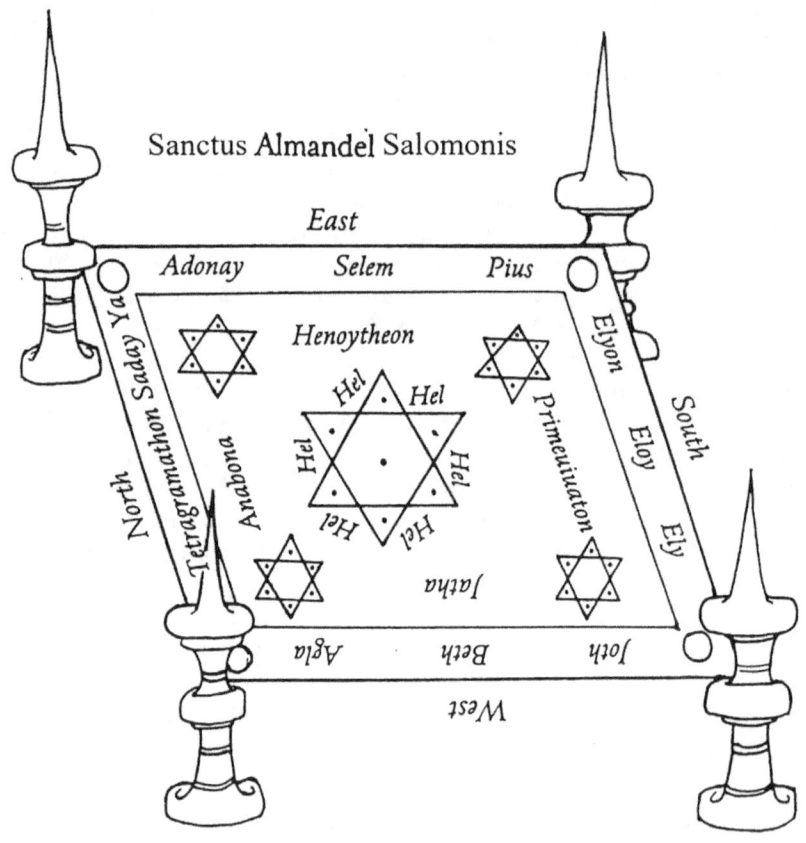

Almandal, from HS 458

Sepher Raziel

Date: C13, pre-1259.
Language: Latin, Castilian, English, Czech, German, French, Italian, Hebrew.
Influences: *Liber Lunae.*
Provenance: The first known copy of *Sepher Raziel* comes from the court of King Alfonso the Wise, and passed through the hands of Queen Christina of Sweden, given to her in 1650. Sloane MS 3846 was owned by Elias Ashmole, as noted by text he added.
MSS: Vatican MS Reg. Latin 1300 (Latin, C13), Halle MS cod. 14 B 36 (C14, Latin), BNF Latin MS 3666 (Late C14/Early C15, Latin), partial in Munich CLM 51 (1487, Latin), Sloane MS 3826 (C16, English), BML Plut. 44.33 (1550, Latin), Sloane MS 3846 (1564, English), fragment in Bodleian Ashmole MS 1790 (1564, English & Latin), partial in Sloane MS 3847 (C16, Latin), partial in Sloane MS 3853 (mid C16, Latin), Lubeck MS Math. 9 (C16, Latin), Yale Osborn MS fa. 7 (late C16, English), Prague NML MS XVII F25 (1595, Czech), Hansestadt Math. 4° 10 (C16/17, German), partial in Additional MS 16390 (Hebrew), MS Lyon 970 (C17/18, French), Leipzig Cod. Mag. 40 (1750, Latin), partial in Alnwick MS 596 (C18, Italian, Latin & English), Dresden MS N. 36 (C18, German), Pennsylvania MS 1685 (late C18, English).
Circle: N/A.
Tools: Ink, reed pen.
Spirit List: Aadon, Aal, Aaniturla, Aaon, Aaron, Abecaisdon, Abedel, Abinel, Ablaieil, Abneyrin, Abnisor, Abrac, Abragin, Abramacyn, Abranocyn, Abrasachysyn, Abrasasyn, Abrastos, Abri, Abris, Abrisaf, Absafyabitan, Absamon, Abson, Acceriel, Acciriron, Acdiel, Achlas, Acia, Aciel, Aczonyn, Addriel, Adi, Adiamenyn, Adiel, Adnibia, Adniel, Adnoiel, Adnyam, Adziriel, Ael, Aesal, Affarfytyriel, Affariel, Affry, Afneirin, Agrasinden, Aguel, Ahiel, Alael, Alapion, Alasqwy, Alatiel, Albafortum, Albedagryn, Albeylyn, Alisaf, Almemel, Almux, Almyon, Alscini, Alserin, Alsfiton, Alson, Altim, Alxim, Alyel, Alzamy, Alzeyeil, Amacia, Amadyeyl, Amael, Amaluch, Amantuliel, Amariel, Ambayerin, Amdalycyn, Ameinyn, Ameyl, Amiol, Amneal, Amrael, Amurael, Amyel, Amynyel, Amytor, Anaya, Anayenyn, Ancarilyn, Ancason, Ancuyel, Andas, Anebynnyl, Anhael, Aniyel, Anmanineylyn, Anqnihim, Anrylin, Antquiel, Anulus, Aol, Apheieyl, Aquyel, Arabyel, Arac, Araqiniel, Araton, Ardiel, Areseferat, Arfaniel, Aribiriel, Arieil, Armaqnieyeyl, Armariel, Armayel, Arobolyn, Arsabon, Artigyel, Aryel, Aryelyn, Arylin, Aryor, Arzaf, Asaphin, Asat, Asdon, Asirac, Aspiramo, Asrieylin, Astagna, Asymeylyn, Aszre, Atragon, Aurion, Ayayeylin, Aymeylyn, Azday, Azigor, Azrageyl, Azraicylin, Azriel, Bacharachyn, Bachmyel, Bactanael, Bacyel, Badeilyn, Bael, Bahoraelin, Baiedalin, Balganarichyn, Baliel, Balriel, Balyer, Banorasti, Baqwylaguel, Barachiel, Barafilin, Baraniel, Barasiel, Barcalin, Bargar, Barhil, Bariel, Barilagni, Barnayeyl, Barquiel, Bastelyn, Basy, Bathaylyn, Batoraielyn, Bearel, Becar, Bee, Beel, Beerel, Belon, Benenil, Bengariel, Beniel, Benit, Beriel, Berion, Berriel, Beryel, Betabaat, Bifealyqnyn, Biraquel, Boel, Borayeyl, Borhai, Bortaz, Bothaz, Boxoraylon, Braaliel, Braliel, Branielin, Briel, Brofilyn, Byeniel, Byny, Cabach, Cabritiel, Cabyn, Cacititlyn, Cadneirin, Cael, Caisaat, Cakaziel, Calcas, Calchihay, Calipon, Calloyel, Calnamia, Camb, Camfilin, Camiel, Camirael, Cananyn, Candanagyn, Canesylyn, Cannyel, Canyel, Capciel, Capeiel, Capiel, Capziel, Caran, Carbiel, Carbiol, Carciel, Carcoyel, Carcyelel, Cardiel, Caribitin, Cariel, Carmiel, Carpariel, Carszeneyl, Cartalion, Cartemat, Caryel, Casiel, Casmuch, Cassilon, Cassurafarttis, Castrubyn, Cathneylyn, Caybemynyn, Cazabriel, Caziel, Cefania, Celabel, Celidoal, Ceradadyn, Ceraphin, Cetabiel, Cethenoylyn, Ceyabos, Ceytatynyn, Chenyon, Cherubyn, Cherudiel, Comaguele, Costiryn, Cullia, Cunnyryel, Cyoly, Cyzamanyn, Dadiel, Daemael, Dalia, Daliel, Dameyel, Dandaniel, Daniel, Danpi, Danroc, Dapsion, Darbiel, Dargoyeyl, Dariculin,

Dariel, Darifiel, Darquiel, Dasfripyel, Debitael, Dedion, Delgna, Denmerzym, Deparael, Dersam, Detriel, Dexxeyl, Doranel, Dragos, Dufuel, Duraniel, Eazerin, Effignax, Effilin, Elieyl, Elisafan, Elisuaig, Ellalyel, Elmia, Elynzy, Emcodeneyl, Emyel, Enplyn, Eralyn, Esmaadyn, Essaf, Esyol, Expaoniel, Expion, Ezuiah, Faceyeyl, Falafon, Falha, Faly, Famnial, Faniel, Fanyel, Farabyn, Farbiel, Farielin, Farionon, Felyypon, Feniturla, Feylarachin, Feyn, Flatoniel, Fonyel, Foylylon, Fuheylyn, Fulitiel, Gabal, Gabanael, Gabgel, Gabion, Gabmion, Gabrael, Gabriel, Gabrynyn, Gadaf, Gadiel, Gael, Galbiet, Galgall, Galliel, Galms, Galnel, Galuf, Galus, Garasyn, Gasca, Gasoryn, Gazriel, Gazril, Gebarbayea, Gebyn, Gedulin, Gemraorin, Geninaturla, Gibryl, Gimon, Gnabriza, Golid, Gromeyl, Guadriel, Guanrinasuch, Gunfiel, Guracap, Guriel, Haayn, Hac, Hacoylyn, Hadzbeyeyl, Hahon, Halilin, Hanin, Hanyel, Hareryn, Hasasisgafon, Hasneyeyl, Hatel, Hayeylin, Haynynael, Hehudael, Hiaeyel, Himeilin, Homycabel, Hoquiel, Horrion, Hosael, Hubayel, Hufrbria, Hyeyl, Hyzy, Iabynx, Impuryn, Indam, Insquen, Israel, Janael, Jarael, Jasyozyn, Jauiel, Jebrayel, Juniel, Kaliel, Karason, Karbiel, Keialin, Kelfeielyn, Kemerion, Kery, Laabiel, Labiel, Labolas, Lacana, Laccudonyn, Lael, Lafiel, Langhasin, Lanifiel, Lantiel, Lariagathyn, Lariel, Lataqnael, Latebaifanysyn, Latgriel, Laudulin, Layzaiosyn, Leal, Lebraieil, Lelalion, Lepiron, Letityelyn, Leuainon, Lezaidi, Libiel, Libral, Locariel, Loch, Loriquiel, Lucifel, Luel, Luliaraf, Lyenyel, Maadon, Maaliel, Maarim, Maasiel, Mabareylyn, Mabsuf, Maccafor, Maccamarif, Macgron, Machin, Macracif, Macria, Madarilyn, Maday, Madrat, Magdiel, Magel, Magnia, Magnyny, Magossangos, Mahamed, Maint, Malaquiran, Malatyn, Malgas, Malgel, Malisan, Malquiel, Malquiel, Mamiazicaras, Mamiel, Mamirot, Mamyel, Mandiel, Manistiorar, Manit, Marcuel, Margabiel, Marhil, Marhum, Mariel, Marilin, Marinoc, Marmanyn, Marmoc, Marneyelin, Masiel, Masulaef, Matiel, Mattriel, Mazica, Maziel, Mefeniel, Mehil, Meliton, Mellifiel, Memieil, Memitilon, Memolyn, Memyiel, Meon, Merigal, Meriol, Metorilin, Miaga, Michael, Micraton, Minael, Miriel, Modiel, Monichion, Montagin, Monteylyn, Morayeil, Moriel, Mortagon, Muracafel, Murion, Mycahe, Mylba, Myriel, Myschiel, Myssa, Naamab, Naasien, Nabiatilyn, Naboon, Nabuel, Nabyalni, Nacery, Nachal, Nactif, Nadib, Nadibael, Naduch, Nafac, Naffrynyn, Naflia, Nagrow, Nahymel, Nangareryn, Nanylin, Nap, Narbell, Nasmyel, Naspaya, Naspiel, Nassa, Nassam, Nastiafori, Nasyel, Natriel, Naxas, Nebubael, Necamia, Necanynael, Necif, Necyl, Nediter, Negri, Nelia, Nenael, Nenel, Nepenielin, Nephyel, Nerad, Neraziel, Nesquiraf, Neyeyl, Nobquin, Nocpis, Nonanrin, Noraraabilin, Noriel, Nuscifa, Nyahpatuel, Nybiel, Nybirin, Nyrysin, Odrael, Oliab, Oliel, Omiel, Ononileon, Onoxion, Orfiel, Oriel, Orinyn, Orychyn, Osfleel, Osmyn, Paafiryn, Paamiel, Pabliel, Pachayel, Pacryton, Pacuel, Pacyta, Pagulan, Paliel, Palitam, Palriel, Paltamus, Palthia, Paltifus, Paly, Panhiniel, Panion, Pansa, Pantaceren, Pantan, Pantaron, Panteron, Papon, Parachbeylyn, Paradiel, Parciot, Parhaya, Pariel, Parna, Partriel, Pasaliel, Paschania, Paticael, Patiel, Patnilin, Paxilon, Paxonion, Pazehemy, Paziael, Pazicaton, Pdgnar, Peciel, Pecyrael, Pegal, Penael, Penat, Pepilon, Phynitiel, Pion, Pirtophin, Pistilin, Pliset, Poniel, Porackmiel, Pyroyinel, Qnatiel, Qnynzi, Quabriel, Quadissa, Qualabye, Quemon, Quesupale, Quian, Quiel, Quilon, Quiron, Quisiel, Quor, Quyel, Qwenael, Raaciel, Raamyel, Rabiel, Rabmia, Rabtilyn, Raconeal, Racyeylyn, Racyno, Radiel, Rafael, Raffeylyn, Ragael, Ragohyel, Raguel, Rahumiel, Rahyeziel, Raliel, Raloyl, Ram, Ramatiel, Ramnel, Rancyl, Ranfiel, Raphael, Rapinis, Rapion, Rartudel, Raseroph, Rasliel, Rasoiel, Rassy, Rastia, Rasziel, Rcynas, Regnia, Relion, Remafidda, Remcatheyel, Resegar, Resfilin, Reycat, Reyn, Rinafonel, Robica, Rofachilion, Rofiniel, Romiel, Roncayl, Ronmeyeyl, Roquiel, Rorafeyl, Rubycyel, Ruffaraneylyn, Rulbelyn, Saamyel, Sababiel, Sacadiel, Sacciniel, Sacdon, Sachiel, Sachquiel, Saciel, Sacstoyeyn, Saddaniel, Sadiel, Saeprel, Safcy, Safe, Saffeyeyl, Safida, Safuel, Sahaman, Sahgragynyn, Sahuhaf, Sahumiel, Salainel, Salion, Saloniel, Salor, Salttri, Samael, Samayelyn, Samhiel, Samiel, Samtiel, Samyel, Samysarach, Sanael, Sandalfon, Sandalson, Sanfael,

Sanficiel, Sansani, Saoriel, Sapiel, Sapsi, Saracus, Sargnamuf, Sarican, Sariol, Sarman, Sarmas, Saron, Sarsac, Sarsaf, Sasci, Sasuagos, Sasuyel, Saton, Satpach, Satquel, Satuel, Satyn, Semeol, Semhahylyn, Semquiel, Sephatia, Serael, Serapiel, Sereriel, Seriel, Simyllyel, Snynyel, Sodiel, Somahi, Sonatas, Soquiel, Soquiel, Sornadaf, Stelmel, Stemehilyn, Suciel, Sugni, Suncacer, Suriel, Syymelyel, Szarhyr, Szeyyeil, Szif, Szucariel, Tabiel, Tablic, Talgnaf, Talgylonyl, Talrailanrain, Tamtiel, Tarael, Taramel, Tarmanydyn, Tartalyn, Tartanelyn, Taryestorat, Tatgiel, Temelion, Tenebriel, Tepyel, Themiton, Thesfealin, Tinsyel, Tiogra, Tiszodiel, Titomon, Tobiel, Torayeil, Toripiel, Traacyel, Tralyelyn, Tubeylyn, Tufiel, Tuniel, Tutiel, Tyel, Tymel, Uaceyl, Uachayel, Uardayheil, Uetamuel, Uiotan, Unaraxxydin, Unascaiel, Unleylyn, Urallim, Uranacha, Urpeniel, Usaryeyel, Uslael, Vaanyel, Vazebelil, Veaboluf, Veal, Veallum, Vehichdunedzineylyn, Verascyer, Veremedyn, Vixalimon, Vtisaryaya, Xatinas, Xysuylion, Yabtasyper, Yael, Yafrael, Yalsenac, Yamaanyl, Yamla, Yanael, Yariel, Yas, Yasmyel, Yassar, Yastamel, Yatayel, Yayac, Yayel, Yaziel, Yebel, Yebiryn, Yecaleme, Yehoc, Yelbrayeyl, Yeocyn, Yesararye, Yesmactria, Ykiel, Ylaraorynil, Ymel, Ymnybron, Ymrael, Yoas, Yodmeyeyl, Yoel, Yryniel, Ysar, Ytael, Ytrut, Yyamnel, Yyel, Zacdon, Zalcycyl, Zalibron, Zamayl, Zamel, Zamiel, Zamirel, Zaquiel, Zarael, Zaratil, Zarfaieil, Zarialin, Zarseyeyl, Zebaliel, Zemeinyn, Zenam, Zesfaieil, Zetael, Zoaziel, Zsmayel, Ztazel, Zupa.

The Text

There were several different works called *Sepher Raziel* in the Middle Ages, which were all completely different.[166] This work is one which influenced other grimoires, originally in Latin and subsequently in other European languages. The number of surviving manuscripts and the variety of languages demonstrates how widely *Sepher Raziel* proliferated.

The preface gives the legend of the origin of *Sepher Raziel* and Solomon gives nine precepts vital for the practice of the magic within. Solomon mentions that seven treatises are contained within it and lists them. These are 'Clavis' (astronomy and the stars), 'Ala' (virtues of some stones, herbs and animals), 'Tractatus Thymiamatus' (suffumigations), 'Treatise of Times' (timings of day and night and part of the year), 'Treatise of Purity and Abstinence', 'Samaim' (the heavens and angels and their operations), and the 'Book of Virtues and Miracles' (figures and properties of magic).

'Clavis' discusses the symbolism and attributions of the seven planets, as well as the zodiacal signs and elements. Other astrological considerations like aspects and the twelve houses are also discussed. 'Ala' ('Wing') details the properties of twenty-four stones (the first wing); twenty-four herbs (the second wing); the six types of beasts (of the four elements, phantoms, and demons), animals (including six birds, six fish, and six animals (the third wing); the associated qualities of the Hebrew letters (the fourth wing). 'Tractatus Thymiamatus' begins with perfumes of the days, discusses the importance of suffumigation, its use in different ways, how conjuration works, and attributions to the twelve zodiacal signs, thirty-six decans, four seasons, four elements and four directions.

The 'Treatise of Times' discusses the times of the year, and the different divisions thereof. It includes a huge spirit list, with angels of the months, the days of the week, the planets over each of the four elements, as well as the planets for each element and season, and the earth and elements in the seasons. The 'Treatise of Purity and of Abstinence' is self-explanatory, and also includes discussion of the Ark of Covenant and the nature of Semiforas and their use. The sixth book is 'Samaim', which lists the heavens and their angels in the four directions.

---

166 For detailed discussion of the different types of *Sepher Raziel*, see Karr & Skinner, 2017.

There are no angels listed for the sixth and seventh heavens; prayers are given for these as they were considered to be occupied by God. The seventh book is the 'Book of Virtues and Miracles', and contains the seven Semiforas, along with the sets of names attributed to each and a description of when Moses used them.

Essential Reading

Karr, Don & Skinner, Stephen (eds) (2017) *Sepher Raziel: Liber Salomonis*. Singapore: Golden Hoard Press. Sourceworks of Ceremonial Magic Volume 6. Excellent study of this important work with the text, and much useful additional contextual material, including on the different *Sepher Raziel* traditions.

The Sworn Book of Honorius (Liber Iuratus Honorii)

Date: Pre 1343.[167]
Language: Latin, English.
Influences: *Ars Notoria*, possibly *Hekhalot* literature,[168] possibly Byzantine orthodox Christianity.[169]
Provenance: First manuscript edition in *Summa Sacra Magice* (1346), with possible earlier historical references
MSS: MS 4° Astron. 3 *Summa Sacre Magice* contains large amounts of the text (1346, Latin) owned by John Dee; Sloane MS 3854 (mid C14); Sloane 313 (late C14) owned by Ben Johnson and John Dee; Royal MS 17 Axlii (mid C16) in Latin and English; Sloane MS 3853 (mid C16) in English and Latin, majority of text with some Agrippa; Sloane MS 3849 (1577) contains excerpts; Sloane MS 3885 (1588) bound with *Practica Nigromanciae* of pseudo-Bacon and other material; MS Germ Fol. 903 (German) *Summa Sacre Magice* contains large amounts of the text (1580s); Leipzig Cod Mag. 16 (German) (c. 1750).
Circle: Yes.
Tools: Censer, gloves, hair shirt, knife, Seal of God, stools, stole, seven swords, wand (hazel/laurel), whistle, white robe.
Spirit List: Abucaba, Abuchaba, Albunalich, Alchibany, Alflas, Amabiel, Amochap, Anael, Asassaiel, Asmoday, Assaibi, Atithael, Atraurbiabilis, Barthan, Baxhathau, Belzebub, Bileth, Bohel, Cafhael, Cafziel, Cambores, Carmehal, Carmox, Cassiel, Caudes, Chaudas, Chide, Corniger, Cynassa, Dardihel, Dehel, Deihel, Dein, Depymo, Depymon, Dragon, Drohas, Eladeb, Euiraber, Exluso, Exmegan, Exmogon, Formione, Gabriel, Gahathus, Garbona, Geneolia, Guth, Guthryn, Habaa, Haibalidech, Hanahel, Harith, Harthan, Hebethel, Hel, Heliothos, Helynon, Hocrohel, Hosyel, Hurathaphel, Hyachonaababur, Hyyci, Ialchal, Iammax, Iarabal, Iesse, Innyhal, Labadu, Maguth, Malafer, Maymon, Megonhamos, Mextyura, Michael, Michrathon, Milalu, Milau, Monyham, Mulcifer, Mychael, Myhel, Naadob, Naasa, Nassar, Nauagen, Nesaph, Oylol, Pahamcocihel, Palas, Parineos, Pasfran, Phagnora, Pheleneos, Proathophas, Quyron, Raphael, Raquiel, Rathion, Ryon, Salguyel, Samael, Samahel, Sambas, Samyel, Sarabocres, Sarapiel, Saterquiel, Satihel, Satquiel, Thaadas, Trachathath, Trocornifer, Yasfla, Ycanohl, Yturahihel, Zach, Zobha.

The Text

The *Sworn Book of Honorius*, or *Liber Iuratus Honorii*, is one of the most significant of the early grimoires. It is also known as the *Liber Sacer* or *Liber Sacratus*. There are numerous medieval references to it, the earliest being a possible mention by William of Auvergne condemning it around 1230 CE.

The earliest known version of the text appears in *Summa Sacre Magice* (1346) and is in a different, and probably more correct, order to that found in the other manuscripts.[170] The other manuscripts are now often referred to as the 'London Honorius' referring to their predominance at the British Library, or the 'Northwestern European' tradition, which includes the German copy of the manuscript. Significant differences include the earliest version

---

167 There is reference to Ganellus lending his copy of *Liber Iuratus* to the defrocked friar Stephanus Pipina in 1343 following the friar's long journey through Spain seeking a copy of it.
168 A number of references show clear parallels to the tradition of Merkavah mysticism.
169 Pointed out by Peterson 2016:17-22.
170 See Peterson, 2016:23.

in Ganellus having material not found in the other manuscripts on the four demon kings (Amaymon, Oriens, Paymon, and Egin), further instructions regarding ritual equipment, and seals of spirits. The core prayers in Ganellus are taken from *Liber Trium Animarum*, not from the *Ars Notoria* as in all the subsequent manuscripts.

John Dee owned copies of *Summa Sacre Magice* (MS 4° Astron. 3) and the *Sworn Book of Honorius* (Sloane MS 313), which influenced his work and provided him with the image of the *Sigillum Dei*, which would feature heavily in his work. There is material in the text which is the same as in the *Lucidation of Necromancy* and the *Heptameron*, indicating its likely influence on those texts.

The text begins with the prologue, and how Honorius, son of Euclid, consulted the angel Hocrohel who provided the material which forms the Sworn Book. The oath is then discussed, with the qualifications of how the book may be passed on. The book moves on to list the topics of the first work, the second work, the third work, and the fourth work. Then the section entitled 'here begins the book' begins the text proper. In this the five parts of the book are delineated: firstly the composition of the Seal of God; secondly the Divine Vision; thirdly the vision of angels; fourthly the binding of spirits; and finally binding the inhabitants of the underworld. The earliest version of the text has these sections in a different order, with the first section at the end. The discussion moves on to there being three types of angel, and three types of people who perform magic, these being pagans, Jews, and Christians. The first two are disparaged, with Christians being the only ones who can achieve divine vision.

The first work or treatise is Concerning the composition of the Seal of the True and Living God (the *Sigillum Dei*). A detailed description of the construction of the seal follows, along with the consecration process including a prayer. Then follows a reminder of the importance of purity and living a good life. Next come the one hundred prayers which are used later in the work. Prayers two to five are to the Virgin Mary, an emphasis which is largely absent from later grimoires. Woven in among the prayers are some from the *Ars Notoria*, these being prayers ten to seventeen and nineteen to forty-four. The Creed (prayer six) and Lord's Prayer (prayer eight) are also present. After prayer forty-four come some details on the use of the previous prayers, followed by the first purification. Note that during the detailed instructions for this, it is mentioned to get a priest to say Matins, Prime,[171] Terce,[172] and a Mass of the Holy Spirit for the practitioner. The prayers begin at number one again, and the first thirty-two plus nine other unnumbered prayers (mostly referred to as Latin prayer or in one instance Hebrew prayer) are all from the *Ars Notoria*. Prayers thirty-three and thirty-four are not from the *Ars Notoria*. The text then moves to the second purification for the Divine Vision. This includes prayers, the hundred names of God, and notes on conduct to ensure success.

The text states the second treatise has twenty-seven topics, which actually refers to the areas under the auspices of the spirits in the section. The material in this treatise is on the natures and offices of angels; concerning the spirits of Saturn, Jupiter, Mars, the Sun, Venus, Mercury, and the Moon; construction of the circle; invocation of the angels; seal and binding; the beginning of the conjuration; the placating.

The third treatise again begins with a list of numerous effects, and then moves into divisions of the spirits of the air; concerning the Spirits of the East (these chapters include descriptions of the spirit types); concerning the Spirits of the West; concerning the Spirits of the South; concerning the Spirits of the North; intermediate spirits (not fully good or evil); concerning the spirits between the East and the South; concerning the spirits between the South and the West; concerning the spirits between the West and the North; end of the

---

171 Service said at sunrise (usually taken as 6:00am).
172 Psalm based service said at the third hour of the day (9:00am).

divisions of the angels and spirits; and beginning of working with them (includes image of the magic circle and its construction);[173] of the approach towards the circle and the raising up of the winds before it; preparation for raising up the spirits (with the process detailed).

The fourth treatise begins with a list of topics concerning the spirits of the Earth. The sections are on the beginning of the way of operating with them. This is a short section which includes the invocation and the magic circle, but also states that Christians rarely work with the earth spirits and it is more of a pagan thing.

The fifth treatise begins with a section which discusses material in the previous four treatises. The sections then begin with the consecration of the ink used for the *Sigillum Dei*, with prayers; concerning the exposition of teachings of the Masses in the first treatise and more exposition of the previous treatises; concerning the beginning of undertaking invocation; the composition of the whistle and exposition of some sayings in the third treatise; the book then ends with a section extolling its own virtue.

Essential Reading

Gösta Hedegård (2002) *Liber Iuratus Honorii: A Critical Edition of the Latin Version of the Sworn Book of Honorius* (Studia Latina Stockholmiensia, 48) Stockholm: Almovist & Wiksell International. Good academic edition which has been superseded by Peterson's edition.

Peterson, Joseph H. (2016) *The Sworn Book of Honorius: Liber Iuratus Honorii*. Lake Worth: Ibis Press. Includes extensive commentary, annotations, and associated useful and relevant material on this extremely important grimoire.

---

173 It is worth noting that the winds are conjured here, as part of the process of bringing the daemons to the circle. Also, the processes in the *Sworn Book of Honorius* are carried out over a period of days: they are not single-shot rituals, as it were.

Summa Sacre Magice (Compendium of Sacred Magic)

Date: 1346.
Language: Latin, German.
Influences: Contains a number of grimoires extant at the time, including the *Sworn Book of Honorius*, *Liber Razielis* (*Book of Raziel*), *De Candariis Salomonis* (*The Talismans of Solomon*) and influences of earlier texts such as *Sepher ha-Razim*, *Shi'ur Qomah* (*Measure of the Body*), *Sepher ha-Yashah* (*Book of the Righteous*), *Tefillat Rav Hmanuna Sava* (*Prayer of Sava the Elder*).
Provenance: Berengar Ganellus, a Catalan scholar of whom virtually nothing is known.
MSS: MS 4° Astron. 3 (1346, Latin) owned by Trithemius and by John Dee, MS Germ Fol. 903 (1570s, German), partial in Halle MS 14 B 36 (c. 1500, Latin).
Circle: Yes.
Tools: Belt cape, crown, hood, overtunic, rings (including planetary), robe (white and black), sash (red), shirt, shoes, sword, tunic, whip, whistle.
Spirit List: Aadrael, Aamel, Aanal, Abaah, Abasdardaon, Abbaoth, Abdebalu, Abdeyadym, Abnalaamar, Abnalaamar, Abnalazafar, Abnalazart, Abnazart, Abrayaon, Abryabrym, Abryahaon, Abucaba, Abzach, Accyel, Achimaal, Achocyb, Acytael, Admoday, Aebrican, Affah, Affyataynt, Agaha, Agaros, Ahadha, Albaryth, Aldynatory, Alegretus, Aleguereth, Algal, Almaza, Almucatyl, Alphlas, Altybany, Amael, Amaymon, Amirafel, Amnalasfar, Amocab, Amynyel, Amyrafel, Anael, Anahel, Andyton, Anech, Annabyel, Anyel, Anzeryer, Aocel, Arator, Arboyl, Arbyal, Ardaguylyel, Ardual, Arebas, Arfur, Arhocib, Ariel, Arpas, Arthan, Aryel, Aryha, Asael, Asamach, Asassayel, Ascymor, Asmoday, Assamach, Assassayel, Astachna, Astaroth, Atragon, Atroel, Atryel, Aysberanta, Aysgaron, Baal, Baalyel, Baanepalpa, Baasocaf, Bablyel, Bacthemael, Bahmyel, Baladau, Balam, Balay, Baldyutabrach, Ballyel, Baltyn, Bamulath, Baqueryel, Barachyel, Barchan, Barkyel, Barofparchas, Baroy, Barquyel, Barrabas, Bartach, Baryel, Bassan, Batyel, Baxatan, Baxatau, Bayatan, Beel, Behemoth, Bel, Belcebuch, Belferyth, Belh, Belphares, Belsebub, Belsefer, Belyal, Berchos, Beryth, Besmet, Besur, Betabaaath, Bethala, Bifrons, Bileth, Boel, Bryson, Byleth, Cacaras, Cadacant, Cafisyel, Calcas, Calce, Calcos, Cambores, Canael, Capberutaoriston, Caphael, Caphciel, Carfyon, Carhyel, Carmeal, Carmyel, Cassynarudya, Castryel, Cathcyel, Caudones, Chahatus, Chodor, Contubal, Corbara, Corniger, Cyray, Dagam, Dagan, Dalquyel, Danael, Darbyel, Dardael, Darothphyel, Darquyel, Debarhama, Demael, Drahas, Dramyel, Dredaryel, Duranyel, Dyane, Ebyrayel, Egyn, Elael, Elberaor, Eleu, Eney, Estahol, Estaolh, Eyeassereye, Falabar, Faomytec, Fassatalucy, Faym, Fegor, Fenyx, Flebilis, Forfornifer, Forforuiferbalzach, Formyone, Fornifer, Furaym, Furcaber, Furcaberbrine, Furcas, Gaberiel, Gaberyel, Gabrael, Gabryel, Gaciel, Gadal, Gadyel, Galtyn, Ganael, Garghaga, Gastyel, Ghadal, Gharam, Gorson, Gramon, Guadudyel, Guerges, Guericos, Hadith, Hadyel, Hamun, Hanael, Hanunyel, Hartan, Haryd, Haryth, Hatrahurbyablis, Hayel, Hebethel, Honosigideus, Horpanyr, Horpenyel, Horyel, Hosael, Hubayel, Humalquyel, Huracaphel/Hurachafel, Huynayl, Irascor, Junyal, Kadarael, Kalamya, Kalbyel, Kamyel, Kaphael, Katara, Kedissa, Kenyel, Kesfyel, Laanab, Laber, Lachmyel, Lagabon, Lampciel, Lanucel, Larthas, Leabarinach, Legabon, Liaras, Liel, Lobquym, Loccana, Lucifer, Lucifiel, Lypalael, Maacyn, Madayl, Maffayl, Mahanyel, Malafar, Malapas, Malquyel, Maltyel, Manyel, Marah, Margabyel, Marog, Marrerym, Masmag, Massadal, Mastyel, Mathateron, Mathyuel, Matnyel, Maymon, Maymona, Meh Artemashe, Mextyhura, Michael, Michyel/Mychyel, Miritno, Misxmo, Modyel, Modyl, Mulciber, Murmur, Myamayon, Mycrathon, Myel, Mylalu, Myrabany, Mysealos, Naadop, Naarach, Naaral, Naassah, Nacbadyel, Nafhyyel, Nagnuel, Nassar, Nathanael, Nathomyel, Necamach, Nelya, Nenael, Nesamach, Nesaph, Nigam, Noryel, Notterorigal, Nulha, Oboel, Ommadyel, Onogoron, Onosigydeus, Onsod,

Orayel, Orienuens, Orychaton, Oryel, Osamyel, Oylol, Paamtotyel, Palas, Pamelon, Pamiel, Pannoniel, Parmyel, Paruasadyel, Paschar, Paymon, Pelayym, Penac, Penael, Penuyel, Penyel, Pestifer, Pluthoal, Proathofas, Procax, Pynceal, Pysoafianta, Raacyel, Raamyel, Rabyel, Ragueguael, Rahumyel, Rakyel, Ramoch, Ramyel, Rapax, Raphael, Raphayel, Raphyel, Raquayel, Razimas, Razyel, Regethal, Requyeyl, Rerabfeceratataz, Resen, Roya, Rucal, Rybyd, Ryon, Saagon, Saaronitbehofz, Saathan, Sackenach, Sacqiel, Saficiel, Sahoryel, Saleh, Salguyel, Saltyn, Samael, Sambas, Samcyel, Samhores, Samhyel, Samiel, Samyel, Sarabotre, Sarbyel, Sardalydy, Saripyel, Sarphyel, Sarpyel, Sascanyel, Satgasbym, Satguyel, Sathan, Sathant, Satpyel, Satquyel, Satyel, Satykyel, Sayel, Scaayroth, Scolberachum, Sebarman, Semylevana, Senanec, Serael, Sofkanyn, Sokyel, Somkas, Sudyr, Suffuyel, Sulphur, Sumchatos, Symygaylon, Symyryssym, Tamach, Tarpalyel, Tarpiel, Taruz, Taryel, Tenachyel, Terror, Tesiach, Thobiel, Toranyel, Torath, Trachatat, Turyel, Tyel, Tyggara, Tytpapaly, Uriel, Uryel, Uyel, Vaanael, Vaanuel, Valyel, Vamuel, Varoy, Vealbyn, Veaseyel, Vecastyel, Vegansores, Vfaltyel, Vflael, Vvaalyel, Vvaslayl, Vvel, Vyonacraba, Yaconablabur, Yammax, Yamyne, Yarabal, Yaslael, Yasrael, Yatyel, Ydydal, Yebelkayam, Yecyssa, Yehel, Yenael, Yerael, Yesse, Yeyel, Yrabal, Ysopatys, Yssytres, Yturayel, Zagam, Zagyron, Zalzoy, Zanyel, Zaym, Zeab, Zebuel, Zepher, Zobha.

The text

Summa Sacre Magice is an incredibly important text from 1346 compiled and written by the Catalan scholar Berengar Ganellus (or Ganell). This eight-hundred page, five-book document is not simply a collection of texts, however, as Ganellus wove the texts together to convey his own perspective of magic. A result of this is that chapters from a particular manuscript may be spread through the book to highlight the theme of the section he was discussing.

Among the earlier or contemporary works Ganellus included in part or whole, are the *Sworn Book of Honorius*, *Liber Razielis* (*Book of Raziel*), *De Candariis Salomonis* (*The Talismans of Solomon*),[174] *Liber Trium Animarum* (*Book of Three Souls*) which is a chapter of fifty-one prayers.[175] Spirit hierarchies and lists occur throughout the text, and it is noteworthy that many of the spirits do not occur in any other grimoires. The conjurations are divided into the Major and Minor Arts, with the Major being calling the four Kings, and the Minor being all other spirits.

The contents of *Summa Sacre Magice* are as follows:[176]

Here begins the table of this book of magical science. The first book contains three tractates in which are taught the excellent art of invoking any spirit, as well as the art both general and specific, etc.

The first chapter of the first tractate is the introduction to the entire book. The second chapter is the general prayer of the procedure. The third chapter is the prayer of the intelligence of Mercury. The fourth chapter is the prayer for the blessing of a place. The fifth chapter concerns the making of a strong circle. The sixth chapter is the prayer proper to Saturn. The seventh chapter is on the proper conjuration. The eighth chapter concerns the particular invocation of Sathan following the general one. The ninth chapter concerns the conjuration proper for all things. The tenth chapter concerns the Semephoras in general. The eleventh chapter is on the names generally powerful in every kind of work. The twelfth chapter is on the winds. The thirteenth chapter is on the names powerful in holy places.

---

174 Mentioned by Trithemius in *Antipalus Maleficiorum*.
175 John Dee numbered the prayers in the margin of the copy he owned.
176 As this work is currently not available in English, included here is a translation of the table of contents, translated from the original Latin by Brian Johnson, with deep gratitude.

The first chapter of the second tractate concerns the witnesses of the first season. The second chapter concerns the conjuration of the witnesses of the second season. The third chapter concerns the conjuration of the witnesses of the third season. The fourth chapter concerns the conjuration of the witnesses of the fourth season. The first chapter of the third tractate concerns the prayer of the witnesses of the third season. The second chapter concerns the prayer of the witnesses for the fourth season. The third chapter concerns the prayer of the witnesses for the second season.

Here begins the second book, in which are defined the rings and other things necessary to the art, and it contains three tractates. The first tractate:

The first chapter of the first tractate is on the first ring of Solomon. The second chapter is on the rings of the seven planets. The third chapter is on the vestments of the art. The fourth chapter is on the Solomonic circlet. The fifth chapter is on the Solomonic whip. The sixth chapter is on the whistle.

The first chapter of the second tractate is on the purifications of the planets. The second chapter is on the prayers of the planets. The third chapter is on the prayers of the spirits of the planets. The fourth chapter is on the Solomonic sword. The fifth chapter is on the table of the Semephoras. The sixth chapter is on the seats of the six spirits. The seventh chapter is on the Semephoras and the altitudes. The eighth chapter is on the fashioning of charaktêres. The ninth chapter is on the forming of images, and on offices. The tenth chapter is on the three rings of Solomon. The eleventh chapter is on the Solomonic seal, and on particular images. The twelfth chapter is on the talismans of Solomon.

The first chapter of the third tractate is on the Solomonic whip, crown, and image. The second chapter is on the five fortifications of conjurations. The third chapter is on the permutation of the Name of Semephoras.

Here begins the third book, and it has two tractates.

The first chapter of the first tractate is on calling spirits within a house. The second chapter is on calling the holy angels in the circle. The third chapter is on the nine methods of invoking spirits.

'The first chapter of the second tractate is on the Almandal. The second chapter is on images and instruction. The third chapter is on the legions of spirits and their offices.

Here begins the fourth book, and it has two tractates.

The first chapter of the first tractate is on the principles of this magic. The second chapter is on the principles to be known of this magic. The third chapter is on consecration. The fourth chapter is on the prayers of the ancient art. The fifth chapter is on the consecration of Honorius. The sixth chapter is on the seal of God. The seventh chapter is on dignification.

The first chapter of the second tractate is on the prayers of the Semephoras. The second chapter is on the 99 prayers of the divided Name of Semephoras. The third chapter is the 'Book of Three Souls'. The fourth chapter is on the powers of the angels, and the legions of the planets. The fifth chapter is on the particular dignification of Venus. The sixth chapter is on the particular dignification of Caput Veneris. The seventh chapter is on the particular dignification of the Moon, as well as the other planets. The eighth chapter is that in which are continued the theory and practice concerning the lunations of the Moon. The ninth chapter is on the ten precepts of the art.

Here begins the fifth book, which contains two tractates.

The first chapter of the first tractate is on the eleven heavens, and the images of the heavens. The second chapter is on the order of things, and the order of the sacred book. The third chapter is on the composition of the tables according to the opinion of Solomon. The fourth chapter is on the extraction of the Name of the spirit according to the teachings of Solomon. The fifth chapter is on the composition of the tables according to Toz Graecus. The sixth chapter is on what is signified by the letters of the four alphabets. The seventh chapter is on the virtue and power of any letter according to the stars. The eighth chapter is on the tables according to other kindred opinions. The ninth chapter is on the tables according to two other opinions.

The first chapter of the second tractate is on the teachings of the art. The second chapter is on the expanded Semephoras. The third chapter is on the method of writing the Name of God, and on the manufacture of the parchment. The fourth chapter is on the offices of particular spirits. The fifth chapter is on the art of enchantment and disenchantment. The sixth chapter is on the teaching of a certain particular working. The seventh chapter is on the working of mother and son. The eighth chapter is on the basis of every letter from the stars. The ninth chapter is on the correction of the tables. The tenth chapter is on the teachings of the art in case of poverty. The eleventh chapter is on the invocation of any spirit in particular. The twelfth chapter is on holy law and sacred liturgy. The thirteenth chapter is on the workings of Rasiel, and the office of a certain spirit at which I hint.[177]

Essential Reading

Gehr, Damaris Aschera (2019) *Beringarius Ganellus and the Summa Sacre Magice*, in *The Routledge History of Medieval Magic*. Excellent study on Ganellus, his background and influences.

Johnson, Brian (trans, ed) (2022) *Naming the Heavens: Orations from the Summa Sacre Magice*. West Yorkshire: Hadean Press. Excellent translation of some of the key material from this hugely important text.

Sofer, Gal (2021) *Wearing Body Parts: Berengar Ganell's Summa Sacre Magice and Shi'ur Qomah*, in *Magic, Ritual, and Witchcraft*, Vol 16.3:304-334. Fascinating exploration of the influence of early and contemporary Jewish texts on the *Summa Sacre Magice*.

Huge thanks are due to Brian Johnson and Andreas Erneus, and the members of the SSM Facebook group for their vital work. Although at the time of writing there is no translation of *Summa Sacre Magice*, when it does become available its influence will be enormous.

---

177 Contents translated from the Latin by Brian Johnson.

ELUCIDATION OF NECROMANCY (LUCIDARIUM ARTIS NIGROMANTICE)

Date: C14 CE.
Language: Latin.
Influences: *Sworn Book of Honorius, Book of Raziel, De Quattor Annulis, Liber Semiphoras, Key of Solomon, Vinculum Salomonis, Astromagia* (possibly *Summa Sacre Magice* as several of these texts are incorporated into it).
Provenance: Attributed to Peter of Abano (1250-1316).
MSS: Ghent MS 1021 (C16), Vad Sig. MS 334 (1533-1566), VAL MS Reg. Lat. 1115 (1569), Dresden MS N166.6 (C18, German).
Circle: Yes.
Tools: Knife, lamen, sword, table, vestments, whistle.
Spirit List: Abalidoth, Abuiori, Abusaba, Albumalith, Altarib, Amabael, Amabiel, Amatiel, Anael, Anasiel, Andras, Anie, Arcan, Arel, Ariel, Assaibi, Astagua, Atragon, Babel, Bacanael, Baciel, Balay, Balidit, Baraburat, Bilef, Boel, Burcat, Cafriel, Caluel, Calzas, Caniel, Capabili, Caphriel, Caracasa, Cariniel, Carsiel, Castiel, Cerabiel, Cheremiel, Cinabal, Commisoros, Corat, Core, Cormax, Ctarari, Curaniel, Dabriel, Dagiel, Damael, Dardiel, Darquiel, Deanulel, Doreniel, Fabriel, Famiel, Flacf, Fraciel, Friaguel, Gabrael, Gabriel, Ganiel, Gardel, Gargatel, Gicael, Gualbarel, Guth, Gutrimis, Habayel, Hadie, Hanail, Hosael, Huratapel, Hutaciel, Huum, Hynyel, Iariahel, Iriel, Ismael, Lama, Laquel, Lobquin, Luel, Madiel, Mael, Maissobri, Maltiel, Maromiel, Masgabriel, Matay, Matil, Matuel, Maymon, Mazatan, Michael, Miel, Milliel, Mitraton, Modiat, Muguth, Nabadiel, Nathasiel, Nelapa, Orphaniel, Pabel, Paffran, Penael, Penat, Peniel, Perna, Postor, Quadisu, Rabit, Rahel, Ralyel, Raniel, Raphael, Raquiel, Raumel, Rayel, Sacriel, Salamia, Sallales, Samael, Sapiel, Saquiel, Sarabotres, Saraphyel, Sariel, Satquiel, Sautaniel, Seraphiel, Serquiel, Soncas, Spugliguel, Succeratos, Suquinos, Tamael, Tamax, Tanaciel, Tarquam, Tataniel, Tegra, Tiel, Tubiel, Tulguaret, Turiel, Tus, Ualiel, Ualnram, Uflael, Umastrail, Unael, Uriel, Varchan, Veaguel, Velel, Venael, Veirmiel, Vetuel, Vianuel, Vrontraba, Yanael, Yaniel, Yayael, Yeresaye, Yslael, Zaniel, Zephyr.

THE TEXT

Although the first known recorded reference to this work is in the *Antipalus Maleficiorum* of Trithemius in 1508, evidence suggests an earlier creation date. The attributed authorship to Peter of Abano would put the text in the late thirteenth or fourteenth century, which fits with the pre-existing influences found in the text.[178] As the precursor to the *Heptameron*, this text is one of the most significant works of the grimoire tradition. The lucid and concise style suggests an educated practitioner as the author, which Peter of Abano certainly was.

The text begins with an introduction by Peter of Abano. The sequence is then: names of the hours; names of the angels of the hours; sigils of the seven angels; names of the angels of the days; names of the four seasons; names of the angels governing the four seasons; concerning the names of the Earth; the names of the Sun and Moon in the four seasons; instructions on all the preceding; the conjuration; conjurations of the seven days of the week; concerning the spirits of the air ruling each day of the week; suffumigations of the planets; prayers to be offered over the fragrances; exorcism and blessing of the fire; the vestment and pentacle; exorcism of the spirits of the air; this following prayer is to be said to the four parts of the world; further instructions; conjuration; the method; now follow instructions on how

---

[178] For discussion of this see Peterson (2021:1-3).

and when the operation should be performed in the art; prayer; the arrangement of the circle; instructions for performing additional experiments; concerning the principles/construction of the circle; how the worker should exercise and present himself in carrying out the aforesaid;[179] prayer for angelic protection; the aerial spirits ruling in the lower heavens, whose names are to be invoked in the circle towards the four regions of the world; the Semiphoras of Moses follow (seven); a concluding prayer, which is added after all the preceding; here follow the Semiphoras of Adam (four); the revelation of the Semiphoras table follows; the prayer to be said over the sacred table (includes table illustration). VAL MS Reg. Lat. 1115 also contains: the arrival of the spirits; license to depart; instructions for performing the experiment; concerning the forms of the spirits (from Agrippa's *Three Books of Occult Philosophy*).

Essential Reading

Peterson, Joseph H. (ed, trans) (2021) *Elucidation of Necromancy*. Fort Worth: Ibis Press. Excellent must-read work giving the different versions of the text and showing its development and influences. It also includes a new translation of the *Heptameron*.

---

[179] Material from this point on is found in Vad. Sig. MS334 but not in Ghent MS 1021.

BOOK OF THE SEVEN RINGS OF THE PLANETS OF MESSALAH

Date: Early C15, probably earlier.
Language: Latin.
Influences: *Sworn Book of Honorius*.
Provenance: Attributed to the Jewish Persian astrologer Misha ibn Attari (740-815) (Messalah).
MSS: Cambridge MS Dd.xi.45 (1441-45 CE), partial in Rawlinson MS D 252 (C15), Kassel 4° MS chem. 66 (C15-16), Darmstadt MS 1410 (1550) the most complete version; partial in Wellcome MS 110 (late C16) which was owned by Frederick Hockley, Rawlinson MS D 253 (1647), partial in Sloane MS 3824 (1649), partial in Sloane MS 3850 (C17).
Circle: Yes.
Tools: Earthen pot, quill pen, rings, sword.

Abanystra, Abhanci, Acroel, Anael, Arcaryamanan/Ortaryaran, Barachiel, Captiel, Carmelan, Cocazim/Corniger, Cyrorax, Gabriel, Gilgheti/Galatia, Michael, Ocarat, Orthorix, Phytones, Raphael, Samael, Satquiel, Uriel, Ypaton.

THE TEXT

This short work is attributed to the Jewish Persian astrologer Misha ibn Attari (740-815) (also known as Messalah and various derivatives of this name). It is mentioned by Trithemius in his *Antipalus Maleficorum* (1508), who called it vain and superstitious. The combination of image magic with rings and the attributed authorship hint at possible earlier Arabic origins.

The text begins with Messalah emphasising how magic works through the grace of God. The metals for making the rings are then described.[180] The construction of the ring of the Sun is given, with its image; followed by the ring of the Moon, the ring of Mars, the ring of Mercury, the ring of Jupiter, the ring of Saturn. Next are the uses for each of the individual rings. Then follows the description of how to behave within the circle and of the planetary timings.

The experiments to use the rings continue the text. The first experiment is with the Sun ring to gain a black horse that will take you anywhere in a moment. The second experiment, of the Moon ring, is to make a river appear, or tree bearing fruits, or fighting ships. The third experiment, of the Mars ring, is to make armed or unarmed men or soldiers or encampments appear, and game mockeries. The fourth experiment, of the Mercury ring, is that no judge or lord shall ever condemn you and you will never upset them. The fifth experiment, of the Jupiter ring, is to make all the coin you have ever given away return, or all that you will be given to come. The sixth experiment, of the Venus ring, is to make any woman you want follow you. The seventh experiment, of the Saturn ring, is to make whomsoever you want to hate each other. The eighth experiment, of the Caput Draconis ring, is to poison whomever you want.

The consecration procedure for the rings is described, along with the exorcism to be spoken during this procedure. The form of the magic circle follows. Next is a discussion of the importance of purity and good behaviour, and mental attitude during the ritual, and discussion of the construction of the rings, stressing that the angel name should be repeated (like a mantra) during the ring construction. A short prayer is given as another way of working with the rings. Storing the rings comes next, along with more on timing and emphasizing how

---

[180] As noted in the subchapter 'The Book of Angels, Rings, Characters and Images of the Planets', the planetary metal attributions here vary considerably from the norm.

tasks during their construction must be done perfectly and within the appropriate planetary hour. Two exorcisms of the Sun are given, more on the performance of the rituals follows with an oration. The ritual includes the sacrifice of an animal, whose body is thrown out of the circle in the direction of the character and name of the angel, who is asked to accept the sacrifice. The consecration is finished after this with the name and character of the angel being written in the blood of the animal with a quill pen on parchment and stored. When the full consecrations are done, the effects of the rings can be obtained more quickly without the full ritual preamble. All the consecrations can be done at the same time, as long as the appropriate timings, sacrifices, and directions are observed. More on being pure and virtuous and the nature of angels continues in the text, which ends with a longer preparatory orison to be used. It should also be mentioned that the text states the rings can be made for another person and work for them as long as they follow the appropriate prayers and ritual structure laid out in the text when using them.

Essential Reading

A partial version of the text is found in Lidaka, Juris (1998) *The Book of Angels, Rings, Characters and Images of the Planets: attributed to Osbern Bokenham* in *Conjuring Spirits* (ed. Fanger, Claire), pp. 32-75. As this text is not published in its complete form, the excellent scholarship of Mihai Vârtejaru has been relied upon. Copies of the texts of several of the manuscripts and his research can be found at his blog at https://studies-vartejaru.blogspot.com.

Book of Consecrations (Liber Consecrationum)

Date: c.1400.
Language: Latin, English.
Influences: Unknown.
Provenance: Anonymous.
MSS:[181] Austin Friars A8, 364 (c.1400); CLM 849 fo.52r-59v, fo.135r-139r (C15); CER184; Trinity College, Cambridge, MS 0.8.29, fo.183-185v (C16); Sloane MS 3853 fo.64-69, fo.188r-198v (mid C16) (Latin & English); Sloane MS 3826 fo.58-65 (English) (C16); Sloane MS 3846 fo.158v-164r (English) early C17); Sloane MS 3850 (early C17).
Circle: Yes.
Tools: Book, laminal, ring, sceptre, sword.
Spirit List: Aegin, Amaimon, Oriens, Paymon.

The Text

The *Book of Consecrations* circulated in medieval Europe and is found mixed in with many other major texts, providing practical instructions which are sympathetic to other grimoires and may be used in conjunction with them. The earliest manuscripts are in Latin, with later versions translated to English, and thus far have generally been found in England, with the exception of the *Munich Handbook of Necromancy*[182] in Germany. Of particular interest is the use of the four demon kings on the laminal, perhaps emphasizing the significance of these beings in earlier grimoires.

The *Book of Consecrations* comprises a series of consecrations for different magical items, The first is the consecration of the book, as it was believed grimoires could lose their magical charge and require reconsecration to ensure the rituals contained within still worked. Clean clothing, holy water, and fasting are all standard for the consecrations. A series of prayers are spoken over the book and it is aspersed with holy water. The consecration and hallowing of the sword follows, with a series of prayers, and anointing of the blade with holy oil. The third consecration and hallowing is of the magical ring. The consecration and hallowing of the laminal and sceptre follow. It is noteworthy that the laminal has the names of the four demon kings of the directions inscribed on it, as well as Tetragrammaton. The text concludes with the preparation and consecration of the magic circle.

Essential Reading

Kieckhefer, Richard (1997) *Forbidden Rites, A Necromancer's Manual of the Fifteenth Century.* Sutton: Stroud. Great academic work on an important text which includes discussion of *Liber Consecratum*.

Speckens, Puk (2019) *Instruments of Consecration: An In-Depth Manuscript Study of the Book of Consecrations in the Vernacular.* Radboud University: Master's Thesis. Excellent study of the *Book of Consecrations*, exploring its presence in different manuscripts, and providing English translations of both Sloane MSS 3850 and 3853.

---

181 The MSS are all in Latin unless otherwise stated.
182 See Kieckhefer 1997.

Munich Handbook of Necromancy

Date: Early to Mid C15.
Language: Latin and German.
Influences: *De Nigromancia, Picatrix, Summa Sacre Magice, Sworn Book of Honorius, Elucidation of Necromancy, Book of Consecrations*.
Provenance: Unknown member of clergy.
MSS: Codex Latinus Monacensis (CLM) 849.
Circle: Yes.
Tools: Basin, crystal, knife, mirror, ring, sword, tripod.
Spirit List: Abgo, Abgoth, Abimalyb, Abuzaba, Acartayl, Acayl, Achalas, Afalion, Agertho, Alhea, Aliberri, Almodab, Alredessym, Althes, Altramat, Alugor, Amabel, Amatyel, Anael, Andyron, Anna, Apolin, Arath, Arbas, Archidemath, Aregero, Assassael, Assayby, Astaroth, Astra, Asyel, Atraa, Atratrayl, Azathi, Baltim, Barbarus, Barmaly, Bartatel, Bartha, Baruth, Basal, Beanke, Bel, Belam, Belferith, Belial, Beliath, Belzebub, Benoham, Berien, Berith, Bireoth, Bohodi, Bos, Brimer, Brulo, Caffriel, Camoy, Cassa, Candas, Captiel, Carab, Cargie, Carmath, Cason, Cassa, Castiel, Cebal, Conas, Constiel, Cormes, Cupid, Curson, Cutroy, Damay, Dardiel, Demefin, Demor, Despan, Dies, Diles, Dilia, Discobermath, Dorayl, Dronoth, Duliatus, Dyabuli, Dyacon, Dydones, Dyrus, Dysi, Dyspil, Ebal, Egippia, Elam, Elemidyri, Emogeni, Ergarrandras, Erlain, Ezirohias, Fabanin, Fabar, Fabath, Fabin, Falmar, Faubair, Febat, Fetolinie, Felsmes, Feremin, Finibet, Floron, Foliath, Fritath, Fyriel, Fyrin, Fyrus, Gaabarayl, Gabriel, Gaeneron, Gaffriel, Gallath, Galtim, Gana, Gatrat, Gebat, Gebel, Gelbid, Gemi, Gemitias, Geremittarum, Gramsatos, Gyton, Haham, Halba, Hanni, Haram, Haybalydoth, Hayton, Hegergibet, Helyberp, Heresim, Hohada, Hohanna, Hyrti, Ignaro, Jubutzis, Lamair, Lamisniel, Lampoy, Lautrayth, Leutaber, Lilith, Lodoni, Lotobor, Lucifer, Lylet, Lyroth, Lytay, Lytim, Madrath, Maloqui, Maraloch, Mascifin, Masair, Mataton, Medirini, Mememil, Memoyr, Metaliteps, Michael, Midain, Millalu, Mirael, Mistal, Mithiomo, Molbet, Moloy, Motmyo, Muriel, Nartim, Nassath, Natheus, Neyilon, Non, Noryoth, Nubar, Ocel, Ohereo, Oliroomim, Onaris, Onor, Onoroy, Oor, Oreoth, Oriens, Ornis, Oronothel, Orooth, Otius, Oymelor, Pacta, Pactas, Panite, Pascami, Pattar, Paymon, Peamde, Peripaos, Pestiferat, Pharachte, Pinen, Pist, Progemon, Pumeon, Pumotor, Quiron, Rabam, Raphael, Rator, Rayma, Reranressym, Reuces, Riasteli, Rimasor, Rimel, Risbel, Rodobayl, Rofanes, Saabotes, Saalalebeth, Saba, Sabael, Sacquiel, Safrit, Salaul, Saltim, Samael, Sammyel, Sanbras, Sanfrielis, Sanyel, Sarpiel, Sarquiel, Sartquiel, Sathan, Satola, Satquiel, Saytam, Satyel, Selentis, Selutabel, Sertugidis, Silitor, Sismael, Sobronoy, Sona, Suburith, Sucax, Sylol, Symofor, Syrama, Syrtroy, Sysabel, Taatus, Tait, Tamafin, Tami, Taob, Taraor, Tarquayl, Tatomofon, Tentetos, Terayl, Tereol, Tereoth, Termines, Thitodens, Thobar, Thomo, Tranayrt, Tryboy, Tvuries, Tubal, Turiel, Tyroces, Tyros, Tyroy, Utanaual, Va, Vanibal, Vatuel, Vijas, Virus, Virytus, Vlmiel, Vm, Vmeloth, Vmon, Vniueny, Vnyrus, Volach, Vom, Vralchim, Vresius, Vrlacafel, Vsyr, Vtimo, Vzmyas, Yfla, Ygrim, Ym, Ynasa, Ytelteos, Zanno, Zelentes, Zymens.

The Text

This text contains elements which associate it more strongly with the medieval perception of witchcraft. Due to its timeframe of fifteenth-century Germany, and the European development of anti-witchcraft literature, this is unsurprising. What does stand out, though, is reference to the instant banishment of conjured creatures such as horses through making the sign of the cross. As a handbook, it contains a wide range of material in distinct text-blocks, making for an interesting miscellany of content. It is noteworthy that sections of the *Book of Consecrations* are in this text. The short manual of astral magic includes conjurations of the days of the week, and seals for the seven archangels of the days of the week with other material in a similar style to the *Elucidation of Necromancy* and *Heptameron*. The use of bones being burned in love conjurations in two instances is interesting and recalls practices from ancient Greek magic.

The text contains the following sections: gaining knowledge of the liberal arts; causing a person to lose their senses; for arousing a woman's love; for gaining dignity and honours; for arousing hatred between friends; for obtaining a banquet; for obtaining a castle, boat, horse; for resuscitating a dead person; for invisibility; obtaining a woman's love; to constrain a man, woman, spirit, or beast; to obtain a horse (another); to obtain a flying throne; finding something in sleep; obtaining a horse (another); the Mirror of Floron; another use of the Mirror of Floron; another way of using a mirror; for invisibility; for discovering a thief or murderer; Mirror of Lilith; crystal gazing to learn uncertain things; crystal gazing for information about a theft; Key of Pluto to open all locks; to obtain information about a theft by gazing into a fingernail; for obtaining information by gazing at a bone; the true art of the basin; twelve names to make spirits appear in a boy's hand; for obtaining information; the *Book of Consecrations*; conjuration of Satan/Mirage; obtaining information from a mirror; short spirit catalogue; for obtaining a woman's love; generic preparation for conjuring spirits; manual of astral magic;[183] obtaining information by gazing into a fingernail; another example of the same; another example of the same; for discovering hidden treasures in sleep; the name Semiforas; to obtain a horse (another); fragment of an experiment for averting harm; for invisibility; favourable and unfavourable days of the month for inscriptions; fragment of a chemical prescription.

Essential Reading

Kieckhefer, Richard (1997) *Forbidden Rites. A Necromancer's Manual of the Fifteenth Century*. Stroud: Sutton. Excellent academic study of MS CLM 849, which is full of interesting information. The one flaw is the lack of a complete English translation of the Latin text.

---

183 Heavily influenced by the Heptameron.

Annulorum Experimenta (Experiments of Rings)

Date: C15.
Language: Latin.
Influences: Arab texts.
Provenance: Attributed to Peter of Abano.
MSS: Bibliothèque Nationale de France MS Lat. 7337 (C15), Augsburg Cod. II.1.4 (C15), London Society of Antiquaries MS 39 (C15), Rawlinson D.252 (C15), Ghent University Bibl. 1021 A (C16), Lübeck MS Math. 9 (1586-90).
Circle: N/A.
Tools: N/A.
Spirit List: Acer, Alibeat, Amanbilch, Anelim, Anna, Anurecha, Astrota, Baratidres, Bardari, Bardiacha, Baroy, Bartifari, Baxo, Bellicorth, Bellicorth, Bergath, Bernerecha, Boad, Bodre, Boriatiacali, Bournay, Bournes, Brachalim, Brachucal, Bragandi, Brandalia, Brandamiroth, Brasilic, Buchyfali, Buthath, Catilaret, Chaumadich, Chulyarib, Craulyaruy, Daratees, Difinicha, Doguenoyth, Dominath, Dordrachuth, Esorum, Estade, Evapria, Farastario, Farnnan, Fartigrat, Fastur, Fervagitim, Fictimetim, Finnuar, Fratradrith, Furinicat, Furterhoth, Garidolicalu, Gariech, Godric, Goralido, Gormi, Gubridali, Guroheit, Habraculith, Hadrigar, Harmuroch, Hastapulo, Hatiarie, Hautricath, Heasil, Herebreth, Heusenebior, Hiradi, Hostibilis, Hyerserus, Iucamilchada, Jeartaag, Jeartaag, Jertubety, Magandarui, Magradarioth, Mancipal, Marcalia, Mare, Maurnach, Moda, Monego, Murath, Naurstic, Noch, Osturies, Pachimisca, Pacos, Panchalitar, Parpabin, Permisbret, Pharai, Predogam, Rariath, Roder, Satyteyr, Saufaole, Sirgith, Sirgith, Sorphail, Staurioci, Stayrabangoriath, Storphalus, Syeth, Tarin, Tennuat, Teriath, Tertin, Tinchir, Tornit, Trellari, Vacerail, Vertegat, Yenuat, Yligai.

The Text

This work is clearly influenced by the Arab to Latin transmission of image magic. The influence of the Mansions of the Moon may come from earlier works like the *Picatrix*. It is noteworthy that the rings are focused heavily on the creation of illusions, more so than in any other texts. There are thirty-nine sets of instructions, of which thirty-five are for rings. The sixteenth Mansion of the Moon does not use a ring, but rather coins wrapped in linen. The fifteenth and twenty-third Mansions of the Moon have silver boxes containing powdered ingredients. The twenty-fourth Mansion uses powdered body parts in a glass jar. It is also significant that almost all the spirit names found in this text do not appear in any other grimoires and are thus seemingly unique. The rings and their production also show an absence of similarities to other ring texts.

The text begins qualifying the twenty-eight Mansions of the Moon and their attribution over the twelve signs of the zodiac.[184] The first eleven Mansions have two rings given for each of them, so there are details given for thirty-nine items. The rings/items have the following powers: to make a river appear in the air (1);[185] to give the appearance of dogs chasing deer, ring to free a chained and imprisoned person (2); to make armed soldiers appear; to make one

---

184 Note: details of the rings are found in 'Appendix VI: Magical Rings', the censing incenses in 'Appendix III: Incense and Oil Recipes', and other materials used in 'Appendix V: Materia Magica', in Volume 2.

185 Two rings are given, the first is silver and the second iron. They have different spirit names and different ingredients are used to cense them with.

hundred soldiers walk for an hour without injury (3); to make a cane appear with fertile vines and branches, second ring to choose which of two fighting men will win (4); that woods with trees and green meadows appear, second ring to make an enemy weak whenever you want (5); that the table may seem to be adorned with fruits and food, second ring that the sick may recover joy and be healed (6); to make a tree appear with fruit or without fruit as you wish, second ring that people see worms eating grapes[186] (7); that oaks appear with different birds and flowers, second ring so that when eating grapes worms seem to be eating them (8); to see a mouse pull millstones from the mill, second ring that a man should leave the house and flee (9); that a bed and linen dresser with beautiful ornaments appear, second ring to find a subtly hidden treasure (10); that an elephant carrying a castle like a man appear, second ring that the house or village is visibly burning (11); that a great and terrible dragon appear, second ring that whatever they do they take off their clothes (12); that a fountain or well is visible in a field (13); to make a castle with your belongings appear wherever you want it (14); that a mountain seems to follow a home (15); that the coins which you spend return with their companions (16); that when people enter the house they dance and rejoice (17); trust experiment to find theft (18); that you have a familiar demon who answers every question asked (19); to have any woman (20); to cause great discord among others (21); to maintain friendship between others (22); to be invisible (23); that your enemies may love you (24); like a horse or other animal actually appears (25); that money is returned from someone by ants (26); that ants appear with money (27); that they believe ants are treasures (28).

Essential Reading

Boudet, Jean-Patrice, & Collard, Franck & Weill-Parot, Nicolas (trans, eds) (2013) *Médecine, Astrologie et Magie entre Moyen Âge et Renaissance: autour de Pietro d'Abano*. Tavarnuzze: Sismel. Fascinating Italian work containing the Latin text of BnF MS Lat. 7337.

---

186 Presumably on the vines.

ENCYCLOPAEDIC ENTRIES 111

BOOK OF WISDOM OF APOLLONIUS OF TYANA (APOTELESMATA APOLLONII)

Date: 1440 (may date back to Late C12).
Language: Greek.
Influences: Arabic texts, *Testament of Adam*.
Provenance: Earliest MS written by the physician Ioannis of Aron. Some copies bound with the *Hygromanteia* and/or the *Testament of Solomon*.
MSS: Bononiensis Univers. 3632 (1440), Parisinus Gr. 2419 (1462), Parisinus Gr. 2316 (C15), Philipps 1577 (C15), Mediolanensis 112 (C16), Metamorphoseos 67 (C16), partial in Parisinus suppl. Gr. 1148 (1539-42), Parisinus suppl. Gr. 20 (C17).
Circle: N/A.
Tools: Amulets, knife, ring.
Spirit List: Aabraēl, Aarith, Abbaēl, Abrasax, Abrētoumē, Agripponer, Akhliarē, Akhnaēl, Akhrikhi, Albuyūn, Alparē, Ammour, Amny, Anēthakh, Apgarēl, 'Aqlyāyl, Arikha, Arkaēl, Arkhēkhnēl, Armoutar, Ašimyal, Asrāfyl, Astiiybl, Asynariēl, 'Atyāyl, Autera, Baglag, Barfynāl, Barikhmē, Beltatouthēl, Beltēl, Bemikhō, Bermariēb, Berphael, Besmil, Bhlyāyl, Da'yāyl, Danaēl, Danysān, Darpoul, Deukhaēl, Ēdrouthe, Eizēri, Enarmerphaēl, Ennoēl, Enthoōr, Fyāl, Fynāl, Gabriēl, Gadril, Galmaēl, Ganaēl, Gasarzan, Gouzaēl, Harbyl, Hayāl, Hrbmayāl, Hyrsabyl, Ida, Isbaēl, Kāakrsayl, Karphaphēl, Katakhaēl, Katharbial, Kemeret, Kesōdour, Khaldēl, Kharakēl, Kharautoune, Kharindēl, Khariz, Kharmasaēl, Kleim, Koulēl, Krmyāyl, Krsayl, Kzfyāl, Liktmoi, Makhdam, Malkhbim, Maltayatbāl, Mandromil, Mathēlial, Mhūr Htlyāyl, Mikhaēl, Mnhyāl, Mtjayāl, Myhimyāyl, Nakhmarēl, Nesdol, Nouēl, Ntyāl, Orniaēl, Orosyphnēd, Ouriēl, Pahkharzēl, Parnikhēl, Pememtēl, Perphaēl, Rahqayāl, 'Rasil, Razhyāl, Rdnāl, 'Rasil, Rhamaēl, Rhaphaēl, Rheradēkh, Rhōmaēl, Rndyāl, Samtēl, Sangasar, Sappour, Sarmeēl, Sfttāyl, Šhyāl, Sinqyyl, Skhindatper, Šmšāyl, Šmšyāyyl, Šqgyāl, Srsyāl, Sūrāyāyl, Sykhnsour, Sympa, Tambēl, Tamhyāl, Telgradekh, Teptadaēl, Tesmarēl, Tlšāyl, Ūasylasyāl, Yūnasyl.

THE TEXT

The text is significant as it demonstrates the continuation of a talismanic tradition running concurrently with the *Hygromanteia* tradition, with clear Arabic influence. It begins with an introduction to the material and the pseudepigraphical attribution to Apollonius of Tyana. There are numerous angel lists for the different categories. This is followed by an amulet for repelling Satan, the blade, and the signet ring. There are many talismans added into different copies of the text, the majority under the heading of the Great Book of Talismans of Apollonius to his Son. These are: an amulet against all obstacles, spell for instant travel, the restraining talisman, the lead amulet, talisman for controlling the flow of a river, planetary angels of the hours, talisman for driving away bugs and flies, to drive away bugs, snake repelling talisman, bath talisman, snake attracting talisman, talisman to drive away flying creatures, talisman for all prey and people, another talisman to ban things from a place, to prevent a river overflowing, another talisman to gather birds, talisman to make an enemy forget everything, talisman to move a person to another place, another talisman to increase well-being, another talisman for retrieving water from the well, another talisman for flowing water, another talisman to make an enemy forget, another talisman to know someone's secrets, another talisman to subdue people, the magic mirror, another talisman for forcing people to sleep endlessly, another talisman for gathering animals of prey, another miraculous talisman that allows control over the bees, another talisman for the destruction of bees, talisman for fishing, if you do not want to have female mice in your land, another talisman to gather mice, another talisman for selling unsaleable goods, another talisman to protect a tree, another talisman for gathering birds, talisman against scorpions, another talisman to gather scorpions, another talisman to gather wasps, a beloved strange talisman (to gather wasps), another talisman for gathering starlings and green fruits, talisman to drive away starlings, talisman for the ravens, another talisman if you want to drive away ravens, a talisman to drive away fleas, talisman to control fleas, another talisman for snakes, talisman against scorpions, talisman against ants, talisman against monkeys, talisman against worms, talisman to increase sales and gain, another talisman which is a great amulet, chastity talisman, talisman for gathering locusts, talisman for gathering doves, talisman against mice, another talisman against trees and fruit, talisman for trees to bring fruit, evocation method.

Essential Reading

Marathakis, Ioannis (trans, ed) (2020) *The Book of Wisdom of Apollonius of Tyana*. Private Publication. Excellent study with copies of all the material from several manuscripts, with valuable contextual material.

Hygromanteia (Magical Treatise of Solomon)

Date: 1440.
Language: Greek.
Influences: *Testament of Solomon, Greek Magical Papyri (PGM), Book of Wisdom of Apollonius.*
Provenance: Earliest edition written by the physician Iōannēs of Aron in 1440.
MSS: Bononiensis Univers. 3632 (1440), Neapolitanus II C.33 (1495), Harley MS 5596 (C15), Taurinensis VII 15 (C15-16) (destroyed by fire), Parisinus Gr. 2419 (1462), Mediolanensis H2 infer. (C16), Athonicus Dion. 282 (C16), Monacensis Gr. 20 (C16), Atheniensis 1265 (C16-19), Gennadianus 45 (C16-17), Princeton Greek MS 131 (C16-18),[187] Petropolitanus Academicus (1684-5), Petropolitanus Nat. Lib. 575 (C17), Petropolitanus Nat. Lib. 646 (C18), Atheniensis 115 (C18), Bernardaceus (late C19) includes *Heptameron*.
Circle: Yes.
Tools: Basin, bell, black-handled knife, censer, cloak, crown, crystal, gloves, lamen, quill, reed pen, ring, shoes, wand (bay).
Spirit List: Abaēl, Abekhe, Abesabeēl, Abiel, Ablikon, Ablokher, Ablote, Abraki, Abrikhos, Adōnan, Agathoēl, Agērakhkiēl, Agimaē, Aginos, Ainath, Ainōth, Akaēl, Akētoēl, Akhlitōn, Akhōniōth, Akhthiob, Akinbola, Akosgō, Akouraph, Akrokh, Alaēl, Alēnos, Alidator, Allēlinel, Almeēl, Altekharix, Altidōn, Amaphriēl, Amatziel, Amikh, Amiōb, Amir, Amphou, Anaēl, Anatokh, Anatziph, Aniel, Anthēros, Apael, Apiaēl, Aplēx, Apodokiel, Apolokhas, Apomios, Apophaēl, Apras, Aprix, Aprixon, Arakiēl, Araps, Arban, Ardaēl, Argemē, Argētan, Argkhykiel, Argousoul, Ariaēl, Ariēl, Ariēm, Arkanēl, Arkidōd, Armētes, Arniēl, Arphanai, Artēr, Asēns, Asge, Askodai, Asmodai, Asouma, Asphrodēl, Asriel, Astarōth, Athathanasi, Atrikh, Atzael, Autodyo, Avizouth, Axigēn, Azakiēl, Azan, Azebou, Azouboul, Babet, Banaēl, Banakhōr, Barakhiēl, Barsephial, Basan, Basigōn, Basin, Batabēl, Batlasar, Bdidimon, Bēara, Bebykis, Beel, Beelzebouēl, Bēkarton, Bekharaēl, Belbee, Belial, Belioukh, Bēnage, Bēodon, Berbiēl, Bergountade, Bergyinita, Bernioēl, Berzebouēl, Besaēl, Biara, Bidouēl, Bikheron, Binae, Bithiel, Bizouk, Blekyn, Blemēn, Bliddōn, Blimōn, Bodimen, Boidonatekan, Bokyēl, Bradaēl, Daktouēl, Dalboth, Daltakosa, Damaron, Deaukon, Denas, Digmasōn, Douniel, Driēl, Driokonta, Ediēl, Eisgonel, Eisierix, Ēkoniel, Ekriroēl, Elbepriz, Ēliditōr, Elioraēl, Elisem, Elsoum, Embel, Emiseēl, Ēmntdbl, Emodias, Emphiloel, Enath, Enokradēs, Ephios, Ephipas, Ephipta, Ēphlakh, Ephorit, Epios, Epithouanon, Ergatige, Ergotas, Ēriton, Ermag, Esmouēl, Ēthiēl, Ēththaēl, Ētouros, Euknitiēl, Exounearge, Ezeēl, Ezimmastraos, Gaabōn, Gaasē, Gabaap, Gabriēl, Gabtel, Gagasi, Galiel, Galios, Galōs, Gameis, Garpa, Gathouel, Gekhaz, Gekhiel, Gelia, Gemē, Genēkiēl, Germiēlēl, Gerphan, Gesteēl, Giamiēl, Giel, Giram, Gisaor, Gitzar, Glesoum, Glosea, Glōssas, Glykidōk, Gnathaēl, Gnōtas, Golgiel, Golgiēl, Gorgeel, Gorgiēl, Gorgopios, Goukoumon, Gouriēl, Gtataphid, Hades, Hēperēēper, Homitoton, Hophetēs, Hopnax, Hyperik, Hypopalt, Iaēl, Ianouēl, Iaper, Iaran, Iasei, Iastaēl, Iazmou, Idoēl, Idouēl, Iekaēl, Ilim, Imeēl, Inōpēx, Iōēl, Iōlapas, Iōn, Iōouph, Iōram, Ioran, Ioroēl, Ioukhan, Ipesidōn, Isphraēl, Issots, Izikator, Jupiter, Kabaēl, Kaginōs, Kaimplanes, Kaiprioukh, Kaite, Kakeenikel, Kakistē, Kalē, Kaliēl, Kaliouth, Kalphael, Kalsiel, Kalsimem, Kandien, Kanistōn, Kanob, Kanops, Kapeēl, Kapnithen, Kapounēl, Karatan, Kariēl, Kariter, Karkinar, Karniēl, Kasaēl, Kasiereph, Katiēl, Katziēl, Kaudien, Keleēl, Kēriam, Kerinoude, Kermaniron, Kernoudēs, Kethapson, Khalēkeel, Khalib, Khalkoum, Khameloul, Kharakiēl, Khariēl, Khartoēl, Khēmeril, Khertosiēl, Khirōt, Khōzei, Khthouniēl, Kinakhas, Kirie, Kispoēl, Kitōēl, Klidator, Klouphar, Kokhbiel, Kondarke, Kontastor, Kopiel, Kopinos, Kortaēl, Koudrouēl, Koulmēnas, Krasiel, Krodalos,

---

187 This manuscript contains a significant amount of *Hygromanteia* material, hence its inclusion. However, it bears the name *Iatrosophion* (*Doctor of Wisdom*).

Krokoutimēs, Kronitiēl, Ktinotothrn, Kydouēl, Kyēl, Kyienotēs, Kynas, Kyrdipol, Kyrsoel, Kysiepotos, Kytos, Labēkos, Labitan, Ladodoēl, Laerpiēl, Lakhkhibiēl, Lamēoul, Lampores, Lapēpote, Lardas, Lastor, Lasyrlampēta, Leinaph, Lemōth, Leontoph, Letziel, Likates, Limer, Lior, Lirik, Lisiel, Liskax, Listithō, Lithidos, Loginar, Louliēl, Loumpēel, Loutzipher, Luna, Lvstērou, Magras, Mainou, Maithoth, Makhōth, Makhoumethou, Makhtheel, Mala, Malaphlion, Maldouōr, Malekapōn, Mamounas, Manasikon, Manēr, Manikos, Mantoēl, Markizaēl, Marmēkhel, Marnikhaēl, Maroēl, Marpikhēl, Mars, Mathniel, Mēanēth, Mēarer, Mēdikit, Medilous, Mekhmeth, Mekisamiēl, Mektimanas, Melaxoēl, Melpiphron, Meltos, Memakhth, Menipade, Mentephoul, Mentiphron, Mercury, Mereēl, Mērtos, Metabiēl, Methaēl, Methridian, Mexiphōn, Miag, Miarer, Miel, Miephiēl, Miesēr, Migadel, Mikhaēl, Misoklēsous, Mizxaoul, Mnasikōn, Mnēdiēl, Mogron, Monikonet, Moroēs, Morōth, Mortzē,[188] Motar, Motzeton, Moubesouēl, Mounokhoth, Mpeltzampēl, Mpiel, Mylin, Nabedikaio, Naboutan, Nagi, Nakhoēl, Naououēl, Naphaēl, Narisou, Nierier, Nigrieph, Nigrophol, Nikem, Nikōn, Nikote, Nintiaph, Niokhel, Niphōn, Nistik, Nōapōkh, Nouriel, Ntasamē, Nyktidōn, Oēnaēl, Oiphalmianethi, Oitos, Ōketar, Okhlor, Oktiel, Omēel, Ompeniel, Oniros, Oniskelia, Onoskelis, Ooneki, Oorgaēl, Ooukh, Opadouēl, Opēral, Operlabostra, Operlaita, Ophtiēl, Opios, Ōprinas, Opseēl, Orapaēl, Orax, Orian, Oriatos, Orikor, Oristeron, Ormiēl, Ornai, Ornia, Orniel, Orphaēl, Orthai, Orthrdile, Osmie, Otraēl, Oualielō, Ouanlēilos, Ougariel, Ouistos, Oukas, Ouktak, Oulodias, Oulphas, Ounipheritousz, Ourieil, Ouroēl, Ourouēl, Ourti, Oustiel, Outaēl, Outolokh, Ouxynoēl, Paēl, Pagarith, Pakhthapiel, Palakon, Palēskax, Paltasar, Paraēs, Paraky, Paraton, Pariel, Pasi, Patiēl, Pēgiab, Pekhtha, Pekoul, Pel, Pēlakouel, Pelaphiēl, Pelēl, Pelgiab, Pelouēl, Pelpiēl, Peltzaphatai, Pēraniēl, Pērathoui, Perdikoim, Perganaēl, Periorath, Periphaēl, Periphrel, Perriorath, Pertan, Pertanael, Pertikeel, Pesēdon, Pharai, Phariem, Pharnimpaēl, Phartouel, Phasaphaēl, Phatagi, Phereēl, Phērmar, Phieblas, Phiel, Philoēl, Phirpheēl, Phniditas, Phobokil, Phorel, Phrentaēl, Phrinaphe, Phrodrinos, Phthiker, Phylonel, Pianō, Piel, Piēz, Piliour, Pimēlaēl, Pimikhaēl, Pinoel, Pixitor, Platanix, Plēxtephō, Pnidōr, Podēkoulator, Poliōn, Pollaikynais, Pontios Pilatos, Porkiki, Potzetan, Prophi, Protizēkatour, Pseēl, Psōlmaton, Ptēlaton, Ptethama, Pthora, Ptixagē, Pyrotorō, Ramatziel, Retziel, Rēx, Rhaetziel, Rhakatlia, Rhakidōn, Rhaphaēl, Rhaphgia, Rhariōph, Rhasaphael, Rhatziele, Rhede, Rhēēl, Rhendipōn, Rhēpēdon, Rherana, Rhetaēl, Rhieridōn, Rhixgioudan, Rhoel, Rhogeēl, Rhōgeēth, Rhokhaēl, Rhomatiēl, Rhoudiel, Rhoustat, Rhoutziēl, Sabalonod, Sabeel, Sabrikel, Sakatiēl, Sakhiel, Sakiboēl, Sakipiēl, Sakobolas, Saliēl, Salmōnem, Salmōnnem, Salouēl, Salphrenas, Salpiel, Saltaēl, Samart, Samōsan, Samouēl, Samtōrte, Sanaēl, Sanipiēl, Santelphōn, Santoteēl, Saphiel, Saraēl, Saraphaēl, Sargile, Sarkhiel, Sarkigia, Sarkya, Sarphaēl, Sarpidie, Sarpiel, Sarpyl, Sarsaēl, Sarsanna, Satanaēl, Saterphoue, Saturn, Sauriēl, Sbirouel, Sechekiēl, Segkhlē, Selia, Selkisameel, Semoēl, Sentioēl, Serpepheēl, Serpidōn, Siar, Sidriēl, Siekhapon, Sigos, Silidō, Silouanēl, Sinaēl, Siotiēl, Siriton, Siteos, Sithlos, Skabadiōd, Skamidinos, Skenaēl, Skhozinoxen, Skitogiri, Skolion, Skonin, Skytokyēl, Sokhar, Soudiel, Spendonim, Sphadōrapo, Sphitzioēl, Sphragiel, Spondōr, Staphiliēl, Stelpha, Stemoēl, Steroēl, Stratiēl, Stratiget, Sun, Symitouēl, Sympilia, Synigērōm, Synopigos, Tablas, Tabtalios, Takhman, Tarat, Tartaroēl, Tartarōni, Tartarouel, Taxouziel, Taxpon, Tektonoēl, Tephraēl, Terkoētz, Tetilol, Thamniēl, Thaphōt, Thapnix, Thēkeēl, Theophil, Theth, Thetodoph, Thonios, Tipidōēl, Tiroēl, Tisizaēl, Todidedos, Tophatiēl, Traxdati, Triabol, Trosiēl, Tzelsiōd, Tzianiz, Tzippat, Tzitzanēel, Tzouel, Tzoukana, Venus, Xerion, Xympōna, Zadiphōr, Zamarpha, Zirtheouēl, Zorzorath.

---

188 This term appears to apply to a class of place-specific beings: i.e., genii loci or ghosts. Its use is thus more as a title without knowing the name of a spirit at any given location.

The Text

The *Hygromanteia* is hugely important, drawing on practices from antiquity and bringing them into the Grimoire tradition. The material in it directly influenced grimoires like the *Key of Solomon* and *Grimorium Verum*, and many other works including the *Book of Secrets of Albertus Magnus*. Significantly, it contains detailed lists of plant use and astrological information, emphasizing the importance of both of these in grimoire practice.

As with the later *Key of Solomon*, there are a number of manuscripts, with variations in the material (chapters) contained in each. The introduction contextualises the grimoire, with an epistle from Solomon to his son Rehoboam about the material contained within. This pseudepigraphical attribution is also seen in the other name of the work, the *Magical Treatise of Solomon*.

The many chapters begin with talismans attributed to the planetary hours/days of the week, with prayers of the planets (planetary gods). It is noteworthy that the classical gods attributed to the planets are subsumed into the sequence, being below God but above the angel and demon conjurations in this work. Information on the signs of the zodiac follows, with talismans of the twelve signs and the days of the Moon. Further astrological information includes a passage on the position of the Moon, the rule of the head and tail of the dragon (Caput and Cauda Draconis) and predictions relating to the dragon in the ninth house. A description of the seven planetary images ensues.

The next section contains the conjurations of the angels, a prayer to God, and the angels and demons of the hours of the days (one of each for every hour of the work, so one hundred and sixty-eight of each). As with the earlier *Testament of Solomon*, the thwarting angel is called with the demon (note that the *Testament of Solomon* was sometimes bound with the *Hygromanteia*). The demonic hierarchy of rulers, with the rulers of the four directions under them and numerous demons under these, is seen throughout the text.

The text moves on with the materia magica, beginning with planetary incenses, characters, seals, alphabets, inks, parchments, herbs (planetary and zodiacal). The black-handled knife, reed pen, quill pen, types of parchment, animal bloods used, wax, and clay are then all discussed. The text jumps back to electional astrology, discussing the Moon, before returning to observations and the preparatory work of the confession, baths and purity, the fast, and garments to be worn.

Tools are revisited next, specifically the crown, lamen, ring, gloves, cloak, shoes, and cotton cloth. The construction of the circle and prayer and three conjurations for the appearance of spirits follow. After this are conjurations for love and finding treasure. Observations on the fast, garments, and lamen continue from here (there is a degree of repetition in this work), with the magic circle being revisited. Conjurations of the four quarters and a general conjuration conclude this part of the text.

The final section comprises a range of miscellaneous techniques focusing heavily on forms of divination. These techniques include imprisoning a spirit in a bottle, evocations of Kalē (Lady of the Mountains) and Mourtzi (the black demon), skull divination, water pot divination, bottle divination, three water divinations, divination by vessel (basin, kettle, and glass), copper bowl divination, mirror divination, crystal divination, egg divination, fingernail divination, necromancy, and invisibility.

ESSENTIAL READING

Marathakis, Ioannis (ed, trans) (2011) *The Magical Treatise of Solomon or Hygromanteia*. Sourceworks of Ceremonial Magic Volume 8. Singapore: Golden Hoard Press. Excellent study of a number of manuscripts of the *Hygromanteia* (including Bononiensis 3632, Harley MS 5596, Atheniensis 115 & 1265, Gennadianus 45), comparing and contrasting their material, with much background and contextual material. One of the most significant grimoire books in a great edition.

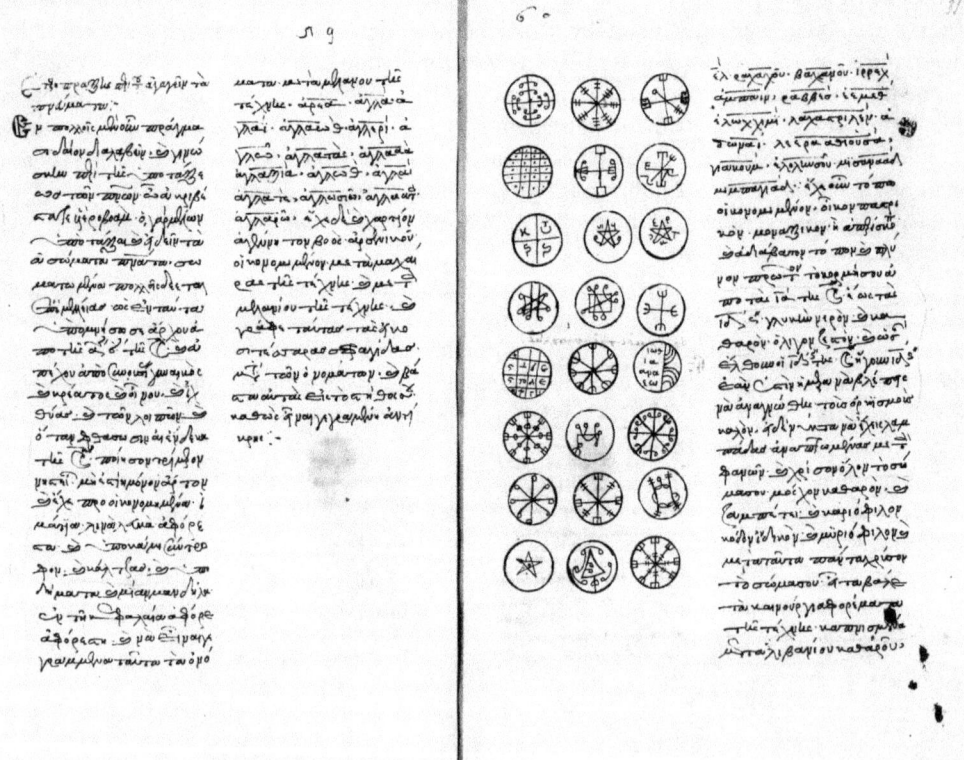

Hygromanteia seals, Harley 5596

The Book of Angels, Rings, Characters and Images of the Planets

Date: 1441-45? (C15).
Language: Latin.
Influences: *Book of the Seven Rings of the Planets* attributed to Messalah, *Liber Lunae*, *De Imaginibus*?
Provenance: Attributed to Osbern Bokenham.
MSS: Cambridge MS Dd.xi.45, Rawlinson MS D253 (part).
Circle: N/A.
Tools: Metal plates, rings, staff (hazel).
Spirit List: Abdalaaa, Agmarob, Alleion, Alos, Alosy, Ames, Ariel, Arnanis, Asiob, Auel, Aycolaytoum, Aynos, Aysmarob, Baal, Barchan, Baysul, Bilet, Cahcaoc, Calacop, Calcaala, Capaton, Carof Caroli, Casfeel, Casiel, Cassael, Caualasyel, Caux, Chatas, Cricios, Daniel, Dardaci, Darial, Dariel, Dilamoi, Dissamata, Ebuzoba, Elcus, Eudelmus, Faccas, Gaidis, Habes, Haiaras, Harmanel, Harnariel, Hayoynois, Hebenel, Hehaha, Hermanel, Heyeyl, Hycandas, Iucuciel, Karmal, Labotapeosy, Lamob, Lassal, Lataleoleas, Lergeom, Loborsomay, Lord of Torments, Mahamtas, Marastac, Maxtarcop, Maya, Maylalu, Michael, Odymon, Orion, Palulnas, Prolege, Raphael, Red Fighter/King, Saffea, Salatiel, Saliciel, Samael, Samatiel, Sariel, Sasaha, Sasta, Sathan, Saycop, Scadexos, Standalcon, Staus, Synaynon, Talanasiel, Taxael, Troion, Uacatara, Vamay, Yaciatal, Ycaachel, Yfasue, Yobial, Zagam, Zombar.

The Text

Although the text is attributed to the Augustinian friar Osbern Bokenham, the evidence does not support this. The name of the author is not known, though a contemporary called William Bokenham has been suggested. This is a curious text; it is noteworthy that there are some attributions which do not match up with any of the more common ones found elsewhere in the grimoire tradition. Additionally, the spirit list is a curious mix, with many unnamed elsewhere combined with the common archangels and several well-known and lesser-known demons.

The manuscript begins with a shortened form of the *Book of the Seven Rings of the Planets* attributed to Messalah, although the text calls him Messayac. The text starts with the ring of the Sun, its construction and uses. Then are the rings of the other six classical planets with their uses. Interestingly, an eighth ring of steel is included for the astrological node Caput Draconis (Head of the Dragon). The next section deals with images of the planets, making coloured wax talismans for the planets and performing conjurations over them, and detailing their use and spirits; an experiment on the morn of the Sabbath (Saturnian) to ruin a man or woman (Trojan Revenge); an experiment on Tuesday to give a person disease; power over demons, which includes a wax figure which becomes an oracle; to make another abominable, making a distorted lead figure to use to torment people; to put others at odds, another image charm; to have the greatest honour, a Jupiterian image charm; a Solar charm to rule over a place; Trojan Revenge variant using decayed wax, which is nastier than the previous version; a true and tried experiment for love; another for the same (note, this is the Moon spirits out of sequence).

The next section deals with using the kameas for a wide range of magical charms. The kamea for Saturn is reversed to its more usual configuration; the Jupiter kamea has rows and columns switched; the Mars, Sun, Venus, Mercury, and Moon kameas are all traditional. The charms are made on thin sheets of metal, these being lead (Saturn), silver (Jupiter, Venus, Mercury, and the Moon), copper (Mars), gold (Sun), with a second Lunar kamea mentioned that is made on lead to create impotence. The text ends with a final note on timings.

Essential Reading

Lidaka, Juris (1998) *The Book of Angels, Rings, Characters and Images of the Planets: attributed to Osbern Bokenham*. In *Conjuring Spirits* (ed. Fanger, Claire), pp. 32-75. Excellent analysis and copy of the text in both English and Latin in an anthology of contextual writings on medieval magic.

Skinner, Stephen & Rankine, David (2018) *A Cunning Man's Grimoire*. Complete transcription of the text of Rawlinson MS D 253 with contextual material. Includes the *Book of Rings* part of the text, with the characters left out in the Bokenham (attributed) text.

LIBER RUNARUM (BOOK OF RUNES)

Date: 1447, possibly earlier.
Language: Latin.
Influences: *Corpus Hermeticum*.
Provenance: Hermetic work of astral magic.
MSS: BAV Pal. Lat. 1439 (C15), Dresden MS N. 100 (1487), Sloane MS 3854 (C15), Vienna MS 12834 (1447).
Circle: N/A.
Tools: N/A.
Spirit List: Antyim, Athelateyl, Behonydiun, Lathleym, Lyeleyl, Mamarayl, Mathmeyl.

THE TEXT

Liber Runarum is a fifteenth-century text in the category of astral or image magic, which attributes a system of medieval runes to the zodiacal signs and elements. The text begins by describing the twelve runes attributed across zodiacal signs. Each rune runs from the last third of a sign into the first two thirds of the next sign. This division of the signs into three parts prompts consideration as to whether there may at some point have been a decan perspective, or if it was drawn from/inspired by Arabic sources. The zodiacal signs follow with several sigils for each (two to five). The text then explains how the figures are extracted from these divisions, and their elemental attributions, along with the alphabet and the signs. Note that the letters J, U and W are missing from the alphabet, giving twenty-three letters and signs.

More explanation of the way to use the signs is given, along with a précis of the qualities of the seven planets for the different types of working to be performed with each in their times. The names of the angels and an explanation of the carving of the signs onto appropriate metals and stones follows. The text concludes with an example of how to work this simple system of magic.

An addendum includes several sets of verses which elaborate on the zodiacal material for the benefit of the practitioner. These are: on the qualities of the signs and triplicities; the order and names of the signs; and the qualities of the planets. Examples of the simple conjurations are also provided.

ESSENTIAL READING

Burnett, Charles & Lucenti, Paolo (eds) (2002) *Hermes Trismegisti Astrologica et Divinitoria*. Brepols: Turnhout. Excellent source work of medieval astrological texts with translations from Arabic, Hebrew, and Latin texts.

Sam Block's excellent website at www.digitalambler.com has a very good piece on *Liber Runarum* which I strongly recommend.

Le Grand Albert (The Big Albert)

Date: 1493.
Language: French.
Influences: Aristotle, Avicenna, Dioscorides, Galen, Hippocrates, Michael Scotus, Polemon, Pliny's *Natural History*, *Three Books of Occult Philosophy*.
Provenance: Latin edition in 1493, with French translation in 1500. Numerous subsequent French reprints, with the most significant and complete being the 1706 and 1774 editions.
MSS: Unknown.
Circle: N/A.
Tools: N/A.
Spirit List: N/A.

The Text

The *Grand Albert* mixes Book of Secrets charms with a medical treatise based on authorities from Antiquity. The charms in the first two parts are largely derived from the *Book of Secrets* attributed to Albertus Magnus. These were earlier works, with earliest known dates of 1493 in Latin and 1500 in French. Books 3 and 4 were added piecemeal in later editions (from 1500 to 1706).

The text begins with an epistle, advice to the reader, the thought of the prince of philosophers, and a prayer.

Book 1 contains thirteen chapters. These are: Of the generation of the embryo, and how man is begotten, how conception comes about, and what menses and semen are, etc. (1); How the fetus is formed. Influences of the celestial powers on the fetus, etc. (2); Influences from the planets. How they act on the body. How often several fetuses are formed in the womb, and how, etc. (3); How imperfect animals are generated. The admirable effects of a woman's hair. Diversity of animals, and where it comes from (4); Of the exit of the fetus. Reasons why women give birth in the sixth month and why one suffers more than the other in childbirth (5); Of a monster of nature, and how it is formed, etc. (6); Signs of conception, etc. (7); The marks to know if a woman is pregnant with a boy or a girl, etc. (8); How to know when a girl has lost her virginity, etc. (9); Signs of chastity and the venom that old women communicate to children by their looks, etc. (10); Of the defect of the womb, and a story that Galen tells of a woman suffocated by the womb, etc. (11); The obstacles and where they come from; and the secrets to conceiving a girl or a boy to a woman (12); Of the nature and digestion of sperm. Thoughts of Avicenna on the sperm (13).

Book 2 contains three chapters. These are: Of the virtue of some herbs, stones, and certain animals, with a table of stars, planets, and a treatise on the marvels of the world (1); Of the virtues of certain stones, etc. (2); Of the virtues of certain animals (3); table of stars and planets, treatise Of the wonders of the world (numerous charms including many candle and lamp-based illusions).

Book 3 contains three chapters. These are: In which we speak of the wonderful and natural secrets (1); virtues and properties of several kinds of droppings[189] (human, dog, wolf, cow, pig, goat, sheep, pigeon, goose, chicken, mouse, small lizard, of urine, of the virtue of

---

[189] This chapter covers the alleged properties of more than just droppings, so the sub-categories are listed.

bones, of saliva, of slugs, earthworms, bugs, old shoes, decayed wood, walnut mesocarp[190] and shells, old tiles and pots, street mud, brine, swallow's nest, soot, cabbage head, spider and web, hare brain, cat brain, oyster shells, hair, and glass) (2); secrets – approved to handle multiple metals, to harden knives and clasps, to harden a file, to harden other things, to make steel hard and sharp, to prevent steel splitting, to soften iron or steel, to soften crystal, to soften iron, to soften iron or steel, to solder all thing even cold iron, to solder iron, for engraving all kinds of metal, to engrave with water, another stronger, for gilding metals silver colour, to yellow tin or copper, for gilding pewter, to give the colour of silver to copper, for gilding iron or steel, to make water to gild iron or steel, to clean iron items (3).

Book 4 has three chapters. Chapter one is described as a treatise on physiognomy.[191] The scope is wider though, including the hair, voice, walk, etc. This appears to have been influenced by the *Liber Physiognomie* of Michael Scotus (1175-1232), who in turn drew on the *Kitab al-Mansuri* (Latinised to *Ad Almansorem*) of the noted Persian physicist, philosopher, and alchemist Abū Bakr Muḥammad ibn Zakariyā al-Rāzī (c.865 – c.925 CE).[192] Chapter two is on favourable and unfavourable days. Chapter three is on the quality of malignant fevers and preparations for them, and includes sections on natural remedies of different forms, lifestyle, and bloodletting.

Essential Reading

Kelly Edmund (2019) *The Grand Albert*. DarkArts Publishing. Reasonable translation.

Thanks to Steve Savedow for giving access to his translation of *Le Grand Albert*, to be published together with his translation of *Le Petit Albert* as a single volume.

---

190 The part between the fruit and the shell.
191 The art of judging character from facial appearance.
192 His name was often Latinised to Rhazes.

Key of Solomon (Clavicula Salomonis)

Date: C15, though there may be earlier manuscripts.[193]
Language: Latin, Italian, English, French, German, Dutch, Hebrew, Czech.
Influences: *Psalms, Sepher ha-Razim, Hygromanteia, Elucidation of Necromancy, Heptameron.*
Provenance: With so many manuscripts, it is to be expected that some of them passed through the hands of well-known figures. Additional MS 3674 was owned by the poet Gabriel Harvey (1550-1630), Baron John Somers (1651-1716), and Sir Joseph Jekyll (1663-1738). Ebenezer Sibly (1752-1799) owned at least three manuscripts, which were sold upon his death to the book-dealer John Denley (1764-1842). Denley employed Frederick Hockley to make copies of manuscripts, though how many is unknown. Aubrey MS 24 was owned by the antiquarian John Aubrey (1626-1697). Pierre Morissoneau, Professor of Oriental Languages at Paris University, is mentioned in at least seven manuscripts from the Rabbi Solomon family. Manuscripts mentioning him were owned by Papus (1865-1916) and Francis Irwin (1828-1892). Mention must be made of Antoine René de Voyer d'Argenson (1722-1787), who collected a number of manuscripts in his huge library of over one hundred thousand volumes, which would later from the basis of the Bibliothèque de l'Arsenal. The military genius Abraham Colorno (1530-1598) translated the *Key of Solomon* into Italian and his work formed the basis of one of the manuscript families.

MSS: Amsterdam BPH 114 (C15, Latin), BN MS 14783 (C15, French & Latin), St Gallen VadSlg MS 334 (C16, Latin), Gregorius Niger Private Collection MS (1558, Latin), Sloane MS 3847 (1572, English), Additional MS 36674 (C16, English), Seville Zayas MS C.XIV.22 (C16, German), Additional MS 10862 (C16, Italian), Brescia Civica Queriniana MS E VI 23 (C16, Italian), Chatsworth MS 73D (C16, Latin), Ghent MS 1021 (C16, Latin), Harry Walton Private Collection MS A901 (1600, Latin), Bodleian Aubrey MS 24 (1674, English & Latin), Wien MS 11344 (C17, Dutch & Latin), Berlin MS Germ. Quarto 474 (C17, Dutch & Latin), Sloane MS 3645 (C17, English), Harley MS 3536 (C17, French), Lansdowne MS 1202 (C17, French), Harvard Houghton MS Fr 554 (C17, French), Wolfenbüttel MS Extravagantes 39 (C17, French), Ferguson MS 142 (C17, German), Berlin Hamilton MS 589 (C17, Italian), Sloane MS 1307 (C17, Italian), Sloane MS 1309 (C17, Italian), Brussels Bibliothèque Royale MS III.1152 (C17, Italian), Wien MS 11262 (C17, Latin), Bergamo MS Lamda II 23 (MM 512) (C17, Latin), BN MS 14075 (C17, Latin), BN MS 15127 (C17, Latin), Bologna MS A.646 (C17, Latin), Additional MS 10862 (C17, Latin), Leipzig MS 841 (C17, Latin), Madrid MS 12707 (C17, Latin), Marseilles MS 983 (Bb 108) (C17, Latin), Nürnberg MS 34 X (C17, Latin), Pommersfelden MS 357 (C17, Latin), Harley MS 3981 (C17/18, French), Lansdowne MS 1203 (C17/18, French), Oriental MS 6360 (C17/18, French), Oriental MS 14759 (C17/18, French), Milano Ambrosiana MS Z 72 sup (C17/18, French), Erlangen MS 853 (C17/18, Latin), Gollancz MS (1700, Hebrew), Wellcome MS 4655 (1725 French), Wellcome MS 4656 (1725, French), Rosenthaliana MS 12 (1729, Hebrew), Additional MS 39666 (1732/82, French), Lenkiewicz Private Collection MS (1732/82, French), Warburg MS FBH 80 (1732/82, French), Leipzig Cod Mag 4 (c.1750, Italian), Leipzig Cod Mag 27 (c.1750, German), Wellcome MS 4668 (1775, Italian & Latin), Harvard Houghton MS Typ 833 (1779, French), Sibley Private Collection MS (1782, English), Bibliothèque Méjanes CGM 1918 (1784, French), John Ryland GB 0133 Eng MS 40 (1789, English), Crawford MS 158 (1789, English), Wellcome MS 983 (1789, French), Wellcome MS 4661 (1796, French), Wellcome MS 4669 (1796, French, 2 MSS), Wellcome MS 4670 (1796, French), John Hay MS BF 1611 (1798, French), John Hay MS M 313 (1798, French), Leipzig MS 790 (C18, Dutch &

---

193 This is an area requiring more study, which is ongoing.

Latin), Kings MS 288 (C18, French), Sloane MS 3091 (C18, French), Jerusalem MS Yahuda 18 (C18, English), Lenkiewicz Private Collection MS (C18, French), Bibliothèque de l'Arsenal MS 2346 (C18, French), Bibliothèque de l'Arsenal MS 2347 (C18, French), Bibliothèque de l'Arsenal MS 2348 (C18, French), Bibliothèque de l'Arsenal MS 2349 (C18, French), Bibliothèque de l'Arsenal MS 2350 (C18, French), Bibliothèque de l'Arsenal MS 2493 (C18, French), Bibliothèque de l'Arsenal MS 2790 (C18, French), Bibliothèque de l'Arsenal MS 2791 (C18, French), Bibliothèque Nationale MS 24244 (C18, French), Bibliothèque Nationale MS 24245 (C18, French), Bibliothèque Nationale MS 25314 (C18, French), Genova MS B VI 35 (C18, French), Harvard Houghton MS Fr 553 (C18, French), Neuchâtel MS A18 (formerly 24079) (C18, French), Wellcome MS 4657 (C18, French), Wellcome MS 4658 (C18, French), Wellcome MS 4659 (C18, French, 2 MSS), Wellcome MS 4660 (C18, French), Wellcome MS 4662 (C18, French), Wellcome MS 4666 (C18, French), Wellcome MS 4667 (C18, French), Wien MS 11517 (C18, French), Yale Mellon MS 85 (C18, French), Harvard Houghton MS Typ 625 (C18, German), Darmstadt MS 1671 (C18, German), Leipzig MS 707 (C18, German), Leipzig MS 710 (C18, German), Leipzig MS 732 (C18, German), Leipzig MS 773 (C18, German), Überlingen MS 164 (C18, German), Jerusalem MS Varia 223 (C18, Italian), Karlsruhe MS 302 (C18, Italian), Leipzig MS 709 (C18, Italian), Leipzig MS 776 (C18, Italian), Milano Ambrosiana MS Z 164 sup (C18, Italian), Münster Nordkirchen MS 169 (C18, Italian), Penn University Van Pelt Codex 515 (C18, Italian), Seville Zayas MS C.XIV.1 (C18, Italian), Bibliothèque Nationale MS 11265 (C18, Latin), Bibliothèque Nationale MS 18510 (C18, Latin), Bibliothèque Nationale MS 18511 (C18, Latin), Evangelische Kirchenbibliotek Codex 31 (C18, Latin), Hamburg Codex Alchim. 739 (C18, Latin), Münich Clm 28942 (C18, Latin), Pisa MS 139 (167) (C18, Latin), St Peterburg MS Q III 645 (C18, Latin), St Peterburg MS Q III 647 (C18, Latin), Edward Hunter Private Collection MS 3 (C18/19, English), Wellcome MS 4663 (1810, Czech), Wellcome MS 4664 (1825, French), Seville Zayas MS C.V.1 (C19, Italian), Upenn MS Codex 1673 (formerly Alnwick MS 584) (Latin), Bodleian Michael MS 276 (Italian), Kobenhavn Thott MS 237 (Latin), Kobenhavn Thott MS 625 (Latin), Stadbibliotek Zittau MS B107 (Italian), Vatican Ar. MS 448 (Arabic).

Circle: Yes.

Tools: Aspergillum, black-handled knives (one with sickle blade), bradawl, callipers, flint lighter, hazel staff, hazel wand, white linen cap, robe, scimitar, stockings and underwear, trumpet, white gloves, light leather shoes, white-handled knife.

Spirit List: Abalidoth,[194] Abaye, Abim, Abroyn, Abuiori, Abumalith, Abuzaha, Africus, Agiel, Agith, Aiel, Amabael, Amabiel, Amadyel, Amtiel, Anael, Anaib, Anathai. Andax, Aniel, Aquiel, Arathron, Arcan, Archasiel, Arpheton, Arragon, Asmalior, Assaiba, Astagna, Astarot, Babel, Babiel, Bachanael, Baciel, Balaym, Balbuch, Baldiel, Balidet, Baliel, Balsaniach, Balthazar, Baraborat, Barchiel, Bartzabel, Becard, Beni Seraphim, Bethor, Bilet, Bulidon, Burchat, Caluel, Calzaz, Capabili, Carabiel, Caracasa, Carmax, Cassiel, Charsiel, Chedusitaniel, Chermiel, Commissoros, Coniel, Corabiel, Corat, Core, Ctarari, Curamiel, Cynabal, Dabriel, Damael, Darquiel, Deamiel, Dolefech, Dormiel, Eleuros, Eliogaphatel, Euphaniel, Famiel, Flaef, Fraciel, Fraigne, Gabrael, Gabriach, Gabriel, Gabriot, Galdel, Gargatel, Gaspar, Gaviel, Graphiel, Guabarel, Guael, Gutrix, Habaiel, Habudiel, Hagiel, Hamoniel, Hanon, Hanum, Hashmodai, He be ruah Schenhakim, Hiel, Hiniel, Hismael, Hufaltiel, Humastrau, Illusabio, Irel, Irly, Iry, Isiael, Ismoli, Jampeluech, Janael, Janiel, Jariahel, Jaxel, Jerescue, Johphiel, Kadiel, Kedemel, Lama, Lobquin, Lucifer, Machasiel, Machatan, Machio, Madiel, Mael, Maguth, Malcha betarsisim, Maltiel, Masgabriel, Mathiel, Mathlai, Matuyel, Maymon, Melchior, Michael, Miel, Milliel, Misig, Missabu, Mitraton,

---

194 The first group of names are found in the Rabbi Solomon text family.

Modiat, Mucechediel, Muriel, Nachiel, Nalapa, Naromiel, Nelapa, Och, Ophaniel, Ophiel, Osael, Ozael, Pabel, Paffran, Penael, Penat, Peniel, Phaleg, Phul, Porna, Radiel, Rael, Rahel, Rahumel, Raniel, Raphael, Rayel, Sachiel, Sacriel, Salales, Samael, Samax, Santanael, Sapiel, Sarabotes, Sched Barsmoth Scharlacham, Seraphiel, Setchiel, Soncas, Sorath, Succeratos, Suquinos, Surgath, Suth, Talaroth, Tamael, Taphthartharat, Tariel, Tarmiel, Tarquam, Tenaciel, Thiel, Tiriel, Tirly, Tonuchon, Topinoch, Tulidomar, Turiel, Tus, Ucimuel, Uriel, Valnum, Varcan, Velel, Venael, Venahel, Veniel, Verchiel, Vianuel, Vionatraba, Vuael, Zaliel, Zazel, Zebul, Abadem,[195] Abbac, Abdac, Abeloy, Abigrabeni, Accusator, Agalaton, Almiras, Amaymon, Amnator, Amos, Arasmali, Aravi, Ariel, Arinalatisten, Artabael, Arthiel, Arvas, Asartim, Asenide, Asmo, Asmodée, Asseme, Astropalem, Astropiel, Atenavim, Athonaval, Audac, Babus, Barachaba, Baruchaba, Beliah, Bellamia, Belpher, Beniel, Berlorim, Beroth, Boncifath, Bored, Calemite, Castormy, Castrac, Chorus, Coac, Cocau, Coeglarth, Consumator, Coribom, Corrosor, Cudos, Daluti, Daniel, Daravisies, Derisor, Desaboday, Detel, Detestator, Devorator, Dilapidator, Diomidis, Discordiæ, Diversator, Donguel, Ebyros, Egeri, Egym, El, Elimygit, Eloy, Emalsood, Emus, Epinamas, Eraticum, Erisset, Ermona, Gebeloy, Genitu, Habaron, Iadonay, Inavis, Incantator, Inopeson, Inora, Istac, Jephormi, Jereté, Jerim, Jes, Jesil, Jihi, Kalemi, Lamstararod, Lapidator, Latistem, Levaria, Luon, Mach, Matagix, Mayton, Meavil, Meidor, Melekh, Metatron, Metinolih, Moas, Necopolitas, Nerombol, Neurim, Noaphoras, Noga, Nostrasil, Noth, Omoras, Otau, Paimon, Periberim, Pirus, Platerion, Poronias, Pusmator, Raziel, Sabanitera, Sabée, Saboles, Saccantos, Samniator, Sator, Saturiel, Seductor, Selateuk, Seminator, Semiticon, Serpora, Soma, Sone, Sonotrabas, Sophina, Suses, Tamis, Tangialem, Teliel, Templator, Tentator, Tevemes, Theut, Thuri, Timaguel, Ton, Trator, Trensidem, Tristator, Tugam, Turons, Uguemenos, Usion, Usor, Venibboth, Vereset, Villaguel, Viloporas, Zeuper, Zeviet, Zucmeni, Achaiah,[196] Agaterop, Agiaton, Ahaiah, Aladjah, Anavel, Aniel, Araton, Ariel, Asaliah, Bahetel, Begud, Belzebut, Boschard, Caliel, Charariel, Chavakiah, Dagoterapter, Damabiah, Daniel, Ejael, Elanthil, Elemiah, Elestor, Eliographatel, Fégol, Frastiel, Frimoth, Galoneti, Glitia, Haaiah, Haamiah, Habuiah, Hacel, Hahael, Hahasiah, Hahviah, Hajaiel, Hakamiah, Hariel, Haziel, Herael, Hymateh, Iabamiah, Iahhel, Iejaliel, Iejazel, Iejiel, Ielahiah, Ieliel, Ierathel, Iminamiah, Irmasiel, Jejazel, Johuiah, Kramaéël, Laviah, Leaviah, Lecabel, Lehaiah, Lelael, Levuiah, Lucifer, Mabahel, Magriel, Mahabiah, Manadel, Mebaiah, Mehiel, Melahel, Menail, Menikel, Mertiel, Michael, Mihael, Mizrael, Mumiah, Nauael, Necariel, Nelchael, Nemamiah, Nitahia, Nithael, Omael, Oriphiel, Pahaliah, Pamachiel, Pojiel, Pomeriel, Ponteriel, Rehael, Rejiel, Resbiroth, Roheel, Rosochim, Saaliah, Sabriel, Satanachi, Sechiah, Sergulas, Seyrechaël, Sirachi, Sitael, Stephanuta, Stepoth, Stumet, Suffuriel, Surgatha, Surgunth, Syrumel, Taiinor, Umabel, Uriel, Vasariah, Vehuel, Vehuiah, Vevaliah.

The Text

The *Key of Solomon* is arguably the most famous and significant of all the grimoires. The first recorded mention is from 1310 in the writing of Peter of Abano, with references in other texts, though the first surviving manuscript is from the fifteenth century. The number of surviving manuscripts in eight different languages hugely outweighs that of any other grimoire, demonstrating its popularity and significance. More than a third of the known manuscripts are French, and several editions of the *Key of Solomon* have been published in French. Despite this, in recent decades most attention has been paid to MacGregor Mather's

---

195 The names from this point are found in the Abraham Colorno text family.
196 The names from this point are those found in the Universal Treatise of Solomon text family.

edition of the *Key of Solomon* in 1889, which was cut-and-pasted from seven manuscripts in the British Library. This edition is flawed by the prejudices of Mathers in what he chose to include, a situation which has been rectified in the more recent editions produced by Joseph Peterson, and by Stephen Skinner and myself.

The many manuscripts of the *Key of Solomon* can be divided into four families, based on their contents.[197] These families are the Rabbi Solomon family, of twenty chapters attributed to Rabbi Solomon; the Abraham Colorno family, divided into two books each of at least seventeen chapters;[198] the Universal Treatise family, divided into four books, commonly having six chapters in book one and ten chapters in book three (this is a major source for the *Grimorium Verum*); the Abognazar family, which contain at least thirty chapters drawn from the other three families, with additional material.

These four families may be further sub-divided into thirteen text-groups. This idea was proposed and documented by Robert Mathiesen and expanded upon by Stephen Skinner and myself in *The Veritable Key of Solomon*. This does not include groups for the *Hygromanteia* or *Sepher Maphteah Shelomoh*, which have their own subchapters in this book as independent works.

The Rabbi Solomon family text begins with instructions on the circle construction drawn from the *Heptameron*. It is the only text family which contains material from the *Heptameron* in it. The twenty chapters are: which skills you must possess if you wish to involve yourselves in the knowledge of Cabalistic secrets (1); what are the most fitting times and places for the operations of the Great Art (2); concerning the materials which are used for the operations, and the way in which to prepare them according to the Cabalah (3); what instruments and utensils are important for the operations of the Great Art (4); what are the Lunar influences and secret qualities affected by the different positions of the Moon in relation to the operations of the Art (5); concerning the manner of working with the figures and characters etc., according to the rules of the Art (includes the Great Pentacle of Solomon) (6); concerning the hours of the day and night for the seven days of the week as they pertain to the planets which control them (7); concerning perfumes appropriate to the seven planets for each day of the week, with the method for crafting them (8); concerning prayers, invocations, and conjurations for each day of the week and concerning the way you recite them (9); concerning prayers in the form of exorcisms in order to consecrate everything used in the operations of the Great Art (10); concerning the colours corresponding to the seven planets (11); names of the seasons and the Angels who preside over each season (12) – this is a very long chapter containing a huge amount of information for each of the days/planets, including prayers, conjurations, characters, planetary hours, perfumes, minerals, plants, animals, colours, and pentacles. There are thirteen pentacles of the Sun,[199] thirteen of the Moon, thirteen of Mars, twelve of Mercury, eleven of Jupiter, eight of Venus, and ten of Saturn. The next chapters are: in which we explain the process of making the pentacles, following the method of the ancient Rabbis, who have been the most skilled in occult and Cabalistic science (13); concerning items which are specifically affected by, appropriate & consecrated to the seven planets and to the spirits who direct their influences (14); concerning the magical rings which the most ancient doctors of the Cabalah used with amazing success (15); concerning the names of the angel for the hours of the day and night of each day of the week (16); concerning mystical dreams and the manner of preparing to have them in accordance with your wishes, and which are used to reveal things that you desire (17); how to

---

197 For a detailed analysis see Skinner and Rankine, 2008:24-32.
198 This is the family that Mathers drew his texts from.
199 Each planet has one double-sided pentacle, except for the Sun which has two.

set quicksilver plates and make talismans out of them (18); in which you will find the designs for the pentacles for each day of the week for each season (19); in which the secrets of great curiosity are revealed (this includes bibliomancy and charms found in later French works) (20). This is followed by a section entitled The Twelve Rings, which is found in several of the *Key of Solomon* manuscripts.

The Abraham Colorno family text says it is divided into four books on the cover; however, the content is set in two books. Book one contains at least nine chapters, with up to thirteen additional chapters being included in some of the manuscripts. These chapters are: concerning Divine Love, which should precede knowledge (1); concerning days, hours, and planetary virtues (2); concerning magical arts (note: includes description of magic circle construction and conjuration) (3); confession, which the exorcist must do and recite (4); prayers and conjurations (5); stronger and more powerful conjurations (6); very powerful conjurations (7); of talismans and pentacles and how you must make them (8); concerning workshops for stolen goods and how they should be performed (9); of the experiment of invisibility, and how it should be performed (10); concerning the operation of love and the way it is performed (11); concerning the operation or work of the apple (12); concerning the operation for love in dreams and how you should emphasize (13); operation and rituals for stirring up hatred and the destruction of enemies (14); how to prepare operations of trickery, mockery, invisibility, and deception (15); how to prepare extraordinary experiments and operations (16); concerning the holy pentacles, talismans, or medallions and their material (17); to hinder a sportsman from killing any game (18); how to make the magic garters (19); how to make the magic carpet proper for interrogating the Intelligences, so as to obtain an answer regarding whatsoever matter one may wish to learn (20); how to render thyself master of a treasure possessed by the spirits (21); of the experiment of seeking favour and love (22).

Book two has eighteen chapters, with up to six additional chapters appearing in some manuscripts. These chapters are: at what hour after the preparation of all things should we give perfection to the working (1); in what manner the master of the art should control and govern himself (2); how the companions and disciples should control and govern themselves (3); concerning the fast, care, and observations (4); concerning baths, and in what manner they should be prepared (5); concerning the locations in which you can comfortably perform the Art and workings (6); of the knife, of the sword, and of the sickle of the Art, the dagger or stylet, the seventeen little lances, the staffs, wands, etc. (7); concerning burning incense and of perfumes (8); of the water and hyssop (9); concerning light and fire (10); concerning clothes, boots, and shoes (11); concerning the pen and the ink (12); concerning pens from the quills of swallows and crows (13); concerning the blood of bats, pigeons, and other animals (14); concerning paper and virgin parchment (15); concerning virgin wax (16); concerning the silken cloth (17); concerning sacrifices to the spirits (18); concerning the needle and other iron instruments (19); concerning characters and the consecration of the magical book (20); how the circle be made and how to enter it, of the formation of the circle (21); concerning the precepts of the Art (22); of the work of images and astronomy, concerning astrological images (23); the blessing of the salt (24).

The Universal Treatise family divides into four short books. Book one begins with the creation of the lamen on virgin parchment or as a magical gem for use in operations. This is followed by a section called 'Concerning spirts and their power', which is a demon spirit list (one of the ancestors of the one in the *Grimorium Verum*); the construction of the wand, and five simple charms. Book two contains a list of the thirteen superior intelligences and their virtues. Book three contains ten chapters, which are: concerning the circle (1); concerning the pentacle (2); concerning the sword (3); concerning the blessed water (4); concerning the robe (5); concerning the fumigations or perfumes (6); concerning the blood and ink (7); concerning the virgin parchment (8); concerning the place and time (9); and regarding invocations and the conjuration of spirits (10). Book four gives seventeen pentacles working with the thirteen intelligences, and their purposes.

Essential Reading

Peterson, Joseph H. (ed) (2010) *The Clavis or Key to the Magic of Solomon*. Lake Worth: Ibis. Excellent edition of the Ebenezer Sibley text copied by Frederick Hockley, which contains a wealth of other material including *The Complete Book of Magic Science*. Presented with Peterson's usual combination of excellent scholarship and fascinating context.

Skinner, Stephen & Rankine, David (2008) *The Veritable Key of Solomon*. Singapore: Golden Hoard Press. Sourceworks of Ceremonial Magic Volume 4. Comprehensive analysis of the four families of *Key of Solomon* texts with examples of three of these, and details of all the chapters across the families. There is also detailed context of the development of the *Key of Solomon* and other works associated with Solomon. Excusing personal bias, this is the book for study of the *Key of Solomon* family of texts.

Skinner, Stephen & Clark, Daniel (eds) (2019) *The Clavis or Key to Unlock the Mysteries of Magic: by Rabbi Solomon*. Singapore: Golden Hoard Press. Beautiful edition of the Sibley manuscript, with huge amount of contextual material about the sources, material, and people connected with the manuscript.

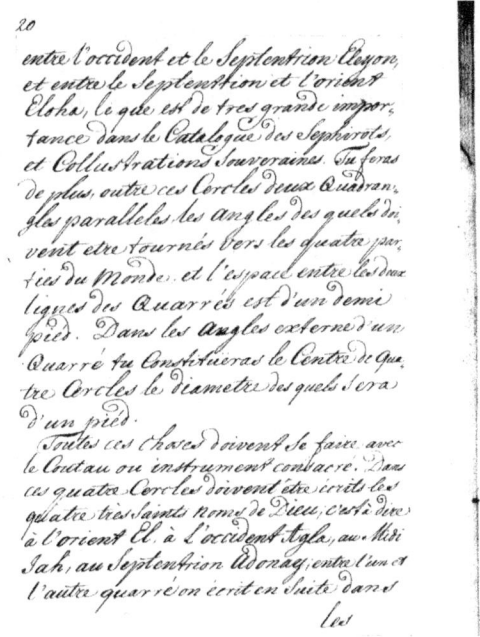 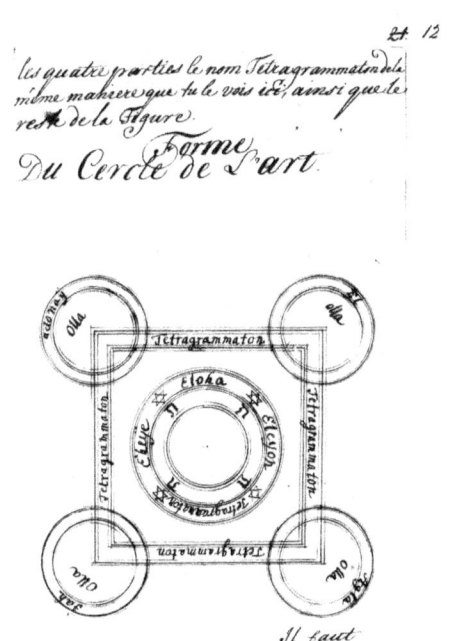

Key of Solomon circle, Kings MS288 circle

Necromancy in the Medici Library

Date: 1494.
Language: Latin.
Influences: *Munich Handbook of Necromancy, Picatrix.*
Provenance: Collection of earlier Arabic and Latin manuscripts.
MSS: MS Plut. 89 sup. 38.
Circle: Yes.
Tools: Robe, sword.
Spirit List: Acar, Afalion, Alphas, Andras, Apolyn, Appolyn, Ara, Arabas, Ascaroth, Ascharoth, Avedie, Azo, Bachimy, Balpala, Basaam, Beduch, Beelzebub, Belferich, Belial, Berich, Bilech, Bille, Boab, Bonoreae, Brulor, Cabelial, Cambea, Camoy, Carcuray, Cupido, Despan, Duliatus, Egym, Fameis, Firïel, Folficay, Foreas, Fulmar, Furfur, Gebel, Geritaton, Gevoia, Gomeris, Gorsor, Isobyl, Lambes, Lampoy, Lanima, Lodovil, Lorich, Lucifer, Maloqui, Mansator, Maraloch, Margoas, Masafin, Melemil, Mirael, Mobabel, Norioth, Nuduch, Oreoth, Oronoch, Otel, Paimon, Paragalla, Pinen, Ponicarpo, Punaton, Puzavil, Radalam, Ras, Reufates, Sacola, Sailmon, Sathan, Siartin, Simias, Sobronoy, Sysmael, Taraor, Tereol, Thyroces, Torcha, Triplex, Tryboy, Tubal, Uriel, Volach, Yudifliges, Zobedam.

The Text

The manuscript (MS Plut. 89 sup. 38) contains a wide range of texts and excerpts in Latin and Italian. Amongst the material are Thebit Bencora, *De Proprietatibus Quarundam Stellarum* (1r-3v); *Incipit Tractatus de Ymaginibus* (3v-8v); *Ptolemaica* (9r-17r); *Picatrix*, excerpts (18r-30r) ; Hermes, *Liber Orationum Planetarum Septem* (76v-77v, 99r-99v); Solomon, *De Quatuor Annulis* (211r-224v); Solomon, *De Figura Almandal* (267v-270r); Hermes/Belenus, *De Imaginibus Septem Planetarum* (280v-282r).

This book focuses on significant grimoire material in the manuscript, especially the spirit catalogue of demons, including a number subsequently found in the *Goetia*. It is worth noting the clear parallels between material contained in this work and the *Munich Handbook of Necromancy*. The final section goes into a lot of detail on timings for conjuration, which is of value. The chapters are: for invisibility; for love; for love, or on the secret arts of the image; for love, or the experiment of the mirror; to make someone lose their senses; for hatred and ill will; so that a woman may not be known by a man; an experiment of Michael Scot, necromancer; on the method of proceeding most quickly, in a short time, to have all sixty-six conscripts subject to one's terms, or to have sixty legions (demon spirit catalogue followed by discussion of timings).

Essential Reading

Johnson, Brian (2020) *Necromancy in the Medici Library*. West Yorkshire: Hadean Press. Excellent study and translation (with the Latin side-by-side) with well-researched contextual material.

Steganographia (Secret Writing)

Date: 1500.
Language: Latin.
Influences: *Sepher Raziel*.
Provenance: Written by Trithemius around 1500. Privately circulated in manuscript form. Published posthumously in 1606 in Frankfurt, with several subsequent editions in 1608, 1621, and after.
MSS: Penarth MS 423D (1591), the copy owned by John Dee; partial copy of Book 1 in Sloane MS 3824 (1649, English).
Circle: N/A.
Tools: N/A.
Spirit List: Abael, Abariel, Aboc, Abrael, Abrulges, Achot, Acreba, Acterar, Adan, Adriel, Agapiel, Aglas, Agor, Agra, Albhadur, Aldrusy, Aleasi, Alferiel, Aliel, Almadiel, Almasor, Almesiel, Almodar, Almoel, Alsuel, Althor, Amandiel, Amasiel, Ambri, Amediel, Amenadiel, Ameta, Amiel, Amoyr, Amriel, Anael, Andros, Andruchiel, Aniel, Anoyr, Ansoel, Apiel, Arach, Arafos, Aratiel, Arbiel, Arcisat, Arean, Arepach, Aridiel, Arifiel, Armadiel, Armany, Armena, Armesiel, Armoniel, Arnen, Arnibiel, Aroan, Aroc, Aroiz, Aroziel, Artinc, Asahel, Asbibiel, Aseliel, Asiniel, Asmadiel, Asmaiel, Asmiel, Asoriel, Asosiel, Asphiel, Asphor, Aspiel, Aspor, Assaba, Astael, Astib, Astor, Asuriel, Asyriel, Athesiel, Athiel, Atriel, Azimel, Azimo, Baabal, Baciar, Badiel, Balsur, Baoxas, Barbil, Barbis, Barchiel, Barfas, Barfos, Bariel, Barmiel, Baros, Barsu, Baruch, Baruchas, Basiel, Bedary, Belsay, Benodiel, Benoham, Betasiel, Bidiel, Bonyel, Borass, Bramsiel, Brufiel, Brymiel, Bucafas, Budar, Budarim, Budiel, Bufar, Bufiel, Bulis, Buniel, Burfa, Buriel, Busiel, Cabariel, Cabarim, Cabiel, Cabron, Cadriel, Calvarnia, Calym, Cambriel, Camiel, Camor, Camory, Camuel, Camyel, Caniel, Capriel, Carasiba, Carba, Cardiel, Carga, Cariel, Carmasiel, Carmiel, Carniel, Carnodiel, Carnol, Caron, Carpiel, Carsiel, Cartael, Casbriel, Casiel, Caspaniel, Caspiel, Cavayr, Cayros, Cazul, Cesael, Chabri, Chamiel, Chamoriel, Chamos, Chanaei. Fursiel, Chansi, Charas, Chariel, Charobiel, Charoel, Charoel, Charsiel, Chasor, Choriel, Chremoas, Chrubas, Chuba, Churibal, Cirecas, Citgara, Clamor, Claniel, Clyssan, Cobusiel, Codriel, Coliel, Cruchan, Cruhiel, Cubi, Cubiel, Cugiel, Culmar, Cumariel, Cumeriel, Cuphal, Cupriel, Cuprisiel, Curasin, Curfas, Curiel, Curifas, Curmas, Cusiel, Cusiel, Cusync, Dadrinos, Dagiel, Damarsiel, Danael, Daniel, Darbori, Decaniel, Delias, Demediel, Demoriel, Diuiel, Dobiel, Dohiel, Dorael, Doriel, Dorothiel, Drabros, Dragon, Dramiel, Drapios, Drasiel, Drubiel, Drusiel, Dubarus, Dubiel, Dubilon, Dusiriel, Earos, Ebra, Edriel, Efiel, Elear, Eliel, Elitel, Emoniel, Emuel, Ermoniel, Espoel, Ethiel, Etimiel, Fabariel, Fariel, Fassua, Femol, Frasmiel, Fubiel, Futiel, Gabir, Gariel, Garnasu, Gediel, Geradiel, Geriel, Geriel, Godiel, Gremiel, Gudiel, Hamas, Hamorphiel, Heresiel, Hermon, Herne, Hidriel, Hissam, Hursiel, Icosiel, Inachiel, Itrasbiel, Itules, Janiel, Jasziel, Keriel, Ladiel, Lamael, Lamas, Lameniel, Lameniel, Laphor, Larael, Larfos, Lariel, Larmol, Larphiel, Las Pharon, Lazaba, Lemodac, Libiel, Lobiel, Lomor, Luciel, Luziel, Macariel, Machariel, Mador, Madriel, Mafayr, Mafrus, Magni, Mahue, Malgaras, Malgron, Malqueel, Maniel, Mansi, Marae, Maras, Maras, Marciaz, Marianu, Mariel, Maroth, Marquus, Maseriel, Mashel, Mastuel, Maziel, Medar, Melas, Melcha, Melchon, Meliel, Menadiel, Menador, Menariel, Merach, Meras, Merasiel, Merosiel, Meroth, Misiel, Molael, Monael, Moniel, Moracha, Morael, Morias, Moriel, Mortaliel, Moziel, Mudirel, Mugael, Munefiel, Murahe, Mursiel, Musiniel, Musiriel, Musor, Musuziel, Myrezyn, Nachiel, Nadrel, Nadroc, Nadrusiel, Nalael, Naras, Narmiel, Narsyel, Narzael, Nasiniel, Nassar, Nastros, Nathriel, Nedriel, Nemariel, Neriel, Nodar, Noquiel, Odiel, Oemiel, Ofisiel, Omael, Omiel, Omyel, Orariel, Oriel, Ormenu, Ornich, Orpeniel, Oryn, Ossidiel, Othiel, Otim, Padiel, Pafiel, Pamersiel,

Pandiel, Pandiel, Pandor, Paniel, Parabiel, Pariel, Parius, Parniel, Parsifiel, Pathier, Pelariel, Pelusar, Penador, Peniel, Phaniel, Phanuel, Pharol, Phutiel, Pirichiel, Pischiel, Potiel, Potiel, Prasiel, Praxeel, Quibda, Quitta, Rabas, Rabiel, Rablion, Raboc, Ramica, Rantiel, Rapsiel, Raysiel, Reciel, Richel, Romiel, Romyel, Rouiel, Sabas, Sadar, Saddiel, Sadiel, Saefarn, Saefer, Saluar, Samiel, Samyel, Sarach, Sarael, Sariel, Sarmiel, Sarviel, Satifiel, Sebach, Sequiel, Sochas, Sodiel, Soleviel, Soriel, Sotheano, Souiel, Suriel, Symiel, Taros, Tediel, Terath, Thalbus, Thanatiel, Tharas, Thariel, Tharson, Thoac, Thurcal, Thuriel, Tigara, Tugaros, Urbaniel, Urisiel, Usiniel, Vadriel, Vadros, Varpiel, Vasenel, Vaslos, Vdiel, Vessur, Vraniel, Vriel, Vsiel, Zabriel, Zachariel, Zamor, Zerael, Zoeniel, Zosiel.

The Text

Steganographia is a text that fascinated Renaissance magicians: Agrippa referred to it and John Dee went to great lengths to acquire a copy of it. The outward theme of the book is one of using spirits to communicate messages instantly over great distances. The caveat was that the receiver would need to be aware of the cryptographic key to the message, as the other theme of the book was cryptography. The value of instantaneous information transmission then would have been huge, a sort of angelic email centuries before the internet.

The book was not written for a general audience. Trithemius himself stressed that the practitioner and recipient of any message both needed to be proficient and pious magicians. He also gave a series of specific guidelines for use in the text, one of which was to only use the methods within if all other conventional avenues had failed.

The large list of spirits and their courts is particularly significant, as Trithemius stressed the need to be sure to use the right spirit to transmit a message. He also stated that when calling a spirit, the practitioner should always mention how many servants the spirit had, as it flattered the spirits and made them more amenable. The spirits listed in books one and two reappear in the *Theurgia-Goetia* and *Ars Paulina* respectively, and these works present a far more accessible methodology for working with these spirits. The books discuss sending messages and the location of the spirits (including the sixteen directions and spirit rulers attributed to each).

For centuries the title and contents of *Steganographia* have led people to believe that is was a work on codes and encryption. In 1996 a German professor, Dr Thomas Ernst, cracked the code. Shortly after and independently, an American mathematician, Dr Jim Reeds, also cracked it. Both emphasize that, as is common for cryptograms, Trithemius had attributed numbers to the letters of the Latin alphabet, but that he had reversed the order of the alphabet, omitting the letters K and Y, and with W and letters for Sch and Tz on the end. Another code found in the book is the use of acrostics to reveal messages in the text.[200] This raises the question of whether the book was simply an encryption text, or whether it was for a dual purpose and also still a manual of spirit communication. This is a topic which is open to debate, but it is interesting to note that the spirit names used in the books are included in later magical texts (*Theurgia-Goetia* and *Ars Paulina*) which have been worked by magicians for centuries.

Essential Reading

McLean, Adam (ed) (1982) *The Steganographia of Johannes Trithemius*. Edinburgh: Magnum Opus. Contains books one and two, rare but worth acquiring.

---

[200] Acrostics, using the first letter of words to form other words, are a well-known practice seen in traditions such as Kabbalah as Notariqon, where some of the most commonly used divine names are acrostics which expand into phrases.

DE NIGROMANCIA (THESAURUS SPIRITUM)

Date: C16, no text dating to C13 lifetime of Roger Bacon known.
Language: Latin, English.
Influences: Uncertain.
Provenance: Attributed to Roger Bacon (1214-92 CE) and Robert Lombard.
MSS: Sloane MS 3885 (C16) (Latin); Additional MS 36674 (late C16) (English); MS Mun A.4.98 (late C16) (Latin/English).
Circle: Yes.
Tools: Finger linen, girdle, lamen, pentacle of Solomon, phylacteries, ring, sceptre, sword, table (laurel), three white-handled knives, white linen robe.
Spirit List: Absoul, Alastiel, Almarazen, Almazon, Amalzatin, Amazael, Anathana, Astaroth, Azael, Aziel, Azriel, Belial, Colitzab'tin, Eliezar, Elobona, Gabriel, Lucifer, Malago, Michael, Raphael, Reguelim, Sabaoth, Saint Cyprian, Sybillia, Troglis, Tyer, Uriel, Urielim.

THE TEXT

De Nigromancia is one of the earlier Cyprian grimoires, evidenced by the numerous references to performing masses of Cyprian, conjuring at his feast, and the treasure-seeking emphasis.

The text begins with a grand oration which references gaining the treasure of the spirits. An introduction explaining the division of the book into four tracts (parts) and a precis of these parts follows. The first tract begins with an emphasis on purity of self and paraphernalia. It then recommends having a priest consecrate the ring, sword, and sceptre used in the practices, stressing their importance. The importance of timing and the wearing of the clean white linen robe follows. The importance of anointing the eyes with chrism (holy anointing oil) to assist in seeing the spirits is stressed. The text interestingly recommends that the sun be shining and there be no clouds, as being more pleasing to the spirits.[201]

Tract two begins with the insistence that a mass of St Cyprian be performed before any conjurations are carried out. The offering of alms is also encouraged to ensure success (a penny is good, a crown is better!). Timing is again referred, stating that between the first and third quarters of the moon are best. From sunset until midday are given as the best times for conjuration at this point (slightly contradicting what was said earlier). A minimum of three days' abstinence and preparation is then emphasized, including eating no meat. The conjurations are stated to be said seven times in each direction, as well as the Our Father seven times in each. It states that whenever the pentacle is shown to the spirits or Tetragrammaton is said, the pentacle should be anointed with sweet balsam. The timing is revisited with instruction to begin during the hour of Venus. May, and specifically 14th May as the Feast of St Cyprian, are recommended. More is said on abstinence and preparatory purification. A description of the vault to be constructed for conjuration if possible is then given. Wine, bread, sweet oils, and a good quantity of straw are placed outside the circle. The circle is drawn in chalk and traced with the sword or sceptre. Discussion of the form of the circle depending on whether working with spirits of air or fire or water follows. For water there must be a phial of rain or spring water present. When the circle is complete, three masses, the first of which should be to St Cyprian, are said in it and the tools suffumigated with frankincense. The consecration is then given. The forms of the magic circle are discussed, with emphasis placed on asperging and suffumigating them. A series of consecrations for the circle is detailed, including one with the Virgin Mary.

---

201 This may be referring to the common notion of the time that most spirits' bodies were made of air, and therefore the absence of water (clouds) was preferable to them.

Tract three discusses planetary work, such as the metals and characters to be used. Days of the Moon and timing are again detailed. The tools are described, specifically the girdle, laminal (plate), phylacteries, ring, sceptre, sword, and white-handled knife. A detailed consecration for the sword is provided, which requires a priest. Consecrations for the other tools are also described, which are all to be done on a Friday.

Tract four moves into the performance of conjuration, again beginning with considerations of timing. It is interesting that the magister enters the circle with the sword in the left hand and sceptre bearing laminal in the right hand. The conjurations are spoken by the magister and instructions for the companions during this are given. A detailed image of the magic circle is shown, followed by a circle for treasure hunting, and the instructions for conjuration for treasure hunting. There are two separate conjurations, one of angels and one of infernal spirits (the latter includes Saint Cyprian in it). A magic circle for finding treasure in water or the sea is then drawn. A conjuration with angels follows, along with another circle for working with water spirits. An ointment for seeing spirits is then described, along with its consecration and the magic circle for use during its preparation. A conjuration of spirits to move the practitioner great distances quickly is next. A conjuration for friendship follows. Then is a conjuration to know a true spirit from any other (to gain a familiar spirit). To cause a thief to return follows, which includes calling the fairy empress Sibylia. An additional prayer ends the text.

Essential Reading

MacDonald, Michael Albion (ed & trans) (1988) *De Nigromancia [attributed to] Roger Bacon*. New Jersey: Heptangle Books. Good facsimile edition drawn from the two manuscripts of the text at the British Library.

The Herpentil Texts

Date: 1505-1805, C16-C19.
Language: Latin, German.
Influences: *Magic Naturalis et Innaturalis*.
Provenance: *Book of the Mightiest Spirits* (1725, German) by J.G. Herpentil; *Almuchabosa Absegalim Alkakib Albaon* (C16, Latin) attributed to Michael Scot (1175-1236); *Magia Ordinis, Artium et Scientiarum abstrusarum* (1725, Latin) by Johannes Kornreuther; *Herpentills Salomonis* (1505, German); *Embodiment of the Unnatural Magic* (C18, German) by J.G. Herpentil; *Libellus St. Gertrudis* (C19?, German).
MSS: *Book of the Mightiest Spirits*: Herzogin Anna Amalia Bibliothek MS F8476 (1725, German). *Almuchabosa Absegalim Alkakib Albaon*: John Rylands, Manchester Latin MS 105 (C16, Latin). *Magia Ordinis, Artium et Scientiarum abstrusarum*: Wellcome MS 3130 (1725, Latin), Augsburg OWB Cod II.2.8.2 (1750, Latin), Wellcome MS 3129 (early C19, German). *Herpentills Salomonis* (published 1505, Latin). *Embodiment of the Unnatural Magic* (published C18, German). *Libellus St. Gertrudis* (booklet 1805?, German).
Circle: Yes.
Tools: Dagger (previously used to kill), mitre, robes, scapula, staff, wand.
Spirit List: Achunhab, Aghizikke, Allenzozoff, Almischak, Almisk, Almuchabzar, Amabosar, Amazeroth, Amileckar, Amisalog, Ascharoth, Aschirikas, Azabhsar, Baltuzaratz, Mebhhazubb, Mezaphzar, Omigiel, Phisazeroth, Qalha, Rabu, Reÿmonzorackon, Suhub.

The Text

The Herpentil texts are a collection of works from late seventeenth to early eighteenth-century Germany. They are short and concise texts which offer a simple, practical system. The texts are united by shared content and fall into two groups based on this shared material. The first group of manuscripts (Class A) are near identical and comprise *The Book of the Mightiest Spirits* by Joseph Herpentil, *Almuchabosa Absegalim Alkakib Albaon* (Compendium of Unnatural Black Magic) by Michael Scot, and *Magia Ordinis, Artium et Scientiarum abstrusarum* (Magic Order of Hidden Arts and Sciences) by Johannes Kornreuther. The second group of manuscripts (Class B) have more variation but still much common material. These are *Herpentills Salomonis*, *The Embodiment of the Unnatural Magic* by Joseph Herpentil, and *Libellus St Gertrudis* by Saint Gertrude of Nivelles. The *Tuba Veneris* pseudepigraphically attributed to John Dee is also in this group.[202]

The *Book of the Mightiest Spirits* by Reverend J.G. Herpentil is more fully titled *Compendium of the Unnatural Magic containing Conjurations and Names of Different Spirits*. It begins with an introduction discussing and qualifying the use of conjuration. The text then provides the circle, wand, mitre, scapula, spirit sigil, ritual numbers and locations, incense recipe, instructions for ritual practice, dealing with unruly spirits, opening prayer, citations and seals, and binding and dismissal of the spirits Amazeroth, Phisazeroth, Reÿmonzorackon, Amileckar, and Allenzozoff; then words for the dismissal of spirits, and an image of the Urim and Thummim.

Almuchabosa Absegalim Alkakib Albaon or *Compendium of Unnatural Black Magic containing citations and sigils of diverse spirits* is attributed to Michael Scot with the (spurious) date of 1204 CE, Prague. The text begins with the qualification of qualities required and cautions regarding the material. It then covers the circle, the wand, the mitre, the scapula, participant numbers, locations, incense recipe, timing, ritual practice, dealing with unruly spirits, opening

---

202 This work has its own subchapter.

prayer, citations, names and sigils of the spirit princes Almuchabzar, Achunhab, Baltuzaratz, and Aghizikke; dismissal of the spirits and words to be spoken on exiting the circle; sigils of Suhub, Rabu, Almisk, and Qalha; citation for the preceding spirits.

Magia Ordinis, Artium et Scientiarum abstrusarum begins with an introduction giving the (false) provenance to an Arab mage in 1495. The text works through the circle, staff, mitre, incense recipe, number of practitioners, and timings; how to deal with reluctant spirits; the words to say on entering the circle; conjurations, sigils, and citations of the spirit princes Mezaphzar, Ascharoth, Azabhsar, Mebhhazubb, and Amisalog; form of conjuration and dismissal.

The *Herpentills Salomonis*, also has an earlier date attributed to it to give it more gravitas, that of 1521. It is first found as part of *Magia Naturalis et Innaturalis* (1612). The foreword gives instructions on preparation, including the preparation of a crucifix and a candle placed in the hand of a dying man. The text then covers the incense recipe and use of incense, the citation, the license to depart,[203] requesting money (not extravagant), dealing with unruly spirits, binding, the license to depart, praying, citation of a spirit, dealing with the spirit, and dismissal.

The *Embodiment of the Unnatural Magic* by Joseph Herpentil has a (spurious) 1519 date. After the foreword are chapters on the magic circle; the wand; instructions on preparing the materials; participant numbers and conditions; ritual instructions; incense recipe; use of the Jupiter seal for treasure; dealing with unruly spirits; how to command the spirits; the names, seals, and citations of the spirit princes Almischak, Aschirikas, Amabosar; greeting and dismissal of the spirits; closing the circle; planetary hours (includes disc showing all the hours of the week); citation; license to depart; and skrying in water calling on Cyprian.

The *Libellus St. Gertrudis* has the subtitle of *The Main Coercion of the spirits at human service, with papal license*, and a (spurious) 1403 CE date. The 1809 foreword, describing the work as engraved on six silver pages, seems a more likely date. The sequence is a string of holy names, universal coercion, commission, bond or call, and dismissal. The number of repetitions of the parts and timings are then given.

Essential Reading

Ortiz, N.A. & Velius, V. (trans & eds) (2016) *A Compendium of Unnatural Black Magic*. Mexico City: Enodia Press. Valuable work providing the translation and original texts with good contextual and provenance material.

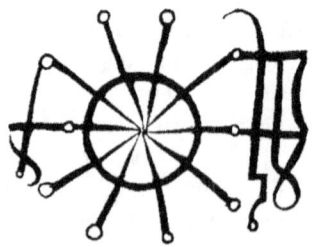

Herpentil Texts - Azabhsar Sigil

---

203 The license to depart has the unusual feature of being the citation read in reverse.

DE SEPTEM SECUNDEIS (SEVEN SECONDARY CAUSES)

Date: 1508.
Language: Latin.
Influences: *Conciliator* of Peter of Abano (published 1472).
Provenance: Written by Johannes Trithemius (1462-1516).
MSS: N/A.
Circle: N/A.
Tools: N/A.
Spirit List: Anael, Gabriel, Michael, Orifiel, Raphael, Samuel, Zachariel.

THE TEXT

De Septem Secundeis is a discussion of Trithemius's view of cycles of history (354-year periods) being ruled by planetary angels under God's command. He discusses historical events and human development through the ages under the dominion of the seven planetary angelic governors.

The sequence of dominion given by Trithemius is Orifiel (Saturn), Anael (Venus), Zachariel (Jupiter), Raphael (Mercury), Samuel (Mars), Gabriel (Moon), Michael (Sun). According to Trithemius we are currently under the rulership of Michael, who took over dominion in November 1789.

ESSENTIAL READING

Lilly, William (trans) (1647) *The worlds catastrophe*. London: J. Partridge. English translation of Trithemius' work. The best source for this work is Joseph Peterson's wonderful website, www.esotericarchives.com

Antipalus Maleficiorum (The Enemy of Witchcraft)

Date: 1508.
Language: Latin.
Influences: Trithemius's (1462-1516) own views.
Provenance: Partial library list from the Abbey of Sponheim, where Trithemius had been abbot. Written in 1506-08, published posthumously in 1605.
MSS: N/A.
Circle: N/A.
Tools: N/A.
Spirit List: N/A.

The Text

The value of *Antipalus Maleficiorum* lies in the list of grimoires and magic books which Trithemius provided in book one, chapter two. He gives the incipit and a brief description of the books, most of which have some mention of demons, angels, or spirits and in a few instances, divination. What is particularly significant to note is how few of those books have survived to the present, though when copies have been found, they have been footnoted (all Latin texts unless otherwise indicated).

Among the books he listed are the *Key of Solomon;* the *Officorum (Book of Offices),*[204] a book in ten parts which imitates the *Picatrix;* the *Picatrix; Sepher Raziel,* referred to as a book of seven works; the *Liber Hermetis (Book of Hermes);*[205] the *Purity of God;*[206] the *Book of the Perfection of Saturn;*[207] a book on demon magic attributed to St Cyprian called *Four Kings;* the *Calculatory Art of Virgil,* dealing with discovering the names and characters of good and bad spirits; the *Book of Simon Magus;* the *Thesaurus Spirituum (Dictionary of Spirits),* attributed to Rupert of Lombardy, with mention of a work on necromancy by this author as well; the *Book of the Actions of Spirits,* attributed to Aristotle,[208] the *Flower of Flowers,* dealing with demon conjurations, names, and characters;[209] the *Almadel,* attributed to Solomon;[210] the *Book of Enoch;* the *Book of the Seven Rings of the Planets,* attributed to Messalah;[211] *The Four Rings of Solomon;*[212] the *Mirror of Joseph;* the *Mirror of Alexander the Great King of Macedonia;* the *Book of Secrets of Hermes of Spain;* a pamphlet on magic attributed to Ganel[213] (a Hungarian or Bulgarian); several demonic tracts attributed to

---

204 Possibly the *Book of Offices of Spirits*.

205 Survives as Harley MS 3731 (1431). An important astrological text which deals with decans and refers back to the early Greek astrologers of the C1-2 CE.

206 Said to be the book given by Raziel to Adam. Note the title is similar to the fifth treatise in *Sepher Raziel,* so there may be a connection.

207 The incipit notes it was found by Abel, son of Adam, which Trithemius criticises heavily.

208 May be found in Sloane MS 3854 (C14-16) f0.105v-110.

209 There is an alchemical manuscript (Wellcome MS 77) of the same name, *Flos Florum,* attributed to pseudo-Arnaldus de Villanova but this is late C16 CE so unlikely to be the same.

210 This refers to one of the Almandal texts (see the subchapter on this work).

211 This text survives in its most complete form in Darmstadt MS 1410 (early C16), Cambridge MS Dd.xi.45 (1441-45), and Rawlinson MS D 253 (1647). Other partial fragments exist in MSS (see subchapter 'Book of the Seven Rings of the Planets').

212 Canterbury, St Augustine's Abbey MSS 1603 (1497); BL Sloane MS 3847 (C16); Leipzig, Stadtsbibliothek MS 739 (C18).

213 Probably Ganellus, and the text would be *Summa Sacre Magice,* which Trithemius is known to have owned.

Tozgrec;²¹⁴ another treatise on demon magic attributed to Michael Scot; a treatise on demon magic attributed to Albertus Magnus; two more treatises on magic attributed to Albertus Magnus; the *Elucidarium Necromantaie*²¹⁵ of Peter of Abano; the *Secret of the Philosophers*;²¹⁶ an unnamed work on the Schemhamphoras, the book *Lamene* by Solomon;²¹⁷ an unnamed book on the names and characters of evil spirits;²¹⁸ a treatise called *Rubeus* (Red), which deals with the operations of demons and which Trithemius compares to *Liber Officorum;* the *Secrets of Albertus* on dealing with evil spirits, falsely attributed to Albertus Magnus; *On the Offices of Spirits,* attributed to Solomon; the *Vinculum Spirituum (Chain of the Spirits),* containing orations and conjurations;²¹⁹ the *Book of the Pentacles of Salomon;*²²⁰ *Of the Stations of the Cult of Venus,* attributed to Tozgrec;²²¹ the *Four Mirrors,* attributed to Tozgrec;²²² the *Image of Venus,* attributed to Tozgrec; the *Book of the Nine Talismans (Candarii)* of Solomon;²²³ *Seven Names of Heaven,* attributed to Mohammed;²²⁴ *Fifteen Names;*²²⁵ the *Book on the Head of Saturn,* which is described as a necromantic work but elsewhere as planetary; the *Liber Praestigiorum Hermetis (Book of Talismans of Hermes);*²²⁶ *Of the Hours of Work,* by Abolemiten; *Of Four Talismans;* the *Composition of Images,* attributed to Hermes, which comprises seven volumes with planetary names i.e., the *Book of the Sun (Liber Solis),* Book of the Moon (Liber Lunae), Book of Mercury (Liber Mercurii), Book of Venus (Liber Veneris), Book of Mars (Liber Martis), Book of Jupiter (Liber Jovis),* and *Book of Saturn (Liber Saturni);*²²⁷ the *Book of the Seven Planetary Images of Geber*²²⁸ *King of India;*²²⁹ the *Liber*

---

214 Tozgrec, said to have been trained by Solomon, also referred to as Toz Graecus, Ioh Grecis, Torzigeus, and a number of other derivations and corruptions of these names.

215 *Elucidation of Necromancy,* see the subchapter on this work.

216 At least eighteen copies exist of this MS, some of them fragmentary: e.g., Bodleian, MS Digby 37 (C14, Latin); MS Rawlinson C.7 (late C14, English); MS Rawlinson D.1066 (C14-15, English); Corpus Christi MS 132 (C15); and Trinity MS O.1.58 (C15). It contains recipes and magic tricks, which may explain Trithemius's negative attitude to it, despite it being organised into seven sections, one for each of the liberal arts.

217 A work on questioning demons; the lamen is worn by the practitioner for protection.

218 Described as *On the Composition of the Names and Characters of the Evil Spirits.* It has been speculated this is an early *Goetia.*

219 ound in Coxe MS 25 (late C15) and Sloane MS 3853 (C16-17 Latin/English). The text is also referred to elsewhere in Sloane MS 3850 (C17) as *Vinculum Salomonis,* putting it in the Solomonic corpus.

220 It is tempting to suggest this as a possible source of the pentacles in the *Key of Solomon* manuscripts.

221 Found in BNM lat. XIV 174 (C14).

222 Found in BNM lat. XIV 174 (C14).

223 Found in MS 4° Astron. 3 (1346), MS Germ Fol. 903 1580s, German), Sloane MS 3850 (C17).

224 Found in Florence BNC II.III.214 (C15).

225 Found in Florence BNC II.III.214, attributed there to Mohammed (C15).

226 York Austin Friars A8 362 (pre-1400), now lost.

227 This collection of works would imply it is the book titled elsewhere as *Liber de imaginibus septem planetarum ex scientia Abel.* All seven volumes are in Vat BARB Lat, 3589 (1430, Occitan). *Liber Lunae* (see subchapter of the same name), *Liber Solis, Liber Martis, Liber Jovis* and *Liber Saturni* are all in Darmstadt HS1410 (1550).

228 Geber was a Latinised name used for the C8-9 CE Arab writer Jābir ibn Ḥayyān, who was not a king of India. This suggests that this work may in fact be *Of the Planetary Seals of Benhensatrus, an Indian King and Philosopher.* Benhensatrus was said to be a king of India and disciple of Apollonius of Tyana. This survives as St Petersburg BAN Q.537 (C16), Dresden MS N.105 (C17, German).

229 Unmarked MS in private collection of Conte de Sarzana (1510).

Praestigiorum Thebit (*Book of Talismans of Thebit*);[230] the *Book of Talismans of Ptolemy*;[231] the *Book of Talismans of Nesbar*;[232] *Of the Composition of the Seven Planetary Images*;[233] *Of the Seals of the Seven Planets*;[234] the *Book of the Wisdom of Bexel of the Rings of the Seven Planets*; the *Book of the Figures of the Seven Planets* by Bexel; the *Book of Ptolemy regarding the Composition of the Talismans, the Rings and the Seals of the Twelve Signs*;[235] the *Seals of the Twelve Signs*, attributed to Arnold de Villanova;[236] the *Arrangement of the Images of the Twenty-four Hours of the Day and Night*, attributed to Balenus; a work attributed to Hermes of four parts, *Of Fifteen Stones*, *Of Fifteen Herbs*, *Of Fifteen Stars*, *Of Fifteen Figures or Characters*;[237] *De Imaginibus* (*Of Images*) of Thebit;[238] *Figures of the Twelve Signs against all Diseases of the Human Body*; *Of the Composition and Power of Images* attributed to Tozgrec; a book on the wisdom of Dorotheus;[239] *Of the Magical Agencies* attributed to al-Razi,[240] which is similar to the *Picatrix*; *Of the Forms and Seals of the Planets*, also attributed to al-Razi; the *Book of Magic Secrets* of Geber;[241] the *Key of the Figures* of Geber; *Of the Astrolabe* of Geber; the *Completion of Magic* of Geber; the *Composition and Effects of the Images of the Planets* by Zeherit the Chaldean;[242] *Miraculous Effects* by Namion; the *Book of Fortuitous Events* by Zabel; *Conjectures* by Balenus (two copies); the *Invention of the Nativity* by Alcandreus;[243] *Book of Talismans* by a certain Thomas, which includes rings for the mansions of the Moon; *Of the Moon* by Balenus; the *Book of the Inclusion of Spirits in the Rings of the Seven Planets*; the *Images of the Seven Planets* by Balenus;[244] the *Book of the Images and Rings of the Seven Planets*, attributed to Hermes;[245] the *Days and Hours of the Seven Planets*, attributed to Hermes; *Of Images which are Engraved on Precious Stones*, attributed to Hermes; the *Twelve Rings of Venus*, attributed to Ptolemy; *Experiments of*

---

230 C12 CE Latin translation of the *De Imaginibus* of Thābit ibn Qurrah. See the subchapter on *Liber Prestigiorum*.

231 See BNF MS 7337 (C15).

232 This may be another manuscript version of *De Imaginibus*, as we know Trithemius had several copies of some works.

233 There are two separate entries for this work, one attributed to Balenus, the Arabic form of Apollonius of Tyana, and the other to Behencasin. MSS of this work are still extant, see Ghent MS 1021A, London SAL 39 (C15, Latin).

234 There are two works with this title, the second has Behencasin in the incipit. He was said to be a student of Apollonius of Tyana. There are several MSS which could relate to or be derived from this, including St Petersburg BAN Q 537 (1512, Latin) and Dresden MS N105 (C17, German).

235 Unmarked MS in private collection of Conte de Sarzana (1510).

236 Arnold de Villanova (c.1240–1311)) was a theologian and alchemist. Dr John Dee owned a manuscript copy of this work.

237 MSS at Bodleian Ashmole MS 341 (C13); BL Harley MS 1612 (C14); Bodleian Ashmole MS 1471 (C14); Erfurt, Collegium Amplonianum, Math. 11 and 53 (both pre-1412); Edinburgh Royal Observatory Cr.3.14 (C15); Corpus Christi MS 125 (C15); Canterbury, St Augustine's Abbey MSS 1277 (1497); Nuremberg, Benedictine Abbey of St Egidien, L11 (pre-1500); BL Sloane MS 3847 (C16).

238 *De Imaginibus* is the same work as *Liber Praestigiorum* already mentioned.

239 Dorotheus was a significant C1 CE Greek astrologer, see 'Introduction'.

240 Muhammad ibn Zakariya al-Razi (854-925 CE) was a Persian physician, astronomer, and alchemist.

241 See footnote above about Geber.

242 Zeherit the Chaldean was said to be the first of the three sages of Chaldean Agriculture.

243 This name is probably derived from *Alchandreana*, the name given to the first body of Arab astrological texts translated into Latin in the C10 CE.

244 MSS copies include BNM lat. XIV.174 (C14), Vatican Pal Lat. 1445B (C14), Vatican Pal Lat. 1375 (1488), BML Plut. 89 sup. 38 (1494), Wiesbaden 79 (1518-19).

245 MS Vat PAL Lat. 1375 (1488).

Miraculous Rings, of the Twenty-eight Mansions of the Moon, attributed to Peter of Abano;[246] *Of the Properties of Fifteen Stars, Stones and Herbs*, attributed to Thabit; *Book of Astonishing Images of Abenhali*,[247] which Trithemius says is mostly Ptolemy;[248] the *Cyranides*; the *Laws of Plato*, attributed to Hinnaxii, son of Zachariah;[249] *Augnempere*, another book by Hinnaxii on Plato; the *Sphere of Pythagoras, Philosophy of Plato and Apulieus*; *Almachbale* by Algabor the Arab; the *Book of Observations of Albedach*, attributed to the Persian king Darius; *Of the Theory and Art of Magic* by Jacob Alkindi.[250]

Essential Reading

As a complete copy of *Antipalus Maleficorum* has not been located, research for this chapter has been largely drawn from Joseph Peterson's website www.esotericarchives.com, and two extremely valuable works: Couliano, Ioan P. (1987) *Eros and Magic in the Renaissance*, and Peuckert, Will-Erich (1956) *Pansophie*. The excellent scholarship of Mihai Vârtejaru was also invaluable in chasing down some of the manuscripts. Copies of the texts of several of the manuscripts and his research can be found at his blog at https://studies-vartejaru.blogspot.com.

---

246 Extant MS include BNF MS 7337 (C15); Leipzig Cod. Mag. 35 (1750, Italian/Latin), containing the first fourteen rings.
247 Abenhali is a shortened form of Albohazen Hali, a C11 CE astronomer and poet, and head of the chancellery of the Zirid prince al-Mu'izz ibn Bādis (1016-1040).
248 This could make the book *Of the Images on the Faces of Signs* of pseudo-Ptolemy; if this is the case there are at least thirty-four MSS of that work.
249 According to van der Lugt (2009) and others, this would seem to be a form of *Liber Vaccae* (C12 CE).
250 There is reference in other texts to Jacob Alkindi being Jewish.

The Art of Drawing Spirits into Crystals

Date: Early C16?
Language: Latin, English.
Influences: Unknown.
Provenance: Written by Johannes Trithemius (1462-1516), translated by Francis Barrett and included in *The Magus* (1801).
MSS: The location of the original Latin manuscript is unknown.
Circle: Yes.[251]
Tools: Crystal/mirror, lamen, pedestal, ring, table, tripod (censer), ebony wand.
Spirit List: Anael, Cassiel, Gabriel, Kings of the Corners of the Earth,[252] Michael, Raphael, Sachiel, Uriel.

The Text

This text was printed as Part IV of Book 2 of *The Magus*. The simple and practical nature of the instructions has made it a popular work amongst modern practitioners. The work begins with instructions on the preparation of the crystal and its stand.

A prayer is given, followed by the procedure for conjuration, questioning, and departure. The angelic rulership of the Planetary Hours for the days of the week concludes the text, with a note about their calculation.

Much of Francis Barrett's seminal work *The Magus* (1801) was plagiarised from the works of Trithemius and Agrippa. In doing so, Barrett made this material available to a wider audience, especially in Britain, and it is noteworthy that *The Magus* was very popular as a source work for cunning folk in the nineteenth century.

Essential Reading

Barrett, Francis (1801) *The Magus*. London: Lackington, Allen & Co. A number of recent editions are available.

---

[251] The circle given here is pictured in some photographs of Alex Sanders.

[252] Not specified in the text, and there is much variation across different grimoires. See the chapter 'Spirit Hierarchies'.

THREE BOOKS OF OCCULT PHILOSOPHY

Date: 1509-10.
Language: Latin.
Influences: *Natural History* of Pliny, the *Bible*, *Sepher Raziel*, *Picatrix*, Albertus Magnus, Marsilio Ficino, Pico della Mirandola, Johannes Reuchlin, Trithemius, Neoplatonic and Hermetic texts.
Provenance: Written by Agrippa in 1509-10. He distributed it in manuscript form, and it was first published in 1533. The first English edition was published in 1651.
MSS: Published text.
Circle: N/A.
Tools: N/A.
Spirit List:[253] Abaddon, Abdizuel, Abrinael, Achaiah, Acteus, Adnachiel, Adramelech, Adriel, Aeacus, Agiel, Aladiah, Alecto, Alheniel, Amaymon, Ambriel, Amelech, Amixiel, Amnediel, Amnixiel, Amutiel, Aniel, Annauel, Ardesiel, Ariel, Asaliah, Asmodel, Asmodeus, Astarath, Ataliel, Azael, Azariel, Azazel, Azeruel, Aziel, Balach, Barbiel, Barchiel, Barzabel, Beelzebub, Behemoth, Bel, Belial, Bethnael, Cahetel, Caliel, Camael, Cerberus, Chaamiah, Chabuiah, Chahuiah, Chamos, Cherub, Chodorlaomor, Ctesiphone, Dagon, Damabiah, Daniel, Dirachiel, Egibiel, Egyn, Eiael, Elemiah, Enediel, Ergediel, Gabiel, Gabriel, Geliel, Geniel, Graphiel, Haaiah, Hachasiah, Hagiel, Hahahel, Hahaiah, Haiaiel, Hakamiah, Hamelial, Hanael, Haniel, Harachel, Hariel, Hasmodai, Haziel, Hecate, Hismael, Iahhel, Iechuiah, Ieiaiel, Ieiazel, Ieilel, Ielahiah, Ieliel, Ierathel, Ihiazel, Iibamiah, Imamiah, Jazeriel, Jeremiel, Johphiel, Jophiel, Judas Iscariot, Kavakiah, Kedemel, Kyriel, Lauiah, Lecabel, Lehachiah, Lelahel, Leuuiah, Leviah, Leviathan, Lucifer, Lycus, Magalesius, Mahazael, Malcha Betharsisim Hed Beruah Schehalim, Malchidiel, Mammon, Mebahel, Mebahiah, Mecheiel, Megera, Mehasiah, Melahel, Melchim, Menkiel, Meririm, Metatron, Michael, Mihael, Mikael, Mimon, Minos, Mizrael, Monadel, Mumiah, Muriel, Nachiel, Nanael, Neciel, Nelchael, Nemamiah, Nicon, Nimbroth, Nithael, Nithhaih, Omael, Ophaniel, Ophis, Oriens, Ormenus, Paymon, Pehaliah, Pluto, Poiel, Pytho, Raehel, Raphael, Rehael, Reiiel, Remma, Requiel, Rhadamancus, Samael, Satan, Schedbarschemoth Schartathan, Scheliel, Schii, Sealiah, Seehiah, Seraph, Serapis, Sitael, Sorath, Tagriel, Taphthartharath, Tharsis, Tiriel, Umahel, Uriel, Vasariah, Vehuel, Vehuiah, Verchiel, Vevaliah, Zadkiel, Zaphkiel, Zazel, Zuriel.

THE TEXT

Three Books of Occult Philosophy is arguably the most influential informational text in the grimoire tradition. It comprises three volumes: Natural Magic, Celestial Magic, and Ceremonial Magic, and drew heavily on works that were extant at the time. Agrippa sought to collect together as much information as he could, and this shows in the amount of quotes and information from Classical sources contained within the books. The importance of this work can be seen in the way material from it turns up in many subsequent grimoires and texts, both in whole chunks or incorporated into the text. Despite its size, this is a book which is worth reading through, as there is so much valuable material in the perspectives Agrippa presents and the heavy use of illustrative quotes from classical sources and the Bible.

---

253 Note that in this work alternative names are given for several of the angels. The alternative names are not listed here as they are the same beings, but they are listed in the chapter 'Spirit List'.

Book one comprises the introduction, which has letters between Agrippa and his teacher Trithemius, and seventy-four chapters. The chapters are: how magicians collect virtues from the three-fold world, is declared in these three books (1); what magic is, what are the parts thereof, and how the professors thereof must be qualified (2); of the four elements, their qualities, and mutual amalgamations (3); of a threefold consideration of the elements (4); of the wonderful natures of fire and earth (5); of the wonderful natures of water, air, and winds (6); of the kinds of compounds, what relation they stand in to the elements, and what relation there is between the elements themselves, and the soul, senses, and dispositions of men (7); how the elements are in the heavens, in stars, in devils, in angels, and lastly in God himself (8); of the virtue of things natural, depending immediately upon elements (9); of the occult virtues of things (10); how occult virtues are infused into the several kinds of things by ideas, through the help of the soul of the world and what things abound most with this virtue (11); how is it that particular virtues are infused into particular individuals, even of the same species (12); whence the occult virtue of things proceeds (13); of the spirit of the world, what it is, and how by way of a medium it unites occult virtues to their subjects (14); how me must find out and examine the virtues of things by way of similitude (15); how the operations of several virtues pass from one thing into another, and are communicated one to the other (16); how by enmity and friendship the virtues of things are to be tried and found out (17); of the inclinations of enmities (18); how the virtues of things are to be tried and found out, which are in them specifically, or in any one individual by way of special gift (19); that natural virtues are in some things throughout their whole substance, and in other things in certain parts or members (20); of the virtues of things which are in them only in their lifetime, and such as remain in them even after death (21); how inferior things are subjected to superior bodies, and how the bodies, the actions and dispositions of men are ascribed to stars and signs (22); how we shall know what stars natural things are under, and what things are under the Sun, which are called Solar (23); what things are Lunar, or under the power of the Moon (24); what things are Saturnine, or under the power of Saturn (25); what things are under the power of Jupiter, and are called Jovial (26); what things are under the powers of Mars, and are called Martial (27); what things are under the power of Venus, and are called Venereal (28); what things are under the power of Mercury, and are called Mercurial (29); that the whole sublunary world, and those things which are in it, are distributed to planets (30); how provinces and kingdoms are distributed to planets (31); what things are under the signs, the fixed stars, and their images (32); of the seals and characters of natural things (33); how by natural things and their virtues we may draw forth and attract influences and virtues of celestial bodies (34); of the blending of natural things, one with another, and their benefits (35); of the union of mixed things, and the introduction of a more noble form, and the senses of life (36); how by some certain natural, and artificial, preparations we may attract certain celestial and vital gifts (37); how we may draw not only celestial and vital, but also certain intellectual and divine gifts from above (38); that we may by some certain matters of the world, stir up the gods of the world and their ministering spirits (39); of bindings, what sort they are, and in what ways they are wont to be done (40); of sorceries, and their power (41); of the wonderful virtues of some kinds of sorceries (42); of perfumes, or suffumigations, their manner and power (43); the composition of some fumes appropriated to the planets (44); of collyries,[254] unctions, love medicines, and their virtues (45); of natural alligations and suspensions (46); of rings, and their compositions (47); of the virtue of places, and what places are suitable to every star (48); of light, colours, candles, and lamps, and to what stars, houses, and elements several colours are ascribed (49); of fascination, and the art thereof (50); of certain observations producing wonderful virtues

---

254 Preparations applied to the face similarly to make-up, but to enhance magical effects.

(51); of the countenance and gesture, the habit, and figure of the body, and to what stars any of these do answer, and of what physiognomy and metoposcopy,[255] and chiromancy, arts of divination, have their grounds (52); of divination and its kinds (53); of diverse certain animals, and other things which have a significance in auguries (54); how auspices are verified by the light of natural instinct, and of some rules of finding them out (55); of the soothsaying of flashes and lightning, and how monstrous and prodigious things are to be interpreted (56); of geomancy, hydromancy, aeromancy, pyromancy, four divinations of elements (57); of the reviving of the dead, and sleeping, and wanting victuals[256] many years together (58); of divination by dreams (59); of madness, and divinations which are made when men are awake, and of the power of a melancholy humor, by which spirits are sometimes induced into men's bodies (60); of the forming of man, of the external senses, and also the inward and the mind, of the threefold appetite of the soul, and passions of the will (61); of the passions of the mind, their origin, difference and kinds (62); how the passions of the mind change the proper body, by changing the accidents and moving the spirit (63); how the passions of the mind change the body by way of imitation from some resemblance, also of the transforming, and translating of men, and what force the imaginative power hath not only over the body, but the soul (64); how the passions of the mind can work out of themselves upon another's body (65); that the passions of the mind are helped by a celestial season, and how necessary the constancy of the mind is in every work (66); how man's mind may be joined with the minds and intelligences of the celestials, and together with them impress certain wonderful virtues upon inferior things (67); how our mind can change, and bind inferior things to that which it desires (68); of speech, and the virtue of words (69); of the virtue of proper names (70); of many words joined together, as in sentences and verses, and of the virtues and constrictions of charms (71); of the wonderful powers of enchantments (72); of the virtue of writing, and of making imprecations and inscriptions (73); of the proportion, correspondence, and reduction of letters to the celestial signs and planets, according to various tongues, and a table showing this (74).

Book two has sixty chapters, with a focus on celestial magic. The chapters are: of the necessity of mathematical learning, and of the many wonderful works which are done by mathematical arts only (1); of numbers, and their power, and virtue (2); what great virtues numbers have, as well in natural things as in supernatural (3); of Unity, and the scale thereof (4); of the number of two, and the scale thereof (5); of the number of three, and the scale thereof (6); of the number of four, and the scale thereof (7); of the number five, and the scale thereof (8); of the number six, and the scale thereof (9); of the number seven, and the scale thereof (10); of the number of eight, and the scale thereof (11); of the number of nine, and the scale thereof (12); of the number ten, and the scale thereof (13); of the number eleven and the number twelve, with a double scale of the number twelve, Cabalistic and Orphic (14); of the numbers which are above twelve, and of their powers and virtues (15); of certain notable numbers, placed in certain gestures (16); of the various notes of numbers observed amongst the Romans (17); of the notes or figures of the Greeks (18); of the notes of the Hebrews and Chaldeans, and certain other notes of magicians (19); what numbers are attributed to letters, and of divining by the same (20); what numbers are consecrated to the Gods, and which are ascribed to what elements (21); of the tables of the planets, their virtues, forms, and what divine names, intelligences, and spirits are set over them (22); of geometric figures and bodies, by what virtue they are powerful in magic, and which are agreeable to each element, and the heavens (23); of musical harmony, of the force and power thereof (24); of sound and harmony,

---

255 Divination based on forehead lines of a person.
256 Food or provisions.

and whence their wonderfulness in operation (25); concerning the agreement of them with the celestial bodies, and what harmony and sound is correspondent to every star (26); of the proportion, measure, and harmony of man's body (27); of the composition and harmony of the human soul (28); of the observation of celestials necessary in every magical work (29); when planets are of most powerful influence (30); of the observation of the fixed stars, and of their natures (31); of the Sun, and Moon, and their magical considerations (32); of the twenty-eight Mansions of the Moon, and their virtues (33); of the true motion of the heavenly bodies to be observed in the eighth sphere, and of the grounds of planetary hours (34); how some artificial things as images, seals, and such like may obtain some virtue from the celestial bodies (35); of the images of the zodiac, what virtues they, being engraved, receive from the stars (36); of the images of the faces, and of those images which are without the zodiac (37); of the images of Saturn (38); of the images of Jupiter (39); of the images of Mars (40); of the images of the Sun (41); of the images of Venus (42); of the images of Mercury (43); of the images of the Moon (44); of the images of the head and tail of the Dragon of the Moon (45); of the images of the Mansions of the Moon (46); of the images of the fixed Behenian stars (47); of geomantic figures, which are the middle between images and characters (48); of images, the figure whereof is not after the likeness of any celestial figure, but after the likeness of that which the mind of the worker desires (49); of certain celestial observations and the practice of some images (50); of characters which are made after the rule and imitation of the celestial, and how with the table thereof they are deduced out of geomantic figures (51); of characters which are drawn from things themselves by a certain likeness (52); that no divination without astrology is perfect (53); of lottery, when and whence the virtue of divining is incident to it (54); of the soul of the world, and of the celestials, according to the traditions of the poets and philosophers (55); the same is confirmed by reason (56); that the soul of the world and the celestial souls are rational and partake of divine understanding (57); of the names of the celestials, and their rule over the inferior world, viz. Man (58); of the seven governors of the world, the planets, and of their various names serving to magical speech (59); that human imprecations do naturally impress their powers upon external things, and how man's mind through each degree of dependency ascends into the intelligible world, and becomes like to the more sublime spirits and intelligences (60).

Book three has sixty-five chapters and focuses on ceremonial magic. The chapters are: of the necessity, power, and profit of Religion (1); of concealing of those things which are secret in religion (2); what dignification is required, that one may be a true magician and a worker of miracles (3); of the two helps of ceremonial magic, which are religion and superstition (4); of the three guides of religion, which bring us to the path of truth (5); how by these guides the soul of man ascends up into the divine nature, and is made a worker of miracles (6); that the knowledge of the true God is necessary for a magician, and what the old magicians and philosophers have thought concerning God (7); what the ancient philosophers have thought concerning the divine Trinity (8); what the true and most orthodox faith is concerning God and the most holy Trinity (9); of divine emanations, which the Hebrews call numerations, others attributes, and the gentiles gods and deities, and of the ten Sephiroth and ten most sacred names of God which rule them, and the interpretation of these (10); of the divine names, and their power and virtue (11); of the influence of the divine names through all the middle causes into these inferior things (12); of the members of God, and of their influence on our members (13); of the gods of the gentiles, and souls of the celestial bodies, and what places were consecrated in times past, and to what deities (14); what our theologians think concerning the celestial souls (15); of intelligences and spirits, and of the threefold kind of them, and of their diverse names, and of infernal and subterranean spirits (16); of these according to the opinion of the theologians (17); of the orders of evil spirits, and of their fall, and diverse natures (18); of the bodies of devils (19); of the annoyance of evil spirits, and the preservation we have by good spirits (20); of obeying a proper Genius, and of the searching out the nature thereof (21); that there is a threefold keeper of man, and from whence each of them proceed (22); of the tongue of angels, and of their speaking amongst themselves, and with us (23); of the names of spirits, and their various imposition; and of the spirits that are set over the stars, signs, corners of the heaven, and the elements (24); how the Hebrew Mekubbals[257] draw forth the sacred names of angels out of the sacred writ, and of the seventy-two angels, which bear the name of God with the tables of Ziruph, and the commutations of letters and numbers (25); of finding out of the names of spirits, and Genii from the disposition of celestial bodies (26); of the calculating art of such names by the tradition of Cabalists (27); how sometimes names of spirits are taken from those things over which they are set (28); of the characters and seals of spirits (29); another manner of making characters, delivered by Cabalists (30); there is yet another fashion of characters, and concerning marks of spirits which are received by revelation (31); how good spirits may be called up by us, and how evil spirits may be overcome by us (32); of the bonds of spirits, and of their adjurations, and castings out (33); of the animistic order, and the heroes (34); of the mortal and terrestrial gods (35); of man, how he was created after the image of God (36); of man's soul and through what means it is joined to the body (37); what divine gifts man receives from above, from the several orders of the intelligences and the heavens (38); how the superior influences, seeing they are good by nature, are depraved in these inferior things, and are made causes of evil (39); that on every man a divine character is imprinted, by the virtue of which man can attain the working of miracles (40); concerning man after death, diverse opinions (41); by what ways the magicians and necromancers do think they can call forth the souls of the dead (42); of the powers of man's soul, in the mind, reason, and imagination (43); of the degrees of souls, and their destruction or immortality (44); of soothsaying and frenzy (45); of the first kind of frenzy, from the Muses (46); of the second kind, from Dionysus (47); of the third kind of frenzy, from Apollo (48); of the fourth kind of frenzy, from Venus (49); of rapture, and ecstasy, and soothsaying, what happens to them which are taken with the falling sickness, or with a swoon or to them in an agony (50); of prophetic dreams (51); of lots and marks possessing the same power as oracles (52); how he that will receive oracles must dispose himself (53); of cleanness, and how it is to be observed (54); of abstinence, fasting, chastity, solitariness, the tranquillity, and ascent of the mind (55); of penitence and alms (56); of those things which being outwardly administered are conducive to expiation (57); of adorations and vows (58); of sacrifices and oblations, and their kinds and manners (59); what imprecations and rites the ancients were wont to use in sacrifices and oblations (60); how these things must be performed, as to God, so as to inferior deities (61); of consecrations and their manner (62); what things may be called holy, what consecrated, and how these become so between us and the deities and of sacred times (63); of certain religious observations, ceremonies, and rites of perfuming, unctions, and suchlike (64); the conclusion of the whole work. Following this is Agrippa's religiously pressured retraction, with sections discussing different types of magic. These are: of magic in general; of natural magic; of mathematical magic; of enchanting magic; of Goetia and necromancy; of theurgy; of Cabalah; and of juggling or legerdemain.

---

257 Old name for rabbis, specifically a rabbi who is highly conversant in Kabbalah.

Essential Reading

Agrippa, Cornelius & Compagni, V. Perrone (ed) (1992) *De Occulta Philosophia Libri Tres*. Leiden; New York: E.J. Brill. The critical Latin edition of the text.

Agrippa, Cornelius & Purdue, Eric (ed, trans) (2021) *Three Books of Occult Philosophy*. Rochester: Inner Traditions. Thorough and scholarly translation of the complete text with extensive notes. The most definitive edition to date.

Agrippa, Cornelius & Tyson, Donald (ed) (2009) *Three Books of Occult Philosophy*. Woodbury: Llewellyn. Good edition of the complete text with copious notes.

Cambridge Book of Magic

Date: 1532-1558.
Language: Latin with some English.
Influences: *Sworn Book of Honorius; Book of Angels, Rings and Characters of the Planets; Munich Handbook of Magic, Heptameron; Opera* of Arnald of Villanova.
Provenance: Attributed to Paul Foreman.
MSS: Cambridge Additional MS 3544.
Circle: Yes.
Tools: Chalk, crown, crystal, knife, mirror, needle, quill, ring, sword.
Spirit List: Abere, Abrodressim, Achibio, Acucabay, Albumasar, Alcall, Alheabesym, Amabiel, Amna, Anael, Anareton, Asasiel, Asmon, Astroth, Asya, Atybe, Balydethe, Barbaras, Barthan, Belial, Belzebub, Beryake, Bleth, Bonaham, Bonohan, Boytheon, Brith, Burada, Cadas, Camna, Capriel, Carmas, Cassiel, Castiel, Castrietur, Chamecayle, Clema, Daba, Daby, Daha, Dardiel, Dedya, Denskalion, Draco, Draganton, Drogancio, Ebenymydykyn, Egipcia, Egipia, Egrip, Elena, Eloy, Enoy, Eyma, Falebery, Farmane, Foros, Gabriel, Gerebay, Giron, Grasmen, Guel, Guth, Guthryn, Hany, Harthan, Hay, Huracapel, Hyhas, Iabedo, Iahanesym, Icamell, Jammas, Kamna, Kyem, Kyos, Lucifer, Maguth, Maheryon, Makyn, Manalaha, Manassa, Masex, Mathatau, Maymon, Mecallytape, Medya, Mee, Mekebin, Michael, Miel, Mumtuel, Mutuel, Mydisyn, Mylay, Namath, Niron, Oamna, Oha, Ohere, Omecalday, Onely, Oyeo, Palfcamyn, Rachiell, Raphael, Sachiel, Samael, Samuel, Saraphiell, Sarborr, Satael, Sathan, Sathiell, Satquiel, Savaa, Scapha, Spyryon, Stelpha, Sybilla, Sylberyolba, Theltrion, Tonther, Uriel, Yeasadis, Yesse, Yron, Zaylethe.

The Text

Although described as a Tudor necromancer's manual, the style and content of the material clearly appear to be that of a cunning man's book of practice. A lot of the material is copied from known earlier sources, and may also be found in later works.

The sections are: of bat's blood (1); the consecration of the characters (2); the consecration over parchment (3); of the construction of the circle (4); an experiment of Sybilla (5); an experiment to call the spirit Mosacus (6); general rule for the working of necromancy (7); the working with a crystal stone (8); to know of things you desire (9); to have a horse (10); a perfect experiment of a glass or mirror (11); that a thief may be bound to return with the thing stolen (12);[258] binding of the thief so that he should bring back immediately the thing stolen (13); to know which thing of yours has been stolen (14); of the crystal stone (15); to remove the guardians of the treasure (16); an experiment of a hoopoe (17); that someone may have an answer from an image (18); of the sunflower, for love (19); for love (20); for the same (21); for the same (22); that a woman should love her husband (23); that a woman should not conceive this year (24); that a woman should conceive (25); that men should sleep at the table (26); to make silver or gold writing (27); if you want to open wax seals (28); that women should follow you (29); for love (30); again for love (31); if you want always to have a penny in your purse (32); for love (33); for the love of a lord (34);[259] for toothache (35); for the same (36); for fevers (37); that no prison will hold you (38); to raise up harnessed men (39); for love (40); that

---

258 This experiment contains the earliest reference found so far to the four demon bishops, though interestingly they are not named as such here. They are still placed under the four kings of the directions as seen later, however.
259 Note that this charm uses the Sator square drawn with the blood of a white dove.

love should be in a man or woman (41); to raise up herbs (42); to know how deceivers work (43); that a woman sleeping with you should tell you what you want (44); that a stolen thing should return (45); if you want someone to sleep for as long as you want (46); that a silver penny should seem to be made of bronze (47); that women should dance in a house (48); that they should lift their skirts up high whilst dancing (49); for the same (50); for the same (51); that women should dance naked in a house (52); to take all manner of beasts on (53); for a thing which has been stolen (54); to win at dice (55); that someone should sleep well (56); that a woman should grant you whatever you wish (57); that a woman should follow you (58); the collection of the plant which is called valerian (59); that a woman should follow you (60); for love (61); a general sentence to be pronounced against rebellious spirits (62); if you want to see wonders (63); of the revenge of Troy (64); if you come before a king or judge (65); who desireth rightfully anything of God (66); this circle suffices with all spirits (67); that no prison will hold you (68); the most secret sign of Solomon (69); the figure of St. Michael (70); to know about those things you desire (71); the sigils of Master Arnold (72);[260] the experiments of the three knights (73); an experiment of Bleth (74); to make to come to thy bed or chamber (75); the sigil of the spirit Mekebin (76); the sigil of the spirit Namath (77); the characters of the planets (78); the sigil of the spirit Castrietur (79); for rebels or spirits which resist (80); if you want to have the spirit called Onely (81); invocation to invoke the spirit called Enoy (82); of the quill or instrument with which they are written (83); of the needle and another instrument of iron (84); of the vellum chart (85); of the quill and the colouring and the other colours and how the rubrics are to be performed (86); of the sheet of silk or linen (87); how the experiments of grace and the petitions should be prepared (88); of the writing of the characters (89); of wands and rods (90); of swords (91).

Essential Reading

Foreman, Paul & Young, Francis (trans) (2015) *The Cambridge Book of Magic*. Texts in Early Modern Magic: Cambridge. Excellent edition providing the entire text with valuable contextual material and useful footnotes.

---

260 From the *de Sigillis* section of Arnald of Villanova's *Opera*.

Galdrabók (Book of Magic)

Date: 1550-1650.
Language: Latin with Runic.
Influences: Mixture of Germanic, Christian, Greek, Jewish, and Gnostic material.
Provenance: The spells in the book were recorded by four unnamed scribes (three Icelandic and the last one Danish) over a period of one hundred and fifty years.
MSS: Sweden ATA ÄMB2.
Circle: N/A.
Tools: Materia magica, mostly with staves carved on them.
Spirit List: Baldur, Balthasar, Beelzebub, Birgur, Caspar, Freyja, Frigg, Fro, Gabriel, Gefjon, Gusta, Hoenir, Loki, Meloiorus, Michael, Njordhr, Odhinn, Raphael, Satan, Tyr, Uriel.

The Text

The *Galdrabók* demonstrates how widely the grimoire tradition spread in Europe. This Icelandic work is unique in the inclusion of Norse deities side by side with demons identified as deities, living in Valholl (Valhalla). The text of the *Galdrabók* comprises of forty-seven spells or charms, collected together in four batches by the four different scribes who recorded spells 1-10, 11-39, 40-44, and a latter part of 44-47. Many of the charms are spoken or written (some historiolae), and incorporate Latin phrases, divine names, spiritual creatures like archangels and demons mixed with Norse deities, as well as the use of bind-runes.[261] Considering Iceland became a Christian country officially at the Althing of 1000 CE, it is worth noting the presence of a number of the Norse gods and use of runes six to seven centuries later in magical works.

The spells are: A prayer for protection against all kinds of dangers (1); for protection against weariness and affliction (2); against trouble with childbearing (3); to staunch blood (4); against headache and insomnia (5); a spell against evil when some other incantations are a problem (6); against fainting or pestilence of livestock (7); to win a girl's love (8); to cause fear in an enemy (9); to get one's wish fulfilled (10); against the hate and poison of friends and enemies (11); against distress at sea, dangerous weapons, and sudden death (12); against harm from an enemy (13); against all kinds of suffering and danger (14); to win the love of a person (15); to cause fear in your enemies (16); to win the favour of powerful men (17); for protection against all kinds of evil (18); to cause fear (19); a washing verse (20); Byrnie prayer (21); days that bring bad luck (22); to be able to count up playing cards, which are face down (23); the 109th Psalm of David (24); a washing verse (25); for the wrath of mighty men (26); to play a joke on someone, so that he cannot hold his foot down the whole day long (27); an antidote for the previous enchantment (28); to hinder a person from coming to your home (29); to kill another's animal (30); against troll-shot (31); to put someone to sleep (32); to find out a thief (33); to bewitch a woman and win her love (34); to find out a thief (35); to find a thief (36); a way to get satisfaction in a legal case (37); for the protection of your horse (38); against troll-shot (39); to find out a thief (40); against wrath (41); against hate (42); to make a woman keep quiet (43); to find out a thief (44); another way to uncover a thief (45); fart runes (46); how can one get the helm of hiding (47).

---

261 A bind-rune is a combination of runes forming a meta-sigil thought to contain the appropriate forces of the different runes, essentially a runic reduction sigil.

Essential Reading

Flowers, Stephen E. (1989) *Galdrabók: An Icelandic Grimoire*. Llewellyn: Maine. Excellent study with whole text of the *Galdrabók* and other manuscripts (including the Huld and Kreddur manuscripts), including very good contextual material.

Le Livre des Esperitz

Date: Mid C16.
Language: French.
Influences: Possible Florence MS Plut. 89 sup. 38.
Provenance: Unknown.
MSS: Trinity College, Cambridge, MS 0.8.29, folios 179-182v.
Circle: N/A.
Tools: N/A.
Spirit Catalogue: Abugor, Agarat, Amon, Amoymon, Artis, Asmoday, Barbas, Barthas, Beal, Berteth, Bezlebut, Bitur, Bucal, Bugan, Bulfas, Bune, Caap, Carmola, Cerbere, Coap, Dam, Distolas, Diusion, Drap, Ducay, Equi, Fenix, Flavos, Forcas, Furfur, Gazon, Gemer, Gorsay, Lucifer, Lucubar, Machin, Malpharas, Orient, Oze, Parcas, Poymon, Salmatis, Samon, Satan, Tudiras, Hoho, Vaal, Vipos.

The Text

This volume is a parchment inserted in a bound collection of manuscripts in the library of Trinity College, Cambridge. This sixteenth-century French grimoire is essentially a spirit list that lists forty-seven/forty-eight spirits or demons, many for the first known time, and provides another step in the ongoing clarification of the provenance and development of the spirit lists used in some of the grimoires, particularly the *Goetia*.

The manuscript falls into the Solmonic tradition, as is made clear by the opening line, which reads 'Here begins the Book of Spirits, which was shown to Solomon the Wise to constrain the Spirits to the earth and make them obey the will of mankind.'

It is significant to note that after the preamble it firsts lists Lucifer, Belzebub, and Satan as the three main rulers of demons, i.e. the L:B:S trinity found in a number of works. Under these are listed the four demon kings or princes of the directions, also found with variations in a number of texts. The main spirit catalogue then follows.

Essential Reading

Boudet, Jean-Patrice (2003) *Les who's who démonologiques de la Renaissance et leurs ancêtres médiévaux*, in Médiévales 44.
Dimech, Alkistis & Grey, Peter (2019) *The Brazen Vessel*. London: Scarlet Imprint. Includes an English translation of the text, however this anthology is not a grimoire.

Sepher Shimmush Tehillim
(Book of the Magical Uses of the Psalms)

Date: 1551.
Language: Hebrew.
Influences: Jewish folk magic and scribal magic, *Book of Psalms*.
Provenance: The collection of the material dates back to at least C10 CE, with it being first published in 1551. Translated from Hebrew into German by Godfrey Selig in 1788. This was translated into English in the late C19 in America as *The Secrets of the Psalms* and spread through traditions like hoodoo and rootwork.
MSS: N/A.
Circle: N/A.
Tools: Materia Magica used with some of the charms.
Spirit List:[262] Chofniel, Mupiel, Schuwniel.

The Text

Sefer Shimush Tehillim grew from Jewish practices in late Antiquity and its influence can be seen in the Grimoire tradition in works like the *Book of Gold*, and its translation into German and then English. Charms are given for all one hundred and fifty of the Psalms found in the *Book of Psalms* in the *Bible*. The Kabbalah is mentioned at various times in the book, to an extent that it could be considered interwoven in the text.

The use of the forty-one divine names and important words from Psalm 91 in the form of a golden menorah with the *Vihi Noam* prayer is reminiscent of the *Sword of Moses*. This particular Psalm (the longest) has charms for each letter of the Hebrew alphabet. There are a number of themes in the charms presented, which number more than one hundred and fifty as some Psalms have more than one charm. These themes are: health and healing (35), protection from perils including at sea (34), overcoming enemies (24), goodwill (17), luck and prosperity (15), petitioning authority (14), overcoming sin or bad behaviour (13), protection in pregnancy and childbirth (9), exorcism (9), marital or family bliss (5), religious piety or overcoming heretics (3), detecting thieves or lost persons (2), visions (2), improving memory and intelligence (2), avoiding repeating mistakes (2). As can be seen the themes are those commonly found throughout the grimoires.

Essential Reading

Peterson, Joseph H. (ed, trans) (2008) *The Sixth and Seventh Books of Moses*. Fort Worth: Ibis Press. Peterson includes a translation of *Sepher Shimmush Tehillim* in this work.
Rebiger, Bill (ed) (2010) *Sefer Shimmush Tehillim: Buch vom magischen Gebrauch der Psalmen*. Tübingen: Mohr Siebeck. Academic edition with translation and commentary.

---

262 Divine Names are used with most of the charms.

Magia Naturalis (Natural Magic)

Date: 1558.
Language: Latin, Italian, French, Dutch, English.
Influences: Pliny the Elder, Theophrastus, other Greek philosophers.
Provenance: Written by the Italian scholar Giambattista della Porta (1535-1615) and published in Naples in 1558. More Latin editions quickly followed, with translations into Italian (1560), French (1565), Dutch (1566) and English (1658).
MSS: N/A.
Circle: N/A.
Tools: N/A.
Spirit List: N/A.

The Text

Although it is sometimes included in the grimoire tradition, *Magia Naturalis* is not a grimoire. It is perhaps more accurately a combination of early science and Book of Secrets material (contemporary charms are referred to in the text). Della Porta argues that magic is part of philosophy, and the wisdom of natural magic is part of that discipline, studied by the wise. The value of this book lies in the discussion of scientific material found in it, such as the book on magnetism, and work on the camera obscura. It is worth noting that later editions of the book included a witch's ointment.[263]

The text is divided into twenty books. These are: of the causes of wonderful things; of the generation of animals; of the production of new plants; of increasing household stuff; of changing metals; of counterfeiting gold; of the wonders of the lodestone; of strange cures; of beautifying women; of distillation; of perfuming; of artificial fires; of tempering steel; of cookery; of fishing, fowling, hunting, etc.; of invisible writing; of strange glasses; of static experiments; of pneumatic experiments; of the chaos.

Essential Reading

This book is easily available online for those interested.

---

263 A salve including psychoactive herbs which induces visions. Also known as flying ointment due to the belief it enabled spirit flight.

Fourth Book of Occult Philosophy

Date: 1559.
Language: Latin, English.
Influences: *Sworn Book of Honorius*, *Three Books of Occult Philosophy*.
Provenance: Although attributed to Cornelius Agrippa, it is more likely it was written by the French Paracelsian Jacques Gohory (1520-76). First published by Malpurgi in 1559 (Latin). Robert Turner translated it into English in 1665.
MSS: None, Published work.
Circle: Yes (in the *Heptameron*).
Tools: Discussed in *Of Occult Philosophy or Of Magical Ceremonies*.
Spirit List: Not included as the *Heptameron* and *Arbatel* have their own subchapters. Spirits mentioned in the *Isagoge* are done in a discursive way, so it is not a spirit list.

The Text

The *Fourth Book of Occult Philosophy* is a combination of six texts, some of which are attributed to Cornelius Agrippa. The texts are: *Of Geomancy*; *Of Occult Philosophy or Of Magical Ceremonies*; the *Heptameron* of Peter of Abano (discussed in its own chapter); *Isagoge: an Introductory Discourse of the nature of such Spirits as are exercised in the Sublunary Bounds* by Geo Pictorius Villinganus; Gerard Cremonensis *Of Astrological Geomancy*. It is an extremely important text providing lucid descriptions of systems and practices in the grimoires. The translation by Robert Turner made this information available in English, from where it would influence a number of later texts and also cunning practices.

Of Geomancy gives a complete description of the practice of geomancy. The *Heptameron* provides a complete system of practice of planetary angelic magic. *Of Occult Philosophy or Of Magical Ceremonies* is allegedly written by Agrippa (probably spuriously) and the material follows on very well from the *Heptameron*. It discusses the creation of good and evil spirit names based on astrological houses and gives lists of simple symbols which may be used in glyphs for spirits. The section then describes the common shapes taken by spirits for each of the classical planets; the construction of pentacles; discussion of the consecrations of the tools and place; discussion of the book of spirits; preparation of the place and the practitioner; how to act in the magic circle; discussion of working with the dead. This final part is highly significant, as it provides more lucid discourse on working with the dead than is seen elsewhere in the grimoires.

The *Isagoge* is in the form of a dialogue between Castor and Pollux. The subtitle, *'their original names, offices, illusions, power, prophecies, miracles, and how they may be expelled and driven away'*, qualifies the nature of the dialogue. The discussion considers the nature of daemons, demons, gods, and spirits, referring to classical authors and saints to illustrate the arguments. *Of Astronomical Geomancy* combines geomancy with astrology to provide an expansion of normal geomancy, with questions attributed to each of the twelve houses. The *Arbatel of Magick* is an extremely important ethical work which includes the Olympic Spirits, and also has its own subchapter.

ENCYCLOPAEDIC ENTRIES

Essential Reading

Agrippa, H.C. & Skinner, Stephen (ed) (1978) *The Fourth Book of Occult Philosophy*. London: Askin Publishers. Excellent edition of this extremely important work with commentary.

Turner, Robert & Tyson, Donald (2009) *Fourth Book of Occult Philosophy: The Companion to Three Book of Occult Philosophy Written by Henry Cornelius Agrippa of Nettesheim*. Woodbury: Llewellyn. Very good edition with extensive commentary.

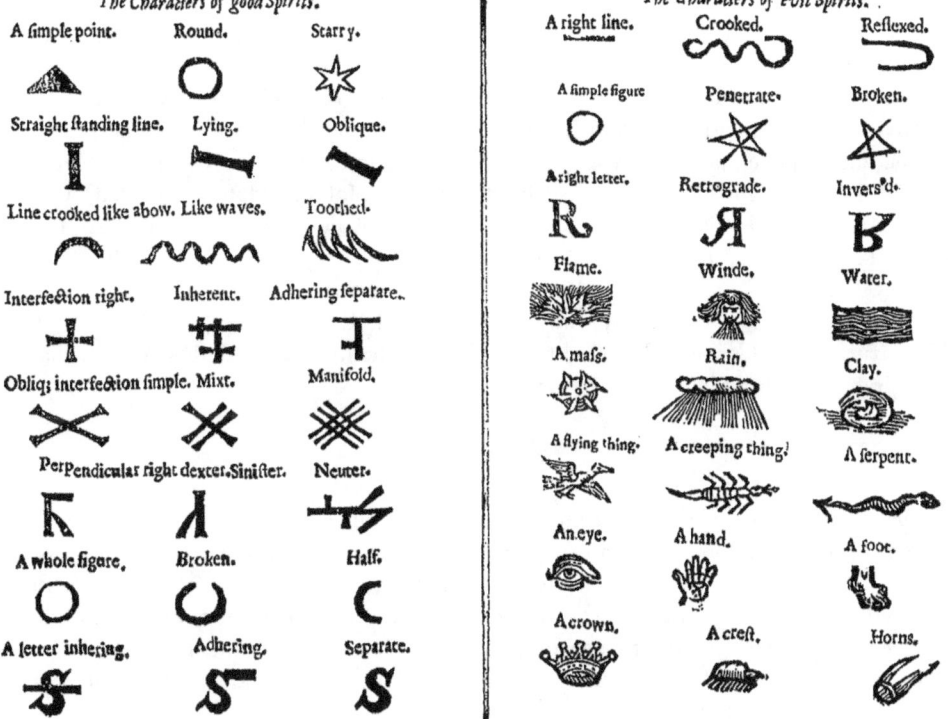

Fourth Book of Occult Philosophy, Characters of Good Spirits and Evil Spirits

Heptameron (Magical Elements)

Date: 1559.
Language: Latin, French, English, German, Italian, Welsh.
Influences: *De Quatuor Annulis, Astromagia, Elucidation of Necromancy, Sworn Book of Honorius, Sepher Raziel, Key of Solomon, Liber Semiphoras.*
Provenance: Attributed to Peter of Abano (1250-1316), probably due to its development from *Elucidation of Necromancy*. Published in Agrippa's *Fourth Book of Occult Philosophy* (which also includes the *Arbatel*) in 1559. Published in French in 1565, and German in 1567. Translated from Latin into English by Robert Turner in 1655. A Welsh work including the *Heptameron* was published in 1830. Additional MS 36674 includes material copied by Dr. John Caius (1510-1573), founder of Caius College, including parts of Agrippa's *De Occulta Philosophia* and the *Heptameron*. UPenn Codex 226 was owned by John Denley.
MSS: Additional MS 36674 (c, 1570, English), Wellcome MS 110 (late C16, Latin), Harley MS 2267 (1600, English), Munich CLM 24936 (1602, Latin), Sloane MS 3824 (1649, English), Bodleian Douce MS 116 (C17, English), Sloane MS 3318 (C17, Italian), Sloane MS 3850 (C17, Latin/English), Vienna MS Lat 11294 (C17, Latin), Pad Cod 235 (1651-1700, Italian), BNF MSS 2792, 24245 (C18, French), BNF MS 17870 (C18, French), UPenn Codex 226 (C18, English).
Circle: Yes.
Tools: Earthen vessel (fire), pentacle, robe, sword.
Spirit List: Aba, Abalidoth, Abuiori, Abumalith, Abuzaha, Acimoy, Africus, Aiel, Amabael, Amabiel, Amatiel, Anael, Anayl, Andas, Aniel, Arcan, Arragon, Asasiel, Assaibi, Astagna, Atel, Auster, Babel, Babiel, Bachanael, Baciel, Balay, Balidet, Baliel, Baraborat, Bilet, Boel, Boreas, Burchat, Caluel, Calzas, Capabili, Caphrael, Caracasa, Cassiel, Castiel, Charsiel, Chedusitaniel, Chermiel, Commissoros, Coniel, Corabael, Corat, Core, Ctarari, Curaniel, Cynabal, Dabriel, Dagiel, Damael, Dardiel, Darmax, Darquiel, Deamiel, Doremiel, Famiel, Flaef, Fraciel, Friagne, Gabrael, Gabriel, Galdel, Gargatel, Gaviel, Guabarel, Guael, Gutrix, Habaiel, Haludiel, Hanun, Humastrau, Huphaltiel, Huratapal, Hyniel, Irel, Isiael, Ismoli, Janael, Janiel, Jariahel, Jazel, Jeresous, Kadie, Lama, Lobquin, Machasiel, Machatan, Madiel, Mael, Maguth, Maltiel, Masgabriel, Mathiel, Mathlai, Matuyel, Mediat, Michael, Miel, Milliel, Missabu, Mitraton, Naromiel, Nelapa, Orphaiel, Osael, Pabel, Paffran, Pemael, Penat, Peniel, Porna, Rachiel, Rael, Rahumel, Raniel, Raphael, Rayel, Sachiel, Sacriel, Sallales, Samael, Samax, Santanael, Sapiel, Sarabotes, Satael, Seraphiel, Setchiel, Soncas, Subsolanus, Suceratos, Suquinos, Suth, Tamael, Tariel, Tarmiel, Tatquam, Tenaciel, Tetra, Thiel, Turiel, Tus, Ucirnuel, Uriel, Ustael, Valnum, Varcan, Velel, Venahel, Vetuel, Vianuel, Vionairaba, Vuael, Zaliel, Zaniel, Zephyrus.

The Text

The *Heptameron* is one of the key grimoire texts, whose influence is found in many subsequent works. It provides a concise system of planetary angelic magic, influenced by earlier works and coalesced into a very workable system. The authorship by Peter of Abano has been disputed, but with the *Elucidation of Necromancy* urtext attributed to him, and given that the *Heptameron* is a development of this work, the attribution is understandable. The *Heptameron* takes material from the former work and reorganises it into a more coherent format, and also sanitises aerial spirits to angels.

The chapters are: of the circle and the composition thereof; of the names of the hours and the angels ruling them; of the four seasons of the year and their angels; the consecrations and benedictions, and first of the benediction of the circle; the benediction of perfumes; the exorcism of the fire upon which the perfumes are to be put; of the garment and pentacle; an oration to be said when the vesture is put on; of the manner of working; an exorcism of the spirits of the Air; a prayer to God, to be said in the four parts of the world, in the circle; visions and apparition; the arrival and welcoming of the spirits; licensing them to depart; considerations of the Lord's day; the conjuration of the Lord's day; considerations of Monday; the conjuration of Monday; considerations of Tuesday; the conjuration of Tuesday; considerations of Wednesday; the conjuration of Wednesday; considerations of Thursday; the conjuration of Thursday; considerations of Friday; the conjuration of Friday; considerations of Saturday; the conjuration of Saturday; tales of the angels of the hours, according to the course of the days.

Essential Reading

Peterson, Joseph H. (ed, trans) (2021) *Elucidation of Necromancy*. Fort Worth: Ibis Press. Excellent must-read work giving the different versions of the text and showing its development and influences, including a new translation of the *Heptameron*.

Tyson, Donald (ed) (2018) *The Fourth Book of Occult Philosophy*. Woodbury: Llewellyn. Good edition of this classic work which includes several important texts including the *Heptameron*.

Lisiewski, Joseph C. (2009) *Ceremonial Magic & the Power of Evocation*. Tempe: Original Falcon. Serious practical work focusing on working with the *Heptameron*.

Stephen Skinner (ed) (1978) *The Fourth Book of Occult Philosophy*. London: Askin Press. Lovely edition of the text with commentary written before the current grimoire revival.

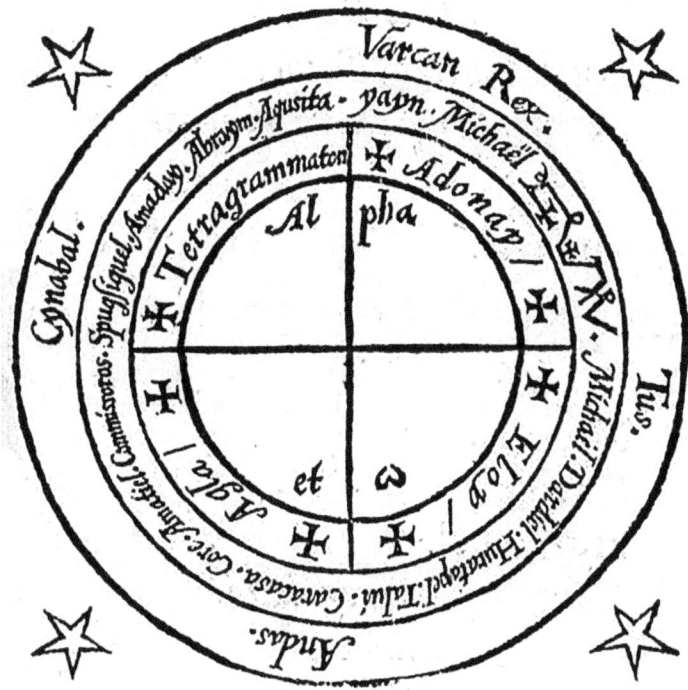

Heptameron, Magic Circle for Sunday, First Hour in Springtime

The Arbatel (Arbatel de Magia Veterum)

Date: 1559.
Language: Latin, English, German.
Influences: Paracelsus, *Three Books of Occult Philosophy*.
Provenance: Possibly written by Jacques Gohory (1520-1576).[264]
MSS: Printed in 1559 in the *Fourth Book of Occult Philosophy*; 1575 in Basel, Switzerland; in English in Sloane 3851, circa 1630-6; translated and printed by Robert Turner in 1655; small section in English in Sloane 3850, dated 1739 on front but earlier;[265] translated and printed in German by Johann Scheible in *Das Kloster*, 1845-49.
Circle: N/A.
Tools: N/A.
Spirit List: Aratron, Bethor, Hagith, Och, Ophiel, Phaleg, Phul.

The Text

The *Arbatel* begins with a list of nine works, of which it is the first. The other eight have never been found, and likely were never written. The text comprises forty-nine aphorisms, divided into seven septenaries. The aphorisms are largely concerned with instructions on living a virtuous and pious life as the key to magical success. The importance of virtue in the magician and the detailed discussion of this theme makes the *Arbatel* an extremely important work, and one worthy of study at the beginning of the path of grimoire practice. It is noteworthy that there are a lot of Biblical quotes used to illustrate points made throughout the text.

Aphorisms 16-21 introduce the seven Olympic Spirits, giving their names, seals, qualities, and their conjuration. A discussion of the different types of secrets follows, leading to the Seal of secrets in aphorism 27. The method of construction of this is given, with instruction on its use as a device for petitioning the angels. The text returns to discussion of good practice, leading a good life, and the theology of magical practice.

The first known mention of the Olympic Spirits is in the works of Paracelsus (1493-1541). He discusses them in his *Liber sextus archidoxis magicae de compositione metallorum* (*Archidoxes of Magic*) and the treatise *De causis morborum invisibilium* (*On the invisible diseases*), which explored possession and mental illness. It is worth noting that the Olympic Spirits are described as being formed from all four of the elements combined (air, fire, water, and earth), rather than the more common view of spirits like angels and demons being made of air or fire.

The text also refers to the 'Biblical Three' archangels, Michael, Gabriel and Raphael, and the idea of spirit hierarchies. The difference between good (calodaemons) and evil (cacodaemons) is also discussed, recalling Neo-Platonic writings (which the author was clearly familiar with). Another recurring theme is repeated references to familiar spirits, in the sense of spirits who work consistently with the magician, rather than necessarily the witchcraft perception of familiar spirits.

Another interesting type of spirit discussed in the *Arbatel* in a way which demonstrates a Paracelsian influence is elemental spirits. The 1566 work *Ex Libro de Nymphis, Sylvanis, Pygmaeis, Salmandris & Gigantibus, etc.* (*On Nymphs, Sylphs, Pygmies and Salamanders, and on the Other Spirits*) discusses the different type of elemental beings in detail. Beings discussed in that work and

---

264 See Peterson (2009:xiv-xvi).
265 The date of 1739/40 is from the sale of the collection of Sir Joseph Jekyll on his death, so the actual date is unknown.

ENCYCLOPAEDIC ENTRIES

found in the *Arbatel* include pygmies and gnomes, nymphs, dryads, sylphs, and sagani.[266]

The *Arbatel* being found in the cunning-man Arthur Gauntlet's book of practice is interesting, as it pre-dates Robert Turner's English edition of the *Arbatel*, indicating that a translated copy of the *Arbatel* was available to Gauntlet, or that he translated it. His edition is significant as it is the only one which contains the drawing of the seal of secrets, not found in any of the printed editions.[267]

Essential Reading

Joseph H. Peterson (ed, trans) (2009) *Arbatel – Concerning the Magic of the Ancients*. Fort Worth: Ibis Press. The definitive work on the *Arbatel*, covered with Peterson's usual scholarly excellence.

Rankine, David (ed) (2011) *The Grimoire of Arthur Gauntlet*. London: Avalonia. Complete transcription of Sloane MS 3851, which has much interesting material, including the *Arbatel* with the only known example of the Seal of Secrets drawn in.

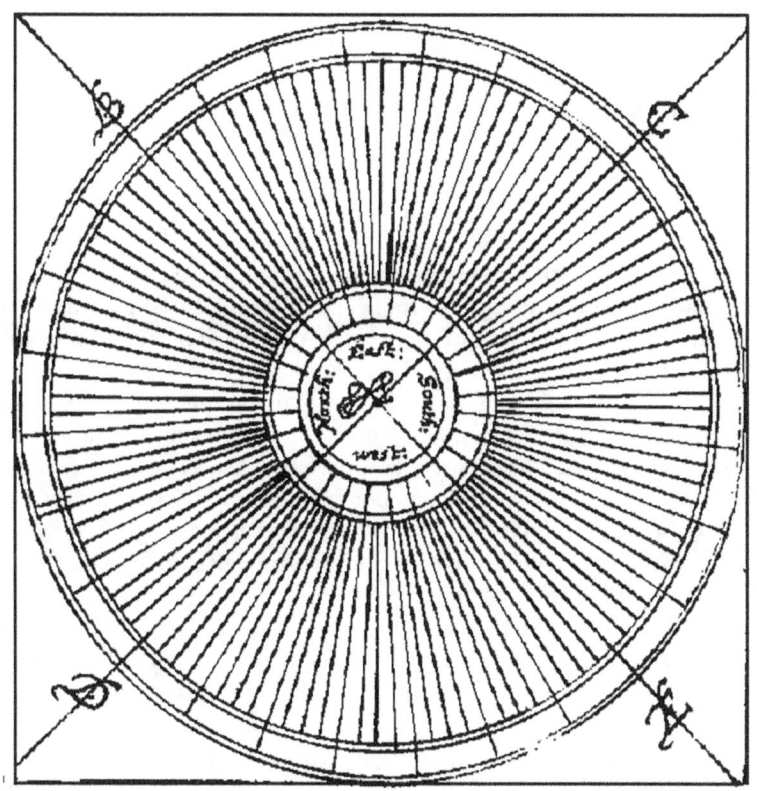

Arbatel, Seal of Secrets

---

266 A 'sagani' is another type of elemental spirit.
267 See Rankine (2011) *The Grimoire of Arthur Gauntlet*.

Secrets of Solomon (Clavicula Salomonis de Secretis)

Date: 1559-1630, possibly earlier.
Language: Latin.
Influences: *Sworn Book of Honorius, Elucidation of Necromancy, Heptameron, Key of Solomon, Three Books of Occult Philosophy*.
Provenance: Uncertain author, manuscripts spread from Venice, possibly written by Francesco Viola, a Dominican monk.
MSS: Venice ASV b.93 (1630), Warsaw MS Rps 3352 II (c17), Dresden SLUB N.91 (late C17), partial in Leipzig Cod. Mag. 136 (1700), some material in Wellcome MS 903 (1709), Toronto GG B134 bound with *Key of Solomon* (1720),[268] Wellcome MS 4667 (mid C18), partial in BNF Lat. 18511 (C18), Warsaw MS Rps 6698 II (1758-1800) (Polish & Latin).
Circle: Yes.
Tools: Bloodstone, lamp, pentacle, robe, sword, wands.
Spirit List: Abumalith, Agaleraptarkimath, Agiaton, Aiel, Amabiel, Anael, Anayl, Araton, Assaibi, Assasiel, Begud, Belzebub, Beschard, Capabali, Cassiel, Castiel, Charariel, Claunth, Dadriel, Doromiel, Elelogaphatel, Elestor, Fabriel, Frimodth, Frulthiel, Fruthmerl, Ftheruthi, Gabriel, Galand, Galdel, Glithrel, Gog Magog, Guadoliel, Gutriel, Hael, Hepath, Heramael, Humeth, Hurchetmigarot, Ianael, Iarihael, Iaxel, Irmasliel, Klepoth, Klio, Lucifer, Madiel, Maganth, Magriel, Masgrabiel, Menail, Merfiel, Michael, Miel, Mustalfiel, Orifiel, Pamechiel, Pantheriel, Periel, Pomeriel, Rabidmadar, Raphael, Resbiroth, Reschin, Ruduel, Sabriel, Sachiel, Sagum, Salkariel, Samael, Sapiel, Satanachi, Segol, Sergulaf, Sergurth, Serphgathana, Sidrigol, Sigambach, Sirkael, Suffugruel, Surgath, Syrach, Tainor, Tamael, Tumael, Turmiel, Uchariel, Uriel, Ustael, Vetael, Vianuel, Zatael, [Aglasis, Brurlefer, Bucon, Hariston, Minotous, Pantagnon, Poculo, Sidragosum,].[269]

The Text

Joseph Peterson describes the book extremely eloquently in the introduction to his edition, 'This text is remarkable in many ways. To some extent it bridges the gaps between folklore, witch trial records, and practical and theoretic magic. Likewise it fills a gap between medieval magic and Wicca. It relies on developing a close relationship with the spirits.'[270]

The introduction from Solomon to his children is significant. Unlike the *Key of Solomon*, where the introduction is from Solomon only to his son Rehoboam, this introduction is also directed at his two daughters. This sets the flavour of the manuscript, where the material is directed at women and men, a rare phenomenon in grimoires. The references in prayers to the 'Most High Governess' with God are interesting, and Peterson argues convincingly these could refer to the goddess Amalthea.[271] Other interesting practices in this work are the singing of charms, and musical accompaniment.

The text specifies the first part is secrets and the second part pentacles. It then describes the character to be created using the practitioner's blood, preferably on a red jasper or bloodstone, for use in the rituals. The practitioner's initials are incorporated into the character.

---

268 The presence of this work in the library of Gerald Gardner leads to speculation as to its possible influence on Wicca, especially as it was bound with a *Key of Solomon* which heavily influenced the tradition. Now in the private collection of Richard and Tamara James.
269 These names are only found in Wellcome MS 983, and subsequently in the *Grimorium Verum*.
270 Peterson, 2018:ii.
271 Peterson, 2018:ii.

Men are told to carry it in their right pocket, and women in the left pocket or between the breasts. A discourse concerning the spirits follows, which emphasises the need to make a pact to gain service from the spirits. It also includes a spirit list and hierarchy. The general forms the spirits take are given, along with descriptions of the ruling three of Lucifer, Belzebub, and Elestor. The seals are also given. There is an interesting note that terrestrial spirits can be seen visibly, but aerial ones are invisible and not as effective, though they can be carried in a ring.

The next section is concerning the secrets, and the charms are: to make it rain; to make it snow; to cause lightning; in order to not be cold; to not be bothered by excessive heat; a wonderful secret for opening all closed things; to win over the love of a young woman; to have coins as often as we please; in order that an enemy will die; to become invisible; to hear the sweetest music; in order that a corpse appear living and able to speak.

The second book, concerning the Pentacles, or Apparitions, follows. Chapters are: concerning the fundamentals of the Art; those things which are to be observed when working in the Art (includes discussion of the Amalthai spirits and the thirteen Intelligences); the power of the superior Intelligences; how we obtain the preceding knowledge, arts, and secrets from the Intelligences; concerning those things which are necessary for invocations and conjurations of the daemons; concerning the circle; concerning the pentacle; concerning the sword; concerning the consecrated water; concerning the garment; concerning the fire and incenses; concerning blood and ink; concerning virgin paper; concerning the place and time; concerning the invocations and conjurations of spirits (includes the preparatory work); concerning the experiments; concerning the pentacles of Orifiel;[272] the pentacles of Magriel; the pentacles of Pamechiel; the pentacles of Pomeriel; the pentacles of Sabriel; the pentacles of Uchariel; the pentacles of Charariel; the pentacles of Pantheriel; the pentacles of Araton; the pentacles of Agiaton; the pentacles of Begud; the pentacles of Tainor.

Book three describes itself as a compendium of the previous knowledge, and goes into a detailed discussion on spirits and their nature. There are sections on the names of the intelligences of the sun and Moon; concerning the Intelligence of the Sun, Michael;[273] concerning the Intelligence of the Moon, Gabriel; concerning the Intelligence of Mars, Samael; concerning the Intelligence of Mercury, Raphael; concerning the Intelligence of Jupiter, Sachiel; concerning the Intelligence of Venus, Anael; concerning the Intelligence of Saturn, Cassiel; concerning the intermediate spirits or the officers of the highest; the Solar Spirits; the Lunar Spirits; the Martial Spirits; the Mercurial Spirits; the Jupiterian Spirits; the Saturnian Spirits; concerning the Stone; concerning the preparation of the stone; concerning the purification of the stone; concerning the consecration of the stone; the baptism of the stone; the practice and procedure of consecration; and first concerning the Pentacle (includes ideas for their creation and also covers consecration.

Essential Reading

Peterson, Joseph H. (ed, trans) (2018) *Secrets of Solomon*. Kasson: Twilit Grotto Press. As always, an excellent work of scholarship presenting the text with much contextual information and introduction.

---

272 Note: the text refers to the following pentacles as being drawn on parchment.
273 The archangels are here referred to as Intelligences.

Pseudomonarchia Daemonum (False Monarchy of Demons)

Date: 1563.
Language: Latin, translated into English, French, and German.
Influences: *Book of the Offices of Spirits*, possibly *Livre des Esperitiz* and MS Plut. 89 sup. 38.
Provenance: Recorded by Johann Weyer as an appendix to his work *De Praestigiis Daemonum* (On the tricks of demons) (1563).
MSS: Published in Basel, Switzerland in 1563. Reginald Scot included the English translation in *Discoverie of Witchcraft* (1584).
Circle: N/A.
Tools: N/A.
Spirit Catalogue: Abalam, Agares, Allocer, Amaymon, Amduscias, Amon, Amy, Andras, Andrealphus, Astaroth, Aym, Baell, Balam, Barbatos, Bathin, Beball, Beliall, Berith, Bifrons, Bileth, Botis, Buer, Bune, Caim, Cimeries, Decarabia, Eligor, Flaures, Focalor, Forneus, Furcas, Furfur, Gaap, Gamigin, Glasya Labolas, Goap, Gomory, Gorson, Gusoin, Haagenti, Halphas, Ipos, Leraie, Lucifer, Malphas, Marbas, Marchosias, Morax, Murmur, Naberius, Orias, Orobas, Ose, Paimon, Phoenix, Procell, Pruflas, Purson, Raum, Ronove, Sabnocke, Saleos, Shax, Sidonay, Sitri, Stolas, Valac, Valefor, Vapula, Vepar, Vine, Vuall, Zagan, Zepar, Zimimar.

The Text

Johann Weyer (1515-88) was a student of Agrippa, giving him access to the magical teachings of not only Agrippa, but also his teacher Trithemius. As a magician who studied medicine and psychiatry, he had a rare and invaluable perspective on the magic of the time. His work *De Praestigiis Daemonum* was a rebuttal of the brutally barbaric witch-hunting manual, *Malleus Maleficarum*. Weyer argued in defence of accused witches, postulating psychological issues like delusion and mental illness rather than the reality of their experience. This approach led to Sigmund Freud calling his book one of the ten most important of all time.

Weyer admitted in the book that he had omitted material and made *Pseudomonarchia Daemonum* unworkable, but its value is still seen in its clear place as a bridge between earlier spirit catalogues and the *Goetia*, which is near identical in the list of demons presented (giving sixty-eight of the seventy-two found in the latter work).

The text itself is a spirit catalogue of sixty-nine demons, with several others being mentioned. It is preceded by an introduction explaining the folly [*sic*] of working with such spirits. After the spirit catalogue, a list of the times of day for conjurations of the spirits depending on their rank is given. The following chapter gives conjurations before exclaiming how profane and wrong such work is!

Essential Reading

Peterson, Joseph H. (2001) *The Lesser Key of Solomon: Lemegeton Clavicula Salomonis*. Maine, Weiser Books. An excellent book exploring the history of the *Goetia*, which also provides the text of *Pseudomonarchia Daemonium* and comparisons of the spirits in it and the *Goetia*.

Stratton-Kent, Jake (2016) *Pandemonium: A Discordant Concordance of Diverse Spirit Catalogues*. West Yorkshire, Hadean Press. Fascinating study exploring the development of spirit catalogues and lists, focusing particularly on that of the *Goetia*, hence with attention given to the development from *Pseudomonarchia Daemonum*.

An Excellent Booke of the Arte of Magicke

Date: 1567.
Language: English.
Influences: *Ars Notoria, Key of Solomon*.
Provenance: Work recorded by Humphrey Gilbert and John Davis. Owned by Gabriel Harvey (1545-1630).
MSS: Additional MS 36674.
Circle: Implied but not mentioned.
Tools: Inks, ring, stone (crystal).
Spirit List: Ægin, Amaimon, Aosal, Assasel, Bleathe, Oriens, Paymon.

The Text

The text is in two sections, the *Excellent Booke* and *Visions*, the latter being a diary of the operations of Gilbert and Davis. This is valuable as a diary of practice and the vision experiences of magicians performing conjurations. The lack of paraphernalia suggests the practitioners were only including details pertinent to the practices without including known information from other sources.

The *Excellent Booke* starts by listing seven different coloured inks required and the need for plenty of sweet powders and perfumes. The spirit Bleathe is recommended for a young beginner to call, and Assasel mentioned with his character. A prayer for dealing with spirits is then given, which is claimed to have been revealed to them by Solomon. The book proper then contains: instructions for behaviour and cleanliness; conjuration of Assasel; conjuration of Oriens; Assasel's call with curse and bond; Aosal's call, curse and bond; the summoning of Oriens and all four kings, curse, bond, and license to depart; general call for all spirits into the stone, general malediction, general bond, general license to depart; the call to make an invisible spirit in a crystal visible in another crystal, curse, deprivation, bond, and names of god written in the stone.

The second part, *Visions*, records the visions seen in the crystal during the operations performed by Gilbert and Davis between 24th February and 6th April 1567. The visions include biblical figures, famous magicians, spirits, creatures, and angels.

Essential Reading

Legard, Phil & Cummins, Alexander (eds) (2020) *An Excellent Booke of the Arte of Magicke*. London: Scarlet Imprint. Excellent edition with much useful contextual information and manuscript copy. Also includes comparative material from several other manuscripts, including an appendix from Illinois MS 0102 (1590) *Crafte of conjureynge and howe to rule the ffierye spiritts of ye planetts & make the devyle appearre* (see subchapter on this grimoire).

The Secret of Secrets (A Cunning Man's Grimoire)

Date: c.1557 with later additions.
Language: English.
Influences: *Annulorum Experimenta, Book of the Seven Rings of the Planets, De Septem Secundeis, Three Books of Occult Philosophy, Heptameron, Sepher Raziel.*
Provenance: May have been written by the magician Thomas Allen (1540-1632), subsequently owned by the conjuror Cornelius of Oxford, cunning man Moses Long, and antiquarian Thomas Hearne (1678-1735).
MSS: Rawlinson MS D.253.
Circle: Yes.
Tools: Black-handled knife, crystal, linen clothes, pentacle, sword, white-handled knife.
Spirit List: Abanixtra, Abdelvam, Abdizuel, Abibo, Abrinael, Acarax, Acia, Acrabiel, Adariat, Admel, Adriel, Advachiel, Advolita, Adzyriel, Æbedel, Alheniel, Alibeat, Amabael, Amabiel, Aman, Amatiel, Ambriel, Amixiel, Amnieiel, Amradiel, Amrrehar, Amutiel, Anacor, Anael, Analos, Anaya, Ancason, Ancor, Antatax, Araton, Ariel, Arnotho, Artus, Asasiel, Asdon, Askariell, Asmodiel, Asqueucon, Ataliel, Avdefiel, Azariel, Azeruel, Aziel, Azvg, Azzial, Banros, Baralama, Barbiel, Barchiel, Bario, Bayag, Beabo, Beandinet, Benkurfsioth, Benyt, Bersada, Bethnael, Betradandi, Betuliel, Birto, Booth, Caisaac, Calatyne, Calilut, Camael, Cambiel, Camelion, Canempria, Caracasa, Carior, Cassiel, Castiel, Casyel, Cauda, Centony, Cherub, Chesetiel, Cliody, Cochabiah, Commissoros, Core, Coriet, Coringer, Ctarari, Dagymiel, Daliarimerat, Dardiel, Davmilbe, Deliel, Dirachiel, Durus, Eanche, Eazsail, Egibiel, Eianliarug, Enediel, Ereleri, Ergediel, Facygrat, Fastarin, Fermagon, Fimiritis, Fortunelich, Fracaday, Gabiel, Gabriel, Gargatel, Gediel, Geliel, Geniel, Georim, Giaray, Gribery, Gualbarel, Guariel, Guesupale, Hamaliel, Hamistradany, Haniel, Hara, Hegur, Hunambilich, Husebreth, Iareahel, Jazeriel, Jophiel, Joviel, Kyriel, Lascra, Lunael, Luneyl, Machatiel, Madimiel, Malchidael, Manopall, Maqua, Martiel, Masniel, Mathapart, Meraitron/Metatron, Mercuriel, Michael, Miel, Missitone, Missyron, Morifiel, Mortatalio, Muratapel, Muriel, Naith, Nares, Nastiafori, Necamya, Neciel, Nogahel, Nyssan, Obtablat, Oriel, Orifiell, Origo, Osturcios, Paltisur, Pasita, Pathmisici, Peliel, Perdagaman, Pergor, Pharap, Philomens, Pomael, Qanor, Qerminat, Quivan, Rachiel, Raphael, Raziel, Requiel, Robica, Rupasta, Sabathiel, Sachiel, Sadael, Samael, Saraphiel, Satael, Sattamiel, Saturniel, Scheliel, Semeliel, Semquiel, Sephatya, Seraiph, Serviel, Seveviel, Soliah, Sornadafs, Sugin, Suriel, Tagriel, Tariel, Tarquam, Teletiel, Termat, Tharsies, Theall, Thomiel, Urasian, Urcifery, Uriel, Ustay, Veneriel, Verchiel, Yariel, Yaziel, Yesmathia, Yparon, Zachariell, Zadchiel, Zaphchel, Zedekiel, Zuriel.

The Text

The Secret of Secrets is a fascinating example of a cunning-man's grimoire. As is usual with such texts, there is a wide range of material drawn from different sources; however, the sources include grimoires not normally seen in these types of texts, where Agrippa and the *Heptameron* are common, but works on magical rings much less so. At least one owner (Moses Long) added notes regarding the importance of working with only angels and doubts about non-angelic conjurations as being un-Christian. This emphasis on Christianity is seen in the large number of prayers included. The practical nature of this text as a working book is emphasised by the set of instructions for the correct order to write the names on seals and pentacles (from the *Heptameron*) not seen elsewhere. There is also an emphasis on astrology, with the inclusion of a number of tables of hours. The section on suffumigations is detailed and very lucid in its explanation of their workings in a way not seen in most grimoires.

The section on rings of the Mansions of the Moon is curious. A number of the rings and charms are missing, possibly due to haste or lack of interest on the part of the copyist (or an incomplete source), these being – tenth, eleventh listed as tenth, twelfth listed as eleventh, twelfth, thirteenth, fifteenth, seventeenth through nineteenth, twenty-first through twenty-third, twenty-eighth listed as twenty-seventh. They are clearly copied from *Annulorum Experimenti*, with some changes of names and minor differences in purposes. The exception is for the twenty-fourth Mansion, which has been copied from the *Three Books of Occult Philosophy* instead. It is interesting to note that the next section on planetary rings is copied from the *Book of the Seven Rings of the Planets*, showing the author had access to two lesser-known earlier texts.

The text contains: Of the Angels & their Power; Man's Power over Spirits; the Preface with Directions & Aphorisms; astrological timing of the operation; that the holy Angels may help thee in thine occasions, say it daily (prayers); making a pentacle to hold in thy hand; a Narration to the seven Planetary Angels; the Seals & Characters of Angels and Spirits & their Use; astrological directions; an experiment to have thy own proper good Angel; the Call for thy proper good Angel; an experiment of three holy Angels, viz. Ancor, Anacor, Analos; a most noble experiment for the glass or crystallomanticall art of the seven Planetary Angels; a true experiment proved in Cambridge AD 1557 of three spirits Durus, Artus, Æbedel; another experiment for the three horsemen said to be approved true; the experiment of Birto; an admonition to the artist; astrological considerations; of essential debilities of the planets; planetary hours; table of the day of the week & Angel (*Heptameron* material, including lucid sequence of angels and names); a table of Hebrew names of the seven Angels set over the planets etc.; spirits of each of the seven planets; five angels & their offices or official names; how long each of the seven planetary angels rules the world; things proper to be done in each hour of the planets; angels & spirits of the twelve signs; angels of the twenty-eight Mansions of the Moon; angels of the four Elements; an experiment of Askariell in a glass or crystal; of fumigations, unguents, collyries, & unctions which cause apparitions of spirits (detailed discussion of incense use); a table of the fumigations for every planet & planetary incense hours called *Thimiamata*;[274] fumigations of diverse sorts, & of different virtues as followeth (includes ointments); of the power and virtue of suffumigations; to gather spirits of the air together; for a vision in the night; names of the angels of the first month;[275] men shall see visions; being therefore to receive an oracle or vision; to make a ring of Saturn for receiving an oracle or true dream, viz. a vision; a ring of the Sun for an oracle; another way to receive a true oracle by the image of the planets; metals, trees, stones, herbs of each of the seven planets (note: Mars is missing); making of the images of the planets; a rule to know when any degree of any sign will come to the ascendant; for an oracle or true dream by a kamea; another way for visions in thy sleep; another true experiment for a vision in thy sleep to find gold or silver; how to work by the twenty-eight Mansions of the Moon; what the twenty-eight Mansions of the Moon are; a table of the twenty-eight Mansions of the Moon; December's observations; a table of hours for the latitude of 51 degrees, 34 minutes (London); simple rural spells – to drive away and consume locusts and worms off from spoiling the corn, and wild beasts and birds consuming and spoiling the corn; to drive away serpents, dragons, and all creeping things and wild beasts; but to drive away wolves, foxes, cats, etc; that hail shall not fall in a place where you would not have it fall; that the Sun appear and shine forth openly

---

274 Greek word for incense.

275 The grimoire author comments he has omitted the angels of the other eleven months as the planetary angels work better. Note also this refers to the Jewish month of Nisan, with the list having been copied from *Sepher Raziel*.

showing to thee its place of being; to quench fire burning a house; that a thief enter not into thy house; rings of the seven planets not as formerly concerned with visions, but for other purposes.

Essential Reading

Skinner, Stephen, & Rankine, David (2018) *A Cunning Man's Grimoire*. Singapore: Golden Hoard. Complete transcription of Rawlinson D.252 with contextual and historical information.

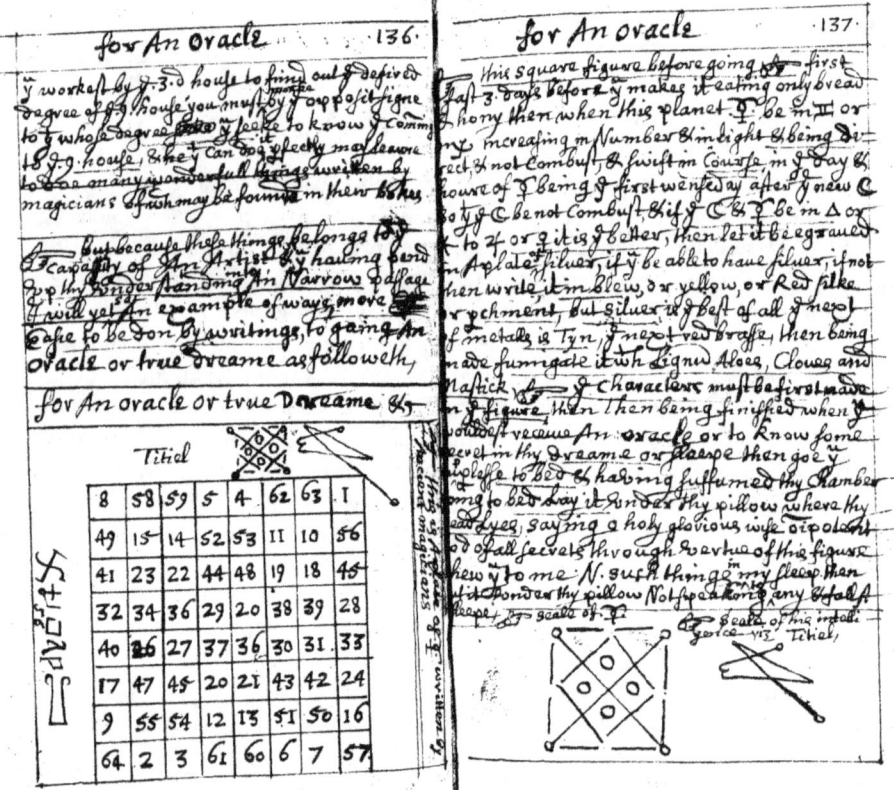

Rawlinson D253

BOOK OF OBERON

Date: 1577-84.
Language: Latin.
Influences: *Arbatel, Enchiridion, Heptameron, Sepher Raziel, Liber Lunae, Key of Solomon, Of the Composition of the Seven Planetary Images, Cambridge Book of Magic, Enchiridion of Pope Leo.*
Provenance: From the text itself, authorship has been suggested by up to four individuals. There are two sets of initials and the names John Porter and John Weston. The manuscript was owned by the painter and occultist Richard Cosway (1740-1821), passing on his death to John Denley (1764-1842), the noted London bookseller and collector of manuscripts. Denley sold it to George W. Graham (1784-1867), a balloonist[276] and member of the Mercurii magical group, where it passed to Robert Cross Smith (1795-1832), better known by his pseudonym of 'Raphael'. Fredrick Hockley (1808-85) acquired the manuscript from Smith's estate. The manuscript disappeared, to resurface in the hands of author Edward Henry William Meyerstein (1889-1952), on his passing being purchased by the booksellers Day's Ltd and thence to the Folger Museum. At some point the manuscript was divided into two parts, and the second part appeared in the collection of artist Robert Lenciwicz (1941-2002), being sold to the B.H. Breslauer Foundation, who donated it to the Folger, restoring the manuscript to completion.
MSS: Folger MS Vb 26.
Circle: Yes.
Tools: Alb, black-handled knife, chair, copper needle, crowns, crystal, fannell, gloves, hazel wand, holy water bucket, lamina, mirror, pentacle of Solomon, rings, robe, rod, sceptre, sprinkler, stole, sword, table, tablecloth, white-handled knife.
Spirit List: Abdizenel, Acrabiel, Africa, Agnix, Alastiel, Alcaroñ, Alingon, Alous, Amadas, Amaymon, Amediell, Amor, Anael, Anguell, Aozol, Ardosiel, Ariel, Arsdortho, Ascariell, Asmoe, Ayeariel, Barbiel, Baron, Battenayer, Benedill, Bentranas, Bethaca, Betuliel, Bilgall, Birachiel, Birto, Boell, Bollo, Booth, Bosco, Bostael, Boytheon, Burfex, Caberyon, Cakiel, Canaphnell, Capeyel, Carmelyon, Cassiel, Castriel, Catys, Cazariel, Chesetiel, Cochabiah, Colkeranon, Dagymiel, Dala, Damadas, Danall, Dangolath, Delforia, Deothan, Dirathon, Doliol, Drypys, Dupanfalo, Dyiaga, Edlodell, Egine, Elogamillo, Eloofe, Emediell, Emenguilla, Enachariorh, Engadiol, Estatell, Etheluill, Euantr, Exoniloelli, Faca, Faon, Fellofell, Fenell, Fervolam, Flodalath, Folla, Fortisan, Fortitudo, Gabriell, Ganyhaon, Gariguanim, Godiell, Handavmusdah, Hemeolon, Hermadafonino, Hermyadell, Hodelfa, Iesaloeella, Iobiell, King of the Pygmies, Isquier, Iuafula, Iulia, Iustitia, Iuuan, Jareahel, Julia, Juliana, Kaelldath, Keryth, Lasys, Laycon, Lesoraell, Lewydission, Lillia, Lymaxillõ, Madimiel, Magniel, Magor, Magrano, Malcranus, Maleus, Malkeo, Maltrans, Mayeryon, Michael, Micoll, Milant, Minquitalem, Muron, Myiasaleti, Nabbasr, Neael, Nogahel, Oberion, Obymero, Odauan, Ohorma, Opathan, Oremaelle, Orience, Ormell, Ornothocos, Orobas, Oropys, Paentagoras, Pandlath, Pandugell, Pantangor, Panteferon, Parathyell, Pascari, Pasill, Paymon, Penedill, Petangor, Portisan, Prudentia, Rabat, Ramalath, Ramasaell, Raphaell, Rasinet, Rasyel, Reatonay, Rendos, Reralath, Restillia, Restun, Reumdatha, Riamiuta, Riarufa, Roauian, Romulon, Rostafalagath, Rufangoll, Sabathiel, Sachiel, Salerica, Saluagan, Samaell, Samiell, Samionim, Sapienta, Saquidaell, Saquiel, Sartamiel, Saziel, Scholiel, Sedamylia, Sedaon, Sedellpha, Segamexe, Selarinum, Semeliel, Seraphius, Severion, Sibilis, Simagon, Spyrion, St. George, Storax, Sumiellam, Suriel, Sylquam, Symeam, Symon Mobris, Tamimiel, Tatalion, Teletiel, Teltrion, Temporantia, Teygra, Timora, Titam, Tobyas, Vah, Vitalot, Viteon, Ydial,

---

276 Ballooning and magic are no strangers, consider Francis Barrett.

Ysus, Zaseres, Zedekiel, [Abech, Acharos, Agaros, Algor, Allogor, Alphasis, Amada, Amon, Annobath, Annoboth, Ansoryor, Aron, Asmoday, Astaroth, Auras, Baall, Baasan, Balath, Barbais, Barbares, Barbaryes, Barbas, Barbates, Barsy, Bartax, Barton, Bartyn, Bason, Bealphares, Belferth, Belial, Bellfarto, Bellzebub, Berith, Bileth, Bilgall, Boab, Bryman, Busin, Cagyne, Caleos, Cambra, Carmerin, Coolor, Cornyx, Corsone, Deydo, Doodall, Doolas, Drewchall, Dyelagoo, Ebeyeth, Emlon, Femell, Fersone, Fessan, Fewrayn, Forcase, Formecones, Friblex, Gamor, Garsone, Gasyaxe, Geenex, Gemmos, Gemon, Gemyem, Geyll, Globa, Gloolas, Goorox, Gordonsor, Gorsyar, Goyle, Gyell, Hanar, Harchase, Hinbra, Hooab, Jambex, Joorex, Kayne, Lambricon, Leban, Lecher, Lewteffar, Lucipher, Madyconn, Mageyne, Mallapas, Marshiones, Mathias, Maxayn, Mistalas, Mosacus, Moyle, Muryell, Neophon, Noocar, Oberyon, Ocarbydatonn, Ogya, Othey, Oze, Ozia, Pamelon, Partas, Pathyn, Paynelon, Porax, Rewboo, Rewsyn, Rodabell, Rombalence, Royne, Ryall, Saranyt, Satan, Semper, Seson, Skor, Sogan, Soonek, Sowrges, Star, Suchay, Suffales, Syeonell, Synoryell, Tamon, Tamor, Tantavalerion, Varbas, Vriell, Vsagoo, Vzago, Zagayne, Zayme],[277] {Abviori, Acimoy, Acuteba, Aiel, Albewe, Alvedio, Alydee, Amabiel, Anayl, Aniel, Arragon, Astagna, Atel, Babel, Baciel, Balay, Baliel, Baraborat, Barkan, Bavhanael, Boel, Buesaba, Burchat, Bybell, Byleth, Bylethor, Caluel, Calzas, Capabil, Caphriel, Carmas, Charsiel, Chedisutaniel, Cherasa, Chermiel, Coniel, Corabiel, Corat, Curaniel, Dabriel, Dagiel, Damael, Dardiel, Darquiel, Deamiel, Doremiel, Etheye, Fabriel, Famiel, Forman, Fraciel, Friagne, Gabrael, Galdel, Gewthem, Gewthren, Guael, Habaiel, Habudiel, Hanuin, Hanyey, Harkam, Hufaltiel, Humastru, Huratapel, Hyniel, Iammas, Ianael, Ianiel, Iariahel, Iaxel, Ierescue, Iriel, Isiael, Itamall, Kadie, Lama, Lobquin, Machasiel, Machatan, Madiel, Mael, Maltiel, Malyke, Manasa, Masgabriel, Mathiel, Mathlai, Matnyel, Millet, Mitraton, Mylalua, Mylu, Naromiel, Nasar, Nelapa, Orphaniel, Osael, Pabel, Palframe, Palframen, Penael, Penat, Peniel, Porna, Rabiel, Rabumel, Rachiel, Rael, Raniel, Rayel, Saba, Sacriel, Salamia, Santaniel, Sapiel, Sarabotres, Satael, Seraphiel, Setchiel, Soncas, Suceratos, Tamael, Tarmiel, Tenaciel, Tetra, Thiel, Turiel, Valnum, Vcirmiel, Velel, Venahel, Vetuel, Viannel, Vionatraba, Vuael, Yron, Ystael, Zaliel, Zaniel},[278] Aeolus, Apollo, Atropos, Aurora, Bacchus, Cerberus, Ceres, Cupid, Diana, Discord, Fortune, Hebe, Hecate, Isis, Juno, Jupiter, Mars, Mercury, Minons, Morpheus, Neptune, Pan, Phoebe, Phoebus, Pluto, Saturn, Venus.[279]

The Text

The text of the manuscript was divided into two sections which were eventually reunited. Confusingly, these have wordings placed on the spine, *Theurgia* and *Key of Solomon*, which give a very different immediate impression of the contents than what is actually found. There is much material copied from other significant works included in the text, and much of the material appears for the first time in this manuscript, to be repeated in other later works, leading to the suggestion that the material was earlier and in circulation before being copied here, though now lost or misplaced. Of particular note is the inclusion of the oldest currently known copy of the *Book of the Offices of Spirits*. This makes the *Book of Oberon* a very significant manuscript in demonstrating the range of texts available in late sixteenth-century England. The text also contains many illustrations of different spirits, making it unusual among grimoires.

---

277 The list of spirits within [] are those named in the *Book of the Offices of Spirits*, which is also part of the material in the *Book of Oberon*.

278 The list of spirits within {} are drawn from the *Heptameron*, with a few interesting differences where attributions from the *Sworn Book of Honorius* have been used, and minor spelling variations.

279 The list of twenty-seven pagan gods given appears to be unique amongst grimoires.

The first part, *Theurgia*, contains the following: prayer; a prayer before you call; another oration; prayer to Jesus; a prayer in affliction; a prayer to God, to be said in the four parts of the world, in the circle; visions and apparitions; here beginneth the little book (excerpt from the *Enchiridion*); conjuration of all types of weapons; [prayer] precious, especially for strength; prayers against all worldly dangers; prayer against arrows; here endeth the little book; the rest as follows; before you call or consecrate: the Lord's Prayer; Hail Mary; another Hail Mary; the creed; Psalm 66; Pslam 54; Psalm 150; Psalm 138; Psalm 51 *misere mei deus*; Psalm 43 *iudica me deus*; Psalm 47 *omnes gentes*; Psalm 121 *leuaui occulos*; the blessing of the fumigations; the exorcism of the fire; concerning the garment and pentacle, and their use; the oration to be said whilst putting on the garment; to consecrate all instruments; five prayers; the Athanasian Creed; the Gospel of St John; how you can speak with your own good angel whenever you wish; prayer for one's angel; the method of the glass or stone; to have a spirit in a glass; experiment of invisibility; the license, or releasing, of any spirit; the consecration of the circle; consecration of the holy water; in order that the spirits don't have the power to harm you; concerning Baron; the experiment of Baron; a bond for a spirit who is rebellious and won't appear; prayer of purification; a *vincle*[280] or call; a conjuration of obedience; a band to bind them into the triangle or ring; the malediction; to speak with a spirit in thy bed; table to know which planet doth rule every hour; planets which be good and evil; signs that be good to work; John's gospel; protection against thieves (includes confession); epilepsy spell; of the intelligences, numbers, and names of the planets; the parchment, ink, pen, and writing; seven planets, twelve signs, thirty days (*Sepher Raziel* extract); of suffumigations, called incenses; to defend treasure from finding; to constrain and bind devils; to see spirits; that one shall prosper in his affairs; to win favour of princes; to see devils or spirits; to bind or loose spirits; upupa (lapwing); to subdue spirits; suffumigating; Semoferas; the Semoferas of Moses; the consecration of the ring; a malediction for the fire; another for the fire for the four kings; with penalty inflicted; a suffumigation that rejoiceth spirits; here followeth a table of everything of every sphere by himself; to make a thief not to depart out of the place where he would steal; the names of the seven sisters of the fairies; to make a thief return what he has stolen (demon bishop conjuration); the offices of spirits;[281] daily planetary angels, fumigations, and conjurations (includes images of angels, seals, and spirits); (list of pagan gods); these be they that make books and write books; a conjuration most necessary to the angels of each day to the obtaining of any spirit thou callest; the order of the circle work; the exorcism of the fire, over which the fumigations are placed; prayer to God which must be said within the circle, to the four parts of the world; prayer before the circle; for opening the circle; entering into the circle; order of the circle; invocation; the consecration and fumigation of the circle; fumigations that rejoiceth spirits; after this, if he does not appear, say this; then say in the four parts; how to call; orders for the excommunication; the necessaries for this art of necromancy; the beginning of circle work; rules; preparing days; place, time, person, and method; an invocation unto the four kings to urge and constrain a spirit; an invocation/last; here beginneth the conjuration of the others; a malediction; a license if he do appear and fulfill, then license him to depart; after you have done; a good constriction for a spirit; for the ground; this must be laid in the earth to urge a late dead man to appear and speak; for hidden treasure; for a keeper of treasure; say three times, if he come not, then say this; when he is come, bind him; to bind the ground, the spirit that keepeth any treasure; then begin again, and dig, etc., then say; an expediment[282] for the ground; the spirit of the North, who is called

---

280 Bond.
281 The *Book of the Offices of Spirits*.
282 Another word for expedient, i.e., an effective way to achieve a result.

King Egin; conjuration of Baron; an experiment of Rome;[283] in order to know about things lost, or accumulated, or hidden in the earth; beginning of the treatise on the experiment for a theft; to make an oil for seeing spirits from the air; an experiment of two hazel rods of one year's growing; this is the office of angels, spirits, and devils, how to see them and overcome them; to see spirits in the air or elsewhere; the secretness of secrets hid; thirty-eight pentacles for diverse purposes, characters of the planets, sigils of planets on the pentacles of Solomon; seals without characters of the seven planets and geomantic signs; fumigation notes from the *Heptameron* and Agrippa; brief notes concerning the course of the Moon (mansions); spirits of the planets; spirits of the signs at the circle; circle work; after the license; observations, after the spirit has appeared; our general request; at the entering of the circle; after you have made the invocation at the circle; instruments of the Art; an experiment approved by Friar Bacon to have a spirit appear; Bilgall (conjuration); for enclosing a spirit in a ring; for having whatever you may covet, lapwing; experiment of Solomon for what you wish; Annabath, Ascariell (conjurations); for making a stolen item return again; an experiment to see in thy sleep whatsoever thou shalt desire; to know whether one suspect be the thief or no; Satan (conjuration); experiment concerning the spirit called Baron; Saint George (conjuration of the thumb); Romulon conjuration; Mosacus conjuration; Orobas; Oberyon conjuration; another way to invoke Oberion; a malediction with a condition; here followeth a constriction; Oberion's circle; circle for the great work, to call the four kings; on the nigromantic doctrine for all useful experiments; concerning the baths.

Part two, titled Key of Solomon, is much shorter and contains charms of the kind commonly associated with cunning practices, including some historiolae. It contains: the Eye of Abraham, for proving persons guilty of theft, that they confess their guilt; for the toothache; this experiment that followeth is to overcome any enemies; for all manner of headache; to find treasure of the earth; ritual for hunting; love experiment, true and proved of many; for shooting write these names; rite using a bread loaf to find a thief; instructions to the steward; this longeth to the priest to use after this manner following; spirit circle; eighteen pentacles; for biting of a dog, adder, or snake that runneth in the wood; another for the same; to cause sleep; terebinthus; to cause conception; another for the same purpose; a special good for women in travail; for the ague; for one that is bewitched; to cause a spirit to appear in thy bed chamber; Magrano conjuration; an excommunication; for a crystal; a conjuration, proven, regarding a theft; experiment for having the spirit Sibilla in the light of a candle; for to take fowls with your hands; for a maid's thought; for love in the day and hour of Venus; against thieves; against thy enemies; against witchcraft; for aches or ague; for sorrow of the teeth; a charm for thieves; in the event of theft; in the event of thefts, proven; experiment for thieves; for to make thieves to stand; to make one fair; for the toothache; to make a maiden to dance; to make one follow thee, for a woman's love; if she is a maid or not; to make love between men and women; if any be angry with thee; also to make thieves to stand as well by night as by day; in the name of the Father; an experiment for thieves; for ulcers, bladder and yard (penis); for fretting of the yard or any other part; a reumen (?); this book of professor William Braius (ring consecration); how to call the king of the pigmies; for the swallow (chelidony stone); the virtue of vervain.

Essential Reading

Harms, Daniel & Clark, James R. & Peterson, Joseph H. (2016) *The Book of Oberon*. Woodbury: Llewellyn. The definitive work presenting the complete manuscript with invaluable contextual material and discussion. This book is a must-have.

---

283 Also known as the Roman experiment of William Bacon.

Book of the Offices of Spirits

Date: 1583? (Probably earlier, early C16).
Language: Latin, English.
Influences: *De Officiis Spirituum* mentioned by Trithemius.
Provenance: Recorded by John Porter in 1583. The manuscript was owned by the painter and occultist Richard Cosway (1740-1821), passing on his death to John Denley (1764-1842) the noted London bookseller and collector of manuscripts. Fredrick Hockley (1808-85) copied the manuscript part of the *Book of the Offices of Spirits* together with the *Key of Rabbi Solomon* from an English translation owned by Robert Palmer (1807-37) (dated 1832, location unknown); the same Palmer manuscript combination was also copied by an unknown female copyist in the mid to late C19 (private collection).
MSS: Folger vb.26 (1577-83), partial reproduction in Sloane MS 3824 (1641) and MS 3853 (mid C16), Robert Palmer (1832), Hockley copy (1864), private copy (mid to late C19).
Circle: N/A.
Tools: N/A.
Spirit Catalogue/List: Abech, Acharos, Africa, Agaros, Algor, Allogor, Alphasis, Amada, Amaymon, Amon, Annobath, Annoboth, Ansoryor, Aron, Asmoday, Astaroth, Auras, Baall, Baasan, Balath, Barbais, Barbares, Barbaryes, Barbas, Barbates, Barsy, Bartax, Barton, Bartyn, Bason, Bealphares, Belferth, Belial, Bellfarto, Bellzebub, Berith, Bileth, Bilgall, Boab, Bryman, Busin, Cagyne, Caleos, Cambra, Carmerin, Coolor, Cornyx, Corsone, Deydo, Doodall, Doolas, Drewchall, Dyelagoo, Egine, Elyeth, Emlon, Falla, Fata, Fersone, Fessan, Fewrayn, Forcase, Formecones, Friblex, Gamor, Garsone, Gasyaxe, Geenex, Gemmos, Gemon, Gemyem, Geyll, Globa, Gloolas, Goorox, Gordonsor, Gorsyar, Goyle, Gyell, Hanar, Harchase, Hinbra, Hooab, Jambex, Joorex, Julya, Kayne, Lambricon, Leban, Lecher, Lewteffar, Lillia, Lucipher, Madycon, Mageyne, Mallapas, Marshiones, Mathias, Maxayn, Mistalas, Mosacus, Moyle, Muryell, Mycob, Neophon, Noocar, Oberyon, Ocarbydaton, Ogya, Orience, Othey, Oze, Ozia, Pamelon, Partas, Pathyn, Paymon, Paynelon, Porax, Restillia, Rewboo, Rewsyn, Rodabell, Rombalence, Royne, Ryall, Saranyt, Satan, Semper, Seson, Skor, Sogan, Soonek, Sowrges, Star, Suchay, Suffales, Syeonell, Synoryell, Tamon, Tamor, Tantavalerion, Temell, Varbas, Venalla, Vriell, Vsagoo, Vzago, Zagayne, Zayme.

The Text

The origin of the *Book of the Offices of Spirits* is not clearly known. It seems likely it was drawn from *De Officiis Spirituum* by Johannes Trithemius (1462-1516). Trithemius referenced this work in his *Antipalus Maleficiorum* (1508), and copies may well have been passed around Europe, but none remain to provide a definitive answer. Johann Weyer (1515-88), himself a student of Agrippa, refers to Trithemius' work in his *Pseudomonarchia Daemonum* (1563), further suggesting an earlier date to the *Book of Offices of Spirits*.

This work is a spirit catalogue, describing the demons as well as the powers they control and can offer. Significantly, the spirit catalogue begins with the ruling trinity of Lucifer, Beelzebub, and Satan, followed by the four directional kings under them, and the demons under them. This hierarchy is often lost or only partly seen in a large number of grimoires, especially later ones.

Essential Reading

Campbell, Colin D. (ed) (2011) *A Book of the Offices of Spirits*. York: Teitan Press. Nice edition of Hockley's copy of the work with notes. Also includes other material from Folger vb.26 that Hockley copied as part of the text.

Harms, Daniel & Clark, James R. & Peterson, Joseph H. (2016) *The Book of Oberon*. Woodbury: Llewellyn. The definitive work presenting the complete manuscript of Folger vb.26 with invaluable contextual material and discussion.

The Enchiridion of Pope Leo III

Date: 1584.
Language: French, Latin.
Influences: *Collectanea Pseudo-Bedæ* (C16), *Three Books of Occult Philosophy*, Ancient Christian Magic (Jesus and King Abgar letters), *Horæ* tradition.
Provenance: First known edition published in Lyon in 1584 (French), reprinted in 1633, 1649, 1660, 1667, and 1740.
MSS: One of the works published in the *Bibliothèque Bleue de Troyes*.
Circle: N/A.
Tools: Earthenware vessel, ink, quill, wand (hazel).
Spirit List: Barachiel, Gabriel, Hael, Hunel, Jendsel, Limoch, Machel, Michael, Ramiach, Raphael, Silti, Stilu, Uriel.

The Text

As with a number of grimoires, the publication date of 1523 given on copies of the *Enchiridion* is spurious and well before its actual publication. 1584 is the first proven edition, following closely from the publication of *Collectanea Pseudo-Bedæ*, which may be the inspiration for the seven mysterious orisons. Another significant presence in the *Enchiridion* is the prayers which are derived from the *Horæ* tradition of Mary-inspired prayers, which also had a strong Charlemagne influence (fitting the claims associated with the grimoire). These influences, along with the collecting of late to high medieval charms and the influence of Agrippa, produce a very interesting grimoire with a heavy religious feel to it.

The text begins with an introduction, referencing the work of Agrippa followed by a seal. There is then the beginning of the Gospel of St John (In the beginning was the Word, etc.). Next follow the seven Penitential Psalms, with magical uses for each, as well as the name and seal of the intelligence to work with for these uses. This leads to text about the creation of the following orisons by Pope Leo III for Charlemagne and their virtues.

The first orison is against all kinds of charms and enchantments. After this are the seven orisons to be said on the days of the week. The mysterious orison and orison against adversities are next, with a brief call to the Virgin, and a very effective orison, an orison of great virtue, and another orison. Continuing, there is an orison against human frailty, one against enemies (with a seal of Michael), an orison, a very useful orison for those who travel, an admirable orison to the cross of the Saviour, an orison of the blessed Virgin, an exhortation to Jesus (including delivery by the Tau cross), orison to make a woman faithful, eternal praise to God.

The text then has a copy of the letter sent by King Abgar of Edessa to Jesus in Jerusalem. Next is a pentacle to conquer your enemies, with instructions on its use and the orison to be said to Jesus. The letter from Jesus back to Abgar continues the text, with an orison of admirable virtues. Following is a letter from Pope Leo III to Charlemagne with orisons, an orison to pass where enemies are, an orison against arrows, an orison for protection from weapons and sorceries, an orison to conjure weapons to be useless, an orison to Jesus the Saviour, another orison, another orison from Pope Leo III to Charlemagne, names of Jesus to be worn to be loved, the words of Adam to be carried to avoid being killed, orison of Saint Augustine to have a revelation, orison of Saint Cyprian to be safeguarded from perils, seal of Gabriel, orison to be carried for divine protection, names of Jesus to carry for safety while travelling, names of the blessed Virgin, orison of Saint Michael for protection on water and against sheep pox, and the figure of the measure of the wound in Jesus' side and instructions for its use.

The next section is on the construction of the pentacles and tools of the art. Other tools follow, with the consecration of the quill, ink, and parchment; blessing of the perfumes, exorcism and blessing of the fire. The virtues of the seven Penitential Psalms and previous orisons are then discussed, with specifics of the purposes to use them for and what is necessary to do so. A section on Mystical Secrets (simple charms) continues from here.

Essential Reading

Cecchetelli, Michael (2011) *Crossed Keys*. London: Scarlet Imprint. This work is valuable as it combines translations of the *Black Dragon* and the *Enchiridion of Pope Leo III*. Context is minimal, including a long quote from A.E. Waite which is outdated and largely inaccurate.

Smith, Edward A. (2012) *Speculum de Arte Magica Papæ & Regis The Enchiridion Leonis Papæ*, Its Origins, Legend, & Memory. York: MA Thesis. Excellent study on the background and content of the *Enchiridion*.

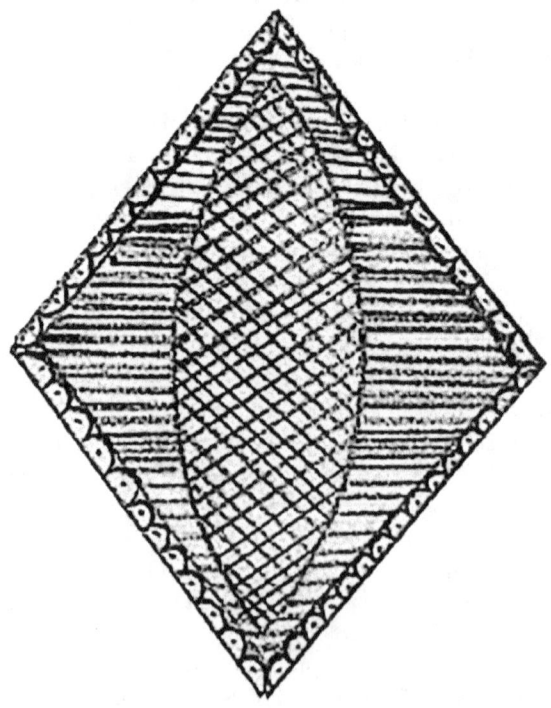

Enchiridion, Wound of Christ

The Discoverie of Witchcraft

Date: 1584.
Language: English.
Influences:[284] Agrippa, Iamblichus, Michael Psellus, Peter of Abano, Roger Bacon, the *Malleus Maleficarum*.
Provenance: Written by Reginald Scot (1541-1599) and first published in 1584. Republished several times, the 1665 edition added more chapters of magical material.
MSS: N/A.
Circle: Yes.
Tools: Belt, cap, carpet, censer, chalk, charcoal, crystal, robe, swords, table, wand.
Spirit List: [Abalam, Agares, Allocer, Amaymon, Amduscias, Amon, Amy, Andras, Andrealphus, Astaroth, Aym, Baell, Balam, Barbatos, Bathin, Beball, Beliall, Berith, Bifrons, Bileth, Botis, Buer, Bune, Caim, Cimeries, Decarabia, Eligor, Flaures, Focalor, Forneus, Furcas, Furfur, Gaap, Gamigin, Glasya Labolas, Gomory, Gusoin, Haagenti, Halphas, Ipos, Leraie, Lucifer, Malphas, Marbas, Marchosias, Morax, Murmur, Naberius, Orias, Orobas, Ose, Paimon, Phoenix, Procell, Pruflas, Purson, Raum, Ronove, Sabnocke, Saleos, Shax, Sidonay, Sitri, Stolas, Valac, Valefor, Vapula, Vepar, Vine, Vuall, Zagan, Zepar],[285] Achilia, Anael, Athanaton, Balkin, Banal, Barma, Bealphares, Boralim, Cassiel, Falaur, Gabriel, Glauron, Hecate, Luridan, Malantha, Michael, Milia, Orgon, Peolphan, Raphael, Sachiel, Samael, Sibylia, Sitrael, Sitrami, Thamaor.

The Text

Reginald Scot wrote this work in an attempt to demonstrate that people who claimed to be witches were deluded, not evil, and did not deserve the persecution they endured. In the process he gathered together a lot of information from earlier grimoires, effectively compiling a grimoire in spite of himself. Much of this large book is concerned with quoting from the *Bible* and ancient philosophers to make his argument about not killing people for believing they are witches. It was also a time period when Catholicism was perceived as a hostile force by many, following the excommunication of King Henry VIII and foundation of the Church of England in 1534. Scot's hostility to the banned Catholicism is evident throughout the text.

The material relevant to the grimoire tradition is scattered in a few places throughout the tome, and it is only these chapters that will be listed due to their relevance. Contained within the book is a copy of Weyer's *Pseudomonarchia Daemonum*. The influence of the *Discoverie of Witchcraft* on the grimoire tradition and cunning folk was extensive, and it is not surprising that the 1665 edition of the book specifically added more grimoire material regarding magic circles and conjurations (some drawn from the *Heptameron*. It is worth noting that Scot specifically refers to certain grimoires in book fifteen chapter thirty-one, these being the *Ars Almadel, Ars Notoria* and books by Solomon and St Cyprian. Chapter forty-two also refers to the *Ars Paulina* and *Ars Notoria*.

The chapters that contain charms and grimoire material follow: Certain Popish and magical cures for them that are bewitched in their privates (Bk 4, ch.8); a strange cure that was done to one molested by an incubus (Bk 4, ch.9); a confutation of all the former follies concerning incubi (Bk 4, ch.10); how men have been bewitched and abused by dreams to

---

284 Scot lists pages of people who influenced the work. Particularly significant and relevant ones are noted here.
285 This is the list of spirits reprinted from *Pseudomonarchia Daemonum*.

search for money (Bk 10, ch.6); the art and order to be used in digging for money, revealed by dreams, and how to procure pleasant dreams (Bk 10, ch.7); sundry receipts and ointments, made and used for the transportation of witches (Bk 10, ch.8); Popish periapts, amulets, and charms (Bk 12, ch.9); how to make holy water, St. Rufus' charm (Bk 12, ch.10); choice of charms against epilepsy, rabies, scorpion sting, toothache, labour, the King's evil, to remove a thorn from the body or a bone in the throat, charms to be said for gathering herbs, for sore eyes, to open locks, against spirits, for horses, and for sour wine (Bk 12, ch.14); the exposition of Iidoni (Bk 15, ch.1); *Pseudomonarchia Dameonum* (Bk 15, ch.2-4); a confutation of the many vanities contained in the previous chapters, especially of commanding devils (Bk 15, ch.5); the names of the planets, their characters, together with the twelve signs of the zodiac (Bk 15, ch.6); the characters of the angels of the seven days with their names, of figures, seals, and periapts (Bk 15, ch.7); an experiment of the dead (Bk 15, ch.8); a license for Sibylia to go and come at all times (Bk 15, ch.9); to know of treasure hidden in the earth (Bk 15, ch.10); an experiment following of Citrael, angels on Sunday (Bk 15, ch.11); how to enclose a spirit in a crystal stone (Bk 15, ch.12); an experiment of Bealphares (Bk 15, ch.13); to bind the spirit Bealphares, and to loose him again (Bk 15, ch.14); the making of the holy water (Bk 15, ch.15); to make a spirit to appear in a crystal (Bk 15, ch.16); an experiment of the dead (Bk 15, ch.17); a bond to bring him to thee (Bk 15, ch.18); a bond to bring him into the crystal stone or glass (Bk 15, ch. 19); when to talk with spirits, and have true answers to find a thief (Bk 15, ch.20); a confutation of conjuration (Bk 15, ch.21); a comparison between popish exorcists and other conjurors (Bk 15, ch.22); a late experiment or conjuration performed at Orleance by Franciscan friars (Bk 15, ch.23); certain conjurations taken out of the pontifical and the missal (Bk 15, ch.27); that Popish priests leave nothing unconjured, a form of exorcism for incense (Bk 15, ch.28); how conjurors have beguiled witches, what books they care about to procure credit to their art (Bk 15, ch.31); all magical arts confuted by an argument concerning Nero, what Cornelius Agrippa and Carolus Gallus[286] have left written thereof and proved by experience (Bk 15, ch.32); of Solomon's conjurations (Bk 15, ch.33); a pleasant miracle wrought by a popish priest (Bk 15, ch.37); of visions, noises, apparitions, and imagined sounds, and of other illusions, of wandering souls: with a confutation thereof (Bk 15, ch.39); Cardanus's[287] opinion of strange noises, how counterfeit visions grow to be credited (Bk 15, ch.40); of theurgy, with a confutation thereof (Bk 15, ch.42). Additional material from 1665 edition: of magical circles, and the reason of their institution (ch.1); how to raise the ghost of one that hanged himself (ch.2); how to raise up the spirits Paymon, Bathin, and Barma, and what wonderful things may be effected by their assistance (Ch.3); how to consecrate all manner of circles, fumigations, fire, magical garments, and utensils (Ch.4); treating more practically of the consecration of circles, fire garments, and fumigations (Ch.5); how to raise and exorcise all sorts of spirits belonging to the airy region (Ch.6); how to obtain the familiarity of the Genius or good angel, and cause him to appear (Ch.7); a form of conjuring Luridan the familiar, otherwise called Belelah (Ch.8); how to conjure the spirit Balkin the master of Luridan (ch.9).

Essential Reading

Scot, Reginald (1886) *The Discoverie of Witchcraft*. London: Elliot Stock. Reprint from 1665 edition giving complete text.
Scot, Reginald (1990) *The Discoverie of Witchcraft*. London: Dover. One of the many editions of this work; it is easily available. It is lacking the Discourse at the end, however.

---

286 Carolus Gallus (1530-1616) was a minister and theology scholar who led a controversial life.
287 Girolamo Cardano (1501-76), Italian polymath and scholar.

Crafte of Conjurynge

Date: 1590.
Language: English with some Latin.
Influences: *Heptameron*.
Provenance: J. Gadow is written on the cover.
MSS: Illinois MS 0102 (1590).
Circle: Yes.
Tools: Crystal, white-handled knife.
Spirit List: Abebon, Aleuia, Analos, Ancor, Anycor, Ascariell, Asmoday, Assriell, Azasell, Babilon, Bariell, Basayn, Beab, Belzebub, Boytheon, Centone, Cerborus, Cudexa, Diatay, Earloy, Ehyn, Enud, Enuie, Fodo, Fummoluolda, Gabriell, Gufsvegia, Harto, Igelsifone, Igilsiton, Igisticon, Looflion, Lucifer, Lumdafquida, Lundoungiwufa, Machaldie, Matuta, Mayryon, Messitone, Michael, Miseton, Naletoritin, Naris, Oberyon, Orebon, Petron, Rabeffie, Raminam, Raphaell, Saday, Sassriell, Satanas, Sathan, Sayapiell, Sermia, Spirion, Teltrion, Tibo, Tibolato, Tibon, Tombam, Uriell, Vitordill, Vpriochi.

The Text

The full title of the text is *Crafte of conjureynge and howe to rule the ffierye spiritts of ye planetts & make the devyle appearre*. As with other English grimoires from this period, there are a lot of unique spirits not named elsewhere, mixed with well-known spirits. Although similar in style and technique to contemporary grimoires, the material largely stands alone, not reproducing earlier work (with the exception of the operation of the demon bishops). The emphasis is heavily on conjuration, with very little simple charm work. The presence of an ointment for spirit vision is an interesting inclusion. The absence of details of paraphernalia and preparation suggest the owner was recording the information they felt necessary, rather than every small detail.

The cover page has sets of magical characters for the planets; next is a pentacle (seal) which is damaged; discussion of beneficial zodiacal signs and considerations follow; more on zodiacal considerations and planetary hours; a Godly prayer (long); infernal rulerships (L:B:S trinity); the pentacle of Solomon (beautifully drawn); magic circle with instructions on use; more prayers and instruction; conjuration; the malediction; conjuration; Solomon's bond; an experiment for a theft to bring a thief again (demon bishops with picture of plate); to gain a familiar spirit to speak with when you will; magic circle; conjuration into a crystal; prayer; how to know of goods that be stolen; conjuration of Askariell; license of Askariell (Latin); a license in English for Askariell (includes seal of Solomon); circle of Ascariell; an experiment of treasure; treasure spirit conjuration; an experiment of Azazell (summoning named dead); license of the spirit (of the dead); another experiment (love); a license for any spirit; and the oration following; the formation of the circle; for binding of spirits that walk (rebellious spirits); to make a spirit appear in a crystal (long sequence); a call of the angels Ancor, Anycor, Analos; the perfect order to consecrate any book; for them that be possessed by any spirit; a prayer for all wicked witches; for health; spirit vision ointment; conjuration; to find gold fortune.

Essential Reading

There are no editions of this manuscript in print at the time of writing.

Archidoxes of Magic

Date: 1591 (posthumously).
Language: Latin.
Influences: Trithemius, Albertus Magnus.
Provenance: Written by Paracelsus (1493-1541) allegedly around 1521.
MSS: First published in Basel in 1591, translated into English in 1656 by Robert Turner.
Circle: N/A.
Tools: Earthenware pot.
Spirit List: N/A.

The Text

The *Archidoxes of Magic* is not a grimoire but was influential on the grimoire tradition. Like Agrippa, Paracelsus trained with Trithemius, giving him access to arguably the greatest magician of that time. Paracelsus wrote extensively, his work influenced by astrology and alchemy, and developed his system of Paracelsian medicine. He was also the most notable author to write on elementals and their nature during the late medieval period. His work *A Book on Nymphs, Sylphs, Pygmies, and Salamanders, and on the Other Spirits* was published posthumously (like most of his works) in 1566 in Latin, and then numerous times in the subsequent centuries.

The text begins by discussing alchemical fire, then the planetary spirits or tinctures. The second treatise is on the Philosopher's Mercury; the third on the construction of the furnace and fire and the tinctures. Paracelsus then moves into discussion of occult philosophy, working through chapters on consecrations, conjurations, characters, visions in dreams, persons and spirits wandering the earth (referencing elementals), the power of the imagination, of treasure and riches hid under the earth, possession by evil spirits, delivering people from possession, of tempests, and of the abuse of magic by those who use it for necromancy and witchcraft.

The next treatise is on the mysteries of the signs of the zodiac. This discusses the use of melothesia in healing and provides arguably the most noteworthy exposition of the Doctrine of Signatures. There follows the well-known amulets with their construction for treatment of different medical conditions. A second treatise on celestial medicines describes the construction of seals for each of the zodiacal seals and their medicinal use. A few common secrets of nature (Book of Secrets-style) follow and end the book: for dealing with mice, protecting sheep, and against flies.

Essential Reading

Paracelsus & Skinner, Stephen (Intr) (2004) *The Archidoxes of Magic*. Berwick: Ibis Press. Good edition of the text with excellent introduction by Stephen Skinner.
Paracelsus & Sigerist, Henry E. (ed) (1996) *Paracelsus Four Treatises*. Baltimore: John Hopkins University Press. Valuable for containing *A Book on Nymphs, Sylphs, Pygmies, and Salamanders, and on the Other Spirits*.

DE HEPTARCHIA MYSTICA

Date: 1592.
Language: English with some Latin.
Influences: Spirit transmission. Cleaned up version of *Compendium Heptarchia Mystica*, written by John Dee in 1588 (Additional MS 36674).
Provenance: Written by John Dee in 1592. Elias Ashmole produced a copy after 1672 when he received the Dee manuscript.
MSS: Additional MS 36674 (1588), Sloane MS 3191 (1592), Sloane MS 3678 (c. 1672).
Circle: N/A.
Tools: Crystal, lamen, ring, rod, *Sigillum Æmeth*, table.
Spirit Catalogue: An, Aoaynnl, Aoidiab, Aue, Avzniln, Babalel, Babepen, Bagenol, Baligon, Banssze, Bbaigao, Bbalpae, Bbanifg, Bbarnfl, Bbasnod, Bbosnia, Befafes, Beigia, Blbopoo, Blisdon, Blvmaza, Bnamgen, Bnapsen, Bnaspol, Bnvages, Bobogel, Bornogo, Bralges, Brorges, Butmono, Byapare, Bynepor, Carmara, Dmal, Eilomfo, El, Elgnseb, Ergdbab, Etevlgl, Gglppsa, Hagonel, Hagonel, Heeoa, I, Ih, Ilmese, Ilr, Ioaespm, Labdgre, Lbbnaav, Leaorib, Leenarb, Liba, Lnanaeb, Michael, Neiciab, Neotpta, Nlinzvb, Nllrlna, Noonman, Nrpcrrb, Nrrcprn, Nrsogoo, Oeeooez, Oesengle, Onedpon, Oogosrs, Raphael, Rocle, Roemnab, Sagaciy, Semiel, Sfamllb, Stimcul, Uriel, Yllmafs.

The Text

Dr John Dee transcribed material from his five books of mystical exercises to produce *De Heptarchia Mystica*, a precis of some of the most significant material from his skrying sessions with Edward Kelly. It uses Dee's standard practice of purification, prayer and skrying, and works as a stand-alone set of planetary rites.

Chapter one is titled Of the Title, and general Contents of this book, some needful testimonies. It contains quotes from angelical communications set as philosophical discussion of God, divine knowledge, and angelic communication. Chapter two is Of John Dee, his principal, and in manner peculiar Interest, to exercise the Doctrine Heptarchial. More quotes regarding spirits and practice are found within, including the character the crystal is placed within, and the nature of the ring to be worn. Chapter three is Some Remembrances of the furniture and Circumstances necessary in the Exercise Heptarchial. It discusses the table and the ring, the assemblies of spirits, the feet rests for the table; the tables made of sweet wood for the kings to be used, the use of the *Sigillum Æmeth*, the composition of the tables, dialogue with Michael and Semiel, the form and creation of the seal of perfection, and the set-up of the table for skrying. Chapter four is Some Notice of peculiar forms, and attire, wherein the kings, princes, and ministers Heptarchical appeared, and of some their Actions, and gestures at their Appearance, &c. This contains the names and sigils of the kings and princes, and the names of their ministers, and the appearance of all of them. Chapter five is *Oratio, ad Deum, singulis diebus, tribus vicibus, ter dicenda*,[288] containing a long prayer to be recited by the practitioner as directed. Chapter six is *Bonorum Angelorum Heptarchicorum, Piae, Deuotaeque Invitationes*,[289] and contains the conjuration for the kings and that for the princes. Chapter seven is Some Recital, and contestation by the peculiar offices, words, and deeds, of the seven Heptarchical Kings and Princes, in their peculiar days, to be used. This gives the associated powers and qualities of the kings and princes with their attributions to the days of the week. The text concludes

---

288 Address to God, each day, three times, spoken thrice.
289 Pious Invitations of the Good Angels of the Heptarchy of God.

with a Table of the forty-nine good angels, comprising a seven-band circle divided into seven, with the names of seven ministers serving under the princes/kings for each of the seven days.

Essential Reading

Turner, Robert (ed) (1986) *The Heptarchia Mystica of John Dee*. Wellingborough: Aquarian Press. Good copy of the material. However, as with the Geoffrey James edition, it is very difficult to obtain.

Joseph Peterson's fantastic website www.esotericarchives.com is recommended for the most up-to-date and accurate version of the material.

THE BOOK OF ABRAMELIN

Date: 1608 (1595-1609).[290]
Language: German, Latin, Hebrew, French.
Influences: *Psalms*, otherwise unknown.
Provenance: Written by Abraham of Worms. First published in 1725 by Peter Hammer in Cologne, also published by Scheible as *The Jewish Book of True Practice* in *Das Kloster* Volume 5 in 1847.
MSS:[291] Codex Guelfibus 10.1 (1608), Codex Guelfibus 13.12 Aug. 4° (1608), Codex Guelfibus 47.13 (1608), SLUB MS N 111 (Latin) (1720), SLUB MS N 161 (1720), Wellcome MS 820 (1726), Bodleian MS Opp. 594 (Hebrew) (1740), Codex Mag. 15 (1750), Wellcome MS 821 (C18), ÖNB Cod. 10579 (Italian) (C18), MS.germ.qu. 1169 (Latin) (C17-18?), ÖNB Cod. 10580 (C18?), MS Dreden N. 111 (C18), BA MS 2351 (French) (1850) – translated from Codex Guelfibus 10.1 by Antoine-René d'Argenson.
Circle: N/A.
Tools: Altar, almond wand,[292] belt, censer, headband, lamp, white robe.
Spirit List:[293] Abhadir, Abusis, Adisak, Adon, Afloton, Afolop, Afray, Agahaly, Agebol, Agilas, Aglafys, Ahabhon, Aherom, Akahim, Akanef, Akesely, Akorok, Alafy, Alluph, Alogil, Aloson, Alpas, Altanor, Ama, Amamil, Amaymon, Amillis, Amolom, Ampholion, Anadir, Anagnostos, Anamalon, Andrachos, Apilki, Apolion, Apormanos, Arakison, Arator, Argax, Argilon, Aril, Arioth, Ariton, Armasia, Arogor, Arolen, Arrabim, Asianon, Asmodi, Asorega, Assmielh, Astaroth, Astolit, Asturel, Baalsori, Badad, Bafamal, Bagalon, Bahal, Bakaron, Balabos, Balachem, Barak, Bariol, Baruel, Batirmiss, Beezlebub, Belial, Beliferes, Bemerot, Bialod, Bilek, Bilifot, Borob, Bruach, Bubanabub, Buriub, Burnahas, Butharuth, Calach, Calamosi, Camalon, Camarion, Camonix, Carasch, Cargosik, Caron, Cayfar, Chaya, Cohen, Concavion, Corilon, Corocon, Cuschi, Daglus, Dagulez, Dalep, Darochim, Debam, Dimurgos, Diopes, Diralisin, Disolel, Dosom, Dramas, Drisoph, Dulid, Earaoe, Ebaron, Eckdulon, Efrigis, Egachir, Ekalak, Ekorok, Elafon, Elamyr, Elonim, Elpinon, Elzegar, Emfatison, Enei, Eralicarison, Eralyx, Ergonion, Ergosil, Erimites, Erkaya, Ermihala, Ethanim, Exenteron, Faguni, Fasma, Faturab, Fernebus, Filaxon, Flabison, Forfaron, Fortesion, Fosfora, Frasis, Gagison, Gagolchon, Gagonix, Galagos, Garininrag, Garsas, Gazaron, Geloma, Gesegas, Gillamon, Giriar, Girmil, Glysy, Golog, Gomogin, Gorilon, Granon, Hachamel, Hageyr, Hagoch, Hagrion, Hahyax, Haragil, Haraoth, Harog, Harosul, Harpinon, Haskub, Hasperim, Hayamen, Helel, Helmis, Hipogon, Hipolepos, Hirih, Holop, Horamar, Hyla, Hyrys, Iamai, Ibulon, Ichdison, Iemuri, Igarag, Igigi, Igilon, Ikon, Ilarak, Ilekel, Iloson, Iotifar, Ipakol, Ipokys, Irasomin, Irmenos, Irminon, Iromas, Iromenis, Isagas, Iuar, Izozon, Jachiel, Kafles, Kalgosa, Kalotes, Kamusel, Karelesa, Kataron, Katsin, Kela, Kemal, Kigios, Kiligil, Kilik, Kilikim, Kirik, Kloracha, Kobada, Kobhan, Kogiel, Kokolon, Kolan, Kore, Kosem, Labisi, Laboneton, Labonix, Lachatyl, Lagasaf, Lagiros, Lamal, Lamargos, Larach, Laralos, Lemalon, Lepacha, Leviathan, Ligilos, Liriol, Liriol, Liroki, Lobel, Lomiol, Losimon, Lotaym, Lucifer, Madail, Mafalach, Maggid, Magog, Magoth, Magyros, Malach, Manties, Mara, Marag, Maranton, Maraos, Marku, Masadul, Matatam, Mebaschel, Mebhaer, Mebhasser, Mechebber, Megalleh, Megalogim, Melabed, Melammed, Memnolik, Mesaf,

---

290 Dating from the excellent essay *Abraham of Worms* by Rick-Arne Kollatsch, 1.10.21.
291 In German unless otherwise stated.
292 The Biblical symbolism of almond is clear here, and it should be noted that the Shekinah is also equated with the almond wand in Kabbalah.
293 There is a curiously large number of palindromic spirit names in this work.

Metofeph, Milon, Mimosa, Mokaschef, Molin, Moreh, Morilon, Moschel, Mynymarup, Myrmo, Nabhi, Nacheran, Nagan, Nagani, Nagar, Nagid, Namalon, Namiros, Nascelon, Nasi, Nasolico, Natales, Negen, Neschamah, Nesisen, Nilima, Nilion, Nimalon, Nimirix, Nogah, Nolom, Nomimon, Notison, Nudeton, Obagiron, Obedamah, Odac, Ogologon, Ohotam, Okirgi, Olassky, Olosirmon, Omagos, Oman, Ombalafa, Opilon, Oriens, Orinel, Ormion, Ormonos, Oroya, Osogyon, Pachahy, Pafesla, Pagalust, Pakid, Pandoli, Panfotron, Parachmon, Parasch, Paraschon, Parelit, Parusur, Pattid, Paymon, Pechach, Peresch, Permases, Petanop, Pliroky, Pother, Presfees, Promachos, Proxonos, Quision, Rachear, Radarap, Ragaras, Rak, Ramiuson, Ramoras, Ranar, Regerion, Rigloen, Rimog, Romages, Romoron, Rosaran, Rotor, Sagarez, Sapipas, Saraph, Sarasim, Sarason, Saris, Sarisel, Sartabachim, Satan, Schaluach, Schaluah, Sched, Schelegon, Scrupulon, Secabim, Semeot, Sibolas, Sigis, Sikastir, Siphon, Sipillipis, Sirgilis, Sobhe, Sochen, Somis, Sorosma, Soterion, Sumuron, Tabbat, Tagora, Takaros, Tarahim, Tareto, Tedean, Texai, Thirama, Tigraphon, Tinakos, Tinira, Tolet, Trapis, Trisacha, Turitil, Ubarim, Udaman, Ugalis, Ugesor, Ugirpon, Ugobog, Unochos, Urgido, Xirmys, Ybarion, Ychigas, Yeyatron, Ygarim, Ylemlis, Yparchos, Yragamon, Ysmiriek, Ysquiron, Zagal, Zalomes, Zugola.

The Text

The *Abramelin* gained notoriety in the Anglophile world through the translation of the French BA MS 2351 by S.L. MacGregor Mathers and publication as *The Sacred Magic of Abramelin the Mage* (1900). Aleister Crowley added to the notoriety of the *Abramelin* through his failed attempt at the practice at Boleskine, on the shores of Loch Ness in Scotland. His translation was based on the latest version of the manuscript, which was incomplete and missing key elements,[294] a clean translation from the original German has only become available in recent years. Although largely unknown to speakers, the German edition published by Peter Hammer in 1725 was known on the Continent, as evidenced in its possession by William Quintscher, a friend of Crowley and member of the Fraternitas Saturni.

The text claims a date of 1458 for writing, however *The Book of Abramelin* first appeared in German in manuscripts dated 1608, which is consistent with the style and hand. Subsequent editions were translated into Latin, Hebrew, and French. Abraham (the author) states that he does not know if his younger son Lamech will become learned (i.e. learn Hebrew), explaining his use of German in the text, as he was bequeathing his writings to his son, with whom he had no contact.

The manuscript is divided into four books. The first book is autobiographical, explaining the composition of the text from oral teachings received from his father and others, combined with material he learned in his travels. Abraham describes the book as a special treasure for his younger son Lamech, and that his older son Joseph received the Kabbalah and the holy tradition (Judaism). Abraham explains how he travelled in search of wisdom, ending up in Egypt, but his search was fruitless. He received inspiration and ended up being directed to Abramelin and receiving his teachings, copying by hand the material contained in Books 3 and 4. Abraham also discusses other masters and holy men he met, none of whom matched Abramelin in his eyes. Along with a list of his achievements using the magic, he discusses further the importance of appropriate behaviour.

---

294 E.g., the operation is given as six months whereas it is eighteen months in the original, many of the magic squares are incomplete in Mathers but complete in the original, etc.

Book 2 is a work of Mixed Kabbalah,[295] containing material Abraham learned from other sources, and which is not directly related to the practice of the Abramelin operation. The chapters are divided into charms for serious diseases; for enmities and war; for friendship, marriage and love; for birthing; against water, fire, tempests, ghosts, and the devil; how to blast rocks, stone cliffs, walls, and doors; how to save houses and buildings in case of earthquake and tempest; how to stand in front of a court and deal with high potentates; in times of hunger and starvation; to make oneself invisible to one's enemies.

Book 3 begins with a discussion of what is real magic, and the importance of the wisdom of the Shekinah (without actually naming her). A discussion of the required qualities to perform the operation follows, along with a chapter on the planetary hours. The following chapters discuss the technicalities of the work: how to behave in the first, second and third six-month periods; what work can be done that will not hinder the operation; choosing the location and preparing the accessories; consecrations; how to call the good and unredeemed spirits; what to request from and how to deal with the spirits. This is followed by the spirit list, along with how to carry out the work, and the way to use Book 4. Book 4 contains the magic letter squares to be used for different purposes. The thirty chapters contain two hundred and forty-six such magic squares.

Essential Reading

Dehn, Georg (ed) & Guth, Steve (trans) (2015) *The Book of Abramelin*. Lake Worth: Ibis. The most comprehensive work on the *Abramelin*, translated from the earliest German manuscripts, giving the complete text. This book completely replaces Mathers's patchy translation of the later (and incomplete) French version of the text.

Mathers, S.L. Mac Gregor (1898) *The Book of the Sacred Magic of Abramelin the Mage*. London: John Watkins. Although flawed and using the later French manuscript, Mathers's treatment of the magic squares and contextual discussions have some value.

---

295 Mixed Kabbalah is a term used to describe simple charms similar to those found in the Book of Secrets tradition. They are distinguished by their consistent use of appropriate Biblical quotes as part of the charms.

The Antiphoner Notebook

Date: Late C16.
Language: English with some Latin.
Influences: *Discoverie of Witchcraft*.
Provenance: Written by an unknown scribe in the late C16 with four additional charms added by another unknown scribe in the C17.
MSS: Bodleian MS Additional B1.
Circle: N/A.
Tools: N/A.
Spirit List: Azaria, Eleazar, Maligare, Raguel, Sabaoth, Sibilia, Uriel, Yris.

The Text

Based on the contents of the work, Klaassen logically suggests that the scribe may have been a cunningman.[296] This collection of charms is a good example of charm books from this time period. A large number of the charms are historiolae (narrative charms) using Jesus, the Apostles, and other Biblical figures.

The text contains: a proven experiment for making a male or female thief return to you in person if he should be in any place within the kingdom of England (1); divination with a crystal (2); a ritual to exorcise demons guarding a treasure (3); charm for ague (4); a prayer against thieves and wicked spirits (5); for to find out a thief (6); another knowledge for to bring out a thief (7); for thieves (8); for quartan fever (9); a prayer for the herber (home) (10); charm for aches (11); a good medicine for fevers (12); a prayer for the bloody flux (13); for a man that may not sleep for sickness (14); a prayer against thieves (15); for fevers (16); if your friend lies sick and you would know whether he will live or die with sickness (17); a prayer to shield from axes (18); for toothache (19); an approved medicine for fevers (20); for women that travel with child (i.e. childbirth) (21); another (22); good prayer for a child that is dead in a woman's womb (23); a good prayer for falling sickness (epilepsy) (24); another (25); a prayer for a growth in a man's eye (26); for toothache (27); for toothache (28); for toothache (29); for pricking of a thorn (30); Three Good Brethren charm (31); to staunch blood (32); for headache (33); for falling sickness (34); for fever (35); protective amulet (36); a prayer for toothache (37); a prayer for toothache (38); for toothache (39); an experiment for wounds (40); a prayer against faeries (41); a prayer for a prick with a sword, dagger, or thorn (42); a prayer for the stitch (43); a prayer for bleeding (44); a prayer against swelling (45); a prayer against worms (46); for staunching of blood (47); Agnus Dei amulet (48);[297] a prayer against shot or a waistcoat of proof (49); protective amulet of Pope Leo (50); a prayer which must never be said, but carried against one, against thieves (51); amulet of Joseph of Arimathea (52); lay indulgence (53); a defensive prayer (54); a prayer of the holy cross (55); this prayer is taken out of the primer (56); a prayer to make [one] taciturn in torture (57); and also (58); counter prayers against these and all other witchcrafts, in the saying whereof witches are vexed (59); to put out the thief's eye (60); another way to find out a thief[298] (61); to spoil a thief or witch or any other enemy and to be delivered from evil (62); for the cramp (63); a horse that is forspoken (64); the nightmare (65); to staunch blood (66); for animals (67); for sick pigs (68); Three Biters charm for women (69); Three Biters charm for men (70); for bloating (71).

---

296 Klaassen 2019:19.
297 Charms 48-62 are all copied from Scot's *Discoverie of Witchcraft*.
298 Shears and sieve divination.

ENCYCLOPAEDIC ENTRIES

ESSENTIAL READING

Klaassen, Frank (ed) (2019) *Making Magic in Elizabethan England: Two Early Modern Vernacular Books of Magic*. Pennsylvania: Penn State University Press. Excellent academic study of the *Antiphoner Notebook* and the *Boxgrove Manual*.

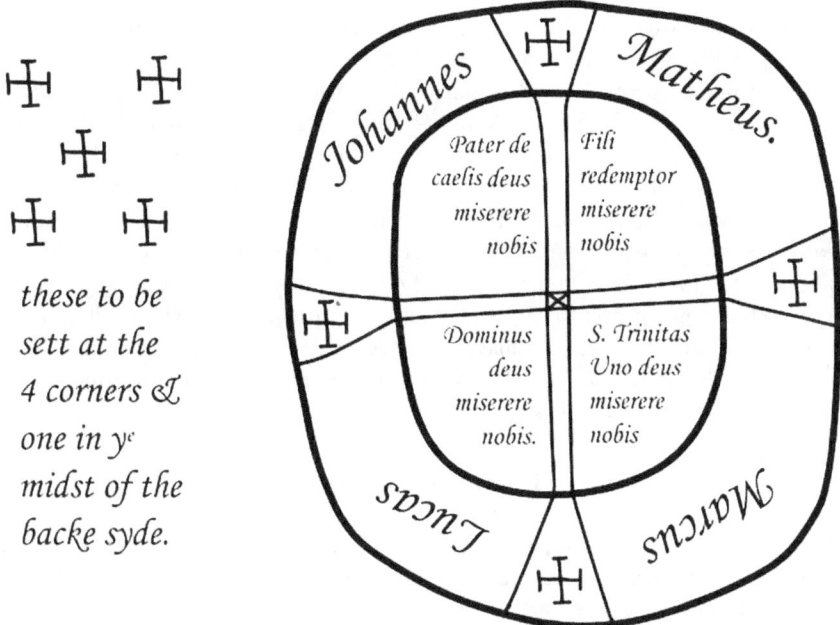

Antiphoner Notebook, Ritual to Exorcise Demon Guarding Treasure

The Boxgrove Manual

Date: 1600.
Language: English.
Influences: *Heptameron, Book of Consecrations, Thesaurus Spirituum, Three Books of Occult Philosophy, Fourth Book of Occult Philosophy.*
Provenance: Owen Clark, a parish clerk in Boxgrove, Sussex, is named as commissioning this manuscript, notarised by local notary George Stent.
MSS: Harley MS 2267.
Circle: Yes.
Tools: Ring, robe, sceptre, sword.
Spirit List: Aba, Abalidoth, Abbadon, Abraym, Agiel, Agusita, Amabiel, Amaday, Amatiel, Amaymon, Anael, Astaroth, Azael, Azazel, Babiel, Baron, Barzabel, Belyall, Belzebub, Bylet, Cadiel, Caracasa, Cassiel, Chedisutamel, Chermiel, Comissores, Coniel, Corat, Core, Doremiel, Egyn, Famiel, Flaef, Gabryel, Graphiel, Hagiel, Hasmoday, Hismael, Hufaltriel, Iophiel, Kedemel, Mahazell, Malchabetharsisim hed Beruah Schehakim, Maltiel, Mammon, Mererym, Michael, Nachiel, Oriens, Paymon, Penael, Penat, Peniel, Porna, Python, Rachiel, Ranael, Raphael, Sachiel, Samael, Santamel, Sathan, Setchiel, Sorath, Spugliguel, Talui, Tamael, Taphtartharath, Tenaciel, Tiriel, Turiel, Varcan, Zazel.

The Text

The *Boxgrove Manual* is synthesised from earlier works like the *Fourth Book of Occult Philosophy*, including the *Heptameron, Book of Consecrations, Thesaurus Spirituum,* and *Three Books of Occult Philosophy*. It includes a number of interesting pentacles different to those found in other works like the *Key of Solomon*. It is significant that this material has been translated into English for use decades before the Turner translations were published. The synthesis of material from several key texts into a workable form with comparative discussion makes this a valuable work demonstrating English grimoire magic circa 1600.

The text contains: pentacle of the apocalyptic Christ (1); what things are attributed to the planets, the Moon (2); Mercury (3); Venus (4); Sun (5); Mars (6); Jupiter (7); Saturn (8); on binding people or things (9); to make lamens or pentacles to call good spirits (10); the name of evil spirits by Cornelius[299] called infernal (11); the divine names of God from manuscript books (12); the divine names of God from Cornelius Agrippa (13); the consecrating of the fumigations (14); the consecration of the water (15); the consecration of the oil (16); the consecration of the fire (17); consecration of the sword (18); consecration of the book and parchment (includes nine prayers) (19); instructions for consecrating the book (20); the method or order to work in this Art (21); to make a pentacle, table, or lamen (22); to make pentacles by holy scripture (23); on pentacles (24); rules for operating (25); figures for Sunday, Monday, Wednesday, and Friday for each season.

Essential Reading

Klaassen, Frank (ed) (2019) *Making Magic in Elizabethan England: Two Early Modern Vernacular Books of Magic*. Pennsylvania: Penn State University Press. Excellent academic study of the *Antiphoner Notebook* and the *Boxgrove Manual*.

---

299 Presumably Cornelius Agrippa.

Tuba Veneris (The Horn of Venus)

Date: c. 1600.
Language: Latin.
Influences: *Heptameron*, *Sworn Book of Honorius*, Agrippa.
Provenance: Attributed to John Dee, actual authorship unknown.
MSS: Warburg MS FBH 510 (1600), Erlangen MS 854 (C17), Munich Cod. Ret. 27005 (C17). Printed in 1794 (in Latin and German).
Circle: Yes.
Tools: Horn (trumpet), Seal of Venus.
Spirit List: Alkyzub, Amabosar, Anael, Belzazel, Falkaroth, Mephgazub, Mogarip.

The Text

The name *Tuba Veneris* has become popular for this text, which more correctly is *Libellus Veneri Nigro Sacer* (The Little Book Sacred to the Black Venus). Although *Tuba Veneris* is attributed to John Dee, the style of the text does not match his other works. A key factor in this short work is the central figure of Black Venus, which it is tempting to equate with the Black Madonna cult or an alchemical motif, or even (it has been suggested) the Shekinah. The manuscript fits into the family of Class B Herpentil texts (discussed elsewhere) but is covered separately due to its notoriety and variations in the material within it from others in the family.

The text begins with an explanation of its contents, the summoning and banishing of six spirits under the dominion of Venus and their seals, the construction of the Seal of Venus, the trumpet, and the magic circle, the consecration of the book and the rites of operation. An introduction which has John Dee's name on it then follows. It should be noted that the number attributed to Venus in this text is six, not the more common seven. This would seem to be based on a comment in Agrippa's work.

The instruction begins with instructions on how to create and consecrate the seal of Venus on a copper hexagon, and to engrave the characters on it with an iron or steel tool. Next come the instructions for the horn, which must be torn live from a bull. In all these instances the timings are based on planetary times for Venus. The creation of the magic circle offers the practitioner the choice of how to prepare the circle. Chalk, charcoal, and a more permanent parchment (one assumes vellum) method are all mentioned, with the author stating a preference for the more permanent parchment variety.

The next chapter details the names, sigils, and invocations of the six spirits under the dominion of Venus. The sigils are made onto discs of green wax mixed with soot. The construction and consecration of the book follows, and then the conjuration procedure and banishing of the spirits. A cautionary after-note about behaviour ends the text.

Essential Reading

Burns, Teresa (trans, ed) & Turner, Nancy (trans) & Vincent Bridges (ed) & Legard, Phil (ed) (2007) *The Consecrated Little Book of Black Venus Attributed to John Dee*. New York: Waning Moon Publications Ltd. Very interesting edition with contextual essays and English translation.

Dee, John & Banner, James (ed) (2010) *Tuba Veneris*. Seattle: Trident Books. Good edition with interesting background material, includes the English, Latin and facsimile of the grimoire. A bibliography of Dee's manuscripts is also included.

Tabula Bonorum Angelorum Invocationes

Date: 1605-8.
Language: Latin, English.
Influences: *Sworn Book of Honorius*, Almandal tradition, *Steganographia*.
Provenance: Dr John Dee (1527-1609) and Edward Kelly (1555-97).
MSS: Sloane MS 3191 (1584-1605) is Dee's original (in Latin), found in his cedar chest in 1662; Elias Ashmole (1617-92) copied Sloane MS 3191 as Sloane MS 3678 (c.1740); Sloane MS 307 (C17) greatly expanded the material; Sloane MS 3821; Rawlinson MS D.1067 (C18); Rawlinson MS D.1363 (C17, also includes Olympic Spirit material at start of MS).
Circle: N/A.
Tools: Unspecified.
Spirit List: Aaan, Aadet, Aaetpio, Aana, Aaoxaif, Aapedoce, Abemo, Aboz, Acar, Acca, Acemliceve, Acepes, Aczinor, Adeta, Adoeoet, Adop, Adre, Æoan, Agelem, Ahaozpi, Aira, Alendood, Alhectega, Amox, Anaa, Anadoin, Anæo, Aomi, Aot, Apeste, Aphar, Arinnaquu, Arzel, Autep, Autotar, Axir, Azizod, Barcen, Bataiva, Berape, Boza, Cenbar, Cepesa, Cezodenes, Dapi, Datete, Detaa, Dexgezod, Dimet, Diom, Diri, Dopa, Ecope, Edelperna, Efermende, Elhiansa, Elzinopo, Emtedi, Enbarc, Endezen, Enheded, Enlarex, Enpeat, Estim, Exarih, Exes, Exgezod, Expeceh, Fipo, Gebal, Gelema, Gemenem, Gezodex, Habioro, Harap, Hetermorda, Hipotga, Iaom, Imted, Jaba, Jahel, Jezexpe, Jezodhehca, Jzazod, Jzodenar, Laidrom, Laoaxarp, Larexen, Larzod, Lefarahpem, Lemage, Leoc, Ligdisa, Magel, Magem, Mesael, Miao, Naaa, Naco, Næoa, Oanæ, Ocenem, Omgege, Omia, Oopezod, Opad, Opemen, Opena, Ormen, Otoi, Oyube, Ozab, Paax, Paco, Pado, Pali, Paoc, Paute, Peden, Pefem, Pemef, Pemox, Pend, Pesac, Phra, Raagios, Rapeh, Relemu, Reniel, Reseni, Rexao, Rexenel, Ries, Sacepe, Saiinou, Saix, Scio, Selgaiol, Shael, Sias, Sispe, Soaixente, Taad, Tedim, Tepau, Toco, Totet, Vasa, Vasge, Vrbeneh, Vrcenbre, Vrgan, Vrvoi, Vrzla, Vsyl, Vtepa, Xcez, Xenelar, Xenes, Zabo, Zazi, ZedocXe, Ziza, Zlar, Zodexge.

The Text

Tabula Bonorum Angelorum Invocationes was the fifth of the five manuscripts of his work found in Dr John Dee's cedar chest some fifty-three years after his death. Apart from the first manuscript (*Libri Mysteriorum I-V*) the rest were bound together by Elias Ashmole into what became Sloane MS 3191. At some point prior to his death or after the discovery of the manuscripts, a person or persons unknown worked the material, expanding it into the complete version found in Sloane MS 307 and subsequent manuscripts.[300] Ashmole preserved much of Dee's work, but it was another Englishman, Meric Causabon, who preserved the memory of Dee's legacy with the publication of his work *A True and Faithful Relation of What Passed for Many Years between Dr John Dee and Some Spirits* (1659).

This work is the core of the active practice of the Enochian material. It begins with the corrected Enochian Tables (not the initial Tables which were amended under instruction from Raphael in 1587). A brief introduction on how to use the Tables follows, with an explanation of the angelic hierarchies in them. The way to derive all the angelic names is explained, including the evil angels, using the Tablet of Union, with some examples of how they are derived.

Next is the method to invoke the angels to visible appearance including the evil angels, and how to constrain them. This is followed by discussion of the general use and significance

---

300 For a discussion of the possible identity of the practitioner, see Skinner & Rankine, 2010:38-42.

of the Tables. The construction of the book of invocations and practice is discussed, followed by the corpus of prayers and invocations to all the angels of the angelic hierarchies of the four Tables.

A small part of Sloane MS 307 was used by the Golden Dawn as Book H in their inner order teachings at the end of the nineteenth century into the early twentieth century.[301] This fraction has formed the basis of much of the Enochian work done since.

Essential Reading

Skinner, Stephen & Rankine, David (2004) *Practical Angel Magic of Dr John Dee's Enochian Tables*. Singapore: Golden Hoard Press. Provides the complete text of Sloane MS 307 and subsequent works, along with a background into possible players involved with the manuscripts and much contextual material.

---

301 See Skinner & Rankine, Appendixes 2 & 3, 2004:269-77 for more on this, including details of Allan Bennett's copy of Book H.

Key of Necromancy

Date: 1609- early C18.
Language: German with some Latin.
Influences: *Heptameron, Key of Solomon, Steganographia, Munich Handbook of Necromancy, Arbatel.*
Provenance: *Nigromantisches Kunst-Buch* published in 1743 by Peter Hammer, *Der Schlüssel von der Zwang der Höllen oder die Beschwörgen under Prozesse des Doctor Johannis Faustae, von der öfters practicirten göttlichen Zauber-Kunst ex Originalibus* published in 1609, and *Experimentir-Buch* (early C18).
MSS: Cornell 4620 Bd. MS 19 (*Experimentir-Buch*).
Circle: Yes.
Tools: Penknife, quill, spear, sword, wonder-rod.
Spirit List: Abalon, Abba, Abentabo, Abican, Abulnatita, Acharib, Achozib, Aegin, Ahesiel, Alatez, Albus, Algar, Alinanat, Alphus, Aluses, Amadiel, Amal, Amaymon, Amiraphales, Anathaniel, Andeles, Anystis, Arathiti, Arathon, Ariel, Aries, Arill, Asmodeus, Astaroth, Asyriel, Aversan, Aybory, Azael, Azazel, Aziel, Balthe, Barbaros, Barich, Barmiel, Baruchas, Bascli, Beelzebub, Belial, Belu, Berith, Bethor, Beymon, Buchermann, Cabariel, Camuel, Capeiel, Caramtias, Carmuth, Carnifex, Cherub, Coronthon, Curson, Daniel, Delen Arathibi, Domas, Donas, Dorothiel, Durstes, Egyn, Etubulnatita, Etybly, Florian, Forcan, Frätata, Frnacrio, Gabanay, Gabriel, Gaimon, Galliane, Gaman, Gatan, Gediel, Hagith, Hellemyr, Hul, Impotiel, Iranal, Jadel, Josla, Jossla, Laamon, Lucifer, Lynion, Mahazael, Malgaram, Marath, Mardach, Masa, Maseriel, Meymonetheby, Michael, Mirus, Muniuer, Mutheon, Nasatz, Nathael, Nerone, Nestorath, Nuleby, Och, Ononias, Oriens, Orina, Oviron, Pacta, Padiel, Parmesiel, Partes, Phiel, Pileth, Pluto, Portas Sambars, Pronsach, Puhsy, Rade, Randat, Raphael, Rauhardt, Raysiel, Saba, Sachan, Samael, Sambaras, Samuel, Sanrich, Saquiel, Saraphlorier, Satan, Serieph, Spracto, Stirel, Stratheam, Sumas, Suria, Sybilla, Symiel, Tegin, Thallus, Tharsis, Tranquinus, Troacrio, Tyman, Urachel, Uribel, Uriel, Usiel, Walachy, Waran, Welur, Welvor, Zabulus.

The Text

This work contains material from three different texts, *Nigromantisches Kunst-Buch* (*Book of the Nigromantic Art*, 1743), *Der Schlüssel von der Zwang der Höllen oder die Beschwörgen under Prozesse des Doctor Johannis Faustae, von der öfters practicirten göttlichen Zauber-Kunst ex Originalibus* (*The Key of the Coercion of Hell or Doctor Johannes Faust's Conjurations and Process, of the commonly practised divine Magical Art from the original*, 1609) and *Experimentir-Buch* (*Book of Experiments*, early C18). These texts are interesting in presenting variations of practices found elsewhere, demonstrating the diversity of the grimoires. They also, like many works, contain gems which should be noted and used in practice.

Volume one contains eleven chapters. These are: dealing with the consecration of the book (1); dealing with the consecration of the tools of the art (2); dealing with the wonder-rod[302] and how it is to be prepared (3); dealing with the ring of Solomon, which is and shall be used for necromancy (4); dealing with the crown of Solomon (5); dealing with the sigils of Solomon, or how to accomplish a beautiful work (6); dealing with the process of conjuration with which all and each of the spirits are and must be called, as well as the conjurations, and how one is to prepare for them (7); prayer to be spoken following the creation of the circle

---

302 A forked hazel rod.

(includes license to depart) (8); dealing with the right practice or use of the necromantic art, on how and in what manner, as well as in which times it is to be performed, or not (includes tables of planetary hours of the week and sigils for the days of the week) (9); the spirits of the necromancy art (for days of the week, the three rulers, the four kings, spirits of the four elements, seven evil spirits, eight prince spirits, and a number of others) (10); dealing with the circles and imprisonment of spirits (four magic circles, and the conjuration process) (11).

Volume two contains twelve chapters. These are: introduction or useful information (1); here follows a strong and powerful conjuration and instructions on the means to summon spirits, kings, and their subordinate princes (2); here follows a conjuration of the aforementioned spirits, and an instruction on how to make the circle, which follows (3); a proved experiment on how to raise a treasure (4); a conjuration for the spirit Waran (5); the art of Nerony over the spirit Remisia (6); a collection of nice remarks from Cornelius Agrippa's Occult Philosophy (7); the preparation of *signaculorum*, taken from ten wonderful experiments (8); an instruction for those who intend to raise hidden treasures (9); short and true report on the seven highest and noble princes (excerpt derived from the *Arbatel* with the seven Olympic spirits) (10); deals with the art of mining and treasure hunting (lists the good and bad days for treasure hunting, methods of preparing candles) (11); deals with various experiments – an experiment of the spirit Sybilla, a beautiful experiment to have a spirit in a crystal, a particular experiment to bring a good spirit into a glass, the figure of Solomon, an experiment to have three spirits bring gold, another beautiful practice for conjuring eight spirits, deals with the *amithusala manus* and how it is to be made (for the coercion of all spirits), *pentaculum Salomonis* (includes pentacle of Raymond Lull) (12).

Essential Reading

Ortiz, Nicolás Álvarez (trans, ed) (2018-19) *The Key of Necromancy* (2 vols). Mexico City: Enodia Press. Fascinating collection of material with good notes, marred only by lack of clear indication which of the source texts the material is drawn from and lack of index.

Magia Naturalis et Innaturalis (Threefold Coercion of Hell)

Date: 1612.
Language: German.
Influences: *Heptameron, Arbatel, Steganographia, De Occulta Philosophia, Semiphoras and Shemhamphorash, Sepher Raziel,* Paracelsus.
Provenance: Attributed to Dr. Johannes Faust (c.1466-c.1541), according to the earliest known MS written in Passau. Published by Scheible in 1849.
MSS: HAAB Q455B (1612); partial in Leipzig Cod. Mag. 6 (1750), Cod. Mag. 22 (1750); Cod. Mag. 30 (1750).
Circle: Yes.
Tools: Brazier, dagger, rod, scourge, sword.
Spirit List: Abdizuel, Abrinel, Abton, Abumalith, Aceruel, Aciel, Acteus, Adadiel, Adaph, Adiel, Adriel, Aecus, Affaibi, Agaton, Ahisdophiel, Alecto, Alheniel, Almadiel, Amadiel, Amaymon, Amixiel, Amniel, Amnixiel, Amodiel, Amutiel, Anael, Anhael, Aniel, Antologan, Apadiel, Apatiel, Aphiel, Apidius, Aratron, Arbiel, Ariel, Asaron, Assardiel, Asteroth, Asterotus, Astromiel, Atatiel, Azael, Azazel, Azeruel, Badon, Barbiel, Barchan, Bazarachiel, Beelzebub, Behemoth, Beherit, Beshor, Bethanael, Beulus, Bidon, Biscerdiel, Bludohn, Brachiel, Bufiel, Buriel, Camiel, Camniel, Carniel, Casadiel, Casbriel, Casphiel, Cassesi, Cassiel, Cerberu, Cerphiel, Chariel, Coachtiel, Coradiel, Coronem, Craffiel, Cresiphone, Cupriel, Cycas, Damniel, Darachiel, Del, Drubriel, Drusiel, Dusiriel, Egibiel, Egyn, Ergediel, Fahassur, Fardiar, Fos, Furiel, Gabriel, Gardiab, Germiciel, Goeme, Habudiel, Hagith, Hamaliel, Hamas, Hamath, Haniel, Harmon, Hassica, Haxiel, Humaliel, Husro, Hydriel, Ibadon, Ipodhar, Ischscabadiel, Jazariel, Jazel, Joiel, Joviel, Kirotiel, Knidadiel, Kunifer, Kyriel, Lameniel, Legion, Leviathan, Lucifer, Lusiel, Magelesius, Mahatan, Mahazael, Malchidael, Marbuel, Megera, Mentanta, Mephistophiel, Merosiel, Metatron, Michael, Mimon, Minos, Monto, Mortaliel, Musuziel, Nadanniel, Narael, Nastros, Nector, Nedriel, Nicon, Och, Ophiel, Oriel, Orion, Oriphiel, Ormenus, Osphadiel, Padiel, Paradiel, Pastorem, Paymon, Peliel, Peliet, Pesariel, Phacamech, Phalec, Phul, Pluto, Primonem, Psohdon, Radamandus, Radiel, Raphael, Rartmaratarium, Raziel, Requiel, Sadon, Salmison, Salvian, Samael, Sambhan, Samiel, Samuel, Sarniel, Satan, Schafforth, Schmaym, Scholiel, Semharis, Soul of Messiah, Sumnidiel, Tagriel, Uriel, Urieus, Urinaphton, Zachariel, Zadkiel, Zaniael, Zaphkiel, Zoyma, Zoyplay, Zuriel.

The Text

Magia Naturalis et Innaturalis has huge significance as the best known and possible source of the Faust book tradition of German grimoires. The text is divided into four books, the second of which is largely an expansion of the first. There are numerous fine colour illustration (one hundred and forty-six). An interesting inclusion in the spirits is the attribution of the four elements to some of the spirits, as well as the spirits of the dead, and how to deal with a poltergeist. Along with the infernal spirits, angels, and Olympic spirits, this gives the book a wide range of spirits to work with.

Book one begins with a preface to the cabbalists, which explores the requisites for the work and how to deal with spirits. Chapter two is Of the Pact with all Spirits and contains the key practice. It includes the creation and consecration of the candles, incense, brazier, and magic circle, along with the operation, namely the conjuration, bond, oath, license to depart, and prayer to be spoken before leaving the circle. Next is Pact with a spirit in certain and specified times (3); termination of the pact (4); dealing with the classifications of the spirits, their names, and of what assistance they can be to men (5); dealing with the hierarchy of all the spirits in the corps of their princes (6); dealing with the spirits, the way to call them, and more importantly, the time of citation at which they can be summoned or called (7); dealing with the grand prince Barbiel (8); dealing with the explanation of the grand prince Barbiel (9); dealing with the main conjuration of Barbiel (10); another conjuration (11); a main conjuration of Barbiel for when he does not want to transform himself (12); dealing with Barbiel's main dismissal and his coercing sigil (13); dealing with the grand prince Mephistophiel (14); dealing with Mephistophiel's confession (15); dealing with the particular conjuration of Mephistophiel (16); dealing with one main conjuration of Mephistophiel (17); dealing with the license to depart of Mephistophiel (18); dealing with the grand prince of hell Apadiel (19); now follow the conjurations of the infernal grand prince Apadiel which are the same that were used with the grand prince Barbiel (20); dealing with Aciel the fourth grand prince of hell (21); dealing with the appearance of Aciel (22); a prayer for the operation of the infernal spirits, specifically Aciel (23); dealing with a particular citation of Aciel (24); dealing with main conjuration of Aciel, when he appears with great rumbling after which he remains silent (25); dealing with the scourge of spirits (26); dealing with the address and questions to the spirit (27); dealing with the coercing sigil of Aciel (28); a conjuration for when Aciel refuses and does not want to turn over the treasure (29); dealing with Aciel when one has him with the money before himself (30); dealing with the last main money and treasure reception of Aciel (31); when the spirit leaves you to dig the treasure (32); dealing with the dismissal and license to depart of Aciel (33); dealing with the coercing sigil of Aciel (34); dealing with when Aciel should bring written answer (35); dealing with the fifth grand prince of hell called Anael (36); dealing with the appearance and coercing sigil of Anael (37); dealing with Ariel, the sixth grand prince of hell (38); dealing with the appearance of Ariel (39); dealing with the citation of Ariel (40); dealing with the bond, dissolution, and license to depart of Ariel (41); dealing with the infernal grand prince Marbuel (42); dealing with the coercing sigil of *sigillum magnum* of Marbuel (43); dealing with Maruel's greetin, coercion and what one can request from him (44); dealing with the particular conjuration of Marbuel (45); the grand prince Marbuel's main conjuration (46); dealing with the bond, dissolution, and dismissal of Marbuel (47); now follow the seven count palatines (48); dealing with the citation of Coradiel (49); dealing with the citation of the count palatine Camniel (50); dealing with the seven counts (51); dealing with what someone can obtain from the count Dirachiel (52); dealing with count Dirachiel's conjurations (53); dealing with the bond, dissolution, and license to depart of Dirachiel (54); dealing with the citation of Amodiel (55); now follow the seven barons in their order (56); now follow the seven noble spirits in their order (57); now follow the seven commoner spirits in their order (58); now follow the seven peasant spirits in their order (59); now follow the seven wise spirits in their order (60); now follow the seven foolish spirits in their order (61); dealing with the four greater free spirits (62); dealing with the general citation of the four free spirits (63); dealing with how one, through Damniel, can get all kinds of garden plants, as you want them to be (64); dealing with how one can get all sorts of beautiful flowers through Damniel (65); dealing with the spirits of the seven liberal arts (66).

Part two, Faust's Cabalae Nigrae, maintains the chapter numbering from part one. They continue: dealing with the seven free spirits, with the way which one can enter a contract with them, on how to be granted their arts and sciences, and to use them for each endeavour (67); now follow the seven great fiery spirits in their order (68); dealing with the fiery spirits, also with a particular explanation on these, on how they can help and serve humans (69); dealing with the citation of the seven greater and five lesser fiery spirits (70); dealing with the eight great aerial spirits in their order (71); the citation of Adatiel (72); the citation of Damniel (73); the citation for this purpose is as follows (74); the citation of Caffiel (75); dealing with all kinds of strengths which Barbiel can provide (76); if you want to be shown all kinds of beautiful summer birds, then cite the aerial spirit Pedatiel with the following words (77); if you want to be taught about alchemy, then cite Coachiel in the following form (78); now follow the water spirits in their order (79);[303] dealing with the citation of Hydriel (80); now follow the earth spirits in their order (includes instruction on the pygmies)[304] (81); dealing with the preparation of the finding-ball (82);[305] now follows another way to prepare the finding-ball (83); still another way to fabricate the finding-ball (84); another different way to make the question and finding-ball (85); dealing with how to make an earth mirror to see every hidden good therein (86); another reinforced mirror, used by the Venetians (87); dealing with a *usu speculi ex electris* (88);[306] dealing with how one should make a magical ell of electrum (89); dealing with how to fabricate crystals out of metals or glass (90); still another way to prepare a crystal or mirror (91); an experiment of a steel mirror, *seu divination specularis* (92);[307] dealing with an experiment so that one can see everything that one desires in the glass (93); dealing with how one can deal with the nine aerial spirits in a glass of water and bring them to appear (94); to make an apparition in the hand (95); still another way to have apparitions in the crystal (96); a further way through which one can now see a thief that has stolen something (97).

Book two is also referred to as the third part of the book. The chapters are: dealing with the spirits of deceased men (1); dealing with the bond, dissolution, and dismissal of Jazariel (2); dealing with the spirit Bazarachiel (3); dealing with the citation of the tribal spirits of deceased me (4); dealing with a lead sigil and how it is to be prepared (5); dealing with how one can expel spirits from treasures (6); dealing with the names and attributes of the false spirits (7); dealing with the false spirit Beulus (8); dealing with the false spirit Laoobis (9); dealing with the false spirit Nestorat (10); dealing with a universal citation for all spirits in general (11); dealing with the black star of Dr Johann Faust (12); dealing with the citation of these spirits (13); dealing with the banishing of a spirit from a building or some other place, which is called a poltergeist (14); dealing with a true explication of the *Herpentills Salomonis*[308] (15); dealing with the citation of a spirit that gives account of all kinds of things (16).

The fourth part is called The Sigils of the Art. The foreword details the seven sigils from the *New Testament* for use in coercion of spirits. The chapters are: Dealing with my precious sigil, which I, Faust, bought from a good friend only for the purpose of unearthing treasures; also I received the chief Bludohn's nasal coercion from my dear Mephistopheles, which I am rightly able to name the ultimate infernal coercion of spirits (1); dealing with the sigils of the throne angels of God (2); a pentacle of Solomon to be hanged (3); to know the position of the treasure or where it is (4); still another lead sigil to be placed over the treasure (5); to lay the Solomonic treasure sigil over a treasure (6); dealing with different characters and sigils, through which one can unearth treasures (7); dealing with four particular secret sigils to dig treasures (8); a magical sigil (9); dealing with a magical ring (10); dealing with four pentacles to be used hanged (11); dealing with two particular pentacles, namely, a cross and the nose-coercion of Lucifer (12); dealing with an arrangement and seat of the throne angels and the seat of the so-called Olympic or planetary angels, or governors (13); comprehending seven particular sigils of the Olympic spirits or pentacles of the seven planetary princes (14); dealing

---

303 Most of the water and earth spirits names seem to have been taken from spirits in *Steganographia*.
304 I.e., earth elementals.
305 A finding-ball is a small metal ball used to locate treasure and lost items, for protection from evil spirits, and sleight of hand.
306 'Enameled glass', i.e. mirror.
307 'Or Mirror Divination'.
308 This grimoire is discussed in the subchapter on the Herpentil texts.

with different sigils and pentacles of Solomon (15); a secret sigil (16); a particular sigil (17); a description of a circle, which can also be done with a conjuration (18); the pentacles of the seven Olympic spirits (19); dealing with the two sigils which consist of the New Testament (20); an approved process of how the two magicians can coerce the spirits Kunifer and Salmison through their sigils so that they have to give written answer to the presented question (21); an approved experiment which I, Dr. Johann Faust, often allowed my student Christopher Wagner to practise (22). There is an appendix at the end which contains the four shields which are to be placed at the four corners of the circle, and the cingulum of Solomon.

Essential Reading

Álvarez, Nicolas Ortiz (ed, trans) (2019) *Magia Naturalis et Innaturalis*. Mexico City: Enodia Press. Good edition which provides an invaluable English translation based on several of the main sources.

The Magical Calendar

Date: 1620.
Language: Latin.
Influences: Harley MS 3420 (original source), *Heptameron*, *Arbatel*, *Archidoxes of Magic* (Paracelsus), *Three Books of Occult Philosophy* (Agrippa), *Tuba Veneris*.
Provenance: Engraving compiled by Johann Baptista Grosschedel von Aicha (author) & Johannes Theodorus de Bry (engraver).
MSS: A number of manuscript copies of the engraving and its contents exist. These include (in Latin unless otherwise stated) – Vienna MS Lat11313 (C17), Wellcome MS 321 (c. 1650, French), Yale Mellon MS 72 (1700), Wellcome MS 2640 (1716), Wellcome MS 2641 (mid C18), Dresden MS N. 67a (C18), Manly Palmer Hall MS 191 (C18, French), Glasgow MS Ferguson 2 (early C19), Rome MS Verginelli-Rota 36 (C19). From the late C18 several books have published this work, most notably T.V.F du Chenteau's *Calendrier Magique et Perpétual*, including additional material from Robert Fludd and others.
Circle: N/A.
Tools: N/A.
Spirit List:[309] Adnachiel, Amabael, Amatiel, Ambriel, Anael, Aquilo, Aratron, Ariel, Asmodel, Auster, Bael, Barbiel, Barchiel, Betor, Camael, Caracasa, Cassiel, Cherub, Comisoros, Ctarari, Egin, Eurus, Gabriel, Gargatel, Gaviel, Gualbarel, Hagit, Hamaliel, Hanael, Malchidiel, Metatron, Michael, Moymon, Muriel, Och, Ophiel, Orphaniel, Phalec, Phul, Poymon, Raphael, Sachiel, Samael, Seraph, Tariel, Tarquam, Tharsis, Uriel, Verchiel, Zadkiel, Zaphkiel, Zephirus, Zuriel.

The Text

Measuring 108 x 60cm, the incredibly detailed copperplate engraving of the Magical Calendar is a treasure-house of magical images and symbolism, coalescing much of the Hermetic, Magical, and Religious thought of the seventeenth century. Ultimately it can be considered an expression of the work of Trithemius, developed through his pupil Agrippa. Much of the material is drawn from Book 2 chapters 4-13 of Agrippa's *Three Books of Occult Philosophy*.

It contains information from alchemy, Christian mysticism, grimoires, Hermeticism, Qabalah, and other sources arranged through the attribution to numerical symbolism of the numbers 1-10 and 12. The material is extremely coherent and the images beautiful, providing a lasting testament to the expanse and cogency of Renaissance magic. The relevance of the Magical Calendar can be seen in the inclusion of material from it in other works like *Janua Magica Reserata*.

Essential Reading

McLean, Adam (ed, trans) (1994) *The Magical Calendar*. Grand Rapids: Phanes Press. This excellent work explores the origins of the calendar and gives all the images from it with English translation.

---

309 Although this is essentially a master table of correspondences, the named spirits are included here for relevance in subsequent influence on other works.

The Grimoire of Arthur Gauntlet

Date: c.1630-6.
Language: English.
Influences: *Heptameron*, *Sworn Book of Honorius*, *Sepher Raziel*, *Arbatel*, *Book of Oberon*, *Key of Solomon* (Addtional MS 36674), *Discoverie of Witchcraft*, Agrippa, William Bacon.
Provenance: Book of Practice of cunningman Arthur Gauntlet. Purchased by John Humphreys, then by Ann Savadge and thence to Elias Ashmole. From Ashmole it passed to Baron Sommers, then Lord Jekyll, ending up with Sir Hans Sloane.
MSS: Sloane MS 3851.
Circle: Yes.
Tools: Basin, black-handled knife, crystal, girdle, pentacle, wand (hazel), white linen robe.
Spirit List: Aachnine, Aba, Abamatra, Abelit, Abrera, Abuiori, Abumalith, Abundant, Abuzaha, Acimay, Acolcrostel, Adtcalea, Affia, Affla, Aiel, Akaba, Alexa, Aliaml, Alis, Alka, Alkates, Allea, Almederie, Alstas, Altibam, Amabael, Amabiel, Amacyon, Amatiel, Amomium, Anaabbus, Anael, Analidoth, Anatnabie, Anayl, Andas, Andragias, Aniel, Aquiel, Aramael, Aratron, Arcan, Arkinlia, Armail, Arragon, Arsdorth, Asariel, Asasiel, Askariel, Asmo. Assaibi, Assassaiel, Astagna, Atanael, Atel, Athay, Aturi, Axel, Babel, Babell, Babiel, Bachanel, Baciel, Baffala, Balay, Balidet, Baliel, Baraborat, Bariel, Baron, Baylon, Bealphares, Belzebub, Bethor, Bilet, Booel, Boytheon, Burchat, Busto, Caldel, Calon, Caluel, Calzas, Cancer, Capabili, Carcasa, Cargutel, Cariel, Carinal, Carmax, Carmelion, Cassal, Cassiel, Castub, Cedas, Cehafa, Cerberus, Charsiel, Chedusitaniel, Chermiel, Cia, Clarari, Cokiel, Commissoros, Con, Coniel, Conuociell, Corabiel, Corat, Core, Cranael, Curaniel, Cynabal, Dabriel, Dagiel, Dala, Damael, Dangolath, Dardiel, Darquiel, Deamiel, Delforia, Denel, Dentalion, Deothan, Diffialofon, Dirath, Donskion, Doremiel, Dupanfolan, Dyiaga, Edlodell, Eillon, Eligamill, Eloofe, Emenguill, Enan, Erusia, Etheluill, Falaur, Famtiell, Faon, Farma, Felofell, Fernola, Fesaloell, Fesoraell, Festinavit, Flaef, Fraciel, Friagne, Frodissma, Fuua, Ga, Gabrael, Gabriel, Gaions, Ganar, Gaoel, Gariguam, Gauiham, Gaviel, Glumfogro, Gratuell, Guabarel, Guael, Guthaca, Gutriz, Haabach, Haasa, Habaiel, Habetell, Habudiel, Hafea, Hagith, Haila, Halt, Handa, Hanun, Hartapel, Hela, Hemeolon, Herb, Hermadafin, Hermiadall, Hodelsa, Hufaltiel, Humastrau, Hundalgunda, Hymiel, Imiual, Inafula, Irel, Iscarath, Isiael, Ismoli, Itna, Janael, Janiel, Jariahel, Jaxel, Jendoad, Jerescue, Julia, Kaberion, Kadie, Kaeldath, Kargiel, Lama, Lambores, Lathaxiell, Letraraamsag, Liachida, Lobquin, Lucifer, Lundrmqnusa, Lymaxill, Machasiel, Machatan, Madiel, Mael, Maguth, Makalice, Mal, Malantha, Malatrin, Malgabriel, Maltiel, Mami, Mammoye, Maros, Massabu, Mastas, Mathiel, Mathlay, Matreton, Matriton, Matuyel, Matuyell, Maymon, Mayrion, Mediat, Memeta, Memibolo, Menera, Michael, Micraton, Miel, Milliel, Minariell, Mitharens, Mitratron, Mulcala, Muron, Musdali, Myiasalet, Naadol, Nata, Nelapa, Oberion, Obnala, Och, Odanan, Offriel, Ohorma, Onat, Onele, Opathan, Ophiel, Orebon, Oremaell, Orphamiell, Osael, Osimimilis, Pabel, Paffran, Pandolath, Parante, Pasas, Penael, Penat, Pendagell, Peniel, Phaleg, Phallus, Phul, Porna, Primac, Princo, Raberion, Rabit, Rachiel, Rael, Ragarad, Ragnel, Raguell, Rahumel, Ramasael, Raniel, Raphiel, Rayel, Reat, Relfato, Rendos, Reralath, Reumdath, Riarnfa, Roauia, Rochell, Rostalagath, Rufangoll, Ruiaminta, Sachiel, Sacriel, Saffiell, Sagamex, Saipaleppe, Salgmel, Saliel, Sallales, Saluagam, Samael, Samax, Sambas, Samiel, Samion, Samuel, Sana, Saniorie, Santanael, Saphea, Sapiel, Satael, Sathan, Satquiell, Saturnion, Scorax, Seberion, Sedamylia, Sedelpha, Sedmaon, Serabotes, Seraphiel, Setchiel, Siaar, Sibilia, Sieate. Sitrael, Sitrami, Soaea, Solseqium, Somoha, Somucha, Soncas, Soquidaell, Spiron, Stifellore, Suceratos, Suquinos, Suth, Taketh, Tamael,

Tamandundiceth, Tamiel, Tanaell, Tariel, Tarmiel, Tarquam, Tartais, Teltrion, Tenaciel, Tetra, Thamaor, Thiel, Tlodalath, Tolana, Turiel, Tus, Uriell, Ustael, Valel, Valerian, Vallo, Valnum, Varcan, Venahel, Veriell, Vervain, Vetuel, Vianuel, Vionatraba, Vraci, Vuael, Walkates, Xoni, Yassaell, Yenesaight, Yesse, Yoasel, Zaliel, Zaniel.

The Text

The *Grimoire of Arthur Gauntlet* (Sloane MS 3851) is an exceptional example of a cunning book of practice. Due to the people and materials he had access to, Arthur Gauntlet composed a book with many interesting and unique features, meriting its inclusion in this book.

Amongst diverse prayers and charms is interspersed material from the *Heptameron*, *Book of Oberon*, *Discoverie of Witchcraft*, *Key of Solomon* and *Sepher Raziel*, particularly conjurations, prayers, and correspondences. A sequence of Psalm charms in Latin are interesting, as they are exact (or near exact in some cases) matches for material found in the later French *Book of Gold*, which could suggest an earlier text source for both. A prayer claimed to be copied from John Dee is also interesting, as it would have been from material lost in the burning of his manuscripts by the unknowing maid (see subchapter on *Tabula Bonorum Angelorum*).

The book contains: Instructions of Ptolomie and Instructions of Cyprian (which describe the importance of personal cleanliness and virtuous behaviour); Jesus turned around will be Jesus to me (conjuration sequence full of Psalms and prayers); license to depart; a prayer to God for good success in matters by John Searle dated 1594; two more licenses to depart; a prayer for thy Genius; charm for success for JF (possibly John Fletcher); love charm of Captain Bubb; charm to not perish; charm against enemies; to make money spent return; to make one sleep at a table; letter charm from St Leo XII to Charlemagne; to make any man to go unhurt upon sword or any sharp thing; for worms; entire text of the *Arbatel*, including the image of the Seal of Secrets; moving and summoning with the prayers appropriate for the day; sign of the Pentacle of Solomon; John 1:1-14; Psalm 91; prayer of benediction; sign of the Pentacle of Solomon (again, with extra text); Psalm 80; Psalm 45; a prayer whereby to have sight of the angels; sign of the Pentacle of Solomon (third version with more text); Luke 1:26-35, 38, 46-54; Psalm 103; *Te deum laudamus*;[310] sign of the Pentacle of Solomon (fourth version with even more text); to call three good angels into a crystal stone or looking glass to thine own sight do as followeth; you may call the angels to yourself according to the method of the next experiment altering very little; how to call three heavenly angels into a looking glass to the visible sight of a child; how you shall make your demands for theft to the three angels; for treasure hidden; for sickness; how you shall bind a spirit for diverse purposes as first for this last experiment for sickness or lameness; how you shall call for a spirit of prophecy; to cause cattle to return to the place from whence they were strayed or stolen; to cause a thief to bring stolen goods again; to cause one that is run away to return; how you shall work for witchcraft; how you shall work to have sight and conference with one good angel; Psalm 51: Psalm 46; Psalm 91 (partial); then read this prayer following three times with great devotion; how you shall call for a good angel; how to call three heavenly angels into a crystal stone or skrying glass to the visible sight of a child; how to call the angels into a glass of water; a prayer preservative always to be carried about man or woman; for theft; for theft; the former experiment (demon bishops); for the accomplishment of the pleasure of the flesh; to gain the love of man or woman; the former experiment; again the former experiment; of the circle and his composition: Peter of Abano;[311] of the names of the hours and angels governing

---

310 Early Christian hymn of praise dating originally to the C4 CE.
311 Excerpt from the *Heptameron* follows.

them; angels of the spring, summer, autumn, and winter; of consecrations and blessings, and first the blessing of the circle; the blessing of fumigations; an exorcism of the fire upon which the fumigations are put; of the garment and pentacle; pentacle; a prayer to be said when the vesture is put on; of the manner of working; an exorcism of the aerial spirits; visions and apparitions; magic circle; considerations for Sunday, angels, and conjuration; considerations of Monday, angels, and conjuration; considerations for Tuesday, angels, and conjuration; considerations of Wednesday, angels, and conjuration; considerations for Thursday, angels, and conjuration; considerations for Friday, angels, and conjuration; considerations for Saturn's day, angels, and conjuration; the fourth book of the hidden philosophy, or of the Magical Ceremonies, written by Cornelius Agrippa;[312] an invocation to call a spirit into a crystal; another conjuration to make a spirit appear in a crystal stone, looking glass or suchlike; the manner to shut a spirit into a crystal stone that will show thee anything thou desirest; the circle for the aforesaid experiment; how to include a spirit in a crystal stone, beryl glass or into any other like instrument; the figure or type proportional following showeth what form must be observed;[313] how to call a spirit into a crystal stone which shall declare the truth of all things thou shalt demand; an experiment of a spirit called Baron which telleth of treasure; an experiment of a spirit called Bealphares,[314] Psalm 22, then say Psalm 51 three times, prayers, conjuration, the bond, and a license for the spirit to depart; magic circle; to have the spirit of a dead body; another experiment of the dead (includes bond and conjuration of the fairy Sibilia); the Roman Secret touching the spirit called Sathan, by William Bacon; to burn or curse a spirit; the consecration of a wand or rod; how he ought to order himself that would call; of the bond of spirits; of perfumes; four magic circles; whosoever hath this following figure and shall use the invocation presently shall make Oberion come; collection of Psalm charms in Latin;[315] here beginneth the Book of the Seven Images of the days; charms for diverse diseases; for the antimonial cup;[316] for to make optical glass; for theft or anything thou desirest; to have conference with spirits, includes the dead, fairie, and familiar spirits; against thieves (includes historiola); the right spell for thieves; against witchcraft; experiments to go invisible; experiment of the herb valerian; experiments of the herb vervain; experiments of the herb called elitrapa; experiments of the herb yarrow; experiments for love; experiments for all games; for toothache; table of planetary hours from an ephemeris.

Essential Reading

Rankine, David (ed) (2011) *The Grimoire of Arthur Gauntlet*. London: Avalonia. This work presents the entire manuscript of Sloane MS 3851, along with numerous notes regarding source and context. The historical background of the manuscript, Arthur Gauntlet and his contemporaries, and owners of the manuscript are all discussed.

---

312 Excerpt from *Fourth Book of Occult Philosophy*.
313 Image of magic circle from *Discoverie of Witchcraft*.
314 From *Discoverie of Witchcraft*, Book XV ch. 13.
315 Interestingly some of these Latin charms match those later found in French in the *Book of Gold*.
316 Such cups were used with wine to induce vomiting; the recipe here is an extreme form of this.

Goetia

Date: 1641.
Language: English.
Influences: *Psalms* (on Rudd's *Goetia*), *Sworn Book of Honorius, Heptameron*, MS Plut. 89 sup. 38, *Le Livre des Esperitez, Pseudomonarchia Daemonum, Book of the Offices of Spirits*.
Provenance: Unknown author. Sloane MS 3825 is the first known copy. Harley MS 6483 by Thomas Rudd, copied by Peter Smart (1712); NWU MS 65 in hand of Thomas Simpkins (1713); Ebenezer Sibley (1752-99)(late C18); copied by Frederick Hockley (1808-85) (1828), copied by Henry Dawson Lea (1809-63) as Wellcome MS 3203, copied by Henry Harries (1821-49) as M11117B.
MSS: Sloane MS 3825 (1641); Sloane 3648 (1649); Sloane 2731 (1686); Harley MS 6483 (1712 from earlier copy); Northwestern University MS 65 (1713); Wellcome MS 3203 (1843); WNL M11117B (1843-6).
Circle: Yes.
Tools: Cap, censer, Hexagon of Solomon, lion-skin belt, Pentacle of Solomon, ring, robe, sceptre, shoes, sword.
Spirit Catalogue: Abalam, Agares, Aim, Alloces, Amduscias, Amon, Amy, Andras, Andrealphus, Andromalius, Asmoday, Astaroth, Bael, Balam, Barbatos, Bathin, Beball, Beleth, Belial, Berith, Bifrons, Botis, Buer, Bune, Caim, Cimeies, Corson, Dantalion, Decarabia, Eligor, Flauros, Focalor, Foras, Forneus, Furcas, Furfur, Gaap, Gamigin, Gemory, Glasya-la bolas, Gusoin, Haagenti, Halphas, Ipos, Leraje, Malphas, Marax, Marbas, Marchosias, Murmur, Naberius, Napula, Orias, Orobas, Ose, Paimon, Phenix, Procel, Purson, Raum, Ronove, Sabnakc, Sallos, Seere, Shax, Sitri, Stolas, Valac, Valefar, Vasago, Vepar, Vine, Vuall, Zagan, Zepar, Ziminiar. The following Shemhamphorash and other angels are found only in Harley MS 6483: Achasiah, Aladiah, Alaliah, Amabael, Amatiel, Anael, Anavel, Andas, Aniel, Ariel, Cahetel, Caliel, Caratasa, Cassiel, Chajakiah, Commissaros, Core, Ctarari, Cynabal, Damabiah, Daniel, Eiael, Elemiah, Gabriel, Gargatel, Gaviel, Guabarel, Haajah, Habujah, Hahahel, Hahajah, Hahasiah, Haiviah, Hajajel, Hakamiah, Hamiah, Hasiel, Hazabel, Haziel, Imamiah, Jahhael, Jehujah, Jejael, Jejalel, Jejazel, Jelahel, Jelahiah, Jeliel, Jerathel, Jezalel, Laviah, Lectabel, Lehahiah, Loviah, Mahasiah, Manadel, Marakel, Mebahel, Mebahiah, Mehiel, Melahel, Michael, Mihael, Mizrael, Mumiah, Nanael, Nelchael, Nemamiah, Nithael, Nithhajah, Omael, Pahaliah, Polial, Rahael, Raphael, Reiajel, Roehel, Sachiel, Samael, Sealiah, Seechiah, Sus, Syrael, Tabamiah, Tariel, Tarquam, Umabel, Varcan Rex, Vasariah, Vehuel, Vehujah, Vevaliah.

The Text

The *Goetia* is the first of the five works collectively bound together as the *Lemegeton*.[317] These works are all separate and are dealt with in separate subchapters to give them the attention they deserve. The five works are all mentioned by name or as types of magic in two consecutive chapters of a work by Agrippa in 1531.[318] Spirit lists found in earlier works seem to be clear precursors to the one found in the *Goetia*. These include the French *Livre des Esperitz*, MS Plut. 89 sup. 38, the *Book of the Offices of Spirits* and Johann Weyer's *Pseudomonarchia Daemonium*, which

---

317 These being *Goetia, Theurgia-Goetia, Ars Pauline, Ars Almadel*, and *Notary Art*. The last two works appear in earlier versions, which is reflected in their earlier position in the time sequence of these chapters.
318 *De incertitudine et vanitate omnium scientarium et artium* (Paris, 1531), *Ars Almadel, Ars Notoria, Ars Pauline, Goetia, Theurgia*.

was reproduced in Walter Scott's *Discoverie of Witchcraft* (all of these works have their own chapter in this work).

The *Goetia* begins with a spirit catalogue[319] of seventy-two spirits, or demons, with descriptions of their appearance, what they can offer the conjuror, and the number of legions they rule. Each description also includes the seal to be used in conjuring the demon. This is followed by the tale of King Solomon binding them all into a brazen vessel and throwing it into a lake in Babylon, only for the Babylonians to fish it out and open it, releasing them all back into the world.

The text proceeds to the practice, beginning with the appropriate times of day to conjure the demons depending on their rank. The magic circle and triangle of conjuration are given, with the hexagram and pentacle of Solomon, and the ring to be worn by the magician. The secret seal and brazen vessel for constraining the spirits follow, along with a list of other tools the magician needs, like the sword, white linen robes, lion-skin girdle, censer, etc. The sequence of conjurations, constraint, methods for dealing with non-compliant spirits, and license to depart follow, forming the last part of the text.

Rudd's *Goetia* has significant additions to the other manuscripts. Rudd assigned the seventy-two angels of the Shemhamphorash as controlling angels of the seventy-two Goetic demons, and as part of this, changed the seals to double seals, with the demonic seal on one side and the angelic seal on the other (the side facing the heart when it is worn as a lamen, with the demonic seal facing outward toward the demon conjured). Each of the angelic seals includes a verse from Psalms around its perimeter.

Rudd also includes additional relevant and useful material from the *Heptameron* in his manuscript. A significant difference is found grammatically in the Rudd manuscript, where the text is changed from the first person (I, me, mine) to the first-person plural (we, us, our), demonstrating that the material was being worked by a group and not a solitary practitioner.

Although the earliest known manuscript of the *Goetia* (Sloane MS 3825) dates to 1641, there is evidence to suggest there may have been earlier copies lost to us now. An interesting association to Rudd's *Goetia* is in the full title of *Liber Malorum Spirituum seu Goetia*. Trithemius in *Antipalus* (1508) refers to a book or manuscript (since lost) called *Liber Malorum Spirituum*, suggesting a possible earlier source for the *Goetia*, which Rudd was aware of.

The *Goetia* is one of the few grimoires found only in English and has gained a degree of notoriety due to Aleister Crowley (1875-1947) publishing MacGregor Mathers's (1854-1918) transcription of it and his comments in his autobiography. Crowley, influenced by the work of Sigmund Freud at the time, postulated the Goetic spirits as psychological constructs, a view which has done no favours to the grimoire tradition, and is just flat-out wrong, as experience of practice soon shows.

Essential Reading

Nottingham, Gary St. Michael (2015) *Liber Terribilis: being an instruction on the Seventy-Two Spirits of the Goetia*. Glastonbury: Avalonia. Good practical introduction to working with the Goetic spirits.

Peterson, Joseph H. (2001) *The Lesser Key of Solomon: Lemegeton Clavicula Salomonis*. Maine, Weiser Books. An excellent book exploring the history of the *Goetia*, with the complete Manuscript of Sloane MS 3825, the earliest known copy. Peterson's work is the definitive study of the earlier manuscripts of the *Goetia*.

---

319 The term Spirit Catalogue is used to qualify where the appearances of the spirits are described and not merely named (Spirit List).

Skinner, Stephen & Rankine, David (2007) *The Goetia of Dr Rudd*. Singapore, Golden Hoard Press. The complete manuscript of Harley MS 6483, with all the seventy-two seals of the Shemhamphorash angels and *Heptameron* material added by Dr Thomas Rudd, with footnotes of all the textual variations in all the major manuscripts. This book also explores the roots of the *Goetia* and associated figures and provides material not found elsewhere from associated texts like Sloane MS 3824. Together with Peterson's edition the two works provide a complete reference to the *Goetia*.

Stratton-Kent, Jake (2016) *Pandemonium: A Discordant Concordance of Diverse Spirit Catalogues*. West Yorkshire, Hadean Press. Fascinating study exploring the development of spirit lists, focusing particularly on that of the *Goetia*.

Goetia, Secret Seal of Solomon

THEURGIA-GOETIA

Date: 1641.
Language: English.
Influences: *Steganographia* Book 1.
Provenance: Unknown author. Sloane MS 3825 is first known copy. Harley MS 6483 by Thomas Rudd, copied by Peter Smart (1712); Northwestern University MS 65 by Thomas Simpkins (1713); Ebenezer Sibley (1752-99)(late C18); copied by Frederick Hockley (1808-85) (1828), copied by Henry Dawson Lea (1809-63) as Wellcome MS 3203, copied by Henry Harries (1821-49) as M11117B.
MSS: Sloane MS 3825 (1641); Sloane MS 3824 (1649); Sloane 3648 (1649); Sloane 2731 (1686); Harley MS 6483 (1712 from earlier copy); Wellcome MS 3203 (1843); WNL M11117B (1843-6).
Circle: N/A.
Tools: Crystal, girdle, Pentacle of Solomon, Table of the Art.
Spirit List: Aariel, Abael, Abariel, Aboc, Abriel, Abrulges, Achot, Acreba, Acteras, Adan, Agapiel, Aglas, Agor, Agra, Albhadur, Aldrusy, Aleasi, Alferiel, Aliel, Almadiel, Almasor, Almesiel, Almodar, Almoel, Althor, Amandiel, Amasiel, Ambri, Amediel, Amenadiel, Ameta, Amiel, Amoyr, Amriel, Anael, Andros, Andruchiel, Aniel, Anoyr, Ansoel, Apiel, Arach, Arafos, Aratiel, Arbiel, Arcisat, Arean, Arepach, Aridiel, Arifiel, Armadiel, Armany, Armena, Armesiel, Armoniel, Arnen, Arnibiel, Aroan, Aroc, Arois, Aroziel, Artino, Asahel, Asbibiel, Aschiel, Asimiel, Asmadiel, Asmaiel, Asmiel, Asoriel, Asosiel, Aspar, Asphiel, Asphor, Aspiel, Assaba, Assuel, Astael, Astib, Astor, Asuriel, Asyriel, Athesiel, Atriel, Azemo, Azimel, Baaba, Bachiel, Baciar, Balsur, Baoxas, Barbil, Barbis, Barchiel, Barfas, Barfos, Bariel, Barmiel, Baros, Barsu, Baruch, Baruchas, Basiel, Bedary, Belsay, Benodiel, Benoham, Betasiel, Bidiel, Bofar, Bonyel, Borasy, Bramsiel, Brufiel, Brymiel, Bucafas, Budar, Budarim, Budiel, Bufiel, Bulis, Buniel, Burfa, Buriel, Busiel, Cabariel, Cabarim, Cabiel, Cabron, Cadriel, Calim, Calvarnia, Cambriel, Camiel, Camor, Camory, Camuel, Camyel, Caniel, Capriel, Carasiba, Carba, Cardiel, Carga, Cariel, Carmasiel, Carmiel, Carniel, Carnodiel, Carnol, Caron, Carpiel, Carsiel, Cartael, Casael, Casbriel, Casiel, Caspaniel, Caspiel, Cavayr, Cayros, Cazul, Chabri, Chamiel, Chamoriel, Chamos, Chanaei. Chansi, Charas, Chariel, Charobiel, Charoel, Charsiel, Chasor, Chremoas, Chrubas, Chuba, Churibal, Cirecas, Citgara, Clamor, Claniel, Clyssan, Cobusiel, Codriel, Coliel, Cruchan, Cruhiel, Cubi, Cubiel, Cugiel, Culmar, Cumariel, Cumeriel, Cuphal, Cupriel, Cuprisiel, Curasin, Curiel, Curifas, Curmas, Cursas, Cusiel, Cusriel, Cusyne, Dadrinos, Dagiel, Damarsiel, Danael, Daniel, Darbori, Decaniel, Deilas, Demediel, Demoriel, Diviel, Dobiel, Dodiel, Dorael, Doriel, Dorochiel, Drabros, Dragon, Dramiel, Drapios, Drasiel, Drubiel, Drusiel, Dubarus, Dubiel, Dubilon, Dusiriel, Earos, Earviel, Ebra, Edriel, Efiel, Elear, Eliel, Elitel, Emoniel, Emuel, Ermoniel, Espoel, Ethiel, Etimiel, Fabariel, Fabiel, Faseua, Femol, Frasmiel, Fursiel, Futiel, Futiel, Gabio, Gariel, Garnasu, Gediel, Geradiel, Geriel, Godiel, Gremiel, Gudiel, Hamas, Hamorphiel, Heresiel, Hermon, Herne, Hidriel, Hissam, Hursiel, Icosiel, Inachiel, Itrasbiel, Itules, Janiel, Jasziel, Keriel, Ladiel, Lamael, Lamas, Lameniel, Laphor, Larael, Larfos, Lariel, Larmol, Larphiel, Las Pharon, Lazaba, Lemodac, Libiel, Lodiel, Lomor, Luciel, Luziel, Macariel, Machariel, Mador, Madriel, Mafayr, Mafrus, Magael, Magni, Mahue, Malgaras, Malgron, Malguel, Maniel, Mansi, Marae, Maras, Mareaiza, Marguns, Marianu, Mariel, Maroth, Maseriel, Mashel, Mastuel, Maziel, Medar, Melas, Melcha, Melchon, Meliel, Menadiel, Menador, Menariel, Merach, Meras, Merasiel, Merosiel, Meroth, Misiel, Molael, Momel, Monael, Moracha, Morael, Morias, Moriel, Mortaliel, Moziel, Mudirel, Munefiel, Murahe, Mursiel, Musiniel, Musiriel, Musor, Musuziel, Myrezyn, Nadrel, Nadroc, Nadrusiel, Nahiel,

Nalael, Naras, Narmiel, Narsial, Narzael, Nasiniel, Nassar, Nastros, Nathriel, Nedriel, Nemariel, Neriel, Nodar, Noguiel, Ochiel, Odiel, Oemiel, Ofisiel, Omiel, Omyel, Orariel, Oriel, Ormenu, Ornich, Orpemiel, Oryn, Ossidiel, Otim, Padiel, Pafiel, Pamersiel, Pandiel, Pandor, Paniel, Parabiel, Pariel, Parius, Parniel, Parsifiel, Pathier, Patiel, Pelariel, Pelusar, Penador, Peniel, Phaniel, Phanuel, Pharol, Pirichiel, Pischiel, Potiel, Prasiel, Praxeel, Quibda, Quitta, Rabas, Rabiel, Rablion, Raboc, Ramica, Ranciel, Rapsiel, Rasiel, Reciel, Richel, Romiel, Romyel, Roriel, Sabas, Sadar, Saddiel, Sadiel, Saefarn, Saefer, Saemiel, Salvor, Samiel, Samyel, Sarach, Sarael, Sariel, Sarviel, Satifiel, Sebach, Sequiel, Sochas, Sodiel, Soleviel, Soriel, Sotheano, Suriel, Symiel, Taros, Tediel, Terath, Thalbus, Thanatiel, Tharas, Thariel, Tharson, Thoac, Thurcal, Thuriel, Tigara, Tugaros, Udiel, Urbaniel, Urisiel, Usiel, Usiniel, Vadriel, Vadros, Varpiel, Vasenel, Vaslos, Vessur, Vraniel, Vriel, Zabriel, Zachariel, Zamor, Zeriel, Zoeniel, Zosiel.

The Text

Much of the material found in *Theurgia-Goetia* has been drawn from Book 1 of the *Steganographia* of Trithemius, with the addition of seals and sigils for all the named spirits. Written in 1500, the *Steganographia* was distributed in manuscript form, not being published until 1608. It is worth noting that the *Steganographia* was published in Latin, and Sloane MS 3824 has a partial English translation of the text in it, together with material from *Theurgia-Goetia*, (and a spirit contract for Padiel) though it is not labelled as such.

The work starts with a discussion of the thirty-one ministering spirits and their nature, emphasised as a mixture of good and evil. The manner of calling them at the appropriate time and from the appropriate direction is stressed heavily. This is followed by the Spirit Compass Rose, a striking image which contains the names of all the major spirits and the direction from which they should each be conjured. The spirit list, with all the seals and numerous servant dukes and their seals, then forms the bulk of the work, with conjurations of the major spirits included (mostly).[320] Again direction of conjuration and timing are stressed heavily, being either by day or night, or in specific planetary hours of these.

Conjurations follow, to the emperors, princes, wandering princes, and dukes. The address to the spirit is given, and the author then explains that the conjuration procedure and equipment used in the *Goetia* should also be used for these conjurations.

Essential Reading

Nottingham, Gary St. Michael (2020) *Ars Theurgia-Goetia: being an account and rendition of the Arte and Praxis of the Conjuration of some of the Spirits of Solomon*. Glastonbury: Avalonia. Good introduction to the little-discussed practice of working with the spirits of the *Theurgia-Goetia*.

Peterson, Joseph H. (2001) *The Lesser Key of Solomon: Lemegeton Clavicula Salomonis*. Maine, Weiser Books. An excellent book exploring the history of the *Goetia*, with the complete Manuscript of Sloane MS 3825, the earliest known copy. Peterson's work is the definitive study of the earlier manuscripts of the *Lemegeton*.

---

320 The conjurations take the same form, so for any missing conjurations it is simply a matter of using another one from the text and replacing the spirit names.

Skinner, Stephen & Rankine, David (2007) *The Goetia of Dr Rudd*. Singapore, Golden Hoard Press. The complete manuscript of Harley MS 6483, this book also explores the roots of the *Goetia* and associated figures and provides material on *Theurgia-Goetia* not found elsewhere from associated texts like Sloane MS 3824 and the *Steganographia*. Together with Peterson's edition the two works provide a complete reference to the *Lemegeton*.

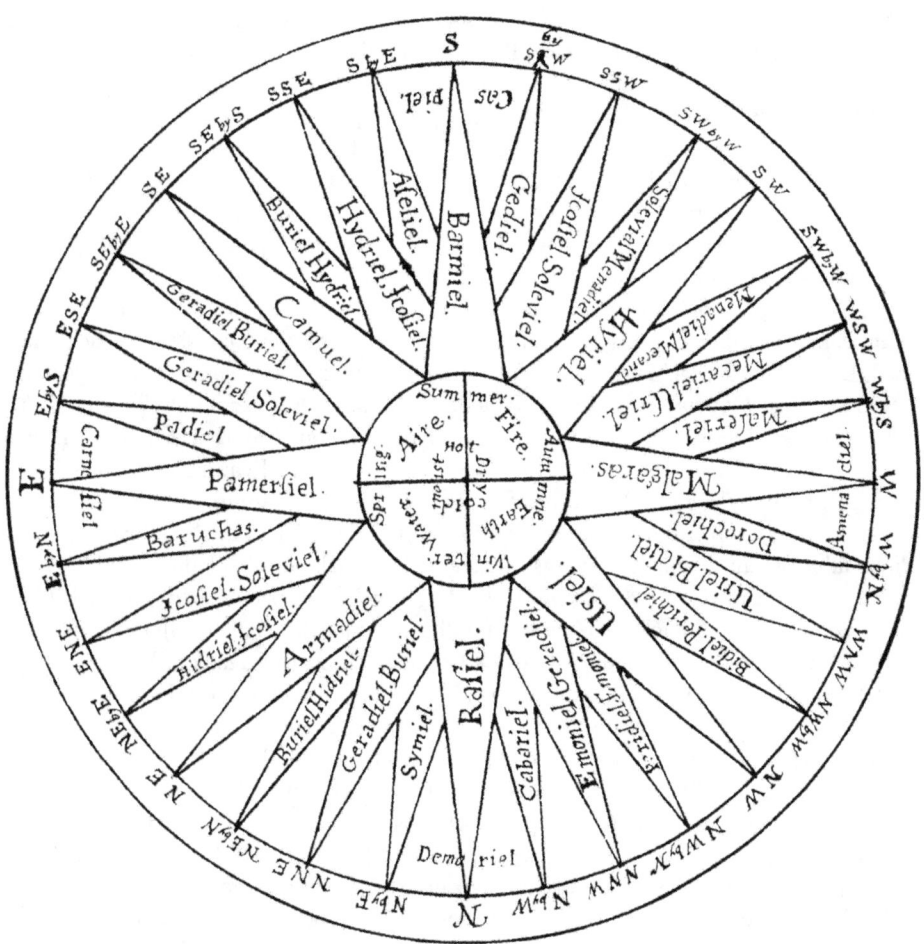

Theurgia Goetia, Spirit Rose Compass

Ars Paulina (The Pauline Art)

Date: 1641.
Language: English.
Influences: *Steganographia* (Book 2), *Archidoxes of Magic*, *Magical Calendar*, John Dee?
Provenance: Unknown author. Sloane MS 3825 is first known copy. Harley MS 6483 by Thomas Rudd, copied by Peter Smart (1712); NWU MS 65 in hand of Thomas Simpkins (1713); Ebenezer Sibley (1752-99) (late C18); copied by Frederick Hockley (1808-85) (1828), copied by Henry Dawson Lea (1809-63) as Wellcome MS 3203.
MSS: Sloane MS 3825 (1641); Sloane MS 3824 (1649); Sloane 3648 (1649); Sloane 2731 (1686); Harley MS 6483 (1712 from earlier copy); Northwestern University MS 65 (1713); Wellcome MS 3203 (1843).
Circle: N/A.
Tools: Crystal, table of practice.
Spirit List: Abasdarhon, Abiel, Abrasiel, Achael, Achiel, Adiel, Adoniel, Adrapon, Adroziel, Aiel, Ajel, Alachuc, Alaphar, Alfrael, Almas, Almerizel, Almodar, Almonoyz, Amalym, Ambriel, Amelson, Ameniel, Amerany, Amisiel, Ammiel, Amonazy, Amriel, Anael, Anapion, Aniel, Aphiel, Appiniel, Araniel, Archiel, Ariel, Armapy, Armiel, Armosiel, Armosy, Arnebiel, Arnmyel, Asel, Asmiel, Assaiel, Astrocon, Astrofiel, Astroniel, Athiel, Ausiul, Aziel, Baajah, Bachiel, Bagiel, Bakiel, Baliel, Bangiel, Bariel, Barmas, Barquiel, Basilon, Baviel, Befranzy, Behel, Bengiel, Beratiel, Beriel, Beshael, Betiel, Bevael, Biael, Bramiel, Brandiel, Brasiel, Brumiel, Bufanotz, Cabiel, Cael, Cahael, Cajael, Cajaiel, Cakiel, Camaron, Cambiel, Camiel, Camosiel, Cardiel, Caremaz, Carman, Cashiel, Casiel, Casmiroz, Cassiel, Casujojah, Cechiel, Cediel, Cegnel, Celiel, Cesiel, Chabiel, Chabrion, Chabriz, Chadiel, Chadros, Chael, Chahel, Chaiel, Chameray, Chamiel, Charaby, Chardiel, Charmy, Charny, Charpon, Charuch, Chasiel, Chazael, Chechiel, Chengiel, Cherasiel, Chermel, Chetiel, Chetivel, Choreb, Choriel, Chrasiel, Chremas, Chroel, Chrusiel, Chrymas, Chushel, Ciajah, Comadiel, Comary, Comiel, Coreziel, Crosiel, Cursiel, Daael, Dachael, Dachiel, Dagiel, Dagnel, Dahiel, Dajiel, Damar, Damasiel, Dameriel, Damery, Damiel, Damyel, Dardariel, Darosiel, Dashiel, Dathiel, Datziel, Daviel, Daziel, Deinatz, Demanoz, Demaor, Demarac, Demarot, Demasor, Denaryz, Diviel, Domaras, Dormason, Drabiel, Dracon, Dramaz, Dramozyn, Drelmech, Dromiel, Druchas, Drufiel, Dubraz, Edriel, Elamyz, Elmoym, Emalon, Emarfiel, Emarion, Emaryel, Emarziel, Emeriel, Enariel, Enatriel, Ermaziel, Ermiel, Evadar, Evandiel, Evanuel, Evarym, Famaras, Famoriel, Farmos, Fenadros, Fenosiel, Fimarson, Framion, Framoth, Franedac, Fremiel, Fromezyn, Fronyzon, Furamiel, Furiel, Fustiel, Futiniel, Gabiel, Gabrael, Gabrinoz, Gadiel, Gahiel, Gamsiel, Gamyel, Ganshiel, Gashiel, Gebiel, Geciel, Gediel, Gehiel, Gemary, Gematzod, Gemezin, Genarytz, Gepheel, Geriel, Gerthiel, Gesiel, Gethiel, Getiel, Gevael, Gezael, Geziel, Giel, Gnachiel, Gnadiel, Gnaheel, Gnakiel, Gnaliel, Gnamiel, Gnaphiel, Gnasiel, Gnathiel, Gneliel, Gnethiel, Gnetiel, Granozyn, Granyel, Haajah, Habalon, Habiel, Hachael, Hadiel, Hael, Hamarytzod, Hamayz, Hameriel, Hardiel, Hariaz, Harmary, Harmiel, Hatiel, Haylon, Hayzoym, Hazaniel, Heckiel, Hediel, Hegnel, Hekiel, Helmas, Hephiel, Hermiel, Herphatz, Heshael, Hetiel, Hevael, Hezael, Heziel, Hobrazym, Hoviel, Hujael, Humaziel, Iassuarim, Ibajah, Irmanotzod, Itael, Itamiel, Itashiel, Jaajah, Jaajeh, Jachiel, Jachoroz, Jadiel, Jael, Jagiel, Jamedroz, Janediel, Janiel, Janofiel, Janothyel, Japhael, Japuriel, Jashiel, Jasphiel, Jastrion, Jatael, Jatroziel, Javael, Javiel, Jebiel, Jechiel, Jefischa, Jenaziel, Jeniel, Jenotriel, Jermiel, Jezel, Jezisiel, Jmonyel, Jonadriel, Josel, Kabriel, Kachiel, Kanorsiel, Kathos, Kheel, Kingael, Kmiel, Kphiel, Kralym, Kranos, Kranoti, Kriel, Kshiel, Lachiel, Ladrotzod, Lamajah, Lamediel, Lameros, Lamerotzod, Lamersy, Lameson, Lamiel, Langael, Lanifiel, Lanoziel, Lantrhots, Lapheriel, Larfuty, Lariel, Larmich, Lashiel, Latiel, Lemaron, Lemozar,

Lemur, Lengael, Leviel, Lustifion, Mabiel, Machmag, Madael, Madiel, Mafriel, Magiel, Magnael, Mahiel, Maiel, Makael, Maneyloz, Manuel, Marachy, Marchiel, Mardiel, Marfiel, Mariel, Marifiel, Maroch, Masiel, Matiel, Maziel, Mechiel, Medusiel, Melanas, Melrotz, Menafiel, Menarchos, Menarym, Menas, Mendrion, Menesiel, Meniel, Menoriel, Mercoph, Meresyn, Meriel, Mesial, Mesriel, Metiel, Metziel, Meviel, Michael, Miel, Mihel, Monasiel, Mursiel, Muviel, Naajah, Nadriel, Nagael, Namael, Nameal, Namedor, Nameron, Nameroyz, Nameton, Naphael, Narcoriel, Nasael, Nastoriel, Nastrus, Nastul, Natheel, Nathmiel, Naveriel, Naveron, Naveroz, Naviel, Nechorym, Nedabor, Nedarym, Nedroz, Nedruan, Nefarym, Nefrias, Neliel, Nerastiel, Nermas, Nestori, Nestoriel, Nestoros, Neszomy, Ol, Omary, Omedriel, Omerach, Oriel, Ormael, Ormas, Ormezyn, Ormyel, Orphiel, Osmadiel, Paajah, Pammon, Pamory, Pamyel, Panael, Pandroz, Pangael, Paniel, Parniel, Parsiniel, Parziel, Pasil, Pasriel, Patiel, Patrozyn, Pegiel, Pemiel, Pemoniel, Penaly, Penargos, Penatiel, Penoles, Periel, Perman, Permaz, Permiel, Permon, Persiel, Phorsiel, Plamiel, Platiel, Praxiel, Prenostix, Putisel, Quabriel, Quenol, Queriel, Quesdor, Quirix, Quosiel, Raajah, Ramaziel, Rameriel, Ramesiel, Raphael, Raphiel, Rathiel, Ratziel, Rayziel, Regael, Rehiel, Remasyn, Rengliel, Riajah, Rimezyn, Romiel, Rudefor, Rymaliel, Sabiel, Sabrathan, Sachael, Sachiel, Sadiel, Sadiniel, Sagel, Sagiel, Sagnel, Sahael, Sahel, Sahiel, Samael, Samelon, Sameon, Sameriel, Sameron, Sameryn, Samiel, Samuel, Sanael, Sangiel, Saniel, Sarandiel, Saraphiel, Sardiel, Sarfiel, Sarmon, Sarmozyn, Sasael, Sasajah, Sasquiel, Satiel, Satziel, Savael, Saviel, Saziel, Sekiel, Senael, Sengael, Seraphiel, Serquanich, Sersael, Serviel, Sethiel, Setiel, Siel, Strubiel, Suiajasel, Tachael, Tachiel, Tagiel, Tahiel, Tajael, Taliel, Tamael, Tameriel, Tamiel, Tangiel, Tarajah, Tarmytz, Tartys, Tashiel, Tavael, Techiel, Tediel, Teliel, Temael, Temas, Tesael, Tezael, Themaz, Theoriel, Thribiel, Thurmytz, Thuros, Tibiel, Tiiel, Trajael, Trasiel, Trubas, Tual, Tuberiel, Tulmas, Turmiel, Turtiel, Tzakiel, Tzangiel, Tzapheal, Tzethiel, Tzisiel, Umariel, Uraniel, Uriel, Vachael, Vagael, Vagel, Vahajah, Vahejah, Vahiel, Vajael, Vameroz, Vamiel, Vanescor, Vanesiel, Vaniel, Vanosyr, Variel, Varmay, Vashiel, Vathmiel, Vatiel, Vaziel, Vemael, Vemasiel, Venesiel, Venomiel, Ventariel, Vequaniel, Voil, Vulcaniel, Xamyon, Xanoriz, Xanthir, Xanthyozod, Xantiel, Xantropy, Xantros, Xemyzin, Xermiel, Xernifiel, Xerphiel, Zaajah, Zaazenach, Zachariel, Zachiel, Zachriel, Zaciel, Zackiel, Zadiel, Zagiel, Zajel, Zamiel, Zardiel, Zasnor, Zasviel, Zavael, Zazyor, Zegiel, Zemoel, Zenoroz, Zethiel, Zeziel, Zodiel, Zoesiel, Zoymiel, Zymeloz.

The Text

The material in the *Ars Paulina* is drawn directly from several sources, giving the 1641 date a good likelihood of accuracy. There is a Latin manuscript which includes a section entitled *Ars Paulina* from the sixteenth century (Bibliotheque Nationale de France MS 7170A), but the short piece bears no resemblance to this text. The associated story of this work is that it was received from St Paul (hence the name), who was able to travel in the heavens freely and hence could assist with angelic communication. Perhaps of greater interest is Vat. Lat. 3180, which contains a section called *Ars Paulina*[321] and also a version of the *Almandal*. This may have been seen by the Italian scholar Julius Caesar Scaliger (1484-1558), who in his work on natural philosophy *Exotericarum Exercitationes* (1557) divided magic into five categories – Trithemian (invention), Theurgic (disposition), Armadel (elocution), Pauline (pronunciation), and Lullian (memory). The juxtaposition of these terms could lead to the supposition that the person who put the *Lemegeton* together read Scaliger and used the terms he mentions.

---

321 Unrelated to the material in this work of the same title.

The spirits in Book 1 are a direct copy of those in *Steganographia* Book 2. The table of practice seems to be based on that used by Dr John Dee, with the planetary seals from *The Magical Calendar* (1620). The seals in Book 2 appear to be derived from Paracelsus's *Archidoxes of Magic*.

The text begins with an introduction of the two parts, the first being focused on working with the twenty-four angels of the hours of the day (and night), and the second on the angels of the three hundred and sixty degrees of the zodiac. Book 1 explains how to draw the seals for working with the angels and their dukes and shows the table of practice, explaining how it is used. It also recommends using appropriate planetary incenses suitable to the nature of the hours. The conjuration sequence is given, with instructions to dismiss as per the usual method, implying that which was given earlier in the collected grimoires in the *Goetia*.

Book 2 discusses the nature of a person's unique attendant spirits, including the Genius of their birth. The angels of the zodiacal signs, and the angelic spirits (called Genii here) of each of the three hundred and sixty degrees of the zodiac are tabulated. Seals for the twelve angelic angels are given with instructions on how to make them using combinations of the classically-assigned planetary metals. The angelic rulers of the four elements, and their associated zodiacal signs are mentioned, before the text ends with a conjuration of the Holy Guardian Angel.

Essential Reading

Peterson, Joseph H. (2001) *The Lesser Key of Solomon: Lemegeton Clavicula Salomonis*. Maine, Weiser Books. An excellent book exploring the history of the *Goetia*, with the complete Manuscript of Sloane MS 3825, the earliest known copy. Peterson's work is the definitive study of the earlier manuscripts of the *Lemegeton*.

Skinner, Stephen & Rankine, David (2007) *The Goetia of Dr Rudd*. Singapore, Golden Hoard Press. The complete manuscript of Harley MS 6483, this book also explores the roots of the *Goetia* and associated figures. Together with Peterson's edition the two works provide a complete reference to the *Lemegeton*.

Of Angels, Demons & Spirits

Date: Early C17.
Language: English with some Latin.
Influences: *De Nigromancia, Almadel, Sworn Book of Honorius, Three Books of Occult Philosophy, Book of Oberon, Book of the Offices of Spirits, Discoverie of Witchcraft, Arbatel, Book of Treasure Spirits, Annulorum Experimenta.*
Provenance: Possibly compiled by Master Kimberly or John Carpenter; subsequently owned by scholar and astrologer Thomas Allen (1540-1632).
MSS: Bodleian e. Mus. 173.
Circle: Yes.
Tools: Basin, book, crown, crystal, lamina, pentacle, ring, sceptre, sword, white-handled knife.
Spirit List: A-Anolita, Abay, Abba, Abermo, Abigellem, Abybo, Achios, Affacill, Affrica, Afoirco, Agal, Agama, Agariel, Agaros, Agyron, Alays, Albanyxa, Aleche, Aleches, Algor, Alibeat, Alkates, Allybyn, Alymos, Alyzaire, Amas, Amay, Amaymon, Ana, Anabiell, Anaell, Anay, Ancor, Andromalchinwce, Andromalcus, Annrafael, Anoboth, Appatay, Appellonii, Aquos, Ara, Arab, Aratron, Aray, Ardo, Ariell, Ariens, Ariplotoson, Arnace, Arvyr, Asazell, Asiell, Askades, Askadeus, Askariell, Asmo, Asmoday, Astarth, Aster, Asteroth, Astole, Astoroth, Asziell, Atesi, Athasan, Atopolin, Ator, Atrox, Atyes, Atythaell, Auras, Aymaeleon, Aymon, Azabal, Azochede, Azoel, Baall, Baba Mutela, Babaty, Babay, Balaam, Balath, Balbo, Balko, Barachaeell, Barachi, Baramptis, Barbas, Barbays, Barthan, Basan, Basquiel, Beabo, Beal, Beelbac, Beldon, Belima, Bell, Belliall, Beluginis, Belugo, Belyall, Belzebub, Benias, Benlam, Beray, Berifer, Bermo, Beryl, Beryth, Bileth, Bilgal, Blyth, Boell, Bolam, Bosco, Bosto, Botheron, Bruschan, Bufflas, Burcham, Busyn, Bybon, Cacaryll, Cagyn, Calkfulgra, Calmus, Camon, Cantivalerion, Caphaell, Capiell, Capuel, Carafax, Carbus, Carmelyon, Caronem, Casiell, Castrietar, Caszepell, Cathan, Catis, Cayma, Caymay, Centony, Ceris, Chadonas, Chanturo, Chule, Corilron, Cornigerum, Cornus, Crea, Crissia, Critaron, Daniell, Dantalion, Daragybya, Dardyell, Deres, Deroper, Detriel, Dileo, Doragybyn, Dracho, Draco, Dracutius, Dradragoban, Draned, Drepis, Ducales, Dulibion, Eaioy, Eansursh, Effrater, Egicam, Egyn, Eiotas, Elerotel, Elyas, Emas, Emull, Ennoy, Entro, Ephradyn, Eptra, Erathon, Erner, Eryneon, Esam, Esay, Esum, Ethamael, Eusule, Falneyl, Farabores, Faraphyell, Festile, Fligoth, Floran, Foca, Focan, Folla, Formasus, Formone, Freese, Fuglep, Gabryell, Galfane, Galian, Gambra, Gaziel, Genitall, Gentuball, Godolyn, Goffela, Golyon, Gordemser, Gorgorydas, Grynaca, Gyal, Hageth, Harataphell, Harthan, He, Hell, Herlam, Hermely, Hinds, Hocraell, Iamfriell, Iammax, Iaspes, Ideus,[322] Iemure, Iesan, Innael, Inquiell, Iperon, Iulia, Iuramiter, Kagaoche, Karus, Kulymzadell, Kuthan, Kyas, Ladilibas, Lamfriell, Lancyell, Lapidator, Laripos, Lepera, Lillia, Lopostarius, Loueson, Loui, Lubyras, Lucifer, Lucyell, Lymer, Maconus, Macryon, Magala, Magram, Malathym, Mallappas, Marayn, Margar, Margon, Marog, Masa, Mayemon, Maymon, Meas, Mekuton, Melse, Membris Liafis, Menanas, Menot, Menser, Meron, Messiton, Messitone, Metelex, Mettuton, Mezebin, Michael, Micriton, Milony, Mirabam, Mircos, Miremicum, Mirus, Misinall, Mistolas, Moas, Mosacus, Moson, Mures, Muryell, Musas, Mychaell, Myhell, Myron, Myssyron, Namath, Naris, Nathan, Navis, Neaphan, Necesolap, Neonem, Nereus, Nerolo, Niloportas, Nocte, Nonis, Nossor, Noxarata, Oberion, Och, Odingeo, Olam, Onahirasterp, Onom, Ophiel, Oralioch, Orces, Orcormislas, Orecha, Oresos, Orgeas, Oriens, Orion, Othey, Oyte, Oze, Ozia, Paavtyell, Pachyn, Palam, Panchasy, Pantetaron, Parcoth, Pariel,

---

[322] The names Asmo and Ideus are next to each other in the text which could be a corruption of Asmodeus.

Partas, Paymon, Perortira, Perth, Pestall, Pestron, Peta, Phalec, Phul, Phytoneum, Piarum, Pistraye, Polacar, Ponilbus, Portasinall, Priamon, Quatuball, Ragnell, Raguel, Ramath, Ranas, Raphael, Rarilzispus, Rarnilpus, Raryhispus, Rasell, Rata, Rather, Raton, Ratoplo, Rayma, Refer, Regessa, Relfem, Relmo, Relsez, Repeli, Restilia, Rignell, Robyell, Roncefall, Ronos, Rowdeys, Ruall, Ruchen, Rufalas, Rurcos, Sabwell, Saciaton, Sadon, Saem, Saine, Salgiell, Salvator, Samaell, Samanus, Samay, Samyell, Sarapiell, Sarypyell, Sathan, Satquiell, Satrapis, Satrox, Saymay, Saymbrie, Scar, Scorpus, Sem, Sema, Semar, Semey, Seper, Sepuros, Serar, Serobattam, Seson, Sever, Sezel, Sgalis, Siadris, Sibilia, Sichone, Silori, Slaugnes, Smargeos, Smue, Sonaco, Sorios, Soyll, Sperabonatos, Spirgon, Stabblait, Storax, Suchay, Sudyr, Suriflyen, Surth, Sycors, Synoryell, Tabat, Taleos, Talgott, Talii, Tamar, Tayly, Terre, Tessaid, Textator, Theal, Theser, Thetor, Toboull, Tobyas, Tobyell, Topora, Trera, Tropayca, Trwdrie, Tyltryon, Ubnell, Uleos, Umbra, Urago, Urricas, Uryall, Uryell, Ustiron, Valgus, Vasmi, Vazago, Veinulla, Velyon, Venus, Verexi, Walkates, Wiel, Yay, Ybles, Ydyal, Yetes, Yfera, Yka, Ykar, Yrtell, Ysaradus, Yska, Yssery, Yssytres, Ysyne, Zacos, Zacui, Zagan, Zagayme, Zaiell, Zalas, Zaphey, Zayme, Zebulo, Zorobaym.

The Text

The text is a fascinating collection drawn from numerous sources, gathered together in a coherent manner for practical work. Whilst the scope of the charms and rites could suggest a cunning practitioner, there is also a breadth of material suggesting a more scholarly approach. The former category includes treasure hunting, uncovering theft, healing, anti-witchcraft, and spirits fulfilling instructions. The latter includes spirits answering questions, and teaching academic disciplines and magic. Additionally, there are the obligatory love and invisibility charms found in most such works.

It is noteworthy that much of the material in this text is held in common with other contemporary English works such as the *Book of Oberon*, the *Book of Treasure Spirits* and Sloane MS 3853. The manuscript contains a very large number of spirit names, both those found in other texts and also unique ones. The mention of a number of the spirits coming from the forest or wood, combined with unique treasure spirits, offers speculation that some of these names might be of old genii loci. The emphasis on magical circles associated with the elements (water, earth, air, and fire) is also a significant unusual feature.

The text contains: Consecration of the Book; the Consecration for the Stone; conjuration for the Wind and the Earth, includes magic circle, prayers and conjurations, and license to depart; the License of Solomon; General License; License of Solomon; calls to Zorobaym and Iuramiter; characters of Asazell and Naris; license of Askariell to depart; for a spirit that walketh; of Asazell and Naris; the circle of defence for the master and his fellows to stand in (includes blessing, large spirit list); a citation of what spirit thou wilt; for to excommunicate spirits that will not appear in their invocation; Alyzaire and his princes; how to treat with spirits; experiment of Elves that is true; call to the Four Kings; an experiment of Askaryell;[323] for theft; again for theft; a partnership for the purpose of knowing; for love; sigil of the Sun, sigil of the Moon; Circle of Earth; these are the spirit names which are to be called; here followeth the names of the seven kings of the seven planets; so that you may know of hidden treasure; letters and characters of the planets; an experiment of Saymay, for treasure in the seas to be brought up, most certainly proved; an experiment for love (wax image); another most true experiment for theft; experiment for the purpose of enclosing the spirit Bilgal in a crystal; experiment of the form of the spatula; Alkates Walkates (solitary crystal skrying

---

323 This section ends with a series of characters for use with any spirit when not using a child skryer.

experiment); call to Cantivalerion; an experiment of the names of them that be suspected for theft or malice; Androyce or Andramalcus (thumbnail divination with young boy); the Olympic spirits and illnesses they treat; for spirits of the water to get treasure out of the sea; for to excommunicate spirits that will not appear; the eight princes of darkness and three more; planetary rulerships; experiment of the three good angels; for the purpose of knowing if any may be vexed by unclean spirits; Serobattam, a good experiment for love or theft; for the love of a woman; for the ague (abracadabra in wing form); on the holy seal of Rabbi Hama (several seals, and then twenty-four seals on permutations of Jesus and Tetragrammaton); an experiment to see spirits what they do; this is the girdle which must be made in parchment and lined with linen; planetary seals;[324] to spoil a thief or witch or any other enemy and to be delivered from the evil; to make a witch confess her evil before you; the experiment of William Bacon to destroy witches; this prayer is to be said before thou dost name the Great Name of God; an experiment for love; an experiment of the secrets of Rome by a spirit that is called Sathan; for hidden treasure; the discharge of Alkates; to avoid spirits that keep any treasure from the ground, that you may have it and enjoy it; consecration of the magical tools; a treatise on calling spirits (includes spirit catalogue, conjurations and license to depart); there be times and hours to be observed and considered (blank); for treasure that is hid, to obtain it (includes excommunication for disobedience); to see a spirit in a crystal by a child or a woman with a child; a license; an experiment to call three spirits into a square new glass; her begins the invocation, and it is called the invocation of the secrets of Solomon; a circle to find treasure; the chapters of all offices of spirits; characters of Oberion and his main servants; spirit list, pentacle of Solomon, sign of Solomon, aquatic circle, spirit list (continued); circles in which the spirits of the Air and of Fire ..., circle of the Earth; circle of the Horse; magical triangles; various circles; the circle of Satan, Barrados, and Belzebue (actually eleven seals); amulet of protection and healing (eight seals); circle of Solomon (with seal of Solomon below); experiments – to assuage anger, to staunch bleeding (five), for bewitchment (four), for horse or bewitched beast (two), for boil or felon, for bite of a mad dog (two); to find treasure that is hid in the ground; a true experiment to find treasure that is hid in the ground; an experiment to cause a thief to come again unto thee in proper person, if he be in England; the Quadrangle for treasure; a license or discharge; magic circle; for treasure that is hid (long conjuration); for them that are bewitched, proved by a hundred; to cause a woman to tell what she hath done in her sleep; the book which is called the Donet[325] or Consecrations (discussion of practice and doctrine of experiments, timings for different classes of spirits): invocation of the kings; an exorcism for the purpose of hate; in the offices of spirits, of the Marquises, regarding Dukes, of Prelates, of Knights, of Earls, of Princes, hours of the day; of the circles, on which days it should be made; the call of Oberion into a crystal stone; most best and most true experiment for the fairies; to see spirits of the Air; a most true and proven experiment for thieves (dreaming with the dead); a short operation for theft; the call or charge of Benias; the preparation of experiments of love as followeth; an experiment for love; the same in English; to make a woman follow thee; for theft; an experiment of a candle for theft provided; for the Mother;[326] that a sword or knife shall not hurt thee; that soldiers may be courageous to fight (actually an illusion spell).[327]

---

324 Curiously all the seals are made of lead, commonly associated with Saturn, except the Venus seal, which is made of copper, the most common attribution for Venus.
325 This may be a copyist's error, as the same text is in Sloane MS 3853 fol. 176-219, as 'A magical book called the Dannel, containing various magical experiments'.
326 Name for a womb condition in early modern English medicine.
327 This is the third ring from *Annulorum Experimenta*.

ESSENTIAL READING

Harms, Daniel & Clark, James R. (2019) *Of Angels, Demons & Spirits*. Woodbury: Llewellyn. Excellent work providing the whole of the manuscript with numerous examples of comparative material and wide-ranging contextual material.

The Book of Gold (Le Livre d'Or)

Date: C17.
Language: French.
Influences: *Sepher Shimmush Twhillim*.
Provenance: Possibly from an earlier Latin text.
MSS: Lansdowne MS 1202, bound after a *Key of Solomon*.
Circle: N/A.
Tools:[328] Bronze drinking vessel, cooking pot, glass, fox skin, glass plate, earthenware pot, ink-pen, tablet.
Spirit List: Caniel, Canielvel, Custel, Eliel, Ha, Issii, Ramul, St. Etienne.

The Text

The *Book of Gold* is a collection of magical charms and prayers for every single Psalm in the *Book of Psalms*. The style is akin to mixed cabalah, in that the emphasis is on using simple items with Biblical verses to achieve desired results for day-to-day life. Although not a grimoire, the prevalence of the Psalms in the Grimoire Tradition makes this work, which was bound with a *Key of Solomon*, a useful adjunct to grimoire practice. The Psalm numeration in this work is based on the Septuagint (Greek) rather than the Masoretic (Hebrew). After the charms of the one hundred and fifty Psalms, the text ends with the Athanasian Creed.

Examining the purposes of the charms, the most common are health issues/healing (27), friendships/for influence (18), luck/improving fortune (15), protection from malice/enemies (15), gaining or removing love (14), vanquishing enemies (12), and protection from or dispelling of enchantments (10). Other uses include pregnancy protection (9), house blessing/protection (9), release/detention in prison (9), killing/destroying enemies (8), protection when travelling (6), child care (5), farm magic (5), ship issues (5), protecting/blessing trees (4), sleep/dream issues (4), combat (2), and detecting thieves (2). A wide variety of simple ingredients are used, the most common being water, oil, and mastic. A range of animal bloods are also used in some of the charms.

The Psalm charms (of which some Psalms have more than one) are: protecting a pregnant woman (1); for gastronomic sickness, to be welcomed by a prince (2); for headache (3); for protection from watery perils and accidents, to gain friendship of great people (4); for protection from malicious people, to gain friendship of lords (5); for curing eye disease (6); for protection from enemies, for vanquishing enemies (7); to prevent children from crying, for holding and moving honeybees (8); to be honoured by a king or prince (9); for killing enemies (10); for preventing slander by enemies (11); for protection from rogues, for making a child amenable to education (12); for appearing majestic (13); for approaching a prince (14); for protection from enchantment (15); for avoiding scandal (16); for healing sick people (17); for assisting pregnancy (18); for healing a sick person (19); for being well-received and honoured (20); for protection from petty and malicious people, for vanquishing enemies (21); for protection when travelling (22); to be loved (23); for helping a sick person sleep (24); for destroying enchantments, for protection from enemies (25); for protecting vine tree, for curing worms for a child (26); for protection from your children and close friends, for reconciliation with enemies (27); for healing a sick man, a house blessing (28); for curing sickness (29); for release from prison (30); for removing desire (31); to ensure conception (32); to heal toothache or fractured bone (33); for access to a prince (34); for safe pregnancy

---

328 The items listed are used as the basis for charms, so from that perspective are considered tools.

(35); for destroying your enemy and his family (36); for healing eye pain (37); for removing bad dreams (38); for preventing miscarriage (39); for controlling an untrustworthy mistress (40); for dispersing enemies (41); to gain access to a king or prince (42); for destroying an enemy (43); for gaining a desired person (44); for armed combat (45); for luck in affairs (46); for seeing a thief (47); to be loved and cherished (48); for killing and distributing a sheep to the poor (49); a protection for haemophilia (50); for pregnancy protection (51); for vanquishing enemies (52); for defence against slander to a prince (53); for preventing an enemy building his house (54); to stop a pregnant woman bleeding (55); for protection from beasts in the desert (56); for destroying the effect of an enchantment (57); for removing sexual enchantment (58); for sorting out business affairs and gaining fortune (59); for reconciling husband and wife (60); for killing or vanquishing an enemy (61); for stopping a child crying (62); for vanquishing enemies (63); for deliverance from need (64); for deliverance from need (65); for healing a sick person (66); for preventing sleep (67); for calming bad weather at sea (68); for healing a named illness (69); for winning your case before a judge (70); for gaining the love of a woman (71); for obtaining your goal or desire (72); for causing an enemy to flee (73); for release from prison, for increasing a merchant's profits (74); for dispelling spirits from a house (75); for dispelling enchantments on a person (76); for vanquishing an enemy (77); for being received honourably (78); for making a woman chaste (79); to stop haemorrhaging (80); to be received honourably (81); for destroying your enemy (82); to gain access to a prince (83); for gaining luck (84); for blessing wine (85); to have fulfillment in your affairs (86); for vanquishing an enemy (87); for curing headache, a house blessing (88); for success in ventures (89); for removing enchantments which separate a man and wife (89); for protection from enchantment and demons, for preventing children being frightened (90); to prevent your enemy from harming you (91); for blessing a house (92); for causing enemies to flee, for increasing the profit of a house or mill (93); for exorcising a demon (94); for dispelling the traps of rich people (95); for dealing with a hated wife (96); for preventing a ship from sailing (97); to be received honourably (98); for protection from the hatred of a mistress (99); for protection of a vineyard, to cure an enchanted man (100); for finding joy and happiness (101); for curing prolonged sickness (102); for gaining a woman you desire, for enflaming the heart of any person (103); for release from prison (104); to sink a ship (105); to keep somebody in prison (106); for approaching a prince or king (107); for erasing an enemy (108); for initiating childbirth (109); for blessing ground for building on (110); for causing an enemy to perish (111); for increasing profits from a house, to have protection for livestock (112); for stopping fishermen catching fish (113); for protecting a child from sickness and peril (114); for preventing drunkenness, for giving healing, for approaching a prince or council (115); for protection from persecution, for helping prisoners (116); for restoring keys to open any room or house (117); for protection from all infirmities (118); for causing an enemy to flee and perish (119); for making yourself unseen (120); for overcoming an enemy (121); for overcoming those who wish you violence (122); for finding your path, a blessing of a house (123); for relief for the sick, for gaining fortune (124); a seed blessing (125); for removing a love enchantment (126); for encouraging a vineyard to fruit, for helping sight (127); for banishing ghosts (128); for blessing a house or field (129); for preventing bad dreams (130); for catching fish (131); for being welcomed everywhere (132); for increasing goods (133); for healing sickness, for healing sick eyes (134); for overcoming an enemy (135); for stopping blood flow (136); for deliverance from prison (137); for penitence from adultery (138); to be saved from poison (139); for protection from scoundrels (140); for release from prison, for bringing a servant back (141); for deliverance from prison (142); for victory in combat, for assisting labour, for rescue from a shipwreck (143); for restoring a husband, for healing sickness (144); for healing sickness including bones (145); for healing sickness (146);

for blessings for a house (147); for banishing demons from a house, for healing a sick woman (148); for healing a sick woman (149); to increase wheat and oil (150).

Essential Reading

Rankine, David (ed) & Barron, Paul Harry (trans) (2010) *The Book of Gold*. London: Avalonia. Complete transcription of the manuscript, giving extensive commentaries on all the individual Psalm charms and origins and comparison to other works. Detailed comparison to the use of Psalms in grimoires is also included, as well as appendixes of comparison and style of contents.

JANUA MAGICA RESERATA

Date: Early to mid C17.
Language: English.
Influences: *Three Books of Occult Philosophy, Arbatel, Magical Calendar*.
Provenance: Written by Dr Thomas Rudd (1583-1656); owned by Elias Ashmole (1617-1692), Sir Joseph Jekyll (1663-1738), Sir Hans Sloane (1660-1753), John Denley (1764-1842), and Frederick Hockley (1808-1885).
MSS: Sloane 3825 (early to mid C17), Harley 6482 (1712).
Circle: N/A.
Tools: N/A.
Spirit List: Abaddon, Abdiziel, Abrinael, Achaiah, Acrabiel, Adriel, Affrica, Aladiah, Amaymon, Ambriel, Amixiel, Amnediel, Amnixiel, Amutiel, Anael, Aniel, Annavel, Aorachiel, Aquariel, Aratron, Ardofiel, Ariel, Asaliah, Asaliel, Asmodel, Asmodeus, Atheniel, Azariel, Aziel, Azoruel, Barbiel, Barchiel, Beelzebub, Belial, Bethor, Betsmael, Botuliel, Caheshel, Caliel, Camael, Cambiel, Cancriel, Capriel, Captiol, Cassiel, Chavakiah, Cherub, Chosetiel, Cochabiel, Cochabijah, Dagymiel, Damabiah, Daniel, Deliel, Diabolus, Dirachiel, Egibiel, Egin, Ejael, Elomiah, Enodiel, Ergodiel, Foca, Gabiel, Gabriel, Geliel, Geminiel, Geniel, Godiel, Haajah, Haamiah, Habuiah, Hagith, Hahahel, Hahaiah, Haiviah, Hajaiol, Hakamiah, Hakasiah, Hamaliel, Hanael, Haniel, Harahel, Hariel, Horiel, Imarniah, Jahhael, Jazoriel, Jejazel, Jelahiah, Jeliel, Jerathel, Jereahiel, Jibamiah, Johujah, Jojabel, Jojaiel, Jojalel, Jolahel, Jophiel, Julia, Kyriel, Lauviah, Laviah, Leoniel, Levaniel, Libriel, Lillia, Lobzabjah, Lochabel, Loviah, Madimiel, Mahasiah, Malchidael, Mammon, Manadel, Masniel, Mathratron, Mebahel, Mebahiah, Mehekiel, Melahel, Meniel, Merizim, Michael, Mihael, Mizrael, Mumiah, Muriel, Nanael, Nemaniah, Nithael, Nithhajah, Nociel, Noganiel, Nolchael, Och, Omael, Ophiel, Ophin, Oriens, Orifiel, Pahaliah, Paymon, Phaleg, Phul, Pisciel, Poiel, Python, Raphael, Raziel, Rehael, Rejaiel, Ressilia, Roehel, Roquiel, Sabathiel, Sachiel, Sagittariel, Samael, Sataniel, Sathan, Schemeschiel, Scorpiel, Seruph, Seshiah, Shemeliel, Sitael, Soaliah, Soheliel, Soul of Messiah, Suriel, Tagriel, Tauriel, Teletiel, Tharsis, Theutus, Tomimiel, Tulia, Umabel, Vafariah, Vehiyah, Venulla, Verginiel, Voerchiel, Vohuel, Vovaliah, Zabdiel, Zabkiel, Zachariel, Zadkiel, Zamael, Zaphkiel, Zedekiel, Zuriel.

THE TEXT

Janua Magica Reserata translates literally as the 'Keys to the Gateway of Magic'. Whilst the opening sections including the 'Beneficial Aphorisms' may seem long-winded, they are worthy of study as contextual material for the mind-set and worldview of a Renaissance magician performing conjurations and expounding on religious and philosophical ideas relevant to that worldview.

The text becomes more practical (though still discursive) from the section 'Of Angels & Spirits', exploring topics like the composition of angels' bodies, and a complex spiritual hierarchy from archangels and angels through various levels to 'spirits of darkness' (demons). There is also a discussion of the personal Evil Angel and its counterpoise to the Guardian Angel.

The next section 'Of the Nine, or Orders of Celestial Angels' begins with a very concentrated summary of the correspondences of the Tree of Life, and a table showing the Kabbalistic correspondences of each of the ten Sephiroth, with god-name, order of angels (Hebrew and English), governing angel or Intelligence, presiding angel, planetary or celestial spheres, and the orders of evil or powers of the Infernal World listed as a counterbalance. Sigils are given for each of the angels of the nine Orbs.

The section on 'The Celestial Hierarchies' concentrates upon the different orders of angels from Seraphim down to the least angel, including the doctrine that individual countries have angels appointed to rule their destiny, a concept that was outlined by Agrippa and which fascinated Dr. John Dee, who expanded it in his *Liber Scientiae, Auxilii, et Victoriae Terrestris*.

The section 'Names of the Celestial Angels or Sacred Intelligences, set over & Governing the Seven Planets' is replete with many tables showing the relationship of angels, planets, various hierarchies, Olympic spirits, elements, zodiacal signs, and directions or functions. The first table shows the important relationship between the seven planets and the seven main angels. The several sets of correspondences between the angels and the twelve zodiacal signs are complemented by the angelic names for each of the twenty-eight Mansions of the Moon. The seventy-two angels of the Shemhamphorash are also given.

The section following 'Of the Hierarchies or Orders of Evil Spirits' gives the equivalent and balancing details of the nine Orders of evil angels or demons, giving their particular order, functions, and degree. It concludes with the names of the four governors of the four quarters, the Demon Princes Oriens, Paymon, Egin, and Amaymon. The hierarchy includes a strange but interesting mixture of old gods like Apollyon, Abaddon, and Beelzebub, various Biblical orders of fallen angels (such as Revengers, Tempters, Ensnarers, and Deceivers), and spirits like Meririm, prince of the aerial powers. It also lists the four demon princes.

The section 'Of Angels Good and Bad Their Degrees and Offices' looks at classical views of demons from Thomas Aquinas to Psellus. This section goes into detail over the different kinds of angels and demons. There is a detailed description of the precise technique for using 'water' in weather magic. The qualities of the spirits of each of the four Elements, or Elementals, and finally the spirits or demons who reside in Hell, charged with the task of tormenting the damned, are outlined.

'Of Incubi and Succubi' draws interesting parallels between them and the Satyrs and Fauns. The section following on the 'Power and Authority that Necromancers and Witches Have over the Devil' begins with a rehearsal of the differences between lawful Natural Magic and Demonic Magic. Natural Magic here includes such things as magic wrought by the burial of certain images. The second kind of magic is associated with the magicians of Pharaoh and Simon Magus. Even Christ's miracles are mentioned as a form of magic utilising a particular demon, in this case Beelzebub. A short section on poltergeists or 'domestical' spirits follows, which associates this phenomenon with hobgoblins and fairy folk like 'Robin Goodfellow'.

Using Latin titles, the section 'Of the Orders of Wicked Demons' looks at the categorisation of demons into nine Orders or Hierarchies. One of the most interesting passages confirms the identity of demons as simply fallen angels, essentially the same kind of creature as angels.

'Of the Bodies of Demons' quotes various, mostly Biblical, authorities on the nature of the bodies of both angels and demons. The prevalent opinion was that their bodies were made of the Elements of air and fire. An interesting sidelight is thrown upon the relationship between angels and demons, where the *Book of Tobit* is quoted as showing how the angel Raphael was able to control the demon Asmodeus.

The last section, 'Some further Considerations...of this Subject touching Spirits' goes deeper into the nature of demonic and angelic bodies, considerations which are important when looking to manifest either of these to visible appearance. This section also contains a more complete list of the different type of spiritual creatures and where traditionally they may be found, including Fairies, Hobgoblins, Elfs, Naiads, Potamides, Nymphs, Oreads, Hamedes, Dryads, Hamadryads, Satyrs, Sylvani, Napta, Agapta, Dodona, Palea, Feniliae,

Gnomes, Sylphs, Pygmies, and Salamanders. The Gnomes were particularly significant as being supposed to be in command of or aware of buried treasure, the location of which was a recurring subject in grimoires.

Essential Reading

Skinner, Stephen & Rankine, David (2005) *Keys to the Gateway of Magic*. Golden Hoard Press. Contains the two versions of the text, combined with conjurations of the four demon kings and the *Nine Celestial Keys* all in one volume, with context, provenance ,and discussion.

The Nine Celestial Keys (of Dr Rudd)

Date: 1641.
Language: English.
Influences: N/A.
Provenance: Written by Dr Thomas Rudd (1583-1656); owned by Elias Ashmole (1617-1692), Sir Joseph Jekyll (1663-1738), Sir Hans Sloane (1660-1753), John Denley (1764-1842), Frederick Hockley (1808-1885).
MSS: Sloane 3825 (f1641), additional in Sloane 3824 (1649), Sloane 3628 (1686-88), Harley 6482 (1712).
Circle: N/A.
Tools: Crystal.
Spirit List: Anael, Cassiel, Gabriel, Haniel, Jophiel, Madimiel, Methattron, Michael, Nogah, Raphael, Raziel, Sachiel, Samael, Uriel, Zadkiel, Zaphkiel.

The Text

This work is a core magical text, concerned from the beginning with practical considerations. It begins with two separate Introductions, which cover similar ground. The first 'Introduction' very clearly explains what happens just before the materialisation of a spirit or angel, indeed the description is like the opening of many of Dr John Dee's actions with spirits:

> [T]he sign of their appearance, most seemeth like a Veil or Curtain of some beautiful Colour, hanging in or about the stone, or Glass, as a bright Cloud, or other pretty kind of Hieroglyphical show, both strange & yet very Delightful to behold.

This is followed by very clear instructions as to what sort of skrying stone should be used and how it should be mounted. This is possibly the clearest description anywhere in print of the precise type and mounting of a shew stone or glass spirit receptacle. These instructions would have been taken for granted by Dr John Dee, and were copied out two hundred years later by Frederick Hockley. It also clearly shows that the stone should be lit by two wax candles on either side or an oil lamp behind.

The main content follows with a 'Key' or Invocation for the main archangels of each of the Nine Hierarchies of angels. Each Key is followed by a 'Replication', an invocation to be used if the first Key has not quite done the job. This section reiterates the advice that invocations for just one type of spiritual creature at a time should be undertaken, and that in no way should you mix up actions of Celestial, Elemental, & Infernal operations.

An important part of this 'Introduction' explains how to tell benevolent angels, & other elemental spirits or powers of light, from those that are infernal or spirits of darkness. This hinges primarily upon appearance, so that spirits of the latter category will betray some form of ugliness or grossness of body, deportment, or speech, whilst the former type will be courteous, friendly and 'well-favoured' or good-looking. This may seem superficial, but the 'Introduction' goes on to show how you can check these initial impressions with specific questions and challenges which cause intruding spirits to vanish, leaving just those spiritual creatures specifically called. Detailed instruction as to how to detect and deal with unwanted intrusions is given.

The 'Second Introduction' gives much the same instructions, and it is followed by 'A Prayer to be said before the moving & Calling forth any of the Celestial Intelligences, to Visible appearance' and a list of which angels are set over each of the nine planetary orbs.

Sloane MS 3628 also contains a copy of the *Nine Celestial Keys*. It comprises five volumes of diary material dated 1686-1688, but it probably predates this material.

The Tenth Key, the single piece that is written in a different hand, is a later addition, which is also to be found amongst miscellaneous pieces in Sloane MS 3824 (fol. 95v-96). This manuscript also contains material on Treasure Spirits following exactly the same style of invocatory formula as all of the material in Sloane MS 3825. Curiously, the version of the *Tenth Key* that is found in Sloane MS 3824 (fol.81-83b) is of greater length and more akin to the *Nine Celestial Keys* in Sloane MS 3825. It seems possible that some later scribe, unfamiliar with the long running tradition of the Nine Hierarchies decided that the tenth Sephirah, Malkuth, also needed a Key of its own.

Essential Reading

Skinner, Stephen & Rankine, David (2005) *Keys to the Gateway of Magic*. Golden Hoard Press. Contains the two versions of the text, combined with conjurations of the four demon kings and Janua Magica Reserata all in one volume, with context, provenance, and discussion.

Book of Treasure Spirits

Date: 1649.
Language: English.
Influences: *Heptameron, Three Books of Occult Philosophy, Book of Oberon, Discoverie of Witchcraft, Goetia, Theurgia-Goetia, Nine Celestial Keys, Steganographia.*
Provenance: Owned by Baron John Somers (1651-1716), Lord Chancellor of England, bequeathed to his brother-in-law Sir Joseph Jekyll (1663-1738), Master of the Rolls, and subsequently purchased by Sir Hans Sloane (1660-1753)
MSS: Sloane MS 3824.
Circle: Yes.
Tools: Copper vessel, crystal, girdle, lamen, sword.
Spirit List: Aba, Abael, Abalidoth, Abarial, Abriel, Abuiori, Abumalith, Abuzaha, Acharon, Acimoy, Acmena, Acnachardus, Adan, Adriel, Africa, Africus, Afsiniel, Agares, Aglas, Agor, Agra, Ahiel, Aiel, Albhadur, Aleasy, Alendir, Alick, Aliel, Aliel, Alilgon, Alphasis, Alpherez, Alsuel, Althor, Amabiel, Amandiel, Amaymon, Amela, Amenadiel, Amiel, Amoyr, Anaboth, Anael, Anayl, Andas, Andromalius, Aniel, Ansoel, Arach, Araiyl, Aratiel, Arcan, Archisal, Arean, Arepach, Ariel, Arnen, Aroan, Aroc, Arois, Aroiz, Arosziel, Arragon, Artino, Asahel, Aseliel, Asimiel, Asmodiah, Asmoel, Aspar, Asphiel, Asphor, Aspiel, Aspor, Assaba, Assaibi, Assoriel, Astagna, Astiel, Astor, Asuriel, Asyriel, Atel, Athiel, Azael, Azazel, Azimel, Azymo, Baal, Babel, Babiel, Bachanael, Bachiar, Baciel, Badiel, Balael, Balam, Balidet, Balserth, Baraborat, Baramper, Barbaros, Barbas, Barbason, Bardiel, Barfas, Barfos, Bariel, Barkam, Barmiel, Baro, Baros, Barsu, Baruson, Basiel, Bataiva, Bealpharos, Beelzebub, Belfarto, Belferit, Belferth, Belial, Belsay, Berith, Betasiel, Bilet, Birto, Bleth, Boel, Booth, Boray, Boreas, Boytheon, Brett, Buchat, Budar, Budiel, Bufar, Bulis, Buniel, Burfo, Busiel, Cabariel, Cabiel, Cabron, Cadriel, Caluel, Calym, Calzas, Camiel, Camret, Camuel, Camyel, Capabel, Caphrael, Carba, Carga, Cariel, Carmiel, Carnesiel, Caron, Carsiel, Caspiel, Cassiel, Castiel, Casul, Cayros, Cerberus, Ceroiel, Cerral, Cesael, Chalcos, Chamos, Chanael, Charas, Charsiel, Chasor, Chedusitaniel, Chermiel, Cherub, Choriel, Cirecas, Citgara, Clidraepe, Clyssan, Coniel, Corabiel, Corat, Cosiel, Cubi, Cubiel, Cugiel, Culdrunal, Culmar, Cuphar, Curaniel, Curfas, Curiel, Cusiel, Cusync, Cutchtpollo, Cynaball, Dabriel, Damael, Danael, Daniel, Dansiation, Dantelion, Darbory, Darmax, Darquiel, Deamiel, Deilas, Demoriel, Diviel, Dobiel, Doremiel, Dorochiel, Dubarus, Dubiel, Earas, Egyn, Elcar, Eliel, Elitel, Emlon, Emuel, Espoel, Ethiel, Etiel, Etimiel, Eurus, Everges, Fabaniel, Famiel, Fariel, Flaef, Foca, Folla, Fraciel, Friagne, Frurodopes, Fubiel, Funaler, Fursiel, Gabrael, Gabriel, Gabril, Galdel, Gariel, Garnaeu, Gedial, Gijel, Godiel, Goral, Gordonizor, Gorson, Guael, Gudiel, Gutrix, Habaniel, Haludiel, Hamas, Hanun, Hasmael, Herne, Hilsam, Humastrau, Huphaltiel, Hur, Huratapel, Hursor, Hyniel, Iriel, Isael, Ismoli, Istael, Isus, Janael, Janiel, Jariahel, Jazel, Jereceue, Jeresous, Jissirpnejd, Jophiel, Jorathon, Joriel, Julia, Kadie, Ladiel, Lama, Lamas, Larfol, Laspharon, Lazaba, Libiel, Lilia, Lobiel, Lobquin, Lomor, Lucifer, Macharioth, Machasiel, Machatan, Madicon, Madiel, Mador, Mael, Magoth, Maguth, Mahazael, Mahuc, Mala, Malgaras, Malqueel, Maltiel, Mamon, Maniel, Maqui, Marae, Marage, Maras, Mariel, Maroth, Maseriel, Masgabriel, Mashiel, Mathiel, Mathlai, Matuyel, Mayerion, Maziel, Mediat, Melas, Melcha, Melid, Merach, Merage, Meras, Meroth, Methratton, Michael, Miche, Miel, Milliel, Mirage, Misiel, Missabu, Mitraton, Moniel, Morael, Morias, Moriel, Moziel, Mugael, Mulpolder, Mureril, Mycob, Nachiel, Nadros, Naras, Naromiel, Narsiel, Nelapa, Neriel, Niophryn, Nodar, Noddarding, Noquiel, Norp, Notus, Oberion, Ocarbidaton, Odiel, Omiel, Omyel, Ophis, Oriel, Oriens, Ornotheos, Orpeniel, Orym, Osiel, Ossidiel, Osysiel, Othiel, Othiy, Pabel, Pabriel, Padiel,

Paffran, Pamersiel, Pandor, Paniel, Paras, Pariel, Parius, Parniel, Pasiel, Pathir, Paymon, Peliel, Pelusar, Pemael, Penat, Peniel, Phadael, Phaniel, Phutiel, Pludir, Pluto, Poliel, Poriel, Porna, Quibda, Rabas, Rabiel, Raboc, Rachiel, Raciel, Rael, Rahumel, Ramica, Raniel, Rantiel, Raphael, Raysiel, Raziel, Roab, Rodmache, Rombulence, Rostilia, Roviel, Sabes, Sachiel, Sacriel, Saddiel, Sadiel, Saefarn, Saefer, Sallales, Salvar, Samael, Samax, Santanael, Sapiel, Sarabotes, Sarach, Sariel, Sathan, Satisiel, Satniel, Scor, Sebach, Sedar, Seere, Sequiel, Seraphiel, Seruph, Setchiel, Sibarbas, Sichard, Sinand, Sirsir, Sitgar, Sobiel, Solykrosyl, Soncas, Sondama, Sonenel, Sonoryan, Sorapis, Soul of Messiah, Soviel, Sperion, Stigamma, Sualata, Suceratos, Sulphur, Suquinos, Suriel, Sursinol, Suth, Sympolsis, Tamael, Tams, Tantavalerion, Tarmiel, Taros, Tassua, Tediel, Temel, Tenaciel, Terach, Tetra, Thalbos, Thaniel, Tharas, Tharsis, Theltryon, Thiel, Thoac, Thurcai, Tugaros, Turiel, Tus, Ucirnuel, Udiel, Um, Umbra, Uraniel, Uriel, Usiniel, Vadros, Valnu, Vassago, Velel, Venahel, Venulla, Vessur, Vetuel, Vianuel, Vionairaba, Vsiel, Vuael, Ysbiloth, Ysquy, Zadkiel, Zamor, Zaniel, Zaphkiel, Zaym, Zeniel, Zephyrus.

The Text

Sloane MS 3824 is a significant document in a number of ways. The unique material in it includes sixty-six pentacles not found elsewhere, many of which are to be carved on different types of wood and other non-metal materials. The use of the divine name Madzilodarp in a conjuration, which is Enochian, may be the first historical example of Enochian being used post-Dee. This is clearly deliberate as there is also a seal of the Enochian king Bataiva later in the manuscript. The number of sources drawn from in compiling this grimoire shows the creator had access to a significant range of source material.

The creator of the manuscript was either multi-lingual or had access to a translator, as seen in the English material from Agrippa's *De Occulta Philosophia* and the *Heptameron*. *De Occulta Philosophia* was not translated into English until 1651, and the *Heptameron* until 1655. Additionally there is material from the *Steganographia* Book one in the manuscript, the only known occurrence of an English translation of this text.[329] There are some interesting differences in the translation of the *Heptameron* material from the later Turner edition. These include 'company' replacing 'servants', and the conjurations being in the 'we' form rather than 'I' suggesting the material was being worked by a group. Another interesting difference is the earthen vessel being replaced by a copper one.

The text contains: A Prayer to be said before the calling forth of Elemental or Infernal Spirits of Darkness; invocation of Lucifer, Beelzebub, and Satan; an operation for the obtaining of Treasure Trove; a general Invocation, conjuration, or constringation;[330] an experiment to cause a thief to return; the consecrations & benedictions;[331] isagogical observations; of the four elements; discussion of types of spirits, including astrological material and the mansions of the Moon; names of the celestial angels, discussion of angels and the composition of their bodies;[332] the Second Part of the Art of King Solomon (*Theurgia-Goetia*); twenty-eight assorted pentacles (many on different woods); page of sigils and charms, binding magic circle

---

329 The use of material from *Steganographia* in *Theurgia-Goetia* has not been included as this refers to the straight translation rather than adaptation.

330 This invocation is interesting as it uses the divine name Madzilodarp, which is Enochian.

331 This section is copied from the *Heptameron*. It is translated from the Latin, with the English edition not being available until it was published six years later.

332 These sections following the *Heptameron* extract are taken from Agrippa's *Three Books of Occult Philosophy*. Ashmole notes in the text that it has been translated from the French edition, which was published before the English edition (published later than this manuscript).

surrounded by seals with conjuration, sigil, four pages of blank double circles, and ten more pentacles, with eight more blank circles;[333] the Tenth Key;[334] seal of the Enochian king Bataiva in a heptagon inside a duodecagon, with what appears to be a reduction sigil in a circle in the centre; twenty-eight more assorted pentacles, with numerous empty circles and single band circles; experiment to call Spirits that guard treasure; material on spirits and fairies,[335] fairy conjuration and types of treasure; choice experiment on how to obtain treasure trove; an experiment of Bret, a carrier to fetch goods from the sea; an experiment of the spirit Birto as hath often been proved at the instant request of Edward the Fourth; conjuration of Bealpharos;[336] an experiment of the spirit Vassago; an experiment of the spirit Agares; an experiment to obtain whatsoever is desired; of the spirit Bleth, who is mostly called upon and appeareth in a glass of water; the names of several spirits, both with and without their characters; the magic circles for the seven spirit kings listed in the previous section; discussion of the demon rulers Lucifer, Beelzebub, and Sathan and the hierarchy under the four kings of the directions, with conjurations; *Trithemius Redivivus* (*Steganographia* Book 1); The Magick and Magicall Elements of the Seven Days of the Week (extract from the *Heptameron*); general conjuration, replication, welcome, and three constraints.

Essential Reading

Rankine, David (2009) *The Book of Treasure Spirits*. London: Avalonia. Partial transcription of the material from Sloane MS 3824, with discussion of treasure hunting magic and the sources of the material found in the text.

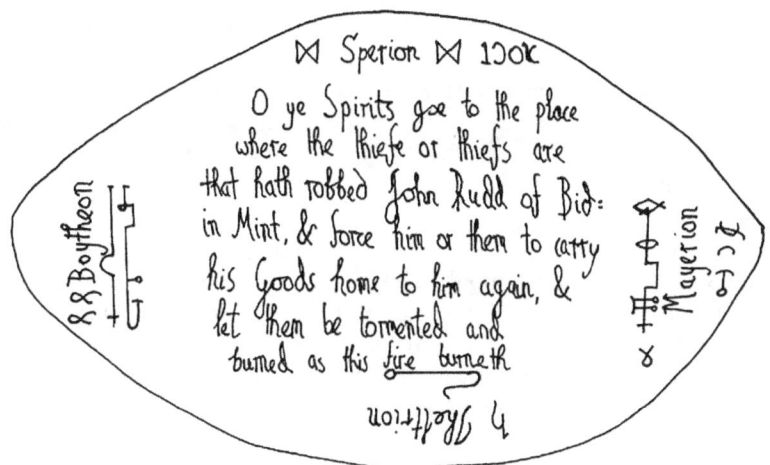

Book of Treasure Spirits, Lead Plate with Demon Bishops

---

333 These blanks were clearly left to be filled in at a later date, but never were.

334 This is an additional conjuration to the set found in the *Nine Celestial Keys*. The use of the Blessed Souls and references to Malkuth makes it clear the author of this piece was applying a Kabbalistic model.

335 Material paraphrased from *Three Books of Occult Philosophy*.

336 This is taken from *Discoverie of Witchcraft*.

Pneumatologia Occulta et Vera
(The Hidden and True Pneumatology)

Date: 1660.
Language: German.
Influences: *Heptameron, Three Book of Occult Philosophy, Abramelin*.
Provenance: Published in *Zauber-Bibliothek* by Georg Conrad Horst (1821-6).
MSS: Manuscript unknown but introduction claims it was located in Salamanca, Spain.
Circle: Yes.
Tools: Bell, crucifix,[337] mirror, rod, wand.
Spirit List: Abaddon, Aetus, Africus, Agiel, Alzazel, Amaliel, Amaymon, Ambriel, Anael, Annachiel, Aomodel, Aratron, Arcan, Ariel, Ariton, Asasiel, Asmodeus, Astaroth, Auster, Azael, Barbiel, Barchiel, Barzabel, Beelzebub, Belial, Bethor, Boreas, Camael, Cassiel, Castael, Chasmodai, Cherub, Dardiel, Egyn, Gabriel, Graphiel, Hagiel, Hagith, Hamabiel, Haniel, Hannael, Hekate, Hismael, Hurtapel, Johphiel, Kedemel, Kyeon, Leviathan, Lycus, Machatan, Machazael, Machidiel, Magoth, Malcha, Mamon, Maymon, Medial, Megalosius, Meierim, Metatron, Michael, Miel, Minos, Nachiel, Och, Ophiel, Oriens, Ormenus, Orphaniel, Paymon, Phaleg, Phuel, Python, Rachiel, Raphael, Sachiel, Samael, Samex, Sarabotref, Saraphiel, Satael, Sathan, Seraph, Sorath, Subsolanus, Suth, Taphartharath, Tharsis, Tiriel, Uriel, Varcan, Verchiel, Zaphiel, Zazel, Zephyrus, Zuriel.

The Text

The *Zauber-Bibliothek* (Magic Library) by Georg Conrad Horst (1821-26) is a six-volume set of works. It is a collection of material from grimoires and witchcraft along with paranormal and theurgic subjects. Within this collection is the *Pneumatologia Occulta*. This gem of a grimoire has some very interesting points which require further consideration. The Hekate prayer found near the beginning of the work is a unique feature, emphasizing the role of the classical Hekate as having power both in the underworld and over spirits (especially the restless dead), making Her an ideal tutelary deity for working with treasure spirits, who are guarding subterranean treasures. The section of information given by the Olympic Spirit Ophiel stands out as an excellent example of a spirit providing information, and the coherence and content of the information makes it very worthy of study.

The 'Introductory Preface' discusses spirits and working with them, referencing Apulieus, Porphyry, and St Cyprian, leading into the Hekate prayer of the sorceress of Lucano (Latin). Discussion continues, referencing Philostratus and Apollonius, and exploring the types of bonds with spirits and how to work with them. Next is a (long) prayer spoken before the work. The Olympic Spirits are listed, along with details of a conjuration of Ophiel by the monk Albertus Bajer (allegedly in 1568) and his revelations about spirits, their natures, and how to work with them (and the brazen bell).

Continuing, the text contains: light to find buried treasure; mirror; divining rod with conjurations for use; days when to use the rod and when spirits should be conjured; instructions for the exorcist when dealing with spirits; lists of spirits (planetary intelligences and spirits, archangels, zodiacal angels, and the nine demonic orders and their rulers); description of realms of hell and torments; how Saturn is over hidden treasures; the forms taken by treasure spirits; elemental rulers, the elements; more spirit names, planetary angels and spirits

---

337 This is the only grimoire which specifies the necessity of wearing the crucifix for all present. Interestingly, it also states the sword is of little use and divine names have more power.

(*Heptameron*); warning about familiar spirits and use of Aratron to control them; procedure for dealing with treasure spirits including incense; description of practices including preparation of practitioners, words spoken before creating the circle; the magic circle, prayers and practices in the circle; how to deal with troublesome spirits; Psalm 91 (used at end of rite).

Essential Reading

At the time of writing there is no English edition of *Pneumatologia Occulta*; thanks are due to Steve Savedow for sharing his forthcoming translation.

Theomagia (or The Temple of Wisdom)

Date: 1662-64.
Language: English.
Influences: Heydon gives a huge list of authorities at the start of the book. Many are classical philosophers, of note in the list are the more contemporary figures of Agrippa (*De Occulta Philosophia*), Kunrath and Michael Scot.
Provenance: Written by John Heydon.
MSS: N/A.
Circle: N/A.
Tools: N/A.
Spirit List: Advachiel, Ambriel, Amnediel, Amnixiel, Amutiel, Aparctias, Aphrieus, Aquilo, Auster, Austra Aphricus, Barchiel, Barzabel, Cambiel, Camiell, Cerviell, Corus, Euroaster, Gabriell, Hamaliel, Hanael, Hasmodai, Hasmodel, Hismael, Jophiell, Kedemel, Kyriel, Malchidael, Metattron, Michaell, Murid, Muriel, Peliell, Raphiell, Raziel, Sabathiell, Sadai, Seheliel, Sorath, Subsolamus, Syrus, Taphthartharath, Verchiel, Zadkiell, Zaphiell, Zazel, Zephirus, Zuriel.

The Text

Theomagia, or The Temple of Wisdom, is a large tome divided into three books, categorised as spiritual, celestial, and elemental. The text begins with an effusive dedication to the noble George Villiers. A long preface setting out Heydon's religious and historical views follows, tracing the wisdom of the ancient world and focusing heavily on Greek and Egyptian mythology (as perceived at the time) through to the Rosicrucians and his own period in time. Admiring testimonial poems then conclude the introduction before the text proper starts.

The book presents the system of Geomancy in a coherent and detailed manner, incorporating a lot of material from Agrippa, including the planetary spirits. There is also material on the Mansions of the Moon drawn from Agrippa. Towards the end of the book there is a thread of Kabbalah added into the material, both practically and discursively.

Book one has fifty-one chapters. These are: how to project a figure, the Rosicrucian way (1);[338] the manner how to frame this Art, and give to each place his name (2); of the signification of these eight figures, and how from them you must make four more (3); how to frame the Witness and the Judge (4); of the names of the seven rulers of the earth, the names of their twelve genii or ideas, and of their sixteen figures (5); of Zazel, and his general and particular significations (6); of Hismael, and his signification (7); of Barzabel, and his signification (8); of Sorath, and his signification, and how he and the rest receive their virtues from above (9); of Kedemel, and her signification (10); of Taphthartharath, and his signification, nature and property (11); of Hasmodai her nature and signification (12); how the seven Rulers of the world be attributed to the figures and the figures to them, both good and evil (13); of the nature, place, countries, general descriptions, and diseases signified by the twelve Ideas (14); how the Ideas are infused into the sixteen figures by the seven Rulers (15); the manner to attribute the Ideas to the figures, and the figures to the Ideas (16); of the four elements, their nature and properties (17); of a threefold consideration of the elements (18); of the wonderful natures of Fire and Earth and their figures (19); of the Water, and of her figures (20); of the Air, and of his figures (21); of the twelve parts of the Earth and the regions, cities, and towns, they contain the natural parts of the body, colours, and winds they signify (22); of the sixteen

---

338 These following chapters are an explanation of the practice of geomancy.

figures and their manifold divisions (23); a table of the aspects of the houses (24); of the Rulers' essential dignities, in the twelve Ideas, that govern the twelve parts of the Earth, incorporated into sixteen figures (25); a very necessary table showing what parts of the body are signified by the sixteen figures, of the seven Rulers in all the twelve houses, of the Earth governed by the twelve Ideas (26); of the qualities of the figures (27); of the colours of the figures (28); a modest defence for Geomancy, and telesmes in the known phenomena of nature (29); of the Sun, and Moon, and their telesmatic considerations (30); of the twenty-eight Mansions of the Moon, and their virtues, in telesmatic figures (31); of the true motion of the heavenly bodies to be observed in the eighth sphere, and of the ground of planetary hours (32); how some artificial things, as telesmes, images, seals, and such like, may obtain some virtue from the celestial and terrestrial bodies (33); of the telesmes made upon metals, what virtues they, being engraved, receive from the stars (34) of the telesmatic images of the faces, and of those images which are without the zodiac (35);[339] of telesmes and how to make them (36); of the telesmes of Saturn, and Zazel (37); of the telesmes of Jupiter, and Hismael (38);[340] of the telesmes of Mars, and Barzabel (39); of the telesmes of the Sun, and Sorath (40); of the talismans of Venus, and Kedemel (41); of the talismans of Mercury, and Taphthartharath (42); of the telesmes of the Moon, and Hasmodel (43); of the images of the head and tail of the Dragon of the Moon (44); of the telesmatic images of the Mansions of the Moon (45); of the images of the fixed behenian stars (46); of images, the figure whereof is not after the likeness of any celestial figure (47); of certain celestial observations and the practice of some telesmatic images (48); of the geomantic and telesmatic characters which are made after imitation of the celestial (49); of telesmatic characters which are drawn from things themselves by a certain likeness (50); that no divination without astromancy and geomancy is perfect (51).

Book two has eighteen chapters. These are: questions concerning the first house and the signification of the Rulers, Ideas, and figures in the same (1); of the second house, and of the signification of all the demands which may be judged in it (2); of the third house, and the demands which may be made therein (3); of the fourth house, and the demands therein contained (4); of the fifth house, and of the demands therein contained (5); of the sixth house, and its questions viz. of sickness, servants, and small cattle (6); significations of the seventh house, viz. of marriages, enemies, wars, lawsuits, and contracts (7); of the eighth house (8); of the ninth house (9); of the tenth house (10); of the eleventh house (11); of the twelfth house, viz. imprisonment, great cattle, witchery, private enemies, labour, and banished men (12); a brief deduction of the accord which the sixteen figures have by the twelve houses (13); of the good or ill houses, and which they be, where the figures be in their place (14); [untitled, on the figures] (15); of the two Witnesses (16); of the Judge (17); [untitled, on spirit communication in dreams with many dream interpretations] (18).

Book three has thirty-six chapters. These are: of several considerations to be observed for the better judgment of a question (1); of the signification of the querent and quesited[341] (2); when a figure is radical, and fit to be judged (3); of the possibility and impossibility of the matter (4); of the person, or matter, furthering or impeding the business (5); of the time wherein a business may be performed (6); of moles, marks, and scars of the querent and quesited (7); judgments proper to the first house (8); questions belonging to the second house (9); judgments pertaining to the third house (10); judgments of the fourth house (11); of judgments belonging to the fifth house (12); judgments belonging to the sixth house (13); of the seventh house (14); judgments proper to the eighth house (15); questions belonging to

---

339 Images of the thirty-six decans.
340 The original says Kedemel here, which is an error.
341 A person sought or inquired about.

the ninth house (16); judgments pertaining to the tenth house (17); how to judge a figure of the day (18); the alphabet of angels and genii, or the writing and language of heaven (19); judgements of the eleventh house (19);[342] judgements belonging to the twelfth house (20); how men receive qualifications from the stars, planets, and angels, and how we may have the society of a Genius (21); what divine gifts man receives from God by Sephiroth, the which transfers them through the several orders of the angels to the planets, and how man receives Aduachiel, the angel Amutuel or Kyriel and converses with them (22); of Camael, and his power and virtue, what diseases Malchidael the spirit cures, how to receive him and of what he teacheth, of Barthiel, and of raising the dead (23); of the sixth name of God Eloha, and of the sixth Sephiroth, and their power and gifts, and how of Verchiel the spirit (24); of the genii Amnixiel or Asmodel, their power in heaven (25); of the use of the Nativity, of Michael the intelligence, and Ambriel (26); of Seheliel the Genius, and Murid the Genius, and Amnediel the Genius (27); of the Temple of Wisdom (28); that knowledge inclines the mind to heresy and atheism, the solution of original guilt (29); of the soul, several opinions (30); that you are with confidence to attend and obey your Genius his commands (31) of the nature of the soul of man (32); of angels, genii, and Ideas (33); that those intellectual or cognoscitive operations we find in ourselves, are not performed by the Evoeliacon[343] (34); the distribution of the faculties of the sensible soul into motion and into sense (35); a very true narration of a gentleman, R.C., who hath the continual society of a guardian Genius (36); of gods, of angels and of spirits, of God's wisdom.

Essential Reading

Heydon, John (2018) *Theomagia, or the Temple of Wisdom*. London: Forgotten Books. Decent reproduction of the book. As an out-of-print book this work is easily available online.

---

342 Two consecutive chapters are both numbered nineteen.
343 Old name for the pineal gland.

The Grimoire of Pope Honorius

Date: 1670.
Language: French and German.
Influences: *Heptameron, Key of Solomon, Three Books of Occult Philosophy, Enchiridion of Pope Leo III.*
Provenance: Catharine la Voisin owned a copy.
MSS: Published in two editions in Rome (1670); Bibliotheque de l'Arsenal MS 2494, bound with *The Grimoire of Armadel* (mid C18); Wellcome 4666, bound with *The Key of Solomon* and *The Grand Grimoire* (mid C18); published in France in 1760 and 1800, being one of the *Bibliothèque Bleue de Troyes* (Blue Library of Troyes) works; Scheible in *Das Kloster* (1845).
Circle: Yes.
Tools: N/A.
Spirit List: Aacoel, Acham, Achariel, Achel, Acquiot, Agarus, Agathoe, Agerol, Aliscor, Altaine, Amaymon, Amiaden, Ampheron, Anasta, Aquiel/Surgat, Ariel, Artis, Asmodai, Astarin, Astaroth, Azdical, Baal, Bahol, Balthazard, Bamulahe, Barbuit, Bareschas, Batemont, Bechet/Bechard, Belem, Belzebuth, Berbigot, Berith, Canfft, Casmiel, Chameron, Croway, Dariston, Donoar, Driades, Dumoson, Egalierap, Egim, Eparine, Estio, Fabbrom, Ferly, Fleruty, Gabriel, Gamoet, Gaspard, Gebepl, Genap, Gewar, Gezery, Hagras, Heleniert, Heneral, Honsi, Ido, Irly, Jilbagor, Johann, Jusatine, Laaval, Leviathant, Lucifer, Machin, Madael, Magoa/Nagoa, Malcha, Mandusin, Margolas, Masiel, Mayrdrus, Melchidael, Melchior, Michael, Migola, Mole, Nabam/Nabara/Guland, Nadel, Naema, Nambroth, Namut, Nape, Nebirots, Nemon, Neront, Nimrod, Odail, Oriel, Oriel, Oriens, Osmony, Oviar, Paymon, Pratham, Premy, Ragiel, Ramath, Ramdoth, Rou, Rouvayet, Sabiel, Sargas, Satanachi, Satanas, Satarin, Scirlin, Seradon, Sibos, Silcharde, Sirachi, Siviant, Soas, Sordinot, St. Petrus, Tarchimache, Tausata, Terly, Tiriel, Tonsin, Xotuda, Zaral, Zazel, Zomal.

The Text

The *Grimoire of Pope Honorius* is a significant seventeenth-century French grimoire with a selection of Book of Secrets charms attached to it called 'The Collection of Secrets'. In combining these two strands of practice, it continued the tradition found in earlier manuscripts where this practice is seen regularly. The countries which dominated the Grimoire tradition were England, France, Italy, and Germany, with the so-called 'black magic' grimoires from the end of this period being largely French and Italian. C.J.S. Thompson noted this, saying, 'During the seventeenth and eighteenth centuries, several small handbooks were printed and circulated in France and Italy professing to record the true magical ritual.'[344]

Inevitably, material crossed borders into other countries, including Spain, and in the early eighteenth century a compilation text called *Agripa Negra* (*Black Agrippa*) proliferated in that country. Dedicated largely to treasure-hunting (as much of the Spanish material was, particularly that of the Cyprian textual tradition), this nineteen-page collection included several conjurations from the *Grimoire of Pope Honorius*, including the King of the East and the spirit Nembrot (Nambroth).[345] A French version of this text called *Agripa Noir* was mentioned in the trial of the Basque cunning-man Gratien Detcheverry in 1750, showing it had returned to the source language it was drawn from.[346]

---

344 Thompson, 1927:256.
345 Davies, 2009:114.
346 Davies, 2003:174.

This process of proliferation is also seen in the nineteenth-century German version of the *Grimoire of Pope Honorius* given by Scheible in his *Das Kloster* (1845). This edition has a number of differences to the earlier French versions, including an extra chapter.

The *Grimoire of Pope Honorius* has never really received the recognition it deserves as arguably the first of the French 'black magic' grimoires, which are characterised by all being published as *Bibliothèque Bleue de Troyes* (Blue Library of Troyes) works. These widely distributed, extremely cheap paperback editions were prevalent across France from the seventeenth to the mid-nineteenth century, and were so-called due to the blue sugar paper they were wrapped in.

As well as material from the *Heptameron*, the content of the *Grimoire of Pope Honorius* also drew on earlier religious influences; in his seminal work on Russian magic, Ryan (1995:295) notes that 'A French Cathar specialist, Rene Nelli, described a very similar prayer current in Languedoc from the twelfth to the twentieth century. It includes Greek and Hebrew words, and Nelli notes that it occurs in the so-called Grimoire of Pope Honorius.'[347] This refers to the Prayer found on pages 15-16 of the 1760 edition of the *Grimoire of Pope Honorius*.

The spirit names used in the *Grimoire of Pope Honorius* are a mixture of significant previous names and others which do not seem to appear in earlier grimoires. Although they vary, it is worth noting that the spirit list in the fifteenth-century *Le Livre des Esperitz* (*The Book of Spirits*)[348] does bear a small degree of similarity to the later *Grimoire of Pope Honorius*, containing the triad of infernal rulers Lucifer, Beelzebub, and Satan (rather than Astaroth) and the four demonic rulers of the cardinal directions. Two of the four names associated with the cardinal directions are the same but transposed on their directional axis, and another one is similar in sound; thus respectively the *Grimoire of Pope Honorius* against the *Livre des Esperitz* has Magoa/Oriens (East), Egim/Amaymon (South), Bayemon/Poymon (West) and Amaymon/Egin (North). The source of these attributions in the *Grimoire of Pope Honorius* is unclear, as those in *Livre des Esperitz* follow the attributions found in earlier sources such as Cecco d'Ascoli's *Commentary on the Sphere of Sacrobosco* (c.1324).

When considering the names of spiritual creatures used in the charms found in the *Grimoire of Pope Honorius*, the influence of Agrippa's *De Occulta Philosophia* may be seen in the charm called 'To make a girl come find you, no matter how wise she may be: operation from a wondrous power from Superior Intelligences'. The intelligences referred to here are probably the planetary intelligences, as the names of both planetary intelligences (Tiriel for Mercury and Malcha for the Moon) and planetary spirits (Zazel for Saturn and possibly a corrupted form of Bartzabel for Mars) are found in this charm.

The *Heptameron* also forms the bulk of the 1744 book *Les Oeuvres Magiques d'Henri Corneille Agrippa* (The Magical Works of Henri Cornelius Agrippa), mentioned in the 1760 edition of the *Grimoire of Pope Honorius*. This book was erroneously described on the cover as being translated by Pierre d'Aban (Peter of Abano). The attribution of de Abano, who is generally credited with being the author of the *Elucidation of Necromancy/Heptameron*, and who died long before Agrippa was born, as the translator of his own work, is a curious mistake, but perhaps was more of a marketing ploy using the more famous (or infamous) magician's name. Certainly there is no material in the book which was actually written by Agrippa at all. A number of the charms found in the *Grimoire of Pope Honorius* are also found in the second part of *Les Oeuvres Magiques d'Henri Corneille Agrippa*, in the section entitled *Occult Secrets*.

There are also numerous charms in the second part of the *Grimoire of Pope Honorius*, emphasising the inclusion of Book of Secrets material, some of which date back to at least the thirteenth century (e.g. the Letter of St Anthony). The charm entitled 'An Enchantment

---

347 Ryan, 1995:295.
348 Trinity College, Cambridge, MS 0.8.29, fol. 179-182v.

to Stop Blood' is previously found in Scot's *Discoverie of Witchcraft* (1584), and was probably copied from this work or some other derivative text. This charm was extremely popular, as it is also found in other works including the Icelandic text called the *Galdrabók*, which was compiled from around 1500-1650.[349] From the mid-sixteenth century there was a huge explosion of Books of Secrets, particularly in Italy and France, which undoubtedly provided much of the material found in later works like the *Grimoire of Pope Honorius*.

The *Grimoire of Pope Honorius* provides reference to the continuing use of grave dirt in this type of magic. The charm entitled 'To see Spirits, of which the air is replete', includes in its ingredients 'some powder from the grave of a dead man, that is to say, some dust, which is touching the coffin'. As this charm occurs in the earliest available edition, i.e. 1670, it provides us with a date at which time grave dirt is being used in French folk magic.[350] Harms provides an excellent discussion of the use of grave dirt in folk magic going back to the Venerable Bede in C8 CE and in Renaissance conjurations.[351] Although grave dirt was used in at least one Anglo-Saxon charm, this was a very specific charm for a woman struggling in childbirth, and required the grave dirt from a dead child of hers, and so is based on a specific familial relationship.[352] Furthermore, the charm 'To use a nail to make someone suffer' uses coffin nails, which have also become popular against witches and for malicious magic in folk traditions across Europe.

As mentioned previously, it is clear that the charms found in the *Grimoire of Pope Honorius* were used in other derivative works, but the extent to which they spread is sometimes surprising. Writing on invisibility spells, the scholar Ioannis Marathakis notes that 'The infamous French Grimoire of Pope Honorius contains a recipe very similar to the first two Greek versions [found in the nineteenth-century Bernardakean Magical Codex].'[353]

The Book of Secrets section of the *Grimoire of Pope Honorius* refers to the *Enchiridion of Pope Leo III* in several places, and different editions contain a variety of charms, some repeated and some not. A complete list of these charms follows. To see spirits, of which the air is replete; to win at gaming; to extinguish a chimney fire; to obtain a hand of glory; garters for travelling without wearying; to be impervious against weapons; conjuration of the Sun; to see in a vision at night (i.e., dream) what you desire to know; to use a nail to make someone suffer; to appear to be accompanied by many; to not be wounded by any weapon; to make a weapon fail; for pleurisy; for fevers; for intermittent fevers; for tertiary fever; for quartan fever; to stop loss of blood; against a sword strike; for when you are going into battle; to extinguish fire; against burns; for headaches; for stomach flux; to prevent eating at the table; to extinguish fire; to prevent copulation; for games; to stop a serpent; for ringworm of the hair; to win at dice; to remove a fish bone from the throat; to not grow weary while walking; to win at all games; to break and destroy all evil spells; the Great Exorcism; to remove all spells and summon the person who caused the evil deed; the Castle of the Fair protection for horse and sheep; guard for whatever you will; another guard (for sheep); guard against mange and scabies and sheep pox; guard against mange; guard for preventing wolves from entering a field where there are sheep; marionettes of protection; guard for horses; guard for the flock; another guard for sheep; new guard for sheep and horses; guard against rabbits; to stop a horse and carriages; counter-charm; for the lambs to return beautiful and strong; against firearms; for ulcerous

---

349 *The Galdrabók*, Flowers, 1989:60.
350 This refers to the European use of grave dirt as opposed to African use. There are references, e.g., to the Caribbean dirt oath, requiring the ingestion of grave dirt, from 1750. See Hughes, 1750:15-16.
351 Harms 2019:62-90.
352 *The Anglo-Saxon Charms*, Grendon, 1909:209.
353 *From the Ring of Gyges to the Black Cat Bone: A Historical Survey of the Invisibility Spells*, Marathakis, 2007.

lesions (sheep); for glanders and colic in horses; to heal sprains and twists in horses; to prevent a flock from touching a harvest; to heal a beast afflicted with haemorrhaging; for mumps; for scabies and ringworm in animals; for haemorrhoids; for epilepsy or falling sickness; for dropsy; for cuts; for iron splinters in the eyes; for white finger; for haemorrhages and blood loss; for relentless diarrhoea; correspondence of ancient and decimal weights; table of medication doses; remedy for gout; for bee stings; for colic; for cholera; for jaundice; for toothache; for sea-sickness; recipes for prolonging life; for sweaty feet; to make three ladies or gentleman come to your room after supper; to make a girl come to find you; to render oneself invisible; to make a person come to you; to make a girl dance nude; to prevent a person from sleeping; to enjoy the use of whomever you will; to prevent a dog from barking; to avoid undergoing interrogation; Guidon's practice for dispossessing; to control (animals); to be impervious; to discover treasure; counter charm; against fire; and for fevers.

ESSENTIAL READING

David Rankine & Paul Harry Barron (2013) *The Complete Grimoire of Pope Honorius*, London: Avalonia. English edition of all the texts, French and German, with in-depth discussion of its provenance, context, and relation to the other French 'black magic' grimoires.

Semiphoras and Shemhamphorash (of King Solomon)

Date: 1686.
Language: Latin, German.
Influences: *Sepher Raziel, Liber Semiphoras, Lucidarium/Heptameron, Three Book of Occult Philosophy.*
Provenance: First published by Andreas Luppius in 1686. Published by Scheible in *Das Kloster* Vol. 3 (1846).
MSS: N/A.
Circle: N/A.
Tools: N/A.
Spirit List:[354] Abdizuel, Abrinael, Abuiony, Achaiah, Adrael, Adriel, Aduachiel, Aladiah, Alheniel, Alscius, Altel, Amael, Amayon, Ambriel, Amixiel, Amnediel, Amnixiel, Amutiel, Anahel, Anazimur, Aniel, Annauel, Ardefiel, Ariel, Arragon, Asaliah, Asmodel, Astagna, Ataliel, Azael, Azariel, Azazel, Azeruel, Aziel, Babiel, Baccanael, Baciel, Baliel, Barael, Barbiel, Barchiel, Barquiel, Baty, Bayel, Beatiel, Betaabat, Bethnael, Boamiel, Boel, Burcat, Cababili, Cabrael, Cahetel, Caliel, Calliel, Calzas, Camael, Caraniel, Carniel, Carpatiel, Carpiel, Carroye, Cerviel, Chaamiah, Chabuiah, Chahuiah, Chanakiah, Charsiel, Cherub, Cnael, Coniel, Damabiah, Damael, Daniel, Deramiel, Dirachiel, Ducaniel, Egibiel, Egyn, Eiael, Elael, Elemiah, Enediel, Erastiel, Ergediel, Fabriel, Famiel, Faniel, Friagne, Gabiel, Gabriel, Gadiel, Gambiel, Geliel, Geniel, Haaiah, Habudiel, Hachasiah, Haciel, Hahahel, Hahaiah, Haiaiel, Hakamiah, Hamaliel, Hanaël, Haniel, Hannu, Harachel, Hariel, Haziel, Hiayel, Holy, Hosael, Hubaiel, Hufaltiel, Husael, Ielahiah, Ihiazel, Imamiah, Jael, Jahhel, Jahyniel, Janael, Jareael, Jasiael, Jazeriel, Jechujah, Jeiazel, Jeilel, Jeli, Jeliel, Jerathel, Jibamiah, Jophiel, Kadie, Kyniel, Kyriel, Lacana, Laviah, Lecahel, Lehachiah, Leiaiel, Lelahel, Leuuiah, Leviah, Lobquin, Loquel, Madiel, Mahasiah, Mahazael, Maianiel, Malchidael, Maltiel, Maniel, Margabiel, Maschasiel, Mathiel, Mebahel, Mebahiah, Mecheiel, Melahel, Menkiel, Metatron, Michael, Mihael, Milliel, Mizrael, Monadel, Mumiah, Muriel, Muscon, Nael, Nahymel, Nanael, Naroniel, Nathan, Neciel, Nelchael, Nelipa, Nemamiah, Nithael, Nithhaih, Omael, Ophaniel, Oriens, Oriphiel, Pahaliah, Papliel, Paschar, Paymon, Peliel, Penac, Peneal, Poiel, Porna, Quadissu, Quelamia, Raehel, Ragnel, Rahumiel, Raphael, Raziel, Rechael, Reiiel, Requiel, Sacriell, Saditel, Samael, Samuel, Saphiel, Sarquiel, Scheliel, Sealiah, Seehiah, Serael, Seruph, Sitael, Sonitas, Staijel, Suceratos, Tagriel, Tariescorat, Tharsis, Thiel, Turiel, Tychagara, Umahel, Unael, Usera, Uslael, Vasans, Vasariah, Vascaniel, Vebol, Vehnel, Vehuiah, Venetal, Verchiel, Vetameil, Vevaliah, Vianiel, Vinnatraba, Volaquiel, Wallum, Yanael, Yeseraije, Zadkiel, Zaniel, Zaphchiel, Zuriel.

The Text

Semiphoras and Shemhamphorash combines a long angelic spirit list with Kabbalah and theology. It falls into the Solomonic tradition as another of the texts with authorship attributed to Solomon. The text has roots in earlier texts like *Liber Semiphoras* (referenced by Roger Bacon in 1260), *Sepher Raziel*, and Agrippa's *Three Books of Occult Philosophy*.

The text begins with 'An Humble Prayer for the Attainment of Wisdom and Understanding'. The capitalization of Wisdom and Understanding[355] hints at the large

---

354 The spirit list of angels in this work is extensive, including the angels of the Shemhamphorash, Mansions of the Moon, Zodiac, Heavens, Directions, and Elements.
355 I.e., the sephiroth of Chokmah and Binah.

amount of Kabbalistic content found in this work. The author ('King Solomon') explains that the names of God can only be spoken in Hebrew. The structure of the world is described through fourfold levels of order and classification, viz. the orders of angels, archangels, elemental angels, and seasons. The fourfold theme is continued in man as the four spiritual faculties, inner senses, moral virtues, and body elements, and in demons as the four elements and directions. The seven different Semiphoras and their powers are then explained. A different set of seven Semiphoras given to Moses follows, along with a prayer. A discussion of divine names, including those given to the Sephiroth, is next, along with the seventy-two angels of the Shemhamphorash.

The next section is on the benefits and use of the Semiphoras, leading into the divine names of the ten Sephiroth, along with their orders of angels and archangels. The following sections are: the nine choirs of angels divide theology into three hierarchies; of the movement of the heavenly powers; what man receives from the orders of angels; what man may obtain from the twelve signs; the planets have seven heights and seven angels;[356] invocation of angels; prayer for use if no spirits turn up.

Essential Reading

Peterson, Joseph H. (ed, trans) (2008) *The Sixth and Seventh Books of Moses.* Fort Worth: Ibis Press. Peterson includes a translation of *Semiphoras and Shemhamphorash* in this excellent work.

---

356 Note the different names given to the same angels are given in the text. The different names may be found in the 'Spirit List' chapter but are not included here as the list is for different spirits.

Book of Saint Cyprian the Sorcerer's Treasure

Date: C17-C20 CE.
Language: Portuguese, Spanish.
Influences: *Heptameron, Three Books of Occult Philosophy, Grimoire of Pope Honorius, Grand Albert, Petit Albert, Grand Grimoire.*
Provenance: Cyprianic literature was initially primarily Iberian (Portuguese and Spanish), spreading across Europe and to South America. Numerous books and pamphlets have been produced in the last two hundred years, major examples of which are listed in the text below.
MSS: The edition which best represents Cyprianic literature as a whole is *O Grande livro de S.Cypriano ou thesouro do feiticeiro*, published by Livraria Económica, C19.
Circle: Yes.
Tools: Black-handled knife, boleante,[357] censer, magic mirror, rod (boxwood), rod (hazel), rods (olive), steel knife, sword.
Spirit List: Aamon, Agaliarept, Agares, Alibis, Aonaes, Aquifolelo, Arpiros, Astarot, Bael, Barabbas, Barbatos, Barechos, Barrabaz, Batel, Bathim, Beelzebub, Beritz, Botis, Buor, Caifaz, Caldeirão (Cauldron), Coanii, Comphac, Dragão (Dragon), Eigo, Erizonas, Extator, Faraiz, Firiel, Flurety, Gabriel, Glosiabolay, Gusovo, Ioray, Lucifer, Lucifuge Rofocale, Machaiel, Malcha, Marbas, Maria Padilha, Matefar, Mechon, Melchiael, Metatron, Michael, Nabirus, Nastrator, Neban, Nembro, Nibiros, Orozamo, Prestas, Pursan, Raphael, Satan, Satanachia, St Anthony, St Barbara, St Cosmas, St Cyprian, St Gregory, St Justina, St Louis, St Lucia, St Manso, St Mateo, St Rita, St Sylvester, Surgatanas, Sytacibor, Thastaro, Tição (Ember), Ulzulino, Zazel.

The Text

The literature associated with Saint Cyprian spans a wide and diverse spectrum. From references in C10 CE texts, to his presence in a number of grimoires, Saint Cyprian was one of the most prominent figures of Renaissance magic and beyond, often viewed as the patron saint of magicians. The influence of Cyprian was particularly strong on the Iberian Peninsula and subsequently South America, and this is evidenced in the books and pamphlets credited to St Cyprian in Portuguese and Spanish. Of these the *Book of Saint Cyprian the Sorcerer's Treasure* (*O Grande livro de S.Cypriano ou thesouro do feiticeiro*) is the most well-known and influential, and is full of prayers, exorcisms, and charms (many using animals and parts of animas, and food and drink). This strand of Cyprianic works does not really include conjurations.

The material in the Livraria Económica edition of the *Book of St Cyprian* is: instructions to priests who are about to heal any ailment (1); new orisons for the open hours (2) the repent [*sic*] and virtues of St Cyprian (3); the signs of malefic influences on creatures (4); regarding ghosts that appear at crossroads, or souls from the spiritual world (5); exorcism to banish the devil from the body (6); disenchantment of treasures (7); system of casting cards (8); method of reading the signs (9); 'Occult Powers, Cartomancy, Orisons and Banishments': how God permits that the Devil torments his creatures (1), the names of the demons who torment God's creatures (2), the way of preparing a sieve for divination (3), to divine with six rosemary sticks (4), ways of reading the cards exactly like St Cyprian did (5), responsory that should be said before casting the cards (6), first magic – the means of obtaining the love of a woman (7), second magic – secret of the hazel wand (8), third magic – enchanted money (9), orison of the

---

357 A rod with nails in it used for chastising demons.

custodian angel (10), an episode of St Cyprian's life (11), Lucifer and the custodian angel (12), orison to assist the sick at the hour of their death (13), great exhortation made by St Cyprian in order to punish Lucifer (14), how St Cyprian began his exhortation to the devil (includes the boleante rod) (15), orison to place precepts on demons (16); 'Orison of the Just Judge'; 'New Treaty on Cartomancy'.

Book 2: 'True Treasure of Black and White Magic or Secrets or Sorcery': cross of St Bartholomew and St Cyprian; great magic of the fava beans (1), magic of the bone of a black cat's head (2), another magic of the black cat (3), another magic of the black cat to cause harm (4), another magic of the black cat and the way of generating a tiny devil with the eyes of a cat (5), method of obtaining a tiny devil by making a pact with the Devil (6), sorcery which is performed with two dolls (7), enchantment and magic of the fern seeds and their properties (8), magic of the four-leaf clover cut on St John's Eve at midnight (9), magic or sorcery that is made with two dolls to do harm to any creature (10), magic of a black dog and its properties (11), second magic or sorcery of the black dog (12), story of St Cyprian and Clotilde (13). 'Mysteries of Sorcery': recipe to force a husband to be faithful (1), recipe to force women to disclose all they have done (2), recipe to become fortunate in all manners of business (3), recipe to make yourself loved by women (4), recipe to make yourself be loved by men (5), secular orison to banish the Devil from a body (6), orison that protects from lightning (7), magic of the grapes and their properties (8), story of Cyprian and Adelaide (9), story of Cyprian and Elvira (10), sorcery with a toad to make someone love against their will (11), sorcery of the toad with his eyes sewn (12), words to be said to the toad after sewing its eyes (13), toad sorcery with mouth sewn for evil purposes (14), toad sorcery to make one love whom they do not desire (15), recipe to win at gambling (16), talisman to make one return to his home quickly rich and happy (17), recipe to convert a good sorcery into an evil one (18), recipe to make a person faithful to their partner (19), recipe to speed up marriages (20), the story of the marvellous ring (21), method of divination by means of magic or magnetism (22), magic of the holly and its virtues cut on the night of St John the Baptist (23), magic of the enchanted vial (24), magic of the needle passed three times through a dead man (25), the magical herb and its properties (26), magic of the black dove (27), the most fateful days of the year, only for evil (28), magic of the egg on night of St John the Baptist (29), sorcery with five nails from a dead man's coffin (30), recipe to bind lovers (31), infallible recipe to get married (32), method of requesting souls in purgatory to do your desire (33), the encounter of St Cyprian and St Gregory (34), sorcery made with a bat to make someone love you (35), another magic of the bat (36), sorcery with mallows picked in a cemetery or churchyard (37), marvellous sorcery of the sprouting potatoes under the night sky (38), remedy against hunchback (39). 'Art of Divining the Passions and Tendencies of People Through Their Skull and Physiognomy'; 'Crossed Cartomancy'; 'Explanation of Dreams and Nocturnal Apparitions'.

'Third and Last Book of St Cyprian or the Treasures of Galicia'. Titled 'Grimoire of St Cyprian or the Prodigies of the Devil'. Contains: the story of Victor Siderol (1); how the grimoire of St Cyprian is uncovered (2); the art of predicting the future (3); a meal under a pile of rocks (4); Siderol becomes wealthy on account of the prize he wins (5); how Siderol is fooled by a woman and asks the Devil for help (6); Siderol decides to publish the Gaul Sorceror (7); how Siderol, starving, asks for the Devil's help and sets out seeking for treasure (8); the curious story in which Siderol sells his unborn children's souls, so the Devil will allow him to find a treasure (9); the strange illness of Siderol, which struck him after he was married and and had given the soul of his first child to the Devil (10); the sadness of Siderol, after ten years of happy marriage, when he realised that he had sold the souls of his eight children (11); Siderol tells his wife the reason of his great sadness (12); how Siderol, with the aid of his wife, managed to rescue his soul and his children's souls (13); the illusion of happiness, or the envy over that which one does not possess (14). 'Treasures of Galicia'. 'Diabolical Spirits That infest houses with loud noises and the remedy to avoid them': on spirits (1), remedy against spirits (2). 'Occult Powers of Hate and Love Discovered by Magician Jannes and Practiced by St Cyprian': owl sorcery for women to captivate men (1), magic of the hedgehog (2), enchantment of the black owl (3), sorcery of the willow root (4), magic of the orange tree flower (5), magic of the hawthorn seeds (6), magic of the navelworts (7), magic of the black donkey (8), recipe to make men marry their lovers (9), sorcery of the stingray to bind a lover (10), magic of the trovisco (daphne) pulled by a black dog (11), magic of the living lizard, dried in the oven (12), magic of the left foot insole (13), magic of the brandão[358] wax (14), magical power of the white bread (15), sorcery of the faithful love (16), infallible remedy to break friendships (17), the meeting of St Cyprian with a sorceress (18), recipe for women to get rid of men they no longer wish to put up with (19), method of continuing the previous magic (20), infallible recipe so as women do not have children (21), another recipe so as not to have children (22), method of operating abortions (23), sorcery of the sweet cake to do harm (24), recipe to heat up cold women (25), the power of the viper head to do either good or evil (26), magic of the pregnant rabbit hung from the ceiling (27), the powerful magic ring (28), method of knowing if an absent person is faithful (29), ingenious way of knowing who are the people who wish you harm (30). 'Art of Divining the Future by the Palm of the Hand'. 'Alchemy or The Art of Making Gold'. 'The Sorceress of Évora or The Story of the Forever-Bride'.

Other Cyprianic texts referenced by Leitão (and hence here) include *Holy Father, Book of King St Cyprian* (*Livro do Rei S. Cipriano*), *Book of St Cyprian Martyr*, *True Book of St Cyprian or The Sorcerer's Private Treasure*, *True and Last Book of St Cyprian*, *Almanac of the Sorceresses or True Almanac of St Cyprian*, *Great and Marvelous Book of St Cyprian*, *Great and True Book of St Cyprian* (Brazilian), *Handbook of the Arruda*[359] *Witch* and a range of later pamphlets. Material in these (with some variations on material in the Livraria Económica edition of the *Book of St Cyprian*) includes:

Prayer of St Cyprian the Sorcerer, which is good for many things (C17); Prayer of St Cyprian of Pedro Ferreira (1701); Prayer of St Cyprian of Domingas Maria (1729); Prayer of St Cyprian of Paulo Caetano Teixeira Leite (1783); 'Prayer of the Just Judge'; assorted Cyprianic charms including: to make Cyprian the protector of a baby boy, a spiritual wash, to have the souls of purgatory give you a vision, and sorcery to violently get a lover (C16); various prayers to drive away the devil; list of treasure locations; list of Latin liturgical hymns, Psalms and litanies; recipes; banishment of enchantments; reasons why God permits that the Devil torments his creatures; cartomancy (techniques and card meanings); origin of the repentance of St Cyprian; prayer to assist the sick at the hour of their death; great exhortation Cyprian made after he became a saint to punish Lucifer; continuation of the exhortation; method of preparing the boleante rod to punish the devil; Lucifer and the angel; occult power (attracting women); the devil and his devilries; the disenchantment of the Moura; in order to make a woman say anything she might have done; art of reading the signs in the coffee grounds; simplified form of material on the spirits, blasting rod and conjuration, the great art of being able to talk to the dead, divination rod, charms from *Grand Grimoire*; material from *Le Grand Albert* and *Le Petit Albert*; to see a missing person in a bowl; magic or witchcraft which forces a person to give us what we desire; to call spirits without conjuration to communicate; sorcery to undo a wedding; using a skull and candles to cause harm, to gain spirits to do what you desire; sorcery for marriage; for fidelity; conjuration for weather illusions, fire, or chasms; spell to achieve what you desire; story of Amandio; what should be understood by sorcery; the extraordinary power of man; pacts with demons; magical tools; magic mirror;

---

358 Large candle.
359 Rue.

the secret cabinet (working room); virtues of plants, stones, and animals; diverse secrets and recipes; planetary hours; the marvels of the world; love talismans; secrets of the *Great Grimoire*; magical power of the mandrake; necromancy and evocation; divination – dreams and explanations, metoposcopy (forehead configuration), cartomancy (including the Portuguese method), chiromancy (palmistry); sorcery of the bat to make oneself loved; the leg of the pedrés chicken; the sorcerous handkerchief; owl leg charm; donkey ears charm; fingernail reading; dreams and nightmares (interpretations); oracle of the single; physiognomy; to cure jaundice; disenchantments; the secrets of Aunty Monica; to acquire fortune; magic of the white mouse; conjuration to force a person to give in to your desires; magic to see a missing person; method of magnetism of a medium; sorcery of the skull; the magic bottle; magic of the enchanting vial; the true idols; fidelity stew; cross of the seven bishops; infernal vinegar to simulate virginity; magic of the owl's leg; lover-binding stew; sweet cake charm; oak gall fidelity charm; sorcery of the miraculous dice; enchanted treasures of the world; flower oracle divination; physiognomy; dream interpretation; prognosis by coffee grounds, clouds, and winds; fish mix to simulate female virginity; horn for money divination; way to know how many lovers a girl has had; how to cure flu in girls; diverse charms; charm to cause harm to a rival; charm to arm those who would interfere in your relationship; charms to banish evil; hare nail charm; ribbon oracle; on Spiritism; prayers to drive away evil spirits; prayers against the temptations of the devil; magic ring (for attraction); charm to deal with a disappointing friend; charm to awaken passion; charm to marry a man you love; to break love; to speak with the devil; exorcism; to recover from bad luck; great magic of the hedgehog; magic of the black donkey; to obtain the happiness of a loved one; teeth of the black goat; the nail of the goat; the heart of the bat; to receive news of someone at sea or far away; evocation of the dead; to drive the devil away; to cripple our enemies; the black sock; assorted philtres; the black spider's web; to speed the return of a loved one; revelation of a theft or lie; wall gecko and orange tree flower charm; magic of the artichokes; magic of the salamander; to discover someone's intentions during a thunderstorm; to undo an illicit bond; charm so seafaring men remember their women; prayer of the hermit of the black cave; charm to contradict the desires of a person; charm to get revenge for love offences; divining owl; viper egg divination; used in charm to know what a lover thinks of you; sorcery of the white owl; toad and hair secrecy charm; charm of three turtledoves to obtain affection that is not reciprocated; charm to make two people hate each other; mysterious writing (automatic writing);[360] the secret of Don Juan (to gain a person one desires); how to make rosewater; bibliomancy; the eyes; the walk.

ESSENTIAL READING

Leitão, José (ed, trans) (2014) *The Book of St. Cyprian: The Sorcerer's Treasure*. West Yorkshire: Hadean Press. Great edition of the text with very extensive and useful commentaries.
Leitão, José (2019) *Opuscula Cypriani: Variations on the Book of Saint Cyprian and Related Literature*. West Yorkshire: Hadean Press. Fantastic reference work covering a huge range of Cyprianic literature.

---

360 This charm calls on several figures including Allan Kardec (Hippolyte Leon Denizard Rivail) (1804-1869), founder of Spiritism, who is also referred to heavily in the section on Spiritism.

Sepher Maphteah Shelomoh (Book of the Key of Solomon)

Date: 1700 (mentioned in 1587).
Language: Hebrew.
Influences: *Heptameron, Sepher Raziel, Key of Solomon*.
Provenance: Left to Hermann Gollancz by his father and published in 1903.
MSS: Gollancz (1700); Rosenthaliana MS 12 (1729); British Library Oriental MSS 6360 and 14759 (C17-18).
Circle: Yes.
Tools: Almadel, knife, pen, scimitar, sickle, sword.
Spirit List: Africus, Armniel, Ashmedai, Astaroth, Auster, Barakon, Barkiel, Beelzebub, Bilit, Bintivash, Boel, Boreas, Cupido, Gabriel, Gog Magog, Hadarmiel, Kaphsiel, Kibaish, Lucifer, Metatron, Michael, Mitmon, Oriens, Pishon, Rapael, Rohi, Samael, Samsanvi, Sangdiel, Sanvi, Satan, Shamshiel, Shanaun, Shangdiel, Shanshimon, Sigron, Subsolanus, Tampalti, Vhshr, Vvishtrom, Zephyrus, Zron.

The Text

Sepher Maphteah Shelomoh is a Jewish version of the *Key of Solomon*, translated into Hebrew, probably from an Italian Latin manuscript. It also contains elements of Arabic magic (e.g. operation of Barakon) and material copied from the *Heptameron* and *Sepher Raziel*.[361] Although the earliest dated reference is 1700, there is mention of a work entitled *Mafhteah Shelomoh* in 1587 in *Shalshelet ha-Qabbalah* by Gedaliah ibn Yahya.

The text contains a number of short 'books' containing the material. These are the 'Book of Prayers and Invocations', twenty-six prayers and invocations; on the composition of the Divine Seal; the preparation of one performing the act; a propitiatory prayer; untitled book containing the various ways to perform the acts and operations, at what hours, on what conditions and by whom, also prayer; the associates and disciples, the conjuration in the case of a boy or girl; how many associates are required; concerning the nine days of preparation; ablution and recital of certain prayers; blessing the salt; the place for performing the act and the prayer; the knife and swords; the sickle; entering the circles; fumigating; the water and hyssop; the lights and fire; the pen and ink; the blood of the bat; virgin and unborn parchment; the wax or mortar for making the candles or images; the needle and iron handle; on various other papers; on the written characters and the silk or linen garment; the Almadel; the seals of the twelve constellations; the wondrous circles; conjurations of Barkiel; 'Book of the images of the twelve hours of the day'; concerning the images of the night; conjuration of the powers of the twelve signs of the zodiac by means of the Almadel; the 'Book of Light', containing the names given to the hours of day and night, the names and seals of the angels for the days of the week, the names of the angels for the four seasons of the year, the names of the Sun and Moon according to the four seasons, followed by conjurations for the days of the week; concerning the spirits of the air that rule during the seven days; fumigation for the aforementioned stars; conjuring the fire in which the incense is put; on the garments and pentacles which must be sewn to the garments; conjuration of the spirits; prayer on donning the garment; names and seals of angels, stars and planets from the *Book of the Angel Raziel*; 'Book of the Seal of Bilit'; conjurations of Bilit; replies of diverse spirits and their seals; concerning the sanctity of the nine talismans (*candari*); names of the angels

---

361 'It contains Christian, Jewish and Arabic elements which either lie unmixed side by side or show in parts a mutual permeation.' Scholem, *Some Sources of Jewish-Arabic Demonology*, 1965:1-13.

that minister before Boel; angels of the twelve stations and of the six firmaments and their workings; a general conjuration; the seven planets and the human body; 'Book of the stations of the Moon'; colours of the planets; 'Book of Practices'; the practice or operation of Simon Magus; a remarkable and true recipe for love by the philosopher Adriano; another recipe, tested and true; recipe for seeing a spirit in a mirror; to conjure or sanctify a ring on the Sabbath day; to escape from prison in a special boat; on going through the air in a cloud; planetary invocations and the method described; seal of the terrestrial spirits; composition of the whistling instrument; on subduing and binding the spirits; on keeping a spirit shut up in a ring; on seeing spirits and conversing with them; on how to become invisible; on prison and fetters; on opening all locks; on obtaining an answer from the spirits; on injuring an enemy; on bringing the good spirit to tell you what you wish, except regarding women and evil-doing, which you must not ask; the operation of Barakon; to discover theft; and a concluding prayer. 'Appendix': further operations and conjurations; specific for malady of the eyes; for one who has swallowed poison; to petition a lord or chief; tradition from Rabbi Shalom; to coerce a king or ruler or whomsoever you wish to do your will.

Essential Reading

Gollancz, Herman (2008) *Sepher Maphteah Shelomoh*. York Beach: Teitan Press. Excellent introduction by Stephen Skinner. Contains the text in Hebrew, no English.

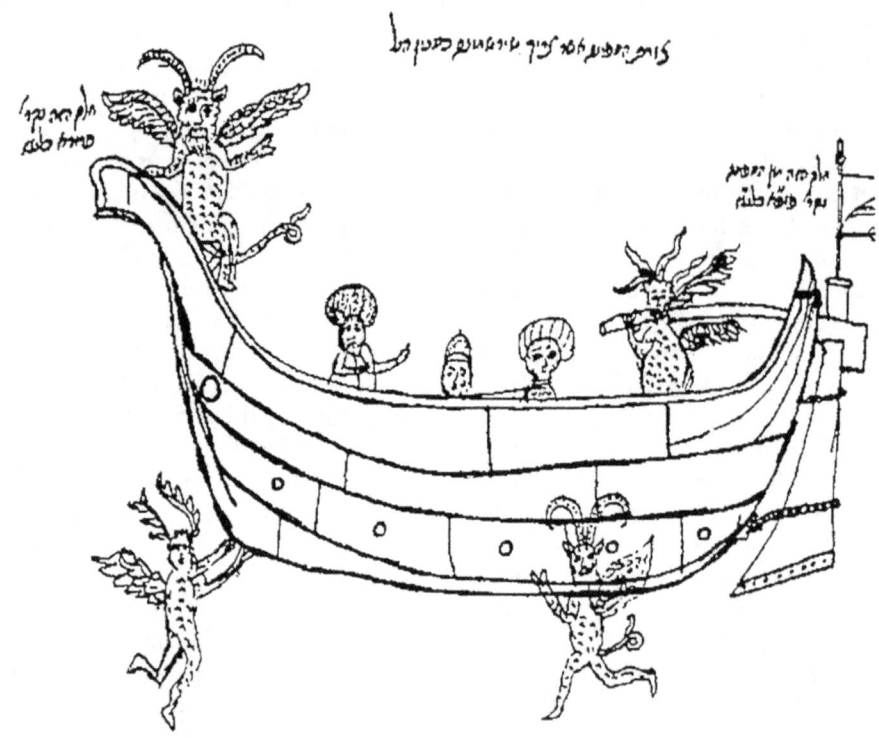

Sepher Mafteah Shelomoh, Special Boat

Sepher Rezial Hemelach (Book of the Angel Rezial)

Date: 1701 (probably C13 or earlier).
Language: Hebrew.
Influences: Torah, *Sepher Yetzirah*, *Sepher ha-Razim*, *Shi'ur Qomah*, Merkavah texts.
Provenance: Published in 1701.
MSS: Additional MS 15299.
Circle: N/A.
Tools: N/A.
Spirit List: A'abedial, A'abiesal, A'aderial, A'akenial, A'akiesal, A'aliehon Avor Kosesor, A'aliekem, A'amal, A'amelial, A'amoal, A'anal, A'anoval, A'aphosal, A'aqerial, A'arebrethiehov, A'areketh, A'aremial, A'aremon, A'aremor, A'ashial, A'avorial, A'avosheh, A'avozial, A'azael, A'azial, A'azrial, Aba Bavoth, Abaddon, Abedieh, Abedoth, Abeka, Abekeleth, Abekeren, Abel Abehem, Abenienok, Aberekial, Aberieh, Aberien, Aberieth, Aberietha, Abiebiem, Abiehod, Abier, Abieriem, Abiyan, Abiyar, Acheseph, Achial, Adelial, Ademial, Adenial, Adenova, Adenoval, Adeq, Aderek, Adi, Adial, Agebial, Agedelen, Agenial, Aha'arehies, Ahedierier, Akal, Akeberon, Akemor, Akesether, Al, Alebera Ayieh, Aleberiyavor, Alebovi, Alemheqenal, Alepheron, Alephi, Alial, Alien, Aliesen, Alieses, Aloheqena, Alphod, Amaph, Amek, Amelial, Amenayi, Amenegenavoth, Amenehi, Amengenan, Amephial, Amereneh, Amial, Amiemial, Amienial, Amok, Amoneh, Amoneher, Amoniem, Amoval, Anavok, Aneboshel, Anechal, Anekier, Anethegenod, Anial, Anoph, Aphenok, Aphephial, Aphethiel, Aphieri, Aphoneh, Aphosien, Aphroditi, Aqoviya, Aralielael, Arebial, Aregala, Arehieh, Aremial, Aremienos, Aremiyiyenos, Arephial, Areq, Arereq, Areterial, Arial, Ariera, Ariyal, Aseberon, Asebiereh, Asephenial, Aseron, Asetheqenal, Asethial, Asethierotz, Ashegeron, Ashekeh, Ashemi, Ashemoli, Ashenor, Ashephek, Ashephor, Asherial, Ashethonal, Ashlekeh, Ashon, Ashoshal, Asiemor, Asmoday, Atemon, Ateredemen, Ateron, Athelega, Atheneni, Athereshov, Athial, Avochial, Avodena, Avokal, Avomerial, Avopheter, Avophieri, Avophori, Avor, Avor Berk, Avor Pheniek, Avoremedial, Avorenial, Avorephenial, Avorial, Avorieni, Avornemok, Avorphenial, Avosethial, Avosetor, Avothoth, Avoyial, Avoyiel, Avoyil, Ayer, Ayied Mesetar, Ayigeda, Ayisemerial, Ayiseteronelien, Ayisethorien, Ayisheteb, Ayizerekebov, Azemerehi, Azial, Azoti, Bal Menael, Baledenien, Bechelial, Bedeqial, Begegal, Begierethov, Behelial, Behial, Bel Ached, Bela'ayi, Bela'ayial, Belehial, Beleqial, Bemechial, Bemerethiyas, Benekial, Bepheliyiya, Bephenial, Beregemi, Bereka, Berekethien, Bereqial, Beresial, Berethobial, Berezial, Berial, Beriekoch, Berietha, Beroqi, Bethemial, Biem, Biememom, Bierekom, Chebial, Cheboval, Chederial, Chedial, Chegeda, Chegeleth, Chegera, Chelial, Chemeh, Chemekial, Chememial, Chemori, Chenial, Chenonial, Cheqierien, Cherial, Chesedial, Chesedora, Chesekos, Chesemal, Cheseniel, Cheshethek, Chetephial, Chezeqial, Cholial, Choshial, Danial, Davoniem, Deberhema, Deghal, Dekadiel, Delegia, Delepheth, Deleqial, Delobial, Demenehi, Demeniya, Demna, Demov, Denetzal, Derapha, Derekethial, Derekial, Deremial, Derial, Deriyavor, Deseleni, Desephor, Diednavor, Diegel, Diegera, Dodenial, Dohel, Domial, Donal, Doqierien, Doreniel, Doth, El, El Bera Avor, El Bera Bavor, El El Ovel, Eliehon, Ga, Ga'aneh, Gabrial, Gabriel, Geba, Gecha, Gechelial, Gechenial, Gedal, Gederial, Gedial, Gelial, Gelietzor, Gemethi, Gemethi, Genesheriesh, Geneshorash, Gephial, Geremetov, Gerezeniyiyeth, Gezorophod, Gielal, Gobial, Golan, Gorenetal, Gorial, Gorshom, Hatha, Hederenial, Hederial, Hehedan, Hekebial, Hekel, Hekieqem, Helesial, Helial, Hememal, Hemiek, Hemon, Herapha, Herekom, Heremod, Heremor, Heriyavor, Herochon, Hesethier, Heshekem, Hetzeniepha, Hetzeniephelehov, Hiegeron, Hoderial, Isa'ayial, Kal, Keberial, Kebier, Kedenial, Kedieneh, Kelah, Kelehon, Kemebial, Kemeshen, Kenogor, Kenophial, Kepheliya, Kephor, Kerebi,

Kerebial, Kerebieb, Keremial, Keresovien, Kerial, Keriethek, Kesial, Kethethial, Kokeb, Kokeb Henogeh, Kokebial, Koledeh, Koretheyavom, Lebermeq, Lega, Lehebial, Lehetial, Leleph, Lemieshotha, Lenegial, Lephial, Lephoch, Leqobethial, Letemoval, Leviathan, Liethial, Liyedi, Lobeqiem, Lonial, Loval, Ma'aroboth, Mavoth, Mazeniem, Mechemed Lov, Mechenial, Mecheniyem, Medegephial, Medonial, Megial, Meherial, Mekeres, Melak Moth, Melekial, Melekieh, Melekiyah, Meletial, Meneshor, Menial, Menothiel, Mepheni Shesher, Mephenial, Mephenieh, Mepheniyeh, Merakephial, Meregebial, Meremeremoth, Meroqaphera, Mesherial, Meshethieb, Mesial, Mesiem, Metatron, Meterial, Methenial, Michael, Michal, Miegal, Miemal, Mieqon, Mieseqoniech, Mikal, Modial, Mol, Moral, Moth, Na, Neberial, Nechelial, Nechemial, Nehenal, Nekebedial, Nemelial, Nemetzial, Nenal, Nenetosh, Nephelial, Neqerial, Neqial, Neqiyet, Nerotheq, Netheleba, Nethenal, Nethenial, Nezal, Nezarel, Nodeh, Nodial, Noherial, Nohetial, Nolegedod, Noredial, Noreh, Norial, Notheneh, Ovamenok, Ovavorial, Pha'avod, Phebehier, Phedal, Phedetem, Phekehier, Phelayiem, Phelelal, Phelemiya, Pheletial, Pheliephal, Phelmiya, Phenal, Phenial, Pheniemor, Pheniyavon, Pheresemon, Phereson, Pheretem, Pheriephohov, Pheriyatz, Pherog, Pheroseh, Pherothial, Pherotial, Pheroval, Pheseker, Pheseqien, Phesetelen, Phesethemer, Phesetzial, Phesker, Phetakieza, Phetapher, Phetebieza, Phethesh, Phetzetzial, Phiekebom, Phielelal, Phkien, Phonekos, Phos, Phothephera, Phoval, Qedemial, Qedeshial, Qediesha, Qedonial, Qelebem, Qenial, Qenod, Qenomial, Qephetzial, Qephien, Qerekoteth, Qeremial, Qerenial, Qeresetom, Qeronieren, Qethenial, Qetieki, Qodial, Qohelorek, Qoherebek, Qoherok, Qokethial, Qomiya, Qorebek, Qorebithieh, Qothial, Raphael, Raphal, Reba, Reba'ayial, Rebenial, Rebiyov Derephes, Rebon, Rechegal, Rechemiel, Rechomial, Rechonal, Redethal, Redophial, Rehal, Rehebial, Rehetial, Rekial, Rememal, Remial, Remiemial, Renerdena, Rephedial, Reqehethov, Rezial, Rieshiehon, Romalov, Romial, Roqial, Rzebeqeteni, Samael, Sandalphon, Sebekial, Sebenial, Sebieren, Sebieren, Sechemor, Secherial, Sekehial, Sekenial, Selechial, Semal, Semekieh, Sememial, Semenial, Semial, Seniegeron, Sephephial, Sepherial, Sephophien, Seraphiel, Serephieth, Seresieth, Sereten, Sereton, Seretov, Sesenial, Seterseti, Setherial, Sethiem, Sha'agien, Sha'aphial, Shebebial, Sheboqothial, Shecheqonek, Sheder, Shehiya, Shekeremen, Shelechial, Shelhebien, Shelishial, Shem Hashem, Shem Qedosh, Shema'ahal, Shema'aial, Shema'ayial, Shemasha, Shemeshial, Shemiechod, Shenial, Shenoch, Sher, Sheral, Sheregemen, Sherial, Shesethenial, Sheshema'a, Shethenesheron, Shethephial, Shobehen, Shokerien, Siederehon, Siegedon, Siegor, Siemephov, Siemoval, Sokeleth, Somekem, Somial, Sophethenien, Soqemeh, Soqial, Soresephi, Techorial, Tehorial, Teredial, Terephial, Teretial, Terial, Teriphon, Tha'akenov, Thederenolial, Thekemial, Thekerial, Thelegial, Thelemenoph, Thelemeteph, Themehor, Themekor, Thena, Thenial, Theniemial, Therebegolial, Theregial, Therekial, Therenech, Therenial, Thereniyal, Therotz, Theshenderenies, Thethederelial, Thieches, Thieleh, Thieretal, Thocheli, Thochereger, Thodeth, Thomenal, Thomial, Thomieni, Thorethah, Thothial, Tier, Tietepech, Tiyal, Tobial, Tomeqem, Ton, Tophiemos, Toreniel, Toti, Turiel, Tzedeqial, Tzegerial, Tzehemial, Tzephial, Tzephnial, Tzereqial, Tzerial, Tzien, Tzoreteq, Tzorial, Voa'anenal, Vobechial, Vobehielael, Vobemethov, Vobeqetemal, Vobereqial, Vobetzelial, Vocheleqiem, Vochenial, Vochesepheth, Vochezeqial, Vogaheh, Voheroqovova, Vokethov, Vomelek, Vomelekial, Vomethenenal, Vophelal, Voqeshial, Vosherephial, Voshovova, Votechenial, Voterephenial, Vothechenial, Vothedoregel, Voyieroval, Voyiheneq, Vozeganen, Yehemial, Yehieh, Yehov, Yehov Hov Ayien, Yibavobavoth, Yida'al, Yiechel Derek, Yiediedial, Yiedod, Yiesorien, Yietzorial, Yihela, Yihelederek, Yihemelieh Mavoth, Yihov Yihov Ayin, Yihova'ayial, Yihoval, Yikenial, Yilereneg, Yilial, Yinal, Yiqemial, Yira'ashial, Yiremoth, Yirial, Yisha'aieh, Yivoash, Yivoba, Yivoqemial, Yizerael, Yoval, Zebdial, Zebedial, Zebenos, Zegdial, Zekorethial, Zemkieth, Zenesial, Zenetoph, Zerezor, Ziena, Zieroval, Zorial.

The Text

In Jewish tradition, *Sepher Rezial* was said to have been given to Adam by the angel Rezial in the Garden of Eden, making it the original book in creation. With such an illustrious pedigree it is unsurprising that there is folklore attached to it, including the belief that having a copy in your home prevents fires there.[362] Although the oldest publicly known copy is from 1701, there are references to *Sepher Rezial* going back to at least the thirteenth century, including discussion of it in the *Zohar*. As such, it stands as a significant source of Jewish magical and Kabbalistic material, the influence of which may have contributed into the grimoire tradition.

Sepher Rezial Hemelach comprises five books covering a wide range of topics including the holy names of God, angelic hierarchies, heaven and hell, interpretations of *Sepher Yetzirah* and Genesis, talismans, gematria, and astronomy and astrology. The five books are: 'The Book of the Vestment', 'The Book of the Great Rezial', 'The Holy Names', 'The Book of the Mysteries, and 'The Book of the Signs of the Zodiac'. The text begins with a foreword by the master proofreader, qualifying the information within with expositions on aspects of the material.

'The Book of the Vestment' comprises two parts. The first part provides the mythical backstory to the book, and part two is the prayer of Adam, which includes spirit lists and magical agricultural practices for the seasons, zodiacal signs, and days of the week.

'The Book of the Great Rezial' comprises three parts which contain practical information woven amongst huge amounts of contemplation/meditation style text. It should be observed that there are 'talismans' in the text which further elucidate some of the concepts. The first part explores threefold symbolism through Hebrew texts like the Torah, in types of wisdom, reverence, and secrets. The Merkavah tradition is mentioned, and the text discusses good practice and lifestyle through the exploration of holy textual themes, through the mysteries of the letters of the Hebrew alphabet, and by gematria.[363] The Shekinah (divine feminine), the qualities of God, and the Kabbalah also form part of this treatise. The second part is called 'Regarding the Power of Ruach', and is a Kabbalistic analysis of the word *ruach* and exposition on the nature of the soul and the world. Part three is titled 'In the Beginning' (*Berashith*),[364] and is divided into two parts. The first part explores the nature and composition of the world, the elements, the zodiac, hell, and Eden. The Qliphoth and the Shekinah are discussed, along with the nature of the Malachim (angelic order of Kings). The second part explores the seals and the firmaments, the power of the planets (especially the cycles of Sun and Moon, the zodiac and the constellations, and celestial measurements.

Book three is 'The Holy Names'. Part one is a detailed Kabbalistic analysis of the Shemhamphorash, including analysis of each of the seventy-two names contained within it. Part two is 'The Commentary' (*Gemarah*), with further analysis of the seventy-two names. Part three is 'The Actions' (*Hepha'avoloth*), which gives veiled instructions on using the power of the Shemhamphorash. Part four is 'The First Action' (*Hepha'avoleh Herashoneh*), and details instructions on the ways to guide with each of the seventy-two names and using the power of the name, and the powers of Metatron and the angelic magistrates.

---

362 Trachtenberg, 1939:315,321-2. (This belief does not hold out in reality, a fact I can unfortunately attest to from personal experience.)
363 It should be mentioned that the *Sepher Yetzirah* (Book of Formation), the original Kabbalistic text, is mentioned repeatedly.
364 The first word of the Bible, and one which is used a lot in Kabbalah and the grimoires.

Book four is 'The Book of the Mysteries' (*Sepher Hereziem*).[365] Part one is a large spirit list of angels. Part two is entitled 'This is the Work of Genesis' (*Zeh Ma'asheh Berashith*) and discusses the realms of the earth, angels over gates, and explores the themes of the Creation in Genesis in a metaphysical exposition. Part three is 'This is the Prayer required to establish Greatness' (*Zeh Hethepheleh Tzeriek Lomer Bekovoneh Gedoleh*). This includes the measure of God, derived from the *Shi'ur Qomah* (Measure of the Body).[366] There is also a large number of prayer sections interspersed with religious teachings.

The fifth book is 'The Book of the Signs of the Zodiac' (*Sepher Hemazeloth*). This includes zodiacal and seasonal angels, timings for amulet engraving, amulets against the evil eye, for childbirth protection for mother and child, for love between a couple, for grace and mercy, and for weapon protection.

Essential Reading

Savedow, Steve (ed, trans) (2000) *Sepher Rezial Hemelach. The Book of the Angel Rezial.* York Beach: Samuel Weiser Inc. Excellent translation from the 1701 text, with scholarly contextual material. This book is a storehouse of magical and mystical Kabbalah.

---

365 Note this is not the same as *Sepher ha-Razim*.
366 This work is a Hekhalot text which details the measurements of the body parts of God, considered heretical for this. See the subchapter on this for more information.

Le Petit Albert (The Little Albert)

Date: 1706.
Language: French.
Influences: Agrippa, Paracelsus, Gerolamo Cardano (1501-76).
Provenance: Published in 1706. Later editions in 1752 and 1782 added to the charms in it. The author is unknown; it was named after Albertus Magnus but this was clearly pseudepigraphical.
MSS: N/A.
Circle: N/A.
Tools:[367] Crown, rings, staff.
Spirit List: N/A.

The Text

The *Petit Albert* is not a grimoire, it does not contain spirits; it is rather a Book of Secrets. Although it was printed in the eighteenth century, it would prove very influential, selling very well and spreading outside of Europe to Hoodoo and the ATRs.

The book begins with a cautionary note, then moves into the section entitled 'The Treasury of Wonderful Secrets'. The introduction to this discusses the importance of planetary timings, explains how the charms are grouped, and also references the *Enchiridion of Pope Leo III*. Many of the charms in the *Petit Albert* are of the kind found in Books of Secrets, dealing with agricultural issues like gaining fish, pigeons, preserving crops, making liqueurs, beauty, health, and other useful charms. There is also much drawn from earlier works, especially those of Agrippa and Paracelsus.

The charms are: for mutual love between the two sexes (nine charms), against the charm of the knotted aiguillette (bound penis), to tie the aiguillette (penis), to moderate the too-great desire for the action of Venus in the woman (sex drive), against the stings of the flesh (to be chaste), to find out if a girl is chaste, another on the same subject, to repair lost virginity, to prevent a woman being bawdy with others, to restore the wrinkled skin of the stomachs of young women after several childbirths, to show daughters or widows during the night the husband they will marry, for the same with regard to men, to guard against cuckolding, to make a naked girl dance in a shirt, to be lucky in games of skill, to enrich oneself by fishing for fish (six charms), to prevent birds from spoiling the crops by eating the grain, to take a large number of birds (four charms), to preserve and multiply pigeons (four charms), against the inconvenience of dogs, another but for rabies, against the inconvenience of wolves, against drunkenness of wine, to restore spoiled wine (three charms), to make excellent vinegar quickly, to make liqueur wines, to make exquisite hippocras (spiced wine) in a short time, to make the real Clairette eau d'Arménie, to have sweet and sweet good-smelling melons, to have beautiful ripe grapes in spring, to make the wheat grow and multiply, to prevent sowing and harvests from being spoiled by animals, to know if the seeds will be abundant next year (two charms), against diseases and other accidents harmful to man.

The next section is on talismans, specifically the talismans of Paracelsus for the days of the week. The kameas of the planets are given, with descriptions of how to use them, their planetary metals, and timings of construction. The kameas do not match up to those found in Agrippa and most other sources. There is included here a table of characters of the planets

---

367 The tools are generally those found in the kitchen for use with herbs and animal body parts in charms.

which is derived from Agrippa. Next is the Cabalistic way of fixing the mercury which is to be used for talismans, to make other talismans according to the Cabalist method, of the peoples who inhabit the four elements, under the names of Salamanders, Gnomes, Sylphs, and Nymphs – discussion of the Paracelsian views (includes the Prayer of the Salamanders), to make perfumes (incenses) of the seven planets for each day of the week, for cabalistic operations (Thursday/Jupiter is missing), for the discovery of treasures, and the way to bring them out of the places where they are hidden, mysterious candle for the discovery of treasures, deceptions of the artificial mandrake, another deception by the head of Saint John, natural subtleties which have something to be admired (four illusion charms), the hand of glory and its effects, to make a criminal insensitive to torture, ointment to expose oneself in fire without being burned, the fiery water which is used for an infinity of great operations, to make the terrible Greek fire, to have peace (two charms), secret of the garters for travellers, secret of the Good Traveller's Staff, to make a horse go more in one hour than another can do in eight hours, to make a furious horse sweet, to make a horse fall as if it were dead, to make oneself invisible by means of a ring, against the Ring of Invisibility, to make other mysterious rings under the auspices of the seven planets, model of the Cabalistic hours of the seven planets (planetary hours), sentiments of wise philosophers on the subject of talismans and mysterious figures, model of a talisman of Mercury, manner of making True Heavenly Water, miraculous properties of Heavenly Water, properties of Balm Oil extracted from Heavenly Water, excellent plague balm, to remove rotten teeth, to cure arquebus shot without ointment or dressings, another more wonderful way (for stab wounds), another against sprained foot, mandrakes, explanation of the two talismans, sympathy powder (for healing), to make gold artificially, another way proven in England, another way following the principles of the famous Aristaeus, mixture of the elixir of Aristaeus, with the true balm of Mercury, to make the precipitated living gold (for healing), to dissolve gold with ease, another more surprising way, to change lead into fine gold, to give tin the sound and hardness of silver, to make borax suitable for melting gold, to counterfeit the real pearls of the Orient, to counterfeit musk which will be excellent, to adulterate ambergris, excellent lozenge composition, to soften ivory, to break ropes with grass, to easily break an iron bar, mysterious ring to heal obsolete ailments, wonderful talisman against poisons and poisonous beasts, explanation of four other talismans, with their models (from the *Key of Solomon*), genuine water of the Queen of Hungary, to remove pimples from the face, to make an exquisite ointment, excellent soap, to make good angel water, wonderful light that puts you to sleep.

The next section is entitled 'Proven Curious Secrets'. It continues with charms: wonderful secret to making the sundial or sympathetic compass by which we can write to a distant friend, to bring a gun to twice its ordinary range, syrup for preserving life, to plant all kinds of tree branches and make them take root, to increase soap, to increase saffron, to increase the crushed pepper by half, to increase white wax, to increase musk, for hair dyeing, beautiful gold varnish, against gravel,[368] to cure it, to clean teeth and gums, against stinking breath, for tertiary and quartan fever.

The next section of charms is called 'Wonderful Secrets' and has a planetary focus to the ailments and their healing: admirable secret to maintaining health, to know if a sick person will live or die, to protect against gout, for fistulas, to remove smallpox spots, for the bladder stone, for colic pains, for difficulty urinating, for oedema, for stomach pain. The text ends with the table of the rising of the Sun over the seventeen provinces and the table of the rising of the Sun over Italy & France.

---

368 A build-up of crystals in the urinary tract.

Essential Reading

Warwick, Tarl (ed). (2016) *The Petit Albert: the Marvelous Secrets of the Little Albert.* Createspace. Reasonable edition of the work.

Steve Savedow will be releasing an edition of *Le Grand Albert* and *Le Petit Albert* in one volume.

Egyptian Secrets of Albertus Magnus (Die Egyptische Geheimnisse)

Date: 1725.
Language: German.
Influences: *Three Books of Occult Philosophy, Grand Albert, Magia Naturalis.*
Provenance: Published in Cologne in 1725, first English edition in 1869.
MSS: N/A.
Circle: N/A.
Tools: Miscellaneous items used in charms.
Spirit List: Asteroth, Balthasar, Beelzebub, Caspar, Gabriel, Lucifer, Melchior, Michael, Moloch, St Francis, Satan, Sephael, Uriel, Zapheel.

The Text

This work, pseudepigraphically attributed to Albertus Magnus, is a voluminous example of a Book of Secrets text containing around nine hundred charms. The emphasis of the charms is on healing and protection of humans, cattle, and horses. There are also a substantial number of combat charms for protection when fighting, and a strong emphasis on protecting home and cattle from witches.

The use of the term 'Egyptian' in the title has nothing to do with Egypt, and refers to the belief at the time that the Roma had their origins there. Although it is implied that lore in this book comes from the Roma, there is no evidence of this either. The German edition had four volumes, but only three have been translated and there is no translation of chapter four available as far as I am aware.

Many of the charms are simple spoken charms with no materia magica component. The Sator magic square is used in a number of charms for diverse purposes, perhaps demonstrating the power attributed to it.

Volume one has the following charms: if a human being or beast is attacked by evil spirits, how to restore him and make him well again (1); if a man or beast is attacked by wicked people, and how to banish them forever from the house (2); for gangrene or mortification (3); for gangrene of man or beast (4); for the sore on any part of the limb, wherever it may be (5); for the worms in the body (6); for the sore on limb or member (7); for griping pain or colic (8); for fever (9); to transplant the rupture of a young man (10); for the sweeny[369] in all limbs and members of man or beast (11); another remedy for the sweeny (12); for erysipelas[370] or St Anthony's fire (13); for epilepsy or fits (14); for scabs (15); for the haish[371] (16); to prevent scars or pockmarks to remain when a person has received burns (17); for the wild fire of man and beast (18); for burns (19); another remedy for the same ailment (20); an ointment for burns (21); to still the blood (22); for swellings (23); another remedy for swellings (24); for a putrid mouth (25); wash for a putrid mouth (26); when a bone is wrenched, dislocated, or sprained (27); another remedy for the same trouble (28); for sore eyes (29); when an animal treads on a nail, speak thus (30); for wounds and stopping of blood (31); to stop the blood (32); when an animal has gangrene (33); when the milk leaves a cow (34); for the erysipelas of animals (35); when a person, adult, or child is swollen (36); for impure air (37); to know when cattle are plagued by witches (38); how to cause that a cow will not bear a steer, but a cow calf (39); when pestilence rages amongst the cattle (40); that no ill may befall the cattle (41); how to wean

---

369 A term for muscular atrophy.
370 Bacterial infection causing red rashes on the skin.
371 Term used to halt horses, like 'whoa'.

calves (42); when the udder and strike of a cow are sore (43); when cattle swell up (44); when cattle or a horse's jawbone is set (45); when cattle are bewitched (46); when a person is troubled with a tumour or desires to remove corns (47); when a sore fails to break open (48); for swelling of the body (49); an ointment for consumptive limbs (50); for the engerling[372] in sheep (51); for one who cannot hold his water (52); when a cow has lost her milk (53); when a cow, having calved, will not clean herself (54); when cattle cannot make water (55); to make a cow give a good supply of milk (56); to cause a cow to become pregnant (57); for rupture of any animal (58); remedy for ulcer or abscess of the lungs, a powder for the cattle (59); an especially approved powder for the gravel[373] (60); a remedy against protruding infant navels, or navels growing too large (61); a very good recipe for colic (62); easy and efficacious remedy for dysentery (63); a simple remedy for worms (64); when the udder of a cow is bewitched (65); when a cow does not change herself (66); to save cattle from putrid fever (67); when cattle are affected by jaundice (68); secret remedy of Paracelsus for healing cancer (69); a performance by which a person will always obtain right before a court (70); another trial to detect a thief (71); experiment to prevent a dog getting mad or rabid (72); approved remedy to prevent horses becoming stiff (73); remedy to cure gout pains in fifteen minutes (74); a remedy for fever (75); ointment for old sores on the feet (76); a secret remedy for gravel (77); for toothache or neuralgia (78); when a man or cattle is plagued by goblins or ill-disposed people (79); for haunted horses and cattle (80); for the swelling of cattle (81); when we are perplexed with what ails cattle (82); when cattle have too much gall (83); when a person is prevented from passing water (84); for fresh wounds (85); for arthritis or pain in the limbs (86); for sore breasts (87); to stay a shot (88); to compel a thief to return stolen property (89); remedy to remove secundines[374] from a cow (90); to make a magnetic compass to discover treasures and ores (91); a marvel to see in a mirror what an enemy does at three miles or more away (92); to destroy sores (93); a remedy against sweeny[375] (94); to prevent firearms from being bewitched (95); secret remedy for sealing cancer (worms) (96); hysterics accompanied by fainting (97); against violent headaches (98); account of an experienced fortune hunter on how treasures beneath the earth rise and fall (99); to prevent pigeons deserting the coop (100); a piece of art which protects a house from fires (101); useful way to make boots waterproof (102); to fasten a thief (103); for violent toothache (104); for splinter or thorn stuck in a leg (105); eye-water that makes the sight clear so glasses are not needed (106); an amulet against cramp (107); for constipation (108); ointment for scurvy (109); remedy to get rid of chicken lice (110); for bad hearing (111); to make a saddle that will press no horse (112); remedy for horse swellings (113); when a person cannot pass water (114); when delivery is too slow (115); after accouchement[376] (116); for consumptive lungs (for cattle) (117); against milk thieves (118); for worms (cattle) (119); for cattle erysipelas (120); how to drive away bed bugs (121); to make oneself invisible (122); to be able to see in the darkest night (123); to make an incombustible oil (124); how to kill bed bugs (125); to banish spiders, flies, gnats, or mosquitoes from a house (126); to destroy mice (127); how to improve all sorts of inferior wines (128); another method to make red wine very good and wholesome (129); how to draw or distil a very good wine (130); to make a gold ring of great protection (131);[377] for rows and fights (132); for the colic (133); for cunning thieves (134); to protect the body from the dangers of all kinds of weapons (135); to tie train

---

372 Beetle larvae.
373 Tonsil stones.
374 Afterbirth and placenta.
375 Atrophy of the shoulder muscles in horses.
376 Old name for childbirth.
377 Charms 131-140 are historiolae, as are several later charms scattered through the text.

oxen (136); to tame a balky and wild horse (137); that nobody may hurt you (138); powerful prayer of protection (139); for epilepsy and palsy (140); for a ruptured child (141); when a cow gives blood in the milk (142); for gout and palsy (143); a particular way to recover stolen goods (144); when the milk leaves the cows (145); for lung rot in cattle (146); for stitch pain in woman or child (147); to drive away swellings (148); to be able to shoot securely (149); ointment for a boil that breaks (150); a remedy to cure coughs (151); another remedy for a cough (152); for sores on any part of the body (153); a sympathetic remedy for fever (154); for pain in the back (155); for colic (156); to cure frosted feet (157); to strengthen the procreative organs (158); to drive away vine fretters and wall lice (159); for intestine colic of horses (160); when cattle is affected by knots (161); when a horse has worms (162); for white swelling and joint water (163); for a decayed horse limb (164); when a person is cut or pounded (165); for suppuration[378] of man or beast (166); for protection while travelling (167); when a horse has swelled legs (168); for a putrid mouth (169); for gravel (170); for infant colic (171); for a plaster (172); for toothache (173); for goitre (174); to heal hernia or rupture (175); to prevent the hearth fire being extinguished (176); when cattle is affected by warts or tumours (177); how to cure a boil or swelling on the face (178); to prevent people doing evil to you (179); a good plaster for open sores (180); for fevers (181); to eradicate rats and mice (182); when a cow loses the milk (183); for griping pains or colic (184); to prevent lameness when the veins are cut or torn (185); to cause the hair to grow wherever you wish (186); to determine whether a sick person will get well again (187); to prevent from being wounded (188); another preventative for the same (189); to drive away lice and nits from the head (190); for gravel, a simple and effective art (191); how to draw poison from the body (192); a good salve for itchy hands (193); to restore manhood (194); another remedy for the above (195); remedy for rabies (196); to clarify wine (197); an approved method to turn conflagrations and epidemics to usefulness (198); truthful discovery of how to discover all diseases by the water (199); how a farmer may be enabled to predict the future state of the weather during the year (200); how to prevent pigeons from leaving the coop (201); when milk is stolen by witchcraft (202); to glue broken glass back together (203); an excellent recipe for pestilence (204); the art of extinguishing fire without water (uses Sator square) (205); for epilepsy (206); how to make yourself bold and amiable (207); how to manage selling cattle you wish to dispose of (208);[379] to vanquish a man (209); against worms in the body of a man (210); a blessing and grace for all (211); for toothache (212); to stay a shot (213); to banish all robbers, murderers and foes (214); to alleviate pains (215); when they shall be released again, speak (216); a good way to stay a thief (217); to cause the return of stolen goods (218); to restore the usefulness of a cow (219); whenever cattle are troubled with diarrhoea (220); to cut a stick to punish a witch that has attacked cattle (221); for fever (uses letter wing formation) (222); for toothache (223); when a beast has erysipelas and the urine is red as blood (224); to protect cattle against the rot (225); for the goblins who deprive cattle of their milk (226); for spots and cataracts on the eyes (227); for griping pains and colic in cattle and horses (228); to cause a cow to give a good supply of milk (229); a drink for sick cattle (230); for pulmonary diseases, consumption, jaundice, and black disease (231); a certain art to kill flies (232); when a man loses his speech or his tonsils fall (233); how earthworm oil is made and the good uses thereof (234); the usefulness of black snails (235); ointment for the cure of the itch (236); how to make the genuine forest ointment for gangrene and sores (237); to make a salve when a man becomes crooked and is believed to be bewitched (238); for a lump on the finger (239); when a person has a cancer on the breast or cheek (240); when a cow's usefulness is taken, to find and mark the perpetrator (241); for hysterics (242); to join

---

378 Festering.
379 From 208-217 is another batch of historiolae charms.

stones or broken glass (243); to repair broken glasses (244); to make a water that will soften all things (245); to soften glass (246); an excellent hardening (247); index to volume 1.

Volume 2 contains: for the swelling of cattle (1); for the fever (2); for cataracts in animals (3); for spots in the eye (4); to heal boils on the hoofs (5); to make a good ointment for burns (6); for falling of the womb and cough (7); to stop the bleeding of a wound (8); to make a blister (9); to eradicate warts (10); to cite a witch (11); in case one suffers from a theft (12); that no witch may leave a church (13); of witches and sorcery (14); to beat witches (15); for sorcery (16); to cause a witch to die within one minute (17); to burn a witch so she receives marks all over her body (18); when a horse is sick or has a blind fistula (19); for influenza, toothache, and headache (20); a magic for one who has been afflicted by illicit love for a female (21); a banishment (22); to stay a rider or several horsemen (23); to cause the return of stolen property (24); to lay spirits by an anathema (25); another anathema (26); for the mange or itch of sleep (27); for the purging of sheep (28); for a rupture (29); for chicken pox (30); to prevent every person from hitting a target (31); to cause rifles or muskets to misfire (32);[380] to prevent a person firing a gun while you are looking in the barrel (33); to make oneself shot-proof (34); to compel a dog, horse, or other animal to follow you (35); to compel a thief to return stolen articles (36); to prevent a person from escaping (37); for a horse that cannot stall (38); to see what others cannot see (39); to draw moles from their holes (40); to obtain money (41); to open locks (42); to understand the song of birds (43); to stop the bleeding of a wound (44); to drive away bed bugs (45); to purchase cheaply and sell at a high price (46); when a horse has some skin growing over the retina (47); to sharpen scythes for mowing (48); for bites of rabid dogs (49); how to discern all secrets and invisible things (50); how a midwife in Nuremberg stopped the blood of patients (51); to make yourself shot-proof (52);[381] another (53); how to make oneself agreeable to all (54); to fasten a person that he may not escape (55); to have good luck in playing, and how to make yourself liked by people (56); to prevent hares from destroying the cabbage (57); to test if a person is chaste (58); how to cause your intended wife to love you (59); when you wish that your sweetheart shall not deny you (60); an Ambrose-stone (61); to stop the blood of one whose name is only known (62); when a horse is constipated (63); for burns (64); an approved representation (thief binding) (65); solution (release) (66); when something is stolen from you, how to cause its return (67); for bed bugs in bedsteads (68); an excellent way to prove whether a person is a witch or not (uses Sator square) (69); if a horse has eaten too much and is swollen (70); when an animal is sprained (71); when a child is bewitched (72); for erysipelas (73); or make for external use (74); for sore feet (75); to compel a thief to return stolen property (76); when a cow has calved or has the fever, to prevent her milk being taken (uses Sator square) (77); to allay pains wherever they be (78); for a constipated cow (79); after this do for the colic as follows (80); for a fractured leg and open sores (81); how to cure a fractured leg (82); speak also thus (83); to cut a stick wherewith to drive away moles and to flog a person (84); when an animal is stupid (85); for worms and colic (86); for lung disease (cattle) (87); for the colic (88); for flush and neuralgic pains of man and beast (89); for the stirring (90); for influenza in the eyes of man or beast (91); a sure remedy for children having measles so that they may not lose their eyesight (92); when a cow is constipated (93); for palsy (94); a verse for the hair worm (95); an approved oil for lame limbs (96); to cure warts (97); to make a herb wine (98); when a woman suffers from not being regular (99); to drive boils and swellings away (100); for the gout or sweeny of man or beast (101); when a cow loses her milk (102); excellent drops for the stomach (103); to prevent anyone taking anything belonging to you (104); for frosted feet (105); when a horse refuses to be shod (106); for the sore on the finger (107); for the salt rheum (108); to transfix a rider (109); solution (110);

---

380 Charms 31-33, which concern firearms, all use voces magicae.
381 Repeat of charm 34 in this volume.

another formula for the same (111); to fix a thief (112); solution (113); to make a mirror in which everything may be discerned (114); when a person has taken a fatal step and how to alleviate (115); a grace for robbers and murderers (116); if a person cannot churn (117); another for the same purpose (118); to fasten a thief upon your estate (119); to regain the stolen property (120); when you have a sprained limb (121); when a cow loses her milk (122); after a cow has lost her milk (123); another remedy for the same ailment (124); how to shoot with accuracy (125); another (126); to make oneself shot-proof (127); to catch fish (128); another (129); to ascertain whether a sick person will die or not (130); how to make blind horses see again and remove the cataract (131); how to obtain a good memory (132); to drive away and vanquish all foes (133); to make a black horse white (134); a certain way to stop the blood (135); for a stubborn horse (136); a remedy for the day of labour pains (137); when a child is attacked (138); to cause the return of stolen goods (139); for under-nourishment of man or beast (140); for toothache (141); to foresee whether a patient dies or recovers (142); to disgust a person who is addicted to gambling (143); if a horse is constipated (144); an excellent eye-water for man and beast (145); to dry up the water in case of gout diseases (146); when a grapevine breaks or warps (147); to produce a light by which hidden treasure may be found in a house (148); to wean a drinker from drinking wine (149); to make a person dislike gambling (150); while travelling (151); that none may vanquish you, and how to open locks (152); for the fever (153); when you have lost your manhood (154); that a horse will not be tired (155); if something is stolen from your house (156); that everyone will buy from you (157); a wolf's blessing (158); when an animal has broken a bone and its blood curdles (159); when a dog is bitten by a mad dog (160); when a horse has sprained its foot (161); when a horse has been pushed and hurt (162); for stopping the blood (163); to cut a fortune wand (164); a blessing for enemies (165); for decayed lungs (cattle) (166); when you put a yoke on an ox for the first time (167); to cast bullets wherewith to have good luck (168); for all sorts of swellings (169); to eradicate caterpillars (170); a black ointment for sore hoofs (171); when cattle cough (172); for swellings (173); a plaster for a sore breast (174); when a man has trodden on a sharp object (175); for the flux (176); when the lungs of cattle swell (177); for the itch or scab (178); for erysipelas (179); to stop bleeding (180); when a woman suffers from a local weakness (181); for St Anthony's Fire (182); for open sores (183); for swellings (184); for coagulated blood (185); what black snails are good for (186); against lockjaw in animals (187); when a person has drunk too much (188); a salve for gouty limbs (189); another remedy for gouty limbs (190); when horses have the itch (191); to drive away lice (192); a drink for horses (193); a plaster for the sore (194); when a rifle or shotgun is bewitched (195); for oedema (196);[382] a good ointment for wounds (197); to prevent eyes from becoming blind (198); a water for all sorts of injuries (199); when a woman arrives at the change of life (200); for swollen shanks or arms (201); to be sure of three certain shots per day (202); to kill powder (203); how to prevent feeling cold in winter (204); to catch many fishes (205); when a horse has overleaped itself (206); an old drink for horses and cattle (207); when labour is difficult (208); yellow jaundice of men and women (209); for sores on men and beasts (210); if you desire to shoot securely, put this under the barrel (211); to be secure against a shot (212); when a person has an open cranium (213); when a horse is foundered (214); when an animal becomes suddenly ill and remains motionless (215); for stoppage of water in man or woman (216); an excellent remedy for apoplexy (217); for colic (horse) (218); when a person suffers from a heavy fall (219); when the lungs and liver of cattle are diseased (220); when a horse has hair worms (221); for swellings (222); for coagulated blood in limbs (223); for proud flesh (224); for swollen knees (225); when the breast of a horse is swollen (226); for all swellings of the breast, heart, and genitals of animals (227); for glanders of horses (228); when a horse

---

382 The older term 'dropsy' has been replaced with the modern term 'oedema' throughout this work.

ENCYCLOPAEDIC ENTRIES 253

has the staggers (229); for the breaking out of sores[383] (horses) (230); another remedy for the same ailment (231); when it becomes difficult to churn (232); an ointment for all kinds of wounds (233); to stop the water in cases of oedema (234); a good ointment (235); to make a good green salve (236); a good ointment for wounds (237); to make a splendid horn salve (238); for a sore (in horse) (239); for old sores which no person could heal (240); for prolapse (241); for St Anthony's fire for cattle (242); to compel the return of stolen goods (243); for constipation of horses (244); for bewitched cattle (245); a certain remedy for stubborn horses (246); for marasmus[384] of children (247); that no person will deny anything to you (248); for lung disease (animals) (249); for an open head (250); that no horse will get blind (251); for the jaundice of horses (252); to stop the blood (253); when a person cannot hold his water (254); for pestilence write over the door (255); for robbers and thieves (256); for the fever (257); to discern the thief who robbed you (258); for sickness of cattle (259); another (260); when cattle are swelled (261); to purify the blood (262); a certain remedy for the eyes (263); when a person cannot pass water (264); when a person has sprained himself (265); for the breaking of sores in horses (266); for the sores (of animals); (267); when a horse has eaten impure stuff (268); another cure for dysentery (269); still another (270); for gangrene (271); for dysentery (272); for the water between skin and flesh (273); when a cow loses her milk (274); when a horse has worms (275); when a horse has a sore hoof (276); when a horse is stabbed and bleeds (277); for the flesh worms of cattle (278); for flux, catarrh, and sorcery (279); when an animal loses its usefulness (280); for distempered horses (281); for bewitched cattle (282); to cure headache (283); an old drink for horses and cattle (284); an amulet for colic (285); when a woman cannot easily bear (286); to heal burns (287); for the cattle (288); to heal injuries on man, cattle, or horse (289); to make yourself invisible (290); to quench a fire (291); to not forget something you hear said (292); when cattle have soft feet (293); when cattle are constipated (294); when a sore on a horse breaks open (295); to still the wild water (boil) (296); for shooting pains (297); for bewitched cattle (298); for sweeny of man or beast (299); when the teeth of cattle are getting soft (300); for cattle sprains (301); that nothing serious may happen to cattle during the entire year (302); to heal swellings (303); for horny excrescences or spavin (304); to make the hair grow wherever you choose (305); to eradicate a tumour and abscess (306); for the swollen foot of a horse (307); for the killing of hoof worms in cattle (308); for erysipelas of cattle (309); for rotten lungs of cattle (310); for swollen udders (311); for inflammation of cattle (312); for shrubby feet of horses (313); a wholesome powder which heals all sort of injuries quickly (314); to heal up wounds (315); a blessing for all (316); to heal open sores (317); for flush and rush of blood (318); when cattle have broken or sprained limbs (319); for colic if we know the name of the patient (320); to prevent the milk from being taken from a cow (321); when a man cannot urinate (322); when cattle are swelling up (323); when a cow loses butter (324); for poisonous air and pestilence (uses Sator square) (325); for rabies (326); to exterminate a tumour (327); when cattle cannot pass urine (328); for all sorts of spots or blisters on the eyes (329); for the windgalls[385] in horses (330); how to heal the same (331); for jaundice (332); for diarrhoea (333); when cattle have drunk too fast after being overheated (334); for wind colic (horse) (335); for diarrhoea (336); to heal injuries (337); for yellow jaundice (338); another remedy for the same ailment (339); for all sorts of sorcery of man and beast (uses Sator square) (340); for milk thieves (341); that the use of a cow may not be taken (342); to prevent bees from flying away (343); an ointment for burns (344); how to make ant's oil and what it is good for (345); for toothache (346); for asthma (347); for freckles (348); a cure for a hard disease (349); for consumption (350); another remedy for

---

383 In some of these remedies sores are called felons, which is a good example of how the meaning of words can change over time.
384 A word for malnutrition or under-nourishment.
385 Fluid swellings behind the fetlock.

consumption (351); for neuralgia and arthritis (352); to cure discharges (353); for gout (354); for matter discharges (355); to prevent witches from entering a stable (356); when the milk of a cow is taken (uses Sator square) (357); that a horse may not become stiff or founder (358); when a horse has eaten feathers (359); to make a blind horse see again (360); to drive worms from the corn (361); to remove itch and lice from cattle (362); when a cow loses her milk (363); when a person or cattle have been bitten by a poisonous animal or poisoned (364); for a weak and dull head (365); to drive mice away from barns (366); for ruptured children (367); to gild tin, glass, or leather (368); truthful prognostics from Egypt (unfortunate days) (369); a remedy for restless persons (370); when a cow loses her use, how to mark the witch (371); index to volume 2.

Volume 3 contains: to quench burning thirst and inward heat (1); for a seated stomach (2); for feverish thirst (3); for bronchitis (4); another remedy for bronchitis (5); another remedy for the same disease (6); still another remedy (7); for white and bloody dysentery (8); for griping pains and straining (9); to secure natural sleep and rest (10); how to stop the blood (horse) (11); to stop bleeding of an absent person (12); another remedy for the same (13); a remedy for nose bleeds (14); for gathered breasts (15)[386]; another for the same trouble (16); to drive away secundines (17); when oedema threatens the system (18); for loose teeth (19); for gravel (kidney stones) (20); how to have a nearly painless and safe childbirth (21); an approved remedy to carry off the secundines (22); an approved remedy for jaundice (23); for jaundice (24); to extinguish moles and marks (25); for swollen feet and pains of the skin (26); for round or maw-worms[387] (27); how to restore nature when arrested by gold or ill-health (skin tumour) (28); a mush for the stomach or bellyaches of infants (29); a good remedy for the four-days' fever (30); a splendid eye-water (31); how to make a good stomach plaster (32); for constipated persons, how to make the bowels open within one hour (33); how to make a gravel water (34); a good recipe for a person suffering from a fall (35); how to distil a water for perspiration (36); for the cough of infants (37); a valuable recipe for pulmonary and other consumptions, also a drink for the breast (38); a good herb wine laxative (39); for erysipelas (40); another approved remedy for erysipelas (41); a good ointment for serious warts (42); to drive away warts (43); to drive away gout and neuralgia (44); to eradicate corns (45); for bloodshot or red eyes (46); for marasmus for young and old folks (47); an excellent stomach tonic (48); an ointment for sore breasts (49); a good relief for a person who met with a fall upon the breast (50); for a youth contracting hernia or rupture (51); for a cough (52); a good black plaster (53); for bad hearing (54); a wash for ladies, to obtain a beautiful physiognomy (55); to facilitate healthy sleep (56); for newly-born children (57); a good pomatum[388] for sore heads (58); an ointment for the itch or mange (59); for mole and liver spots (60); how to beautify the face (61); an ointment for the face for seat and gold (62); a domestic injection (63); for straining pains (64); when a person cannot pass water (65); how to retain the passing labour pains (66); for the after-pains (of labour) (67); for the flooding (urine problems) (68); for putrid mouths of the scurvy (69); a gargle for a putrid mouth (70); how to wean a child without producing pains in the breasts (71); a good powder for marasmus of children (72); a good stomach plaster for a bewitched child (73); a good plaster for an obscure disease (74); an excellent ointment for erysipelas (75); another recipe for the same ailment (76); for erysipelas (77); a good remedy for gout (78); for tympanitis[389] and oedema (79); a good powder for the gravel (80); an excellent purifier for womb disease (81); to prevent that any harm may come to cattle (82); for loose teeth of cows (83); when the livers of cows rot (84); for bewitched cattle (85); when a cow is plagued with erysipelas (86); another remedy for the

---

386 Old term for breast abscesses.
387 Parasitic worms which infect the stomachs or intestines of mammals.
388 Another word for pomade, a scented oil applied to the hair.
389 Enflamed eardrum.

disease (87); another (88); still another (89); when cattle is plagued with too much bile (90); when cattle swell up (91); when cattle are raw or sore (92); how to wean calves (93); for the worms of cattle (94); another remedy for the same (95); how Madame de Vellberg[390] had her powder prepared (96); when cattle die suddenly (97); when cattle are plagued by worms in sore parts or wounds (98); when sheep die (99); when an animal belches up, and the ailment is unknown (100); when animals are bilious (101); another remedy for the same ailment (102); when a cow will not purify after calving (103); another for the same disease (104); still another (105); when cattle cannot pass urine (106); when a witch besets the animals (107); for the swellings of beasts (108); a powder for open and sore feet (109); to cause a cow to give plenty of milk (110); when an epidemic is raging among cattle (111); for the sudden dying of cattle (112); for the superabundance of blood in sheep or cattle (113); for the witches (animal protection (114); another for the witches (115); another remedy for the same disease (116); when cattle have dysentery (117); a powder for the lung rot of cattle (118); a drink (for cattle lung rot) (119); when the vomit rages among cattle (120); when cattle are sick and the disease is not known (121); a remedy to apply to cows during Christmas in order to make them give plenty of milk (122); a remedy for the vomit (of animals) (123); what to give calving cow soon after calving to make her give much milk (124); when a cow is hard to calf (125); remedy against all injuries and diseases of horses (126); another remedy for irritation and bristles (127); another remedy for the same ailment (128); another remedy (129); still another remedy (130); another remedy for the above disease (131); when the hoofs of cattle fall off (132); a grand art to stop the cramp (133); when the udder of a cow is bewitched (134); for worms of cattle (135); a powder for the rot of cattle (136); to discern what ails cattle (137); for all sorts of palsy (138); prescription for epilepsy (139); a good prescription for fractures of men and beasts (140); an ointment for fistula (141); for irritable and bristly horses (142); another remedy for the same (143); how to heal raw flesh spots within twenty-four hours (horses) (144); when a horse is sore and oozes blood (145); when a horse swells up (146); for the swelling of a horse's shoulder-blade (147); when the shoulder-blade is swelled or sprained (148); a plaster for the above swellings (149); when a horse is injured by pressure (150); when the shanks of a horse are swollen, and the flux appears (151); if a horse is injured by pressure, swellings, or tumours which have to be cut (152); when a horse becomes scabby (153); when a horse's urinary organs are obstructed (154); when a horse has an itch or old sore (155); when a horse cannot pass urine (156); to purify the urine (horse) (157); for horse jaundice (158); for colic (horses) (159); for erysipelas of man and beast (160); for the gripes and colic of horses and cattle (161); for yellow knots (horse) (162); when a horse is restless (163); when one of the eyes of a horse threatens to get blind (164); for colic of human beings (165); for cataracts in horse's eyes (166); how to discover the disease of a horse (167); an excellent eye-water for man and beast (168); when a horse is restless (169); when a horse is constipated (170); to remove a bullet, thorn, or splinter (171); for labour pains or falling of the womb (172); when a horse is charmed or bewitched (173); when a cow is constipated (174); for the spleen or milt disease (cattle) (175); a sure remedy for bristly horses (176); for the lung rot of cattle (177); for decayed lungs of cattle (178); for biliousness (cattle) (179); another remedy for too much gall (180); for the thrush of cattle (181); for St Anthony's fire (182); when cattle have thrush in their mouth (183); an ointment for various kinds of pimples and boils and smallpox (184); for the fits of children (185); for the bad hearing of horses (186); to make a sad person mirthful when the ailment is caused by the blood (187); for frozen hands or feet (188); when a cow has a sore on it foot (189); for a heavy cough originating from the kidneys (190); when an animal treads on a nail (191); for the womb disease or colic when the patient is not present and only the name is known (192); for the heart blood (193); for

---

390 Information on a historical character bearing this name is lacking. As Vellberg is a German town, one might assume she was a German lady.

the swelling up of cattle (194); blood stopping (195); for cataracts in the eyes of horses (196); for cancer (197); for obstruction of urine (198); how to make wild game and other animals stand (199); when a man or animal is in danger of going blind (200); for a fractured leg of a horse, when it is recent (201); when a horse falls upon or wrenches his backbone (202); to heal proud flesh (203); how to prevent a horse from contracting glanders (204); for all sorts of injuries of horses under the saddle (205); an ointment for the eyes of horses (206); when a horse leans its head to one side it is an indication of a worm in the ear (207); for bony excrescences of horses (208); to prevent a traveller from ill befalling him (209); when a cow loses her milk, how to cause its return (210); a good way to stop the constipation of cattle (211); a good salve for the eyes (212); when a horse does not eat (213); remedy against the biting of rabid dogs (214); an art, how to quench fire without water (uses Sator square) (215); a preventative which must be carried on the body, for the arts and wiles of Gypsies (216); how to fix a thief so that he must stand still (217); an extraordinary quick banishment (218); dissolved again (a banishment) (219); how to cause a thief to return stolen goods (220); to be given to cattle against witchcraft and diabolical mischief (uses Sator square) (221); to prevent a wound from hurting (222); how to stay the pains of a fresh wound (223); an art, how to stop the blood, which is good at all times (224); an amulet to carry on your person (225); a preventative from all harm from weapons (226); security from firearms and animals (227); a perfect security against shot (228); rejecting ball and bullet (229); how to heal the broken legs of sheep and other animals (230);[391] for the cough (231); how to free yourself of all ropes and fetters (232); when a person goes out to battle and speaks the following, he will be secure against swords and other weapons (233); a protection for all those who carry this blessing with them (234); how to shoot securely (235); to prevent mice from doing any injury in barns, bins, and stables (236); a good way to fix thieves (237); when the urine of a person is mixed with blood (238); how to remove neuralgia in an arm or foot by a vapour bath (239); to secure children against jaundice, rheumatism, and epilepsy during their entire lifetime (240); to stop sanguineous discharges (241); to prevent children having measles from becoming blind (242); how to draw out a thorn or splinter (243); for aches in the back and loins (244); for cramp in the stomach (245); when a person has the gravel (246); that no wolf or dog may bite or bark at you (247); miscellaneous parchments (incudes assorted folk beliefs); of antipathies, of actives and passives, of stones, fishes, rivers, etc., of the wonderful celestial and terrestrial influences, etc.; of the occult virtues of things which are only inherent in them in their lifetime, and such as remain in them even after death; of sorceries – their wonderful and truthful power – of witchcraft, etc.; to cause several kinds of dreams, a way to cause merry and funny dreams, to make dark and troublesome dreams; to soften the teeth and make them sound and white; of the wonders of natural magic – sympathetic and occult; a good plaster for swollen fingers; when a horse is stubborn being shod; when a cow will not be cleansed after calving; how to raise a cow calf and not a bull calf; when cattle are dying of knavish tricks; when during a wet season cows eat moist grass and become rotten and threaten to die; how to discover whether cattle are troubled by witches; against milk thieves; another preventative for the same; index to volume 3.

Essential Reading

Magnus, Albertus (2012) *Egyptian Secrets of Albertus Magnus*. Createspace: Theophania publishing. Reasonable reproduction of this text.

A very good copy is available on Joseph Peterson's www.esotericarchives.com.

---

391 Charms 215-230 are all spoken historiolae charms with a few amulets in-between.

The Grimoire of Armadel

Date: Mid C18?
Language: French with some Latin.
Influences: *Arbatel, Heptameron, Grimoire of Pope Honorius*, Agrippa
Provenance: Owned by Antoine-René de Voyer (1722-1787), King Charlex X for Bibliotheque de l'Arsenal.
MSS: Bibliotheque de l'Arsenal MS 826 (C18), MS 2494 (C18), uncategorised German MS (C18).
Circle: Yes.
Tools: Lamen.
Spirit List: Alepta, Anael, Angels of Love & Charity, Aratron, Asmodeus, Astarot, Belzebut, Betel, Betor, Brufor, Camael, Caphael, Cassiel, Dalete, Gabriel, Gimela, Haniel, Hemostophile, Hetael, Hethatia, Laune, Leviathan, Lucifer, Michael, Och, Ophiel, Phalet, Phul, Raphael, Sachiel, Samael, Spirits of Force and Counsel, Spirits of Joy, Tetathia, Thavael, Uriel, Vau-el, Zadkiel, Zainael, Zaphkiel.

The Text

The *Grimoire of Armadel* is one of the most interesting and largely ignored works in the Solomonic Grimoire tradition. MacGregor Mathers' mistake-ridden translation of this work was first published in 1980, decades after his death. As with other works in the Solomonic tradition it is essentially planetary in nature, containing both the classical planetary archangels and the Olympic spirits.

Along with *The Sacred Magic of Abra-Melin the Mage*, this was the only other manuscript which Mathers translated from the Parisian Bibliotheque de l'Arsenal (labelled MS 88 by him). Why he should have chosen this particular manuscript out of all those available is unclear, though the striking images may have drawn his attention, as they do of anyone who has seen it. Like the *Abra-Melin*, it seems likely that the *Grimoire of Armadel*, though written in French and Latin, may also have had German roots (suggested by numerous words badly translated from German to French, and the unseen German manuscript). These German roots are also suggested by the inclusion of spirits found in the *Abra-Melin* and the Faust books.

Although Mathers translated MS 88, this number is now assigned to a fourteenth-century text, and his work matches that translated from MS 2494 (formerly 88 SAF). The manuscript is comprised of six parts, being *The Grimoire of the Cabalah of Armadel* (117 pages) which Mathers translated; *The Grimoire of Pope Honorius* (45 pages); *The elements to operate in the magical sciences* (107 pages) by Pierre Maissonneaux, Cabalistic Philosopher; the *Heptameron* and the *Magical Elements* (56 pages) of Peter of Abano; *A little treatise on the way of conjuring up celestial and terrestrial spirits* (34 pages); and *A Grimoire to ward off the spirit of a place* (20 pages).

On examination, the *Grimoire of Armadel* does not appear to be a complete work, though the inclusion of material from the *Heptameron*, the *Arbatel*, the *Grimoire of Pope Honorius* and Agrippa's works implies the author was widely-read. With the *Heptameron* and the *Grimoire of Pope Honorius* bound in the same manuscript, the inclusion of material from them becomes much more clear and logical. When taken in conjunction with these works, the practice becomes clearer, as the omissions are largely covered within them.

There is a second manuscript of the *Grimoire of Armadel* in the Bibliotheque de l'Arsenal, numbered MS 826, which has a different chapter sequence. Both manuscripts are dated to the eighteenth century CE, and although the authorship of them is unknown, both were formerly in the collection of Marquis de Palmy, Antoine-René de Voyer (1722-1787). De

Voyer was a diplomat and noted bibliophile who collected over one hundred thousand works in his lifetime. He forbade the dispersal of his library after his death, and it was purchased by King Charles X (prior to his ascension to the French throne) and formed the nucleus of the Bibliotheque de l'Arsenal.

Gabriel Naude recorded the use of the term 'Armadel' as a type of magic in *The History of Magick* (1625). He criticised the Italian scholar Julius Caesar Scaliger (1484-1558) for his description among his assertions in his work on natural philosophy *Exotericarum Exercitationes* (1557). Scaliger divided magic into five categories – Trimethian (invention), Theurgic (disposition), Armadel (elocution), Pauline (pronunciation), and Lullian (memory). The topics given recall the tradition of the Notary Art. The association of the name Armadel with a type of magic in the mid-sixteenth century is significant and should not be ignored.

One interesting feature of the *Grimoire of Armadel* is the visibly permeating level of Qabalistic influence in it, seen nowhere else in Solomonic grimoires to this extent (except *The Nine Celestial Keys*). The Qabalistic material is set within the context of Biblical scripture. The text is full of Qabalistic references, such as the 'Paths of Wisdom', and the 'diabolic Qliphoth'.

Amongst this material is an intriguing group of spirits whose names are derived from the first nine letters of the Hebrew alphabet – Alepta (Aleph), Betel (Beth), Gimela (Gimel), Dalété (Daleth), Hetael (He), Vau-el (Vau), Zainael (Zain), Hethatia (Cheth) and Tetathia (Teth). These spirits are all associated with significant biblical events, and we can speculate as to why it should be the first nine letters. The number being nine brings the Aiq Beker square used for sigil creation to mind as a tempting possible connection, considering the flavour of the grimoire, but this is purely speculation. For working with these spirits, it is worth remembering that in texts like the *Zohar* the Hebrew letters are described as all female. These spirits make the spirit list in this book very diverse. There are classical archangels, previously unknown angels, Olympic spirits, demons, alphabet spirits, and concept spirits. The concept spirits, or Spirits of the Paths of Wisdom, are the Spirits of Force and Counsel, Spirits of Joy, and the Angels of Love & Charity. With the Qabalistic influence we could suggest speculative association with the three pillars of the Tree of Life based on concepts attributed to them – Black Pillar (Force & Counsel), White Pillar (Love & Charity), Grey or Middle Pillar (Joy). The third group being the Angels of Love & Charity implies that the three groups are all of an angelic nature.

The text contains: 'The Magic of Armadel' – conjuration; license to depart; conjuration. 'The Theosophy of our Forefathers or their Sacred and Mystic Theology'[392] – as regardeth the planets, the Sanhedrin (Zadkiel); the circumcision of Jesus at Nazareth (Thavael); by the flowing of Jordan (Caphael); the son of Zacharias in the desert (Samael); in the fields of Babylon (Uriel); the spirit of Elisha (Michael); of the life of Elijah (Gabriel); the wisdom of Solomon (Raphael); the explorer and leader Joshua (Hetael); the vision of 'Man' (Vau-ael); the rod of Moses (Zainael); Moses in the interior of the desert (Hethatia); the cave of Ephron (Tetahatia); the going forth of Abraham from Ur of the Chaldees and from Haran (Alepta); the wisdom of our forefather Adam (Betel); the beholding of the Serpent (Gimela); the vision of formation – Adam (Dalété); the vision of Eden, or the terrestrial paradise (Phalet); concerning Phitone or the abuses of necromancy (Samael); concerning the communication of the Genii (Camael); concerning the transformation of the Genii (Haniel); concerning the nature of the Genii (Anael). 'The Sacro-Mystic Theology of our Fathers' – concerning the science of the regeneration of Adam and his children by Pelech (Ophiel); concerning the devils and how they may be bound and compelled to visible appearance (Asmodeus, Leviathan); concerning the devils and how they can become visible (Hemostophile); concerning the devils and how

---

[392] Each of these sections has a seal and angel or spirit associated with it (given in brackets) and type of magic.

they may be bound and become visible (Brufor); concerning the ways of knowing the devils and of banishing them (Launé); concerning the devils and their life (Betor); concerning the ways of knowing the good angels, and of consulting them (Zadkiel, Sachiel); concerning the life of Man (Phul, Gabriel); concerning the creation of the souls of men (Aratron); concerning the evangelic rebellion and expulsion (Lucifer, Belzebut, Astarot); concerning the life of the angels before the Fall (Zaphkiel and his spirits); concerning the creation of all the angels (Och and his spirits); concerning God, the Preserver, the Destroyer, and the Creator (Gabriel and his spirits); concerning God in his Trine personality (Michael and his spirits); concerning God the universally One (Cassiel); concerning the paths of wisdom (Spirit of Force and Counsel, Spirits of Joy, Angels of Love and Charity). 'The Rational Table or the Qabalistical Light, penetrating whatsoever things be most hidden among the celestials, the terrestrials, and the infernals'; the vision of anointing; the vision of dust; the preparation of the soul (I); the preparation of the soul (II); the characters of Michael.

Essential Reading

Mathers, S.L. MacGregor (trans) (1980) *The Grimoire of Armadel*. Newburyport: Red Wheel/Weiser. Despite its errors, it is the main English-language version of the text available. It is to be hoped an edition drawing on both manuscripts and with further research will become available at some point.

Grimoire of Armadel, Zadkiel Seal

Ars Phytonica

Date: 1750.
Language: German.
Influences: *PGM, Hygromanteia.*
Provenance: German edition of undated Latin text *Tractatus de Arte Phytonica.*
MSS: Leipzig Cod. Mag. 97.
Circle: Yes.
Tools: Headband, horn-handled knife, skull, vessel.
Spirit List: Angerion, Astaroth, Beelzebub, Cornigerion, Cortornifer, Forfornifer, Gaseon, Inanialchi, Lucifer, Namil.

The Text

This technique of using a skull as a spirit vessel, although rare in the grimoires, is also found in two manuscripts of the *Hygromanteia*, and has precedents in the *PGM*. There are many stories and examples from Antiquity (discussed in *Appendix XIII: Of Future Times*).

Some of the names of the four spirits written on the skull are unique, not being seen in any other grimoires. Examining earlier texts, it is worth noting that Cornigerion is very similar to Corniger, a terrestrial spirit king of the south in the *Sworn Book of Honorius* and *Summa Sacre Magice*, where Forfornifer also occurs. Another close name similarity of Cornigerion is Cornigerum an angel of Mars in *Of Angels, Demons & Spirits*.

The time constraints, purification, preparation, location, and tools are described. The circle construction (a simple line drawn with the knife) is then given along with a conjuration of the four spirits. The spirits are then questioned and licensed to depart. The items are then collected and the skull returned to its hiding place. An explanation which elaborates on the procedure follows, with the explanation that the spirits will speak as strong winds.

Essential Reading

Acher, Frater & Sabogal, José Gabriel Alegria (2020) *Clavis Goêtica: Keys to Chthonic Sorcery*. West Yorkshire: Hadean Press. Fascinating and highly recommended work expanding the developing field of goêtic practice with the manuscript of *Ars Phytonica* (in German and English) set in historical and practical context.

GRAND GRIMOIRE/RED DRAGON (LE GRAND GRIMOIRE/DRAGON ROUGE)

Date: 1750?
Language: French, Italian (*Il Vero Drago Rosso*, The True Red Dragon), German (*Der Wahrhaftige Feurige Drache*, The True Fiery Drache), Spanish.
Influences: *Key of Solomon, Pseudomonarchia Daemonum, Grimoire of Pope Honorius, Dictionnaire Infernal*.
Provenance: First published in French, possibly c. 1750, with numerous later editions following, including 1823, 1845.
MSS: N/A.
Circle: Yes.
Tools: Blasting rod, censer, knife, wand (hazel).
Spirit List: Aamon, Abigar, Agaliarept, Agares, Astarot, Ayperos, Bael, Barbatos, Bathim, Belzebut, Botis, Buer, Fleurety, Forau, Glasyabolas, Gusoyn, Loray, Lucifer, Lucifuge Rofocale, Marbas, Nebiros, Nuberus, Pruslas, Pursan, Sargatanas, Satanachia, Valefar.

THE TEXT

This work is another of the 'black magic' grimoires of the Bibliothèque Bleue imprint which proliferated through France and beyond. The list of eighteen ministering demons is clearly taken from *Pseudomonarchia Daemonum*, with some corruption of names. The one name of these not found in that text is Pruflas, who is, however, found in the *Dictionnaire Infernal*, published in 1818. Many of the charms in the second book are from the *Grimoire of Pope Honorius*.

The text begins with a chapter extolling the virtues of the book and hyping its contents. Chapter two deals with preparation for ritual including dietary patterns and a prayer, and the purchasing of a hematite[393] stone. It is also specified that the rite is performed by two people, a skryer or seer being the second person. A solitary place for the rite is specified, to which the practitioner takes a goat kid to sacrifice. The kid is offered to God as a sacrifice with a short declaration. It is then skinned and the rest of it burned. The ashes remaining from this are thrown at the rising sun with another declaration. The skin is kept to make the magic circle on. The wand is then cut, and the blade taken to a blacksmith to make two sharp iron caps for the tines of the wand. These are fitted after being magnetised with a lodestone, as a prayer is spoken. The following evening all the paraphernalia is then taken to the site and the magic circle constructed. The incense and ashes (from the sacrifice fire) are offered to God. Two orations and an offering of the incense with brandy are made. Three conjurations to Lucifer are made,[394] followed by the grand invocation, and then Lucifuge Rofocale appears. There is then a query and response session with him, with timings to appear agreed and him signing the spirit contract. Next follows a conjuration of Lucifer, who declares seven articles regarding conduct and is dismissed. A spirit then offers to lead the conjurer to treasure, and the conjurer, armed with the blasting rod and bloodstone, goes and collects the treasure. The conjurer then returns to the circle where the assistants are still waiting, gives Lucifer license to depart, and gives thanks to God.

The second book concerns the making of pacts with spirits and their use. The names and offices of the demons are then given as a spirit list of three rulers, six subordinates, and

---

[393] The text says bloodstone or ematille. As ematille is hematite, which through its iron content is associated with blood, this seems more likely than bloodstone (heliotrope), however bloodstone is used in other texts including the earlier *Secrets of Solomon*.
[394] Although these are named to Lucifer, it is Lucifuge Rofocale who appears.

eighteen spirits beneath them. The triangle of the pacts is shown, which is the same as the magic circle shown earlier, along with the signs and characters of the demons. The qualities of the six subordinate spirits are given, as these are the ones whom the conjurer chooses from to make a pact. A hazel wand is made as described before, and the process described for making the pact. The practitioner performs the great invocation, and then the spirit of Lucifuge Rofocale (or other summoned spirit) appears and there is a question and response session. The pact is signed and followed by another question and response session. The spirit leads the practitioner to treasure, which they gather and return to the circle and dismiss the spirit. A prayer to God and oration for protection from evil spirits follows.

The next section is entitled 'The Magic Secret, or the Art of Speaking with the Dead'. The practitioner attends midnight mass at Christmas, and at the moment the priest lifts the Host, bows down and says '*Resurgent mortuit et ac me veniut*'. On saying this they head to the cemetery and offer a prayer at the first tomb they see to the infernal powers. After a moment of silence the request is made for the dead spirit, a handful of earth is then taken and spread as the practitioner asks in a low voice for the dead spirit to awaken to come and answer questions. The practitioner then bends a knee to the ground, facing East, and at the first sign of sunrise makes a cross of St Andrew with the bones of the dead man (taken from the tomb) and throws them at the first church they see. The practitioner then takes five thousand nine-hundred steps in a western direction, and lays down straight as if to sleep on the ground, with the palms against the thighs. They then look to the Moon and call the dead spirit with the words '*Ego sum te peto, et videre queo*'. The dead spirit then appears and answers questions, and is licensed to depart. The practitioner then returns to the tomb and makes a cross on it with the knife held in the left hand.

The next section is called 'Secrets of the Magic Art'. It begins with a paragraph on how to make the Philosopher's Stone! Next is instruction on how to make a divining rod (hazel); then charms to enchant firearms; to win any time one plays the lottery; to speak with spirits on the Eve of St John; to be insensible to torture; to compel a person to dance completely naked; to make oneself invisible; to make oneself favourable to judges; to be impervious to firearms; to make the garter of twenty miles per hour; a plaster to travel ten miles per hour; the composition of the ink for making pacts; Solomon's Mirror; a table of auspicious and inauspicious days; the Secret of the Black Hen; and the great invocation to summon spirits taken from *Key of Solomon*.

A section entitled 'Other Magic Secrets' ends the book. This has a small grouping of charms, viz.: to prevent a woman from conceiving; to find out if a woman is fertile; to make three young women, or spirits, come to your room after dinner; to be lucky in every enterprise; to make a woman disclose her secrets; to see and do the supernatural; to make everything in an apartment appear black; glue to attach crystals; glue to repair porcelain vases; to create reciprocal love between a man and a woman; ring love charm; apple of love charm.

Essential Reading

Gretchen, Ruby (trans) (2004) *The Grand Grimoire*. Boston: Trident Books. Good edition of the text; however it is drawn from the later Italian text.

Lamda, Aaman (trans) & Overman, Arundell (ed) (2020) *The Complete Illustrated Grand Grimoire, or the Red Dragon*. Amazon: Aaman Lamda. Detailed interlinear translation presenting the original French and translation with contextual material.

Wentworth, Joshua (trans) (2011) *The Red Dragon*. York Beach: Teitan Press. More comprehensive edition drawing from two texts and with useful notes.

La Véritable Magie Noire (True Black Magic)

Date: 1790.
Language: French.
Influences: *Key of Solomon, Three Books of Occult Philosophy.*
Provenance: Published circa 1790, with another edition around 1830. The pseudo-epigraphical attribution of Iroé Grego (Toz Grecus) is derived from the *Key of Solomon*.
MSS: N/A.
Circle: Yes.
Tools: Arctave (craft or quill knife), black-handled knife, boline, dagger, hat, hazel wand, lancet, robe, shoes, sword, staff, white-handled knife.
Spirit List: Anaël, Asmodée, Aymemon, Cocamiel, Donquel, Egim, Genoria, Holmadiel, Lucifer, Macariel, Nogariel, Ocbelia, Paymon, Parosiel, Savania, Socadia, Theliel.

The Text

La Véritable Magie Noire is an interesting work in the *Bibliothèque Bleue* imprint, which contains a condensed version of the *Key of Solomon* with some unique features. According to Peterson its use of the term arctave (craft knife) is the source of the word athame used in Wicca.[395]

Like the *Key of Solomon*, the text begins with the preamble of Solomon addressing his son Roboam and giving the context of the book. It is divided into two books of twenty-two and six chapters. The six chapters in book two includes forty-five pentacles.

The chapters in book one are: the love of God (1); the hours and virtues of the planets (2); in which times the Arts must be accomplished and perfected, when they are prepared (3); of all the instruments necessary for the Art (4); the experiment of theft, and how one performs it (5); the experiment of invisibility (6); the experiment of love and how it is performed (7); the experiment of influence and favour (8); experiments of hatred and destruction (9); how to perform operations involving mockery and ridicule (10); the manner of preparing extraordinary experiments (11); how the exorcist should conduct himself (12); how you should make the asperser and exorcised water (13); incenses and suffumigations (14); the silk cloth (15); the quill pen of a male goose (16); the blood of a pigeon and other animals (17); the quill pen of a swallow (18); how the virgin parchment should be prepared (19); the caul of a new-born child (20); the characters written in the experiments (21); virgin wax or virgin earth (22).

The chapters in book two are: of the pentacles, and how they are prepared (1); what must be observed for the use of the pentacles (2), the circle which is used for the consecration of the pentacles, the most great and unique pentacle coloured green and red (*Sigillum Dei*), then the pentacles. This comprises: the first seven pentacles are those of Saturn, which must be black; the seven pentacles of Jupiter, made in celestial blue; the six pentacles of Mars, made in red; the seven pentacles of the Sun, made in gold; the five pentacles of Venus, made in green; the five pentacles of Mercury, made in red and green; and six pentacles of the Moon, made in gold even though it is not lunar. After that are: what the exorcist must do and say (3); important remark about the bath (4); exorcism of the water (5); the clothing of the exorcist (6); conclusion.

Essential Reading

Peterson, Joseph H. (ed, trans) (2017) *True Black Magic, La Véritable Magie Noire*. Kasson: Twilit Grotto Press. Complete edition of the French original text with English translation.

---

395 Peterson 2017:i.

A Most Rare Compendium of the Whole Magical Art

Date: c. 1795.
Language: German and Latin.
Influences: *Arbatel, Ars Notoria, Abramelin, Liber Octo Quaestionem, Three Books of Occult Philosophy, Pseudomonarchia Daemonum.*
Provenance: Austrian manuscript of unknown origin.
MSS: Wellcome MS 1766.
Circle: Yes.
Tools: Censer, glass, girdle, glove, mirror, sword, wand.
Spirit List: Alhuzy, Aloggiell, Alogiel, Alraundl, Amakbuel, Ariton, Asa, Asmodai, Astarot, Baimon,[396] Barachias, Belial, Belzebub, Bileth, Calephas, Cassiel, Cerberus, Chuz, Dagol, Drisop, Eihanim, Eliles, Eloson, Eloson, Envy, Gabriel, Gogalchon, Hemor, Iahacobah, Ifftan, Iglion, Iohonah, Ioloma, Kilik, Lapador, Leviaten, Lucifer, Machialel, Magoth, Maranal, Marbar, Medon, Merech, Michael, Nabhi, Nelion, Nudaton, Oriens, Paimon, Parufar, Polipis, Pruflas, Ramaison, Raphael, Rigaton, Samael, Saman, Sathan, Simehon Hacephi, Sumuran, Thamni, Tifereth,[397] Tiphoar, Tirama, Turiril, Uriel, Vesol, Wamidal, Witch of Endor, Zagal, Zagrion, Zugula.

The Text

A Most Rare Compendium is a unique manuscript, whose creator drew material from a number of sources, combining them with stunning colour images. As Tilton and Cox note,[398] much of the material was gathered in the Zetzner edition of Agrippa's *Opera* (1630). The *Abramelin* material could have been drawn from the Hammer edition (1725) or a manuscript, though the former seems likely based on the heavy use of published material. One noteworthy element of the text is the significant amount of material regarding the use of psychoactive plants in suffumigations, copied from *Aufschlüsse zur Magic (Disclosures on the Subject of Magic*, 1788-92) by the Catholic mystic Karl von Eckhartausen (1752-1803).

The work begins with warnings about spirits, and then gives characters for some of the major demon rulers, interestingly including Lilith (called Eliles and Liles in the text in different places). Then follows a page of characters of elemental spirits, and one of good spirits, and images of the symbols to be drawn on the inside and outside of the gloves worn by the magician, and of the magic circle. More striking images follow, including the attempted burning of Shadrach, Meshach, and Abednego. Several pages on narcotics and their use break up the images, followed by a striking image of Ashtaroth and other demons interspersed with other images.

The text continues with details of practice including prayer, suffumigation, and conjuration. Discussion of pacts, forms of divination, and the six types of demon and their characteristics leads into a general discussion of black magic. Then there is another conjuration and considerations for practice. The functions of the different orders of angels with details of a combined planetary incense for white magic are discussed.

A detailed instruction on how to construct a mirror for black magic is the subject of the next section. Another discussion continues on the types of magic and the benefits of magic.

---

396 This is clearly a copyist's error for Paimon as the list is from *Abramelin*.
397 The substitution of the sixth Sephira of the Tree of Life, Tifereth, for James the Lesser is an odd one.
398 Tilton & Cox, 2017:11.

Another section of images of demons and scenes occurs, with notes on topics like the creation of the *shedim* (evil spirits) through the masturbation of Adam.

The main written text begins with explanation of how to break a pact, and a concise description of the steps of a magical operation and useful instruction on things to avoid in spirit contact. The text returns to the differences in types of magic and the pitfalls for those practicing magic, ending with a warning not to practise without experience and knowledge.

Essential Reading

Tilton, Hereward & Cox, Merlin (eds & trans) (2017) *Touch Me Not. A Most Rare Compendium of the Whole Magical Art*. Somerset: Fulgur. Beautifully produced edition containing the full manuscript in glorious colour, with the original text and translation, and useful footnotes and endnotes as well as a valuable introduction.

A Collection of Magical Secrets & A Treatise of Mixed Cabalah

Date: 1796.
Language: French.
Influences: *Enchiridion of Pope Leo*, *Key of Solomon*.
Provenance: Collection of charms and conjurations of largely unknown provenance.
MSS: Wellcome MS 4669.
Circle: Yes.
Tools: Crystal, materia magica for charms, mirror, pentacles, white-handled knife.
Spirit List: Abor, Abraca, Abracola, Acansarny, Adeel, Adus, Alabxatas, Aller, Anael, Artos, Aspides, Assa, Astaroth, Athanora, Aysenel, Bileth, Caba, Camael, Canbtat, Carmelion, Cassiel, Castal, Castaon, Cobia, Diel, Ebrion, Estel, Faral, Fulcinifer, Gabriel, Gabrion, Gabzav, Gadym, Gulas, Haniel, Huriel, Janifeth, Kaberion, Lastul, Laufer, Laufial, Letistel, Lipos, Lucibel, Melchior, Meso, Metatron, Mezarim, Michael, Orish, Pelvm, Quul, Raphael, Raziel, Sachiel, Salatiel, Salixos, Samael, Sathara, Severion, Sibady, Sisoy, Ssanday, Stimel, Thobiel, Tronax, Tuel, Uriel, Veycis, Zadkiel, Zaphkiel.

The Text

This text is bound together with two *Key of Solomon* manuscripts, from the Abraham Colorno and Universal treatise text families. The style of much of the material is similar to that found in other books of secrets and mixed cabalah. There are some experiments, however, which stand out, and due to their unique nature this text is included in this work. They include angelic dream incubation and distant healing. There are a lot of charms for locating stolen or lost items, and a lot of operations to gain a familiar spirit.

The reference in the subtitle to the secrets being taken from Peter of Abano and Cornelius Agrippa is spurious, as the material bears no relation to their work. As was often the case, this is clearly done to give a fake pedigree to the material. There are a number of rings described in the text, and reference to making them during particular Mansions of the Moon is noteworthy, as is the wondrous ring of Lucibel.

A Collection of Magical Secrets begins with magical operations for difficult objects. These are: in order to discover a wish; in order to make a thief give back the stolen item; in order to find stolen objects; another for finding stolen objects; another for stolen things; to find a stolen item and to know all hidden things; a charm for love; another charm for love; to obtain anything you wish from a person; another for the same effect.

The next part is called 'Secrets taken from Agrippa'.[399] The charms are: to make yourself loved; to make a child drink their mother's milk; to dispel stormy weather; to cure toothache, headache, or jaw ache; for a continual fever; for a cramp; for toothache; water for wounds and to remove splinters; to make yourself loved; to stop a nosebleed; to remove splinters without using any iron; to give back colour to someone who is as jaundiced as saffron; for headaches; to extract teeth without using any iron; to whiten your teeth; to give someone a better memory; for toothache; against weapons; perfect quenching for weapons; to gild without gold; for malaria and other fevers; to give vigour to the stomach; to prevent hair from turning white; to castrate animals without using any iron; to prevent a woman becoming pregnant when you have intercourse with her; another for the same effect; to make yourself loved by a woman; for the same; for the same with powder; to make love to a woman for a long time without ejaculating; to be appealing for love; to get any information you wish from a spirit; properties

---

399 They are not.

of the herb called honesty; to have a familiar spirit called Ebrion at your disposal; to make any spirit familiar; to receive a reply from the spirit of Jupiter in a dream; to gain knowledge of everything through the medium of an egg; to have a familiar spirit; another to have a familiar spirit; for love; to have a familiar spirit; to receive a reply during sleep; to stop nose-bleeds, women's wounds, and haemorrhages; to get any information you wish from a familiar spirit; to stem the flow of blood; to brush flies away; another for the same objective; against rain; against fleas, lice, and bedbugs; to make a woman give immediate birth; for love; another; to win at games; for games; for love; another; to be invisible; to see a spirit on your hand; for love; to heal a sick man from the evils mentioned in the following circle; to be transported to any place that you wish to go in a boat or vessel; to receive a reply from a spirit (Huriel); second method to have a reply from the spirit Huriel; observations on the two preceding procedures; to hold the spirit Mezarim in a ring, who rules over sciences; another to have a familiar spirit; Dr. Etienne's procedure for speaking with a spirit; to receive a reply from a spirit in a mirror; to make the wonderful ring of Lucibel; to be invisible; amulet useful against different kinds of difficulties; experiment to know what the time is; to win at games; for games of chance; to receive goodwill and favours from someone; for the same; to receive affection from kings and other great people; for love; for the same; to be loved either by a woman or by everyone else; to make a good angel appear, who will reply to any questions asked on him.

The *Treatise of Mixed Cabalah* is divided into four parts, all entitled 'Concerning Miscellaneous Cabalah'. Part one begins with a discussion of the ten sephiroth and the relationship of the human and divine; the order of the days during which you should work; names of the angels appointed to the days mentioned above; and Psalms and prayers. Part two deals with the seals or pentacles to be made and worn. The sections are: concerning the materials suitable for these rituals; concerning the method for making the pentacle or heptacle; properties of the verses and scripture verses for illnesses and infirmities. Part three is a technique for dream incubation with archangels (includes seals and prayers for each day), Part four is a divination technique called the 'Book of Fate', with one hundred and twelve answers, and the answer is determined by random number choice.

Essential Reading

Rankine, David & Skinner, Stephen (2009) *A Collection of Magical Secrets & A Treatise of Mixed Cabalah*. London: Avalonia. English translation of the text with contextual material and discussion of sources.

Clavis Inferni sive Magia Alba et Nigra Approbata Metatrona (The Key of Hell with White and Black Magic approved by Metatron)

Date: 1797.
Language: Latin, Greek, and Hebrew with numerous magical alphabets.
Influences: *Hepatmeron, Goetia, Arbatel*, the images of Albrecht Durer (1471-1528).
Provenance: Unknown author, possibly owned by Robert Curzon (1810-1873).
MSS: Wellcome 2000.
Circle: Yes.
Tools: Golden seal.
Spirit List: Aratron, Bethor, Egyn, Gabriel, Hagith, Haniel, Kamael, Maymon, Metatron, Michael, Och, Ophiel, Paymon, Phaleg, Phul, Raphael, Sachiel, Tzadkiel, Uriel, Urieus.

The Text

Clavis inferni (sive magia alba et nigra approbata Metatrona), or *The Key of Hell with white and black magic approved by Metatron*, is a unique manuscript. The images are coloured and striking, and the text is a mixture of Greek, Hebrew, and Latin (reversed and also contracted in places), with symbols from a lot of magical alphabets thrown in. It is a very short work, comprising twenty-one pages.

The reference to Saint Cyprian in the title might suggest this grimoire being part of the Cyprianic tradition of grimoires, but the content is far more Solomonic in nature; however, exploration of the symbolism found throughout does hint at connections to the sorcerous saint and his symbols.

The text is a concise conjuration process of prayer, summoning, binding, and banishment. The golden seal appears to be a lamen to be worn during the conjuration. The striking colour images of the four demon kings with their animals and sigils is unique amongst grimoires, and adds to the exotic flavour of this grimoire. Significantly, the appropriate divine names and archangels for working with each of the demon kings are also given.

Essential Reading

Stephen Skinner & David Rankine (2009) *The Grimoire of St. Cyprian – Clavis Inferni*. Golden Hoard Press. The complete manuscript with the cipher text deciphered and translated, set in the context of the Cyprianic tradition.

THE MAGUS (OR CELESTIAL INTELLIGENCER)

Date: 1801.
Language: English.
Influences: Draws heavily on the works of Agrippa (*Three Books of Occult Philosophy*), Paracelsus, Trithemius, *Heptameron*, *Key of Solomon*.
Provenance: Published by Francis Barrett in 1801.
MSS: Wellcome MS 1072, Barrett's copy of The Magus, bound with *Directions for the Invocation of Spirits*, by a student of Francis Barrett (1802).
Circle: Yes.
Tools: Bible, lamen, lamp, pen pentacle of Solomon, ring, robe, sceptre, sword.
Spirit List:[400] Aba, Abdizuel, Abel, Abiladoth, Abrinael, Abuhaza, Abuiori, Abumalith, Acteus, Adnachiel, Adriel, Aehaiah, Agiel, Aiel, Aladiah, Amabael, Amabiel, Amatiel, Amaymon, Ambriel, Amnediel, Amnixiel, Amutiel, Anael, Andas, Aniel, Anixiel, Annauel, Antichrist, Apollyon, Aquiel, Arcan, Ardesiel, Ariel, Arragon, Asaliah, Asasiel, Asmodel, Asmodeus, Assaibi, Astagna, Atheniel, Atliel, Azael, Azariel, Azazel, Azeruel, Aziel, Babiel, Bachanae, Baciel, Balay, Balidet, Baliel, Baraborat, Barbiel, Barchiel, Barzabel, Beelzebub, Behemoth, Belial, Bethnael, Bilet, Blaef, Burchat, Cahethel, Caliel, Calvel, Calzas, Camael, Capabili, Caracasa, Carmax, Cassiel, Cbedusitaniel, Cetarari, Charsiel, Chavakiah, Chermiel, Cherub, Commissoros, Coniel, Corat, Core, Corobael, Curaniel, Cynabal, Dabriel, Damabiah, Damael, Daniel, Dardiel, Darquiel, Deamiel, Dirachiel, Doremiel, Egibiel, Egin, Eiael, Elemiah, Enediel, Ergediel, Famiel, Fraciel, Friagne, Gabiel, Gabriel, Galdel, Gargatel, Gaviel, Geliel, Geniel, Graphiel, Guabarel, Guel, Gutrix, Haaiah, Haamiah, Habiel, Habuiah, Hagiel, Hahahel, Hahaiah, Hahaziah, Hahuiah, Haiaiel, Hakamiah, Haludiel, Hamaliel, Hanael, Haniel, Hanun, Harahel, Hariel, Hasiel, Hasmodai, Hismael, Humastraw, Huphaltiel, Huratapel, Hyniel, Iahhael, Iehuiah, Ieiaiel, Ieiazel, Ieilael, Ielahiah, Ieliel, Ierathel, Ihiazel, Iibamiah, Imamiah, Irel, Isiael, Ismoli, Janak, Janiel, Jarihael, Jazel, Jazeriel, Jeruscue, Johphiel, Kadie, Kedemel, Kyriel, Lama, Lauiah, Lecabel, Lehahiah, Lelahel, Leuuiah, Leviah, Leviathan, Lobguin, Lucifer, Lycus, Machasiel, Machatan, Madiel, Mael, Maguth, Mahasiah, Mahazael, Malcha Betharsisim Hed Beruah Schehalim, Malchidial, Maltiel, Mammon, Manadel, Masgabriel, Mathiel, Mathlai, Matuyel, Maymon, Mebahel, Mebahiah, Mediat, Megalesius, Mehekiel, Meil, Melahel, Meniel, Merattron, Meririm, Metatron, Michael, Mihael, Milliel, Mimon, Missabu, Mizrael, Muriel, Nachiel, Nanael, Naromiel, Neciel, Nelapa, Nelchael, Nemamiah, Nicon, Nithael, Nithhaiah, Numiah, Omael, Ophaniel, Ophis, Oriphael, Ormenus, Osael, Pabel, Pahaliah, Passran, Paymon, Penael, Peniel, Poiel, Porosa, Pytho, Rachiel, Rael, Ranie, Raphael, Rayel, Rehael, Reiiel, Requiel, Rhaumel, Roehel, Sachiel, Sacriel, Sallales, Samael, Samax, Santanael, Saphiel, Sarabotes, Satael, Satan, Schedbarschemoth Schartathan, Scheliel, Sealiah, Seehiah, Seraph, Seraphiel, Setchiel, Sitael, Sorath, Suceratos, Suneas, Suquinos, Suth, Tagriel, Tamuel, Taphartharath, Tariel, Tarmiel, Tarquam, Tenaciel, Tharsis, Theutus, Thiel, Tiriel, Turiel, Tus, Ucirmiel, Umabel, Urieus, Ustael, Uvael, Valnum, Varcan, Vasariah, Vehuel, Vehuiah, Velel, Venahel, Verchiel, Vetuel, Vevaliah, Vianuel, Vionatraba, Zachariel, Zadkiel, Zaliel, Zaniel, Zaphiel, Zazel, Zuriel.

---

400 Note these spirits are all named in the text, though they are not mentioned in conjurations. The list is to demonstrate which spirits are still being referenced.

The Text

The Magus, subtitled *A Complete System of Occult Philosophy*, is a major work of three volumes which drew heavily on the works of previous magicians and presented it in an accessible format. It was extremely popular with British cunning folk in the nineteenth century as a repository of magical information and techniques. It also made the material contained within more easily available to the public for the first time. Book one focuses on natural magic, including talismans and conjuration. Book two focuses on Qabalah and ceremonial magic, and book three is a magical biography. It is interesting to note that *The Magus* is one of the texts which specifically mentions taking the Bible into the magic circle.

The introduction looks at the virtues of the stars and discusses natural magic. Book one begins with ten chapters, which deal with natural magic, the fall of man and the virtue of the soul; natural magic through sympathy with animals, plants, metals, and stones, and the serpent; amulets, charms, and enchantments; unctions, philtres, and potions; of magical suspensions and allegations; of antipathies; what has virtue when living and what retains it when dead; the wonderful virtues of some precious stones; of the mixtures of natural things and producing monstrous animals; and on the art of fascination, binding, sorceries, lights, candles, and lamps. A section on alchemy follows, which begins with an epistle to Museus and note to the reader.

Part two of book one has forty-six chapters: of the four elements and their natural qualities; of the properties and wonderful nature of fire and earth; of the water and air; of compound or mixed bodies, how the elements relate to the soul, senses, and disposition of man; that the elements are in the heavens, the stars, devils, angels, intelligences, and God; that the wisdom of God works through second causes; of the spirit of the world; of the seals and characters impressed by celestials upon natural things; the virtue of perfumes and suffumigations and to what planets they are attributed; of the composition of perfumes of the seven planets; of the composition and magic virtue of rings; that the passions of the mind are assisted by celestials and that constancy of mind is necessary; how man's mind may be joined with intelligences and celestials; showing the necessity of mathematical knowledge and the power of numbers in talismans; the great virtues of numbers; of the scale of unity; of the number two, and scale; of the number three, and scale; of the number four, and scale; of the number five, and its scale; of the number six, and the scale; of the number seven, and the scale; of the number eight, and the scale; of the number nine, and the scale; of the number ten, and the scale; of the numbers eleven and twelve, with the Cabalistical scale; of the notes of the Hebrews and Chaldeans, and other notes of magicians (Hebrew alphabet); the magic tables of the planets (kameas), their form and virtue and what intelligences and spirits are set over them; of the observations of the celestials necessary in magical work; when the planets are of most powerful influence; observations on the fixed stars; of the Sun and Moon and their magical considerations; of the twenty-eight Mansions of the moon and their virtues; how images, seals, etc. may gain virtue from celestial bodies; of the images of the zodiac and what virtues they, being engraved, bring from the stars (includes diagram of geomantic characters); of the images of Saturn; of the images of Jupiter; of the images of Mars; of the images of the Sun; of the images of Venus; of the images of Mercury; of the images of the Moon; of the images of the head and tail of the dragon of the Moon;[401] of the images of the Mansions of the Moon; how man's mind can influence the external and become like sublime spirits; conclusion on talismanic magic and its practice.

---

401 I.e., Caput Draconis and Cauda Draconis, the North and South Nodes of the Moon, respectively.

Book two, part one has twenty chapters, and notes that it draws heavily on the work of Trithemius. The chapters are on magnetism; of sympathetic medicine; the power of sympathy; of the armary unguent; on the power of natural spirits, of astral spirits upon which necromancy is based; of witchcraft; of the vital spirit; of the magical power; of the exciting or stirring up the magical virtue; of the magical virtue of the soul. Part two is on Cabala and ceremonial magic. The chapters are: on the Cabala; preparation necessary to become a true magician; that the knowledge of God is necessary; of divine emanations and the ten sephiroth; of the power and virtue of the divine names; of intelligences and spirits and infernals and subterranean spirits; of the order of evil spirits; of the annoyance of infernal spirits and preservation from good spirits; that there is a threefold keeper of man; of the tongue of angels; of the names of spirits, and those set over the stars, signs, corners of the earth, and the elements; of the seventy-two angels; of finding the names of spirits and genii from the disposition of the celestial bodies; of the calculating art of such names by the Cabalists; of the characters and seals of spirits; another way of making characters (list of magical alphabets); another kind of characters only received by revelation; of the bonds of spirits, and their adjurations and casting out; by what means the souls of the dead are called forth; of prophetic dreams.

Book two, part two does not have chapter numbers and starts with an introduction entitled 'The perfection and key of the Cabala or ceremonial magic'. The sections are on the magic pentacles and their composition; of the consecration of all magical instruments and materials; the consecration of water; consecration of fire; consecration of oil; of the benediction of lights, lamps, wax, etc.; the consecration of places, ground, and circle; of the invocation of evil spirits, and the binding of and constraining them to appear; an invocation of the good spirits; the particular form of the lamen; of oracles by dreams; of the method of raising evil or familiar spirits by a circle, likewise the souls and shadows of the dead. Part two ends and is followed by a section on the composition of the magic circle, which draws heavily on the *Heptameron*. This includes benediction of the perfumes; exorcism of fire; of the habit (robe) of the exorcist; of the pentacle of Solomon; an oration when the vestment is put on; the manner of working; a general exorcism of the spirits of air; a prayer to God to be said in the four directions in the circle; the oration; of the appearance of the spirits; the considerations and conjurations for every day of the week.

A section entitled 'The Magic and Philosophy of Trithemius of Sponheim' follows. It begins with a letter from Barrett to a friend who is one of his students. Next comes a caution to the inexperienced; of the making of the crystal and the form of preparation for a vision (these are the text of the *Art of Drawing Spirits into Crystals*); and a list of planetary hours and their angel rulers. This finishes book two, and book three is entitled 'Biographia Antiqua' and is biographies of various famous magicians of the past.

Essential Reading

Barrett, Francis (2000) *The Magus*. Boston: Weiser Books. Very good reproduction of the complete text of the original, includes colour plates of the demons as found in the original printing. There are many reproductions of this work easily available.

Grimorium Verum (True Grimoire)

Date: 1817.
Language: French, Italian.
Influences: *Key of Solomon, Secrets of Solomon, Grand Grimoire, Grimoire of Pope Honorius*.
Provenance: The major editions were published by Alibeck (1817) and Blocquel (c. 1830) in French, and Bestetti (1868) and Muzzi (1880) in Italian, both of those derived from Blocquel.
MSS: Lansdowne MS 1202 bound with a *Key of Solomon* and the *Book of Gold*.[402]
Circle: Yes.
Tools: Asperser, black-handled knife, bottle, burin, elder staff, hazel wand, ladle, lamen, lancet, mirror, Pentacle of Solomon, quill knife.
Spirit List: Ador, Adricanorum, Aglasis, Agliarept, Aliseon, Alphrois, Aluiel, Alymdrictels, Amaltea, Ameclo, Amisor, Anael, Anazarda, Anereton, Angrecton, Aroc, Arogani, Asophiel, Astaroth, Atalsloym, Atemis, Ayperos, Azigola, Baltazard, Baniel, Baros, Barsechas, Bechaud, Beelzebuth, Beldor, Benez, Betu, Brazo, Bretull, Brulefer, Bucon, Bulerator, Cadat, Cadomir, Caldurech, Calmiron, Calniso, Calvodium, Cameron, Cameso, Caron, Casmiel, Cerberus, Chameron, Charusihoa, Chenibranbo, Clauneck, Clistheret, Colehon, Crisolsay, Cumana, Cureviorbas, Dalmaley, Dalmay, Danochar, Delmusan, Donmeo, Dorsamot, Dragin, Dumaso, Dumosson, Elelogap, Elespontiaca, Elivisa, Epaneson, Eptalelon, Eritrean, Erly, Eslevor, Esmony, Estiot, Euchey, Fabelleronthon, Fito, Fleruty, Frangam, Frigia, Frimost, Frucissière, Frutimière, Fubentroty, Gabriel, Gaspard, Glassyabolas, Guland, Hael, Halmon, Haristum, Hayras, Heramael, Hicpacth, Hone, Horiel, Huictiigaras, Humots, Ibasil, Ilnostreon, Irly, Khil, Klepoth, Labilafs, Lamboured, Lameck, Lamideck, Ledrion, Lemon, Lhavala, Liamintho, Libussa, Lodir, Lucifer, Lucifuge Rofocale, Madilon, Madoin, Malcha, Mandousin, Maractatam, Mareso, Martiro, Melany, Melchidael, Melchior, Meon, Merfilde, Merloy, Merroe, Michael, Minosons, Mitraton, Morail, Musisin, Naberus, Naydrus, Nebiros, Nidar, Nisa, Noard, Noelma, Omot, Or, Oriet, Osumy, Ouyar, Pancia, Parandome, Paron, Peatham, Peloym, Pentagnony, Person, Peunt, Phorsy, Pleorim, Praredun, Premy, Proculo, Sagatana, Salmay, Sambetta, Saradon, Saroy, Satanakia, Satanicæ, Scirlin, Segal, Segrael, Sergulath, Sergutthy, Sesle, Sidragosum, Siranday, Sirchade, Sodirno, Solymo, Surgat, Sustugriel, Syrach, Tabrasol, Tarchimache, Tarihimal, Tely, Terly, Theu, Tiburtina, Timo, Tiriel, Trimasel, Uriel, Valuerituf, Velous, Venus, Vermias, Vesturiel, Viordy, Vulnavij, Zalay, Zazel.

The Text

The *Grimorium Verum* (True Grimoire) is an example of a published grimoire, with editions in French and Italian, and a later manuscript example bound with other works in French. As one of the later grimoires (1817), the style has been simplified to a more practical style, simplifying material in places drawn from earlier works like the *Key of Solomon*, and reproducing from others like the *Grimoire of Pope Honorius* and the *Grand Grimoire*.

It is clear that the *Grimorium Verum* owes much of its contents to the Universal Treatise manuscript family, the third of the four families of *Key of Solomon* manuscripts.[403] Examination of two of the French manuscripts in this family, the late eighteenth-century Wellcome 4669, Book 1 (fol. 77-87) and the seventeenth-century Lansdowne 1202, Book 3 (fol. 105-114) makes

---

402 Rankine (2010), *The Book of Gold*.
403 See *The Veritable Key of Solomon*, Skinner & Rankine, 2008:24-25.

it clear how heavily the *Grimorium Verum* draws from them. There is also a significant portion of material drawn from the *Secrets of Solomon* contained in it.

The later Italian editions begin with a preamble, found in some *Key of Solomon* manuscripts, of King Solomon explaining to his son Roboam how the contents of this wondrous material were delivered to him.

The work proper begins by declaring the triumvirate of powers of Lucifer, Beelzebuth, and Astaroth. This is followed by details of the construction of the lamen to be carried, interestingly giving the differences for men and women, emphasizing that both practised the work. The image of the great wheel of the sphere of the Planets is next, which is a circle of seven rings divided into twenty-four segments, which provides the attribution of the planetary hours (more commonly found in tabular form).

The nature of pacts is discussed, along with the areas of rulership for the three powers. Lucifer is attributed Europe and Asia, Africa to Beelzebuth, and the Americas to Astaroth. The common forms these powers take and that they can assume other forms continues the discussion. Next is the spirit list, with the seals of the individual spirits, and the powers they can provide. Note that some of the seals are missing in different editions.

The practical elements of invocation, oration, and conjuration, the magic circle and the tools with their construction, continue the text, forming the corpus of essential instruction required to work this grimoire. Interestingly, this section includes an Oration of the Salamanders, published by the Count de Gabalis in 1670, and subsequently included by Eliphas Levi in *Transcendental Magic*. It is interesting to note there are several spirits named in this section which occur previously in *Pseudomonarchia Daemonum/Goetia* and *Theurgia-Goetia*.

Part 2 is described as 'Rare and Surprising Secrets of Magic' and consists of charms similar to those found in Mixed Kabbalah and Books of Secrets. Interestingly, there is emphasis here on the archangels Anael (the Mirror of Solomon) and Uriel (divination by the word of Uriel) in the initial charms. The third charm is divination by means of an egg. From the fourth charm on, most of the charms have been copied from the *Grimoire of Pope Honorius*. Included in the Italian editions as Part 3 are the conjurations for the spirits from Thursday to Sunday.

Part 4 is a short piece entitled the 'Great Kabbalah of the Green Butterfly', which details how to catch the green butterflies and perform a conjuration from the *Red Dragon* to Astaroth. A list of fourteen powers Astaroth can offer concludes. The Italian editions have a Part 5 with more charms.

The *Grimorium Verum* has become very popular in the last few years, and this is largely due to the work of Jake Stratton-Kent, who has written voluminously and lucidly on his work with this grimoire, making it highly accessible.

Essential Reading

Peterson, Joseph H. (2007) *Grimorium Verum*. Scott's Valley: Createspace. Collection of translations gathering the French and Italian material together in one place in English. As always, Peterson's work is the definitive reference source for the material.

Stratton-Kent, Jake (2010) *The True Grimoire*. Scarlet Imprint. Detailed and fascinating practical study of the content and practice of the *Grimorium Verum*, setting it within the practices of the Goetic originating in ancient Greek practice.

Dictionnaire Infernal (Infernal Dictionary)

Date: 1818.
Language: French.
Influences: *Livre des Esperitz, Pseudomonarchia Daemonum, Grand Grimoire*, assorted mythologies including Breton, German, Greek, Indian, Russian, and Scandinavian, John Milton's *Paradise Lost*.
Provenance: Written by Collin Jacques de Plancy (1793-1881) and published in 1818. Numerous editions have been published since, with the most significant in 1863, including sixty-nine illustrations by Louis Le Breton.
MSS: N/A.
Circle: N/A.
Tools: N/A.
Spirit List: Abalam, Abigor, Abraxas, Adramalech, Aguares, Alastor, Alocer, Amduscias, Amon, Andras, Asmodee, Astaroth, Azazel, Bael, Balan, Barbatos, Bebal, Behemoth, Belphegor, Belzebuth, Berith, Bhairava, Buer, Caacrinolaas, Cali, Caym, Cerbere, Deimos, Eurynome, Flaga, Flavros, Forcas, Furfur, Ganga, Garuda, Gomory, Haborum, Ipes, Lamia, Lechies, Leonard, Lucifer, Malphas, Mammon, Marchosias, Melchom, Moloch, Nybbas, Orobas, Paimon, Picollus, Pruflas, Puck, Rahovart, Ribesal, Ronwe, Scox, Stolas, Tap, Tomgarsuk, Ukobach, Volac, Wall, Xaphan, Yan-gan-y-tan, Zaebos

The Text

The *Dictionnaire Infernal* is an A-Z of superstition and magical beliefs. It is not merely a list of demons, but also contains a huge collection of entries on different forms of divination, occult personalities, folklore, and much more. De Plancy revised the editions over a forty-five-year period as his beliefs changed due to becoming an ardent Roman Catholic. The 1863 edition, with its illustrations of all the demons, has been used as an image source ever since. The European reaction to the 'difference' of Indian cosmology is seen in the demonization of Indian deities, clearly reflecting the cultural bias of the time.

Essential Reading

De Plancy, C. J. (1818-1863) *Dictionnaire Infernal*. This public domain work is easily available in both English and French online.

Black Pullet (La Poule Noire)

Date: 1820.
Language: French.
Influences: *Key of Solomon*.
Provenance: Claiming a 1740 date, the first edition was 1820, and this book was popularised as part of the Bibliothèque Bleue imprint. It was also reprinted as the *Black Screech-Owl*. In recent decades a number of English editions have been published.
MSS: N/A.
Circle: Yes.
Tools: Rings, Talismans, Wand.
Spirit List: Discord, Envy, Fortune, Glory, Nemesis, Odous, Venus.

The Text

The *Black Pullet* takes the form of a first-person narrative, combining the life experiences of the character with the details of the magic he was taught. The narrator describes himself as an officer in the French army on an expedition in Egypt. His unit was attacked by Arabs and all his companions killed, with him receiving several wounds. He crawled to a pyramid and saw an old Muslim man come out of the pyramid. He attracted his attention and was taken into the pyramid and healed by the old man. A father-son bond quickly developed between them and the old man revealed that he was the last bearer of the secrets of magic and taught them to him.

The old man taught him that he must focus on love, and love of God, and renounce hate and negative virtues, which he did. He then began by explaining about the four types of elementals. His teaching commenced with an oration of the sages, to be addressed to God. The old man then described a creation myth and took the narrator on a spirit journey, witnessing and encountering powerful beings like Discord, Glory, and Fortune. He then guided the narrator through an initiation.

The narrator was shown a series of rings and talismans, worn over the heart when the ring is worn, which achieve different purposes and their use is described (including the voces magicae to be spoken). The first of these conjures the celestial and infernal powers. The second set grants the love of anyone of beauty. The third set grants the bearer all the treasures that exist. The fourth set enables the bearer to know all secrets from anywhere. The fifth set causes a person to divulge their most hidden thoughts. The sixth set activates as many spirits as needed to conduct an action or stop someone else's. The seventh set has the power to destroy anything, command the elements, and preserve friends from accidents. The eighth set makes the bearer invisible to all, even the spirits, and to see hidden things. The ninth set transports the bearer to any part of the world without danger. The tenth set opens any locks. The eleventh set enables the bearer to see in a building from outside, read the thoughts of people, and do them good or injury as desired. The twelfth set destroys any projects against the bearer and forces hostile spirits to submit. The thirteenth set gives the bearer all virtues and talents and the ability to render bad quality things into good. The fourteenth set gives knowledge of the virtues and properties of all vegetables and minerals, and the universal medicine. The fifteenth set subdues any animals to the bearer's will and allows them to understand them, as well as to be able to kill any animal at a distance. The sixteenth set reveals the good or bad intentions of everyone met and leaves a mark on the face of the ill-intentioned. The seventeenth set gives all talents and a profound understanding and ability in all arts. The eighteenth set enables winning at lotteries and games of chance. The nineteenth set enables the bearer to direct the infernal powers against enemies. The twentieth set enables the bearer to know the plans of the infernal powers and thwart them if desired. The rings are described as being made of bronzed steel, and the talismans in different colours of satin embroidered with gold or silver.[404] The old man then gave the prayers that must be said before and after each conjuration. The next part of the narrative goes into details of the black hen, its powers, and how to make it. The old man informed the narrator that he would die soon, as he was two hundred and seventy years old and his time has come. After the death of the old man the narrator and his familiar spirit returned to France and he verified the power of the black hen again.

Essential Reading

Anon (1972) *The Black Pullet: Science of Magical Talisman*. New York: Samuel Weiser Inc. There have been numerous editions of this book published in recent years, which is ironic for such a fantastical and impractical work.

---

404 Note: twenty-two talisman satin colours are given; however, although there are twenty-two illustrations, the first two are of the wand and the magic circle, and there are twenty ring/talisman pairs described.

COMPLETE BOOK OF MAGIC SCIENCE

Date: c. 1834-50.
Language: English.
Influences: *Heptameron*, Agrippa *Three Books of Occult Philosophy*, *Arbatel*.
Provenance: Created by Frederick Hockley. The manuscript has a fake date of 1573 attributed to it on the cover.
MSS: Weiser MS.
Circle: Mentioned but not described.
Tools: Girdle, lamen, white robe.
Spirit List: Abuiori, Abumalith, Acimoy, Anael, Arragon, Asasiel, Assaibi, Astagna, Atel Aniel, Babiel, Bachanael, Balidet, Baraborat, Bilet, Burchat, Cabzars, Caimax, Capabili, Cassiel, Castiel, Chedusitaniel,[405] Coniel, Corabiel, Corat, Curaniel, Cynabat, Dagiel, Damael, Deamiel, Friagne, Furiel, Gabriel, Guael, Gutrix, Habiel, Habudiel, Hadie, Hanum, Hunaspel, Huphaltiel, Isiael, Ismoli, Janael, Janiel, Jaxel, Jerabel, Jerescue, Lama, Lobquin, Machatan, Mael, Maguth, Maltiel, Masgabriel, Mathlai, Maymon, Michael, Midael, Missabis, Mitraton, Miztiel, Orphaniel, Osael, Pabel, Pabiel, Paspon, Penael, Peniel, Poenar, Porno, Rael, Raphael, Sachiel, Salamla, Samael, Senaciel, Soncas, Suquinos, Suth, Tamiel, Tarmiel, Thiel, Uriel, Ustael, Venabel, Vianiel, Vionatraba, Vrael, Zadkiel, Zaniel, Zebul, Zubiel.

THE TEXT

A Complete Book of Magic Science is a practical conjuration manual compiled by Frederick Hockley from several sources. It is a concise condensation of a lot of material into a workable form, which assumes a level of foreknowledge (and presumably equipment). It was later reproduced with minor amendments as the *Secret Grimoire of Turiel*.

The text goes straight into practical considerations, with 'Observations and Method of Working in the Art'. This includes blessings of the circle and lights; benedictions of the lamen, pentacles, vestments, ground, and perfumes; consecration of the girdle; exorcism of the fire; oration on putting on the vestments, prayer for the commencement of the work; names and offices of the ruling, presiding, and ministering spirits; prayer; invocation; interrogation; form of a bond of the spirits; license to depart; invocations of the spirits of the seven planets with the seals of the spirits; planetary incense recipes; and pentacles of the planets.

ESSENTIAL READING

Bergman, Dietrich (ed) (2008) *A Complete Book of Magic Science*. York Beach: Teitan Press. Good edition which compares and contrasts the material with the *Secret Grimoire of Turiel*, and also explores the influence of Hockley's material on the Hermetic Order of the Golden Dawn.

Peterson, Joseph H. (ed) (2010) *The Clavis or Key to the Magic of Solomon*. Lake Worth: Ibis. Excellent edition of the Ebenezer Sibley text copied by Frederick Hockley, which contains a wealth of other material including *The Complete Book of Magic Science*. Presented with Peterson's usual combination of excellent scholarship and fascinating context.

---

405 This name is separated into Chedu and Sitaniel in the text, but in the original it is the one name.

Verus Jesuitarum Libellus (The True Petition of the Jesuits)

Date: 1846.
Language: Latin, English.
Influences: St Cyprian references and treasure emphasis suggests the influence of Cyprianic books.
Provenance: Unknown.
MSS: Published in *Das Kloster*, translated into English by Herbert Irwin (1875) and subsequently his copy owed by A.E. Waite, the same being in John G. White collection W 091.92 V618.
Circle: N/A.
Tools: N/A.
Spirit List: Abbadon, Abiul, Ahesin, Almaziel, Amguel, Anathamia, Anisel, Ariel, Astaroth, Barfael, Baufa, Beelzebub, Belial, Berith, Calizabin, Calizantin, Chamus, Chinicham, Dromdrom, Ezea, Ezebul, Lapasis, Laya, Lissa, Lomta, Lucifer, Luna, Maluzim, Masa, Mephistopheles, Merapis, Michael, Milea, Milpeza, Moubnel, Palasa, Peripalabim, Pimpam, Pluto, Poia, Satan, Usiel, Wunsolary, Zayariel.

The Text

Verus Jesuitarum Libellus, also known as *Libellus Magicus*, is a small work claiming a 1508 date. As is often the case, this is clearly not so, as can be seen from the content and style of the manuscript. The work bears the flavour of Books of Cyprian, with its emphasis on treasure, and also reference to Cyprian in the text. The earliest date which can be definitively given to it is 1846, when it was published in *Das Kloster*, though as this was a compilation of existing texts it seems safe to assume an earlier date for it.

The work begins with a sequence of seven conjurations followed by a discharge, which actually reads as another conjuration. Next is a short conjuration of Usiel,[406] the Angelic Citation of St Cyprian, a conjuration of spirits guarding hidden treasure, a list of divine names to say when the spirit appears visibly, and two conjurations to compel obedience. The text then moves into a spirit list of the principal spirits of hell and their offices, followed by a conjuration of infernal spirits, and the Dismissal of Cyprian.

Essential Reading

Stephen J. Zietz's online transcription of the work is recommended.

---

406 It has been suggested this is a miscopying of Uriel.

THE SIXTH AND SEVENTH BOOKS OF MOSES

Date: 1849 first published, may be centuries older with pamphlets dating to at least 1734.
Language: German, English.
Influences: *Hebrew Bible, Babylonian Talmud, Heptameron, Sepher Raziel, Arbatel, Three Books of Occult Philosophy, Verus Jesuitarum Libellus*.
Provenance: Scheible collected all the variants he could locate and published them in 1849 in German. First English edition published in 1880 in New York.
MSS: Various pamphlets, mostly gathered by Scheible.
Circle: Yes.
Tools: Chalk, ram horn, seals.
Spirit List: Achusaton, Adoij, Adola, Adoyahel, Adramelech, Aeburatiel, Ageh, Agrippa, Aha, Ahae, Ahaij, Ahel, Ahenatos, Aimeh, Alymon, Amarzyom, Anoch, Anyam, Arael, Aromicha, Ascher, Asijma, Astarte, Asteroth, Auet, Awal, Awijel, Azijelzm, Azoth, Banch, Barechel, Bealherith, Betodah, Bymuan, Chabalym, Chahanya, Chamyel, Chanije, Channanijah, Chaylon, Chayo, Chuscha, Cijbor, Donahan, Driffon, Echad, Eead, Ehym, Elijon, Elohaym, Eloheij, Emol, Esor, Fatenovenia,Gabriel, Habu, Hadlam, Hael, Hahowel, Hamaya, Haseha, Hayozer, Hemohon, Holyl, Hoschiah, Ijud, Ileh, Iseij, Jael, Jaho, Jeha, Jehuel, Jka, Jomar, Karohel, Kawa, Kijgij, Kijlij, Kijmah, Kyptip, Lahehor, Lemar, Leviathan, Leykof, Lima, Luija, Luil, Maakyel, Magaripp, Mazbaz, Meho, Melech, Michael, Mijl, Moloch, Mupiel, Nisroch, Niva, Och, Ofel, Ohel, Oseny, Parymel, Patecha, Patteny, Phuel, Ragat, Raphael, Rawa, Reta, Roah, Ruweno, Safyn, Sahon, Salatheel, Samohayl, Sarwiel, Sazlij, Schaddaij, Schaddyl, Schadym, Schamayl, Schawayt, Scheol, Schijwin, Schimuel, Schumntel, Sedul, Semanglaf, Sephiroth,[407] Sewachar, Sezah, Sinna, Symnay, Sywaro, Taftyah, Taftyarohel, Taihn, Tehom, Tehor, Thamy, Theoska, Thoaijl, Tijlaij, Tuwahel, Tywael, Uhal, Umijchob, Uriel, Urikon, Uwula, Veal, Veduij, Waed, Wezynna, Wijch, Yagar, Yagelor, Yahel, Yalyon, Yamb, Yamdus, Yaron, Yeehah, Yeschaijah, Yeschnath, Yhahel, Yhaij, Yheloruvesopijhael, Yles, Yloij, Ymah, Ymij, Ymmat, Ymoeloh, Yomelo, Yvaij, Zacharael, Zarall, Zarenar, Zawar, Zeno, Zeolam, Zowanos, Zwyolech.

THE TEXT

The *Sixth and Seventh Books of Moses* are so named to describe their alleged provenance as the material given to Moses by God which enabled him to defeat the Egyptian Pharaoh's priest-magicians. The title implies their sacred nature as following from the Pentateuch (Five Books of Moses) which form the first five books of the Torah.

Johann Scheible, a Stuttgart book dealer and antiquarian, collected together dozens of grimoires which he published in the twelve-volume set *Das Kloster* from 1845-49. Amongst these many works he gathered together all the variants he could find of pamphlets that had been circulating for decades to compile his edition of the *Sixth and Seventh Books of Moses*. Translated into English and published in New York in 1880, the book would become one of the most significant texts influencing the traditions of Pennsylvania Dutch, Hoodoo, and rootwork in America (and beyond).

The text begins with a piece entitled 'The magic of the Israelites' which was added by Scheible for the second edition, written by Jospeh Ennemoser.[408] This essay discusses the uses

---

407 Considering the meaning of Sephiroth in Kabbalah, this seems likely to have been a copyists' error.
408 Taken from his book *Geschichte der Magic* (1844). Leipzig.

and occurrences of magic throughout the Bible (Old and New Testament), and sets a pious tone for the practical material that follows.

The *Sixth Book* begins by declaring the efficacy of the work to summon and deal with angels and spirits. The introduction records the message from God regarding the following seals and tables, which is full of divine names to demonstrate the virtue and power contained thereof. The seven seals and their conjurations continue the text, with reference to their special powers, These are (in order): to gain treasure from the ground, to have great fortune and blessing, to be beloved and defeat your enemies, to avoid misery and have fortune and a long life, to heal sickness, for dreams and visions, and to reveal the contents of a mine.

The *Seventh Book* contains twelve tables with short conjurations, which also give powers to their bearer. The first seal is of the Spirits of Air, and relieves the bearer from necessity. The second is of the Spirits of Fire, with no specified benefit. Third is the Spirits of Water and supplies the treasures of the deep. Fourth is the Treasures of Earth and gives the treasures of the earth. Fifth is the Spirits of Saturn, bringing good luck. Sixth is the Spirits of Jupiter for assistance with lawsuits and disputes. Seventh is the Spirits of Mars, bringing good fortune in quarrels. Eighth is the Spirits of the Sun, to attain honour and wealth, and give gold and treasure. Ninth is the Spirits of Venus, to make the bearer beloved and know secrets through dreams, and to help with businesses. Tenth is the Spirits of Mercury, giving wealth in chemistry and treasures from mines. Eleventh is the Spirits of the Moon, giving luck and fortune, and treasures of the sea. The twelfth seal is the Seal of Shemhamphorash and compels spirits to appear immediately and serve when placed on the other Tables.

The 'General Citation' follows, detailing the procedure for using the Seals and Tables, including prayers, and the form of the magic circle. A list of 'Ministering Familiars or Mysteries' follows, which includes some notable demons, which must be cited by the twelfth Table during solar or lunar eclipses. The book ends with the 'Generation Seal', to be held in the right hand, but not read, during the citation.

Another text following here is *The Magical Kabbalah of the Sixth and Seventh Books of Moses*. This contains a further set of seals attributed to Moses and Aaron, Eleazer and others, with names like Breastplate and Helmet. A whole range of abilities are associated with these. There are further sequences of Hebrew names attributed to the magical acts of Moses, and prayers and actions (especially horn blowing) to be performed in their use. Other excerpts from pamphlets include spirit lists and conjurations.

Essential Reading

Peterson, Joseph H. (ed, trans) (2008) *The Sixth and Seventh Books of Moses.* Fort Worth: Ibis Press. Peterson gathers together all the relevant material in excellent scholarly fashion and includes a translation of *Sepher Shimmush Tehillim* as well.

BLACK DRAGON (LE VÉRITABLE DRAGON NOIR)

Date: 1887.
Language: French.
Influences: *Heptameron, Grimoire of Pope Honorius, Grimorium Verum.*
Provenance: Published in French in 1887.
MSS: N/A.
Circle: Yes.
Tools: Chalk, charcoal, knife, lamp, stang, table.
Spirit List: Acham, Amaymon, Astaroth, Balthazard, Bayemon, Bechard, Cassiel, Egym, Ferly, Frimost, Gaspard, Guland, Irly, Lucifer, Magoa, Melchior, Silcharde, Surgat, Terly.

THE TEXT

The *Dragon Noir* (*Black Dragon*) is highly derivative of the *Grimoire of Pope Honorius*. Of the five parts of the *Dragon Noir*, the 'Evocations', some of the 'Spells and Counter-Spells', the 'Marvellous Secrets', and the 'Hand of Glory', all are entirely derived from the *Grimoire of Pope Honorius*. 'The Black Hen' is previously found in the *Grimorium Verum*, making the *Dragon Noir* seem of little unique value in the later content. However, the instructions in the preface are extremely lucid and well worth study. A number of the charms make use of the cemetery, which is worth mentioning.

The text begins with a conjuration of the book, accompanied by a cautionary note on the use of magic for personal gain. The preface discusses the practicalities of work, and begins discussing the chalk or charcoal used, and how to make the right charcoal to use. Then it discusses the importance of bathing, and how the magic circle should be twelve feet across and have no breaks in it. The knife and stang are next, with detailed instructions on the use of the stang. It is noted that only the conjurer should ever speak, and that the demon should not be allowed to depart without a pledge being agreed. The text emphasises this must not be any body fluid or item which has been close to the body, and must be agreeable to both. The importance of caution in pacts and ensuring the license to depart and prayers are spoken before leaving the circle are also stressed. More good advice is given on practice, with comments on the contents of the other sections and a caution again against avarice.

Part one of the book is entitled 'Evocations'. It begins with conjuration and the banishment, along with the pentacle from the *Heptameron*. The conjurations of the four kings of the directions follow, along with one for hidden treasure, conjurations of the demons for the days of the week with their seals and times to perform the conjuration. Next is the great exorcism.

Part two of the book is 'Spells and Counter-Spells'. This begins with a spell to lift a spell and summon the harm-causer; to destroy evil spells cast against animals; the sympathetic mirror to reflect spells and reveal the caster; periwinkle talisman to heal, break spells, or be used as a talisman; to take care returning from the home of a person you wish to heal; to lift a spell or rid a house of demons; to destroy a spell with a black cock; to divert a person; to ward off a bad encounter; to make a person suffer; and to immobilise and make a person suffer.

Part three of the book is 'Marvellous Secrets', and is drawn almost entirely from the *Grimoire of Pope Honorius*. They begin with the castle of beauty protection for horse and sheep; against colic, wounds, and infections of horses; in order that lambs become healthy and strong; to cure a cancer or other illness accessible to the eyes and fingers; against burns; to recover stolen objects; to see in a vision at night (i.e., dream) what you desire to know; to stop a serpent; to stop a horse and carriages; counter-spell; to appear to be accompanied by many; to render oneself invisible; garters for travelling without wearying; to not grow weary while walking; to prevent eating at the table; to win at gambling; to win at gambling; to win at dice; to win at gaming; to win every time on lotteries; to be loved; to make a girl come whom you find modest; to make a girl dance nude; to not be wounded by any weapon; for going into battle; against firearms; to charm firearms; and to make a weapon fail.

Part four deals with the hand of glory. In this instance it is a mandrake root rather than the hand of a murderer, and the process for preparing and using it is described. It also includes the black hen charm. Part five is 'Orisons for Different Purposes'. It starts with acts of grace, to protect yourself from evil spirits. Then are Latin versions of prayers, the 'Pater Noster', the 'Ave Maria', '*Veni Creator*' (with translation), and '*Symbolum Apostolorum*'. The books end with a table of favourable and unfavourable days.

Essential Reading

Cecchetelli, Michael (2011) *Crossed Keys*. London: Scarlet Imprint. This work is valuable as it combines translations of the *Black Dragon* and the *Enchiridion*. Although there is little context, there is an interesting section on the author's experience of working the grimoire.

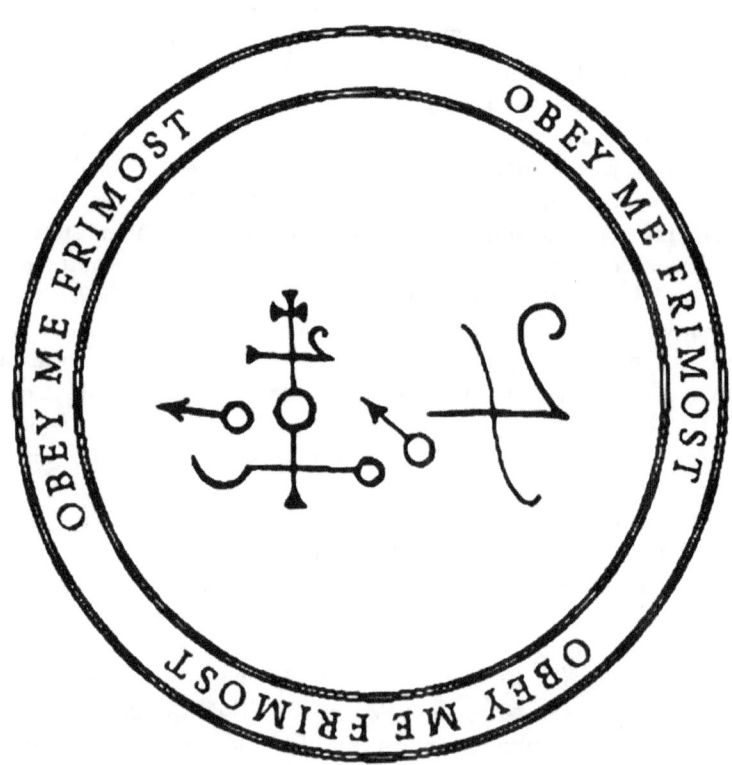

Black Dragon, Frimost Circle

Grimoire Sympathia

Date: 1906.
Language: English.
Influences: Unknown.
Provenance: Written by John Thomas (1826-1908) under the name Charubel.
MSS: N/A.
Circle: N/A.
Tools: N/A.
Spirit List: Adolrwngfa, Adruel, Agathel, Amphrenomel, Amruel, Amvelrah, Amvradel, Aphhimoo, Aphruel, Arhugal, Arphoriel, Arrutel, Aruel, Arumaphobiel, Arvirevel, Athruel, Avmahujah, Avruthel, Avvihugal, Bathrael, Cedragel, Dergabel, Duwarchua, Elnerah, Ephlehimah, Evagel, Gromogel, Harvalam, Hoomel, Hoovahmah, Ishmarathel, Luvarmel, Mevathma, Moru, Murroo, Nephro, Ovalackbah, Rovamhal, Soomathuel Divoomathel, Tharophim, Tichmavah, Trivoo, Trooaval, Vivooel, Zara.

The Text

The full title of this book explains its purpose: *Grimoire Sympathia. The Workshop of the Infinite. Healing without Medicine using the Spiritual Essence of Plants, Minerals and Precious Stones*. This work marks a change in the grimoires as the twentieth century dawned. Ex-Methodist minister John Thomas was a curious character who produced a unique work which, despite its differences, still maintains something of the essence of the grimoire tradition.

John Thomas was clairvoyant, and it was through his psychic gifts that he derived the sigils[409] and names used in his system. In addition to these, this work is also full of digressions about magical topics, making it a worthwhile read as there are many insights contained within it.

The first section of the book contains discussion of the natural world and its operation. There is an emphasis on the feminine side of divinity as the nurturer, the provider, and as the force behind the magic in this work. The subsequent sections discuss the Word of God, the Body and Soul, and Intellect and Imagination, followed by a conclusion.

The introduction explains the process that led the author to developing the material he presented. For each of the chapters on plants, he discusses the background of the plant, its lore, and use as a remedy, as well as the sigil and word of invocation (spirit name) with details of how to use these to receive their healing benefits. Some chapters also give invocations and digress into the psychology associated with the plant. The plant chapters are on the lichen, mosses, ferns, adder's tongue, mare's tail, the ash tree, brook lime, lilac, devil's bit scabious, oak (long chapter), buttercup, anemone, clematis, monkshood (aconite), peony, Christmas rose (black hellebore), St John's wort, poppy, corn poppy, crane's bill (herb Robert), wood sorrel, lime tree, marsh mallow, orange tree, fir tree, yew tree, mountain ash (rowan) (long chapter), digression into the nature of wood nymphs, alder tree, elder tree, birch tree, poplar tree, elm tree, box tree, holly tree, ivy, and heather.

The next section is on the psychological properties of minerals. This begins with a long chapter on gold, its nature and uses (sigil but no name given). This is followed by iron and copper, and then moves into precious stones. The stones considered are topaz, amethyst, coral, rock crystal (quartz), emerald, diamond (for which he was apparently not allowed to give the name and sigil), ruby, turquoise, sapphire, garnet, and carbuncle (deep red garnet).

---

409 It must be said that the sigils are crisp, clean, and appealing.

The book ends with an index of all the plants, metals, and stones contained, with a handy entry for each on its healing uses. A second index lists all the healing ailments and which plant or mineral to use for it.

Essential Reading

Charubel (2003) *Grimoire Sympathia: The Workshop of the Infinite*. Thame: I-H-O Books. Good reprint of the 1906 original, providing all the material.

The Supreme Black, Red & Infernal Magic Of The Chaldeans And Egyptians

Date: 1916.
Language: Spanish.
Influences: *Key of Solomon, Enchiridion of Pope Leo, Red Dragon, Grimorium Verum, Book of St Cyprian*.
Provenance: Attributed (falsely) to Jonas Sufurino, edition produced by Francisco Moreno (1852-1919, Argentina).
MSS: N/A.
Circle: Yes.
Tools: Lancet, ring, sceptre.
Spirit List: Achajah, Astaroth, Belzebuth, Cathethel, Jeliel, Jesabel, Lucifer, Luzbel, Maria Padhilla, Mehahel, Satanas, Vehniah.

The Text

This text is an interesting one, resembling the style of Agrippa's *De Occulta Philosophia* and *The Magus* in its discursive element, with elements of grimoire practice and Book of Secrets-style charms included. The focus on the triumvirate of Lucifer, Beelzebub, and Astaroth points to texts like the *Grimorium Verum* as possible influences. The inclusion of Maria Padhilla as queen of hell is particularly interesting, suggesting a cross-over with Quimbanda practice (although she does appear in Cyprianic literature so this could also be the source).

The text contains: part one: 'Supreme Red Magic' — Solomon and High Magic Introduction; advice from Solomon to his son Rehoboam and to those who will dedicate themselves to magic (1); how men learned magic (2); the talismans (3); invocations, evocations, and spells of Solomon —- invocation to the Celestial Spirits (4); the secret of the sphinxes (5); the paradoxical questions to the sphinxes and their answer (6); part two: 'Alchemy' — cookbook of the true magician: secret to obtain perpetual youth (1); glorious water for the preparation of potable gold (2); magic unions (3); part three: 'Chaldean and Egyptian Magic' — philtres, enchantments, spells and charms; charms, produced by the virtues and qualities of toads (1); enchantments produced by the fern seed and its properties (2); to obtain the protection and help of the demon without making a covenant with him (3); spells by means of a bat (4); part four: 'The Secrets of Queen Cleopatra' — recipes and ointments; part five: 'Philosophy of Magic' — the Cabala and the unknown forces; the Ternary and the Immutable Laws of Nature (1); the laws of Analogy according to the Sephiroth (2); significance and value of numbers (3); part six: 'The Ether' — life and death; the Astral Light (1); effects of the Astral Light and the Will (2); body and soul (3); what is the human being and how the Will is exercised (4); synergy and theurgy of the macrocosm and the microcosm (5); imagination and sympathetic attraction (6); mysteries of fertilization and attraction (7); Man in relation to the stars (8); influence of the constellations and planets (9); how to make the horoscope (10); mysteries of virginity and virgin blood (11); fluid larvae and Elemental Spirits (12); why did Simon the Magician fly and how people can fly (13); how and why is magical power lost (14).

Essential Reading

Moreno, Francisco & Savedow, Steve (ed, trans) (2022) *The Supreme Black, Red & Infernal Magic Of The Chaldeans And Egyptians*. West Yorkshire: Hadean Press. Interesting translation with commentary, the text shows cross-fertilisation with other traditions and practices.

Secret Grimoire of Turiel

Date: 1960.
Language: English.
Influences: *Arbatel, Heptameron, Key of Solomon, Complete Book of Magic Science* (Hockley).
Provenance: Modern compilation presented with a backstory to try and provide credibility.
MSS: N/A.
Circle: Yes.
Tools: Forked wand, girdle, knife, lamen, pentacles, sword, wand.
Spirit List: Abinzaba, Abuori, Aiedat, Amabiel, Anael, Aratron, Arragon, Asasiel, Astel, Babiel, Bachiel, Baraborat, Bethor, Bileth, Burchat, Capabile, Castiel, Chassiel, Chedusitanich, Coiznas, Conieh, Corael, Corat, Doremiel, Estael, Gabraei, Gabriel, Hagith, Haludiel, Hubaril, Huphatrieb, Inhabit, Kadiel, Machasiel, Madios, Mael, Maltiel, Mathlai, Mizabu, Modiat, Naromiel, Och, Ophiel, Orael, Pabael, Peajel, Penael, Penat, Phul, Praleg (Phaleg), Rachiel, Rael, Ramel, Raphael, Sachieh, Sachiel, Sallales, Samael, Satael, Seraphiel, Setchiel, Suceratos, Sugmonos, Tarmiel, Tenariel, Teriapel, Thamael, Thiel, Turiel, Uriel, Ustael, Valnum, Vianathraba, Zebarel, Zoniel.

The Text

The book begins with an introduction setting up a fake provenance for itself. The author tells the story of receiving the text from a defrocked priest, who sold him the severely worn Latin original dating to 1518 and a clean English translation. Considering that aside from the bulk of the material being from Hockley's *Complete Book of Magic Science*, the other sources are all works published in the late nineteenth and early twentieth century, this is clearly spurious.[410]

The text proper begins with observations and the method of invoking. It explains the preparation; gives the first Morning Prayer; the blessing of the light; consecration of the sword; benediction of the lamens, pentacles, garment, and perfume; and the exorcism of fire. Next are the invocations of the planets by their day, each with a planetary magic circle and conjuration. This is followed by the Olympic Spirits with their seals and perfumes.

The second part includes the oration to be said when putting on the vestments; the knife, lamen, prayer, names and offices of the spirits, and the messengers and intelligences of the seven planets,[411] Then follows invocation, interrogations, and license to depart, and a form of a bond of spirits given by Turiel (with seal of Turiel).

Essential Reading

Malchus, Marius (2011) *The Secret Grimoire of Turiel*. Theophania Publishing. Reasonable edition of this modern compilation, though the spelling is awful.

---

410 The *Arbatel* material is taken from A.E.Waite's *Book of Black Magic and Pacts*, and the *Key of Solomon* from the MacGregor Mathers edition.

411 These are spirits found in earlier works such as the *Heptameron* with completely different (random?) attributions. The way they are done suggests a lack of knowledge on the part of the author.

Sworn and Secret Grimoire

Date: 2021.
Language: English.
Influences: *Greek Magical Papyri, Picatrix, Arbatel, Petit Albert, Complete Book of Magical Science, Secret Grimoire of Turiel.*
Provenance: Written by Jake Stratton-Kent.
MSS: N/A.
Circle: Yes.
Tools: Girdle, hazel forked wand, hazel wand, lamen, pentacles, robe, sword.
Spirit List: Abinzaba, Abuori, Aiediat, Amabiel, Anael, Aphrodite, Aratron, Ares, Arragon, Asasiel, Asbil, Astel, Ba'il, Babiel, Bachiel, Baraborat, Bethor, Bijail, Bileth, Bitail, Burchat, Capabile, Castiel, Chassiel, Chedusitaniel, Colzras, Coniel, Corael, Corat, Doremiel, Estael, Gabrael, Gabriel, Hagith, Haludiel, Harqil, Hermes, Hubaril, Huphatriel, Kadiel, Machasiel, Madios, Mael, Maltiel, Mathlai, Mene, Mizabu, Modiat, Naromiel, Och, Ophiel, Orael, Pabael, Penael, Penat, Penjel, Phaleg, Phul, Rachiel, Rael, Ramel, Raphael, Rufijail, Sachiel, Saljail, Sallales, Samael, Satael, Saturn, Seraphiel, Setchiel, Sol, Suceratos, Sugmonos, Tarmiel, Tenariel, Teriapel, Thamael, Thiel, Turiel, Uranel, Uriel, Ustael, Valnum, Venoel, Vianathraba, Zebarel, Zeus, Zoniel.

The Text

The book begins with an introduction and an overview of the *Secret Grimoire of Turiel*. Book one has two parts. Part one has: observations and method of invoking related with great pains and diligent research, detailing the consecrations of the tools, invocations of the days with pentacles, the Olympic spirits with their qualities and incenses (drawn ultimately from Agrippa's *Three Books of Occult Philosophy*), precepts and aphorisms from the *Arbatel*, license to depart; Part two is: of the invocations, conjurations and exorcisms; of the bond of spirits.

Book two focuses on the planetary days and hours. The sections are on the planetary days, gods of time, Egyptian and Hermetic decans, alternative invocations: Sabean planetary magic, hymns to the planetary gods, and tables of planetary hours for the day and night.

The appendices detail two examples of ritual frames for evocation, examining the stages and their practices. A short contextual discussion of the grimoires and the author's experiences ends the work.

Essential Reading

Stratton-Kent, Jake (2021) *The Sworn and Secret Grimoire*. West Yorkshire: Hadean Press. Excellent well-written and sourced introduction to grimoire practice as a self-contained work.

Spirit List

Throughout the grimoires a huge number of spiritual creatures of different types are named, and sometimes described. This list combines them all in one place. The abbreviations are used to identify which grimoires each of the listed spirits may be found in. For early pre-grimoire compilation texts such as *Ancient Christian Magic*, the *Greek Magical Papyri* and *Supplementum Magicum*, where a spirit occurs more than once, each individual papyrus reference is listed. Specific name epithets for deities are given, but not the descriptive epithets applied to them (e.g., dart-shooter, crested one, etc.).

If a spirit name is followed by another in brackets, this indicates it is another name for the bracketed spirit. Where there is a question mark, this is a suggested attribution based on similarity of the name and a matching description in the spirit catalogue, generally pointing at an earlier from of the spirit, from the *Book of the Offices of Spirits* to the *Goetia* or *Pseudomonarchia Daemonum*, for example.

If a specific edition of rescension is listed, the associated spirit names given in the list are only those which differ from other editions, e.g., the extra material in the Rudd edition of the *Goetia*.

When there are two or more variant spellings of a name, this indicates divergence over the same or different manuscripts of the same grimoire. Many of these are clearly copying errors.

If there is more than one entry for a name, this may indicate different spirits of the same name, e.g., an angel and a demon. This is not to definitively state they are not the same being, but rather that different entries offer that option.

When a time is given, such as 'hour six', it refers to the Planetary Hour of the day or night, as indicated. There is an instance in *Theurgia-Goetia* where the twenty-four-hour period is divided into fifteen hours, and so the Hour reads as 'X of fifteen'. In the same grimoire, there are also demon dukes who serve on alternate years, given as Y1 or Y2. In the case of the seven archangels ruling the hours, this has been tabulated separately in Volume 2, 'Appendix XII: Timings' for convenience.

The spirits are named according to the grimoire in which they are found, so terms like 'devil' and 'genii' are used in places. As such, the use of the word genii in the *Art Pauline* represents a spirit, not the type of genii associated with Arabic magic and folklore. Also, when a spirit is named and its type not specified as angel, demon, fairy, etc., I have remained with spirit rather than making assumptions as to their nature in the text.

Some texts give names in conjurations and practices without it being clear if they are divine names, names of spirits, voces magicae, etc. In these instances, I have not included the names in the list as they are not specified as being spirits. Likewise, I have not listed the unnamed angels in the Bible such as those in Revelation or the angel of the Lord (which is used numerous times without being clear if it refers to the same being across those uses).

The classical gods listed below, from the list in the *Book of Oberon*, are reproduced as per the manuscript. This means some of the attributions may seem curious to the modern eye, and some of the goddesses are incorrectly called gods. Nonetheless, I have recorded as found rather than altering them to suit modern sensibilities. The *Hygromanteia* lists many different names for the planetary gods in their prayers, which are included in the list for completion and comparison.

I have included classifications not specifically listed in grimoires that were in works from the timeframe such as the attributions of the seven deadly sins in the anonymous *The Lantern of Light* (1409-10) and Peter Binsfield's *Princes of Hell* in *De confessionibus maleficorum et sagarum* (1589) for a more comprehensive list.

Name	Type	Grimoires
A		
Aaan	Enochian Angel – South, over second lesser Angle	*TBA*
Aaazial	Angel – Third Heaven, serving Ibnial	*ShR*
Aabdial	Angel – First Encampment, first Heaven	*ShR*
A'abedial	Angel – Malachim, under Avorphenial	*SRH*
A'abiesal	Angel – Malachim, under Pheseker	*SRH*
Aabiō/Aabōn/Aabon (Jupiter)	Jupiter – Alternative Name	*Hyg*
Aabr	Angel – Fifth Encampment, first Heaven	*ShR*
Aabraēl/Kyabraiēl	Angel – Winter	*BoW*
Aacoel/Aacol	Demon – South	*GoPH*
A'aderial	Angel Prince – East Gate	*SRH*
Aadet	Enochian Angel – West, over first lesser Angle	*TBA*
Aadmun	Angel – Sixth Encampment, first Heaven	*ShR*
Aadnnial	Angel Encampment Head – sixth Heaven, East	*ShR*
Aadon	Angel – Iyar	*SR*
Aadrael	Angel – First Heaven, East	*SSM*
Aaetpio	Enochian Senior – South	*TBA*
Aagial	Angel Prince – fourth Heaven, Water	*ShR*
A'akenial	Angel – Malachim, Tammuz	*SRH*
A'akiesal	Angel – Malachim, under Pheseker	*SRH*
Aal	Angel – Mercury/Wednesday	*SR*
Aali	Angel – Fifth Encampment, first Heaven Angel – Third Step, second Heaven	*ShR*
A'aliehon Avor Kosesor	Angel Prince – Malachim, Spring	*SRH*

A'aliekem	Angel of Knowledge	SRH
Aalzial	Angel – Seventh Encampment, first Heaven	ShR
A'amal	Angel Prince – Gate of Spirit of East	SRH
Aamel	Angel – First three signs	SSM
A'amelial	Angel – Malachim, Flames of Fire	SRH
Aamial	Angel – Sixth Encampment, first Heaven Angel – Seventh Step, second Heaven Angel – Eighth Step, second Heaven Angel Prince – Fourth Heaven, Water	ShR
Aamnial	Angel – Eighth Step, second Heaven	ShR
A'amoal	Angel – Malachim, Veil of the Firmament	SRH
Aana	Enochian Angel – South, over second lesser Angle	TBA
Aanal	Spirit	SSM
A'anal	Angel Magistrate – Sowing Soil Angel – Malachim, Summer Angel Prince – Gate of Spirit of West	SRH
Aanbal	Angel – Second Step, second Heaven	ShR
A'anial	Angel – Moon, Gemini, Virgo Angel – Malachim, Spring and Nisan Angel Minister – Malachim, first Dwelling Angel Prince – Gate of Spirit of West Archangel – Malachim, over the Shem	SRH
Aaniturla	Angel – Mercury/Wednesday	SR
Aannial	Angel – Fourth Step, second Heaven Angel Encampment Head – sixth Heaven, East	ShR
A'anoval	Angel – Malachim, Nisan	SRH
Aanshal	Angel – First Step, second Heaven	ShR
Aaon	Angel – Mercury/Wednesday	SR
Aaoxaif	Enochian Senior – East	TBA
Aapedoce	Enochian Senior – South	TBA
A'aphosal	Angel – Malachim, sixth Host	SRH
Aaqb	Angel – Fifth Encampment, first Heaven	ShR
A'aqerial	Angel – Malachim, Flames of Fire	SRH
Aaqial	Angel – Third Heaven, serving Rhtial	ShR

ABBREVIATIONS

Aaqrial	Angel – Eleventh Step, second Heaven Angel – Third Heaven, serving Dtqial	*ShR*
A'arebrethiehov	Angel Prince	*SRH*
A'areketh	Angel Magistrate – Sowing Soil	*SRH*
A'aremial	Angel Prince – Craftiness	*SRH*
A'aremon	Angel – Malachim, under Pheseker Angel – Malachim, sixth Host	*SRH*
A'aremor	Angel – Malachim, sixth Host	*SRH*
Aariel/Ariel/Adriel	Demon Duke – South-West Day	*Stg, ThG, BoTS*
Aarith/Abrēth	East Wind – Autumn	*BoW*
Aaron	Angel – Iyar	*SR*
Aars (Rubaeel, Greek) and (Shams, Greek)	Spirit King – Mars/Sun	*Pic*
A'ashial	Angel Prince – Malachim, Spring Nights	*SRH*
Aaulph	Angel – West Wind	*ShR*
Aaur	Angel – Seventh Encampment, first Heaven	*ShR*
Aauzial	Angel – Sixth Encampment, first Heaven	*ShR*
A'avorial	Angel Minister – Malachim	*SRH*
A'avosheh	Angel – Malachim, under Dohel	*SRH*
A'avozial	Angel Magistrate – Throne of Glory Angel – Malachim, under Pheseker Angel – Malachim, sixth Host	*SRH*
A'azael/A'aza	Angel Magistrate – Wisdom	*SRH*
Aazial	Angel – Second Step, second Heaven	*ShR*
A'azial	Archangel – Malachim, over the Shem Angel Prince – Summer	*SRH*
Aazmal	Angel – Tenth Step, second Heaven	*ShR*
A'azrial	Spirit Prince – North	*SRH*
Aazrial	Angel – Eighth Step, second Heaven Angel Encampment Head – fifth Heaven, East	*ShR*
A'azrial (Ahedierier)	Angel – Ruler of Preservation of Crops	*SRH*
Aazy	Angel – Fifth Encampment, first Heaven	*ShR*
Aba	Angel Minister of Air – Friday	*Hmn, BM, GAG, tM*
Abaah	Demon King under Belzebub	*SSM*
Abaal	Angel	*SM*: P. Med. I.20

Aba Bavoth	Angel Prince – Autumn Spirit Prince – Ocean in Autumn	*SRH*
Abaddon/Apollyon/ Abbadon	Demon Prince – Furyes Demon Minister Demon of Sloth Minister of Death	HB Job 28:22,[412] Rev 9:10; *3BOP, BM,* *JMR, SRH, PO, tM,* *VJL*
Abadem	Angel Minister	*KoSA*
Abael	Angel	*ACM:* Oriental 6794
Abaēl/Sabbaēl	Angel – Tuesday Hour seventeen	*Hyg*
Abaēl/Abaēli	Angel – Saturday Hour four	*Hyg*
Abael	Duke – West by North after Midnight	*Stg, ThG, BoTS*
Abalam	Demon King	*PmD, DoW, Goe, DI*
Abalidoch/Abalidoth	Spirit Attendant – Venus Angel Minister of Air – Friday, Venus	*EoN, Hmn, BM,* *KoSR, GAG, tM*
Abalon	Spirit – West	*KoN*
Abamatra	Angel	*GAG*
Abaōth	God (Hebrew)	PGM III:1-64
Abanystra	Angel – Venus	*B7R*
Abariel/Abaris/ Abarial	Demon Duke – North-West Day	*Stg, ThG, BoTS*
Abasdardaon	Angel – Second Season by Night	*SSM*
Abasdarhon/ Abasdarho	Angel Ruler – Night Hour five	*Stg, ArP*
Abay	Spirit	*oADS*
Abaye	Angel – Sunday/Sun	*KoSR*
Abba	Angel – First Encampment, first Heaven Angel	*ShR, NA*
Abba	Spirit	*oADS, KoN*
Abbac	Angel – Trickery	*KoSA*
Abbachiaox	Angel – Cherubim	*ACM:* Oriental 6796
Abbaēl/Ababa	Angel – Summer	*DoW*
Abbaoth	Angel of Abyss – Autumn	*SSM*
Abdac	Angel – Trickery	*KoSA*
Abdalaa	Demon King – Moon	*BARC*
Abdaph	Spirit Prince – Surgery	*MNeI*

---

[412] Only the reference where Abaddon is personified in the Bible is listed, not the instances where it is identified as hell (sheol).

ABBREVIATIONS

Abdebalu	Spirit	*SSM*
Abdelvam	Angel – Nisan	*tSoS*
Abdeyadym	Angel Superior – three signs of third Season	*SSM*
Abdiziel/Abdizenel/ Abdizuel	Angel – Mansion twelve and Leo	*3BOP, BoO, tSoS, JMR, SaS, tM*
Abdizuel/Abdicuel	Commoner Spirit, Fire	*MNeI*
Abdulas	Bottom part of Bandalos	*Pic*
Abebon/Abibon	Spirit	*CoC*
Abecaisdon	Angel – Tishrei	*SR*
Abech	Demon – South	*BOS, BoO*
Abedel	Angel – Nisan	*SR*
Abedieh	Angel – Malachim, under Plemiya	*SRH*
Abedoth	Spirit – East in Autumn	*SRH*
Abeka	Angel – Malachim, under Avorphenial	*SRH*
Abekeleth	Angel Prince	*SRH*
Abekeren	Spirit – Spring	*SRH*
Abekhe/Abekhkhe/ Abelkhe/Akhbekhe	Demon – East	*Hyg*
Abêl	Angel	*SM:* P. Med. I.20
Abel Abehem	Angel Prince – Malachim, Tammuz	*SRH*
Abelit	Wind Spirit	*GAG*
Abeloy	Angel Minister	*KoSA*
Abemo	Enochian Angel – East, serving third lesser Angle	*TBA*
Abenienok	Angel – Malachim, under Ayigeda	*SRH*
Abentabo	Demon Servant – Sunday	*KoN*
Abere	Spirit of the Thumb	*CBoM*
Aberekial	Angel Prince – Adar	*SRH*
Aberieh	Angel Magistrate – Malachim	*SRH*
Aberien/Aberiek	Spirit – North in Summer	*SRH*
Aberieth	Spirit – East in Autumn	*SRH*
Aberietha	Angel – Malachim, under Ayigeda	*SRH*
Abermo	Spirit – Book Making	*oADS*
Abesabeēl/Abesabeel	Angel	*Hyg*

Abezithibod	Demon	*ToS*
Abgo	Demon	*MHN*
Abgoth	Demon	*MHN*
Abhadir	Servant Spirit	*Abm*
Abhanci/Abanystra/Abanixtra/Abhanzizi	Angel – Venus	*B7R, tSoS*
Abial	Angel – First Encampment, first Heaven	*ShR*
Abibal	Angel – Second Encampment, first Heaven	*ShR*
Abibo	Spirit	*tSoS*
Abican	Spirit – East	*KoN*
Abiebiem	Angel Prince – Summer	*SRH*
Abiehod	Angel, serving above sixth Degree	*SRH*
Abiel	Angel	*Hyg*
Abiel	Genii – 15° Cancer, 15° Leo	*ArP*
Abier Abieriem	Angel Prince – Malachim, Summer	*SRH*
Abigellem	Spirit – Minister of Love	*oADS*
Abigrabeni	Angel Minister – Love and Fornication	*KoSA*
Abim	Angel – Moon	*KoSR*
Abimalyb	Spirit Assistant – Saturday	*MHN*
Abimud	Angel – Sixth Step, second Heaven	*ShR*
Abinel	Angel – Jupiter/Thursday	*SR*
Abinzaba	Spirit – four Quarters of the Universal Mansions Spirit – Moon	*SGT, SSG*
Abiout	Angel Guardian	*ACM*: Hay 10391
Abiul	Angel	*VJL*
Abiyan	Spirit – East	*SRH*
Abiyar	Angel – Malachim, under Dohel	*SRH*
Abizouth/Azibouth/Abēzouth	Demon – North	*Hyg*
Ablaieil	Angel – Venus/Friday	*SR*
Ablikon/Ablēkou	Demon – North	*Hyg*
Ablimas	Left part of Didas	*Pic*
Ablokher	Angel	*Hyg*
Ablote	Spirit	*Hyg*

Abnalaamar	Punishing Wind	*SSM*
Abnalazafar	Punishing Wind	*SSM*
Abnalazart	Punishing Wind	*SSM*
Abnazart	Punishing Wind	*SSM*
Abneyrin	Angel – Venus/Friday	*SR*
Abnisor	Angel – Sivan	*SR*
Aboc/Aboce	Demon Duke – North-East	*Stg, ThG*
Abonay	Angel – Seventh Altitude (Libra)	*Alm*
Abor	Angel – Jupiter	*CoMS*
Aboz	Enochian Angel – North, over first lesser Angle	*TBA*
Abrac	Angel – Ab	*SR*
Abraca	Spirit – Mirror	*CoMS*
Abracola	Spirit – Mirror	*CoMS*
Abragin	Angel – Iyar	*SR*
Abraki	Demon	*Hyg*
Abrakiim	Angel – Moon	*LL*
Abramacyn	Angel – Moon/Monday	*SR*
Abramatim/Abramathin	Angel – Moon	*LL*
Abrancasai	Angel – Moon	*LL*
Abranodomilim	Angel – Moon	*LL*
Abranonin	Angel - Moon	*LL*
Abras	Angel – Moon	*LL*
Abrasachysyn	Angel – Moon/Monday	*SR*
Abrasasyn	Angel – Moon/Monday	*SR*
Abrashim	Angel – Moon	*LL*
Abrasiel/Abrasul	Angel – Day Hour seven	*Stg, ArP*
Abrasks	Angel Prince – fourth Heaven, Fire	*ShR*
Abrastos	Angel – Water	*SR*
Abrax	Archangel	*ACM*: Cologne 20826
Abraxas/Abrasax/Abracax/Abrasaxsax/Abrasaks	Gnostic Archon/Spirit Lord of the Mountains/Birds	PGM I:262-347, III:1-164, III:187-262, III:424-466, III:633-731,

Abraxas/Abrasax/ Abracax/ Abrasaxsax/Abrasaks (con't.)		PGM IV:296-466, IV:1496-1595, IV:3255-3274, V:96-172, V:304-369, VII:201-202, VII:643-651, VIII:1-63, IX:1-14, X:36-50, XIc:1-9, XII:14-95, XII:201-269, XIII:1-343, XIXa:1-54, XXIII:1-70, XXVIIIa:1-7, XXXIIa:1-25, XXXVI:35-68, XXXVI:134-160, XXXVI:333-360, XLV:1-8, LVIII:15-39, LXI:159-196, LXI:197-216, LXVII:1-24, LXVIII:1-20, LXIX:1-3, LXXX:1-5, LXXXI:1-10, LXXXIX:1-27, XCII:1-16, CXVI:1-17, PDM XIV:376-394, XIV:695-700; *SM*: P. Lund IV.12, PSI I.28, P. Köln Inv. 3323, T. Louvre I,nv. E 27145, P. Mich. Inv. 6925, T. Köln Inv. 1, O. Köln Inv. 409, T. Köln Inv. 4, O. Bodl. II.2180, P. Merton II.58, P. Oxy. LVI.3834, Oxy. 924; *ACM*: Berlin 5565, Bodl C(P)4, Berlin 8503, Cairo EM 49547; BoW, DI
Abrasaxael	Angel over Lightning	*ACM*: BN Turin
Abraxiel	Angel	*ACM*: Oriental 6172
Abryaon	Angel Superior – three signs of third Season	*SSM*

ABBREVIATIONS

Abrayel	Angel	*LL*
Abrētoumē	Angel – Plant Ruler	*BoW*
Abrh	Angel – Eighth Step, second Heaven	*ShR*
Abri	Angel – Tishrei	*SR*
Abrial	Angel – Seventh Step, second Heaven	*ShR*
Abriel	Duke – West by North Afternoon	*Stg, ThG, BoTS*
Abrih	Angel – Fourth Encampment, first Heaven	*ShR*
Abrikhos/Ablykhos	Demon – Wednesday Hour fifteen	*Hyg*
Abrinael	Angel – Mansion twenty-four	*3BOP, tSoS, JMR, SaS, tM*
Abrinel/Aprinaelis	Noble Spirit – Fire	*MNeI*
Abris	Angel – Sivan	*SR*
Abrisaf	Angel – Shebat	*SR*
Abrita	Angel – Second Encampment, first Heaven	*ShR*
Abrkial	Angel Prince – fifth Heaven, Month of Adar Angel Encampment Head – sixth Heaven, East	*ShR*
Abrodressim	Spirit of the Thumb	*CBoM*
Abroyn	Angel – Moon	*KoSR*
Abrulges/Abrulge	Demon Duke – East	*Stg, ThG*
Abryabrym	Angel Superior – second Season by Day	*SSM*
Abryahaon	Angel – Sun, three signs of second Season	*SSM*
Absafyabitan	Angel – Iyar	*SR*
Absamon	Angel – Iyar	*SR*
Abson	Angel – First Heaven, West	*SR*
Absoul	Angel – Treasure seeking	*dN*
Abton	Plutonian Spirit	*MNeI*
Abucaba/Habuchada	Punishing Wind Daemon Minister – Moon, West	*SSM, SBH*
Abuchaba	Daemon – Moon, serving West Wind; West	*SBH*
Abugor/Abigor/Abigar (Eligor)	Demon Duke	*LdE, GG, DI*
Abuioni	Angel – Second Heaven, North	*SaS*

Abuiori/Abviori	Angel – Second Heaven Wednesday, North Ministering Spirit – Mercury	EoN, Hmn, KoSR, BoO, GAG, BoTS, tM, CBMS
Abulal	Angel	SoM
Abulnatita	Demon Servant – Saturday	KoN
Abumalith	Angel Minister of Air – Saturday Spirit – Saturn Presiding Spirit – Saturn	Hmn, KoSR, SoS, GAG, BoTS, MNeI, tM, CBMS
Abundant	Wind Spirit	GAG
Abuori	Intelligence – Moon	SGT, SSG
Aburm	Angel – Third Encampment, first Heaven	ShR
Abusi	Angel	SoM
Abusis	Servant Spirit	Abm
Abuzaba	Spirit Assistant – Monday	MHN
Abuzaha/Abusaba	Angel Minister of Air – Monday Spirit Attendant – Moon	EoN, Hmn, KoSR, GAG, BoTS, M
Abybo	Spirit – Woods	oADS
Abzach	Demon Senior	SSM
Acansarny	Spirit – Mirror	CoMS
Acar	Demon Count	NML
Acar	Enochian Angel – South, serving fourth lesser Angle	TBA
Acarax/Carax (Ocarat)	Angel – Sun	tSoS
Acartayl	Angel – Autumn	MHN
Acayl	Angel – Autumn	MHN
Acca	Enochian Angel – East, serving fourth lesser Angle	TBA
Acceriel	Angel – Water	SR
Acciriron	Angel – Saturn/Saturday	SR
Accusator	Angel Minister – Love and Fornication	KoSA
Accyel	Angel Lord – Nights of the Year	SSM
Acdiel	Angel – Fire	SR
Acemliceve	Enochian Senior – North	TBA
Acepes	Enochian Angel – South, over third lesser Angle	TBA
Acer	Spirit – sixth Mansion of Moon Ring	AE

Aceruel/Azeruel	Peasant Spirit, Fire	*MNeI*
Achab	Angel	*ACM*: H. Kopt. 679
Achael	Biblical Elder Spirit – Gate of the West	*ACM*: Berlin 11347, Oriental 6796, L. Anastasi 9
Achael	Genii – 24° Cancer, 24° Leo	*ArP*
Achajah	Salamander Head (two of six)	*SBRM*
Achal	Angel – Fourth Encampment, first Heaven	*ShR*
Achalas	Spirit	*MHN*
Acham	Demon – Thursday, Treasure-seeking	*GoPH, BD*
Acharah	Angel	*ACM*: H. Kopt. 679
Acharib	Spirit Prince – Metals	*KoN*
Achariel	Demon – South	*GoPH*
Acharon/Acheron	Spirit King	*BoTS*
Acharos/Aharas/Aharus	Demon Duke	*BOS, BoO*
Achasiah/Achaiah/Aehaiah	Angel – Shem seven	*KoSU, 3BOP, GoeR, JMR, SaS, tM*
Achel	Intelligence – France	*GoPH*
Acheseph	Angel – Malachim, under Plemiya Angel Magistrate – Malachim	*SRH*
Achial	Angel – Seventh Encampment, first Heaven Angel Prince – Gate of Spirit of North	*ShR, SRH*
Achibio	Spirit of the Thumb	*CBoM*
Achiel	Genii – 21° Cancer, 21° Leo	*ArP*
Achilia	Fairy Queen, sister one of three	*DoW*
Achimaal	Spirit – East	*SSM*
Achios	Devil – third Hour of Day	*oADS*
Achithim	Angel – Moon	*LL*
Achlas	Angel – Iyar	*SR*
Achmuda	Angel – Seventh Encampment, first Heaven	*ShR*
Achocyb	Spirit	*SSM*
Achorbou	Angel – Seraphim who Cover their Bodies	*ACM*: H. Kopt. 686
Achot/Achet	Demon Duke – North by East Day	*Stg, ThG*
Achoubael	Spirit	*ACM*: Oriental 6796

Achozib	Spirit – East	*KoN*
Achrichiour	Third of seven Pole Lords of Heaven	PGM IV:475-829
Achsp	Angel – Third Heaven, serving Rhtial	*ShR*
Achunhab	Spirit Prince	*AAAA*
Achusp	Angel – Fourth Encampment, first Heaven	*ShR*
Achusaton	Angel – Thrones	*67M*
Acia	Angel – Nisan	*SR, tSoS*
Aciel	Angel – Fifth Heaven, East	*SR*
Aciel	Demon – Prince-Elector, Sun and Taurus Wise Spirit Prince Palatine/Great Prince	*MNeI*
Acimoy/Acimay	Archangel – Mars	*Hmn, BoO, GAG, BoTS, CBMS*
Achachardus/ Acnachardus	Spirit King	*BoTS*
Acolcrostel	Angel – Jupiter	*GAG*
Acquiot	Demon – Sunday	*GoPH*
Acrabiel (Aduachiel)	Angel – Scorpio Spirit – Scorpio	*3BOP, BoO, tSoS, SaS*
Acreba	Demon Duke – South Night	*Stg, ThG*
Acroel	Angel – Sun	*B7R*
Acronis (Ashbeel, Greek)	Spirit King – Saturn	*Pic*
Acteras/Acterar/ Acterer	Demon Duke – South Day	*Stg, ThG*
Acteus	Demon – Bringer of Calamity/ Instigator of Misfortune Demon – Telchine	*3BOP, MNeI, tM*
Acucabay	Spirit Helper – Monday	*CBoM*
Acuteba (Abuzaha?)	Angel Minister of Air – Monday	*BoO*
Acytael/Accytael	Angel Subordinate – Moon	*SSM*
Aczinor	Enochian Senior – North	*TBA*
Aczonyn	Angel – Moon/Monday	*SR*
Adadiel	Demon – Count Palatine	*MNeI*
Adan	Demon Duke – North-West Night	*Stg, ThG, BoTS*
Adariat	Spirit – sixth Mansion of Moon Ring	*tSoS*
Addriel	Angel – Adar	*SR*

Adeel	Spirit – Mirror	*CoMS*
Adekaēl/Ademaēl/ Ademael (Luna)	Luna – Alternative Name	*Hyg*
Adelial	Angel – Malachim, under Ayigeda	*SRH*
Ademial	Angel – Malachim, under Pheseker	*SRH*
Adenial	Angel – Malachim, Kislev	*SRH*
Adenova	Angel – Malachim, under Avorphenial	*SRH*
Adenoval	Angel – Malachim, under Avorphenial	*SRH*
Adeq	Angel – Malachim, under Ayigeda	*SRH*
Aderek	Angel, serving above sixth Degree	*SRH*
Adeta	Enochian Angel – West, over first lesser Angle	*TBA*
Adi	Angel – Sivan Angel – Malachim, under Ayigeda	*SR, SRH*
Adial	Angel – Malachim, under Avorphenial	*SRH*
Adiamenim	Angel – Moon	*LL*
Adiamenyn	Angel – Moon/Monday	*SR*
Adiel	Angel – Sivan	*SR*
Adiel	Demon Baron, Air	*MNeI*
Adiel	Genii – 27° Cancer, 27° Leo	*ArP*
Adikhaēl (Mars)	Mars – Alternative Name	*Hyg*
Adilas	Spirit – Love/Sexual Attraction	*Pic*
Adir	Angel – Second Encampment, first Heaven	*ShR*
Adisak	Servant Spirit	*Abm*
Adlial	Angel – Second Encampment, first Heaven	*ShR*
Admoday (Asmoday?)	Demon Prince	*SSM*
Adnial	Angel – Eleventh Step, second Heaven	*ShR*
Adnibia	Angel – Iyar	*SR*
Adniel/Admiel	Angel – Nisan	*SR, tSoS*
Adnyam	Angel – Tammuz	*SR*
Adobgoud	Demon – Thursday Hour ten	*Hyg*
Adoeoet	Enochian Senior – South	*TBA*
Adoij	Spirit – Saturn	*67M*
Adola	Ministering Familiar/Mystery	*67M*

Adolrwngfa	Plant Spirit – Yew	*GS*
Adon	Speechless Spirit	*ACM*: Berlin 8503
Adon	Servant Spirit	*Abm*
Adonael	Angel Angel over the Coming in and Going Forth of the Father	*ToS*; *ACM*: BN Turin
Adonaeth	Angel	*ToS*
Adonaios (Hades)	Greek Underworld Ruler God	PGM I:262-347, IV:1496-1595, LXVII:1-24, XCII:1-16, PDM XVI:1-75; *SM*: P. Mich. Inv. 6925, T. Köln Inv. 1, T. Köln Inv. 2, O. Köln Inv. 409
Adōnan	Angel	*Hyg*
Adone	Angel Ruler – twelve Hours of Day	*ACM*: P. Mich. 1190
Adoniel	Angel – Kislev Angel – Mercury	*SR, CoMS*
Adoniel/Adomel	Angel – Night Hour twelve	*Stg, ArP*
Adonis	Greek God of Beauty	PGM IV:296-466; *SM*: T. Cairo Mus. JdE 48217, T. Louvre Inv. E 27145, P. Mich. Inv. 6925, T. Köln Inv. 1, O. Köln Inv. 409, P. Merton II.58
Adop	Enochian Angel – South, over first lesser Angle	*TBA*
Ador	Spirit	*GV*
Adoyahel	Angel – Thrones	*67M*
Adq	Angel – Second Encampment, first Heaven	*ShR*
Adrael	Angel – First Heaven, East	*SaS*
Adramelech/Adramalech	Ministering Familiar/Mystery High Chancellor of Hell and Wardrobe Steward	*3BOP, 67M, DI*
Adrasteia	Greek Goddess of Fate (also used as epithet for Nemesis)	PGM VII:490-504

Adricanorum	Spirit	*GV*
Adulal	Angel	*SoM*
Adrapon/Adrapan/Adyapon	Angel – Night Hour nine	*Stg, ArP*
Adre	Enochian Angel – South, serving fourth lesser Angle	*TBA*
Adriel	Spirit	PGM VII:423-428
Adriel	Angel – North	*SR*
Adriel	Angel – Mansion seventeen	*3BOP, tSoS, JMR, SaS, tM*
Adriel	Commoner Spirit	*MNeI*
Adrk	Angel – Sixth Step, second Heaven	*ShR*
Adroziel	Angel – Night Hour four	*Stg, ArP*
Adruel	Plant Spirit – Box Tree	*GS*
Adrun	Angel – Seventh Step, second Heaven	*ShR*
Adtcalea	Angel – Venus	*GAG*
Adtriel	Angel – West	*SR*
Aduma	Angel – Fifth Encampment, first Heaven	*ShR*
Adunial	Angel – Eighth Step, second Heaven	*ShR*
Adus	Spirit – Mirror	*CoMS*
Adut	Angel – Third Encampment, first Heaven Angel – Fifth Encampment, first Heaven	*ShR*
Advolita	Spirit – third Mansion of Moon Ring	*tSoS*
Adykhēl (Mars)	Mars – Alternative Name	*Hyg*
Adzdiel	Angel – Third Heaven, Venus	
Adziriel/Adzyriel	Angel – Nisan	*SR, tSoS*
Aē	Name of Khephra	PGM IV:930-1114
Aeacus/Aecus	Infernal Judge	*3BOP, MNeI*
Aeburatiel	Angel – Potestates	*67M*
Aegin	Spirit – North, Treasures	*KoN*
Ael	Spirit – Gate of the West	*ACM*: L. Anastasi 9
Ael	Angel – Jupiter/Thursday	*SR*
Aēnoēl	Angel – Saturn	*Hyg*
Æbedel	Air/Wood Spirit	*tSoS*
Æoan	Enochian Angel – North, over third lesser Angle	*TBA*

Aeolus	God – Winds	*BoO*
Aerthoē	Name of Helios in twelfth Hour	PGM IV:1596-1715
Aesal	Angel – Marchesvan	*SR*
Aetus	Demon – Originators of All Harm (one of six)	*PO*
Afalion, Afalyon	Spirit – Hot Spirit – Love	*MHN, NML*
Afarot (Raphael)	Archangel	*ToS*
Affacill	Spirit – Minister of Love	*oADS*
Affarfytyriel	Angel – Jupiter/Thursday	*SR*
Affah	Planetary Spirit – Moon	*SSM*
Affariel	Angel – Earth	*SR*
Affayelin	Angel – Day Hour two	*LL*
Affia	Angel – Saturn	*GAG*
Affla (Affia?)	Angel – Saturn	*GAG*
Affry	Angel – Iyar	*SR*
Affyataynt	Angel of Seas/Waters – Winter	*SSM*
Afloton	Servant Spirit	*Abm*
Afneirin	Angel – Venus/Friday	*SR*
Afoirco	Angel before Throne of God	*oADS*
Afolop	Servant Spirit	*Abm*
Afray	Servant Spirit	*Abm*
Africa/Affrica/Afficia/Afrid	Fairy – fifth of seven sisters	*oADS, BoO, JMR*
Africus/Afrus	South-West Wind – over Angels of Wednesday and Saturday	*Hmn, KoSR, BoTS, SMS, PO*
Afsimiel	Demon Duke – South-East Night	*BoTS*
Agaesin	Spirit – East	*Hyg*
Agaha	Planetary Spirit – Venus	*SSM*
Agahaly	Servant Spirit	*Abm*
Agal	Spirit – Minister of Love	*oADS*
Agalaton	Angel Minister – Love and Fornication	*KoSA*
Agaleraptarkimath/Agateraptarkimath	Demon Duke	*SoS*

ABBREVIATIONS

Agalierap/ Agalierapts/ Aglierapt/Agaliarept (Agaleraptarkimath)	Demon Demon General	*GV, GG, BoSC*
Agama	Spirit – Minister of Love	*oADS*
Agapiel/Asapiel	Demon Duke – Hour five of fifteen	*Stg, ThG*
Agares/Agarus/ Agarat/ Agaros/Aguares	Spirit Demon Duke – East	*SSM, LdE, BOS, BoO, PmD, DoW, oADS, Goe, BoTS, GoPH, GG, BoSC, DI*
Agariel	Spirit – Water	*oADS*
Agaterop	Demon Chief – under Belzebut	*KoSU*
Agathel	Stone Spirit – Coral	*GS*
Agathoe	Demon Prince	*GoPH*
Agathos Daimon/ Agathodaimon ('Good God/Spirit')	God/Spirit	PGM IV:1596-1715, IV:2373-2440, IV:3125-3171, VII:490-504, XII:201-269, XIII:734-1077, XXXVI:211-230, PDM XIV:1-92, XIV:93-114, XIV:117-149, XIV:428-450, XIV:563-574, XIV:585-593, XIV:1110-1129, XV:1-21, LXI:159-96
Agaton	Treasure Spirit	*MNeI*
Agathoēl/Agathouēl	Angel – Friday Hour one	*Hyg*
Agebial	Angel Minister – Malachim	*SRH*
Agedelen	Angel – Malachim, under Avorphenial	*SRH*
Ageh	Spirit – Mars	*67M*
Agchonion	Demon – Decan thirty-three	*ToS*
Agdln	Angel – First Encampment, first Heaven	*ShR*
Agebol	Servant Spirit	*Abm*
Agelem	Enochian Angel – West, over third lesser Angle	*TBA*
Agenial	Angel – Malachim, Flames of Fire	*SRH*

Agērakhiēl	Angel	Hyg
Agerol	Demon	GoPH
Agertho	Spirit of the Thumb	MHN
Aghizikke	Spirit Prince	AAAA
Agiaton	Superior Intelligence – Water	SoS
Agiel	Planetary Intelligence – Saturn	KoSR, 3BOP, BM, PO, tM
Agilas	Servant Spirit	Abm
Agimaē	Angel	Hyg
Aginos	Spirit	Hyg
Agla/Egla (Mars)	Mars – Alternative Name	Hyg
Aglafys	Servant Spirit	Abm
Aglas	Demon Duke – South by West Night	Stg, ThG, BoTS
Aglasis	Demon	SoSW, GV
Aglaton	Superior Intelligence	KoSU
Aglgltun	Angel – Eleventh Step, second Heaven	ShR
Aglipal (Sun)	Sun – Alternative Name	Hyg
Agmarob	Angel – Sun	BARC
Agmial	Angel – Seventh Encampment, first Heaven	ShR
Agnix	Angel – Mansion three and Aries	BoO
Agor	Demon Duke – West Day	Stg, ThG, BoTS
Agōran (Venus)	Venus – Alternative Name	Hyg
Agounsael/Agoun (Saturn)	Saturn – Alternative Name	Hyg
Agra	Angel – Third Heaven, serving Rhtial	ShR
Agra	Demon Duke – South by West Night	Stg, ThG, BoTS
Agramouēl/Agrammaēl/Agrakoēl (Luna)	Luna – Alternative Name	Hyg
Agrasinden	Angel – Moon/Monday	SR
Agrial	Angel – Second Encampment, first Heaven Angel – Seventh Step, second Heaven	ShR
Agrippa	Ministering Familiar/Mystery	67M
Agrippas	Demon	ACM: Berlin 8313

Agrpponer/ Apriponar	Angel – Plant Ruler	*BoW*
Agrital	Angel Prince – fourth Heaven, Fire	*ShR*
Aguel	Angel – Adar	*SR*
Agusita	Angel – Spring	*BM*
Agyron	Demon Prince of Darkness	*oADS*
Aha	Angel – Dominations	*67M*
Aha	Spirit – Fire	*67M*
Ahabhon	Servant Spirit	*Abm*
Aha'arehies	Spirit – North	*SRH*
Ahadha	Supportive Planetary Spirit – Sun	*SSM*
Ahaeb	Angel	*67M*
Ahaij	Spirit – Mercury	*67M*
Ahaozpi	Enochian Senior – East	*TBA*
Ahedierier	Angel – Ruler of Preservation of Crops	*SRH*
Ahel	Spirit – Moon	*67M*
Ahenatos	Spirt – Earth	*67M*
Aherom	Servant Spirit	*Abm*
Ahesiel	Demon Prince – East under Oriens	*KoN*
Ahesin	Angel	*VJL*
Ahgiih	Angel – Seventh Encampment, first Heaven	*ShR*
Ahiel	Angel – Jupiter/Thursday	*SR*
Ahisdophiel	Demon – Count Palatine	*MNeI*
Ahyw Psqtyh	Angel King – Ruler of the twelve Princes	*SoM*
Aiakos	Underworld Judge	PGM IV:1390-1495
Aial	Angel – Fifth Step, second Heaven	*ShR*
Aidesos (Jupiter)	Jupiter – Alternative Name	*Hyg*
Aiediat	Intelligence – Mercury	*SGT, SSG*
Aiel	Angel Fourth Heaven Sunday – North, Spring Angel – Aries Spirit – Sun	*Hmn, KoSR, SoS, BoO, GAG, ArP, BoTS, tM*
Aierōnthi	First of seven Pole Lords of Heaven	PGM IV:475-829
Aikrit	Angel – Second Encampment, first Heaven	*ShR*

Ailial	Angel – Third Heaven, serving Dlqial	ShR
Aimanaton (Mars)	Mars – Alternative Name	Hyg
Aimeh	Ministering Familiar/Mystery	67M
Aimik	Angel – Third Encampment, first Heaven	ShR
Ainik	Angel – Third Encampment, first Heaven	ShR
Aion	Greek/Mithraic God of Time	PGM I:42-195, I:262-347, IV:475-829, IV:1115-1166, IV:1167-1226, IV:2241-2358, IV:3125-3171, V:96-172, V:459-489, VII:370-373, XII:201-269, XIII:1-343, XIII:734-1077; SM: P. Ant. II.66
Aioutha	Spirit – Moon	ACM: L. Anastasi 9
Aisturti	Angel – Second Encampment, first Heaven	ShR
Ainath	Demon – North	Hug
Aira	Enochian Angel – North, serving first lesser Angle	TBA
Aithridōr	Demon – Tuesday Hour two	Hyg
Aitmial	Angel – Second Encampment, first Heaven	ShR
Ajel	Genii – 3° Leo	ArP
Akaba	Angel – Venus	GAG
Akaēl/Okaēl	Angel – Tuesday Hour six, South	Hyg
Akaēl	Demon – Wednesday Hour twenty	Hyg
Akahim	Servant Spirit	Abm
Akal	Angel – Third Encampment, first Heaven Angel – Malachim, under Dohel	ShR, SRH
Akalata	Angel	ACM: H. Kopt. 679
Akanef	Servant Spirit	Abm
Akanitē (Jupiter)	Jupiter – Alternative Name	Hyg
Akar/Arkigē/Arkygi	Demon – West	Hyg
Akaultu	Angel	SoM
Akeberon	Spirit – East in Spring, Summer	SRH

ABBREVIATIONS

Akemor	Angel – Malachim, under Dohel	*SRH*
Akentael	Angel over the Stars	*ACM*: BN Turin
Akesely	Servant Spirit	*Abm*
Akesether	Angel – Malachim, under Ayigeda	*SRH*
Akētoēl	Angel – Monday Hour fifteen	*Hyg*
Akhistal	Demon – Monday Hour eleven	*Hyg*
Akhliarē/Akhkabar	East Wind in Spring	*BoW*
Akhlē (Mars)	Mars – Alternative Name	*Hyg*
Akhlitōn/Ekhleton/Akhiēton/Akhlitōl	Demon – Tuesday Hour thirteen, sixteen	*Hyg*
Akhnaēl	Angel – Plant Ruler	*BoW*
Akhogisth	Demon – South	*Hyg*
Akhōniōth/Akhōniōkh/Akhonioth	Demon – South	*Hyg*
Akhrikhi	North Wind – Sun	*BoW*
Akhripal (Sun)	Sun – Alternative Name	*Hyg*
Akhthiob/Akhthiōth/Akhthēsōb/Akhthiokh	Demon – West	*Hyg*
Akhyzi/Arkhi	Spirit – East	*Hyg*
Akinbola	Angel	*Hyg*
Aknsp	Angel – Third Heaven, serving Rhtial	*ShR*
Akorok	Servant Spirit	*Abm*
Akosgō/Aggosko	Spirit – West	*Hyg*
Akouraph/Akouēraph/Akourphirixio	Demon – North	*Hyg*
Akpp	Angel – Tenth Step, second Heaven	*ShR*
Akr	Angel – Seventh Encampment, first Heaven	*ShR*
Akrael	Angel over Sea	*ACM*: BN Turin
Akramata	Holy Creature of the Throne (two of four)	*ACM*: H. Kopt. 686
Akrokh/Akrōk	Demon – Saturday Hour fourteen	*Hyg*
Aktarya/Actarie/Aqtaraja	Spirit	*Pic*

Aktiōphis/Aktiōphi	Moon Goddess	PGM IV:2441-2621, IV:2622-2707, IV:2708-2784, IV:2891-2942, VII:981-993, PDM XIV:675-694
Akton	Demon – Decan twenty-four	*ToS*
Akuel	Angel	*ACM*: Moen 3
Akutael	Angel	*ACM*: BN Turin
Akynakiēl/Akinatiēl/Akinakiēl	Angel – Monday Hour fifteen	*Hyg*
Akzan	Angel Encampment Head – sixth Heaven, West	*ShR*
Al	Angel – First Encampment, first Heaven Angel – Malachim, under Avorpheniel/under Dohel	*ShR, SRH*
Alaashh	Angel – Third Encampment, first Heaven	*ShR*
Alaazr	Angel – Third Step, second Heaven	*ShR*
Alabanaēl (Mars)	Mars – Alternative Name	*Hyg*
Alabxatas	Angel – Joy and Divination	*CoMS*
Alachuc/Alachus	Angel – Night Hour eleven	*Stg, ArP*
Aladiah/Aladiel/Aladjah	Angel – Shem ten	*KoSU, 3BOP, GoeR, JMR, SaS, tM*
Aladim	Angel – Moon	*LL*
Alael	Angel – First Heaven, North	*SR*
Alaēl	Demon – West and Aries	*Hyg*
Alafy	Servant Spirit	*Abm*
Alal	Angel – First Encampment, first Heaven	*ShR*
Alaliah/Asaliah	Angel – Shem forty-seven	*KoSU, 3BOP, GoeR, JMR, SaS, tM*
Alamyr (Jupiter)	Jupiter – Alternative Name	*Hyg*
Alaphar	Angel – Night Hour eleven	*Stg, ArP*
Alapion	Angel – Mercury, over Earth	*SR*
Alasignō/Alsignō (Jupiter)	Jupiter – Alternative Name	*Hyg*
Alastiel	Spirit Prince – West	*dN, BoO*
Alastor	Demon Executioner	*DI*
Alatez	Demon Count Palatine – West	*KoN*

Alath	Demon – Decan twenty-one	*ToS*
Alatiel	Angel – Mercury, over Water	*SR*
Alays	Night Devil	*oADS*
Albafortum	Spirit	*SR*
Albalal	Name of God	PGM IV:930-1114
Alband/Albanaēl (Mars)	Mars – Alternative Name	*Hyg*
Albanyxa/Albanixta/ Albanixa	Angel – Venus	*oADS*
Albaryth	Demon Deputy Ruler – North-East	*SSM*
Albedagryn	Angel – Sun/Sunday	*SR*
Albewe	Spirit Minister – Saturn	*BoO*
Albeylyn	Angel – Mars/Tuesday	*SR*
Albumalith	Spirit Attendant – Saturn	*EoN*
Albhadur	Demon Duke – North Day	*Stg, ThG, BoTS*
Albowarees	Spirit – Love/Sexual Attraction	*Pic*
Albumasar	Spirit Helper – Saturday	*CBoM*
Albunalich	Daemon Attendant – Saturn, North	*SBH*
Albus	Spirit	*KoN*
Albuyūn	Angel – Hour nine/Sagittarius	*BoW*
Alcall	Spirit Helper – Sunday	*CBoM*
Alcaroñ/Acharon/ Acheron	Spirit King	*BoO*
Alchibany/Alcybany	Daemon – Saturn, serving South-West Wind, North	*SBH*
Alcritrgasos	Spirit Familiar	*BoTS*
Aldrusy/Adrnsy/ Adrnsis	Demon Duke	*Stg, ThG*
Aldynatory/ Aldinatory	Demon King	*SSM*
Aleasi/Aleasy	Demon Duke – North Night	*Stg, ThG, BoTS*
Alebera Ayieh	Angel Prince – Autumn	*SRH*
Aleberiyavor	Angel Prince – Malachim, Tishri	*SRH*
Alebovi	Angel – Malachim, under Avorphenial	*SRH*
Aleche	Spirit – South	*oADS*
Aleches	Spirit – West	*oADS*

Alecto	Fury	3BOP, MNeI
Alegretus	Spirit	SSM
Aleguereth	Demon Senior	SSM
Alemheqenal	Angel Prince – Gate of Spirit of West	SRH
Alendir	Spirit	BoTS
Alendood	Enochian Senior – South	TBA
Alēnos/Ēlinos	Angel – Sunday Hour twenty-three	Hyg
Alepheron	Spirit – South in Summer	SRH
Alephi	Angel – Malachim, under Avorphenial/ under Dohel	SRH
Alepta	Spirit	GoA
Aleuia	Spirit	CoC
Alexa	Angel – Jupiter	GAG
Alferiel	Demon Duke – North-East	Stg, ThG
Alflas	Daemon – Saturn, serving South-West Wind, North	SBH
Alfrael	Angel – Day Hour ten	Stg, ArP
Algal	Spirit	SSM
Algar	Spirit – West	KoN
Algor	Demon – East	BOS, BoO, oADS
Alhea/Alheabesyn	Spirit of the Thumb	MHN, CBoM
Alhectega	Enochian Senior - North	TBA
Alheniel	Commoner Spirit	MNeI
Alial	Angel – Third Encampment, first Heaven Angel – Third Step, second Heaven Angel Prince – Fourth Heaven, Fire Angel Encampment Head – Sixth Heaven, East Angel – Malachim, under Ayigeda/under Dohel	ShR, SRH
Aliaml	Angel – Jupiter	GAG
Alianos (Sun)	Sun – Alternative Name	Hyg
Alibeat/Alibiat	Spirit – Third Mansion of Moon Ring	AE, oADS, tSoS
Aliberri	Spirit of the Thumb	MHN
Alibis	Spirit – Tuesday	BoSC
Alick	Spirit – Presidentail Counsellor, South	BoTS

Alidator/Alēdator/ Alidapar	Demon- Saturday	*Hyg*
Aliel	Demon Duke – West by South Day	*Stg, ThG, BoTS*
Aliel/Liel	Duke – West by North pre-Midnight	*Stg, ThG, BoTS*
Alien	Angel – Malachim, under Avorphenial	*SRH*
Aliesen	Angel Magistrate – Malachim	*SRH*
Alieses	Angel – Malachim, under Plemiya	*SRH*
Alilgon	Spirit – Presidential Counsellor	*BoTS*
Alimiel (Arymyel)	Angel – Chora one	*ArA*
Alinanat	Demon King – Sunday	*KoN*
Alingon	Demon	*BoO*
Aliopon (Venus)	Venus – Alternative Name	*Hyg*
Alioub (Saturn)	Saturn – Alternative Name	*Hyg*
Alis	Angel – Saturn	*GAG*
Alisaf	Angel – Marchesvan	*SR*
Aliscor/Aliseon	Spirit	*GoPH, GV*
Aliss	Angel – Fourth Encampment, first Heaven	*ShR*
Alka	Angel – Venus	*GAG*
Alkadeus	Spirit	*oADS*
Alketes	Spirit	*GAG*
Alkyone	Nymph – Pleiades	PGM IV:2241-2358
Alkyzub	Spirit – Venus	*TV*
Allayn	Angel – Seventh Altitude (Libra)	*Alm*
Allazool	Angel	*ToS*
Allea	Angel – Venus	*GAG*
Alleion	Angel – Sun	*BARC*
Allekto ('Unceasing')	One of the Furies (Erinyes)	PGM IV:2785-2890
Allēlinel	Angel	*Hyg*
Allenzozoff	Spirit Prince	*BoMS*
Allocer/Alloces/ Alocer	Demon Duke	*PmD, DoW, Goe, DI*
Alleborith	Demon – Decan thirty	*ToS*
Allēopōn/Aliōpan (Venus)	Venus – Alternative Name	*Hyg*
Aller	Spirit – Mirror	*CoMS*

Allogor (Eligos/ Eligor?)	Demon Duke	BOS, BoO
Alluph	Servant Spirit	Abm
Allybyn/Alybyn	Spirit Prince – under Alyzaire	oADS
Almadiel	Demon Duke – Night Hour two	Stg, ThG
Almadiel	Earth Spirit	MNeI
Almanos/Almanath/ Almynat (Mars)	Mars – Alternative Name	Hyg
Almas/Ahuas	Angel – Day Hour eleven	Stg, ArP
Almarazin	Angel – Treasure seeking	dN
Almasor/Almator/ Almatiel	Demon Knight	Stg, ThG
Almaza	Demon Senior	SSM
Almaziel	Angel	VJL
Almazon	Spirit – Venus	dN
Almederie	Spirit	GAG
Almeēl	Angel	Hyg
Almemel	Angel – Saturn, over Water	SR
Almeos	Angel – Eleventh Altitude (Aquarius)	Alm
Almerizel/Almerisel	Angel – Day Hour eleven	Stg, ArP
Almesiel/Amesiel/ Alinesiel	Demon Duke – West	Stg, ThG
Alminial	Angel – Fourth Encampment, first Heaven	ShR
Almiras	Angel – Master of Invisibility	KoSA
Almischak (Almisck?)	Spirit Prince	EUM
Almisck/Almisckakos	Spirit	AAAA
Almodab	Spirit King – Monday	MHN
Almodar	Demon Duke – Y1	Stg, ThG
Almodar	Angel – Night Hour two	Stg, ArP
Almoel	Demon Duke – North-West Night	Stg, ThG, BoTS
Almonoyz/ Almonoyzod	Angel – Night Hour three	Stg, ArP
Almucatyl	Angel – Saturn	SSM
Almuchabzar	Spirit Prince	AAAA
Almux	Angel – Sivan	SR
Almyon	Angel – Saturn/Saturday	SR

ABBREVIATIONS

Al-Nash's Daughters	Spirits of Three Tail Stars of Ursa Major	*Pic*
Alnay	Angel – Fifth Altitude (Leo)	*Alm*
Alnitkal	Angel Encampment Head – sixth Heaven, West	*ShR*
Alnu	Angel – First Encampment, first Heaven	*ShR*
Alogil/Alogill/ Alogiel/ Aloggiell	Servant Spirit	*Abm, MRC*
Aloheqena	Angel Prince – Gate of Spirit of West	*SRH*
Alos	Angel – Sun	*BARC*
Aloson/Eloson	Servant Spirit	*Abm, MRC*
Alosy	Angel – Sun	*BARC*
Alou/Aloi (Jupiter)	Jupiter – Alternative Name	*Hyg*
Alous	Spirit King	*BoO*
Alousi/Alhuzy	Prince of Ishim and Apostle	*3BOP, MRC*
Alparē/Adpare	Angel – Plant Ruler	*BoW*
Alpas	Servant Spirit	*Abm*
Alpha[413]	Angel – Ninth Altitude (Sagittarius)	*Alm*
Alphaneos	Angel – Eleventh Altitude (Aquarius)	*Alm*
Alpharaym	Angel – Second Altitude (Taurus)	*Alm*
Alphariza/Aphiriza (Alpharaym)	Angel – Chora two	*ArA*
Alphas/Malapas (Malphas)	Demon President	*NML*
Alphasis/Alphassis	Demon Messenger – West Spirit Messenger – West	*BOS, BoO, BoTS*
Alpherez	Treasure Spirit	*BoTS*
Alphlas	Punishing Wind	*SSM*
Alphod	Angel – Malachim, under Avorphenial	*SRH*
Alphrois	Spirit	*GV*
Alphus/Alphis	Spirit – North, War and Martial Power	*KoN*
Alpi	Angel – First Encampment, first Heaven Angel – Third Encampment, first Heaven	*ShR*

---

[413] Alpha is more commonly used as part of a divine name, with Omega, as the first and last (letters of the Greek alphabet).

Alpial	Angel – Second Encampment, first Heaven Angel – Fourth Step, second Haven	ShR
Alpntus	Angel – Fifth Encampment, first Heaven	ShR
Alprt	Angel – Seventh Encampment, first Heaven	ShR
Alraundl	Evil Treasure Spirit	MRC
Alredessym	Spirit of the Thumb	MHN
Alscini	Angel – First Heaven, South	SR
Alscius	Angel – First Heaven, West	SaS
Alsdq	Angel – Tenth Step, second Heaven	ShR
Alserin	Angel – Venus/Friday	SR
Alsfiton	Angel – Saturn/Saturday	SR
Alson	Angel – Marchesvan	SR
Alstas	Wind Spirit	GAG
Altaine	Demon Prince	GoPH
Altanor	Servant Spirit	Abm
Altarib	Angel – Winter	EoN, tSoS
Altekharix/ Tekharyx/ Tekharēr	Angel – Saturday Hour twelve	Hyg
Altel	Angel – Fourth Heaven, East	SaS
Altheros	Spirit	ACM: Cairo 45060
Althes	Demon	MHN
Althor	Duke – West by North pre-Noon	Stg, ThG, BoTS
Altibam	Wind Spirit	GAG
Altidōn	Demon – Friday Hour eleven	Hyg
Altim	Angel – Tishrei	SR
Altramat	Demon	MHN
Altybany	Punishing Wind	SSM
Aluiel	Spirit	GV
Alun	Angel – First Encampment, first Heaven	ShR
Aluses	Demon Duke – West, used by Faust)	KoN
Alvedio	Angel Minister of Air – Wednesday	BoO
Alxim	Angel – Iyar	SR
Alydee	Spirit Minister – Saturn	BoO

ABBREVIATIONS

Alyel	Angel – Mars/Tuesday	SR
Alymdrictels	Spirit	GV
Alymon	Angel – Potestates	67M
Alymos	Angel – Twelfth Altitude (Pisces)	Alm
Alymos	Spirit Prince – under Alyzaire	oADS
Alyzaire	Spirit Prince – East Altitude	oADS
Alzamy	Angel – Tebet	SR
Alzeyeil	Angel – Venus/Friday	SR
Ama	Servant Spirit	Abm
Amaamilim	Angel – Moon	LL
Amabael	Angel – Winter	EoN, Hmn, KoSR, tSoS, MC, GAG, GoeR, tM
Amabel (Amabael?)	Angel – Winter	MHN
Amabiel/Amabihel/Amaliel	Angel – Tuesday Spirit – Mars Angel Minister of Air – Friday Presiding Spirit – Mars	SBH, EoN, Hmn, KoSR, CBoM, SoS, BoO, BM, tSoS, GAG, PO, tM, SGT, SSG
Amabosar	Spirit – Venus Spirit Prince	TV, EUM
Amachem	Spirit	ACM: Hay 10391
Amacia	Angel – Ab	SR
Amacyon	Angel – Sun	GAG
Amada	Demon Duke	BOS, BoO
Ama-das/Amadai	Spirit – Sun	BoO
Amaday	Angel – Spring	BM
Amadiel/Amediel	Peasant Spirit, Fire	MNeI
Amadyel	Angel – Sunday/Sun	KoSR
Amadyeyl	Angel – Mars/Tuesday	SR
Amael	Angel – Third Heaven, East	SR, SSM, SaS
Amakbuel	Gatekeeper of Hell	MRC
Amal	Demon King – Tuesday	KoN
Amaltea	Spirit – Sibyl (seven of ten)	GV
Amaluch	Angel – Adar	SR
Amalym/Amatim	Angel – Day Hour eight	Stg, ArP
Amalzatin	Angel – Treasure seeking	dN

Amamil	Servant Spirit	*Abm*
Amanael	Spirit – Dawn	*ACM*: L. Anastasi 9
Amanbilch/ Amanbith/ Hunambilich	Spirit – twenty-fifth Mansion of the Moon Ring	*AE, tSoS*
Amandiel	Demon Duke – North-West Day	*Stg, ThG, BoTS*
Amanou	Angel Guardian	*ACM*: Hay 10391
Amap	Angel – Fourth Encampment, first Heaven	*ShR*
Amaph	Angel – Malachim, under Plemiya Angel Magistrat – Malachim	*SRH*
Amaphriēl	Angel	*Hyg*
Amarael	Spirit – Dawn	*ACM*: L. Anastasi 9
Amariel	Angel Ruler – Sivan	*SR*
Amarzyom	Angel – Thrones	*67M*
Amas	Spirit – Minister of Love	*oADS*
Amasiel/Armasiel	Demon Under Duke	*Stg, ThG*
Amatiel/Amtiel	Angel – Spring	*EoN, Hmn, KoSR, BM, MC, GAG, GoeR, tM*
Amatyel	Angel – Spring	*MHN*
Amatziel	Angel	*Hyg*
Amay	Demon	*oADS*
Amaymon/ Amemon/ Mayrary/ Aymoymon/ Moymon/Amaimon/ Amayon/Aymemon/ Mayemon	Demon King – North or South, Noon, or East Demon Duke	*ToSC, SSM, Abm, BoC, KoSA, 3BOP, oADS, BOS, BoO, LdE, PmD, EBAM, DoW, BM, MC, Goe, BoTS, JMR, GoPH, SaS, MNeI, KoN, PO, VMN, tM, BD*
Amazael	Angel – Treasure seeking	*dN*
Amazeroth	Spirit Prince	*BoMS*
Ambaēl	Angel – Monday Hour twenty-one	*Hyg*
Ambayerin	Angel – Venus/Friday	*SR*
Ambri	Demon Duke – South	*Stg, ThG*
Ambriel	Angel – Gemini Angel – Night Hour twelve Genius – Albus	*Stg, 3BOP, tSoS, MC, ArP, JMR, SaS, Thm, PO, tM*

ABBREVIATIONS

Amdalycyn	Angel – Moon/Monday	*SR*
Amduscias/Amducias	Demon Duke	*PmD, DoW, Goe, DI*
Ameclo	Spirit	*GV*
Amediel	Demon Duke – Hour seven of fifteen	*Stg, ThG*
Amediell	Angel – Mansion eight and Cancer	*BoO*
Ameinyn	Angel – Mercury/Wednesday	*SR*
Amek	Angel – Malachim, under Dohel	*SRH*
Amekranebecheo Thōyth	Name of Helios in third Hour	PGM IV:1596-1715
Amelech	Evil Spirit	*3BOP*
Amelial	Angel Minister – Malachim	*SRH*
Amelson/Amelzon/Amelzom	Angel – Night Hour eight	*Stg, ArP*
Amenadiel/Ameradiel	Demon Emperor – West	*Stg, ThG, BoTS*
Amenayl	Angel – Malachim, under Plemiya	*SRH*
Amenegenavoth	Angel – Malachim, Flames of Fire	*SRH*
Amenehi	Angel Magistrate – Malachim	*SRH*
Amengenan	Angel Minister – Malachim	*SRH*
Ameniel	Angel – Day Hour one	*Stg, ArP*
Amephial	Angel – Malachim, under Dohel	*SRH*
Amerany	Angel – Night Hour one	*Stg, ArP*
Amereneh	Spirit – North in Spring	*SRH*
Amerial	Angel – Malachim, Ayer	*SRH*
Ames	Angel – Mars	*BARC*
Ameta/Amel	Demon Duke – North-West Day	*Stg, ThG, BoTS*
Ameyl	Angel – Sun/Sunday Angel	*SR, LL*
Amguel	Demon Prince	*VJL*
Amiaden	Demon Prince	*GoPH*
Amial	Angel – Fourth Encampment, first Heaven Angel Magistrate – Malachim	*ShR, SRH*
Amiel	Demon Duke – South-West Night Demon Duke – West Night	*Stg, ThG, BoTS*
Amiemial	Angel – Malachim, under Ayigeda	*SRH*
Amienial	Angel – Malachim over Fire and Flames	*SRH*

Amikal	Angel – Third Encampment, first Heaven	ShR
Amikh/Amēkh	Demon – Friday Hour ten	Hyg
Amikhilim	Angel – Moon	LL
Amileckar	Spirit Prince	BoMS
Amillis	Servant Spirit	Abm
Aminal	Angel – Eleventh Step, second Heaven	ShR
Aminual	Angel – Third Heaven, serving Dlqial	ShR
Amiōb	Angel	Hyg
Amiol	Angel – Mercury/Wednesday	SR
Amir/Amor/Akōr/Amōr	Demon – Thursday Hour six	Hyg
Amirafel	Spirit – South	SSM
Amiraphales	Spirit – Mountains and Bridges	KoN
Amiras	Top part of Barhoyas	Pic
Amisalog	Spirit Prince	MOAS
Amisiel	Angel – Day Hour five	Stg, ArP
Amisor	Angel	GV
Amixiel/Anixiel	Angel – Mansion three	3BOP, tSoS, JMR, SaS, MNeI, tM
Amlial	Angel Encampment Head – sixth Heaven, West	ShR
Amman	Spirit	ACM: Hay 10391
Ammiel/Mumiel	Angel – Night Hour seven	Stg, ArP
Ammon	Egyptian Creator God	PGM IV:2967-3006, IV:3007-3086, V:172-212, XII:96-106, LVII:1-37, CXXII:1-55; SM: P. Berol. Inv. 21243
Ammour/Amlyr	Angel – Plant Ruler	BoW
Amnalasfar	Punishing Wind	SSM
Amnator	Angel Minister – Love and Fornication	KoSA
Amnchial	Angel – Third Heaven, serving Ibnial	ShR
Amneal	Angel – Mercury/Wednesday	SR
Amnediel	Angel – Mansion eight	3BOP, tSoS, JMR, SaS, Thm, tM
Amngnan	Angel – Third Heaven, serving Dlqial	ShR

Amnhr	Angel – Fourth Encampment, first Heaven	*ShR*
Amnial	Angel – Second Step, second Heaven	*ShR*
Amniel	Demon Baron Foolish Spirit	*MNeI*
Amnixiel	Angel – Mansion twenty-eight Genius – Letitia	*3BOP, tSoS, JMR, SaS, Thm, tM*
Amnixiel	Commoner Spirit	*MNeI*
Amny	North Wind – Spring	*BoW*
Amocab	Punishing Wind	*SSM*
Amochap/Amocap	Daemon – Moon, serving West Wind; West	*SBH*
Amodiel	Demon Count Free Spirit – Whoring	*MNeI*
Amoel	Angel Minister	*ACM*: P. Mich. 593
Amok	Angel – Malachim, under Avorphenial/ under Dohel	*SRH*
Amolom	Servant Spirit	*Abm*
Amomium	Angel – Saturn	*GAG*
Amon	Egyptian King of the Gods	HB Jer 46:25
Amon/Aamon	Demon Marquis – East	*LdE, BOS, BoO, PmD, DoW, Goe, GG, BoSC, DI*
Amonayelin	Angel – Day Hour two	*LL*
Amonazy/Amonzy	Angel – Night Hour six	*Stg, ArP*
Amoneh/Amoniem	Spirit – North in Spring	*SRH*
Amoneher	Angel – Malachim, under Plemiya	*SRH*
Amor	Spirit of Love	*BoO*
Amos	Angel Minister – Love and Fornication	*KoSA*
Amoval	Angel – Malachim, under Plemiya	*SRH*
Amox	Enochian Angel – South, serving second lesser Angle	*TBA*
Amoyr	Demon Duke – West by South Night	*Stg, ThG, BoTS*
Ampatzout	Demon	*TosC*
Ampheron	Demon	*GoPH*
Amphiaraos	Greek Underworld God	PGM IV:1390-1495
Ampholion	Servant Spirit	*Abm*
Amphou	Demon – Saturday Hour twenty-one	*Hyg*

Amphou/Aphōn	Demon – Saturday Hour twenty	*Hyg*
Amphrenomel	Plant Spirit – Ivy	*GS*
Ampira (Mars)	Mars – Alternative Name	*Hyg*
Ampyzanoliem (Mars)	Mars – Alternative Name	*Hyg*
Amrael	Angel – Tammuz	*SR*
Amrial	Angel – Fifth Step, second Heaven	*ShR*
Amriel	Demon Duke – Y2	*Stg, ThG*
Amriel	Angel – Night Hour three	*Stg, ArP*
Ammrrehar	Spirit – Ring of seventh Mansion of the Moon	*tSoS*
Amruel	Plant Spirit – Heather	*GS*
Amstial	Angel Encampment Head – sixth Heaven, West	*ShR*
Amuath	Angel	*H.O.* Lange Text
Amuhael	Angel	*SoM*
Amuk	Angel – First Encampment, first Heaven	*ShR*
Amun/Amoun	Egyptian Creator God	PGM I.42-195, III:424-466, IV:154-285, XII:376-396, XXI:1-29, PDM XIV:150-231, XIV:239-295, XIV:395-427, XIV:585-593, XIV:695-700, XIV:1097-1103, Suppl. 60-101, Suppl. 138-149; *ACM*: P. Mich. 136
Amuntuliel	Angel – Ab	*SR*
Amurael	Angel – Venus, over Earth	*SR*
Amutiel	Angel – Mansion nineteen	*3BOP, tSoS, JMR, SaS, Thm, tM*
Amutiel/Amudiel	Noble Spirit, Fire	*MNeI*
Amvelrah	Plant Spirit – Birch	*GS*
Amvradel	Stone Spirit – Emerald	*GS*
Amy/Auns	Demon President	*PmD, DoW, Goe*
Amyel	Angel – Bisertilis Angel – Jupiter/Thursday	*SR*

Amymaryil	Angel – Day Hour two	*LL*
Amynyel	Angel – Fire	*SSM, SR*
Amyrafel	Spirit	*SSM*
Amyter	Angel – Ab	*SR*
An	Spirit – Son of Sons of Light	*dHM*
Ana/Anas	Spirit Prince – under Alyzaire	*oADS*
Anaa	Enochian Angel – South, over second lesser Angle	*TBA*
Anaabbus	Wind Spirit	*GAG*
Anabbeyl	Angel – Tenth Altitude (Capricorn)	*Alm*
Anabiell	Angel	*oADS*
Anabo	Angel – Eighth Altitude (Scorpio)	*Alm*
Anaboel	Angel Steward	*ACM*: Hay 10122
Anacor/Hanacor	Angel	*NA, tSoS*
Anadir	Servant Spirit	*Abm*
Anael/Amael/Anaël/ Anaêl/Anaell	Angel/Archangel – Venus, Friday, Sun, Love Angel – Tebet Ruler of Day Hour two fourth Heaven Sunday – West, Spring Angel Commander first Heaven, South first Heaven, Moon Intelligence – Venus	*SM*: P. Med. I.20; *ACM*: P. Prague 1; H. Kopt. 544, Berlin 11347; Hay 10434, Bodl C(P)4, Würzburg 42, Hay 10391, Cairo 45060, P. Mich. 593, L. Anastasi 9; *SSM, SR, SBH, EoN, Hmn, Hyg, B7R, KoSR, SoS, MHN, tSoS. dSS, Stg, ADS, CBoM, oADS, BoO, DoW, TV, BM, MC, GAG, GoeR, ArP, JMR, 9CK, BoTS, SaS, GoA, GV, VMN, PO, CoMS, tM, CBMS*
Anaēl/Banaēl/ Thanaēl	Angel – Saturday Hour twenty-four	*Hyg*
Anael	Demon Duke – South by West Night Demon – Prince-Elector, Venus	*Stg, ThG, BoTS, MNeI*
Anael	Spirit Messenger – Moon Presiding Spirit – Venus	*SGT, SSG*

Anæo	Enochian Angel – North, over third lesser Angle	TBA
Anag Biathi	Angel	PGM XIII:343-646
Anagnostos	Servant Spirit	Abm
Anaheed/Anihid (Zahra/Zuhra, Persian)	Spirit Queen – Venus	Pic, SSG
Anahel/Avahel	Angel – Fifth Heaven, West Angel Prince – third Heaven Angel – Fourth Heaven, West	SSM, SaS
Anaib	Angel – First Heaven, South	KoSR
Anailim	Angel – Moon	LL
Analos	Angel	CoC, tSoS
Anamalon	Servant Spirit	Abm
Ananael	Angel Angel Minister	ACM: Bodl C(P)4, Cairo 45060, P. Mich. 593, L. Anastasi 9
Ananke	Greek Goddess of Necessity	SM: P. Gaál
Anaoth	Angel	ACM: Moen 3
Anaphyn	Angel – Tenth Altitude (Capricorn)	Alm
Anapion/Amapion	Angel – Night Hour seven	Stg, ArP
Anapuel	Angel	ACM: Oriental 5899
Anareton	Spirit	CBoM
Anas	Angel – Twelfth Altitude (Pisces)	Alm
Anasiel	Angel – Jupiter/Thursday	EoN
Anasta	Demon – South	GoPH
Anataliel	Angel	ACM: Oriental 5899
Anatel	Spirit – Gate of the East	ACM: L. Anastasi 9
Anathael	Angel Minister	ACM: P. Mich. 593
Anathai	Angel – Moon	KoSR
Anathamia	Angel	VJL
Anathana	Angel – Treasure seeking	dN
Anathanael	Angel	KoN
Anatiel	Angel – Venus	CoMS
Anatnabie	Wind Spirit	GAG

Anatokh/Anapōkh/ Anapokh	Demon – North	*Hyg*
Anatreth	Demon – Decan twenty-five	*ToS*
Anatziph	Angel	*Hyg*
Anaur	Angel – Third Encampment, first Heaven	*ShR*
Anavel/Annavel/ Annauel	Angel – Shem sixty-three	*KoSU, 3BOP, GoeR, JMR, SaS, tM*
Anavok	Angel – Malachim, under Dohel	*SRH*
Anax	Spirit	*ACM: Cairo 45060*
Anay	Angel – Eighth Altitude (Scorpio) Angel – Twelfth Altitude (Pisces)	*Alm*
Anay	Spirit Prince – under Alyzaire	*oADS*
Anaya	Angel – Nisan	*SR, tSoS*
Anayenyn	Angel – Moon/Monday	*SR*
Anayl/Anaol	Angel first Heaven Monday – South Spirit – Moon	*Hmn, SoS, BoO, GAG, BoTS*
Anaym	Angel – Eighth Altitude (Scorpio)	*Alm*
Anayton	Demon King	*SSM*
Anazarda	Spirit	*GV*
Anazimur	Throne Angel (five of seven)	*SaS*
Anbur	Angel – Second Encampment, first Heaven	*ShR*
Ancarilyn	Angel – Mercury/Wednesday	*SR*
Ancason	Angel – Nisan	*SR, tSoS*
Ancor/Hancor	Angel	*NA, CoC, tSoS*
Ancor	Spirit – Iron Artificer	*oADS*
Ancuyel	Angel – Jupiter/Thursday	*SR*
Andalashim	Angel – Moon	*LL*
Andalasin	Angel – Moon	*LL*
Andalees	Spirit – Love/Sexual Attraction	*Pic*
Andas/Andax/ Andras	Angel Minister of Air – Sunday Spirit Attendant – Sun Angel – Sivan	*EoN, Hmn, KoSR, SR, GAG, GoeR, BoTS, tM*
Andeles	Demon Companion – Thursday	*KoN*
Andgnur	Angel Prince – fifth Heaven, Month of Kislev	*ShR*
Andonin	Angel – Moon	*LL*

Andrachos	Servant Spirit	*Abm*
Andragias	Demon	*GAG*
Andraphor/Adraphor (Sun)	Sun – Alternative Name	*Hyg*
Andras/Vandras	Demon Marquis	*NML, PmD, DoW, Goe, DI*
Andrealphus/ Andralfas/ Androalphus	Demon Marquis	*LdE, PmD, DoW, Goe*
Andromalchinwe	Spirit Prince – under Alyzaire	*oADS*
Andromalcus	Spirit	*oADS*
Andromalius	Demon Earl	*Goe, BoTS*
Androphag/ Androphaēl	Demon – Monday Hour fifteen, sixteen	*Hyg*
Androphagēs/ Androphai	Demon – Monday Hour seventeen	*Hyg*
Androphai	Demon – Monday Hour eighteen	*Hyg*
Andros	Demon Duke – Day Hour three and Night Hour three	*Stg, ThG*
Androyce/ Andramalcus	Spirit of the Thumb	*oADS*
Andruchiel/ Andrucha/ Andruchas	Demon Chief Duke	*Stg, ThG*
Andyron	Demon	*MHN*
Andyton	Spirit	*SSM*
Aneboshel	Angel – Malachim, under Dohel	*SRH*
Anebynnyl	Angel – Sun/Sunday	*SR*
Anech	Spirit – South	*SSM*
Anechal	Angel Prince – Gate of Spirit of West	*SRH*
Anekier	Angel – Malachim, under Ayigeda	*SRH*
Anelim/A-Anolita	Spirit – third Mansion of Moon Ring	*AE, oADS*
Anēphōr	Demon – Friday Hour twenty-four	*Hyg*
Anepo (Great Anubis)	Title of Anubis	PDM XIV:295-308, XIV:805-840
Anereton	Angel	*GV*
Anet	Demon	*ToSC*

ABBREVIATIONS

Anēthakh/Ainkhath	Angel – Plant Ruler	*BoW*
Anethegenod	Angel Prince – Kislev	*SRH*
Angara	Spirit King – Mars	*Pic, SSG*
Angarozan	Angel – Moon	*LL*
Angels of Love and Charity	Angel	*GoA*
Angerion	Spirit – Skull Divination	*ArPh*
Angial	Angel – Third Heaven, serving Dlqial	*ShR*
Angrecton	Angel	*GV*
Anguell	Angel	*BoO*
Anhael	Angel – Fifth Heaven, West	*SR, MNeI*
Anial	Angel Prince – Gate of Spirit of North	*SRH*
Aniel	Angel	PDM XIV:489-515, XIV:516-527
Aniel/Kaniel	Angel – Friday Hour seven	*Hyg*
Aniel	Angel – Shem thirty-seven	*KoSU, 3BOP, GoeR, JMR, SAS, tM*
Aniel/Aquiel	Angel – Fourth Heaven Sunday, North, Spring Angel fourth Heaven – North Ministering Spirit – Sun	*EoN, Hmn, KoSR, BoO, GAG, BoTS, MNeI, SaS, tM, CBMS*
Aniel	Demon Duke – South by East Day, West Day	*Stg, ThG, BoTS*
Aniel	Genii – 6° Cancer, 6° Leo	*ArP*
Aninei	Angel – Moon	*LL*
Aniquel	Demon Prince	*SoM*
Anisel	Demon Prince	*VJL*
Anisi (Jupiter)	Jupiter – Alternative Name	*Hyg*
Aniyel	Angel – Tebet	*SR*
Ankanitei/Anikaninte (Jupiter)	Jupiter – Alternative Name	*Hyg*
Anlel	Angel	*ACM*: BN Turin
Anmanineylyn	Angel – Moon/Monday	*SR*
Anmri	Angel – Fourth Encampment, first Heaven	*ShR*
Anna/Annam/Aman	Spirit – second Mansion of Moon Ring	*AE, tSoS*
Anna/Amna	Spirit of the Thumb	*MHN, CBoM*
Annabyel/Amiabyel	Angel Subordinate – Mars	*SSM*

Annobath	Demon Lord and Governor	BOS, BoO
Annoboth/Anaboth/ Annabath/ Annobathe	Demon – North Spirit – Presidential Counsellor, North	BOS, BoO, oADS, BoTS
Annrafael	Spirit	oADS
Anoch	Angel – Cherubim/Seraphim	67M
Anodaē	Demon – Sunday Hour one	Hyg
Anodoin	Enochian Senior – South	TBA
Anōph/Anoph/Anpe (Jupiter)	Jupiter – Alternative Name	Hyg
Anoph	Angel – Malachim, under Avorphenial	SRH
Anoster	Demon – Decan twenty-nine	ToS
Anouth	Names of Bes	PGM VII:222-249, VIII:64-110, CII:1-17
Anoyr	Demon Duke – East	Stg, ThG
Anqiu	Angel – Fifth Encampment, first Heaven	ShR
Anqnihim	Angel – Sun/Sunday	SR
Anrach	Angel – Fifth Altitude (Leo)	Alm
Anramuel	Angel – Right Hand of God	ACM: H. Kopt. 686
Anrylin	Angel – Venus/Friday	SR
Ansoel/Ansol	Demon Duke – North-West Night	Stg, ThG, BoTS
Ansoryor/Antyor	Demon Lord	BOS, BoO
Antatax/Tantax	Angel – Sun	tSoS
Antēouz (Sun)	Sun – Alternative Name	Hyg
Anthēros/ Stanthyros/ Stautheros	Demon – Friday Hour fourteen	Hyg
Anthychoy	Angel – Third Altitude (Gemini)	Alm
Antichrist	Demon Chief	tM
Antikon/Antiour (Sun)	Sun – Alternative Name	Hyg
Antologan	Pygmy Prince	MNeI
Antoor/Antur/ Ancora	Spirit – Sun	Pic
Antquiel	Angel – Jupiter/Thursday	SR
Antrakuel	Angel – Left Hand of God	ACM: H. Kopt. 686

Antyim/Antyym/ Ancytym	Angel – Mercury	*LR*
Antzi (Jupiter)	Jupiter – Alternative Name	*Hyg*
Anubis/Anoubis/ Anoup	Egyptian Jackal-headed God, Ruler of Underworld and Daemons	PGM I:247-262, IV:1-25, IV:94-153, IV:296-466, IV:1390-1495, VII:319-334, VII:540-578, XII:469-473, XII:474-479, XII:480-495, XVIIa:1-25, XXXII:1-19, XXXVI:333-360, CXVII fr.9, PDM XIV:1-92, XIV:150-231, XIV:239-295, XIV:395-427, XIV:528-553, XIV:554-562, XIV:585-593, XIV:627-635, LXI:1-30, Suppl. 60-101, Suppl. 101-116, Suppl. 117-130, Suppl. 138-149, Suppl. 185-208; *SM*: PSI I.28, T. Cairo Mus. JdE 48217, T. Louvre Inv. E 27145, P. Mich. Inv. 6925, T. Köln Inv. 1, P. Monac. II.28; *ACM*: Schmidt P., GMPP: 1-25, 93-154, Oxy. 1150, Berlin 11347
Anuk	Angel – First Encampment, first Heaven Angel – Seventh Encampment, first Heaven	*ShR*
Anulus	Angel – Second Heaven, West	*SR*
Anup	Angel – First Encampment, first Heaven	*ShR*
Anurecha	Spirit – Ring of seventh Mansion of the Moon	*AE*
Anyam	Angel – Potestates	*67M*

Anycor (Anacor)	Angel	*CoC*
Anyel	Angel – Fifth Heaven, North Angel – Second Season by Day	*SSM*
Anylos/Hanylos	Angel	*NA*
Anystis	Demon Count – North under Egyn	*KoN*
Anzeryer	Demon Senior	*SSM*
Aoaynnl	Spirit Minister, serving King Baligon	*dHM*
Aocel	Spirit of Treasure – South	*SSM*
Aoidiab	Spirit Minister, serving Prince Bornogo	*dHM*
Aol	Angel – Mercury/Wednesday	*SR*
Aōlōi (Jupiter)	Jupiter – Alternative Name	*Hyg*
Aomi	Enochian Angel – North, over fourth lesser Angle	*TBA*
Aonaes	Spirit of the twenty-four Waves	*BoSC*
Aooda/Ahude	Spirit	*Pic*
Aorachiel/ Adnachiel/ Aduachiel/ Advachiel/ Annachiel	Angel – Sagittarius Genius – Acquisito	*3BOP, tSoS, MC, JMR. SaS, Thm, PO, tM*
Aosal	Spirit	*EBAM*
Aot	Enochian Evil Spirit	*TBA*
Aou	Angel	*ACM*: H. Kopt. 679
Aozol	Spirit King	*BoO*
Apadiel	Demon – Prince-Elector, Mars and Caput Algol Wise Spirit Prince Palatine	*MNeI*
Apael	Angel	*Hyg*
Aparctias	North Wind	*Thm*
Apatiel/Apactiel	Peasant Spirit	*MNeI*
Apeste	Enochian Angel – South, serving first lesser Angle	*TBA*
Apgarēl/Aptarēl	Spirit	*BoW*
Aphael	Angel over Snow	*ACM*: BN Turin
Aphar	Enochian Angel – North, over second lesser Angle	*TBA*

Apheieyl	Angel – Venus/Friday	*SR*
Aphenok	Angel Magistrate – Malachim	*SRH*
Aphephial	Angel Prince – Knowledge	*SRH*
Aphethiel	Angel – Malachim ruling Dangerous Creatures	*SRH*
Aphhimoo	Plant Spirit – Marsh Mallow	*GS*
Aphiel	Genii – 9° Cancer, 9° Leo	*ArP*
Aphiel	Spirit Prince – Hunting	*MNeI*
Aphieri	Angel – Malachim, under Plemiya	*SRH*
Aphoneh	Angel – Malachim, under Avorphenial	*SRH*
Aphosien	Spirit – South in Autumn	*SRH*
Aphrieus	South-West by West Wind	*Thm*
Aphrodite/ Aphrodite-Urania	Greek Love Goddess	PGM IV:835-849, IV:1265-1274, IV:1716-1870, IV:2441-2621, IV:2891-2942, IV:3209-3054, VII:215-218, VII:862-918, XII:201-269, XIII:646-734, CXXII:1-55; *SM*: T. Köln Inv. 1, P. Berol. Inv. 21243; *ACM*: Oxy. 1060, H.O.Lange Text; *SSG*
Aphrodite (Zahra, Roman)	Spirit Queen – Venus	*Pic*, *SSG*
Aphroditi	Angel – Malachim, under Plemiya	*SRH*
Aphropaic	Gnostic Light-Virgin	*ACM*: NH Codex VIII
Aphruel	Stone Spirit – Carbuncle (Deep Red Garnet)	*GS*
Apiaēl/Opiael/ Optaēl/ Opiakēl	Angel – Saturday Hour eighteen	*Hyg*
Apidius	Spirit Prince – Architecture and Construction	*MNeI*
Apiel	Angel Minister	*ACM*: P. Mich. 593

Apiel	Demon Duke – North by East Night	*Stg, ThG*
Apik	Angel – First Encampment, first Heaven	*ShR*
Apilki	Servant Spirit	*Abm*
Apis	Egyptian Bull God	HB Jer 46:15; PGM CXXVIa:1-21; *SM*: P. Ant. II.66
Aplēx/Plyx/Plēx	Demon – Thursday Hour eleven	*Hyg*
Apnial	Angel – Fifth Encampment, first Heaven	*ShR*
Apnos (Jupiter)	Jupiter – Alternative Name	*Hyg*
Apodokiel/ Apodokiēl/ Apodokyēl/ Apodokōel	Angel – Mercury	*Hyg*
Apolen/Apolii	Demon	*ToSC*
Apolin/Apolyn/ Appolyn	Spirit/Demon	*MHN, NML*
Apolion	Servant Spirit	*Abm*
Apollo	Greek God of Healing, Music, and Prophecy God – Wisdom	PGM I:262-347, II:64-184, III:187-262, III:282-409, VI:1-47, VII:727-739, X:36-50, XIII:1-343, XIII:646-734, XXIIa:2-9; *ACM*: H.O.Lange Text; BoO
Apolokhas/Plolakhe/ Plotokhai/Mplolakhe	Demon – West	*Hyg*
Apolyn	Demon	*NMI*
Apomios/Atomos/ Atomeos	Demon – Saturday Hour sixteen	*Hyg*
Apophaēl	Demon – Monday Hour seventeen	*Hyg*
Apophantes	Gnostic Spirit	*ACM*: NH Codex VIII
Apophis/Aphyphis/ Apep	Chaos Serpent	PGM XIII:1-343, XIV:585-593
Apormanos	Servant Spirit	*Abm*
Appatay	Night Devil	*oADS*
Appellonii	Devil – Ursa Major	*oADS*

Appiniel/Appinel	Angel – Night Hour five	*Stg, ArP*
Aprial	Angel – Third Heaven, serving Dlqial	*ShR*
Apras	Spirit	*Hyg*
Aprix/Aprax/Apriz/Apax	Demon – Friday Hour sixteen	*Hyg*
Aprixon	Demon – Tuesday Hour twelve, thirteen	*Hyg*
Aprksi	Angel Ruler – Sixth Heaven, West	*ShR*
Aproōz/Aprōx	Demon – Tuesday Hour thirteen	*Hyg*
Apshrial	Angel Encampment Head – sixth Heaven, East	*ShR*
Aptial	Angel – First Encampment, first Heaven	*ShR*
Aqilih	Angel – First Encampment, first Heaven	*ShR*
'Aqlyāyl	Angel – Venus	*BoW*
Aqoviya	Angel – Malachim, under Avorphenial	*SRH*
Aqrapirim	Angel – Moon	*LL*
Aqrba	Angel – Second Encampment, first Heaven	*ShR*
Aqrial	Angel Encampment Head – sixth Heaven, East	*ShR*
Aquariel (Cambiel)	Angel – Aquarius Spirit – Aquarius	*3BOP, tSoS, JMR, SaS*
Aquashimadi	Angel – Moon	*LL*
Aqudu	Angel Encampment Head – sixth Heaven, West	*ShR*
Aquiel	Demon – Sunday	*GoPH*
Aquifolelo	Spirit – Sunday	*BoSC*
Aquilo	Wind – North	*MC, Thm*
Aquos	Night Devil	*oADS*
Aquyel	Angel – Tishrei	*SR*
Ara	Demon Duke and Marquis Spirit – Minister of Love	*NML, oADS*
Arab	Spirit – Minister of Love	*oADS*
Arabas/Accabas/Irabas (Orobas)	Demon Prince	*NML*
Araboth	Angel Chief – seventh Heaven	*SaS*
Arabyel	Angel – Elul	*SR*
Arac	Angel – Kislev	*SR*

Arach	Demon Duke – West by South Night	*Stg, ThG, BoTS*
Aracha	Angel – Cherubim, Sun	*ACM*: L. Anastasi 9
Arachael	Angel – Cherubim, Sun	*ACM*: L. Anastasi 9
Arael	Angel/Archangel	*ToS*; *ACM*: Oriental 5899, L. Anastasi 9; 67M
Arafos	Demon Duke – North by East Night	*Stg, ThG*
Arakiēl/Arkiēl/Arakēl	Angel – Wednesday Hour two	*Hyg*
Arakison	Servant Spirit	*Abm*
Aral	Angel – First Encampment, first Heaven	*ShR*
Aralielael	Angel – Malachim over Fire and Flames	*SRH*
Aram	Spirit – Moon	*ACM*: L. Anastasi 9
Aramael	Angel – Mars	*GAG*
Aranael	Angel	*ACM*: Oriental 5899
Aranial	Angel – First Encampment, first Heaven	*ShR*
Araniel/Aramiel	Angel – Day Hour five	*Stg, ArP*
Araps	Demon – Sunday Hour twenty	*Hyg*
Arariqniel	Angel – Kislev	*SR*
Ararmachēs	Fourth of Seven Egyptian Fates of Heaven	PGM IV:475-829
Aras/Bara (Hindi) (Sams)	Angel – Sun	*SSG*
Arasmali	Angel Minister – Love and Fornication	*KoSA*
Aratachael	Spirit – Stars	*ACM*: L. Anastasi 9
Arath	Demon	*MHN*
Aratha	Spirit – Gate of the East	*ACM*: L. Anastasi 9
Arathael	Spirit – Gate of the East	*ACM*: L. Anastasi 9
Arathiti	Demon Companion – Thursday	*KoN*
Aratiel	Demon Duke – South by East Day	*Stg, ThG, BoTS*
Araton	Angel – Nisan	*SR, tSoS*
Araton	Superior Intelligence – Fire	*KoSU, SoS*
Arator	Demon Senior Servant Spirit	*SSM, Abm*
Aratron/Arathron/Arathon	Olympic Spirit – Saturn	*KoSR, Arb, MC, GAG, JMR, MNeI, oADS, KoN, GoA, PO, ClI, SGT, SSG*

ABBREVIATIONS

Aravi	Angel Minister – Love and Fornication	*KoSA*
Arax/Araz	Demon – Sunday Hour sixteen	*Hyg*
Aray	Spirit – Minister of Love	*oADS*
Arayl/Arayel	Demon Duke – North Night	*Stg, ThG, BoTS*
Arban/Azaphē	Demon – Monday Hour four	*Hyg*
Arboab	Spirit – Woods	*oADS*
Abras/Arbes	Spirit	*MHN*
Abraym/Abraem	Angel – Spring	*BM, BoO*
Arbial	Angel – Sixth Encampment, first Heaven	*ShR*
Arbiel	Demon Duke – Day Hour ten	*Stg, ThG*
Arbiel	Water Spirit	*MNeI*
Arboab	Spirit	*tSoS*
Arboyl	Demon Senior	*SSM*
Arbrathiabra	Angel – Lunar, Night Hour twelve	PGM VII:862-918
Arbyal	Spirit	*SSM*
Arcan	Angel – King of Air on Monday Spirit King – Moon	*EoN, Hmn, KoSR, GAG, PO, tM*
Arcaryamanan/ Ortaryaran	Angel – Cauda Draconis	*B7R*
Archasiel	Angel – Saturn	*KoSR*
Archidemath	Demon	*MHN*
Archiel/Sarchiel	Angel – Day Hour two	*Stg, ArP*
Archon	Decan Spirit	*ACM*: Cologne 10235
Arcisat/Arcifat/ Archisat	Demon Duke – South-West Day	*Stg, ThG, BoTS*
Ardaēl	Angel	*Hyg*
Ardaghos	Left part of Daghdiyos	*Pic*
Ardaguylyel	Angel of Seas/Waters – Winter	*SSM*
Ardiel	Angel – Bisertilis	*SR*
Ardo	Beast before God (sixth of six)	*oADS*
Ardofiel/Ardosiel/ Ardesiel/Ardefiel/ Avdefiel	Angel – Mansion ten Angel – Leo	*3BOP, BoO, tSoS, JMR, SaS, tM*
Ardq	Angel – Fourth Encampment, first Heaven	*ShR*
Ardual	Spirit – East	*SSM*

Arduda	Angel – Seventh Encampment, first Heaven	ShR
Arean/Aream	Demon Duke – South by East Day	Stg, ThG, BoTS
Arebas	Spirit of War – West	SSM
Arebial	Angel – Malachim, under Pheseker Angel – Malachim, sixth Host	SRH
Aregela	Angel – Malachim, under Dohel	SRH
Aregero	Spirit of the Thumb	MHN
Arehieh	Spirit – North in Autumn	SRH
Arel	Angel	SoM
Aremial	Angel – Malachim, sixth Host	SRH
Aremienos	Angel – Malachim, under Pheseker	SRH
Aremiyiyenos	Angel – Malachim, sixth Host	SRH
Arepach	Demon Duke – North Night	Stg, ThG, BoTS
Arephial	Angel Minister – Malachim Angel – Malachim, Flames of Fire	SRH
Arephiel (Luna)	Luna – Alternative Name	Hyg
Areq	Angel – Malachim, under Ayigeda/under Phelmiya	SRH
Arereq	Angel – Malachim, under Plemiya	SRH
Ares	Greek War God	PGM IV:474, IV:830, IV:835-849, IV:2967-3006, XII:401-44, XIII:646-734; SSG
Ares (Greek/Roman) (Rubijail)	Angel – Mars	SSG
Arēsiēl	Angel – Monday Hour thirteen	Hyg
Areterial	Spirit – Winter	SRH
Arfaniel	Angel – Earth	SR
Arfigyel	Angel – Saturn, over Air	SR
Arfose	Good Spirit	SoM
Arfur	Demon Prince	SSM
Argax	Servant Spirit	Abm
Argemē	Spirit	Hyg

ABBREVIATIONS

Argētan/Aritan/ Argitau/ Argitan	Demon – Saturday Hour fifteen	*Hyg*
Argilon	Servant Spirit	*Abm*
Argkhykiel	Angel	*Hyg*
Argla	Angel – Third Encampment, first Heaven	*ShR*
Argousoul/Artisoul	Demon – North	*Hyg*
Arhawthaas	Spirit – Regal Sympathy	*Pic*
Arhocib	Spirit – West	*SSM*
Arhos	Back part of Didas	*Pic*
Arhugal	Stone Spirit – Garnet	*GS*
Ariaēl/Arainēl/ Ariyl/ Arnoēl	Demon – Sun	*Hyg*
Arial	Spirit – East in Autumn	*SRH*
Arias	Angel ruling Sweet-smelling Herbs	*SoM*
Aribiriel	Angel – Mercury/Wednesday	*SR*
Aridiel/Ariaiel	Demon Duke – South	*Stg*, *ThG*
Arieil	Angel – Sun/Sunday	*SR*
Arieisin	Angel – Moon	*LL*
Ariêl	Angel	*SM*: P. Med. I.20; *ACM*: Hay 10122
Ariēl/Araēl/Aroul/ Oureēl/Ouriēl	Angel – Sun	*Hyg*
Ariel/Nariel	Angel Prince – South, Leo, Fire, South Wind	*JMR*, *GoPH*, *SaS*, *tM*
Ariel (Verchiel for Leo)	Angel – Fourth Heaven, North Angel – Leo Angel – Aries Spirit – Leo Spirit – Aries	*EoN*, *3BOP*, *BoO*, *tSoS*, *JMR*, *SaS*
Ariel	Angel – Shem forty-six	*KoSU*, *3BOP*, *GoeR*, *JMR*, *SAS*, *tM*
Ariel/Ariell	Angel Minister – Love and Fornication Spirit – Minister of Love	*KoSA*, *oADS*
Ariel	Genii – 12° Cancer, 12° Leo	*ArP*
Ariel	Governor – Earth Angel Ruler – Earth, governs Azael	*3BOP*, *tSoS*, *MC*, *KoN*, *BoTS*, *PO*

Ariel	Demon Governor/Prince Demon – Prince-Elector, Mercury Wise Spirit Prince Palatine/Great Prince Sea Spirit – Middle	*SoM, SSM, BARC, MNeI, VJL*
Ariēm	Demon – West and Aries	*Hyg*
Ariera	Angel – Malachim, under Ayigeda	*SRH*
Aries	Spirit – Sea and Water, East	*KoN*
Arifiel/Arisiel	Demon Duke – East	*Stg, ThG*
Arihaylim	Angel – Moon	*LL*
Arikha/Arēkha	West Wind – Autumn	*BoW*
Aril	Servant Spirit	*Abm*
Arill	Spirit Prince – Treasure	*KoN*
Arimatha	Spirit – Moon	*ACM*: L. Anastasi 9
Arinalatisten	Angel Minister – Love and Fornication	*KoSA*
Arinatael	Spirit – Gate of the West	*ACM*: L. Anastasi 9
Arinnaquu	Enochian Senior – South	*TBA*
Arioth	Servant Spirit	*Abm*
Ariphaēl (Luna)	Luna – Alternative Name	*Hyg*
Ariplotoson	Spirit – Minister of Love	*oADS*
Ariste	Name of Artemis	PGM IV:1390-1495
Ariton	Demon Duke	*Abm, PO, MRC*
Ariyal	Angel – Malachim, Sunday and Tuesday	*SRH*
Arakēl/Rhkaēl	Angel – Winter, Lord of the Towers	*BoW*
Arkanēl/Orkanil/ Akaēl	Demon – South	*Hyg*
Arkatiēl	Angel – Monday Hour thirteen	*Hyg*
Arkhēkhnēl/ Arkhokhnēl	Spirit	*BoW*
Arkhēpal (Sun)	Sun – Alternative Name	*Hyg*
Arkidōd/Artidos/ Arkidōi/Sarkidōn	Demon – Monday Hour twenty-four	*Hyg*
Arkinlia	Angel – Venus	*GAG*
Armadiel	Demon Duke – North-East Demon Duke – North under Egyn	*Stg, ThG, KoN*
Armail	Angel – Mars	*GAG*
Armany	Demon Duke – East	*Stg, ThG*

Armapy/Armapi	Angel – Night Hour nine	*Stg, ArP*
Armaqnieyeyl	Angel – Sun/Sunday	*SR*
Armariel	Angel – Water	*SR*
Armasia	Servant Spirit	*Abm*
Armat	Angel Encampment Head – sixth Heaven, East	*ShR*
Armayel	Angel – Sun/Sunday	*SR*
Armena	Demon Duke – North Day	*Stg, ThG, BoTS*
Armētes	Demon – West	*Hyg*
Arnen/Annen	Demon Duke – North-West Day	*Stg, ThG, BoTS*
Armesiel/Armisiel	Demon Duke – Day Hour ten	*Stg, ThG*
Armial	Angel – Sixth Encampment, first Heaven	*ShR*
Armiel/Anniel	Angel – Night Hour eleven	*Stg, ArP*
Armitēl/Armatēl	Angel – Monday Hour thirteen	*Hyg*
Armniel	Demon	*SMS*
Armoēl	Angel – Friday Hour eleven	*Hyg*
Armon	Angel – Second Altitude (Taurus) Angel – Chora two	*Alm, ArA*
Armoniel	Demon Chief Duke	*Stg, ThG*
Armosiel	Angel – Night Hour four	*Stg, ArP*
Armosy/Armasi/Armesi	Angel – Day Hour ten	*Stg, ArP*
Armoutar	Angel – Plant Ruler	*BoW*
Armozel/Armiel	Gnostic Spirit of Light	*ACM*: NH Codex VIII
Armud	Angel – Third Encampment, first Heaven	*ShR*
Armunis	Angel – Sixth Encampment, first Heaven	*ShR*
Armut	Angel – Eleventh Step, second Heaven	*ShR*
Arnace	Devil – Third Hour of Day	*oADS*
Arnael	Angel over Hearing	*ACM*: BN Turin
Arnanis	Angel – Mars	*BARC*
Arnech	Angel – Fourth Altitude (Cancer)	*Alm*
Arnibiel	Demon Duke – North	*Stg, ThG*
Arnibiel	Angel – Day Hour six	*Stg, ArP*
Arniēl/Arkiēl	Angel – Saturday Hour twelve, thirteen	*Hyg*

Arnmyel/Ammyel	Angel – Day Hour four	Stg, ArP
Arnotho (Ornotheos)	Spirit Prince	tSoS
Arnub	Angel – First Encampment, first Heaven	ShR
Aroan/Ayoan	Demon Duke – South by West Night	Stg, ThG, BoTS
Arobolyn	Angel – Venus/Friday	SR
Aroc/Arois	Demon Duke – West Night	Stg, ThG, BoTS, GV
Arogani	Spirit	GV
Arogor	Servant Spirit	Abm
Arois/Aroiz/Aroias	Demon Duke – West Day	Stg, ThG, BoTS
Arolen	Servant Spirit	Abm
Aromicha	Angel – Dominations	67M
Aron/Aran	Demon Lord	BOS, BoO
Arophtobel	Archangel	ACM: BN Turin
Arotosael	Demon – Decan three	ToS
Arouēr ('Horus the Great')	Title of Horus	PGM VII:664-685
Aroziel/Arosziel	Demon Duke – West by North pre-Midnight	Stg, ThG, BoTS
Arpas	Demon Senior	SSM
Arpda	Angel – Second Step, second Heaven	ShR
Arphael	Angel Minister	ACM: P. Mich. 593
Arphanai/Arphanaēl	Angel – Sunday Hour two	Hyg
Arphel	Angel – Ninth Altitude (Sagittarius)	Alm
Arpheton	Angel – Saturn	KoSR
Arphin/Arphēn (Saturn)	Saturn – Alternative Name	Hyg
Arphoriel	Metal Spirit – Iron	GS
Arpiros	Demon	BoSC
Arpsan	Demon – Tuesday Hour sixteen	Hyg
Arq	Angel – Second Encampment, first Heaven	ShR
Arqni	Angel – Third Heaven, serving Rhtial	ShR
Arrabim	Servant Spirit	Abm
Arragon/Atragon	Angel – Fifth Heaven Tuesday, East Angel – Fifth Heaven, East Presiding Spirit – Mars	EoN, Hmn, KoSR, BoO, GAG, BoTS, SaS, tM, CBMS

ABBREVIATIONS 341

Arragon	Spirit – Venus	*SGT, SSG*
Arrutel	Plant Spirit – Moss	*GS*
Arsaferal	Angel – Marchesvan	*SR*
Arsdortho/Arsdorth	Spirit	*BoO, GAG*
Arsenouphis	Egyptian (originally Kushite) God	*SM*: PSI I.28, T. Köln Inv. 1
Artabael	Angel Minister – Love and Fornication	*KoSA*
Artagēl	Demon – Sunday Hour twenty-one	*Hyg*
Artēr/Armetēs/ Armētēs/ Armetos	Demon – West	*Hyg*
Arsabon	Angel – Tishrei	*SR*
Artemis/Artemi/ Artemisia/Artemisos	Greek Huntress/Moon Goddess	PGM III:424-466, IV:2441-2621, IV:2708-2784, IV:2785-2890, XXVIIIa:1-7, XXVIIIb:1-9, XXVIIIc:1-11, PDM XIV:239-295; *SM*: T. Köln Inv. 1, H. O. Lange Text; HB Acts 19:24, 19:27-28, 19:34-35
Arthamiel	Archangel	*ACM*: BN Turin
Arthan	Spirit	*SSM*
Arthiel	Angel Minister	*KoSA*
Artidēl	Demon – Monday Hour twenty-three	*Hyg*
Artino	Demon Duke – West by North pre-Noon	*Stg, ThG, BoTS*
Artis (Botis)	Demon – Prince	*LdE, GoPH*
Artlidi	Angel – Twelfth Step, second Heaven	*ShR*
Artmiktun	Angel – Twelfth Step, second Heaven	*ShR*
Artolan	Angel – Six of seven over the seven Baths	*ACM*: H. Kopt. 686
Artolar	Angel – Seven of seven over the seven Baths	*ACM*: H. Kopt. 686
Artole	Angel – Five of seven over the seven Baths	*ACM*: H. Kopt. 686
Artos	Angel – Joy and Divination	*CoMS*
Artus	Air/Wood Spirit	*tSoS*
Aurel	Angel	*ACM*: Oriental 5899

Aruel	Plant Spirit – Wall Fern	*GS*
Arumaphobiel	Plant Spirit – Christmas Rose (Black Hellebore)	*GS*
Arumbol	Spirit Familiar	*BoTS*
Arunur	Angel – Second Encampment, first Heaven	*ShR*
Arush	Angel – Second Encampment, first Heaven	*ShR*
Arvas	Angel Minister – Love and Fornication	*KoSA*
Arvirevel	Plant Spirit – Wood Sorrel	*GS*
Arvyr	Night Devil	*oADS*
Aryel	Spirit	*SSM*
Aryel	Angel – Iyar	*SR*
Aryelyn	Angel – Moon/Monday	*SR*
Aryha	Supportive Planetary Spirit – Moon	*SSM*
Arylin	Angel – Moon/Monday	*SR*
Arymyel	Angel – First Altitiude (Aries)	*Alm*
Asuel	Angel	*ACM*: Oriental 5899, Oriental 5525, Würzburg 42, Oriental 6794, Oriental 6796
Arzaf	Angel – Marchesvan	*SR*
Arzel	Enochian Angel – East, over first lesser Angle	*TBA*
Asa	Spirit	*MRC*
Asaf	Angel – Tammuz	*SR*
Asahel	Demon Duke – South by East Day	*Stg, ThG, BoTS*
Asaibi	Spirit Attendant – Saturn	*EoN*
Asaliel/Ataliel/Atliel	Angel – Mansion fifteen	*3BOP, tSoS, JMR, SaS, tM*
Asamach	Storm Spirit – West	*SSM*
Asamuth	Spirit	*ACM*: H. O. Lange Text
Asaphin	Angel – Moon/Monday	*SR*
Asariel/Aerell/Asaciell	King of the Dead/Keeper of the Bones of the Dead	*GAG*

Asaron	Spirit – King of Luck	MNeI
Asaroth	Guardian Angel Cherub of the Air	ACM: Yale 1800, H. Kopt. 686
Asartim	Angel Minister – Love and Fornication	KoSA
Asael	Spirit – Middle	SSM
Asasiel/Asassiel	Angel – Thursday Spirit – Jupiter Presiding Spirit – Jupiter	SBH, Hmn, CBoM, tSoS, GAG, tM, CBMS, PO, SGT, SSG
Asassayel	Angel Subordinate – Jupiter	SSM
Asatael/Astiel	Demon Duke – North Day	Stg, ThG, BoTS
Asazell/Aszazell	Spirit Lord	oADS
Asbeor	Good Spirit	SoM
Asbibiel	Demon Duke – North-East	Stg, ThG
Asbon (Jupiter)	Jupiter – Alternative Name	Hyg
Ascariell/Askariell/Askariel/Assachell	Demon Spirit – over the Dead	BoO, CoC, tSoS
Ascaroth (Astaroth?)	Demon	NML
Ascharoth (Astaroth)	Spirit Prince	MoAS
Ascher	Ministering Familiar/Mystery	67M
Aschiel/Aseliel	Demon King – South by East	Stg, ThG, BoTS
Aschirikas	Spirit Prince	EUM
Ascymor	Angel – Mars	SSM
Asdon	Angel – Nisan	SR, tSoS
Aseberon	Spirit – East in Spring	SRH
Asebiereh	Angel – Malachim, under Dohel	SRH
Asel	Angel	ACM: H. Kopt. 679
Asel	Genii – 3° Cancer	ArP
Asenide	Angel Minister – Love and Fornication	KoSA
Asēns/Askyros/Askēn/Askinos/Askeros	Demon – Sunday Hour eighteen	Hyg
Asentael	Angel over the Stars	ACM: BN Turin
Aseoulouēl/Asekhouēl (Mercury)	Mercury – Alternative Name	Hyg
Asephenial	Angel – Malachim, Monday	SRH
Asēr/Asyr (Mars)	Mars – Alternative Name	Hyg

Aseron	Angel Prince – Gate of Spirit of East	*SRH*
Asetheqenal/ Asetheqena	Angel Prince – Gate of Spirit of West	*SRH*
Asethial	Angel – Malachim, under Avorphenial	*SRH*
Asethierotz	Angel – Malachim, under Ayigeda	*SRH*
Asge	Spirit	*Hyg*
Asgorēs	Demon – Thursday Hour nine	*Hyg*
A'shael	Angel	*SoM*
Ashbeel/Asbil	Spirit King – Saturn	*Pic, SSG*
Ashbh	Angel – First Encampment, first Heaven	*ShR*
Ashbur	Angel – Second Encampment, first Heaven	*ShR*
Ashdda	Angel – Ninth Step, second Heaven	*ShR*
Ashedial	Angel – Friday	*SRH*
Ashegeron	Angel – Malachim, Winter Nights	*SRH*
Ashekeh	Angel – Malachim, under Avorphenial	*SRH*
Ashemi	Angel – Malachim, under Avorphenial	*SRH*
Ashemoli	Angel Prince – Torah	*SRH*
Ashenor	Angel – Malachim, under Ayigeda	*SRH*
Ashephek	Angel – Malachim, under Dohel	*SRH*
Ashephor	Angel – Malachim, under Ayigeda	*SRH*
Asherah[414]	Canaanite Wisdom Goddess	HB Deut 7:5, 12:3, 16:21, Judg 3:7, 1 Kgs 14:15, 14:23, 15:13, 16:33, 18:19, 2 Kgs 17:10, 17:16, 18:4, 21:7, 23:4-7, 23:14, 2 Chr 14:2, 15:16, 24:18, 31:1, 33:3, 34:3-4, 34:7, Isa 17:8, Jer 17:2, Mic 5:13
Asherial	Angel – Saturday	*SRH*
Ashethonal	Angel – Malachim, under Dohel	*SRH*
Ashima	Goddess of Samaria	HB Amos 8:14

---

414 Note although some of the Biblical references to Asherah are as 'asherah', the sacred tree, this was associated with her and implies her, so these are included in the source list.

Ashlba	Angel – Second Encampment, first Heaven	*ShR*
Ashlekeh	Angel – Malachim, under Ayigeda	*SRH*
Ashmdaa	Angel – Fourth Step, second Heaven	*ShR*
Asiemor	Angel Magistrate – Malachim, fifth Throne	*SRH*
Asmedai (Asmodeus)	Demon King – South	*SMS*
Ashon	Angel – Malachim, under Dohel	*SRH*
Ashoshal	Angel – Malachim, Summer Nights	*SRH*
Ashpr	Angel – Third Encampment, first Heaven	*ShR*
Ashpur	Angel – Second Encampment, first Heaven	*ShR*
Ashrial	Angel Encampment Head –Sixth Heaven, West	*ShR*
Ashtib	Angel – Second Encampment, first Heaven	*ShR*
Ashtnuil	Angel – Third Encampment, first Heaven	*ShR*
Asianon	Servant Spirit	*Abm*
Asidaus	Demon – Sunday Hour one	*Hyg*
Asiel	Demon	*ToSC*
Asijma	Ministering Familiar/Mystery	*67M*
Asimiel	Demon Duke – South-East Night	*Stg, ThG, BoTS*
Ašimyal/Asmyāl	Angel – July/Cancer	*BoW*
Asiob	Angel – Sun	*BARC*
Asirac	Angel – Tebet	*SR*
Askades (Askadeus?)	Spirit	*oADS*
Askadeus	Spirit	*oADS*
Askariell/Askariel/ Ascariell/Askaryell	Demon Spirit – Woods	*oADS, BoO, GAG*
Askiri	Angel – Third Encampment, first Heaven	*ShR*
Asklepios	Greek Healing God	PGM VII:628-642, VII:993-1009
Askodai	Demon – North	*Hyg*
Askyēl	Angel – Wednesday Hour two	*Hyg*
Aslaqwy	Angel – Tebet	*SR*
Asmaaual	Angel Prince – fourth Heaven, Water	*ShR*

Asmadiel/Amadiel	Demon Duke – Day Hour five and Night Hour five	*Stg, ThG*
Asmaiel	Demon Duke – North-East	*Stg, ThG*
Asmalior	Spirit	*KoSR*
Asmiel	Demon Duke – North by East Day	*Stg, ThG*
Asmiel/Ansmiel	Angel – Day Hour three	*Stg, ArP*
Asmigdn	Angel – Twelfth Step, second Heaven	*ShR*
Asmōdas/Astmodri	Demon – Thursday Hour thirteen	*Hyg*
Asmo	Angel Minister – Love and Fornication Spirit – Minister of Love	*KoSA, oADS*
Asmo	Spirit	*GAG*
Asmodeus/Asmodee/ Asmodée/Asmodeo/ Asmodai/Asmodi/ Asmoday	Demon King – Ursa Major Demon King – East/South Demon King (formerly Order of Thrones) Demon Prince – Revengers of Evil Demon of Lust Demon Duke Demon – South, Sunday Hour one Spirit – North Terrestrial Spirit	HB Tob 3:8, 3:17, 8:3-4; *ToS, ACM*: Yale 1800, Oriental 6795; *SSM, ToSC, SBH, Hyg, Abm, KoSA, LdE, 3BOP, BOS, BoO, KoN, CoC, Goe, oADS, JMR, GoPH, SRH, GoA, PO, VMN, MRC, tM, DI*
Asmodel/Aomodel	Angel – Taurus	*3BOP, tSoS, MC, JMR, SaS, Thm, PO, tM*
Asmodiah	Spirit	*BoTS*
Asmodiel	Free Spirit – Murder	*M.NeI*
Asmoe/Asmoo	Demon Senator	*BoO*
Asmon	Infernal Spirit	*CBoM*
Asmoy	Good Spirit	*SoM*
Asophiel	Spirit	*GV*
Asorega	Servant Spirit	*Abm*
Asoriel/Aforiel/ Assoriel	Demon Duke – West Day	*Stg, ThG, BoTS*
Asosiel	Demon Duke – Y2	*Stg, ThG*
Asouma	Spirit	*Hyg*
Aspar/Aspor	Demon Duke – West Night	*Stg, ThG, BoTS*
Asphiel	Demon Duke – South by East Night	*Stg, ThG, BoTS*
Asphor	Duke – West by North Afternoon	*Stg, ThG, BoTS*

ABBREVIATIONS 347

Asphrodēl/ Asphrodiel/ Asphodēl	Angel – Friday Hour twenty	*Hyg*
Aspides	Spirit	*CoMS*
Aspiel	Demon Duke – South-West Night Demon Duke – West Night	*Stg, ThG, BoTS*
Aspiō	Demon – Thursday Hour eighteen	*Hyg*
Aspiramo	Angel – Tishrei	*SR*
Asppial	Angel Prince – fourth Heaven, Water	*ShR*
Aspraēl/Appraēl	Angel – Friday Hour thirteen	*Hyg*
Asqryhw	Angel Prince – Middle Five	*SoM*
Asqueucon	Angel – Nisan	*tSoS*
Asrael	Angel	*SoM*
Asrāfyl	Angel	*BoW*
Asriel	Demon	*Hyg*
Asrieylin	Angel – Moon/Monday	*SR*
Assa	Intelligence	*CoMS*
Assaba/Affaba	Demon Duke – South by West Day	*Stg, ThG, BoTS*
Assaibi/Affaibi	Angel Minister of Air – Saturday Daemon Attendant – Saturn, North Spirit – Saturn Presiding Spirit – Saturn	*SBH, Hmn, KoSR, SoS, GAG, BoTS, MNeI, tM, CBMS*
Assamach	Spirit	*SSM*
Assardiel	Demon Baron	*MNeI*
Assasel (Azazel?)	Spirit King – Ruler of the Dead	*EBAM*
Assassaiel/Assassael/ Assassayel/Assasiel	Angel – Jupiter Spirit – Jupiter	*SSM, SBH, SoS, MHN, GAG*
Assayby	Spirit Ruler – Saturday	*MHN*
Asseme	Angel Minister	*KoSA*
Asser	Angel – Eleventh Altitude (Aquarius)	*Alm*
Assi/Assih/Apragsih	Angel Messenger	*SoM*
Assaiel/Asaiel	Angel Prince – Earth	*ArP*
Asshy	Angel Prince – Top Three	*SoM*
Assmielh	Servant Spirit	*Abm*
Assriell	Demon	*CoC*
Asstraelos/Astraelos	Spirit	PGM XXXVI:256-264

Assuel/Alsuel	Demon Duke – West by South Day	*Stg, ThG, BoTS*
Astagna/Astachna/ Astagua/Astragna	Angel – Fourth Heaven, West Angel – Fifth Heaven Tuesday, West Angel – Fifth Heaven, West Ministering Spirit – Mars	*SR, SSM, EoN, Hmn, KoSR, BoO, GAG, BoTS, SaS, tM, CBMS*
Astarin	Spirit	*GoPH*
Astarot/Astaroth/ Asteroth/Astarōth/ Astarath/ Astroth/Ascharoth/ Ascaroth/Astoroth/ Astharoth	Demon King – Wednesday Demon Prince – Accusers/Inquisitors Demon King – East, ruling Earthly Spirits/South Demon Duke/Governor Demon Count – Americas Demon – South/West Grand Prince – Hell Infernal Treasure Spirit Ministering Familiar/Mystery	*ToSC, SSM, Hyg, MHN, Abm, KoSR, dN, 3BOP, CBoM, BOS, BoO, NML, PmD, DoW, BM, Goe, JMR, oADS, GoPH, MNeI, KoN, SMS, ArPh, GoA, ES, GV, MRC, CoMS, PO, VJL, GG, 67M, BoSC, DI, BD, SBRM*
Astarte/Ashtarte	Canaanite Queen of Heaven	HB Judg 2:13, 10:6, 1 Sam 7:3-4, 12:10, 31:10, 1 Kgs 11:5, 11:33, 2 Kgs 23:13, Jer 7:18, 44:17-19, 44:25
Astarte	Ministering Familiar/Mystery	*67M*
Astarth (Astaroth?)	Spirit – Venus	*oADS*
Astas	Alternative name of Metatron	*SQ*
Astel	Spirit – Saturn	*SGT, SSG*
Aster	Spirit – Minister of Love	*oADS*
Asteraoth	Angel	*ToS*
Asterotus	Spirit – Prince of Poltergeists	*MNeI*
Astib	Demon Duke – South Night	*Stg, ThG*
Astirup	Angel – Second Encampment, first Heaven	*ShR*
Astiiybl/Asfyāl	Angel – June/Orion	*BoW*
Astoēl	Angel – Thursday Hour twelve	*Hyg*
Astogen (Venus)	Venus – Alternative Name	*Hyg*
Astial	Angel – First Encampment, first Heaven	*ShR*
Astole	Devil – Cancer, Storms	*OADS*
Astolit	Servant Spirit	*Abm*
Astor/Aitor	Demon Duke – South-West Day	*Stg, ThG, BoTS*

Astra	Spirit	*MHN*
Astrimi	Angel – Twelfth Step, second Heaven	*ShR*
Astrocon	Angel – Night Hour eight	*Stg, ArP*
Astrofiel/Astrafael/Altrafiel	Angel – Day Hour twelve	*Stg, ArP*
Astromiel	Spirit Prince – Mining	*MNeI*
Astroniel	Angel – Day Hour nine	*Stg, ArP*
Astropalem	Angel Minister – Love and Fornication	*KoSA*
Astropiel	Angel Minister – Love and Fornication	*KoSA*
Astrota/Vestiote	Spirit – second Mansion of the Moon Ring	*AE*
Asttial	Angel – Eleventh Step, second Heaven	*ShR*
Astun	Angel – Third Encampment, first Heaven Angel Prince – fourth Heaven, Fire	*ShR*
Asturel	Servant Spirit	*Abm*
Asuriel	Demon Duke – North-West Night	*Stg, ThG, BoTS*
Asturin	Angel – Second Encampment, first Heaven	*ShR*
Asya	Spirit Helper – Saturday	*CBoM*
Asyel/Asiell	Spirit	*MHN, oADS*
Asymeylyn	Angel – Mars/Tuesday	*SR*
Asymvr	Angel Overseer (five of seven) – first Heaven	*ShR*
Asyn	Spirit Familiar	*BoTS*
Asynariēl/Askaraēl	Angel – Autumn	*BoW*
Asyriel	Demon King – South-West Demon Prince – South under Amaymon	*Stg, ThG, BoTS, KoN*
Asziell	Angel – North	*oADS*
Aszre	Angel – Nisan	*SR*
Ataf	Angel over Pains, Sharp Pains, Inflammation, Dropsy	*SoM*
Atalsloym	Spirit	*GV*
Atanael	Angel – Saturn	*GAG*
Atanianous/Antinianous	Demon	*ToSC*
Atargatis	Syrian Fertility Goddess	HB 2 Mac 12:26

Atasser/Ataser (Saturn)	Saturn – Alternative Name	*Hyg*
Atatiel	Spirit	*NMeI*
Atdshu	Angel – Third Encampment, first Heaven	*ShR*
Atel/Abel	Angel fourth Heaven Sunday – East Ministering Spirit – Sun	*EoN, Hmn, BoO, GAG, BoTS, tM, CBMS*
Atemis	Spirit – Sibyl (three of ten)	*GV*
Atemon	Angel Prince	*SRH*
Atenavim	Angel Minister – Love and Fornication	*KoSA*
Ateredemen	Angel – Malachim, Summer Nights	*SRH*
Ateron/Anoron	Angel Prince – Gate of Spirit of East	*SRH*
Aterouēl	Angel – Plant Ruler	*BoW*
Atesi	Spirit – Minister of Love	*oADS*
Atgla	Angel – Third Encampment, first Heaven	*ShR*
Atha	Spirit – Dawn	*ACM*: L. Anastasi 9
Athael	Spirit – Moon, Dawn	*ACM*: L. Anastasi 9
Athanael	Angel	*ACM*: Oriental 6796
Athanaton	Spirit – East	*DoW*
Athanora	Spirit – Mirror	*CoMS*
Athariel	Spirit	*ACM*: Cairo 45060
Athasan	Devil – third Hour of Day	*oADS*
Athathanasi	Demon – Moon	*Hyg*
Athay	Angel – Jupiter	*GAG*
Athelateyl/Atelateyl/ Acelateyl/Acelaceyl/ Acelayl	Angel – Saturn	*LR*
Athelega	Angel – Malachim, under Dohel	*SRH*
Athena	Greek Wisdom Goddess	PGM IV:2967-3006, VII:643-651; *ACM*: H. O. Lange Text
Atheneni	Angel – Malachim, under Avorphenial	*SRH*
Atheniel/Alheniel	Angel – Mansion twenty-seven	*3BOP, tSoS, JMR, SaS, tM*
Athereshov	Angel – Malachim, under Dohel	*SRH*
Athesiel	Demon Duke – Hour eleven of fifteen	*Stg, ThG*
Athial	Spirit Prince – Ocean in Summer	*SRH*

Athiel	Angel	*ACM*: BN Turin
Athiel	Genii – 18° Cancer, 18° Leo	*ArP*
Athonaval	Angel	*KoSA*
Athrak	Angel – Sun	*ACM*: P. Mich. 1190
Athruel	Plant Spirit – Brook Lime	*GS*
Atithael/Athithael	Spirit – Moon	*SBH*
Atiyefas	Left part of Bandalos	*Pic*
Atkial	Angel – Tenth Step, second Heaven	*ShR*
Atniel/Athiel	Demon Duke – West by South Day	*Stg, ThG, BoTS*
Atnni	Angel – First Encampment, first Heaven	*ShR*
Atnox/Atnos (Jupiter)	Jupiter – Alternative Name	*Hyg*
Atopolin	Spirit – Minister of Love	*oADS*
Ator	Treasure Spirit	*oADS*
Atr	Angel – Fifth Encampment, first Heaven	*ShR*
Atraa	Angel – Winter	*MHN*
Atragon	Angel – Fourth Heaven, East	*SR, SSM*
Atratrayl	Angel – Winter	*MHN*
Atraurbiabilis	Daemon – Mars, subject to East Wind; South	*SBH*
Atrax	Demon – Decan sixteen	*ToS*
Atriel	Demon Duke – West by South Night	*Stg, ThG, BoTS*
Atrikh/Hotrikhos/ Erikhos/Otrikhos	Demon – Friday Hour eighteen	*Hyg*
Atroel/Atiohel	Angel Senior – Moon	*SSM*
Atropos	One of the Moirai (Fates)	PGM II:64-184, IV:2785-2890
Atropos	God – Death	*BoO*
Atrox	Spirit – Minister of Love	*oADS*
Atryel	Angel – Fifth Heaven, East	*SSM*
Atuesuel	Angel	*SoM*
Atum/Athom	Egyptian Crator Sun God	PDM XIV:239-295, XIV:585-593, XIV:636-669, LXI:63-78; PGM XXXVI:333-360
Aturbi	Wind Spirit	*GAG*

'Atyāyl	Angel – Sun	*BoW*
Atybe	Spirit of the Thumb	*CBoM*
Atyes	Devil – Early Morning	*oADS*
Atyor	Angel – Tebet	*SR*
Atythaell	Angel	*oADS*
Atzael	Angel	*Hyg*
Atziniel (Jupiter)	Jupiter – Alternative Name	*Hyg*
Aual	Angel Prince – fourth Heaven, Fire	*ShR*
Aubr	Angel – Seventh Encampment, first Heaven	*ShR*
Aubshal	Angel – Third Encampment, first Heaven	*ShR*
Audac	Angel – Trickery	*KoSA*
Audhal	Angel – Third Step, second Heaven	*ShR*
Audial	Angel – Second Encampment, first Heaven	*ShR*
Aue	Spirit – Son of Sons of Light	*dHM*
Auel	Demon King	*BARC*
Auet	Spirit – Sun	*67M*
Augrbbu	Angel – Third Encampment, first Heaven	*ShR*
Auhial	Angel – Third Encampment, first Heaven	*ShR*
Aul	Angel	*SoM*
Aumial	Angel – Fourth Step, second Heaven	*ShR*
Aumigra	Angel – Seventh Encampment, first Heaven	*ShR*
Aumrhi	Angel – Fourth Encampment, first Heaven	*ShR*
Aumtun	Angel – Twelfth Step, second Heaven	*ShR*
Aunbib	Angel – Fourth Step, second Heaven	*ShR*
Aupri	Angel – Fourth Encampment, first Heaven	*ShR*
Aur	Angel – Second Encampment, first Heaven	*ShR*
Auras	Demon – North	*BOS, BoO, oADS*
Aurial	Angel – Third Encampment, first Heaven	*ShR*
Auriel	Angel	*ACM*: BN Turin
Aurion	Angel – Saturn/Saturday	*SR*
Aurit	Angel – Fourth Encampment, first Heaven	*ShR*

Aurnh	Angel – First Encampment, first Heaven	*ShR*
Aurnial	Angel – Fourth Encampment, first Heaven	*ShR*
Aurpnial	Angel Encampment Head – sixth Heaven, West	*ShR*
Aurpnil	Angel Overseer (one of seven) – First Heaven	*ShR*
Ausiul/Ansuil/Ausim	Angel – Aquarius	*ArP*
Auster	South Wind – over Angels of Thursday	*Hmn, MC, Thm, BoTS, SMS, PO*
Austra Aphricus	South-West by South Wind	*Thm*
Autep	Enochian Angel – East, over second lesser Angle	*TBA*
Autera/Atebou	East Wind – Summer	*BoW*
Authrounios	Gnostic Administrator Spirit	*ACM*: NH Codex VIII
Autiour (Sun)	Sun – Alternative Name	*Hyg*
Autodyo	Demon – Sunday Hour one	*Hyg*
Autotar	Enochian Senior – East	*TBA*
Autothith	Demon – Decan thirty-four	*ToS*
Autut	Angel – Third Encampment, first Heaven	*ShR*
Avedie	Demon King and Duke	*NML*
Aversan/Overthan (Ornias?)	Spirit	*KoN*
Aymaeleon	Unknown Throned Angel (?)	*oADS*
Avmahujah	Metal Spirit – Copper	*GS*
Avochial	Angel – Malachim, under Dohel	*SRH*
Avodena	Angel – Malachim, under Avorphenial	*SRH*
Avokal	Angel – Malachim, under Ayigeda	*SRH*
Avophieri	Angel – Malachim, under Plemiya	*SRH*
Avophori	Angel Magistrate – Malachim	*SRH*
Avornemok	Angel – Malachim, under Ayigeda	*SRH*
Avor	Spirit – West in Winter	*SRH*
Avor Berek	Spirit – Earth in Winter	*SRH*
Avoremedial	Angel – Malachim, Autumn	*SRH*
Avomerial	Angel – Malachim, under Plemiya	*SRH*

Avorenial	Angel – Malachim, under Plemiya Angel Magistrate – Malachim	*SRH*
Avorephenial	Angel – Malachim, under Ayigeda	*SRH*
Avorial	Angel Prince – Autumn Angel – Malachim, Winter, Sunday Angel – Malachim, under Dohel Angel – Malachim, Tebeth/ Nisan	*SRH*
Avorieni	Angel – Malachim, under Plemiya	*SRH*
Avorphenial	Angel Magistrate – Malachim, first Throne	*SRH*
Avor Pheniek	Angel Prince – Malachim, Nisan	*SRH*
Avopheter	Angel Prince – Spring	*SRH*
Avosethial	Angel – Malachim, under Avorphenial	*SRH*
Avosetor	Angel – Malachim, under Ayigeda	*SRH*
Avothoth	Angel – Malachim, under Ayigeda/under Dohel	*SRH*
Avoyial	Angel – Malachim, under Pheseker	*SRH*
Avoyiel	Angel – Malachim, Flames of Fire	*SRH*
Avoyil	Angel Minister – Malachim	*SRH*
Avruthel	Plant Spirit – Rowan Stone Spirit – Amethyst	*GS*
Avvihugal	Plant Spirit – Poplar	*GS*
Avzia (Metatron)	Angel of the Presence	*SoM*
Avzniln	Spirit Minister, serving Prince Hagonel	*dHM*
Awal/Awel	Spirit – Venus	*67M*
Awdoras	Spirit – Love/Sexual Attraction	*Pic*
Awijel	Spirit – Earth	*67M*
Axel	Angel – Jupiter	*GAG*
Axigēn	Spirit	*Hyg*
Axinous	Demon – West	*Hyg*
Axir	Enochian Angel – North, serving third lesser Angle	*TBA*
Ay[415]	Angel – Seventh Altitude (Libra)	*Alm*
Ayayeylin	Angel – Venus/Friday	*SR*
Aybory	Demon Servant – Saturday	*KoN*
Aycolaytoum	Demon – Jupiter	*BARC*

---

415 Used elsewhere as a divine name.

ABBREVIATIONS

Ayeariel	Angel – Mansion four and Taurus	*BoO*
Ayied Mesetar	Angel Prince – Spring	*SRH*
Ayigeda	Angel Magistrate – Malachim, second Throne	*SRH*
Ayinmoos	Spirit – Regal Sympathy	*Pic*
Ayisemerial	Angel – Malachim, Tishri	*SRH*
Ayiseteronelien	Angel, serving above sixth Degree	*SRH*
Ayisethorien	Angel – Malachim, under Ayigeda	*SRH*
Ayisheteb	Angel – Malachim, under Ayigeda	*SRH*
Ayizerekebov	Angel – Malachim, under Dohel	*SRH*
Aym/Aim/Haborim/Haborym	Demon Duke	*PmD, DoW, Goe, DI*
Aymeylyn	Angel – Moon/Monday	*SR*
Aymon	Spirit – East	*oADS*
Aynos	Angel – Mars	*BARC*
Aysberanta	Planetary Spirit Lord – Moon	*SSM*
Aysenel	Spirit – Mirror	*CoMS*
Aysgaron	Angel – Fourth Season by Night	*SSM*
Aysmarob	Angel – Sun	*BARC*
Azabal	Spirit – Water	*oADS*
Azabhsar	Spirit Prince	*MOAS*
Azael/Azaēl	Archangel Angel – Treasure seeking	*ToS*; PGM XXXVI:161-177; *ACM*: L. Anastasi 9; *dN*
Azael	Demon Prince – North Demon Prince – Water/Earth	*3BOP, SaS, BM, BoTS, MNeI, KoN, PO, tM*
Azafarin	Angel – Moon	*LL*
Azakiēl	Archangel	*Hyg*
Azan	Demon – Monday Hour five	*Hyg*
Azanōr/Azaēr/Azaēl (Jupiter)	Jupiter – Alternative Name	*Hyg*
Azardin	Angel – Moon	*LL*
Azareil	Angel – Day Hour two	*LL*
Azaria	Spirit	*AN*

Azariēl	Angel	PGM XXXVI:161-177
Azariel	Angel – Mansion four	3BOP, tSoS, JMR, SaS, tM
Azathi	Demon	MHN
Azazel/Alzazel	Demon King – North Demon Prince – West Demon Prince – Air/Water	HB Lev 16:26, 3BOP, JMR, SaS, BM, BoTS, MNeI, KoN, PO, tM, DI
Azasell/Azazell	Spirit – Lord of Dead Bodies	CoC
Azaziel	Angel	SM: P. Heid. Inv. Lat. 5
Azday	Angel – Kislev	SR
Azdical	Demon – West	GoPH
Azebou/Azibou/ Azēbou/ Abbēzou	Demon – North	Hyg
Azemerehi	Angel Magistrate – Malachim	SRH
Azemo/Azimo/ Azymo	Demon Duke – South-East Night	Stg, ThG, BoTS
Azeruel	Commoner Spirit, Fire	MNeI
Aziabel	Demon Prince	SoM
Azial	Angel – Sixth Encampment, first Heaven Angel – Malachim, sixth Host	ShR, SRH
Aziēl	Angel	PGM XXXVI:161-177
Aziel	Angel – Mansion twenty-five	3BOP, tSoS, JMR, SaS, tM
Aziel	Spirit – West	KoN
Aziel	Demon Prince	SoM
Aziel	Angel – Treasure seeking	dN
Aziel	Genii – 30° Cancer, 30° Leo	ArP
Azigola	Spirit	GV
Azigor	Angel – Sivan	SR
Azijelm	Ministering Familiar/Mystery	67M
Azimel	Demon Duke – West by South Day	Stg, ThG, BoTS
Azizod	Enochian Angel – South, over fourth lesser Angle	TBA

Azlibn	Angel – Third Heaven, serving Dlqial	*ShR*
Azliel	Angel	*SoM*
Azo/Oze (Ose)	Demon President	*NML*
Azochede	Spirit	*oADS*
Azoel	Spirit – Treasure	*oADS*
Azoruel/Azeruel	Angel – Mansion sixteen	*3BOP, tSoS, JMR, SaS, tM*
Azoth	Angel – Dominations	*67M*
Azoti	Angel – Malachim, under Ayigeda	*SRH*
Azouboul/Azaboul/Azabol	Demon – Thursday Hour ten	*Hyg*
Azrageyl	Angel – Sun/Sunday	*SR*
Azraieylin	Angel – Venus/Friday	*SR*
Azriel	Angel – Adar	*SR*
Azriel	Spirit	*dN*
Azuti	Angel – Second Encampment, first Heaven	*ShR*
Azvg	Angel – Nisan	*tSoS*
Azzial	Spirit – Ring of second Mansion of the Moon	*tSoS*

B		
Baaba/Baabal	Demon Duke – South Night	*Stg, ThG*
Baajah	Genii – 15° Capricorn, 15° Aquarius	*ArP*
Baal[416]	Canaanite Weather God Phoenician Ruler God	*HB* Num 25:3, Deut 4:3, Judg 2:11, 2:13, 3:7, 6:25, 6:31-32, 8:33, 9:4, 10:6, 10:10, 1 Sam 7:4, 12:10, 1 Kgs 16:31-32 18:18-19, 18:22, 18:25-26, 18:40, 19:18, 22:54, 2 Kgs 3:2, 10:18-28, 11:18, 17:16, 23:4-5, 2 Chr 23:17, 24:7, 28:2, 33:3, 34:4,

---

416 The Bible refers to plural Baals, as well as the singular, as a generic term for foreign gods or versions of Baal. The singular and plural listings are included here.

Baal (con't.)		HB Ps 106:28, Jer 2:8, 2:23, 2:28, 7:9, 11:17, 12:16, 19:5, 23:13, 23:27, 32:35, Hos 2:15, 2:18-19, 11:2, 13:1, Zeph 1:4, Rom 11:4, 15:30; *SM*: T. Berol Inv. 13412
Baal/Baall/Bael/ Baell/ Beal/Veal/Bel	Demon King – East Spirit Messenger – East	*SSM, MHN, BARC, 3BOP, LdE, BOS, BoO, oADS, MC, PmD, DoW, Goe, BoTS, GoPH, GG, BoSC, DI*
Baalsori	Servant Spirit	*Abm*
Baalyel	Angel – Fourth Heaven, East	*SSM*
Baalzebub (Beelzebub)	Phoencian God	HB 2 Kgs 1:2, 1:4, 1:6, 1:16
Baanepalpa	Angel of Seas/Waters – Summer	*SSM*
Baasan	Demon King – West	*BOS, BoO*
Baashial	Angel – Third Heaven, serving Ibnial	*ShR*
Baasocaf	Demon King	*SSM*
Baayel/Ba'il	Spirit King – Sun	*Pic, SSG*
Babalel	Angel King – Tuesday	*dHM*
Baba Mutela	Treasure Spirit	*oADS*
Babaty	Treasure Spirit	*oADS*
Babay	Treasure Spirit	*oADS*
Babel	Angel – Second Heaven Wednesday, South	*EoN, Hmn, KosR, BoO, GAG, BoTS*
Babell	Angel	*GAG*
Babepen	Spirit Minister, serving Prince Brorges	*dHM*
Babet/Babete/ Bateb/ Sabet	Demon – Venus Demon Chief	*Hyg*
Babibaktar	Demon – Venus Demon Chief	*Hyg*
Babiel	Angel – Third Heaven Friday, West Angel – Third Heaven, West Ministering Spirit – Venus	*Hmn, KoSR, BM, GAG, BoTS, SaS, tM, CBMS*

Babiel	Spirit Messenger – Jupiter	*SGT, SSG*
Babilon	Demon	*CoC*
Bablyel	Angel – Fifth Heaven, West	*SSM*
Babus	Angel Minister – Love and Fornication	*KoSA*
Babylon	Mother of Harlots	HB Rev 17:5-6, 18:2-8
Bacanel/Baccanael	Angel – First Heaven, West	*EoN, SaS*
Bacchios (Bacchus)	Greek God of Vegetation and Frtuifulness	PGM VII:459-461
Bacchus	God – Wine and Excess	*BoO*
Bachanael/ Barchanel/ Bachanae	Angel first Heaven Monday – West Ministering Spirit – Moon	*Hmn, KoSR, BoO, GAG, BoTS, tM, CBMS*
Bacharachyn	Angel – Moon/Monday	*SR*
Bachiel/Badiel	Demon Duke – West by South Night	*Stg, ThG, BoTS*
Bachiel	Genii – 20° Taurus, 20° Gemini, 21° Pisces	*ArP*
Bachiel	Spirit – Saturn	*SGT, SSG*
Bachimy/Albermi/ Cabeïm (Aim)	Demon Duke	*NML*
Bachmyel	Angel – Water	*SR*
Baciar/Basiar/ Bacier/ Bachiar	Demon Duke – North Day	*Stg, ThG, BoTS*
Baciel	Angel – Fourth Heaven, Sunday, East Angel – Fourth Heaven, East, Spring	*EoN, Hmn, KoSR, BoO, GAG, BoTS, SaS, tM*
Bacthemael	Angel – First Heaven, West	*SSM*
Bacyel	Angel – Fourth Heaven, North	*SR*
Badad	Servant Spirit	*Abm*
Badadeyl	Angel	*LL*
Badakiēl	Angel	PGM X:36-50
Badalimaas	Spirit – Regal Sympathy	*Pic*
Badaylin	Angel – Moon	*LL*
Badeilyn	Angel – Moon/Monday	*SR*
Badon	Spirit Prince – Philosophy	*MNeI*
Badrayeylyn	Angel – Day Hour two	*LL*

Bael	Angel before Heavenly Pillars	*ACM*: BN Turin, Cairo 45060
Bael	Angel – Earth	*SR*
Bafamal	Servant Spirit	*Abm*
Baffala	Angel – Venus	*GAG*
Bagalon	Servant Spirit	*Abm*
Bagenol	Angel Prince – Friday	*dHM*
Bagiel	Genii – 12° Virgo, 22° Virgo	*ArP*
Baglag	North Wind – Autuhmn	*BoW*
Bahal	Servant Spirit	*Abm*
Bahatores	Spirit – Love/Sexual Attraction	*Pic*
Bahalim	Angel – Day Hour two	*LL*
Bahimoos	Spirit – Regal Antipathy	*Pic*
Bahmyel/Bamyel	Angel of Seas/Waters - Spring	*SSM*
Bahol (Astaroth)	Demon	*GoPH*
Bahoraelin	Angel – Venus/Friday	*SR*
Bahram (Persian) (Rubijail)	Angel – Mars Mars	*SSM*, *SSG*
Baiedalin	Angel – Moon/Monday	*SR*
Bainchooch/ Bainchōōōch	Egyptian Spirit of Darkness	PGM IV:930-1114, IX:1-14, XIXa:1-54, XCV:1-8; *ACM*: P. Mich.1190
Bai Solbai	Name of Helios in sixth Hour	PGM IV:1596-1715
Bakaron	Servant Spirit	*Abm*
Bakiel	Genii – 10° Gemini	*ArP*
Baktiotha	Spirit Lord – Serpents	*ACM*: P. Mich. 1190
Bal	Spirit	*ACM*: Cairo 45060
Balaam	Spirit	*oADS*
Balabos	Servant Spirit	*Abm*
Balach	Evil Spirit	*3BOP*
Balachem	Servant Spirit	*Abm*
Baladau	Spirit	*SSM*
Balam	Spirit – East	*SSM*
Balam/Balan	Demon King	*PmD*, *DoW*, *Goe*, *DI*
Balath/Batath	Demon – West	*BOS*, *BoO*, *oADS*

Balay/Balaym	Angel – First Heaven, North Angel – First Heaven, Monday, North	*SSM, EoN, Hmn, KoSR, BoO, GAG, BoTS, tM*
Balbo	Spirit	*oADS*
Balbuch	Spirit	*KoSR*
Baldiel	Angel – Saturn	*KoSR*
Baldur	Norse God	*Gbk*
Baldyutabrach/Baldiutabrach	Demon Chief – West	*SSM*
Baledenien	Spirit – South in Summer	*SRH*
Balganarichyn	Angel – Moon/Monday	*SR*
Baliadē (Luna)	Luna – Alternative Name	*Hyg*
Balidit/Balidet	Spirit Attendant – Saturn Angel Minister of Air – Saturday	*EoN, Hmn, KoSR, GAG, BoTS, tM, CBMS*
Baliel/Balael	Angel – Marchesvan Angel first Heaven, Monday, North Angel second Heaven, South	*SR, Hmn, KoSR, BoO, GAG, BoTS, tM*
Baliel	Genii – 10° Libra	*ArP*
Baligon (Carmara)	Angel King – Friday	*dHM*
Balkanaritin	Angel – Moon	*LL*
Balkin	Spirit – Lord of the Northern Mountains	*DoW*
Balknaritim	Angel – Moon	*LL*
Balko	Spirit – Forest	*oADS*
Ballyel	Angel – First Heaven, North	*SSM*
Bal Menael	Angel Prince – Moon in Summer	*SRH*
Balpala (Napula)	Demon Duke	*NML*
Balquiel	Angel – Fifth Heaven, Mars	*SR*
Balsamēs (Bainchooch)	Phoenician Sun God	PGM IV:930-1114, XII:480-495
Balsaniach	Spirit	*KoSR*
Balsur	Demon Duke – West	*Stg, ThG*
Baltasar/Baltasera/Baktasar/Baitarssa	Demon – Venus Demon Chief	*Hyg*
Balthazard/Baltazard/Balthasar (Balthazar)	Spirit – Magi Kings (first of three)	*KoSR, ES, GoPH, GV, BD*

Balthe	Spirit	*KoN*
Balthial	Angel	*ToS*
Baltim/Balthym/ Balthim/Baltym	Spirit	*MHN*
Baltuzaratz	Spirit Prince	*AAAA*
Baltyn	Demon Senior	*SSM*
Balydethe	Spirit Helper – Saturday	*CBoM*
Balyer	Angel – Second Heaven, South	*SR*
Bamulahe	Demon – North	*GoPH*
Bamulath	Spirit – South	*SSM*
Banaēl/Bannaēl	Angel – Saturday Hour twenty-three	*Hyg*
Banakhōr/Banakhos	Demon – West	*Hyg*
Banal	Spirit – Necromantic	*DoW*
Bandalos	Spirit of the Sun	*Pic*
Bandoras	Spirit – Regal Sympathy	*Pic*
Baneh	Angel	*67M*
Bangiel	Genii – 13° Libra	*ArP*
Baniel	Spirit	*GV*
Banithe	Spirit	*ACM*: Hay 10391
Banorsasti	Angel – Shebat	*SR*
Banros	Spirit – ninth Mansion of the Moon Ring	*tSoS*
Banssze	Spirit Minister, serving Prince Brorges	*dHM*
Bantal	Spirit	*ACM*: Hay 10391
Banuel	Biblical Elder	*ACM*: Berlin 11347, Oriental 6796
Baoxas	Demon Duke – North-East	*Stg, ThG*
Baqueryel	Angel – Second Heaven, South	*SSM*
Baqwylaguel	Angel – Kislev	*SR*
Barabbas	Spirit Lord	*BoSC*
Baraborat/Baraburat	Angel – Second Heaven Wednesday, East Presiding Spirit – Mercury	*EoN, Hmn, KoSR, BoO, GAG, BoTS, tM, CBMS*
Baraborat	Spirit – Mercury	*SGT, SSG*
Barachaba	Angel	*KoSA*
Baracheell/Barachyell	Angel	*oADS*

ABBREVIATIONS

Barachi	Spirit	*oADS*
Barachiah/Barachias (Bartholomew)	Prince of Ishim and Apostle	*3BOP, MRC*
Barachiel	Angel – Air Angel – Sun Angel – First Altitiude (Aries)	*Alm, SR, B7R, EPL*
Barachyel	Angel Senior – Mars Angel – Fourth Season by Day	*SSM*
Barael	Throne Angel (three of seven)	*SaS*
Baraēl	Angel – Monday Hour four	*Hyg*
Barak	Servant Spirit	*Abm*
Barakhiēl/Barakhēel	Angel	*Hyg*
Barakon	Spirit	*SMS*
Baralama	Spirit – eleventh (twelfth) Mansion of the Moon ring	*tSoS*
Baramper	Treasure Spirit	*BoTS*
Baramptis	Demon	*oADS*
Baraniel	Angel – Earth	*SR*
Barasiel	Angel – Moon, over Air	*SR*
Baratidres/Baratidris/Baratudes	Spirit – seventh Mansion of the Moon Ring	*AE*
Barbais	Demon – East	*BOS, BoO*
Barbaras	Spirit	PGM XXIIa:18-27
Barbaras/Barabas	Demon – South	*CBoM*
Barbares/Barbaros	Demon Earl Demon Count – East	*BOS, BoO, BoTS, KoN*
Barbaritha	Title of Adonis	PGM IV:206-466
Barbarouch/Barbaraoth	Spirit – Power of Darkness	*ACM*: Berlin 8322, Hay 10391, Oriental 6796
Barbarus	Demon Count and Duke	*MHN*
Barbas/Corbas (Marbas?)	Demon Chief – East Spirit – Presidential Counsellor	*BOS, BoO, oADS, BoTS*
Barbasan/Barbason	Treasure Spirit	*BoTS*
Barbates/Barbares (Barbatos?)	Demon Lord and Viscount	*BOS, BoO*

Barbatos/Barbas/ Batal	Demon Prince – Sagittarius Demon Count/Earl and Duke	*LdE, PmD, DoW, Goe, GG, BoSC, DI*
Barbaryes	Demon Prince	*BOS, BoO*
Barbays	Spirit – East	*oADS*
Barbelo	Gnostic Hermaphroditic First Emanation	*ACM*: NH Codex VIII
Barbiel	Angel – Mansion nine Angel – Leo/Scorpio Angel – First Heaven, South	*3BOP, BoO, tSoS, JMR, SaS, PO, tM*
Barbiel	Demon – Prince-Elector, Saturn Wise Spirit Prince Palatine	*MNeI*
Barbil	Demon Duke – South Day	*Stg, ThG*
Barbis	Demon Duke – South Night	*Stg, ThG*
Barbuel	Demon Prince	*SoM*
Barbuit	Demon	*GoPH*
Barcalin	Angel – Venus/Friday	*SR*
Barcayl	Angel	*LL*
Barcen	Enochian Angel – East, over third lesser Angle	*TBA*
Barchan	Demon – Sun	*BARC*
Barchan	Demon King under Belzebub Mirror Spirit – Wedneday	*SSM, MNeI*
Barchiel/Barbiel	Angel - Scorpio/Pisces Angel – Moon/Pisces Genius – Rubeus	*KoSR, 3BOP, tSoS, MC, JMR, SaS, Thm, PO, tM*
Barchiel/Brachiel/ Brackiel	Demon Duke – Day Hour six Demon Under Duke	*Stg, ThG*
Barchiel	Angel – Chora four	*ArA*
Bardari/Badari	Spirit – sixth Mansion of Moon Ring	*AE*
Bardiacha	Spirit – eighteenth Mansion of the Moon Ring	*AE*
Barechel	Ministering Familiar/Mystery	*67M*
Barechos/Berechos	Spirit	*BoSC*
Bareschas	Angel	*GoPH, GV*
Barfael	Demon Prince	*VJL*
Barfas/Barface	Demon Duke – West Day	*Stg, ThG, BoTS*
Barfos	Demon Duke – North-West Night	*Stg, ThG, BoTS*

Barfynāl	Angel – February/Aquarius	*BoW*
Bargar	Angel – Iyar	*SR*
Bargees (Rafael, Persian)	Spirit King – Jupiter	*Pic*
Barhawt/Barhawat/Barhaot	Spirit – seventh Heaven	*Pic*
Barhil	Angel – Sun/Sunday	*SR*
Barhoyas	Spirit of Mercury	*Pic*
Bariana	Spirit	*ACM*: Hay 10391
Bariba	Angel – Sixth Encampment, first Heaven	*ShR*
Barich	Angel	*KoN*
Bariel	Archangel	*ACM*: BN Turin
Bariel/Bariell	Demon Duke – South by West Day Demon	*Stg, CoC, GAG, ThG, BoTS*
Bariel	Angel – Mercury/Wednesday Angel Ruler – Day Hour eleven	*SR, Stg, ArP*
Barikhmē/Bakhenmous	Angel – Sea Ruler in Spring	*BoW*
Barilagni	Angel – Bisertilis	*SR*
Bariol	Servant Spirit	*Abm*
Barionin	Angel – Moon	*LL*
Barkan/Barkam (Varcan)	Angel King – Sunday	*BoO, BoTS*
Barkiel	Angel	*SMS*
Barkyel	Angel – three signs of third Season	*SSM*
Barma	Spirit	*DoW*
Barmaly	Angel – Tuesday	*MHN*
Barmas/Baymasos	Angel – Night Hour five	*Stg, ArP*
Barmiel	Demon Prince – South Demon Prince – South under Amaymon	*Stg, ThG, BoTS, KoN*
Barmolees	Spirit – Regal Antipathy	*Pic*
Barnayeyl	Angel – Venus/Friday	*SR*
Barnidōn/Barnēdōn (Mercury)	Mercury – Alternative Name	*Hyg*
Baroba	Angel – Malachim, under Pheseker Angel – Malachim, sixth Host	*SRH*
Barolas	Spirit – Love/Sexual Attraction	*Pic*

Baron/Baraham/ Bareth/ Barachin/Baaran/ Baryth	Demon Prince – North	BoO, BM, GAG
Baros/Baras	Demon Duke – West by South Night	Stg, ThG, , BoTS, GV
Barouch	Angel – Underworld	PGM CXXIV:1-43; ACM: P. Mil. Vogl. Inv. 1251, H. Kopt. 681
Baroy/Baray/Borai/ Bayag	Spirit Spirit – first Mansion of Moon Ring	SSM, AE, tSoS
Barquiel/Barquyel	Angel – Fifth Heaven, East Angel – First Heaven, South	SR, SSM, SaS
Barquiel/Bargniel	Angel Ruler – Hour seven	Stg, ArP
Barrabas/Barrabaz	Spirit	SSM, BoSC
Barsafael	Demon – Decan two	ToS
Barsephial/ Barsaphēala	Demon – North	Hyg
Barsfilin	Angel – Mercury/Wednesday	SR
Barsu/Barfu	Demon Duke – North-West Day	Stg, ThG, BoTS
Barsy	Demon Ruler and Captain	BOS, BoO
Bartach	Angel – Fifth Heaven, West	SSM
Bartatel	Angel – Summer	MHN
Bartax	Demon Ruler	BOS, BoO
Bartha/Bartham	Spiriti King	MHN
Barthan	Daemon King – Sun, East Spirit King – Sunday	SBH, CBoM, oADS
Barthaylin	Angel – Moon	LL
Bartifari	Spirit – third Mansion of Moon Ring	AE
Barton/Harton	Demon Duke	BOS, BoO
Bartyn	Demon Duke	BOS, BoO
Baruch	Demon Under Duke	Stg, ThG
Baruchaba	Angel	KoSA
Baruchas	Demon King – East by North Demon Prince – North under Egyn	Stg, ThG, KoN
Baruchiachel	Angel	ToS
Baruel	Servant Spirit	Abm

Baruson	Spirt messenger – West	*BoTS*
Baruth	Demon	*MHN*
Baryel	Angel – Fourth Season by Day	*SSM*
Barzabel	Planetary Spirit – Mars Ruler – Puer, Rubeus Co-Ruler – Cauda Draconis	*KoSR, 3BOP, BM, Thm, PO, tM*
Basaam	Demon King	*NML*
Basal	Spirit	*MHN*
Basan	Spirit	*Hyg*
Basayn	Spirit	*CoC*
Bascli/Basclip	Demon Prince – West under Beymon	*KoN*
Bashathan	Daemon – Sun, subject to North Wind	*SBH*
Basiel	Demon Duke – West Night	*Stg, ThG, BoTS*
Basigōn/Basigōr/ Basigor/Basegor	Demon – West	*Hyg*
Basilon/Busiton	Angel – Day Hour ten	*Stg, ArP*
Basin	Spirit	*Hyg*
Baslamos	Front part of Didas	*Pic*
Bason/Baasan/ Barson/ Basan	Demon King – West	*BOS, BoO, oADS*
Basquiel	Angel	*oADS*
Basras	Spirit – Regal Antipathy	*Pic*
Bassan	Demon Senior	*SSM*
Bast/Bastet	Egyptian Cat Goddess of Pleasure and Protection	PGM XII:376-396, PDM XIV:841-850
Bastelyn	Angel – Mars/Tuesday	*SR*
Basy	Angel – First Heaven, North	*SR*
Basyaccor	Angel	*NA*
Batabēl	Demon	*Hyg*
Bataiva/Bataivah	Enochian King – East	*TBA, BoTS*
Batel	Spirit – Friday	*BoSC*
Bathaylyn	Angel – Moon/Monday	*SR*
Bathiabēl	Angel – Lunar, Night Hour eleven	PGM VII:862-918
Bathin/Barthin/ Bathym/Bathim/ Mathim/Marthim	Demon Duke	*PmD, DoW, Goe, GG, BoSC*

Bathrael	Plant Spirit – Lichen	*GS*
Bathuel	Angel	*ACM*: Hay 10434
Bathurael	Great Father Spirit	*ACM*: BN Turin
Bathuriel	Spirit	*ACM*: Cairo EM 49547, Oriental 6796
Batirmiss	Servant Spirit	*Abm*
Batirolees	Spirit – Love/Sexual Attraction	*Pic*
Batiydyas	Spirit – Regal Sympathy	*Pic*
Batoraielyn	Angel – Venus/Friday	*SR*
Batraiel	Angel – Day Hour two	*LL*
Batriel	Angel – Second Heaven, South	*SR*
Battenayer/Battenaye	Spirit	*BoO*
Baty	Angel – Second Heaven, South	*SaS*
Batyel	Angel – Fourth Heaven, North	*SSM*
Baubo	Greek Goddess of Mirth	PGM IV:2708-2784, VII:664-685, VII:686-702, VII:862-918; *SM*: T. Köln Inv. 1, P. Reinach II.88
Baufa	Familiar Spirit	*VJL*
Baviel	Genii – 24° Scorpio, 24° Sagittarius	*ArP*
Baxatan	Spirit	*SSM*
Baxatau	Spirit Punishing Wind	*SSM*
Baxhathau/Baxhatau	Spirit – Sun, East	*SBH*
Baxo/Baio/Bayd	Spirit – tenth Mansion of the Moon Ring	*AE*
Bayalos	Spirit – Enmity	*Pic*
Bayatan	Spirit	*SSM*
Bayel	Angel – Fifth Heaven, North	*SaS*
Bayemon/Bayemont (Paymon)	Demon King – West	*GoPH, BD*
Baylon	Demon	*GAG*
Baysul	Demon – Moon	*BARC*
Bazarachiel	Tribal Spirit Prince – the Dead	*MNeI*
Bazazeth	Angel	*ToS*

Bbaigao	Spirit Minister, serving Prince Butmono	*dHM*
Bbalpae	Spirit Minister, serving Prince Butmono	*dHM*
Bbanifg	Spirit Minister, serving Prince Butmono	*dHM*
Bbarnfl	Spirit Minister, serving Prince Butmono	*dHM*
Bbasnod	Spirit Minister, serving Prince Butmono	*dHM*
Bbital	Angel – Seventh Encampment, first Heaven	*ShR*
Bbosnia	Spirit Minister, serving Prince Butmono	*dHM*
Bbsbau	Angel – Fifth Step, second Heaven	*ShR*
Bdidimon	Spirit	*Hyg*
Beab/Beabo	Spirit Spirit – Woods	*CoC, oADS, tSoS*
Beal/Beall	Spirit	*oADS*
Bealberith	Ministering Familiar/Mystery	*67M*
Belphares/ Bealphares/ Bealpear/Bialphar	Spirit	*SSM, BOS, DoW, GAG*
Beandinet	Spirit – fourteenth Mansion of the Moon ring	*tSoS*
Beanke/Beanre	Spirit of the Thumb	*MHN*
Bēara	Demon – North	*Hyg*
Bearel	Angel – Jupiter/Thursday	*SR*
Beatiel	Angel – Fourth Heaven, East	*SaS*
Beball/Bebal/Baball	Demon King	*PmD, DoW, Goe, DI*
Bebykis	Demon – South	*Hyg*
Becar	Angel – Marchesvan	*SR*
Bechaud/Beschard/ Bechard/Bechet/ Bechar/Becard	Demon Duke Demon – Friday Demon – under Sirach	*KoSR, KoSU, SoS, GoPH, GV, BD*
Bechelial	Angel Prince – South Gate, Firmament	*SRH*
Bedary/Bedarys	Demon Duke – East	*Stg, ThG*
Beddah (Utarid, Indian)	Spirit King – Mercury	*Pic*
Bedeqial	Angel – Malachim, Tishri	*SRH*
Beduch/Bamone (Bitru)	Demon Marquis	*NML*
Bedunim/Bunedreim	Angel	*SoM*

Bee	Angel – Mercury/Wednesday	SR
Beel	Demon King under Beelzebub – East	SSM
Beel	Angel – Jupiter/Thursday Angel – Saturn	SR, Hyg
Beelbac	Spirit – Pleiades (seven of seven)	oADS
Beelzebub / Bellzebub/ Belzebut/ Belzebuth/ Beelzeboul/ Bellsabube/ Belzebub/Berzeboul/ Bell/Beelzebul/ Bielzouz/ Belsebub/Zeboul/ (Charon)	Demon Ruler Demon Prince – False Gods, Asia Demon Prince – Africa Demon Prince – Americas Demon Prince – East Demon Prince – Darkness Demon Duke/Governor Demon – Saturn, South Demon of Gluttony Daemon Prince Grand Prince – Hell	ToS, HB Matt 10:25 12:24, 12:27, Mark 3:22, Luke 11:15, 11:18-19; SSM, SBH, Hyg, MHN, Abm, NML, KoSU, Gbk, 3BOP, CBoM, LdE, SoS, BOS, BoO, CoC, BM, GAG, JMR, oADS, BoTS, GoPH, MNeI, KoN, SMS, ArPh, GoA, ES, GV, BoSC, PO, MRC, tM, GG, DI, VJL, SBRM
Beerel	Angel – Mercury/Wednesday	SR
Befafes	Angel Prince – Tuesday	dHM
Befranzy/Befranzij	Angel – Night Hour nine	Stg, ArP
Begeal	Angel Prince – Gate of Spirit of East	SRH
Begehalodin	Angel – Moon	LL
Begierethov	Spirit – East in Winter	SRH
Begud	Superior Intelligence – Water	KoSU, SoS
Behel	Genii – 23° Libra	ArP
Behelial	Angel Prince – Gate of Spirit of East	SRH
Behemnos	Angel	NA
Behemoth	Primal Chaos Creature Demon Chief/Monster Chief of Hell Punishing Wind	HB Job 40:16; SSM, 3BOP, MNeI, tM, DI
Beherit	Grand Prince – Hell	MNeI
Behial	Angel Prince – Gate of Spirit of North	SRH
Behonydiun/ Behonydin/ Behonydyn	Angel – Venus	LR
Beigia	Son of Light, subject to Prince Hagonel	dHM

ABBREVIATIONS

Bekharaēl/Beraēl/Beriēl	Angel – Saturday Hour seventeen	*Hyg*
Bēkarton	Demon – East	*Hyg*
Bel (Marduk)	Babylonian God of Order	HB Isa 46:1, Jer 50:2, 51:44, Dan 14:3-22
Bel	Spirit	*ACM*: Oriental 6796; *SSM*
Bela'ayi	Angel Prince – North Gate	*SRH*
Bela'ayial	Angel Prince – North Gate	*SRH*
Bel Ached	Spirit – Earth in Summer	*SRH*
Belam/Bolam	Infernal Spirit	*MHN, oADS*
Belaratat/Belaraēl	Angel – Saturday Hour seventeen	*Hyg*
Belbee/Belbie/Belbēs/Belbial	Demon – West	*Hyg*
Belbel	Demon – Decan eight	*ToS*
Belcebuch (Beelzebub)	Spirit – North	*SSM*
Beldon	Spirit – Pleiades (three of seven)	*oADS*
Beldor	Spirit	*GV*
Belehial	Angel Prince – South Gate, Firmament	*SRH*
Belem	Demon – North	*GoPH*
Beleqial	Angel Minister – Malachim	*SRH*
Belet	Demon	*ToSC*
Beleth/Bileth/Byleth	Demon King Demon – South Spirit – Four Quarters of the Universal Mansions	*BoO, PmD, DoW, Goe, SGT*
Belfarto/Belferit	Spirit Messnger – East	*BoTS*
Belferith/Belferich	Demon	*MHN, NML*
Belferth	Demon Messenger – West	*BOS, BoO, BoTS*
Belferyth (Belferith)	Spirit	*SSM*
Belgahaladim	Angel – Moon	*LL*
Belh	Demon Minister – Beelzebub	*SSM*
Beliah	Angel Minister – Love and Fornication	*KoSA*

Belial/Beliall/ Belyall/ Belyal/Bellyall/Beliar	Demon King – West Demon Prince – Vessels of Iniquity/Wrath Demon Prince or Duke – South Demon Viceroy Infernal Treasure Spirit Spirit Messenger – West Demon King (was Order of Thrones) Spirit – Minister of Love	HB 2 Cor 6:15; *SSM, Hyg, MHN, Abm, dN, NML, 3BOP, CBoM, BOS, BoO, PmD, DoW, BM, Goe, oADS, JMR, BoTS, KoN, MRC, PO, tM, VJL*
Beliath	Spirit	*MHN*
Beliferes	Servant Spirit	*Abm*
Belima	Spirit – Minister of Love	*oADS*
Belioukh/Bilioul/ Belioul	Demon – South	*Hyg*
Bell	Demon Prince – Earth Spirit – Treasure and Familiars Spirit – Minister of Love	*oADS*
Bellamia	Angel Minister	*KoSA*
Bellfarto/Bellferit	Demon Messenger – East	*BOS, BoO*
Bellicorth/Bellicaert	Spirit – ninth Mansion of the Moon Ring	*AE*
Belon	Angel – Saturn/Saturday	*SR*
Belouch	Spirit – Power of Darkness	*ACM*: Berlin 8322
Belphegor/ Baalphegor	Demon Ambassador – France Demon of Sloth	*DI*
Belpher	Angel Minister – Love and Fornication	*KoSA*
Belsay	Demon Duke – North Night	*Stg, ThG, BoTS*
Belsefer	Spirit	*SSM*
Beltatouthēl	East Wind – Winter	*BoW*
Beltēl	Spirit	*BoW*
Beltoliel/Beltouliel/ Beltokhiel (Saturn)	Saturn – Alternative Name	*Hyg*
Belu	Spirit – Herbs	*KoN*
Beluginis	Demon	*oADS*
Belugo	Demon	oADS
Belzazel	Spirit – Venus	*TV*
Bemechial	Angel – Malachim, Flames of Fire	*SRH*
Bemerethiyas	Angel Magistrate – Malachim	*SRH*
Bemerot	Servant Spirit	*Abm*
Bemikhō/Bemaōr	South Wind – Winter	*BoW*

Bēnage	Demon – East	*Hyg*
Benedill	Spirit	*BoO*
Benekial	Angel – Malachim, Flames of Fire	*SRH*
Benenil	Angel – Mercury/Wednesday	*SR*
Benez	Spirit	*GV*
Bengariel	Angel – Mercury, over Air	*SR*
Bengiel	Genii – 11° Pisces	*ArP*
Benias`	Spirit	*oADS*
Beniel	Angel – Jupiter/Thursday Angel Minister	*SR, KoSA*
Beni Seraphim	Intelligence – Venus	*KoSR*
Benit/Benyt	Angel – Nisan	*SR, tSoS*
Benkurfsioth	Spirit – ninth Mansion of the Moon Ring	*tSoS*
Benlam/Renlam	Treasure Spirit	*oADS*
Benodiel	Demon Chief Duke	*Stg, ThG*
Benoham/Bonoham	Spirit of the Thumb	*MHN, CBoM*
Benoham	Demon Duke – East	*Stg, ThG*
Benouēl/Benoēl (Luna)	Luna – Alternative Name	*Hyg*
Bentranas	Spirit	*BoO*
Bēodon	Demon – South	*Hyg*
Bepheliyiya	Angel – Malachim, sixth Host	*SRH*
Bephenial	Spirit Prince – Ocean in Winter	*SRH*
Beqshdeilim	Angel – Moon	*LL*
Berape	Enochian Angel – South, serving second lesser Angle	*TBA*
Beratiel/Beraliel	Angel Ruler – Day Hour twelve	*Stg, ArP*
Beray	Spirit	*oADS*
Berbiēl	Angel – Saturday Hour fourteen	*Hyg*
Berbigot	Demon	*GoPH*
Berchos	Angel – three signs of fourth Season	*SSM*
Beregemi	Angel – Malachim, under Ayigeda	*SRH*
Bereka	Angel – Malachim, under Dohel	*SRH*
Berekethian	Angel – Malachim, under Dohel	*SRH*
Berekial	Angel – Malachim, Tebeth	*SRH*

Beremon	Angel – Second Altitude (Taurus)	*Alm*
Bereqial	Archangel – Jupiter, Leo, Winter Angel – Malachim, Autumn Angel Minister – Malachim, sixth Dwelling Angel – Malachim, Ab	*SRH*
Beresial	Angel Prince – Malachim over the Gates of the Sky	*SRH*
Berethobial	Angel – Malachim, under Dohel	*SRH*
Berezial	Angel – Malachim, Tebeth	*SRH*
Bergath	Spirit – third Mansion of Moon Ring	*AE*
Bergountade	Angel	*Hyg*
Bergyinita	Angel	*Hyg*
Berharim	Angel – Day Hour two	*LL*
Berial	Angel – Malachim, Winter	*SRH*
Berich/Belfayt (Berith)	Demon King and Duke	*NML*
Beriekoch	Spirit – East in Winter	*SRH*
Beriel	Angel – Mercury, over Earth	*SR*
Beriel	Genii – 11° Taurus	*ArP*
Berien/Beryen	Spirit	*MHN*
Berietha	Angel – Malachim, under Ayigeda	*SRH*
Berifer	Spirit – Minister of Love	*oADS*
Berik/Berim/Beria (Saturn)	Saturn – Alternative Name	*Hyg*
Berion	Angel – Mercury/Wednesday	*SR*
Berith/Brith/Beale/Beall/Bofry/Bolfry/Bolfri	Demon Duke Demon – South Demon Prince Spirit – Presidentail Counsellor, South	*MHN, CBoM, BOS, BoO, PmD, DoW, Goe, BoTS, KoN, GoPH, DI, VJL*
Beritz	Spirit	*BoSC*
Berlorim	Angel Minister – Love and Fornication	*KoSA*
Bermarieb/Berbareth	Angel – Plant Ruler	*BoW*
Bermo	Spirit – Minister of Love	*oADS*
Bernerecha/Berudjech	Spirit – tenth Mansion of the Moon Ring	*AE*
Bernioēl/Berniōēl	Angel	*Hyg*

Beroqi	Angel – Malachim, under Avorphenial	*SRH*
Beroth	Angel	*KoSA*
Berphaēl	Angel – Summer	*DoW*
Berriel	Angel – Sun, over Air	*SR*
Bersada	Spirit – fourth Mansion of Moon Ring	*tSoS*
Bersebour	Demon King	*ACM*: Yale 1791
Berteth (Berith)	Demon Duke	*LdE*
Beryake	Spirit of the Thumb	*CBoM*
Beryel	Angel – Adar	*SR*
Beryl	Spirit – Minister of Love	*oADS*
Beryth	Spirit Spirit – South	*SSM*, *oADS*
Berzebouēl (Beelzebub)	Demon – West and Aries	*Hyg*
Bes/Besas/Besa	Egyptian Apotropaic Dwarf God	PGM VII:222-249, VIII:64-110, CII:1-17; *SM*: P. Oxy. XXXVI.2753
Besaēl	Angel – Saturday Hour three	*Hyg*
Besbyki	Name of Helios in tenth Hour	PGM IV:1596-1715
Beshael	Genii – 25° Capricorn, 25° Aquarius	*ArP*
Besmet	Spirit – West	*SSM*
Besmil/Bemil	Spirit	*BoW*
Besur	Spirit	*SSM*
Betaabat/Betabbat/Betabaaath	Angel – Second Heaven, East	*SR*, *SSM*, *SaS*
Betaeel/Bitail	Spirit King – Venus	*Pic*, *SSG*
Betaniēl/Bataniēl/Bataaniēl	Angel – Friday Hour twenty-three	*Hyg*
Betasiel/Betasid	Demon Duke – North Day	*Stg*, *ThG*, *BoTS*
Betel	Spirit	*GoA*
Beth	Angel Guardian	*ACM*: Hay 10391
Betha	Angel Guardian	*ACM*: Hay 10391
Bethala	Demon Chief – South-East	*SSM*
Bethanael/Bethnael	Noble Spirit, Fire	*MNeI*
Bethaz	Angel – Sun/Sunday	*SR*

Betheca	Spirit	*BoO*
Bethemial	Spirit Prince – Sea in Spring	*SRH*
Bethor/Betor/ Beshor/ Tehor/Thetor	Olympic Spirit – Jupiter	*KoSR, Arb, MC, GAG, JMR, MNeI, oADS, KoN, GoA, PO, ClI, 67M, SGT, SSG*
Betiel	Genii – 20° Aries	*ArP*
Betodah	Angel	*67M*
Betu	Demon	*GV*
Beulus	False Spirit – Lord of Roots and Flowers	*MNeI*
Bevael	Genii – 14° Scorpio, 14° Sagittarius	*ArP*
Bghial	Angel Prince – fourth Heaven, Water	*ShR*
Bhairava/Beyrevra	Indian Demon/God	*DI*
Bhchml	Angel Encampment Head – sixth Heaven, West	*ShR*
Bhdrk	Angel Encampment Head – sixth Heaven, West	*ShR*
Bhlyāyl	Angel – Sun	*BoW*
Bhnirial	Angel Encampment Head – sixth Heaven, East	*ShR*
Biael	Genii – 1° Aries	*ArP*
Bialod	Servant Spirit	*Abm*
Bianakith	Demon – Decan thirty-six	*ToS*
Biara/Bbiara/Bēara/ Biaroth	Demon – North	*Hyg*
Bidiel/Bydiel	Demon Wandering Prince	*Stg, ThG*
Bidon	Spirit Prince – Painting	*MNeI*
Bidouēl/Bediēl	Angel – Sunday Hour ten	*Hyg*
Biēl	Angel – Sunday Hour eleven	*Hyg*
Biem	Angel Prince – North Gate	*SRH*
Biememom	Angel – Malachim, sixth Host	*SRH*
Bierekom	Angel, serving above sixth Degree	*SRH*
Bifealyqnyn	Angel – Moon/Monday	*SR*
Bifrons/Bifrovs	Demon Earl	*SSM, PmD, DoW, Goe*
Bifulica	Angel – Moon	*LL*
Bihynolsaser	Spirit – Love/Sexual Attraction	*Pic*

Bikheron/ Bekharnou/ Bilerou/Bekherou	Demon – West	*Hyg*
Bikitaroos	Spirit – Love/Sexual Attraction	*Pic*
Bilech	Demon King	*NML*
Bilek	Servant Spirit	*Abm*
Bilet/Bileth/Byleth/ Bilit/ Bylet/Bilef	Angel Minister of Air – Monday Daemon Minister – Moon, West Demon King Demon – South Ministering Spirit – Saturn Spirit – South Spirit Attendant – Moon	*SSM, SBH, EoN, Hmn, BARC, BOS, KoSR, BoO, BM, GAG, oADS, BoTS, SMS, KoN, MRC, CoMS, tM, CBMS, SSG*
Bilgall/Bylgall/Bilgal	Demon	*BOS, BoO, oADS*
Bilifot	Servant Spirit	*Abm*
Bille (Bune)	Demon Duke	*NML*
Bimadam	Angel	PGM XXVI:1-42
Binae	Spirit – East	*Hyg*
Bintivash	Demon	*SMS*
Birachiel	Angel – Mansion six and Gemini	*BoO*
Biraquel	Angel Ruler – Ab	*SR*
Bireoth	Benign Spirit	*MHN*
Birga (Persian) (Rufijail)	Angel – Jupiter	*SSG*
Birgur	Norse Deity (?)	*Gbk*
Birto	Spirit	*BoO, tSoS, BoTS*
Biscerdiel/Discerdiel	Free Spirit – Quarrel	*MNeI*
Bisseros	Angel – Sixth Altitude (Virgo)	*Alm*
Bitaael/Bitail	Spirit Advisor – Venus	*Pic, SSG*
Bithiel	Angel	*Hyg*
Bitsmael/Bethnael	Angel – Mansion twenty-one	*3BOP, tSoS, JMR, SaS, tM*
Bitur (Sitri)	Demon Marquis	*LdE*
Biual	Angel Encampment Head – sixth Heaven, West	*ShR*
Bizoul/Bizikē/Biziē/ Bizēk/Bixikē	Demon – Friday Hour two	*Hyg*
Blbopoo	Spirit Minister, serving Prince Brorges	*dHM*

Bkpi	Angel – Fifth Step, second Heaven	*ShR*
Bleathe (Bleth?)	Spirit	*EBAM*
Blekyn	Demon – Wednesday Hour sixteen	*Hyg*
Blemēn/Blemeg/ Blemigkh	Demon – Wednesday Hour seventeen	*Hyg*
Bleth (Bileth?)	Spirit	*BoTS*
Bliddōb	Angel	*Hyg*
Blimōn	Angel	*Hyg*
Blisdon	Angel Prince – Wednesday	*dHM*
Blnial	Angel – Third Heaven, serving Ibnial	*ShR*
Blqur	Angel – Fourth Encampment, first Heaven	*ShR*
Bludohn (Pluto)	Exiled Angel	*MNeI*
Blvmaza	Angel King – Monday	*dHM*
Blyth	Spirit	*oADS*
Bmriut	Angel – Twelfth Step, second Heaven	*ShR*
Bnamgen	Spirit Minister, serving Prince Brorges	*dHM*
Bnapsen	Angel King – Saturday	*dHM*
Bnaspol	Angel King – Wednesday	*dHM*
Bnrial	Angel Prince – fourth Heaven, Water	*ShR*
Bnsh	Angel – Fifth Encampment, first Heaven	*ShR*
Bnvages	Spirit Minister, serving Prince Brorges	*dHM*
Boab/Boal/Boall	Demon President Demon Prelate	*NML, BOS, BoO*
Boad	Spirit – third Mansion of Moon Ring	*AE*
Boaēl (Luna)	Luna – Alternative Name	*Hyg*
Boamiel	Angel – First Heaven, East	*SaS*
Bobogel	Angel King – Sunday	*dHM*
Bodimen/Bodēmēl/ Bodimēl/Bedmeēl	Demon – West	*Hyg*
Bodre/Bodith	Spirit – fifth Mansion of the Moon Ring	*AE*
Bodyees	Spirit – Love/Sexual Attraction	*Pic*
Bodykil	Demon – West	*Hyg*
Boel	Angel Subordinate – Saturn	*SSM*
Boel	Angel – Elul Angel – Mercury/Wednesday	*SR, SMS*

Boel	Throne Angel (seven of seven)	*SaS*
Boell	Demon Senator	*BoO*
Bofar/Bufar	Demon Duke – South by East Night	*Stg, ThG, BoTS*
Bohel/Boel/Boell	Spirit – Saturn Angel – Saturn	*SBH, EoN, oADS, BoTS*
Bohodi	Spirit of the Thumb	*MHN*
Boidonatekan/ Boidōn/ Boidon/Bēodon	Demon – South	*Hyg*
Bok	Demon	*ACM*: H. Kopt. 681
Bokarpar/Bokarpa/ Bokarpan	Demon – East	*Hyg*
Bokiel/Boilēl	Angel – Thursday Hour fourteen	*Hyg*
Bokyēl	Angel – Thursday Hour thirteen, fourteen	*Hyg*
Bollo	Spirit	*BoO*
Boncifath	Angel Minister – Love and Fornication	*KoSA*
Bonohan	Spirit of the Thumb	*CBoM*
Bonoreae	Demon Marquis and Duke	*NML*
Bonyel/Boniel/ Banier	Demon Duke – North by East Day	*Stg, ThG*
Booel/Boel	Archangel – Saturn	*Hmn, BoO, GAG*
Booth	Spirit	*BoO, tSoS, BoTS*
Borachial/Barachiel	Angel – Chora one	*ArA*
Boralim	Spirit – South	*DoW*
Borasy/Borass/Boras	Demon Duke – West Day	*Stg, BoO, BOS, ThG, BoTS*
Borayeyl	Angel – Venus/Friday	*SR*
Borbai	Angel – Sivan	*SR*
Borcolin	Angel – Moon	*LL*
Boreas	North Wind – over Angels of Sunday	*Hmn, BoTS, SMS, PO*
Bored	Angel Minister	*KoSA*
Boriatiacali/ Boriatiacath	Spirit – twelfth Mansion of the Moon Ring	*AE*
Boriel	Angel of Flaming Face	*ACM*: P. Mich. 1190
Bornogo	Angel Prince – Sunday	*dHM*
Borob	Servant Spirit	*Abm*

Boros	Angel	*NA*
Bortaz	Angel – Fifth Heaven, West	*SR*
Bos	Demon	*MHN*
Bosco	Spirit Spirit – Forest	*BoO, oADS*
Bostael	Spirit	*BoO*
Bosto	Spirit	*oADS*
Bothothel/Bobel	Demon – Decan thirteen	*Tos*
Botis/Otis	Demon President and Earl	*PmD, DoW, Goe, GG, BoSC*
Botuliel/Betuliel (Hamaliel)	Angel – Virgo Spirit – Virgo	*3BOP, BoO, tSoS, JMR, SaS*
Bouēl/Boel	Angel Lord	PGM IV:930-1114, PDM XIV:150-231, XIV:459-475, XIV:489-515, XIV:516-527, XIV:1163-1179
Boul	Demon – West	*ToSC*
Bournay/Vournay	Spirit – ninth Mansion of the Moon Ring	*AE*
Bournes/Bonrnos	Spirit – ninth Mansion of the Moon Ring	*AE*
Boxoraylon	Angel – Saturn/Saturday	*SR*
Boytheon/Beytheon/ Bethereon/Betheron/ Botheron	Demon Bishop – South or West	*CBoM, BoO, CoC, GAG, oADS, BoTS*
Boza	Enochian Angel – North, over first lesser Angle	*TBA*
Braa (Shams, Indian)	Spirit King – Sun	*Pic*
Braaliel	Angel – Fourth Heaven, East	*SR*
Brachalim/Bratalim/ Biataliz	Spirit – first Mansion of the Moon Ring	*AE*
Brachiel	Water Spirit	*MNeI*
Brachucal	Spirit – eleventh Mansion of the Moon Ring	*AE*
Bradaēl/Bradiēl/ Bradēl/ Bradyē	Angel – Sunday Hour twenty-two	*Hyg*

Bragandi/ Bitradandibi/ Betradandi	Spirit – fifth Mansion of Moon Ring	AE, tSoS
Bralges	Angel Prince – Monday	dHM
Braliel	Angel – Fourth Heaven, East	SR
Bramiel/Bromiel	Angel – Night Hour four	Stg, ArP
Bramsiel	Demon Chief Duke	Stg, ThG
Brandalia/Sicandilis	Spirit – seventh Mansion of the Moon Ring	AE
Brandamiroth/ Branda/ Beaudamuet	Spirit – fourteenth Mansion of the Moon Ring	AE
Brandiel	Angel – Night Hour nine	Stg, ArP
Branielin	Angel – Moon/Monday	SR
Brasiel	Angel – Day Hour six, Day Hour nine	Stg, ArP
Brasilic/Brafilis	Spirit – fifth Mansion of the Moon Ring	AE
Braut	Angel – Twelfth Step, second Heaven	ShR
Brazo	Spirit	GV
Bret/Brett	Treasure Spirit	BoTS
Bretull	Demon	GV
Brgal	Angel – Twelfth Step, second Heaven	ShR
Brgmi	Angel – Second Encampment, first Heaven	ShR
Briel	Angel – Jupiter/Thursday	SR
Brieus	Angel	ToS
Brimas	Spirit of Saturn	Pic
Brimer	Spirit	MHN
Brimo/Brimō	Greek Vengeance Goddess	PGM IV:2241-2358, IV:2441-2621, IV:2943-2966, VII:686-702, CXXIIIa:1-70; SM: P. Reinach II.88, P. Mil. Vogl. Inv. 1245-50, 1252-53
Briyanos	Spirit – Love/Sexual Attraction	Pic
Brkial	Angel – Third Step, second Heaven Angel – Eighth Step, second Heaven	ShR

Brkib	Angel – Second Encampment, first Heaven	ShR
Brofilyn	Angel – Mars/Tuesday	SR
Brohoyas	Spirit – Love/Sexual Attraction	Pic
Brorges	Angel Prince – Saturday	dHM
Brqial	Angel – Eighth Step, second Heaven	ShR
Brshsal	Angel – Third Heaven, serving Ibnial	ShR
Brtubial	Angel – Third Encampment, first Heaven	ShR
Bruach	Servant Spirit	Abm
Brufiel/Brusiel/Burfiel	Demon Duke – Day Hour eleven and Night Hour eleven	Stg, ThG
Brufor	Demon	GoA
Brulo/Brulor	Demon	MHN, NML
Brumiel	Angel – Day Hour one	Stg, ArP
Bruq	Angel – First Encampment, first Heaven	ShR
Bruschan	Night Devil	oADS
Bryman/Myniciorom/Mycioron	Demon Earl	BOS, BoO
Brymiel/Byrmiel/Brimiel	Demon Duke	Stg, ThG
Bryson	Angel – First Heaven, West	SSM
Btuar	Angel – Fifth Encampment, first Heaven	ShR
Bubanabub	Servant Spirit	Abm
Bubukuk	Angel – Twelfth Step, second Heaven	ShR
Bucafas	Demon Duke – East	Stg, ThG
Bruslefer/Brulefer	Demon	SoSW, GV
Bualu/Bual	Angel	SoM
Bucal (Procel)	Demon Duke	LdE
Buchat	Angel – Fourth Heaven Sunday, West	BoTS
Buchermann	Spirit Prince – Arts	KoN
Buchyfali/Buchifali/Bictisaly	Spirit – third Mansion of the Moon Ring	AE
Bucon/Bucons	Demon	SoSW, GV
Budar/Buder	Demon Duke – South-West Night	Stg, ThG, BoTS
Budarim/Budarym	Demon Duke – South	Stg, ThG

ABBREVIATIONS

Buddha (Hindi) (Utarid)	Angel – Mercury	*SSG*
Budiel	Demon Duke – South-East Day	*Stg, ThG, BoTS*
Buer/Buor	Demon President/Prince	*PmD, DoW, Goe, GG, BoSC, DI*
Buesaba	Angel – Sunday	*BoO*
Bufanotz/Bufanotzod	Angel – Night Hour eight	*Stg, ArP*
Bufflas (Suffales)	Spirit – East	*oADS*
Bufiel/Busiel	Demon Duke – Night Hour seven	*Stg, ThG*
Bufiel	Earth Spirit	*MNeI*
Bugan	Demon King	*LdE*
Buhram (Rubaeel, Persian)	Spirit King – Mars	*Pic*
Buldumech	Demon – Decan eighteen	*ToS*
Bulfas	Demon Prince	*LdE*
Bulerator	Spirit	*GV*
Bulidon	Angel – Saturn	*KoSR*
Bulis	Duke – West by North pre-Midnight	*Stg, ThG, BoTS*
Bune/Bime	Demon Duke	*LdE, PmD, DoW, Goe*
Bunes	Spirit	*ACM*: Cairo 45060
Buniel	Demon Duke – South-West Day	*Stg, ThG, BoTS*
Burada	Spirit	*CBoM*
Burcham	Devil – Cancer, Storms	*OADS*
Burchat/Burcat	Angel – Fourth Heaven Sunday, West, Spring Angel – Fourth Heaven, West Presiding Spirit – Sun	*EoN, Hmn, KoSR, BoO, GAG, SaS, tM, CBMS*
Burchat	Spirit Messenger – Sun	*SGT, SSG*
Burfa	Demon Duke – North-West Night	*Stg, ThG, BoTS*
Burfex//Bursex/Burphax	Fairy Queen	*BoO*
Buriel	Demon Wandering Prince	*Stg, Thg*
Buriel	Chief Earth Spirit	*MNeI*
Buriub	Servant Spirit	*Abm*
Burnahas	Servant Spirit	*Abm*
Burtias	Angel – Fourth Encampment, first Heaven	*ShR*

Busiel	Duke – West by North Afternoon	*Stg, ThG, BoTS*
Busin	Demon – South	*BOS, BoO*
Busto	Spirit	*GAG*
Busyn	Spirit – South	*oADS*
Butharuth	Servant Spirit	*Abm*
Buthath	Spirit – third Mansion of Moon Ring	*AE*
Butmono/Bvtmono	Angel Prince – Thursday	*dHM*
Bval	Angel Overseer (seven of seven) – first Heaven	*ShR*
Bvmdi	Angel – First Encampment, first Heaven	*ShR*
Byapare	Spirit Minister, serving Prince Brorges	*dHM*
Bybon	Spirit	*oADS*
Byell	Angel – Sunday	*BoO*
Byeniel	Angel – Earth	*SR*
Bylethor	Angel Minister of Air – Monday	*BoO*
Bymnan/Bymnam	Angel – Potestates	*67M*
Bynepor	Angel King – Thursday	*dHM*
Byny	Angel – Ab	*SR*
Bythath	Spirit, Sits over the Abyss	*PGM XXVI*:1-42

C

Caap (Gaap)	Demon Prince	*LdE*
Caba	Spirit – Mirror	*CoMS*
Cabach	Angel – Ab	*SR*
Cabariel/Gabariel	Demon Duke – West Demon Duke – West under Beymon	*Stg, ThG, BoTS, KoN*
Cabarim/Cabarym	Demon Duke – North	*Stg, ThG*
Cabelial	Demon King	*NML*
Caberyon/Caveryon/Gaberyon	Fairy Advisor	*BoO*
Cabiel	Demon Duke – West Day	*Stg, ThG, BoTS*
Cabiel	Genii – 21° Virgo	*ArP*
Cabriel	Angel – First Heaven, East	*SaS*
Cabrifiel	Angel – Jupiter/Thursday	*SR*
Cabron	Duke – West by North Afternoon	*Stg, ThG, BoTS*

ABBREVIATIONS

Cabyn	Angel – Mars/Tuesday	*SR*
Cacaras	Spirit – Middle	*SSM*
Cacaryll (Saranyt)	Spirit – North	*oADS*
Cachaoc	Angel – Moon	*BARC*
Cacitilyn	Angel – Mars/Tuesday	*SR*
Cadacant	Spirit	*SSM*
Cadas	Spirit Helper – Sunday	*CBoM*
Cadat	Angel	*GV*
Cadiel	Angel – Venus, West	*BM*
Cadnaelin	Angel – Day Hour two	*LL*
Cadneirin	Angel – Venus/Friday	*SR*
Cadomir	Spirit	*GV*
Cadriel	Duke – West by North after Midnight	*Stg, ThG, BoTS*
Cael	Angel – Adar Angel – Cancer	*SR, ArP*
Cafhael/Caphael/ Caphaell/Kaphael/ Kaphaell	Spirit – Sun Angel	*SBH, SSM, oADS*
Cafisyel	Spirit	*SSM*
Cafziel	Spirit – Saturn	*SBH*
Cagyne/Cogin/ Cagyn	Demon – West	*BOS, BoO, oADS*
Cahael	Genii – 23° Scorpio, 23° Sagittarius	*ArP*
Cahetel/Caheshel/ Cahethel/Cabetel/ Bahetel	Angel – Shem eight	*KoSU, 3BOP, GoeR, JMR, SAS, tM*
Caifaz/Caiphas	Spirit	*BoSC*
Caim/Caym/Camio	Demon President	*PmD, DoW, Goe, DI*
Caimax	Ministering Spirit – Saturn	*CBMS*
Caisaat/Caisaac	Angel – Nisan	*SR, tSoS*
Cajael	Genii – 30° Pisces	*ArP*
Cajaiel	Genii – 20° Pisces	*ArP*
Cakaziel	Angel – Venus, over Air	*SR*
Cakiel	Genii – 9° Aries	*ArP*
Cakiel	Angel – Mansion five and Taurus	*BoO*
Calach	Servant Spirit	*Abm*

Calacop	Angel – Sun	*BARC*
Calamosi	Servant Spirit	*Abm*
Calatyne/Galatyne/ Galatyn	Angel – Saturn	*tSoS*
Calcaala	Angel – Moon	*BARC*
Calcas	Angel – Fourth Heaven, East	*SR, SSM*
Calce	Demon Senior	*SSM*
Calchihay	Angel – Kislev	*SR*
Calcos	Demon Senior	*SSM*
Caldeirão	Demon	*BoSC*
Caldurech	Angel	*GV*
Calemite	Angel	*KoSA*
Caleos	Demon – West	*BOS, BoO*
Cali (Kali)	Demon Queen – Indian Hell	*DI*
Caliel	Angel – Shem eighteen	*KoSU, 3BOP, GoeR, JMR, SAS, tM*
Calim/Calym	Demon Duke – South-East Night	*Stg, ThG, BoTS*
Calipon	Angel – Saturn/Saturday	*SR*
Calitut	Spirit – fourteenth Mansion of the Moon ring	*tSoS*
Calizabin	Angel	*VJL*
Calizantin (Calizabin?)	Angel	*VJL*
Calkfulgra	Night Devil	*oADS*
Calliel	Angel – Second Heaven, South	*SaS*
Calloyel	Angel – Second Heaven, South	*SR*
Calmiron	Spirit	*GV*
Calmus	Spirit	*oADS*
Calnamia	Angel – Mercury/Wednesday	*SR*
Calniso	Spirit	*GV*
Calon	Angel – Moon	*GAG*
Caluel/Laquel	Angel – Second Heaven Wednesday, South Angel – Thursday/Jupiter	*EoN, Hmn, KoSR, BoO, GAG, BoTS, tM*
Calvarnia/ Caluarnia/ Catvarnia	Demon Duke – North-East	*Stg, ThG*

ABBREVIATIONS

Calvodium	Spirit	GV
Calzas/Calzaz/ Cabzars	Angel – Fifth Heaven Tuesday, East Angel – Fifth Heaven, East Presiding Spirit – Mars	EoN, Hmn, KoSR, BoO, GAG, BoTS, SaS, tM, CBMS
Camael	Archangel – Mars Ruler of Order of Powers (Potestates)	NA, tSoS, MC, JMR, GoA, CoMS, PO, tM
Camael	Genii – 4° Aquarius	ArP
Camalon	Servant Spirit	Abm
Camarion	Servant Spirit	Abm
Camaron	Angel – Day Hour twelve	Stg, ArP
Camb	Angel – Ab	SR
Cambea	Demon Count	NML
Cambiel/Gambiel/ Gabiel	Angel – Aquarius Angel – Night Hour eight Genius – Tristitia	Stg, 3BOP, tSoS, ArP, JMR, SaS, Thm
Cambores	Punishing Wind Daemon – Venus, subject to East and West Winds; between South and West	SSM, SBH
Cambra	Demon – South	BOS, BoO
Cambriel	Demon Duke – Hour eight of fifteen	Stg, ThG
Cameron	Spirit	GV
Cameso	Spirit	GV
Camfilin	Angel – Mercury/Wednesday	SR
Camiel/Camael	Demon Duke – West, Day Hour nine	Stg, ThG, BoTS
Camiel/Bariel	Angel – Day Hour five	Stg, ArP
Camiel	Water Spirit	MNeI
Camirael	Angel – Venus, over Air	SR
Camna	Spirit of the Thumb	CBoM
Camniel	Demon – Count Palatine Wise Spirit	MNeI
Camon	Spirit – Minister of Love	oADS
Camonix	Servant Spirit	Abm
Camor/Camory	Demon Duke – South	Stg, ThG
Camory/Camort	Demon Duke – South	Stg, ThG
Camosiel	Angel – Day Hour six	Stg, ArP
Camoy/Canay	Demon	MHN, NML
Camret	Spirit Duke – Treasure	BoTS

Camuel	Demon King – South-East Demon Prince – East under Oriens	*Stg, ThG, BoTS, KoN*
Camyel/Camyvel	Demon Duke – South-East Day	*Stg, ThG, BoTS*
Canael	Spirit – North	*SSM*
Cananyn	Angel – Mercury/Wednesday	*SR*
Canaphnell	Angel	*BoO*
Canariel	Angel – Day Hour two	*LL*
Canbtat	Spirit – Mirror	*CoMS*
Cancer	Wind Spirit	*GAG*
Cancriel (Muriel)	Angel – Cancer Spirit – Cancer	*3BOP, tSoS, JMR, SaS*
Candanagyn	Angel – Moon/Monday	*SR*
Candanegin	Angel – Moon	*LL*
Candas	Spirit Assistant – Sunday	*MHN*
Canempria	Spirit – eleventh (twelfth) Mansion of the Moon ring	*tSoS*
Canesylyn	Angel – Venus/Friday	*SR*
Canfft	Demon	*GoPH*
Caniel	Angel – Third Heaven, West	*EoN*
Caniel/Camel	Demon Duke – South Night	*Stg, ThG*
Caniel	Intelligence	*BoG*
Canielvel	Intelligence	*BoG*
Cannamdin	Angel – Moon	*LL*
Cannyel	Angel – Mars/Tuesday	*SR*
Cantivalerion/ Galgathell/Golgathell (Tantavalerion)	Spirit Emperor	*oADS*
Canyel	Angel – Tebet	*SR*
Caon	Demon – North	*DoW*
Capabile	Spirit Messenger – Sun	*SGT, SSG*
Capabili/Capabil/ Cababili/Capabel	Angel – Fourth Heaven Sunday, West, Spring Angel – Fourth Heaven, West Spirit – Sun Ministering Spirit – Sun	*EoN, Hmn, KoSR, SoS, BoO, GAG, BoTS, SaS, tM, CBMS*
Capaton	Angel – Mars	*BARC*
Capberutaoriston	Planetary Spirit Lord – Saturn	*SSM*

Capciel	Angel – Venus, over Fire Angel – Seventh Heaven, Saturn	*SR*
Capcyel (Cassiel)	Archangel – Saturn	*BoO*
Capeiel	Angel – Saturn/Saturday	*SR, KoN*
Caphael	Angel Subordinate - Sun Angel	*SSM, GoA*
Caphar	Angel	*NA*
Caphciel/Caphcyel	Angel Ruler – Saturn	*SSM*
Caphriel/Caphrael/ Capriel	Archangel – Saturn	*EoN, Hmn, CBoM, BoO, BoTS*
Capiel/Capiell	Angel – Fourth Heaven, East Angel	*SR, oADS*
Capriel (Haniel)	Angel – Capricorn Spirit – Capricorn	*3BOP, tSoS, JMR, SaS*
Capriel	Demon Duke – East	*Stg, ThG*
Captiel	Angel – Saturday/Saturn Angel – Chora four	*B7R, MHN, ArA*
Captiol	Angel – Saturn	*JMR*
Capuel	Angel	*oADS*
Capziel (Cassiel)	Archangel – Saturn	*SR*
Carab/Careb	Spirit	*MHN*
Carabiel	Angel – Moon	*KoSR*
Carafax	Angel	*oADS*
Caramtias	Demon King (formerly Order of Thrones)	*KoN*
Caran	Angel – Sun/Sunday	*SR*
Caraniel	Angel – Third Heaven, East	*SaS*
Carasch	Servant Spirit	*Abm*
Carasiba	Demon Duke – North-East	*Stg, ThG*
Caratasa/Caracasa	Angel – Spring	*EoN, Hmn, KoSR, BM, tSoS, MC, GAG, GoeR. tM*
Carba	Duke – West by North pre-Noon	*Stg, ThG, BoTS*
Carbiel	Angel – Jupiter/Thursday	*SR*
Carbiol	Angel – Iyar	*SR*
Carbus	Spirit	*oADS*
Carciel	Angel – Elul	*SR*
Carcoyel	Angel – Second Heaven, East	*SR*

Carcuray	Wicked Spirit	*NMI*
Carcyelel	Angel – Adar	*SR*
Cardiel	Demon Knight	*Stg, ThG*
Cardiel	Angel – Adar Angel – Night Hour eleven	*SR, Stg, ArP*
Caremaz/Carmax/ Caremax	Angel – Night Hour five	*Stg, ArP*
Carfyon	Angel Superior – first three signs	*SSM*
Carga/Cargo	Demon Duke – South-West Day	*Stg, ThG, BoTS*
Cargie	Spirit	*MHN*
Cargosik	Servant Spirit	*Abm*
Carhyel	Angel – Fire	*SSM*
Caribifin	Angel – Mercury/Wednesday	*SR*
Cariel	Angel – Fire Angel – Mars	*SR, GAG*
Cariel	Demon Duke – South-East Day	*Stg, ThG, BoTS*
Carinal	Angel – Mars	*GAG*
Cariniel	Angel – Second Heaven, East	*EoN*
Carman/Charmas	Angel – Night Hour eleven	*Stg, ArP*
Carmara/Marmara	Angel King – Monday	*dHM*
Carmas	Spirit Helper – Tuesday	*CBoM*
Carmath	Spirit Assistant – Tuesday	*MHN*
Carmax/Cormax/ Carmas/Carmab	Angel Minister of Air – Tuesday Spirit Attendant – Mars	*EoN, Hmn, KoSR, BoO, GAG, BoTS, tM*
Carmehal/Carmeal	Punishing Wind Daemon – Mars, subject to East Wind; South	*SSM, SBH*
Carmelan/ Cameleon/ Camelion/Camillion	Angel – Moon	*B7R, tSoS*
Carmelyon/ Carmelion (Carmelan)	Fairy Advisor and Angel – Moon	*oADS, BoO, GAG, CoMS*
Carmerin/ Carmeryn/ Cayenam (Gemory?)	Demon Lord	*BOS, BoO*
Carmiel/Carmyel	Angel – Second Heaven, East Angel – Third Heaven, North	*SR, SSM*

Carmiel/Carimiel	Demon Duke – West Day	*Stg, ThG, BoTS*
Carmola	Demon Marquis	*LdE*
Carmox	Daemon Minister – Mars, South	*SBH*
Carmuth	Demon Servant – Tuesday	*KoN*
Carnesiel/Carmasiel	Demon Emperor – East	*Stg, ThG, BoTS*
Carniel	Angel – Third Heaven, North	*SaS*
Carniel	Demon Duke – Night Hour ten	*Stg, ThG*
Carniel	Earth Spirit	*MNeI*
Carnifex	Spirit Prince – West	*KoN*
Carnnamdin	Angel – Moon	*LL*
Carnodiel	Demon Duke – Day Hour three	*Stg, ThG*
Carnol/Carnel	Demon Duke – North	*Stg, ThG*
Carof Caroli	Angel – Sun	*BARC*
Caron	Demon Duke – West Night	*Stg, ThG, BoTS*
Caron	Servant Spirit	*Abm, GV*
Caronem	Spirit – Sea Treasure	*oADS*
Carpatiel	Angel – First Heaven, West	*SaS*
Carpiel	Angel – Fourth Heaven, East	*SaS*
Carpiel/Carpid	Demon Duke – South Day	*Stg, ThG*
Carroye	Angel – Second Heaven, East	*SaS*
Carsiel	Angel – Fourth Heaven, South	*EoN*
Carsiel	Duke – West by North pre-Noon	*Stg, ThG, BoTS*
Carszeneyl	Angel – Mars/Tuesday	*SR*
Cartael	Demon Duke – North-East	*Stg, ThG*
Cartalion	Angel – Sivan	*SR*
Cartemat	Angel – Iyar	*SR*
Casadiel	Demon Count	*MNeI*
Casael/Cesael	Duke – West by North Afternoon	*Stg, ThG, BoTS*
Casbriel	Demon Duke – Night Hour five	*Stg, ThG*
Casbriel	Earth Spirit	*MNeI*
Casdiel	Foolish Spirit	*MNeI*
Casfeel	Angel – Jupiter	*BARC*
Casfrubyn	Angel – Moon/Monday	*SR*
Cashiel	Genii – 4° Capricorn	*ArP*

Casiel	Genii – 3° Sagittarius	*ArP*
Casiel/Casyel	Angel – Mars Angel – Nisan	*BARC, SR, tSoS*
Casiel	Demon Duke – West Day	*Stg, ThG, BoTS*
Casmiel	Spirit	*GoPH, GV*
Casmiroz/Casmiros	Angel – Night Hour eleven	*Stg, ArP*
Casmuch	Angel – Sivan	*SR*
Cason	Demon Duke	*MHN*
Caspaniel/Caspaniet	Demon Duke – Day Hour eleven	*Stg, ThG*
Casphiel/Capfiel	Demon – Count Palatine Foolish Spirit	*MNeI*
Caspiel	Demon Emperor – South	*Stg, ThG, BoTS*
Cassa	Angel – Spring	*MHN*
Cassal	Angel – Moon	*GAG*
Cassesi	Spirit – Air	*MNeI*
Cassiel/Caffriel/ Cassael/ Caphriel/Cafriel	Archangel – Saturn, Earth, Saturday, Treasure-seeking Angel Prince – Seventh Heaven Intelligence – Saturn	*SBH, EoN, Hmn, BARC, KoSR, CBoM, SoS, MHN, BM, ADS, BoO, DoW, tSoS, MC, GAG, GoeR, ArP, JMR, 9CK, BoTS, SaS, MNeI, GoA, MRC, CoMS, PO, tM, CBMS, BD*
Cassiel	Demon Duke – South-West Day	*BoTS*
Cassilon	Angel – Saturn/Saturday	*SR*
Cassurafarttis	Angel – Ab	*SR*
Cassynarudya	Demon King	*SSM*
Castaon	Spirit – Mirror	*CoMS*
Castiel/Cassiel/ Casiell/ Castael	Angel – Thursday Spirit – Jupiter Presiding Spirit – Jupiter	*EoN, Hmn, CBoM, SoS, MHN, tSoS, GAG, oADS, tM, CBMS, PO, SGT, SSG*
Castormy	Angel Minister	*KoSA*
Castrac	Angel – Trickery	*KoSA*
Castriel	Spirit King	*BoO*
Castrietur/Castrietar	Spirit	*CBoM, oADS*
Castryel	Spirit – East	*SSM*

Castub	Angel – Sun	*GAG*
Casujojah/Casuijah/Casuisah	Angel – Capricorn	*ArP*
Casul	Demon Duke – West Night	*BoTS*
Caszepell	Angel	*oADS*
Catepha/Calephas (Thadeus)	Prince of Ishim and Apostle	*3BOP, MRC*
Cathan	Spirit	*oADS*
Cathathel	Salamander Head (five of six)	*SBRM*
Cathcyel	Angel – Fifth Heaven, South	*SSM*
Cathneylyn	Angel – Moon/Monday	*SR*
Catilaret/Calciaret	Spirit – fourth Mansion of the Moon Ring	*AE*
Catys/Catis/Catacis	Angel – Book Writer	*BoO, oADS*
Caualasyel	Angel – Sun	*BARC*
Cauda/Caudam	Spirit – sixth Mansion of Moon Ring	*tSoS*
Caudes	Daemon – Sun, subect to North Wind; East	*SBH*
Caudones	Punishing Wind	*SSM*
Caux	Angel – Sun	*BARC*
Cavayr/Couayr/Cavayx	Demon Duke – North-East	*Stg, ThG*
Caybemynyn	Angel – Moon/Monday	*SR*
Cayfar	Servant Spirit	*Abm*
Cayma	Spirit – Minister of Love	*oADS*
Caymay	Spirit – Sea Treasure	*oADS*
Cayros	Duke – West by North after Midnight	*Stg, ThG, BoTS*
Cazariel	Angel – Mansion thirteen and Virgo	*BoO*
Caziel	Angel – Moon, over Water	*SR*
Cazuk/Cazsul	Demon Duke – West by North Night	*Stg, ThG*
Cebal	Spirit	*MHN*
Cechiel	Genii – 29° Aries	*ArP*
Cedas/Galba	Lord of Angels and Winds	*GAG*
Cediel	Genii – 22° Libra	*ArP*
Cedragel	Plant Spirit – Alder	*GS*
Cefania	Angel – Sivan	*SR*

Cegnel	Genii – 6° Aries	*ArP*
Cehafa	Angel – Moon	*GAG*
Celabel	Angel – Mars/Tuesday	*SR*
Celidoal	Angel – Bisertilis	*SR*
Celiel	Genii – 1° Virgo	*ArP*
Cemas	Angel	*NA*
Cemeil/Cemeyl	Angel – Moon	*LL*
Cenbar	Enochian Angel – East, over third lesser Angle	*TBA*
Centone/Centony/ Sentony	Spirit Spirit – Woods	*CoC, oADS, tSoS*
Cepesa	Enochian Angel – South, over third lesser Angle	*TBA*
Cerabiel	Angel – First Heaven, West	*EoN*
Ceradadyn	Angel – Moon/Monday	*SR*
Ceraphin	Angel – Air	*SR*
Cerbere (Naberius)	Demon Marquis	*LdE, DI*
Cerberus/Cerberu/ Cerborus	Porter of Hell, Demon Fury	*3BOP, BoO, CoC, GAG, BoTS, MNeI, MRC, GV*
Ceres	Goddess – Corn	*BoO*
Ceris	Spirit – Minister of Love	*oADS*
Ceroiel	Angel	*BoTS*
Cerphiel	Archangel – Netzach	*MNeI*
Cerrel	Angel	*BoTS*
Cerviel/Cerviell	Angel – Netzach	*SaS, Thm*
Cesiel	Genii – 3° Scorpio	*ArP*
Cetabiel	Angel – Adar	*SR*
Cethenoylyn	Angel – Mars/Tuesday	*SR*
Ceyabos	Angel – Bisertilis	*SR*
Ceytatynyn	Angel – Sun/Sunday	*SR*
Cezodenes	Enochian Angel – East, serving first lesser Angle	*TBA*
Chabalym	Angel – Cherubim/Seraphim	*67M*
Chabiel	Genii – 20° Scorpio, 20° Sagittarius	*ArP*
Chabri	Demon Duke	*Stg, ThG*

Chabrion	Angel – Night Hour twelve	*Stg, ArP*
Chabriz/Chabril	Angel – Night Hour two	*Stg, ArP*
Chabroel	Spirit	*ACM*: Cairo 45060
Chadiel	Genii – 16° Taurus, 16° Gemini, 26° Taurus, 26° Gemini	*ArP*
Chadonas	Devil – Ursa Major	*oADS*
Chadraoun	Angel	PGM XXVI:1-42
Chadros	Angel – Day Hour eleven	*Stg, ArP*
Chael	Genii – 21° Capricorn, 21° Aquarius	*ArP*
Chahanya	Spirit – Water	*67M*
Chahatus	Punishing Wind	*SSM*
Chahel	Genii – 26° Aries	*ArP*
Chahelype	Angel	*NA*
Chaiel	Genii – 2° Libra	*ArP*
Chajakiah/ Chavakiah/ Chauakiah/Kavakiah	Angel – Shem thirty-five	*KoSU, 3BOP, GoeR, JMR, SAS, tM*
Chalcos	Treasure Spirit	*BoTS*
Chamachal	Spirit	*ACM*: Hay 10391
Chamarmariao	Spirit before the Fourteen Firmaments	*ACM*: BN Turin
Chamaudich/ Camarideth/ Chamaridach/	Spirit – third Mansion of the Moon Ring	*AE*
Chamecayle	Spirit of the Thumb	*CBoM*
Chameray	Angel – Night Hour ten	*Stg, ArP*
Chameron	Spirit	*GoPH, GV*
Chamiel/Chomiel	Demon Duke – North	*Stg, ThG*
Chamiel	Genii – 1° Aquarius	*ArP*
Chamoriel/ Chamorid	Demon Duke – Day Hour two	*Stg, ThG*
Chamos/Chomas	Demon Duke – South by East Night	*Stg, 3BOP, ThG, BoTS*
Chamus	Demon Minister	*VJL*
Chamyel	Angel – Thrones	*67M*
Chanaei/Chanoel/ Chanael	Demon Duke – North Day	*Stg, ThG, BoTS*
Chanije	Ministering Familiar/Mystery	*67M*

Channanijah	Ministering Familiar/Mystery	67M
Chansi	Demon Duke – South Day	Stg, ThG
Chanturo	Devil – Noon	oADS
Charaby/Charby	Angel – Night Hour five	Stg, ArP
Charariel	Superior Intelligence – Mercury	KoSU, SoS
Charas	Demon Duke – South by East Day	Stg, ThG, BoTS
Chardiel/Cardiel	Angel – Day Hour two	Stg, ArP
Chariel	Demon Duke – South, Day Hour twelve	Stg, ThG
Chariel	Water Spirit	MNeI
Charmy/Charmis/Charnis	Angel – Day Hour nine	Stg, ArP
Charny	Angel – Day Hour ten	Stg, ArP
Charobiel	Demon Chief Duke	Stg, ThG
Charochin	Angel – Moon	LL
Charoel/Caroel	Demon Duke – Y2 Demon Duke – Day Hour four and Night Hour four	Stg, ThG
Charon	Underworld Ferryman	PGM IV:1390-1495; ACM: P. EM. 10263
Charpon/Charpen	Angel – Day Hour one	Stg, ArP
Charsiel	Angel – Fourth Heaven Sunday, South, Spring Angel – Fourth Heaven, South	Hmn, KoSR, BoO, GAG, BoTS, SaS, tM
Charsiel	Demon Chief Duke	Stg, ThG
Charuch	Angel – Day Hour six	Stg, ArP
Charusihoa	Spirit	GV
Chasiel	Genii – 29° Taurus, 30° Scorpio, 30° Sagittarius	ArP
Chasmodai/Hasmodai/Hasmoday	Planetary Spirit – Moon Ruler – Populus, Via	KoSR, 3BOP, BM, Thm, PO, tM
Chasor/Charos/Claros	Demon Duke – West by South Day	Stg, ThG, BoTS
Chassiel	Intelligence – Sun	SGT, SSG
Chatas	Demon – Sun	BARC
Chaudas/Caudas	Daemon Minister – Sun, East	SBH
Chaya	Servant Spirit	Abm

Chaylon	Angel – Cherubim/Seraphim	*67M*
Chayo	Angel – Thrones	*67M*
Chazael	Genii – 17° Pisces, 19° Taurus, 19° Gemini, 27° Pisces	*ArP*
Chdial	Angel Prince – fourth Heaven, Water	*ShR*
Chebial	Angel Minister – Malachim	*SRH*
Cheboval	Angel – Malachim, Flames of Fire	*SRH*
Chechiel	Genii – 29° Libra	*ArP*
Chederial	Angel Prince – Gate of Spirit of East	*SRH*
Chedial	Angel – Malachim, Flames of Fire	*SRH*
Chedusitanich	Spirit – Jupiter	*SGT, SSG*
Chedusitaniel/ Chedisutaniel/ Chedisutamel	Angel third Heaven Friday – East	*Hmn, KoSR, BoO, BM, GAG, BoTS, tM, CBMS*
Chegeda	Angel – Malachim, under Ayigeda	*SRH*
Chegeleth	Angel – Malachim, under Ayigeda	*SRH*
Chegera	Angel – Malachim, under Ayigeda	*SRH*
Chekemial	Angel – Malachim, under Pheseker	*SRH*
Chelial	Angel – Malachim, under Avorphenial	*SRH*
Chemamoht	Angel	*NA*
Chemeh	Angel – Malachim, under Avorphenial	*SRH*
Chemekial	Angel, serving above sixth Degree	*SRH*
Chememial	Angel – Malachim, under Pheseker Angel – Malachim, sixth Host	*SRH*
Chemori	Angel – Malachim, under Avorphenial	*SRH*
Chemosh	Semitic God	HB Judg 11:24, 1 Kgs 11:7, 11:33, 2 Kgs 23:13, Jer 48:7, 48:13, 48:46
Chengiel	Genii – 19° Libra	*ArP*
Chenial	Angel – Virgo	*SRH*
Chenibranbo	Spirit	*GV*
Chenonial	Angel Prince – Gate of Spirit of North	*SRH*
Chenyon	Angel – Saturn/Saturday	*SR*
Cheqierien	Angel Prince	*SRH*
Cherasa	Spirit Minister – Saturn	*BoO*

Cherasiel/Cheraliel/Cherahel	Angel – Night Hour six	*Stg, ArP*
Cheremiel	Angel – Third Heaven, South	*EoN*
Cherial	Angel Minister – Malachim	*SRH*
Cherinael	Spirit – Gate of the West	*ACM*: L. Anastasi 9
Chermel/Chermes	Angel – Night Hour nine	*Stg, ArP*
Chermiel	Angel – Third Heaven Friday, South	*Hmn, KoSR, BoO, BM, GAG, BoTS, tM*
Cheroubin	Spirit – Gate of the West	*ACM*: L. Anastasi 9
Cherub	Angel President/Governor – Air Angel Ruler – Air, governs Samael	*3BOP, tSoS, MC, BoTS, JMR, KoN, SaS, PO, tM*
Cherubyn	Angel – Air	*SR*
Cherudiel	Angel – Jupiter/Thursday	*SR*
Chesediel/Chesedial	Angel – Venus Angel Minister – Malachim, third Dwelling Angel – Malachim, under Phelmiya	*SRH*
Chesedora	Angel – Malachim, under Avorphenial	*SRH*
Chesekos	Angel Prince	*SRH*
Chesemal	Angel – Malachim, sixth Host	*SRH*
Cheseniel	Angel – Malachim, under Dohel	*SRH*
Chesethek	Angel – Malachim, under Ayigeda	*SRH*
Chetephial	Angel – Malachim, under Pheseker Angel – Malachim, sixth Host	*SRH*
Chetiel	Genii – 18° Virgo	*ArP*
Chetivel	Genii – 28° Virgo	*ArP*
Chezeqial	Angel Prince – Gate of Spirit of North	*SRH*
Chgl	Angel – Second Encampment, first Heaven	*ShR*
Chgra	Angel – Second Encampment, first Heaven	*ShR*
Chichrōalithō	Fifth of seven Pole Lords of Heaven	PGM IV:475-829
Chide	Spirit Minister	*SBH*
Chinicham	Familiar Spirit	*VJL*
Chlian	Angel – First Encampment, first Heaven	*ShR*
Chlilal	Angel – Ninth Step, second Heaven	*ShR*

Chilial	Angel – Third Heaven, serving Dlqial	*ShR*
Chlshial	Angel – Fifth Encampment, first Heaven	*ShR*
Chlsial	Angel – Fourth Encampment, first Heaven	*ShR*
Chlual	Angel Prince – fourth Heaven, Water	*ShR*
Chmmial	Angel – Sixth Encampment, first Heaven	*ShR*
Chmqial	Angel Prince – fourth Heaven, Water	*ShR*
Chnial	Angel Encampment Head – sixth Heaven, West	*ShR*
Chnoum/Chneōm (Khnum)	Egyptian Creator God	PGM VII:429-458, XII:179-181
Chodor	Spirit – West	*SSM*
Chodorlaomor	Evil Spirit	*3BOP*
Chofniel/Chosniel	Angel	*SST*
Cholial	Angel Minister – Malachim Angel – Malachim, Flames of Fire	*SRH*
Chōnsou (Khonsu)	Egyptian Moon God	PGM VII:300
Chooch	Spirit (God)	*ACM*: Cairo 45060
Chorborbath	Angel – Lunar, Night Hour six	PGM VII:862-918
Choreb	Angel – Day Hour ten	*Stg, ArP*
Choriel/Choriol/Choriel/Chorion	Angel – Day Hour twelve, Night Hour seven	*Stg, ArP, BoTS*
Chorus	Angel Minister	*KoSA*
Chosetiel/Chesetiel (Aorachiel)	Angel – Sagittarius Spirit – Sagittarius	*3BOP, BoO, tSoS, JMR, SaS*
Choshial	Angel Prince – Gate of Spirit of South	*SRH*
Choucho	Gnostic Archon – third Aeon	*ACM*: Bruce Codex
Chouncheoch	Gnostic Archon – second Aeon	*ACM*: Bruce Codex
Chous	Gnostic Archon – first Aeon	*ACM*: Bruce Codex
Chrasiel/Charsiel	Angel – Night Hour one	*Stg, ArP*
Chremas	Angel – Hour one	*Stg, ArP*
Chremoas/Chremo	Demon Chief Duke	*Stg, ThG*
Chrepsenthaēs	First of seven Egyptian Fates of Heaven	PGM IV:475-829
Chrhal	Angel – Third Heaven, serving Dlqial	*ShR*
Chrial	Angel – Tenth Step, second Heaven	*ShR*

Christuel	Biblical Elder/Angel	*ACM*: Oriental 5899, Berlin 11347, Oriental 6796
Chroel	Angel – Day Hour eight	*Stg, ArP*
Chrubas	Demon Duke – North by East Day	*Stg, ThG*
Chrusiel/Crusiel	Angel – Night Hour three	*Stg, ArP*
Chrymas/Chrymos	Angel – Night Hour five	*Stg, ArP*
Chsdial	Angel – Fourth Encampment, first Heaven	*ShR*
Chshndrnus	Angel Prince – fifth Heaven, Month of Shevat	*ShR*
Chsial	Angel Prince – fourth Heaven, Fire	*ShR*
Chsnial	Angel – Third Encampment, first Heaven	*ShR*
Chtnial	Angel Prince – fourth Heaven, Water	*ShR*
Chtpial	Angel – Sixth Encampment, first Heaven	*ShR*
Chu	Power of Death	*ACM*: Cairo Bone A/B
Chuba/Chubor	Demon Duke – North-East	*Stg, ThG*
Chule	Devil – Cancer, Storms	*OADS*
Churibal	Demon Duke – North	*Stg, ThG*
Chuscha	Angel – Thrones	*67M*
Chushel	Genii – 1° Capricorn	*ArP*
Chustual	Angel – Sixth Encampment, first Heaven	*ShR*
Chuz	Spirit	*MRC*
Chyma	Angel	*NA*
Chymchy	Good Spirit	*SoM*
Chzal	Angel – Seventh Encampment, first Heaven	*ShR*
Cia	Angel – Saturn	*GAG*
Ciajah	Genii – 24° Capricorn, 24° Aquarius	*ArP*
Cijbor	Ministering Familiar/Mystery	*67M*
Cimeies/Cimeries	Demon Marquis – Africa	*PmD, DoW, Goe*
Circe	Greek Demi-Goddess Enchantress	PGM XXIII:1-70
Ciricas/Cirecas	Demon Duke – South by West Night	*Stg, ThG, BoTS*
Citgara	Demon Duke – South-East Day	*Stg, ThG, BoTS*
Ciyoos	Right part of Brimas	*Pic*
Clamor/Chamor	Demon Chief Duke	*Stg, ThG*

ABBREVIATIONS

Claniel/Chaniel	Demon Duke – Day Hour one and Night Hour one	*Stg, ThG*
Claunth/Clauneck/Claunech/Chauntha/Chaunta/Elantiel/Elantil	Demon – under Sirach	*KoSU, SoS, GV*
Clema	Spirit of the Thumb	*CBoM*
Clidraepe	Spirit	*BoTS*
Cliody	Spirit – twentieth Mansion of the Moon Ring	*tSoS*
Clistheret/Glithrel/Clisthert/Sirumel/Selytarel	Demon Duke	*SoS, GV*
Clyssan/Elysam	Demon Duke – West Day	*Stg, ThG, BoTS*
Cnael	Angel – Fifth Heaven, East	*SaS*
Coac	Angel Minister – Trickery	*KoSA*
Coachtiel/Coachdiel	Peasant Spirit, Air	*MNeI*
Coanii	Angel	*BoSC*
Coap	Demon Prince	*LdE*
Cobia	Spirit – Mirror	*CoMS*
Cobusiel	Demon Duke – Y1	*Stg, ThG*
Cocau	Angel Minister – Love and Fornication	*KoSA*
Cocamiel	Spirit – Mercury	*VMN*
Cocazim/Corniger	Angel – Mars	*B7R*
Cochabiel/Cochalijah/Cochabiah/Coahabiath (Raphael)	Archangel – Mercury	*3BOP, BoO, tSoS, JMR, SaS*
Codriel	Demon Duke – West	*Stg, ThG*
Coeglarth	Angel Minister – Love and Fornication	*KoSA*
Cohen	Servant Spirit	*Abm*
Coiznas/Colznas	Spirit Messenger – Venus	*SGT, SSG*
Cokiel	Demon	*GAG*
Colehon	Spirit	*GV*
Coliel/Cotiel	Demon Duke – South by West Day	*Stg, ThG*
Colitzab'tin	Angel – Treasure seeking	*dN*

Colkeranon/ Colkeran	Spirit	BoO
Comadiel	Angel – Day Hour three	Stg, ArP
Comaguele	Angel – Sun/Sunday	SR
Comary/Cmary	Angel – Night Hour nine	Stg, ArP
Comeil	Angel – Moon	LL
Comial/Lomiel	Angel – Day Hour eleven	Stg, ArP
Commissoros/ Commissaros/ Comisoros/ Comissores	Angel – Spring	EoN, Hmn, KoSR, BM, tSoS, MC, GAG, GoeR, tM
Comphac	Angel	BoSC
Con	Angel – Sun	GAG
Conas	Spirit Assistant – Wednesday	MHN
Concavion	Servant Spirit	Abm
Conieh/Coniel	Spirit Messenger – Jupiter	SGT, SSG
Coniel	Angel – Third Heaven Friday, West Angel – Third Heaven, West Presiding Spirit – Venus	Hmn, KoSR, BoO, BM, GAG, BoTS, SaS, tM, CBMS
Consumator	Angel – Hatred and Destruction	KoSA
Contubal	Demon Minister – Beelzebub	SSM
Conupciell	Demon	GAG
Coolor (Volac?)	Demon Prince	BoS, BoO
Corabael/Corabiel	Angel first Heaven Monday – West Ministering Spirit – Moon	Hmn, KoSR, BoO, GAG, BoTS, tM, CBMS
Corabiel	Angel – South	SR
Coradiel	Demon – Count Palatine Peasant Spirit, Air	MNeI
Corael	Spirit – Jupiter	SGT, SSG
Corat/Chorat	Angel – Third Heaven Friday, East Presiding Spirit – Venus	Hmn, KoSR, BoO, BM, GAG, BoTS, tM, CBMS
Corat	Spirit – Sun	SGT, SSG
Corbara	Demon Senior	SSM
Corcornifer	Spirit	SSM

ABBREVIATIONS

Core	Angel – Spring	*EoN, Hmn, KoSR, BM, tSoS, GAG, GoeR, tM*
Coreziel	Angel – Night Hour four	*Stg, ArP*
Coribom	Angel Minister – Love and Fornication	*KoSA*
Coriet	Spirit – eleventh (twelfth) Mansion of the Moon ring	*tSoS*
Corilon	Servant Spirit	*Abm*
Corilron	Spirit – Minister of Love	*oADS*
Coringer (Cornigerum)	Angl – Mars	*tSoS*
Cormelyon	Angel – Moon	*oADS*
Cormes	Demon	*MHN*
Corniger	Spirit / Terrestrial Spirit – King of South	*SSM, SBH*
Cornigerion	Spirit – Skull Divination	*ArPh*
Cornigerum/Cornegerum	Angel – Mars	*oADS*
Cornus	Spirit – Bird Capturers	*oADS*
Cornyx	Demon Captain	*BOS, BoO*
Corocon	Servant Spirit	*Abm*
Coroczay	Angel – Seventh Altitude (Libra)	*Alm*
Coronem	Spirit	*MNeI*
Coronis (Ashbeel, Roman)	Spirit King – Saturn	*Pic*
Coronthon	Spirit	*KoN*
Corowe	Good Spirit	*SoM*
Corrosor	Angel – Hatred and Destruction	*KoSA*
Corson/Gorson/Gorzon	Demon King – West	*PmD, Goe, BoTS*
Corsone (Purson?)	Demon Count/Earl	*BOS, BoO*
Cortonifer	Spirit – Skull Divination	*ArPh*
Corus	West by North – West Wind	*Thm*
Corviel	Angel – Venus	*JMR*
Costiryn	Angel – Mars/Tuesday	*SR*
Craffiel	Demon Baron, Air	*MNeI*
Cramos	Angel	*NA*

Cranael	Angel – Sun	*GAG*
Craulyaruy	Spirit – fourth Mansion of Moon Ring	*AE*
Crea	Treasure Spirit	*oADS*
Crest of Dragons	Demon	*ToS*
Cricios	Angel – Jupiter	*BARC*
Crisolsay	Spirit	*GV*
Crissia	Devil – Ursa Major	*oADS*
Critaron	Demon Prince of Darkness	*oADS*
Crosiel	Angel – Day Hour seven	*Stg, ArP*
Croway	Spirit	*GoPH*
Cruchan	Demon Chief Duke	*Stg, ThG*
Cruhiel	Demon Duke – Day Hour nine	*Stg, ThG*
Ctarari/Clarari/ Cetarari	Angel – Winter	*EoN, Hmn, KoSR, tSoS, MC, GAG, GoeR, tM*
Ctesiphone/ Cresiphone	Fury	*3BOP, MNeI*
Cubi	Demon Duke – West Night	*Stg, ThG, BoTS*
Cubiel	Demon Duke – South by East Day	*Stg, ThG, BoTS*
Cudexa	Spirit	*CoC*
Cudos	Angel Minister – Love and Fornication	*KoSA*
Cugiel	Demon Duke – West Night	*Stg, ThG, BoTS*
Culdrunal	Spirit	*BoTS*
Cullia	Angel – Tishrei	*SR*
Culmar	Demon Duke – North Night	*Stg, ThG, BoTS*
Cumana	Spirit – Sibyl (four of ten)	*GV*
Cumariel	Demon Duke – Hour twelve of fifteen	*Stg, ThG*
Cumeriel	Demon Duke – East	*Stg, ThG*
Cunnyryel	Angel – Jupiter/Thursday	*SR*
Cuphal/Cupher/ Cuphar	Demon Duke – West Day	*Stg, ThG, BoTS*
Cupid/Cupido	God – Love Spirit – Love	*BoO, MHN, NML, SMS*
Cupriel/Eupriel	Demon Duke – Night Hour three	*Stg, ThG*
Cupriel	Earth Spirit	*MNeI*
Cuprisiel	Demon Knight	*Stg, ThG*

Curaniel/Curamiel	Angel first Heaven Monday – South Ministering Spirit – Jupiter	*EoN, Hmn, KoSR, BoO, GAG, BoTS, tM, CBMS*
Curasin/Curasyn	Demon Under Duke	*Stg, ThG*
Cureviorbas	Spirit	*GV*
Curiel	Demon Duke – South by East Night, North by East Night	*Stg, ThG, BoTS*
Curifas	Demon Duke – West	*Stg, ThG*
Curmas/Curmis	Demon Duke	*Stg, ThG*
Cursas/Curfas	Duke – West by North pre-Midnight	*Stg, ThG, BoTS*
Cursiel	Angel – Day Hour two	*Stg, ArP*
Curson	Spirit – East	*KoN*
Cuschi	Servant Spirit	*Abm*
Cusiel	Demon Duke – South-West Day/Night	*Stg, ThG, BoTS*
Cusriel/Cusrel	Demon Duke – South-West Night	*Stg, ThG*
Custel	Intelligence	*BoG*
Cusyne	Duke – West by North pre-Midnight	*Stg, ThG*
Cutchtpollo	Spirit	*BoTS*
Cutroy/Cotroy	Spirit	*MHN*
Cycas	Demon – Instigator of Misfortune	*MNeI*
Cynabal/Cynaball/ Cinaball/Cynabat/ Sinabal/Cinabal	Angel Minister of Air – Sunday Spirit Attendant – Sun Ministering Spirit – Saturn	*EoN, /Hmn, KoSR, BoO, GAG, GoeR, BoTS, tM, CBMS*
Cynassa	Daemon Minister – Venus; between South and West	*SBH*
Cyoly	Angel – Second Heaven, South	*SR*
Cypris	Titel of Aphrodite	PGM VII:385-389
Cyray	Demon Senior	*SSM*
Cyrorax	Angel – Sun	*B7R*
Cyzamanyn	Angel – Moon/Monday	*SR*

D		
Daael	Genii – 27° Capricorn, 27° Aquarius	*ArP*
Daaihu	Angel – Third Step, second Heaven	*ShR*
Daba	Spirit of the Thumb	*CBoM*
Dabnotirorin	Angel – Moon	*LL*

Dabriel/Dadriel	Angel first Heaven Monday – South	*EoN, Hmn, KoSR, SoS, BoO, GAG, BoTS, tM*
Daby	Spirit of the Thumb	*CBoM*
Dachael	Genii – 22° Aries, 26° Scorpio, 26° Sagittarius	*ArP*
Dachiel	Genii – 16° Scorpio, 16° Sagittarius	*ArP*
Dadiel	Angel – Elul Angel – Tishrei	*SR*
Dadrinos	Demon Duke – North	*Stg, ThG*
Daemael	Angel – Fourth Heaven, East	*SR*
Dagan/Dagam	Demon Senior – West	*SSM*
Daghayos	Spirit gatherer of Gharnos	*Pic*
Daghdiyos	Spirit of Mars	*Pic*
Dagiel/Daguiel	Archangel – Venus	*EoN, Hmn, BoO, CBMS*
Dagiel/Dagael	Demon Duke – North by East Day	*Stg, ThG*
Dagiel	Genii – 13° Pisces, 23° Pisces	*ArP*
Daglus	Servant Spirit	*Abm*
Dagnel	Genii – 13° Taurus	*ArP*
Dagol (Dagon?)	Demon Prince	*MRC*
Dagon	Syrian Grain God	HB Judg 16:23, 1 Sam 5:2-5, 5:7, 1 Chr 10:10
Dagon	Demon	*3BOP*
Dagoterapter	Demon – authority over underground treasures	*KoSU*
Dagulez	Servant Spirit	*Abm*
Dagymiel (Barchiel)	Angel – Pisces Spirit – Pisces	*3BOP, BoO, tSoS, JMR, SaS*
Daha	Spirit of the Thumb	*CBoM*
Dahdees	Back part of Barhoyas	*Pic*
Dahidas	Spirit gatherer of Damahos	*Pic*
Dahidmas	Spirit gatherer of Daghdiyos	*Pic*
Dahifas	Right part of Bandalos	*Pic*
Dahimas	Top part of Bandalos	*Pic*
Dahiel	Genii – 14° Virgo, 24° Virgo	*ArP*
Dahtarees	Spirit gatherer of Didas	*Pic*

ABBREVIATIONS

Dainut	Angel – Third Encampment, first Heaven	ShR
Daitoos	Spirits – Love/Sexual Attraction	Pic
Dajiel	Genii – 22° Taurus, 22° Gemini	ArP
Dakhli/Dakhēl (Mars)	Mars – Alternative Name	Hyg
Daktouēl	Angel	Hyg
Dala	Spirit – Jupiter	BoO, GAG
Dalboth/Dalphos/ Dalboa/Dalphōth/ Diaphothēl	Angel – Thursday Hour 10	Hyg
Dalep	Servant Spirit	Abm
Dalete	Spirit	GoA
Dalia	Angel – Sivan	SR
Daliarimerat	Spirit – sixth Mansion of the Moon ring	tSoS
Daliel	Angel – Shebat Angel – Moon, over Fire	SR
Dalmaley	Angel	GV
Dalmay	Angel	GV
Dalquiel	Angel Prince – third Heaven and Fire	SaS
Dalquyel	Angel Subordinate – Saturn	SSM
Daltakosa	Angel	Hyg
Daluti	Angel	KoSA
Dam	Demon Count	LdE
Damabiah	Angel – Shem sixty-five	KoSU, 3BOP, GoeR, JMR, SAS, tM
Damadas	Spirit	BoO
Damael	Angel – Fifth Heaven Tuesday, East Angel – Fifth Heaven, East Presiding Spirit – Mars	EoN, Hmn, KoSR, BoO, GAG, BoTS, SaS, tM, CBMS
Damahos	Spirit of Jupiter	Pic
Damar/Damer/ Dumar	Angel – Night Hour eleven	Stg, ArP
Damaron/ Damourouph	Demon – North	Hyg
Damarsiel	Demon Knight	Stg, ThG
Damasiel	Angel – Night Hour twelve	Stg, ArP

Damasōn/Damasin/Damason	Demon – South	*Hyg*
Damay/Damayn	Spirit	*MHN*
Damayis	Right part of Didas	*Pic*
Dameriel	Angel – Night Hour eleven	*Stg, ArP*
Damery	Angel – Night Hour twelve	*Stg, ArP*
Dameyel	Angel – Mercury, over Fire	*SR*
Damiel	Angel – Day Hour five	*Stg, ArP*
Damniel	Free Air Spirit – Theft	*MNeI*
Damyel/Damiel	Angel – Day Hour nine	*Stg, ArP*
Danael	Angel – Venus	*SSM*
Danaēl/Adōnaēl	Angel – Winter	*BoW*
Danael	Duke – West by North Afternoon	*Stg, ThG, BoTS*
Danall	Demon Senator	*BoO*
Dandaniel	Angel – Sun, over Fire Angel – Fourth Heaven, Sun	*SR*
Danepta	Spirit – third Mansion of Moon Ring	*AE*
Dangolath	Spirit – Jupiter	*BoO, GAG*
Danial	Angel Prince – Moon in Winter	*SRH*
Daniel	Angel – Shem fifty	*KoSU, 3BOP, GoeR, JMR, SAS, tM*
Daniel/Daniell	Angel – Sun/Sunday Angel – Sun Angel – Earth Angel Minister	*SR, BARC, KoSA, oADS*
Daniel	Demon Duke – South-East Day	*Stg, ThG, BoTS*
Daniel	Spirit – West	*KoN*
Danoup/Chrator Berbali Balbith Iaō	Pair of Mighty Man and God in charge of every need	PGM XIII:1-343
Danpi	Angel – Elul	*SR*
Danroc	Angel – Tammuz	*SR*
Dansiation	Demon Prince	*BoTS*
Dantalion/Dantaylion/Dantalion/Dentalion	Demon Duke	*GAG, Goe, oADS, BoTS*
Danysān	Angel – Hour seven/Libra	*BoW*

ABBREVIATIONS

Dapi	Enochian Angel – West, serving fourth lesser Angle	*TBA*
Dapson	Angel – Saturn/Saturday	*SR*
Darachiel	Demon Count	*MNeI*
Daragybya	Spirit	*oADS*
Daratees	Spirit – sixth Mansion of Moon Ring	*AE*
Daravisies	Angel Minister – Love and Fornication	*KoSA*
Darbiel/Darbyel	Angel – First Heaven, South	*SSM, SR*
Darbori/Darbory	Duke – West by North pre-Midnight	*Stg, ThG, BoTS*
Dardaci	Angel – Sun	*BARC*
Dardariel	Angel Ruler – Night Hour eleven	*AeP*
Dardiel/Dardiell/ Dardihel/Dardaell/ Bardiel/ Dardyell/Daydiel	Angel – Sunday Spirit – Sun	*SSM, SBH, EoN, Hmn, MHN, CBoM, oADS, BoO, tSoS, GAG, BoTS, PO, tM*
Darees	Left part of Damahos Left part of Barhoyas	*Pic*
Dargoyeyl	Angel – Sun/Sunday	*SR*
Darial	Demon – Mercury	*BARC*
Dariculin	Angel – Moon/Monday	*SR*
Dariel	Angel – Shebat	*SR*
Dariel	Demon King	*BARC*
Dariston	Demon	*GoPH*
Darifiel	Angel – Mercury, over Fire	*SR*
Darmas	Top part of Damahos	*Pic*
Darochim	Servant Spirit	*Abm*
Darogan/Itarogan	Demon	*ToSC*
Darosiel	Angel – Day Hour one	*Stg, ArP*
Darothphyel	Angel – Fourth Season by Night	*SSM*
Darpoul/Darpour	West Wind – Winter	*BoW*
Darquiel/Darquyel/ Datquyel	Angel – First Heaven, South Angel – First Heaven, Monday – South	*SSM, SR, EoN, Hmn, KoSR, BoO, GAG, BoTS, tM*
Dasfripyel	Angel – Mars/Tuesday	*SR*
Dashiel	Genii – 17° Capricorn, 17° Aquarius	*ArP*
Datete	Enochian Angel – South, serving third lesser Angle	*TBA*

Dathirl	Genii – 12° Gemini	*ArP*
Datziel	Genii – 15° Libra	*ArP*
Daubit	Angel – Second Encampment, first Heaven	*ShR*
Daveithe	Gnostic Spirit of Light	*ACM*: NH Codex VIII, P. Mich. 1190
Daviel	Genii – 28° Gemini	*ArP*
Davithea	Angel – Gatherer of Angels	*ACM*: Oriental 6794
Davmilbe/Parinilbe	Spirit – twentieth Mansion of the Moon Ring	*tSoS*
Davoniem	Angel – Malachim, under Dohel	*SRH*
Dawn (Eos)	Greek Dawn Goddess	*ACM*: H. O. Lange Text
Da'yāyl	Angel – Moon	*BoW*
Daziel	Genii – 25° Libra	*ArP*
Dbal	Angel – Seventh Encampment, first Heaven	*ShR*
Dbbal	Angel – Seventh Encampment, first Heaven	*ShR*
Dbbaur	Angel Encampment Head – sixth Heaven, West	*ShR*
Dbrial	Angel Encampment Head – sixth Heaven, East	*ShR*
Dchgial	Angel – Second Encampment, first Heaven	*ShR*
Deamiel/Deanuel	Angel first Heaven Monday – East Presiding Spirit – Moon	*EoN, Hmn, KoSR, BoO, GAG, BoTS, tM, CNMS*
Death	Personification of Death	HB Rev 6:8
Deaukon/Deankon/ Deagkion/Deaukōn/ Diaukoēl	Angel – Friday Hour nineteen	*Hyg*
Debam	Servant Spirit	*Abm*
Debarhama	Angel Superior – fourth Season by Day	*SSM*
Debehal	Angel	*NA*
Deberhema	Angel Prince – Malachim, Winter	*SRH*
Debitael	Angel – Venus, over Fire	*SR*
Decaniel	Demon Duke – North-East	*Stg, ThG*

Decarabia/Carabia	Demon Marquis	*PmD, DoW, Goe*
Deception	Demon – Pleiades one	*ToS*
Dedael	Biblical Elder	*ACM*: Berlin 11347, Oriental 6796
Dedion	Angel – Saturn/Saturday	*SR*
Dedya	Demon – South	*CBoM*
Deghal	Angel Prince – Ayer	*SRH*
Dehel	Angel	*NA, SBH*
Deibenim	Angel – Moon	*LL*
Deihel	Angel	*SBH*
Deilas/Delias	Demon Duke – West Night	*Stg, ThG, BoTS*
Deimos/Deumus	Indian Demon/Goddess	*DI*
Dein	Angel	*SBH*
Deinatz/Dematron	Angel – Night Hour five	*Stg, ArP*
Dekadial	Angel Magistrate – Sowing Soil	*SRH*
Del	Infernal Spirit	*MNeI*
Delen Arathibi	Demon Companion – Thursday	*KoN*
Delepheth	Angel – Malachim, under Ayigeda	*SRH*
Deleqial	Angel Prince – Malachim, over Flames, Burning House, Sinking of the Sky	*SRH*
Delforia	Fairy Lady/Empress	*BoO, GAG*
Delgna	Angel – Tammuz	*SR*
Deliel/Doliol (Cambiel)	Angel – Aquarius Spirit – Aquarius	*3BOP, BoO, tSoS, JMR, SaS*
Deliel	Angel – Chora four	*ArA*
Delmusam	Spirit	*GV*
Delobial	Angel – Malachim, under Dohel	*SRH*
Demael	Angel – Fourth Heaven, East	*SSM*
Demanoz/Deminoz	Angel – Night Hour three	*Stg, ArP*
Demaor/Demnnameals/Demannor	Angel – Night Hour nine	*Stg, ArP*
Demarac/Demerec	Angel – Day Hour twelve	*Stg, ArP*
Demarot/Demaros	Angel – Day Hour eight	*Stg, ArP*
Demediel	Demon Knight	*Stg, ThG*
Demefin	Spirit	*MHN*

Demeham	Angel	NA
Demenehi	Angel Magistrate – Malachim	SRH
Demeniya	Angel – Malachim, under Plemiya	SRH
Demesor/Demesar	Angel – Day Hour eleven	Stg, ArP
Demna	Angel – Malachim, under Avorphenial	SRH
Demor/Denior	Spirit	MHN
Demoriel	Demon Emperor – North	Stg, ThG, BoTS
Demov	Angel – Malachim, under Ayigeda	SRH
Denaryz/Denaryzod	Angel – Night Hour twelve	Stg, ArP
Denas	Demon	Hyg
Denel	Angel – Saturn	GAG
Denetzal	Angel Prince – Gate of Spirit of East	SRH
Denmerzym	Angel – Sun/Sunday	SR
Denskalion (Dantalion?)	Infernal Spirit	CBoM
Deothan	Spirit – Sun	BoO, GAG
Deparael	Angel – Venus, over Fire	SR
Depymo	Angel	NA, SBH
Depymon	Angel	NA, SBH
Deramiel	Angel – Third Heaven, North	SaS
Derapha	Angel Prince – Winter	SRH
Derekethiel	Angel Prince	SRH
Derekial	Angel Prince – South Gate	SRH
Deremial	Angel Prince – Gate of Spirit of North	SRH
Deres	Spirit – Minister of Love	oADS
Dergabel	Stone Spirit – Ruby	GS
Derial/Redial	Spirit Prince – West	SRH
Derisor	Angel – Trickery	KoSA
Deriyavor	Spirit – West in Winter	SRH
Deroper	Spirit – Minister of Love	oADS
Dersam	Angel – Sivan	SR
Desaboday	Angel Minister – Love and Fornication	KoSA
Deseleni	Spirit – North in Summer	SRH
Desephour	Spirit – North in Winter	SRH
Desoude	Jupiter – Alternative Name	Hyg

Despan	Demon	*MHN, NML*
Detaa	Enochian Angel – West, over first lesser Angle	*TBA*
Detel	Angel Minister	*KoSA*
Detestator	Angel – Trickery	*KoSA*
Detriel	Angel – Sun/Sunday	*SR*
Detriel	Beast before God (fifth of six)	*oADS*
Devorator	Angel – Hatred and Destruction	*KoSA*
Dexgezod	Enochian Angel – East, over fourth lesser Angle	*TBA*
Dexxeyl	Angel – Mars/Tuesday	*SR*
Deydo/Deyoo	Demon Earl	*BOS, BoO*
Deyhel	Angel	*NA*
Deyn	Angel	*NA*
Dghial	Angel Prince – fifth Heaven, Month of Iyar	*ShR*
Dgrial	Angel – Second Encampment, first Heaven	*ShR*
Dgugra	Angel – Second Encampment, first Heaven	*ShR*
Diam	Angel – Seventh Encampment, first Heaven	*ShR*
Diana/Dyane	Greek Virgin Goddess of the Moon Goddess – Woods and Chases	*SSM, BoO*
Diana (Roman) (Zuhara	Angel – Venus	*SSG*
Diatay	Spirit	*CoC*
Diatiphē	Name of Helios in eighth Hour	PGM IV:1596-1715
Dibqial	Angel – Third Heaven, serving Ibnial	*ShR*
Didas	Spirit of Venus	*Pic*
Didial	Angel – Fifth Encampment, first Heaven	*ShR*
Didnaur	Angel Prince – fifth Heaven, Month of Sivan	*ShR*
Didriuk	Angel – Fifth Encampment, first Heaven	*ShR*
Diednavor	Angel Prince – Sivan	*SRH*
Diegel	Angel – Malachim, under Avorphenial	*SRH*
Diegera	Angel – Malachim, under Ayigeda	*SRH*

Diel	Spirit – Mirror	*CoMS*
Diema	Good Spirit	*SoM*
Dies	Demon	*MHN*
Diffialofon	Angel – Jupiter	*GAG*
Difinicha/Diffiton/Disamata	Spirit – tenth Mansion of the Moon Ring	*AE*
Digl	Angel – First Encampment, first Heaven	*ShR*
Digmasōn	Demon – South	*Hyg*
Digra	Angel – Second Encampment, first Heaven	*ShR*
Dike	Greek Goddess of Justice	PGM IV:2785-2890
Dikhil (Mars)	Mars – Alternative Name	*Hyg*
Dilamoi	Angel – Moon	*BARC*
Dilapidator	Angel – Hatred and Destruction	*KoSA*
Dileo	Demon	*oADS*
Diles	Demon	*MHN*
Dilia	Demon	*MHN*
Dimet	Enochian Angel – West, over second lesser Angle	*TBA*
Dimhn	Angel – Fifth Encampment, first Heaven	*ShR*
Dimtmr	Angel – Seventh Encampment, first Heaven	*ShR*
Dimurgos	Servant Spirit	*Abm*
Dinmur	Angel – Fifth Encampment, first Heaven	*ShR*
Diom	Enochian Angel – South, serving third lesser Angle	*TBA*
Diomidis	Angel Minister	*KoSA*
Dione	Aphrodite title	PGM IV:2708-2784
Dionysus	Greek God of Wine and Ecstasy	HB 2 Mac 6:6, 14:3
Diopes	Servant Spirit	*Abm*
Dioscuri (Castor and Pollux)	Patron Gods of Sailor	HB 28:11
Diqna	Angel – Fifth Encampment, first Heaven	*ShR*
Diqomilim	Angel – Moon	*LL*
Dirachiel	Angel – Mansion six	*3BOP, tSoS, JMR, SaS, tM*

Diralisin	Servant Spirit	*Abm*
Dirathon/Dirath	Spirit – Venus	*BoO, GAG*
Diraz	Angel – Fifth Encampment, first Heaven	*ShR*
Diri	Enochian Angel – East, serving second lesser Angle	*TBA*
Diriyoos	Right part of Brimas	*Pic*
Discobermath	Demon	*MHN*
Discord	God – Strife and Debate	*BoO*
Discord	Spirit – Discord	*BP*
Discordiæ	Angel – Hatred and Destruction	*KoSA*
Disolel	Servant Spirit	*Abm*
Dissamata	Angel – Sun	*BARC*
Distolas (Stolas)	Demon Marquis	*LdE*
Distress	Demon – Pleiades four	*ToS*
Ditrun	Angel – Seventh Encampment, first Heaven	*ShR*
Diusion/Dicision (Purson)	Demon King	*LdE*
Diviel/Diuiel	Duke – West by North Afternoon	*Stg, ThG, BoTS*
Diversator	Angel – Hatred and Destruction	*KoSA*
Diviel	Angel – Day Hour four	*Stg, ArP*
Diwas	Spirit – Enmity	*Pic*
Dknsur	Angel – Fifth Encampment, first Heaven	*ShR*
Dkrial	Angel – Tenth Step, second Heaven	*ShR*
Dlgial	Angel – Second Encampment, first Heaven	*ShR*
Dlglial	Angel Encampment Head – sixth Heaven, East	*ShR*
Dlkt	Angel – Second Encampment, first Heaven	*ShR*
Dlqial	Angel Prince three of three – third Heaven Angel – Second Step, second Heaven	*ShR*
Dlrial	Angel Encampment Head – sixth Heaven, East	*ShR*
Dmal	Angel Encampment Head – sixth Heaven, West	*ShR*
Dmal	Son of Light, subject to Prince Hagonel	*dHM*

Dmimial	Angel – First Step, second Heaven	ShR
Dmna	Angel – First Encampment, first Heaven	ShR
Dmnai	Angel – Fourth Encampment, first Heaven	ShR
Dmnshr	Angel – Seventh Encampment, first Heaven	ShR
Dmual	Angel – Eleventh Step, second Heaven Angel Encampment Head – sixth Heaven, East	ShR
Dmula	Angel – Fifth Encampment, first Heaven	ShR
Dmumial	Angel – Second Encampment, first Heaven	ShR
Dnhl	Angel Overseer (three of seven) – first Heaven	ShR
Dobiel	Demon Duke – South-East Day/Night	Stg, ThG, BoTS
Dodenial	Angel – Sun	SRH
Dodiel/Dobiel	Demon Duke – West Night	Stg, ThG, BoTS
Doguenoyth/ Dognenoÿth/ Doguenioth	Spirit – eighth Mansion of the Moon Ring	AE
Dohel	Angel Magistrate – Malachim, third Throne	SRH
Dolefech	Spirit	KoSR
Domaras/Domaros/ Domarof	Angel – Night Hour one	Stg, ArP
Domas	Demon Servant – Tuesday	KoN
Domial	Angel, serving above sixth Degree	SRH
Dominath/Derminte	Spirit – twelfth Mansion of the Moon Ring	AE
Donahan	Archangel	67M
Donal	Angel Prince – South Gate	SRH
Donas	Demon Servant – Wednesday	KoN
Donēm	Angel – Moon	Hyg
Donguel	Angel Prince – Love	KoSA
Donmeo	Spirit	GV
Donoar/Danochar	Spirit	GoPH, GV
Donquil	Angel Prince – Love	VMN

Donskion (Dansiation?)	Demon Prince	*GAG*
Doodall/Doodal	Demon Knight	*BOS, BoO*
Doolas	Demon Prince	*BOS, BoOq*
Dopa	Enochian Angel – North, serving third lesser Angle; South, over first lesser Angle	*TBA*
Doqierien	Angel Prince	*SRH*
Dorael	Demon Duke – North-East	*Stg, ThG*
Doragybyn	Spirit	*oADS*
Doranel	Angel – Third Heaven, North	*SR*
Dorayl	Good Spirit	*MHN*
Dordrachuth/Derdachut	Spirit – twelfth Mansion of the Moon Ring	*AE*
Doremiel/Dormiel/Doreniel	Angel third Heaven Friday – North	*EoN, Hmn, KoSR, BoO, BM, GAG, BoTS, tM*
Doremiel	Spirit Messenger – Mercury	*SGT, SSG*
Doreniel/Dorenial	Angel Minister – Malachim, fourth Dwelling Angel – Malachim, under Ayigeda Angel Prince – South Gate/East Gate	*SRH*
Doriel/Dēriel (Sun)	Sun – Alternative Name	*Hyg*
Doriel/Diriel	Demon Duke – North	*Stg, ThG*
Dormason/Dorbason/Darnason	Angel – Night Hour one	*Stg, ArP*
Dorochiel/Dorothiel	Demon Prince – West by North Demon Prince – West under Beymon	*Stg, ThG, BoTS, KoN*
Doromiel	Spirit – Venus	*SoS*
Doroos	Rear part of Brimas	*Pic*
Doruel	Angel – six of twenty-one on the Left	*ACM*: Berlin 10587
Dorsamot	Spirit	*GV*
Dosom	Servant Spirit	*Abm*
Doth	Angel – Malachim, under Dohel	*SRH*
Douniel/Doniēl/Dōniēl/Doneēl/Donoēl	Angel – Sun	*Hyg*
Drabiel/Darbiel	Angel – Day Hour ten	*Stg, ArP*

Drabros/Drabos	Demon Duke	*Stg, ThG*
Dracho	Spirit – Minister of Love	*oADS*
Draco	Demon – South Spirit – Minister of Love	*CBoM, oADS*
Dracon	Angel – Night Hour six	*Stg, ArP*
Dracutius	Spirit – Minister of Love	*oADS*
Dradragoban	Spirit	*oADS*
Dragão	Demon	*BoSC*
Dragaton/Draganton	Demon – South	*CBoM*
Dragin	Spirit	*GV*
Dragon	Angel	*SBH*
Dragon	Demon Duke	*Stg, ThG*
Dragos	Angel – Bisertilis	*SR*
Drahas	Punishing Wind	*SSM*
Dramas	Servant Spirit	*Abm*
Dramaz/Dramazed	Angel – Night Hour six	*Stg, ArP*
Dramiel	Demon Duke – Day Hour five	*Stg, ThG*
Dramkaite/ Dramkaphte	Demon – Thursday Hour fifteen	*Hyg*
Dramozyn/ Dramozin/ Dremozin	Angel – Night Hour eight	*Stg, ArP*
Dramyel	Angel – Third Heaven, North	*SSM*
Draned	Spirit – Minister of Love	*oADS*
Drap/Deas	Demon Duke	*LdE*
Drapios/Darpios/ Drapias	Demon Duke	*Stg, ThG*
Drasiel/Drassiel	Demon Chief Duke	*Stg, ThG*
Dredaryel	Angel of Seas/Waters – Autumn	*SSM*
Drelmech	Angel – Day Hour three	*Stg, ArP*
Drepis Eryneon	Spirit – Book Making	*oADS*
Drewchall	Demon Prince/King	*BOS, BoO*
Driades	Demon Prince	*GoPH*
Driēl/Draēl/ Hydroēl/ Hydrōēl	Angel – Wednesday Hour thirteen	*Hyg*

ABBREVIATIONS

Driffon	Ministering Familiar/Mystery	*67M*
Driokonta/Driakonta	Demon – North	*Hyg*
Drisoph/Drisop	Servant Spirit	*Abm, MRC*
Drmial	Angel Encampment Head – sixth Heaven, East	*ShR*
Drogancio	Demon – South	*CBoM*
Drohas	Daemon – Mercury, serving West and Southwest Winds; between the West and North	*SBH*
Dromdrom	Familiar Spirit	*VJL*
Dromiel	Angel – Night Hour twelve	*Stg, ArP*
Dronoth	Demon	*MHN*
Drubiel	Demon Duke – Night Hour eleven	*Stg, ThG*
Drubriel	Earth Spirit	*MNeI*
Druchas/Drucas/ Orucas/ Drachas	Angel – Night Hour nine, Night Hour eleven	*Stg, ArP*
Drudial	Angel – Twelfth Step, second Heaven	*ShR*
Drufiel/Drusiel	Angel – Day Hour seven	*Stg, ArP*
Drumial	Angel – Third Heaven, serving Rhtial	*ShR*
Drusiel	Demon Duke – Night Hour nine, Day Hour one and Night Hour one	*Stg, ThG*
Drusiel	Earth Spirit	*MNeI*
Drypys	Angel – Book Writer	*BoO*
Drsmiel	Angel over Pains, Sharp Pains, Inflammation, Dropsy	*SoM*
Drumial	Angel – Fifth Encampment, first Heaven	*ShR*
Dshnchia	Angel – Fifth Encampment, first Heaven	*ShR*
Dshuua	Angel – Second Encampment, first Heaven	*ShR*
Dubarus	Demon Duke – North Day	*Stg, ThG, BoTS*
Dubiel	Demon Duke – West Night	*Stg, ThG, BoTS*
Dubilon	Demon Duke – North	*Stg, ThG*
Dubraz	Angel – Night Hour seven	*Stg, ArP*
Ducales	Night Devil	*oADS*
Ducaniel	Angel – First Heaven, South	*SaS*
Ducay	Demon Marquis	*LdE*

Dufuel	Angel – Mercury/Wednesday	SR
Dukmsal	Angel Encampment Head – sixth Heaven, West	ShR
Duliatus	Spirit – Hot Spirit – Love	MHN, NML
Dulibion	Spirit – Pleiades (fourth of seven)	oADS
Dulid	Servant Spirit	Abm
Dumaso	Spirit	GV
Dumial	Angel – Sixth Step, second Heaven	ShR
Dumoson/ Dumosson/ Dumoston	Spirit	GoPH, GV
Dunrnia	Angel – Second Encampment, first Heaven	ShR
Dupanfalo/ Dupanfalon	Spirit – Moon	BoO, GAG
Duranyel/Duraniel	Angel – First Heaven, South	SSM, SR
Durayl	Angel	LL
Durial	Angel – Third Heaven, serving Dlqial	ShR
Durstes	Spirit – Treasure	KoN
Durus	Air/Wood Spirit	tSoS
Dusiriel	Demon Duke – Day Hour eight	Stg, ThG
Dusiriel	Water Spirit	MNeI
Duwarchua	Plant Spirit – Oak	GS
Dyabuli	Spirit King – Tuesday	MHN
Dyacon	Good Spirit	MHN
Dydones	Demon	MHN
Dyelagoo	Demon Prince	BOS, BoO
Dyiaga/Dejiaga	Spirit - Mercury	BoO, GAG
Dyrus	Demon	MHN
Dysi	Spirit of the Thumb	MHN
Dyspil/Dyspyl	Spirit – Water	MHN

E

Eaioy	Spirit	*oADS*
Eanche	Spirit – Ring of seventh Mansion of the Moon	*tSoS*
Eansursh	Spirit – Minister of Love	*oADS*
Earaoe	Servant Spirit	*Abm*
Earloy	Spirit	*CoC*
Earny	Spirit Familiar	*BoTS*
Earos/Paras/Ewas	Demon Duke – West by South Night	*Stg, ThG, BoTS*
Earviel/Faviel	Demon Duke – West by South Day	*Stg, ThG, BoTS*
Eazerin	Angel – Venus/Friday	*SR*
Ebal	Infernal Spirit	*MHN*
Ebaron	Servant Spirit	*Abm*
Ebenymydykyn	Spirit of the Thumb	*CBoM*
Ebeyeth/Eleth	Demon King	*BOS, BoO*
Ebra/Ebras	Demon Duke – East	*Stg, ThG*
Ebriêl	Angel	*SM*: P. Med. I.20
Ebrion	Familiar Spirit	*CoMS*
Ebuhuel	Angel	*SoM*
Ebuzoba	Demon – Moon	*BARC*
Ebyrayel	Angel – three signs of fourth Season	*SSM*
Ebyros	Angel Minister	*KoSA*
Ecabel	Angel – Fifth Altitude (Leo)	*Alm*
Echad	Angel – Cherubim/Seraphim	*67M*
Echommiē	Fifth of Seven Egyptian Fates of Heaven	PGM IV:475-829
Eckdulon	Servant Spirit	*Abm*
Ecope	Enochian Angel – South, serving second lesser Angle	*TBA*
Edam	Demon – Sunday Hour one	*Hyg*
Edanōth	Angel – Over Sea	PGM XXVI:1-42
Edelperna	Enochian King – South	*TBA*
Ēder (Mars)	Mars – Alternative Name	*Hyg*
Ediēl/Dydiēl/Eudēl/Aēdiēl	Angel – Tuesday Hour four	*Hyg*
Edlodell	Spirit – Venus	*BoO, GAG*

Edriel	Demon Duke – Day Hour two	*Stg, ThG*
Edriel	Angel – Day Hour twelve	*Stg, ArP*
Êdrouthe	Angel – Plant Ruler	*BoW*
Eead	Spirit – Air	*67M*
Eēkhleton	Demon – Tuesday Hour fifteen	*Hyg*
Eemaktinos	Demon – Monday Hour nine	*Hyg*
Efermende	Enochian Angel – East, serving first lesser Angle	*TBA*
Effignax	Angel – Elul	*SR*
Effilin	Angel – Venus/Friday	*SR*
Effrater	Treasure Spirit	*oADS*
Efiel	Duke – West by North pre-Noon	*Stg, ThG*
Efrigis	Servant Spirit	*Abm*
Egachir	Servant Spirit	*Abm*
Egalierap	Demon	*GoPH*
Egeri	Angel Minister – Love and Fornication	*KoSA*
Egibiel	Angel – Mansion eighteen	*3BOP, tSoS, JMR, SaS, tM*
Egibiel	Commoner Spirit	*MNeI*
Egicam	Treasure Spirit	*oADS*
Egin/Egine/Egyn/ Oegim/Egim/Egym/ Equi/Aegin/Ægin	Demon King – South or North, Midnight	*SSM, LdE, BoC, NML, KoSA, 3BOP, BOS, EBAM, oADS, BoO, BM, MC, BoTS, JMR, GoPH, SaS, MNeI, KoN, PO, VMN, ClI, tM, BD*
Egipcia	Spirit of the Thumb	*CBoM*
Egippia/Egipia	Spirit of the Thumb	*MHN, CBoM*
Egodraosis (Sun)	Sun – Alternative Name	*Hyg*
Egrip	Spirit of the Thumb	*CBoM*
Eheomynt	Angel – Eighth Altitude (Scorpio)	*Alm*
Ehym	Angel – Cherubim/Seraphim	*67M*
Ehyn	Spirit	*CoC*
Eia	Spirit	*ACM*: Cairo 45060
Eiael	Angel	*ACM*: Hay 10122

Eiael/Ejael	Angel – Shem sixty-seven	*KoSU, 3BOP, GoeR, JMR, SAS, tM*
Eianliarug	Spirit – fourth Mansion of Moon Ring	*tSoS*
Eidiel	Angel	*ACM*: Würzburg 42
Eieio	Spirit	*ACM*: Cairo 45060
Eiemēn (Sun)	Sun – Alternative Name	*Hyg*
Eigo	Demon	*BoSC*
Eililōph (Mercury)	Mercury – Alternative Name	*Hyg*
Eillon	Angel – Sun	*GAG*
Eilomfo	Spirit Minister, serving Prince Befafes	*dHM*
Eiotas	Spirit – Pleiades (two of seven)	*oADS*
Eiphiel	Spirit	*ACM*: Cairo 45060
Eisgonel/Ēsginel/ Eisginel	Demon – South	*Hyg*
Eistierix/Ispynrix/ Ipnērix/Hypnirix/ Eispniryx	Demon – Wednesday Hour three	*Hyg*
Eizēri	Spirit	*BoW*
Ekalak	Servant Spirit	*Abm*
Ekenel	Spirit	*ACM*: Cairo 45060
Ēkēsyōr	Demon – West	*Hyg*
Eknel	Spirit	*ACM*: Cairo 45060
Ēkoniēl/Likoniēl/ Ikoniēl/ Eikoniēl	Angel – Monday Hour twenty-two	*Hyg*
Ekorok	Servant Spirit	*Abm*
Ekriroēl	Angel – Friday Hour five	*Hyg*
Ektaser (Saturn)	Saturn – Alternative Name	*Hyg*
El[417]	Angel Minister – Love and Fornication Angel Prince – West Gate	*KoSA, SRH*
El	Spirit – Son of Sons of Light	*dHM*
Eladeb	Daemon Minister – Mercury, between the West and North	*SBH*
Elael	Angel – First Heaven, North	*SSM, SaS*

---

[417] One of the instances where a divine name is given as an angelic one, and in the context one has to wonder why!

Elafon/Elason/Eloson	Servant Spirit	*Abm, MRC*
Elam	Spirit	*MHN*
Elamyr	Servant Spirit	*Abm*
Elamyz/Elamiz/Elamis	Angel – Night Hour eleven	*Stg, ArP*
Elbaoukh/Elbioukh (Sun)	Sun – Alternative Name	*Hyg*
Elbepriz/Elbeperix/Elprix/Albaperx	Demon – West	*Hyg*
El Bera Bavor/El Bera Avor	Angel Prince – Malachim, Autumn	*SRH*
Elberaor	Angel Ruler Superior – third Season by Day	*SSM*
Elcus	Angel – Mars	*BARC*
Elear/Elcar	Demon Duke – South-East Day	*Stg, ThG, BoTS*
Eleazar	Spirit	*AN*
Ēlēkēl	Demon – Mercury	*Hyg*
El El Ovel	Angel Prince – North Gate	*SRH*
Eleleth	Gnostic Spirit of Light	*ACM*: NH Codex VIII, P. Mich. 1190
Êlêlyth	Angel	*SM*: P. Med. I.20
Elemidyri	Spirit of the Thumb	*MHN*
Elena	Spirit	*CBoM*
Eliopaghatel/Elelogaphatel/Elelogap	Demon – Authority over underground treasures	*KoSU, SoS, GV*
Elemiah/Elomiah	Angel – Shem four	*KoSU, 3BOP, GoeR, JMR, SAS, tM*
Elerotel	Spirit – Water	*oADS*
Elespontiaca	Spirit – Sibyl (eight of ten)	*GV*
Elestor/Clestor/Elector	Demon Count – America	*SoS, KoSR, KoSU*
Eleu	Demon Senior	*SSM*
Eleuros	Angel – Venus	*KoSR*
Elgnseb	Spirit Minister, serving Prince Blisdon	*dHM*
Elhiansa	Enochian Senior – North	*TBA*

Eliach	Spirit	*ACM*: Oriental 6796
Ēliditōr/Alidapōr/ Klidētōr/Klēndatōr	Demon – Saturday Hour one	*Hyg*
Eliehon	Angel Prince – Summer	*SRH*
Eliel	Demon Duke – West by South Night	*Stg, ThG, BoTS*
Eliel	Intelligence	*BoG*
Elieyl	Angel – Sun/Sunday	*SR*
Eliezar	Spirit	*dN*
Eligor/Eligos/ Abigor/ Alugor	Demon Duke	*MHN, PmD, DoW, Goe*
Elijon	Spirit – Earth	*67M*
Eliles (Lilith)	Demon	*MRC*
Elimygit	Angel	*KoSA*
Eliogaphatel	Spirit	*KoSR*
Eliorael	Angel	*Hyg*
Eliphamasay/ Eliphamasai/ Eliphanasai	Archangel Angel – Chora three	*NA, ArA*
Elisafan	Angel – Tammuz	*SR*
Elisem/Eliasem/ Aliasem/Eliesem	Demon – Friday Hour nine	*Hyg*
Elisuaig	Angel – Marchesvan	*SR*
Elitel	Demon Duke – West Day	*Stg, ThG, BoTS*
Elivisa	Spirit	*GV*
Ellalyel	Angel – Sun, over Fire	*SR*
Elmia	Angel – Mercury/Wednesday	*SR*
Elmoym	Angel – Day Hour two	*Stg, ArP*
Elnerah	Plant Spirit – Mare's Tail	*GS*
Elobona	Spirit – Venus	*dN*
Elogamillo/Eligamill	Spirit – Saturn	*BoO, GAG*
Elohaym	Angel – Potestates	*67M*
Eloheij	Ministering Familiar/Mystery	*67M*
Elomnit/Elomnia/ Elomina	Archangel Angel – Chora three	*NA, ArA*
Elonim	Servant Spirit	*Abm*

Eloofe	Spirit – Venus	*BoO, GAG*
Elouch	Spirit – Power of Darkness	*ACM*: Berlin 8322
Eloy	Angel Spirit of the Thumb	*KoSA, CBoM*
Elpel/Elbioul (Sun)	Sun – Alternative Name	*Hyg*
Elpinon	Servant Spirit	*Abm*
Elsoum	Spirit	*Hyg*
Eltzen/Eltzin	Demon – North	*ToSC*
Elubatel	Angel	*SoM*
Elyas	Devil – Noon	*oADS*
Elynzy	Angel – Kislev	*SR*
Elzegar	Servant Spirit	*Abm*
Elzinopo	Enochian Senior – North	*TBA*
Emalon/Enalom	Angel – Night Hour one	*Stg, ArP*
Emalsood	Angel Minister – Love and Fornication	*KoSA*
Emarfiel	Angel – Day Hour four	*Stg, ArP*
Emarion/Etharion	Angel – Night Hour twelve	*Stg, ArP*
Emaryel/Emariel	Angel – Night Hour two	*Stg, ArP*
Emarziel/Emerziel	Angel – Night Hour ten	*Stg, ArP*
Emas	Spirit – Minister of Love	*oADS*
Embel	Angel	*Hyg*
Emcodeneyl	Angel – Mars/Tuesday	*SR*
Emediell	Angel – Mansion two and Aries	*BoO*
Emenguilla/Emenguill	Spirit – Jupiter	*BoO, GAG*
Emeriel	Angel – Night Hour eleven	*Stg, ArP*
Emfatison	Servant Spirit	*Abm*
Emiel	Angel	*ACM*: Hay 10122
Emiseēl/Mesoēl/Misoel/Messoēl	Angel – Thursday Hour nine	*Hyg*
Ēmitoton	Demon – Tuesday Hour eleven	*Hyg*
Emlon	Demon Messenger – South	*BOS, BoO, BoTS*
Ēmntdbl	Demon – West and Aries	*Hyg*
Emodias	Demon – Thursday Hour thirteen	*Hyg*

ABBREVIATIONS 427

Emogeni	Demon	*MHN*
Emol	Spirit – Mars	*67M*
Emoniel	Demon Wandering Prince	*Stg, ThG*
Emphiloel/Ephēloēl/ Ephēloēm/ Emphilonēm/ Emphiloēl/Imphiōēl	Angel – Moon	*Hyg*
Emphinoēl	Angel – Friday Hour three	*Hyg*
Emtedi	Enochian Angel – West, over second lesser Angle	*TBA*
Emuel	Duke – West by North Afternoon	*Stg, ThG, BoTS*
Emull	Spirit – Minister of Love	*oADS*
Emus	Angel Minister – Love and Fornication	*KoSA*
Emyel	Angel – Venus, over Water	*SR*
Enachariorh/ Macharioth	Spirit King	*BoO*
Enaezraēl	Angel	*PGM* XXXVI:161-177
Enamerphiēl/ Marphēl	Angel – Summer	*DoW*
Enariel/Gnaviel	Angel – Night Hour six	*Stg, ArP*
Enaritar	Demon – Saturday Hour nineteen	*Hyg*
Enath	Demon – North	*Hyg*
Enatriel/Etnatriel	Angel – Night Hour four	*Stg, ArP*
Enbarc	Enochian Angel – East, over third lesser Angle	*TBA*
Endezen	Enochian Angel – West, serving third lesser Angle	*TBA*
Ēndōr/Eder (Mars)	Mars – Alternative Name	*Hyg*
Enei	Servant Spirit	*Abm*
Enenuth	Demon – Decan twenty-six	*ToS*
Enepsigos	Demon – Moon	*ToS*
Eneriel	Angel – eight of twenty-one on the Left	*ACM*: Berlin 10587
Eney	Demon King under Beelzebub – South	*SSM*
Engadiol	Angel – Mansion fourteen and Virgo	*BoO*
Enheded	Enochian Angel – West, serving first lesser Angle	*TBA*

Enlarex	Enochian Angel – West, over fourth lesser Angle	*TBA*
Ennael	Angel	*ACM*: Yale 1800
Ennoēl	Spirit	*BoW*
Ennoy	Spirit	*oADS*
Ēnōan/Enia (Sun)	Sun – Alternative Name	*Hyg*
Enodas	Demon	*ToSC*
Enodiel/Enediel	Angel – Mansion two	*3BOP, tSoS, JMR, SaS, tM*
Enoy	Spirit	*CBoM*
Enokradēs	Spirit	*Hyg*
Enpeat	Enochian Angel – East, serving fourth lesser Angle	*TBA*
Enphanchouph	Name of Helios in fifth Hour	PGM IV:1596-1715
Enplyn	Angel – Mars/Tuesday	*SR*
Entatzik (Saturn)	Saturn – A;ternative Name	*Hyg*
Entauros	Demon – Monday Hour eighteen, twenty	*Hyg*
Enthoōr/Enthoa	Angel – Spring	*BoW*
Entro	Angel before Throne of God	*oADS*
Enud	Demon	*CoC*
Enuie (Envy)	Demon	*CoC*
Envy	Demon	*ToS, MRC*
Envy	Spirit – Envy	*BP*
Eorasichē	Seventh of seven Pole Lords of Heaven	PGM IV:475-829
Ēoth	Angel – Sunday Hour six	*Hyg*
Eouka (Mars)	Mars – Alternative Name	*Hyg*
Eparine/Eparineson	Spirit	*GoPH, GV*
Ephemeranion	Angel – Tongue of God	*ACM*: H. Kopt. 686
Ephesach	Gnostic Revelatory Spirit	*ACM*: NH Codex VIII
Ephialtes	Member of the Greek Gigantes	PGM IV:474, IV:830
Ephios/Aphios	Demon – Saturday Hour eight	*Hyg*
Ephipas/Ephiēlas/ Ephippas/Asphēplas	Demon – Wednesday Hour ninteen	*Hyg*
Ephipta/Ephēpta/ Ephilta	Demon – South	*Hyg*

Ephippas	Demon – Arabia	*ToS*
Ephlehimah	Plant Spirit – Lilac	*GS*
Ephnix	Archangel	*ACM*: BN Turin
Ephorit/Ephryx/ Ephirit/ Ephēx	Demon – Friday Hour twelve	*Hyg*
Ēphlakh/Ēphal	Demon – South	*Hyg*
Ephradyn/Elphedus	Spirit – Water	*oADS*
Epiē	Demon – Thursday Hour eighteen	*Hyg*
Epinimas	Angel Minister – Love and Fornication	*KoSA*
Epios/Epiē	Demon – Thursday Hour nineteen	*Hyg*
Epithouanon/ Epithoamon/ Opithoua/ Opithounianos/ Spithouanos/ Opēthoumenos/ Opothoumenos	Demon- Sun	*Hyg*
Eptalelon	Spirit	*GV*
Eptiel	Biblical Elder	*ACM*: Berlin 11347, Oriental 6796
Eptra	Treasure Spirit	*oADS*
Eralicarison	Servant Spirit	*Abm*
Eralyn	Angel – Mars/Tuesday	*SR*
Eralyx	Servant Spirit	*Abm*
Eraphael	Angel over the Day	*ACM*: BN Turin
Erastiel	Angel – Fifth Heaven, South	*SaS*
Erathon	Night Devil	*oADS*
Eraticum	Angel	*KoSA*
Erebos	Greek Night Goddess	PGM IV:1390-1495; *SM*: T. Köln Inv. 1
Ereschigal/ Eresgshingal (Ereshkigal)	Sumerian Underworld Goddess	PGM IV:296-466, IV:2441-2621, IV:2708-2784, IV:2891-2942, V:304-369, V:370-446, VII:317-318, VII:862-918,

Ereschigal/ Eresgshingal (Ereshkigal) (con't.)		PGM: VII:981-993, LXX:4-25, PDM XIV:150-231, XIV:675-694; *SM*: PSI I.28, T. Cairo Mus. JdE 48217, T. Louvre Inv. E 27145, P. Mich. Inv. 6925, T. Köln Inv. 1, Audollent DT.38
Ēreth (Venus)	Venus – Alternative Name	*Hyg*
Ergarrandras	Spirit	*MHN*
Ergediel	Commoner Spirit, Fire	*MNeI*
Ērgatige/Ērgatge/ Irgotie/ Ērogtige	Demon – Tuesday Hour twenty-three	*Hyg*
Ergdbab	Spirit Minister, serving Prince Blisdon	*dHM*
Ergodiel/Ergediel	Angel – Mansion fourteen	*3BOP, tSoS, JMR, SaS, tM*
Ergonion	Servant Spirit	*Abm*
Ergosil	Servant Spirit	*Abm*
Ergotas/Ergōtas	Demon – Thursday Hour nine	*Hyg*
Eriel	Angel over Water	*ACM*: BN Turin, Oriental 6796
Erimites	Servant Spirit	*Abm*
Erisset	Angel Minister – Love and Fornication	*KoSA*
Eritrean	Spirit – Sibyl (five of ten)	*GV*
Erizonas	Angel	*BoSC*
Erkaya	Servant Spirit	*Abm*
Erlain	Spirit	*MHN*
Erly/Ferly	Spirit	*GoPH, GV*
Ermag/Ermager/ Hermag/Asormagē	Demon – Friday Hour five	*Hyg*
Ermaziel/Ermoziel/ Ermosiel	Angel – Day Hour two	*Stg, ArP*
Ermichthathōps	Sixth of seven Pole Lords of Heaven	PGM IV:475-829
Ermiel	Angel – Day Hour eight	*Stg, ArP*
Ermihala	Servant Spirit	*Abm*
Ermona	Angel Minister – Love and Fornication	*KoSA*

ABBREVIATIONS 431

Ermoniel	Demon Duke – Day Hour one	*Stg, ThG*
Ermukratos	Gnostic Spirit of Light	*ACM*: P. Mich. 1190
Erner	Spirit – Minister of Love	*oADS*
Eros	Greek Love God	PGM IV:1716-1870, VII:478-490, XII:14-95, LII:20-26
Erou Rombriēs	Seventh of Seven Egyptian Fates of Heaven	PGM IV:475-829
Erphanouel	Spirit	*ACM*: Cairo 45060
Error	Demon – Pleiades six	*ToS*
Erusia	Spirit	*GAG*
Erynhel	Angel – Third Altitude (Gemini)	*Alm*
Esam	Spirit – Minister of Love	*oADS*
Esay	Night Devil	*oADS*
Eschakleō	God of the Abyss of Primal Waters	PGM XIII:1-343
Ēsenephys/Senephthys	Isis-Nephthys Composite Deity	PGM XII:201-269, LXII:1-24, CXXII:1-55
Eslevor	Spirit	*GV*
Esmaadyn	Angel – Sun/Sunday	*SR*
Esmouēl/Esmaēl/Estmaēl/Ismatiēl/Amael	Angel – Tuesday Hour twenty-three	*Hyg*
Esor	Angel – Cherubim/Seraphim	*67M*
Esorum	Spirit – sixth Mansion of Moon Ring	*AE*
Esparte	Daughter of the Devil	*ACM*: P. Mich. 1190
Espoel	Demon Duke – West by South Day	*Stg, ThG, BoTS*
Essaf	Angel – Ab	*SR*
Estade	Spirit – third Mansion of Moon Ring	*AE*
Estael	Intelligence – Jupiter	*SGT, SSG*
Estahol	Spirit – West	*SSM*
Estaolh	Spirit	*SSM*
Estatell/Alkatell/Alkates	Spirit	*BoO*
Estel	Spirit – Mirror	*CoMS*
Estim	Enochian Angel – North, serving fourth lesser Angle	*TBA*

Estio/Estiot	Spirit	*GoPH, GV*
Estoge (Venus)	Venus – Alternative Name	*Hyg*
Esum	Spirit – Minister of Love	*oADS*
Esyel	Angel – Saturn, over Earth	*SR*
Etevlgl	Spirit Minister, serving Prince Befafes	*dHM*
Ethael	Biblical Elder	*ACM*: Berlin 11347, Oriental 6796
Ethamael	Angel – Superior	*oADS*
Ethanim/Ethamim/Eihanim	Servant Spirit	*Abm, MRC*
Etheluill	Spirit – Venus	*BoO, GAG*
Etheye	Spirit Minister – Saturn	*BoO*
Ēthiēl/Athiēl/Athouēl/Athoēl	Angel – Sunday Hour twenty	*Hyg*
Ethiel	Demon Duke – North-West Night	*Stg, ThG, BoTS*
Ēththaēl	Angel – Sunday Hour four	*Hyg*
Etiel	Demon Duke – West by North pre-Noon	*BoTS*
Etimiel/Etymiel/Elimiel	Demon Duke – West Day	*Stg, ThG, BoTS*
Eilophnaendōr (Mercury)	Mercury – Alternative Name	*Hyg*
Erkigē	Demon – West	*Hyg*
Ētiton	Angel – Monday Hour nineteen	*Hyg*
Ētouros/Entauros	Demon – Monday Hour nineteen	*Hyg*
Etubulnatita	Demon Servant – Saturday	*KoN*
Euantr/Enan	Spirit – Venus	*BoO, GAG*
Euchey	Angel	*GV*
Eudelmus	Angel – Mars	*BARC*
Euiraber	Terrestrial Spirit – Attendant in South	*SBH*
Euknitiēl	Demon – Monday Hour twenty-three	*Hyg*
Euphaniel	Angel – Venus	*KoSR*
Euroaster/Euronotus	South-East by South Wind	*Thm*
Eurus/Auster	Wind – East	*MC, BoTS*
Eurynome	Corpse-eating Daemon	*DI*
Eusule	Devil – Noon	*oADS*

Evadar/Enadar	Angel – Day Hour six	*Stg, ArP*
Evagel	Stone Spirit – Quartz	*GS*
Evandiel	Angel – Night Hour nine	*Stg, ArP*
Evanuel/Evamiel/ Evannel	Angel – Night Hour three	*Stg, ArP*
Evapria/Empro	Spirit – twelfth Mansion of the Moon Ring	*AE*
Evarym/Evarim	Angel – Day Hour seven	*Stg, ArP*
Everges	Treasure Spirit	*BoTS*
Exarih	Enochian Angel – West, serving third lesser Angle	*TBA*
Exchauruht	Angel	*NA*
Exenteron	Servant Spirit	*Abm*
Exes	Enochian Evil Spirit	*TBA*
Exgezod	Enochian Angel – East, over fourth lesser Angle	*TBA*
Exhauthes	Angel	*NA*
Exiel	Angel – Guardian of Mary (two of three)	*ACM*: H. Kopt. 686
Exluso	Angel	*NA, SBH*
Exmegan	Angel	*NA, SBH*
Exmogon	Angel	*NA, SBH*
Exoniloelli	Spirit – Moon	*BoO*
Exoueargē	Demon – West	*Hyg*
Expaoniel	Angel – Venus, over Water	*SR*
Expeceh	Enochian Angel – West, serving fourth lesser Angle	*TBA*
Expion	Angel – Saturn/Saturday	*SR*
Extator	Angel	*BoSC*
Eyeassereye	Angel – Second Heaven, West	*SSM*
Eyma	Spirit of the Thumb	*CBoM*
Ezay	Angel – Fifth Altitude (Leo)	*Alm*
Ezea	Angel	*VJL*
Ezebul	Angel	*VJL*
Ezeēl/Ezekiēl/Ēoēl/ Iōēl/ Dezeēl	Angel – Monday Hour eight	*Hyg*

Ezimmistraos	Demon	*Hyg*
Ezirohias	Spirit of the Thumb	*MHN*
Ezriēl	Angel	PGM XXXVI:161-177
Ezuiah	Angel – Sun/Sunday	*SR*

F

Fabanin	Spirit	*MHN*
Fabar	Demon	*MHN*
Fabariel/Fabatiel	Demon Duke – North-West Day	*Stg, ThG, BoTS*
Fabath	Demon	*MHN*
Fabbrom/Fabelleronthon	Spirit	*GoPH, GV*
Fabiel/Fubiel	Duke – West by North pre-Noon	*Stg, ThG, BoTS*
Fabin	Good Spirit	*MHN*
Fabriel	Angel – Fourth Heaven, East	*EoN, SaS*
Fabriel	Spirit – Sun	*SoS*
Faccas	Demon – Mercury Angel – Jupiter	*BARC*
Faceyeyl	Angel – Sun/Sunday	*SR*
Facygrat	Spirit – twentieth Mansion of the Moon Ring	*tSoS*
Faguni	Servant Spirit	*Abm*
Fahassur	Spirit – Air	*MNeI*
Falabar	Spirit	*SSM*
Falafon	Angel – Adar	*SR*
Falebery/Falibery	Spirit	*CBoM*
Falha	Angel – Sun/Sunday	*SR*
Falmar	Spirit	*MHN*
Falaur	Demon King – North	*DoW, GAG*
Falkaroth	Spirit – Venus	*TV*
Falneyl/Salnet	Spirit Prince – under Alyzaire	*oADS*
Faly	Angel – Fifth Heaven, West	*SR*
Famaras/Famaris	Angel – Day Hour twelve	*Stg, ArP*

ABBREVIATIONS

Fameis/Fronone (Forneus?)	Demon Marquis	*NML*
Famiel	Angel – Third Heaven Friday, South Angel – Third Heaven, South	*EoN, Hmn, KoSR, BoO, BM, GAG, BoTS, SaS, tM*
Famoriel	Angel – Night Hour two	*Stg, ArP*
Famtiell	Angel – Mars	*GAG*
Faniel	Angel – Jupiter/Thursday Angel – Third Heaven, North	*SR, SaS*
Fanyel	Angel – Adar	*SR*
Faomytec	Angel – Sun in signs of fourth Season	*SSM*
Faon/Dilifaon	Spirit – Mercury	*BoO, GAG*
Farabyn	Angel – Mars/Tuesday	*SR*
Faraiz	Demon	*BoSC*
Faral	Spirit – Mirror	*CoMS*
Faraphyell	Angel	*oADS*
Farastario	Spirit – Ring of seventh Mansion of the Moon	*AE*
Farbarakin	Angel – Moon	*LL*
Farbiel	Angel – Fifth Heaven, East	*SR*
Farcelin	Angel – Day Hour two	*LL*
Fardiar	Spirit	*MNeI*
Fariel	Angel – Day Hour two	*LL*
Farielin	Angel – Moon/Monday	*SR*
Farionon	Angel – Mercury/Wednesday	*SR*
Farma	Wind Spirit	*GAG*
Farmane	Spirit King – Thursday	*CBoM*
Farmos/Fermos	Angel – Day Hour seven	*Stg, ArP*
Farnnan	Spirit – third Mansion of Moon Ring	*AE*
Farnnial	Angel – Mercury/Wednesday	*SR*
Faroos	Back part of Damahos	*Pic*
Fartigrat/Factogret	Spirit – twentieth Mansion of the Moon Ring	*AE*
Fasma	Servant Spirit	*Abm*
Faseua/Fassua/Fascua	Demon Duke – South-West Night	*Stg, ThG, BoTS*

Fassatalucy	Demon King	*SSM*
Fastarin	Spirit – Ring of seventh Mansion of the Moon	*tSoS*
Fastur	Spirit – fourth Mansion of Moon Ring	*AE*
Fatenovenia	Spirit	*67M*
Faturab/Faturasso	Servant Spirit	*Abm*
Faubair	Spirit	*MHN*
Faym	Demon Senior	*SSM*
Febat	Demon	*MHN*
Fecolinie	Spirit of the Thumb	*MHN*
Fégol	Demon – under Sirach	*KoSU*
Fegor	Spirit – North	*SSM*
Fellofell/Felofell	Spirit – Saturn	*BoO, GAG*
Felsmes	Demon	*MHN*
Felyypon	Angel – Saturn/Saturday	*SR*
Femalos	Spirit – Love/Sexual Attraction	*Pic*
Femell/Fenell/ Temell/ Semell	Demon Messenger – East	*BOS, BoO*
Femol/Femel	Demon Duke – South	*Stg, ThG*
Fenadros/Fenadroz/ Fenadross	Angel – Night Hour nine	*Stg, ArP*
Fenell	Spirit	*BoO*
Feniturla	Angel – Mercury/Wednesday	*SR*
Fenosiel/Tenostiel	Angel – Day Hour twelve	*Stg, ArP*
Fenyx/Fenix (Phenix)	Demon Marquis	*SSM, LdE*
Feremin	Spirit	*MHN*
Feresin	Angel – Moon	*LL*
Ferly	Spirit	*GoPH, BD*
Fernebus	Servant Spirit	*Abm*
Fersone/Tersone (Purson?)	Demon King	*BOS, BoO*
Fervagitim/Fermagon	Spirit – eleventh Mansion of the Moon Ring	*AE, tSoS*
Fervolam/Fernola	Spirit – Sun	*BoO, GAG*
Fessan/Tessan	Demon – North	*BOS, BoO*

ABBREVIATIONS

Festile/Festilen/Festilem	Spirit	oADS
Festinavit	Angel – Mars	GAG
Fewrayn/Fewrayne	Demon Governor/Marquis	BOS, BoO
Feylarachin	Angel – Moon/Monday	SR
Feyn	Angel – Mercury/Wednesday	SR
Fictimetim/Foromaloh/Firmelti/Fortunelich	Spirit – fifth Mansion of the Moon Ring	AE, tSoS
Filaxson	Servant Spirit	Abm
Fimarson/Emarson	Demon Duke – Day Hour twelve	ArP
Fimiritis	Spirit – fourteenth Mansion of the Moon ring	tSoS
Finibet	Demon	MHN
Fipo	Enochian Angel – West, serving third lesser Angle	TBA
Firïel	Spirit	NML
Fisfilin	Angel – Mercury/Wednesday	SR
Fito	Spirit – Sibyl (six of ten)	GV
Flabison	Servant Spirit	Abm
Flacf	Spirit Attendant – Jupiter	EoN
Flaef/Blaef	Angel Minister of Air – Friday	Hmn, KoSR, BM, GAG, tM
Flaga	Scandinavian Fairy	DI
Flauros/Flaures/Haures/Flavos/Flavros	Demon Duke	LdE, PmD, DoW, Goe, DI
Flebilis	Demon Chief – West	SSM
Fleruty/Fleurty/Flurety (Ftheruthi?)	Demon Demon Lieutenant General	GoPH, GG, GV, BoSC
Fligoth	Spirit – Bird Capturers	oADS
Flodalath/Tlodalath	Spirit – Sun	BoO, GAG
Floga	Lunar Spirit	MNeI
Flor	Spirit	MNeI
Floran	Spirit	oADS
Florian (Floron?)	Spirit King – Treasure, North	KoN
Floron	Spirit	MHN

Foca/Faca/Fata	Fairy – third of Seven Sisters	oADS, BoO, JMR, BoTS,
Focalor/Focator/Forcalor	Demon Duke	PmD, DoW, Goe
Focan	Spirit – Minister of Love	oADS
Fodo	Demon	CoC
Folficay	Wicked Spirit	NMI
Foliath	Demon	MHN
Folla/Fola/Tolla/Falla	Fairy – fourth of Seven Sisters	oADS, BoO, JMR, BoTS
Fonyel	Angel – Jupiter, over Fire	SR
Foras/Foreas/Fortas/Sartas	Demon President	NML, Goe
Forcan	Spirit	KoN
Forcase/Forcas/Forras (Foras?)	Demon Prince	BOS, BoO, DI
Forfaron	Servant Spirit	Abm
Forfornifer	Spirit Spirit – Skull Divination	SSM, ArPh
Forforuiferbalzach	Demon Senior	SSM
Forman	Spirit King – Jupiter	BoO
Formasus	Spirit	oADS
Formecones	Demon Prince	BOS, BoO
Formione/Formone/Formyone	Demon King under Beelzebub Daemon King – Jupiter Angel King – between East and South	SSM, SBH, oADS
Forneus/Gorners	Demon Marquis	PmD, DoW, Goe
Fornifer	Demon Senior Spirit – East	SSM
Foros	Spirit of the Thumb	CBoM
Fortesion	Servant Spirit	Abm
Fortisan	Demon	BoO
Fortitudo	Spirit of Strength	BoO
Fortune	God – Uncertainty	BoO
Fortune	Spirit – Fortune	BP
Fos	Spirit – Air	MNeI
Fosfora	Servant Spirit	Abm

ABBREVIATIONS

Foylylon	Angel – Saturn/Saturday	*SR*
Fraciel	Angel – Fifth Heaven Tuesday, North	*EoN, Hmn, KoSR, BoO, GAG, BoTS, tM*
Fraigne	Angel – Fifth Heaven, Tuesday, East	*KoSR*
Framion	Angel – Day Hour eight	*Stg, ArP*
Framoth/Framoch	Angel – Night Hour seven	*Stg, ArP*
Franedac/Frandedac	Angel – Night Hour one	*Stg, ArP*
Frangam	Spirit	*GV*
Frasis	Servant Spirit	*Abm*
Frasmiel	Demon Duke	*Stg, ThG*
Frastiel.Feultiel	Demon – under Sirach	*KoSU*
Frätata	Demon Servant – Friday	*KoN*
Fratradrith/ Fratradat/ Fracaday	Spirit – sixth Mansion of the Moon Ring	*AE, tSoS*
Freese	Spirit – Minister of Love	*oADS*
Fremiel/Fresmiel	Angel – Night Hour four	*Stg, ArP*
Freyja	Norse Sorcery Goddess	*Gbk*
Friagne/Friaguel	Angel – Fifth Heaven Tuesday, East Angel – Fifth Heaven, East	*EoN, Hmn, BoO, GAG, BoTS, SaS, tM, CBMS*
Friblex/Friplex/ Triblex	Demon Duke and Marquis	*BOS, BoO*
Frigg	Norse Mother Goddess	*Gbk*
Frigia	Spirit – Sibyl (nine of ten)	*GV*
Frimodth/Frimost/ Frimoth	Demon Duke Demon – Tuesday Demon – under Sirach	*KoSU, SoS, GV, BD*
Fritath	Demon	*MHN*
Frnacrio	Spirit – South	*KoN*
Frö	Norse Deity (?)	*Gbk*
Frodissma	Demon	*GAG*
Fromezyn/Fromezin	Angel – Night Hour two	*Stg, ArP*
Fronyzon/Fromyzon/ Fronzon/Fromzom/ Fremzon	Angel – Night Hour three	*Stg, ArP*

Frulthiel/Frucissière/ Frulhel/Frastiel	Demon Duke	*SoS*, *GV*
Frurodopes	Spirit	*BoTS*
Fruthmerl/ Frutimière/ Glitia	Demon Duke	*SoS*, *GV*
Ftheruthi	Demon Duke	*SoS*
Fubentroty	Spirit	*GV*
Fuglep	Treasure Spirit	*oADS*
Fuheylyn	Angel – Mars/Tuesday	*SR*
Fulcinifer	Spirit – Mirror	*CoMS*
Fulitiel	Angel – Saturn, over Water	*SR*
Fulmar	Demon	*NMI*
Fummoluolda	Demon	*CoC*
Funaler	Spirit	*BoTS*
Furamiel/Fumarel	Angel – Night Hour eleven	*Stg*, *ArP*
Furaym	Spirit	*SSM*
Furcaber	Spirit	*SSM*
Furcaberbrine	Demon Senior	*SSM*
Furcas	Demon Knight or Prince	*SSM*, *LdE*, *PmD*, *DoW*, *Goe*
Furfur/Furtur	Demon Earl or Count	*LdE*, *NML*, *PmD*, *DoW*, *Goe*, *DI*
Furiel/Furtiel	Angel – Day Hour three Presiding Spirit – Venus	*Stg*, *ArP*, *CBMS*
Furinicat	Spirit – eleventh Mansion of the Moon Ring	*AE*
Fursiel/Furciel	Demon Duke – North Day	*Stg*, *ThG*, *BoTS*
Furtherhoth/ Furtoihot/ Fiatant	Spirit – first Mansion of the Moon Ring	*AE*
Fustiel	Angel – Day Hour five	*Stg*, *ArP*
Futiel/Phutiel	Duke – West by North after Midnight	*Stg*, *ThG*, *BoTS*
Futiel/Futid	Demon Duke – Night Hour eight	*Stg*, *ThG*
Futiel	Earth Spirit	*MNeI*
Futiniel/Futinel	Angel – Day Hour five	*Stg*, *ArP*
Fyāl	Angel – Cancer	*BoW*

Fynāl/Fytāyl	Angel – August/Leo	*BoW*
Fyriel	Spirit	*MHN*
Fyrin/Syrim	Spirit – Water	*MHN*
Fyrus	Demon	*MHN*

G

Ga	Angel – Malachim, under Pheseker	*SRH*
Ga	Angel – Sun	*GAG*
Gaabōn/Gaaboul/ Gaabēoul/Ganaboul	Demon – South	*Hyg*
Gaaharayl	Angel – Autumn	*MHN*
Ga'aneh	Angel – Malachim, under Avorphenial	*SRH*
Gaap/Goap/Tap/ Taob	Demon President and Prince Demon King – South	*MHN, PmD, Goe, DI*
Gaasē/Gaasi/Gagasi	Spirit – East	*Hyg*
Gaashial	Angel Encampment Head – sixth Heaven, East	*ShR*
Gabaap/Bagōap/ Bagoap/Bagoakh	Demon – North	*Hyg*
Gabal	Angel – Mercury/Wednesday	*SR*
Gabanael	Angel – Bisertilis	*SR*
Gabanay	Demon King – South under Amaymon	*KoN*
Gabēd (Luna)	Luna – Alternative Name	*Hyg*
Gaberiel	Angel Ruler – third Season by Day	*SSM*
Gaberyel	Angel – three signs of third Season	*SSM*
Gabgel	Angel – Bisertilis	*SR*
Gabiel	Angel – Mansion five	*3BOP, tSoS, JMR, SaS, tM*
Gabiel	Genii – 13° Aries	*ArP*
Gabiel/Gobiel	Angel – Chora four	*ArA*
Gabio/Gabir/Gabas	Demon Duke – South Night	*Stg, ThG*
Gabion	Angel – Saturn/Saturday	*SR*
Gabmion	Angel – Iyar	*SR*
Gabraei /Gabrael	Spirit – Moon	*SGT, SSG*
Gabrael	Angel first Heaven Monday – East	*SR, EoN, Hmn, KoSR, BoO, GAG, BoTS, tM*

Gabriach (Gabriel?)	Spirit	*KoSR*
Gabrial (Gabriel)	Angel Prince – Moon in Spring, Cancer, Scorpio, Aquarius Angel – Harvest Ruler Angel – Malachim, Autumn Angel Minister – Malachim, fifth Dwelling Angel Prince – East Gate Angel – Malachim, Tishri/ Tebeth	*SRH*
Gabriel/Gabriell/ Gabriēl/Gabriēl/ Gabril/Gabryel/ Gabryell	Archangel – Moon, Water, Monday, Aquarius, Mars, North Wind, Midnight Winds, first Heaven, East, Autumn Archangel – Yesod Angel Commander Angel – Moon, over Fire Angel – Shebat Angel – Autumn Ruler of Order of Angels Angel – First Altitiude (Aries) Angel – Chora one Fourth Heaven Sunday – East, Spring First Heaven Monday – East Intelligence – Moon Archangel – Malachim, over the Shem Angel Prince – Winter	HB Dan 8:16, 9:21, Luke 1:19, 1:26; PGM I:262-347, III:1-164, III:282-409, III:494-611, IV:1716-1870, VII:1009-1016, VII:1017-1026, X:36-50, XXIIa:18-27, XXXVI:295-311, XLIII:1-27, XC:1-13, CVI:1-10; *SM*: P. Berol inv. 21165, P. Heid. Inv. G 1101, P. Heid. Inv. Lat. 5, P. IFAO s.n., P. Med. I.20; *ACM*: P. EM. 10263, Cairo C4 Text, P. Prague 1; P. Mich. 136, H. Kopt. 544, Oriental 5899, Berlin 11347, Oriental 5525, P. Mich. 1190, BN Turin, H. Kopt. 684, H. Kopt. 581; Hay 10376, Hay 10434, Oriental 5986, P. Lichačev, Bodl C(P)4, Oriental 6172, Aberdeen Text, Cairo IAFO, Würzburg 42, H. O. Lange Text, P. Mich. 3023A, P. Mich. 3472, Cairo 45060, Oriental 6796, P. Mich. 593,

Gabriel/Gabriell/ Gabriēl/Gabriēl/ Gabril/Gabryel/ Gabryell (con't.)			*ACM*: L. Anastasi 9, H. Kopt. 686; *SoM, dCL, Alm, SSM, NA, SR, LL, SBH, EoN, BoW, Hmn, Hyg, B7R, KoSR, Gbk, 3BOP, CBoM, SoS, MHN, dN, CoC, tSoS, dSS, ADS, DoW, oADS, BoO, BM, MC, Thm, GAG, GoeR, ArP, ArA, JMR, BoTS, MNeI, KoN, GoA, GoPH, SaS, SMS, ES, BoSC, SRH, EPL, PO, ClI, GV, MRC, CoMS, tM, , CBMS 67M*
Gabriel		Spirit – Sun Spirit – Moon	*SGT, SSG*
Gabril (Gabriel)		Angel – First Heaven, Monday – East	*BoTS*
Gabrinoz/Gabrynoz		Angel – Night Hour two	*Stg, ArP*
Gabrion		Angel – Joy and Divination	*CoMS*
Gabriot		Spirit	*KoSR*
Gabryel		Angel – First Heaven, East	*SSM*
Gabrynyn		Angel – Mars/Tuesday	*SR*
Gabtel/Gabtzel		Angel – Wednesday Hour twenty-four	*Hyg*
Gabzav		Angel – Joy and Divination	*CoMS*
Gaciel		Spirit – East	*SSM*
Gadaf		Angel – Ab	*SR*
Gadal		Spirit	*SSM*
Gadiel/Gadyel		Angel – FSourth Heaven, South Angel – Fifth Heaven, South	*SR, SSM, SaS*
Gadiel		Genii – 15° Aries	*ArP*
Gadril		Spirit	*BoW*
Gadym		Angel – Joy and Divination	*CoMS*
Gael		Angel – Saturn, over Air Angel – Fourth Heaven, East	*SR*
Gaeneron (Gomory?)		Demon Duke	*MHN*
Gaffriel (Caffriel)		Angel – Hour five	*MHN*
Gaforin		Angel – Moon	*LL*

Gagasi	Demon – East	*Hyg*
Gagison	Servant Spirit	*Abm*
Gagolchon/ Gogalchon	Servant Spirit	*Abm, MRC*
Gagonix	Servant Spirit	*Abm*
Gahathus/Gahatus	Daemon – Sun, subect to North Wind; East	*SBH*
Gahiel	Genii – 22° Pisces	*ArP*
Gaidis	Angel – Mars	*BARC*
Gaimon	Spirit Prince – Invisibility Coat	*KoN*
Gaions	Angel – Sun	*GAG*
Galaēl/Galabēr (Luna)	Luna – Alternative Name	*Hyg*
Galagos	Servant Spirit	*Abm*
Galand/Guland/ Galant	Demon Duke Demon – Saturday	*SoS, GoPH, GV, BD*
Galbiet	Angel – Jupiter/Thursday	*SR*
Galdel/Caldel	Angel fifth Heaven Tuesday – South Spirit – Mars	*Hmn, KoSR, SoS, BoO, GAG, BoTS, tM*
Galfane	Devil King	*oADS*
Galgall	Angel – Tammuz	*SR*
Galgidōn/Galgēdōn	Demon – Friday Hour eleven	*Hyg*
Galian	Spirit	*oADS*
Galiel/Galieliōr/ Galierōth/Galieliar	Demon – Thursday Hour twenty-three	*Hyg*
Gallagil (Luna)	Luna – Alternative Name	*Hyg*
Gallath	Demon	*MHN*
Galliane	Spirit Lord	*KoN*
Galliel	Angel – Water	*SR*
Galmaēl/Gamaēl	Angel – Spring	*BoW*
Galms	Angel – Iyar	*SR*
Galnel	Angel – Kislev	*SR*
Galoneti	Demon – under Sirach	*KoSU*
Galōs/Galos	Demon – North	*Hyg*
Galtim/Galtym/ Galtyra	Spirit	*MHN*

Galtyn	Demon Senior	*SSM*
Galuf	Angel – Tammuz	*SR*
Galus	Angel – Iyar	*SR*
Gamael	Genii – 26° Capricorn, 26° Aquarius	*ArP*
Gaman	Spirit	*KoN*
Gambra	Spirit – South	*oADS*
Gameis/Gamphais/ Gamphaēs/Ganbais/	Demon – North	*Hyg*
Gamiel	Angel – Kislev	*SR*
Gamiel (Apadiel)	Prince Palatine	*MNeI*
Gamigin/Gamgyn	Demon Marquis	*PmD, DoW, Goe*
Gamoet	Demon	*GoPH*
Gamor	Demon – South	*BOS, BoO*
Gamsiel/Gramsiel	Angel – Night Hour eight	*Stg, ArP*
Gamyel/Jamiel	Angel – Day Hour six	*Stg, ArP*
Gana	Demon	*MHN*
Ganael	Spirit – North	*SSM*
Ganaēl/Anaēl	Angel – Summer, Lord of the Towers	*BoW*
Ganar	Angel – Sun	*GAG*
Ganarsu/Ganarfu/ Garnasu	Demon Duke – North-West Day	*Stg, ThG, BoTS*
Ganga/Gramma	Indian Demon	*DI*
Ganiel	Angel – Summer	*EoN*
Ganten/Gatinēl	Angel – Wednesday Hour twenty-four	*Hyg*
Ganuel	Biblical Elder	*ACM*: Berlin 11347, Oriental 6796
Ganyhaon/Gauiham	Spirit – Sun	*BoO, GAG*
Gaoel	Angel – Saturn	*GAG*
Gaporim	Angel – Moon	*LL*
Gararouēl (Sun)	Sun – Alternative Name	*Hyg*
Garasyn	Angel – Bisertilis	*SR*
Garbona	Angel	*NA, SBH*
Gardel	Angel – Fifth Heaven, South	*EoN*
Gardiab	Spirit	*MNeI*

Gargatel/Cargutel	Angel – Summer	EoN, Hmn, KoSR, tSoS, MC, GAG, GoeR, tM
Garghaga	Planetary Spirit – Saturn	SSM
Garidolicalu	Spirit – eleventh Mansion of the Moon Ring	AE
Gariech/Garieth/ Garior/ Carior	Spirit – fifth Mansion of the Moon Ring	AE, tSoS
Gariel	Duke – West by North after Midnight	Stg, ThG, BoTS
Gariguanim/ Gariguam	Spirit – Saturn	BoO, GAG
Garinirag/Gariniray	Servant Spirit	Abm
Garmaniel	Angel – Guardian of Mary (one of three)	ACM: H. Kopt. 686
Garon	Spirit Familiar	BoTS
Garpa	Demon	Hyg
Garron	Demon – West	DoW
Garsas	Servant Spirit	Abm
Garsone/Garson	Demon King	BOS, BoO
Garta	Name of Pre	PDM XIV:528-553
Garuda	Indian Giant Bird Mount	DI
Gasarzan/Sasarzan	Spirit	BoW
Gasca	Angel – Tebet	SR
Gaseon	Spirit	ArPh
Gashgorzim	Angel – Moon	LL
Gashiel	Genii – 16° Capricorn, 16° Aquarius	ArP
Gasial (Saturn)	Saturn – Alternative Name	Hyg
Gasoryn	Angel – Moon/Monday	SR
Gaspard/Gaspar/ Caspar (Gasper/ Casper)	Spirit – Magi King (third of three)	KoSR, ES, Gbk, GoPH, GV, BD
Gasretos	Demon – West	Hyg
Gasyaxe	Demon Ruler	BOS, BoO
Gatan	Demon King (formerly Order of Thrones)	KoN

Gathouel/Gathoue/ Agathouēl/ Agathoēil/ Agathoel/Agathoēl	Angel – Venus	*Hyg*
Gatrat	Angel – Spring	*MHN*
Gastyel	Angel – Fire	*SSM*
Gaupr	Angel – First Encampment, first Heaven	*ShR*
Gaviel/Guariel	Angel – Summer	*Hmn, KoSR, tSoS, MC, GAG, GoeR, tM*
Gazaron	Servant Spirit	*Abm*
Gaziel	Spirit – Wealth	*oADS*
Gazriel	Angel – Fire	*SR*
Gazril	Angel – Shebat	*SR*
Gba	Angel – Second Encampment, first Heaven	*ShR*
Gblial	Angel – Third Step, second Heaven	*ShR*
Gbrial (Gabriel)	Angel Prince – Fourth Heaven, Fire	*ShR*
Gchlial	Angel – Sixth Step, second Heaven	*ShR*
Gdgl	Angel – Fifth Encampment, first Heaven	*ShR*
Gdial	Angel – Second Encampment, first Heaven Angel – Fourth Encampment, first Heaven Angel – Third Heaven, serving Rhtial	*ShR*
Gdrial	Angel – Seventh Encampment, first Heaven	*ShR*
Gdudial	Angel – Ninth Step, second Heaven	*ShR*
Gê (Gaia)	Greek Earth Goddess	*SM*: P. Oxy. Inv. 72/65 (a)
Geb	Egyptian Earth God	PDM XIV:295-308, XIV:366-375, XIV:594-620, XIV:805-840, XIV:1026-1045, LXI:79-94, LXI:106-111
Geba	Angel – Malachim, under Ayigeda	*SRH*
Gebal	Enochian Angel – North, serving second lesser Angle	*TBA*
Gebarbayea	Angel – Sun/Sunday	*SR*

Gebat/Gebath	Demon	*MHN*
Gebeche Banai/Gedo Bonay/Gedobonai	Archangel	*NA*
Gebel	Good Spirit	*MHN*
Gebel	Demon	*NMI*
Gebepl	Demon	*GoPH*
Gebiel	Genii – 12° Pisces	*ArP*
Geboloy	Angel	*KoSA*
Gebyn	Angel – Mercury/Wednesday	*SR*
Gecha	Angel – Malachim, under Ayigeda	*SRH*
Gechelial	Angel, serving above sixth Degree	*SRH*
Gechenial	Angel Prince – South Gate	*SRH*
Geciel	Genii – 19° Aries	*ArP*
Gedal	Angel – Malachim, under Plemiya	*SRH*
Gederial	Angel Prince – East Gate	*SRH*
Gedial	Angel Prince – Malachim over Winter Nights Angel Minister – Malachim ruling Rain Angel Prince – Gate of Spirit of South Angel Magistrate – Malachim	*SRH*
Gediel/Gedediel/Gedial	Demon King – South by West Demon Prince – South under Amaymon	*Stg, ThG, BoTS, KoN*
Gediel	Genii – 13° Virgo, 23° Virgo	*ArP*
Gediel (Hanaël)	Angel – Capricorn Spirit – Capricorn	*3BOP, tSoS, SaS*
Gediel	Angel – Chora four	*ArA*
Gedobonai/Gedobenai	Angel – Chora three	*ArA*
Gedoniya	Angel – Malachim, under Pheseker	*SRH*
Gedulin	Angel – Venus/Friday	*SR*
Geenex	Demon Knight	*BOS, BoO*
Gefjon	Norse Agriculture Goddess	*Gbk*
Gefowe	Good Spirit	*SoM*
Gēgaor/Gēgorgē	Demon – Tuesday Hour twenty-four	*Hyg*
Gehnamos	Angel	*NA*
Gehiel	Genii – 27° Taurus	*ArP*
Gekhaz	Angel	*Hyg*

Gekhiel	Angel	*Hyg*
Gelamaguar	Angel	*NA*
Gelbid/Gevoia	Demon	*MHN, NML*
Gelema	Enochian Angel – West, over third lesser Angle	*TBA*
Gelia	Angel	*Hyg*
Gelial	Angel Magistrate – Malachim	*SRH*
Geliel	Angel – Mansion twenty-two	*3BOP, tSoS, JMR, SaS, tM*
Geliel (Peliet)	Noble Spirit, Fire	*MNeI*
Gelietzor	Angel – Malachim, Tishri	*SRH*
Geloma	Servant Spirit	*Abm*
Gelomiros (Gelomyoro)	Angel – Chora three	*ArA*
Gelomyoro	Angel – Eighth Altitude (Scorpio)	*Alm*
Gelonucoa/ Gelomiros/ Gelomicros	Archangel	*NA*
Getlstamōt/ Gelstamat (Mercury)	Mercury – Alternative Name	*Hyg*
Gemary	Angel – Day Hour three	*Stg, ArP*
Gemary/Gemari/ Clemary	Angel – Night Hour five	*Stg, ArP*
Gematzod/ Gemotzol/ Gemtzod	Angel – Night Hour six	*Stg, ArP*
Gemē	Spirit	*Hyg*
Gemenem	Enochian Angel – South, serving second lesser Angle	*TBA*
Gementhi	Angel – Malachim, under Plemiya	*SRH*
Gemer/Gemen (Buer)	Demon King	*LdE*
Gemethi	Angel – Malachim, under Avorphenial Angel Magistrate – Malachim	*SRH*
Gemezin/Gemozin	Angel – Night Hour four	*Stg, ArP*
Gemi	Angel – Wednesday	*MHN*
Geminiel (Ambriel)	Angel – Gemini Spirit – Gemini	*3BOP, tSoS, JMR, SaS*

Gemitias	Demon	*MHN*
Gemmos	Demon Lord	*BOS*, *BoO*
Gemon	Demon Captain	*BOS*, *BoO*
Gemraorin	Angel – Moon/Monday	*SR*
Gemyem (Gemory?)	Demon Duke	*BOS*, *BoO*
Genahyha	Angel	*NA*
Genap	Demon	*GoPH*
Genarytz/ Genaritzos/ Genaritzod	Angel – Night Hour seven	*Stg*, *ArP*
Genēkiēl/Genikiēl/ Kikiēl/ Genikyēl	Angel – Monday Hour twenty-three	*Hyg*
Geneolia	Spirit Minister	*SBH*
Genesheriesh	Angel – Malachim, Nisan	*SRH*
Geneshorash	Angel – Malachim, Spring	*SRH*
Geniel	Angel – Mansion one	*3BOP, tSoS, JMR, SaS, tM*
Genier (Jupiter)	Jupiter – Alternative Name	*Hyg*
Geniniturla	Angel – Mercury/Wednesday	*SR*
Genira	Angel – Moon	*LL*
Genitall	Spirit – Minister of Love	*oADS*
Genithokim	Angel – Moon	*LL*
Genitu	Angel Minister – Love and Fornication	*KoSA*
Genna	Deity of Generative Power	PGM XIII:1-343, XIII:343-646
Genon	Angel – Chora two	*ArA*
Genoria	Spirit – Mercury	*VMN*
Gentuball	Demon Prince of Darkness	*oADS*
Gepheel	Genii – 14° Libra	*ArP*
Gephial	Angel – Malachim, under Avorphenial	*SRH*
Gerabcai	Archangel	*NA*
Geradiel/Garadiel	Demon Wandering Prince	*Stg*, *ThG*
Geran/Girphan	Demon – Monday Hour seven	*Hyg*
Gerbiēl/Geabiēl	Angel – Saturday Hour thirteen	*Hyg*
Gerebay	Spirit of the Thumb	*CBoM*

Gereel	Spirit	*ACM*: Cairo 45060
Geremetov	Angel – Malachim, under Plemiya	*SRH*
Geremittarum	Demon	*MHN*
Gereon/Geon	Angel – Second Altitude (Taurus)	*Alm*
Gerezeniyiyeth	Angel – Malachim, sixth Host	*SRH*
Gerguolyhon	Angel	*NA*
Geriel/Geriol	Demon Duke – South, East by North	*Stg*, *ThG*
Geriel	Genii – 11° Gemini	*ArP*
Gerienon/Gereimon	Angel – Chora two	*ArA*
Geritaton	Wicked Spirit	*NMI*
Germiciel	Demon Baron, Air	*MNeI*
Germiēlēl	Angel – Tuesday Hour ten	*Hyg*
Germyohal	Angel	*NA*
Geron (Gereon)	Angel – Chora two	*ArA*
Gerphan/Stirphan	Demon – Monday Hour nine	*Hyg*
Gerthiel	Angel – Night Hour twelve	*Stg*, *ArP*
Gesegas	Servant Spirit	*Abm*
Gesiel	Genii – 2° Aries	*ArP*
Gesteēl/Gistiēl/ Gestiēl	Angel – Tuesday Hour nine	*Hyg*
Gethiel	Genii – 12° Taurus	*ArP*
Getiel	Genii – 21° Taurus, 21° Gemini	*ArP*
Gevael	Genii – 24° Libra	*ArP*
Gewar	Demon	*GoPH*
Gewthem	Spirit Minister – Jupiter	*BoO*
Gewthren	Spirit Minister – Jupiter	*BoO*
Geyll	Demon Earl	*BOS*, *BoO*
Gezede	Angel	*NA*
Gezery	Demon	*GoPH*
Gezael	Genii – 25° Scorpio, 25° Sagittarius	*ArP*
Geziel	Genii – 15° Scorpio, 15° Sagittarius	*ArP*
Gezodex	Enochian Angel – East, over fourth lesser Angle	*TBA*
Gezorophed	Spirit – North in Autumn	*SRH*
Gglppsa	Spirit Minister, serving King Baligon	*dHM*

Ghadal	Spirit – South	*SSM*
Ghadees	Back part of Bandalos	*Pic*
Gharam	Spirit – East	*SSM*
Gharnos	Spirit of the Moon	*Pic*
Ghidyos	Bottom part of Daghdiyos	*Pic*
Ghiylos	Upper part of Didas	*Pic*
Ghyrto	Spirit Familiar	*BoTS*
Giamiēl	Angel	*Hyg*
Gianiak (Mars)	Mars – Alternative Name	*Hyg*
Giaray	Spirit – first Mansion of Moon Ring	*tSoS*
Gibryl	Angel – Sun/Sunday	*SR*
Gicael	Angel – Fifth Heaven, East	*EoN*
Giel/Gielmon/Gielmōn	Angel – Saturday Hour five	*Hyg*
Giel	Angel – Gemini	*ArP*
Giel	Genii – 21° Aries	*ArP*
Gielal	Angel – Malachim, under Plemiya	*SRH*
Gigkōrgi	Demon – Tuesday Hour twenty-four	*Hyg*
Gijel	Treasure Spirit	*BoTS*
Gilbiēl/Gelbiēl	Angel – Saturday Hour fourteen	*Hyg*
Gilgheti/Galatia	Angel – Saturn	*B7R*
Gillamon	Servant Spirit	*Abm*
Gimela	Spirit	*GoA*
Gimon	Angel – Kislev	*SR*
Giriar	Servant Spirit	*Abm*
Girmil	Servant Spirit	*Abm*
Giron	Infernal Spirit	*CBoM*
Girshum	Angel – First Encampment, first Heaven	*ShR*
Gisaor/Gilaōr	Demon – Tuesday Hour twenty-four	*Hyg*
Gitzar/Gatazar/Iatzar/Gatzar/Gatazar	Demon – Wednesday Hour ten	*Hyg*

ABBREVIATIONS

Glasya-la bolas/ Glassyabolas/ Caassimolar/ Caacrinolaas/ Glosiabolay	Demon President	*PmD*, *DoW*, *Goe*, *GV*, *GG*, *BoSC*, *DI*
Glaurah	Demon – East	*DoW*
Glauron	Spirit – North	*DoW*
Glesoum	Spirit	*Hyg*
Glgla	Angel – Seventh Encampment, first Heaven	*ShR*
Glibiōd/Glibiōth/ Glēbiōd (Sun)	Sun – Alternative Name	*Hyg*
Glikidōl	Angel – Friday Hour fifteen	*Hyg*
Glitia	Demon – under Sirach	*KoSU*
Globa	Demon Duke	*BOS*, *BoO*
Gloolas (Glasya-la-bolas?)	Demon King/Prince	*BOS*, *BoO*
Glosea/Glōsea	Angel	*Hyg*
Glory	Spirit – Glory	*BP*
Glōssas/Glotas/ Glōstas/ Gotasēl	Angel – Thursday Hour five	*Hyg*
Gloukiēl	Demon – Mercury	*Hyg*
Glumfogro	Demon	*GAG*
Glykidōk/Glykidōr/ Glykidōl/Glykoēdōēl	Angel – Friday Hour sixteen	*Hyg*
Glysy	Servant Spirit	*Abm*
Gmti	Angel – First Encampment, first Heaven Angel – Fourth Encampment, first Heaven	*ShR*
Gnabriza	Angel – Tishrei	*SR*
Gnachiel	Genii – 6° Libra	*ArP*
Gnadiel	Genii – 13° Scorpio	*ArP*
Gnaheel	Genii – 13° Sagittarius	*ArP*
Gnakiel	Genii – 7° Scorpio, 7° Sagittarius, 10° Taurus	*ArP*
Gnaliel	Genii – 4° Gemini	*ArP*
Gnamiel	Genii – 8° Capricorn, 12° Libra, 14° Capricorn	*ArP*

Gnaphiel	Genii – 5° Virgo	*ArP*
Gnashiel	Genii – 8° Aquarius, 14° Aquarius	*ArP*
Gnasiel	Genii – 4° Pisces, 11° Virgo	*ArP*
Gnathaēl/Agathnēl	Angel – Tuesday Hour seven	*Hyg*
Gnathiel	Genii – 10° Pisces	*ArP*
Gneliel	Genii – 4° Taurus	*ArP*
Gnethiel	Genii – 13° Leo	*ArP*
Gnetiel	Genii – 9° Gemini	*ArP*
Gnōntas/Gnōtas	Demon – Saturday Hour sixteen	*Hyg*
Gnōtas	Demon – Saturday Hour seventeen	*Hyg*
Gnts	Angel – Third Heaven, serving Rhtial	*ShR*
Gōb	Angel – Thursday Hour eighteen, twenty	*Hyg*
Gobēl	Angel – Thursday Hour nineteen	*Hyg*
Gobial	Angel Minister – Malachim	*SRH*
Gōdasōr/Godasost/ Gōdasēl (Sun)	Sun – Alternative Name	*Hyg*
Godiel/Godiell (Hanael)	Angel – Capricorn	*BoO, JMR*
Godiel	Demon Duke – North-West Night, West Day	*Stg, ThG, BoTS*
Godolyn	Demon	*oADS*
Godric/Ghodiat	Spirit – fifth Mansion of the Moon Ring	*AE*
Goera	Spirit Familiar	*BoTS*
Goeme	Spirit – Air	*MNeI*
Goffela	Treasure Spirit	*oADS*
Gog Magog	Spirit	*SoS, SMS*
Gokysael (Saturn)	Saturn – Alternative Name	*Hyg*
Golan	Angel – Malachim, under Avorphenial	*SRH*
Golgiel/Gorpel/ Gorgiel/ Gogliēl	Angel – Friday Hour twenty-two	*Hyg*
Golgiēl/Gorgoēl/ Golgoēl	Angel – Saturday Hour fifteen	*Hyg*
Golid	Angel – Elul	*SR*
Golog	Servant Spirit	*Abm*
Golyon	Demon	*oADS*

ABBREVIATIONS

Gomedēn/ Gōmedēm/ Gōmedim (Luna)	Luna – Alternative Name	*Hyg*
Gomeris/Caym (Gomory)	Demon Duke	*NML*
Gomogin	Servant Spirit	*Abm*
Gomory/Gemory/ Gremory	Demon Duke	*PmD, DoW, Goe, DI*
Gonsollados	Spirit Familiar	*BoTS*
Goorox	Demon Earl	*BOS, BoO*
Goral	Spirit	*BoTS*
Goralidio/Boralidio/ Gzigotalibet	Spirit – fourteenth Mansion of the Moon Ring	*AE*
Gordonsor/ Gordonsar/ Gordonizor/ Gordemser	Demon – West Spirit – Presidential Counsellor, West	*BOS, BoO, oADS, BoTS*
Gorenetal	Angel – Malachim, sixth Host	*SRH*
Gorgeel	Angel – Friday Hour twenty-three	*Hyg*
Gorgiēl/Gorphil/ Gorfil/ Garphiēl	Angel – Tuesday Hour thirteen	*Hyg*
Gorgopios	Demon – Saturday Hour ten	*Hyg*
Gorgorydas	Devil – Cancer, Storms	*OADS*
Gorhon	Good Spirit	*SoM*
Gorilon	Servant Spirit	*Abm*
Gorial/Gezerial	Angel – Malachim over Fire and Flames	*SRH*
Gorino	Spirit Familiar	*BoTS*
Gormi/Geormi/ Georim	Spirit – sixth Mansion of the Moon Ring	*AE, tSoS*
Gorsay	Demon Duke	*LdE*
Gorshom	Angel – Malachim, under Avorphenial	*SRH*
Gorsor/Gorson (Gusoin)	Demon Duke	*SSM, MNL*
Gorsyar	Demon King	*BOS, BoO*
Goth	Angel – Thursday Hour twenty	*Hyg*

Goukoumon/ Goukoumōr/ Gokōm/Gonagoum/ Ioukoumōn	Demon –Wednesday Hour two	*Hyg*
Gouriēl/Gouliōn/ Goulion/Gouliōth	Demon – Friday Hour one	*Hyg*
Gouzaēl	Angel – Summer	*DoW*
Gouzgoupos	Demon – Saturday Hour nine	*Hyg*
Goyle	Demon – North	*BOS, BoO*
Gozeēs/Zōgeis	Spirit – East	*Hyg*
Graaih	Angel Encampment Head – sixth Heaven, West	*ShR*
Gramon	Demon Senior	*SSM*
Gramsatos	Angel – Spring	*MHN*
Granon	Servant Spirit	*Abm*
Granozyn/Granozy	Angel – Night Hour two	*Stg, ArP*
Granyel	Angel – Day Hour two	*Stg, ArP*
Graphiel	Planetary Intelligence – Mars	*KoSR, 3BOP, BM, PO, tM*
Grasmen	Demon – South	*CBoM*
Gratuell	Spirit	*GAG*
Grchta	Angel – Second Encampment, first Heaven	*ShR*
Gremiel/Germiel/ Germel	Demon Duke – Day Hour nine and Night Hour nine	*Stg, ThG*
Gromeyl	Angel – Mars/Tuesday	*SR*
Gromogel	Plant Spirit – Peony	*GS*
Grynaca	Night Devil	*oADS*
Gryol	Spirit Familiar	*BoTS*
Gsqial	Angel Encampment Head – sixth Heaven, West	*ShR*
Gtataphid/Itadiph	Demon – Wednesday Hour five	*Hyg*
Guabarel/Gualbarel	Angel – Autumn	*EoN, Hmn, KoSR, tSoS, MC, GoeR, tM*
Guabriel	Angel	*NA*
Guadoliel	Spirit – Venus	*SoS*
Guadriel	Angel – Shebat	*SR*

ABBREVIATIONS

Guadudyel	Angel Superior – fourth Season by Night	*SSM*
Guael/Guel	Angel – Fifth Heaven Tuesday, East	*Hmn, KoSR, BoO, GAG, BoTS, tM, CBMS*
Guamasyemahe	Angel	*NA*
Guanrinasuch	Angel – Tebet	*SR*
Gubridali/Gribery	Spirit – sixth Mansion of the Moon Ring	*AE, tSoS*
Gubril/Gebril	Angel	*SoM*
Gudiel	Duke – West by North Afternoon	*Stg, ThG, BoTS*
Guel	Spirit	*CBoM*
Guerges	Spirit	*SSM*
Guericos	Angel – First three signs	*SSM*
Guesupale	Angel – Nisan	*tSoS*
Gufsvegia	Demon	*CoC*
Gulan	Angel – First Encampment, first Heaven	*ShR*
Gulas	Angel – Joy and Divination	*CoMS*
Gulial	Angel – Fourth Encampment, first Heaven	*ShR*
Gunfiel	Angel – Jupiter/Thursday	*SR*
Gunuel	Angel	*ACM*: Oriental 5986
Guracap	Angel – Bisertilis	*SR*
Gurial	Angel Encampment Head – sixth Heaven, East	*ShR*
Guriel	Angel – Shebat Angel – Adar	*SR*
Guroheit	Spirit – first Mansion of Moon Ring	*AE*
Gushpnial	Angel – Third Heaven, serving Rhtial	*ShR*
Gusoin/Gusoyn/Gazon/Gusovo	Demon Duke	*LdE, PmD, DoW, Goe, GG, BoSC*
Gusta	Norse Deity (?)	*Gbk*
Guth	Daemon Attendant – Jupiter Spirit King – Jupiter Angel Minister – between East and South Spirit Helper – Thursday	*SBH, EoN, CBoM*
Guthaca	Angel – Venus	*GAG*

Guthryn/Gutrhyn	Daemon Attendant – Jupiter Angel Minister – between East and South Spirit Helper – Thursday	SBH, CBoM
Gutrimis	Spirit Attendant – Jupiter	EoN
Gutrix/Gutriel/Gutriz	Angel Minister of Air – Thursday Spirit – Jupiter Presiding Spirit – Jupiter	Hmn, KoSR, SoS, GAG, BoTS, tM, CBMS
Guziel	Evil Angel	SoM
Gyal	Night Devil	oADS
Gyell/Gyel	Demon Count/Earl Night Devil	oADS, BOS, BoO
Gyneri (Jupiter)	Jupiter – Alternative Name	Hyg
Gyran/Stirphan	Demon – Monday Hour nine	Hyg
Gyton	Demon	MHN
Gzrial	Angel – Fifth Encampment, first Heaven	ShR

H

Ha	Intelligence – Jupiter	BoG
Haabach	Angel – Saturn	GAG
Haagenti	Demon President	PmD, DoW, Goe
Haajah/Haaiah	Angel – Shem twenty-six	KoSU, 3BOP, GoeR, JMR, SAS, tM
Haajah	Genii – 18° Capricorn, 18° Aquarius	ArP
Haasa	Angel – Venus	GAG
Haayn	Angel – Mars/Tuesday	SR
Habaa/Abaa/Abba	Daemon King – Mercury; between the West and North	SBH, oADS
Habaiel/Habayel/Habiel/Habaniel	Angel first Heaven Monday – West Ministering Spirit – Moon	EoN, Hmn, KoSR, BoO, GAG, BoTS, tM, CBMS
Habalon/Hubalom	Angel – Night Hour five	Stg, ArP
Habaron	Angel	KoSA
Habes	Angel – Mars	BARC
Habetell	Wind Spirit	GAG
Habiel	Genii – 23° Aries	ArP
Habioro	Enochian Senior – East	TBA
Habracha	Angel	NA

Habraculith	Spirit – fifth Mansion of Moon Ring	*AE*
Habu	Angel – Dominations	*67M*
Habudiel	Archangel	*MNeI*
Habujah/Habuiah/Chabuiah	Angel – Shem sixty-eight	*KoSU, 3BOP, GoeR, JMR, SAS, tM*
Hac	Angel – Sivan	*SR*
Hacel	Demon – Languages and Writing	*KoSU*
Hachael	Genii – 23° Taurus, 23° Gemini	*ArP*
Hachamel	Servant Spirit	*Abm*
Hachar	Angel	*NA*
Haciel	Angel – Fourth Heaven, North	*SaS*
Hacoylyn	Angel – Moon/Monday	*SR*
Hacsemim	Angel – Moon	*LL*
Hadarmiel	Angel	*SMS*
Hadees	Top part of Gharnos	*Pic*
Hades	Greek God – Underworld	PGM XII:201-269; *Hyg*
Hadie	Angel – Third Heaven, West	*EoN*
Hadie	Ministering Spirit – Venus	*CBMS*
Hadiel	Genii – 14° Pisces	*ArP*
Hadith	Supportive Planetary Spirit – Saturn	*SSM*
Hadlam	Angel – Potestates	*67M*
Hadrigar/Sadrigar/Obegar/Adriagar	Spirit – sixth Mansion of the Moon Ring	*AE*
Hadyel	Angel – Third Heaven, West	*SSM*
Hadzbeyeyl	Angel – Sun/Sunday	*SR*
Hael	Intelligence	*EPL*
Hael	Angel – Potestates	*67M*
Hael	Genii – 3° Aries	*ArP*
Hael	Demon	*SoS, GV*
Hafea	Angel – Venus	*GAG*
Hageyr	Servant Spirit	*Abm*
Haghedes	Top part of Daghdiyos	*Pic*
Hagiel	Planetary Intelligence – Venus	*KoSR, 3BOP, BM, PO, tM*

Hagith/Hagit/Agith/ Hageth	Olympic Spirit – Venus	*KoSR, Arb, MC, GAG, JMR, MNeI, oADS, KoN, PO, ClI, SGT, SSG*
Hagman	Alternative name of Metatron	*SQ*
Hagoch	Servant Spirit	*Abm*
Hagonel	Angel Prince – Monday Spirit – Son of Sons of Light	*dHM*
Hagras/Hayras/ Havras	Spirit	*GoPH, GV*
Hagrion	Servant Spirit	*Abm*
Hagyhoty	Angel	*NA*
Hagyr	Good Spirit	*SoM*
Hahahel/Hahael	Angel – Shem forty-one	*KoSU, 3BOP, GoeR, JMR, SAS, tM*
Hahahjah/Hahaiah/ Ahaiah	Angel – Shem twelve	*KoSU, 3BOP, GoeR, JMR, SAS, tM*
Haham	Spirit of the Thumb	*MHN*
Hahasiah/Hakasiah/ Hachasiah/Hahaziah	Angel – Shem fifty-one	*KoSU, 3BOP, GoeR, JMR, SAS, tM*
Hahon	Angel – Tebet	*SR*
Hahowel	Archangel	*67M*
Hahyax	Servant Spirit	*Abm*
Haiaras	Angel – Mars	*BARC*
Haibalidech	Daemon Attendant – Saturn, North	*SBH*
Haila	Angel – Jupiter	*GAG*
Haiviah/Hahuiah/ Haaiah/Hahviah/ Chahuiah	Angel – Shem twenty-four	*KoSU, 3BOP, GoeR, JMR, SAS, tM*
Hajajel/Hajaiol/ Haiaiel/ Hajaiel	Angel – Shem seventy-one	*KoSU, 3BOP, GoeR, JMR, SAS, tM*
Hakamiah	Angel – Shem sixteen	*KoSU, 3BOP, GoeR, JMR, SAS, tM*
Halamas/Hallamas	Angel	*NA*
Halamothona	Angel	*NA*
Halay	Angel – Sixth Altitude (Virgo)	*Alm*
Halba	Spirit of the Thumb	*MHN*

ABBREVIATIONS

Halilin	Angel – Venus/Friday	*SR*
Hallamon	Angel	*NA*
Halmasython	Angel	*NA*
Halmon	Spirit	*GV*
Halphas/Malthas	Demon Earl	*PmD, DoW, Goe*
Halt	Angel – Jupiter	*GAG*
Haludiel/Habudiel	Angel – Fourth Heaven Sunday, South, Spring Angel – Fourth Heaven, South Ministering Spirit – Sun	*Hmn, KoSR, BoO, GAG, BoTS, SaS, tM, CBMS*
Haludiel	Intelligence – Sun	*SGT, SSG*
Hamaliel/Hameliel/Hamabiel	Angel – Virgo Genius – Conjunctio	*3BOP, tSoS, MC, JMR, SaS, MNeI, Thm, PO, tM*
Hamarytzod	Angel – Night Hour eleven	*Stg, ArP*
Hamas	Demon Duke – South-West Night	*Stg, ThG, BoTS*
Hamas	Mirror Spirit – Tuesday	*MNeI*
Hamasy	Angel	*NA*
Hamath	Mirror Spirit – Sunday	*MNeI*
Hamaya	Angel – Dominations	*67M*
Hamayz/Hamoyzod/Hamayzod	Angel – Night Hour four	*Stg, ArP*
Hameriel	Angel – Night Hour five	*Stg, ArP*
Hamiah/Haamiah/Chaamiah	Angel – Shem thirty-eight	*KoSU, 3BOP, GoeR, JMR, SAS, tM*
Hamistradany	Spirit – fifth Mansion of Moon Ring	*tSoS*
Hamoniel	Angel – Mercury/Virgo	*KoSR*
Hamos	Angel	*NA*
Hamorphiel	Demon Duke – East	*Stg, ThG*
Hamst	God of the Gods of Darkness	PDM XIV:851-855
Hamun	Angel – First Heaven, South	*SSM*
Hamyhel	Angel	*NA*
Hamynos	Angel	*NA*
Hamynosya	Angel	*NA*

Hanael/Haniel/ Hanahel/ Hanaël/Hannael/ Hanail	Archangel – Venus Archangel – Netzach Angel – First Heaven, South Spirit – Venus Angel – Capricorn Ruler of Order of Principalities Genius – Carcer	*SSM, SBH, EoN, 3BOP, tSoS, MC, JMR, 9CK, SaS, MNeI, Thm, GoA, CU, CoMS, PO, tM*
Hanar	Demon Prince	*BOS, BoO*
Hanatar	Angel	*NA*
Hanatayhar	Angel	*NA*
Hancomagos	Angel	*NA*
Handaroos	Spirit – Love/Sexual Attraction	*Pic*
Handavmusdah/ Handa/ Handarmus	Spirit – Mercury	*BoO, GAG*
Handighyos	Front part of Daghdiyos	*Pic*
Haniel	Angel	*SoM*
Hanin	Angel – First Heaven, South	*SR*
Hanni (Amy?)	Demon President	*MHN*
Hanon	Angel – Moon	*KoSR*
Hannu	Angel – First Heaven, South	*SaS*
Hanun/Hanuin/ Hanum/ Harnim	Angel first Heaven Monday – South Ministering Spirit – Jupiter	*Hmn, KoSR, BoO, GAG, BoTS, tM, CBMS*
Hanunyel	Angel – Fourth Heaven, North	*SSM*
Hany	Spirit Helper – Wednesday	*CBoM*
Hanyel	Angel – Elul Angel – Fifth Heaven, North	*SR*
Hanyey	Angel Minister of Air – Wednesday	*BoO*
Hapochohon	Angel	*NA*
Hapy/Hapi	Egyptian God of the Nile Flood	*PDM XIV:309-334*
Haqoilim	Angel – Moon	*LL*
Hara	Spirit – fourth Mansion of Moon Ring	*tSoS*
Harabar	Angel	*NA*
Haragil	Servant Spirit	*Abm*
Haram	Positive Spirit	*MHN*
Haraman	Angel	*NA*

Haraoth	Servant Spirit	*Abm*
Harap	Enochian Angel – North, over second lesser Angle	*TBA*
Harataphell	Angel	*oADS*
Harays	Angel	*NA*
Harbathanōps Iaoai	Good Daimon	PGM IV:930-1114
Harbyl	Angel – November/Scorpio	*BoW*
Harchase	Demon King	*BOS, BoO*
Hardiel	Angel – Night Hour twelve	*Stg, ArP*
Hareryn	Angel – Venus/Friday	*SR*
Hariaz	Angel – Night Hour eleven	*Stg, ArP*
Hariston/Haristum	Demon	*SoSW, GV*
Harith/Haryth	Punishing Wind Daemon – Jupiter, serving North and East Winds, between East and South	*SSM, SBH*
Harkam (Arcan)	Angel – King of Air on Monday	*BoO, BoTS*
Harkentechta/Harchentechtha	Form of Horus	PGM IV:1928-2005, 2241-2358
Harmanel	Angel – Mars	*BARC*
Harmary/Hamary	Angel – Day Hour twelve	*Stg, ArP*
Harmiel	Angel – Day Hour seven	*Stg, ArP*
Harmon	Mirror Spirit – Monday	*MNeI*
Harmosiel	Angel	*ACM*: Cairo EM 49547
Harmozel	Angel Trumpeter	*ACM: Yale 1791*
Harmuroch	Spirit – sixth Mansion of the Moon Ring	*AE*
Harnariel	Angel – Mars	*BARC*
Harog	Servant Spirit	*Abm*
Haroos (Utarid, Roman)	Spirit King – Mercury	*Pic*
Harpax	Demon – Decan twenty-eight	*ToS*
Harpinon	Servant Spirit	*Abm*
Harpokrates	Greco-Egyptian God of Silence	PGM III:633-731, IV:930-1114, PDM XIV:750-771, LXI:159-196
Harsanaraht	Angel	*NA*

Hartan/Harthan	Demon King under Belzebub Daemon King – Moon, West Spirit King – Monday	*SSM, SBH, CBoM, oADS*
Har-Thoth	Egyptian Composite God	PDM LXI:63-78
Hartiyoon/Anehutyora	Spirit	*Pic*
Hartninay	Angel – Moon	*LL*
Harto	Spirit	*CoC*
Haruz (Iranian) (Utarid)	Angel – Mercury	*SSG*
Harvalam	Stone Spirit – Turquoise	*GS*
Haryd	Supportive Planetary Spirit – Jupiter	*SSM*
Haryolomo	Angel	*NA*
Hasa	Angel	*NA*
Hasasisgafon	Angel – Tebet	*SR*
Haseha	Angel – Thrones	*67M*
Hasiel/Horiel/Haziel	Angel – Shem nine	*KoSU, 3BOP, GoeR, JMR, SAS, tM*
Hasiqtas	Alternative name of Metatron	*SQ*
Haskub	Servant Spirit	*Abm*
Hasmael	Angel	*BoTS*
Hasmodel	Genius – Amissio Angel – Taurus	*Thm*
Hasneyeyl	Angel – Venus/Friday	*SR*
Hasperim	Servant Spirit	*Abm*
Hasqevatz	Alternative name of Metatron	*SQ*
Hasqos	Alternative name of Metatron	*SQ*
Hassica	Spirit – Air	*MNeI*
Hassyhethas	Angel	*NA*
Hastapulo/Astanulo/Rupasta	Spirit – sixth Mansion of Moon Ring	*AE*
Hastas	Alternative name of Metatron	*SQ*
Hatanazar	Angel	*NA*
Hatha	Angel – Malachim, under Ayigeda	*SRH*
Hathanaym	Angel	*NA*

Hathor	Egyptian Cow-Headed Fertility and Love Goddess	PDM XIV:1026-1045; *ACM*: Schmidt P.
Hatiarie	Spirit – fourth Mansion of Moon Ring	*AE*
Hatiel	Genii – 27° Scorpio, 27° Sagittarius	*ArP*
Hatosul	Servant Spirit	*Abm*
Hatrahurbyablis	Punishing Wind	*SSM*
Hautricath/ Hariothet/ Hantireath	Spirit – third Mansion of the Moon Ring	*AE*
Havechylem	Angel	*NA*
Haxiel	Archangel	*MNeI*
Hay	Spirit Helper – Saturday	*CBoM*
Hayāl	Angel – Hour four/Cancer	*BoW*
Hayamen	Servant Spirit	*Abm*
Haybalydoth	Spirit Assistant – Saturday	*MHN*
Hayel	Angel – Fifth Heaven, North	*SR, SSM*
Hayeylin	Angel – Venus/Friday	*SR*
Haylon	Angel – Night Hour three	*Stg, ArP*
Haynynael	Angel – Fourth Heaven, North	*SR*
Hayoynois	Angel – Mars	*BARC*
Hayozer	Angel – Dominations	*67M*
Hayton	Spirit Ruler – Saturday	*MHN*
Hayzoym/Hayzoim	Angel – Night Hour one	*Stg, ArP*
Hazabel/Harahel/ Harchel/Harachel/ Herael	Angel – Shem fifty-nine	*KoSU, 3BOP, GoeR, JMR, SAS, tM*
Hazamyhathos	Angel	*NA*
Hazaniel	Angel – Night Hour ten	*Stg, ArP*
Hazaryobal	Angel	*NA*
Hazathor	Angel	*NA*
Haziel/Hariel	Angel – Shem fifteen	*KoSU, 3BOP, GoeR, JMR, SAS, tM*
Hazihadas	Angel	*NA*
Hazyhaccor	Angel	*NA*
Hdrial	Angel – First Step, second Heaven	*ShR*

Hdrnial	Angel Encampment Head – sixth Heaven, East	ShR
Hdrzywlw	Angel Prince – Lower Four	SoM
He	Spirit – Minister of Love	oADS
Headless One	Spirit (possibly Bes)	PGM V:96-172, VII:222-249, VIII:64-110, CII:1-17
Heasil/Teasil/ Veasid/ Eazsail	Spirit – Ring second Mansion of the Moon	AE, tSoS
Hebe	Greek Goddess of Youth	PGM VII:993-1009
Hebe	God – Youth	BoO
Hebenel	Angel – Sun	BARC
Hebero	Angel	NA
Hebethel	Punishing Wind Daemon – Moon, serving West Wind; West	SSM, SBH
Hecate/Hekate	Goddess – Charmery and Invocance (Magic)	3BOP, BoO, DoW, PO
Hechondos	Angel	NA
Heckiel	Genii – 26° Libra	ArP
Hederenial	Angel – Malachim, Tishri	SRH
Hederial	Angel – Malachim, Friday	SRH
Hediel	Genii – 24° Pisces	ArP
Heeoa	Son of Light, subject to Prince Hagonel	dHM
Hegergibet	Demon	MHN
Hegnel	Genii – 13° Gemini	ArP
Hegrozamyhel	Angel	NA
Hegur	Spirit – seventh Mansion of the Moon ring	tSoS
Hehaha	Angel – Sun	BARC
Hehedan	Angel Prince – Tishri	SRH
Hehudael	Angel – Kislev	SR
Heizamamim	Angel – Moon	LL
Heka/Hike	Egyptian God of Magic	PDM XIV:150-231
Hekate	Demon – Pleiades seven	ToS

Hekate/Hecate/ Hekate-Artemis	Greek Goddess of Magic and the Underworld	PGM III:1-164, IV:1390-1495, IV:2006-2125, IV:2241-2358, IV:2441-2621, IV:2622-2707, IV:2708-2784, IV:2785-2890, IV:2943-2966, XXXVI:187-210, LXX:4-25, XCIII:1-6, CXIV:1-14, CXVII fr.14; *SM*: T. Köln Inv. 1, Audollent DT.38, P. Monac. II.28
Hekebial	Angel – Malachim, Wednesday	*SRH*
Hekel	Angel – Malachim, under Ayigeda	*SRH*
Hekiel	Genii – 16° Libra	*ArP*
Heknet	Egyptian Vulture-Headed Goddess	PDM XIV:295-308, XIV:805-840
Hel	Angel	*NA, SBH*
Hela	Angel – Sun	*GAG*
Helees	Front part of Barhoyas	*Pic*
Helel	Servant Spirit	*Abm*
Heleniert	Demon – South	*GoPH*
Helenothos	Angel	*NA*
Helesial	Angel – Malachim, under Phelmiya Angel Magistrate – Malachim	*SRH*
Helial	Angel – Malachim, under Ayigeda	*SRH*
Helioros	Helios-Horus Composite God	PGM I.42-195
Helios	Greek Sun God	PGM I.42-195, I.195-222, I:222-231, II.1-64, II-64-184, III:1-164, III:187-262, III:263-275, III:410-423, III:424-466, III:467-478, III:479-483, III:494-611, III:633-731, IV:88-93, IV:154-285,

Helios (con't.)		PGM IV:296-466, IV:835-849, IV:1275-1322, IV:1596-1715, IV:1928-2005, IV:2241-2358, IV:2785-2890, IV:2967-3006, IV:3086-3124, V:1-53, V:172-212, V:213-303, V:370-446, Va:1-3, VI:1-47, VII:505-528, VII:528-539, VII:727-739, VII:981-993, VII:1017-1026, VIII:64-110, XII:160-178, XII:201-269, XII:270-350, XII:401-44, XIII:1-343, XIII:646-734, XXIIa:18-27, XXIII:1-70, XXIVa:1-25, XXXIIa:1-25, XXXVI:211-230, LXII:1-24, LXVIII:1-20, LXXXI:1-10, CXXII:1-55, PDM XXXVI:211-230, LXI:159-196, LXI:197-216; *SM*: P. Berol. Inv. 21243, P. Berol. Inv. 21227; *ShR*
Helios (Roman) (Sams)	Angel – Sun	*SSG*
Helios-Mithras	Greek Solar Composite God	PGM IV:475-829
Heliothos	Angel	*SBH*
Hell	Treasure Spirit	*oADS*
Hellemyr	Spirit Lord	*KoN*
Hellison/Helison (Helyson)	Angel – Chora one	*ArA*

Helmas/Hehuas	Angel – Day Hour eleven	*Stg, ArP*
Helmis	Servant Spirit	*Abm*
Heloy[418]	Angel – Third Altitude (Gemini)	*Alm*
Helphleges	Angel	*NA*
Helsa	Angel	*NA*
Helyberp	Demon	*MHN*
Helyffan	Angel – First Altitiude (Aries)	*Alm*
Helymaht	Angel	*NA*
Helymoht	Angel	*NA*
Helymyhot	Angel	*NA*
Helynon	Angel	*NA, SBH*
Helyson	Angel – First Altitiude (Aries)	*Alm*
Helythos	Angel	*NA*
Hememal	Angel Prince – Gate of Spirit of East	*SRH*
Hemeolon	Spirit Prince	*BoO, GAG*
Hemiek	Angel – Malachim, under Ayigeda	*SRH*
Hemohon	Archangel	*67M*
Hemon	Angel Prince – South Gate	*SRH*
Hemor	Demon	*MRC*
Hemostophile	Demon	*GoA*
Hena	Angel	*NA*
Heneral	Demon	*GoPH*
Hēperdemyde (Luna)	Luna – Alternative Name	*Hyg*
Hēperēēper	Demon – South	*Hyg*
Hephaistos	Greek Smith and Fire God	PGM VII:376-384, XII:160-178, XII:401-44
Hephesimireth	Demon – Decan thirty-one	*ToS*
Hephiel	Genii – 17° Scorpio, 17° Sagittarius	*ArP*
Hera	Greek Goddess of Marriage	PGM IV:2967-3006, LII:1-9
Herakles	Greek Demi-God Hero	PGM XII:401-44; *SM*: T. Cairo Mus. JdE 36059

---

418 This name appears more commonly as a divine name.

Heramael/ Hèramael/ Eramael	Demon	*SoS, GV*
Herapha	Angel Prince – Winter	*SRH*
Herb	Angel – Moon	*GAG*
Herebreth/Hesebret/ Husebreth	Spirit – twentieth Mansion of the Moon Ring	*AE, tSoS*
Herekom	Angel – Malachim, under Ayigeda	*SRH*
Heremegos	Angel	*NA*
Heremod	Angel – Malachim, under Pheseker	*SRH*
Heremor	Angel – Malachim, sixth Host	*SRH*
Heresiel	Demon Duke – Hour fourteen of fifteen	*Stg, ThG*
Heresim	Spirit of the Thumb	*MHN*
Heriey	Egyptian Goddess of Destruction	PDM XIV:1-92
Heriyavor	Angel – Malachim, under Avorphenial	*SRH*
Herlam	Spirit	*oADS*
Hermadafinuni/ Hermadafin	Spirit – Saturn	*BoO, GAG*
Hermanel	Angel – Mars	*BARC*
Hermanubis	Composite Deity of Hermes and Anubis	PGM IV:3125-3171
Hermekate	Composite Deity of Hekate and Hermes	PGM III:1-64, IV:2441-2621
Hermely	Spirit	*oADS*
Hermes (Greek) (Utarid)	Angel – Mercury	*SSG*
Hermes (Hermes-Thoth/ Hermes-Thouoth)	Greek Magic and Messenger God	PGM III:1-164, IV:296-466, IV:835-849, IV:850-929, IV:1390-1495, IV:2241-2358, IV:2359-2372, IV:2373-2440, IV:2441-2621, IV:2967-3006, V:172-212, V:213-303, V:370-446, VII:540-578, VII:664-685, VIII:1-63, XII:144-152, XII:401-44,

ABBREVIATIONS

Hermes (Hermes-Thoth/ Hermes-Thouoth) (con't.)		PGM: XIII:1-343, XIII:646-734, XVIIb:1-23, XXIII:1-70, XXIVa:1-25, XXXII:1-19, LI:1-27, LXII:47-51, LXVII:1-24, CIX:1-8, CXXII:1-55; *SM*: PSI I.28, T. Cairo Mus. JdE 48217, T. Louvre Inv. E 27145, P. Mich. Inv. 6925, T. Köln Inv. 1, Audollent DT.38, T. Cairo Mus. JdE 36059; *ACM*: P. Oxy. Inv. 50.4B 23/J, P. Berol. Inv. 21243, P. Berol. Inv. 21243; HB: Acts 13:12; *SSG*
Hermiel	Angel – Day Hour four	*Stg, ArP*
Hermon	Demon Duke	*Stg, ThG*
Hermyadell/ Hermiadell	Spirit – Sun	*BoO, GAG*
Herne	Demon Duke – North-West Day	*Stg, ThG, BoTS*
Herochon	Angel – Malachim, under Ayigeda	*SRH*
Heron	Greco-Roman-Egyptian God	PGM V:213-303
Heros	Angel – Sixth Altitude (Virgo)	*Alm*
Herphatz/Herphatzal	Angel – Night Hour five	*Stg, ArP*
Heseculaty	Angel	*NA*
Heseleagy	Angel	*NA*
Hesethier	Angel – Malachim, under Phelmiya Angel Magistrate – Malachim	*SRH*
Heshael	Genii – 28° Capricorn, 28° Aquarius	*ArP*
Heshekem	Angel Prince	*SRH*
Hesonas	Angel	*NA*
Hestia	Greek Goddess of the Hearth	PGM VII:376-384, XII:401-44
Hetael	Spirit	*GoA*
Hetermorda	Enochian Senior – East	*TBA*

Hethatia	Spirit	*GoA*
Hetiel	Genii – 30° Aries	*ArP*
Hetzeniepha	Angel – Malachim, under Ayigeda	*SRH*
Hetzeniephelehov	Angel – Malachim, under Ayigeda	*SRH*
Heusenebior/ Herusenebior	Spirit – tenth Mansion of the Moon Ring	*AE*
Hevael	Genii – 15° Virgo	*ArP*
Heyeyl	Angel – Moon	*BARC*
Hezael	Genii – 18° Aries	*ArP*
Hezegrathos	Angel	*NA*
Heziel	Genii – 29° Gemini	*ArP*
Hepath/Hicpacth/ Hiepacth/Hiepact/ Hepoth	Demon Duke	*SoS, GV*
Hgdiab	Angel – Seventh Step, second Heaven	*ShR*
Hhgrit	Angel – East Wind	*ShR*
Hiatregilos	Angel	*NA*
Hiayel/Hiaeyel	Angel – First Heaven, North	*SR, SaS*
Hidriel/Hydriel	Demon Wandering Prince	*Stg, Thg*
Higron/Hiegeron	Alternative title of Metatron Angel Prince	*SQ, SRH*
Hiel	Spirit – Mars	*KoSR*
Himeilin	Angel – Venus/Friday	*SR*
Hinbra/Umbra	Demon – North	*BOS, BoO*
Hinds	Spirit – Minister of Love	*oADS*
Hiniel	Angel – Fifth Heaven, Tuesday, North	*KoSR*
Hipogon	Servant Spirit	*Abm*
Hipolepos	Servant Spirit	*Abm*
Hipotga	Enochian Senior – East	*TBA*
Hiqron	Alternative name of Metatron	*SQ*
Hiradi	Spirit – fourth Mansion of Moon Ring	*AE*
Hiraminim	Angel – Moon	*LL*
Hirih/Herich/Hirich	Servant Spirit	*Abm*
Hismael/Hysmaell	Planetary Spirit – Jupiter Ruler – Acquisito, Letitia Co-Ruler – Caput Draconis	*KoSR, 3BOP, BM, Thm, tM*

ABBREVIATIONS

Hissam/Hisiam	Demon Duke – North-West Day	*Stg, ThG, BoTS*
Hiyadees	Spirit – Love/Sexual Attraction	*Pic*
Hiyakos	Spirit – Love/Sexual Attraction	*Pic*
Hiylos	Bottom part of Didas	*Pic*
Hiytes	Bottom part of Barhoyas	*Pic*
Hmk	Angel – Second Encampment, first Heaven	*ShR*
Hmnkial	Angel Encampment Head – sixth Heaven, East	*ShR*
Hnial	Angel Encampment Head – sixth Heaven, East	*ShR*
Hoasaresin	Angel	*LL*
Hobrazym/Hobrazim	Angel – Night Hour eight	*Stg, ArP*
Hocraell	Angel	*oADS*
Hodelfa/Hodelsa	Fairy Lady	*BoO, GAG*
Hoderial	Angel Prince – Gate of Spirit of South	*SRH*
Hoenir	Norse Warrior God	*Gbk*
Hohada	Spirit of the Thumb	*MHN*
Hohanna	Spirit of the Thumb	*MHN*
Holmadiel	Spirit – Mercury	*VMN*
Holop	Servant Spirit	*Abm*
Holy	Angel – Second Heaven, South	*SaS*
Holyl	Angel – Potestates	*67M*
Holy Spirit	Spirit of Divine Force and Action	*HB* Gen 1:1-2, Ps 139:7-8, 143:10, Ez 36:27, Zech 4:6, Is 61:1, Matt 1:18, 1:20, 12:31-32, 28:19-20, Mark 13:11, Luke 1:35, 3:21-22, 11:13, John 1:33, 14:26, 15:26, Acts 1:8, 2:3-4, 2:33, 2:38, 4:31, 5:32, 9:31, 10:47, 11:15, 13:2, 13:4, 13:9, 13:52, 19:2, 19:6, 21:4, 21:11,

Holy Spirit (con't.)		HB Rom 8:14-27, 9:1, 1 Cor 2:10-14, 3:16, 7:40, 12:3-11, 2 Cor 3:17-18, 1 Th 1:6, 1 Tim 4:1, Ts 3:5, Heb 3:7, 9:8, 10:15, Pet 1:2, 1:12, 1 John 5:6-8, Jude 1:19-20, Rev 2:7, 2:17, 2:29, 3:6, 3:13, 3:22, 14:13, 22:17
Homitoton/Homitot/ Omitot	Demon – Tuesday Hour twelve	*Hyg*
Homycabel	Angel – Sun, over Earth	*SR*
Honosigideus	Spirit	*SSM*
Honsi/Hone	Spirit	*GoPH, GV*
Hooab	Demon Prince	*BOS, BoO*
Hoomel	Plant Spirit – Ash	*GS*
Hoovahmah	Plant Spirit – Elder	*GS*
Hophetēs/Ophitan/ Ophitas/Ophytan	Demon – Wednesday Hour fourteen	*Hyg*
Hopnax/Opnax/ Opnaz/ Apnax	Demon – Wednesday Hour twenty-four	*Hyg*
Hoquiel	Angel – Saturn, over Water	*SR*
Horamar	Servant Spirit	*Abm*
Horiel	Spirit	*GV*
Hormosiel	Angel	*ACM*: Hay 10122
Hormus (Utarid, Greek)	Spirit King – Mercury	*Pic*
Hormuz/Ormazf (Iranian) (Rufijail)	Angel – Jupiter	*SSG*
Hornan	Demon – Tuesday Hour seventeen	*Hyg*
Horpanyr	Angel Master – Planets in first three signs	*SSM*
Horpenyel	Angel – Moon	*SSM*
Horrion	Angel – Saturn/Saturday	*SR*
Hor-Amoun	Egyptian Compound God	PDM XIV:1-92

Horus/Horos/Hor	Egyptian Falcon God	PGM I:42-195, III:633-731, IV:296-466, IV:930-1114, IV:1928-2005, IV:3125-3171, VII:490-504, XIII:343-646, XXXVI:295-311, XXXVI:333-360, PDM XII:6-20, XIV:428-450, XIV:1-92, XIV:239-295, XIV:528-553, XIV:563-574, XIV:585-593, XIV:636-669, XIV:1026-1045, XIV:1097-1103, XIV:1219-1227, LXI:79-94, LXI:106-111, Suppl. 60-101, Suppl. 130-138, Suppl. 168-184, Suppl. 185-208; *SM*: Inscr. Mus. Louvre 204, SM: PSI I.28, P. Berol. Inv. 21243; *ACM:* Oxy. 1060, Oslo 1.5, P. Mich. 136, Berlin 5565, Berlin 8313; Schmidt 1, Schmidt 2
Horus-Apollo	Greco-Egyptian Sun God	*SM*: P. Köln Inv. 851
Horyel	Angel Sun – Signs of third Season	*SSM*
Hosael	Angel – Fourth Heaven, South Angel – Fifth Heaven, South	*SR, SSM, SaS*
Hoschiah	Angel	*67M*
Hostibilis	Spirit – eighteenth Mansion of the Moon Ring	*AE*
Hostyhol	Angel	*NA*
Hosuatyn	Angel	*NA*
Hosyel/Hosiel	Angel	*NA, SBH*
Hosymagalon	Angel	*NA*

Hoviel	Genii – 25° Virgo	*ArP*
Hozor	Angel	*NA*
Hraguel	Angel	*ACM*: Würzburg 42
Hraphael	Angel	*ACM*: Hay 10122
Hrbmayāl	Angel – Mercury	*BoW*
Hrmaial	Angel Prince – fourth Heaven, Fire	*ShR*
Hrmnaa	Angel – Fifth Encampment, first Heaven	*ShR*
Hrmur	Angel – Sixth Encampment, first Heaven	*ShR*
Hrophot	Angel	*ACM*: Würzburg 42
Hsaaial	Angel – First Step, second Heaven	*ShR*
Hshtk	Angel – Second Encampment, first Heaven	*ShR*
Hsniplpt	Angel – Second Encampment, first Heaven	*ShR*
Hstr	Angel – Fourth Encampment, first Heaven	*ShR*
Htnial	Angel – Third Heaven, serving Rhtial	*ShR*
Hubaiel/Hubayel	Angel – First Heaven, West	*SSM, SaS*
Hubaril	Spirit Messenger – Saturn	*SGT, SSG*
Hubayel	Angel – First Heaven, South	*SR*
Hud	Angel – Fifth Encampment, first Heaven	*ShR*
Hud Hud	Angel – Eighth Step, second Heaven	*ShR*
Hudial	Angel Prince – fourth Heaven, Fire	*ShR*
Hudih	Angel – Fourth Step, second Heaven	*ShR*
Hufrbria	Angel – Third Heaven, East	*SR*
Hujael	Genii – 2° Taurus	*ArP*
Humaliel	Spirit	*MNeI*
Humalquyel	Angel – Fifth Heaven, South	*SSM*
Humastrau	Angel first Heaven Monday – North	*Hmn, KoSR, BoO, GAG, BoTS, tM*
Humaziel/Humasiel	Angel – Night Hour six	*Stg, ArP*
Humeth/Humots/Humet	Demon Duke	*SoS, GV*
Hunaspel	Ministering Spirit – Saturn	*CBMS*
Hundalgunda	Demon	*GAG*
Hunel	Intelligence	*EPL*

Hunmura	Angel – Fifth Encampment, first Heaven	*ShR*
Huphaltiel/Hufaltiel/ Hufaltriel	Angel – Third Heaven Friday, West Angel – Third Heaven, West Ministering Spirit – Venus	*Hmn, KoSR, BoO, BM, GAG, BoTS, SaS, tM, CBMS*
Huphatrieb	Intelligence – Jupiter	*SGT, SSG*
Hupniaun	Angel – Sixth Encampment, first Heaven	*ShR*
Huratapal/ Huratapel/ Hartapel/Hartapiell/ Hurtapel/ Hurathaphel/ Huracapel/ Huracaphel/ Hurachafel/ Hurathayel/ Muratapel	Angel – Sunday Spirit – Sun	*SSM, SBH, EoN, Hmn, CBoM, BoO, tSoS, GAG, BoTS, PO, tM*
Hurchetmigarot/ Huictiigaras/ Huictugaras/ Huictiigara	Demon Duke	*SoS, GV*
Hur	Spirit	*BoTS*
Hurmuz (Rafael, Barbarian)	Spirit King – Jupiter	*Pic*
Hursiel/Husiel	Demon Knight	*Stg, ThG*
Hursor	Spirit	*BoTS*
Husael	Angel – Third Heaven, East	*SaS*
Husro	Spirit – Air	*MNeI*
Hutaciel	Angel – Third Heaven, West	*EoN*
Huum	Angel – First Heaven, South	*EoN*
Huynayl	Angel – Venus	*SSM*
Hyachonaababur/ Yachonaababur	Daemon – Mars, subject to East Wind; South	*SBH*
Hycandas	Demon – Sun	*BARC*
Hydōr (Mars)	Mars – Alternative Name	*Hyg*
Hydriel	Chief Water Spirit	*MNeI*
Hyeyl	Angel – Sun/Sunday	*SR*
Hyerserus/ Hiererferus	Spirit – seventh Mansion of the Moon Ring	*AE*
Hygalaēl (Luna)	Luna – Alternative Name	*Hyg*

Hyhas	Spirit of the Thumb	CBoM
Hyielispak (Mercury)	Mercury – Alternative Name	Hyg
Hyla	Servant Spirit	Abm
Hyliotilopos (Luna)	Luna – Alternative Name	Hyg
Hymaeth/Hymateh	Demon Chief – under Belzebut	KoSU
Hyne	Angel	NA
Hyniel/Hymiel/Hynyel	Angel – Fifth Heaven Tuesday, North	EoN, Hmn, BoO, GAG, BoTS, tM
Hyperik/Hēperēēpar/Hēpereēr	Demon – South	Hyg
Hypha	Demon – South	Hyg
Hypopalt/Hypokhtal/Hēpoltagi/Hipoulpe	Demon – South	Hyg
Hyquirros	Angel	NA
Hyros	Angel – Tenth Altitude (Capricorn)	Alm
Hyrsabyl	Angel – Hour six/Gemini/ Spica	BoW
Hyrti/Hyiti	Spirit Assistant – Thursday	MHN
Hyrys	Servant Spirit	Abm
Hyesemigadōn	Unknown chthonic god	PGM IV:206-466
Hymon	Angel	NA
Hysichar	Angel	NA
Hysoreōnō (Mercury)	Mercury – Alternative Name	Hyg
Hyyci/Hyici	Daemon Minister – Mercury; between the West and North	SBH
Hyzy	Angel – Kislev	SR

	I	
I	Son of Light, subject to Prince Hagonel	dHM
Iaashal	Angel – Third Step, second Heaven	ShR
Iabedo	Spirit of the Thumb	CBoM
Iabiel	Angel over Pains, Sharp Pains, Inflammation, Dropsy	SoM
Iabuk	Angel Prince – fourth Heaven, Fire	ShR
Iabutiau	Angel – Fifth Step, second Heaven	ShR

Iabynx	Angel – Marchesvan	*SR*
Iaciz	Angel – Moon	*LL*
Iadonay	Angel Minister – Love and Fornication	*KoSA*
Iaēl/Ariēl/Iarēl	Angel – Sunday Hour nineteen	*Hyg*
Iagrou/Iagouto (Mercury)	Mercury – Alternative Name	*Hyg*
Iahanesym	Spirit of the Thumb	*CBoM*
Iakiak	Angel	*ACM*: Oriental 6796
Iakōr/Iakor (Venus)	Venus – Alternative Name	*Hyg*
Ialal	Angel – Fifth Step, second Heaven	*ShR*
Ialchal/Iarabal/Yalcal	Daemon – Sun, subject to North Wind; East	*SBH*
Iamai	Servant Spirit	*Abm*
Ianbou/Ēamboum	Demon – West	*Hyg*
Iameth	Angel	*ToS*
Iamfriell	Spirit	*oADS*
Iammas (Samax?)	Angel – King of Air on Tuesday	*BoO*
Iammax/Iamax/Tamax	Daemon King – Mars, South Spirit King – Mars	*SBH, EoN, oADS*
Iamnuk	Angel – Fourth Encampment, first Heaven	*ShR*
Iangas	Angel – Moon	*LL*
Ianiēl	Angel – Saturday Hour twenty-one	*Hyg*
Ianouēl/Iannouēl	Angel – Saturday Hour twenty	*Hyg*
Iaom	Enochian Angel – North, over fourth lesser Angle	*TBA*
Iaoth	Angel	*ToS*
Iaper/Ēaper	Demon – West	*Hyg*
Iaran/Eniran/Niran/Anēran	Demon – Tuesday Hour twenty-one	*Hyg*
Iarabel	Daemon – Sun, subject to North Wind	*SBH*
Iarbath	Deity (identity uncertain, may be Seth or Tetragrammaton)	*SM*: P. Mich inv. 6666
Iareahel (Levaniel)	Angel – Moon	*tSoS*
Iareth (Venus)	Venus – Alternative Name	*Hyg*
Iariehel	Angel – Second Heaven, North	*EoN*
Iarn	Angel – Fourth Encampment, first Heaven	*ShR*

Iasei/Iasi	Angel	Hyg
Iasēph/Iastēr (Venus)	Venus – Alternative Name	Hyg
Iaspes	Spirit – Iron Artificer	oADS
Iassurim/Iasguim/ Jasguarim/Jasgnarim	Angel Ruler – Night Hour ten	Stg, ArP
Iastaēl	Angel	Hyg
Iax	Angel	ToS
Iazmou	Demon – West	Hyg
Ibadon	Spirit Prince – Astrology	MNeI
Ibajah	Genii – 1° Libra	ArP
Ibasil	Spirit	GV
Ibnial	Angel Prince one of three – third Heaven	ShR
Ibulon	Servant Spirit	Abm
Icamell	Spirit Helper – Tuesday	CBoM
Ichdison	Servant Spirit	Abm
Icho	Spirit	ACM: Hay 10391
Ichsi	Angel Prince – fourth Heaven, Fire	ShR
Ichspt	Angel – First Encampment, first Heaven	ShR
Ichthion	Demon – Decan thirty-two	ToS
Ichzial	Angel – Fourth Step, second Heaven	ShR
Icosiel	Demon Wandering Prince	Stg, ThG
Ida/Paida	Angel – Spring	BoW
Idaat	Angel – Fifth Encampment, first Heaven	ShR
Ideus	Spirit – Minister of Love	oADS
Ido	Demon Prince	GoPH
Idoēl/Ēdiēl	Angel – Sunday Hour eleven	Hyg
Idouēl/Nidouēl/Idoēl	Angel – Friday Hour two	Hyg
Idrial	Angel – Third Heaven, serving Ibnial	ShR
Idual	Angel – Seventh Encampment, first Heaven	ShR
Iegoulas/Iagelas/ Ēgegoulas	Demon – North	Hyg
Iekaēl/Iesakaēl	Angel	Hyg
Iemure	Spirit – Minister of Love	oADS
Iemuri	Servant Spirit	Abm

ABBREVIATIONS

Ieropael	Demon – Decan seventeen	*ToS*
Iesaloeella/Fesaloell	Spirit – Moon	*BoO, GAG*
Iesan	Treasure Spirit	*oADS*
Iesoraell/Fesoraell	Spirit – Saturn	*BoO, GAG*
Iesse	Daemon – Jupiter, serving North and East Winds; between East and South	*SBH*
Ifftan	Demon	*MRC*
Igaraf	Servant Spirit	*Abm*
Igelsifone	Spirit	*CoC*
Igigi	Servant Spirit	*Abm*
Igilon/Iglion	Servant Spirit	*Abm, MRC*
Igilsiton	Spirit	*CoC*
Igiman	Alternative name of Metatron	*SQ*
Igisticon	Spirit	*CoC*
Ignaro	Spirit Assistant – Thursday	*MHN*
Ignyel	Demon – South	*Hyg*
Ih	Son of Light, subject to Prince Hagonel	*dHM*
Ihal	Angel – Tenth Step, second Heaven	*ShR*
Ihual	Angel – Third Step, second Heaven	*ShR*
Iiqr	Angel – Fifth Encampment, first Heaven	*ShR*
Ijud	Ministering Familiar/Mystery	*67M*
Ikarizi (Venus)	Venus – Alternative Name	*Hyg*
Ikmtu	Angel – Fourth Encampment, first Heaven	*ShR*
Ikon	Servant Spirit	*Abm*
Ikptini	Angel – Twelfth Step, second Heaven	*ShR*
Ikstr	Angel – Second Encampment, first Heaven	*ShR*
Ikti	Angel – First Encampment, first Heaven	*ShR*
Ilarak	Servant Spirit	*Abm*
Ildng	Angel Prince – fifth Heaven, Month of Cheshvan	*ShR*
Ileh	Spirit – Moon	*67M*
Ilekel	Servant Spirit	*Abm*
Ilial	Angel – Second Encampment, first Heaven	*ShR*

Ilim	Spirit	*Hyg*
Illusabio	Spirit	*KoSR*
Ilmese	Spirit – Son of Sons of Light	*dHM*
Ilnostreon	Spirit	*GV*
Iloson	Servant Spirit	*Abm*
Ilr	Son of Light, subject to Prince Hagonel	*dHM*
Imamiah/Iminamiah	Angel – Shem fifty-two	*KoSU, 3BOP, GoeR, JMR, SAS, tM*
Imeēl/Mnimeōēl/Mnēmeēl/Mnimeēl	Angel – Thursday Hour six	*Hyg*
Imhotep the Great/Iymhotep	Egyptian High Priest and Architect	PDM XII:21-49, XIV:93-114, Suppl. 168-184
Imiual	Angel – Mars	*GAG*
Impotiel	Spirit Ruler – Cripples and Paralysed	*KoN*
Impuryn	Angel – Mars/Tuesday	*SR*
Impyra (Mars)	Mars – Alternative Name	*Hyg*
Imumial	Angel – Second Encampment, first Heaven	*ShR*
Imted	Enochian Angel – West, over second lesser Angle	*TBA*
Inachiel	Demon Duke – Y1	*Stg, ThG*
Inanialchi	Spirit	*ArPh*
Inavis	Angel Minister – Love and Fornication	*KoSA*
Incantator	Angel Minister – Trickery	*KoSA*
Indam	Angel – Fire	*SR*
Indous	Angel	*Hyg*
Inhabit	Spirit – four Quarters of the Uiversal Mansions	*SGT*
Iniran/Nēran	Demon – Tuesday Hour twenty	*Hyg*
Innael	Angel	*oADS*
Innyhal/Innial	Daemon – Mars, subject to East Wind; South	*SBH*
Inopeson	Angel Minister – Love and Fornication	*KoSA*
Inōpēx/Kynopex/Kinopex	Demon – North	*Hyg*
Inora	Angel Minister – Love and Fornication	*KoSA*

Inquiell	Angel	oADS
Insquen	Angel – Tebet	SR
Ioaespm	Spirit Minister, serving King Baligon	dHM
Iobiell	Angel	BoO
Iochael	Biblical Elder	ACM: Berlin 11347, Oriental 6796
Ioēl	Angel	PGM XXXVI:161-177
Iōēl	Angel – Monday Hour nine	Hyg
Iōlapas	Angel	Hyg
Ioloma	Spirit	MRC
Iōn/Iōnēl/Ēonēniēl	Angel – Sunday Hour twenty-four	Hyg
Iōnan (Sun)	Sun – Alternative Name	Hyg
Iōouph/Iōkhth/Kokhth	Angel – Sunday Hour six	Hyg
Iōraēl/Ērae	Angel – Sunday Hour four	Hyg
Iōram	Angel	Hyg
Ioran/Iōran/Ēōra	Angel – Sunday Hour eight	Hyg
Ioray	Demon	BoSC
Ioroēl/Oroēl/Olaēl	Demon – West	Hyg
Iōthath	Name of Hermes-Thoth	PGM CI:1-53
Iotifar	Servant Spirit	Abm
Iouēl	Angel	PGM XXXVI:161-177
Ioukhan/Nioukhan	Demon – Saturday Hour twenty	Hyg
Ioukhan/Ēoukhan	Demon – Saturday Hour nineteen	Hyg
Ipakol	Servant Spirit	Abm
Iperon/Iparon	Angel – Mercury	oADS
Ipesidōn/Pesidōn/Pesēdon/Pesidon	Demon – North	Hyg
Iphiaph	Angel, fourth Heaven	PGM XXVI:1-42
Ipodhar	Spirit	MNeI
Ipokys	Servant Spirit	Abm
Ipos/Ipes/Ayperos/Ayporos	Demon Earl and Prince	PmD, DoW, Goe, GV, GG, DI
Irascor	Demon Senior	SSM

Irasomin	Servant Spirit	*Abm*
Irazēl (Venus)	Venus – Alternative Name	*Hyg*
Irel/Iriel	Angel fifth Heaven Tuesday – West	*EoN, Hmn, KoSR, BoO, GAG, BoTS, tM*
Irly	Spirit	*KoSR, GoPH, GV, BD*
Irmanotz/ Irmanotzod	Angel – Night Hour twelve	*Stg, ArP*
Irmasliel/Trimasel/ Trimasael/Irmasial/ Irmasi/Trmael	Demon – under Satanachi	*KoSU, SoS, GV*
Irmenos	Servant Spirit	*Abm*
Irminon	Servant Spirit	*Abm*
Iromas	Servant Spirit	*Abm*
Iromenis	Servant Spirit	*Abm*
Irraēl	Angel	PGM IV:1716-1870
Irshial	Angel Prince – fourth Heaven, Fire	*ShR*
Iry	Spirit	*KoSR*
Isa'ayial	Angel Minister – Malachim, ruling Rain	*SRH*
Isagas	Servant Spirit	*Abm*
Isbaēl	Angel – Plant Ruler	*BoW*
Iscarath	Spirit	*GAG*
Ischscabadiel/ Jschscabadiel	Demon Count	*MNeI*
Iseij	Spirit – Moon	*67M*
Ishaaial	Angel – Second Step, second Heaven	*ShR*
Ishmarathel	Plant Spirit – Holly	*GS*
Ishmi	Angel – First Encampment, first Heaven	*ShR*
Ishmrial	Angel – First Step, second Heaven	*ShR*
Isiael/Iaiel	Angel fifth Heaven Tuesday – West Ministering Spirit – Mars	*Hmn, KoSR, BoO, GAG, BoTS, tM, CBMS*
Isis/Isi	Egyptian Goddess of Magic	PGM IV:94-153, IV:1390-1495, IV:2241-2358, IV:2373-2440, IV:2967-3006, IV:3125-3171, V:213-303,

ABBREVIATIONS 485

Isis/Isi (con't.)		PGM VII:429-458, VII:490-504, VII:540-578, VIII:1-63 XII:14-95, XII:144-152, XII:201-269, XII:365-375, XXIVa:1-25, XXXVI:134-160, XXXVI:283-294, XXXVI:295-311, XXXVI:333-360, LVII:1-37, LIX:1-15, CI:1-53, CXXII:1-55, PDM XIV:1-92, XIV:150-231, XIV:239-295, XIV:395-437, XIV:428-450, XIV:528-553, XIV:554-562, XIV:563-574, XIV:585-593, XIV:594-620, XIV:636-669, XIV:750-771, XIV:851-855, XIV:1219-1227, LXI:106-111, LXI:112-127, LXI:159-196, Suppl. 101-116, Suppl. 130-138, Suppl. 138-149, Suppl. 162-168, Suppl. 185-208; *SM*: T. Genav. Inv. 269, P. Berol. Inv. 21243; *ACM*: Schmidt P., GMPP:94-153, P. Mich. 136, Berlin 5565, Berlin 8313, Schmidt 1, Schmidt 2, Mich. 4932, Yale 1013A
Isis	God – Fruit	*BoO*
Isis-Sothis	Isis identified with Sirius	PGM VII:490-504

Ismael	Spirit Attendant – Mars	*EoN*
Ismoli	Angel Minister of Air – Tuesday Ministering Spirit – Saturn	*Hmn, KoSR, GAG,* *BoTS, tM, CBMS*
Isobyl	Wicked Spirit	*NMI*
Isphraēl	Angel – Thursday Hour three	*Hyg*
Isquier/Ysquisy/ Ysquy	Spirit King	*BoO*
Israel	Angel Minister	*ACM*: P. Mich. 593
Israel	Angel – Shebat Angel – Malachim, Saturday	*SR*
Isrial	Angel Prince – fourth Heaven, Water	*ShR*
Issii/Isy	Intelligence	*BoG*
Isstos/Hoistros/ Hoistos/ Oistas	Demon – Sunday Hour thirteen	*Hyg*
Istac	Angel – Trickery	*KoSA*
Istraēl	Angel	PGM IV:1716-1870
Itael	Genii – 8° Aries	*ArP*
Itamas (Ismoli?)	Angel Minister of Air – Tuesday	*BoO*
Itanal	Demon Servant – Tuesday	*KoN*
Itimon	Alternative name of Metatron	*SQ*
Itmon	Alternative name of Metatron	*SQ*
Itna	Angel – Jupiter	*GAG*
Itrasbiel	Demon Duke – East	*Stg, ThG*
Ittalainma	Angel ruling Animals	*SoM*
Itules	Demon Duke – East	*Stg, ThG*
Iuafula/Inafula	Fairy Lady	*BoO, GAG*
Iuar	Servant Spirit	*Abm*
Iucamilchada/ Hannistada	Spirit – fifth Mansion of Moon Ring	*AE*
Iucuciel	Angel – Jupiter	*BARC*
Iudal	Demon – Decan five	*ToS*
Iulia/Julia/Julya	Fairy Lady	*BoO, GAG*
Iuqmial	Angel – Sixth Step, second Heaven	*ShR*
Iuramiter	Angel	*oADS*
Iussh	Angel – First Encampment, first Heaven	*ShR*

Iustitia	Spirit of Justice	*BoO*
Iutnh	Angel – First Encampment, first Heaven	*ShR*
Iuuan/Fuua/Tuua	Spirit – Mercury	*BoO, GAG*
Iuun	Angel – First Encampment, first Heaven	*ShR*
Ixion	King of the Lapiths of Thessaly	PGM XXIII:1-70
Iylyoos (Shams, Roman)	Spirit King – Sun	*Pic*
Iymedōn (Sun)	Sun – Alternative Name	*Hyg*
Izamiel	Genii – 10° Aquarius	*ArP*
Izashiel	Genii – 10° Capricorn	*ArP*
Izikator	Demon – Venus	*Hyg*
Izozon	Servant Spirit	*Abm*

J

Jaajah	Genii – 3° Capricorn	*ArP*
Jaajeh	Genii – 3° Aquarius	*ArP*
Jaba	Enochian Angel – North, serving fourth lesser Angle	*TBA*
Jabniel	Angel Prince – third Heaven and Fire	*SaS*
Jachehay	Angel – Moon	*LL*
Jachiel	Genii – 30° Virgo	*ArP*
Jachiel	Servant Spirit	*Abm*
Jachoroz	Angel – Night Hour nine	*Stg, ArP*
Jadel	Demon Servant – Monday	*KoN*
Jadiel	Genii – 22° Scorpio, 22° Sagittarius	*ArP*
Jael	Angel – Libra	*ArP*
Jael	Angel – Fifth Heaven, West	*SaS*
Jael	Angel – Cherubim on Mercy Seat	*67M*
Jagiel	Genii – 21° Libra	*ArP*
Jahacob/Tifereth (Jamesthe Lesser)	Prince of Ishim and Apostle	*3BOP, MRC*
Jahacobah/Iahacobah (James)	Prince of Ishim and Apostle	*3BOP, MRC*
Jahel	Enochian Angel – North, serving second lesser Angle	*TBA*

Jahhael/Iahhael/Iahhel	Angel – Shem sixty-two	*KoSU, 3BOP, GoeR, JMR, SAS, tM*
Jaho	Spirit – Saturn	*67M*
Jahyniel	Angel – Fifth Heaven, North	*SaS*
Jambex/Lambex	Demon Marquis, Captain and Governor	*BOS, BoO*
Jamedroz/Jamearoz/Jamodroz	Angel – Night Hour eight	*Stg, ArP*
Jammas	Spirit King – Tuesday	*CBoM*
Jampeluech	Spirit	*KoSR*
Jamyrum	Angel	*NA*
Janael	Angel – First Heaven, West	*SR, SaS*
Janael/Ianael/Janak	Angel first Heaven Monday – East Spirit – Moon Presiding Spirit – Moon	*Hmn, KoSR, SoS, BoO, GAG, BoTS, tM, CBMS*
Janediel	Angel – Day Hour nine	*Stg, ArP*
Janiel/Ianiel	Angel fifth Heaven Tuesday – South Ministering Spirit – Jupiter	*Hmn, KoSR, BoO, GAG, BoTS, tM, CBMS*
Janiel	Demon Duke – North-East	*Stg, ThG*
Janiel	Genii – 2° Sagittarius	*ArP*
Janifeth	Spirit – Mirror	*CoMS*
Janofiel/Janosiel	Angel – Day Hour eight	*Stg, ArP*
Janothyel/Janoshyel	Angel – Night Hour three	*Stg, ArP*
Janozothin	Angel – Moon	*LL*
Japhael	Genii – 7° Aries	*ArP*
Japuriel/Japuviel	Angel – Night Hour four	*Stg, ArP*
Jarael/Jareael	Angel – Second Heaven, North	*SR, SaS*
Jariahel/Iariahel/Jarihael/Iarihael	Angel – Second Heaven Wednesday, North Spirit – Mercury	*Hmn, KoSR, SoS, BoO, GAG, BoTS, tM*
Jasamana	Angel	*NA*
Jashiel	Genii – 23° Capricorn, 23° Aquarius	*ArP*
Jasiael	Angel – Fifth Heaven, West	*SaS*
Jasphiel	Angel – Night Hour four	*Stg, ArP*
Jastrion/Pastrion	Angel – Night Hour eight	*Stg, ArP*
Jasyozyn	Angel – Moon/Monday	*SR*
Jasziel/Iasziel	Demon Duke – North-East	*Stg, ThG*

ABBREVIATIONS

Jatael	Genii – 19° Pisces, 29° Pisces	*ArP*
Jatroziel/Jatrziul/Jatroziul	Angel – Night Hour eleven	*Stg, ArP*
Jauiel	Angel – Jupiter/Thursday	*SR*
Javael	Genii – 28° Taurus	*ArP*
Javiel	Genii – 18° Taurus, 18° Gemini	*ArP*
Jazariel	Demon Count Chief – Tribal Spirits, Pisces and Libra, thirteenth Mansion of the Moon	*MNeI*
Jazel/Jaxel/Iaxel	Angel – Fifth Heaven Tuesday, West Spirit – Mars Ministering Spirit – Mars	*Hmn, KoSR, SoS, BoO, GAG, BoTS, MNeI, tM, CBMS*
Jeartaag	Spirit – ninth Mansion of the Moon Ring	*AE*
Jebrayel	Angel – Jupiter/Thursday	*SR*
Jeha	Spirit – Mars	*67M*
Jebiel	Genii – 10° Sagittarius	*ArP*
Jechar	Angel	*NA*
Jechiel	Genii – 20° Virgo	*ArP*
Jehon	Angel	*NA*
Jecushuo	Angel	*NA*
Jefischa/Jefisiel/Jdfischa	Angel Ruler – Night Hour four	*Stg, ArP*
Jeha	Spirit – Moon	*67M*
Jehuel	Ministering Familiar/Mystery	*67M*
Jehujah/Johujah/Iehuiah/Jechujah/Iechuiah/Jehuiah	Angel – Shem thirty-three	*KoSU, 3BOP, GoeR, JMR, SAS, tM*
Jejael/Jojaiel/Ieiaiel/Iejiel/Leiaiel	Angel – Shem twenty-two	*KoSU, 3BOP, GoeR, JMR, SAS, tM*
Jejalel/Jojabel/Ieilael/Jeialel/Ieilel/Iejaliel	Angel – Shem fifty-eight	*KoSU, 3BOP, GoeR, JMR, SAS, tM*
Jejazel/Ihiazel	Angel – Shem forty	*KoSU, 3BOP, GoeR, JMR, SAS, tM*
Jelahel/Jolahel/Lelahel/Lelael	Angel – Shem six	*KoSU, 3BOP, GoeR, JMR, SAS, tM*

Jelahiah/Ielahiah	Angel – Shem forty-four	*KoSU, 3BOP, GoeR, JMR, SAS, tM*
Jeli	Angel – Second Heaven, South	*SaS*
Jeliel/Ieliel	Angel – Shem two	*KoSU, 3BOP, GoeR, JMR, SAS, tM*
Jeliel	Salamander Head (four of six)	*SBRM*
Jemamoht	Angel	*NA*
Jemehiz	Angel	*NA*
Jenaziel/Janaziel	Angel – Night Hour two	*Stg, ArP*
Jendoad	Angel – Venus	*GAG*
Jendsel	Intelligence	*EPL*
Jeniel	Genii – 2° Scorpio	*ArP*
Jenotriel	Angel – Day Hour six	*Stg, ArP*
Jephormi	Angel Minister – Love and Fornication	*KoSA*
Jerabel	Ministering Spirit – Mercury	*CBMS*
Jerathel/Ierathel	Angel – Shem twenty-seven	*KoSU, 3BOP, GoeR, JMR, SAS, tM*
Jereceue (Jerescue?)	Angel – Issim	*BoTS*
Jeremiel/Ieremiel	Archangel	*SM: P. Heid. Inv. Lat. 5, 3BOP*
Jeresous/Ierescue/Jerescue	Angel – Second Heaven Wednesday, West Presiding Spirit – Mercury	*Hmn, KoSR, BoO, GAG, BoTS, tM, CBMS*
Jereté	Angel	*KoSA*
Jerim	Angel Minister – Love and Fornication	*KoSA*
Jermiel	Angel – Day Hour four	*Stg, ArP*
Jeroham	Angel	*NA*
Jertubety	Spirit – fourth Mansion of the Moon Ring	*AE*
Jes	Angel Minister – Love and Fornication	*KoSA*
Jesabel	Salamander Head (three of six)	*SBRM*
Jesamanay	Angel	*NA*
Jesbar	Angel	*NA*
Jesenemay	Angel	*NA*
Jesil	Angel Minister – Love and Fornication	*KoSA*

ABBREVIATIONS

Jesus/Christ/Iēsous	Demi-God of Christianity	PGM IV:3007-3086, XII:190-192, XIII:1-343, CXXIIIa:1-70, PGM CXXVIII:1-11; *ACM: EM 10263, Cologne 851, Amsterdam 173, Berlin 21230, Rainer 5, Vienna K8303, Berlin 8313, Yale 1792, P. Mich. 3023A, Oriental 6796*
Jethomezos	Angel	*NA*
Jethosama	Angel	*NA*
Jezalel/Jazoriel/Jazeriel	Angel – Mansion thirteen	*3BOP, tSoS, GoeR, JMR, SaS, tM*
Jezel	Genii – 28° Aries	*ArP*
Jezexpe	Enochian Angel – North, serving fourth lesser Angle	*TBA*
Jezisiel	Genii – 6° Taurus	*ArP*
Jezodhehca	Enochian King – North	*TBA*
Jihi	Angel Minister – Love and Fornication	*KoSA*
Jilbagor	Demon	*GoPH*
Jissirpnekd	Spirit	*BoTS*
Jka	Spirit – Sun	*67M*
Jmonyer/Imonyel/Imoniel	Angel – Night Hour seven	*Stg, ArP*
Joel	Angel – West	*SR*
Johanah/Iohonah (John)	Prince of Ishim and Apostle	*3BOP, MRC*
Johann/John	Spirit	*GoPH*
Johphiel/Jophiel	Planetary Intelligence – Jupiter	*KoSR, 3BOP, PO, tM*
Joiel	Archangel	*MNeI*
Jojalol/Jeiazel/Ieiazel/Iejazel	Angel – Shem thirteen	*KoSU, 3BOP, GoeR, JMR, SAS, tM*
Jomar	Ministering Familiar/Mystery	*67M*
Jomaraht	Angel	*NA*

Jonadriel	Angel – Night Hour seven	*Stg, ArP*
Joorex/Ioorex	Demon Ruler	*BOS, BoO*
Jophiel/Iophiel/ Jophiell	Archangel – Jupiter/Zodiac Archangel – Chokmah/Binah	*3BOP, tSoS, MC, 9CK, SaS, BM, Thm, BoTS*
Jorathon	Spirit King	*BoTS*
Joriel	Duke – West by North pre-Midnight	*BoTS*
Joroyhel	Angel	*NA*
Jorvahol (Gabriel)	Archangel – Moon	*JMR*
Josel/Sosol	Angel – Scorpio	*ArP*
Josey	Angel	*NA*
Josla	Demon Servant – Saturday	*KoN*
Jossla	Demon Servant – Saturday	*KoN*
Joviel (Zadkiel)	Archangel – Jupiter Archangel – Chokmah and Binah	*3BOP, tSoS, JMR, MNeI*
Jubutzis	Demon	*MHN*
Judas Iscariot	Demon	*3BOP*
Julia/Julya/Iulia	Fairy – sixth of Seven Sisters	*oADS, BoO, JMR, BoTS*
Juliana (Venulla)	Fairy – seventh of Seven Sisters	*BoO, JMR*
Juniel	Angel – Jupiter/Thursday	*SR*
Juno	Goddess – Riches and Treasures	*BoO*
Junyal	Punishing Wind	*SSM*
Jupiter	God – Virtues/Riches	*Hyg, BoO*
Jusatine	Demon Prince	*GoPH*
Jzazod	Enochian Angel – South, over fourth lesser Angle	*TBA*
Jzodenar	Enochian Angel – North, serving first lesser Angle	*TBA*

K

Kāakrsayl	Angel – Jupiter	*BoW*
Kabaēl/Kiakbiēl/ Akbaēl	Angel – Monday Hour twenty-one	*Hyg*
Kaberion	Angel	*GAG, CoMS*
Kabriel/Kbriel	Angel – Night Hour twelve	*Stg, ArP*

Kachiel	Genii – 9° Libra	*ArP*
Kadarael	Angel – First Heaven, East	*SSM*
Kadie/Kadiel	Angel – Third Heaven Friday, West Angel – Third Heaven, West	*Hmn, KoSR, BoO,* *GAG, BoTS, SaS, tM*
Kadiel	Intelligence – Jupiter	*SGT, SSG*
Kadōn (Sun)	Sun – Alternative Name	*Hyg*
Kadukuliti	Angel	*SoM*
Kaelldath/Kaeldath	Spirit – Moon	*BoO, GAG*
Kafinas	Spirit – Regal Sympathy	*Pic*
Kafles	Servant Spirit	*Abm*
Kagaoche	Spirit – Minister of Love	*oADS*
Kaginōs	Angel	*Hyg*
Kaimplanes/ Kemlanes/ Keiplanēs	Spirit – East	*Hyg*
Kaipolēs/Kaipollēs (Luna)	Luna – Alternative Name	*Hyg*
Kaiprioukh/ Kypridoun/ Kypreidoukh	Demon – West	*Hyg*
Kairos	God of Time	PGM XIII:1-343, XIII:343-646
Kaite/Kaitē/Kaēte	Demon – Thursday Hour seventeen	*Hyg*
Kakeenikel/ Kanianel/ Kanikel/Kaēkeēl	Angel – Friday Hour four	*Hyg*
Kakem/Kakym (Venus)	Venus – Alternative Name	*Hyg*
Kakistē/Kakēstē/ Kakeisten	Spirit – East	*Hyg*
Kal	Angel Prince – Gate of Spirit of West	*SRH*
Kalamya	Angel – Sun	*SSM*
Kalbyel	Angel – Second Heaven, South	*SSM*
Kalē	Fairy Queen, Lady of the Mountains	*Hyg*
Kalemi	Angel Minister – Love and Fornication	*KoSA*
Kalgosa	Servant Spirit	*Abm*
Kalidad	Angel – Thursday Hour twenty-three	*Hyg*

Kaliēl/Kalēēl	Angel – Thursday Hour four	*Hyg*
Kaliouth/Kalithoul/ Kathēthoul/Kapipoul	Demon – South	*Hyg*
Kalonos/Kalēnos/ Kalinos (Mars)	Mars – Alternative Name	*Hyg*
Kalotes	Servant Spirit	*Abm*
Kalphael/ Kalbalgeēl/ Kalbatel/Kalbalgiel/ Kalbagiēl	Angel – Wednesday Hour eight	*Hyg*
Kalsiel	Angel	*Hyg*
Kalsimem	Angel	*Hyg*
Kalubusi	Angel	*SoM*
Kaluku	Angel	*SoM*
Kamar (Silyaeel, Arabic)	Spirit King – Moon	*Pic*
Kamna	Spirit of the Thumb	*CBoM*
Kamusel	Servant Spirit	*Abm*
Kamyel	Angel – Third Heaven, West	*SSM*
Kandien	Angel	*Hyg*
Kanipza/Kanipta (Jupiter)	Jupiter – Alternative Name	*Hyg*
Kanistōn	Demon – Tuesday Hour two	*Hyg*
Kanob/Kanōb	Angel	*Hyg*
Kanops/Kiknyt/ Kyknitas/Kyknit/ Kynops	Demon – Monday Hour twenty-two	*Hyg*
Kanorsiel/Kanorfiel/ Hanorfiel	Angel – Night Hour eight	*Stg, ArP*
Kapeēl/Ageēl/ Koupeēl/ Agiēl	Angel – Wednesday Hour eighteen	*Hyg*
Kaphiban (Luna)	Luna – Alternative Name	*Hyg*
Kaphsiel (Cassiel)	Angel – Saturn	*SMS*
Kapnithen/ Kapnithel/ Kapnitholel	Demon – Friday Hour twenty-one	*Hyg*

Kapounēl/Kaponiēl/ Marnikhaēl/ Marmikhaēl	Angel – Saturday Hour ten	*Hyg*
Karaaēl	Angel – Thursday Hour twenty-two	*Hyg*
Karap	Demon	*ToSC*
Karason	Angel – Sun, over Air	*SR*
Karassaēl	Angel – Thursday Hour twenty-one	*Hyg*
Karatan/Karatēn/ Karaton	Demon – Wednesday Hour eight	*Hyg*
Karbiel	Angel – Marchesvan	*SR*
Kardiel	Angel	*ACM*: Oriental 5899, Berlin 11347
Karelesa	Servant Spirit	*Abm*
Kargiel	Angel – Venus	*GAG*
Kariēl/Tariēl/ Tereateēl	Angel – Monday Hour six	*Hyg*
Kariphasiēl	Angel – Friday Hour five	*Hyg*
Kariter/Karitel/ Karetar	Demon – South	*Hyg*
Karkinar	Demon – Three-way Crossroads	*Hyg*
Karmal	Demon – Mars	*BARC*
Karnabiel	Angel Guardian	*ACM*: Hay 10391
Karnabot	Angel Guardian	*ACM*: Hay 10391
Karniēl/Marniēl	Angel – Tuesday Hour twenty	*Hyg*
Karohel	Angel – Dominations	*67M*
Karphaphēl	Spirit	*BoW*
Karsaēl	Angel – Thursday Hour twenty	*Hyg*
Karus/Kaius	Spirit	*oADS*
Kasaēl/Iamoēl/ Iasmiēl/ Iasmēl	Angel – Tuesday Hour two	*Hyg*
Kasiereph/ Kasiotpos/ Kasiōr	Demon – Monday Hour fifteen	*Hyg*
Kasierōph	Demon – Monday Hour sixteen	*Hyg*
Kasioptos	Demon – Monday Hour fourteen	*Hyg*
Kasis	Angel	*ACM*: H. Kopt. 679

Kastiel/Astiel	Demon	*ToSC*
Katakhaēl	Angel	*BoW*
Katanikotael	Demon – Decan eleven	*ToS*
Katara	Planetary Spirit – Mercury	*SSM*
Kataron	Servant Spirit	*Abm*
Katharbial/Katharbia	Angel – Plant Ruler	*BoW*
Kathos	Angel – Day Hour seven	*Stg, ArP*
Katiēl/Kastrikē/Katriēl	Angel – Sunday Hour nine	*Hyg*
Katonēs	Angel – Saturday Hour nine	*Hyg*
Katsin	Servant Spirit	*Abm*
Kattiēl	Angel	PGM XXXVI:161-177
Katuel/Ketuel	Angel	*SoM*
Katzaēl/Kantiēl/Katziēl/Katiēl/Matziēl	Angel – Wednesday Hour twenty-one	*Hyg*
Kaudien	Angel	*Hyg*
Kawa	Spirit – Saturn	*67M*
Kawisu	Angel	*SoM*
Kayne	Demon Duke	*BOS, BoO*
Kazētok (Mercury)	Mercury – Alternative Name	*Hyg*
Kbir	Angel – Second Encampment, first Heaven	*ShR*
Kdial	Angel – First Encampment, first Heaven	*ShR*
Kdir	Angel – Fifth Encampment, first Heaven	*ShR*
Kdumial	Angel – Fourth Step, second Heaven	*ShR*
Kearldim	Angel – Moon	*LL*
Keberial	Angel – Malachim, Marheshvan	*SRH*
Kebier	Angel – Malachim, under Ayigeda	*SRH*
Kebutzi	Angel	*SoM*
Kedemel	Planetary Spirit – Venus Ruler – Amissio, Puella Co-Ruler – Caput Draconis	*KoSR, 3BOP, BM, Thm, PO, tM*
Kedenial	Angel – Malachim, Tammuz	*SRH*
Kedesōd/Kedesod (Jupiter)	Jupiter – Alternative Name	*Hyg*

Kedieneh	Angel – Malachim, under Avorphenial	*SRH*
Kedissa	Angel – Third Heaven, East	*SSM*
Kēdōēl	Angel – Thursday Hour seventeen	*Hyg*
Keialin	Angel – Venus/Friday	*SR*
Kela	Servant Spirit	*Abm*
Kelah	Angel Prince – South Gate, Firmament	*SRH*
Keleēl/Kolkil/ Kelekeēl/ Kelekiēl/Kyliēl	Angel – Monday Hour five	*Hyg*
Kelehon	Angel, serving above sixth Degree	*SRH*
Kelfeielyn	Angel – Venus/Friday	*SR*
Kemal	Servant Spirit	*Abm*
Kemebial	Angel Minister – Malachim	*SRH*
Kemeret	Spirit	*BoW*
Kemerion	Angel – Mercury/Wednesday	*SR*
Kemeshen	Angel – Malachim, under Ayigeda	*SRH*
Kemouêl	Angel	*SM*: P. Med. I.20
Kenel	Spirit	*ACM*: Cairo 45060
Kenēnēt	Demon – Monday Hour twenty-one	*Hyg*
Kēnoēl (Venus)	Venus – Alternative Name	*Hyg*
Kenogor	Spirit – West in Summer	*SRH*
Kenophial	Angel – Malachim, under Ayigeda	*SRH*
Kenyel	Angel – Third Heaven, South	*SSM*
Keobkh	Demon – Monday Hour seventeen	*Hyg*
Keoulēs (Luna)	Luna – Alternative Name	*Hyg*
Kepheliya	Angel – Malachim, under Pheseker	*SRH*
Kephor	Spirit – North in Winter	*SRH*
Kepiok	Demon – Saturday Hour three	*Hyg*
Kerberos (Cerberus)	Underworld Dog Guardian	PGM IV:1872-1927, IV:2241-2358, IV:2785-2890; *SM*: PSI I.28
Kerebi	Angel – Malachim, under Avorphenial	*SRH*
Kerebial	Angel – Malachim, Winter	*SRH*
Kerebieb	Angel – Malachim, under Ayigeda	*SRH*

Keremial	Angel Minister – Malachim over Rain Angel Prince – East Gate, Firmament	*SRH*
Keresovien	Angel Magistrate – Malachim	*SRH*
Keria	Angel	*ACM*: H. Kopt. 679
Kerial	Angel – Malachim, under Avorphenial	*SRH*
Kēriam/Keriae/ Keriakos/Keriak	Demon – Saturday Hour four	*Hyg*
Keriel/Kiriel	Demon Duke – South Day	*Stg, ThG*
Keriethek	Angel – Malachim, under Ayigeda	*SRH*
Kerinoude/ Keridonal/ Kerinoudalos/ Klinenotē	Demon – Tuesday Hour six	*Hyg*
Kermaniron/ Karipher/ Karkanipher/ Karkanpher/ Kanieleē	Angel – Friday Hour six	*Hyg*
Kernoudēs/Karnodē	Demon – Tuesday Hour five	*Hyg*
Kery	Angel – Kislev	*SR*
Keryth	Spirit	*BoO*
Kesfyel	Angel – three signs of third Season	*SSM*
Kesial	Angel – Malachim, under Avorphenial	*SRH*
Kēsiepopos	Demon – Monday Hour seventeen	*Hyg*
Kesōdour/Masoder	South Wind – Summer	*BoW*
Kethapson/ Kaiphapsō/ Ēthapson/ Kaithapso/ Phapsō	Demon – South	*Hyg*
Kethethial	Angel Prince – Understanding	*SRH*
Kewan {Persian} (Isbil)	Angel – Saturn	*SSG*
Khaldēl/Khandēl	Angel – Plant Ruler	*BoW*
Khalēkeel	Demon	*Hyg*
Khalib/Khalion/ Khabēl/ Khalēon	Demon- Mercury	*Hyg*
Khalkidōn	Angel – Friday Hour sixteen	*Hyg*

ABBREVIATIONS

Khalkoum	Spirit	*Hyg*
Khalkydōēl	Angel – Friday Hour fourteen	*Hyg*
Khameloul/ Khameoul/ Lamēoul/Lamaoul	Demon – South	*Hyg*
Khamōth/Khalmōth	Demon – Tuesday Hour eighteen, seventeen	*Hyg*
Kharakhēl	Spirit	*BoW*
Kharakiēl/ Khalkikhēl/ Akharkyēl	Angel – Wednesday Hour twelve	*Hyg*
Kharautoune/ Kharaphtoune	Angel – Plant Ruler	*BoW*
Khariel/Khariēl/ Kharaēl/Khazēēl	Angel- Moon	*Hyg*
Khariēl/Kheriel/ Skahriel/Khalriēl/ Khereēl	Angel – Thursday Hour seven	*Hyg*
Kharindēl/Khariēdēl	Angel – Plant Ruler	*BoW*
Khariōmō (Luna)	Luna – Alternative Name	*Hyg*
Kharioun/Kharou	Demon – Mercury	*Hyg*
Khariz/Kharia	Spirit	*BoW*
Kharmasaēl	Spirit	*BoW*
Khartoēl/Khartōēl	Angel – Thursday Hour eleven	*Hyg*
Khaselōn/Khasilon (Mercury)	Mercury – Alternative Name	*Hyg*
Kheel	Genii – 16° Aries	*ArP*
Kheirim/Kherēm	Demon – Saturday Hour two	*Hyg*
Khēmeril/Khimeril/ Khymeriēl	Angel – Thursday Hour sseventeen	*Hyg*
Khephra/Khephri/ Chpyris/Chphyris/ Scarab	Egyptian Solar Beetle God	PGM VII:579-590, XII:96-106, XIII:1-343, PDM XXI:1-29
Khertosiēl/ Khartisēel/ Khaltosiēl/ Khartisiel/ Khattēsiēl	Angel – Wednesday Hour five	*Hyg*

Khiet (Mars)	Mars – Alternative Name	*Hyg*
Klio/Khil/Klic/Kleim	Demon	*SoS, GV*
Khimeriēl	Angel – Thursday Hour fifteen	*Hyg*
Khirōt/Kheirōn/Khvron	Demon – Wednesday Hour eighteen	*Hyg*
Khoibi (Mars)	Mars – Alternative Name	*Hyg*
Khonsu	Egyptian Moon God	PDM XIV:239-295
Khorēzē/Khorizē (Mars)	Mars – Alternative Name	*Hyg*
Khoukan	Demon – Thursday Hour twenty-four	*Hyg*
Khōzei	Spirit – East	*Hyg*
Khroos	Bottom part of Brimas	*Pic*
Khthouniēl/Khthonēēl/Khthoniēl/Khthoneēl/Khōnael	Demon – Sun	*Hyg*
Kibaish	Demon	*SMS*
Kidmoos	Spirit – Love/Sexual Attraction	*Pic*
Kiephaēl/Kisphaēl/Kophphaēl	Angel – Thursday Hour three	*Hyg*
Kiepni	Angel – Thursday Hour twenty-four	*Hyg*
Kigios	Servant Spirit	*Abm*
Kijgij	Ministering Familiar/Mystery	*67M*
Kijlij	Spirit – Moon	*67M*
Kijmah	Spirit – Venus	*67M*
Kildh	Angel – First Encampment, first Heaven	*ShR*
Kiligil	Servant Spirit	*Abm*
Kilik	Servant Spirit	*Abm, MRC*
Kilikim	Servant Spirit	*Abm*
Kimphas	Power of Death	*ACM*: Cairo Bone A/B
Kinakhas/Kynakhas/Keinakhas	Demon – North	*Hyg*
Kingael	Genii – 7° Taurus, 7° Gemini	*ArP*
King of the Pygmies	Ruler – Earth Elementals	*BoO*

Kinouel (Venus)	Venus – Alternative Name	*Hyg*
Kinpharaph/ Kēpharaph	Angel – Thursday Hour eleven	*Hyg*
Kipol	Angel – Thursday Hour twenty-three	*Hyg*
Kipos/Kēpōs/ Kypōs/ Kythos	Demon – Saturday Hour eleven	*Hyg*
Kirie	Demon – Saturday Hour six	*Hyg*
Kirik	Servant Spirit	*Abm*
Kirotiel	Peasant Spirit	*MNeI*
Kismosan	Angel – Saturday Hour nine	*Hyg*
Kispoēl	Angel – Thursday Hour twenty-one, twenty-two	*Hyg*
Kitōēl/Koutael/ Koutaēl	Demon – West	*Hyg*
Kiwan (Ashbeel, Persian)	Spirit King – Saturn	*Pic*
Kleim/Klēm	Angel – Ruler of Sea in Spring	*BoW*
Klepoth/Kleppoth	Demon Duke	*SoS, GV*
Klidator/Klēdator/ Klideutor	Demon – Saturn	*Hyg*
Klinoēl/Klinos/ Klēnoēl	Angel – Sunday Hour twenty-three	*Hyg*
Klinonitos/Klinotios	Demon – Tuesday Hour seven	*Hyg*
Klinos	Demon – Monday Hour one	*Hyg*
Klmiia	Angel Overseer (four of seven) – First Heaven	*ShR*
Klmniia	Angel – Fourth Step, second Heaven	*ShR*
Klnh	Angel – Fifth Encampment, first Heaven	*ShR*
Kloracha	Servant Spirit	*Abm*
Klotho	One of the Moirai (Fates)	PGM II:64-184, IV:2241-2358, IV:2785-2890
Klothod ('Battle')	Demon – Pleiades three	*ToS*
Klouphar/Kinphar/ Kiphar	Angel – Thursday Hour twelve	*Hyg*
Klptun	Angel – Twelfth Step, second Heaven	*ShR*
Klubial	Angel – Third Encampment, first Heaven	*ShR*

Kmiel	Genii – 11° Capricorn	*ArP*
Kmshial	Angel – Third Step, second Heaven	*ShR*
Kmshu	Angel – Second Encampment, first Heaven	*ShR*
Kneph	Egyptian Builder God	PGM CXI:1-15; *SM*: P. Wash. Univ. II.74
Knidadiel/ Kniedadiel	Demon Baron	*MNeI*
Kniedatiel (Knidadiel?)	Foolish Spirit	*MNeI*
Kniphōr	Demon – Friday Hour twenty-four	*Hyg*
Kntun	Angel – Sixth Step, second Heaven	*ShR*
Knur	Angel – Fifth Encampment, first Heaven	*ShR*
Kobada	Servant Spirit	*Abm*
Kobhan	Servant Spirit	*Abm*
Kogiel	Servant Spirit	*Abm*
Kokeb	Angel Magistrate – Malachim	*SRH*
Kokeb Henogeh	Angel – Malachim, under Phelmiya	*SRH*
Kokebiel	Angel Prince – South	*SRH*
Kokhbiel	Angel	*Hyg*
Kokolon	Servant Spirit	*Abm*
Kolan	Servant Spirit	*Abm*
Koledeh	Angel – Malachim, under Avorphenial	*SRH*
Kommes (Kenmu)	Egyptian Decan God (Decan seventeen)	PGM II:64-184
Kondarke/Kōndar	Angel – Thursday Hour twenty-three	*Hyg*
Kondiroēl/Kondiēnēl	Angel – Saturday Hour twenty-two	*Hyg*
Kontastor	Demon	*Hyg*
Kōpakil	Demon – West	*Hyg*
Kopēnos/Kopinos	Demon – Thursday Hour fourteen	*Hyg*
Kopiel/Kopiēl/ Kopēl/ Kopeēl	Angel – Monday Hour four	*Hyg*
Kopil	Angel – Monday Hour three	*Hyg*
Kopinos/Skopinos	Demon – Thursday Hour sixteen	*Hyg*

ABBREVIATIONS

Kore (Persephone)	Greek Chthonic Goddess	PGM IV:206-466, IV:1390-1495, IV:2241-2358, IV:2708-2784, IV:2943-2966
Kore	Servant Spirit	*Abm*
Koretheyavom	Angel – Malachim, under Phelmiya	*SRH*
Kortaēl/Kourtaēl	Angel – Wednesday Hour seventeen	*Hyg*
Kosem	Servant Spirit	*Abm*
Kotraēl	Angel – Thursday Hour twenty-three	*Hyg*
Kouchos	Power of Death	*ACM*: Cairo Bone A/B
Koudraēl	Angel – Thursday Hour twenty-two	*Hyg*
Koudrouēl	Angel – Saturday Hour twenty-one	*Hyg*
Koulēl	Spirit	*BoW*
Koulmēnas	Demon	*Hyg*
Koupeēl/Koupaēl	Angel – Wednesday Hour seventeen	*Hyg*
Koure (Kore)	Title of Persephone	*SM*: T. Cairo Mus. JdE 48217, T. Louvre Inv. E 27145, P. Mich. Inv. 6925, T. Köln Inv. 1, Audollent DT.38
Kourtaēl	Angel – Wednesday Hoursixteen	*Hyg*
Kphiel	Genii – 7° Pisces	*ArP*
Kpniia	Angel – Sixth Encampment, first Heaven	*ShR*
Kpun	Angel – First Encampment, first Heaven	*ShR*
Kraēl	Angel – Mars	*Hyg*
Kraipophōn (Venus)	Venus – Alternative Name	*Hyg*
Kralym/Kralim	Angel – Night Hour five	*Stg, ArP*
Kramaéēl	Demon – under Satanachi	*KoSU*
Kranos/Kronos/Kromos	Angel – Day Hour nine	*Stg, ArP*
Kranoti/Krunoti/Kruneli	Angel – Day Hour ten	*Stg, ArP*
Krasiel	Angel	*Hyg*
Krba	Angel – Third Encampment, first Heaven	*ShR*
Krbi	Angel – First Encampment, first Heaven	*ShR*

Krbtun	Angel – Third Encampment, first Heaven	ShR
Krdi	Angel – South Wind	ShR
Krhal	Angel Encampment Head – sixth Heaven, West	ShR
Kriel	Genii – 8° Virgo	ArP
Krigenos/Krigenēs (Venus)	Venus – Alternative Name	Hyg
Krimka	Angel Prince – fourth Heaven, Fire	ShR
Krinel	Demon	ToSC
Krkus	Angel – Sixth Step, second Heaven	ShR
Kriophoros ('Ram-bearer')	Hermes title	ShR
Kriptophon/ Kryptophoron (Venus)	Venus – Alternative Name	Hyg
Krital	Angel – Second Encampment, first Heaven	ShR
Krm	Angel – Fifth Encampment, first Heaven	ShR
Krmyāyl	Angel – Jupiter	BoW
Krodalos/ Kakloudalos/ Kerinoudal/ Kerinoudalos/ Kelouaulos	Demon – Friday Hour 6	Hyg
Krokotimēs	Spirit	Hyg
Kronitiēl/Krotiēl	Angel – Monday Hour 24	Hyg
Kronos	Greek Titan God of Time	PGM IV:835-849, IV:2241-2358, IV:2785-2890, IV:2967-3006, IV:3086-3124, XII:201-269, XII:401-44, XIII:646-734, PDM XVI:1-75; ACM: H. O. Lange Text
Kronos (Greek/ Roman) (Isbil)	Angel – Saturn	SSG
Krqta	Angel – Seventh Step, second Heaven	ShR
Krsayl	Angel – Wednesday	BoW
Krsun	Angel – Fourth Encampment, first Heaven	ShR

ABBREVIATIONS

Krth	Angel – First Encampment, first Heaven	*ShR*
Kshiel	Genii – 11° Aquarius	*ArP*
Ksil	Angel – First Encampment, first Heaven	*ShR*
Ktbral	Angel – First Step, second Heaven	*ShR*
Ktētoēl/Ktēnoēl/Ektonoēl	Angel – Saturn	*Hyg*
Ktinotothen/Ktētonthen	Angel – Saturn	*Hyg*
Ktioēl (Venus)	Venus – Alternative Name	*Hyg*
Kukkuel	Angel	*ACM*: P. Lichačev
Kluymzadel	Spirit – Pleiades (five of seven)	*oADS*
Kumeatel	Demon – Decan fourteen	*ToS*
Kunifer	Spirit	*MNeI*
Kunospaston	Demon – Sea	*ToS*
Kurtael	Demon – Decan nine	*ToS*
Kuthan	Night Devil	*oADS*
Kuzziba	Angel – Fourth Step, second Heaven	*ShR*
Kyas	Night Devil	*oADS*
Kybaēl	Angel – Thursday Hour three	*Hyg*
Kydoēl	Angel – Thursday Hour eighteen	*Hyg*
Kydouēl/Kedouēl/Kidouēl	Angel – Thursday Hour nineteen	*Hyg*
Kyēl	Angel – Friday Hour eleven	*Hyg*
Kyem	Demon – South	*CBoM*
Kyeon	Demon – Originators of All Harm (five of six)	*PO*
Kyienotēs	Demon – Tuesday Hour seven	*Hyg*
Kylikos/Ablikōr	Demon – Thursday Hour twenty-two	*Hyg*
Kynas/Kiōnas/Kyonas/Kēone	Demon – East	*Hyg*
Kynēpro	Demon – East	*Hyg*
Kyniel	Angel – Third Heaven, South	*SaS*
Kynogyr/Kēntogir	Demon – Wednesday Hour six	*Hyg*
Kynops/Kanōps/Kenōps	Demon – Monday Hour twenty-three	*Hyg*

Kyos	Demon – South	*CBoM*
Kyphthō/Kypthonios	Demon – Saturday Hour nine	*Hyg*
Kypris	Epithet of Aphrodite	*SM*: P. Merton II.58
Kyptip	Angel – Potestates	*67M*
Kyrdipol/Kispōl	Angel – Thursday Hour twenty-four	*Hyg*
Kyriel	Angel – Mansion twenty	*3BOP, tSoS, JMR, SaS, Thm, tM*
Kyriel/Kiriel	Noble Spirit, Fire	*MNeI*
Kyrmaēn (Mercury)	Mercury – Alternative Name	*Hyg*
Kyrsoel/Kērsoēl/ Kyrsoēl/Kyrsonaēl/ Kausnoēl/ Kyrssoniēl	Angel- Venus	*Hyg*
Kysiepotos/ Kysiepetos	Demon – Monday Hour sixteen	*Hyg*
Kythere/Kythereia	Epithet of Aphrodite	PGM IV:2891-2942
Kytos	Demon – Saturday Hour twelve	*Hyg*
Kzfyāl/Krfyāl	Angel – January/Capricorn	*BoW*

L		
Laabiel	Angel – Adar	*SR*
Laamon	Spirit – South	*KoN*
Laanab	Spirit – Middle	*SSM*
Laaval	Demon – North	*GoPH*
Labadu	Terrestrial Spirit – Prince	*SBH*
Labam/Labak/ Laban (Venus)	Venus – Alternative Name	*Hyg*
Labatel/Lebatei/ Lebutal	Angel	*SoM*
Labatu	Angel	*SoM*
Labdgre	Spirit Minister, serving Prince Hagonel	*dHM*
Labdiel	Angel	*ACM*: Oriental 5899
Labēkos	Demon – South	*Hyg*
Labelas	Angel – Moon/Monday	*SR*
Labelas	Angel – Moon	*LL*
Laber	Demon King under Beelzebub – North	*SSM*

ABBREVIATIONS

Labiel	Angel – Adar	*SR*
Labiel	Angel – Jupiter/Thursday	*SR*
Labilafs	Spirit	*GV*
Labisi	Servant Spirit	*Abm*
Labitan/Lazitan/ Latzētan/Latzitan	Demon – South	*Hyg*
Laboneton	Servant Spirit	*Abm*
Labonix	Servant Spirit	*Abm*
Labtiel	Biblical Elder	*ACM*: Berlin 11347, Oriental 6796
Labusi	Angel	*SoM*
Lacana	Angel – Fourth Heaven, West Angel – Fifth Heaven, West	*SR, SaS*
Laccudonyn	Angel – Moon/Monday	*SR*
Lachatyl	Servant Spirit	*Abm*
Lachesis/Lachis	One of the Moirai (Fates)	PGM II:64-184, IV:2785-2890
Lachiel	Genii – 1° Pisces	*ArP*
Lachmyel	Angel – Second Season by Day	*SSM*
Ladiel	Demon Duke – West Night	*Stg, ThG, BoTS*
Ladilibas	Spirit – Pleiades (six of seven)	*oADS*
Ladodoēl	Angel	*Hyg*
Ladokon/Ladikon (Venus)	Venus – Alternative Name	*Hyg*
Ladrotz/Ladrotzod	Angel – Night Hour twelve	*Stg, ArP*
Laerpiēl	Angel – Wednesday Hour fifteen	*Hyg*
Lafaqnael	Angel – Moon, over Earth	*SR*
Lafiel	Angel – Jupiter/Thursday	*SR*
Lagabon	Spirit	*SSM*
Lagasaf	Servant Spirit	*Abm*
Lagha	Angel – Moon	*LL*
Laghoo	Angel – Moon	*LL*
Lagiros	Servant Spirit	*Abm*
Lahagenim	Angel – Moon	*LL*
Lahehor	Angel – Thrones	*67M*
Laiagelm	Angel – Moon	*LL*

Laiaselesyn	Angel – Moon	*LL*
Laidrom	Enochian Senior – North	*TBA*
Lailam	God of Winds and Spirits	PGM XXIIa:18-27
Lairayozim	Angel – Moon	*LL*
Lakhkhibiēl/ Lakhibeēl	Archangel	*Hyg*
Lalakim	Angel – Day Hour one	*LL*
Laltōēl	Angel – Thursday Hour eleven	*Hyg*
Lama	Angel – Fifth Heaven Tuesday, West Presiding Spirit – Mars	*EoN, Hmn, KoSR, BoO, GAG, BoTS, tM, CBMS*
Lamael	Demon Duke – West, North-East	*Stg, ThG*
Lamaho	Angel	*NA*
Lamair	Spirit	*MHN*
Lamajah	Genii – 5° Capricorn	*ArP*
Lamal	Servant Spirit	*Abm*
Lamargos	Servant Spirit	*Abm*
Lamas	Demon Duke – North Night	*Stg, ThG, BoTS*
Lambes	Demon King and President	*NML*
Lambores	Wind (?) Spirit	*GAG*
Lamboured	Spirit	*GV*
Lambricon/ Lambracaron	Demon King – North	*BOS, BoO*
Lamechiel	Angel	*ToS*
Lameck	Angel	*GV*
Lamediel/Lamodiel	Angel – Night Hour four	*Stg, ArP*
Lamehc	Angel	*NA*
Lamei	Decan Spirit	*ACM*: Cologne 10235
Lameniel/Lemeniel/ Leminid	Demon Duke – Day Hour five Demon Chief Duke	*Stg, ThG*
Lameniel	Water Spirit	*MNeI*
Lamēoul	Demon – South	*Hyg*
Lameros	Angel – Day Hour five	*Stg, ArP*
Lamerotzod/ Lamerotz	Angel – Night Hour six	*Stg, ArP*

Lamersy	Angel – Night Hour eleven	*Stg, ArP*
Lameson	Angel – Day Hour nine	*Stg, ArP*
Lamia	Demon Queen – Libya	*DI*
Lamiar	Angel	*Hyg*
Lamideck	Angel	*GV*
Lamiel/Laniel	Angel – Day Hour eleven	*Stg, ArP*
Lamisniel/Lanisiyel/Lamfriell	Spirit	*MHN, oADS*
Lamitrorosh	Angel – Day Hour one	*LL*
Lamob	Angel – Sun	*BARC*
Lampcyel	Angel Superior – Saturn	*SSM*
Lampores	Demon – East	*Hyg*
Lampoy	Demon	*MHN, NML*
Lamstararod	Angel Minister – Love and Fornication	*KoSA*
Lanach	Archangel	*ACM*: BN Turin
Lanagotim	Angel – Moon	*LL*
Lanalay	Angel – Fifth Altitude (Leo)	*Alm*
Landabamy	Angel	*NA*
Lancyell	Angel	*oADS*
Langael	Genii – 4° Sagittarius	*ArP*
Langbali	Angel – Day Hour one	*LL*
Lanifiel	Angel – Day Hour eleven	*Stg, ArP*
Lanima/Pruunas	Demon Count	*NML*
Lanoziel/Lenaziel	Angel – Night Hour six	*Stg, ArP*
Lanporish	Angel – Day Hour one	*LL*
Lantiel	Angel – Bisertilis	*SR*
Lantrhots/Lantrhos/Lantrhes	Angel – Day Hour eight	*Stg, ArP*
Lanucel	Spirit – East	*SSM*
Lapasis	Demon Minister	*VJL*
Laoaxarp	Enochian Senior – West	*TBA*
Laoobis	False Spirit – Lord of Hunting	*MNeI*
Lapador	Spirit	*MRC*
Lapēei	Demon – East	*Hyg*
Lapēpote/Laptope	Angel	*Hyg*

Lapheriel	Angel – Night Hour ten	*Stg, ArP*
Laphor/Lapor	Demon Duke – East	*Stg, ThG*
Lapidator	Angel – Hatred and Destruction Spirit – Minister of Love	*KoSA, oADS*
Laquel	Angel – Second Heaven, South	*EoN*
Larabusin	Angel – Moon	*LL*
Larach	Servant Spirit	*Abm*
Larael	Demon Duke – North by East Day	*Stg, ThG*
Laralos	Servant Spirit	*Abm*
Lardas	Demon	*Hyg*
Larexen	Enochian Angel – West, over fourth lesser Angle	*TBA*
Larfos	Duke – West by North Afternoon	*Stg, ThG, BoTS*
Larfuty/Larfuti	Angel – Day Hour eight	*Stg, ArP*
Lariagathyn	Angel – Moon/Monday	*SR*
Lariel	Angel – Saturn, over Earth	*SR*
Lariel	Demon Duke – North-East	*Stg, ThG*
Lariel	Genii – 10° Aries	*ArP*
Laripos	Spirit – Minister of Love	*oADS*
Larmich	Angel – Day Hour four	*Stg, ArP*
Larmol/Larmel	Demon Duke – South Chief Duke	*Stg, ThG*
Larphiel/Lerphiel	Demon Duke – Hour six of fifteen	*Stg, ThG*
Larthas	Spirit	*SSM*
Larzod	Enochian Angel – East, over first lesser Angle	*TBA*
Lasarak	Demon	*ToSC*
Lascivious or Lecherous Spirit	Demon	*ToS*
Lascra	Spirit – fourth Mansion of Moon Ring	*tSoS*
Lashepet	Angel – Day Hour one	*LL*
Lashepim	Angel – Day Hour one	*LL*
Lashiel	Genii – 5° Aquarius	*ArP*
Las Pharon/Lasphoron	Demon Duke – North-West Night	*Stg, ThG, BoTS*
Lassal	Angel – Moon	*BARC*

Lastor/Lastōr	Demon – Thursday Hour eighteen	*Hyg*
Lastor/Lastōr	Demon – Thursday Hour seventeen	*Hyg*
Lastul	Spirit – Mirror	*CoMS*
Lasyrlampēta/ Laeoure/ Lapite/Lapēte/ Laesir/ Lapire	Demon – East	*Hyg*
Lasys	Angel – Book Writer	*BoO*
Latabusi	Angel	*SoM*
Lataleoleas	Angel – Mars	*BARC*
Latebaifanysyn	Angel – Moon/Monday	*SR*
Latgriel	Angel – Earth	*SR*
Lathaxiell	Angel – Jupiter	*GAG*
Lathleym/Lachleym/ Llachleym/Lachlym	Angel – Jupiter	*LR*
Latiel	Genii – 1° Taurus, 1° Gemini	*ArP*
Latistem	Angel Minister – Love and Fornication	*KoSA*
Latzandonim	Angel – Moon	*LL*
Latzepher/Latzipher	Demon	*ToSC*
Laudulin	Angel – Venus/Friday	*SR*
Laufer	Spirit – Mirror	*CoMS*
Laufiel	Spirit – Mirror	*CoMS*
Laune	Demon	*GoA*
Lauriel	Angel Minister of Raphael	*ACM*: BN Turin
Lautrayth	Spirit	*MHN*
Laviah/Laviel/ Lauiah	Angel – Shem eleven	*KoSU, 3BOP, GoeR, JMR, SAS, tM*
Lawisu	Angel	*SoM*
Laya	Familiar Spirit	*VJL*
Layafurin	Angel – Moon	*LL*
Laycon	Angel – Book Writer	*BoO*
Layziosyn	Angel – Moon/Monday	*SR*
Lazaba	Demon Duke – North Night	*Stg, ThG, BoTS*
Lbnaav	Spirit Minister, serving King Baligon	*dHM*
Lbial	Angel – Third Encampment, first Heaven	*ShR*

Lchsun	Angel – Seventh Encampment, first Heaven	*ShR*
Leabarinach	Angel Superior – second Season by Night	*SSM*
Leal	Angel – Mercury/Wednesday	*SR*
Leaorib	Spirit Minister, serving Prince Bornogo	*dHM*
Leban	Demon Knight	*BOS, BoO*
Lebatei	Angel	*SoM*
Lebermeq	Angel Prince – Malachim, Summer Nights	*SRH*
Lebes (Lybes)	Angel – Chora one	*ArA*
Lebokar/Labēkos/ Labekas	Demon – South	*Hyg*
Lebraieil	Angel – Venus/Friday	*SR*
Lebusi	Angel	*SoM*
Lecher	Demon – West	*BOS, BoO*
Lechies	Russian Satyr Demon	*DI*
Lectabal/Lochabel/ Lecabel	Angel – Shem thirty-one	*KoSU, 3BOP, GoeR, JMR, SAS, tM*
Ledrion	Angel	*GV*
Leenarb	Spirit Minister, serving Prince Bornogo	*dHM*
Lefarahpem	Enochian Senior – West	*TBA*
Lega	Angel – Malachim, under Ayigeda	*SRH*
Legabon	Spirit – North	*SSM*
Legioh	Evil Spirit	*SoM*
Legion	Name given by demon for a group possessing a person	HB Mark 5:9, Luke 8:30
Legion	Infernal Spirit	*MNeI*
Lehahiah/ Lobzabjah/ Lehachiah/ Lechachiah/ Lehaiah	Angel – Shem thirty-four	*KoSU, 3BOP, GoeR, JMR, SAS, tM*
Lehebial	Angel – Wednesday	*SRH*
Lehetial	Angel – Taurus	*SRH*
Leinaph	Angel	*Hyg*
Lelael	Angel – Crown of Light	*ACM*: H. Kopt. 686
Lelalion	Angel – Saturn/Saturday	*SR*
Leleph	Angel – Malachim, under Avorphenial	*SRH*

Lelisphak (Mercury)	Mercury – Alternative Name	*Hyg*
Lemage	Enochian Angel – West, over third lesser Angle	*TBA*
Lemalon	Servant Spirit	*Abm*
Lemar	Angel Angel – Dominations	*NA, 67M*
Lemaron	Angel – Night Hour three	*Stg, ArP*
Lemay	Angel	*NA*
Lemieshotha	Angel – Malachim, under Dohel	*SRH*
Lēmnei	Angel – Lunar, Night Hour three	PGM VII:862-918
Lemodac	Demon Duke – Day Hour twelve and Night Hour twelve	*Stg, ThG*
Lemon	Spirit	*GV*
Lemōth	Demon – Tuesday Hour eighteen	*Hyg*
Lemozar/Lemozor	Angel – Night Hour eight	*Stg, ArP*
Lemur	Angel – Day Hour ten	*Stg, ArP*
Lemythan	Angel	*NA*
Lenegial	Angel – Malachim, sixth Host	*SRH*
Lenel/Nenel/Oelenel	Demon	*ToSC*
Lengael	Genii – 4° Scorpio	*ArP*
Leoc	Enochian Angel – West, serving second lesser Angle	*TBA*
Leonard	Demon Sabbath Grand Master	*DI*
Leoniel (Veorchiel)	Angel – Leo Spirit – Leo	*3BOP, tSoS, JMR, SaS*
Leontoph/Leotoph/Leotaph	Demon – North	*Hyg*
Lepacha	Servant Spirit	*Abm*
Lepera	Treasure Spirit	*oADS*
Lephial	Angel – Malachim, under Dohel	*SRH*
Lephoch	Angel – Malachim, under Ayigeda	*SRH*
Lepiron	Angel – Saturn/Saturday	*SR*
Leqobethial	Angel Minister – Malachim, ruling Rain	*SRH*
Lerai/Leraje/Leraye/Leraic/Loray/Oray	Demon Marquis	*PmD, DoW, Goe, GG*
Lergeom	Angel – Sun	*BARC*

Lēstērou	Demon	Hyg
Letemoval	Angel – Malachim, under Phelmiya	SRH
Lēthetioud/ Lētethoud (Sun)	Sun – Alternative Name	Hyg
Letityelyn	Angel – Mars/Tuesday	SR
Letraraamsag	Wind (?) Spirit	GAG
Letziel	Angel	Hyg
Leuainon	Angel – Saturn/Saturday	SR
Leutaber/Zeugaber	Spirit	MHN
Leuviah/Lauviah/ Leuuiah/Levuiah	Angel – Shem nineteen	KoSU, 3BOP, GoeR, JMR, SAS, tM
Levanael/Jareahel (Gabriel)	Archangel – Moon	3BOP, BoO, JMR, SaS
Levaria	Angel Minister – Love and Fornication	KoSA
Leviathan/ Leviathant/ Leviaten	Demon King – South Demon of Envy Chief of Hell Great Fish	HB Job 40:25, Ps 74:14, 104:26, Isa 27:1; Abm, 3BOP, GoPH, MNeI, GoA, SRH, MRC, PO, tM, 67M
Leviel	Genii – 17° Aries	ArP
Lewsydission	Spirit King	BoO
Lewteffar/Falcas	Demon Prince	BOS, BoO
Leykof	Angel	67M
Lezaidi	Angel – Tammuz	SR
Lgch	Angel – Second Encampment, first Heaven	ShR
Lhavala	Spirit	GV
Lhba	Angel – Fifth Encampment, first Heaven	ShR
Lhgial	Angel Prince – fourth Heaven, Fire	ShR
Lhtqup	Angel – Fifth Encampment, first Heaven	ShR
Liachida	Minister of Seat of Hell	Hmn, GAG
Liamintho	Spirit	GV
Lia	Spirit – Son of Sons of Light	dHM
Liaras	Demon Prince	SSM
Libbal	Angel Prince – fourth Heaven, Water	ShR
Libiel	Angel – Saturn, over Fire	SR
Libiel/Libieli	Demon Duke – West Night	Stg, ThG, BoTS

Libral	Angel Prince – fourth Heaven, Water Angel – Shebat	*ShR, SR*
Libriel (Zuriel)	Angel – Libra Spirit – Libra	*3BOP, tSoS, JMR*
Librnk	Angel – Fifth Encampment, first Heaven	*ShR*
Libussa	Spirit – Sibyl (two of ten)	*GV*
Liel	Angel – Second Heaven, South	*SSM*
Liethial	Angel Minister – Malachim over Rain	*SRH*
Ligdisa	Enochian Senior – West	*TBA*
Ligilos	Servant Spirit	*Abm*
Ligmiēl/Ligmiel	Angel – Tuesday Hour ten	*Hyg*
Ligorō/Lithridōn/Lithgorot	Demon – Tuesday Hour two	*Hyg*
Likates/Lykotas/Lēkotas/Likate	Demon – East	*Hyg*
Liktmoi/Lektmoi	Spirit	*BoW*
Lilith	Demon	HB Isa 34:14; *MHN*
Lilles/Eliles (Lilith)	Demon	*MRC*
Lillia/Lilia	Fairy – first of Seven Sisters	*oADS, BoO, JMR, BoTS*
Lima	Spirit – Jupiter	*67M*
Limer/Jhimer/Khimeri/Khēmar	Demon – Friday Hour nineteen	*Hyg*
Limoch	Demon – Jupiter	*EPL*
Limod (Sun)	Sun – Alternative Name	*Hyg*
Linnial	Angel – Sixth Encampment, first Heaven	*ShR*
Lioikon (Venus)	Venus – Alternative Name	*Hyg*
Lior	Demon – Thursday Hour twenty-four	*Hyg*
Lipos	Spirit	*CoMS*
Lirik/Lyrik	Demon – Saturday Hour two	*Hyg*
Liriol	Servant Spirit	*Abm*
Liroki	Servant Spirit	*Abm*
Lisiel/Lysiel/Lēsyrilē	Angel – Sunday Hour fifteen	*Hyg*
Liskax/Paliskax/Palēskax/Peliskar	Demon – South	*Hyg*
Lissa	Familiar Spirit	*VJL*

Listithō/Listrothō/ Lestrētho/Listritho	Demon – South	*Hyg*
Lithidos	Demon – Tuesday Hour one	*Hyg*
Lithikōn/Lithikon (Venus)	Venus – Alternative Name	*Hyg*
Lithitioul (Sun)	Sun – Alternative Name	*Hyg*
Lix Tetrax/Tephras	Demon	*ToS*
Liyedi	Angel – Malachim, Winter Nights	*SRH*
Llp	Angel – First Encampment, first Heaven	*ShR*
Lmial	Angel Prince – fourth Heaven, Water	*ShR*
Lmushy	Angel – Third Encampment, first Heaven	*ShR*
Lnanaeb	Spirit Minister, serving Prince Bornogo	*dHM*
Lobel	Servant Spirit	*Abm*
Lobeqiem	Angel Prince – Gate of Spirit of West	*SRH*
Lobirik (Saturn)	Saturn – Alternative Name	*Hyg*
Loborsomay	Angel – Sun	*BARC*
Lobquin/Lobquain	Angel – Fifth Heaven Tuesday, West Angel – Fifth Heaven, West Ministering Spirit – Mars	*EoN, Hmn, KoSR, BoO, GAG, BoTS, SaS, tM, CBMS*
Lobquym	Angel – Fourth Heaven, West	*SSM*
Locariel	Angel – Sun, over Earth	*SR*
Loccana	Angel – Fourth Heaven, West	*SSM*
Loch	Angel – Ab	*SR*
Lodiel/Lobiel	Duke – West by North after Midnight	*Stg, ThG, BoTS*
Lodir	Spirit	*GV*
Lodoni/Lodovil	Demon	*MHN, NML*
Loginar/Loginaph	Demon – Wednesday Hour twenty-one	*Hyg*
Logos	Angel	*NA*
Lohep	Angel	*ACM*: H. Kopt. 679
Loki	Norse Trickster God	*Gbk*
Lomiol	Servant Spirit	*Abm*
Lomor	Duke – West by North Afternoon	*Stg, ThG, BoTS*
Lomta	Familiar Spirit	*VJL*
Lonial	Angel – Malachim, under Pheseker	*SRH*

ABBREVIATIONS

Lonuel	Angel – twenty of twenty-one on the Left[419]	*ACM*: Berlin 10587
Looflion/Loofhon	Spirit	*CoC*
Lopostarius	Spirit – Minister of Love	*oADS*
Loquel	Angel – First Heaven, West	*SaS*
Lord of Torments	Demon – Jupiter	*BARC*
Lorich	Demon	*NML*
Loriqniel	Angel – Mercury, over Air	*SR*
Losimon	Servant Spirit	*Abm*
Lotaym	Servant Spirit	*Abm*
Lotobor	Spirit	*MHN*
Louchme	Spirit – Underworld Ruler	*ACM*: Berlin 8322
Loueson	Spirit – Minister of Love	*oADS*
Loui	Spirit – Minister of Love	*oADS*
Loukan/Khoukan	Demon – Wednesday Hour sixteen	*Hyg*
Louliēl/Laleēl/ Loulier/ Louliel/Khaleēl	Angel – Wednesday Hour twenty-two	*Hyg*
Louloukaksa	Angel – Guardian of Mary (three of three)	*ACM*: H. Kopt. 686
Loumpēel	Demon	*Hyg*
Lounael/Lunael/ Lunajah/Lunaiah/ Levaiah (Gabriel)	Archangel – Moon	*3BOP, tSoS, JMR*
Loupet	Demon	*ToSC*
Loutzipher/ Loutzēpher	Demon – Wednesday Hour one, East	*Hyg*
Loval	Angel Prince – South Gate, Firmament	*SRH*
Loviah/Leviah/ Leaviah	Angel – Shem seventeen	*KoSU, 3BOP, GoeR, JMR, SAS, tM*
Lpum	Angel – Second Encampment, first Heaven	*ShR*
Ltmial	Angel – Fourth Encampment, first Heaven	*ShR*
Ltsrpal	Angel – Third Heaven, serving Rhtial	*ShR*
Lubras	Angel – Twelfth Altitude (Pisces)	*Alm*
Lubyras/Lubras	Spirit Prince – under Alyzaire	*oADS*
Lucibel (Lucifer)	Ruler – Fallen Angels	*CoMS*

---

419 Although the text states there are twenty-one angels, it only lists twenty.

Luciel/Lusiel	Demon Duke – Day Hour eleven	*Stg, ThG*
Lucifel	Angel – Sun, over Earth	*SR*
Lucifer/Lucipher/ Lucyfer	Demon Ruler/King Demon Emperor – Europe and Asia Demon King – Monday Demon Prince of Darkness Demon of Pride Grand Prince – Hell Great Prince and Prince Palatine	*SSM, MHN, Abm, NML, KoSR, KoSU, LdE, 3BOP, CBoM, dN, BOS, BoO, PmD, CoC, oADS, DoW, SoS, GAG, BoTS, GoPH, MNeI, KoN, SMS, ES, ArPh, GoA, GV, BoSC, VMN, MRC, DI, tM, GG, VJL, BD, SBRM*
Lucifiel (Lucifer)	Ruler of Demons – North-East	*SSM*
Lucifuge Rofocale	Demon Duke	*GG, GV, BoSC*
Lucubar	Demon Duke	*LdE*
Lucyell	Angel	*oADS*
Luel/Louêl	Angel – Shebat Angel – Second Heaven, South	*SM*: P. Vindob. Inv. G 42406, *SR, EoN*
Luija/Luiji	Spirit – Mars	*67M*
Luil	Spirit – Mars	*67M*
Luliaraf	Angel – Tammuz	*SR*
Lumdafquida	Demon	*CoC*
Luna	Goddess – Moon	*Hyg*
Luna	Familiar Spirit	*VJL*
Lundoungiwufa	Demon	*CoC*
Lundrmqnusa	Demon	*GAG*
Luneyl	Spirit – first Mansion of Moon Ring	*tSoS*
Luon	Angel Minister – Love and Fornication	*KoSA*
Luridan/Belelah	Familiar Spirit	*DoW*
Lusiel	Water Spirit	*MNeI*
Lustifion/Lustision	Angel – Night Hour eight	*Stg, ArP*
Lusor	Spirit Familiar	*BoTS*
Luvarmel	Plant Spirit – Monkshood (Aconite)	*GS*
Luzbel (Lucifer)	Infernal Ruler	*SBRM*
Luziel/Luriel	Demon Duke – West	*Stg, ThG*
Lybes	Angel – First Altitiude (Aries)	*Alm*

Lycus	Demon – Bringer of Calamity Demon – Telchine Demon – Originators of All Harm (four of six)	*3BOP, PO, tM*
Lyeleyl/Lyeleym/Llyeleyl	Angel – Moon	*LR*
Lyenyel	Angel – Third Heaven, South	*SR*
Lykogorot	Demon – Tuesday Hour one	*Hyg*
Lylet/Bylet/Bylent	Demon	*MHN*
Lymaxillõ/Lymaxill	Spirit – Mars	*BoO,*
Lymer/Leymer	Spirit – Iron Artificer	*oADS*
Lynion	Spirit – South	*KoN*
Lypalael	Angel of Seas/Waters – Summer	*SSM*
Lyroth	Spirit	*MHN*
Lyssamomaēl	Angel – Saturday Hour nine	*Hyg*
Lytay/Lytoy/Litor	Spirit	*MHN*
Lytim	Demon	*MHN*
Lytrophar/Liarophar (Sun)	Sun – Alternative Name	*Hyg*

M		
Maachin	Angel – Second Heaven, East	*SR*
Maacyn	Angel – Second Heaven, East	*SSM*
Maadon	Angel – Tammuz	*SR*
Maah (Silyaeel, Persian)	Spirit King – Moon	*Pic*
Maakyel	Angel – Cherubim/Seraphim	*67M*
Maaliel	Angel – Marchesvan	*SR*
Maarim	Angel – Marchesvan	*SR*
Ma'aroboth	Angel Minister – Malachim, ruling Rain	*SRH*
Maasiel	Angel – Sivan	*SR*
Maat	Egyptian Goddess of Truth and Balance and Justice	PDM XIV:805-840
Mabareylyn	Angel – Mars/Tuesday	*SR*
Mabiel	Genii – 25° Leo	*AeP*
Mabsuf	Angel – Sivan	*SR*

Machaldie	Spirit	*CoC*
Machiel	Angel – Day Hour two	*LL*
Machin (Bathin)	Demon Duke	*LdE, GoPH*
Macariel	Spirit – Venus	*VMN*
Macariel/Mecariel	Demon Wandering Prince	*Stg, ThG*
Maccafor	Angel – Sivan	*SR*
Macgron	Angel – Saturn/Saturday	*SR*
Mach	Angel	*KoSA*
Machadon	Angel	*NA*
Machalay	Angel	*NA*
Machar	Angel	*NA*
Macharael	Angel	*ACM*: Moen 3
Machariel	Demon Duke – Hour one of fifteen	*Stg, ThG*
Macharioth	Spirit King	*BoTS*
Machasiel	Angel fourth Heaven Sunday – South, Spring	*Hmn, KoSR, BoO, GAG, BoTS, tM*
Machasiel	Intelligence – Sun	*SGT, SSG*
Machatan	Angel – Saturday	*Hmn, KoSR, BoO, GAG, BoTS, PO, tM, CBMS*
Machatiel	Angel – Saturday	*tSoS*
Machel	Demon – Jupiter	*EPL*
Machiael	Spirit	*BoSC*
Machio	Angel – Saturn	*KoSR*
Machmag	Angel – Night Hour seven	*Stg, ArP*
Machoumet	Demon	*ToSC*
Maconus	Demon	*oADS*
Macracif	Angel – Elul	*SR*
Macria	Angel – Ab	*SR*
Macromechon	Angel	*NA*
Madael	Demon – North	*GoPH*
Madael	Genii – 17° Cancer	*ArP*
Madail	Servant Spirit	*Abm*
Madarilim	Angel – Moon	*LL*
Madarilyn	Angel – Moon/Monday	*SR*

ABBREVIATIONS

Maday	Angel – Tammuz	SR
Madayl	Spirit – North	SSM
Madees	Spirit – Love/Sexual Attraction	Pic
Madicon	Spirit Messenger – South	BoTS
Madiel	Angel – First Heaven Monday, East Angel Prince – Water Spirit – Moon	EoN, Hmn, KoSR, SoS, BoO, GAG, ArP, BoTS, SaS, tM
Madilon	Spirit	GV
Madimiel (Samael)	Archangel – Mars	3BOP, BoO, tSoS, JMR, 9CK, SaS
Madios	Spirit – Moon	SGT, SSG
Madloos	Spirit – Regal Sympathy	Pic
Madoēl (Sun)	Sun – Alternative Name	Hyg
Madoin	Spirit	GV
Mador	Demon Duke – North, West Night	Stg, ThG, BoTS
Madrat	Angel – Ab	SR
Madrath	Spirit King – Thursday	MHN
Madriel	Demon Duke – East	Stg, ThG
Madualim	Angel – Day Hour two	LL
Madyconn/Madycon	Demon Messenger – South	BOS, BoO
Mael	Angel – First Heaven Monday, North Angel Prince – Water Angel Ministering Spirit – Moon	ACM: Oriental 5899, Hmn, KoSR, BoO, GAG, ArP, BoTS, tM, CBMS
Mael	Intelligence – Saturn	SGT, SSG
Mafalach	Servant Spirit	Abm
Mafatyn	Angel – Moon/Monday	SR
Mafayr	Demon Duke – North-East	Stg, ThG
Maffayl	Spirit	SSM
Mafriel/Masriel	Angel – Night Hour eleven	Stg, ArP
Mafrus	Demon Duke – North by East Night	Stg, ThG
Magael/Mugael	Duke – West by North pre-Noon	Stg, ThG, BoTS
Magala	Treasure Spirit	oADS
Magalesius	Demon – Bringer of Calamity	3BOP
Magandarui/Gammagandarui	Spirit – sixth Mansion of Moon Ring	AE

Maganth	Spirit – Jupiter	*SoS*
Magaripp	Ministering Familiar/Mystery	*67M*
Magdiel	Angel – Marchesvan	*SR*
Magel	Angel – Bisertilis	*SR*
Magel	Enochian Angel – West, over third lesser Angle	*TBA*
Magelesius	Demon – Instigator of Misfortune	*MNeI*
Magem	Enochian Angel – West, serving second lesser Angle	*TBA*
Mageyne	Demon Ruler	*BOS, BoO*
Maggid	Servant Spirit	*Abm*
Maghees	Right part of Damahos	*Pic*
Maghnamos	Front part of Bandalos	*Pic*
Maghras	Right part of Daghdiyos	*Pic*
Magiel	Genii – 16° Leo, 26° Cancer	*ArP*
Magnael	Genii – 8° Cancer, 14° Cancer	*ArP*
Magni/Maqui	Demon Duke – North-West Day	*Stg, ThG, BoTS*
Magnia/Magnyny	Angel Ruler – Elul	*SR*
Magoa/Nagoa	Demon King – East	*GoPH, BD*
Magog	Servant Spirit	*Abm*
Magor/Magoth/Maguth	Spirit King	*BoO*
Magossangos	Angel – Bisertilis	*SR*
Magot/Magoth	Demon Duke Spirit King	*ToSC, Abm, BoTS, PO, MRC*
Magram	Treasure Spirit	*oADS*
Magrano/Magrany	Herb (?) Spirit	*BoO*
Magradarioth	Spirit – 1ninth Mansion of the Moon Ring	*AE*
Magras/Maggos/Mankōs/Mogrlos	Demon – Saturday Hour twenty-two	*Hyg*
Magriel	Superior Intelligence – Firmament	*KoSU, SoS*
Maguth/Magruth	Angel Minister of Air – Thursday Daemon Attendant – Jupiter Angel Minister – between East and South Presiding Spirit – Jupiter Spirit Helper – Thursday	*SBH, Hmn, KoSR, CBoM, GAG, BoTS, tM, CBMS*
Magyros	Servant Spirit	*Abm*

ABBREVIATIONS 523

Mah (Persian) (Saljail)	Angel – Moon	*SSG*
Mahamel	Angel – Fourth Heaven, South	*SR*
Mahamtas	Angel – Mars	*BARC*
Mahandas	Back part of Daghdiyos	*Pic*
Mahanyel	Angel – Fourth Heaven, South	*SSM*
Mahasiah/ Mehasiah/ Mahabiah	Angel – Shem five	*KoSU, 3BOP, GoeR, JMR, SAS, tM*
Mahatan	Archangel	*MNeI*
Mahazael/Mahazell/ Machazael	Demon Prince – South Demon Prince – Earth/Fire	*3BOP, SaS, BM, BoTS, MNeI, KoN, PO, tM*
Mahiel	Genii – 28° Leo	*ArP*
Mahodees	Spirit gatherer of Barhoyas	*Pic*
Mahue/Mahuc	Demon Duke – West by South Day	*Stg, ThG, BoTS*
Mahurel (Egin)	Demon King – North	*JMR*
Maianiel	Angel – Fifth Heaven, South	*SaS*
Maiel	Angel Angel – First Heaven, North	*ACM*: Hay 10122, *EoN*
Maiel	Genii – 23° Cancer	*ArP*
Maiman	Spirit	*ACM*: Hay 10391
Mainou/Mainōn	Angel	*Hyg*
Maint	Angel – Tebet	*SR*
Maissobri/Misabu	Spirit Attendant – Moon	*EoN*
Maithoth/Mailoth/ Mailōth/Maēloth	Demon – Tuesday Hour three	*Hyg*
Makael	Genii – 11° Cancer	*ArP*
Makalice	Demon	*GAG*
Makatak/Makkatak	Demon	*ToSC*
Makhdam	South Wind – Spring	*BoW*
Makhōth/Makhoth	Demon – North	*Hyg*
Makhoumethou/ Moukhoumethou/ Makhoumatou	Demon – North	*Hyg*
Makhtheel	Angel	*Hyg*
Maktiel	Angel ruling Trees	*SoM*
Makyn	Spirit of the Thumb	*CBoM*

Mal	Angel – Jupiter	*GAG*
Mala	Angel	*Hyg*
Mala	Spirit – Presidentail Counsellor, South	*BoTS*
Malach	Servant Spirit	*Abm*
Malafar/Malafer	Spirit Terrestrial Spirit – Attendant in West	*SSM, SBH*
Malago	Spirit	*dN*
Malakēs	Demon – Wednesday Hour seventeen	*Hyg*
Malanes/Malakis	Demon – Wednesday Hour sixteen	*Hyg*
Malantha	Demon King – North	*DoW, GAG*
Malapas (Malphas?)	Spirit	*SSM*
Malaphlion	Spirit	*Hyg*
Malaquiran	Angel – Nisan	*SR*
Malathym	Angel – Saturn	*oADS*
Malatrin	Angel – Venus	*GAG*
Malcha/Malcha Betarsisim	Planetary Intelligence – Moon	*KoSR, GoPH, GV, PO, BoSC*
Malcha Betharsisim Hed Beruah Schehalim/ Malchabetharsisim hed Beruahschehakim/ Hed Be ruah Schenhakim	Planetary Intelligence of Intelligences – Moon	*KoSR, 3BOP, BM, tM*
Malchidael/ Malchidiel/ Machidael	Angel – Aries Genius – Puer	*3BOP, tSoS, MC, JMR, SaS, MNeI, Thm, PO, tM*
Malcranus	Demon Messenger	*BoO*
Maldouōr	Demon – Three-way Crossroads	*Hyg*
Malekapōn/ Maliskar/ Malēskar/Melēskar	Demon – South	*Hyg*
Maleus (Maltrans?)	Demon Messenger	*BoO*
Malgaras/Malgaram	Demon King – West Demon Prince – West under Beymon	*Stg, ThG, BoTS, KoN*
Malgas	Angel – Nisan	*SR*
Malgel	Angel – Elul	*SR*

ABBREVIATIONS

Malgron	Demon Duke – North by East Day	*Stg, ThG*
Malguel/Malguels/ Malugel/Malqueel	Demon Duke – South-West Day	*Stg, ThG, BoTS*
Maligare	Spirit	*AN*
Malisan	Angel – Tebet	*SR*
Malkeo/Malkes	Spirit	*BoO*
Malkhbim/ Makhbeim	West Wind – Spring	*BoW*
Mallapas/Mallapar / Mallappas (Malphas)	Demon – South	*BOS, BoO, oADS*
Maloqui	Demon	*MHN, NML*
Malphas	Demon President	*PmD, DoW, Goe, DI*
Malpharas (Malphas)	Demon Seigneur	*LdE*
Malqniel	Angel – Fire	*SR*
Malquiel	Angel – Adar	*SR*
Malquyel	Angel – Fire	*SSM*
Maltayatbāl/Mltytyāl	Angel – December/ Sagittarius	*BoW*
Maltiel/Maltyel	Angel – Third Heaven Friday, West Angel – Third Heaven, West Ministering Spirit – Venus	*SSM, EoN, Hmn, KoSR, BoO, BM, GAG, BoTS, SaS, tM, CBMS*
Maltiel	Intelligence – Jupiter	*SGT, SSG*
Maltrans	Demon Messenger	*BoO*
Maluzim	Angel	*VJL*
Malyke	Spirit Minister – Saturn	*BoO*
Mamarayl	Angel – Mars	*LR*
Mamenim	Angel – Moon	*LL*
Mami	Angel – Venus	*GAG*
Mamiazicaras	Angel – Sivan	*SR*
Mamiel	Angel – Shebat	*SR*
Mamirot	Angel – Ab	*SR*
Mammon/Mamon	Demon Prince – Tempters and Ensnarers Demon of Greed	*3BOP, BM, JMR, BoTS, PO, tM, DI*
Mammoye	Spirit	*GAG*
Mamounas/ Mamonas/ Mamōn/Mamona	Demon – Monday Hour one	*Hyg*

Mamyel	Angel – Fifth Heaven, North	*SR*
Manachoth	Spirit who Established the Fourteen Firmaments	*ACM*: BN Turin
Manadel/Monadel	Angel – Shem thiry-six	*KoSU, 3BOP, GoeR, JMR, SAS, tM*
Manael	Angel	*ACM*: Moen 3
Manalaha	Spirit	*CBoM*
Manasa/Manassa	Spirit Helper Angel Minister of Air – Friday	*BoO*
Manasikon	Spirit	*Hyg*
Mancipal/Mantipal/Mamopal	Spirit – seventh Mansion of the Moon Ring	*AE*
Mancoraas	Spirit – Love/Sexual Attraction	*Pic*
Manderilin	Angel – Moon	*LL*
Mandiel	Angel – Kislev	*SR*
Mandromil/Mandrobyl	Angel – Ruler of Sea in Autumn	*BoW*
Mandusin/Mandousin	Spirit	*GoPH, GV*
Manenim	Angel – Moon	*LL*
Manēr/Manaēl/Maniēs/Maniēr/Manaēn	Demon – Sunday Hour seven	*Hyg*
Maneyloz/Maneylozor/Maney	Angel – Night Hour four	*Stg, ArP*
Mangororam	Angel – Moon	*LL*
Manhorees	Spirit – Love/Sexual Attraction	*Pic*
Maniel	Angel – Fourth Heaven, North	*SaS*
Maniel	Duke – West by North pre-Noon	*Stg, ThG, BoTS*
Manikos/Manikōs	Demon – Saturday Hour twenty-one	*Hyg*
Manistiorar	Angel – Marchesvan	*SR*
Manit	Angel – Iyar	*SR*
Manopall	Spirit – seventh Mansion of the Moon ring	*tSoS*
Manopiqon	Angel – Day Hour two	*LL*
Mansator	Wicked Spirit	*NMI*
Mansi	Demon Duke – South Day	*Stg, ThG*

Manties	Servant Spirit	*Abm*
Mantoris	Spirit – Love/Sexual Attraction	*Pic*
Mantouēl/ Mantatoēl/ Mantoēl/Matonēl/ Madadoel	Angel – Mercury	*Hyg*
Manuel	Angel Angel – Gate of the East, West	*ACM*: P. Mich. 3472, Oriental 6796, L. Anastasi 9
Manuel/Mamiel	Angel – Day Hour seven	*Stg, ArP*
Manurayis	Spirit – Love/Sexual Attraction	*Pic*
Manyel	Angel of Abyss – Winter	*SSM*
Maphēkleē	Angel – Saturday Hour eleven	*Hyg*
Maqua	Angel – Nisan	*tSoS*
Mar	Demon	*ACM*: H. Kopt. 681
Mara	Servant Spirit	*Abm*
Marachy	Angel – Night Hour twelve	*Stg, ArP*
Maractatam	Spirit	*GV*
Marae	Demon Duke – North-West Night	*Stg, ThG, BoTS*
Marag	Servant Spirit	*Abm*
Marage	Spirit Messnger – Amaymon and Oriens	*BoTS*
Marah	Supportive Planetary Spirit – Mercury	*SSM*
Maraht	Angel	*NA*
Marakel/Meniel/ Menkiel/Menikel	Angel – Shem sixty-six	*KoSU, 3BOP, GoeR, JMR, SAS, tM*
Maraloch	Spirit	*MHN, NML*
Maranal	Demon	*MRC*
Maranos	Bottom part of Gharnos	*Pic*
Maranton	Servant Spirit	*Abm*
Maraos	Servant Spirit	*Abm*
Maras	Demon Duke – South, West by South Night	*Stg, ThG*
Mara Simya ('Blind God', Sabian)	Spirit King – Mars	*Pic*
Marastac	Demon King – Jupiter	*BARC*
Marath	Demon Prince – South under Amaymon	*KoN*

Marax/Morax/ Foraii/ Forau	Demon Earl and President	*PmD, DoW, Goe, GG*
Marbas/Marbar/ Barbas/Barthas	Demon President or Prince	*LdE, PmD, DoW, Goe, MRC, GG, BoSC*
Marbuel	Demon Prince Demon – Prince-Elector, Moon Wise Spirit Prince Palatine/Great Prince	*SoM, MNeI*
Marcalia/Marcalis/ Martalio	Spirit – seventh Mansion of the Moon Ring	*AE*
Marchiel	Angel – Night Hour seven	*Stg, ArP*
Marchosias/ Marchocias	Demon Marquis	*PmD, DoW, Goe, DI*
Marcuel	Angel – Marchesvan	*SR*
Mardach	Demon King – Thursday	*KoN*
Mardero	Demon – Decan twenty	*ToS*
Marduel/Merdiel	Angel – Night Hour one	*Stg, ArP*
Marduk	Babylonian God of Order	HB Jer 50:2
Mare	Spirit – seventh Mansion of the Moon Ring	*AE*
Mareaiza/Marciaz/ Morcaza	Demon Duke – South Night	*Stg, ThG*
Marēbat (Luna)	Luna – Alternative Name	*Hyg*
Mareekh (Rubaeel, Arabic)	Spirit King – Mars	*Pic*
Mareso	Spirit	*GV*
Mareupel	Spirit	*ACM*: Hay 10391
Marfiel	Angel – Day Hour four	*Stg, ArP*
Margabiel/ Margabyel	Angel – Fifth Heaven, North Angel – Fourth Heaven, North	*SR, SSM, SaS*
Margala	Treasure Spirit	*oADS*
Margar	Treasure Spirit	*oADS*
Margoas/Margodas/ Mardoas/Margutas (Marchosias)	Demon Marquis	*NML*
Margolas	Demon	*GoPH*
Margon	Treasure Spirit	*oADS*

ABBREVIATIONS

Marguns/Marquus	Demon Duke – South Night	*Stg, ThG*
Marhil	Angel – Sun/Sunday	*SR*
Marhum	Angel – Tishrei	*SR*
Marianu	Demon Duke – North by East Night	*Stg, ThG*
Maria Padilha	Pomba Gira, Queen of Hell	*BoSC, SBRM*
Mariel	Demon Duke – South by East Day	*Stg, ThG, BoTS*
Mariel	Angel	*ACM*: Moen 3
Mariel	Angel – Kislev Angel – Day Hour eight	*SR, Stg, ArP*
Marifiel	Angel – Night Hour eight	*Stg, ArP*
Marilin	Angel – Venus/Friday	*SR*
Marinoc	Angel – Iyar	*SR*
Marinthael	Spirit	*ACM*: L. Anastasi 9
Marinus	Angel – Eleventh Step, second Heaven	*ShR*
Marioth	Angel	*ACM*: H. O. Lange Text
Mariphonou	Demon – Monday Hour ten	*Hyg*
Marit	Angel Prince – fourth Heaven, Fire	*ShR*
Markizaēl	Angel	*Hyg*
Marku	Servant Spirit	*Abm*
Marmanyn	Angel – Mars/Tuesday	*SR*
Marmar	Spirit, first Heaven	PGM XXVI:1-42; *ACM*: Oriental 6796
Marmarael	Angel	*ACM*: Moen 3
Marmarao/ Marmariō	Angel	*ToS*; PGM IV:1167-1226
Marmarath/ Marmaraoth/ Marmariooth/ Marmaroi/ Marmaraōth/ Marmorouth	Angel	*ToS*; PGM IV:296-466, VII:593-619; *ACM*: BN Turin, Hay 10391
Marmariel	Angel	*ACM*: Moen 3
Marmaroulach/ Marmarouach	Spirit	*ACM*: Oriental 6796
Marmēkhel	Angel	*Hyg*
Marmoc	Angel – Tebet	*SR*

Marneyelin	Angel – Moon/Monday	SR
Marnikhaēl/ Mesnikhaēl	Angel – Saturday Hour eleven	Hyg
Maroch	Angel – Day Hour five	Stg, ArP
Maroēl/Marouēl/ Mourouēl	Angel – Wednesday Hoursixteen	Hyg
Marog	Spirit – Middle Spirit – Swiftness	SSM, oADS
Maromiel/Naromiel	Angel – Fourth Heaven, South	EoN
Maros	Demon Prince	GAG
Maroth	Demon Duke – South-West Night	Stg, ThG, BoTS
Maroutha	Spirit – Gate of the South	ACM: L. Anastasi 9
Marouthael	Spirit – Gate of the South	ACM: L. Anastasi 9
Marpikhēl	Angel	Hyg
Marrerym	Spirit	SSM
Mars	God – Battle and Changing the Nature of Beasts	Hyg, BoO
Marshiones	Demon Duke	BOS, BoO
Marthael	Angel	ACM: Moen 3
Marthiel	Angel	ACM: Moen 3
Martiel (Samael)	Angel – Mars	3BOP, tSoS
Martiro	Spirit	GV
Maruel	Angel – three of twenty-one on the Left Angel – Fourth Heaven, South	ACM: Berlin 10587, EoN
Mary (Virgin)	Female Saint/Mother of Jesus	ACM: P. Berlin 21911, P. G. Vitelli 365, Oslo 1.5, P. Mich. 1190, Oriental 6796
Masa	Demon Servant – Friday	KoN
Masa	Spirit – Minister of Love Familiar Spirit	oADS, VJL
Masadul	Servant Spirit	Abm
Masair	Spirit	MHN
Mascifin/Masafin	Demon	MHN, NML
Maschasiel	Angel – Fourth Heaven, South	SaS

ABBREVIATIONS

Maseriel	Dmon King – West by South Demon Prince – South under Amaymon	*Stg, ThG, BoTS, KoN*
Masex	Spirit Helper – Friday	*CBoM*
Masgabriel/ Malgabriel/ Masgrabiel	Angel – Fourth Heaven Sunday, North, Spring Spirit – Sun Ministering Spirit – Sun	*EoN, Hmn, KoSR, SoS, BoO, GAG, BoTS, tM, CBMS*
Mashel/Mashiel	Demon Duke – South by West Day	*Stg, ThG, BoTS*
Masiel	Angel – Adar	*SR*
Masiel	Demon – West	*GoPH*
Masiel	Genii – 7° Leo	*ArP*
Masmag	Spirit – Middle	*SSM*
Masniel/Magniel (Zuriel)	Angel – Libra Spirit – Libra	*3BOP, BoO, tSoS, JMR, SaS*
Massadal	Spirit – West	*SSM*
Massatholon	Angel	*NA*
Mastas	Angel – Mars	*GAG*
Masthel	Angel – twelve of twenty-one on the Left	*ACM*: Berlin 10587
Mastuel/Nastuel/ Naustuel	Demon Duke – Day Hour seven and Night Hour seven	*Stg, ThG*
Mastyel	Angel – Fourth Heaven, North	*SSM*
Masualef	Angel – Tishrei	*SR*
Matagix	Angel Minister	*KoSA*
Matatam	Servant Spirit	*Abm*
Mataton	Angel – Saturday	*MHN*
Matattiah/Mathias/ Machialel (Matthias)	Prince of Ishim and Apostle	*3BOP, MRC*
Matay	Angel – Second Heaven, East	*EoN*
Matees	Bottom part of Damahos	*Pic*
Matefar	Demon	*BoSC*
Mathapart	Spirit	*tSoS*
Mathatau	Angel – Saturday	*CBoM*
Mathateron	Angel – Second Heaven, West	*SSM*
Mathēlial/ Mathēhalaēl	South Wind – Autumn	*BoW*
Mathias	Demon Lord	*BOS, BoO*

Mathiel	Angel – Fifth Heaven Tuesday, North Angel – Fifth Heaven, North Presiding Spirit – Mercury	*Hmn, KoSR, BoO, GAG, SaS, BoTS, tM, CBMS*
Mathlai/Mathlay	Angel – Second Heaven Wednesday, East	*Hmn, KoSR, BoO, GAG, BoTS, tM, CBMS*
Mathlai	Spirit – Mercury	*SGT, SSG*
Mathmeyl/ Machmeyl/ Machymeyl/ Machmereyl/ Mathmereyl	Angel – Sun	*LR*
Mathyuel	Demon Minister – Beelzebub	*SSM*
Matiel	Angel – Fourth Heaven, North	*SR*
Matil	Angel – Fifth Heaven, North	*EoN*
Matinos	Spirit – Love/Sexual Attraction	*Pic*
Mathniel	Angel	*Hyg*
Matiel/Maliel	Angel – Night Hour nine	*Stg, ArP*
Matnairelin	Angel – Moon	*LL*
Matnyel	Angel – Fifth Heaven, North	*SSM*
Matreton	Angel – Saturn	*GAG*
Matriton	Spirit	*GAG*
Mattriel	Angel – Elul	*SR*
Matuta	Spirit	*CoC*
Matuyel/Matnyel	Angel fourth Heaven Sunday – North, Spring	*Hmn, KoSR, BoO, GAG, BoTS, tM*
Maugoran/Masgoran (Venus)	Venus – Alternative Name	*Hyg*
Maurnach/Muicnath	Spirit – seventh Mansion of the Moon Ring	*AE*
Maut	Angel – First Encampment, first Heaven	*ShR*
Mavoth	Angel – Malachim, under Avorphenial	*SRH*
Maxayn/Marayn	Demon – East	*BOS, BoO, oADS*
Maxtarcop	Angel – Saturn	*BARC*
Maya	Angel – Sun	*BARC*

ABBREVIATIONS 533

Mayeryon/ Maheryon/ Maorys/Mahireon/ Mahereon/Mayrion/ Mayerion/Marion/ Mayryon/Macryon	Demon Bishop – North	*CBoM, BoO, CoC, GAG, oADS, BoTS*
Maylalu	Demon – Moon	*BARC*
Maymon	Daemon King – Saturn, North Spirit King – Saturn Angel – King of Air on Saturday Spirit King – Saturday Presiding Spirit – Saturn	*SSM, SBH, EoN, Hmn, KoSR, CBoM, oADS, GAG, PO, tM, CBMS*
Maymon	Demon King	*ClI*
Maymona/ Maymonare	Demon Governor, Wind of Albaryth	*SSM*
Mayrdrus/Naydrus	Spirit	*GoPH, GV*
Mayrion/the Black One (Mayrion, Demon Bishop?)	Demon King - Saturn	*BARC*
Mayton	Angel Minister	*KoSA*
Mazatan	Angel – Saturn/Saturday	*EoN*
Mazbaz	Angel – Potestates	*67M*
Mazeniem	Spirit – West in Spring	*SRH*
Mazica	Angel – Tammuz	*SR*
Maziel	Genii – 20° Cancer	*ArP*
Maziel	Duke – West by North after Midnight	*Stg, ThG, BoTS*
Mbriel	Angel ruling Winds	*SoM*
Mbum	Angel – Fifth Step, second Heaven	*ShR*
Mchshina	Angel – Seventh Encampment, first Heaven	*ShR*
Mdnial	Angel – Third Encampment, first Heaven	*ShR*
Meachuel	Angel	*SoM*
Mēanēth/Mianethi/ Mianēth	Demon – South	*Hyg*
Mēarer	Demon – East	*Hyg*
Meas	Spirit – Minister of Love	*oADS*
Meavel	Angel Minister – Love and Fornication	*KoSA*
Mebahel/Mabahel	Angel – Shem fourteen	*KoSU, KoSU, 3BOP, GoeR, JMR, SAS, tM*

Mebahiah/Mebaiah	Angel – Shem fifty-five	*KoSU, 3BOP, GoeR, JMR, SAS, tM*
Mebaschel	Servant Spirit	*Abm*
Mebhaer	Servant Spirit	*Abm*
Mebhasser	Servant Spirit	*Abm*
Mebhhazubb	Spirit Prince	*MOAS*
Mecallytape	Spirit of the Thumb	*CBoM*
Mechelyptos	Angel	*NA*
Mechiel	Genii – 1° Leo, 4° Leo	*ArP*
Mechebber	Servant Spirit	*Abm*
Mechemed Lov	Spirit – Earth in Spring	*SRH*
Mechenial	Angel Prince – Gate of Spirit of South	*SRH*
Mecheniyem	Spirit – West in Spring	*SRH*
Mechon	Angel	*BoSC*
Mechran	Third of seven Egyptian Fates of Heaven	PGM IV:475-829
Mechuel/Meachuel	Angel	*SoM*
Medagamos	Angel	*NA*
Medar/Meder/Medal	Demon Duke – North	*Stg, ThG*
Medegephial	Angel Prince – Gate of Spirit of North	*SRH*
Mederini	Spirit of the Thumb	*MHN*
Mediat/Modiat/Medial/Modial	Angel – King of Air on Wednesday Spirit King – Mercury	*EoN, Hmn, KoSR, GAG, PO, tM*
Mediesin	Angel – Moon	*LL*
Mēdikit/Midomet/Midikēt/Mēdōkit/Midokot	Demon – Wednesday Hour four	*Hyg*
Medon (Matthew)	Prince of Ishim and Apostle	*3BOP, MRC*
Medonial	Angel – Sagittarius	*SRH*
Medusiel	Angel – Day Hour six	*Stg, ArP*
Medya	Demon Mistress – South	*CBoM*
Mee	Spirit of the Thumb	*CBoM*
Mefeniel	Angel – Jupiter/Thursday	*SR*
Megaira ('Grudge')	One of the Furies (Erinyes)	PGM IV:2785-2890

Megalosius/ Megalesius/ Megalezius	Demon – Originators of All Harm (two of six) Demon – Telchine	PO, tM
Megalleh	Servant Spirit	Abm
Megalogim	Servant Spirit	Abm
Megalos	Angel	NA
Megehon	Angel	NA
Megera	Fury	3BOP, MNeI
Megial	Angel – Malachim, under Dohel	SRH
Megnon	Angel	NA
Megonhamos	Angel	SBH
Mehahel	Salamander Head (six of six)	SBRM
Meh Artemashe/ Mehah Artemasheh	Planetary Spirit Lord – Venus	SSM
Meherial	Angel, serving above sixth Degree	SRH
Mehiel/Mehekiel/ Mecheiel	Angel – Shem sixty-four	KoSU, 3BOP, GoeR, JMR, SAS, tM
Mehil	Angel – Sun/Sunday	SR
Meho	Spirit – Sun	67M
Meidor	Angel Minister – Love and Fornication	KoSA
Meinget/Mingot	Demon	ToSC
Mekaktinos/	Demon – Monday Hour eleven	Hyg
Mekebin	Spirit	CBoM
Mekēnes (Mercury)	Mercury – Alternative Name	Hyg
Mekeres	Angel – Malachim, under Ayigeda	SRH
Mekhmeth/ Makhmithe/ Mekheme/Melmeth	Demon – Sunday Hour twenty-two	Hyg
Mekisamiēl	Angel	Hyg
Mektimanas	Demon – Monday Hour ten	Hyg
Mekuton	Angel	oADS
Melabed	Servant Spirit	Abm
Melahel	Angel – Shem twenty-three	KoSU, 3BOP, GoeR, JMR, SAS, tM
Melak Chebeleh	Angel of Destruction	SRH
Melak Moth	Angel of Death	SRH

Melammed	Servant Spirit	*Abm*
Melanas	Angel – Night Hour twelve	*Stg, ArP*
Melany	Spirit	*GV*
Melas	Demon Duke – South by East Night	*Stg, ThG, BoTS*
Melaxoēl/Melaxōēl	Angel	*Hyg*
Melcha/Milcha	Demon Duke – North Day	*Stg, ThG, BoTS*
Melchidael/ Machidael/ Melchiael	Angel – Mercury	*GoPH. GV, BoSC*
Melchim	Demon	*3BOP*
Melchior/Meloiorus	Spirit – Magi Kings (second of three)	*KoSR, ES, Gbk, GoPH, CoMS, GV, BD*
Melchom	Demon Paymaster	*DI*
Melchon	Demon Duke – North-East	*Stg, ThG*
Melech	Angel – Potestates	*67M*
Melekh	Angel	*KoSA*
Melekieh	Angel – Malachim, Flames of Fire	*SRH*
Melekial	Angel Minister – Malachim, ruling Rain Angel Magistrate – Malachim	*SRH*
Melekiyah	Angel Minister – Malachim	*SRH*
Melekial	Angel – Malachim over Fire and Flames Angel – Malachim over Rain Angel – Malachim, under Ayigeda	*SRH*
Melemil	Spirit	*NML*
Meletial	Angel Prince – Gate of Spirit of West	*SRH*
Melidous/Meladous	Demon – West	*Hyg*
Meliel	Demon Duke – West Day	*Stg, ThG, BoTS*
Melifon	Angel – Saturn/Saturday	*SR*
Meliton	Holy Creature of the Throne (one of four)	*ACM*: H. Kopt. 686
Melkailin	Angel – Day Hour two	*LL*
Mellifiel	Angel – Mercury, over Water	*SR*
Melpiphron/ Meltiphōn/ Meltiphrōn/ Mentephron	Demon – Thursday Hour one	*Hyg*
Melrotz/Melrotzod	Angel – Night Hour three	*Stg, ArP*
Melse	Devil – Ursa Major	*oADS*

ABBREVIATIONS

Meltos/Mēltoal/ Mētoar/ Miktaēr	Demon – South	*Hyg*
Meltphrōn	Demon – Thursday Hour twenty-four	*Hyg*
Memakha	Demon – Monday Hour five	*Hyg*
Memakhth/ Demakhth	Demon – Monday Hour six	*Hyg*
Membridōkh	Demon – West	*Hyg*
Membris Liafis	Spirit – Book Making	*oADS*
Mememil/Melemil	Spirit	*MHN*
Memeta	Angel – Saturn	*GAG*
Memibolo	Demon	*GAG*
Memieil	Angel – Jupiter/Thursday	*SR*
Memitilon	Angel – Saturn/Saturday	*SR*
Memnolik	Servant Spirit	*Abm*
Memolyn	Angel – Mars/Tuesday	*SR*
Memoyr/Memoir	Spirit	*MHN*
Memyiel	Angel – Moon, over Water	*SR*
Menadiel	Demon Wandering Prince	*Stg, ThG*
Menador/Menander	Demon Duke – North	*Stg, ThG*
Menafiel	Angel – Day Hour eleven	*Stg, ArP*
Menail	Demon – under Sirach	*KoSU*
Menaktinos	Demon – Monday Hour ten	*Hyg*
Menanas	Treasure Spirit	*oADS*
Menarchos/ Menerchos	Angel – Day Hour two	*Stg, ArP*
Menariel/Menaziel	Demon Knight	*Stg, ThG*
Menarym/Menarim	Angel – Night Hour three	*Stg, ArP*
Menas/Menos	Angel – Day Hour nine	*Stg, ArP*
Mendrion	Angel Ruler – Night Hour seven	*Stg, ArP*
Mene/Mēnē	Greek Goddess of Months	PGM IV:2241-2358, IV:2441-2621, IV:2785-2890, VII:756-794
Mene (Hekate)	Greek Lunar Goddess	*SSG*
Menebain	Angel – Lunar, Night Hour one	PGM VII:862-918

Menera	Wind Spirit	*GAG*
Menescheēs	Second of seven Egyptian Fates of Heaven	PGM IV:475-829
Meneshor	Spirit – South in Spring	*SRH*
Menesiel/Memesiel	Angel – Night Hour seven	*Stg, ArP*
Menial	Angel – Malachim, under Phelmiya Angel Magistrate – Malachim	*SRH*
Meniel	Angel – Night Hour five	*Stg, ArP*
Menipade	Spirit	*Hyg*
Mēnopa	Demon – Sunday Hour nineteen	*Hyg*
Menoriel/Menorik/ Menoyik/Menorike	Angel – Night Hour six	*Stg, ArP*
Menot	Spirit – Minister of Love	*oADS*
Menothiel	Angel – Malachim, under Ayigeda	*SRH*
Menser	Spirit – Minister of Love	*oADS*
Mentanta	Spirit – Air	*MNeI*
Mentephoul	Angel	*Hyg*
Mentiphron/ Mentephrōn/ Mentephron	Demon – East	*Hyg*
Mēntokau (Venus)	Venus – Alternative Name	*Hyg*
Mentzatzia (Saturn)	Saturn – Alternative Name	*Hyg*
Meon	Angel – Jupiter, over Water	*SR*
Meon	Spirit	*GV*
Meōps (Mercury)	Mercury – Alternative Name	*Hyg*
Meos	Angel – Joy and Divination	*CoMS*
Mephenial	Angel Prince – Tebeth Spirit – North in Winter	*SRH*
Mephenieh	Spirit – West in Winter	*SRH*
Mepheni Shesher	Spirit – South in Spring	*SRH*
Mepheniyeh	Spirit – West	*SRH*
Mephgazub	Spirit – Venus	*TV*
Mephistopheles	Demon Prince	*VJL, SoM*
Mephistophiel (Mephistopheles)	Demon – Prince-Elector, Jupiter Wise Spirit Prince Palatine	*MNeI*
Mephython	Angel	*NA*

ABBREVIATIONS

Merach	Duke – West by North pre-Noon	*Stg, ThG, BoTS*
Merage	Spirit Messenger – Egyn	*BoTS*
Merakephial	Angel – Right Hand of the Lord	*SRH*
Merapis	Demon Minister	*VJL*
Mēran (Jupiter)	Jupiter – Alternative Name	*Hyg*
Meras	Demon Duke – South-East Night	*Stg, ThG, BoTS*
Merasiel/Manasael	Demon Chief Duke	*Stg, ThG*
Mercheimeros	Second of seven Pole Lords of Heaven	PGM IV:475-829
Mercoph/Mezcoph	Angel – Night Hour two	*Stg, ArP*
Mercuriel (Raphael)	Archangel – Mercury	*3BOP, tSoS, JMR*
Mercury	God – Languages, Sciences and Eloquence	*Hyg, BoO*
Mercy	Angel – Second Altitude (Taurus)	*Alm*
Mereēl/Mourkēēl/ Mourkē/Mouriēl/ Mouzkēr	Angel – Friday Hour and	*Hyg*
Meregebial	Angel Prince – Gate of Spirit of North	*SRH*
Meremeremoth/ Meremeravoth	Angel – Malachim over Rain	*SRH*
Merepōn (Mercury)	Mercury – Alternative Name	*Hyg*
Mererym	Demon – Air	*BM*
Meresyn	Angel – Day Hour one	*Stg, ArP*
Merfiel/Merfilde/ Merfide/Mersilde/ Mertiel/Inertiel/ Jeurtiel	Demon Duke Demon – under Sirach	*KoSU, SoS, GV*
Meribat (Luna)	Luna – Alternative Name	*Hyg*
Meriel	Angel – Night Hour twelve	*Stg, ArP*
Merigal	Angel – Mercury/Wednesday	*SR*
Merael	Biblical Elder	*ACM*: Berlin 11347, Oriental 6796
Meriol	Angel – Mercury/Wednesday	*SR*
Meririm/Meierim	Demon Prince – Aerial Powers/South	*3BOP, JMR, PO, tM*
Merkim/Merkoum	Demon – Saturday Hour seventeen	*Hyg*
Merkou	Demon – Saturday Hour eighteen	*Hyg*
Merloy	Spirit	*GV*
Meroēl/Maroēl	Angel – Wednesday Hour fifteen	*Hyg*

Meron	Spirit – Irritates Men	oADS
Meroqaphera	Angel – Left Hand of the Lord	SRH
Merosiel/Marosiel	Demon Duke – Night Hour one	Stg, ThG
Merosiel	Earth Spirit	MNeI
Meroth	Demon Duke – West by North after Midnight	Stg, ThG, BoTS
Merpon (Mercury)	Mercury – Alternative Name	Hyg
Merran/Mērōn (Jupiter)	Jupiter – Alternative Name	Hyg
Merroe	Angel	GV
Mērtos/Myretos/Miretos/Mēretos	Demon – West	Hyg
Meruel	Angel – Bearer of Crown of Shoots from the Tree of Life	ACM: H. Kopt. 686
Mesael	Enochian Angel – North, serving fourth lesser Angle	TBA
Mesaf	Servant Spirit	Abm
Mesaou/Mēsaou/Mēstan (Jupiter)	Jupiter – Alternative Name	Hyg
Mesargiltō	Fourth of seven Pole Lords of Heaven	PGM IV:475-829
Mesemiasim	Angel	ACM: H. O. Lange Text
Mesherial	Angel Minister – Malachim Angel – Malachim, Flames of Fire	SRH
Meshethieb	Angel – Malachim, under Ayigeda	SRH
Mesial/Mesiel	Angel – Day Hour eight Angel Prince – Gate of Spirit of North	Stg, ArP, SRH
Mesiem	Angel Prince – East Gate, Firmament	SRH
Mesriel/Mefriel	Angel – Day Hour ten	Stg, ArP
Messay	Angel	NA
Messitone/Messiton	Spirit Spirit – Woods	CoC, oADS
Metabiēl	Angel – Monday Hour twenty	Hyg
Metaliteps	Spirit of the Thumb	MHN
Metathiax	Angel	ToS

ABBREVIATIONS

Metatron/ Methratton/ Metattron/Meraitron	Archangel – Voice of God Archangel – Kether, Malkuth Ruler of Order of Seraphim Ruler of Primum Mobile	*SQ, KoSA, 3BOP, tSoS, MC, JMR, 9CK, BoTS, SaS, MNeI, Thm, SMS, SRH, PO, CII, CoMS, tM, BoSC*
Metelex	Treasure Spirit	*oADS*
Meterial	Angel Minister – Malachim over Rain	*SRH*
Methaēl/Mithniēl/ Methēēl/Methniēl/ Mēthniēl	Angel – Tuesday Hour twenty-one	*Hyg*
Methagdal (Ahedierier)	Angel – Ruler of Preservation of Crops	*SRH*
Methenial	Angel – Malachim ruling Dangerous Creatures Spirit – South in Autumn	*SRH*
Methridan/ Mykhridam/ Mekhmea/ Mēthridanou	Demon – Sunday Hour twenty-three	*Hyg*
Metiel	Genii – 2° Cancer, 22° Leo	*ArP*
Metinolih	Angel	*KoSA*
Metmouriēl	Angel	PGM XXXVI:161-177
Metofeph	Servant Spirit	*Abm*
Metorilin	Angel – Mercury/Wednesday	*SR*
Mettuton	Angel	*oADS*
Metziel	Genii – 10° Leo	*ArP*
Meuchiel	Angel	*ACM*: Moen 3
Mevathma	Plant Spirit – Cranesbill (Herb Robert)	*GS*
Meviel	Genii – 29° Cancer	*ArP*
Mexiphōn	Demon – Monday Hour ten, eleven, twelve	*Hyg*
Mextyura/Mextyhura	Punishing Wind Daemon – Saturn, serving South-West Wind, North	*SSM, SBH*
Meymonotheby	Demon King – Saturday	*KoN*
Mezaphzar	Spirit Prince	*MOAS*
Mezarim	Spirit – Rules Sciences	*CoMS*
Mezebin	Spirit	*oADS*

Mezetin	Angel – Moon	*LL*
Mhrial	Angel – Sixth Step, second Heaven	*ShR*
Mhūr Htlyāyl	Angel – Monday, Jupiter Hour	*BoW*
Mhyhwgtzy	Angel Prince – Middle Five	*SoM*
Miag/Main/Miegi	Demon – Wednesday Hour nine	*Hyg*
Mial	Angel Prince – fourth Heaven, Fire	*ShR*
Miao	Enochian Angel – North, over fourth lesser Angle	*TBA*
Miarer/Mēarer/Miaror	Spirit – East	*Hyg*
Michael/Mikhaēl/Michaell/Mychyal	Archangel – Sun, Fire, Sunday, Monday, Moon, Air, Mercury, Wednesday, Saturn, East Wind, Morning Winds, South, Gemini, Virgo Archangel – Hod Chief Angel – Fourth Heaven Ruler of Order of Virtues/Archangels Angel – Sun, over Water Intelligence – Sun Archangel – Malachim, over the Shem	HB: Dan 10:21, 12:1, Rev 12:7; PGM I:262-347, III:1-164, III:187-262, III:282-409, IV:1-25, IV:1716-1870, IV:2241-2358, IV:2708-2784, VII:255-259, VII:593-619, VII:973-980, VII:1009-1016, VII:1017-1026, X:36-50, XIII:734-1077, LXXX:1-5, XXIIa:18-27, XXXVI:161-177, XXXVI:295-311, XLIII:1-27, XLIV:1-18, LXXXIII:1-20, XC:1-13, CVI:1-10, PDM XIV:627-635; *ToS, SM*: P. Berol inv. 21165, P. Princ. II.107, P. Heid. Inv. G 1101, P. Heid. Inv. Lat. 5, P. IFAO s.n., P. Med. I.20, P. Noviomagensis Inv. 2, Cairo C4 Text; *ACM*: P. Prague 1; ACM: GMPP:1-25, H. Kopt. 544, Berlin 11347, Oriental 5525, P. Mich. 1190,

ABBREVIATIONS 543

Michael/Mikhaēl/ Michaell/Mychyal (con't.)		*ACM*: BN Turin, H. Kopt. 518; Hay 10434, Oriental 5986, P. Lichačev, Bodl C(P)4, Berlin 10587, Oriental 6172, Berlin 8503, Aberdeen Text, Cairo IAFO, Würzburg 42 H. Kopt. 681, Berlin 8322, Moen 3, P. Mich. 3023A, P. Mich. 3472, Hay 10391, Oriental 6794, Oriental 6796, P. Mich. 593, L. Anastasi 9, H. Kopt. 686; *SoM, dCL, Alm, SSM, NA, SR, BoW, SBH, EoN, Hmn, Hyg, B7R, KoSR, Gbk, CBoM, SoS, BARC, MHN, dN, CoC, tSoS, dSS, ADS, 3BOP, oADS, BoO, DoW, dHM, BM, MC, Thm, GAG, GoeR, ArP, BoTS, JMR, 9CK, ES, GoPH, SaS, MNeI, KoN, SMS, BoSC, SRH, GoA, EPL, CII, MRC, GV, CoMS, tM, CBMS, PO, 67M, VJL*
Michael/Mikael	Angel – Shem forty-two	*KoSU, 3BOP, GoeR, JMR, SAS, tM*
Michal	Angel – Harvest Ruler Angel Prince – South	*SRH*
Miche	Spirit	*BoTS*
Michrathon	Spirit – Saturn	*SBH*
Michyel	Angel Subordinate – Moon	*SSM*
Micob/Mycob/ Micoll/ Micol/Aricol	Fairy Queen	*BoO, BoTS*

Name	Description	Source
Micraton	Angel – Saturn/Saturday Angel – Air	SR, GAG
Micriton	Spirit – Forest	oADS
Midael	Angel – Moon	CBMS
Midain	Good Spirit	MHN
Miegal	Angel – Malachim, under Avorphenial	SRH
Miel	Spirit	ACM: Oriental 6796
Miel	Angel – Wednesday Angel – Thursday/Jupiter Angel Prince – Air Spirit – Mercury	EoN, Hmn, KoSR, CBoM, SoS, tSoS, GAG, ArP, PO, tM
Miel/Miēl	Angel – Wednesday Hour eleven	Hyg
Miemal	Angel – Malachim, under Avorphenial	SRH
Mieqon	Angel Prince	SRH
Mieseqoniech	Angel Prince	SRH
Miesēr/Mesyr/Mēesir	Demon – North	Hyg
Miephiēl/Amphiēl/Masphiēl/Miemphiēl/Emphiēl	Angel – Wednesday Hour three	Hyg
Miet (Mercury)	Venus – Alternative Name	Hyg
Migadel/Mēgadel	Demon – East	Hyg
Migal	Angel – First Encampment, first Heaven Angel – Third Encampment, first Heaven	ShR
Migola	Demon Prince	GoPH
Mihael	Angel – Shem forty-eight	KoSU, 3BOP, GoeR, JMR, SAS, tM
Mihel	Genii – 5° Cancer	ArP
Mihos	Egyptian Lion God	PDM XIV:239-295
Mihr (Persian) (Sams)	Angel – Sun	SSG
Mijl	Spirit – Moon	67M
Mikal (Michael)	Angel Minister – Malachim, seventh Dwelling	SRH
Mikael	Angel	ACM: Moen 3
Mikroel	Angel	ACM: Moen 3
Milalu	Daemon Minister – Moon, West	SBH

Milant	Spirit	*BoO, GoPH*
Milau/Mylau	Daemon – Moon, serving West Wind; West	*SBH*
Milcom	Ammonite God	HB 1 Kgs 11:5, 11:33, 2 Kgs 23:13, 1 Chr 20:2, Jer 49:1, 49:3, Zeph 1:6
Milea	Demon Minister	*VJL*
Milia	Fairy Queen, Sister (second of three)	*DoW*
Millalu (Milalu?)	Spirit Assistant – Monday	*MHN*
Milliel/Millet	Angel – Second Heaven Wednesday, South	*EoN, Hmn, KoSR, GAG, BoTS, SaS, M*
Milon	Servant Spirit	*Abm*
Milony	Spirit	*oADS*
Milpeza	Demon Secretary	*VJL*
Milyoras	Spirit – Love/Sexual Attraction	*Pic*
Mimgogm	Angel – Moon	*LL*
Mimmechabatouthel	Spirit	*ACM*: Cairo 45060
Mimon	Demon – Bringer of Calamity/ Instigator of Misfortune Demon – Telchine	*3BOP, MNeI, tM*
Mimosa	Servant Spirit	*Abm*
Min	Egyptian Fertility/Harvest God	PGM III:1-64
Minael	Angel – Kislev	*SR*
Minalos	Back part of Gharnos	*Pic*
Minariell	Angel – Mercury	*GAG*
Minianto	Spirit	*ACM*: Hay 10391
Minons/Minos	Judge of Hell Demon – Originators of All Harm (six of six)	*3BOP, BoO, MNeI, PO*
Minotous/Minosons/Minoson	Demon	*SoSW, GV*
Minquitalem	Spirit	*BoO*
Miobiou	Demon – Monday Hour eighteen	*Hyg*
Miōt (Mercury)	Mercury – Alternative Name	*Hyg*
Miqon	Alternative name of Metatron	*SQ*
Mirabam	Demon Prince of Darkness	*oADS*

Miracl	Spirit	*MHN*
Mirael	Spirit	*NML*
Mirage	Spirit Messenger – Paymon	*BoTS*
Mircos	Spirit – Seducer of Women	*oADS*
Miremicum	Spirit – Causes Women to Love	*oADS*
Miriel	Angel – Shebat Angel – Mercury	*SR, BARC*
Miritno	Demon Senior	*SSM*
Mirotheos/Mirotheas	Gnostic Spirit – Realm Guide	*ACM*: NH Codex VII
Mirrih (Arabic) (Rubijail)	Angel – Mars	*SSG*
Mirus	Demon King, under Beymon	*KoN*
Misaēl	Angel	PGM IV:1716-1870
Misaou (Jupiter)	Jupiter – Alternative Name	*Hyg*
Miseton	Spirit	*CoC*
Misiel/Alisiel	Demon Duke – West Day	*Stg, ThG, BoTS*
Misig	Angel – Venus	*KoSR*
Misinall	Devil – Noon	*oADS*
Misoel	Angel – seven of twenty-one on the Left	*ACM*: Berlin 10587
Misoklēsous	Demon – West and Aries	*Hyg*
Missabis	Ministering Spirit – Saturn	*CBMS*
Missabu/Massabu	Angel Minister of Air – Monday	*Hmn, KoSR, GAG, BoTS, tM*
Missitone	Spirit	*tSoS*
Missyron/Myssyron	Spirit	*tSoS*
Mistal	Spirit	*MHN*
Mistalas/Mistolas	Demon – West	*BOS, BoO, oADS*
Misthan/Misan (Jupiter)	Jupiter – Alternative Name	*Hyg*
Misxmo	Demon Senior	*SSM*
Mitharens	Angel – Saturn	*GAG*
Mithiomo	Demon	*MHN*

ABBREVIATIONS

Mithra/Mithras	Roman Warrior God	PGM III:424-466, V:1-53, PDM Suppl. 185-208; *SM*: PSI I.28; *ACM*: MRN Amulet
Mitmon	Angel	*SMS*
Miton	Alternative name of Metatron	*SQ*
Mitraton/Merattron	Angel – Second Heaven Wednesday, West Presiding Spirit – Mercury	*EoN, Hmn, KoSR, BoO, GAG, BoTS, GV, tM, CBMS*
Mizabu	Spirit – Four Quarters of the Universal Mansions Spirit – Moon	*SGT, SSG*
Mizrael	Angel	*ACM*: Cairo EM 49547
Mizrael	Angel – Shem sixty	*KoSU, 3BOP, GoeR, JMR, SAS, tM*
Miztiel	Ministering Spirit – Jupiter	*CBMS*
Mizxaoul	Demon – West and Aries	*Hyg*
Mkmikal	Angel – Tenth Step, second Heaven	*ShR*
Mksabu	Angel – Fifth Step, second Heaven	*ShR*
Mksial	Angel – Seventh Encampment, first Heaven	*ShR*
Mlaga	Angel – Mercury/Wednesday	*SR*
Mlechial	Angel	*NA*
Mlgdm	Angel – Fifth Encampment, first Heaven	*ShR*
Mlkial	Angel – Second Encampment, first Heaven Angel – Fourth Encampment, first Heaven Angel – Fourth Step, second Heaven Angel Prince – fourth Heaven, Fire Angel Encampment Head – sixth Heaven, East	*ShR*
Mlkih	Angel – Fifth Encampment, first Heaven Angel – Third Heaven, serving Dtqial	*ShR*
Mlmial	Angel Encampment Head – sixth Heaven, East	*ShR*
Mltchial	Angel – Third Heaven, serving Ibnial	*ShR*
Mnasikōn	Angel	*Hyg*

Mnēdiēl/Mniēl/ Mēniēl/ Omniēl/Ēmiēl	Angel – Monday Hour seven	*Hyg*
Mnevis	Egyptian Bull God	PGM IV:2967-3006
Mnhal	Angel Prince – fourth Heaven, Water	*ShR*
Mnhral	Angel Encampment Head – sixth Heaven, East	*ShR*
Mnhyāl	Angel – Hour 1ten/Capricorn	*BoW*
Mnitial	Angel – Second Encampment, first Heaven	*ShR*
Mnmlk	Angel – Fifth Encampment, first Heaven	*ShR*
Mnurial	Angel Prince – fourth Heaven, Fire	*ShR*
Moas/Maos	Angel Minister – Love and Fornication Spirit – Minister of Love	*KoSA, oADS*
Mobabel	Wicked Spirit	*NMI*
Mobles	Vervain Herb Spirit	*BoO*
Moda	Spirit – fifth Mansion of the Moon Ring	*AE*
Modial	Angel Prince – East Gate	*SRH*
Modiat	Intelligence – Mercury	*SGT, SSG*
Modiel/Modyel	Angel – First Heaven, East Demon King under Beelzebub – West	*SSM, SR*
Mogarip	Spirit – Venus	*TV*
Mogron/Moigrōn	Demon – Saturday Hour twenty-three	*Hyg*
Moira (Moirai)	Greek Fate Triple Goddesses	PGM XIII:1-343, XIII:343-646, XVIIb:1-23; *ACM*: H. O. Lange Text
Mokaschef	Servant Spirit	*Abm*
Mol	Angel – Malachim, under Avorphenial	*SRH*
Molael	Demon Duke – North by East Night	*Stg, ThG*
Molbet	Demon Prince	*MHN*
Mole	Demon Prince	*GoPH*
Molech/Moloch	Canaanite God	HB Lev 18:26, 20:2-5, 2 Sam 23:10, 1 Kgs 11:7, Jer 32:35, Acts 7:43
Molin	Servant Spirit	*Abm*

Moloch	Ministering Familiar/Mystery Demon Prince	*ES, 67M, DI*
Moloy	Spirit	*MHN*
Momel/Moniel	Duke – West by North pre-Midnight	*Stg, ThG, BoTS*
Monael	Demon Duke – North-East	*Stg, ThG*
Monasiel	Angel – Day Hour one	*Stg, ArP*
Monego/Anego/Apnego	Spirit – tenth Mansion of the Moon Ring	*AE*
Monichion	Angel – Saturn/Saturday	*SR*
Monikonet	Demon – Thursday Hour fifteen	*Hyg*
Monosy	Angel – Fifth Altitude (Leo)	*Alm*
Montagin	Angel – Moon/Monday	*SR*
Montaginim	Angel – Moon	*LL*
Monteylyn	Angel – Mars/Tuesday	*SR*
Monto	Spirit – Air	*MNeI*
Montoaran (Venus)	Venus – Alternative Name	*Hyg*
Monyham	Angel	*NA, SBH*
Moracha	Demon Duke – Y1	*Stg, ThG*
Morael	Demon Duke – North Night	*Stg, ThG, BoTS*
Morail/Menail	Demon Duke	*SoS, GV*
Moral	Angel Prince – Alul	*SRH*
Morayeil	Angel – Venus/Friday	*SR*
Moreh/Morech/Merech	Servant Spirit	*Abm, MRC*
Moria/Mōria/Mōrēl/Mōriēl	Demon – Saturday Hour six	*Hyg*
Morias	Demon Duke – West Night	*Stg, ThG, BoTS*
Moriel	Demon Duke – South-East Night	*Stg, ThG, BoTS*
Morifiel	Spirit	*tSoS*
Morilon	Servant Spirit	*Abm*
Moroēs	Demon – West and Aries	*Hyg*
Morōth	Angel	*Hyg*
Morpheus	God – Opener of Dreams	*BoO*
Mortagon	Spirit	*SR*
Mortaliel	Demon Duke – Day Hour one	*Stg, ThG*

Mortaliel	Water Spirit	*MNeI*
Mortatalio	Spirit – seventh Mansion of the Moon ring	*tSoS*
Mortzē	Genius Loci	*Hyg*
Moru	Plant Spirit – Devil's Bit Scabious	*GS*
Mosacus	Spirit	*CBoM, BOS, BoO, oADS*
Moschel	Servant Spirit	*Abm*
Moson	Devil – Cancer, Storms	*OADS*
Mosul	Angel Minister	*ACM*: P. Mich. 593
Motar	Spirit	*Hyg*
Moth	Angel – Malachim, under Ayigeda	*SRH*
Motmyo	Demon	*MHN*
Motzeton	Angel	*Hyg*
Moubesouēl/ Moubeoul/ Mebiol/Mebioul/ Moubleou	Demon – West	*Hyg*
Moubnel	Demon Prince	*VJL*
Mounokhoth	Demon – West and Aries	*Hyg*
Mourkē	Angel – Friday Hour seven	*Hyg*
Mouriatha	Angel, sixth Heaven	PGM XXVI:1-42
Mou Rōph	Name of Helios in eleventh Hour	PGM IV:1596-1715
Moutokran (Venus)	Venus – Alternative Name	*Hyg*
Moyle	Demon Marquis	*BOS, BoO*
Moziel	Duke – West by North after Midnight	*Stg, ThG, BoTS*
Mparmparoēl	Demon- Moon	*Hyg*
Mpeltzampēl	Demon	*Hyg*
Mpiel	Demon	*Hyg*
Mpnial	Angel Prince – fifth Heaven, Month of Tevet	*ShR*
Mpnur	Angel – Fourth Step, second Heaven	*ShR*
Mqpa	Angel – Fifth Encampment, first Heaven	*ShR*
Mrbnial	Angel – Eighth Step, second Heaven	*ShR*
Mrgial	Angel – Eighth Step, second Heaven	*ShR*
Mrgywal	Angel Prince – Lower Four	*SoM*

Mrial	Angel Encampment Head – sixth Heaven, East	*ShR*
Mriut	Angel – Second Step, second Heaven	*ShR*
Mrmin	Angel Prince – fourth Heaven, Fire	*ShR*
Mrmraut	Angel Prince – fourth Heaven, Fire	*ShR*
Mrmrin	Angel – Seventh Encampment, first Heaven	*ShR*
Mrmual	Angel – Tenth Step, second Heaven	*ShR*
Mrnisal	Angel – Eighth Step, second Heaven	*ShR*
Mrsum	Angel – Second Encampment, first Heaven	*ShR*
Msgial	Angel Encampment Head – sixth Heaven, West	*ShR*
Mshtub	Angel – Second Encampment, first Heaven	*ShR*
Msrial	Angel – Third Heaven, serving Dlqial	*ShR*
Msrush	Angel – Fifth Encampment, first Heaven	*ShR*
Mtjayāl	Angel – Hour eight/Scorpio	*BoW*
Mtnal	Angel – Eighth Step, second Heaven	*ShR*
Mtnisl	Angel ruling Wild Beasts	*SoM*
Mual	Angel – First Encampment, first Heaven	*ShR*
Mucechediel	Angel – Jupiter	*KoSR*
Mudirel	Demon Chief Duke	*Stg, ThG*
Muguth	Spirit Attendant – Jupiter	*EoN*
Muhr (Shams, Persian)	Spirit King – Sun	*Pic*
Mukal	Angel Encampment Head – sixth Heaven, West	*ShR*
Muktial	Angel Prince – fourth Heaven, Fire	*ShR*
Mulcala	Angel – Moon	*GAG*
Mulciber	Spirit	*SSM*
Mulcifer	Terrestrial Spirit – Attendant in North	*SBH*
Mulpolder	Spirit	*BoTS*
Multas	Right part of Gharnos	*Pic*
Mumiah/Numiah	Angel – Shem seventy-two	*KoSU, 3BOP, GoeR, JMR, SAS, tM*
Mumtuel	Angel	*CBoM*
Munefiel	Demon Duke – Hour thirteen of fifteen	*Stg, ThG*

Muniuer	Spirit – Theft	KoN
Mupiel	Angel – Potestates	SST, 67M
Muracafel	Angel – Sun, over Water	SR
Murahe/Marale	Demon Duke – North by East Night	Stg, ThG
Mural	Angel Prince – fifth Heaven, Month of Elul	ShR
Murath	Spirit – first Mansion of Moon Ring	AE
Mureril	Treasure Spirit	BoTS
Mures	Spirit – Irritates Men	oADS
Muriel/Murid	Angel – Wednesday, Moon, Cancer Genus – Populus, Via	KoSR, MHN, 3BOP, tSoS, MC, JMR, SaS, Thm, tM
Murion	Angel – Saturn/Saturday	SR
Murmur/Murmus	Demon Duke and Earl	SSM, PmD, DoW, Goe
Muron	Woodland Spirit	BoO, GAG
Murophael	Angel	ACM: Oriental 5899
Murroo	Plant Spirit – Poppy	GS
Mursiel	Demon Duke – Y2	Stg, ThG
Mursiel	Angel – Day Hour three	Stg, ArP
Murus/Mirus/Nurus	Spirit	oADS
Muryell	Demon – North	BOS, BoO, oADS
Mus	Angel – Fifth Encampment, first Heaven	ShR
Musas	Spirit – Irritates Men	oADS
Musasin/Musifin/Musofin/Musisin/Resochin/Rosochim/Roschim (Reschin)	Demon – under Sirach	KoSU, GV
Muscon	Angel – Second Heaven, West	SaS
Musdali	Spirit	GAG
Mushial	Angel – Third Heaven, serving Rhtial	ShR
Mushtary (Rafael, Arabic)	Spirit King – Jupiter	Pic
Musiniel	Demon Duke – Day Hour twelve	Stg, ThG
Musiriel	Demon Duke – West	Stg, ThG
Musor	Demon Duke – North by East Day	Stg, ThG
Mustalfiel	Spirit – Venus	SoS

ABBREVIATIONS   553

Mustari (Arabic) (Rufijail)	Angel – Jupiter	*SSG*
Musuziel/Musiel	Demon Duke – Day Hour four	*Stg, ThG*
Musuziel	Water Spirit	*MNeI*
Mut	Egyptian Mother Goddess	PDM XIV:1026-1045
Mutar	Angel – Second Encampment, first Heaven	*ShR*
Mutheon	Spirit	*KoN*
Mutuel	Angel	*CBoM*
Muviel	Genii – 19° Leo	*ArP*
Myamayon	Angel – three Signs of Spring	*SSM*
Mycahe	Angel – Sun/Sunday	*SR*
Mychael/Mychaell (Michael?)	Spirit – Mercury Spirit	*SBH, oADS*
Mycrathon	Angel Subordinate – Saturn	*SSM*
Mydisyn	Spirit of the Thumb	*CBoM*
Myel/Myhel/Mihel/Miel/Myhell	Angel – Mercury Spirit – Mercury	*SSM, SBH, oADS*
Myhimyāyl/Mthmyāyl	Angel – April/Aries	*BoW*
Myhon	Angel	*NA*
Myhotheophy	Angel	*NA*
Myiasaleti/Myiasalet	Spirit – Mars	*BoO, GAG*
Mylalu	Punishing Wind	*SSM*
Mylalua	Angel – Sunday	*BoO*
Mylay	Spirit Helper – Monday	*CBoM*
Mylba	Angel – Second Heaven, South	*SR*
Mylin/Moli/Mōlē/Mely/Molen	Demon – Froday Hour twenty	*Hyg*
Mylon	Spirit Familiar	*BoTS*
Mylu (Missabu?)	Angel Minister of Air – Monday	*BoO*
Mynaēl/Minaēl	Angel – Monday Hour 1ten	*Hyg*
Mynuel	Angel – Third Altitude (Gemini)	*Alm*
Mynymarup	Servant Spirit	*Abm*
Myraan (Jupiter)	Jupiter – Alternative Name	*Hyg*

Myrabany	Demon Minister – Beelzebub	*SSM*
Myragkous/ Miragkous/ Myrakos	Demon	*ToSC*
Myratziel/Miratzeel/ Myrakiel	Demon	*ToSC*
Myretagyl	Angel	*NA*
Myrezyn/Myresyn	Demon Duke – East	*Stg, ThG*
Myriel	Angel – Fire	*SR*
Myrmo	Servant Spirit	*Abm*
Myron	Spirit – Forest	*oADS*
Mysahel	Angel	*NA*
Myschiel	Angel – Shebat	*SR*
Mysealos	Demon Senior	*SSM*
Myssa	Angel – Elul	*SR*
Myssyron/Messyron	Spirit – Woods	*oADS*
Mzpwpyasayal	Angel Prince – Angels of Anger	*SoM*

N		
Na	Angel Prince	*SRH*
Naaa	Enochian Angel – South, over second lesser Angle	*TBA*
Naadob	Daemon – Jupiter, serving North and East Winds; between East and South	*SBH*
Naadol	Wind Spirit	*GAG*
Naadop	Punishing Wind	*SSM*
Naajah	Genii – 6° Capricorn, 6° Aquarius	*ArP*
Naamab	Angel – Sivan	*SR*
Naamwsnyqttyal	Angel Prince – Angels of Fury	*SoM*
Naanh	Angel – First Encampment, first Heaven	*ShR*
Naarach	Spirit – North	*SSM*
Naaral	Spirit – Middle	*SSM*
Naasa	Daemon – Venus, subject to East and West Winds; between South and West	*SBH*
Naasien	Angel – Sivan	*SR*
Naassah	Punishing Wind	*SSM*

Nabadiel	Angel – Fourth Heaven, South	*EoN*
Nabam/Nabara	Demon – Saturday	*GoPH*
Nabbasr/Nabbas	Spirit	*BoO*
Nabedikaio	Angel	*Hyg*
Nabel/Nabal	Demon	*ToSC*
Naberius/Naberus/ Nuberus/Cerberus/ Nabirus/Nibiros	Demon Marquis Demon Field Marshal	*PmD, DoW, Goe, GV, GG, BoSC*
Nabhi	Servant Spirit	*Abm, MRC*
Nabiafilyn	Angel – Mercury/Wednesday	*SR*
Naboon	Angel – Sivan	*SR*
Naboutan	Spirit	*Hyg*
Nabrishotht	Cherub of Amenti	PDM XIV:395-437
Nabuel	Angel – Marchesvan	*SR*
Nabyalni	Angel – Moon/Monday	*SR*
Nacbadyel	Angel – Fifth Heaven, South	*SSM*
Naccamarif	Angel – Elul	*SR*
Nacery	Angel – Elul	*SR*
Nachal	Angel – Ab	*SR*
Nacheran	Servant Spirit	*Abm*
Nachiel	Planetary Intelligence – Sun	*KoSR, 3BOP, BM, PO, tM*
Naco	Enochian Angel – East, serving third lesser Angle	*TBA*
Nactif	Angel – Ab	*SR*
Nadanniel (Lucifer)	Exiled Angel	*MNeI*
Nadel	Demon – South	*GoPH*
Nadib	Angel – Iyar	*SR*
Nadibael	Angel – Marchesvan	*SR*
Nadrel	Demon Duke – East	*Stg, ThG*
Nadriel/Madriel	Angel – Day Hour nine	*Stg, ArP*
Nadroc/Madrock/ Nadros	Demon Duke – West	*Stg, ThG, BoTS*
Nadrusiel/Nadusiel	Demon Duke – Y1	*Stg, ThG*
Naduch	Angel – Kislev	*SR*
Nael	Angel – Fifth Heaven, West	*SaS*

Naema	Demon – West	*GoPH*
Naendōr (Mercury)	Mercury – Alternative Name	*Hyg*
Næoa	Enochian Angel – North, over third lesser Angle	*TBA*
Nafac	Angel – Elul	*SR*
Naffrynyn	Angel – Mars/Tuesday	*SR*
Nafhyyel	Angel – Fifth Heaven, South	*SSM*
Naflia	Angel – Tebet	*SR*
Nagael	Genii – 2° Gemini	*ArP*
Nagan	Servant Spirit	*Abm*
Nagani	Servant Spirit	*Abm*
Nagar	Servant Spirit	*Abm*
Nagi	Demon – East	*Hyg*
Nagid	Servant Spirit	*Abm*
Nagiēl	Angel – Saturday Hour twenty-one	*Hyg*
Nagnuel	Angel – First Heaven, South	*SSM*
Nagrow	Angel – Tammuz	*SR*
Nahiel/Naliel/Nachiel	Duke – West by North pre-Midnight	*Stg, ThG, BoTS*
Nahymel	Angel – First Heaven, South	*SR, SaS*
Naias Meli	Highest God	*ACM*: Oslo 1.5
Naith	Spirit – eighth Mansion of the Moon ring	*tSoS*
Nakhmarēl/Nēkhmarēl	Spirit	*BoW*
Nakhoēl/Nakhōēl/Nakhiēl	Angel – Tuesday Hour eleven	*Hyg*
Nakistos/Kakiston/Kakistōn	Demon – Tuesday Hour one	*Hyg*
Nalael	Demon Duke – North by East Night	*Stg, ThG*
Nalapa	Angel – Thursday/Jupiter	*KoSR*
Naletoritin	Spirit	*CoC*
Nalkatan	Angel – Day Hour two	*LL*
Naltrothothr	Spirit	*ACM*: Cairo 45060
Namael	Angel – Night Hour twelve	*Stg, ArP*
Namalon	Servant Spirit	*Abm*
Namath	Spirit	*CBoM, oADS*

Nambrot/Nambroth/ Nimbroth	Demon King – Tuesday / Saturday Demon Baron – Libya and Mount Etna	*3BOP, GoPH*
Nameal	Angel – Night Hour nine	*Stg, ArP*
Namedor/ Namendor/ Ivamendor	Angel – Night Hour six	*Stg, ArP*
Namer	Spirit	*ACM*: Hay 10391
Nameron	Angel – Day Hour ten	*Stg, ArP*
Nameroyz/ Nameroizod	Angel – Night Hour ten	*Stg, ArP*
Nameton/Namelon	Angel – Night Hour five	*Stg, ArP*
Namil	Spirit	*ArPh*
Namiros	Servant Spirit	*Abm*
Namut	Demon	*GoPH*
Nanael/Nauael	Angel – Shem fifty-three	*KoSU, 3BOP, GoeR, JMR, SAS, tM*
Nangareryn	Angel – Moon/Monday	*SR*
Nanea	Mesopotamian Goddess of Love and War	HB 2 Mac 1:13, 1:15
Nanoel	Spirit – Dawn	*ACM*: L. Anastasi 9
Nanylin	Angel – Venus/Friday	*SR*
Naoth/Nathath	Demon – Decan nineteen	*ToS*
Naououēl/Natoēl/ Natouēl/Oenotoēl	Angel – Sunday Hour sixteen	*Hyg*
Nap	Angel – Marchesvan	*SR*
Napalaikon/ Nampalaikon	Demon	*ToSC*
Nape	Demon Prince	*GoPH*
Naphaēl	Angel	*Hyg*
Naphael	Genii – 5° Scorpio, 5° Sagittarius	*ArP*
Napour	Demon	*ToSC*
Narael	Spirit – King of Luck	*MNeI*
Naras	Demon Duke – South by West Day	*Stg, ThG, BoTS*
Narbell	Angel – Mars/Tuesday	*SR*
Narcoriel/Narcriel	Angel Ruler – Night Hour eight	*Stg, ArP*
Nariēl	Angel	PGM XXXVI:161-177

Naris/Nares	Spirit Lord Devil Spirit – over Dead	*CoC, oADS, tSoS*
Narkisou	Demon – West and Aries	*Hyg*
Narmiel	Demon Duke	*Stg, ThG*
Naromiel/Naroniel	Angel – Fourth Heaven Sunday, South, Spring Angel – Fourth Heaven, South	*Hmn, KoSR, BoO, BoTS, SaS, tM*
Naromiel	Intelligence – Moon	*SGT, SSG*
Narp	Spirit	*BoTS*
Narsial/Narsiel	Duke – West by North after Midnight	*Stg, ThG, BoTS*
Nartim/Siartin	Demon	*MHN, NML*
Narzael/Narzal	Demon Duke – North by East Night	*Stg, ThG*
Nasael	Genii – 3° Virgo	*ArP*
Nasar	Angel Minister of Air – Friday	*BoO*
Nasatz	Demon Servant – Friday	*KoN*
Nascelon	Servant Spirit	*Abm*
Nasi	Servant Spirit	*Abm*
Nasiniel	Demon Duke – Day Hour eight	*Stg, ThG*
Nasmyel	Angel – Bisertilis	*SR*
Nasolico	Servant Spirit	*Abm*
Naspaya	Angel – Tebet	*SR*
Naspiel	Angel – Marchesvan	*SR*
Nassa	Angel – Elul	*SR*
Nassar	Punishing Wind Daemon Minister – Venus Daemon subject to East and West Winds; between South and West	*SSM, SBH*
Nassar/Massak	Demon Duke – North-East	*Stg, ThG*
Nassam	Angel – Shebat	*SR*
Nassath	Spirit Assistant – Friday	*MHN*
Nastiafori	Angel – Nisan	*SR, tSoS*
Nastoriel	Angel – Night Hour eleven	*Stg, ArP*
Nastrator	Angel	*BoSC*
Nastros	Demon Duke – Night Hour twelve	*Stg, ThG*
Nastros	Earth Spirit	*MNeI*

Nastrus/Naustrus	Angel – Day Hour seven	*Stg, ArP*
Nastul	Angel – Night Hour one	*Stg, ArP*
Nasyel	Angel – Shebat	*SR*
Nata	Angel – Moon	*GAG*
Natales	Servant Spirit	*Abm*
Nathael	Spirit – Alchemy, West	*KoN*
Nathan	Angel – Second Heaven, East	*SaS*
Nathan	Demon Prince – Water	*oADS*
Nathanael	Angel	*ACM*: Yale 1013A
Nathanel	Demon Prince – South-East	*SSM*
Nathaniel (Seruph)	Angel President – Fire	*JMR, SaS*
Nathasiel	Angel – Fourth Heaven, South	*EoN*
Natheel	Genii – 11° Aries	*ArP*
Natheus	Demon Prince	*MHN*
Nathmiel/Nathniel	Angel – Day Hour six	*Stg, ArP*
Nathomyel	Angel – Fifth Heaven, South	*SSM*
Nathriel	Demon Duke – Hour nine of fifteen	*Stg, ThG*
Natriel	Angel – Shebat	*SR*
Nauagen/Navagen	Angel	*NA, SBH*
Naurstic/Muinstich	Spirit – seventh Mansion of the Moon Ring	*AE*
Naveriel	Angel – Night Hour twelve	*Stg, ArP*
Naveron	Angel – Day Hour ten	*Stg, ArP*
Naveroz/Mavezoz	Angel – Night Hour eleven	*Stg, ArP*
Naviel	Genii – 4° Libra	*ArP*
Navis	Demon	*oADS*
Naxas	Angel – Marchesvan	*SR*
Nayzaday	Angel – Ninth Altitude (Sagittarius)	*Alm*
Nbimal	Angel Prince – fourth Heaven, Water	*ShR*
Nbrial	Angel Prince – fourth Heaven, Water	*ShR*
Nchlial	Angel – Sixth Encampment, first Heaven	*ShR*
Neael	Angel – Mansion eleven and Leo	*BoO*
Nchlial	Angel – Third Heaven, serving Dlqial	*ShR*
Nearach	Servant Spirit	*Abm*
Neater	Spirit	*ACM*: Cairo 45060

Neban	Spirit – Saturday	*BoSC*
Neberial	Spirit – Autumn	*SRH*
Nebirots/Nebiros	Demon – Saturday	*GoPH, GG, GV*
Nebo (Nabu)	Babylonian Vegetation God	HB Isa 46:1
Nebound	Angel – Lunar, Night Hour two	PGM VII:862-918
Neboutosoualēth	Light-Bringing Goddess, Epithet of Hekate	PDM XIV:93-114
Nebubael	Angel – Marchesvan	*SR*
Necamach	Spirit – West	*SSM*
Necamia/Necamya	Angel – Nisan	*SR, tSoS*
Necanyael	Angel – Jupiter, over Fire	*SR*
Necariel	Superior Intelligence	*KoSU*
Necesolap	Spirit – Minister of Love	*oADS*
Nechelial	Angel – Malachim, under Pheseker Angel – Malachim, sixth Host	*SRH*
Nechemial	Angel Prince – Gate of Spirit of South	*SRH*
Nechiel	Angel	*ACM*: BN Turin
Nechorym/Nechorin/Necorin/Nechoxin	Angel – Night Hour five	*Stg, ArP*
Necif	Angel – Ab	*SR*
Necopolitas	Angel Minister – Love and Fornication	*KoSA*
Nector	Spirit – Air	*MNeI*
Necyl	Angel – Sun/Sunday	*SR*
Nedabor/Nedabar	Angel – Day Hour six	*Stg, ArP*
Nedarym/Nedarim	Angel – Night Hour eight	*Stg, ArP*
Nediter	Angel – Tammuz	*SR*
Nedriel	Demon Duke – Night Hour six Demon Under Chief	*Stg, ThG*
Nedriel	Earth Spirit	*MNeI*
Nedroz/Nedros	Angel – Night Hour two	*Stg, ArP*
Nedruan/Jvedruan/Nedrum	Angel – Night Hour four	*Stg, ArP*
Nefarym/Nefarin/Nesarin	Angel – Day Hour nine	*Stg, ArP*
Nefthada	Demon – Decan twenty-three	*ToS*
Nefrias/Nefryas	Angel – Night Hour twelve	*Stg, ArP*

Negen	Servant Spirit	*Abm*
Negmos/Nēgmos/ Nygmos/Ougmos	Demon – Sunday Hour fifteen	*Hyg*
Negri	Angel – Tebet	*SR*
Nehenal	Angel Prince – Deliverance of the Lord	*SRH*
Nehilim	Angel – Moon	*LL*
Neiciab	Spirit Minister, serving Prince Bornogo	*dHM*
Neilin	Angel – Moon	*LL*
Neith	Egyptian War Goddess	PGM VII:335-347, XIXa:1-54; *SM*: P. Oxy. LVI.3834
Nekebedial	Angel Prince – Gate of Spirit of South	*SRH*
Nelapa/Nelipa	Angel – Second Heaven Wednesday, South	*EoN, Hmn, KoSR, BoO, GAG, BoTS, SaS, tM*
Nelchael/Nolchael	Angel – Shem twenty-one	*KoSU, 3BOP, GoeR, JMR, SAS, tM*
Nelēphel (Mercury)	Mercury - Alternative Name	*Hyg*
Nelia/Nelya	Angel – Second Heaven, South	*SR, SSM*
Neliel	Genii – 2° Pisces	*ArP*
Nelion	Spirit	*MRC*
Nemamiah/ Nemaniah	Angel – Shem fifty-seven	*KoSU, 3BOP, GoeR, JMR, SAS, tM*
Nemariel	Demon Knight	*Stg, ThG*
Nembro	Spirit – Wedneday	*BoSC*
Nemelial	Angel – Summer	*SRH*
Nemesis	Greek Goddess of Retribution	PGM VII:490-504
Nemesis	Spirit – Retribution	*BP*
Nemetzial	Angel – Malachim, Tammuz, Summer	*SRH*
Nemon	Demon	*GoPH*
Nemormoth	Angel – Lunar, Night Hour four	PGM VII:862-918
Nemouēl	Angel	PGM CXXIIIa:1-70
Nenael	Angel – Second Heaven, North	*SR, SSM*
Nenal	Angel Prince – North Gate, Firmament	*SRH*
Nenel	Angel – Second Heaven, North	*SR*
Nenetosh	Angel Prince	*SRH*

Neonem	Spirit Prince	oADS
Neophon/Neaphan	Demon – East	BOS, BoO, oADS
Neotpta	Spirit Minister, serving Prince Befafes	dHM
Nepenielin	Angel – Moon/Monday	SR
Nephael	Angel over Aid	ACM: BN Turin
Nēphan (Mercury)	Mercury – Alternative Name	Hyg
Nēphdahpid/ Ntadadiph/ Ētadiadiph	Demon – Wednesday Hour five	Hyg
Nephelial	Angel Prince – Gate of Spirit of South	SRH
Nepheriēri	Name of Aphrodite	PGM IV:1265-1274
Nephro	Plant Spirit – Corn Poppy	GS
Nephthys/Nephtho	Egyptian Protective Goddess	PGM IV:94-153, XIa:1-40, XXIII:1-70; PDM XII:21-49, XIV:1-92, XIV:239-295, XIV:1219-1227, LXI:100-105, Suppl. 130-138, Suppl. 138-149; SM: P. Berol. Inv. 21243; ACM: Berlin 5565
Nephyel	Angel – Saturn, over Air	SR
Nēprodoukh	Demon – West	Hyg
Neptune	God – Seas and Waters	BoO
Neqerial	Angel Prince – South Gate, Firmament	SRH
Neqial	Angel – Malachim, under Ayigeda	SRH
Neqiyet	Angel Minister – Malachim, over Water	SRH
Nerad	Angel – Kislev	SR
Nerael	Biblical Elder	ACM: Berlin 11347, Oriental 6796
Nerastiel/Nerostiel	Angel – Day Hour twelve	Stg, ArP
Neraziel	Angel – Venus, over Air	SR
Nereus	Spirit – Reviver of Dead	oADS
Neriel/Neriol	Demon Duke – South-East Day	Stg, ThG, BoTS
Nermas/Hermas	Angel – Night Hour eleven	Stg, ArP
Nerolo	Spirit – Minister of Love	oADS

Nerombel	Angel	*KoSA*
Nerone	Spirit	*KoN*
Neront	Demon	*GoPH*
Nerotheq	Angel – Malachim, under Avorphenial	*SRH*
Nesamach	Spirit	*SSM*
Nesanel/Nesanel	Angel	*SoM*
Nesaph	Punishing Wind Daemon – Jupiter, serving North and East Winds; between East and South	*SSM, SBH*
Nesbiros/Nebiros (Resbiroth?)	Demon	*GG, GV*
Neschamah	Servant Spirit	*Abm*
Nesdol	Spirit	*BoW*
Neseliēl/Seliēl/Seliniēl	Angel – Friday Hour five	*Hyg*
Nesisen	Servant Spirit	*Abm*
Nesquiraf	Angel – Ab	*SR*
Nestorat	False Spirit – Lord of Love	*MNeI*
Nestorath	Spirit – East	*KoN*
Nestori	Angel – Day Hour seven	*Stg, ArP*
Nestoriel/Nestorel	Angel – Day Hour one, Night Hour twelve	*Stg, ArP*
Nestoros/Nestozoz/Neztozoz	Angel – Night Hour three	*Stg, ArP*
Neszomy/Neszomi	Angel – Night Hour five	*Stg, ArP*
Netheleba	Angel Prince	*SRH*
Nethenal	Angel – Malachim, under Avorphenial	*SRH*
Nethenial	Angel – Malachim, under Avorphenial	*SRH*
Neurim	Angel Minister – Love and Fornication	*KoSA*
Neyeyl	Angel – Sun/Sunday	*SR*
Neyilon	Spirit	*MHN*
Neysa	Angel	*NA*
Nezal	Angel	*SRH*
Nezeral	Angel	*SRH*
Nhial	Angel – Second Encampment, first Heaven	*ShR*
Niar (Mercury)	Mercury – Alternative Name	*Hyg*

Nicon	Demon – Bringer of Calamity/ Instigator of Misfortune Demon – Telchine	3BOP, MNeI, tM
Nidar	Spirit	GV
Nier/Nietz (Jupiter)	Jupiter – Alternative Name	Hyg
Niemiesem	Angel – Malachim, under Pheseker	SRH
Nieriel/Nierier	Demon – Thursday Hour twenty-one	Hyg
Nierier	Demon – Thursday Hour twenty	Hyg
Nigam	Planetary Spirit – Jupiter	SSM
Nigrieph/Nigrisph	Demon – Saturday Hour twenty-three, twenty-four	Hyg
Nigrophol	Demon	Hyg
Nikem/Nekem/ Enikym/ Enikēm	Demon – Saturday Hour five	Hyg
Nikokip/Nikokep	Demon – Thursday Hour fifteen	Hyg
Nikōn	Demon – Sunday Hour fifteen	Hyg
Nikote/Nikotel/ Nēkote	Demon – West	Hyg
Niktidōn	Demon – Monday Hour eleven	Hyg
Nilima	Servant Spirit	Abm
Nilion	Servant Spirit	Abm
Niloportas	Spirit – Minister of Love	oADS
Nimalon	Servant Spirit	Abm
Nimirix	Servant Spirit	Abm
Nimmus	Angel – Sixth Encampment, first Heaven	ShR
Nimrod	Demon – Tuesday	GoPH
Nintiaph	Demon – Sunday Hour sixteen	Hyg
Ninshia	Angel – Fifth Encampment, first Heaven	ShR
Niōekh	Demon – Monday Hour nineteen	Hyg
Niokhel/Niokkh	Demon – Monday Hour eighteen	Hyg
Niophryn	Spirit – Presidential Counsellor	BoTS
Niphōn/Nyphōn/ Nēphōn/Nephron	Demon – Friday Hour seventeen	Hyg
Niplial	Angel Encampment Head – sixth Heaven, East	ShR
Niron	Infernal Spirit	CBoM

Nisa	Spirit	*GV*
Nisroch	Assyrian Agriculture God	HB 2 Kgs 19:37, Isa 37:38
Nisroch	Ministering Familiar/Mystery	*67M*
Nistik/Nestibe/ Nēsta/ Nysteba	Demon – Sunday Hour eleven	*Hyg*
Nithael	Angel – Shem fifty-four	*KoSU, 3BOP, GoeR, JMR, SAS, tM*
Nithhajah/Nithlajah/ Nithhaiah/Nitahia	Angel – Shem twenty-five	*KoSU, 3BOP, GoeR, JMR, SAS, tM*
Nitisilom (Sun)	Sun – Alternative Name	*Hyg*
Nitriaphi/Netriaph/ Nēstriaph/Nētriaphrē	Demon – Sunday Hour seventeen	*Hyg*
Niva	Spirit – Jupiter	*67M*
Njordhr	Norse Sea God	*Gbk*
Nkbrial	Angel Prince – fourth Heaven, Water	*ShR*
Nkmra	Angel – Third Heaven, serving Rhtial	ShR
Nlinzvb	Spirit Minister, serving Prince Blisdon	*dHM*
Nllrlna	Spirit Minister, serving King Baligon	*dHM*
Nmdial	Angel – Third Heaven, serving Ibnial	*ShR*
Nnrial	Angel Encampment Head – sixth Heaven, West	*ShR*
Noaphoras	Angel Minister – Love and Fornication	*KoSA*
Nōapōkh/ Nouapōkh/ Nouopokh	Demon – West	*Hyg*
Noard	Spirit	*GV*
Nobquin	Angel – Fourth Heaven, West	*SR*
Noch/Choth	Spirit – twentieth Mansion of the Moon Ring	*AE*
Nocpis	Angel – Iyar	*SR*
Nocte	Spirit – Book Making	*oADS*
Nodar	Demon Duke – South-East Day/Night	*Stg, ThG, BoTS*
Noddarding	Spirit	*BoTS*
Nodeh	Angel Minister – Malachim	*SRH*
Nodial	Angel – Malachim, under Ayigeda	*SRH*

Noeiel/Neciel	Angel – Mansion eleven	3BOP, tSoS, JMR. SaS, tM
Noelma	Spirit	GV
Noga	Angel Minister – Love and Fornication	KoSA
Nogael	Archangel	9CK
Nogah	Servant Spirit	Abm
Nogariel	Spirit – Venus	VMN
Nogathiel/Nogahel (Anael)	Archangel – Venus	3BOP, BoO, tSoS, JMR, SaS
Noguiel/Noquiel	Demon Duke – West by South Night	Stg, ThG, BoTS
Noherial	Angel Prince – Gate of Spirit of East	SRH
Nohetial	Angel – Malachim over Rain	SRH
Nokhoēl	Angel – Tuesday Hour ten	Hyg
Nokt (Mars)	Mars – Alternative Name	Hyg
Nolegedod	Spirit – North in Autumn	SRH
Noliem/Noliel (Mars)	Mars – Alternative Name	Hyg
Nolom	Servant Spirit	Abm
Nomēn/Nokēn (Mercury)	Mercury – Alternative Name	Hyg
Nomimon	Servant Spirit	Abm
Non	Spirit	MHN
Nona	Demon – West	Hyg
Nonanrin	Angel – Venus/Friday	SR
Nonis	Spirit – Book Making	oADS
Noocar	Demon Lord	BOS, BoO
Noonman	Spirit Minister, serving Prince Befafes	dHM
Noraraabilin	Angel – Venus/Friday	SR
Noredial	Angel – Malachim, sixth Host	SRH
Noreh	Angel – Malachim, Flames of Fire	SRH
Noreil	Angel – Day Hour two	LL
Norial	Angel – Malachim over Fire and Flames Angel Prince – Gate of Spirit of East Angel Prince – Spring	SRH
Noriel/Moriel	Angel Ruler – Tammuz	SR
Noryel	Angel – Fire	SSM

Noryoth/Moryoth/Norioth	Demon	*MHN, NML*
Nossor	Beast before God (third of six)	*oADS*
Nostrasil	Angel Minister – Love and Fornication	*KoSA*
Noth	Angel	*KoSA*
Notheneh	Angel – Malachim, under Avorphenial	*SRH*
Notiōliosēm/Notiliōseis/Nopliosēm (Sun)	Sun – Alternative Name	*Hyg*
Notison	Servant Spirit	*Abm*
Notterorigal	Angel Governor – third Season by Night	*SSM*
Notus	South Wind	*BoTS*
Nouēl	Spirit	*BoW*
Nouēt (Mars)	Mars – Alternative Name	*Hyg*
Nouphiēr	Angel – Lunar, Night Hour five	PGM VII:862-918
Nourêl/Nouriel	Angel	*SM*: P. Med. I.20, *Hyg*
Nous/Phrenes	God of Mind/Wits	PGM XIII:1-343, XIII:343-646
Noxarata	Spirit – Minister of Love	*oADS*
Npli	Angel Prince – fourth Heaven, Fire	*ShR*
Nppmiut	Angel – Eleventh Step, second Heaven	*ShR*
Nqrial	Angel – Fifth Step, second Heaven	*ShR*
Nrhal	Angel Encampment Head – sixth Heaven, West	*ShR*
Nrntq	Angel – First Encampment, first Heaven	*ShR*
Nrpcrrb	Spirit Minister, serving Prince Blisdon	*dHM*
Nrrcprn	Spirit Minister, serving Prince Hagonel	*dHM*
Nrsogoo	Spirit Minister, serving Prince Hagonel	*dHM*
Nrumial	Angel Prince – fourth Heaven, Fire	*ShR*
Nsbrial	Angel Prince – fourth Heaven, Fire	*ShR*
Nshchial	Angel – Ninth Step, second Heaven	*ShR*
Nshmial	Angel – Second Step, second Heaven	*ShR*
Nshr	Angel – Fifth Encampment, first Heaven	*ShR*
Ntasamō	Demon	*Hyg*

Ntekhariz/ Ntekharigx	Angel – Saturday Hour eleven	Hyg
Ntial	Angel – First Encampment, first Heaven	ShR
Ntnal	Angel – First Encampment, first Heaven	ShR
Ntpial	Angel – Second Encampment, first Heaven	ShR
Ntyāl	Angel – Hour eleven/Aquarius, Sun	BoW
Nubar	Demon	MHN
Nudeton/Nudaton	Servant Spirit	Abm, MRC
Nudniia	Angel – Sixth Encampment, first Heaven	ShR
Nuduch/Andrialfis Paelsis (Andrealphus)	Demon	NML
Nuhrial	Angel – Seventh Encampment, first Heaven	ShR
Nuit/Nut (Mother of Gods)	Egyptian Goddess of Heavens	PGM XII:201-269, PDM XIV:150-231, XIV:295-308, XIV:805-840
Nuleby	Demon Servant – Sunday	KoN
Nulha	Angel – Second Heaven, South	SSM
Nurial	Angel Prince – fourth Heaven, Fire	ShR
Nuscita	Angel – Sivan	SR
Nyahpatuel	Angel – Adar	SR
Nybbas	Demon Dream and Vision Manager	DI
Nybiel	Angel – Saturn, over Fire	SR
Nybirin	Angel – Mars/Tuesday	SR
Nyktedon	Demon – Monday Hour ten	Hyg
Nyktidōn/Niktidōn/ Nyktēdon	Demon – Monday Hour twelve, thirteen, fourteen	Hyg
Nyphan (Mercury)	Mercury – Alternative Name	Hyg
Nyrysin	Angel – Mars/Tuesday	SR
Nyssan	Angel – Nisan	tSoS

O		
Oamna	Spirit of the Thumb	CBoM
Oanæ	Enochian Angel – North, over third lesser Angle	TBA

Obach	Spirit – Air over Ocean	*SM*: T Köln inv.7
Obagiron	Servant Spirit	*Abm*
Obedamah	Servant Spirit	*Abm*
Oberion/Oberyon/ Oberon/Obyron/ Obriun	Fairy King Demon King – Sun and Moon	*BOS, BoO, CoC, GAG, oADS, BoTS*
Obizuth	Demon	*ToS*
Obnala	Angel – Saturn	*GAG*
Oboel	Angel – Saturn	*SSM*
Obohees	Spirit – Love/Sexual Attraction	*Pic*
Obtablat	Spirit – third Mansion of Moon Ring	*tSoS*
Obymero/Abrinno	Angel – Book Writer	*BoO*
Ocarat/Cyrorax	Angel – Sun	*B7R*
Ocarbydatonn/ Ocarcydaton/ Ocarbidaton	Demon Messenger – South Spirit Messenger – South	*BOS, BoO, BoTS*
Ocbelia	Spirit – Venus	*VMN*
Ocel	Demon	*MHN*
Ocenem	Enochian Angel – East, serving third lesser Angle	*TBA*
Och	Olympic Spirit – Sun	*KoSR, Arb, MC, GAG, JMR, MNeI, oADS, KoN, GoA, PO, ClI, 67M, SGT, SSG*
Ochael	Angel	*ACM*: Oriental 5899
Ochiel/Othiel	Demon Duke – South by East Night	*Stg, ThG, BoTS*
Odac	Servant Spirit	*Abm*
Odail	Demon – North	*GoPH*
Odan	Demon – North	*Hyg*
Odauan/Odanan	Spirit – Sun	*BoO, GAG*
Odēl/Odie (Saturn)	Saturn – Alternative Name	*Hyg*
Odhinn	Norse All-Father God	*Gbk*
Odiel	Demon Duke – South by East Night	*Stg, ThG, BoTS*
Odingeo	Treasure Spirit	*oADS*
Odrael	Angel – First Heaven, East	*SR*
Odymon	Angel – Sun	*BARC*
Ödyr (Mars)	Mars – Alternative Name	*Hyg*

Oeeooez	Spirit Minister, serving King Baligon	*dHM*
Oel	Demon	*ToSC*
Oemiel/Oeniel	Demon Duke – North-East	*Stg*, *ThG*
Oēniēl	Angel – Tuesday Hour twelve	*Hyg*
Oesengle	Spirit Minister, serving Prince Hagonel	*dHM*
Ofel (Ophiel?)	Spirit – Jupiter	*67M*
Offriel	Demon	*GAG*
Ofisiel/Ofisel/Osysiel	Duke – West by North pre-Midnight	*Stg*, *ThG*, *BoTS*
Ogologon	Servant Spirit	*Abm*
Ogya	Demon Prince	*BOS*, *BoO*
Oha	Spirit of the Thumb	*CBoM*
Ohereo/Ohere	Spirit of the Thumb	*MHN*, *CBoM*
Ohorma	Spirit – Mars	*BoO*, *GAG*
Ohotam	Servant Spirit	*Abm*
Oiphal	Demon – South	*Hyg*
Oiphalmianethi	Demon – South	*Hyg*
Oitos	Angel	*Hyg*
Okēēl	Angel – Tuesday Hour twelve	*Hyg*
Ōketar/Okytar	Demon – Saturday Hour eighteen	*Hyg*
Okhlor/Okhlos/ Okhlios/ Hokhlos	Demon – Thursday Hour two	*Hyg*
Okirgi/Akirgi/Akrey	Servant Spirit	*Abm*
Oklokiēl	Demon – Mercury	*Hyg*
Oknan	Angel – Tuesday Hour twelve	*Hyg*
Okokes/Akokeph	Demon – Thursday Hour thirteen	*Hyg*
Okpē/Oket (Saturn)	Saturn – Alternative Name	*Hyg*
Okritera	Demon – Saturday Hour nineteen	*Hyg*
Oktiel	Angel	*Hyg*
Ol	Angel – Leo	*ArP*
Olabēr (Jupiter)	Jupiter – Alternative Name	*Hyg*
Olalborim	Angel – Seraphim who Cover their Faces	*ACM*: H. Kopt. 686
Olam	Spirit	*oADS*

Olamtêr/Olamptēr	Angel	*ACM*: P. Mil. Vogl. Inv. 1251; PGM CXXIV:1-43
Olassky	Servant Spirit	*Abm*
Oliab	Angel – Tebet	*SR*
Oliel	Angel – Sun, over Air	*SR*
Oliroomim	Spirit	*MHN*
Olithiel	Angel/Biblical Elder	*ACM*: Oriental 5899, Berlin 11347, Oriental 6796
Oliyos	Spirit – Love/Sexual Attraction	*Pic*
Olosirmon	Servant Spirit	*Abm*
Olous	Familiar Spirit	*BP*
Omadoēl (Sun)	Sun – Alternative Name	*Hyg*
Omael	Angel – Shem thirty	*KoSU, 3BOP, GoeR, JMR, SAS, tM*
Omagos	Servant Spirit	*Abm*
Oman	Servant Spirit	*Abm*
Omary/Omery	Angel – Day Hour eleven	*Stg, ArP*
Ombalafa	Servant Spirit	*Abm*
Omecalday	Spirit of the Thumb	*CBoM*
Omedriel	Angel – Night Hour one	*Stg, ArP*
Omēel/Omiēl	Angel – Thursday Hour eight	*Hyg*
Omēr/Omyr (Mars)	Mars – Alternative Name	*Hyg*
Omerach/Omezach	Angel – Day Hour five	*Stg, ArP*
Omgege	Enochian Angel – North, serving second lesser Angle	*TBA*
Omia	Enochian Angel – North, over fourth lesser Angle	*TBA*
Omiel	Angel – Jupiter/Thursday	*SR*
Omiel/Omael	Demon Duke – South-West Night Demon Duke – West by North pre-Noon	*Stg, ThG, BoTS*
Omigiel	Spirit	*HS*
Ommadyel	Angel Ruler – third Season by Day	*SSM*
Omoras	Angel Minister – Love and Fornication	*KoSA*
Omot	Spirit	*GV*
Ompeniel	Angel	*Hyg*

Omyel/Omiel	Demon Duke – South-East Day	*Stg, ThG, BoTS*
Onahirasterp	Spirit – Minister of Love	*oADS*
Onaris	Demon	*MHN*
Onay	Angel – Sixth Altitude (Virgo)	*Alm*
Onedpon	Spirit Minister, serving Prince Befafes	*dHM*
Onely/Onele	Angel	*CBoM, GAG*
Onigeui/Onigevonitzep (Jupiter)	Jupiter – Alternative Name	*Hyg*
Oniros/Onēros/Onēros	Demon – Thursday Hour three	*Hyg*
Oniskelia/Onoskelid/Noskelēs/Nesikēldō (Onoskelis)	Demon – East	*Hyg*
Onistos/Onistōs	Demon – Monday Hour thirteen	*Hyg*
Önitzēr (Luna)	Luna – Alternative Name	*Hyg*
Onogoron/Onogeron	Planetary Spirit – Sun	*SSM*
Onokh/Anokh	Demon – Thursday Hour twelve	*Hyg*
Onom/Onon	Treasure Spirit	*oADS*
Ononias	Demon Margrave – Africa, under Amaymon	*KoN*
Ononiteon	Angel – Saturn/Saturday	*SR*
Onor	Spirit	*MHN*
Onoroy	Spirit	*MHN*
Onosigydeus	Demon King	*SSM*
Onoskelis	Demon Demon – Three-way Crossroads	*ToS, Hyg*
Onoxion	Angel – Saturn/Saturday	*SR*
Onsod	Supportive Planetary Spirit – Mars	*SSM*
Ontatoēl	Angel – Monday Hour nineteen	*Hyg*
Oōgēn (Sun)	Sun – Alternative Name	*Hyg*
Ooogosrs	Spirit Minister, serving Prince Blisdon	*dHM*
Ooneki	Spirit – East	*Hyg*
Oopezod	Enochian Angel – South, serving third lesser Angle	*TBA*
Oor/Dor	Spirit	*MHN*

Oorgaēl/Organiēl/Organiel	Angel – Monday Hour sixteen	*Hyg*
Oou (Saturn)	Saturn – Alternative Name	*Hyg*
Ooukh/Ouōkh	Demon – Thursday Hour fourteen	*Hyg*
Ōoulan (Venus)	Venus – Alternative Name	*Hyg*
Opad	Enochian Angel – South, over first lesser Angle	*TBA*
Opadouēl/Padouēl/Opadiēl/Pandonēl	Angel – Tuesday Hour nineteen	*Hyg*
Opathan	Spirit – Sun	*BoO, GAG*
Opena	Enochian Angel – North, serving third lesser Angle	*TBA*
Opēral/Operal/Ōperal	Demon – East	*Hyg*
Operdouka	Angel – Moon	*Hyg*
Operlaita	Angel	*Hyg*
Operlabostra	Angel	*Hyg*
Opermen	Enochia/OuAngel – South, serving first lesser Angle	*TBA*
Opet	Mother of Fire (Title of Nuit)	PDM XIV:150-231
Ophaniel	Throne Angel (one of seven) Archangel – Chokmah Angel Ruler – Cherubim Angel – Moon	*KoSR, 3BOP, SaS, tM*
Ophiel/Phiel	Olympic Spirit – Mercury	*KoSR, Arb, MC, GAG, JMR, MNeI, oADS, KoN, GoA, PO, ClI, SGT, SSG*
Ophis	Demon Chief	*3BOP, BoTS, tM*
Ophtiēl/Ophkhinēl/Ophriēl	Angel – Saturday Hour nineteen	*Hyg*
Opilon	Servant Spirit	*Abm*
Opios/Apios/Apiōs	Demon – Sunday Hour fourteen	*Hyg*
Oplon (Venus)	Venus – Alternative Name	*Hyg*
Ōprinas/Oprinas	Demon – West	*Hyg*
Opseēl/Opsiēl	Angel – Sunday Hour thirteen	*Hyg*
Or	Angel	*GV*
Orael	Intelligence – Saturn	*SGT, SSG*

Oragon	Angel	NA
Oralioch	Spirit – Minister of Love	oADS
Orapaēl	Demon	Hyg
Orariel	Demon Duke – North-East	Stg, ThG
Orasiel	Angel – Head of God	ACM: H. Kopt. 686
Orasita (Jupiter)	Jupiter – Alternative Name	Hyg
Orax	Demon – Sunday Hour seventeen	Hyg
Orayel	Angel – three signs of fourth Season	SSM
Orbeēth	Angel – Lunar, Night Hour seven	PGM VII:862-918
Orces	Spirit – Minister of Love	oADS
Orcormislas	Devil – Noon	oADS
Oreatēr	Angel – Thursday Hour fourteen	Hyg
Orebon	Demon	CoC, GAG
Orecha	Devil – Noon	oADS
Orek/Orikor	Spirit – East	Hyg
Oremaelle/Oremaell	Spirit – Mars	BoO, GAG
Oreoth	Demon	MHN, NML
Oresos	Devil – Noon	oADS
Orfiel	Angel – Jupiter/Thursday	SR
Organ	Demon – Thursday Hour nineteen, twenty	Hyg
Orgau	Demon – Thursday Hour twenty	Hyg
Orgeas	Night Devil	oADS
Orgogorgoniotrian	One of the Erinys	PGM IV:1390-1495
Orgon	Spirit – West	DoW
Oriamēl	Demon – Sun	Hyg
Orian/Orpsan/Ornau	Demon – Tuesday Hour seventeen	Hyg
Orias	Demon Marquis	PmD, DoW, Goe
Oriatēr	Angel – Thursday Hour fifteen	Hyg
Oriatos/Oriniēl/Oriatōr/Oriator/Khmeriēl	Angel – Thursday Hour sixteen	Hyg
Oriel	Angel	ACM: Hay 10122
Oriel/Oriet	Demon Duke – South Demon Duke – West Day Demon – East	Stg, ThG, BoTS, GoPH, GV

ABBREVIATIONS

Oriel	Angel Ruler – Nisan Angel – Water, Earth	*SR, tSoS, MNeI*
Oriel	Angel Ruler – Day Hour ten	*Stg, ArP*
Oriens/Ories/ Orience/ Orient/Urieus/ Urinuo/ Samuel/Ariens	Demon King – East, Sunrise Demon Duke	*ToSC, MHN, Abm, BoC, 3BOP, EBAM, oADS, BOS, BoO, LdE, BM, oADS, BoTS, JMR, SaS, GoPH, MNeI, KoN, SMS, PO, ClI, MRC, tM*
Orienuens/ Oriennens (Oriens)	Demon King – East	*SSM*
Orifiel	Superior Intelligence – Primum Mobile	*SoS*
Orifiel/Orifiell/ Oriphael/ Oriphael	Archangel – Saturn Superior Intelligence Intelligence – Saturn	*KoSU, SaS, MNeI, tSoS, dSS, JMR, tM*
Origen (Jupiter)	Jupiter – Alternative Name	*Hyg*
Origo	Spirit – fourteenth Mansion of the Moon ring	*tSoS*
Orikor	Demon – East	*Hyg*
Orina	Demon Knight	*KoN*
Orinel	Servant Spirit	*Abm*
Orinyn	Angel – Venus/Friday	*SR*
Orion/Ōriōn	Greek Hunter Giant/Constellation	PGM I:1-42, IV:2708-2784
Orion	Archangel	*MNeI*
Orion	Demon King Demon	*BARC, oADS*
Orish	Spirit – Mirror	*CoMS*
Oriskos	Angel – Teeth of God	*ACM*: H. Kopt. 686
Oristeron/Oristerōn	Angel	*Hyg*
Orkhat	Demon – Thursday Hour sixteen	*Hyg*
Orkip/Orkyp (Saturn)	Saturn – Alternative Name	*Hyg*
Orkitaeph/Orjitaph/ Orkistaph/Orkytas	Demon – Wednesday Hour twenty	*Hyg*
Ormael/Mael	Angel – Night Hour four	*Stg, ArP*
Ormas/Oymas	Angel – Day Hour ten	*Stg, ArP*

Ormell/Orymell	Demon Senator	*BoO*
Ormen	Enochian Angel – North, serving first lesser Angle	*TBA*
Ormenu/Ormenus	Demon Duke – East, Demon – Bringer of Calamity/ Instigator of Misfortune Demon – Telchine Demon – Originators of All Harm (three of six)	*Stg, 3BOP, ThG, MNeI, tM*
Ormezyn/Ormezin/ Ormesin	Angel – Night Hour two	*Stg, ArP*
Ormiēl/Orkiēl/ Orkyēl	Angel – Sunday Hour seventeen	*Hyg*
Ormion	Servant Spirit	*Abm*
Ormonos	Servant Spirit	*Abm*
Ormyel	Angel – Day Hour four	*Stg, ArP*
Ornai	Demon – Sunday Hour two	*Hyg*
Orniaēl	Angel – Plant Ruler	*BoW*
Ornias/Ontos/ Ornia/ Ornēas/Orneas	Demon Spirit – East	*ToS, Hyg*
Ornich/Orvich/ Orrich/ Orich	Demon Duke – East, Day Hour six	*Stg, ThG*
Orniel/Orniēl/ Ornēel/ Ornil/Ornoēl/ Orkiēl/ Orkiol	Demon – Jupiter	*Hyg*
Orniēl	Angel – Thursday Hour seventeen	*Hyg*
Ornis	Spirit	*MHN*
Ornochynta	Angel – Sixth Altitude (Virgo)	*Alm*
Ornothocos/ Ornotheos	Spirit Prince	*BoO, BoTS*
Orobas/Obus	Demon Prince	*BoO, PmD, DoW, Goe, DI*
Oroiael	Gnostic Spirit of Light	*ACM*: NH Codex VIII
Oronoch	Demon	*NML*
Oronothel	Spirit	*MHN*

Orooth	Spirit – Water	*MHN*
Oropel	Demon – Decan four	*ToS*
Oropys	Angel – Book Writer	*BoO*
Orosyphnēd	Angel – Spring	*BoW*
Orouēl/Ouriēl/Ourroēl	Angel – Wednesday Hour one	*Hyg*
Orowor	Good Spirit	*SoM*
Oroya	Servant Spirit	*Abm*
Orozamo	Angel	*BoSC*
Orpemiel/Orpeniel	Demon Duke – South-East Day	*Stg*, *ThG*, *BoTS*
Orpha	Angel	*ACM*: MRN Amulet
Orphaēl/Orphniēl	Angel – Thursday Hour eighteen	*Hyg*
Orphaniel/Orphamiell/Orphamiel	Archangel – Moon Ruler of Order of Cherubim Ruler – Fixed Stars Angel – Finger of God's Right Hand	*ACM*: MRN Amulet, Cairo EM 49547, Oriental 6796, H. Kopt. 686; *EoN*, *Hmn*, *BoO*, *MC*, *GAG*, *CBMS*, *PO*
Orphiel	Angel – Day Hour two	*Stg*, *ArP*
Orphōn (Saturn)	Saturn – Alternative Name	*Hyg*
Orphor/Orphōr/Arphōr	Demon – Thursday Hour seven	*Hyg*
Orsita (Jupiter)	Jupiter – Alternative Name	*Hyg*
Ortanoēl	Demon – Moon	*Hyg*
Orthai/Ornai/Orne	Spirit – East	*Hyg*
Orthorix/Arcaryamanan	Angel – Caput Draconis	*B7R*
Orthrdile/Orthrideēl/Osthridie	Demon – Tuesday Hour eleven	*Hyg*
Orychaton	Demon Minister – Beelzebub	*SSM*
Orychyn	Angel – Air	*SR*
Oryel	Angel – Fifth Heaven, South Angel – Fourth Season by Day	*SSM*
Oryn	Demon Duke – North-East	*Stg*, *ThG*
Osael/Osiel	Angel fifth Heaven Tuesday – South Ministering Spirit – Jupiter	*EoN*, *Hmn*, *KoSR*, *BoO*, *GAG*, *BoTS*, *tM*, *CBMS*

Osamyel	Angel – three signs of third Season	*SSM*
Osergariach Nomaphi	Hermes True Name of fifteen Letters	PGM VIII:1-63
Osfleel	Angel – Jupiter/Thursday	*SR*
Osimimilis	Demon	*GAG*
Osiris/Ousiri/ Ouseiri/ Osir/Osiris Unnefer/ Osiris Wennefer/ Osiris Nophrioth	Egyptian Fertility/ Underworld God	PGM I:247-262, III:165-186, III:424-466, IV:1-25, IV:94-153, IV:154-285, IV:930-1114, IV:2006-2125, IV:2241-2358, IV:2967-3006, IV:3125-3171, VII:255-259, VII:319-334, VII:429-458, VII:540-578, VII:643-651, VII:973-980, VII:993-1009, VIII:64-110, XII:144-152, XII:201-269, XII:270-350, XII:365-375, XXIII:1-70, XXIVa:1-25, XXXVI:134-160, XXXVI:283-294, XXXVI:295-311, XXXVI:333-360, LVII:1-37, LVII:1-14, LXXII:1-36, CI:1-53, CII:1-17, CXVII fr.7, CXXII:1-55, CXXVIa:1-21, PDM XII:21-49, XIV:1-92, XIV:150-231, XIV:239-295, XIV:428-450, IX:451-458, XIV:528-553, XIV:554-562, XIV:563-574,

ABBREVIATIONS 579

Osiris/Ousiri/ Ouseiri/ Osir/Osiris Unnefer/Osiris Wennefer/Osiris Nophrioth(con't.)		PDM XIV:574-585, XIV:585-593, XIV:627-635, XIV:636-669, XIV: 1110-1129, LXI:112-127, Suppl. 60-101, Suppl. 101-116, Suppl. 117-130, Suppl. 130-138, Suppl. 162-168, Suppl. 168-184, Suppl. 185-208; SM: PSI I.28, P. Köln Inv. 3323, T. Louvre Inv. AF 6716, P. Monac. II.28, P. Berol. Inv. 21243, P. Noviomagensis Inv. 2, P. Ant. II.66; ACM: Schmidt P., GMPP, Mich. 4932f
Osiris-Khenty-Amenti	Egyptian Composite God	PDM XIV:150-231
Osiris-Michael	Composite God-Angel	PGM XXIIb:27-31
Osiris-Mnevis	Egyptian Composite God	PGM VII:429-458
Osiris-Phre (Re)	Egyptian Composite Ruler God	PGM I:247-262
Osmadiel	Angel Ruler – Day Hour eight	*Stg, ArP*
Osmie/Semie	Demon – Sunday Hour eight	*Hyg*
Osmony/Esmony	Spirit	*GoPH, GV*
Osmyn	Angel – Kislev	*SR*
Osogyon	Servant Spirit	*Abm*
Osor Mnevis	Sacred Bull of Apis (two of three)	PGM XIXa:1-54
Osor Nobechis/Buchis	Sacred Bull of Apis (one of three)	PGM XIXa:1-54
Osor Nophris/Onuphis/Osoronnophris	Sacred Bull of Apis (three of three)	PGM V:96-172, XIXa:1-54, LXII:1-24
Osphadiel	Demon – Count Palatine	*MNeI*
Ospheggeamiou (Moon)	Luna – Alternative Name	*Hyg*
Ossidiel/Osfidiel	Demon Duke – North-West Night	*Stg, ThG, BoTS*

Osturies/Asureides/ Osturcios	Spirit – fifth Mansion of Moon Ring	*AE, tSoS*
Osul	Angel Minister	*ACM*: P. Mich. 593
Osurmy	Spirit	*GV*
Otau	Angel Minister – Love and Fornication	*KoSA*
Otel	Demon	*NML*
Otheos	Angel	*NA*
Othey/Othiy	Demon – North Spirit – Presidential Counsellor, North	*BOS, BoO, oADS, BoTS*
Othride	Demon – Tuesday Hour ten	*Hyg*
Othridie	Demon – Tuesday Hour nine	*Hyg*
Otim/Orym/Orijm	Demon Duke – West Night	*Stg, ThG, BoTS*
Otius	Demon Governor and Count	*MHN*
Otoi	Enochian Angel – East, serving fourth lesser Angle	*TBA*
Otos	Member of the Greek Gigantes	PGM IV:474, IV:830
Otraēl/Araēl	Angel – Friday Hour twelve	*Hyg*
Oualielō/Oualielos/	Demon – Thursday Hour twenty-two	*Hyg*
Ouanlēilos/Ouaniēle	Demon – Thursday Hour twenty-one	*Hyg*
Ouchou	Demon	*ACM*: H. Kopt. 681
Ougariel	Angel – Moon	*Hyg*
Ougran/Ougraph (Saturn)	Saturn – Alternative Name	*Hyg*
Ouiditouma (Venus)	Venus – Alternative Name	*Hyg*
Ouistos	Demon – Monday Hour fifteen	*Hyg*
Ouistos/Onistros	Demon – Monday Hour fourteen	*Hyg*
Oukas/Oulkas/ Oukkas	Demon – South	*Hyg*
Oukros/Ouēros	Demon – Thursday Hour three	*Hyg*
Ouktak/Outaēt/ Outak	Demon – Thursday Hour eight	*Hyg*
Ouleos/Oulatos	Demon	*ToSC*
Ouliat	Power of Death	*ACM*: Cairo Bone A/B
Ouliob (Saturn)	Saturn – Alternative Name	*Hyg*
Oukisem/Onkysem	Demon – Friday Hour twenty-three	*Hyg*

Oulodias/Ouloudias/Oulōdias/Ouloudiēl	Angel – Wednesday Hour seven	*Hyg*
Oulphas/Noulphas/Louphas/Ouphaas	Demon – North	*Hyg*
Oumesthōth	Name of Helios in Hour seven	PGM IV:1596-1715
Ounipheritousz/Ounipher/Ouniphrēr	Demon – Friday Hour twenty-four	*Hyg*
Ououle (Venus)	Venus – Alternative Name	*Hyg*
Oupiel	Biblical Elder	*ACM*: Berlin 11347, Oriental 6796
Ourael	Angel	*ACM*: Hay 10122
Ouranos	Primordial Greek Sky God	PGM IV:2967-3006
Ouraphon (Saturn)	Saturn – Alternative Name	*Hyg*
Ourieil	Angel	*Hyg*
Ourouēl/Ouril/Ouriēl	Angel – Mars	PGM IV:1716-1870; *BoW, Hyg*
Ourti	Demon – South	*Hyg*
Ousiel	Angel	*ACM*: Hay 10122
Oustiel	Demon	*Hyg*
Outaēl	Demon – Thursday Hour seven	*Hyg*
Outanon/Outiton/Outitōm	Angel – Monday Hour nineteen	*Hyg*
Outat/Outap/Outp (Mars)	Mars – Alternative Name	*Hyg*
Outēkai	Demon – South	*Hyg*
Outolokh/Ontokhōr	Demon – Monday Hour twelve	*Hyg*
Outolōkh	Demon – Monday Hour thirteen	*Hyg*
Outolōon	Demon – Monday Hour eleven	*Hyg*
Outoupōn/Outopon (Luna)	Luna – Alternative Name	*Hyg*
Outriel	Angel	*ACM*: Hay 10122
Ouxynoēl/Oxinoēl	Angel – Saturday Hour twenty-two	*Hyg*
Ouzouēl	Angel – Wednesday Hour one	*Hyg*
Ovalackbah	Plant Spirit – Elm	*GS*
Ovamenok	Angel – Malachim, under Phelmiya	*SRH*
Ovavorial	Angel – Aries	*SRH*
Oviar/Ouyar	Spirit	*GoPH, GV*

Oviron	Demon Companion – Thursday	*KoN*
Ovoval (Yiediedial)	Angel Prince – West	*SRH*
Oxioēl/Ouxounouēl	Angel – Saturday Hour twenty-three	*Hyg*
Oyeo	Spirit of the Thumb	*CBoM*
Oylol/Oilol	Punishing Wind Daemon – Moon, serving West Wind; West	*SSM, SBH*
Oymclor	Spirit	*MHN*
Oymelor	Spirit	*MHN*
Oyte	Spirit – Minister of Love and Maker of Friendship	*oADS*
OYube	Enochian Angel – East, serving second lesser Angle	*TBA*
Ozab	Enochian Angel – North, over first lesser Angle	*TBA*
Ozael	Spirit – Mars	*KoSR*
Oze/Ose/Oso	Demon Marquis/President Demon – South	*LdE, BOS, BoO, PmD, DoW, Goe, oADS*
Ozia	Demon – North	*BOS, BoO, oADS*

P

Paafiryn	Angel – Mars/Tuesday	*SR*
Paajah	Genii – 9° Capricorn, 9° Aquarius	*ArP*
Paamiel	Angel – Adar	*SR*
Paamtotyel/Paanitotyel	Angel Subordinate – Jupiter	*SSM*
Paaur	Angel – First Encampment, first Heaven	*ShR*
Paavtyell	Angel	*oADS*
Paax	Enochian Angel – West, serving first lesser Angle	*TBA*
Pabaēl	Angel – Monday Hour twenty-one	*Hyg*
Pabael	Spirit Messenger – Moon	*SGT, SSG*
Pabel	Angel – Fourth Heaven Sunday, West, Spring Presiding Spirit – Sun	*EoN, Hmn, KoSR, BoO, GAG, BoTS, tM, CBMS*
Pabiel	Ministering Spirit – Jupiter	*CBMS*
Pabliel	Angel – Fifth Heaven, West	*SR*

ABBREVIATIONS

Pabriel (Gabriel)	Angel – Fourth Heaven Sunday, East	*BoTS*
Pachahy	Servant Spirit	*Abm*
Pachamisca/ Pathimsiti/ Pathmisici	Spirit – fifth Mansion of Moon Ring	*AE, tSoS*
Pachayel	Angel – Jupiter/Thursday	*SR*
Pachyn	Spirit – South	*oADS*
Paco	Enochian Angel – West, serving third lesser Angle	*TBA*
Pacos/Pacoth/ Pelcorp	Spirit – thirteenth Mansion of the Moon Ring	*AE*
Pacryton	Angel – Saturn/Saturday	*SR*
Pacta	Angel – Thursday	*MHN*
Pacta	Demon Servant – Wednesday	*KoN*
Pactas	Spirit Assistant – Wednesday	*MHN*
Pacuel	Angel – Tebet	*SR*
Pacyta	Angel – Nisan	*SR*
Padiel	Demon King – East by South Demon Prince – East under Oriens Demon – Count Palatine Foolish Spirit	*Stg, ThG, BoTS, MNeI, KoN*
Pado	Enochian Angel – South, over first lesser Angle	*TBA*
Paēl	Angel – Thursday Hour twenty	*Hyg*
Paentagoras	Spirit	*BoO*
Pafesla	Servant Spirit	*Abm*
Paffran/Palframe	Angel Minister of Air – Tuesday Spirit Attendant – Mars	*EoN, Hmn, KoSR, BoO, GAG, BoTS, tM*
Pafiel/Pasiel	Duke – West by North after Midnight	*Stg, ThG, BoTS*
Pagarith	Demon	*Hyg*
Paglust	Servant Spirit	*Abm*
Pagulan	Angel – Tishrei	*SR*
Pahaliah/Pehaliah	Angel – Shem twenty	*KoSU, 3BOP, GoeR, JMR, SAS, tM*
Pahamcocihel/ Pahamcociel	Spirit – Jupiter	*SBH*

Paimon/Paymon/ Panym/ Poymon/ Pagmon/Plyomn/ Peymon/Beymon/ Azael	Demon King – West, Sunset, North Demon Duke	*SSM, MHN, LdE, Abm, BoC, NML, KoSA, 3BOP, BOS, oADS, BoO, PmD, DoW, BM, MC, Goe, oADS, BoTS, JMR, GoPH, SaS, MNeI, KoN, PO, ClI, VMN, MRC, tM, DI*
Pakathiel	Angel	*ACM*: Moen 3
Pakerbēth	Epithet of the God Seth	PGM I:262-347
Pakhthaphiel	Angel	*Hyg*
Pakid	Servant Spirit	*Abm*
Palakon	Demon – East	*Hyg*
Palam	Spirit	*oADS*
Palas	Punishing Wind Daemon – Mercury, serving West and Southwest Winds; between the West and North	*SSM, SBH*
Palasa	Familiar Spirit	*VJL*
Palēskax	Demon – South	*Hyg*
Palfcamyn	Spirit Helper – Tuesday	*CBoM*
Palframen	Angel Minister of Air – Tuesday	*BoO*
Pali	Enochian Angel – South, serving fourth lesser Angle	*TBA*
Paliel	Angel – Ab Angel – Marchesvan	*SR*
Palriel	Angel – Jupiter, over Earth	*SR*
Palitam	Angel – Marchesvan	*SR*
Paltamus	Angel – Sivan	*SR*
Paltaphote/ Paltaphate	Demon	*ToSC*
Paltasar	Demon Chief	*Hyg*
Palthia	Angel – Iyar	*SR*
Paltiel Tzamal	Demon	*ToSC*
Paltifus/Paltisur	Angel – Nisan	*SR, tSoS*
Palulnas	Angel – Sun	*BARC*
Paly	Angel – Fifth Heaven, West	*SR*

Pamactuel	Superior Intelligence	*KoSU*
Pamathiel	Angel	*ACM*: Moen 3
Pamechiel	Superior Intelligence – Jupiter	*SoS*
Pamelon	Spirit Demon Ruler	*SSM, BOS, BoO*
Pamersiel	Demon Duke – East	*Stg, ThG, BoTS*
Pamiel	Spirit – Middle	*SSM*
Pammon	Angel – Night Hour six	*Stg, ArP*
Pamory	Angel – Day Hour nine	*Stg, ArP*
Pamphilius	Angel	*NA*
Pamphirius	Angel	*dCL*
Pamyel/Pamiel	Angel Ruler – Night Hour nine	*Stg, ArP*
Pan	Greek Fertility God	PGM IV:2145-2240, IV:2241-2358, IV:2441-2621
Pan	God – Shepherds and Beasts	*BoO*
Panael	Genii – 5° Taurus	*ArP*
Panaplor	Angel – Moon	*LL*
Panatheneos	Angel	*NA*
Panchalitar	Spirit – fourth Mansion of the Moon Ring	*AE*
Panchasy	Devil – Ursa Major	*oADS*
Pancia	Angel	*GV*
Pandiel	Demon Duke – North-East	*Stg, ThG*
Pandlath/Pandolath	Spirit – Jupiter	*BoO, GAG*
Pandoēl	Angel – Monday Hour two	*Hyg*
Pandoli	Servant Spirit	*Abm*
Panion	Angel – Saturn/Saturday	*SR*
Pandor	Demon Duke – West Night	*Stg, ThG, BoTS*
Pandroz/Pondroz/ Poudros/Pendroz	Angel – Night Hour seven	*Stg, ArP*
Pandugell/Pendagell	Spirit – Venus	*BoO, GAG*
Panfotron	Servant Spirit	*Abm*
Pangael	Genii – 5° Pisces	*ArP*
Panhiniel	Angel – Jupiter/Thursday	*SR*
Paniel	Duke – West by North pre-Midnight	*Stg, ThG, BoTS*

Paniel	Genii – 5° Gemini	*ArP*
Panite/Panyte	Demon	*MHN*
Pankharzēl	Spirit	*BoW*
Panmōth	Angel – Lunar, Night Hour eight	PGM VII:862-918
Pannoniel	Spirit – East	*SSM*
Panon	Demon – Sea	*ToSC*
Pansi	Angel – Tebet	*SR*
Pantaceren	Angel – Air	*SR*
Pantagnon/ Pentagnony/ Pentagnogny/ Pentagnegni	Demon	*SoSW, GV*
Pantan	Angel – Adar	*SR*
Pantangor	Spirit	*BoO*
Pantaron	Angel – Adar	*SR*
Panteferon	Angel	*BoO*
Pantēkolatron	Demon – Jupiter	*Hyg*
Panteron	Angel – Adar	*SR*
Pantetaron	Angel	*oADS*
Panthanay	Angel – Third Altitude (Gemini)	*Alm*
Pantheriel	Superior Intelligence – Moon	*SoS*
Paoc	Enochian Angel – East, serving second lesser Angle	*TBA*
Paonel	Angel	*ACM*: Moen 3
Papliel	Angel – Fourth Heaven, West	*SaS*
Paplin	Angel	*ACM*: H. Kopt. 679
Papon	Angel – Saturn/Saturday	*SR*
Papothiel	Angel	*ACM*: Moen 3
Parabiel	Demon Duke – North-East	*Stg, ThG*
Parachbeylyn	Angel – Mars/Tuesday	*SR*
Parachmon	Servant Spirit	*Abm*
Paradiel	Angel – Mercury, over Fire	*SR*
Paradiel	Demon Count/Baron Foolish Spirit	*MNeI*
Paraēs	Angel	*Hyg*
Paragalla	Demon Marquis and Count	*NML*

Paraky	Spirit	Hyg
Paramera	Holy Creature of the Throne (four of four)	ACM: H. Kopt. 686
Parammon	Surname of Hermes	PGM V:172-212
Parandome	Spirit	GV
Parante	Angel – Jupiter	GAG
Parapiēl	Angel – Wednesday Hour fourteen, fifteen	Hyg
Paras	Demon Duke – North Night	Stg, ThG, BoTS
Parasch	Servant Spirit	Abm
Paraschon	Servant Spirit	Abm
Parathyell	Angel	BoO
Paraton/Paratōn/Tharatōn	Demon – East	Hyg
Parcas	Demon Prince	LdE
Parciot	Angel – Iyar	SR
Parcoth	Beast before God (first of six)	oADS
Parel/Parelkoziu	Demon	ToSC
Parelit	Servant Spirit	Abm
Parheya	Angel – Adar	SR
Pariel	Angel – Jupiter/Thursday Angel before Throne of God	SR, oADS
Pariel	Demon Duke – South-East Day Demon	Hyg, Stg, ThG, BoTS
Parineos	Angel	SBH
Parinos/Parēnos (Venus)	Venus – Alternative Name	Hyg
Parithoel	Angel	ACM: Moen 3
Parius	Demon Duke – West Day	Stg, ThG, BoTS
Parkiēn	Demon – East	Hyg
Parmesiel (Pamersiel?)	Demon Prince – East under Oriens	KoN
Parmyel	Spirit	SSM
Parniel	Demon Duke – South by East Day	Stg, ThG, BoTS
Parniel	Angel – Day Hour three	Stg, ArP
Parnikhēl/Parēkhēl	Spirit	BoW
Paron	Spirit	GV
Parosiel	Spirit – Lord of Treasures	VMN

Parpabin	Spirit – first Mansion of Moon Ring	*AE*
Parsifiel/Persifiel	Demon Chief Duke	*Stg, ThG*
Parsiniel/Prasiniel/Parlimiel	Angel – Day Hour eleven	*Stg, ArP*
Partas/Parras	Demon – South	*BOS, BoO, oADS*
Partes	Spirit Prince – Treasure	*KoN*
Parthoel	Angel	*ACM*: Moen 3
Partriel	Angel – Earth	*SR*
Paruasadyel	Angel – Third Heaven, South	*SSM*
Parusur/Parufar	Servant Spirit	*Abm, MRC*
Paruthel	Angel	*ACM*: Moen 3
Paryneos	Angel	*NA*
Parziel	Genii – 6° Virgo	*ArP*
Pasas	Angel – Mars	*GAG*
Pascami	Spirit Assistant – Tuesday	*MHN*
Pascari/Pastarie/Pastary	Demon Senator	*BoO*
Paschania	Angel – Tammuz	*SR*
Paschar	Angel – Jupiter Throne Angel (six of seven)	*SSM, SaS*
Pasfran	Daemon Minister – Mars, South	*SBH*
Pasi	Spirit	*Hyg*
Pasil/Pasiel/Pasel	Angel – Pisces	*ArP*
Pasill/Fasall	Demon	*BoO, oADS*
Pasita	Angel – Nisan	*tSoS*
Paspon	Ministering Spirit – Saturn	*CBMS*
Pasqonit	Alternative name of Metatron	*SQ*
Pasriel/Pastiel	Angel – Day Hour seven	*Stg, ArP*
Pastor	Archangel – Jupiter	*BoO*
Pastorem	Spirit	*MNeI*
Patecha	Angel – Dominations	*67M*
Pathier/Pathir	Demon Duke – North-West Night	*Stg, ThG, BoTS*
Pathyn	Demon – South	*BOS, BoO*
Paticael	Angel – Moon, over Fire	*SR*

Patiēl	Angel – Adar Angel – Tuesday Hour fourteen	*SR*, *Hyg*
Patiel/Potiel	Demon Duke – West by South Day	*Stg*, *ThG*, *BoTS*
Patiel	Genii – 7° Libra	*ArP*
Patience	Angel – Third Altitude (Gemini)	*Alm*
Patnilin	Angel – Venus/Friday	*SR*
Patra	Angel – Tenth Altitude (Capricorn)	*Alm*
Patriel	Angel	*ACM*: Hay 10122
Patriēl	Angel – Saturday Hour twenty	*Hyg*
Patrozyn/Patrozin	Angel – Night Hour five	*Stg*, *ArP*
Patteny	Angel – Dominations	*67M*
Pattid	Servant Spirit	*Abm*
Patymel	Angel – Thrones	*67M*
Patyr	Angel	*NA*
Paute	Enochian Angel – East, over second lesser Angle	*TBA*
Paxilon	Angel – Saturn/Saturday	*SR*
Paxonion	Angel – Saturn/Saturday	*SR*
Paynelon/Pamelon/Pamelons	Demon Knight	*BOS*, *BoO*
Pazehemy	Angel – Kislev	*SR*
Paziael	Angel – Venus, over Earth	*SR*
Pazicaton	Angel – Moon, over Water	*SR*
Pchdrun	Angel Prince – fifth Heaven, Month of Tishrei	*ShR*
Pchdwttgm	Angel Prince – Middle Five	*SoM*
Pdgnar	Angel – Ab	*SR*
Pdhal	Angel – Ninth Step, second Heaven Angel Prince – fourth Heaven, Water	*ShR*
Pdutial	Angel – Second Encampment, first Heaven	*ShR*
Peace	Angel – Second Altitude (Taurus)	*Alm*
Peajel/Penjel	Spirit Messenger – Venus	*SGT*, *SSG*
Peamde	Demon	*MHN*
Pechach	Servant Spirit	*Abm*
Pechiel	Angel	*ACM*: H.O. Lange Text

Pechoel	Angel	ACM: Moen 3
Peciel	Angel – Jupiter/Thursday	SR
Pecyrael	Angel – Sun, over Water	SR
Peden	Enochian Evil Spirit	TBA
Pefem	Enochian Evil Spirit	TBA
Pegal	Angel – Mercury/Wednesday	SR
Pēgiab	Demon – South	Hyg
Pegiel	Genii – 14° Aries	ArP
Pekhtha	Angel	Hyg
Pēklērōth (Mars)	Mars – Alternative Name	Hyg
Pekoul	Spirit	Hyg
Pel/Pal/Pelē	Angel – Sunday Hour seven	Hyg
Pēlakouel/Palaklotēēlē/Pilaktoēl/Pelatoēl	Angel – Venus	Hyg
Pelaphiēl	Angel – Saturday Hour seven	Hyg
Pelariel/Pesariel	Demon Duke – Day Hour three	Stg, ThG
Pelayym	Angel Governor – third Season by Night	SSM
Peleki/Pelēkē	Angel – Sunday Hour two, three	Hyg
Pelēl/Peliēl/Pariēl/Periēl/Pelēēl	Angel – Sunday Hour eighteen	Hyg
Pelgiab/Pēgiab/Pilgiap	Demon – South	Hyg
Peliel/Peliell	Angel – Sun/Mercury Archangel – Geburah and Tiphereth	tSoS, JMR, Thm, BoTS, MNeI
Peliet	Noble Spirit, Fire	MNeI
Pelkadōn (Sun)	Sun – Alternative Name	Hyg
Pelkhaous/Pelkhaoul/Pelkasyr (Jupiter)	Jupiter – Alternative Name	Hyg
Pelon	Demon	ToSC
Pelouēl/Perouēl	Angel – Sunday Hour two, three	Hyg
Peloym	Spirit	GV
Pelpiēl	Angel	Hyg

Peltzaphatai/ Peltzapouth/ Peltzateēth/ Peltzapouth	Spirit – East	*Hyg*
Pelusar	Duke – West by North pre-Midnight	*Stg, ThG, BoTS*
Pelvm	Angel – Joy and Divination	*CoMS*
Pemadel	Angel	*ACM*: Moen 3
Pemael/Penael	Angel – Third Heaven Friday, North Ministering Spirit – Venus	*EoN, Hmn, KoSR, BoO, BM, GAG, BoTS, tM, CBMS*
Pemef	Enochian Evil Spirit	*TBA*
Pememtēl	Spirit	*BoW*
Pemiel	Angel – Day Hour six	*Stg, ArP*
Pemnamouel	Angel	*ACM*: Moen 3
Pemoel	Angel	*ACM: Moen 3*
Pemoniel	Angel – Night Hour seven	*Stg, ArP*
Pemox	Enochian Angel – East, serving fourth lesser Angle	*TBA*
Penac	Angel – Third Heaven, North	*SSM, SaS*
Penador/Penader	Demon Duke – Y2	*Stg, ThG*
Penael	Angel – Third Heaven, North	*SR, SSM*
Penael	Spirit Messenger – Venus	*SGT, SSG*
Penaly	Angel – Day Hour ten	*Stg, ArP*
Penargos/Penergos	Angel – Night Hour three	*Stg, ArP*
Penat	Angel – Third Heaven Friday, North	*SR, EoN, Hmn, KoSR, BoO, BM, GAG, BoTS, tM*
Penat	Intelligence – Venus	*SGT, SSG*
Penatiel/Penaliel	Angel – Day Hour twelve	*Stg, ArP*
Pend	Enochian Evil Spirit	*TBA*
Penael	Angel – Third Heaven, North	*SSM, SaS*
Penedill	Spirit	*BoO*
Peniel	Angel – Third Heaven Friday, North Ministering Spirit – Venus	*EoN, Hmn, KoSR, BoO, BM, GAG, BoTS, tM, CBMS*
Peniel	Demon Duke – West Night	*Stg, ThG, BoTS*
Penoles	Angel – Night Hour one	*Stg, ArP*

Penuyel	Angel Governor Master – third Season by Night	SSM
Pēoēroth (Mars)	Mars – Alternative Name	Hyg
Peolphan/Peolphon	Demon King – North	DoW
Pephkeion	Demon – East	Hyg
Pepilon	Angel – Saturn/Saturday	SR
Perchamiel	Angel	ACM: Moen 3
Pēraniēl/Paraniēl/Peraniēl/Paraēl	Angel – Wednesday Hour nineteen	Hyg
Pērathē	Demon – Sunday Hour two	Hyg
Pērathoui/Pērrath/Pyrath	Demon – Sunday Hour three	Hyg
Perdikoim/Perdikēm/Perdikoum/Operdikym/Pidykēm/Pēldēim	Angel – Moon	Hyg
Peresch	Servant Spirit	Abm
Perganaēl/Perganiēl/Perianiēl/Piēganeēl	Angel – Tuesday Hour eight	Hyg
Pergor	Spirit – eighth Mansion of the Moon ring	tSoS
Periberim	Angel Minister	KoSA
Periel	Angel	ACM: Moen 3
Periel	Spirit – Saturn	SoS
Periel	Genii – 8° Scorpio, 8° Sagittarius	ArP
Periorath	Demon – East	Hyg
Peripalabim	Angel	VJL
Peripaos	Good Spirit	MHN
Periphaēl	Angel	Hyg
Periphrel/Preniphel/Pernipher/Perniphel/Pernipheēl	Angel – Thursday Hour two	Hyg
Perman	Angel – Day Hour eleven	Stg, ArP
Permaz	Angel – Night Hour two	Stg, ArP
Permases	Servant Spirit	Abm
Permiel	Angel – Day Hour four	Stg, ArP
Permisbret/Permilbo	Spirit – twentieth Mansion of the Moon Ring	AE

Permon	Angel – Day Hour six, Night Hour eleven	*Stg, ArP*
Peronias	Angel Minister – Love and Fornication	*KoSA*
Perortira	Spirit – Minister of Love	*oADS*
Perriorath/Periorath	Spirit – East	*Hyg*
Persephassa	Form of Persephone	PGM IV:1390-1495
Persephone	Greek Underworld Goddess	PGM IV:296-466, IV:2441-2621, IV:2785-2890, VII:981-993, XII:1-13; *SM*: PSI I.28, T. Cairo Mus. JdE 48217, T. Louvre Inv. E 27145, P. Mich. Inv. 6925, Audollent DT.38
Persiel	Angel – Day Hour three	*Stg, ArP*
Persomphon	Gnostic Archon – first Aeon	*ACM*: Bruce Codex
Person	Spirit	*GV*
Pertan/Partan/Partanē/Tetan	Angel – Tuesday Hour fifteen	*Hyg*
Pertanael	Angel	*Hyg*
Perth	Angel before Throne of God	*oADS*
Perthathaniel	Angel	*ACM*: Moen 3
Pertikeel/Peltikoēl	Angel – Mercury	*Hyg*
Pesac	Enochian Angel – South, over third lesser Angle	*TBA*
Pesariel	Water Spirit	*MNeI*
Pesēdon	Demon – North	*Hyg*
Peskinther	Angel	*ACM*: Moen 3
Pestall	Spirit – Minister of Love	*oADS*
Pestefirat	Demon	*MHN*
Pestifer	Spirit	*SSM*
Pestron	Spirit – Sea Treasure	*oADS*
Peta	Spirit – Minister of Love	*oADS*
Petangor	Spirit	*BoO*
Petanop	Servant Spirit	*Abm*

Petbe	Thunder Deity	*ACM*: H. O. Lange Text
Petreēl/Pitriel	Angel – Saturday Hour fourteen	*Hyg*
Petron	Spirit	*CoC*
Peunt	Spirit	*GV*
Pgrial	Angel – Fourth Step, second Heaven	*ShR*
Pha'avod	Angel – Malachim, under Avorphenial	*SRH*
Phabriêl	Angel	*SM*: P. Med. I.20
Phacamech	Spirit	*MNeI*
Phadael	Angel	*BoTS*
Phael	Angel Minister	*ACM*: P. Mich. 593
Phagnora	Angel	*SBH*
Phakanel	Demon	*ToSC*
Phaleg/Phalet/ Phalec/ Praleg/Thallus/ Thallis	Olympic Spirit – Mars	*KoSR, Arb, MC, GAG, JMR, MNeI, oADS, KoN, GoA, PO, ClI, SGT, SSG*
Phallus	Wind Spirit	*GAG*
Phaloumpol/ Phalopor (Venus)	Venus – Alternative Name	*Hyg*
Phamothēel	Angel	*Hyg*
Phaniel	Demon Duke – South-East Night	*Stg, ThG, BoTS*
Phanuel	Angel over Produce	*ACM*: Oriental 5899, BN Turin, Bodl C(P)4, P. Mich. 3023A, P. Mich. 3472
Phanuel/Panuel	Demon Duke – Day Hour four	*Stg, ThG*
Phaphaēl	Angel – Monday Hour eleven	*Hyg*
Pharactc	Demon	*MHN*
Pharai/Pharos/ Pharōs	Demon – Wednesday Hour twenty-two	*Hyg*
Pharai/Pharay/ Pharap	Spirit – first Mansion of Moon Ring	*AE, tSoS*
Pharakounēth	Name of Helios in first Hour	PGM IV:1596-1715
Pharan	Demon	*ToSC*
Phareht	Angel	*NA*

Pharene	Angel	NA
Phariel	Angel	*ACM*: BN Turin
Phariem	Angel	*Hyg*
Pharnimpaēl	Angel	*Hyg*
Pharol	Demon Duke – North-East	*Stg, ThG*
Phartouel	Demon – Three-way Crossroads	*Hyg*
Phasaphaēl/ Pharsaēl/ Pharaphouēl	Angel – Monday Hour two	*Hyg*
Phatael	Angel	*Hyg*
Phatai/Phatagi	Demon – East	*Hyg*
Phateneynehos	Angel	*NA*
Phausiel	Angel	*ACM*: H. Kopt. 686
Phebehier	Angel – Malachim, under Phelmiya	*SRH*
Phedal	Angel Prince – Gate of Spirit of West	*SRH*
Phedetem	Angel – Malachim, under Phelmiya	*SRH*
Pheheneos	Angel	*NA*
Phekehier	Angel Magistrate – Malachim	*SRH*
Phelayiem	Angel – Malachim, Autumn Nights	*SRH*
Phelelal	Angel Prince – Gate of Spirit of West	*SRH*
Phelemiya	Angel Magistrate – Malachim	*SRH*
Pheleneos	Angel	*SBH*
Pheletial	Angel Prince – Gate of Spirit of West	*SRH*
Pheliephal	Spirit Prince – Sea in Summer	*SRH*
Phelmiya	Angel Magistrate – Malachim, fourth Throne	*SRH*
Phenal	Angel Prince – Gate of Spirit of North	*SRH*
Phenial	Angel Prince – Malachim, Autumn Nights Angel – Malachim, under Ayigeda/under Pheseker Angel Prince – Gate of Spirit of North Angel – Malachim, sixth Host Angel – Malachim, Elul Angel – Gemini	*SRH*
Pheniemor	Spirit – South in Summer	*SRH*
Phenix/Phoenix	Demon Marquis	*PmD, DoW, Goe*
Pheniyavon	Angel – Malachim, sixth Host	*SRH*

Phēous Phōouth	Name of Helios in ninth Hour	PGM IV:1596-1715
Phereēl	Demon – West and Aries	*Hyg*
Pheresemon	Angel – Malachim, under Pheseker Angel – Malachim, sixth Host	*SRH*
Phereson	Angel – Malachim, under Phelmiya	*SRH*
Pheretem	Angel Magistrate – Malachim	*SRH*
Pheriephohov	Angel – Malachim, under Phelmiya	*SRH*
Pheriyatz	Angel – Malachim, under Avorphenial	*SRH*
Phērmar/Pherma/Phimas	Demon – South	*Hyg*
Pherog	Angel – Malachim, under Ayigeda	*SRH*
Pheroseh	Angel – Malachim, under Avorphenial	*SRH*
Pherothial	Angel – Malachim, under Ayigeda	*SRH*
Pherotial	Angel – Malachim, under Ayigeda	*SRH*
Pheroval	Angel Prince – Gate of Spirit of South	*SRH*
Pherphaēl/Pherbaēl	Angel – Autumn	*BoW*
Pheseker	Angel – Malachim, sixth Host	*SRH*
Pheseqien	Angel Prince	*SRH*
Phesetelen	Angel, serving above sixth Degree	*SRH*
Phesethemer	Angel – Malachim, under fPheseker Angel – Malachim, sixth Host	*SRH*
Phesetzial	Angel – Malachim, under Pheseker	*SRH*
Phesker	Angel Magistrate – Malachim, sixth Throne	*SRH*
Phetakieza	Angel – Malachim, under Phelmiya	*SRH*
Phetapher	Angel – Malachim, under Avorphenial	*SRH*
Phetebieza	Angel Magistrate – Malachim	*SRH*
Pheth	Demon – Decan twenty-seven	*ToS*
Phethesh	Angel – Malachim, under Ayigeda	*SRH*
Phetzetzial	Angel – Malachim, sixth Host	*SRH*
Phidēl	Angel – Friday Hour twenty	*Hyg*
Phieblas	Demon – North	*Hyg*
Phiekebom	Angel – Malachim, sixth Host	*SRH*
Phiel	Angel Minister	*ACM*: P. Mich. 593
Phiel	Demon	*Hyg*

Phielelal	Angel Prince – Gate of Spirit of West	*SRH*
Philoēl/Emphiloēl/ Amphiloēl	Angel – Friday Hour three	*Hyg*
Philopael	Biblical Elder	*ACM*: Berlin 11347, Oriental 6796
Phirpheēl/ Pherpheriēl/ Phrereēl/Pherphireēl	Angel – Tuesday Hour three	*Hyg*
Phisaēl/Phisnaēl	Angel – Thursday Hour twenty-one	*Hyg*
Phisazeroth	Spirit Prince	*BoMS*
Phisiel	Angel – Thursday Hour nineteen	*Hyg*
Phlegothes	Angel	*NA*
Phniditas/ Phnidiotas/ Phnidōtas	Demon – Wednesday Hour seven	*Hyg*
Phnunoboeol	Angel	*ToS*
Phobokil/Phbokil/ Phbokēl/Phthokeiēl	Demon – West	*Hyg*
Phoboulēl	Angel – Plant Ruler	*BoW*
Phoebe	God – Moon	*BoO*
Phoebus (Apollo)	God – Sun	*BoO*
Phoibos/Phobos	Apollo epithet	PGM II:1-64, II:64-184, III:282-409, VI:1-47, XIII:343-646
Phokien	Angel – Malachim, under Avorphenial	*SRH*
Phonekos	Angel – Malachim, under Pheseker	*SRH*
Phoraeim	Angel – Seraphim who Cover their Faces	*ACM*: H. Kopt. 686
Phorel	Demon – West and Aries	*Hyg*
Phorsiel/Phersiel	Angel – Night Hour four	*Stg, ArP*
Phorsy	Spirit	*GV*
Phos	Angel – Malachim, under Pheseker	*SRH*
Phōs-Auge (Light-Radiance)	God of Cosmos and Fire	PGM XIII:1-343, XIII:343-646
Phosegma	Angel	*NA*
Phosmo	Angel	*NA*
Phoste	Angel	*NA*

Phothephera	Angel – Malachim, under Ayigeda	SRH
Phothos	Angel	NA
Photuel	Angel	SM: P. Heid. Inv. Lat. 5
Phourani	Angel Guardian	ACM: Hay 10391
Phourat	Angel Guardian	ACM: Hay 10391
Phoval	Angel Magistrate – Malachim, seventh Throne	SRH
Phōx	Four-Faced Daimon	PDM XIV:93-114
Phra	Enochian Angel – North, over second lesser Angle	TBA
Phre/Phreth/Pre	Sun God (Re)	PGM IV:850-929, IV:1275-1322, VII:319-334, XXIII:1-70, PDM XIV:117-149, XIV:295-308, XIV:355-365, XIV:459-475, XIV:475-488, XIV:489-515, XIV:528-553, XIV:636-669, XIV:805-840, XIV:1026-1045, Suppl. 60-101
Phrektiouz/ Phriktouzgon (Venus)	Venus – Alternative Name	Hyg
Phrentaēl	Demon	Hyg
Phrinaphre/ Phloaniphe/ Philinolor/Phlinaphe	Demon – Monday Hour twenty-one	Hyg
Phrodrinos/ Phrodenos/ Phondenos/ Phrodainos	Demon – Sunday Hour twenty-four	Hyg
Phryktouel/Phrikout (Sun)	Sun – Alternative Name	Hyg
Phthas	Egyptian Name of Hephaistos	PGM XXIII:1-70
Phthenoth	Demon – Decan thirty-five	ToS
Phthiker/Phēstisiker/ Phēssisēker	Demon – West	Hyg

ABBREVIATIONS 599

Phukta	Spirit who Divides the Days and Hours	*ACM*: P. Mich. 190
Phul/Phuel/Hul	Olympic Spirit – Moon	*KoSR, Arb, MC, GAG, JMR, MNeI, oADS, KoN, GoA, PO, ClI, 67M, SGT, SSG*
Phylianēre	Demon – Monday Hour twenty	*Hyg*
Phylonel/Philouēl/Philoēl/Phēlouēl/Pholoul/Philoel	Angel – Sun	*Hyg*
Phynitiel	Angel – Saturn, over Fire	*SR*
Physis	Greek Primordial Goddess of Nature	PGM IV:3209-3054
Phytones/Phytoneus/Phytoneum/Philoneum/Phitones/Philomens/Philomons/Philonions	Angel – Jupiter	*B7R, tSoS, oADS*
Piak	Angel – three of seven over the seven Baths	*ACM*: H. Kopt. 686
Pial	Angel – Twelfth Step, second Heaven	*ShR*
Pianō	Angel	*Hyg*
Piarum	Spirit – Invisibility	*oADS*
Picollus	Prussian Demon – Foreteller of Important Deaths	*DI*
Pidaēl	Angel – Tuesday Hour five	*Hyg*
Piel/Pisel/Porē	Angel – Sunday Hour five	*Hyg*
Piēz/Pnyx/Pnix/Pnēx	Demon – Sunday Hour nine	*Hyg*
Pikhaoul (Jupiter)	Jupiter – Alternative Name	*Hyg*
Piktoēl	Angel – Tuesday Hour five	*Hyg*
Pileth (Bileth?)	Demon King (formerly Order of Thrones)	*KoN*
Piliour/Pelōr/Pelios/Peliōr/Pelēor	Demon – Sunday Hour twelve	*Hyg*
Pimēlaēl	Angel	*Hyg*
Pimikhaēl	Angel	*Hyg*
Pimpam	Familiar Spirit	*VJL*
Pinen	Demon	*MHN, NML*

Pinoel/Pantoēl/ Pistdoēl/ Pindōēl	Angel – Monday Hour three	*Hyg*
Pion	Angel – Saturn/Saturday	*SR*
Piorirōth (Mars)	Mars – Alternative Name	*Hyg*
Piout/Pioutōn (Mercury)	Mercury – Alternative Name	*Hyg*
Piphathi	Demon – Sunday Hour two	*Hyg*
Pirael	Biblical Elder	*ACM*: Berlin 11347, Oriental 6796
Pirichiel/Pyrichiel	Demon Wandering Prince	*Stg, Thg*
Pirtophin	Angel – Mars/Tuesday	*SR*
Pirus	Angel Minister – Love and Fornication	*KoSA*
Pischiel/Psichiel	Demon Duke – Hour two of fifteen	*Stg, ThG*
Pisciel (Barchiel)	Angel – Pisces Spirit – Pisces	*3BOP, tSoS, JMR, SaS*
Pishon	Angel Alternative name of Metatron	*SQ, SMS*
Pisqon	Alternative name of Metatron	*SQ*
Pisqonit	Alternative name of Metatron	*SQ*
Pist	Demon	*MHN*
Pistraye	Devil – Noon	*oADS*
Pithankouz/Pēthakou (Sun)	Sun – Alternative Name	*Hyg*
Pithiel	Angel	*ACM*: Oriental 5899
Pitiēl	Angel, fifth Heaven	PGM XXVI:1-42
Pitpri	Angel – Second Encampment, first Heaven	*ShR*
Pixitor/Pizitōr/ Pizitor/ Pēzētos/Pizētor	Demon – Friday Hour fifteen	*Hyg*
Pkhur	Angel – Fourth Encampment, first Heaven	*ShR*
Plamiel/Pamiel	Angel – Day Hour twelve	*Stg, ArP*
Platanix/Pletanix	Angel – Saturday Hour nine	*Hyg*
Platerion	Angel Minister – Love and Fornication	*KoSA*
Platiel/Phatiel// Phaytiel/ Phaliel	Angel – Night Hour five	*Stg, ArP*

Plaual	Angel Prince – fourth Heaven, Fire	*ShR*
Plēlaton	Demon – Tuesday Hour eight	*Hyg*
Plemos	Power of Death	*ACM*: Cairo Bone A/B
Plenanix/Pletaniēl	Angel – Saturday Hour eight	*Hyg*
Plēneut	Demon – Tuesday Hour nine	*Hyg*
Pleorim	Spirit	*GV*
Plēsym/Plēssim (Mars)	Mars – Alternative Name	*Hyg*
Plēxtephō/ Plixtephtra/ Plēxtephra/ Plēxtebras	Demon – East	*Hyg*
Pliroky	Servant Spirit	*Abm*
Pliset	Angel – Iyar	*SR*
Pludir	Spirit	*BoTS*
Pluthoal	Demon Senior	*SSM*
Pluto/Plouton	Roman Underworld God	PGM IV:1390-1495; *SM*: T. Cairo Mus. JdE 48217, T. Louvre Inv. E 27145, P. Mich. Inv. 6925, T. Köln Inv. 1, Audollent DT.38
Pluto	God – Hell Demon Prince Spirit of Darkness	*3BOP, BoO, BoTS, MNeI, KoN, VJL*
Pneumathon	Angel – Third Altitude (Gemini)	*Alm*
Pnial	Angel – Sixth Encampment, first Heaven Angel – Eighth Step, second Heaven	*ShR*
Pnidōr/Phnidōr	Demon – Wednesday Hour eleven	*Hyg*
Pnimur	Angel – Third Step, second Heaven	*ShR*
Poia	Familiar Spirit	*VJL*
Pobrax (Mercury)	Mercury – Alternative Name	*Hyg*
Podēkoulator/ Podikolator	Demon – Jupiter	*Hyg*
Poenar	Ministering Spirit – Venus	*CBMS*
Polacar	Spirit – Minister of Love	*oADS*

Poliel/Poiel/Pojiel	Angel – Shem fifty-six	*KoSU, 3BOP, GoeR, JMR, SAS, tM*
Poliōn/Polyonēl	Angel – Friday Hour twenty-four	*Hyg*
Poilipos/Polipis (Philip)	Prince of Ishim and Apostle	*3BOP, MRC*
Pollaikynais/Polaskon	Spirit – East	*Hyg*
Pomael	Spirit	*tSoS*
Pomelyhon	Angel	*NA*
Pomeriel	Superior Intelligence – Mars	*KoSU, SoS*
Ponicarpo	Demon Duke	*NML*
Poniel	Angel – Third Heaven, North	*SR*
Ponilbus	Spirit – Minister of Love	*oADS*
Ponteriel/Pentacriel/Pantëriel	Superior Intelligence	*KoSU*
Pontikoēl	Demon – Jupiter	*Hyg*
Pontios Pilatos/Pontius Pilate	Demon – Jupiter	*Hyg*
Porackmiel	Angel – Water	*SR*
Porax	Demon Prince	*BOS, BoO*
Porkiki	Demon – East Spirit – West	*Hyg*
Porna/Porosa/Parna/Porno/Perna	Angel – Third Heaven Friday, South Angel – Third Heaven, South	*SR, EoN, Hmn, KoSR, BoO, BM, GAG, BoTS, SaS, tM, CBMS*
Portasinall	Spirit – Minister of Love	*oADS*
Portas Sambaras	Demon Servant – Tuesday	*KoN*
Portisan	Demon	*BoO*
Postor	Angel Prince – Thursday	*EoN*
Pother	Servant Spirit	*Abm*
Potiel/Poriel	Demon Duke – North-West Day	*Stg, ThG, BoTS*
Potzetan	Spirit	*Hyg*
Potzeties/Potzetios	Demon	*ToSC*
Poulasskē	Spirit – East	*Hyg*
Power	Demon – Pleiades five	*ToS*
Ppal	Angel – Twelfth Step, second Heaven	*ShR*
Pptsh	Angel – Second Encampment, first Heaven	*ShR*

Praatup	Angel – Fifth Encampment, first Heaven	*ShR*
Praiithel	Angel	*ACM*: Moen 3
Pral	Angel – Ninth Step, second Heaven	*ShR*
Praredun/Praredum	Spirit	*GV*
Prasiel	Demon Duke – Year two of two	*Stg, ThG*
Pratham/Peatham	Spirit	*GoPH, GV*
Praxeel/Proxel	Demon Duke – Year one of two	*Stg, ThG*
Praxiel	Angel – Night Hour two	*Stg, ArP*
Prchgal	Angel – Eleventh Step, second Heaven	*ShR*
Prdial	Angel – Third Heaven, serving Rhtial	ShR
Predogam/Perdogamma/Perdo/Perdagaman	Spirit – sixth Mansion of Moon Ring	*AE, tSoS*
Premy	Spirit	*GoPH, GV*
Prenostix	Angel – Night Hour six	*Stg, ArP*
Preradōn	Angel	*Hyg*
Presfees	Servant Spirit	*Abm*
Prestas	Demon	*BoSC*
Prial	Angel – Second Encampment, first Heaven Angel Prince – fourth Heaven, Water	*ShR*
Priamon	Spirit – Sea Treasure	*oADS*
Prian	Angel – First Encampment, first Heaven	*ShR*
Pribial	Angel – Fourth Step, second Heaven	*ShR*
Priel	Angel	*ACM*: Moen 3
Prikael	Angel	*ACM*: Moen 3
Prikinu	Angel – Fourth Encampment, first Heaven	*ShR*
Primac	Prince – ninth Bond of the Apologian Seat	*Hmn, GAG*
Primonem	Spirit	*MNeI*
Prince	Angel – Second Altitude (Taurus)	*Alm*
Princo	Angel – Saturn	*GAG*
Priolam	Angel – Day Hour two	*LL*
Priphiel	Angel	*ACM*: Moen 3
Priroel	Angel	*ACM*: Moen 3
Prnigal	Angel – Twelfth Step, second Heaven	*ShR*

Prnin	Angel Encampment Head – sixth Heaven, West	*ShR*
Prnus	Angel – Fourth Encampment, first Heaven	*ShR*
Proathofas/ Proathophas	Punishing Wind Daemon – Mars, subject to East Wind; South	*SSM, SBH*
Procax	Demon Senior	*SSM*
Procell/Procel/ Crocell	Demon Duke	*PmD, DoW, Goe*
Proculo	Demon	*SoSW, GV*
Proeiel	Angel	*ACM*: Moen 3
Progemon	Demon	*MHN*
Prohos	Angel	*NA*
Prolege	Angel – Mars	*BARC*
Promachos	Servant Spirit	*Abm*
Promiel	Angel – ten of twenty-one on the Left	*ACM*: Berlin 10587
Promsacha Aleeiō	God of the Abyss of Primal Waters	PGM XIII:343-646
Pronoia	Greek Goddess of Providence	PGM LVII:1-37
Pronsach	Demon Companion – Thursday	*KoN*
Prophi/Prophoē/ Prorōi/ Prophai	Demon – Tuesday Hour fifteen	*Hyg*
Prophiel	Angel	*ACM*: Moen 3
Prophōn	Demon – Tuesday Hour fourteen	*Hyg*
Prorōi	Demon – Tuesday Hour fifteen	*Hyg*
Proteth/Prote	Gnostic Archon – first Aeon	*ACM*: Bruce Codex
Prothiel	Angel	*ACM*: Moen 3
Protizēkatour/ Prōtizēkati/ Prostozikator/ Protitzikator/Proti	Demon – Venus	*Hyg*
Proxonos	Servant Spirit	*Abm*
Prsial	Angel Prince – fourth Heaven, Water	*ShR*
Prsumun	Angel – Sixth Encampment, first Heaven	*ShR*
Prual	Angel – Eighth Step, second Heaven	*ShR*
Prudentia	Spirit of Prudence	*BoO*

ABBREVIATIONS

Pruflas/Bufas/Pruslas	Demon Prince and Duke	*PmD, DoW, MRC, GG, DI*
Prug	Angel – Second Encampment, first Heaven	*ShR*
Prukh	Angel – First Encampment, first Heaven	*ShR*
Prupial	Angel – Seventh Encampment, first Heaven	*ShR*
Prush	Angel – Fifth Encampment, first Heaven	*ShR*
Prutial	Angel – Second Encampment, first Heaven	*ShR*
Prziel	Evil Angel	*SoM*
Przirum	Angel – Second Step, second Heaven	*ShR*
Psal	Angel Prince – fourth Heaven, Water	*ShR*
Psalketios	Angel – Friday Hour seventeen	*Hyg*
Psatael	Angel	*ACM*: Yale 1800
Psdiel	Evil Angel	*SoM*
Pseēl	Angel – Monday Hour thirteen	*Hyg*
Pserathael	Angel	*ACM*: Oriental 5899
Pshoi	Egyptian unknown deity (of the abyss	PGM IV:138-143
Pshshial	Angel – Sixth Encampment, first Heaven Angel – Second Step, second Heaven	*ShR*
Psiksuk	Angel – Twelfth Step, second Heaven	*ShR*
Psilaphael	Biblical Elder	*ACM*: Berlin 11347, Oriental 6796
Pskial	Angel – Third Heaven, serving Dlqial	*ShR*
Pskr	Angel Overseer (six of seven) – First Heaven	*ShR*
Psohdon	False Spirit	*MNeI*
Psōlmaton/Psalmatros/Psalmatios	Angel – Friday Hour seventeen	*Hyg*
Psotomis	Power of Death	*ACM*: Cairo Bone A/B
Psourouthioun	Holy Creature of the Throne (three of four)	*ACM*: H. Kopt. 686
Pspial	Angel – Third Step, second Heaven	*ShR*
Pstmr	Angel – Sixth Encampment, first Heaven	*ShR*

Psyche	Greek Goddess of the Soul	PGM IV:475-829, IV:1716-1870, XII:14-95, XIII:1-343, XIII:343-646
Ptah	Egyptian Builder God	PDM XII:21-49, XIII:734-1077, Suppl. 168-184
Ptchial	Angel – Ninth Step, second Heaven	*ShR*
Ptchih	Angel – Seventh Step, second Heaven	*ShR*
Pthakiēl	Demon – West	*Hyg*
Ptēlaton/Plēlatan	Demon – Tuesday Hour nine	*Hyg*
Ptethama/ Ptetharme/ Potetharmi/ Ptaparme	Demon – South	*Hyg*
Pthora	Demon – West	*Hyg*
Ptixagē	Spirit	*Hyg*
Ptkia	Angel – Fourth Encampment, first Heaven	*ShR*
Ptrupi	Angel – First Encampment, first Heaven	*ShR*
Ptual	Angel – Seventh Encampment, first Heaven	*ShR*
Ptunial	Angel – Fifth Step, second Heaven	*ShR*
Pual	Angel Prince – fourth Heaven, Fire	*ShR*
Pubun	Angel – First Encampment, first Heaven	*ShR*
Puchon	Evil Spirit	*SoM*
Puck/Puckar (Odin)	Malefic Spirit	*DI*
Puhsy	Spirit, under Paymon	*KoN*
Pukbus	Angel – Sixth Encampment, first Heaven	*ShR*
Pumeon	Good Spirit	*MHN*
Pumotor/Pumiotor	Spirit	*MHN*
Punaton	Wicked Spirit	*NMI*
Purson/Pursan/ Curson	Demon King	*MHN, PmD, DoW, Goe, GG, BoSC*
Purtnial	Angel – Seventh Encampment, first Heaven	*ShR*
Pusmator	Angel Minister – Love and Fornication	*KoSA*
Putisel/Putifel	Angel – Day Hour five	*Stg, ArP*

Puzavil	Wicked Spirit	*NMI*
Puziel	Evil Angel	*SoM*
Pynceal	Spirit	*SSM*
Pypour (Sun)	Sun – Alternative Name	*Hyg*
Pyrgetōn/Pyrgetos/ Pyrgenon (Venus)	Venus – Alternative Name	*Hyg*
Pyripton (Mercury)	Mercury – Alternative Name	*Hyg*
Pyrotorō/Pritoōr/ Tyrrytōr	Demon – Tuesday Hour eight	*Hyg*
Psoafianta	Angel of Seas/Waters – Autumn	*SSM*
Pythian Serpent/Illou	Serpent of Foreknowledge	PGM XIII:1-343, XIII:343-646, XIII:646-734
Pytho/Python	Demon Prince – Spirits of Lies	*3BOP, BM, JMR, PO, tM*

	Q	
Qalha	Spirit	*AAAA*
Qamar (Arabic) (Saljail)	Angel – Moon	*SSG*
Qanor	Angel – Nisan	*tSoS*
Qarmayndim	Angel – Moon	*LL*
Qchnial	Angel – Sixth Encampment, first Heaven	*ShR*
Qdmial	Angel – Sixth Encampment, first Heaven	*ShR*
Qdshial	Angel – Eighth Step, second Heaven	*ShR*
Qedemial	Angel – Malachim, under Pheseker	*SRH*
Qedeshial	Angel Prince – Gate of Spirit of South	*SRH*
Qediesha	Angel Prince – Gate of Spirit of East	*SRH*
Qedonial	Angel – Malachim, under Pheseker	*SRH*
Qelebem	Angel Prince – Gate of Spirit of East	*SRH*
Qenial	Angel, serving above sixth Degree Angel Prince – Gate of Spirit of South	*SRH*
Qenomial	Angel – Malachim, under Ayigeda	*SRH*
Qephetzial	Angel – Caricorn, Aquarius	*SRH*
Qephien	Angel – Malachim, under Avorphenial	*SRH*
Qerekoteth	Angel Magistrate – Malachim	*SRH*

Qeremial	Angel – Malachim, sixth Host	SRH
Qerenial	Angel Prince – Gate of Spirit of West	SRH
Qeresetom	Angel – Malachim, under Phelmiya	SRH
Qerminat	Spirit – eleventh (twelfth) Mansion of the Moon ring	tSoS
Qeronieren	Angel – Malachim, sixth Host	SRH
Qethenial	Angel – Malachim, under Pheseker Angel – Malachim, sixth Host	SRH
Qetieki	Angel – Malachim, under Avorphenial	SRH
Qitr	Angel – Sixth Step, second Heaven	ShR
Qlaaial	Angel Encampment Head – sixth Heaven, East	ShR
Qlilial	Angel – Third Heaven, serving Rhtial	ShR
Qmnial	Angel Prince – fourth Heaven, Water	ShR
Qnal	Angel – Tenth Step, second Heaven	ShR
Qnatiel	Angel – Ab	SR
Qnumial	Angel – Second Encampment, first Heaven	ShR
Qnynzi	Angel – Ab	SR
Qodial	Angel Prince – Gate of Spirit of West	SRH
Qohelorek	Spirit – West in Spring	SRH
Qoherebek	Spirit – Summer	SRH
Qoherok	Spirit – East in Summer	SRH
Qokethial	Angel – Malachim over Rain	SRH
Qomiya	Angel – Malachim, under Ayigeda	SRH
Qonedek	Spirit – East	SRH
Qorebek	Spirit – East in Summer	SRH
Qorebithieh	Angel Prince	SRH
Qothial	Angel Minister – Malachim, over Water	SRH
Qrba	Angel – Fifth Encampment, first Heaven Angel – Ninth Step, second Heaven	ShR
Qrstus	Angel – Fourth Encampment, first Heaven	ShR
Qrukns	Angel – Seventh Encampment, first Heaven	ShR
Qrumial	Angel – Seventh Encampment, first Heaven	ShR
Qrunidn	Angel – Sixth Encampment, first Heaven	ShR

ABBREVIATIONS

Qshtial	Angel Encampment Head – sixth Heaven, East	*ShR*
Qsmial	Angel – Third Heaven, serving Ibnial	*ShR*
Qspial	Angel Prince – fourth Heaven, Water	*ShR*
Qstsdial	Angel – Third Heaven, serving Ibnial	*ShR*
Qswaappghyal	Angel Prince – Angels of Wrath	*SoM*
Qtgnypry	Angel Prince – Middle Five	*SoM*
Qtibia	Angel – First Encampment, first Heaven	*ShR*
Qtchnial	Angel – Third Heaven, serving Dlqial	*ShR*
Qtipur	Angel – Seventh Step, second Heaven	*ShR*
Quabriel	Angel – Air	*SR*
Quabriel/Vadriel	Angel Ruler – Day Hour nine	*Stg, ArP*
Quabriel/Uvabriel	Angel – Night Hour three	*Stg, ArP*
Quadissa/Quadisu/Quadissuu	Angel – Third Heaven, East	*SR, EoN, SaS*
Qualabye	Angel – Elul	*SR*
Quamshilindim	Angel – Moon	*LL*
Quantuball	Demon Prince of Darkness	*oADS*
Quato	Good Spirit	*SoM*
Qudshial	Angel Prince – fourth Heaven, Fire	*ShR*
Quelamia	Throne Angel (four of seven)	*SaS*
Quemon	Angel – Iyar	*SR*
Quenol/Uvenel	Angel – Night Hour one	*Stg, ArP*
Queriel	Angel – Day Hour four	*Stg, ArP*
Quesdor/Uvesolor	Angel – Night Hour five	*Stg, ArP*
Quesupale	Angel – Nisan	*SR*
Quial	Angel – Sixth Step, second Heaven	*ShR*
Quian	Angel – Second Heaven, North	*SR*
Quibda	Demon Duke – North Night	*Stg, ThG, BoTS*
Quiel	Angel – Fifth Heaven, North	*SR*
Quiheth	Good Spirit	*SoM*
Quilon	Angel – Saturn/Saturday	*SR*
Quirix/Vuirix/Uvirix	Angel – Day Hour twelve	*Stg, ArP*
Quiron	Angel – Saturn/Saturday	*SR*
Quiron	Spirit Assistant – Thursday	*MHN*

Quisiel	Angel – Jupiter/Thursday	SR
Quision	Servant Spirit	Abm
Quitta/Quita/Quinta	Demon Duke – East by North	Stg, ThG
Quivan	Angel – Nisan	tSoS
Qumial	Angel – Second Encampment, first Heaven	ShR
Qunaqrial	Angel – Fifth Step, second Heaven	ShR
Quntzilim	Angel – Moon	LL
Quor	Angel – Nisan	SR
Quorthonn	Evil Spirit	SoM
Quosiel	Angel – Day Hour two	Stg, ArP
Qup	Angel – Fifth Encampment, first Heaven	ShR
Quul	Spirit – Mirror	CoMS
Quyel	Angel – Jupiter, over Earth	SR
Quyron	Daemon Minister – Mercury; between the West and North	SBH
Quz	Angel – Sixth Step, second Heaven	ShR
Qwenael	Angel – Iyar	SR

R		
Ra/Re	Egyptian Creator and Sun God	PGM III:633-731, IV:94-153, 2145-2240, XII:153-160, PDM XIV:150-231, XIV:239-295, XIV:309-334, XIV:335-355, XIV:355-365, LXI:63-78; Suppl. 138-149
Raaciel	Angel – Tebet	SR
Raba	Alternative name of Metatron	SQ
Racyel	Angel – Fifth Heaven, East	SSM
Raadnial	Angel Prince – fourth Heaven, Water	ShR
Raagios	Enochian King – West	TBA
Raajah	Genii – 12° Aquarius	ArP
Raamyel	Angel – Marchesvan Angel – First Heaven, East	SSM, SR

Ra'asiel	Angel	*SoM*
Raba	Alternative name of Metatron	*SQ*
Rabacyel	Angel Prince – third Heaven and Fire	*SaS*
Rabam	Spirit	*MHN*
Rabas	Demon Duke – South-West Day	*Stg, ThG, BoTS*
Rabat/Rabas	Spirit	*BoO*
Rabchlou	Angel	*PGM* XXXVI:161-177
Rabdos ('Staff')	Demon	*ToS*
Rabees	Front part of Gharnos	*Pic*
Rabeffie	Demon	*CoC*
Raberion	Angel (Mars?)	*GAG*
Rabfilyn	Angel – Mars/Tuesday	*SR*
Rabidmadar	Spirit Secretary	*SoS*
Rabiēēl	Angel	*PGM* XXXVI:161-177
Rabiel	Angel – Mercury, over Earth	*SR*
Rabiel	Demon Duke – West by South Night, West Day	*Stg, ThG, BoTS*
Rabit	Angel – Third Heaven, West Angel – Saturn	*EoN, GAG*
Rablion	Demon Duke – East	*Stg, ThG*
Rabmia	Angel – Mercury/Wednesday	*SR*
Raboc	Demon Duke – West Night	*Stg, ThG, BoTS*
Rabuel	Angel	*ACM*: P. Lichačev
Rabyel	Angel – Third Heaven, West	*SSM*
Rachiel/Rachiell	Angel – Friday	*Hmn, CBoM, tSoS, BoO, GAG, PO*
Rachiel	Presiding Spirit – Venus	*SGT, SSG*
Rachion	Angel	*NA*
Raconeal	Angel – Saturn/Saturday	*SR*
Racyeylyn	Angel – Mars/Tuesday	*SR*
Racynas	Angel – Tishrei	*SR*
Racyno	Angel – Kislev	*SR*
Radalam	Demon	*NML*
Radarap	Servant Spirit	*Abm*

Rade	Demon King – Monday	*KoN*
Radiel	Angel – Kislev Angel – Sunday/Sun	*SR, KoSR*
Radiel	Demon Count	*M.NeI*
Rael	Biblical Elder	*ACM*: Berlin 11347, Oriental 6796
Rael	Angel – Second Heaven Wednesday, North Ministering Spirit – Mercury	*Hmn, KoSR, BoO, GAG, BoTS, tM, CBMS*
Rael	Intelligence – Venus	*SGT, SSG*
Rafael	Angel – Fire Angel – Air	*SR*
Rafael/Raphaeel/Rufijail	Spirit King – Jupiter	*Pic, SSG*
Raffeylyn	Angel – Mars/Tuesday	*SR*
Ragael	Angel – Adar	*SR*
Ragarad	Spirit	*GAG*
Ragaras	Servant Spirit	*Abm*
Ragat	Angel – Cherubim/Seraphim	*67M*
Ragehyel	Angel – Air	*SR*
Ragiel	Demon – Friday	*GoPH*
Ragnel/Ragnell	Angel – Venus Angel – Fourth Heaven, East	*SR, SaS, oADS, GAG*
Ragueguael	Angel – Fourth Heaven, East	*SSM*
Raguel/Raguell	Angel	*ACM*: P. Prague 1, Oriental 5525; Hay 10122, Oriental 6796; *AN, GAG, oADS*
Rahab	Primordial Sea Monster	HB Ps 89:11, Isa 51:9
Rahel	Angel – Second Heaven, North Angel – Thursday/Jupiter	*EoN, KoSR*
Rahovart	Demon Tormentor of Evil	*DI*
Rahqayāl	Angel – Jupiter	*BoW*
Rahu	Spirit	*AAAA*
Rahumel/Rabumel/Rhaumel/Rahumiel/Rahumyel	Angel – Fourth Heaven, North Angel – Fifth Heaven Tuesday, North Angel – Fifth Heaven, North	*SSM, Hmn, KoSR, BoO, GAG, BoTS, SaS, tM*

Rahumiel	Angel – Fourth Heaven, North	*SR*
Rahyeziel	Angel – Tebet	*SR*
Rak	Servant Spirit	*Abm*
Ra-Khephri-Atum	Egyptian Composite Solar God	PDM XIV:309-334
Rakuel	Angel	*ACM*: Bodl C(P)4, Moen 3
Rakyel	Angel Subordinate – Venus	*SSM*
Raliel	Angel – Jupiter/Thursday	*SR*
Ralkh	Angel – First Encampment, first Heaven	*ShR*
Ralyel	Angel – Fifth Heaven, South	*EoN*
Ram	Angel – Nisan	*SR*
Ramalath	Spirit	*BoO*
Ramana	Angel – Eighth Altitude (Scorpio)	*Alm*
Ramasaell/Ramasael	Spirit – Moon	*BoO, GAG*
Ramath	Spirit	*oADS*
Ramath	Demon – North	*GoPH*
Ramatiel	Angel – Mercury, over Air	*SR*
Ramatziel	Angel	*Hyg*
Ramaziel	Angel – Night Hour two	*Stg, ArP*
Ramdoth	Demon – South	*GoPH*
Ramel	Spirit Messenger – Mercury	*SGT, SSG*
Rameriel/Rameziel/ Ramesiel	Angel – Day Hour five	*Stg, ArP*
Ramesiel	Angel – Night Hour one	*Stg, ArP*
Ramiach	Intelligence	*EPL*
Ramica	Demon Duke – North Day	*Stg, ThG, BoTS*
Raminam	Demon	*CoC*
Ramiuson/Ramaison	Servant Spirit	*Abm, MRC*
Ramnel	Angel – Jupiter/Thursday	*SR*
Ramoch	Spirit – South	*SSM*
Ramoras	Servant Spirit	*Abm*
Rampel	Angel ruling Deep Waters and Mountains	*SoM*
Ramul	Intelligence	*BoG*
Ramyel	Angel – Third Heaven, North	*SSM*
Ranar	Servant Spirit	*Abm*

Ranas	Devil – third Hour of Day	oADS
Ranciel/Rantiel	Demon Duke – South by West Day	Stg, ThG, BoTS
Rancyl	Angel – Sun/Sunday	SR
Randat	Demon Servant – Monday	KoN
Ranfiel	Angel – Shebat	SR
Raniel/Rabiel/ Ramael/ Ranael	Angel – Third Heaven Friday, North	EoN, Hmn, KoSR, BoO, BM, GAG, BoTS, tM
Rapax	Demon Prince	SSM
Rapeh	Enochian Angel – North, over second lesser Angle	TBA
Raphael/Raphaell/ Raphiell	Archangel – Mercury, Air, Wednesday, Fire, Sun, Venus, Jupiter, West Wind, Evening Winds, second Heaven, East, Leo Archangel – Tiphereth Archangel – Geburah and Tiphereth Angel Commander Ruler of Order of Archangels/Virtues third Heaven Friday – North Intelligence – Mercury Angel Prince – Gate of Spirit of North Archangel – Malachim, over the Shem Angel Prince – Winter	HB Tob 3:17, 5:4, 5:10, 6:11-18, 7:9, 8:3-4, 9:1, 9:5, 11:4, 11:7, 12:5-20; PGM III:1-164, III:187-262, VII:1009-1016, VII:1017-1026, X:36-50, XXVI:1-42, XXXVI:161-177, XLIII:1-27, XC:1-13, CVI:1-10, CXXIIIa:1-70; ToS, SM: P. Berol inv. 21165, P. Heid. Inv. G 1101, P. Heid. Inv. Lat. 5, P. Med. I.20, P. Mil. Vogl. Inv. 1245-50, 1252-53; ACM: H. Kopt. 544, Berlin 11347, Oriental 5525, BN Turin; Hay 10434, Oriental 5986, Bodl C(P)4, P. Prague 1, Berlin 10587, Moen 3, P. Mich. 3472, Oriental 6794, Oriental 6795, Oriental 6796, P. Mich. 593, L. Anastasi 9, H. Kopt. 686; SoM, dCL, SSM, NA, SR, SBH, EoN, Hmn, B7R,

ABBREVIATIONS 615

Raphael/Raphaell/ Raphiell (con't.)		BARC, KoSR, Gbk, CBoM, SoS, MHN, dN, CoC, tSoS, dSS, ADS, 3BOP, oADS, BoO, DoW, BM, dHM, Thm, GAG, MC, Goe, BoTS, ArP, JMR, 9CK, SaS, MNeI, KoN, BoSC, GoA, SMS, SRH, EPL, PO, ClI, MRC, 67M, CoMS, tM, CBMS
Raphael	Spirit Messenger – Mercury Presiding Spirit – Mercury	SGT, SSG
Raphal	Angel – Harvest Ruler	SRH
Raphayel	Angel – Fire	SSM
Raphiel	Angel – Sun	GAG
Raphiel	Genii – 8° Taurus, 8° Gemini	ArP
Raphyel	Angel Subordinate – Jupiter	SSM
Rapinis	Angel – Tebet	SR
Rapion	Angel – Elul	SR
Rapsiel/Rapsel	Demon Duke – West	Stg, ThG
Raquayel	Angel Ruler – third Season by Day	SSM
Raquiel	Spirit – Venus	SBH, EoN
Rardem	Vervain Herb Spirit	BoO
Rarith/Bario	Spirit – eighth Mansion of the Moon Ring	AE, tSoS
Rarilzispus/ Raryhispus	Spirit – Seducer of Women	oADS
Rarnilpus	Spirit – Seducer of Women	oADS
Rartmaratarium	Treasure Spirit	MNeI
Rartudel	Angel – Jupiter/Thursday	SR
Ras	Demon President	NML
Rasaidin	Angel – Moon	LL
Rasamen	Angel	NA
Rasaym	Angel	NA
Raschear	Servant Spirit	Abm
Rasell	Angel	oADS

Raseroph	Angel – Elul	*SR*
Rasfia	Angel – Mercury/Wednesday	*SR*
Ra-Shu	Egyptian Composite God	PDM Suppl. 162-168
Rasiel/Raysiel	Demon Duke – North Demon Duke – North under Egyn	*Stg, ThG, BoTS, KoN*
Rasil	Angel – Venus	*BoW*
Rasinet/Rasynet	Demon Messenger	*BoO*
Rasliel	Angel – Marchesvan	*SR*
Rasoiel	Angel – Fire	*SR*
Rassy	Angel – Elul	*SR*
Rasyel	Demon Messenger	*BoO*
Rasziel	Angel – Elul	*SR*
Rata	Spirit – Minister of Love	*oADS*
Rath/Radinos	Demon	*ToS*
Rathan	Angel – Seventh Altitude (Libra)	*Alm*
Rathanael	Angel	*ToS*
Rather	Spirit – Minister of Love	*oADS*
Rathiel	Genii – 9° Virgo	*ArP*
Rathion	Angel	*SBH*
Raton	Spirit – Seducer of Women	*oADS*
Ratoplo	Spirit – Minister of Love	*oADS*
Rator	Demon	*MHN*
Ratziel	Genii – 8° Pisces	*ArP*
Rauhardt	Spirit – Rules Tyrants	*KoN*
Raum/Raim	Demon Earl	*PmD, DoW, Goe*
Raumel	Angel – Fifth Heaven, North	*EoN*
Rawa	Spirit – Mercury	*67M*
Rayel/Rael	Angel fifth Heaven Tuesday – North	*EoN, Hmn, KoSR, BoO, GAG, BoTS, tM*
Rayma	Demon Spirit – Minister of Love	*MHN, oADS*
Rayziel/Raisziel/Raisiel	Angel – Night Hour four, Night Hour seven	*Stg, ArP*
Razhyāl	Angel – Hour one/Aries	*BoW*

ABBREVIATIONS

Raziel/Razyel/Rezial	Archangel – Saturn Archangel – Chokmah Ruler of Order of Cherubim	*SSM, KoSA, tSoS, JMR, 9CK, SaS, MNeI, Thm, SRH, CoMS*
Razimas	Spirit – East	*SSM*
Rbaaial	Angel – Sixth Step, second Heaven	*ShR*
Rbal	Angel Prince – fourth Heaven, Fire	*ShR*
Rbnia	Angel – Ninth Step, second Heaven	*ShR*
Rbsal	Angel Prince – fourth Heaven, Water	*ShR*
Rchbia	Angel – Seventh Encampment, first Heaven	*ShR*
Rchbial	Angel – Third Encampment, first Heaven	*ShR*
Rchgl	Angel – First Encampment, first Heaven	*ShR*
Rdnāl	Angel – Hour two/Taurus	*BoW*
Rdqial	Angel – Eleventh Step, second Heaven	*ShR*
Rdrial	Angel Prince – fourth Heaven, Water	*ShR*
Reanei	Angel – Moon	*LL*
Reat	Angel – Venus	*GAG*
Reatonay/Reatony	Spirit	*BoO*
Reba	Angel Prince – Gate of Spirit of East	*SRH*
Reba'ayial	Angel, serving above sixth Degree	*SRH*
Rebenial	Angel Prince – Moon in Autumn	*SRH*
Rebial	Angel Prince – Malachim, Tebeth	*SRH*
Rebiyov Derephes	Angel Prince – Winter	*SRH*
Rebon	Angel Prince – Winter	*SRH*
Rechegal	Angel – Malachim, under Avorphenial	*SRH*
Rechomial	Angel Prince – Gate of Spirit of North	*SRH*
Rechonal	Angel – Malachim, under Ayigeda	*SRH*
Reciel/Raciel	Demon Duke – South by West Night	*Stg, ThG, BoTS*
Redethal	Angel – Malachim, under Ayigeda	*SRH*
Red Fighter/Red King	Demon King – Mars	*BARC*
Redophial	Angel – Malachim, Winter Nights	*SRH*
Rees (Rubaeel, Roman)	Spirit King – Mars	*Pic*
Refacbilion	Angel – Saturn/Saturday	*SR*

Refer	Spirit – Minister of Love	oADS
Regael	Genii – 11° Sagittarius	ArP
Regay	Angel	NA
Regerion	Servant Spirit	Abm
Regessa	Treasure Spirit	oADS
Regethal	Spirit – North	SSM
Regnia	Angel – Iyar	SR
Reguelim	Angel	dN
Rehael/Rohael/Rechael	Angel – Shem thirty-nine	KoSU, 3BOP, GoeR, JMR, SAS, tM
Rehal	Angel Prince – Mystery of the Shekinah	SRH
Rehebial	Angel Prince	SRH
Rehetial	Angel Prince – Malachim, over Horseman and Horse of Fire	SRH
Rehiel	Genii – 11° Scorpio	ArP
Reiajel/Rejaiel/Reiiel/Rechael/Rejiel	Angel – Shem twenty-nine	KoSU, 3BOP, GoeR, JMR, SAS, tM
Re-Kephri-Atum	Egyptian Universal Sun God (Composite)	PGM III:633-731
Rekial	Angel – Malachim, under Ayigeda Angel Prince – Gate of Spirit of West	SRH
Relemu	Enochian Angel – North, serving second lesser Angle	TBA
Relfato	Angel – Jupiter	GAG
Relfem	Devil – Early Morning	oADS
Relion	Angel – Saturn/Saturday	SR
Relmo	Spirit – Minister of Love	oADS
Relsez	Devil – Early Morning	oADS
Remafidda	Angel – Tammuz	SR
Remasyn/Remasin/Remafin	Angel – Day Hour eight	Stg, ArP
Remcatheyel	Angel – Sun/Sunday	SR
Rememal	Angel Prince – Gate of Spirit of East	SRH
Remial	Angel Prince – Gate of Spirit of North	SRH
Remiemial	Angel – Malachim, under Ayigeda	SRH
Remisia/Remisian	Spirit	KoN

Remma	Evil Demon	3BOP
Rendos	Spirit – Mars	BoO, GAG
Renerdena	Angel – Malachim, under Ayigeda	SRH
Rengliel	Genii – 10° Scorpio	ArP
Reniel	Enochian Angel – West, serving fourth lesser Angle	TBA
Repeli	Treasure Spirit	oADS
Rephan	Composite of Syrian God and Goddess (Renpu and Kan)	HB Acts 7:43
Rephedial	Angel – Malachim over Fire and Flames	SRH
Reqehethov	Angel – Malachim, under Avorphenial	SRH
Requiel	Noble Spirit, Fire	MNeI
Requyeyl	Angel – Venus	SSM
Rerabfecerataz	Planetary Spirit Lord – Mercury	SSM
Reralath	Spirit – Moon	BoO, GAG
Reranressym	Spirit of the Thumb	MHN
Resaym	Angel	NA
Resbiroth	Demon Duke – under Elestor	KoSU, SoS
Reschin	Demon Duke	SoS
Resegar	Angel – Iyar	SR
Resen	Spirit – South	SSM
Reseni	Enochian Angel – North, serving first lesser Angle	TBA
Resfilin	Angel – Venus/Friday	SR
Resphodōm (Venus)	Venus – Alternative Name	Hyg
Ressilia/Restillia/Restilia/Rostillia	Fairy – second of seven sisters	oADS, BoO, JMR, BoTS
Restun	Spirit King	BoO
Reta	Spirit – Venus	67M
Retziel	Angel	Hyg
Reuces	Spirit – Hot	MHN
Reufates/Reufo	Spirit – Love	NML
Reumdatha/Reumdath	Spirit – Saturn	BoO, GAG
Rewboo/Kewboo	Demon Prince	BOS, BoO
Rewsyn	Demon Duke	BOS, BoO

Rexao	Enochian Angel – North, serving third lesser Angle	*TBA*
Rexenel	Enochian Angel – West, over fourth lesser Angle	*TBA*
Reycat	Angel – Ab	*SR*
Reÿmonzorackon,	Spirit Prince	*BoMS*
Reyn	Angel – Mars/Tuesday	*SR*
'Rfyāl	Angel – March	*BoW*
Rgbial	Angel – Fifth Encampment, first Heaven	*ShR*
Rhaamet/Raimet	Demon	*ToSC*
Rhadamncus/ Radamandus	Infernal Judge	*3BOP, MNeI*
Rhaetziel	Angel	*Hyg*
Rhakatlia/Rhakalia	Angel	*Hyg*
Rhakidōn/Rhaekrō/ Rhakitō/Rhakirō/ Rhaektron	Demon – Tuesday Hour twenty-two	*Hyg*
Rhamatiēl	Angel – Monday Hour sixteen	*Hyg*
Rhandouēl	Angel	*Hyg*
Rhanitza (Jupiter)	Jupiter – Alternative Name	*Hyg*
Rhaphaēl / Rhaphael/ Sarphaēl (Raphael)	Angel – Thursday Hour one, Jupiter Luna – Alternative Name	*BoW, Hyg*
Rhaphgia/ Rhaphygia/ Rhapidōn	Angel	*Hyg*
Rhariōph/ Rhaphiōph/ Phariōth/Phrariōth	Demon – Friday Hour four	*Hyg*
Rhasaphael	Angel	*Hyg*
Rhatziele	Angel	*Hyg*
Rhede	Demon – South	*Hyg*
Rhēēl	Demon	*Hyg*
Rhendipōn/ Rhendipon/ Rhedepoon/ Rhedipon/ Rhenpidon	Demon – South	*Hyg*
Rhēpēdon	Spirit	*Hyg*

Rheradēkh/ Rhirathokh	Angel – Plant Ruler	*BoW*
Rherana	Spirit	*Hyg*
Rhēsiel	Angel – Thursday Hour twenty	*Hyg*
Rhesphodōm/ Rhesphidok (Venus)	Venus – Alternative Name	*Hyg*
Rhetaēl	Angel – Saturday Hour six	*Hyg*
Rhieridōn/Rhisdron	Spirit – East	*Hyg*
Rhixgioudan/ Rhēxēouda	Demon – North	*Hyg*
Rhixtheoul	Demon – South	*Hyg*
Rhoapt	Demon	*ToSC*
Rhoel	Angel	*Hyg*
Rhōgeēth	Angel	*Hyg*
Rhogēl	Angel	*Hyg*
Rhokhaēl/Rhakhaēl	Angel – Monday Hour twelve	*Hyg*
Rhōmaēl	Spirit	*BoW*
Rhomatiēl/ Rhamaēl/ Rhamatiēl/ Rhōmatiēl/ Rhamaiēl	Angel – Monday Hour seventeen	*BoW, Hyg*
Rhoudiel/Rhoudiēl	Angel – Friday Hour fourteen	*Hyg*
Rhoudiēl	Angel – Friday Hour thirteen	*Hyg*
Rhoustat/Rhoktat/ Rhroutar	Demon – Wednesday Hour twenty-three	*Hyg*
Rhoutziēl/Rhitzioēl/ Rhizoēl/Trizioēl/ Rhipsioēl	Angel – Tuesday Hour twenty-three	*Hyg*
Rhtial	Angel Prince two of three – third Heaven Angel – Seventh Encampment, first Heaven	*ShR*
Riajah	Genii – 12° Capricorn	*ArP*
Riamiuta/Ruiaminta	Spirit – Venus	*BoO, GAG*
Riarufa/Riarnfa	Spirit – Moon	*BoO, GAG*
Riasteli	Spirit	*MHN*
Ribesal/Rubezal	Silesian Weather Spectre	*DI*
Richel	Demon Duke – North by East Night	*Stg, ThG*

Ries	Enochian Evil Spirit	*TBA*
Rieshiehon	Angel, serving above sixth Degree	*SRH*
Rignell	Spirit – Venus	*oADS*
Rigolen/Rigaton	Servant Spirit	*Abm, MRC*
Rimezyn/Remezyn/ Remesin/Rimesin	Angel – Night Hour four	*Stg, ArP*
Rimog	Servant Spirit	*Abm*
Rimasor	Spirit	*MHN*
Rimel	Spirit – Water	*MHN*
Rinafonel	Angel – Mercury, over Water	*SR*
Ripipis	Angel – Second Step, second Heaven	*ShR*
Risbel/Ristel	Spirit	*MHN*
Rixtheoul/ Rēxthelou/ Rhyxtheoul	Demon – South	*Hyg*
Rkilal	Angel – Second Encampment, first Heaven	*ShR*
Rlbial	Angel – Third Heaven, serving Ibnial	*ShR*
Rmgdl	Angel – Fifth Encampment, first Heaven	*ShR*
Rmial	Angel – Seventh Encampment, first Heaven	*ShR*
Rnchial	Angel Encampment Head – sixth Heaven, East	*ShR*
Rndyāl/Randyāl	Angel – Hour three/Gemini/ Orion	*BoW*
Rnzial	Angel – First Step, second Heaven	*ShR*
Roab	Treasure Spirit	*BoTS*
Roah	Angel – Dominations	*67M*
Roauian/Roauia	Fairy Lady	*BoO, GAG*
Robica	Angel – Nisan	*SR, tSoS*
Robyell	Angel	*oADS*
Rochell	Angel	*GAG*
Rocle	Spirit – Son of Sons of Light	*dHM*
Rodabell/Rodybell/ Rodobell/Radabelbes	Demon Messenger – North	*BOS, BoO*
Roder/Veder/Bober	Spirit – thirteenth Mansion of the Moon Ring	*AE*
Rodobayl/Rodobail	Spirit	*MHN*

Rodmache	Spirit	*BoTS*
Roehel/Raehel/ Roheel	Angel – Shem sixty-nine	*KoSU, 3BOP, GoeR, JMR, SAS, tM*
Roeled	Demon – Decan fifteen	*ToS*
Roemnab	Spirit Minister, serving Prince Bornogo	*dHM*
Rofanes	Demon	*MHN*
Rofiniel	Angel – Jupiter/Thursday	*SR*
Rohi	Demon	*SMS*
Romages	Servant Spirit	*Abm*
Romalov	Angel – Malachim, under Avorphenial	*SRH*
Rombalence/ Ramblane	Demon King – West Spirit Messenger – West	*BOS, BoO, BoTS*
Romial	Angel – Pisces	*SRH*
Romiel	Demon Duke – North by East Day	*Stg, ThG*
Romiel	Angel – Adar Angel – Day Hour twelve	*SR, Stg, ArP*
Romoron	Servant Spirit	*Abm*
Romulon	Demon Soldier	*BoO*
Romyel/Remyel	Demon Duke – Day Hour six and Night Hour six	*Stg, ThG*
Roncayl	Angel – Sun/Sunday	*SR*
Roncefall	Spirit – Minister of Love	*oADS*
Ronmeyeyl	Angel – Sun/Sunday	*SR*
Ronos	Angel before Throne of God	*oADS*
Ronove/Roneve/ Ronwe	Demon Marquis and Earl	*PmD, DoW, Goe, DI*
Roqial	Angel – Harvest Ruler	*SRH*
Roqniel	Angel – Fire	*SR*
Roquiel/Requiel	Angel – Mansion twenty-three	*3BOP, tSoS, JMR, SaS, tM*
Rorafeyl	Angel – Mars/Tuesday	*SR*
Rorex	Angel	*ToS*
Roriel/Rouiel/ Roniel/ Roviel	Demon Duke – West by South Day	*Stg, ThG, BoTS*
Rosaran	Servant Spirit	*Abm*

Rostafalagath/ Rostalagath/ Rastafalagath	Spirit – Mercury	*BoO, GAG*
Rotor	Servant Spirit	*Abm*
Rou (Rouvayet?)	Spirit	*GoPH*
Roubēl	Angel	*PGM* XXXVI:161-177
Rouēl	Angel – Venus	*Hyg*
Roumbouthiēl/ Roubouthiēl	Angel	*PGM* XXXVI:161-177
Rouvayet	Spirit	*GoPH*
Rovamhal	Plant Spirit – Buttercup	*GS*
Rowdeys	Night Devil	*oADS*
Roya	Punishing Wind	*SSM*
Royne	Demon Earl	*BOS, BoO*
Rpdial	Angel – Eleventh Step, second Heaven	*ShR*
Rppial	Angel – Third Step, second Heaven	*ShR*
Rqhti	Angel – First Encampment, first Heaven	*ShR*
Rshial	Angel – First Step, second Heaven	*ShR*
Rsput	Angel – Fourth Encampment, first Heaven	*ShR*
Ruah	Alternative name of Metatron	*SQ*
Ruax	Demon – Decan one	*ToS*
Rubaeel/Robaeel/ Rubijail	Spirit King – Mars	*Pic, SSG*
Rubycyel	Angel – Jupiter/Thursday	*SR*
Rucal	Demon Senior	*SSM*
Ruchen	Night Devil	*oADS*
Rudefor/Rudozor	Angel – Night Hour six	*Stg, ArP*
Ruduel	Spirit – Mercury	*SoS*
Ruel	Angel	*ACM*: Oriental 5899
Rufalas	Night Devil	*oADS*
Rufangoll	Spirit	*BoO, GAG*
Ruffaraneylyn	Angel – Mars/Tuesday	*SR*
Rulbelyn	Angel – Mars/Tuesday	*SR*
Ruluxidye	Angel – Fourth Altitude (Cancer)	*Alm*
Rumapi	Angel – First Encampment, first Heaven	*ShR*

Rumiel	Angel – One of twenty-one on the Left	*ACM*: Berlin 10587
Runuel	Angel – seventeen of twenty-one on the Left	*ACM*: Berlin 10587
Rupasta	Spirit – sixth Mansion of Moon Ring	*tSoS*
Ruphos	Angel – Egypt	*ACM*: Vienna K 8304
Rurcos	Spirit – Seducer of Women	*oADS*
Ruweno	Archangel	*67M*
Ryall/Reyall/Ruall (Vuall)	Demon – West	*BOS, BoO, oADS*
Rybyd	Supportive Planetary Spirit – Venus	*SSM*
Rymaliel/Rimaliel	Angel – Night Hour one	*Stg, ArP*
Rymor	Spirit Familiar	*BoTS*
Ryon	Punishing Wind Daemon – Jupiter, serving North and East Winds; between East and South	*SSM, SBH*
Rzial	Angel – Seventh Step, second Heaven	*ShR*

S

Saabotes	Spirit King – Friday	*MHN*
Saagon	Angel Lord – Nights of the Year	*SSM*
Saal (Saturn)	Saturn – Alternative Name	*Hyg*
Saalalebeth	Spirit Assistant – Thursday	*MHN*
Saamyel	Angel – Tammuz	*SR*
Saaronitbehofz/ Szaaronitbehofz	Planetary Spirit Lord – Sun	*SSM*
Saathan	Demon Governor, Wind of Lucifer	*SSM*
Saba	Spirit King – Wednesday / Demon King – Wednesday	*MHN, KoN*
Saba (Mediat?)	Angel – King of Air on Wednesday	*BoO*
Sababiel	Angel – Tishrei	*SR*
Sabael	Angel	PDM XIV:627-635
Sabael	Angel over the Good	*ACM*: BN Turin
Sabael	Angel – Wednesday	*MHN*
Sabaēl (Luna)	Luna – Alternative Name	*Hyg*
Saball	Angel Chief – sixth Heaven by Night	*SaS*

Sabalonod	Demon – East	*Hyg*
Sabanitera	Angel	*KoSA*
Sabaoth[420]	Angel	*dN, AN*
Sabas	Demon Duke – South by West Day	*Stg, ThG, BoTS*
Sabathiel/Sabathiell (Cassiel)	Archangel – Saturn	*3BOP, BoO, tSoS, JMR, SaS, Thm*
Sabayhon	Angel	*NA*
Sabée	Angel Minister – Love and Fornication	*KoSA*
Sabeel/Sabaēl/Sabatiēl/Sabrēēl/Sabagiēl/Beiēl	Angel – Mars	*Hyg*
Sabial	Angel – Fourth Encampment, first Heaven	*ShR*
Sabiel	Demon – East	*GoPH*
Sabiel	Genii – 25° Cancer	*ArP*
Sabnacke/Sabnach/Sabnac/Sabnock/Salmac	Demon Marquis	*PmD, DoW, Goe*
Saboles	Angel	*KoSA*
Sabrael	Angel	*ToS*
Sabrathan/Sabrachan/Sabrachon	Angel Ruler – Night Hour one	*Stg, ArP*
Sabriēl/Sabēel/Sanbriel	Angel – Sun	*Hyg*
Sabrikel/Sabboliker/Sablēker	Demon – West	*Hyg*
Sabriel	Superior Intelligence – Sun	*KoSU, SoS*
Sabwell	Demon Prince of Darkness	*oADS*
Sacadiel	Angel – Bisertilis	*SR*
Saccantos	Angel Minister	*KoSA*
Sacciniel	Angel – Jupiter/Thursday	*SR*
Sacdon	Angel – Tishrei	*SR*
Sacepe	Enochian Angel – South, over third lesser Angle	*TBA*
Sachael	Genii – 3° Gemini, 30° Taurus	*ArP*

---

420 This divine name being used as an angelic name is unusual, to say the least.

Sachan	Demon Companion – Thursday	*KoN*
Sachieh	Spirit Messenger – Saturn	*SGT*
Sachiel	Angel – Kislev	*SR*
Sachiel/Sochiel	Archangel – Jupiter, Earth, Thursday, Friday first Heaven Monday – West third Heaven Friday – South Intelligence – Jupiter Presiding Spirit – Moon	*Hmn, KoSR, SoS, ADS, CBoM, BoO, DoW, BM, tSoS, MC, GAG, GoeR, ArP, JMR, 9CK, BoTS, GoA, ClI, CoMS, PO, tM, CBMS*
Sachiel	Presiding Spirit – Jupiter Presiding Spirit – Venus	*SGT, SSG*
Sachiel	Genii – 1° Cancer, 3° Taurus, 5° Cancer	*ArP*
Sachmoune (Sekhmet)	Egyptian Lioness-Headed War Goddess	PGM VII:359-369
Sachoiel	Angel – thirteen of twenty-one on the Left	*ACM*: Berlin 10587
Sachquiel	Angel – Jupiter/Thursday	*SR*
Saciaton	Demon Prince – Hell	*oADS*
Saciel	Angel Ruler – Tisirin	*SR*
Sackenach	Angel – Second Season by Night	*SSM*
Sacqiel	Angel – Second Season by Day	*SSM*
Sacquiel	Angel – Friday	*MHN*
Sacriel/Sacriell	Angel – Fifth Heaven Tuesday, South Angel – Fifth Heaven, South	*EoN, Hmn, KoSR, BoO, GAG, BoTS, SaS, tM*
Sacromatyhel	Angel	*NA*
Sacstoyeyn	Angel – Moon/Monday	*SR*
Sadael	Spirit	*tSoS*
Sadai	Angel	*Thm*
Sadama	Angel	*NA*
Sadar	Demon Duke – North Day	*Stg, ThG, BoTS*
Saday	Spirit	*CoC*
Saddaniel	Angel – Sun, over Fire	*SR*
Saddiel	Demon Duke – North-West Night	*Stg, ThG, BoTS*
Sadiel	Angel – Third Heaven, South	*SR*
Sadiel	Demon Duke – South by West Night/Day	*Stg, ThG, BoTS*
Sadiel	Genii – 17° Leo	*ArP*

Sadiniel/Sadimel	Angel – Day Hour three	Stg, ArP
Saditel	Angel – Third Heaven, South	SaS
Sadon	Mirror Spirit – Saturday Spirit – Seducer of Women	MNeI, oADS
Saefarn	Demon Duke – North-West Day	Stg, ThG, BoTS
Saefer	Demon Duke – North-West Day	Stg, ThG, BoTS
Saem	Spirit – Minister of Love	oADS
Saemiel/Sarmiel	Demon Duke – West by South Night	Stg, ThG, BoTS
Saeosin	Angel – Moon	LL
Saeprel	Angel – Fifth Heaven, North	SR
Saesechel	Angel – Over Serpents	PGM XXVI:1-42
Safaole/Sanefarle	Spirit – eighth Mansion of the Moon Ring	AE
Safcy	Angel – Tishrei	SR
Saffea	Angel – Moon	BARC
Saffeyeyl	Angel – Sun/Sunday	SR
Saffiell	Angel – Saturn	GAG
Saficiel	Spirit – Middle	SSM
Safida	Angel – Tammuz	SR
Safrax	Angel – Eleventh Altitude (Aquarius)	Alm
Safrit	Demon	MHN
Safuel	Angel – Iyar	SR
Safyn	Angel – Potestates	67M
Sagaciy	Spirit Minister, serving Prince Befafes	dHM
Sagarez	Servant Spirit	Abm
Sagatana/Sagathana/Sargatanas	Demon	GG, GV
Sagel	Genii – 16° Cancer	ArP
Sagiel	Angel – Day Hour seven	Stg, ArP
Sagiel	Genii – 14° Leo, 26° Leo	ArP
Sagittariel/Sagitariel (Aorachiel)	Angel – Sagittarius Spirit – Sagittarius	3BOP, tSoS, JMR, SaS
Sagman	Alternative name of Metatron	SQ
Sagnel	Genii – 12° Aries	ArP
Saguar	Angel	NA

ABBREVIATIONS

Sagum	Spirit – Venus	*SoS*
Sahacabary	Angel	*NA*
Sahael	Genii – 3° Libra	*ArP*
Sahaman	Angel – Kislev	*SR*
Sahees	Right part of Barhoyas	*Pic*
Sahel	Genii – 5° Leo	*ArP*
Sahgragynyn	Angel – Moon/Monday	*SR*
Sahiel	Genii – 28° Cancer	*ArP*
Sahon	Angel	*67M*
Sahoryel	Angel – Fourth Heaven, South	*SSM*
Sahuhaf	Angel – Shebat	*SR*
Sahumiel	Angel – Shebat	*SR*
Saiinou	Enochian Senior – West	*TBA*
Sailmon/Zamon (Sabnock?)	Demon Duke and President and Count	*NML*
Saine	Spirit – Minister of Love	*oADS*
Saint Anthony	Saint	*BoSC*
Saint Barbara	Saint	*BoSC*
Saint Blaise	Saint	*BoSC*
Saint Cosmas	Saint	*BoSC*
Saint Cyprian	Saint	*ACM*: H. Kopt. 684; *dN*; *BoSC*
Saint Etienne/Stephen	Saint	*BoG*
Saint Francis	Saint	*ES*
Saint George	Saint	*BoO*
Saint Gregory	Saint	*BoSC*
Saint Justina	Saint	*BoSC*
Saint Leontius	Saint	*ACM*: Rylands 100
Saint Louis	Saint	*BoSC*
Saint Lucia	Saint	*BoSC*
Saint Manso	Saint	*BoSC*
Saint Mateo/Matao	Saint	*BoSC*
Saint Petrus/Peter	Saint	*GoPH*

Saint Philoxenus	Saint	*ACM*: Oxy. 1150, Oxy. 1926, Harris 54
Saint Phocas	Saint	*ACM*: Oxy. 1060
Saint Rita	Saint	*BoSC*
Saint Serenus	Saint	*ACM*: Berlin 954
Saint Sylvester	Saint	*BoSC*
Saint Zachariah	Saint	*ACM*: Cairo IAFO
Saipaleppe	Angel – Saturn	*GAG*
Saix	Enochian Angel – West, serving first lesser Angle	*TBA*
Sakatiel/Bakatoēl	Angel – Saturn	*Hyg*
Sakhiel	Angel	*Hyg*
Sakhmet/Sekhmet	Egyptian Lioness-Headed War Goddess	PDM XIV:150-231, XIV:309-334, XIV:355-365
Sakiboēl	Angel	*Hyg*
Sakipiēl/Sakapiel/ Sakatiēl/Sabapiēl	Angel – Saturday Hour one	*Hyg*
Sakobolas/Sabolōn/ Salbo/Sabalonod	Spirit – East	*Hyg*
Salainel	Angel – Venus, over Earth	*SR*
Salamex	Gnostic Light in Thought	*ACM*: NH Codex VIII
Salamia/Salamla	Archangel fourth Host – Sunday	*EoN, Hmn, BoO, GAG, CBMS*
Salani	Angel	*ACM*: H. Kopt. 679
Salatheel	Angel	*67M*
Salathiel	Angel Commander	*ACM*: H. Kopt. 686
Salatiel	Angel – Mars Angel – Jupiter	*BARC, CoMS*
Salaul	Spirit	*MHN*
Saleeny (Silyaeel, Roman)	Spirit King – Moon	*Pic*
Saleh	Planetary Spirit – Mars	*SSM*
Saleos/Sallos/ Zaleos/ Zaebos	Demon Earl/Duke	*PmD, DoW, Goe, DI*

Salerica/Salarica	Demon Senator	*BoO*
Saliciel	Angel – Mars	*BARC*
Salgiel (Salguyel?)	Angel	*oADS*
Salgmel	Angel – Venus	*GAG*
Salguyel/Salguiel	Spirit – Venus	*SSM, SBH*
Saliēl/Saloēl	Angel – Saturday Hour two	*Hyg*
Salkariel	Spirit – Jupiter	*SoS*
Saliel	Angel – Mars	*GAG*
Salion	Angel – Saturn/Saturday	*SR*
Sallales/Salales	Angel Minister of Air – Wednesday Spirit Attendant – Mercury	*EoN, Hmn, KoSR,* *GAG, tM*
Salixos	Angel – Joy and Divination	*CoMS*
Sallales	Intelligence – Mercury	*SGT, SSG*
Salmatis/Estor (Sabnack)	Demon Marquis	*LdE*
Salmay	Angel	*GV*
Salmison	Spirit	*MNeI*
Salmōnem	Demon	*Hyg*
Salmōnnem	Demon	*Hyg*
Salnet	Angel – Twelfth Altitude (Pisces)	*Alm*
Salny	Angel – Tenth Altitude (Capricorn)	*Alm*
Salon	Angel – Sivan	*SR*
Saloniel	Angel – Venus, over Water	*SR*
Salouēl/Selgiēl/Sagiēl/Sergiēl/Saragilouēil/Saphgēil/Sariēl	Angel- Moon	*Hyg*
Salphrenas	Demon – West and Aries	*Hyg*
Salpiax	Spirit	*ACM*: H. O. Lange Text
Salpiel/Saltiēl/Saltiel	Angel – Tuesday Hour sixteen	*Hyg*
Saltaēl/Salaēl/Sassaēl	Angel – Wednesday Hour twenty-three	*Hyg*
Saltim	Spirit Duke	*MHN*
Salttri	Angel – Elul	*SR*
Saltyn	Demon Senior	*SSM*

Saluagan	Spirit – Jupiter	*BoO, GAG*
Salvator	Angel before Throne of God	*oADS*
Salvian	Pygmy Prince	*MNeI*
Salvor/Solvar	Demon Duke – West by South Night	*Stg, ThG, BoTS*
Samaeel/Salyaeel/ Saljail (Silyaeel, Greek)	Spirit King – Moon	*Pic, SSG*
Samael /Samaell/ Zamael/Samuel/ Kamael/Camael/ Camiel	Archangel – Mars, Tuesday, Monday, Earth, West, Aries, Scorpio Archangel – Geburah Ruler of Order of Powers Angel Prince – Fifth Heaven Angel Prince – Water Angel Prince – Summer fourth Heaven Sunday – East, Spring third Heaven Friday – South Intelligence – Mars	*EoN, Hmn, SSM, SR, SBH, B7R, BARC, KoSR, 3BOP, CBoM, SoS, MHN, tSoS, dSS, Stg, oADS, BoO, DoW, BM, MC, Thm, GAG, GoeR, ArP, JMR, 9CK, SaS, KoN, BoTS, SMS, SRH, GoA, MRC, CII, CoMS, tM, CBMS*
Samael	Demon Prince – East Demon Prince – Fire/Air	*3BOP, SaS, BoTS, MNeI, KoN, PO, tM*
Samael	Spirit – Saturn Presiding Spirit – Mars	*SGT, SSG*
Samahel (Samael)	Spirit – Mars	*SBH*
Samail (Iranian) (Saljail)	Angel – Moon	*SSG*
Samal (Yiediedial)	Angel Prince – West Angel – Malachim, Spring	*SRH*
Samam/Saman (Simon the Canaanite)	Prince of Ishim and Apostle	*3BOP, MRC*
Samanus	Spirit	*oADS*
Samarahos	Angel	*NA*
Samart	Angel	*Hyg*
Samas/Shamash	Canaanite Solar God	*PGM V:1-53*
Samatiel	Angel – Mars	*BARC*
Samax/Samex	Angel – King of Air on Tuesday	*Hmn, KoSR, GAG, BoTS, PO, tM*
Samay	Spirit – Sea Treasure	*oADS*
Samayelyn	Angel – Mars/Tuesday	*SR*

ABBREVIATIONS

Sambas/Zambas	Punishing Wind Daemon – Mercury, serving West and Southwest Winds; between the West and North Wind Spirit	*SSM, SBH, GAG*
Sambetta	Spirit – Sibyl (one of ten)	*GV*
Sambhan	Mirror Spirit – Friday	*MNeI*
Sambaras	Demon Servant – Wednesday	*KoN*
Samcyel	Angel – Fifth Heaven, East	*SSM*
Samelon/Semelon	Angel – Night Hour five	*Stg, ArP*
Samelos	Angel	*NA*
Sameon	Angel – Day Hour six	*Stg, ArP*
Sameriel/Semeriel/Someriel	Angel – Night Hour seven	*Stg, ArP*
Sameron	Angel – Day Hour twelve	*Stg, ArP*
Sameryn/Samerin	Angel – Night Hour five	*Stg, ArP*
Samhiel	Angel – Shebat	*SR*
Samhores	Spirit	*SSM*
Samhyel	Angel – Third Heaven, South	*SSM*
Samiel	Angel – Adar	*SR*
Samiel	Spirit – North	*SSM*
Samiel	Demon Duke – North-East, Day Hour seven	*Stg, ThG*
Samiel	Genii – 7° Aquarius	*ArP*
Samiel	Water Spirit	*MNeI*
Samiell	Angel – Mansion one and Aries	*BoO*
Samionim/Samion	Spirit – Saturn	*BoO, GAG*
Sammyel (Samael?)	Angel – Monday	*MHN*
Samna	Spirit Familiar	*BoTS*
Samniator	Angel – Hatred and Destruction	*KoSA*
Samohayl	Archangel	*67M*
Samon	Demon King	*LdE*
Samōsan/Samosan	Angel – Saturday Hour eight	*Hyg*
Samouēl/Samaēl/Samoēl	Angel – Tuesday Hour one	*Hyg*
Samsanvi	Demon	*SMS*

Samtēl	Spirit	*BoW*
Samtiel	Angel – Elul	*SR*
Samtōrte	Angel	*Hyg*
Samuel	Angel – Venus Angel – Third Heaven, South	*GAG, SaS, MNeI*
Samyel	Angel Subordinate – Mars Angel – Third Heaven, South	*SSM, SR*
Samyel	Spirit – Moon	*SSM, SBH, oADS*
Samyel/Samiel/ Samyell	Demon Chief Duke	*Stg, ThG*
Samyos	Angel	*NA*
Samysarach	Angel – Sivan	*SR*
Sana	Angel – Venus	*GAG*
Sanael	Angel – Eleven of twenty-one on the Left	*ACM*: Berlin 10587
Sanaēl/Salaēl	Angel – Sunday Hour twelve	*Hyg*
Sanael	Angel – Third Heaven, South	*SR*
Sanael	Genii – 3° Pisces	*ArP*
Sanaleph (Mars)	Mars – Alternative Name	*Hyg*
Sanasara (Hindi) (Isbil)	Angel – Saturn	*SSG*
Sanbras	Spirit Assistant – Wednesday	*MHN*
Sandalfon	Angel – Air	*SR*
Sandalphon	Archangel – Binder of the Crowns, Deliverer of the Merkavah Angel – Malachim, Adir	*SRH*
Sandalson	Angel – Saturn/Saturday	*SR*
Sandamyhar	Angel	*NA*
Sanfael	Angel – Jupiter/Thursday	*SR*
Sanficiel	Angel – Fifth Heaven, East	*SR*
Sanfrielis	Demon	*MHN*
Sangasar	Spirit	*BoW*
Sangdiel	Demon	*SMS*
Sangeron	Alternative name of Metatron	*SQ*
Sangiel	Genii – 4° Virgo	*ArP*
Saniel/Samiel	Angel Ruler – Day Hour six	*Stg, ArP*
Saniorie	Angel – Venus	*GAG*

Sanipeēl/Sanypiēl/Sknipieēl	Angel – Saturday Hour sixteen	*Hyg*
Sanrich	Spirit Lord	*KoN*
Sansani	Angel – Marchesvan	*SR*
Sansoniel	Demon	*ToSC*
Santanael/Santaniel/Santamel	Angel third Heaven Friday – South	*Hmn, KoSR, BoO, BM, GAG, BoTS, tM*
Santelphōn	Angel	*Hyg*
Santoteēl	Angel	*Hyg*
Sanvi	Demon	*SMS*
Sanyel	Angel – Tuesday	*MHN*
Saoriel	Angel – Fourth Heaven, South	*SR*
Saoth	Speechless Spirit	*ACM:* Berlin 8503
Saoumiēl	Angel	PGM XXXVI:161-177
Saparatzel/Sapatel	Demon	*ToSC*
Saphathorael	Demon – Decan twelve	*ToS*
Saphea	Angel – Jupiter	*GAG*
Saphianim	Angel – Moon	*LL*
Saphiel	Angel	*Hyg*
Saphinoēl	Angel – Friday Hour three	*Hyg*
Sapi	Angel – Spring	*BoW*
Sapiel	Angel – Water	*SR*
Sapiel/Saphiel	Angel – Fourth Heaven Sunday, North, Spring Angel – Fourth Heaven, North Spirit – Sun	*EoN, Hmn, KoSR, SoS, BoO, GAG, BoTS, SaS, tM*
Sapientia	Spirit of Wisdom	*BoO*
Sapipas	Servant Spirit	*Abm*
Sappathai	Unicorn Spirit	*ACM:* Oriental 6796
Sappōra/Satora/Saptora/Saphporen	Demon – West	*Hyg*
Sappour/Saptouri	West Wind – Summer	*BoW*
Sapsi	Angel – Elul	*SR*
Saqtas	Alternative name of Metatron	*SQ*
Saquidaell/Soquidaell	Spirit – Mars	*BoO, GAG*

Saquiel	Angel – Third Heaven, South	*EoN*
Saquiel (Zadkiel)	Archangel – Jupiter	*BoO*
Saqyos	Alternative name of Metatron	*SQ*
Sarabotre/Sarabotes/ Sarabotres/ Sarabocres/ Sarabotref/ Farabores/ Tres	Demon King under Belzebub Spirit King – Venus Angel – King of Air on Friday Daemon King – Venus; between South and West	*SSM, SBH, EoN, Hmn, oADS, KoSR, BoO, GAG, BoTS, PO, tM*
Sarach	Demon Duke – North Night	*Stg, ThG, BoTS*
Saracus	Angel – Tammuz	*SR*
Saradon/Seradon/ Sarietur	Spirit – Treasure	*GoPH, GV*
Sarael	Angel – eighteen of twenty-one on the Left	*ACM*: Berlin 10587
Saraēl/Teraēl	Angel – Sunday Hour fourteen	*Hyg*
Sarael	Archangel	*ACM*: P. Prague 1
Sarael	Demon Duke – North-East	*Stg, ThG*
Sarajemin	Angel – Moon	*LL*
Saranana/ Saromana/ Saranava	Angel Angel – Chora three	*NA, ArA*
Sarandiel	Angel Ruler – Night Hour twelve	*Stg, ArP*
Saranyt	Demon – North	*BOS, BoO*
Saraph	Servant Spirit	*Abm*
Saraphaēl	Demon – West and Aries	*Hyg*
Saraphiell/Saraphiel/ Sarapiel/Sarapiell	Angel – Wednesday Angel – Day Hour five Spirit	*CBoM, tSoS, Stg, oADS, ArP, PO*
Saraphlorier	Demon King – Friday	*KoN*
Saraphuel	Angel	*ACM*: Oriental 5525, Würzburg 42, Oriental 6794, Oriental 6796, P. Mich. 593
Saraphyel	Angel – Fifth Heaven, North	*EoN*
Sarapiel/Saripiel	Spirit – Mercury	*SBH*

Sarapis/Osarapis	Greco-Egyptian Sun God	PGM IV:154-285, IV:1596-1715, V:1-53, V:447-458, XIII:343-646, XIXa:1-54, XCVIII:1-7; *SM*: P. Köln inv. 1982, PSI I.28
Sarasim	Servant Spirit	*Abm*
Sarason	Servant Spirit	*Abm*
Saratiel	Demon	*ToSC*
Sarbitha	Daughter of Agathodaimon	PDM XIV:563-574
Sarborr	Spirit King – Friday	*CBoM*
Sarbyel	Angel – Fifth Heaven, East	*SSM*
Sardalydy	Angel – Fourth Season by Night	*SSM*
Sardiel/Saraiel/Sarajel	Angel – Night Hour nine	*Stg*, *ArP*
Sarfiel/Serfiel	Angel – Day Hour eight	*Stg*, *ArP*
Sargas	Demon	*GoPH*
Sarghatoom	Spirit – Moon in Aquarius	*Pic*
Sargile	Angel	*Hyg*
Sarnamuf	Angel – Tebet	*SR*
Sarican	Angel – Tishrei	*SR*
Sariel	Angel Angel – Marchesvan, Tebet, Adar, Mercury, Jupiter, South	*ACM*: BN Turin; *SR*, *BARC*
Sariel/Seriel	Demon Duke – South by East Night Day South by West Day	*Stg*, *ThG*, *BoTS*
Saripyel	Angel – Mercury	*SSM*
Saris	Servant Spirit	*Abm*
Sarinael	Spirit – Gate of the West	*ACM*: L. Anastasi 9
Sarisel	Servant Spirit	*Abm*
Sarkigia	Angel	*Hyg*
Sarkhiel	Angel	*Hyg*
Sarkya	Spirit	*Hyg*
Sarman	Angel – Tebet	*SR*
Sarmas	Angel – Marchesvan	*SR*

Sarmeēl/Saphmeēl	Spirit	*BoW*
Sarmon/Satmon	Angel – Night Hour six	*Stg, ArP*
Sarmozyn/ Sarmezyn/ Sarmezyrs/Samrezin	Angel – Night Hour three	*Stg, ArP*
Sarniel	Earth Spirit	*MNeI*
Sarnochoibal	Angel – Lunar, Night Hour ten	PGM VII:862-918
Sarōk/Sarom/Saron (Saturn)	Saturn – Alternative Name	*Hyg*
Saromalay	Angel	*NA*
Saron	Angel – Saturn/Saturday	*SR*
Saroy	Spirit	*GV*
Sarphaēl	Angel	*Hyg*
Sarphanoēl	Demon – North	*Hyg*
Sarphyel	Angel – Fourth Heaven, North	*SSM*
Sarpiel	Angel – Wednesday	*Hyg, MHN*
Sarpidie/Sarapidi/ Sarapidie/Sarpidiel	Demon – Tuesday Hour four	*Hyg*
Sarpyel	Angel Subordinate – Mercury	*SSM*
Sarpyl	Angel	*Hyg*
Sarquiel	Angel – Friday Angel – Third Heaven, East	*MHN, SaS*
Sarsac	Angel – Tammuz	*SR*
Sarsaēl/Skorsaēl	Angel – Thursday Hour twenty-two	*Hyg*
Sarsaf	Angel – Iyar	*SR*
Sarsanna	Demon – Three-way Crossroads	*Hyg*
Sartabachim	Servant Spirit	*Abm*
Sartquiel/Satraquel	Angel – Saturday	*MHN*
Sarviel	Demon Duke – Night Hour four	*Stg, ThG*
Sarwiel	Ministering Familiar/Mystery	*67M*
Saryel	Angel – Tuesday	*MHN*
Sarypyell	Angel	*oADS*
Sasael	Angel	*ACM*: BN Turin
Sasael	Genii – 7° Cancer	*ArP*
Sasaha	Angel – Sun	*BARC*
Sasajah	Genii – 7° Capricorn	*ArP*

Sasamalyhon	Angel	*NA*
Sascanyel	Angel – Third Heaven, South	*SSM*
Sasci	Angel – Marchesvan	*SR*
Sasmiasas	Spirit	*ACM*: H.O.Lange Text
Sasquiel	Angel Ruler – Day Hour five	*Stg, ArP*
Sassriell	Demon	*CoC*
Sasta	Angel – Moon	*BARC*
Sasuagos	Angel – Bisertilis	*SR*
Sasuyel	Angel Ruler – Iyar	*SR*
Satad (Saturn)	Saturn – Alternative Name	*Hyg*
Satael	Angel – Tuesday	*Hmn, CBoM, BoO, tSoS, GAG, PO, tM*
Satael	Presiding Spirit – Mars	*SGT, SSG*
Satael/Tasael	Demon	*ToSC*
Satan/Sathan/ Satanas	Demon Ruler/King Demon Prince – Deluders Demon Prince – Air Demon Governor Demon of Wrath Grand Prince – Hell Daimon Spirit – Venus Devil – Cancer, Storms	HB Job 1:6-12, 2:1-7, Matt 4:5-11, 12:26, Mark 1:13, 3:23-26, Luke 4:2-13,[421] 10:18, 11:18, 13:16, 22:3, John 13:27, Acts 5:3, 1 Cor 5:5, 7:5, 2 Cor 2:11, 11:14, 12:7, 1 Th 2:18, 2 Th 2:9, 1 Tim 1:20, 5:15, Pet 5:8, Rev 2:9, 2:12-13, 2:24, 3:9, 12:9, 19:19-20, 20:2; PGM IV:1227-1264; *ACM*: GMPP:1227-64, BN Turin, Cologne 10235, Hay 10391, L. Anastasi 9; *SSM, MHN, Abm, BARC, NML, LdE, Gbk, 3BOP, CBoM, BOS, BoO, CoC, BM, oADS, ES, GAG, BoTS, JMR, GoPH, MNeI, KoN, SMS,*

---

[421] Although he is referred to here as 'the devil', the reference is included for completion.

Satan/Sathan/ Satanas (con't.)		*BoSC, PO, tM, VJL, SBRM*
Satanachi/ Satanachia/ Satanaki	Demon Leader – under Lucifer Demon Duke Demon General-in-Chief	*KoSU, SoS, GoPH, GG, GV, BoSC*
Satanael	Speechless Spirit	*ACM*: Berlin 8503, H. Kopt. 686
Satanaēl/Santaēl/ Sataēl	Angel – Wednesday Hour twenty	*Hyg*
Satanicæ	Demon	*GV*
Sataniel/Sartamiel/ Sattamiel (Muriel)	Angel – Cancer Spirit – Cancer	*3BOP, BoO, tSoS, JMR, SaS*
Satarin	Spirit	*GoPH*
Satēr (Venus)	Venus – Alternative Name	*Hyg*
Saterphou	Angel	*Hyg*
Saterquiel	Spirit – Saturn	*SBH*
Satgasbym	Angel Governor – third Season by Night	*SSM*
Satguyel	Angel – Jupiter	*SSM*
Sathamaht	Angel	*NA*
Sathant	Spirit	*SSM*
Sathare	Spirit – Mirror	*CoMS*
Sathiell	Angel – Thursday	*CBoM*
Satiel	Genii – 2° Leo	*ArP*
Satifiel	Demon Duke – West Day	*Stg, ThG, BoTS*
Satihel/Satiel	Spirit – Mars Angel – Mars	*SBH, EoN*
Satis	Egyptian War and Fertility Goddess	*PGM* III:1-64
Satola/Sacola	Demon	*MHN, NML*
Saton	Angel – Iyar	*SR*
Sator	Angel Minister – Love and Fornication	*KoSA*
Satpach	Angel – Elul	*SR*
Satpyel	Angel – Fifth Heaven, North	*SSM*
Satquiel/Satquiell/ Satquel/Satquyel/ Sathquyel/ Sabquiell	Angel Ruler – Jupiter Archangel – Jupiter/Saturn Angel – Sixth Heaven, Jupiter Angel – Third Heaven, East Angel – Second Heaven, Mercury Spirit – Jupiter	*SSM, SR, SBH, EoN, B7R, CBoM, MHN, oADS, KON, GAG*

ABBREVIATIONS

Satrapis	Demon	oADS
Satrox	Spirit – Minister of Love	oADS
Satuel	Angel – Kislev	SR
Saturiel	Angel Minister	KoSA
Saturn	God – Treasure/Gold and Lead Roman Time God and Titan	Hyg, BoO, SSG
Saturniel (Zaphkiel)	Archangel – Saturn	3BOP, tSoS, JMR
Saturnion	Demon	GAG
Satyel	Angel Subordinate – Mars	SSM
Satykyel	Angel – three signs of third Season	SSM
Satyn	Angel – Shebat	SR
Satyteyr/Satiter/Scitetie/Sacassaeyt	Spirit – sixth Mansion of the Moon Ring	AE
Satziel	Genii – 6° Scorpio, 6° Sagittarius	ArP
Sauriēl	Angel – Sun	Hyg
Sautaniel	Angel – Third Heaven, South	EoN
Savaa	Spirit King – Wednesday	CBoM
Savael	Genii – 29° Leo	ArP
Savania	Spirit – Mercury	VMN
Saviel	Genii – 19° Gemini, 20° Leo	ArP
Sayapiell	Spirit	CoC
Saycop	Angel – Sun	BARC
Sayel	Angel – First three signs	SSM
Saymay	Spirit – Sea Treasure	oADS
Saymbrie	Devil – third Hour of Day	oADS
Saytam	Spirit King – Sunday	MHN
Saziel	Genii – 5° Libra	AeP
Saziel	Spirit King	BoO
Sazlij	Spirit – Saturn	67M
Sbbial	Angel – Third Heaven, serving Dlqial	ShR
Sbibal	Angel – Fourth Encampment, first Heaven	ShR
Sbirouel/Sbirouēl	Demon – Mars	Hyg
Sblh	Angel – First Encampment, first Heaven	ShR
Scaayroth	Angel Superior – three signs of fourth Season	SSM

Scadexos	Angel – Mars	*BARC*
Scapha	Demon – South	*CBoM*
Schaddaij	Ministering Familiar/Mystery	*67M*
Schaddyl	Angel – Thrones	*67M*
Schadym	Angel – Cherubim/Seraphim	*67M*
Schaeter/ Schaemoth/ Schartagan (Floga)	Lunar Spirit	*MNeI*
Schafforth	Infernal Spirit	*MNeI*
Schal	Angel – Third Heaven, serving Ibnial	*ShR*
Schaluach	Servant Spirit	*Abm*
Schaluah	Servant Spirit	*Abm*
Schamayl	Angel – Potestates	*67M*
Schawayt	Angel – Thrones	*67M*
Sched	Servant Spirit	*Abm*
Schedbarschemoth Schartathan	Planetary Spirit of Spirits – Moon	*KoSR, 3BOP, tM*
Schelegon	Servant Spirit	*Abm*
Scheol	Angel – Potestates	*67M*
Schii	Evil Spirit	*3BOP*
Schimuel	Angel – Thrones	*67M*
Schlemeshiel (Michael)	Archangel – Sun	*JMR*
Schmaym	Archangel	*MNeI*
Scholiel/Scheliel/ Seheliel	Angel – Mansion seven and Gemini	*3BOP, BoO, tSoS, MNeI*
Schruri	Angel – First Encampment, first Heaven	*ShR*
Schumnyel/ Schunmyel (Schuwniel?)	Angel – Potestates	*67M*
Schuwniel/ Schrewniel	Angel	*SST*
Scio	Enochian Angel – South, serving first lesser Angle	*TBA*
Scirlin/Scyrlin	Demon Intermediary	*GoPH, GV*
Scor/Scarus/Scar	Spirit – East Treasure Spirit	*oADS, BoTS*

ABBREVIATIONS

Scorax/Storax	Angel – Sun	*oADS, GAG, CoMS*
Scorpiel (Barchiel)	Angel – Scorpio Spirit – Scorpio	*3BOP, tSoS, JMR, SaS*
Scorpus	Spirit – Bird Capturers	*oADS*
Scrupulon	Servant Spirit	*Abm*
Sdrial	Angel – Sixth Encampment, first Heaven Angel Encampment Head – sixth Heaven, East	*ShR*
Sdrkin	Angel Encampment Head – sixth Heaven, West	*ShR*
Sealiah/Soaliah/Saaliah	Angel – Shem forty-five	*KoSU, 3BOP, GoeR, JMR, SAS, tM*
Sebach	Demon Duke – North Night	*Stg, ThG, BoTS*
Sebarman	Angel Lord – Nights of the Year	*SSM*
Sebekial	Angel – Malachim, under Phelmiya Angel Magistrate – Malachim	*SRH*
Sebenial	Angel – Malachim over Rain	*SRH*
Seberien	Angel – Malachim, under Pheseker	*SRH*
Seberion	Fairy Counsellor	*GAG*
Sebieren	Angel – Malachim, sixth Host	*SRH*
Sebt-Hor	Unkown Spirit	*ACM*: Hay 10434
Secabim	Servant Spirit	*Abm*
Sechay	Angel	*NA*
Sechekiēl	Angel	*Hyg*
Sechemor	Spirit – West in Autumn	*SRH*
Secherial	Angel, serving above sixth Degree	*SRH*
Sechrer	Spirit	*ACM*: Cairo 45060
Secramalan	Angel	*NA*
Secray	Angel	*NA*
Sedamylia	Fairy Lady	*BoO, GAG*
Sedaon/Sedmaon	Spirit – Jupiter	*BoO, GAG*
Sedellpha/Sedelpha	Spirit – Mars	*BoO, GAG*
Sediō/Sedio (Jupiter)	Jupiter – Alternative Name	*Hyg*
Seductor	Angel – Hatred and Destruction	*KoSA*
Sedul	Spirit – Saturn	*67M*

Seechiah/Seekiah/ Seehiah/Sechiah	Angel – Shem twenty-eight	*KoSU, 3BOP, GoeR, JMR, SAS, tM*
Seere/Seer	Demon Prince – East	*Goe, BoTS*
Segamexe/Sagamex	Fairy Lady	*BoO, GAG*
Segol/Segal/Fegot	Demon Duke	*SoS, GV*
Segkhlē	Spirit	*Hyg*
Segrael	Spirit	*GV*
Sehan	Angel	*NA*
Seheliel	Angel	*Thm*
Sekehial	Angel Prince – Gate of Spirit of West	*SRH*
Sekenial	Angel Minister – Malachim, ruling Rain	*SRH*
Sekhmet-Isis	Composite Egyptian Goddess	PDM XIV:585-593
Sekiel	Genii – 11° Leo	*ArP*
Selak/Selam (Mercury)	Mercury – Alternative Name	*Hyg*
Selarinum/Seliare	Spirit	*BoO*
Selateuk	Angel Minister – Love and Fornication	*KoSA*
Selechial	Angel Minister – Malachim	*SRH*
Selene	Greek Moon Goddess	PGM I.42-195, II.1-64, III:410-423, III:424-466, IV:835-849, IV:2441-2621, IV:2622-2707, IV:2708-2784, IV:2785-2890, IV:2967-3006, V:370-446, VI:1-47, VII:429-458, VII:664-685, VII:862-918, XII:201-269, XIII:1-343, XIII:646-734, XIII:734-1077, XVIIb:1-23, LII:1-9, LXII:1-24
Selene (Roman) (Saljail)	Angel – Moon	*SSG*
Selentis	Demon	*MHN*
Selgaiol	Enochian Senior – West	*TBA*
Selia	Spirit	*Hyg*

Selieēl	Angel – Saturday Hour five	*Hyg*
Selkisameel	Angel	*Hyg*
Selutabel/Belutabel	Spirit	*MHN*
Sem	Spirit – Minister of Love	*oADS*
Sema	Spirit – Minister of Love	*oADS*
Semahabel	Angel	*NA*
Semal	Angel – Malachim, Nisan, Monday, Spring	*SRH*
Semanglaf	Angel – Potestates	*67M*
Semanuel	Angel	*ACM*: L. Anastasi 9
Semar	Spirit	*oADS*
Semea	Syrian Goddess	PGM III:1-64
Semegay	Angel	*NA*
Semekieh	Angel, serving above sixth Degree	*SRH*
Sememial	Angel – Malachim, Tebeth, Winter	*SRH*
Semenial	Angel Prince – Autumn	*SRH*
Semeol	Angel – Mercury/Wednesday	*SR*
Semeot	Servant Spirit	*Abm*
Semesilam/Semesilamps	Name of Hermes	PGM XIII:1-343, XIII:343-646
Semey	Spirit – Minister of Love	*oADS*
Semezehel	Angel	*NA*
Semhahylyn	Angel – Moon/Monday	*SR*
Semharis	Mirror Spirit – Thursday	*MNeI*
Semial	Angel – Malachim, Nisan	*SRH*
Semiel	Angel of the Tables	*dHM*
Seminator	Angel – Hatred and Destruction	*KoSA*
Semiticon	Angel	*KoSA*
Semoēl/Senoēl	Angel – Thursday Hour fifteen	*Hyg*
Semohy	Angel	*NA*
Semper/Semp (Vepar?)	Demon – East	*BOS, BoO*
Semquiel	Angel – Nisan	*SR, tSoS*
Semylevana	Spirit	*SSM*
Semynaphaz	Angel	*NA*
Senaciel	Presiding Spirit – Venus	*CBMS*

Senael	Genii – 2° Virgo	*ArP*
Senanec	Spirit – Middle	*SSM*
Senazamar	Angel	*NA*
Sene/Sone	Angel	*KoSA*
Sēnēl	Angel – Moon	*Hyg*
Sengael	Genii – 8° Leo	*ArP*
Senigron/Seniegeron	Alternative title of Metatron Angel Prince	*SQ, SRH*
Senthenips	Name of Helios in fourth Hour	PGM IV:1596-1715
Sentioēl	Angel	*Hyg*
Sēntōr	Demon – Monday Hour nineteen	*Hyg*
Seper	Spirit	*oADS*
Sephael (Raphael)	Archangel	*ES*
Sephatia/Sephatya	Angel – Nisan	*SR, tSoS*
Sephephial	Angel Prince – Intelligence	*SRH*
Sepherial	Angel – Malachim, under Pheseker Angel – Malachim, sixth Host	*SRH*
Sephiroth	Angel – Potestates	*67M*
Sephophien	Spirit – West	*SRH*
Sepuros	Spirit – Minister of Love	*oADS*
Sequiel	Demon Duke – North Day	*Stg, ThG, BoTS*
Serael	Angel – Fourth Heaven, North Angel – Fifth Heaven, North	*SR, SSM, SaS*
Seraph/Seruph/Serieph	Angel President/Governor – Fire Angel Ruler – Fire, governs Mahazael	*3BOP, tSoS, MC, BoTS, JMR, KoN, SaS, PO, tM*
Seraphiel	Angel – Fifth Heaven Tuesday, North Angel – Fifth Heaven, North Angel – Wednesday Angel Prince – Air Angel Prince – Gate of Spirit of North	*EoN, Hmn, KoSR, BoO, GAG, ArP, SRH, BoTS, SaS, tM*
Seraphiel	Presiding Spirit – Mercury	*SGT, SSG*
Seraphius	Spirit	*BoO*
Serapiel	Angel – Fourth Heaven, North	*SR*
Serapis	Greco-Egyptian Sun God	*ACM*: H. O. Lange Text
Serapis/Sorapis	Demon Prince	*3BOP, BoTS*

ABBREVIATIONS

Serar	Treasure Spirit	*oADS*
Serasopho	Angel	*NA*
Serephieth	Angel Magistrate – Malachim	*SRH*
Sereriel	Angel – Nisan	*SR*
Seresieth	Angel – Malachim, under Phelmiya	*SRH*
Sereten	Angel Magistrate – Malachim	*SRH*
Sereton	Angel Prince	*SRH*
Seretov	Angel – Malachim, under Phelmiya	*SRH*
Sergulas/Sergulaf/ Sergulath	Demon – Machines	*KoSU, SoS, GV*
Sergurph/Sergutthy/ Serguthy/Sugunth/ Serguty	Demon	*SoS, GV*
Seriel	Angel – Kislev	*SR*
Sermia	Demon	*CoC*
Seroael	Angel	*ACM*: Oriental 5899, Berlin 11347
Serobattam/ Serobadam	Spirit – Pleiades (one of seven)	*oADS*
Serpepheēl/ Serpēphiēl/ Serpephēel/ Serpephouēl/ Persepheēl	Angel- Jupiter	*Hyg*
Serphgathana	Demon Duke	*SoS*
Serpidōn/Selpidōn/ Selpiou/Pelpiouēl	Angel – Monday Hour eighteen	*Hyg*
Serpora	Angel Minister – Love and Fornication	*KoSA*
Serquanich/ Sarquamech	Angel Ruler – Night Hour three	*Stg, ArP*
Serquiel	Angel – Third Heaven, East	*EoN*
Sersael	Genii – 10° Cancer	*ArP*
Sertugidis	Demon	*MHN*
Seruhc	Angel	*NA*
Servehyhon	Angel	*NA*
Serviel	Angel Angel – Day Hour three	*tSoS, Stg, ArP*

Sesenial	Angel Minister – Malachim Angel – Malachim, Flames of Fire	*SRH*
Sesle	Spirit	*GV*
Seson/Sefon	Demon – East	*BOS, BoO, oADS*
Setariel	Demon	*ToSC*
Setchiel	Angel third Heaven Friday – East	*Hmn, KoSR, BoO, BM, GAG, BoTS, tM*
Setchiel	Spirit – Jupiter	*SGT, SSG*
Setel	Archangel	*ACM*: L. Anastasi 9
Setereseti	Angel – Malachim, under Phelmiya	*SRH*
Seth/Sēth/Seith/ Seth-Typhon	Egyptian Chaos God	PGM III:1-164, VII:359-369, XII:121-143, XXXVI:1-34, XXXVI:69-101, XLVI:4-8, LVII:1-37, CXXVIa:1-21, PDM XIV:585-593, Suppl. 60-101; *SM*: P. Palau Rib. Inv. 3
Setherial	Angel – Malachim, under Phelmiya Angel Magistrate – Malachim	*SRH*
Sethiel	Genii – 13° Cancer	*ArP*
Sethiem	Angel Prince	*SRH*
Setiap (Venus)	Venus – Alternative Name	*Hyg*
Setiel	Genii – 22° Cancer	*ArP*
Sever	Spirit – Minister of Love	*oADS*
Severion	Fairy Advisor	*BoO, CoMS*
Seveviel	Angel – Nisan	*tSoS*
Sewachar	Angel – Cherubim/Seraphim	*67M*
Seyrechaël	Demon – Under Sirach	*KoSU*
Sezah	Angel – Potestates	*67M*
Sezel	Spirit – Bones of the Dead	*oADS*
Sfamllb	Spirit Minister, serving Prince Blisdon	*dHM*
Sfttāyl	Angel – Friday, Hour of the Moon	*BoW*
Sgalis	Treasure Spirit	*oADS*
Sgrial	Angel – Third Heaven, serving Dlqial Angel Prince – fourth Heaven, Water	*ShR*

Sha'agien	Angel – Malachim, Spring Nights	*SRH*
Shaaipial	Angel – Third Heaven, serving Ibnial	*ShR*
Shaamam	Angel – Moon	*LL*
Sha'aphial	Angel Prince – Nisan	*SRH*
Shaapial	Angel Prince – fifth Heaven, Month of Nisan Angel Encampment Head – sixth Heaven, East	*ShR*
Shaaqmuh	Angel – Fourth Step, second Heaven	*ShR*
Shaasial	Angel Prince – fourth Heaven, Water	*ShR*
Shael	Enochian Angel – East, serving third lesser Angle	*TBA*
Shafriel	Angel	*ACM*: Yale 882A
Shams/Sams (Arabic)/Ba'il/Yebil	Spirit King – Sun	*Pic*, *SSG*
Shamshiel	Angel	*SMS*
Shanamael	Spirit	*ACM*: Cairo 45060
Shanaun	Demon	*SMS*
Shangdiel	Demon	*SMS*
Shanshar (Ashbeel, Indian)	Spirit King – Saturn	*Pic*
Shanshimon	Demon	*SMS*
Shapl	Name of Sirius	PDM Suppl. 162-168
Sharhitzinim	Angel – Moon	*LL*
Sharailim	Angel – Moon	*LL*
Shawal	Angel Prince – fourth Heaven, Water	*ShR*
Shax/Chax/Scox	Demon Marquis	*PmD*, *DoW*, *Goe*, *DI*
Shbaaqni	Angel – Fourth Encampment, first Heaven	*ShR*
Shbial	Angel – Fifth Encampment, first Heaven	*ShR*
Shbiudaa	Angel – Fifth Encampment, first Heaven	*ShR*
Shbkiria	Angel – Sixth Encampment, first Heaven	*ShR*
Shbqial	Angel – Tenth Step, second Heaven	*ShR*
Shchial	Angel – Eleventh Step, second Heaven	*ShR*
Shdqi	Angel – Third Heaven, serving Rhtial	*ShR*
Shdqial	Angel Prince – Fourth Heaven, Fire	*ShR*

Shdrlial	Angel – Twelfth Step, second Heaven	*ShR*
Shebebial	Angel – Malachim, under Pheseker Angel – Malachim, sixth Host	*SRH*
Sheboqothial	Angel – Malachim over Sea and Life in it	*SRH*
Shecheqonek	Angel – Malachim, Summer Nights	*SRH*
Sheder	Angel – Malachim, Winter Nights	*SRH*
Shehiya	Angel – Malachim, under Phelmiya	*SRH*
Shekeremen	Angel – Malachim, Spring Nights	*SRH*
Shelechial	Angel – Malachim, Flames of Fire	*SRH*
Shelhebien	Angel – Malachim, under Ayigeda	*SRH*
Shelishial	Angel – Harvest Ruler	*SRH*
Shema'ahal	Angel Prince – Gate of Spirit of South	*SRH*
Shema'aial	Spirit Prince – North	*SRH*
Shema'ayial	Angel Prince – Gate of Spirit of South	*SRH*
Shemeliel/Semeliel/ Semeschia/ Semechiel/ Semishiah (Michael)	Archangel – Sun	*3BOP, BoO, tSoS, JMR, SaS*
Shemeshial	Angel Prince – Gate of Spirit of East	*SRH*
Shem Hashem	Angel Prince – Gate of Spirit of West	*SRH*
Shemiechod	Angel, serving above sixth Degree	*SRH*
Shem Qedosh	Angel Prince – Gate of Spirit of West	*SRH*
Shenial	Angel – Capricorn	*SRH*
Shenoch	Angel – Malachim, under Ayigeda	*SRH*
Sher	Angel – Malachim, under Ayigeda	*SRH*
Sheral	Angel Prince – Gate of Spirit of North	*SRH*
Sheregemen	Angel – Malachim, Spring Nights	*SRH*
Sherial	Angel Prince – South	*SRH*
Shesethenial	Angel Prince – Gate of Spirit of South	*SRH*
Sheshema'a	Angel – Malachim, under Avorphenial	*SRH*
Shethakam	Angel – Moon	*LL*
Shethenesheron	Angel – Malachim, Autumn Nights	*SRH*
Shethephial	Angel Prince – Gate of Spirit of North	*SRH*
Shgrial	Angel – Fourth Step, second Heaven	*ShR*
Shial	Angel – Ninth Step, second Heaven	*ShR*

ABBREVIATIONS

Shiraium	Angel Encampment Head – Sixth Heaven, West	*ShR*
Shkinttk	Angel – Fifth Encampment, First Heaven	*ShR*
Shknial	Angel – Fifth Encampment, first Heaven	*ShR*
Shlate Late Balate	White Crocodile Spirit	PDM XIV:574-585
Shlhbin	Angel – Second Encampment, first Heaven	*ShR*
Shlmial	Angel – Eleventh Step, second Heaven	*ShR*
Shlqial	Angel – Third Heaven, serving Dlqial	*ShR*
Shmial	Angel – Eighth Step, second Heaven	*ShR*
Shmihud	Angel – Sixth Step, second Heaven	*ShR*
Shmshial	Angel – Seventh Encampment, first Heaven	*ShR*
Shnnal	Angel – Second Step, second Heaven	*ShR*
Shobehen	Angel – Malachim, sixth Host	*SRH*
Shokerien	Angel – Malachim, under Pheseker	*SRH*
Shpiqual	Angel – Third Heaven, serving Rhtial	*ShR*
Shplial	Angel – Sixth Encampment, first Heaven	*ShR*
Shptial	Angel – Seventh Encampment, first Heaven Angel Prince – fourth Heaven, Water	*ShR*
Shptpa	Angel – Tenth Step, second Heaven	*ShR*
Shqd Chwzy	Angel Prince – Lower Four	*SoM*
Shrial	Angel Encampment Head – sixth Heaven, West and East	*ShR*
Shrmial	Angel – Sixth Encampment, first Heaven	*ShR*
Shshmaa	Angel – First Encampment, first Heaven	*ShR*
Shtqial	Angel – SSeventh Step, second Heaven	*ShR*
Shtryshwyh	Angel Prince – Top Three	*SoM*
Shu	Egyptian God of the Air	PDM XII:21-49, XIV:335-355, XIV:636-669, LXI:79-94, Suppl. 60-101
Shukdun	Angel – Sixth Encampment, first Heaven	*ShR*
Shuprial	Angel Encampment Head – sixth Heaven, West	*ShR*
Shwtgyayh	Angel Prince – Top Three	*SoM*

Šhyāl	Angel – Mercury, Hour of Mercury	*BoW*
Shytynychwm	Angel Prince – Middle Five	*SoM*
Siaar	Wind Spirit	*GAG*
Siadris	Treasure Spirit	*oADS*
Siak	Angel – Four of seven over the seven Baths	*ACM*: H. Kopt. 686
Siar	Demon – Saturday Hour thirteen	*Hyg*
Siar/Siarsatouz (Venus)	Venus – Alternative Name	*Hyg*
Sias	Enochian Angel – East, serving first lesser Angle	*TBA*
Siat (Mars)	Mars – Alternative Name	*Hyg*
Sibarbas	Spirit – Presidential Counsellor	*BoTS*
Sibady	Spirit	*CoMS*
Sibilia/Sibilis/ Sibbells/ Sybilia/Sybilla	Fairy Empress Fairy Queen	*dN, CBoM, BoO, DoW, KoN, AN, GAG, oADS*
Sibolas	Servant Spirit	*Abm*
Siboraz/Siobez (Mercury)	Mercury – Alternative Name	*Hyg*
Sibos	Demon	*GoPH*
Sichard	Spirit	*BoTS*
Sichone	Treasure Spirit	*oADS*
Sidonay/Sydonay/ Sidonai (Asmoday)	Demon King	*PmD, DoW*
Sidragosum	Demon	*SoSW, GV*
Sidriēl/Sidēr/Sidrēl	Angel – Wednesday Hour fourteen	*Hyg*
Sidrigol	Spirit – Saturn	*SoS*
Sieate	Spirit	*GAG*
Siederehon	Spirit – East in Winter	*SRH*
Siegedon	Angel Prince	*SRH*
Siegor	Spirit – West in Summer	*SRH*
Siekhapon	Demon Chief	*Hyg*
Siel	Genii – 23° Leo	*ArP*
Sielkin	Angel – Saturday Hour five	*Hyg*
Siemephov	Spirit – West in Summer	*SRH*
Siemoval	Angel – Malachim, Summer	*SRH*

Sigambach	Spirit	*SoS*
Sigēp/Siet (Saturn)	Saturn – Alternative Name	*Hyg*
Sigis	Servant Spirit	*Abm*
Signō (Jupiter)	Jupiter – Alternative Name	*Hyg*
Sigos/Sigior/Sigōr	Demon – Thursday Hour twelve	*Hyg*
Sigron	Angel	*SMS*
Sikastir	Servant Spirit	*Abm*
Sikbrdm	Angel – Seventh Step, second Heaven	*ShR*
Silidō/Silidōn/ Silēdōn/ Sylēd	Demon – Sunday Hour four	*Hyg*
Silitor/Silitol	Spirit	*MHN*
Silori	Demon	*oADS*
Silouanēl/Sēnouanēl	Demon – Mercury	*Hyg*
Silti/Silli	Intelligence	*EPL*
Silyaeel	Spirit King – Moon	*Pic*
Simagon	Spirit King	*BoO*
Simehon Hacephi/ Symehon Facehpi (Peter)	Prince of Ishim and Apostle	*3BOP, MRC*
Simias/Gumas (Orias)	Demon Marquis	*NML*
Simoēl	Angel – Thursday Hour thirteen, fourteen	*Hyg*
Simyllyel	Angel – Moon, over Earth	*SR*
Sinae/Sina (Sun)	Sun – Alternative Name	*Hyg*
Sinaēl/Senaēl	Angel – Monday Hour ten	*Hyg*
Sinaēl/Synaēl	Angel – Monday Hour nine	*Hyg*
Sinand	Spirit	*BoTS*
Sinna	Ministering Familiar/Mystery	*67M*
Sinqyyl	Angel – Moon	*BoW*
Siotiēl/Sitioēl	Angel – Thursday Hour thirteen	*Hyg*
Siphon	Servant Spirit	*Abm*
Sipillipis	Servant Spirit	*Abm*
Siqmh	Angel – First Encampment, first Heaven	*ShR*
Sirachi/Sirach/ Syrach	Demon Leader – under Lucifer	*KoSU, SoS, GoPH, GV*

Siranday	Spirit	*GV*
Sirgilis	Servant Spirit	*Abm*
Sirgith	Spirit – ninth Mansion of the Moon Ring	*AE*
Siriton/Sirtōr/Syritōr	Demon – Monday Hour twenty	*Hyg*
Sirkael/Silcharde/Sircharde	Demon Duke Demon – Thursday	*SoS, GoPH, GV, BD*
Siroph (Venus)	Venus – Alternative Name	*Hyg*
Sirpēl	Demon – Mars	*Hyg*
Sirsir	Spirit	*BoTS*
Sisiaho	Unknown God	PDM XIV:528-553
Sisinaei	Angel – Keeper of Hell	*ACM*: P. Mich. 1190
Sismael	Demon	*MHN*
Sisoy	Angel – Joy and Divination	*CoMS*
Sispe	Enochian Angel – South, serving fourth lesser Angle	*TBA*
Siteos/Sitros/Sytros	Demon- Sunday Hour five	*Hyg*
Sitgar	Demon Duke – South-East Night	*BoTS*
Sithlos/Sythlos	Demon – Tuesday Hour ten	*Hyg*
Sitoel	Angel – Thursday Hour twelve	*Hyg*
Sitoriel	Angel – Cross of Light over God's Head	*ACM*: H. Kopt. 686
Sitrael	Demon King – North	*DoW, GAG*
Sitrami	Demon King – North	*DoW, GAG*
Sitri/Sytry/Bitru	Demon Prince	*PmD, DoW, Goe*
Sitros/Sytros	Demon – Sunday Hour three	*Hyg*
Sityap (Venus)	Venus – Alternative Name	*Hyg*
Siviant	Demon	*GoPH*
Sizarhyr	Angel – Sivan	*SR*
Skabadiōd/Sabadiod/Sabadēod/Sabaōth	Demon – North	*Hyg*
Skamidinos	Demon – Monday Hour seven	*Hyg*
Skamidōn	Demon – Monday Hour six	*Hyg*
Skar/Skaros	Demon – Saturday Hour twelve	*Hyg*
Skenaēl/Sēnaēl	Angel – Monday Hour eleven	*Hyg*
Skēutoēl	Demon – Wednesday Hour six	*Hyg*

ABBREVIATIONS   655

Skhindatper/ Skhedapar	Angel – Ruler of the Sea in Winter	*BoW*
Skhozinoxen	Spirit – East	*Hyg*
Skiaēl	Angel – Thursday Hour eight	*Hyg*
Skitogiri/Skyntogēr	Demon – Wednesday Hour six	*Hyg*
Skolion/Skōlion/ Skoliōn	Demon – Monday Hour two	*Hyg*
Skonaphor/ Skonaroph/ Skounareph (Mars)	Mars – Alternative Name	*Hyg*
Skonin/Smoēn/ Skōēn	Demon – Tuesday Hour fourteen	*Hyg*
Skor	Demon King/Prince	*BOS, BoO*
Sksial	Angel – Ninth Step, second Heaven	*ShR*
Sktbaq	Angel – Fifth Step, second Heaven	*ShR*
Skyegephom/ Sygkyrom	Demon – Saturday Hour seven	*Hyg*
Skyepika	Angel – Saturday Hour sixteen	*Hyg*
Skytouēl/Skirtouēl/ Skyrtoel/Kyrtoēl	Angel – Friday Hour ten	*Hyg*
Skytokyēl/Skytomiēl/ Skitamiēl/Skotomiēl	Angel – Wednesday Hour nine	*Hyg*
Slaugnes	Devil – Cancer, Storms	*OADS*
Slbidm	Angel – Sixth Encampment, first Heaven	*ShR*
Slchial	Angel – Seventh Encampment, first Heaven	*ShR*
Sliyobaroon/ Saljubarun/ Celyuberon	Spirit – fifth Heaven	*Pic*
Smrgeos	Spirit, Bringer of Sorrow	*oADS*
Smiail	Angel Prince – fourth Heaven, Water	*ShR*
Smial	Angel Encampment Head – sixth Heaven, East	*ShR*
Smikal	Angel – Tenth Step, second Heaven	*āShR*
Smkial	Angel – Ninth Step, second Heaven	*ShR*
Smkih	Angel – Sixth Step, second Heaven	*ShR*
Smnial	Angel – Third Heaven, serving Dlqial	*ShR*
Šmšāyl	Angel – Mars	*BoW*

Šmšyāyyl	Angel – Friday, Hour of Saturn	*BoW*
Smue	Spirit – Minister of Love	*oADS*
Snial	Angel Encampment Head – sixth Heaven, East	*ShR*
Snigman	Alternative name of Metatron	*SQ*
Sntael	Spirit – Gate of the West	*ACM*: L. Anastasi 9
Snynyel	Angel – Jupiter/Thursday	*SR*
Soaea	Angel – Venus	*GAG*
Soas	Demon	*GoPH*
Soaixente	Enochian Senior – West	*TBA*
Sobek/Souchos	Egyptian Crocodile God of the Nile	PGM XII:201-269, PDM XIV:1-92
Sobhe	Servant Spirit	*Abm*
Sobronoy	Demon	*MHN, NML*
Socadia	Spirit – Venus	*VMN*
Sochas	Demon Duke – South Day	*Stg, ThG*
Sochen	Servant Spirit	*Abm*
Sochot	Angel – Seraphim who Cover their Bodies	*ACM*: H. Kopt. 686
Socthac	Angel	*NA*
Sodiel	Angel – Marchesvan	*SR*
Sodiel	Demon Duke – North-West Night	*Stg, ThG, BoTS*
Soe	Angel – Moon	*LL*
Sofiel	Angel ruling Garden Fruit (Vegetables)	*SoM*
Sofkanyn	Holy Powerful Angel (third Season)	*SSM*
Sogan/Sogom	Demon Marquis	*BOS, BoO*
Soheliel/Seheliel	Angel – Mansion seven	*JMR, SaS, tM*
Sokar	Egyptian God of the Dead	PDM XII:21-49
Sokeleth	Angel – Malachim, under Avorphenial	*SRH*
Sokhar	Spirit	*Hyg*
Sokyel	Angel – First Heaven, West	*SSM*
Sol	Roman Sun God	*SSG*
Solarcham	Angel	*NA*
Soleviel/Soleriel	Demon Wandering Prince	*Stg, ThG*
Soliah (Michael)	Archangel – Sun	*3BOP, tSoS, JMR*
Solomon	Angel – Seraphim who Cover their Feet	*ACM*: H. Kopt. 686

Solomon/Salaman	Biblical Mage/King	PGM XCIV:17-21; *ACM*: Oslo 1.5
Solothiel	Angel	*ACM*: Berlin 11347
Solseqium (Heliotrope)	Stone Spirit	*GAG*
Solykosyl	Spirit	*BoTS*
Solymo	Spirit	*GV*
Soma	Angel Minister – Love and Fornication	*KoSA*
Soma (Hindi) (Saljail)	Angel – Moon	*SSG*
Somahi	Angel – Tebet	*SR*
Somekem	Angel Prince – Gate of Spirit of West	*SRH*
Somial	Angel – Malachim, Adir	*SRH*
Somis	Servant Spirit	*Abm*
Somkas	Angel – Fourth Heaven, West	*SSM*
Somoha	Angel – Moon	*GAG*
Somucha	Angel – Moon	*GAG*
Somuel	Angel – nine of twenty-one on the Left	*ACM*: Berlin 10587
Sona	Spirit	*MHN*
Sonaco	Spirit – Minister of Love	*oADS*
Sonatas	Angel – Fourth Heaven, West	*SR*
Soncas/Sonitas	Angel – Fifth Heaven Tuesday, West Angel – Fifth Heaven, West Ministering Spirit – Mars	*EoN, Hmn, KoSR, BoO, GAG, BoTS, SaS, tM, CBMS*
Sondama/Sondanna	Spirit	*BoTS*
Sonenel	Treasure Spirit	*BoTS*
Sonoryan	Spirit	*BoTS*
Sonotrobas	Angel Minister – Love and Fornication	*KoSA*
Soomathuel Divoomathel	Stone Spirit – Topaz	*GS*
Soonek/Loonex	Demon Earl	*BOS, BoO*
Sophia	Gnostic Divine Feminine	*ACM*: NH Codex VIII
Sophina	Angel Minister – Love and Fornication	*KoSA*
Soqemeh	Angel – Malachim, under Avorphenial	*SRH*
Soquiel/Soquial	Angel – First Heaven, South, West Angel Prince – West Gate	*SR, SRH*

Sorath	Planetary Spirit – Sun Ruler – Fortuna Major, Fortuna Minor	*KoSR, 3BOP, BM,* *Thm, PO, tM*
Sordazal	Angel	*NA*
Sordinot/Sodirno	Spirit	*GoPH, GV*
Soresephi	Angel Magistrate – Malachim	*SRH*
Soriel/Souiel	Duke – West by North Afternoon/after Midnight	*Stg, ThG, BoTS*
Sorios/Soyrio	Spirit	*oADS*
Sornadaf/Sornadafs	Angel – Nisan	*SR, tSoS*
Sorosma	Servant Spirit	*Abm*
Sorphail/Corsayl	Spirit – second Mansion of Moon Ring	*AE*
Sōrtērkha (Luna)	Luna – Alternative Name	*Hyg*
Sotad/Sotadē (Saturn)	Saturn – Alternative Name	*Hyg*
Soterion	Servant Spirit	*Abm*
Sotheano/Sotheans	Demon Duke – East	*Stg, ThG*
Soudiel	Angel	*Hyg*
Soul of Messiah	Archangel – Malkuth	*3BOP, SaS, BoTS, MNeI*
Souleel	Angel	*ACM*: Aberdeen Text
Soum (Silyaeel, Indian)	Spirit King – Moon	*Pic*
Souphi	Name of Helios in second Hour	PGM IV:1596-1715
Soupiel	Demon	*ToSC*
Souriel/Souriēl	Archangel, third Heaven	PGM III:1-164, X:36-50, XXVI:1-42, XXXVI:161-177, XLIII:1-27, CVI:1-10; *SM*: P. Berol inv. 21165
Sourouchchata	Spirit	*ACM*: Berlin 8321
Sowrges/Nowrges	Demon Marquis	*BOS, BoO*
Soyll	Spirit – North	*oADS*
Sparou/Sparonē/Sparto (Luna)	Luna – Alternative Name	*Hyg*

Spekouēl/ Spertikouēl/ Speltikoēl/Spetēkoēl/ Spetikoēl	Angel – Mercury	*Hyg*
Spendonim/ Spindonēm/ Spitiēm	Angel – Moon	*Hyg*
Sperabonatos	Spirit – Minister of Love	*oADS*
Sphadōrapo/ Sphendarap/ Sphindorap/ Sphedorap	Demon – North	*Hyg*
Sphalikon/ Sphelēkon/ Sphelikon (Mercury)	Mercury – Alternative Name	*Hyg*
Sphandor	Demon – Decan seven	*ToS*
Sphendonael	Demon – Decan six	*ToS*
Sphitzioēl/Sphikoēl/ Sphiskēnoēl/ Sphykinoēl/ Sphianoēl	Angel – Wednesday Hour six	*Hyg*
Sphragiel/Phragiel/ Pharagiel	Demon – West	*Hyg*
Sphysiroēl	Demon – Mars	*Hyg*
Spipial	Angel Encampment Head – sixth Heaven, East	*ShR*
Spirit of the Antichrist	Spirit embodying Satan	HB 1 John 4:3, Rev 11:7, 19:20
Spirits of Force and Counsel	Spirit	*GoA*
Spirits of Joy	Spirit	*GoA*
Spnig	Angel – Twelfth Step, second Heaven	*ShR*
Spondōr/Spindōr/ Spyldar/Spilēdōr	Demon – Saturday Hour three	*Hyg*
Spora	Deity of Procreation	PGM XIII:1-343, XIII:343-646
Spracto	Demon Margrave – East under Oriens	*KoN*
Sprial	Angel – Sixth Encampment, first Heaven	*ShR*

Spugliguel/ Spugligueell/ Sutiguol	Angel – Spring	*EoN, BM, tSoS*
Spum	Angel – Third Step, second Heaven	*ShR*
Spyryon/Spyrion/ Speryon/Spireon/ Sperion/Sireon/ Spirdon/Spiron/ Spirgon/Spirion	Demon Bishop – West or East	*CBoM, BoO, CoC, GAG, oADS, BoTS*
Šqgyāl/Mgtyāl	Angel – September/Virgo	*BoW*
Squatu	Spirit Familiar	*BoTS*
Srael	Angel – Fifteen of twenty-one on the Left	*ACM*: Berlin 10587
Sraguel	Angel	*ACM*: Hay 10122
Sramael	Angel – Fourteen of twenty-one on the Left	*ACM*: Berlin 10587
Sraphoel	Angel	*ACM*: Hay 10122
Srk	Angel – Fifth Encampment, first Heaven	*ShR*
Srpial	Angel – Seventh Encampment, first Heaven	*ShR*
Srsial	Angel Prince – fourth Heaven, Water	*ShR*
Srsyāl	Angel – Hour twelve/Pisces	*BoW*
Srugial	Angel – Seventh Encampment, first Heaven	*ShR*
Srukit	Angel – North Wind	*ShR*
Srura	Angel – Seventh Encampment, first Heaven	*ShR*
Ssanday	Spirit – Mirror	*CoMS*
Stablotthis/Stabblait	Spirit – Third Mansion of Moon Ring	*AE, oADS*
Staijel	Angel – First Heaven, North	*SaS*
Stal	Angel – Eleventh Step, second Heaven	*ShR*
Standalcon	Angel – Saturn	*BARC*
Staphiliēl/ Stouphouēl/ Stariēl/Stauphnēl	Angel – Friday Hour eighteen	*Hyg*
Star	Demon – East	*BOS, BoO*
Staurioci/Stanirioci/ Sumryoyy	Spirit – Fourteenth Mansion of the Moon Ring	*AE*
Staus	Angel – Jupiter	*BARC*

Stayrabangoriath/ Vamgonatus/ Scaagrabax	Spirit – Second Mansion of the Moon Ring	*AE*
Stelmel	Angel – Bisertilis	*SR*
Stelpha/Stelph	Demon – Saturday Hour ten, eleven Demon – South	*Hyg, CBoM*
Stemehylyn	Angel – Moon/Monday	*SR*
Stemēnos (Mercury)	Mercury – Alternative Name	*Hyg*
Stemoēl	Angel	*Hyg*
Stephanuta	Demon Leader – under Elestor	*KoSU*
Stepoth	Demon – under Sirach	*KoSU*
Steroēl/Stryroēl/ Steriēl/ Stiroēl/Storoēl	Angel – Tuesday Hour twenty-two	*Hyg*
Stifellore	Angel – Jupiter	*GAG*
Stigamma	Spirit	*BoTS*
Stirel	Demon Count – North under Egyn	*KoN*
Stilu	Intelligence	*EPL*
Stimcul	Son of Light, subject to Prince Hagonel	*dHM*
Stimel	Spirit – Mirror	*CoMS*
Stoel	Angel – Breath of God's Nostrils	*ACM*: H. Kopt. 686
Stolas/Stolus	Demon Prince	*PmD, DoW, Goe, DI*
Storax/Sycoracem	Fairy Advisor and Angel – Sun	*oADS, BoO*
Storphalus	Spirit – first Mansion of Moon Ring	*AE*
Stratiēl/Stragiēl/ Straggiēl	Angel – Tuesday Hour eighteen	*Hyg*
Stratheam	Spirit – Jupiter	*KoN*
Stratiget/Stragiton/ Straget	Demon – Friday Hour thirteen	*Hyg*
Strength	Angel – Third Altitude (Gemini)	*Alm*
Strial	Angel – Fourth Encampment, first Heaven Angel – Sixth Step, second Heaven	*ShR*
Strife	Demon – Pleiades two	*ToS*
Strtu	Angel – Fourth Encampment, first Heaven	*ShR*
Strubiel	Angel – Day Hour four	*Stg, ArP*
Stumet	Demon – Under Sirach	*KoSU*
Sualata	Spirit	*BoTS*

Subba	Spirit	*ACM*: Hay 10391
Subsolanus/ Subsolamus	East Wind – Over Angels of Tuesday	*Hmn, Thm, SMS, PO*
Suburith	Spirit	*MHN*
Sucax	Demon Marquis	*MHN*
Suceratos	Angel – Fourth Heaven Sunday, West, Spring Angel – Fourth Heaven, West	*EoN, Hmn, KoSR, BoO, GAG, SaS, tM*
Suceratos	Spirit Messenger – Sun	*SGT, SSG*
Suchay	Demon – West	*BOS, BoO, oADS*
Suciel	Angel – Marchesvan	*SR*
Sudyr	Spirit Demon	*SSM, oADS*
Suel	Angel – four of twenty-one on the Left	*ACM*: Berlin 10587
Suffales	Demon – East	*BOS, BoO*
Suffuriel/Suffugruel/ Sustugriel/ Sustugriel/ Suffugiel/Suffugidel	Demon – under Satanachi	*KoSU, SoS, GV*
Suffuyel	Angel of Abyss – Spring	*SSM*
Sugmonos	Intelligence – Mercury	*SGT, SSG*
Sugni/Sugin	Angel – Nisan	*SR, tSoS*
Suhub	Spirit	*AAAA*
Suiajasel/Suiaiaseh	Angel – Sagittarius	*ArP*
Sulphur	Demon Senior Treasure Spirit	*SSM, BoTS*
Sumas	Demon Margave – Astronomy	*KoN*
Sumchatos	Angel – Fifth Heaven, West	*SSM*
Sumiellam/Sumiella/ Samiel	Spirit – Mercury	*BoO, GAG*
Sumnidiel	Peasant Spirit, Air	*MNeI*
Sumuron/Sumuran	Servant Spirit	*Abm, MRC*
Sun	God – Sun	*Hyg*
Suncacer	Angel – Fifth Heaven, West	*SR*
Suquinos/Suguinos	Angel Minister of Air – Wednesday Spirit Attendant – Mercury Ministering Spirit – Saturn	*EoN, Hmn, KoSR, GAG, tM, CBMS*

Sūrāyāyl	Angel – Monday, Hour of Venus	*BoW*
Surfah/Surfa/Astarte (Zahra, Indian)	Spirit Queen – Venus	*Pic*, *SSG*
Surgath/Surgat/ Surgatha/Surgatanas	Demon Duke Demon – Sunday Demon – under Sirach Demon Brigadier	*KoSR*, *KoSU*, *SoS*, *GoPH*, *GV*, *BoSC*, *BD*
Surgunth/Surgunt	Demon – Under Satanachi	*KoSU*
Suria	Demon King – West	*KoN*
Suriel	Angel Angel Commander	*ACM*: H. Kopt. 544, Berlin 11347, Oriental 5525, Hay 10434, Oriental 5986, Bodl C(P)4, Cairo IAFO, P. Mich. 3472, Oriental 6794, Oriental 6796, P. Mich. 593, H. Kopt. 686
Suriel (Asmodel)	Angel – Taurus Spirit – Taurus	*3BOP*, *BoO*, *tSoS*, *JMR*, *SaS*
Suriel	Angel – Tishrei	*SR*
Suriel	Demon Duke – West by North pre-Noon	*Stg*, *ThG*, *BoTS*
Suriflyen	Night Devil	*oADS*
Sursinol	Spirit	*BoTS*
Surth	Beast before God (fourth of six)	*oADS*
Suruel	Angel	*ACM*: P. Lichačev
Susael	Angel – Nineteen of twenty-one on the Left	*ACM*: Berlin 10587
Suses	Angel Minister – Trickery	*KoSR*
Susial	Angel – Third Heaven, serving Rhtial	*ShR*
Susip/Susab/Zauceb	Spirit – Sixth Heaven	*Pic*
Suth	Angel – King of Air on Thursday Presiding Spirit – Jupiter	*Hmn*, *KoSR*, *GAG*, *BoTS*, *PO*, *tM*, *CBMS*
Suua	Angel – Second Encampment, first Heaven	*ShR*
Swatlees	Spirit – Enmity	*Pic*
Syar (Venus)	Venus – Alternative Name	*Hyg*
Sycors	Spirit	*oADS*

Syeonell/Lyeonell	Demon Count/Earl	*BOS, BoO*
Syeth	Spirit – Ninth Mansion of the Moon Ring	*AE*
Sygip (Saturn)	Saturn – Alternative Name	*Hyg*
Sygō (Jupiter)	Jupiter – Alternative Name	*Hyg*
Sygrie	Demon – Saturday Hour twenty-three	*Hyg*
Sykhnsour	North Wind – Winter	*BoW*
Sylberyolba	Spirit of the Thumb	*CBoM*
Syliēl	Angel	*PGM X:36-50*
Sylol	Spirit Assistant – Monday	*MHN*
Sylquam	Demon Messenger	*BoO*
Symeam	Angel – Book Writer	*BoO*
Symiel/Simiel	Demon Duke – North by East Demon Duke – North under Egyn	*Stg, ThG, KoN*
Symitouēl	Angel – Friday Hour ten	*Hyg*
Symnay	Angel – Potestates	*67M*
Symofor/Simofor	Spirit	*MHN*
Symon Mobris	Angel – Book Writer	*BoO*
Sympa	Angel – Spring	*BoW*
Sympilia/Sibylia (Sibilia?)	Fairy Queen	*Hyg*
Symposis	Spirit	*BoTS*
Symygaylon	Demon King	*SSM*
Symyryssym	Demon King	*SSM*
Synaynon	Angel – Sun	*BARC*
Synigērōm/ Singyrōm/ Synigeirōm	Demon – Saturday Hour seven	*Hyg*
Synopigos/ Pinopygos/ Kinopigos/Pēnopigos	Demon – Sunday Hour nineteen	*Hyg*
Synoryell	Demon – North	*BOS, BoO, oADS*
Syol	Spirit Familiar	*BoTS*
Syrael/Sitael	Angel – Shem three	*KoSU, 3BOP, GoeR, JMR, SAS, tM*
Syrama/Sirama	Spirit	*MHN*
Syritēr	Demon – Monday Hour twenty-one	*Hyg*

Syrōph/Syriphas (Venus)	Venus – Alternative Name	*Hyg*
Syrumel/Slittareth	Demon – under Sirach	*KoSU*
Syrus/Trachias	North West by North Wind	*Thm*
Sysabel/Sisabel	Spirit – Water	*MHN*
Sysmael	Demon	*NML*
Sytacibor	Angel	*BoSC*
Sytroy	Spirit	*MHN*
Sywaro	Archangel	*67M*
Syymelyel	Angel – Jupiter/Thursday	*SR*
Szeyyeil	Angel – Venus/Friday	*SR*
Szif	Angel – Tebet	*SR*
Szucariel	Angel – Tishrei	*SR*

T

TaadS	Enochian Angel – West, over first lesser Angle	*TBA*
Taanbun	Angel Prince – Fifth Heaven, Month of Tammuz	*ShR*
Ta'aniel	Angel	*SoM*
Taatus	Spirit Assistant – Sunday	*MHN*
Taay	Angel – Fifth Encampment, first Heaven	*ShR*
Taazma	Angel – Third Heaven, serving Rhtial	*ShR*
Tabamiah/Jibamiah Iibamiah/Iabamiah	Angel – Shem seventy	*KoSU, 3BOP, GoeR, JMR, SAS, tM*
Tabat	Treasure Spirit	*oADS*
Tabbat	Servant Spirit	*Abm*
Tabiel	Angel – Shebat	*SR*
Tabiym	Angel – Over Rivers	PGM XXVI:1-42
Tablas/Taklas/ Toiblas/ Tabblai	Demon – Wednesday Hour twelve	*Hyg*
Tablic	Angel – Ab	*SR*
Tabrasol	Spirit	*GV*

Tabtalios/Tantalēs/ Tabtalēr/Tabaltalis/ Tautaliē	Demon – Friday Hour seven	*Hyg*
Tachael	Genii – 18° Pisces	*ArP*
Tachiel	Genii – 28° Pisces	*ArP*
Tael	Angel	*ACM*: Hay 10122
Tafel	Angel	*SoM*
Taftyah	Angel – Potestates	*67M*
Taftyarohel	Angel – Potestates	*67M*
Tagiel	Genii – 12° Scorpio, 21° Scorpio, 21° Sagittarius	*ArP*
Tagishun	Angel – Twelfth Step, second Heaven	*ShR*
Tagora	Servant Spirit	*Abm*
Tagriel	Angel – Mansion twenty-six	*3BOP, tSoS, JMR, SaS, tM*
Tagriel	Noble Spirit, Fire Foolish Spirit	*MNeI*
Tagrtat	Spirit, He of Eternity	PDM XIV:459-475, XIV:489-515, XIV:516-527
Tahegilihos	Angel	*NA*
Tahiel	Genii – 17° Taurus, 17° Gemini, 27° Gemini	*ArP*
Tahimarees	Spirit gatherer of Bandalos	*Pic*
Tahitoos	Spirit gatherer of Brimas	*Pic*
Taijn	Spirit – Moon	*67M*
Taimon (Saturn)	Saturn – Alternative Name	*Hyg*
Tainor/Tainet	Superior Intelligence – Earth	*KoSU, SoS*
Tait	Angel – Spring	*MHN*
Tajael	Genii – 29° Virgo	*ArP*
Takaros	Servant Spirit	*Abm*
Taketh	Demon	*GAG*
Takhman	Demon – Friday Hour twenty-two	*Hyg*
Takhmnan	Demon – Friday Hour twenty-three	*Hyg*
Takuel	Angel	*ACM*: Moen 3
Talanasiel	Angel – Sun	*BARC*
Talaroth	Angel – Venus	*KoSR*

Talbusi/Talubsi	Angel	*SoM*
Taleos (Caleos)	Spirit – West	*oADS*
Talgnaf	Angel – Shebat	*SR*
Talgott	Spirit – Minister of Love and Maker of Friendship	*oADS*
Talgylnenyl	Angel – Sun/Sunday	*SR*
Taliel	Genii – 1° Sagittarius	*ArP*
Talii	Spirit – Minister of Love	*oADS*
Talkidiōth/Talkidonios	Angel – Friday Hour thirteen	*Hyg*
Talrailanrain	Angel – Venus/Friday	*SR*
Talui	Angel – Spring	*BM*
Tamach	Spirit – East	*SSM*
Tamael	Angel – Third Heaven Friday, East Spirit – Venus	*Hmn, KoSR, SoS, BoO, BM, GAG, BoTS, tM*
Tamael	Genii – 11° Libra	*ArP*
Tamafin	Spirit	*MHN*
Tamandundiceth	Demon	*GAG*
Tamar	Spirit – South	*oADS*
Tambēl/Tambil	Spirit	*BoW*
Tamees	Front part of Damahos	*Pic*
Tameriel/Tamariel/Famariel	Angel – Night Hour two	*Stg, ArP*
Tameriel/Jamiriel/Jamriel	Angel – Night Hour nine	*Stg, ArP*
Tamhyāl/Tmhyal	Angel – May/Taurus	*BoW*
Tami/Tamy/Tamer	Spirit	*MHN*
Tamiel	Presiding Spirit – Venus	*CBMS*
Tamiel	Genii – 13° Aquarius	*ArP*
Tamis	Angel Minister – Love amd Fornication	*KoSA*
Tammuz	Sumerian Shepherd/Fertility God	HB Ex 8:14
Tamon	Demon King	*BOS, BoO*
Tamor/Chamor	Demon Prince	*BOS, BoO*
Tampalti	Demon	*SMS*
Tams	Spirit – Presidential Counsellor, West	*BoTS*

Tamtiel	Angel – Bisertilis	SR
Tamus	Front part of Brimas	Pic
Tanaell	Spirit	GAG
Tangialem	Angel Minister	KoSA
Tangiel	Genii – 10° Virgo	ArP
Tantavalerion/ Golgathell	Demon Emperor	BOS, BoO
Taphartharath/ Taphthartharath/ Taphtartharath	Planetary Spirit – Mercury Ruler – Albus, Conjunctio	KoSR, 3BOP, BM, Thm, PO, tM
Tarael	Angel – Jupiter/Thursday	SR
Tarahim	Servant Spirit	Abm
Tarajah	Genii – 9° Pisces	ArP
Taramel	Angel – Third Heaven, East	SR
Taraor	Spirit	MHN, NML
Tarat/Garastri/ Garakt/ Gērat/Garatrē	Demon – Sunday Hour ten	Hyg
Tarbin/Tarbustaym/ Torbin	Spirit – second Mansion of the Moon Ring	AE
Tarchimache/ Tarchimach	Demon	GoPH, GV
Tareto	Servant Spirit	Abm
Tarfanyelyn	Angel – Mars/Tuesday	SR
Tariel	Angel – Summer	Hmn, KoSR, tSoS, MC, GAG, GoeR, tM
Tariescorat	Angel – Third Heaven, East	SaS
Tarihimal/ Tharithimal	Demon	GV
Tarmanydyn	Angel – Moon/Monday	SR
Tarmiel	Angel – Second Heaven Wednesday, East	Hmn, KoSR, BoO, GAG, BoTS, tM, CBMS
Tarmiel	Spirit – Mercury	SGT, SSG
Tarmytz/Tarmitzod	Angel – Night Hour seven	Stg, ArP
Taros/Tarof	Demon Duke – West Day	Stg, ThG, BoTS
Tarpalyel	Angel – First Heaven, West	SSM

Tarpiel	Angel – Fourth Heaven, East	*SSM*
Tarquam/Tarranan	Angel – Autumn	*EoN, Hmn, KoSR, tSoS, MC, GAG, GoeR, tM*
Tarquayl (Tarquam?)	Angel – Autumn	*MHN*
Tarseus	Demon	*ToSC*
Tartais	Angel – Venus	*GAG*
Tartalyn	Angel – Mars/Tuesday	*SR*
Tartaroēl/Taritaēl/Tartarouēl	Demon – Sunday Hour twenty-one	*Hyg*
Tartarōni/Tartarouil/Tartarouēl/Tartaroēl	Demon – North	*Hyg*
Tartarouchos	Underworld God	*ACM*: Berlin 8314
Tartarouel/Tartaroēl	Demon – Moon	*Hyg*
Tarterouēl/Tartarouēl	Demon – Tuesday Hour five	*Hyg*
Tartys/Taktis/Taklis	Angel Ruler – Night Hour two	*Stg, ArP*
Taruz	Angel Lord – Nights of the Year	*SSM*
Taryel	Angel – Third Heaven, East	*SSM*
Taryestorat	Angel – Third Heaven, East	*SR*
Tashiel	Genii – 13° Capricorn, 22° Capricorn, 22° Aquarius	*ArP*
Tasmon (Saturn)	Saturn – Alternative Name	*Hyg*
Tatalion/Tataleon (Dantalion?)	Demon	*BoO, oADS*
Tatgiel	Angel – Sivan	*SR*
Tatir (Venus)	Venus – Alternative Name	*Hyg*
Tatomofon	Spirit	*MHN*
Tatriel	Spirit	*ACM*: Oriental 6796
Taulasin	Demon – Wednesday Hour twelve	*Hyg*
Tauriel	Angel	*ACM*: Oriental 5899, Berlin 11347
Tauriel (Asmodel)	Angel – Taurus Spirit – Taurus	*3BOP, tSoS, JMR, SaS*
Tausata	Demon Prince	*GoPH*
Tavael	Genii – 27° Aries	*ArP*

Tawados	Spirit – Love/Sexual Attraction	*Pic*
Taxael	Angel – Mars	*BARC*
Taxouziel	Angel	*Hyg*
Taxpon/Taxeponi/ Taxipōn/Taxepōn/ Takhseponē	Demon – Wednesday Hour thirteen	*Hyg*
Tayly	Spirit – Minister of Love and Maker of Friendship	*oADS*
Tayriomim	Angel – Moon	*LL*
Tazouel	Angel	*Hyg*
Tbgial	Angel – Tenth Step, second Heaven	*ShR*
Tbl	Angel – Second Encampment, first Heaven	*ShR*
Tdhdial	Angel – Third Heaven, serving Ibnial	*ShR*
Techorial	Angel Prince – Gate of Spirit of South	*SRH*
Tedean	Servant Spirit	*Abm*
Tediel	Demon Duke – South-East Night	*Stg, ThG, BoTS*
Tediel	Genii – 12° Sagittarius	*ArP*
Tedim	Enochian Angel – West, over second lesser Angle	*TBA*
Teer (Utarid, Persian)	Spirit King – Mercury	*Pic*
Tefnut	Egyptian Goddess of Moisture	PDM XIV:366-375
Tegin	Spirit – Treasure	*KoN*
Tegra	Angel Prince – Wednesday	*EoN*
Tehiel	Genii – 30° Libra	*ArP*
Tehom	Angel – Dominations/ Thrones	*67M*
Tehorial	Angel Prince – Gate of Spirit of South	*SRH*
Teibinenim	Angel – Moon	*LL*
Tekauriel	Angel – God's Mouth	*ACM*: H. Kopt. 686
Tēkhōr/Tēkhar/ Teikhir	Demon – Saturday Hour thirteen	*Hyg*
Tektonoēl/Taktoniēl	Angel – Tuesday Hour five	*Hyg*
Teletiel (Malehidael)	Angel – Aries Spirit – Aries	*3BOP, BoO, tSoS,* *JMR, SaS*
Telgradekh/ Tetrdekh/ Telgrade	Angel – Autumn, Lord of the Towers	*BoW*

ABBREVIATIONS 671

Teliel	Angel Prince – Love	*KoSA*
Teliel	Genii – 1° Scorpio	*ArP*
Teltrion/Theltrion/ Theltryom/ Theltryon/ Tyltyon	Demon Bishop – East or South	*CBoM, BoO, CoC, GAG, oADS, BoTS*
Tely	Spirit	*GV*
Telzē	Angel – Over Snow	PGM XXVI:1-42
Temael	Genii – 2° Capricorn	*ArP*
Temas/Temal	Angel – Day Hour 11	*Stg, ArP*
Temel	Spirit Messenger – East	*BoTS*
Temelion	Angel – Saturn/Saturday	*SR*
Temeluchos	Angel – Punishes Perjurers	*ACM*: Berlin 10587
Templator	Angel Minister – Love and Fornication	*KoSA*
Temporantia	Spirit of Temperance	*BoO*
Tenachyel	Spirit	*SSM*
Tenaciel	Angel – Third Heaven Friday, East	*Hmn, KoSR, BoO, BM, GAG, BoTS, tM*
Tenariel	Spirit – Venus	*SGT, SSG*
Tenebiel	Angel – Adar	*SR*
Tēnneostge (Jupiter)	Jupiter – Alternative Name	*Hyg*
Tennuat/Temiorpt	Spirit – first Mansion of the Moon Ring	*AE*
Tentator	Angel – Hatred and Destruction	*KoSA*
Tentetos	Spirit	*MHN*
Tepau	Enochian Angel – East, over second lesser Angle	*TBA*
Tephraēl/Tepha	Demon – Tuesday Hour twenty	*Hyg*
Teptadaēl	Angel – Winter	*BoW*
Tepyel	Angel – Saturn, over Earth	*SR*
Terath/Terach	Demon Duke – North Day	*Stg, ThG, BoTS*
Teratouōn/Teratuon (Mercury)	Mercury – Alternative Name	*Hyg*
Terayl	Angel – Winter	*MHN*
Teredial	Angel – Malachim, under Pheseker	*SRH*
Tereol	Spirit/Demon	*MHN, NML*
Tereoth	Good Spirit	*MHN*

Terephial	Angel Prince – Gate of Spirit of East	*SRH*
Teretial	Angel Minister – Malachim, ruling Rain	*SRH*
Terial	Angel – Malachim, Tammuz	*SRH*
Teriapel	Intelligence – Venus	*SGT, SSG*
Teriath/Ateriath	Spirit – twelfth Mansion of the Moon Ring	*AE*
Teriphon/Teriephon	Angel – Malachim, under Pheseker Angel – Malachim, sixth Host	*SRH*
Terkoëtz	Angel	*Hyg*
Terly/Tirly	Spirit	*KoSR, GoPH, GV, BD*
Termat	Spirit – ninth Mansion of the Moon Ring	*tSoS*
Termines	Good Spirit	*MHN*
Terre	Spirit	*oADS*
Terror	Demon Senior	*SSM*
Tertin/Terin	Spirit – fifth Mansion of the Moon Ring	*AE*
Tesael	Genii – 2° Aquarius	*ArP*
Tesiach	Spirit – South	*SSM*
Tesmarēl	Spirit	*BoW*
Tessaid (Fessan/Tessan)	Spirit – North	*oADS*
Tetathia	Spirit	*GoA*
Tetilol/Tetilōt/Tetalol/Tetilotēl/Petilōl	Angel – Friday Hour twenty-one	*Hyg*
Tētorō	Demon – Tuesday Hour seven	*Hyg*
Tetra	Archangel – Mercury	*Hmn, BoO, GAG*
Tetriēl	Angel – Saturday Hour fifteen	*Hyg*
Tevemes	Angel	*KoSA*
Texai	Servant Spirit	*Abm*
Textator	Spirit – Minister of Love	*oADS*
Teygra/Tygra	Demon Senator	*BoO*
Tezael	Genii – 9° Taurus	*ArP*
Tgmlial	Angel – Third Heaven, serving Dlqial	*ShR*
Tgrial	Angel – Third Encampment, first Heaven	*ShR*
Thaadas/Taadas	Daemon Minister – Sun, East	*SBH*
Tha'akenov	Angel Prince – Tammuz	*SRH*

Thacserar	Angel	*NA*
Thaisara	Presence in the Heavenly Pillars	*ACM*: BN Turin
Thalamora	Presence in the Heavenly Pillars	*ACM*: BN Turin
Thalbus/Thalbos	Demon Duke – West Night	*Stg, ThG, BoTS*
Thamael	Spirit – Venus	*SGT, SSG*
Thamaor	Demon King – North	*DoW, GAG*
Thamniēl/ Thamanaēl/ Thamaniēl/Thamiēl	Angel – Sunday Hour twenty-one	*Hyg*
Thamy	Angel – Potestates	*67M*
Than	Angel	*NA*
Thanael	Angel	*ACM*: Hay 10122
Thanatiel/Tanatiel	Demon Duke – Hour three of fifteen	*Stg, ThG*
Thanay	Angel – Fourth Altitude (Cancer)	*Alm*
Thaoth	Angel – Feet of God	*ACM*: H. Kopt. 686
Thaotha	Angel – Feet of God	*ACM*: H. Kopt. 686
Thaphōt/Phaphot/Phaphōt	Demon – Thursday Hour four	*Hyg*
Thapnix/Thapnyx/Thapniz	Demon – Friday Hour eight	*Hyg*
Tharas	Demon Duke – North Day	*Stg, ThG, BoTS*
Thariel	Demon Duke – North Night	*Stg, ThG, BoTS*
Tharinela	Angel	*NA*
Tharophim	Plant Spirit – St John's Wort	*GS*
Tharsis/Tharsies	Angel President/Governor – Water Angel Ruler – Water, governs Azazel	*3BOP, tSoS, MC, BoTS, JMR, KoN, SaS, PO, tM*
Tharson	Demon Under Duke	*Stg, ThG*
Thastaro (Astaroth?)	Spirit – Thursday	*BoSC*
Thathiel	Biblical Elder	*ACM*: Berlin 11347, Oriental 6796
Thauruel	Angel over the Clouds	*ACM*: BN Turin
Thavael	Angel	*GoA*
Theal/Theall	Spirit – Woods Spirit	*oADS, tSoS*
Thebaēl	Angel – Saturday Hour three	*Hyg*
Thebot	Evil Spirit	*SoM*

Theielēphoēl (Luna)	Luna – Alternative Name	*Hyg*
Thēkeēl/Thekiēl/Thokyēl	Angel – Friday Hour fifteen	*Hyg*
Thekerial	Angel Minister – Malachim, over Water	*SRH*
Thelegial	Angel – Malachim, under Avorphenial	*SRH*
Thelemenoph	Angel Minister – Malachim	*SRH*
Thelemeteph	Angel – Malachim, Flames of Fire	*SRH*
Theliel	Angel Prince – Love	*VMN*
Themahehugos	Angel	*NA*
Themamoht	Angel	*NA*
Themaz/Themax	Angel – Night Hour eight	*Stg, ArP*
Themekor	Spirit – South in Autumn	*SRH*
Themis	Greek Goddess of Justice	PGM V:172-212
Themiton	Angel – Saturn/Saturday	*SR*
Themos	Angel	*NA*
Thenial	Angel Minister – Malachim, ruling Rain	*SRH*
Theophil	Angel	*Hyg*
Theoriel/Theor	Angel – Day Hour eight	*Stg, ArP*
Theoska	Archangel	*67M*
Theotodoph/Thetidoph/Thetidōph	Demon – Monday Hour three	*Hyg*
Thederenolial	Angel Prince – Sea	*SRH*
Thekemial	Angel – Malachim, under Pheseker	*SRH*
Themehor	Spirit – South in Winter	*SRH*
Thena	Angel – Malachim, under Avorphenial	*SRH*
Thenial	Angel – Malachim over Rain	*SRH*
Theniemial	Angel – Malachim, under Ayigeda	*SRH*
Theodony	Angel	*NA*
Theos[422]	Angel	*NA*
Thephehohal	Angel	*NA*
Therebegolial	Spirit Prince – Sea in Winter	*SRH*
Therechamzon	Angel	*NA*

---

422 As *Theos* is Greek for God, it is possible the presence of this name in an angel list is not indicative of it being an angel.

Theregial	Angel – Malachim, under Dohel	*SRH*
Therekial	Angel – Malachim over Sea and Life in it	*SRH*
Therenech	Angel – Malachim, under Ayigeda	*SRH*
Therenial	Angel – Malachim, sixth Host	*SRH*
Thereniyal	Angel Prince – Gate of Spirit of East	*SRH*
Theriel	Angel before Heavenly Pillars	*ACM*: BN Turin
Therotz	Angel – Malachim, Spring Nights	*SRH*
Thesara	Angel	*NA*
Theser	Spirit – Minister of Love	*oADS*
Thesfealin	Angel – Venus/Friday	*SR*
Theshenderenies	Angel Prince – Shevet	*SRH*
Thesoha	Presence in the Heavenly Pillars	*ACM*: BN Turin
Thetēdōr/Athetdōr	Demon – Monday Hour three	*Hyg*
Theteus	Demon Chief	*tM*
Theth	Demon – Three-Way Crossroads	*Hyg*
Thethederelial	Spirit Prince – Sea in Autumn	*SRH*
Thetynchos	Angel	*NA*
Theu	Spirit	*GV*
Theumatha	Demon	*ACM*: Hay 10414
Theut	Angel Minister – Love and Fornication	*KoSA*
Thezemon	Angel	*NA*
Thieches	Angel – Malachim, under Dohel	*SRH*
Thiel	Angel – Second Heaven Wednesday, North	*Hmn, KoSR, BoO, GAG, BoTS, SaS, tM*
Thiel	Intelligence – Venus	*SGT, SSG*
Thielaphoēl (Luna)	Luna – Alternative Name	*Hyg*
Thieleh	Angel – Malachim, under Ayigeda	*SRH*
Thieretal	Angel Prince – Gate of Spirit of East	*SRH*
Thimiael	Angel	*ACM*: Hay 10122
Thirama/Tirama	Servant Spirit	*Abm, MRC*
Thitodens	Demon	*MHN*
Thoac/Phoac/Phoacs	Demon Duke – North Day	*Stg, ThG, BoTS*
Thoaijl	Ministering Familiar/Mystery	*67M*
Thobar	Demon	*MHN*

Thobiel	Angel	*SSM, CoMS*
Thocheli	Angel – Malachim, under Avorphenial	*SRH*
Thochereger	Angel Prince – Ab	*SRH*
Thodeth	Angel Prince – Gate of Spirit of East	*SRH*
Thol	Angel – Light of God's Eyes	*ACM*: H. Kopt. 686
Thomenal	Angel – Malachim, Flames of Fire	*SRH*
Thomial	Angel Minister – Malachim	*SRH*
Thomiel	Spirit – Gemini	*tSoS*
Thomieni	Angel – Malachim, under Phelmiya	*SRH*
Thomo	Demon	*MHN*
Thonios/Thorios	Demon – Saturday Hour nine	*Hyg*
Thoramodor	Angel	*NA*
Thoran	Angel – Light of God's Eyes	*ACM*: H. Kopt. 686
Thoranor	Spirit Familiar	*BoTS*
Thorethah	Angel Magistrate – Sowing Soil	*SRH*
Thoth/Thōouth/Thouth/Thath/Thayth (Hermes-Thoth)	Egyptian God of Magic	PGM I:262-347, III:282-409, III:467-478, IV:1-25, IV:94-153, IV:296-466, V:1-53, V:213-303, VII:490-504, VII:540-578, VII:919-924, VIII:1-63, XII:96-106, XII:107-121, XII:153-160, XII:160-178, XII:270-350, LXXX:1-5, PDM XII:21-49, XIV:1-92, XIV:150-231, XIV:309-334, XIV:395-427, LXI:63-78, Suppl. 101-116, Suppl. 149-162, Suppl. 168-184; *SM*: T. Cairo Mus. JdE 48217, T. Louvre Inv. E 27145, P. Mich. Inv. 6925,

ABBREVIATIONS 677

Thoth/Thōouth/ Thouth/ Thath/Thayth (Hermes-Thoth) (con't.)		*SM*: T. Köln Inv. 1; *ACM*: GMPP:1-25, P. Mich. 136
Thothial	Angel Minister – Malachim, over Water	*SRH*
Thouri/Thoeris (Tauret)	Egyptian Hippopotamus Goddess of Childbirth and Fertility	PGM XIXa:1-54
Thouriēl	Archangel	PGM IV:1716-1870
Thpial	Angel – Third Heaven, serving Ibnial	*ShR*
Thrakai/Thrakaim	Spirit who Hung the Heavens	*ACM*: BN Turin
Thrial	Angel Encampment Head – sixth Heaven, East	*ShR*
Thribiel	Angel – Day Hour eight	*Stg, ArP*
Thriel	Angel	*ACM*: BN Turin, P. Mich. 593
Throel	Angel before Heavenly Pillars	*ACM*: BN Turin
Thurcal	Demon Duke – North Night	*Stg, ThG, BoTS*
Thuri	Angel Minister – Love and Fornication	*KoSA*
Thuriel/Thirciel/ Thirsiel	Demon Duke – Day Hour ten and Night Hour ten	*Stg, ThG*
Thurmytz/ Thurmytzod/ Thurmytzol	Angel – Night Hour three	*Stg, ArP*
Thuros/Thuroz	Angel – Day Hour four	*Stg, ArP*
Thyeloēl (Luna)	Luna – Alternative Name	*Hyg*
Thymenephri	Angel – Lunar, Night Hour nine	PGM VII:862-918
Thyroces	Demon	*NMI*
Thykiēl	Angel – Friday Hour fourteen	*Hyg*
Thzrial	Angel – Third Heaven, serving Ibnial	*ShR*
Tiamial	Angel – First Encampment, first Heaven	*ShR*
Tibiel	Genii – 20° Libra	*ArP*
Tiburtina	Spirit – Sibyl (ten of ten)	*GV*
Tichmavah	Plant Spirit – Fir	*GS*
Tichnondaēs	Sixth of Seven Egyptian Fates of Heaven	PGM IV:475-829
Tiel	Angel – Second Heaven, North	*EoN*
Tier	Angel – Malachim, under Ayigeda	*SRH*

Tietepech	Angel Prince – Gate of Spirit of West	SRH
Tigara	Demon Duke – South Day	Stg, ThG
Tigraphon	Servant Spirit	Abm
Tigrh	Angel Overseer (two of seven) – First Heaven	ShR
Tiiel	Genii – 19° Virgo	ArP
Tijlaij	Spirit – Mars	67M
Tilh	Angel – Second Encampment, first Heaven	ShR
Timaguel	Angel	KoSA
Timnhrq	Angel Encampment Head – sixth Heaven, West	ShR
Timo	Spirit	GV
Timora	Spirit of Fear	BoO
Timugu	Angel – Fourth Encampment, first Heaven	ShR
Tinakos	Servant Spirit	Abm
Tinchir	Spirit – sixth Mansion of Moon Ring	AE
Tinios (Jupiter)	Jupiter – Alternative Name	Hyg
Tiniaē/Tiniak (Mars)	Mars – Alternative Name	Hyg
Tinira	Servant Spirit	Abm
Tinsyel	Angel – Jupiter, over Fire	SR
Tiogra	Angel – Mercury/Wednesday	SR
Tiphoar/Tiphon (Typhon?)	Evil Spirit	MRC
Tipidōēl/Trapidōēl/Trapidōn/Trapēdōēl	Angel – Monday Hour fourteen	Hyg
Tir (Persian) (Utarid)	Angel – Mercury	SSG
Tiriel/Firiel	Planetary Intelligence- Mercury	KoSR, 3BOP, BM, GoPH, GV, PO, tM, BoSC
Tirli	Angel – First Encampment, first Heaven	ShR
Tiroēl/Tyroēl/Teroēl/Tirōēl	Angel – Wednesday Hour ten	Hyg
Tirum	Angel – Third Encampment, first Heaven	ShR
Tisizaēl	Angel	Hyg
Tiszodiel	Angel – Marchesvan	SR

Titam/Titan/ Tytam/ Tytarit	Fairy Queen	*BoO*
Titomon	Angel – Saturn/Saturday	*SR*
Tiyal	Angel Prince – North Gate, Firmament	*SRH*
Tiyana (Zahra, Greek)	Spirit Queen – Venus	*Pic*
Tiymas	Left part of Gharnos	*Pic*
Tkt	Angel – First Encampment, first Heaven	*ShR*
Tkurks	Angel – Seventh Encampment, first Heaven	*ShR*
Tlbaap	Angel – Third Heaven, serving Dlqial	*ShR*
Tibo	Spirit	*CoC*
Tibolato	Spirit	*CoC*
Tibon	Spirit	*CoC*
Tição	Demon	*BoSC*
Tlgial	Angel – First Encampment, first Heaven	*ShR*
Tlhbn	Angel – Twelfth Step, second Heaven	*ShR*
Tlial	Angel – Second Encampment, first Heaven	*ShR*
Tlšāyl	Angel – Saturn	*BoW*
Tmkial	Angel – Sixth Step, second Heaven	*ShR*
Tmnial	Angel – Third Heaven, serving Rhtial	*ShR*
Tmpnih	Angel Encampment Head – sixth Heaven, West	*ShR*
Tmr	Angel – Second Encampment, first Heaven	*ShR*
Tmsmael	Evil Angel over Pains, Sharp Pains, Inflammation, Dropsy	*SoM*
Tnimial	Angel – Second Encampment, first Heaven	*ShR*
Tobial	Angel Magistrate – Malachim, under Phelmiya	*SRH*
Tobiel	Angel – Air	*SR*
Tobyas/Tobias	Spirit	*BoO, oADS*
Tobyell	Angel	*oADS*
Toco	Enochian Angel – West, serving first lesser Angle	*TBA*
Todedē	Demon – Tuesday Hour eighteen	*Hyg*

Todidedos/Todede/ Todedē/Todexgi/ Touddedēn	Demon – Tuesday Hour nineteen	*Hyg*
Toikeos (Jupiter)	Jupiter – Alternative Name	*Hyg*
Tolana	Spirit	*GAG*
Tolet	Servant Spirit	*Abm*
Tombam	Spirit	*CoC*
Tomekem	Angel Prince – Gate of Spirit of West	*SRH*
Tomgarsuk	Greenland Fishing Spirit	*DI*
Tomimiel/Tamimiel (Ambriel)	Angel – Gemini	*3BOP, BoO, JMR, SaS*
Tomōn (Saturn)	Saturn – Alternative Name	*Hyg*
Ton	Angel Minister – Love and Fornication Angel – Malachim, under Avorphenial	*KoSA, SRH*
Tonalianos/ Touldōraph/ Touktoraph/ Togodoraph/ Tondopharioan (Sun)	Sun – Alternative Name	*Hyg*
Toniel	Angel – Moon, over Earth	*SR*
Tonsin	Demon Prince	*GoPH*
Tonther	Spirit of the Thumb	*CBoM*
Tonuchon	Spirit	*KoSR*
Toorigōth (Mars)	Mars – Alternative Name	*Hyg*
Tophatiēl/Toratoēl/ Tauphatiēl	Angel – Friday Hour nine	*Hyg*
Tophiemos	Angel – Malachim, sixth Host	*SRH*
Tophue	Archangel	*ACM*: BN Turin
Topinoch	Spirit	*KoSR*
Topora	Spirit – Minister of Love	*oADS*
Toranyel	Angel – Third Heaven, East	*SSM*
Torath	Angel – Third Heaven, East	*SSM*
Torayeil	Angel – Sun/Sunday	*SR*
Torcha	Demon Marquis and Duke	*NML*
Toreniel	Angel Prince – Gate of Spirit of West	*SRH*
Toripiel	Angel – Jupiter/Thursday	*SR*
Torothora	Angel – Seraphim who Cover ther Feet	*ACM*: H. Kopt. 686

Tos	Top part of Brimas	*Pic*
Totet	Enochian Angel – East, serving first lesser Angle	*TBA*
Toti	Angel – Malachim, under Pheseker	*SRH*
Tougel	Demon	*ToSC*
Touid/Touēd (Venus)	Venus – Alternative Name	*Hyg*
Toumiel	Angel	*SM*: P. Heid. Inv . G 1101
Toutimar (Venus)	Venus – Alternative Name	*Hyg*
Tqu	Angel – Fifth Encampment, first Heaven	*ShR*
Traacyel	Angel – Jupiter/Thursday	*SR*
Trachathath/ Trachatat	Punishing Wind Daemon – Venus, subject to East and West Winds; between South and West	*SSM, SBH*
Trajael	Genii – 8° Libra	*ArP*
Tralyelyn	Angel – Mars/Tuesday	*SR*
Tranayrt/Tramayrt	Spirit	*MHN*
Tranquinus	Spirit Prince – Illness	*KoN*
Trapis	Servant Spirit	*Abm*
Trasiel/Frasiel	Angel – Day Hour six	*Stg, ArP*
Trator	Angel Minister – Love and Fornication	*KoSA*
Traxdati/Traxdatē/ Praxdate	Demon – West	*Hyg*
Trellari/ Trellanyeunat/ Treleatye/Ereleri	Spirit – ninth Mansion of the Moon Ring	*AE, tSoS*
Tremael	Angel Minister	*ACM*: P. Mich. 593
Tremuel	Angel	*ACM*: Bodl C(P)4, Oriental 6172
Trera	Spirit – Minister of Love	*oADS*
Tresndiem	Angel Minister	*KoSA*
Trgch	Angel – Second Encampment, first Heaven	*ShR*
Trgiaob	Angel ruling Wild Fowls and Creeping Things	*SoM*
Triabol/Troibol/ Triabokh	Demon – North	*Hyg*

Triphis (Noble Lady)	Egyptian Lioness-Headed Goddess	PDM XIV:528-553, XIV:585-593, XIV:1026-1045
Triplex/Complex	Demon Duke and Marquis	*NML*
Tripun	Angel – Sixth Encampment, first Heaven	*ShR*
Trisacha	Servant Spirit	*Abm*
Tristator	Angel – Trickery	*KoSA*
Trivoo	Plant Spirit – Lime Tree	*GS*
Trkial	Angel – Tenth Step, second Heaven	*ShR*
Trmial	Angel – Sixth Encampment, first Heaven	*ShR*
Troacrio/Tamariel	Demon Prince, under Amaymon	*KoN*
Trocornifer	Terrestrial Spirit – Attendant in East	*SBH*
Troglis	Spirit – Infernal Treasure	*dN*
Troion	Demon King	*BARC*
Tronax	Spirit – Mirror	*CoMS*
Trooaval	Stone Spirit – Sapphire	*GS*
Tropayca	Night Devil	*oADS*
Trophos	Power of Death	*ACM*: Cairo Bone A/B
Trosiēl/Prosiēl/ Arōsiēl/ Prosionēl	Angel – Wednesday Hour four	*Hyg*
Trquih	Angel – First Encampment, first Heaven	*ShR*
Trsiel	Angel ruling Rivers	*SoM*
Trspu	Angel – Fourth Encampment, first Heaven	*ShR*
Trsunial	Angel – Ninth Step, second Heaven	*ShR*
Trtm	Angel – Second Encampment, first Heaven	*ShR*
Truaur	Angel – First Encampment, first Heaven	*ShR*
Trubas	Angel – Day Hour nine	*Stg, ArP*
Truhun	Angel – Second Encampment, first Heaven	*ShR*
Trurgr	Angel Prince – fifth Heaven, Month of Av	*ShR*
Trwdrie	Night Devil	*oADS*
Tryboy/Triay	Demon	*MHN, NML*
Tsel	Angel	*ACM*: H. Kopt. 544
Tsial	Angel – Third Heaven, serving Ibnial	*ShR*
Ttbal	Angel – Third Heaven, serving Ibnial	*ShR*

ABBREVIATIONS

Ttghh	Angel – Fifth Encampment, first Heaven	*ShR*
Tual	Angel – Taurus	*ArP*
Tub	Angel – Fifth Encampment, first Heaven	*ShR*
Tubal	Spirit – Hot Spirit – Love	*MHN, NML*
Tubatlu	Angel	*SoM*
Tuberiel	Angel – Night Hour six	*Stg, ArP*
Tubeylyn	Angel – Mars/Tuesday	*SR*
Tubial	Angel – Fourth Encampment, first Heaven Angel Encampment Head – sixth Heaven, East	*ShR*
Tubiel	Angel – Summer	*EoN, tSoS*
Tubo	Angel	*SoM*
Tubull	Devil – Ursa Major	*oADS*
Tudiras Hoho	Demon Marquid	*LdE*
Tuel	Spirit – Mirror	*CoMS*
Tufiel	Angel – Jupiter, over Earth	*SR*
Tugam	Angel Minister – Love and Fornication	*KoSA*
Tugaros/Tuaros	Demon Duke – South-East Night	*Stg, ThG, BoTS*
Tulatu	Angel	*SoM*
Tulef	Evil Spirit	*SoM*
Tulguaret/Tolquaret	Angel – Autumn	*EoN, tSoS*
Tulidomar	Angel – Saturn	*KoSR*
Tulmas/Tusmas	Angel – Day Hour seven	*Stg, ArP*
Tumiel (Turiel?)	Spirit – Sun	*SoS*
Tupopsta	Spirit	*ACM*: Hay 10391
Tupumus	Angel – Sixth Encampment, first Heaven	*ShR*
Tuqpial	Angel – Ninth Step, second Heaven Angel Prince – fourth Heaven, Fire	*ShR*
Tuqpirs	Angel Ruler – sixth Heaven, East	*ShR*
Turiel	Spirit Messenger – Jupiter	*SGT, SSG*
Turiel/Turyel	Angel – Venus Angel – Summer, third Heaven Friday – West third Heaven – West Archangel – Malachim, over the Shem	*SSM, EoN, Hmn, KoSR, MHN, BM, GAG, BoTS, SaS, SRH, tM*
Turitil	Servant Spirit	*Abm, MRC*

Turmiel	Angel – Day Hour eleven	*Stg, ArP*
Turmiel	Spirit – Mercury	*SoS*
Turons	Angel Minister – Love and Fornication	*KoSA*
Turtiel	Angel – Night Hour one	*Stg, ArP*
Tus/Tuz/Sus	Angel Minister of Air – Sunday Spirit Attendant – Sun	*EoN, Hmn, KoSR, GAG, GoeR, BoTS, tM*
Tutiel	Angel – Jupiter/Thursday	*SR*
Tuwahel	Archangel	*67M*
Tuwalu	Angel	*SoM*
Tuwisu	Angel	*SoM*
Tvuries/Tuveries (Cimeries?)	Demon Marquis	*MHN*
Twtrysy	Angel Prince – Lower Four	*SoM*
Tychagara	Throne Angel (two of seven)	*SaS*
Tyche	Greek Goddess of Fortune	PGM IV:3125-3171, VII:505-528, L:1-18, LVII:1-37
Tyel	Angel – Second Heaven, North	*SSM, SR*
Tyer	Angel – Treasure seeking	*dN*
Tyggara	Angel – Mercury	*SSM*
Tymel	Angel – Jupiter/Thursday	*SR*
Tyman	Spirit – Invisibility	*KoN*
Tymor	Spirit Familiar	*BoTS*
Tyneos (Jupiter)	Jupiter – Alternative Name	*Hyg*
Typhi	Epithet of Aphrodite	PGM XII:201-269
Typhon	Egyptian Demon Spirit	PGM IV:154-285, IV:1331-1389, IV:3255-3274, VII:467-477, XII:365-375, XXXIIa:1-25, XXXVI:1-34, XXXVI:69-101, XXXVI:295-311, XXXVI:333-360, LXVIII:1-20, LXXII:1-36, CXXVIa:1-21,

Typhon (con't.)		PDM LVIII:1-14, LXI:197-216
Typhonbon	Demon – Thursday Hour one	*Hyg*
Typhon-Seth (Seth)	Egyptian Chaos God	PDM XIV:675-694; *SM*: P. Ant. II.66
Tyr	Norse God	*Gbk*
Tyroces	Spirit	*MHN*
Tyros	Demon	*MHN*
Tyroy	Spirit – Water	*MHN*
Tysyel	Spirit Familiar	*BoTS*
Tytpapaly	Angel – Fifth Heaven, West	*SSM*
Tywael	Archangel	*67M*
Tzadadraban	Angel – sets Torah in the Heart	*SQ*
Tzakētoēl	Angel – Friday Hour seventeen	*Hyg*
Tzakiel	Genii – 7° Virgo	*ArP*
Tzanas/Tzana (Mars)	Mars – Alternative Name	*Hyg*
Tzangiel	Genii – 9° Sagittarius	*ArP*
Tzaphiel	Genii – 6° Pisces	*ArP*
Tzebeqeteni/ Tzebeqetheni	Angel – Malachim, under Phelmiya Angel Magistrate – Malachim	*SRH*
Tzedeqial	Angel – Mercury, Sagittarius, Pisces Angel – Malachim, Summer Angel Prince – Spring, Tammuz Angel Minister – Malachim, second Dwelling Angel Prince – Gate of Spirit of East	*SRH*
Tzegerial	Angel Minister – Malachim	*SRH*
Tzehemial	Angel – Malachim, sixth Host	*SRH*
Tzelsiōd/Kelsiōd/ Kelsido	Spirit – East	*Hyg*
Tzephial	Angel – Malachim, Tebeth	*SRN*
Tzephnial	Spirit Prince – Ocean in Spring	*SRH*
Tzerepones	Demon	*ToSC*
Tzeremial	Angel – Malachim, under Pheseker	*SRH*
Tzereqial	Angel – Malachim, Tammuz	*SRH*
Tzerial	Angel Prince – Gate of Spirit of South	*SRH*

Tzermaēn/Tzermaēl (Mercury)	Mercury – Alternative Name	Hyg
Tzetahotim	Angel – Moon	LL
Tzethiel	Genii – 9° Scorpio	ArP
Tzianiz	Angel	Hyg
Tzianphiel/ Tzeanphiel/ Entzianphiel	Demon	ToSC
Tzien	Angel Prince – West Gate	SRH
Tzippat/Tzēpatēr/ Tzipat/ Tzipater	Demon – Thursday Hour five	Hyg
Tzisiel	Genii – 6° Gemini	ArP
Tzitzanēel	Demon	Hyg
Tzoreteq	Angel Prince – Gate of Spirit of West	SRH
Tzorial	Angel – Harvest Ruler Angel – Malachim, Flames of Fire Angel – Malachim, Tishri Angel – Libra	SRH
Tzoukana	Angel	Hyg
Tzqtzwrwmtyal	Angel Prince – Angels of Rage	SoM

U		
Uabalkanarithin	Angel – Moon	LL
Uacatara	Angel – Moon	BARC
Uaceyl	Angel – Mars/Tuesday	SR
Uachayel	Angel – Venus/Friday	SR
Ualiel	Angel – First Heaven, North	EoN
Ualnram	Angel – First Heaven, North	EoN
Uardeyheil	Angel – Venus/Friday	SR
Ūasylasyāl/Šyšyāyl	Angel – October/Libra	BoW
Ubarim	Servant Spirit	Abm
Ubelutusi	Angel	SoM
Ubisi/Ublisi	Angel	SoM
Ubnell	Angel	oADS
Uchariel	Superior Intelligence – Venus	SoS

Ucirnuel/Vcirmiel/ Ucirmiel/Ucimuel	Angel – Second Heaven Wednesday, North	Hmn, KoSR, BoO, BoTS, tM
Udaman	Servant Spirit	Abm
Udiel	Demon Duke – West Day	Stg, ThG, BoTS
Uetamuel	Angel – Second Heaven, North	SR
Ugalis	Servant Spirit	Abm
Ugesor	Servant Spirit	Abm
Ugirpon	Servant Spirit	Abm
Ugobog	Servant Spirit	Abm
Uguemenos	Angel Minister	KoSA
Uhal	Spirit – Venus	67M
Uiotan	Angel – Water	SR
Uiutn	Angel Encampment Head – sixth Heaven, West	ShR
Ukobach	Demon – Infernal Boiler Oil Maintainer	DI
Uleos/Ulios	Spirit	oADS
Ulzulino	Spirit of Evil	BoSC
Um	Spirit – Presidential Counsellor, North	BoTS
Umabel	Angel – Shem sixty-one	KoSU, 3BOP, GoeR, JMR, SAS, tM
Umariel/Vmariel/ Amariel	Angel – Night Hour five	Stg, ArP
Umastrail	Angel – First Heaven, North	EoN
Umbra	Spirit – North Treasure Spirit	oADS, BoTS
Umijchob	Ministering Familiar/Mystery	67M
Umnuel	Biblical Elder	ACM: Berlin 11347, Oriental 6796
Unael	Angel – First Heaven, North	SaS
Unascaiel	Angel – First Heaven, North	SR
Unaraxxydin	Angel – Sun/Sunday	SR
Unknown God	Unknown God	HB Acts 17:23
Unleylyn	Angel – Mars/Tuesday	SR
Unochos	Servant Spirit	Abm
Uorayeylin	Angel – Day Hour two	LL
Upathna	Angel – Fourth Encampment, first Heaven	ShR

Urachel/Urachiel	Spirit – Necromancy, under Oriens	*KoN*
Urallim	Angel – First Heaven, North	*SR*
Uranacha	Angel – Fifth Heaven, East	*SR*
Uraniel/Vraniel	Angel – Night Hour ten	*Stg, ArP*
Uraniel	Angel – Day Hour five	*Stg, ArP*
Uraniel	Spirit – Mercury	*SSG*
Uranos	Greek Sky God	*ACM*: H. O. Lange Text
Urasian	Spirit – Ring of second Mansion of the Moon	*tSoS*
Urbaniel/Vrbaniel	Demon Duke – Hour fifteen of fifteen	*Stg, ThG*
Urbaniel	Duke – West by North after Midnight	*BoTS*
Urcifery	Spirit – third Mansion of Moon Ring	*tSoS*
Urgido	Servant Spirit	*Abm*
Uri	Angel Ruler – twelve Hours of Night	*ACM*: P. Mich. 1190
Uribel	Demon Servant – Sunday	*KoN*
Uriel/Uriell/Uryell/ Nariel/Ouriel/Nuriel	Archangel – Earth, East, Saturn Angel – Fourth Heaven Sunday, South, Spring Noonday Winds Angel before Throne of God	PGM XC:1-13, CVI:1-10; *ToS, SM*: P. Berol inv. 21165, P. Heid. Inv. G 1101, P. Heid. Inv. Lat. 5, P. Med. I.20; *ACM*: P. Prague 1, Oriental 5899, BN Turin, Berlin 10587, Moen 3, P. Mich. 3472, Oriental 6794, Oriental 6796, P. Mich. 593, L. Anastasi 9; *SR, SSM, EoN, Hmn, B7R, KoSR, dN, NML, Gbk, CBoM, CoC, oADS, ADS, 3BOP, dHM, AN, tSoS, MC, GAG, ArP, BoTS, 9CK, MNeI, KoN, ES, GoA, GV, SaS, EPL, PO, CII, MRC, CoMS, tM, 67M, CBMS*
Uriel	Superior Intelligence – Saturn	*KoSU, SoS*

Uriel	Intelligence – Moon Presiding Spirit – Mercury	*SGT, SSG*
Urielim	Angel	*dN*
Urikon	Ministering Familiar/Mystery	*67M*
Urinaphton	Pygmy King	*MNeI*
Urisiel/Usiel	Demon Duke – South	*Stg, ThG*
Urpeniel	Angel – Water	*SR*
Urricas	Spirit – Minister of Love	*oADS*
Uruel	Angel	*ToS*
Uryall	Spirit – North	*oA*
Uryel (Uriel)	Angel Senior – Venus	*SSM*
Usaryeyel	Angel – Mars/Tuesday	*SR*
Usera	Angel – First Heaven, North	*SaS*
Usiel/Vsiel	Demon Prince – North-West Demon Prince – West under Beymon	*Stg, ThG, BoTS, KoN,* *VJL*
Usiniel/Usimiel/ Vsimiel	Demon Duke – North-West Day	*Stg, ThG, BoTS*
Usion	Angel Minister – Love and Fornication	*KoSA*
Usor	Angel – Hatred and Destruction	*KoSA*
Ustael/Ystiel/Vstael/ Uslael/Uflael	Angel – Fourth Heaven Sunday, West Spirit – Sun Presiding Spirit – Sun	*EoN, Hmn, SoS, BoO,* *GAG, BoTS, SaS, tM,* *CBMS*
Ustael	Spirit Messenger – Moon	*SGT, SSG*
Ustay	Spirit – Ring of seventh Mansion of the Moon	*tSoS*
Ustiron	Beast before God (second of six)	*oADS*
Utanaual	Spirit Assistant – Tuesday	*MHN*
Utarid (Arabic) / Arquil/Harquil	Spirit King – Mercury	*Pic, SSG*
Uwula	Ministering Familiar/Mystery	*67M*
Uyel	Angel – Mercury	*SSM*

V		
Va	Spirit	*MHN*
Vaal/Vual	Demon King	*LdE*
Vaanael	Angel – First Heaven, East	*SSM*

Vaanuel	Angel – Second Heaven, North	*SSM*
Vaanyel	Angel – Fourth Heaven, South	*SR*
Vacerail/Varoayl	Spirit – second Mansion of Moon Ring	*AE*
Vachael	Genii – 30° Gemini	*ArP*
Vadriel	Demon Duke – East	*Stg, ThG*
Vadros/Vadras	Demon Duke – West	*Stg, ThG, BoTS,*
Vagael	Genii – 18° Scorpio, 18° Sagittarius	*ArP*
Vagel	Genii – 24° Aries	*ArP*
Vah	Spirit	*BoO, GoPH*
Vahajah	Genii – 15° Pisces	*ArP*
Vahejah	Genii – 25° Pisces	*ArP*
Vahiel	Genii – 14° Taurus, 14° Gemini, 24° Taurus, 24° Gemini	*ArP*
Vajael	Genii – 28° Scorpio, 28° Sagittarius	*ArP*
Valac/Valu/Volac/Volach	Demon President	*MHN, PmD, DoW, Goe, DI*
Valefar/Valefor/Malephar/Malaphar	Demon Duke	*PmD, DoW, Goe, GG*
Valerian	Herb Spirit	*GAG*
Valgus/Malchus	Devil – Keeper of the Infernal Gates	*oADS*
Vallo	Spirit	*GAG*
Valnum	Angel first Heaven Monday – North	*Hmn, KoSR, BoO, GAG, BoTS, tM*
Valnum	Intelligence – Saturn	*SGT, SSG*
Valuerituf	Spirit	*GV*
Valyel	Angel – Second Heaven, South	*SSM*
Vamay	Angel – Moon	*BARC*
Vameroz/Vameros/Vomeros	Angel – Night Hour two	*Stg, ArP*
Vamiel	Genii – 29° Capricorn, 29° Aquarius	*ArP*
Vamuel	Angel – Fourth Heaven, South	*SSM*
Vanescor/Venescor/Venescar/Vanesior	Angel – Night Hour five	*Stg, ArP*
Vanesiel	Angel – Day Hour four	*Stg, ArP*
Vanibal	Spirit Assistant – Sunday	*MHN*
Vaniel	Genii – 4° Aries	*ArP*

ABBREVIATIONS

Vanish	Alternative name of Metatron	*SQ*
Vanosyr/Vanoir/Vanoie	Angel – Night Hour three	*Stg, ArP*
Vantif	Alternative name of Metatron	*SQ*
Vantovi	Alternative name of Metatron	*SQ*
Vapula/Nappula/Napula/Valpula	Demon Duke/President	*PmD, DoW, Goe*
Varbas/Carbas/Darbas	Demon King/Prince	*BOS, BoO*
Varcan/Varkan/Verkan/Varchan	Angel – King of Air on Sunday Spirit King – Sun	*EoN, Hmn, KoSR, BoO, GAG, GoeR, PO, tM*
Varcan	Angel – King of Air, Venus[423]	*BM*
Variel	Genii – 17° Libra	*ArP*
Varmay	Angel – Day Hour seven	*Stg, ArP*
Varoy	Spirit	*SSM*
Varpiel/Verpiel	Demon Duke – Day Hour eight and Night Hour eight	*Stg, ThG*
Vasa	Enochian Angel – West, serving fourth lesser Angle	*TBA*
Vasago/Vassago/Vsagoo/Vazago/Usagoo	Demon Prince Spirit – Presidential Counsellor, North	*BOS, BoO, Goe, oADS, BoTS*
Vasariah/Vafariah	Angel – Shem thirty-two	*KoSU, 3BOP, GoeR, JMR, SAS, tM*
Vasans	Angel – First Heaven, North	*SaS*
Vascaniel	Angel – Third Heaven, South	*SaS*
Vasenel/Vasenal	Demon Duke – Day Hour seven	*Stg, ThG*
Vasge	Enochian Angel – South, serving first lesser Angle	*TBA*
Vashiel	Genii – 19° Capricorn, 19° Aquarius	*ArP*
Vaslos/Vastos/Vafros	Demon Duke – North by East Day	*Stg, ThG*
Vasmi	Spirit – Minister of Love	*oADS*
Vastamel	Angel – Third Heaven, South	*SR*
Vathmiel/Vachmiel	Angel Ruler – Day Hour four	*Stg, ArP*
Vatiel	Genii – 27° Libra	*ArP*

---

423 This appears to be a copyist's error, as Varcan is Solar in the *Heptamer*on which this text draws from.

Vatuel	Spirit	*MHN*
Vau-el	Spirit	*GoA*
Vazebelil	Spirit	*SR*
Vaziel	Genii – 16° Virgo, 26° Virgo	*ArP*
Veaboluf	Angel – Marchesvan	*SR*
Veaguel	Angel – Fourth Heaven, North	*EoN*
Veal	Spirit – Sun	*67M*
Vealbyn	Angel – First Heaven, North	*SSM*
Veallum	Angel – First Heaven, North	*SR*
Veaseyel	Angel – Fifth Heaven, North	*SSM*
Vebol	Angel – Second Heaven, North	*SaS*
Vecastyel	Angel – Fourth Heaven, South	*SSM*
Veduij	Spirit – Saturn	*67M*
Vegansores	Angel Lord – Planets in Spring	*SSM*
Vehichdunedzineylyn	Angel – Sun/Sunday	*SR*
Vehniah	Salamander Head (one of six)	*SBRM*
Vehuel/Vohuel	Angel – Shem forty-nine	*KoSU, 3BOP, GoeR, JMR, SAS, tM*
Vehujah/Vehiyah/Vehuiah	Angel – Shem one	*KoSU, 3BOP, GoeR, JMR, SAS, tM*
Veirmiel	Angel – Second Heaven, North	*EoN*
Velel/Valel	Angel – Second Heaven Wednesday, North	*EoN, Hmn, KoSR, BoO, GAG, BoTS, tM*
Velous	Angel	*GV*
Velyon	Night Devil	*oADS*
Vemael	Angel – Day Hour eight	*Stg, ArP*
Vemasiel	Angel – Night Hour nine	*Stg, ArP*
Venahel/Venael/Venabel	Angel – Second Heaven Wednesday, North Ministering Spirit – Mercury	*EoN, Hmn, KoSR, BoO, GAG, BoTS, tM, CBMS*
Veneriel/Vendriel (Anael)	Archangel – Venus	*3BOP, tSoS, JMR*
Venesiel	Angel – Day Hour seven	*Stg, ArP*
Venetal	Angel – Second Heaven, North	*SaS*
Venibbeth	Angel	*KoSA*
Venoel	Spirit – Mercury	*SSG*

Venomiel	Angel – Night Hour two	*Stg, ArP*
Ventariel	Angel – Night Hour seven	*Stg, ArP*
Venulla/Venulia/ Venila/ Venalla/Veinilla	Fairy – seventh of Seven Sisters	*oADS, BoO, JMR, BoTS*
Venus	Goddess – Love	*Hyg, BoO, oADS, GV*
Venus	Spirit – Voluptuousness	*BP*
Veorchiel/Verchiel	Angel – Leo Angel Ruler – Sun and Leo Genius – Fortuna Major, Fortuna Minor	*KoSR, 3BOP, tSoS, MC, JMR, SaS, Thm, PO, tM*
Vepar/Separ	Demon Duke	*PmD, DoW, Goe*
Vequaniel/Vegvaniel	Angel Ruler – Day Hour three	*Stg, ArP*
Verascyer	Angel – Fourth Heaven, South	*SR*
Verciseri	Spirit – third Mansion of Moon Ring	*AE*
Veremedyn	Angel – Sun/Sunday	*SR*
Vereon	Angel – Second Altitude (Taurus)	*Alm*
Vereset	Angel Minister – Love and Fornication	*KoSA*
Verexi	Treasure Spirit	*oADS*
Verginiel (Hamaliel)	Angel – Virgo	*JMR*
Veriell	Angel – Mercury	*GAG*
Vermias	Spirit	*GV*
Vertegat	Spirit – seventh Mansion of the Moon Ring	*AE*
Veruel	Angel – First Heaven, South	*EoN*
Vervain	Herb Spirit	*GAG*
Vessur/Vesour	Demon Duke – West by South Day	*Stg, ThG, BoTS*
Vesturiel	Spirit	*GV*
Vetameil	Angel – Second Heaven, North	*SaS*
Vetuel/Vetael	Angel – First Heaven Monday, South Spirit – Moon	*Hmn, KoSR, SoS, BoO, GAG, tM*
Vevaliah/Vovaliah	Angel – Shem forty-three	*KoSU, 3BOP, GoeR, JMR, SAS, tM*
Veycis	Spirit – Mirror	*CoMS*
Vezol	Spirit	*MRC*
Vfaltyel	Angel – Third Heaven, West	*SSM*
Vflael	Angel – Fifth Heaven, West	*SSM*

Vhshr	Demon	*SMS*
Vianathraba	Spirit – Sun	*SGT, SSG*
Vianuel/Viannel/ Vianiel	Angel – Fifth Heaven Tuesday, South Angel – Fifth Heaven, South Spirit – Mars Ministering Spirit – Jupiter	*EoN, Hmn, KoSR, SoS, BoO, GAG, BoTS, SaS, tM, CBMS*
Vidoraas	Spirit – Regal Antipathy	*Pic*
Vijas	Demon	*MHN*
Villaguel	Angel	*KoSA*
Viloporas	Angel Minister – Love and Fornication	*KoSA*
Vine	Demon King and Earl	*PmD, DoW, Goe*
Vionairaba/ Vionatraba	Angel – Fourth Heaven Sunday, East, Spring Angel – Fourth Heaven, East	*Hmn, KoSR, GAG, BoTS, SaS, tM, CBMS*
Viordy	Spirit	*GV*
Virginiel (Hamaliel)	Angel – Virgo Spirit – Virgo	*3BOP, tSoS, SaS*
Virus	Demon	*MHN*
Virytus	Demon	*MHN*
Vitalot	Spirit	*BoO, GoPH*
Viteon	Woodland Spirit	*BoO*
Vitordill	Spirit	*CoC*
Vivooel	Plant Spirit – Adder's Tongue	*GS*
Vixalimon	Angel – Saturn/Saturday	*SR*
Vlmiel	Angel – Summer	*MHN*
Vm	Demon	*MHN*
Vmeloth	Good Spirit	*MHN*
Vmon	Demon	*MHN*
Vniueny	Demon	*MHN*
Vnyrus	Demon	*MHN*
Voa'anenal	Angel Prince – Gate of Spirit of South	*SRH*
Vobechial	Angel Prince – West Gate	*SRH*
Vobehielael	Angel – Malachim ruling Dangerous Creatures	*SRH*
Vobemethov	Angel Magistrate – Malachim	*SRH*
Vobeqetemal	Angel Prince – West Gate	*SRH*

Vobereqial	Angel Prince – Gate of Spirit of East	*SRH*
Vobetzelial	Angel Prince – North Gate	*SRH*
Vocheleqiem	Angel Prince – North Gate, Firmament	*SRH*
Vochenial	Angel Prince – East Gate/North Gate, Firmament	*SRH*
Vochesepheth	Angel – Malachim, under Avorphenial	*SRH*
Vochezeqial	Angel Prince – Gate of Spirit of North	*SRH*
Vogaheh	Angel Minister – Malachim, over Water	*SRH*
Vohereqovova	Angel – Malachim, under Avorphenial	*SRH*
Voil/Violl	Angel – Virgo	*ArP*
Vokethov	Angel – Malachim, under Avorphenial	*SRH*
Volach (Valac)	Demon President	*NML*
Volaquiel	Angel – Fourth Heaven, North	*SaS*
Vom	Demon	*MHN*
Vomelek	Angel – Malachim, under Phelmiya	*SRH*
Vomelekial	Angel Prince – Gate of Spirit of South	*SRH*
Vomethenenal	Angel Prince – Gate of Spirit of North	*SRH*
Vophelal	Angel Prince – Gate of Spirit of West	*SRH*
Voqeshial	Angel Prince – Gate of Spirit of South	*SRH*
Vosherephial	Angel Prince – Gate of Spirit of East	*SRH*
Voshovova	Angel – Malachim, under Ayigeda	*SRH*
Votechenial	Angel – Malachim, Flames of Fire	*SRH*
Voterephenial	Angel Prince – West Gate	*SRH*
Vothechenial	Angel Minister – Malachim	*SRH*
Vothedoregel	Angel – Malachim, Autumn Nights	*SRH*
Voyieroval	Angel – Tuesday	*SRH*
Voyiheneq	Angel Prince – Gate of Spirit of East	*SRH*
Vozeqanen	Angel, serving above sixth Degree	*SRH*
Vpriochi	Spirit	*CoC*
Vraci	Angel – Mars	*GAG*
Vrael	Ministering Spirit – Moon	*CBMS*
Vralchim	Demon	*MHN*
Vraniel	Duke – West by North pre-Midnight	*Stg, ThG*
Vrbeneh	Enochian Angel – East, serving second lesser Angle	*TBA*

Vrcenbre	Enochian Angel – East, over third lesser Angle	*TBA*
Vresius	Demon	*MHN*
Vrgan	Enochian Angel – South, serving third lesser Angle	*TBA*
Vriel	Demon Wandering Prince	*Stg, ThG*
Vriel/Uriel	Demon Duke – South by West Night, North Day	*Stg, ThG, BoTS*
Vriell/Vriall/Uriell/Uriall	Demon – North	*BOS, BoO*
Vrlacafel	Angel – Sunday	*MHN*
Vronatraba	Angel – Fourth Heaven, East	*EoN*
Vrvoi	Enochian Angel – West, serving second lesser Angle	*TBA*
Vrzla	Enochian Angel – East, over first lesser Angle	*TBA*
Vsyl	Enochian Angel – West, serving second lesser Angle	*TBA*
Vsyr	Spirit	*MHN*
Vtepa	Enochian Angel – East, over second lesser Angle	*TBA*
Vtimo	Demon	*MHN*
Vtisaryaya	Angel – Tishrei	*SR*
Vuael/Uvael	Angel first Heaven Monday – North	*Hmn, KoSR, BoO, GAG, BoTS, tM*
Vuall/Vual/Nuall/Wal/Wall	Demon Duke	*PmD, DoW, Goe, DI*
VulcanielVulcamiel/Vntramiel	Angel – Night Hour five	*Stg, ArP*
Vulnavij	Spirit	*GV*
Vvaij	Ministering Familiar/Mystery	*67M*
Vvalyel	Angel – First Heaven, North	*SSM*
Vvaslayl	Angel – First Heaven, North	*SSM*
Vvel/Vuel	Angel Senior – Jupiter	*SSM*
Vvishtrom	Demon	*SMS*
Vyel	Angel Senior – Venus	*SSM*
Vyonacraba	Angel – Fifth Heaven, East	*SSM*

Vzago/Urago (Vassago?)	Demon – North	*BOS, BoO, oADS*
Vzmyas	Demon	*MHN*

W

Waed	Angel – Potestates	*67M*
Wahsaft (Rafael, Indian)	Spirit King – Jupiter	*Pic*
Walachy	Demon Count – South under Amaymon	*KoN*
Walkadeus/Walkades	Spirit	*oADS*
Walkates	Spirit	*GAG*
Wallum	Angel – First Heaven, North	*SaS*
Wamidal/Vamidal	Evil Spirit	*MRC*
Wandolas	Spirit – Love/Sexual Attraction	*Pic*
Waran	Spirit	*KoN*
Wegulo	Angel	*SoM*
Wel	Angel – Day Hour one	*LL*
Welor	Good Spirit	*SoM*
Welur	Demon Count – East under Oriens	*KoN*
Welvor	Demon Count – Orient	*KoN*
Wepwawet	Egyptian Jackal/Wolf-Headed War God	PDM XIV:239-295, XIV:585-593; *ACM*: Schmidt P.
Wethor	Evil Spirit	*SoM*
Wewor	Good Spirit	*SoM*
Wezynna	Angel – Dominations	*67M*
White Wolf	Horus or Apollo epithet	*ACM*: Cologne 851
Wickedness	Female Spirit	HB Zec 5:8
Wiel	Angel	*oADS*
Wihasfati (Hindi) (Rufijail)	Angel – Jupiter	*SSG*
Wijch/Wrjch	Spirit – Sun	*67M*
Winged Dragon	Demon	*ToS*
Wipoliyaqwa	Angel – Moon	*LL*

Wisdom (Shekinah)	Divine Feminine Hypostasis	HB Job 28:1-28, Prv 1:20-33, 3:13-18, 4:7-9, 7:4, 8:1-36, 9:1-18, 14:1, Wis 1:4-6, 6:12-23, 7:12-15, 7:22-30, 8-10, 11:1, Ben 4:11-19, 6:18-31, 14:20-27, 15:1-8, 24, 51:13-26, Bar 3:15, 3:21-23, 3:29-32, 3:37-38
Witch of Endor	Spirit – Teacher of Witches	*MRC*
Woreth	Good Spirit	*SoM*
Woryon	Evil Spirit	*SoM*
Wunsolary	Familiar Spirit	*VJL*

X		
Xamyon/Zamion	Angel – Day Hour six	*Stg, ArP*
Xanael	Spirit	*ACM*: Cairo 45060
Xanoriz/Xanoryz/Hanoriz	Angel – Night Hour eight	*Stg, ArP*
Xanthir	Angel – Night Hour nine	*Stg, ArP*
Xanthis	Daimon	PGM XII:453-465
Xanthyozod/Zanthyozod	Angel – Night Hour three	*Stg, ArP*
Xantiel/Xautiel	Angel – Day Hour three	*Stg, ArP*
Xantropy/Zantropy/Zantropis	Angel – Night Hour five	*Stg, ArP*
Xantros/Zantros/Zentros	Angel – Day Hour ten	*Stg, ArP*
Xaphan	Demon – Second Order	*DI*
Xatinas	Angel – Tebet	*SR*
Xcez	Enochian Evil Spirit	*TBA*
Xemyzin/Zemizin/Lemizin	Angel – Night Hour two	*Stg, ArP*
Xenelar	Enochian Angel – West, over fourth lesser Angle	*TBA*
Xenes	Enochian Evil Spirit	*TBA*
Xerion	Demon – West and Aries	*Hyg*

ABBREVIATIONS

Xermiel/Zarmiel	Angel – Day Hour nine	*Stg, ArP*
Xernifiel/Xernisiel	Angel – Night Hour eight	*Stg, ArP*
Xerphiel	Angel – Night Hour six	*Stg, ArP*
Xexor	Evil Spirit	*SoM*
Xiphiel	Biblical Elder	*ACM*: Berlin 11347, Oriental 6796
Xirmys	Servant Spirit	*Abm*
Xomoy	Good Spirit	*SoM*
Xoni	Angel – Jupiter	*GAG*
Xonor	Good Spirit	*SoM*
Xotuda	Demon Prince	*GoPH*
Xympōna	Demon – West and Aries	*Hyg*
Xysorym	Evil Spirit	*SoM*
Xysuylion	Angel – Saturn/Saturday	*SR*

Y

Yabtasyper	Angel – Bisertilis	*SR*
Yaciatal	Demon – Sun	*BARC*
Yaconablabur	Punishing Wind	*SSM*
Yadalim	Angel – Moon	*LL*
Yadiel	Angel	*SoM*
Yael	Angel – Fourth Heaven, West	*SR*
Yafrael	Angel – Fire	*SR*
Yagar	Angel – Cherubim/Seraphim	*67M*
Yagelor	Angel – Cherubim/Seraphim	*67M*
Yahel	Angel – Thrones	*67M*
Yak	Angel – two of seven over the seven Baths	*ACM*: H. Kopt. 686
Yaldabaoth	Gnostic Archon – third Aeon	*ACM*: Bruce Codex
Yalsenac	Angel – Marchesvan	*SR*
Yalyon	Angel – Cherubim/Seraphim	*67M*
Yamaanyl	Angel – Sun/Sunday	*SR*
Yamaghash	Angel – Moon	*LL*
Yamb	Spirit – Venus	*67M*
Yamdus	Angel	*67M*

Yamiel	Angel – North	*SR*
Yamla	Angel – Elul	*SR*
Yammax	Demon King under Belzebub	*SSM*
Yamoora/Memora/Jamur	Spirit	*Pic*
Yamyne	Angel – three signs of third Season	*SSM*
Yanael	Angel – Second Heaven, North Angel – First Heaven, East	*SR, EoN, SaS*
Yanayel	Spirit King – Mars	*Pic*
Yan-gan-y-tan	Breton Demon – Evil Omens	*DI*
Yaniel	Angel – Fifth Heaven, South	*EoN*
Yao	Angel – One of seven over the seven Baths	*ACM*: H. Kopt. 686
Yaoel	Angel over Every Place	*ACM*: BN Turin
Yao Sabaoth Adonai/Yao Sabaoth/Iao Sabaoth/ Yasabaoth Adonai/Yao Adonai/Aio Sabaoth Adonai/Iao Sabaoth Adonai	Jewish God Gnostic Ruler of the Four Corners of the Earth	PGM V:304-369, VII:619-627, XII:201-269, XII:270-350, PDM XIV: 1110-1129, PGM XXVI:1-42, XXXVI:35-68, XXXVI:187-210,
Yao Sabaoth Adonai/Yao Sabaoth/Iao Sabaoth/ Yasabaoth Adonai/Yao Adonai/Aio Sabaoth Adonai/Iao Sabaoth Adonai (con't.)		PGM XXXVI:333-360; *ACM*: GMPP: 1227-64, Oxy. 1060, Oslo 1.5, P. Mich. 136, Vienna K7093, Cologne 20826, Freer 10, MRN Amulet, Oriental 5525, H. Kopt. 518, Mich. 4932f, AM 1981.940, P. Mich. 3472, Oriental 6796
Yarabal	Punishing Wind	*SSM*
Yarceth	Angel – Fourth Altitude (Cancer)	*Alm*
Yariel	Angel – Nisan	*SR*
Yaron	Angel – Cherubim/Seraphim	*67M*
Yas	Angel – Fourth Heaven, West	*SR*
Yasfla	Daemon Attendant – Saturn, North	*SBH*

Yaslael	Angel – Fourth Heaven, West	*SSM*
Yasmyel	Angel – Bisertilis	*SR*
Yasrael	Angel – Fire	*SSM*
Yassaell	Angel – Sun	*GAG*
Yassar	Angel – Elul	*SR*
Yasue	Demon – Mars	*BARC*
Yatayel	Angel – Earth	*SR*
Yatham	Angel – Fourth Altitude (Cancer)	*Alm*
Yatyel	Angel of Abyss – Summer	*SSM*
Yatzarpnishim	Angel – Moon	*LL*
Yay	Spirit	*oADS*
Yayac	Angel – Sivan	*SR*
Yayael	Angel – Fifth Heaven, West	*EoN*
Yayel	Angel – Bisertilis	*SR*
Yaziel	Angel – Nisan	*SR*
Ybarion	Servant Spirit	*Abm*
Ybles	Devil – Noon	*oADS*
Ycaachel	Angel – Mars	*BARC*
Ycanohl/Ichanol	Daemon Minister – Mars, South	*SBH*
Ychigas	Servant Spirit	*Abm*
Ydial	Spirit King	*BoO*
Ydyal	Spirit	*oADS*
Ydydal	Spirit – East	*SSM*
Yeasadis	Spirit Helper – Wednesday	*CBoM*
Yebel	Angel – Jupiter/Thursday	*SR*
Yebelkayam	Angel – Second Heaven, North	*SSM*
Yebiryn	Angel – Moon/Monday	*SR*
Yebrunkhilim	Angel – Moon	*LL*
Yecaleme	Angel – Sun/Sunday	*SR*
Yecyssa	Angel – Second Season by Night	*SSM*
Yedmeyeyl	Angel – Sun/Sunday	*SR*
Yeehah	Angel – Potestates	*67M*
Yehel	Angel – Fourth Heaven, West	*SSM*
Yehemial	Angel Prince – Autumn	*SRH*

Yehoc	Angel – Iyar	SR
Yehov Hov Ayien	Angel Prince – Spring	SRH
Yehov Yehieh	Angel – Harvest Ruler	SRH
Yelbrayeyl	Angel – Sun/Sunday	SR
Yenesaight	Wind Spirit	GAG
Yenael	Angel – Second Heaven, North	SSM
Yenuat/Ymas	Spirit – ninth Mansion of the Moon Ring	AE
Yeocyn	Angel – Sun/Sunday	SR
Yerael	Angel – Second Heaven, North	SSM
Yeremiel	Angel over Bowls	ACM: BN Turin
Yesararye	Angel – Second Heaven, West	SR
Yeschaijah	Sprit – Water	67M
Yeschnath	Angel	67M
Yeseraije	Angel – Second Heaven, West	SaS
Yesmactria	Angel – Nisan	SR
Yessaye	Angel – Second Heaven, West	EoN
Yesse	Punishing Wind Spirit of the Thumb Wind Spirit	SSM, CBoM, GAG
Yetes	Spirit – Minister of Love	oADS
Yeyatron	Servant Spirit	Abm
Yeyel	Angel – Fourth Heaven, West	SSM
Yfera/Ysera	Devil King	oADS
Yfla	Spirit Assistant – Saturday	MHN
Ygarim	Servant Spirit	Abm
Ygrim	Demon	MHN
Yhahel	Archangel	67M
Yhaij	Spirit – Moon Ministering Familiar/Mystery	67M
Yheloruvesopijhael	Spirit – Venus	67M
Yhethamay	Angel – Third Altitude (Gemini)	Alm
Yibavobavoth	Spirit Prince – Earth in Winter	SRH
Yida'al	Angel Prince – North Gate, Firmament	SRH
Yiechel Derek	Spirit – South	SRH
Yiediedial/Yiedierial	Angel Prince – West	SRH

ABBREVIATIONS

Yiedod	Angel – Love	*SRH*
Yiesorien	Angel Magistrate – Sowing Soil	*SRH*
Yietzorial	Archangel – Malachim, over the Shem	*SRH*
Yihela/Yihelal	Angel Prince – Gate of Spirit of West	*SRH*
Yihelederek	Spirit – South in Winter	*SRH*
Yihemelieh Mavoth	Spirit Prince – Earth in Summer	*SRH*
Yihova'ayial	Angel – Malachim, Thursday	*SRH*
Yihoval	Angel Prince – Testimony	*SRH*
Yihov Yihov Ayin	Spirit Prince – Earth in Spring	*SRH*
Yikenial	Angel Prince – Malachim, Words of Fire	*SRH*
Yilereneg	Angel Prince – Marheshvan	*SRH*
Yilial	Angel Prince – South Gate, Firmament	*SRH*
Yinal	Angel Prince – North Gate, Firmament	*SRH*
Yipos (Ipos)	Demon Count	*LdE*
Yiqemial	Angel – Autumn	*SRH*
Yira'ashial	Angel Prince – Gate of Spirit of East	*SRH*
Yiremoth	Angel – Autumn	*SRH*
Yirial	Angel – Malachim, Shebet	*SRH*
Yisha'aieh	Angel – Malachim over Rain	*SRH*
Yisriel	Angel	*SoM*
Yivoash	Angel – Malachim, under Avorphenial	*SRH*
Yivoba	Angel Magistrate – Sowing Soil	*SRH*
Yivoqemial	Angel, serving above sixth Degree	*SRH*
Yizerael	Angel – Malachim over Fire and Flames	*SRH*
Yka	Night Devil	*oADS*
Ykar	Night Devil	*oADS*
Ykiel	Angel – Jupiter, over Water	*SR*
Ylaraorynil	Angel – Mercury/Wednesday	*SR*
Ylemlis	Servant Spirit	*Abm*
Yles	Ministering Familiar/Mystery	*67M*
Yligai/Lignr/Hliÿar	Spirit – seventh Mansion of the Moon Ring	*AE*
Yllmafs	Spirit Minister, serving Prince Hagonel	*dHM*
Yloij	Spirit – Mercury	*67M*
Ym	Spirit	*MHN*

Ymah	Spirit – Mercury	67M
Ymel	Angel – Jupiter/Thursday	SR
Ymij	Spirit – Sun	67M
Ymmat	Angel – Cherubim/Seraphim	67M
Ymnybron	Angel – Saturn/Saturday	SR
Ymoeloh	Archangel	67M
Ymrael	Angel – Jupiter/Thursday	SR
Ynasa	Spirit Assistant – Friday	MHN
Yoas	Angel – Elul	SR
Yoasel	Angel – Mars	GAG
Yobial	Demon – Mars	BARC
Yoel	Gnostic Indestructible Spirit	ACM: NH Codex VIII, H. Kopt. 544, P. Mich. 593
Yoel	Angel – Bisertilis	SR
Yofiel (Metatron)	Angel – Prince of the Torah Angel – Prince of the Presence Angel – Glory from Above	SQ, SoM
Yohau	Angel	ACM: H. Kopt. 679
Yoiriel	Angel	ACM: BN Turin
Yomelo	Angel – Potestates	67M
Yonael	Angel – Two of twenty-one on the Left	ACM: Berlin 10587
Yoniel	Angel – five of twenty-one on the Left	ACM: Berlin 10587
Yonuel	Angel – sixteen of twenty-one on the Left	ACM: Berlin 10587
Yoranael	Spirit	ACM: Cairo 45060
Yostaa	Demon – Sunday Hour eleven	Hyg
Yothael	Spirit	ACM: Cairo EM 49547
Youlach	Spirit	ACM: Oriental 6796
Yoval	Angel Prince – West	SRH
Yparchos	Servant Spirit	Abm
Ypaton/Yparon/Iparon	Angel – Mercury	B7R, tSoS
Yrabal	Spirit	SSM
Yragamon	Servant Spirit	Abm
Yris	Spirit	AN

Yron	Spirit Helper – Wednesday Angel – Minister of Air on Wednesday	*CBoM, BoO*
Yrtell	Spirit – Minister of Love	*oADS*
Yryniel	Angel – Jupiter, over Water	*SR*
Yrzon	Evil Spirit	*SoM*
Ysar	Angel – Sivan	*SR*
Ysbiloth	Spirit	*BoTS*
Ysfagor	Spirit Familiar	*BoTS*
Yska	Devil – Ursa Major	*oADS*
Yslael	Angel – Fifth Heaven, West	*EoN*
Ysmiriek	Servant Spirit	*Abm*
Ysopatys	Spirit	*SSM*
Ysquiron	Servant Spirit	*Abm*
Ysquy/Isquy	Spirit King	*BoTS*
Ysraradus	Devil – Early Morning	*Alm*
Yssa	Angel – Eighth Altitude (Scorpio)	*Alm*
Yssery	Devil – third Hour of Day	*oADS*
Yssytres/Yssyteres	Angel Senior – Sun Angel	*SSM, oADS*
Ysus/Isus	Spirit King	*BoO, BoTS*
Ysyne	Night Devil	*oADS*
Ytach	Angel – Sixth Altitude (Virgo)	*Alm*
Ytael	Angel – Adar	*SR*
Ytelteos	Demon	*MHN*
Ythasym	Angel	*NA*
Ytrut	Angel – Tishrei	*SR*
Yturayel	Angel Subordinate – Mars	*SSM*
Yturihihel/Yturaihel	Spirit – Mars	*SBH*
Yudifliges	Demon Duke	*NML*
Yūnasyl	Angel – Hour five/Leo	*BoW*
Yvaij	Spirit – Moon	*67M*
Ywote	Evil Spirit	*SoM*
Yyamnel	Angel – Water	*SR*
Yyel	Angel – Fourth Heaven, West	*SR*
Yzazel	Good Spirit	*SoM*

Z		
Zaajah	Genii – 30° Capricorn, 30° Aquarius	*ArP*
Zaan	Angel – Ninth Altitude (Sagittarius)	*Alm*
Zaarsa	Alternative name of Metatron	*SQ*
Zaazenach	Angel Ruler – Night Hour six	*Stg, ArP*
Zabdiel	Angel – North	*SR*
Zabo	Enochian Angel – North, over first lesser Angle	*TBA*
Zabon	Angel – Ninth Altitude (Sagittarius)	*Alm*
Zabriel	Demon Duke – East	*Stg, ThG*
Zabulus	Demon Duke	*KoN*
Zacdon	Angel – Elul	*SR*
Zach	Daemon Minister – Mercury; between the West and North	*SBH*
Zacharael	Archangel	*67M*
Zachariel/Zachariell	Angel – Jupiter, Second Heaven	*tSoS, dSS, JMR, SaS, MNeI, tM*
Zachariel/Zachriel	Demon Duke – Hour ten of fifteen	*Stg, ThG*
Zachariel	Angel – Night Hour seven	*Stg, ArP*
Zachiel/Zathiel	Angel – Day Hour five	*Stg, ArP*
Zachiel	Angel Prince – sixth Heaven	*SaS*
Zachiel	Genii – 17° Virgo, 27° Virgo, 29° Scorpio, 29° Sagittarius	*ArP*
Zachriel/Zackriel	Angel – Night Hour twelve	*Stg, ArP*
Zaciel	Genii – 5° Aries	*ArP*
Zackiel	Genii – 19° Scorpio, 19° Sagittarius	*ArP*
Zacos	Night Devil	*oADS*
Zacui	Spirit – Minister of Love	*oADS*
Zadama	Angel	*NA*
Zadanay	Angel – Ninth Altitude (Sagittarius)	*Alm*
Zadaynahc	Angel	*NA*
Zadiel	Genii – 25° Aries	*ArP*
Zadiphōr/Zaphan/Zēphar/Xyphran	Demon – Sunday Hour six	*Hyg*

ABBREVIATIONS 707

Name	Description	Sources
Zadkiel/Tzadkiel/ Zabkiel/Zabdiel/ Zedekiel/Zadkiell/ Zadchiel/Sedekiel/ Sedetiel	Archangel – Jupiter Archangel – Chesed Ruler of Order of Dominations	*ACM*: L. Anastasi 9, H. Kopt. 686; *3BOP, BoO, MC, JMR, 9CK, BoTS, GoA, SaS, MNeI, tSoS, Thm, ClI, CoMS, tM, CBMS*
Zagal/Zagol	Servant Spirit	*Abm, MRC*
Zagan/Zagon/ Zagam	Demon King and President Demon – Venus Spirit – Minister of Love	*SSM, BARC, LdE, PmD, DoW, Goe, oADS*
Zagayne/Saygayne/ Laygayne/Zagayme (Zagan)	Demon – West	*BOS, BoO, oADS*
Zagiel	Genii – 15° Gemini, 25° Taurus, 25° Gemini	*ArP*
Zaglytai/Zaglaton (Venus)	Venus – Alternative Name	*Hyg*
Zagrion	Spirit	*MRC*
Zaguhel	Angel	*NA*
Zagyron	Demon Minister – Beelzebub	*SSM*
Zahbuk	Angel over Pains, Sharp Pains, Inflammation, Dropsy	*SoM*
Zahra/Zuhra (Arabic)	Spirit Queen – Venus	*Pic, SSG*
Zaiell	Spirit – Minister of Love	*oADS*
Zainael	Spirit	*GoA*
Zajel	Genii – 28° Libra	*ArP*
Zalas	Night Devil	*oADS*
Zalay	Angel	*GV*
Zalcycyl	Angel – Mars/Tuesday	*SR*
Zalibron	Angel – Saturn/Saturday	*SR*
Zaliel	Angel – Fifth Heaven Tuesday, South	*Hmn, KoSR, BoO, GAG, BoTS, tM*
Zallamay	Angel	*NA*
Zalomes	Servant Spirit	*Abm*
Zalzoy	Demon Senior	*SSM*
Zamael (Samael)	Intelligence – Mars	*tM*
Zamanzathas	Angel	*NA*

Zamarpha/ Zōmarpha/ Zamarphas/ Ēamarpha	Demon – North	Hyg
Zamayl	Angel – Sun/Sunday	SR
Zamel	Angel – First Heaven, South	SR
Zamiel	Angel – Shebat	SR
Zamiel	Genii – 20° Capricorn, 20° Aquarius	ArP
Zamirel	Angel – Mercury/Wednesday	SR
Zamor	Demon Duke – West Night	Stg, ThG, BoTS
Zaniael	Spirit	MNeI
Zaniel/Zatael/Zanyel	Angel first Heaven Monday – West Presiding Spirit – Moon	SSM, EoN, Hmn, KoSR, SaS, SoS, BoO, GAG, BoTS, tM, CBMS
Zanno/Zaimo	Spirit	MHN
Zantof	Alternative name of Metatron	SQ
Zantu	Alternative name of Metatron	SQ
Zaphey	Spirit – Sea Treasure	oADS
Zaphiell	Angel – Capricorn first part	Thm
Zaphkiel/Tzaphkiel/ Zaphiel/Zaphchiel/ Zaphchel/Zapheel	Archangel – Saturn Archangel – Binah Ruler of Order of Thrones	3BOP, tSoS, MC, JMR, 9CK, SaS, ES, BoTS, MNeI, GoA, CoMS, PO, tM
Zaquiel	Angel – Fifth Heaven, East	SR
Zara	Plant Spirit – Clematis	GS
Zarael	Angel – Sun/Sunday	SR
Zarafil	Angel – Sun/Sunday	SR
Zaral	Demon – North	GoPH
Zarall	Angel – Cherubim on Mercy Seat	67M
Zarathiel	Angel	ACM: H. Kopt. 544
Zardiel	Angel – Day Hour four	Stg, ArP
Zarenar	Angel	67M
Zarfaieil	Angel – Sun/Sunday	SR
Zarialin	Angel – Venus/Friday	SR
Zarneach	Angel – Eleventh Altitude (Aquarius)	Alm
Zarseyeyl	Angel – Sun/Sunday	SR

Zartiel	Biblical Elder	*ACM*: Berlin 11347, Oriental 6796
Zasamaht	Angel	*NA*
Zaseres	Spirit King	*BoO*
Zasnor/Zasnoz	Angel – Day Hour nine	*Stg, ArP*
Zasviel	Angel – Day Hour four	*Stg, ArP*
Zatahel	Angel	*NA*
Zavael	Genii – 16° Pisces, 26° Pisces	*ArP*
Zawar	Angel – Thrones	*67M*
Zawish (Rafael, Greek)	Spirit King – Jupiter	*Pic*
Zayariel	Spirit	*VJL*
Zayleth/Zaybothe	Spirit Helper – Monday	*CBoM*
Zayme/Layme/Zaym	Demon – West	*SSM, BOS, BoO, oADS, BoTS*
Zazel/Zaphehiel	Planetary Spirit – Saturn Ruler – Tristitia, Carcer Co-Ruler – Cauda Draconis	*KoSR, 3BOP, BM, Thm, GoPH, GV, PO, tM, BoSC*
Zazi	Enochian Angel – South, over fourth lesser Angle	*TBA*
Zaziēl	Angel	PGM X:36-50
Zazyor/Zasior	Angel – Day Hour ten	*Stg, ArP*
/Zbdial	Angel – First Step, second Heaven	*ShR*
Zbitur	Angel – Fifth Encampment, first Heaven	*ShR*
Zchzchal	Angel Prince – fourth Heaven, Water	*ShR*
Zeab	Demon Governor Punishing Wind	*SSM*
Zebarel	Spirit – Jupiter	*SGT, SSG*
Zebdial	Angel – Malachim, under Avorphenial	*SRH*
Zebedial	Spirit Prince – North Angel Prince – Autumn	*SRH*
Zebena (Ahedierier)	Angel – Ruler of Preservation of Crops	*SRH*
Zebenos	Angel – Malachim, sixth Host	*SRH*
Zeberouēl/ Tzibirouēl/ Berouēl	Demon – Mars	*Hyg*
Zebourthaunēn	Archangel	PDM XIV:93-114

Zebrican	Spirit Vizier – Affah	*SSM*
Zebuel	Demon Minister – Beelzebub	*SSM*
Zebul	Angel – Thursday/Jupiter Angel Chief – sixth Heaven by Day	*KoSR, SaS, CBMS*
Zebulo	Spirit – Irritates Men	*oADS*
Zechar	Angel	*NA*
Zechas	Angel	*NA*
Zedebomoy	Angel – Eighth Altitude (Scorpio)	*Alm*
Zedekiel/Zetekiel/Setekiel	Angel Angel Commander	*ACM*: H. Kopt. 544, Berlin 11347, H. Kopt. 686
ZedocXe	Enochian Evil Spirit	*TBA*
Zefael	Angel – Shebat	*SR*
Zegdial	Angel – Malachim, under Ayigeda	*SRH*
Zegiel	Genii – 15° Taurus	*ArP*
Zēkhithoel (Luna)	Luna – Alternative Name	*Hyg*
Zekorethial	Angel – Malachim over Sea and Life in it	*SRH*
Zelentes	Demon	*MHN*
Zemeinyn	Angel – Mercury/Wednesday	*SR*
Zemkieth	Angel – Malachim, under Ayigeda	*SRH*
Zemoel	Angel – Day Hour eleven	*Stg, ArP*
Zenam	Angel – Sivan	*SR*
Zenay	Good Spirit	*SoM*
Zenesial	Angel Prince – West Gate	*SRH*
Zenetoph	Angel Prince	*SRH*
Zeno	Spirit – Jupiter	*67M*
Zenoroz/Xenoroz	Angel – Night Hour nine	*Stg, ArP*
Zenoviyem	Angel – Malachim, under Pheseker	*SRH*
Zeolam/Seolam	Angel – Potestates	*67M*
Zepar	Demon Duke	*PmD, DoW, Goe*
Zepher	Demon Senior	*SSM*
Zephyr/Zephyrus/Zephirus	West Wind – over Angels of Monday, Friday	*EoN, Hmn, MC, Thm, BoTS, SMS, PO*
Zereqetha (Ahedierier)	Angel – Ruler of Preservation of Crops	*SRH*
Zerezor	Spirit – West in Autumn	*SRH*

Zeriel/Zeniel	Demon Duke – West by South Day	*Stg, ThG*
Zerobehel	Angel	*NA*
Zerubehel	Angel	*NA*
Zesfaieil	Angel – Venus/Friday	*SR*
Zethiel	Genii – 18° Libra	*ArP*
Zētōn (Mercury)	Mercury – Alternative Name	*Hyg*
Zeuper	Angel Minister – Love and Fornication	*KoSA*
Zeus/Zas	Greek Sky and Ruler God	HB 2 Mac 6:2, Acts 14:12-13; PGM I:262-347, II:1-64, II:64-184, III:187-262, IV:467-468, IV:475-829, IV:831-832, IV:835-849, IV:1390-1495, IV:1596-1715, IV:2441-2621, IV:2708-2784, IV:2785-2890, IV:2967-3006, IV:3209-3054, V:1-53, V:459-489, VI:1-47, VII:199-201, XII:160-178, XIII:646-734, XIII:734-1077, LXII:47-51, XXIIa:9-10, XXIII:1-70, PDM XIV:489-515, *SM*: P. Berol. Inv. 21227; *ACM*: GMPP:1-25; *SSG*
Zeus (Greek) (Rufijail)	Angel – Jupiter	*SSG*
Zeus-Helios	Greek Composite Solar God	*SM*: P. Reinach II.88
Zeus-Iao-Zen-Helios	Composite God	PGM CV:1-5
Zeviet	Angel Minister – Love and Fornication	*KoSA*
Zezaymanay	Angel	*NA*
Zeziel	Angel – Night Hour six	*Stg, ArP*
Zhal	Angel Prince – fourth Heaven, Water	*ShR*
Zhsmael	Angel over Pains, Sharp Pains, Inflammation, Dropsy	*SoM*

Ziena	Angel Prince	*SRH*
Zieroval	Angel – Thursday	*SRH*
Zimimar/Ziminiar/ Ziminar/Ziminay	Demon King – North	*PmD*, *Goe*
Zirtheouēl	Demon – South	*Hyg*
Ziva	Alternative name of Metatron	*SQ*
Ziza	Enochian Angel – South, over fourth lesser Angle	*TBA*
Zizaubiō	Angel – Pleiades	PGM VII:795-845
Zkrial	Angel – First Encampment, first Heaven Angel – Third Heaven, serving Rhtial	*ShR*
Zlar	Enochian Angel – East, over first lesser Angle	*TBA*
Zlqial	Angel – Sixth Step, second Heaven	*ShR*
Zmbut	Angel – Second Encampment, first Heaven	*ShR*
Zoaziel	Angel – Fifth Heaven, East	*SR*
Zobedam	Demon	*NML*
Zobha	Punishing Wind Daemon – Mercury, serving West and Southwest Winds; between the West and North	*SSM*, *SBH*
Zodexge	Enochian Angel – East, over fourth lesser Angle	*TBA*
Zodiel/Zodrel	Angel – Night Hour four	*Stg*, *ArP*
Zoeniel	Demon Duke – West	*Stg*, *ThG*
Zoesiel/Zoetiel	Angel – Day Hour three	*Stg*, *ArP*
Zogothoul (Luna)	Luna – Alternative Name	*Hyg*
Zomal	Demon	*GoPH*
Zombar	Demon King – Mercury	*BARC*
Zoniel	Spirit Messenger – Saturn	*SGT*, *SSG*
Zorconifer	Demon Senior	*SSM*
Zorial	Angel – Cancer	*SRH*
Zorobaym	Spirit imprisoned in the Book	*oADS*
Zoroel	Angel	*ToS*
Zorokothora Melchisidek	Gnostic Transporter of Light	*ACM*: Bruce Codex

Zorzorath/Zorzori/Zorzorēth	Demon – Friday Hour three	*Hyg*
Zosiel	Demon Duke – Hour four of fifteen	*Stg, ThG*
Zostihon	Angel	*NA*
Zouriēl	Angel	PGM XXXVI:295-311
Zowanos/Zowanus	Archangel	*67M*
Zoyma	Spirit	*MNeI*
Zoymiel	Angel – Day Hour nine	*Stg, ArP*
Zoyplay	Spirit	*MNeI*
Zrgri	Angel – Third Heaven, serving Rhtial	*ShR*
Zron	Demon	*SMS*
Zsmayel	Angel – Water	*SR*
Zsniel	Angel over Pains, Sharp Pains, Inflammation, Dropsy	*SoM*
Ztazel	Angel – Moon, over Air	*SR*
Zubiel	Ministering Spirit – Jupiter	*CBMS*
Zucmeni	Angel Minister – Love and Fornication	*KoSA*
Zugola/Zugula	Servant Spirit	*Abm, MRC*
Zuhal (Ashbeel, Arabic)	Spirit King – Saturn	*Pic, SSG*
Zunnum	Angel – Sixth Encampment, first Heaven	*ShR*
Zupa	Angel – Fifth Heaven, West	*SR*
Zuriel	Angel – Libra Genius – Puella	*3BOP, tSoS, MC, JMR, SaS, MNeI, Thm, PO, tM*
Zuwoy	Evil Spirit	*SoM*
Zygothoel (Luna)	Luna – Alternative Name	*Hyg*
Zymeloz/Zimeloz	Angel – Night Hour eight	*Stg, ArP*
Zymens	Demon	*MHN*
Zynconzon	Angel	*NA*
Zywolech	Archangel	*67M*
Zzial	Angel – Seventh Encampment, first Heaven	*ShR*

Glossary

Note I have not included medical terms in this glossary. Such terms are footnoted when they first occur.

Altitude: term for a spirit grouping/hierarchy.
Astral: used to describe image magic, specifically associated with the stellar constellations of the zodiac.
Charaktêres: character forms used as magical signs.
Decan: 10° arc in the zodiac. There are thirty-six decans, three in each sign.
Defixiones: a curse tablet, usually written on a lead tablet.
Gateway Image: the form in which a spiritual creature is commonly described and perceived to assume during engagement with it.
Historiola: a narrative charm, usually spoken, and commonly on a mythic or biblical theme.
Hymnology: the repetitious use of prayer and strings of divine names for angelic adjuration.
Iatromagical: on the threshold of magic and medicine and combining elements of both.
Kamea: a magic number square with the columns, rows and diagonals all totalling the same number. Attributed to the planets by the square size (Saturn 3x3, Jupiter 4x4, Mars 5x5, Sun 6x6, Venus 7x7, Mercury 8x8, Moon 9x9) and also used as the basis of creating sigils of spirit names with the Hebrew alphabet.
Lamella: thin metal sheet, often used as basis of defixiones and phylacteries.
Phylactery: protective charm written usually on parchment (or occasionally very thin metal sheets) wrapped up and bound to the arm.
Sator Square: a magic letter square (one of the most popular) of the form:

S	A	T	O	R
A	R	E	P	O
T	E	N	E	T
O	P	E	R	A
R	O	T	A	S

Schwindeschema: disappearing pattern, refers to an inverted letter triangle which reduces the number of letters from the original word down to a single letter. The most famous of these is Abracadabra.
Semiphoras: a prayer/orison containing a string of Hebrew divine names (and sometimes also **voces magicae**).
Spirit Catalogue: a spirit list that includes more information about the spirits, usually being the description (gateway image) and tasks/skills the spirits will perform or possess.
Spirit List: as the name suggests, the list of spirits found in a text.
Urtext: the original form of a text, from which subsequent versions are derived.
Voces Magicae: also called *barbarous words* or *nomina magica*, refers to words which do not have an intelligible meaning in the language of texts but are considered to contain an inherent power.

Bibliography

Manuscripts

Abbey Library, Steitenstetten
  MS 273
Abbey Library, Vorau
  Cod. Voraviensis 186 (CCCXIX)
Aberdeen University, Aberdeen
  Unclassified papyrus
Alnwick Castle, Alnwick
  MS 596
Altes Museum, Berlin
  P. Berlin 8318
Ambrosian Library, Milan
  MS 1030
  MSS Z 72 sup, Z 164 sup
  Mediolanensis H2 infer.
Andreas Convent, Mt Athos
  MS 73
Archaeological Society, Athens
  P.S.A. Athen. 70
Archiquinnasio Municipal Library, Bologna
  MSS A.165, A.646
Ashmolean Museum, Oxford
  O. Ashm. Shelton 194
  O. Bodl. II.2180
  P. Ant. II.65, II.66, III.140
  P. Ash. 1981.940
  P. Oxy. XLII 3068, inv. 50.4B 23/J, inv. 72/65 (a), XXXVI.2753, XLVI.3298, LVI.3834, LVI.3835
Augsburg University, Augsburg
  OWB Cod.II.1.4, Cod.II.2.8.2
  4° Codex 55
Augustine Monastery, Klosterneuburg
  CCl 121, CCl 759
  Cod. 950
Austrian National Library, Vienna
  Codex philos. Graec. MS 108
  Codex Vincob 3400
  Inv. no. 8031, 8033, 8034, 8035, K 8303
  MSS 3317, 11262, 11281, 11321, 11340, 11374, 11517, 12834, 13859, 15482
  MSS Lat. 11294, 11313
  ÖNB Cod. 10579, 10580
  P. Amst. I.26
  P. Gr. 1, 323, 328, 331, 332, 334, 335, 337, 339, 19929, 29272, 29273

P. Rainer 5
P. Vienna K 70, K 7093, K 8302, K 8638
P. Vindob. G16685, inv. G 42406

Avranches Municipal Library, Avranches
    MS 235
Baden State Library, Karlsruhe
    MS 302
Bavarian Regional Library, Munich
    CGM 407
    CLM 51, 268, 276, 849, 17711, 24936, 28858, 28942, 30010
    Cod. Ret. 27005
    Monacensis Gr. 20
    MSS 22, 40
    P. Coptic 5
    P. Mon. Gr. Inv. 216
Benedictine Abbey of St Egidien, Nuremberg
    MS L11
Bergamo Civic Library, Bergamo
    MS Lamda II 23 (MM 512)
Berlin State Museum, Berlin
    BGU III.955, III.956, IV.1026
    Germ. Fol. 903
    P. Amh. ii
    P. Berol inv. 954, 5025, 5026, 5565, 7504, 8313, 8319, 8324, 9096, 9566, 9909, 10587, 11737, 11858, 13895, 21227, 21243
    P. Monac. II.28
    P. Oxy. inedit
Bernardakēdes Private Library, Greece
    Bernardaceus
Bibliothèque de l'Arsenal (Library of the Arsenal), Paris
    BA MSS 824, 826, 1033, 2346, 2347, 2348, 2349, 2350, 2351, 2493, 2494, 2790, 2791, 2792
Bibliothèque Nationale de France (National Library of France), Paris
    Allemand MS 160
    Anciens fonds Grec. MSS 38, 2419
    Audollent DT.38
    Collection Jacques Mosseri VI 13.2
    BNF Greek MS 9
    BNF MSS 1565, 7170A, 7337, 7373, 11265, 14075, 14783, 15127, 17870, 18510, 18511, 24244, 24245, 25314
    MSS Lat. 3666, 7152, 7153, 7154, 7340, 9336, 10272, 10273, 13016, 13017, 17871
    Parisinus Graec. MS 2316, 2419
    Parisinus Suppl. Gr. 20, 1148
    P. Bibl. Nat. Sup. Gr. No. 574
    Supp. Graec. MS 500
Bodleian Library, Oxford
    Additional B1
    Ashmole MSS 187, 341, 1406, 1416, 1471, 1515, 1790, 2871

Aubrey MS 24
Bodley 951, 8908
Canonicus Lat. 500
Crawford MS 158
Digby MSS 29, 37, 218, 226, 228
Douce MS 116
E Mus. 173
Liturg. 160
Michael MSS 273, 276
MSS Heb. 18/30, Heb. D 62/50, Heb. E 67/32-33, Heb. F 45
MS OPP.594
P. Oxy. 412, 886, 887, 959, 1383, 1384, 1477, 1478, 2061, 2062, 2063
Rawlinson MS C.7
Rawlinson MSS D.252, D.254, D.1066, D.1067, D.1363

Bologna University Library, Bologna
Bononiensis Uni. MS 3632
P. Bon. 3

British Library, London
Additional MSS 10862, 15299, 16390, 18027, 36674, 39666, 43725
Bruce Codex
Coptic MS C (P) 4
Harley MSS 80, 181, 585, 1420, 1612, 2267, 3420, 3536, 3731, 3981, 5596, 6482, 6483
Kings MS 288
Lansdowne MSS 795, 1202, 1203
MSS 10384, 10675
Oriental MSS 1013A, 4721, 5525, 5897, 5899, 5986, 6172, 6360, 6577, 6794, 6795, 6796, 10678 (formerly Gaster MS 178), 14759
P. Lit. Lond. 171
P. Oxy. 924, 1060
Royal MSS Cxviii, 17 Axlii, 1 Dv-viii 12 Dxvii
Sloane MSS 307, 313, 513, 1302, 1305, 1307, 1309, 1712, 1727, 2383, 2731, 3008, 3091, 3191, 3318, 3628, 3645, 3648, 3678, 3679, 3805, 3821, 3822, 3824, 3825, 3826, 3846, 3847, 3849, 3850, 3851, 3853, 3854, 3885, 4042, 4061

British Museum, London
P. Brit. Mus. Inv. 10588
P. London 46, 47, 121, 122, 123, 124, 125, 147, 148
P. London Demotic 10070
P. London Hay 10122, 10376, 10414, 10434

Cadbury Research Library, Birmingham
P. Harris 54

Cambridge University, Cambridge
Add. 405
K.K 1.1
P. Michael 27
Trinity 0.9.7
T-S NS 70.130, NS 298/72
T-S K 1/13. K 1/97, K 1/98, K 1/102, K 1/145, K 21/95, NS 135, NS 246/26, T-S Arabic 12/207, 31/183, 33/9, 43/84, 43/223, 43/260, 45/12

Catherine Library of the Seminary, Pisa
    MS 139 (167)
Catholic University, Nijmegen
    P. Noviomagensis Inv. 2
Catholic University of Milan, Milan
    P. Coll. Youtie II.91
    P. Med. inv. 71.58
Catholic University of the Sacred Heart, Madrid
    P. Med. Inv. No. 23
Chester Beatty Library, Dublin
    P. Merton II.58
Chetham's Library, Manchester
    MS Mun A.4.98
Chicago Oriental Institute, Chicago
    P. 13767
Cistercian Monastery Library, Heilsbronn
    MSS 153 (Erlangen 65 (337))
Cleveland Library, New York
    W 091.92 V618
Coimbra University Library, Coimbra
    MS 2559
Collection of the Egyptian Museum, Berlin
    P. Berlin 8314, 8322, 8325
    P. Berol. 11347, 13232, 21165, 21227, 21230, 21260, 21269, 21911
    P. Turner 49
    T. Berol. inv. 13412
Collegium Amplonianum, Erfurt
    MSS Math. 11, 14, 53
    Quarto 28a, 380
Columbia University, New York
    George A. Pimpton 180
Coptic Museum, Cairo
    Nag Hammadi Codex VII, Codex VIII
    P. 4959, 4960
Cornell University, New York
    4620 Bd. MS 19
Corpus Christi College, Cambridge
    MS 243
Corpus Christi University, Oxford
    MSS 125, 132
Count Schönburn's Library, Pommersfelden
    MS 357
Darmstadt University, Darmstadt
    MSS 362, 1410, 1671
Dionysius Monastery, Mt Athos
    Athonicus Dion. 282
    MS 132
Dresden Library, Dresden
    MSS N. 36, N. 67a, N. 100, N. 105, N.111

SLUB MSS N. 91, N. 111, N. 161

Dropsie College, Philadelphia
  Genizah Collection 437
Duchess Anna Amalia Library, Weimar
  HAAB Q455B
  MSS F. 374/2, F. 8476
Duke August Library, Wolfenbüttel
  Codex Guelfibus 10.1, 13.12 Aug. 4°, 47.13, 47.15 Aug. 4°
  MS Extravagantes 39
Duke of Devonshire's Library, Chatsworth
  MS 73D
Durazzo Library, Genova
  MS B VI 35
Dzanasia Museum, Tblisi
  Zereteli-Tiflis 24
Edinburgh Royal Observatory, Ebinburgh
  Cr.3.14
Egypt Exploration Society, London
  P. Ant. II.65, II.66, III.140
  P. Oxy. 50.4 B23 J(1-3)b, 1566, 2753
Egyptian Museum, Cairo
  Bones Cairo A & B
  O. Cairo inv. CP 25/8/37/1-2
  P. Cairo 10263, 45060, 49547, 67188
  P. Oxy. 39 5B 125/A
  T. Cairo Mus. JdE 36059, 48217
Egyptian Museum, Turin
  P. Cairo 10434, 10563, 60139, 60140, 60636
Egyptology Foundation of Queen Elisabeth, Brussels
  P. Brux.
E. Moen Collection, Baarn
  O. Moen 34
  P. Moen 3
  T. Moen s.n.
Erlangen University, Erlangen
  MSS 853, 854
  P. Erlangen 15, 37
Erno Gaál Collection, Budapest
  P. Gaál.
  P. (Mag.) Gaál. Ined.
Evangelical Church Library, Hamburg
  MS Codex 31
Firenze University, Florence
  Ambrosiana B8 Sup.
  Florence 5845
  MSS Magliabechi XX 20, XX 21
  MSS II.iii.24, II.iii.214
  Plut. 17 Cod. III

Plut. 44.13, Plut. 44.33
Plut. 89 sup. 35, Plut. 89 sup. 38
Folger Shakespeare Library, Washington D.C.
Folger MS Vb26
Freer Gallery, Smithsonian, Washington D.C.
Freer frag. 10
French Institute of Oriental Archaeology, Cairo
Amulet text
Papyrus text (unclassified)
P. IFAO III.50
P. IFAO s.n.
P. Oxy. 1077
Freiburg University Library, Freiburg
HS. 458
P. Un. Bibl. Freib.
G.A. Michaïlidis Collection, Cairo
P. Michael 27
Giessen University Library, Giessen
P. Iand. 87
Geneva Public & University Library, Geneva
MS Genève 145
P. Genav. inv. 186, inv. 293
T. Genev. inv. 269
Gennadius Library, Athens
Gennadianus 45
Genoa University, Genoa
PUG I.6
Ghent University, Ghent
MS 1021A
Glasgow University Library, Glasgow
MSS Ferguson 2, 50, 142
P. Oxy. 1121
Graz University Library, Graz
MSS 680, 1016
Greco-Roman Museum of Alexandria, Alexandria
P. Alex. Inv. 941
Hamburg Library, Hamburg
Codex Alchim. 739
Math 4° 10
Harvard University, Cambridge MA
Houghton MSS Fr 553, 554
Houghton MSS Typ 625, 833
Hermitage Museum, St Petersburg
Amulet Text
Hiedelberg University Library, Heidelberg
P. Heid, 2170
P. Heid. inv. G 1101, G 1359, G 1386
P. Heid. inv. Lat 5
P. Heid. Kopt. 518, 564, 679, 681, 682, 684, 686

Historical & Ethnological Society of Greece, Athens
	Atheniensis 115
H.O. Lange Collection, Copenhagen
	Unclassified text
Holkham Hall, Norfolk
	MS 99
Hungarian Academy, Budapest
	MS 224
Illinois University, Illinois
	MS 0102
Institute for Archaeology, Köln
	O. Köln inv. 409
	P. Köln inv. 35, 851, 1886, 1982, 2283, 2861, 3323, 5512, 5514, 20826, VI.257
	T. Köln inv. 1, 2, 3, 7, 8, 10
Institute for Classical Studies, Copenhagen University, Copenhagen
	P. Haun. III.50, III.51
	Institute of Papyrology, Florence University, Florence
	PSI I.29, inv. 319
Institute of Papyrology, Sorbonne University, Paris
	P. Reinach II.88, II.89 inv 2176
Institute of Papyrology, University of Milan, Milan
	O. Mil. Vogl. inv. 85
	P. Mil. Vogl. inv. 1245, 1246, 1247, 1248, 1249, 1250, 1251, 1252, 1253, 1254, 1255, 1256, 1257, 1258, 1259, 1260, 1261, 1262, 1263
	P. Vitelli 365
Institute of Papyrology of the University of Lugduno-Batavae, Leiden
	P. Warren 21
Italian Society for Papyrus Research, Florence
	P. Flor. (no number)
Jagiellonian University Library, Cracow
	MSS 793 (DD.III.36), 2076
Jewish Theological Seminary Library, New York
	ENA 2643.5, 2673.23, 2750, 3373
	ENA NS 2.11, 89
	MSS 12, 14, 1892, 1990, 2130, 8115
John Hay Library, Brown University, Providence
	MS BF 1611
	MS M 313
John Rylands Library, Manchester
	Gaster MS 177
	GB 0133 Eng MS 40
	Latin MS 105
	P. Oxy. 1150
	P. Rylands 100, 103, 104
Karl Schmidt Collection, Berlin
	P. Schmidt 1, 2
Kassel University Library, Halle
	MS 4° Astron. 3
MSS 4° Chem. 66, 4° Chem. 96

　　　　　　MS Codex 14 B 36
Laurentian Medici Library, Florence
　　　　P. Laur. Inv. 54, III.57, III.58, III/472, IV.148, IV.149
　　　　P. Med. I.20
　　　　PSI I.28
Leipzig City Library, Leipzig
　　　　MS 829
Leipzig University, Leipzig
　　　　Codex Magica 4, 6, 12, 15, 16, 22, 27, 30, 35, 40, 60, 96, 97, 136
　　　　Cod. Vulcaniani 45
　　　　MSS 707, 709, 710, 732, 739, 773, 776, 790, 841
　　　　P. Gr. 9.418, 9.429
Lenin State Library, Moscow
　　　　Guenzberg MSS 90, 131
Leopold-Sophien Library, Überlingen
　　　　MS 164
Library of the Academy of Lincei, Rome
　　　　MS Verginelli-Rota 36
Library of the Episcopal Seminary, Padua
　　　　Cod. 235
Liverpool Institute of Archaeology, Liverpool
　　　　Unclassified papyrus text
London Society of Antiquaries, London
　　　　MS 39
Louvre Museum, Paris
　　　　Inscr. 204
　　　　No. 2396 (P. Mimault fragments 1-4), 3378
　　　　P. Louvre E14.250, E3229
　　　　T. Louvre inv. AF 6716
　　　　T. Louvre inv. E 27145
Lübeck University, Germany
　　　　MS Math. 9
Lund University Library, Lund
　　　　P. Lund Univ. Bibl. IV.12 inv. No. 32
Lyons Municipal Library, Lyons
　　　　Lyons MSS 328, 970
Manly Palmer Hall Collection, Los Angeles
　　　　MS 191
Marseilles Municipal Library, Marseilles
　　　　MS 983 (Bb 108)
Martin Luther University, Halle
　　　　ULSA B14 B.36
McMaster University Library, Hamilton
　　　　MS 107
Méjanes Library, Aix-en-Provence
CGM 1918
Merton College, Oxford
　　　　Medieval 999
Metamorphoseos Monastery, Metoera

Metamorphoseos M67
Moen Collection, Amsterdam
   Text amulet
Münster University Library, Münster
   MS 169
Museum of the Near East, Egypt & the Mediterranean, Rome
   Inv. 181/665
National Library of Denmark, Copenhagen
   Thott MSS 237, 625
National Library of Greece, Athens
   Atheniensis 1265
National Library of Israel, Jerusalem
   AMST Ros 1808 A9
   Heb. 8° 476
   JNUL MS 381
   MS Varia 223
   MS Yah. Var. 34
   MS Yehuda 18
National Library, Naples
   Neapolitanus II C.33
National Library of Poland, Warsaw
   MSS Rps 3352 II, Rps 6698 II
   National Library of Spain, Madrid
   MS 12707
National Library of Wales, Aberystwyth
   M11117B
   Penarth MS 423D
National Museum, Prague
   MS 2483 (XI A 19)
   MS XVII F25
   P. GR. I, 18; I, 21
National Museum of Antiquities, Leiden
   P. Lugd. Bat. J383, J384, J395, XIX 20, XXV 9
Neuchâtel Public Library, Neuchâtel
   MS A18 (formerly 24079)
Northwestern University, Illinois
   MS 65
Nuremberg University, Nuremberg
   MS 34 X
Oslo University Library, Oslo
   P. Oslo I, 1; I, 2; I, 3; I, 4; I, 5; III, 75
Oxford University Libraries, Oxford
   MSS 1102, 1791, 1816, 1915, 1960, 2257
   Heb. C 65
Royal Palace Library, Madrid
   Real Biblioteca MS h-I-16
Papyrological Institute, Leiden
   T. Leid. Demarée
Papyrology Seminary, Barcelona

P. Palau Rib. inv. 3, inv. 126, inv. 200
Pierpont Morgan Library, New York
    M662B 22
Pisa University, Pisa
    P. Cazzaniga nos 1-6, no. 7, nos 8-13
Prague University Library, Prague
    MS 267 (I.F.35), 1866
Princeton Theological Seminary, Princeton
    P. Oxy. 925
Princeton University, Princeton
    P. Princ. II.76, II.107, III.159
Private Collection, Edward Hunter
    Key of Solomon MS
Private Collection, Gregorius Niger
    Key of Solomon MS
Private Collection, Harry Walton
    MS A901
Private Collection, London
    Hay 10391
Private Collection, Toronto
    MS B GG134
Private Collection, Unknown
    Former Lenkiewicz Key of Solomon, 2 MSS
    Gollancz MS
    Grimoire of Armadel MS (German)
    Sibley Key of Solomon MS
Queriniana Civic Library, Brescia
    MS E VI 23
Raleigh, North Carolina
    Rev. A. B. Hunter 39
Regional and University Library, Strasbourg
    Copt. MS 135
    P. Gr. 574, 1167, 1179
Ritman Library, Amsterdam
    BPH 114
Robert Nahman Collection
    Text amulet
Rosenthal Library, University of Amsterdam, Amsterdam
    MS 12
Royal Library, Brussels
    MS III.1152
Royal Library, Copenhagen
    Gl. Kgl. S.3499
Royal Swedish Academy of Letters, History and Antiquities, Stockholm
    MS ATA ÄMB2
Sachsen-Anhalt Library, Halle
    MS 14 B. 36
    Stolb. Wernig Za 74
Sackler Library, Oxford

P. Oxy. 1926
Saint Augustine's Abbey, Canterbury
　　MSS 1277, 1603
Saint Nicholas Hospital Library, Bernkastel-Kues
　　CC 216, 322
Schocken Library, Jerusalem
　　Kabbalah MS 3
Science Academy, St. Petersburg
　　Antonine 238
　　BAN Q.537
　　Petropolitanus Academicus
　　Petropolitanus Nat. Lib. 575, 646
　　P. Lichačev
　　MSS Q III 645, III 647
Scots Abbey, Vienna
　　Vind. 140 (61)
Selly Oak Colleges Central Libray, Birmingham
　　P. Harris 56
Seville University, Seville
　　Zayas MSS C.V.1, C.XIV.1, C.XIV.22
Society of Antiquaries of London, London
　　MS SAL 39
State Library of Prussian Cultural Heritage, Berlin
　　MS Germ Fol. 903
　　MS Germ. Quarto 474
　　Hamilton MS 589
　　Phillips MS 1577
State and University Library, Hamburg
　　Mag. Fol. 188
　　P. Hamb. I.22
State Library, Zittau
　　MS B107
State Library of Czechoslovakia, Prague
　　P. Prag. I.6, P. Prag. 1 Wessely
St Gallen University, St Gallen
　　VadSlg MS 334
Study Library, Salzburg
　　Cod. M I 24
Thuringian State Library, Weimar
　　MS O 95
Trinity College, Cambridge
　　MSS 0.1.58, 0.8.29, 0.9.7
　　MS 1419
Turin National University Librrary, Turin
　　MS E.V. 13
University College Institute of Archaeology, London
　　　Edward Collection
　　P. Haw. 312
University Library, Amsterdam

P. Amst. Inv. 16
P. Amst I.15, 173
University of California, Berkeley
P. Tebt. II.275
Univeristy of Michigan Library, Ann Arbor
Cryptogr. P.
P. Fay. 5
P. Mich. 136, 593, 1190, 1523, 3023A, 3472, 3565, 4932f; III, 154; III, 155; III, 156; inv. 6666
University of Pennsylvania, Philadelphia
MS 1685
MS Codex 1673 (formerly Alnwick MS 584)
Van Pelt Codex 515
University Papyrus Collection, Heidelberg
P. Heid. G. 1386
Unknown Locations
Conte de Sarzana MS ZZ
Coxe 25
Old Coptic Schmidt Papyrus
Sasson MS 522
Uppsala University Library, Uppsala
P. Ups. 6
Vadian Collection, St Gallen
MS VSG 334
Vatican Library, Rome
Coptic Papyrus 1
MS AR 448
MS BA lat. 3180, 3185, 6482
MS BARB lat. 3589
MSS BAV Pal. lat. 957, 1375, 1401, 1439, 1445B
MSS BAV Reg lat 1106, 1115, 1283a, 1300
MS Bibl. Vat. Gr. 1209
MS BNM lat. XIV 174
Venice National Library, Venice
ASV b.93
BNM lat. XIV 174
Victoria Museum of Egyptian Antiquities, Uppsala
P. Holm.
Warburg Library, London
MSS FBH 80, 510
Warsaw University, Warsaw
P. Vars. 4
Washington University, Washington
P. Wash. Univ. inv. 139, inv. 181, inv. 242, II.74
Weiser Collection, USA
Hockley Rabbi Solomon MS
Wellcome Library, London
Wellcome MSS 110, 116, 321, 517, 820, 821, 983, 1026, 1072, 1581. 1766, 2000, 2640, 2641, 3129, 3130, 3203, 4653, 4654, 4655, 4656, 4657, 4658, 4659, 4660,

4661, 4662, 4663, 4664, 4665, 4666, 4667, 4668, 4669, 4670
Wiesbaden University, Wiesbaden
  MS 79
Wisconsin University Library
  Duveen MS D388
Woodbrooke College, Birmingham
  P. Harr. 55
Worldheart Foundation, Amsterdam
  BPH 242
Würzberg University Library, Würzberg
  P. Anastasi 9
  P. Berlin 8503
  Würzberg 42
Yale University Library, Yale
  Mellon MSS 1, 72, 85
  Osborn MS fa. 7
  P. Yale inv. 989, inv. 1206, 882A, 1784, 1791, 1792, 1800, 2124, II.130, II.134

Printed Sources

Aakhus, Patricia (2012). Astral Magic and Adelard of Bath's *Liber Prestigiorum*; or Why Werewolves Change at the Full Moon. *Culture and Cosmos* 16.1–2: 151–61
Acher, Frater & Sabogal, José Gabriel Alegria (2020). *Clavis Goêtica: Keys to Chthonic Sorcery*. West Yorkshire: Hadean Press
Agrippa, Henry Cornelius (1550). *De Occulta Philosophia Libri Tres*. Basel: Lugduni
Agrippa, H. C. (1559). *Liber Quartus de Occulta Philosophia, seu de Cerimoniis Magicis. Cui accesserunt, Elementa Magica Petri De Abano, Philosophi*. Marburg
Agrippa, H. C. (1578). *Opera*. Basel: Thomas Guarin
Agrippa, H. C. (1651). *Three Books of Occult Philosophy* (John French, trans.). London: Gregory Moule
Agrippa, H. C. (1978). *Fourth Book of Occult Philosophy* (Stephen Skinner, ed.). London: Askin Publishers
Agrippa, H. C. (1992). *De Occulta Philosophia Libri Tres* (V. Perrone Compagni, ed.). Leiden; New York: E.J. Brill
Agrippa, H. C. (2011). *Three Books of Occult Philosophy* (Donald Tyson, ed.). Woodbury: Llewellyn
Alexander, Philip S. (2003). Sepher ha-Razim and the Problem of Black Magic in Early Judaism. In Todd Klutz (ed.), *Magic in the Biblical World* (pp. 170–90). T&T Clark International
Álvarez, Nicolas Ortiz (ed., trans.) (2019). *Magia Naturalis et Innaturalis*. Mexico City: Enodia Press
Anon. (1892). *Les Clavicules de Salomon*. Paris: Chamuel
Anon. (1909). *Le Dragon Noir Ou Les Forces Infernales Soumises à L'homme*. Paris: Librairie Générale Des Sciences Occultes
Anon. (1972). *The Black Pullet: Science of Magical Talisman*. New York: Samuel Weiser Inc.
Arnovick, Leslie K. (2006). *Written Reliquaries: the Resonance of Orality in Medieval English Texts*. Amsterdam: John Benjamins Publishing Co.

Kiesel, William (ed.) (2002). *Picatrix (Ghayat al-Hakim) Goal of the Wise* (Hashem Atallah, trans.). Seattle: Ouroboros Press. Two volumes

Attrell, Dan & Porreca, David (eds., trans.) (2019). *Picatrix: A Medieval Treatise on Astral Magic*. University Park: Pennsylvania State University Press

Aubrey, John (1890). *Miscellanies Upon Various Subjects*. London: Reeves & Turner

Avilés, Alejandro G. Weiserrcia (1994). *Two Astromagical Manuscripts of Alfonso X the Wise*. University of Murcia.

Baker, Colin F. & Polliack, Meira (eds.) (2001). *Arabic and Judeo-Arabic Manuscripts in the Cambridge Genizah Collections*. Cambridge: Cambridge University Press

Baker, Jim (2014). *The Cunning Man's Handbook: The Practice of English Folk Magic 1550-1900*. London: Avalonia

Bang, Anton Christian (1901). *Norske Hexeformularer og Magiske Opskrifter*. Kristiana: J Dybwad

Banner, James & Davis, John (eds.) (1998). *The Great Grimoire of Pope Honorius* (Kineta Ch'ien & Matthew Sullivan, trans.). Washington: Trident Books

Barrett, Francis (1801). *The Magus*. London: Lackington, Allen & Co.

Barrett, Francis (2000). *The Magus*. Boston: Weiser Books

Barry, Kieran (1999). *The Greek Qabalah*. York Beach: Samuel Weiser

Beard, C. R. (1933). *The Romance of Treasure Trove*. London: Sampson, Low, Marston & Co.

Beinert, Richard A. (2003). *Windows on a Medieval World: Medieval Piety as Reflected in the Lapidary Literature of the Middle Ages*. Newfoundland: St Johns

Bergman, Dietrich (ed.) (2008). *A Complete Book of Magic Science*. York Beach: Teitan Press

Bergman, Jan (1982). Ancient Egyptian Theogony in a Greek Magical Papyrus. In M. Heerma van Voss, E. J. Sharpe & R. J. Z. Werblowsky (eds.), *Studies in Egyptian Religion* (pp. 28–37). Leiden: E. J. Brill

Betz, Hans Dieter (1991). Magic and Mystery in the Greek Magical Papyri. In Christopher A. Faraone and Dirk Obbink (eds.), *Magika Hiera: Ancient Greek Magic & Religion* (pp. 244–59). Oxford: Oxford University Press

Betz, Hans Dieter (ed.) (1996). *The Greek Magical Papyri in Translation*. Chicago: University of Chicago Press

Blanchard, R. (1996). *The Black Dragon*. California: IGOS

Bohak, Gideon (1999). Greek, Coptic, and Jewish Magic in the Cairo Genizah. *Bulletin of the American Society of Papyrologists* 36: 27–44

Bohak, Gideon (2008). *Ancient Jewish Magic: A History*. Cambridge: Cambridge University Press

Bohak, Gideon & Bellusci, Alessia (2019). The Greek Prayer to Helios in *Sefer ha-Razim*, in Light of New Textual Evidence. In Ljuba Merlina Bortolani, William Furley, Svenja Nagel, and Joachim Friedrich Quack (eds.), *Cultural Plurality in Ancient Magical Texts and Practices* (pp. 259–75). Tubinen: Mohr Siebeck

Bos, Gerrit, Charles Burnett & Paolo Lucentini (eds.) (2002). *Hermetis Trismegisti Astrologica et Diuinatoria*. Brepols: Turnhout

Boudet, Jean-Patrice (2001). Les Condamnations de la Magie à Paris en 1398. *Revue Mabillon* 12.73: 121–57

Boudet, Jean-Patrice (2003). Les who's who démonologiques de la Renaissance et leurs ancêtres médiévaux. *Médiévales* 44: 117–40

Boudet, Jean-Patrice, Franck Collard & Nicolas Weill-Parot (eds., trans.) (2013). *Médecine, Astrologie et Magie entre Moyen Âge et Renaissance: autour de Pietro d'Abano*. Tavarnuzze: Sismel

Boudet, Jean-Patrice & Véronèse, Julien (2006). Le Secret dans la Magie Rituelle Médiévale. *Micrologus* 14: 101–50

Bremmer, Jan N. & Veenstra, Jan R. (eds.) (2002). *The Metamorphosis of Magic from Late Antiquity to the Early Modern Period*. Leuven: Peeters

Bridges, Vincent, Teresa Burns & Phil Legard (eds.) (2007). *The Consecrated Little Book of Black Venus Attributed to John Dee* (Teresa Burns & Nancy Turner, trans.). New York: Waning Moon Publications, Ltd.

Briggs, Katharine (1953). Some Seventeenth Century Books of Magic. *Folklore* 64.4: 445–62

Briggs, Katharine (1959). *The Anatomy of Puck: An Examination of Fairy Beliefs among Shakespeare's Contemporaries and Successors.* London: Routledge & Kegan Paul

Briggs, Katharine (1962). *Pale Hecate's Team: An Examination of the Beliefs on Witchcraft and Magic among Shakespeare's Contemporaries and His Immediate Successors.* London: Routledge & Kegan Paul

Brown, P. (1972). Sorcery, Demons and the Rise of Christianity: from Late Antiquity into the Middle Ages. In Peter Brown (ed.), *Religion and Society in the Age of Saint Augustine* (pp. 119–46). London: Faber & Faber

Brucker, Gene A. (1963). Sorcery in Early Renaissance Florence. *Studies in the Renaissance* 10: 7–24

Burnett, Charles (1996). *Magic and Divination in the Middle Ages: Texts and Techniques in the Islamic and Christian Worlds.* Aldershot: Variorium

Burnett, Charles (ed., trans.) (1998). *Adelard of Bath, Conversations with his Nephew.* Cambridge: Cambridge University Press

Burnett, Charles & Ryan, W.F. (eds.) (2006). *Magic and the Classical Tradition.* London: Warburg Institute

Butler, E. M. (1952). *The Fortunes of Faust.* Cambridge: Cambridge University Press

Butler, E. M. (1980). *Ritual Magic.* Cambridge: Cambridge University Press

Campbell, Colin D. (ed.) (2011). *A Book of the Offices of Spirits.* York: Teitan Press

Campbell, Josie P. (1986). *Popular Culture in the Middle Ages.* Wisconsin: Popular Press

Casaubon, Meric (ed.) (1974). *A True and Faithful Relation of What Passed for Many Years Between Dr John Dee and some Spirits.* London: Askin Publishers

Cecchetelli, Michael (2011). *Crossed Keys.* London: Scarlet Imprint

Charubel (2003). *Grimoire Sympathia: The Workshop of the Infinite.* Thame: I-H-O Books

Chicosky, Alison (2022). *The Secrets of Helios: Unlocking the Practical Uses of PGM IV:1596-1715.* West Yorkshire: Hadean Press

Clucas, Stephen (2006). John Dee's Angelic Conversations and the Ars Notoria. In Stephen Clucas (ed.), *John Dee: Interdisciplinary Studies in English Renaissance Thought* (pp. 231–73). Dordrecht: Springer

Cohen, Martin Samuel (1983) *Shi'ur Qomah: Liturgy and Theurgy in Pre-Kabbalistic Jewish Mysticism.* Tubingen: J.C.B. Mohr

Cohen, Martin Samuel (1985). *Shi'ur Qomah: Text and Recensions.* Tubingen: J.C.B. Mohr

Coletânea (2007). *São Cipriano, o Bruxo.* Rio de Janeiro: Pallas

Collins, Derek (2008). *Magic in the Ancient Greek World.* Oxford: Blackwell Publishing Ltd.

Collisson, Marcus (2010). *On the Operation of Dæmons.* Singapore: Golden Hoard Press

Conybeare, F. C. (1898). The Testament of Solomon. *The Jewish Quarterly Review* 11.1: 1–45

Couliano [Culiano], Ioan P. (1981). Magia Spirituale e Magia Demonica nel Rinascimento. *Rivista de Storia e Letteratura Religiosa* 17: 360–408

Couliano, Ioan P. (1987). *Eros and Magic in the Renaissance* (Margaret Cook, trans.). Chicago: Chicago University Press

D'Aban, Pierre (1744). *Les Oeuvres Magiques d'Henri Corneille Agrippa.* Paris: Liege

Daiches, Samuel (1913). *Babylonian Oil Magic in the Talmud and in the Later Jewish Literature.* London: Jews' College

Daniel, Robert W. (1991). Intrigue in the Cloister: PGM LXVI. *Zeitschrift für Papyrologie und Epigraphik* 89:119–120

Daniel, Robert W. & Maltomini, Franco (1990). *Supplementum Magicum Volume 1*. Koln: Westdeutscher Verlag

Daniel, Robert W. & Maltomini, Franco (1992). *Supplementum Magicum Volume 2*. Koln: Westdeutscher Verlag

Davidson, Gustav (1967). *A Dictionary of Angels, Including the Fallen Angels*. New York: Free Press

Davies, Owen (1996). Healing Charms in Use in England and Wales 1700-1950. *Folklore* 107: 19–32

Davies, Owen (2003). *Cunning-Folk: Popular Magic in English History*. London: Hambledon & London

Davies, Owen (2004). French Charmers and Their Healing Charms. In Jonathan Roper (ed.), *Charms and Charming in Europe* (pp. 91–112). Basingstoke: Palgrave Macmillan

Davies, Owen (2009). *Grimoires: A History of Magic Books*. Oxford: Oxford University Press

Davis, Robert C. (1927). *Shipbuilders of the Venetian Arsenal*. Johns Hopkins University Press

Debus, Allen G. (2002). *The Chemical Philosophy: Paracelsian Science and Medicine in the Sixteenth and Seventeenth Centuries*. Devon: Dover

De Claremont, Lewis (1936). *The Ancient's Book of Magic*. Oracle

Dee, John (2010). *Tuba Veneris* (James Banner, ed.). Seattle: Trident Books

De Givry, E. G. (1931). *Sorcery, Magic and Alchemy*. London: George G. Harrap & Co. Ltd.

Dehn, Georg (ed.) (2006). *The Book of Abramelin* (Steven Guth, trans.). Lake Worth: Ibis

Delatte, Armand (1927–39). *Anecdota Atheniensia*. Liège: H. Vaillant-Carmanne, and Paris: Edouard Champion

Dennis, Rabbi Geoffrey W. (2007). *The Encyclopaedia of Jewish Myth, Magic and Mysticism*. Llewellyn: Minnesota

d'Este, S. & Rankine, David (2008). *Wicca Magical Beginnings*. London: Avalonia

d'Este, S. & Rankine, David (2011). *The Cosmic Shekinah: A Historical Study of the Goddess of the Old Testament and Kabbalah*. Glastonbury: Avalonia

d'Este, S. & Rankine, David (eds.) (2013). *The Faerie Queens: A collection of essays exploring the myths, magic and mythology of the Faerie Queens*. Glastonbury: Avalonia

Dieleman, Jacco (2005). *Priests, Tongues, and Rites: The London-Leiden Manuscripts and Translation in Egyptian Ritual (100-300 CE)*. Leiden: Brill

Dillinger, Johannes (2012). *Magical Treasure Hunting in Europe and North America: A History*. New York: Palgrave Macmillan

Dimech, Alkistis & Grey, Peter (2019). *The Brazen Vessel*. Cornwall: Scarlet Imprint

Duffy, Eamon (1992). *The Stripping of the Altars: Traditional Religion in England, c. 1400–c. 1580*. New Haven: Yale University Press

Duling, D.C. (1975). Solomon, Exorcism, and the Son of David. *Harvard Theological Review* 68.3: 235–252

Duling, D.C. (1984). The Legend of Solomon the Magician in Antiquity. *Proceedings of the Eastern Great Lakes Biblical Society* 4: 1–27

Duling, D.C. (1985). The Eleazar Miracle and Solomon's Magical Wisdom in Flavius Josephus's *Antiquitates Judaicae* 8.42-49. *HTR* 78.1–2: 1–25

Duling, D. C. (1988). The Testament of Solomon: Retrospect and Prospect. *Journal for the Study of the Pseudepigrapha* 1.2: 87–112

Dumas, F. R. (2008). *Grimoires et Rituels Magiques*. Paris: Le Pre aux Clercs

Eamon, William (1994). *Science and the Secrets of Nature: Books of Secrets in Medieval and Early Modern Culture*. Princeton: Princeton University Press

Eleazar of Worms (1701). *Sepher Raziel*. Amsterdam: Coutinho

Evans, Joan (1922). *Magic Jewels of the Middle Ages and Renaissance*. Oxford: Clarendon Press

Fabricius, Johann Albert (1713). *Codex Pseudepigraphus Veteris Testamenti*. Hamburg: Felgineri

Fanger, Claire (ed.) (1998). *Conjuring Spirits: Texts and Traditions of Medieval Ritual Magic*. University Park: Pennsylvania State University Press
Fanger, Claire (ed.) (2012). *Invoking Angels: Theurgic Ideas and Practices, Thirteenth to Sixteenth Centuries*. University Park: Pennsylvania State University Press
Fanger, Claire (2012). Libra Nigromantici: The Good, the Bad, and the Ambiguous in John of Morigny's Flowers of Heavenly Teaching. *Magic, Ritual and Witchcraft*, Winter 2012: 164–189
Fanger, Claire (2015). *Rewriting Magic: An Exegesis of the Visionary Autobiography of a Fourteenth Century French Monk*. University Park: Pennsylvania State University Press
Faraone, Christopher (1988). Hermes but No Marrow: Another Look at a Puzzling Magical Spell. *Zeitschrift für Papyrologie und Epigraphik* 72: 279–286
Faraone, Christopher (1999). *Ancient Greek Love Magic*. Cambridge: Harvard University Press
Faraone, Christopher A. & Obbink, Dirk (1991). *Magika Hiera: Ancient Greek Magic and Religion*. Oxford: Oxford University Press
Feingold, Mordechai (1984). The Occult Tradition in the English Universities of the Renaissance: A Reassessment. In Brian Vickers (ed.), *Occult and Scientific Mentalities in the Renaissance* (pp. 73–94). Cambridge: Cambridge University Press
Flint, Valerie I. J. (1991). *The Rise of Magic in Early Medieval Europe*. New Jersey: Princeton University Press
Flint, Valerie I. J. (1999). The Demonisation of Magic and Sorcery in Late Antiquity: Christian Redefinitions of Pagan Religions. In Bengt Ankarloo & Stuart Clark (eds.), *Witchcraft and Magic in Europe: Ancient Greece and Rome* (pp. 277–348). Philadelphia: University of Pennsylvania Press
Flowers, Stephen E. (1989). *Galdrabók: An Icelandic Grimoire*. Llewellyn: Maine
Forbes, Thomas R. (1971). Verbal Charms in British Folk Medicine. *Proceedings of the American Philosophical Society* 115.4: 293–316
French, Sarah K. (trans.) (2004). *The Enchiridion of Pope Leo III*
Freudenthal, Gad & Mandosio, Jean-Marc (2014). Old French into Hebrew in Twelfth-Century Tsarfat: Medieval Hebrew Versions of Marbode's Lapidary. *Aleph* 14.1: 11–187
Gager, John G. (1992). *Curse Tablets and Binding Spells from the Ancient World*. Oxford: Oxford University Press
Gaster, Moses (ed., trans.) (1896). *The Sword of Moses: an Ancient Book of Magic*. London
Gaster, Moses (1910). English Charms of the Seventeenth Century. *Folklore* 21.3: 375–8
Gaster, Moses (1990). *Studies and Texts in Folklore, Magic, Medieval Romance, Hebrew Apocrypha and Samaritan Archaeology*. New Jersey: KTAV Publishing
Gettings, Fred (1981). *Dictionary of Occult, Hermetic and Alchemical Sigils*. London: Routledge & Kegan Paul
Gibson, Marion (2003). *Witchcraft and Society in England and America 1550-1750*. London: Continuum
Gilbert, R.A. (ed.) (1983). *The Magical Mason: Forgotten Hermetic Writings of William Wynn Westcott, Physician and Magus*. Wellingborough: Aquarian Press
Giralt, Sebastià (2017). The Liber Lune and the Liber Solis attributed to Hermes in the MS Vatican, B.A.V., Barb. lat. 3589. *Journal of Medieval and Humanistic Studies* 33: 103–126
Gollancz, Hermann (ed.) (2008). *Sepher Maphteah Shelomoh* (Book of the Key of Solomon). York Beach: Teitan Press
Graf, Fritz (1997). *Magic in the Ancient World*. Cambridge: Harvard University Press
Greenfield, Richard (1988). *Traditions of Belief in Late Byzantine Demonology*. Amsterdam: Hakkert
Greenup, A. W. (ed.) (1912). *Sepher ha-Levanah: the Book of the Moon*. London
Grinsell, L. V. (1967). Barrow Treasure, in Fact, Tradition, and Legislation. *Folklore* 78.1: 1–38

Grypeou, Emmanouela (2016). Talking Skulls: On Some Personal Accounts of Hell and their Place in Apocalyptic Literature. *Zeitschrift für Antikes Christentum* 20.1: 109–126

Grypeou, Emmanouela (2019). Talking Heads: Necromancy in Jewish and Christian Accounts from Mesopotamia and Beyond. *Collectanea Christiana Orientalia* 16: 1–30

Guidon (2011). *Magic Secrets* (P. Pissier, trans.). Hinckley: Society for Esoteric Endeavour

Hamill, John (ed.) (1986). *The Rosicrucian Seer: Magical Writings of Frederick Hockley*. Wellingborough: Aquarian Press

Hammer, P. (ed.) (1743). *Nigromantisches Kunst-Buch, handelnd von der Glücks-Ruthe, dem Ring und der Krone Salomonis, den Fürsten-Geheimnissen, den dienstbaren Krystall- und Schatz-Geistern und andern wunderbaren Arcanen*. Köln am Rhein: Peter Hammer's Erben

Hansen, Joseph (ed) (1901) *Quellen und Untersuchungen zur Geschichte des Hexenwahns und der Hexenverfolgung im Mittelalter*. Bonn: Carl Georgi

Harari, Yuval (1997). *Harba de-Moshe (The Sword of Moses): A New Edition and a Study*. Jerusalem: Academon

Harkness, Deborah E. (1999). *John Dee's Conversations with Angels: Cabala, Alchemy, and the End of Nature*. Cambridge: Cambridge University Press

Harms, Daniel (2019). 'Thou Art Keeper of Man and Woman's Bones' – Rituals of Necromancy in Early Modern England. *Thanatos* 8.1: 62–90

Harms, Daniel & Clark, James R. (2019). *Of Angels, Demons & Spirits*. Woodbury: Llewellyn

Harms, Daniel, James R. Clark & Joseph H. Peterson (2016). *The Book of Oberon: A Sourcebook of Elizabethan Magic*. Woodbury: Llewellyn

Harms, Daniel (2013). Spirits at the Table: Fairie Queens in the Grimoires. In Sorita d'Este & David Rankine (eds.), *The Faerie Queens* (pp. 44–61). London: Avalonia

Hedegård, Gösta (2002). *Liber Iuratus Honorii: A Critical Edition of the Latin Version of the Sworn Book of Honorius*. Stockholm: Almquist & Wiksell International

Hernández, Raquel Martin (2012). Reading Magical Drawings in the Greek Magical Papyri. In Paul Schubert (ed.), *Actes du 26ᵉ Congrès International de Papyrologie* (pp. 491–98). Geneva: Librairie Droz S.A.

Hesiod (2005). *Works of Hesiod and the Homeric Hymns* (Daryl Hines, trans.). Chicago: University of Chicago Press

Heydon, John (2018). *Theomagia, or the Temple of Wisdom*. London: Forgotten Books

Hockley, Frederick (2008). *A Complete Book of Magic Science Containing the method of constraining and exorcising spirits to appearance and consecration of Magic Circles* (Dietrich Bergman, ed.). York Beach: Teitan

Hohman, J. G. (1820). *Pow-wows; or, Long Lost Friend: A Collection of Mysterious and Invaluable Arts and Remedies, for Man as well as Animals, with many Proofs*. Pennsylvania: Hohman

Howe, Ellic (1972). *The Magicians of the Golden Dawn*. Wellingborough: Aquarian Press

Howe, Ellic (ed.) (1985). *The Alchemist of the Golden Dawn: The Letters of the Revd W. A. Ayton to F. L. Gardner and Others 1886-1905*. Wellingborough: Aquarian Press

Hull, J. M. (1974). *Hellenistic Magic and the Synoptic Tradition*. London: SCM

Huson, Paul (2001). *Mastering Herbalism: A Practical Guide*. Maryland: Madison Books

Jackson, H. M. (1988). Notes on the Testament of Solomon. *Journal for the Study of Judaism* 19.1: 19–60

James, Geoffrey (1997). *Angel Magic: the Ancient Art of Summoning and Communicating with Angelic Beings*. St. Paul: Llewellyn

Jeffers, Ann (1996). *Magic and Divination in Ancient Palestine and Syria*. Leiden: Brill

Johnson, Brian (ed., trans.) (2019). *Testament of Solomon: Recension C*. West Yorkshire: Hadean Press

Johnson, Brian (ed., trans.) (2020). *Necromancy in the Medici Library*. West Yorkshire: Hadean Press

Johnson, Brian (ed., trans.) (2022). *Naming the Heavens: Orations from the Summa Sacre Magice*. West Yorkshire: Hadean Press

Josephus, Flavius (1987). *The Works of Josephus, Complete and Unabridged* (William Whiston, trans.). Peabody: Hendrickson Publishers

Judge, E. A. (1987). The Magical Use of Scripture in the Papyri. In Edgar W. Conrad & Edward G. Newing (eds.), *Perspectives on Language and Text* (pp. 339–349). Indiana: Eisenbrauns

Karr, Don & Skinner, Stephen (eds.) (2010). *Sepher Raziel: Liber Salomonis*. Singapore: Golden Hoard Press

Kassell, Lauren (2006). 'All This Land Full Fill'd of Faerie,' or Magic and the Past in Early Modern England. *Journal of the History of Ideas* 67.1: 107–22

Kassell, Lauren (2005). The Economy of Magic in Early Modern England. In Margaret Pelling & Scott Mandelbrote (eds.), *The Practice of Reform in Health, Medicine, and Science, 1500–2000: Essays for Charles Webster* (pp. 43–57). Aldershot: Ashgate

Kelly, Edmund (2019). *The Grand Albert*. DarkArts Publishing

Kieckhefer, Richard (1997). *Forbidden Rites: A Necromancer's Manual of the Fifteenth Century*. Sutton: Stroud

Kieckhefer, Richard (2001). *Magic in the Middle Ages*. Cambridge: Cambridge University Press

Kiesel, William (ed.) (2002). *Picatrix: Ghayat Al-Hakim*. Seattle: Ouroboros Press

Kiesel, William (2015). *Magic Circles in the Grimoire Tradition*. Seattle: Ouroboros Press

Kiesewetter, Carl (1893). *Faust in der Geschichte und Tradition*. Leipzig: Spohr

King, B. J. H. (trans.) (1984). *The Grimoire of Pope Honorius III*. Northampton: Sut Anubis Books

Klaassen, Frank (2003). Medieval Ritual Magic in the Renaissance. *Aries* 3.2: 166–99

Klaassen, Frank (2013). *The Transformations of Magic: Illicit Learned Magic in the Later Middle Ages and Renaissance*. University Park: Pennsylvania State University Press

Klaassen, Frank (ed.) (2019). *Making Magic in Elizabethan England: Two Early Modern Vernacular Books of Magic*. University Park: Pennsylvania State University Press

Klutz, Todd (ed.) (2003). *Magic in the Biblical World: from the Rod of Aaron to the Ring of Solomon*. London: T&T Clark International

Klutz, Todd (2005). *Rewriting the Testament of Solomon: Tradition, Conflict and Identity in a Late Antique Pseudepigraphon*. New York: T & T Clark

Kollatsch, Rick-Arne (2021, October 1). *Abraham of Worms*. Humanities Commons. https://hcommons.org/deposits/objects/hc:41822/datastreams/CONTENT/content?fbclid=IwAR3rl5KHalY-MW35yDyxQ6r7P4DAda3x36_U-1Q8PcJFqx9Llw66H1PHtCA

Kraus, Thomas J. (ed.) (2007). *Ad Fontes: Original Manuscripts and Their Significance for Studying Early Christianity*. Leiden: Brill

Kuntz, Darcy (ed.) (2006). *Ars Notoria: the Magical Art of Solomon…Englished by Robert Turner*. Sequim: Holmes

Lamda, Aaman (trans) & Overman, Arundell (ed) (2020) *The Complete Illustrated Grand Grimoire, or the Red Dragon*. Amazon: Aaman Lamda

Lang, Benedek (2008). *Unlocked Books: Manuscripts of Learned Magic in the Medieval Libraries of Central Europe*. University Park: Pennsylvania State University

Laycock, Donald & Skinner, Stephen (1978). *The Complete Enochian Dictionary*. London: Askin

Lea, H. C. (1957). *Materials Towards A History Of Witchcraft* (3 volumes). New York: Thomas Yoseloff

Lecouteux, Claude (2002). *Le Livres des Grimoires*. Paris: Editions Imago

Lecouteux, Claude (2012). *A Lapidary of Sacred Stones: Their Magical and Medicinal Powers Based on the Earliest Sources*. Vermont: Inner Traditions

Legard, Phil & Cummins, Alexander (eds.) (2020). *An Excellent Booke of the Arte of Magicke*.

London: Scarlet Imprint

Lehrich, C. I. (2003). *The Language of Demons and Angels: Cornelius Agrippa's Occult Philosophy*. Leiden: Brill

Leitão, José (ed., trans.) (2014). *The Book of St. Cyprian: The Sorcerer's Treasure*. West Yorkshire: Hadean Press

Leitão, José (2019). *Opuscula Cypriani: Variations on the Book of Saint Cyprian and Related Literature*. West Yorkshire: Hadean Press

Leitch, Aaron (2005). *Secrets of the Magical Grimoires*. Woodbury: Llewellyn

Lesses, Rebecca (1996). Speaking with Angels: Jewish and Grêco-Egyptian Revelatory Adjurations. *The Harvard Theological Review* 89.1: 41–60

Levi, Eliphas (1913). *The History of Magic*. London: William Rider & Son

Levi, Eliphas (1959). *The Key of the Mysteries*. London: Rider & Co.

Lidaka, Juris (1998). The Book of Angels, Rings, Characters and Images of the Planets: attributed to Osbern Bokenham. In Claire Fanger (ed.), *Conjuring Spirits* (pp. 32–75). University Park: Pennsylvania State University Press

Lilly, William (1647). *The World's Catastrophe*. London: J. Partridge

Lisiewski, Joseph (2004). *Ceremonial Magic & the Power of Evocation*. Temple: New Falcon

Love, Edward O. D. (2016). *Code-switching with the Gods: The Bilingual (Old Coptic-Greek) Spells of PGM IV and their Linguistic, Religious, and Socio-Cultural Context in Late Roman Egypt*. Berlin: DeGruyter

Luck, Georg (1985). *Arcana Mundi: Magic and the Occult in the Greek and Roman Worlds*. Baltimore: Johns Hopkins University Press

Luibheld, C. (trans.) (1987). *Pseudo-Dionysus: The Complete Works*. New York: Paulist Press

MacDonald, Michael Albion (ed., trans.) (1988). *De Nigromancia [attributed to] Roger Bacon*. New Jersey: Heptangle Books

MacLeod, Mindy & Mees, Bernard (2006). *Runic Amulets and Magic Objects*. Suffolk: Boydell Press

Magdalino, Paul & Mavroudi, Maria (eds.) (2006). *The Occult Sciences in Byzantium*. Geneva: La Pomme d'Or

Magnus, Albertus (1599). *The Secrets of Albertus Magnus. Of the Vertues of Hearbes, Stones, and Certaine Beasts. Whereunto Is Newly Added, a Short Discourse of the Seauen Planets Gouerning the Natiuities of Children. Also a Booke of the Same Author, of the Maruellous Things of the Worlde, and of Certaine Effects Caused by Certaine Beasts*. London: W. Iaggard

Magnus, Albertus (2012). *Egyptian Secrets of Albertus Magnus*. Createspace: Theophania Publishing

Maguire, Henry (ed.) (1995). *Byzantine Magic*. Washington: Dunbarton Oaks

Marathakis, Ioannis (2007). *Anazetontas ten Kleida tou Solomonta*. Athens: Eidikos Typos

Marathakis, Ioannis (2007). *From the Ring of Gyges to the Black Cat Bone: A Historical Study of the Invisibility Spells*. Hermetics Resource Site. www.hermetics.org/Invisibilitas.html

Marathakis, Ioannis (ed., trans.) (2011). *The Magical Treatise of Solomon or Hygromanteia*. Singapore: Golden Hoard Press

Marathakis, Ioannis (ed., trans.) (2020). *The Book of Wisdom of Apollonius of Tyana*. Private publication

Malchus, Marius (2011). *The Secret Grimoire of Turiel*. Theophania Publishing

Margalioth, Mordecai (1966). *Sepher ha-Razim*. Jerusalem: Yedioth Achronot

Mathers, S. L. MacGregor (trans.) (1889). *The Key of Solomon the King (Clavicula Salomonis)*. London: Redway

Mathers, S. L. MacGregor (trans.) (1898). *The Sacred Magic of Abramelin the Mage*. London: Watkins

Mathers, S. L. MacGregor (trans.) (1980). *The Grimoire of Armadel*. Newburyport: Red Wheel/

Weiser
Mathiesen, Robert (1995). Magic in Slavic Orthodoxa: The Written Tradition. In Henry Maguire (ed.), *Byzantine Magic* (pp. 155–177). Washington, D.C.: Dumbarton Oaks
Mathiesen, Robert (2007). The Key of Solomon: Towards a Typology of the Manuscripts. *Societas Magica Newsletter* 17: 1–9
McCown, C. C. (ed.) (1922). *The Testament of Solomon*. Leipzig: J.C. Hinrichs'sche Buchhandlung
McCown, C. C. (1933). The Christian Tradition as to the Magical Wisdom of Solomon. *JPOS* 2: 1–24
McLean, Adam (ed.) (1982). *The Steganographia of Johannes Trithemius*. Edinburgh: Magnum Opus
McLean, Adam (ed.) (1990). *A Treatise on Angel Magic*. Grand Rapids: Phanes Press
McLean, Adam (ed., trans.) (1994). *The Magical Calendar*. Grand Rapids: Phanes Press
Meyer, Marvin W. & Smith, Richard (eds.) (1999). *Ancient Christian Magic: Coptic Texts of Ritual Power*. Princeton: Princeton University Press
Michaud, L. G. (1865). *Biographie Universelle Ancienne et Moderne XIV*. Paris: Delagrave & Co.
Migne, Jacques Paul (1858). *Dictionnaire des Apocryphes*. Paris: Migne
Mirecki, Paul A. & Meyer, Marvin W. (2002). *Magic and Ritual in the Ancient World*. Leiden: Brill
Morgan, Michael A. (1983). *Sepher ha-Razim: The Book of the Mysteries*. USA: Society of Biblical Literature
Mowat, Barbara A. (2001). Prospero's Book. *Shakespeare Quarterly* 52.1: 1–33
Naudaeus, Gabriel (1657). *The History of Magic: By way of Apology, for all the Wise Men who have unjustly been reputed Magicians, from the Creation, to the present Age* (J. Davies, trans.). London: John Streater
Naveh, Joseph & Shaked, Shaul (1998). *Amulets and Magic Bowls: Aramaic Incantations of Late Antiquity*. Jerusalem: Magnes Press
Nigosian, Solomon A. (2004). *From Ancient Writings to Sacred Texts: The Old Testament and Apocrypha*. Maryland: JHU Press
Nigosian, Solomon A. (2008). *Magic and Divination in the Old Testament*. Portalnd: Sussex Academic Press
Nottingham, Gary St. Michael (2015). *Liber Terribilis: being an instruction on the Seventy-Two Spirits of the Goetia*. Glastonbury: Avalonia
Nottingham, Gary St. Michael (2020). *Ars Theurgia-Goetia: being an account and rendition of the Arte and Praxis of the Conjuration of some of the Spirits of Solomon*. Glastonbury: Avalonia
Nowotny, K. A. (1949). The Construction of Certain Seals and Characters in the Work of Agrippa of Nettesheim. *Journal of the Warburg and Courtauld Institutes* 12: 46–57
Ogden, Daniel (2002). *Magic, Witchcraft and Ghosts in the Greek and Roman World*. Oxford: Oxford University Press
Olsan, Lea T. (1992). Latin Charms of Medieval England: Verbal Healing in a Christian Oral Tradition. *Oral Tradition* 7: 116–42
Olsan, Lea T. (2003). Charms and Prayers in Medieval Medical Theory and Practice. *Social History of Medicine* 16.3: 343–366
Olsan, Lea T. (2004). Charms in Medieval Memory. In Jonathan Roper (ed.), *Charms and Charming in Europe* (pp. 59–87). New York: Palgrave
Olsan, Lea T. (2009). The Corpus of Charms in the Middle English Leechcraft Remedy Books. In Jonathan Roper (ed.), *Charms, Charmers and Charming: International Research on Verbal Magic* (pp. 214–37). New York: Palgrave Macmillan
Ortiz, Nicolás Álvarez (ed., trans.) (2018–19). *The Key of Necromancy* (2 vols.). Mexico City: Enodia Press
Ortiz, N. A. & Velius, V. (eds., trans.) (2016). *A Compendium of Unnatural Black Magic*. Mexico City: Enodia Press

Page, Sophie (2004). *Magic in Medieval Manuscripts*. British Library: London
Page, Sophie (2013). *Magic in the Cloister: Pious Motives, Illicit Interests, and Occult Approaches to the Medieval Universe*. University Park: Pennsylvania State University Press
Page, Sophie & Rider, Catherine (eds.) (2019). *The Routledge History of Medieval Magic*. Abingdon: Routledge
Paracelsus (1996). *Four Treatises of Theophrastus von Hohenheim Called Paracelsus* (Henry H. Sigerist, ed.). Baltimore: Johns Hopkins University Press
Paracelsus (2004). *The Archidoxes of Magic* (Stephen Skinner, intr.). Berwick: Ibis Press
Peters, John P. (2009). *The Psalms as Liturgies*. Charleston: BiblioLife
Peterson, Joseph H. (ed.) (2001). *The Lesser Key of Solomon: Lemegeton Clavicula Salomonis*. Maine: Weiser Books
Peterson, Joseph H. (ed.) (2003). *John Dee's Five Books of Mystery*. York Beach: Weiser Books
Peterson, Joseph H. (ed., trans.) (2007). *Grimorium Verum*. California: CreateSpace
Peterson, Joseph H. (ed., trans.) (2008). *The Sixth and Seventh Books of Moses*. Fort Worth: Ibis Press
Peterson, Joseph H. (ed., trans.) (2009). *Arbatel: Concerning the Magic of the Ancients*. Fort Worth: Ibis Press
Peterson, Joseph H. (ed.) (2010). *The Clavis or Key to the Magic of Solomon*. Lake Worth: Ibis
Peterson, Joseph H. (ed., trans.) (2016). *The Sworn Book of Honorius: Liber Iuratus Honorii*. Lake Worth: Ibis Press
Peterson, Joseph H. (ed., trans.) (2017). *True Black Magic (La Véritable Magie Noire)*. Kasson: Twilit Grotto Press
Peterson, Joseph H. (ed., trans.) (2018). *Secrets of Solomon*. Kasson: Twilit Grotto Press
Peterson, Joseph H. (ed., trans.) (2021). *Elucidation of Necromancy*. Fort Worth: Ibis Press
Peuckert, Will-Erich (1956). *Pansophie: Ein Versuch zur Geschichte der Weissen und Schwarzen Magie*. Berlin: Erich Schmidt
Pingree, David (1984). The Diffusion of Arabic Magical Texts in Western Europe. In Biancamaria Scarcia Amoretti (ed.), *La diffusione delle Scienze Islamiche nel Medio Evo Europeo*, pp. 57–102). Rome: Leone Caeteni Foundation
Pingree, David (ed.) (1986). *Picatrix: The Latin Version of the Ghayat al-Hakim*. London: Warburg Institute
Pollington, Stephen (2003). *Leechcraft: Early English Charms, Plantlore and Healing*. Norfolk: Anglo-Saxon Books
Rankine, David (2006). *Heka: The Practice of Ancient Egyptian Ritual & Magic*. London: Avalonia
Rankine, David (ed.) (2009). *The Book of Treasure Spirits*. London: Avalonia
Rankine, David (ed.) (2010). *The Book of Gold* (Paul Harry Barron, trans.). London: Avalonia
Rankine, David (ed.) (2011). *The Grimoire of Arthur Gauntlet*. Glastonbury: Avalonia
Rankine, David (ed.) (2013). *The Complete Grimoire of Pope Honorius* (Paul Harry Barron, trans.). Glastonbury: Avalonia
Rankine, David (2020). *Sepher Yetzirah Magic*. West Yorkshire: Hadean Press
Rankine, David (2019). *Conjuring the Planetary Intelligences*. West Yorkshire: Hadean Press
Rankine, David (2022, 2005). *Climbing the Tree of Life*. Glastonbury: Avalonia
Rebiger, Bill (ed.) (2010). *Sefer Shimmush Tehillim: Buch vom magischen Gebrauch der Psalmen*. Tübingen: Mohr Siebeck
Rebiger, Bill (2013). Non-European Traditions of Hekhalot Literature. The Yemenite Evidence. In Ra'anan S. Boustan et al. (eds.), *Envisioning Judaism. Studies in Honour of Peter Schäfer on the Occasion of his Seventieth Birthday* (pp. 685–713). Tübingen: Mohr Siebeck
Reff, Daniel T. (2005). *Plagues, Priests and Demons*. Cambridge: Cambridge University Press
Regan, Vajra (2018). The *De Consecratione Lapidum*: A Previously Unknown Thirteenth Century

Version of the Liber Almandal Salamonis. *Journal of Medieval Latin* 28: 277–333
Riddle, John M. (ed.) (1977). *Marbode of Rennes' (1035-1123) De Lapidibus* (C. W. King, trans.). Wiesbaden: Franz Steiner
Riva, Fernando (2020). 'Est Iste Liber Maximi Secreti': Alfonso X's *Liber Razielis* and the Secrets of Kingship. *Neophilologus* 104.4: 485–502
Ritner, Robert K. (1993). *The Mechanics of Ancient Egyptian Magical Practice*. Chicago: University of Chicago
Rohrbacher-Sticker, Claudia (1995). A Hebrew Manuscript of *Clavicula Salomonis*, Part II. *British Library Journal* 21: 128–136
Rohrbacher-Sticker, Claudia (1993/4). Mafteah Shelomoh: A New Acquisition of the British Library. *Jewish Studies Quarterly* 1.3: 263–70
Roper, Jonathan (ed.) (2004). *Charms and Charming in Europe*. Basingstoke: Palgrave Macmillan
Runyon, Carroll 'Poke' (2003). *The Book of Solomon's Magic*. Silverado: CHS
Ryan, W. F. (1999). *The Bathhouse at Midnight: Magic in Russia*. University Park: Pennsylvania State University Press
Savage-Smith, Emilie (ed.) (2004). *Magic and Divination in Early Islam*. Aldershot: Ashgate
Savedow, Steve (ed., trans.) (2000). *Sepher Rezial Hemelach: The Book of the Angel Rezial*. York Beach: Samuel Weiser
Savedow, Steve (2022). *Goetic Evocation*. West Yorkshire: Hadean Press
Schäfer, P. (1990). Jewish Magic Literature in Late Antiquity and Early Middle Ages. *Journal of Jewish Studies* 41: 75–91
Scheible, Johann (1845–49). *Das Kloster: Weltlich und geistlich. Meist aus der ältern deutschen Volks-, Wunder-, Curiositäten-, und vorzugsweise komischen Literatur* (12 volumes). Stuttgart: Verlag des Herausgebers
Scheible, Johann (1849). *Bibliothek der Zauber*. Bucher: Geheimnissund Offenbarungs
Scheible, Johann (1873–4). *Bibliotheca Magica*. Bucher: Geheimnissund Offenbarungs
Schiffman, L. H., & Swartz, M. D. (1992). *Hebrew and Aramaic Incantation Texts from the Cairo Genizah*. Sheffield: JSOT Press
Scholem, Gershom (1965). Some Sources of Jewish-Arabic Demonology. *Journal of Jewish Studies* 16: 1–13
Scot, Reginald (1584). *The Discouerie of Witchcraft*. London: W. Brome
Scot, Reginald (1886). *The Discoverie of Witchcraft* (reprinted from 1665 edition). London: Elliot Stock
Scot, Reginald (1990). *The Discoverie of Witchcraft*. London: Dover
Scully, Sally (1995). Marriage or a Career? Witchcraft as an Alternative in Seventeenth Century Venice. *Journal of Social History* 2: 857–76
Shah, Idries (1956). *Oriental Magic*. London: Rider
Shah, Idries (1957). *The Secret Lore of Magic*. London: Frederick Muller Ltd.
Shaked, Shaul (ed.) (2005). *Officina Magica: Essays on the Practice of Magic in Antiquity*. Leiden: Brill
Shulvass, Moses Avigdor (1973). *The Jews in the World of the Renaissance*. Leiden: Brill
Simon (2007). *Papal Magic: Occult Practices Within the Catholic Church*. New York: Harper
Skemer, Don C. (2006). *Binding Words: Textual Amulets in the Middle Ages*. University Park: Pennsylvania State University Press
Skinner, Stephen (2006). *The Complete Magician's Tables*. Singapore: Golden Hoard Press
Skinner, Stephen (2021). *Techniques of Greco-Egyptian Magic*. Singapore: Golden Hoard Press
Skinner, Stephen (2021). *Techniques of Solomonic Magic*. Singapore: Golden Hoard Press
Skinner, Stephen & Rankine, David (2004). *Practical Angel Magic of John Dee's Enochian Tables*. Singapore: Golden Hoard Press
Skinner, Stephen & Rankine, David (2005). The *Keys to the Gateway of Magic*. Singapore: Golden

Hoard Press
Skinner, Stephen & Rankine, David (2007). *The Goetia of Dr Rudd*. Singapore: Golden Hoard Press
Skinner, Stephen & Rankine, David (2008). *The Veritable Key of Solomon*. Singapore: Golden Hoard Press
Skinner, Stephen & Rankine, David (eds.) (2009). *A Collection of Magical Secrets & A Treatise of Mixed Cabalah* (Paul Harry Barron, trans.). London: Avalonia
Skinner, Stephen & Rankine, David (2009). *The Grimoire of St Cyprian: Clavis Inferni*. Singapore: Golden Hoard Press
Skinner, Stephen, & Rankine, David (eds.) (2018). *A Cunning Man's Grimoire*. Singapore: Golden Hoard Press
Skinner, Stephen & Clark, Daniel (eds.) (2019). *The Clavis or Key to Unlock the Mysteries of Magic: by Rabbi Solomon*. Singapore: Golden Hoard Press
Society for the Diffusion of Useful Knowledge, The (1842). *The Biographical Dictionary of the Society for the Diffusion of Useful Knowledge*. London: Longman, Brown, Green, and Longmans
Sofer, Gal (2021). Wearing God, Consecrating Body Parts: Berengar Ganell's *Summa Sacre Magice* and *Shi'ur Qomah*. *Magic, Ritual, and Witchcraft* 16.3: 304–34
Sperber, Daniel (1994). *Magic and Folklore in Rabbinic Literature*. Jerusalem: Bar-Ian
Smith, Edward A. (2012). *Speculum de Arte Magica Papæ & Regis: The Enchiridion Leonis Papæ, Its Origins, Legend, & Memory* [MA thesis, University of York].
Speckens, Puk (2019). *Instruments of Consecration: An In-Depth Manuscript Study of the Book of Consecrations in the Vernacular* [MA thesis, Radboud University].
Stephens, Walter (2002). *Demon Lovers: Witchcraft, Sex and the Crisis of Belief*. Chicago: University of Chicago Press
Stratton-Kent, Jake (2010). *Geosophia: The Argo of Magic*. London: Scarlet Imprint
Stratton-Kent, Jake (2010). *The True Grimoire*. London: Scarlet Imprint
Stratton-Kent, Jake (2016). *Pandemonium: A Discordant Concordance of Diverse Spirit Catalogues*. West Yorkshire: Hadean Press
Stratton-Kent, Jake (2021). *The Sworn and Secret Grimoire*. West Yorkshire: Hadean Press
Sufurino, Jonás (2022). *The Supreme Black, Red & Infernal Magic of The Chaldeans And Egyptians* (Steve Savedow, ed. & trans.). West Yorkshire: Hadean Press
Summers, Montague (1995). *Witchcraft and Black Magic*. London: Senate
Swartz, M. D. (1992). *Mystical Prayers in Ancient Judaism*. Tübingen: Mohr
Symonds, John Addington (2001). *Renaissance in Italy: The Catholic Reaction. Part 1*. Boston: Adamant Media Corporation
Taillepied, Noël (1588). *Traicté de l'apparition des esprits*. Paris: G. Bichon
Thomas, Keith (1973). *Religion and the Decline of Magic*. London: Penguin
Thompson, C. J. S. (1927). *Mysteries and Secrets of Magic*. London: John Lane
Thompson, R. Campbell (2000). *Semitic Magic: Its Origins and Development*. Maine: Samuel Weiser
Thorndike, Lynn (1923). *A History of Magic and Experimental Science* (12 volumes). New York: Columbia University Press
Tilton, Hereward & Cox, Merlin (eds., trans.) (2017). *Touch Me Not: A Most Rare Compendium of the Whole Magical Art*. Somerset: Fulgur
Torijano, Pablo (2002). *Solomon the Esoteric King*. Leiden: Brill
Trachtenberg, Joshua (1939). *Jewish Magic and Superstition: A Study in Folk Religion*. New York: Behrman House
Turner, Dawson (1846). On Treasure-Trove and Invocation of Spirits. *Norfolk Archaeology* 1: 46–64
Turner, Robert (trans.) (1657). *Ars Notoria: The Notory Art of Solomon, Shewing the Cabalistical Key of*

Magical Operations. London: J. Cotrell

Turner, Robert (ed.) (1986). *The Heptarchia Mystica of John Dee*. Wellinborough: Aquarian Press

Turner, Robert (1989). *Elizabethan Magic: the Art and the Magus*. Shaftsbury: Element Books

Tyson, Donald (ed.) (2009). *Fourth Book of Occult Philosophy: The Companion to Three Book of Occult Philosophy Written by Henry Cornelius Agrippa of Nettesheim* (Robert Turner, trans.). Woodbury: Llewellyn

Tyson, Donald (ed.) (2018). *The Fourth Book of Occult Philosophy*. Woodbury: Llewellyn

Veenstra, Jan R. (1998). *Magic and Divination in Burgundy and France: Text and Context of Laurens Pignon's* Contre le Divineurs. Leiden: Brill

Veenstra, Jan R. (2002). *The Holy Almandal: Angels and the Intellectual Aims of Magic*. Leuven: Peeters

Venitiana del Rabina, Antonio (ed.) (2004). *The Grand Grimoire* (Gretchen Ruby, trans.). Boston: Trident Books

Véronèse, Julien (2007). *L'Ars Notoria au Moyen Age: Introduction et edition critique*. Firenze: SISMEL, Edizioni del Galluzzo

Véronèse, Julien (2012). *L'Almandal et l'Almadel latins au Moyen Âge : introduction et édition critique*. Firenze: SISMEL, Edizioni del Galluzzo

Waegeman, Maryse (1987). *Amulet and Alphabet: Magical Amulets in the First Book of Cyranides*. Leiden: Brill

Waite, A. E. (1886). *The Mysteries of Magic: A Digest of the Writings of Eliphas Levi*. London: George Redway

Waite, A. E. (1911). *The Book of Ceremonial Magic*. London: William Rider & Son

Waite, A. E (1911). *The Secret Tradition in Goetia*. London: Rider

Waite, A. E. (writing as Grand Orient) (1972). *Complete Manual of Occult Divination: The Book of Destiny* (2 vols.). New York: University Books Inc.

Waite, A. E. (1972). *The Book of Black Magic and of Pacts*. York Beach: Samuel Weiser

Walker, Daniel P. (1981). *Unclean Spirits: Possession and Exorcism in France and England in the Late Sixteenth and Early Seventeenth Centuries*. London: Scholar

Warnock, Christopher & Greer, John Michael (trans.) (2018). *The Complete Picatrix: The Occult Classic of Astrological Magic*. Lulu.com

Warwick, Tarl (ed.) (2016). *The Petit Albert: the Marvelous Secrets of the Little Albert*. Createspace

Wentworth, Joshua (trans.) (2011). *The Red Dragon*. York Beach: Teitan Press

Yates, Frances A. (1969). *Giordano Bruno and the Hermetic Tradition*. New York: Vintage

Yates, Frances A. (1983). *The Occult Philosophy in the Elizabethan Age*. London: Ark

www.ingramcontent.com/pod-product-compliance
Lightning Source LLC
Chambersburg PA
CBHW081140290426
44108CB00018B/2396